G000256013

BRITISH ATHLETICS
1995

Compiled by the
National Union of Track Statisticians

Editor: Rob Whittingham
Assistant Editors: Peter Matthews, Ian Hodge,
Liz Sissons

Published by: Umbra Softwa...
Unit 1, Bredbury Busi...
Bredbury Park Way, Bredbu...
Tel: 0161 406 6320   Fax: 0161 40b...

ISBN 1 898258 01 5

Front Cover: COLIN JACKSON. If you win everything you appear on the front cover.

All photos by: All photographs provided by Mark Shearman,
22 Grovelands Road, Purley, Surrey CR2 4LA
Tel: 0181-660 0156   Fax: 0181-660 3437
His help is greatly appreciated.

Distributed by: Old Bakehouse Publications,
The Old Bakehouse, Church Street,
Abertillery, Gwent NP3 1EA
Tel: 01495 212600   Fax: 01495 216222

Printed in
Great Britain by: J.R. Davies (Printers) Limited,
The Old Bakehouse, Church Street, Abertillery, Gwent NP3 1EA
Tel: 01495 212600   Fax: 01495 216222

CONTENTS

NATIONAL UNION OF TRACK STATISTICIANS AND COMPILERS

Honorary President: Norris D McWhirter CBE

Vice Presidents: Peter E May   Leonard F Gebbett Richard Hymans
                  Martin H James Patrick E Brian   Colin Young   Andrew Huxtable

Honorary Members: Roberto L Quercetani, John Bromhead, Jimmy Green, Ted O'Neill

Executive Committee: Les Crouch (Chairman)   Dr Shirley E Hitchcock (Hon Sec)
                      John M Powell (Treasurer)

Stanley Greenberg	Peter J Matthews	Melvyn F Watman	Lionel Peters
Elizabeth Sissons	Bob Sparks	Alfred P Wilkins	Justin Clouder
Sally Gandee	Dr. Tim Grose	David Lynch	Stuart Mazdon

Members:

Joe Barrass	Cliff Gould	Wilf Morgan
Glen Bishop	William Green	Bill Myers
Arnold Black	Roger W H Gynn	Anthony O'Neill
John Brant	Ian Hodge	D K R (Bob) Phillips
Ian Buchanan	Melvyn Jones	Thomas Pollak
David Burton	Alan Keys	Martin Rix
Mark Butler	Alan Lindop	Richard A Simmons
Mark Cawte	Peter Lovesey	Ian R Smith
Geoffrey Clarke (Hon.Aud.)	John Lunn	Sandy Sutherland
Andrew Clatworthy	Tim G Lynch-Staunton	Ian Tempest
Dave Cocksedge	David Martin	Dave Terry
Eric Cowe	Peter V Martin	Dr Chris Thorne
Alan A Currie	Anthony G Miller	John L J Walsh
Brenda Currie	Steve Mitchell	Malcolm Warburton
John T Glover	Keith Morbey	Rob Whittingham

Compilation

General Editor - Rob Whittingham

Assistant Editors - Ian Hodge, Peter Matthews, Liz Sissons

Records - Bob Sparks All Time Lists and Index - Martin Rix, Tony Miller
Results - Stuart Mazdon, Pat Brian

Men's Lists - Ian Hodge (HJ,PV and overall), Joe Barrass (sprints),
Tim Grose (800m to 10,000m), Steve Mitchell (5000m, 10,000m), John Walsh (Marathon),
Shirley Hitchcock (hurdles), Bill Myers (LJ,TJ),Tony O'Neill (throws).

Under 20 & Under 17 Men - Ian Hodge with above compilers and Melvyn Jones

Under 15 Men - Ian Hodge and Tony O'Neill   Under 13 Men - Mark Cawte

Women's Lists - Liz Sissons, Tony Miller (Under 17),
John Brant (Under 15), Bill Green (Under 13), Sally Gandee (Veterans).

Walks - John Powell   Relays - Keith Morbey   Multi-Events - Alan Lindop   Road - Dave Walsh

Also acknowledgements for specific help to Alan and Brenda Currie (Wales), John Glover and
Alan Keys (Northern Ireland), Arnold Black (Scotland) and various other NUTS members.

ABBREVIATIONS & NOTES

A	-	mark set at altitude over 1000m
a	-	automatic timing only known to one tenth of a second
D	-	performance made in a Decathlon
dh	-	downhill
e	-	estimated time
et	-	extra trial
ex	-	exhibition
h	-	heat
H	-	performance made in a Heptathlon
hc	-	handicap race
i	-	indoor
jo	-	jump off
m	-	position in race when intermediate time taken
mx	-	performance in mixed race
O	-	performance made in an Octathlon
o	-	over age
P	-	performance made in a Pentathlon

Q	-	qualifying round
q	-	quarter final
r	-	race number
s	-	semi final
t	-	track
u	-	unofficial time
un	-	unconfirmed performance
w	-	wind assisted (> 2.0 m/sec)
W	-	wind assisted (over 4m/sec in decathlon/heptathlon)
x	-	relay team may include outside age-group members
+	-	intermediate time
*	-	legal performance where best is wind assisted
"	-	photo electric cell time
#	-	Unratified (may not be ratifiable)
&	-	as yet unratified
§	-	now competes for another nation
¶	-	drugs ban

AGE GROUP DESIGNATIONS

Men's events:

U13 - Under 13	(born 1.9.81 or later)
U15 - Under 15	(born 1.9.79 to 31.8.81)
U17 - Under 17	(born 1.9.77 to 31.8.79)
U20 - Under 20	(born 1.1.75 to 31.8.77)
V - Veteran	(age 40 or over)

Women's events:

U13 - Under 13	(born 1.9.81 or later)
U15 - Under 15	(born 1.9.79 to 31.8.81)
U17 - Under 17	(born 1.9.77 to 31.8.79)
U20 - Under 20	(born 1.1.75 to 31.8.77)
V - Veteran	(age 35 or over)

Care must be taken with very young age groups for athletes with an unknown date of birth from Northern Ireland since their age groups differ slightly.

Italics indicates the athlete competes for a British club but is not eligible to represent Britain.

MULTI - EVENTS

Pentathlon, Heptathlon and Decathlon lists show the complete breakdown of individual performances in the following order:

Pentathlon (women) - 100mH, SP, HJ, LJ, 800m; Junior: LJ, SP, 75mH, HJ, 800m
Heptathlon (women) - 100mH, HJ, SP, 200m (1st day); LJ, JT, 800m (2nd day) (80mH - Inters)
Decathlon (men)   - 100m, LJ, SP, HJ, 400m (1st day); 110mH, DT, PV, JT, 1500m (2nd day)

Totals which include performances made with following winds in excess of 4 m/s are denoted by W. The date shown is the second day of competition.

RANKING LISTS:

These show the best performances in each event recorded during the 1994 season.
For each performance the following details are shown:

Performance; wind reading (where appropriate);   name (with, where appropriate, age-group category); date of birth (DDMMYY);   position in competition;   venue;   date.

The following numbers are used, although strength of performance or lack of information may vary the guidelines -

50 perfomances   100 athletes for each standard event

Age Groups - 40 Under 20, 30 Under 17, 20 Under 15, 10 Under 13

In the junior men, athletes are shown in older age groups if their performances merit this, e.g. an U15 can appear in the U17 list etc. For junior women, athletes are shown in their age group as per womens rules. Although juniors of any age will be shown in the main list on merit.

INDEX

Club details and previous personal bests, where better than those recorded in 1994, are shown in the index for all athletes in the main lists.

VENUES

Major venues for athletics - the name by which the stadium is denoted is shown in capitals:

LONDON (xx)

BP   Battersea Park
Col   Colindale (Metropolitan Police track)
CP   Crystal Palace, Nat. Sports Cen. Norwood
Elt   Sutcliffe Park, Eltham
EL   East London, Mile End
Ha   New River Sports Centre, Haringey
He   Barnet Copthall Stadium, Hendon
Hu   Hurlingham

Nh   Terence McMillan, Newham, Plaistow
PH   Parliament Hill Fields, Camden
SP   Southwark Park
TB   Tooting Bec
WC   White City Stadium
WF   Waltham Forest, Walthamstow
WL   West London Stadium

ABERDEEN, Chris Anderson Stadium, Balgowrie
ALDERSHOT Military Stadium (Army)
ANDOVER, Charlton Sports Centre
ANTRIM Forum
BARKING, Mayesbrook Park
BARRY, Jenner Park
BASILDON, Gloucester Park
BASINGSTOKE, Down Grange
BEBINGTON, The Oval, Wirral
BEDFORD, Newnham Track, Barkers Lane
BELFAST, Mary Peters Track
BIRMINGHAM, Alexander Stadium, Perry Park
         (Un) University Track, Edgbaston
BLACKBURN, Witton Park
BLACKPOOL, Stanley Park
BOLTON
BOURNEMOUTH, Kings Park
BRACKNELL, John Nike Stadium, Bracknell SC
BRAUNTON, North Devon Athletic Track
BRIERLEY HILL, The Dell, Dudley
BRIGHTON Sports Arena, Withdean
BRISTOL, Whitchurch Stadium
BROMLEY, Norman Park
CAMBRIDGE, Milton Road
CANNOCK, Festival Stadium, Pye Green Road
CARLISLE, Sheepmount Stadium
CHELTENHAM, Prince of Wales Stadium
CLECKHEATON, Pr. Mary Pl. Fields, Spenbro
COATBRIDGE
COLWYN BAY, Eirias Park Arena
CORBY, Rockingham Triangle
COSFORD (RAF), Indoor and outdoor arenas
COVENTRY, Warwick Univ., Kirby Corner Rd
CRAWLEY Leisure Centre, Haslett Avenue
CREWE, Cumberland Road Sports Ground
CROYDON Arena
CUDWORTH, Dorothy Hyman Sports Centre
CWMBRAN Sports Centre
DARTFORD, Central Park
DERBY, Moorways Stadium
EDINBURGH, Meadowbank Sports Centre
ENFIELD, Q. Eliz. II Stadium, Carterhatch Lane
GATESHEAD International Stadium
GLASGOW, Crown Point
         Indoors: Kelvin Hall
GRANGEMOUTH Stadium, Falkirk
GRIMSBY, K George V Stadium, Weelsby Rd
HARLOW Sports Centre
HARROW, Bannister Sports Centre, Hatch End
HIGH WYCOMBE, Handy Cross Track
HOO, Deangate Stadium, Rochester
HORNCHURCH Stadium, Havering, Upminster
HORSHAM, Broadbridge Heath Sports Centre
HULL, Costello Stadium
ILFORD, Cricklefields Athletic Ground
IPSWICH, Northgate Sports Centre
ISLEWORTH, Borough Road College
JARROW, Monckton Stadium

JERSEY, Greve D'Azette, Jersey, CI
KINGSTON, K Meadow, Kingston-u-Thames
KIRKBY Sports Centre, Liverpool
LEAMINGTON, Edmonscote Track
LEEDS, Carnegie College
LEICESTER, Saffron Lane Sports Centre
LINCOLN, Yarborough Sports Centre
LIVERPOOL, Wavertree Track
LOUGHBOROUGH, Ashby Rd Stadium (Univ)
LUTON, Stockwood Park
MANCHESTER, Wythenshawe Park
MANSFIELD, Berry Hill Athletcs Track
MELKSHAM, Christie Miller Sports Centre
MIDDLESBROUGH, Clairville Stadium
MOTSPUR PARK
NORWICH, Norfolk Athletics Track, Earlham
NOTTINGHAM, Harvey Hadden Stadium
OXFORD, Iffley Road (University)
PERIVALE Park Tr, Ruislip Rd,Greenford, Mx
PETERBOROUGH, Embankment Track
PITREAVIE Playing Fields, Dunfermline
PLYMOUTH, Brickfields Stad,Devonport(R.N)
PORTSMOUTH, Mountbatten Cen, Alex. Park
         (RN) Stadium, Burnaby Road
READING, Palmer Park
REDDITCH, Abbey Stadium
ROTHERHAM, Herringthorpe Stadium
ST. IVES, St. Ivo Outdoor Centre
SHEFFIELD, Don Valley Stadium
         (W) Woodburn Road, Attercliffe
SOLIHULL, Tudor Grange Park
SOUTHAMPTON, Shirley Sports Centre
SOUTHEND, Southchurch Park Stadium
STOKE, Northwood C,Hanley, Stoke-on-Trent
STRETFORD, Longford Park
SUNDERLAND, Silksworth
SUTTON COLDFIELD,Wyndley Leisure Cent.
SWANSEA, Morfa Stadium, Landore
SWINDON, Thamesdown Tr., County Ground
THURROCK, Blackshots Stadium, Grays
WARLEY, Hadley Playing Fields, Smethwick
WARRINGTON, Victoria Park, Knutsford Rd
WATFORD, Woodside Stadium, Garston
WELWYN, Gosling Stad, Welwyn Garden City
WIGAN, Robin Park
WINDSOR, Vansittart Road Track
WISHAW Stadium
WOKING, Blackmore Crescent, Sheerwater
WOLVERHAMPTON Stadium, Aldersley Road
WOODFORD, Ashton P Fields,Woodford Br.
WORTHING, West Park, Shaftesbury Avenue
WREXHAM, Queensway Sports Complex
YATE, Broadlane Track, Gloucester
YEOVIL Recreation Centre, Chilton Grove

Note also, in Ireland
DUBLIN (B) Belfield
         (M) Morton Stad. (Santry)

6

INTRODUCTION - by Rob Whittingham

Another year has passed and a new annual is ready. As always I start my introduction by thanking the people who have made significant effort to ensure the book is as accurate as possible. Peter Matthews found time between writing three book to check all the senior lists and make countless amendments. Ian Hodge provided the majority of the men's junior lists and obtained hundreds of new dates of birth for the database. Tony Miller checked all the lists and provided some extra useful information. Liz Sissons, as always, produced all the senior women's lists. Martin Rix supplied the 'all time' information and as ever Alan Lindop provided the extra data on the multi events. Arnold Black spent a great deal of time checking data against his Scottish lists. It is only through efforts like this and the work of all the compilers that the annual is as comprehensive as it is now.

As usual I received great help from Geoff Blamire, Michael Kubiena and Julie Fletcher at Umbra Software. Marty, by her own words, had an easy year and *only* checked the typesetting.

I am always trying to expand the content of the book and this year have increased the 'all time' lists. Followers of the mile may be particularly pleased with the lists included.

Unfortunately I have to report that this year's annual may contain some inconsistencies. It has been the practice to use ATFS abbreviations for countries throughout the book, however since the ATFS now use the IAAF abbreviations a few of these have appeared. I intend to convert to the IAAF codes fully next year. Traditionally, foreigners who have competed for a British club have also been included in the lists, although not in the counts. This year a large number of foreign athletes have used Britain as a training camp and joined local clubs for the occasional competition. I have tried to exclude these from the lists, although a few may still remain. In future only foreign athletes who are genuinely resident in Britain will appear on the lists.

This latest edition of the annual includes a short version of the T.S.B. junior rankings. These new lists will be produced during 1995 by the T.S.B. and it is hoped that they will be 1000 deep for each age group - U20, U17 and U15 for both men and women by the end of the season. The rankings are achieved by scoring all the events against the Hungarian scoring tables, with slight modifications to take account of junior performances. As with any list produced using tables there are bound to be problems and areas where the tables do not completely produce optimum results. However, with rankings to this depth a relatively simple method is required and the Hungarian tables are the most up to date. Although not perfect, it is hoped that the ranking lists will produce great interest from junior athletes. The T.S.B. are to be praised for their bold initiative. If possible I intend to publish the full ranking lists in next years annual.

My thanks to the B.A.F. for their financial assistance.

Any corrections are welcome.

Rob Whittingham
March 1995   7 Birch Green   Glossop   SK13 8PR

BAF & OTHER ADDRESSES

British Athletic Federation
225A Bristol Road
Edgbaston
Birmingham
B5 7UB
Tel: 021 440 5000

AAA of England
225A Bristol Road
Edgbaston
Birmingham
B5 7UB
Tel: 021 440 5000

SCOTLAND
Scotland A.F.
Caledonia House
South Gyle
Edinburgh
Tel: 031 317 7320

WALES
A.A. of Wales
Morfa Stadium Landore
Swansea
West Glamorgan SA1 7DF
Tel: 0792 456237

NORTHERN IRELAND
Northern Ireland A.A.F.
Honorary Secretary: J.Allen
House of Sport
Upper Malone Road
Belfast BT9 5LA
Tel: 0232 381222

Midland Counties A.A.
Edgebaston House
3 Duchess Place
Hagley Road
Birmingham
B16 8NM
Tel: 021 452 1500

North of Engnd A.A.
Studio 106, EMCO House
5/7 New York Road
Leeds LS2 7PJ
Tel: 0532 461835

South of England A.A.
Suite 36 City of London Fruit Exchange
Brushfield St
London E1 6EU
Tel: 071 247 2963

Commonwealth Games Councils:
England
General Secretary: Miss A.Hogbin
1 Wandsworth Plain
London SW18 1EH
Tel: 081 871 2677

Northern Ireland
Honorary Secretary: R.J.McColgan MBE
22 Mountcoole Park, Cave Hill
Belfast BT14 8JR
Tel: 0232 716558

Scotland
Honorary Secretary: G.A.Hunter OBE
139 Old Dalkeith Road
Little France
Edinburgh EH16 4SZ
Tel: 031 664 1070

Wales
Honorary Secretary: M.John MBE
Pennant
Blaenau, Ammanford
Dyfed SA18 3BZ
Tel: 0269 850390

British Athletics League
Honorary Secretary: M.Ison
7 Green Hill Avenue
Luton
Beds LU2 7DN
Tel: 0582 26283

National Young Athletes' League
Honorary Secretary: R.Sales
78 Orchard Road
South Ockendon
Essex RM15 6HH
Tel: 0708 852178

Supporters Club - British Athletics Club
Honorary Secretary: Mrs M.Pieri
11 Railway Road
Newbury, Berks RG14 7PE
Tel: 0635 33400

Sports Council
The Sports Council
16 Upper Woburn Place
London WC1H OQP
Tel: 071 388 1277

Athletics Weekly
Editor: David Clarke
Bretton Court, Bretton
Peterborough PE3 8DZ
Tel: 0733 261144

National Union of Track Statisticians
Secretary: Dr. S. Hitchcock
2 Chudleigh Close
Bedford
MK40 3AW

MAJOR OUTDOOR FIXTURES IN 1995

MAY

13-14	County Championships	Various
13-14	District Championships (Scotland)	Various
28	Walks International v HUN v ROM v UKR v POL	Ozd, HUN

JUNE

17-18	Area Championships	Various
17	Welsh Championships	Newport
23-24	Scottish Championships	
24-25	European Cup	Villeneuve d'Ascq, FRA
24-25	GB U20 v NOR	Lillehammer, NOR

JULY

1	Northern Ireland Championships	Antrim
1-2	AAA Under 20 Championships	Bedford
7	IAAF Grand Prix	London (CP)
7-8	TSB English Schools Championships	Nottingham
9	Welsh Games	Cwmbran
9	U20 Wales v HOL v BEL	Holland
13-23	World Veterans Championships	Buffalo, USA
15-16	AAA Championships inc World Trial	Birmingham
22-23	Wal v Sco v NI v TUR v ISR	Cardiff
23	TSB Challenge	Sheffield
27	GB v USA	Edinburgh
27-30	European Junior Championships	Nyiregyhaza, HUN
29	U23 GB v ITA v SPA v FRA	France

AUGUST

5-6	GB v RUS v GER v SWZ (Combined Events)	Vladimor, RUS
4-13	World Championships	Gothenburg, SWE
27	McDonald's Games	London (CP)
28-8Sep	World Student Games	Fukuoka, JAP

SEPTEMBER

9	GRE Gold/Jubilee Cup Final	Stoke
10	GRE Plate Final	Stoke

BEST AUTHENTIC PERFORMANCES (MEN)

(as at 31 Dec 1994)

W = World, E = European, C = Commonwealth, A = UK All-Comers, N = UK, J = Junior

100 m	W	9.85		Leroy Burrell	USA	6 Jul 94	Lausanne
	E,C,N	9.87		Linford Christie	Eng	15 Aug 93	Stuttgart
	A	10.03		Jon Drummond	USA	15 Jul 94	London (CP)
	WJ	10.05	#	Davidson Ezinwa	NIG	3 Jan 90	Bauchi
		10.08	A	Obadele Thompson	BAR	16 Apr 94	El Paso
	EJ	10.14		Sven Matthes	GER	13 Sep 88	Berlin
	NJ	10.21		Jamie Henderson		6 Aug 87	Birmingham
200 m	W,E	19.72	A	Pietro Mennea	ITA	12 Sep 79	Mexico City
	C	19.85		Frank Fredericks	NAM	20 Aug 93	Stuttgart
	A	19.85		Michael Johnson	USA	6 Jul 90	Edinburgh
	N	19.87	A&	John Regis		31 Jul 94	Sestriere
		19.94		John Regis		20 Aug 93	Stuttgart
	WJ	20.07	#	Lorenzo Daniel	USA	18 May 85	Starkville
		20.13		Roy Martin	USA	16 Jun 85	Indianapolis
	EJ	20.37		Jürgen Evers	GER	28 Aug 83	Schwechat
	NJ	20.54		Ade Mafe		25 Aug 85	Cottbus
300 m	W	31.48		Danny Everett	USA	3 Sep 90	Jerez de la Frontera
		31.48		Roberto Hernández	CUB	3 Sep 90	Jerez de la Frontera
	E,C,A,N	31.67		John Regis	Eng	17 Jul 92	Gateshead
	WJ	32.08		Steve Lewis	USA	28 Sep 88	Seoul
	EJ,NJ	32.53		Mark Richardson		14 Jul 91	London (Ha)
400 m	W	43.29		Butch Reynolds	USA	17 Aug 88	Zürich
	E	44.33		Thomas Schönlebe	GER	3 Sep 87	Rome
	C	44.17		Innocent Egbunike	NIG	19 Aug 87	Zürich
	A	43.98		Michael Johnson	USA	10 Jul 92	London (CP)
	N	44.47		David Grindley		3 Aug 92	Barcelona
	WJ	43.87		Steve Lewis	USA	28 Sep 88	Seoul
	EJ	45.01		Thomas Schönlebe	GER	15 Jul 84	Berlin
	NJ	45.36		Roger Black		24 Aug 85	Cottbus
600 m	W	1:12.81		Johnny Gray	USA	24 May 86	Santa Monica
	E,C,A,N	1:14.95		Steve Heard	Eng	14 Jul 91	London (Ha)
	NJ	1:16.79		Andrew Lill		24 Jul 90	Mansfield
800 m	W,E,C,N	1:41.73	"	Sebastian Coe	Eng	10 Jun 81	Florence
	A	1:43.22		Steve Cram		31 Jul 86	Edinburgh
	WJ	1:44.9	y#	Jim Ryun	USA	10 Jun 66	Terre Haute
		1:44.3		Joaquim Cruz	BRA	27 Jun 81	Rio de Janeiro
	EJ	1:45.45		Andreas Busse	GER	7 Jun 78	Ostrava
	NJ	1:45.64		David Sharpe		5 Sep 86	Brussels
1000 m	W,E,C,N	2:12.18		Sebastian Coe	Eng	11 Jul 81	Oslo
	A	2:12.88		Steve Cram		9 Aug 85	Gateshead
	WJ,EJ	2:18.31		Andreas Busse	GER	7 Aug 77	Dresden
	NJ	2:18.98		David Sharpe		19 Aug 86	Birmingham
1500 m	W	3:28.86		Noureddine Morceli	ALG	6 Sep 92	Rieti
	E,C,N	3:29.67		Steve Cram	Eng	16 Jul 85	Nice
	A	3:30.72		Noureddine Morceli	ALG	15 Jul 94	London (CP)
	WJ	3:34.92		Kipkoech Cheruiyot	KEN	26 Jul 83	Munich
	EJ,NJ	3:36.6		Graham Williamson		17 Jul 79	Oslo

Event	Cat	Time	Name	Country	Date	Venue
1 Mile	W	3:44.39	Noureddine Morceli	ALG	5 Sep 93	Rieti
	E,C,N	3:46.32	Steve Cram	Eng	27 Jul 85	Oslo
	A	3:49.49	Steve Cram		12 Sep 86	London (CP)
	WJ	3:51.3	Jim Ryun	USA	17 Jul 66	Berkeley
	EJ,NJ	3:53.15	Graham Williamson		17 Jul 79	Oslo
2000 m	W	4:50.81	Saïd Aouita	MAR	16 Jul 87	Paris
	E,C,N	4:51.39	Steve Cram	Eng	4 Aug 85	Budapest
	A	4:55.20	Steve Cram		28 Aug 88	London (CP)
	WJ,EJ	5:04.4	Harald Hudak	GER	30 Jun 76	Oslo
	NJ	5:06.56	Jon Richards		7 Jul 82	Oslo
3000 m	W	7:25.11	Noureddine Morceli	ALG	2 Aug 94	Monaco
	E,A,N	7:32.79	Dave Moorcroft		17 Jul 82	London (CP)
	C	7:28.96	Moses Kiptanui	KEN	16 Aug 92	Cologne
	WJ	7:38.20	Ismael Kirui	KEN	27 Aug 93	Berlin
	EJ	7:43.20	Ari Paunonen	FIN	22 Jun 77	Cologne
	NJ	7:48.28	Jon Richards		9 Jul 83	Oslo
2 Miles	W,C	8:09.01	Moses Kiptanui	KEN	30 Jul 94	Hechtel
	E	8:13.2 i	Emiel Puttemans	BEL	18 Feb 73	Berlin
	E,A,N	8:13.51	Steve Ovett		15 Sep 78	London (CP)
	WJ	8:25.2	Jim Ryun	USA	13 May 66	Los Angeles
	EJ,NJ	8:28.31	Steve Binns		31 Aug 79	London (CP)
5000 m	W	12:56.96	Haile Gebrsilassie	ETH	4 Jun 94	Hengelo
	E,C,N	13:00.41	Dave Moorcroft	Eng	7 Jul 82	Oslo
	A	13:06.72	William Sigei	KEN	15 Jul 94	London (CP)
	WJ	13:02.75	Ismael Kirui	KEN	16 Aug 93	Stuttgart
	EJ,NJ	13:27.04	Steve Binns		14 Sep 79	London (CP)
10 km	W,C	26:52.23	William Sigei	KEN	22 Jul 94	Oslo
	E	27:13.81	Fernando Mamede	POR	2 Jul 84	Stockholm
	A	27:30.3 #	Brendan Foster		23 Jun 78	London (CP)
		[27:30.6	Brendan Foster		23 Jun 78	London (CP)]
	N	27:23.06	Eamonn Martin		2 Jul 88	Oslo
	WJ	27:11.18	Richard Chelimo	KEN	25 Jun 91	Hengelo
	EJ	28:22.48	Christian Leuprecht	ITA	4 Sep 90	Koblenz
	NJ	29:21.9	Jon Brown		21 Apr 90	Walnut
20 km	W	56:55.6	Arturo Barrios	MEX	30 Mar 91	La Flèche
	E	57:18.4	Dionisio Castro	POR	31 Mar 90	La Flèche
	C,N	57:28.7	Carl Thackery	Eng	31 Mar 90	La Flèche
	A	58:39.0	Ron Hill		9 Nov 68	Leicester
1 Hour	W	21,101 m	Arturo Barrios	MEX	30 Mar 91	La Flèche
	E	20,944 m	Jos Hermens	HOL	1 May 76	Papendal
	C,N	20,855 m	Carl Thackery	Eng	31 Mar 90	La Flèche
	A	20,472 m	Ron Hill		9 Nov 68	Leicester
	NJ	18,221 m	Eddie Twohig		16 Jun 81	Leamington
25 km	W	1:13:55.8	Toshihiko Seko	JAP	22 Mar 81	Christchurch, NZ
	E	1:14:16.8	Pekka Päivärintä	FIN	15 May 75	Oulu
	C,A,N	1:15:22.6	Ron Hill	Eng	21 Jul 65	Bolton
30 km	W	1:29:18.78	Toshihiko Seko	JAP	22 Mar 81	Christchurch, NZ
	E,C,A,N	1:31:30.4	Jim Alder	Sco	5 Sep 70	London (CP)
Half Marathon	W,C	59:47	Moses Tanui	KEN	3 Apr 93	Milan
	A	60:02	Benson Masya	KEN	18 Sep 94	Tyneside
	E	60:03	Vincent Rousseau	BEL	23 Jan 94	Tokyo
	N	60:59	Steve Jones		8 Jun 86	Tyneside
	WJ	62:11	Melk Mothuli	RSA	3 Oct 93	Brussels
	NJ	66:48	Alan Wilson		29 May 83	Kirkintilloch

Marathon	W	2:06:50	Belayneh Dinsamo	ETH	17 Apr 88	Rotterdam
	E	2:07:12	Carlos Lopes	POR	20 Apr 85	Rotterdam
	C,N	2:07:13	Steve Jones	Wal	20 Oct 85	Chicago
	A	2:08:16	Steve Jones		21 Apr 85	London
	WJ	2:12:49	Negash Dube	ETH	18 Oct 87	Beijing
		2:12:49	Tesfayi Dadi	ETH	9 Oct 88	Berlin
	NJ	2:23:28	Eddie Twohig		28 Mar 82	Wolverhampton
2km St	W,C	5:14.43	Julius Kariuki	KEN	21 Aug 90	Rovereto
	E	5:18.36	Alessandro Lambruschini	ITA	12 Sep 89	Verona
	A	5:19.68	Samson Obwocha	KEN	19 Jul 86	Birmingham
	N	5:19.86	Mark Rowland		28 Aug 88	London (CP)
	WJ,EJ	5:25.01	Arsenios Tsiminos	GRE	2 Oct 80	Athens
	NJ	5:29.61	Colin Reitz		18 Aug 79	Bydgoszcz
3km St	W,C	8:02.08	Moses Kiptanui	KEN	19 Aug 92	Zürich
	E	8:07.62	Joseph Mahmoud	FRA	24 Aug 84	Brussels
	A	8:15.53	Patrick Sang	KEN	10 Sep 93	London (CP)
	N	8:07.96	Mark Rowland		30 Sep 88	Seoul
	WJ	8:19.21	Daniel Njenga	KEN	11 Jun 94	Tokyo
	EJ	8:29.50	Ralf Pönitzsch	GER	19 Aug 76	Warsaw
	NJ	8:29.85	Paul Davies-Hale		31 Aug 81	London (CP)
110m H	W,E,C,N	12.91	Colin Jackson	Wal	20 Aug 93	Stuttgart
	A	13.03	Colin Jackson		4 Sep 94	Sheffield
	WJ	13.23	Renaldo Nehemiah	USA	16 Aug 78	Zürich
	EJ,NJ	13.44	Colin Jackson		19 Jul 86	Athens
200m H	WECAN	22.63	Colin Jackson	Wal	1 Jun 91	Cardiff
	NJ	23.2	Jon Ridgeon		19 Sep 86	Thurrock
		24.02	Paul Gray		13 Sep 87	London (CP)
400m H	W	46.78	Kevin Young	USA	6 Aug 92	Barcelona
	E	47.48	Harald Schmid	GER	8 Sep 82	Athens
		47.48 #	Harald Schmid	GER	1 Sep 87	Rome
	C	47.10	Samuel Matete	ZAM	7 Aug 91	Zürich
	A	47.67	Kevin Young	USA	14 Aug 92	Sheffield
	N	47.82	Kriss Akabusi		6 Aug 92	Barcelona
	WJ	48.02	Danny Harris	USA	17 Jun 84	Los Angeles
	EJ	48.74	Vladimir Budko	RUS	18 Aug 84	Moscow
	NJ	50.22	Martin Briggs		28 Aug 83	Schwechat
High Jump	W	2.45	Javier Sotomayor	CUB	27 Jul 93	Salamanca
	E	2.42	Patrik Sjöberg	SWE	30 Jun 87	Stockholm
		2.42 i#	Carlo Thränhardt	GER	26 Feb 88	Berlin
	(C,N)	2.38 i#	Steve Smith	Eng	4 Feb 94	Wuppertal
	C,N,WJ,EJ,NJ	2.37	Steve Smith		20 Sep 92	Seoul
	C	2.37	Troy Kemp	BHM	26 Jun 93	Pau
	C,N	2.37	Steve Smith		22 Aug 93	Stuttgart
	A	2.41	Javier Sotomayor	CUB	15 Jul 94	London (CP)
	WJ,EJ	2.37	Dragutin Topic	CRO	12 Aug 90	Plovdiv
Pole Vault	W,E	6.15 i#	Sergey Bubka	UKR	21 Feb 93	Donetsk
		6.14	Sergey Bubka	UKR	31 Jul 94	Sestriere
	C	5.90	Okkert Brits	RSA	10 Sep 94	London (CP)
	A	6.05	Sergey Bubka	UKR	10 Sep 93	London (CP)
	N	5.65	Keith Stock	Eng	7 Jul 81	Stockholm
	WJ,EJ	5.80	Maksim Tarasov	RUS	14 Jul 89	Bryansk
	NJ	5.50	Neil Winter		9 Aug 92	San Giuliano
Long Jump	W	8.95	Mike Powell	USA	30 Aug 91	Tokyo
	E	8.86 A	Robert Emmiyan	ARM	22 May 87	Tsakhkadzor

Long	C	8.41		Craig Hepburn	BHM	17 Jun 93	Nassau
Jump	A	8.54		Mike Powell	USA	10 Sep 93	London (CP)
	N	8.23		Lynn Davies		30 Jun 68	Berne
	WJ	8.34		Randy Williams	USA	8 Sep 72	Munich
	EJ	8.24		Volodymyr Ochkan	UKR	21 Jun 87	St. Petersburg
	NJ	7.98		Stewart Faulkner		6 Aug 88	Birmingham
Triple	W	17.97		Willie Banks	USA	16 Jun 85	Indianapolis
Jump	E	17.92		Khristo Markov	BUL	31 Aug 87	Rome
	C,N	17.57	A	Keith Connor	Eng	5 Jun 82	Provo
	A	17.61		Yoelvis Quesada	CUB	10 Sep 94	London (CP)
	WJ,EJ	17.50		Volker Mai	GER	23 Jun 85	Erfurt
	NJ	16.58		Tosi Fasinro		15 Jun 91	Espoo
Shot	W	23.12		Randy Barnes	USA	20 May 90	Los Angeles
	E	23.06		Ulf Timmermann	GER	22 May 88	Khaniá
	C,N	21.68		Geoff Capes	Eng	18 May 80	Cwmbrân
	A	22.28	#	Brian Oldfield	USA	18 Jun 75	Edinburgh
		21.72		Ulf Timmermann	GER	5 Aug 89	Gateshead
	WJ	21.05	i#	Terry Albritton	USA	22 Feb 74	New York
		20.65	#	Mike Carter	USA	5 Jul 79	Boston
		20.38		Terry Albritton	USA	27 Apr 74	Walnut
	EJ	20.20		Udo Beyer	GER	6 Jul 74	Leipzig
	NJ	18.21	i#	Matt Simson		3 Feb 89	Cosford
		18.11		Matt Simson		27 Aug 89	Varazdin
Discus	W,E	74.08		Jürgen Schult	GER	6 Jun 86	Neubrandenburg
	C	67.80		Adewale Olukoju	NIG	11 May 91	Los Angeles
	A	68.32		John Powell	USA	30 Aug 82	London (CP)
	N	65.16	#	Richard Slaney		1 Jul 85	Eugene
		64.32		Bill Tancred		10 Aug 74	Woodford
	WJ	65.62	#	Werner Reiterer	AUS	15 Dec 87	Melbourne
	(WJ),EJ	63.64		Werner Hartmann	GER	25 Jun 78	Strasbourg
	NJ	55.10		Glen Smith		31 Aug 91	Brierley Hill
Hammer	W,E	86.74		Yuriy Sedykh	UKR/RUS	30 Aug 86	Stuttgart
	C	77.58		Sean Carlin	AUS	11 Feb 94	Adelaide
	A	85.60		Yuriy Sedykh	UKR/RUS	13 Jul 84	London (CP)
	N	77.54		Martin Girvan		12 May 84	Wolverhampton
	WJ,EJ	78.14		Roland Steuk	GER	30 Jun 78	Leipzig
	NJ	67.48		Paul Head		16 Sep 84	Karlovac
Javelin	W,E,A	95.66		Ján Zelezny	CS	29 Aug 93	Sheffield
	C,N	91.46		Steve Backley	Eng	25 Jan 92	Auckland
	WJ,EJ	80.94		Aki Parviainen	FIN	5 Jul 92	Jyväskylä
	NJ	79.50		Steve Backley		5 Jun 88	Derby
Pent.	W,A	4123		Bill Toomey	USA	16 Aug 69	London (CP)
	E	4079		Rein Aun	EST	17 Jul 68	Tartu
	C,N	3841		Barry King	Eng	20 May 70	Santa Barbara
Dec.	W,	8891		Dan O'Brien	USA	5 Sep 92	Talence
	E,C,N	8847		Daley Thompson	Eng	9 Aug 84	Los Angeles
	A	8663		Daley Thompson		28 Jul 86	Edinburgh
	WJ,EJ	8397		Torsten Voss	GER	7 Jul 82	Erfurt
	NJ	8082		Daley Thompson		31 Jul 77	Sittard
(1986 Javelin)							
	E,C,N	8811	#	Daley Thompson	Eng	28 Aug 86	Stuttgart
	WJ,EJ	8114	#	Michael Kohnle	GER	25 Aug 89	Varazdin
	NJ	7488	#	David Bigham		9 Aug 90	Plovdiv

13

4x100m	W	37.40		United States		8 Aug 92	Barcelona
		37.40		United States		21 Aug 93	Stuttgart
	E,N	37.77		UK National Team		22 Aug 93	Stuttgart
	C	37.83		Canada		22 Aug 93	Stuttgart
	A	38.39		UK National Team		5 Aug 89	Gateshead
	WJ	39.00	A	United States		18 Jul 83	Colorado Springs
	EJ	39.21	#	UK National Team		20 Sep 92	Seoul
	(EJ)	39.25		West Germany		28 Aug 83	Schwechat
	NJ	39.21		UK National Team		20 Sep 92	Seoul
4x200m	W	1:18.68		Santa Monica T.C.	USA	17 Apr 94	Walnut
	E	1:21.10		Italy		29 Sep 83	Cagliari
	C	1:20.79		Jamaica		24 Apr 88	Walnut
	A,N	1:21.29		UK National Team		23 Jun 89	Birmingham
	NJ	1:27.46	i	UK National Team		28 Jan 89	Glasgow
		1:27.6		Borough of Enfield		13 Jun 82	London (He)
4x400m	W	2:54.29		United States		22 Aug 93	Stuttgart
	E,C,N	2:57.53		UK National Team	Eng	1 Sep 91	Tokyo
	A	3:00.93		UK National Team		19 Jun 92	Edinburgh
	WJ	3:01.90		United States		20 Jul 86	Athens
	EJ,NJ	3:03.80	#	UK National Team		12 Aug 90	Plovdiv
	(EJ)	3:04.58		East Germany		23 Aug 81	Utrecht
4x800m	WECAN	7:03.89		UK National Team	Eng	30 Aug 82	London (CP)
	NJ	7:35.3		Liverpool Harriers		14 Aug 90	Leeds
4x1500m	W,E	14:38.8		West Germany		17 Aug 77	Cologne
	C	14:40.4		New Zealand		22 Aug 73	Oslo
	A	15:04.7		Italy		5 Jun 92	Sheffield
	N	14:56.8	a#	UK National Team		23 Jun 79	Bourges
		15:04.6		UK National Team		5 May 76	Athens
	NJ	16:04.3		Blackburn Harriers		15 Sep 79	Luton
4x1mile	W,E	15:49.08		Ireland		17 Aug 85	Dublin (B)
	C	15:59.57		New Zealand		1 Mar 83	Auckland
	A	16:21.1		UK National Team		10 Jul 93	Oxford
	N	16:17.4		Bristol A.C.		24 Apr 75	Des Moines
	WJ,EJ,NJ	16:56.8		BMC Junior Squad		10 Jul 93	Oxford

Track Walking

1500 m	W,E	5:12.0		Algis Grigaliunas	LIT	12 May 90	Vilnius
	C	5:19.1		Dave Smith	AUS	7 Feb 83	Melbourne
	N	5:19.22	i	Tim Berrett §		9 Feb 90	East Rutherford
1 mile	W,E	5:36.9		Algis Grigaliunas	LIT	12 May 90	Vilnius
	C	5:54.6	i	Marcel Jobin	CAN	16 Feb 80	Houston
	N	5:56.39	i	Tim Berrett §		2 Feb 90	New York
	(C),A,(N)	5:59.1		Darrell Stone	Eng	2 Jul 89	Portsmouth
	NJ	6:09.2		Phil Vesty		23 Jun 82	Leicester
3000 m	W,E	10:47.11		Giovanni DeBenedictis	ITA	19 May 90	S. G. Valdarno
	C	10:56.22		Andrew Jachno	AUS	7 Feb 91	Melbourne
	A	11:19.00	i	Axel Noack	GER	23 Feb 90	Glasgow
		11:19.9		Tim Berrett	CAN	20 Apr 92	Tonbridge
	N	11:24.4		Mark Easton		10 May 89	Tonbridge
	WJ,EJ	11:13.2		Jozef Pribilinec	SVK	28 Mar 79	Banská Bystrica
	NJ	11:54.23		Tim Berrett §		23 Jun 84	London (CP)
5000 m	W,E	18:11.41	i	Ronald Weigel	GER	13 Feb 88	Vienna
		18:17.22		Robert Korzeniowski	POL	3 Jul 92	Reims
	C	18:52.20	i	Dave Smith	AUS	7 Mar 87	Indianapolis
		18:52.87		Dave Smith	AUS	21 Feb 86	Canberra
	A	18:56.27	i	Axel Noack	GER	23 Feb 90	Glasgow

5000 m	(A),N	19:35.0	Darrell Stone		16 May 89	Brighton
	WJ,EJ	19:19.3	Mikhail Shchennikov	RUS	9 Aug 86	Chemnitz
	NJ	20:16.40	Philip King		26 Jun 93	Lubeck
10 km	W,E	38:02.60	Jozef Pribilinec	SVK	30 Aug 85	Banská Bystrica
	C	38:06.6	Dave Smith	AUS	25 Sep 86	Sydney
	A	39:26.02	Guillaume Leblanc	CAN	29 Jun 90	Gateshead
	N	40:06.65	Ian McCombie		4 Jun 89	Jarrow
	WJ,EJ	38:54.75	Ralf Kowalsky	GER	24 Jun 81	Cottbus
	NJ	41:52.13	Darrell Stone		7 Aug 87	Birmingham
1 Hour	W	15,577 m	Bernardo Segura	MEX	7 May 94	Fana
	E	15,447 m	Jozef Pribilinec	SVK	6 Sep 86	Hildesheim
	C	15,300 m	Dave Smith	AUS	6 Sep 86	Hildesheim
	A	14,383 m	Anatoliy Solomin	UKR	26 Aug 77	Edinburgh
	N	14,324 m #	Ian McCombie		7 Jul 85	London (SP)
		14,158 m	Mark Easton		12 Sep 87	Woodford
	NJ	13,487 m	Darrell Stone		12 Sep 87	Woodford
20 km	W	1:17:25.6	Bernardo Segura	MEX	7 May 94	Fana
	E	1:18:35.2	Stefan Johansson	SWE	15 May 92	Fana
	C	1:20:12.3	Nick A'Hern	AUS	8 May 93	Fana
	A	1:24:07.6 #	Phil Vesty		1 Dec 84	Leicester
		1:24:22.0	José Marín	SPA	28 Jun 81	Brighton
	N	1:23:26.5	Ian McCombie		26 May 90	Fana
	WJ,EJ	1:22:42	Andrey Perlov	RUS	6 Sep 80	Donetsk
	NJ	1:31:34.4	Gordon Vale		28 Jun 81	Brighton
2 Hours	W,E	29,572 m	Maurizio Damilano	ITA	4 Oct 92	Cuneo
	C	28,800 m #	Guillaume Leblanc	CAN	16 Jun 90	Sept Iles
		27,123 m	Willi Sawall	AUS	24 May 80	Melbourne
	A,N	27,262 m #	Chris Maddocks		31 Dec 89	Plymouth
	(A)	26,265 m	Jordi Llopart	SPA	28 Jun 81	Brighton
	(N)	26,037 m	Ron Wallwork		31 Jul 71	Blackburn
30 km	W,E	2:01:44.1	Maurizio Damilano	ITA	4 Oct 92	Cuneo
	C	2:04:55.7	Guillaume Leblanc	CAN	16 Jun 90	Sept Iles
	A,N	2:11:54 #	Chris Maddocks		31 Dec 89	Plymouth
	(A)	2:17:26.4	Jordi Llopart	SPA	28 Jun 81	Brighton
	(N)	2:19:18	Chris Maddocks		22 Sep 84	Birmingham
50 km	W,E	3:41:28.2	René Piller	FRA	7 May 94	Fana
	C	3:43:50.0	Simon Baker	AUS	9 Sep 90	Melbourne
	A	4:03:52	Gerhard Weidner	GER	1 Jun 75	Woodford
	N	4:05:44.6	Paul Blagg		26 May 90	Fana

Road Walking - Fastest Recorded Times

5000m	W,E	18:21		Robert Korzeniowski	POL	15 Sep 90	Bad Salzdetfurth
	A,C	19:51	hc	Andy Penn	Eng	30 Jan 93	Coventry
		20:50		Chris Maddocks	Eng	1 Jan 88	Plymouth
	N	19:29		Andi Drake		27 May 90	Søfteland
	NJ	20:54.3		Ian Ashforth		5 May 85	Cascina
10 km	W,E	38:34		Valdas Kazlauskas	LIT	10 Jun 89	Hildesheim
	C	39:09		Dave Smith	AUS	3 Sep 86	Bad Salzdetfurth
	A,N	40:16.6		Chris Maddocks		30 Apr 89	Burrator
	NJ	41:46		Darrell Stone		26 Sep 87	Paris
20 km	W,E	1:18:13		Pavol Blazek	SVK	16 Sep 90	Hildesheim
	C	1:19:22		Dave Smith	AUS	19 Jul 87	Hobart
	A	1:21:42		Jose Marin	SPA	29 Sep 85	St. John's, IoM
	N	1:22:03		Ian McCombie		23 Sep 88	Seoul

	WJ	1:21:33		Carlos Mercenario	MEX	5 Oct 86	St. Léonard
	EJ	1:21:39.1		Ralf Kowalsky	GER	7 Aug 81	Jena
	NJ	1:26:13		Tim Berrett §		25 Feb 84	Dartford
30 km	W,E	2:02:41		Andrey Perlov	RUS	18 Feb 89	Sochi
	C	2:05:59		Dave Smith	AUS	10 May 86	Canberra
	A	2:07:46.7		Simon Baker	AUS	31 Jul 86	Edinburgh
	N	2:07:56		Ian McCombie		27 Apr 86	Edinburgh
	NJ	2:30:46		Phil Vesty		31 Jul 82	London (VP)
50 km	W,E	3:37:41		Andrey Perlov	RUS	5 Aug 89	St. Petersburg
	C	3:43:13		Simon Baker	AUS	28 May 89	L'Hospitalet
	A	3:47:31		Hartwig Gauder	GER	28 Sep 85	St. John's IoM
	N	3:51:37		Chris Maddocks		28 Oct 90	Burrator
	WJ,EJ	4:07:23		Aleksandr Volgin	RUS	27 Sep 86	Zhytomyr
	NJ	4:18:18		Gordon Vale		24 Oct 81	Lassing

RECORDS set in 1994

100 m	WJ	10.08	A	Obadele Thompson	BAR	16 Apr 94	El Paso
	W	9.85		Leroy Burrell	USA	6 Jul 94	Lausanne
	A	10.03		Jon Drummond	USA	15 Jul 94	London (CP)
200 m	N	19.87	A&	John Regis		31 Jul 94	Sestriere
1500 m	A	3:30.72		Noureddine Morceli	ALG	15 Jul 94	London (CP)
3000 m	W	7:25.11		Noureddine Morceli	ALG	2 Aug 94	Monaco
2 Miles	W,C	8:09.01		Moses Kiptanui	KEN	30 Jul 94	Hechtel
5000 m	W	12:56.96		Haile Gebrsilassie	ETH	4 Jun 94	Hengelo
	A	13:06.72		William Sigei	KEN	15 Jul 94	London (CP)
10 km	W,C	26:52.23		William Sigei	KEN	22 Jul 94	Oslo
Half	E	60:23		Vincent Rousseau	BEL	23 Jan 94	Tokyo
Marathon	A	60:02		Benson Masya	KEN	18 Sep 94	Tyneside
3km St	WJ	8:19.21		Daniel Njenga	KEN	11 Jun 94	Tokyo
110m H	A	13.03		Colin Jackson		4 Sep 94	Sheffield
High J	A	2.41		Javier Sotomayor	CUB	15 Jul 94	London (CP)
Pole	C	5.85		Okkert Brits	RSA	8 Jul 94	Lille
Vault	C	5.85		Okkert Brits	RSA	18 Jul 94	Nice
	W,E	6.14		Sergey Bubka	UKR	31 Jul 94	Sestriere
	C	5.90		Okkert Brits	RSA	10 Sep 94	London (CP)
Triple	A	17.61		Yoelvis Quesada	CUB	10 Sep 94	London (CP)
Hammer	C	77.58		Sean Carlin	AUS	11 Feb 94	Adelaide
4x200m	W	1:18.68		Santa Monica T.C.	USA	17 Apr 94	Walnut
1 HrWT	W	15,577 m		Bernardo Segura	MEX	7 May 94	Fana
20 kmWT	W	1:17:25.6		Bernardo Segura	MEX	7 May 94	Fana
50 kmWT	W,E	3:45.24.2		Thierry Toutain	FRA	2 Apr 94	Fraconville
	W,E	3:41:28.2		René Piller	FRA	7 May 94	Fana

WOMEN'S EVENTS

100 m	W	10.49		Florence Griffith Joyner	USA	16 Jul 88	Indianapolis
	E	10.77		Irina Privalova	RUS	6 Jul 94	Lausanne
	C	10.78		Merlene Ottey	JAM	30 May 90	Seville
		10.78		Merlene Ottey	JAM	3 Sep 94	Paris
	A	11.02		Merlene Ottey	JAM	14 Jul 89	London (CP)
	N	11.10		Kathy Smallwood/Cook		5 Sep 81	Rome
	WJ,EJ	10.88	#	Marlies Oelsner/Göhr	GER	1 Jul 77	Dresden
		10.89		Kathrin Krabbe	GER	20 Jul 88	Berlin
	NJ	11.27	A	Kathy Smallwood/Cook		9 Sep 79	Mexico City
200 m	W	21.34		Florence Griffith Joyner	USA	29 Sep 88	Seoul
	E	21.71		Marita Koch	GER	10 Jun 79	Chemnitz
		21.71	#	Marita Koch	GER	21 Jul 84	Potsdam
		21.71		Heike Drechsler	GER	29 Jun 86	Jena
		21.71	#	Heike Drechsler	GER	29 Aug 86	Stuttgart
	C	21.64		Merlene Ottey	JAM	13 Sep 91	Brussels
	A	22.23		Merlene Ottey	JAM	9 Sep 94	London (CP)
	N	22.10		Kathy Cook		9 Aug 84	Los Angeles
	WJ,EJ	22.19		Natalya Bochina	RUS	30 Jul 80	Moscow
	NJ	22.70	A	Kathy Smallwood/Cook		12 Sep 79	Mexico City
300 m	W,E	34.1	#	Marita Koch	GER	6 Oct 85	Canberra
		34.8	+	Marita Koch	GER	8 Sep 82	Athens
		35.00	+	Marie-José Pérec	FRA	27 Aug 91	Tokyo
	C,A,N	35.46		Kathy Cook		18 Aug 84	London (CP)
	(A)	35.46		Chandra Cheeseborough	USA	18 Aug 84	London (CP)
	WJ,EJ,NJ	36.2		Donna Murray/Hartley		7 Aug 74	London (CP)
	WJ,EJ	36.24		Grit Breuer	GER	29 Aug 90	Split
	NJ	36.46		Linsey Macdonald		13 Jul 80	London (CP)
400 m	W,E	47.60		Marita Koch	GER	6 Oct 85	Canberra
	C,N	49.43		Kathy Cook	Eng	6 Aug 84	Los Angeles
	A	49.33		Tatjána Kocembová	CS	20 Aug 83	London (CP)
	WJ,EJ	49.42		Grit Breuer	GER	27 Aug 91	Tokyo
	NJ	51.16		Linsey Macdonald		15 Jun 80	London (CP)
600 m	W,E	1:23.5		Doina Melinte	ROM	27 Jul 86	Poiana Brasov
	C	1:26.0		Charlene Rendina	AUS	12 Mar 79	Adelaide
	A	1:25.90		Delisa Walton-Floyd	USA	28 Aug 88	London (CP)
	N	1:26.18		Diane Edwards/Modahl		22 Aug 87	London (CP)
	NJ	1:27.33		Lorraine Baker		13 Jul 80	London (CP)
800 m	W,E	1:53.28		Jarmila Kratochvílová	CS	26 Jul 83	Munich
	C,N	1:57.42		Kirsty McDermott/Wade	Wal	24 Jun 85	Belfast
	A	1:57.14		Jarmila Kratochvílová	CS	24 Jun 85	Belfast
	WJ	1:57.18		Wang Yuan	CHN	8 Sep 93	Beijing
	EJ	1:57.45	#	Hildegard Ullrich	GER	31 Aug 78	Prague
	(EJ)	1:59.17		Birte Bruns	GER	20 Jul 88	Berlin
	NJ	2:01.11		Lynne MacDougall/McIntyre		18 Aug 84	London (CP)
1000 m	W,E	2:30.6	#	Tatyana Providokhina	RUS	20 Aug 78	Podolsk
	(W,E)	2:30.67		Christine Wachtel	GER	17 Aug 90	Berlin
	C,A,N	2:33.70		Kirsty McDermott/Wade	Wal	9 Aug 85	Gateshead
	WJ,EJ	2:35.4	a	Irina Nikitina	RUS	5 Aug 79	Podolsk
	NJ	2:38.58		Jo White		9 Sep 77	London (CP)
1500 m	W	3:50.46		Qu Yunxia	CHN	11 Sep 93	Beijing
	E	3:52.47		Tatyana Kazankina	RUS	13 Aug 80	Zürich
	C,N,(EJ),NJ	3:59.96		Zola Budd/Pieterse	Eng	30 Aug 85	Brussels
	A	3:59.31		Ravilya Agletdinova	BLR	5 Jun 83	Birmingham
	WJ	3:59.81		Wang Yuan	CHN	11 Sep 93	Beijing
	EJ	4:04.39		Zola Budd/Pieterse		28 May 84	Cwmbrân

17

Event	Cat	Mark	Name	Nat	Date	Place
1 Mile	W,E	4:15.61	Paula Ivan	ROM	10 Jul 89	Nice
	C,N,WJ,EJ,NJ	4:17.57	Zola Budd/Pieterse	Eng	21 Aug 85	Zürich
	A	4:19.59	Mary Slaney	USA	2 Aug 85	London (CP)
2000 m	W,E,A	5:25.36	Sonia O'Sullivan	IRE	8 Jul 94	Edinburgh
	C,N	5:26.93	Yvonne Murray	Sco	8 Jul 94	Edinburgh
	WJ,EJ,NJ	5:33.15	Zola Budd/Pieterse		13 Jul 84	London (CP)
3000 m	W	8:06.11	Wang Junxia	CHN	13 Sep 93	Beijing
	E,A	8:21.64	Sonia O'Sullivan	IRE	15 Jul 94	London (CP)
	C,N,NJ	8:28.83	Zola Budd/Pieterse	Eng	7 Sep 85	Rome
	WJ,EJ	8:28.83 #	Zola Budd/Pieterse		7 Sep 85	Rome
	(WJ)	8:36.45	Ma Ningning	CHN	6 Jun 93	Jinan
	(EJ)	8:40.08	Gabriele Szabo	ROM	10 Aug 94	Helsinki
5000 m	W,E	14:37.33	Ingrid Kristiansen	NOR	5 Aug 86	Stockholm
	C,A,N,WJ,EJ,NJ	14:48.07	Zola Budd/Pieterse	Eng	26 Aug 85	London (CP)
10 km	W	29:31.78	Wang Junxia	CHN	8 Sep 93	Beijing
	E	30:13.74	Ingrid Kristiansen	NOR	5 Jul 86	Oslo
	C,A	30:52.51	Elana Meyer	RSA	10 Sep 94	London (CP)
	N	30:57.07	Liz McColgan		25 Jun 91	Hengelo
	WJ	31:15.38 &	Sally Barsosio	KEN	21 Aug 93	Stuttgart
		31:40.56	Delilah Asiago	KEN	16 Jun 91	Tokyo
	EJ	32:12.51 #	Marleen Renders	BEL	4 Sep 87	Rome
		32:25.74	Olga Nazarkina	RUS	23 Aug 89	Varazdin
1 Hour	W,E	18,084 m	Silvana Cruciata	ITA	4 May 81	Rome
	C,A,N	16,460 m i	Bronwyn Cardy-Wise	Wal	8 Mar 92	Birmingham
		16,272 m	Zina Marchant	Eng	30 Mar 88	London (TB)
20 km	W	1:06:48.8	Izumi Maki	JAP	19 Sep 93	Amagasaki
	E	1:06:55.5 #	Rosa Mota	POR	14 May 83	Lisbon
	C,A,N	1:21:43.0 #	Eleanor Adams/Robinson	Eng	16 Oct 82	London (He)
25 km	W,E	1:29:29.2	Karolina Szabó	HUN	22 Apr 88	Budapest
	C,A,N	1:42:36.9 #	Eleanor Adams/Robinson	Eng	16 Oct 82	London (He)
30 km	W,E	1:47:05.6	Karolina Szabó	HUN	22 Apr 88	Budapest
	C,A,N	2:03:53.0 #	Eleanor Adams/Robinson	Eng	16 Oct 82	London (He)
Half Marathon	W,E	67:59	Uta Pippig	GER	20 Mar 94	Kyoto
	C,A,N	68:42	Liz McColgan	Sco	11 Oct 92	Dundee
Distance unverified		66:40	Ingrid Kristiansen	NOR	5 Apr 87	Sandnes
Downhill (.16%)		67:11	Liz McColgan	Sco	26 Jan 92	Tokyo
	WJ	69:05	Delilah Asiago	KEN	5 May 91	Exeter
	NJ	77:52 #	Kathy Williams		28 Mar 82	Barry
		78:00	Karen Whapshott/Downer		4 Apr 82	Fleet
Marathon	W,E,A	2:21:06	Ingrid Kristiansen	NOR	21 Apr 85	London
	C	2:23:51	Lisa Martin/Ondieki	AUS	31 Jan 88	Osaka
	N	2:25:56	Véronique Marot		23 Apr 89	London
	WJ	2:30:15	Gu Dongmei	CHN	4 Apr 93	Tianjin
	NJ	2:58:58	Tracy Howard		9 May 82	London
2km St	W,E	6:11.84	Marina Pluzhnikova	RUS	25 Jul 94	St. Petersburg
	C,A,N	7:04.7mx&	Sally Young	Eng	14 Jul 93	Sutton
		7:13.3 (2'6")	Sally Young		11 Aug 93	Watford
	NJ	7:52.8 (2'6")	Victoria Wilkinson		25 Sep 93	Leeds
100mH	W,E	12.21	Yordanka Donkova	BUL	20 Aug 88	Stara Zagora
	C	12.78 A	Julie Rocheleau/Baumann	CAN	21 May 88	Provo
	A	12.51	Ginka Zagorcheva	BUL	12 Sep 86	London (CP)
	N	12.82	Sally Gunnell		17 Aug 88	Zürich
	WJ	12.84	Aliuska López	CUB	16 Jul 87	Zagreb

18

Event	Cat	Mark		Athlete	Country	Date	Place
100mH	EJ	13.00	#	Gloria Kowarik	GER	16 Jun 83	Chemnitz
		13.00	#	Lyudmila Kristosenko	UKR	16 Jul 85	Krasnodar
		13.10		Monique Ewanje-Epée	FRA	23 Aug 85	Cottbus
		13.10		Heike Tillack	GER	18 Jul 86	Athens
	NJ	13.25		Diane Allahgreen		21 Jul 94	Lisbon
400mH	W,E,C,N	52.74		Sally Gunnell	Eng	19 Aug 93	Stuttgart
	A	53.69		Sandra Farmer-Patrick	USA	10 Sep 93	London (CP)
	WJ	55.20		Leslie Maxie	USA	9 Jun 84	San Jose
	EJ	55.53	#	Radostina Shtereva	BUL	21 Jul 84	Potsdam
		55.62		Radostina Shtereva	BUL	20 May 84	Sofia
	NJ	58.02		Vyvyan Rhodes		28 Jun 92	Birmingham
High Jump	W,E	2.09		Stefka Kostadinova	BUL	30 Aug 87	Rome
	C	1.99	i	Debbie Brill	CAN	23 Jan 82	Edmonton
		1.98		Debbie Brill	CAN	2 Sep 84	Rieti
		1.98		Vanessa Ward	AUS	12 Feb 89	Perth
		1.98		Alison Inverarity	AUS	17 Jul 94	Ingolstadt
	A	2.03		Ulrike Meyfarth	GER	21 Aug 83	London (CP)
		2.03		Tamara Bykova	RUS	21 Aug 83	London (CP)
	N	1.95		Diana Elliott/Davies		26 Jun 82	Oslo
	WJ,EJ	2.01	#	Olga Turchak	KAZ	7 Jul 86	Moscow
		2.01		Heike Balck	GER	18 Jun 89	Chemnitz
	NJ	1.91		Lea Haggett		2 Jun 91	Khaniá
Pole Vault	W	4.11	#	Sun Caiyun	CHN	21 Mar 93	Guangzhou
		4.05		Sun Caiyun	CHN	21 May 92	Nanjing
	E	4.08	i	Nicole Rieger	GER	1 Mar 94	Karlsruhe
		4.01	&	Marina Andreyeva	RUS	18 Jun 94	Voronezh
	C,N	3.65		Kate Staples	Eng	11 Jun 94	Sheffield
	A	3.70		Caroline Ammel	FRA	4 Sep 94	Southampton
	WJ	4.05		Sun Caiyun	CHN	21 May 92	Nanjing
	EJ	3.90	&	Nicole Rieger	GER	21 Jul 91	Berlin
	NJ	3.44	&	Clare Ridgley		10 Sep 94	Holzminden
		3.40		Clare Ridgley		2 Jul 94	Bedford
Long Jump	W,E	7.52		Galina Chistyakova	RUS	11 Jun 88	St. Petersburg
	C,N	6.90		Beverly Kinch	Eng	14 Aug 83	Helsinki
	A	7.14		Galina Chistyakova	RUS	24 Jun 89	Birmingham
	WJ,EJ	7.14	#	Heike Daute/Drechsler	GER	4 Jun 83	Bratislava
		6.98		Heike Daute/Drechsler	GER	18 Aug 82	Potsdam
	NJ	6.90		Beverly Kinch		14 Aug 83	Helsinki
Triple Jump	W,E	15.09		Anna Biryukova	RUS	21 Aug 93	Stuttgart
	C,N	14.22	#	Ashia Hansen	Eng	29 Aug 94	Welwyn
		14.09		Ashia Hansen		17 Sep 94	Bedford
	A	14.70		Anna Biryukova	RUS	4 Sep 94	Sheffield
	WJ	14.36		Ren Ruiping	CHN	1 Jun 94	Beijing
	EJ	14.32		Yelena Lysak	RUS	18 Jun 94	Voronezh
	NJ	13.05		Michelle Griffith		16 Jun 90	London (CP)
Shot	W,E	22.63		Natalya Lisovskaya	RUS	6 Jun 87	Moscow
	C	19.74		Gael Mulhall/Martin	AUS	14 Jul 84	Berkeley
	A	21.95		Natalya Lisovskaya	RUS	29 Jul 88	Edinburgh
	N	19.36		Judy Oakes		14 Aug 88	Gateshead
	WJ,EJ	20.54		Astrid Kumbernuss	GER	1 Jul 89	Orimattila
	NJ	17.10		Myrtle Augee		16 Jun 84	London (CP)
Discus	W,E	76.80		Gabriele Reinsch	GER	9 Jul 88	Neubrandenburg
	C	68.72		Daniele Costian	AUS	22 Jan 94	Auckland
	A	73.04		Ilke Wyludda	GER	5 Aug 89	Gateshead
	N	67.48		Meg Ritchie		26 Apr 81	Walnut
	WJ,EJ	74.40		Ilke Wyludda	GER	13 Sep 88	Berlin
	NJ	54.78		Lynda Whiteley		4 Oct 82	Brisbane

Hammer	W,E	67.34	#	Svetlana Sudak	BLR	4 Jun 94	Minsk
		66.84		Olga Kuzenkova	RUS	23 Feb 94	Adler
	C	62.38	&	Debbie Sosimenko	AUS	19 Feb 94	Melbourne
	A,N	59.92	&	Lorraine Shaw		2 Apr 94	London (Col)
		59.58		Lorraine Shaw		11 Jun 94	Sheffield
	WJ,EJ	65.48		Mihaela Melinte	ROM	26 Feb 94	Bucharest
	NJ	55.44	&	Lyn Sprules		19 Jul 94	Haslemere
		54.48		Lyn Sprules		2 Jul 94	Bedford
Javelin	W,E	80.00		Petra Felke	GER	8 Sep 88	Potsdam
	C,N	77.44		Fatima Whitbread	Eng	28 Aug 86	Stuttgart
	A	75.62		Fatima Whitbread		25 May 87	Derby
	WJ,EJ	71.88		Antoaneta Todorova	BUL	15 Aug 81	Zagreb
	NJ	60.14		Fatima Whitbread		7 May 80	Grays
Hept.	W	7291		Jackie Joyner-Kersee	USA	24 Sep 88	Seoul
	E	7007		Larisa Nikitina	RUS	11 Jun 89	Bryansk
	C	6695		Jane Flemming	AUS	28 Jan 90	Auckland
	A	6419		Birgit Clarius	GER	21 Jul 91	Sheffield
	N	6623		Judy Simpson		30 Aug 86	Stuttgart
	WJ,EJ	6465		Sybille Thiele	GER	28 Aug 83	Schwechat
	NJ	5833		Joanne Mulliner		11 Aug 85	Lons-le-Saunier
4x100m	W,E	41.37		East Germany		6 Oct 85	Canberra
	C	41.94		Jamaica		1 Sep 91	Tokyo
		41.94		Jamaica		22 Aug 93	Stuttgart
	A	41.87		East Germany		5 Aug 89	Gateshead
	N	42.43		UK National Team		1 Aug 80	Moscow
	WJ,EJ	43.33	#	East Germany		20 Jul 88	Berlin
		43.48		East Germany		31 Jul 88	Sudbury
	NJ	44.16		UK National Team		12 Aug 90	Plovdiv
4x200m	W,E	1:28.15		East Germany		9 Aug 80	Jena
	C,N	1:31.57		UK National Team	Eng	20 Aug 77	London (CP)
	A	1:31.49		Russia		5 Jun 93	Portsmouth
	NJ	1:42.2		London Olympiades AC		19 Aug 72	Bracknell
4x400m	W,E	3:15.17		U.S.S.R.		1 Oct 88	Seoul
	C	3:21.21		Canada		11 Aug 84	Los Angeles
	A	3:20.79		Czechoslovakia		21 Aug 83	London (CP)
	N	3:22.01		UK National Team		1 Sep 91	Tokyo
	WJ,EJ	3:28.39		East Germany		31 Jul 88	Sudbury
	NJ	3:35.10		UK National Team		25 Aug 85	Cottbus
4x800m	W,E	7:50.17		U.S.S.R.		5 Aug 84	Moscow
	C	8:20.73		UK National Team	Eng	5 Jun 93	Portsmouth
	A	7:57.08		Russia		5 Jun 93	Portsmouth
	N	8:19.9	m	UK National Team		5 Jun 92	Sheffield
	NJ	8:53.1		Havering AC		24 May 80	Birmingham
4x1500m	W	17:18.10	#	Villanova Univ	USA/IRE	27 Apr 90	Philadelphia
	(W),E	17:22.30		Providence Univ	IRE	26 Apr 91	Philadelphia
	N	18:16.2		Cambridge & Oxford Univs		27 Apr 90	Philadelphia
4x1mile	WECAN	19:17.3		BMC National Squad	Eng	10 Jul 93	Oxford

Track Walking

1500 m	W,C	5:50.51		Kerry Junna-Saxby	AUS	20 Jun 91	Sydney
	E	5:53.0		Sada Eidikyte	LIT	12 May 90	Vilnius
	A	6:04.5	i	Beate Anders/Gummelt	GER	4 Mar 90	Glasgow
1 Mile	W, E	6:16.72	i	Sada Eidikyte	LIT	12 May 90	Vilnius
		6:19.39		Ileana Salvador	ITA	15 Jun 91	Siderno
	C	6:47.9		Sue Cook	AUS	14 Mar 81	Canberra

1 Mile	A	6:30.7	i	Beate Anders/Gummelt	GER	4 Mar 90	Glasgow
	(A),N	7:14.3		Carol Tyson		17 Sep 77	London (PH)
	NJ	7:31.6		Kate Horwill		22 Aug 93	Solihull
3000 m	W,E	11:44.00	i	Alina Ivanova	RUS	7 Feb 92	Moscow
		11:48.24		Ileana Salvador	ITA	29 Aug 93	Padua
	C	11:51.26		Kerry Junna-Saxby	AUS	7 Feb 91	Melbourne
	A	12:32.37		Yelena Nikolayeva	RUS	19 Jun 88	Portsmouth
	N	12:49.16		Betty Sworowski		28 Jul 90	Wrexham
	WJ,EJ	12:29.98	i	Susana Feitór	POR	6 Mar 93	Braga
	WJ	12:39.1		Wang Yan	CHN	30 Mar 86	Beijing
	EJ	12:53.61	+	Oksana Shchastnaya	RUS	7 Aug 87	Birmingham
	NJ	13:03.4		Vicky Lupton		18 May 91	Sheffield
5000 m	W,E	20:07.52	#	Beate Anders/Gummelt	GER	23 Jun 90	Rostock
	(W),C	20:17.19		Kerry Junna-Saxby	AUS	14 Jan 90	Sydney
	(E)	20:28.62	&	Sari Essayah	FIN	9 Jul 94	Tuusula
		20:50.03		Ileana Salvador	ITA	6 Sep 89	Macerata
	A	21:08.65		Yelena Nikolayeva	RUS	19 Jun 88	Portsmouth
	N	21:57.68	#	Lisa Langford		25 Jun 90	Antrim
		22:02.06		Betty Sworowski		28 Aug 89	Gateshead
	WJ	20:37.7		Jin Bingjie	CHN	3 Mar 90	Hefei
	EJ	21:01.8		Susana Feitór	POR	8 May 93	Fana
	NJ	22:36.81		Vicky Lupton		15 Jun 91	Espoo
10 km	W,E	41:56.23		Nadezhda Ryashkina	UKR	24 Jul 90	Seattle
	C	41:57.22		Kerry Junna-Saxby	AUS	24 Jul 90	Seattle
	A	45:47.0		Sue Cook	AUS	14 Sep 83	Leicester
	N	45:53.9		Julie Drake		26 May 90	Fana
	WJ	42:55.38		Cui Yingzi	CHN	27 Sep 91	Tangshan
	EJ	46:28.6		Flyura Akhmetzhanova	RUS	13 Oct 85	Alushta
	NJ	47:04		Vicky Lupton		30 Mar 91	Sheffield
1 Hour	W	12,771 m		Victoria Herazo	USA	20 Oct 91	Cambridge, Mass
	E	12,644 m		Giuliana Salce	ITA	25 Apr 86	Ostia
	C	12,555 m		Sue Cook	AUS	29 Jun 85	Canberra
	A,N,NJ	11,590 m		Lisa Langford		13 Sep 86	Woodford
20 km	W,E	1:35:29.5		Madeleine Svensson	SWE	10 Jul 91	Borås
	C,N	1:58:37.8		Margaret Lewis	Eng	15 Sep 71	Sotteville
	WJ	1:48:18.6		Sue Liers/Westerfield	USA	20 Mar 77	Kings Point
50 km	W,E	5:13:49.8		Zofia Turosz	POL	13 Oct 85	Warsaw
	C,N	5:26:59		Sandra Brown	Eng	27 Oct 90	Etrechy

Road Walking - Fastest Recorded Times

3000 m	W,E	12:13	Yelena Nikolayeva	RUS	8 May 88	Søfteland
	C	12:16	Kerry Junna-Saxby	AUS	23 Sep 87	Bad Salzdetfurth
	A,N	13:11	Lisa Langford		20 May 90	Romford
	NJ	13:49	Gillian Edgar		31 May 81	Søfteland
5000 m	W,C	20:25	Kerry Junna-Saxby	AUS	10 Jun 89	Hildesheim
	E	20:26	Ileana Salvador	ITA	5 Apr 92	Barcelona
	A,N	21:36	Vicky Lupton		18 Jul 92	Sheffield
	WJ,EJ	21:46	Tatyana Shchastnaya	RUS	29 Jul 90	Moscow
	NJ	22:43	Vicky Lupton		29 Jun 91	Örnsköldsvik
10 km	W,E	41:29.4	Ileana Salvador	ITA	10 Jul 93	Livorno
	C	41:29.8	Kerry Junna-Saxby	AUS	27 Aug 88	Canberra
	A	43:27	Graciella Mendoza	MEX	8 Oct 89	Hull
	N	45:28	Vicky Lupton		10 Jul 93	Livorno
	WJ	41:57	Gao Hongmiao	CHN	8 Sep 93	Beijing
	EJ	43:30	Susana Feitór	POR	15 Jan 94	Grandola
	NJ	47:30	Vicky Lupton		17 Mar 91	Sheffield
20 km	W,C	1:29:40	Kerry Junna-Saxby	AUS	13 May 88	Värnamo

	E	1:30:42	Olga Kardopoltseva	BLR	29 Apr 90	Kaliningrad
	A,N	1:40:45	Irene Bateman		9 Apr 83	Basildon
	WJ,EJ	1:34:31	Tatyana Titova	RUS	4 Oct 87	Alushta
	NJ	1:52:03	Vicky Lupton		13 Oct 91	Sheffield
50 km	WECAN	4:50:51	Sandra Brown	Eng	13 Jul 91	Basildon

RECORDS set in 1994

100 m	E	10.77		Irina Privalova	RUS	6 Jul 94	Lausanne
	C	10.78		Merlene Ottey	JAM	3 Sep 94	Paris
200 m	A	22.23		Merlene Ottey	JAM	9 Sep 94	London (CP)
2000 m	W,E,A	5:25.36		Sonia O'Sullivan	IRE	8 Jul 94	Edinburgh
	C,N	5:26.93		Yvonne Murray	Sco	8 Jul 94	Edinburgh
3000 m	E,A	8:21.64		Sonia O'Sullivan	IRE	15 Jul 94	London (CP)
	EJ	8:40.08		Gabriele Szabo	ROM	10 Aug 94	Helsinki
10 km	C,A	30:52.51		Elana Meyer	RSA	10 Sep 94	London (CP)
H. Mar	W,E	67:59		Uta Pippig	GER	20 Mar 94	Kyoto
100mH	NJ	13.25		Diane Allahgreen		21 Jul 94	Lisbon
2k St.	W,E	6:11.84		Marina Pluzhnikova	RUS	25 Jul 94	St. Petersburg
High J	C	1.98		Alison Inverarity	AUS	17 Jul 94	Ingolstadt
Pole	C,A,N	3.61	#	Kate Staples	Eng	30 May 94	Corby
Vault	E	3.96	&	Nicole Rieger	GER	2 Jun 94	Bad Bergzabern
	E	3.96	&	Andrea Müller	GER	5 Jun 94	Worms
	NJ	3.30	#	Clare Ridgley		11 Jun 94	Sheffield
	C,A,N	3.65		Kate Staples	Eng	11 Jun 94	Sheffield
	E	4.00	&	Nicole Rieger	GER	12 Jun 94	Duisberg
	E	4.01	&	Marina Andreyeva	RUS	18 Jun 94	Voronezh
	NJ	3.35	#	Clare Ridgley		25 Jun 94	London (CP)
	NJ	3.40		Clare Ridgley		2 Jul 94	Bedford
	NJ	3.41	&	Clare Ridgley		10 Jul 94	Southampton
	A	3.70		Caroline Ammel	FRA	4 Sep 94	Southampton
	NJ	3.44	&	Clare Ridgley		10 Sep 94	Holzminden
Triple	WJ	14.36		Ren Ruiping	CHN	1 Jun 94	Beijing
Jump	C,N	13.87		Michelle Griffith	Eng	11 Jun 94	Sheffield
	C,N	14.08		Michelle Griffith	Eng	11 Jun 94	Sheffield
	EJ	14.32		Yelena Lysak	RUS	18 Jun 94	Voronezh
	C,N	14.22	#	Ashia Hansen	Eng	29 Aug 94	Welwyn
	A	14.70		Anna Biryukova	RUS	4 Sep 94	Sheffield
	C,N	14.09		Ashia Hansen		17 Sep 94	Bedford
Discus	C	68.72		Daniele Costian	AUS	22 Jan 94	Auckland
Hammer	C	60.30		Debbie Sosimenko	AUS	29 Jan 94	Sydney
	C	61.46		Debbie Sosimenko	AUS	12 Feb 94	Sydney
	W,E	66.84		Olga Kuzenkova	RUS	23 Feb 94	Adler
	C	62.38	&	Debbie Sosimenko	AUS	19 Feb 94	Melbourne
	WJ,EJ	65.48		Mihaela Melinte	ROM	26 Feb 94	Bucharest
	A,N	59.92	&	Lorraine Shaw		2 Apr 94	London (Col)
	NJ	52.28	#	Lyn Sprules		18 May 94	Guildford
	W,E	67.34	#	Svetlana Sudak	BLR	4 Jun 94	Minsk
	A,N	59.58		Lorraine Shaw		11 Jun 94	Sheffield
	NJ	53.92	#	Lyn Sprules		25 Jun 94	London (CP)
	NJ	54.48		Lyn Sprules		2 Jul 94	Bedford
	NJ	55.44	&	Lyn Sprules		19 Jul 94	Haslemere
5000 mW	E	20:34.76	&	Sari Essayah	FIN	3 Jul 94	Kokemäki
Track	E	20:28.62	&	Sari Essayah	FIN	9 Jul 94	Tuusula
10 kmW Road	EJ	43:30		Susana Feitór	POR	15 Jan 94	Grandola

NATIONAL RECORDS OF THE UNITED KINGDOM (MEN)

(as at 31 Dec 94)

These are the best authentic performances for the four countries of the U.K.
E = England S = Scotland W = Wales NI = Northern Ireland

100 m	E	9.87		Linford Christie	15 Aug 93	Stuttgart, GER
	S	10.11		Allan Wells	24 Jul 80	Moscow, RUS
	W	10.29		Colin Jackson	28 Jul 90	Wrexham
	NI	10.46		Mark Forsythe	17 Jun 89	Tel Aviv, ISR
200 m	E	19.87	A&	John Regis	31 Jul 94	Sestriere, ITA
		19.94		John Regis	20 Aug 93	Stuttgart, GER
	S	20.21		Allan Wells	28 Jul 80	Moscow, RUS
	NI	20.81		Paul McBurney	24 Aug 94	Victoria, CAN
	W	20.84		Jamie Baulch	24 Aug 94	Victoria, CAN
300 m	E	31.67		John Regis	17 Jul 92	Gateshead
	S	32.44		David Jenkins	4 Jul 75	London (CP)
	NI	33.77		Simon Baird	24 Jun 85	Belfast
	W	34.4		Jeff Griffiths	2 Jul 80	Cwmbrân
		34.57	i	Gareth Davies	20 Feb 93	Birmingham
400 m	E	44.47		David Grindley	3 Aug 92	Barcelona, SPA
	S	44.93		David Jenkins	21 Jun 75	Eugene, USA
	W	45.98		Iwan Thomas	23 Aug 94	Victoria, CAN
	NI	46.49		Paul McBurney	22 Aug 94	Victoria, CAN
600 m	E	1:14.95		Steve Heard	14 Jul 91	London (Ha)
	S	1:15.4		Tom McKean	21 Jul 91	Grangemouth
	W	1:18.02		Glen Grant	2 Aug 78	Edmonton, CAN
	NI	1:18.3	i	Joe Chivers	14 Dec 74	Cosford
		1:20.1		Kenneth Thompson	24 May 80	Belfast
800 m	E	1:41.73	"	Sebastian Coe	10 Jun 81	Florence, ITA
	S	1:43.88		Tom McKean	28 Jul 89	London (CP)
	W	1:45.44		Neil Horsfield	28 Jul 90	Wrexham
	NI	1:46.94		Mark Kirk	20 Jul 87	Belfast
1000 m	E	2:12.18		Sebastian Coe	11 Jul 81	Oslo, NOR
	S	2:16.82		Graham Williamson	17 Jul 84	Edinburgh
	W	2:17.36		Neil Horsfield	9 Aug 91	Gateshead
	NI	2:19.05		Mark Kirk	5 Aug 87	Oslo, NOR
1500 m	E	3:29.67		Steve Cram	16 Jul 85	Nice, FRA
	S	3:33.83		John Robson	4 Sep 79	Brussels, BEL
	W	3:35.08		Neil Horsfield	10 Aug 90	Brussels, BEL
	NI	3:35.83		Gary Lough	15 Jul 94	London (CP)
1 Mile	E	3:46.32		Steve Cram	27 Jul 85	Oslo, NOR
	S	3:50.64		Graham Williamson	13 Jul 82	Cork, IRE
	W	3:54.29		Neil Horsfield	8 Jul 86	Cork, IRE
	NI	3:55.0		Jim McGuinness	11 Jul 77	Dublin (B), IRE
2000 m	E	4:51.39		Steve Cram	4 Aug 85	Budapest, HUN
	S	4:58.38		Graham Williamson	29 Aug 83	London (CP)
	NI	5:02.61		Steve Martin	19 Jun 84	Belfast
	W	5:05.32		Tony Simmons	4 Jul 75	London (CP)
3000 m	E	7:32.79		Dave Moorcroft	17 Jul 82	London (CP)
	S	7:45.81		John Robson	13 Jul 84	London (CP)
	W	7:46.40		Ian Hamer	20 Jan 90	Auckland, NZ
	NI	7:49.1		Paul Lawther	27 Jun 78	Oslo, NOR

2 Miles	E	8:13.51	Steve Ovett	15 Sep 78	London (CP)
	S	8:19.37	Nat Muir	27 Jun 80	London (CP)
	W	8:20.28	David James	27 Jun 80	London (CP)
	NI	8:30.6	Paul Lawther	28 May 77	Belfast
5000 m	E	13:00.41	Dave Moorcroft	7 Jul 82	Oslo, NOR
	W	13:09.80	Ian Hamer	9 Jun 92	Rome, ITA
	S	13:17.9	Nat Muir	15 Jul 80	Oslo, NOR
	NI	13:39.11	Terry Greene	31 Jul 86	Edinburgh
10 km	E	27:23.06	Eamonn Martin	2 Jul 88	Oslo, NOR
	W	27:39.14	Steve Jones	9 Jul 83	Oslo, NOR
	S	27:43.03	Ian Stewart	9 Sep 77	London (CP)
	NI	28:40.03	John McLaughlin	29 May 83	Edinburgh
20 km	E	57:28.7	Carl Thackery	31 Mar 90	La Flèche, FRA
	S	59:24.0	Jim Alder	9 Nov 68	Leicester
1 Hour	E	20,855 m	Carl Thackery	31 Mar 90	La Flèche, FRA
	S	20,201 m	Jim Alder	9 Nov 68	Leicester
	W	18,587 m	Malcolm Edwards	15 Sep 89	Westhofen, GER
25 km	E	1:15:22.6	Ron Hill	21 Jul 65	Bolton
	S	1:15:34.3	Jim Alder	5 Sep 70	London (CP)
30 km	S	1:31:30.4	Jim Alder	5 Sep 70	London (CP)
	E	1:31:56.4	Tim Johnston	5 Sep 70	London (CP)
	W	1:33:49.0	Bernie Plain	1 Dec 73	Bristol
Half	W	1:00:59	Steve Jones	8 Jun 86	Tyneside
Marathon	E	1:01:03	Nick Rose	18 Sep 85	Philadelphia, USA
	NI	1:02:16	Jim Haughey	20 Sep 87	Philadelphia, USA
	S	1:02:19 #	Mike Carroll	3 Jun 90	Irvine
		1:02:28	Allister Hutton	21 Jun 87	Tyneside
Marathon	W	2:07:13	Steve Jones	20 Oct 85	Chicago, USA
	E	2:08:33	Charlie Spedding	21 Apr 85	London
	S	2:09:18	Allister Hutton	21 Apr 85	London
	NI	2:13:06	Greg Hannon	13 May 79	Coventry
2km St	E	5:19.86	Mark Rowland	28 Aug 88	London (CP)
	S	5:21.77	Tom Hanlon	11 Jun 92	Caserta, ITA
	W	5:23.6	Roger Hackney	10 Jun 82	Birmingham
	NI	5:31.09	Peter McColgan	5 Aug 86	Gateshead
3km St	E	8:07.96	Mark Rowland	30 Sep 88	Seoul, SKO
	S	8:12.58	Tom Hanlon	3 Aug 91	Monaco, MON
	W	8:18.91	Roger Hackney	31 Jul 88	Hechtel, BEL
	NI	8:27.93	Peter McColgan	25 Jun 91	Hengelo, HOL
110m H	W	12.91	Colin Jackson	20 Aug 93	Stuttgart, GER
	E	13.00	Tony Jarrett	20 Aug 93	Stuttgart, GER
	S	13.86	Kenneth Campbell	23 Aug 94	Victoria, CAN
	NI	14.19	C.J. Kirkpatrick	16 Jun 73	Edinburgh
200m H	W	22.63	Colin Jackson	1 Jun 91	Cardiff
	E	22.79	John Regis	1 Jun 91	Cardiff
	S	23.76	Angus McKenzie	22 Aug 81	Edinburgh
	NI	24.81	Terry Price	31 Aug 92	Belfast
400m H	E	47.82	Kriss Akabusi	6 Aug 92	Barcelona, SPA
	NI	49.60	Phil Beattie	28 Jul 86	Edinburgh
	W	50.01	Phil Harries	5 Jun 88	Derby
	S	50.79	Mark Davidson	18 Jun 89	Sittard, HOL

High	E	2.38	i	Steve Smith	4 Feb 94	Wuppertal, GER
Jump		2.37		Steve Smith	20 Sep 92	Seoul, SKO
		2.37		Steve Smith	22 Aug 93	Stuttgart, GER
	S	2.31		Geoff Parsons	26 Aug 94	Victoria, CAN
	W	2.24		John Hill	23 Aug 85	Cottbus, GER
	NI	2.20		Floyd Manderson	14 Jul 85	London (CP)
		2.20		Floyd Manderson	21 Jun 86	London (CP)
		2.20		Floyd Manderson	16 Aug 86	Leiden, HOL
Pole	E	5.65		Keith Stock	7 Jul 81	Stockholm, SWE
Vault	W	5.50		Neil Winter	9 Aug 92	San Giuliano, ITA
		5.50		Neil Winter	6 Aug 94	Crawley
	NI	5.25		Mike Bull	22 Sep 73	London (CP)
	S	5.21		Graham Eggleton	10 Jul 82	Grangemouth
Long	W	8.23		Lynn Davies	30 Jun 68	Berne, SWZ
Jump	E	8.15		Stewart Faulkner	16 Jul 90	Belfast
	NI	8.14		Mark Forsythe	7 Jul 91	Rhede, GER
	S	7.67		David Walker	14 Sep 68	Portsmouth
Triple	E	17.57	A	Keith Connor	5 Jun 82	Provo, USA
Jump		17.44		Jon Edwards	16 Aug 93	Stuttgart, GER
	S	16.17		John Mackenzie	17 Sep 94	Bedford
	W	15.90		David Wood	16 Sep 84	Karlovac, CRO
	NI	15.78		Michael McDonald	31 Jul 94	Corby
Shot	E	21.68		Geoff Capes	18 May 80	Cwmbrân
	W	20.33	&	Paul Edwards	9 Jul 91	Roehampton
		19.85		Paul Edwards	2 Jul 89	Walton
	S	18.93		Paul Buxton	13 May 77	Los Angeles, USA
	NI	16.35		Michael Atkinson	18 Jul 81	Dublin (B), IRE
		16.35		John Reynolds	16 Aug 86	Leiden, HOL
Discus	E	65.16	#	Richard Slaney	1 Jul 85	Eugene, USA
		64.32		Bill Tancred	10 Aug 74	Woodford
	S	59.84	#	¶Colin Sutherland	10 Jun 78	San Jose, USA
		58.58		Darrin Morris	22 Jun 91	Enfield
	W	57.12		Paul Edwards	10 Aug 88	London (Col)
	NI	50.44		John Moreland	18 Jun 94	Antrim
Hammer	NI	77.54		Martin Girvan	12 May 84	Wolverhampton
	E	77.30		David Smith	13 Jul 85	London (CP)
	S	75.40		Chris Black	23 Jul 83	London (CP)
	W	68.64		Shaun Pickering	7 Apr 84	Stanford, USA
Javelin	E	91.46		Steve Backley	25 Jan 92	Auckland, NZ
	W	81.70		Nigel Bevan	28 Jun 92	Birmingham
	NI	70.34		Damien Crawford	20 Jul 91	Hayes
	S	69.20		Roddy James	28 Apr 89	Des Moines, USA
Decathlon	E	8847		Daley Thompson	9 Aug 84	Los Angeles, USA
	S	7885	h	Brad McStravick	6 May 84	Birmingham
		7856		Brad McStravick	28 May 84	Cwmbrân
	NI	7874		Colin Boreham	23 May 82	Götzis, AUT
	W	7308	h	Clive Longe	29 Jun 69	Kassel, GER
		7268		Paul Edwards	14 Aug 83	Bonn, GER
4x100m	E	37.98		D. Braithwaite, J. Regis, M. Adam, L. Christie (UK)	1 Sep 90	Split, CRO
	S	39.24		D. Jenkins, A. Wells, C. Sharp, A. McMaster	12 Aug 78	Edmonton, CAN
	W	40.0	ay	T. Davies, L. Davies, K. Jones, R. Jones	13 Aug 66	Kingston, JAM

4x100m	NI	40.8	M. Bull, G. Carson,			
			J. Chivers, J. Kilpatrick	13 Jun 70	Edinburgh
		40.94	D. Marrs, S. Baird,			
			N. Watson, M. Forsythe	19 Jul 88	Tarragona, SPA
4x400m	E	2:57.53	R. Black, D. Redmond,			
			J. Regis, K. Akabusi (UK)	1 Sep 91	Tokyo, JAP
	W	3:03.68	P. Maitland, J. Baulch,			
			P.Gray, I.Thomas	27 Aug 94	Victoria, CAN
	S	3:04.68	M. Davison, T. McKean,			
			D. Strang, B. Whittle	3 Feb 90	Auckland, NZ
	NI	3:11.81	??, ??,			
			??, ??	1 Sep 85	Tel Aviv, ISR

Track Walking

3000 m	E	11:24.4		Mark Easton	10 May 89	Tonbridge
	W	11:45.77		Steve Johnson	28 Jun 87	Cwmbrân
	S	11:54.96	i	Martin Bell	13 Feb 93	Birmingham
		12:04.6		Martin Bell	16 Jul 88	Barry
	NI	13:35.6		Arthur Agnew	18 Jun 77	Belfast
5000 m	E	19:22.29	i	Martin Rush	8 Feb 92	Birmingham
		19:35.0		Darrell Stone	16 May 89	Brighton
	W	20:08.04	i	Steve Barry	5 Mar 83	Budapest, HUN
		20:22.0		Steve Barry	20 Mar 82	London (WL)
	S	20:13.0		Martin Bell	2 May 92	Enfield
	NI	25:06.2		G. Smyth	13 Jul 80	London (He)
10 km	E	40:06.65		Ian McCombie	4 Jun 89	Jarrow
	W	41:13.62		Steve Barry	19 Jun 82	London (CP)
	S	42:07.42		Martin Bell	28 Jun 92	Corby
	NI	48:42.41		Stephen Murphy	31 Jul 83	Edinburgh
20 km	E	1:23:26.5		Ian McCombie	26 May 90	Fana, NOR
	W	1:26:22.0		Steve Barry	28 Jun 81	Brighton
	S	1:44:37.0		Derek Howie	19 Aug 78	Brighton
30 km	E	2:11:54	#	Chris Maddocks	31 Dec 89	Plymouth
		2:19:18		Chris Maddocks	22 Sep 84	Birmingham
50 km	E	4:05:44.6		Paul Blagg	26 May 90	Fana, NOR
1 Hour	E	14,324 m	#	Ian McCombie	7 Jul 85	London (SP)
		14,158 m		Mark Easton	12 Sep 87	Woodford
	W	13,987 m		Steve Barry	28 Jun 81	Brighton
	S	13,393 m		Bill Sutherland	27 Sep 69	London (He)
2 Hours	E	27,262 m	#	Chris Maddocks	31 Dec 89	Plymouth
		26,037 m		Ron Wallwork	31 Jul 71	Blackburn

Road Walking

10 km	E	40:17	Chris Maddocks	30 Apr 89	Burrator
	W	40:35	Steve Barry	14 May 83	Southport
	S	42:08	Martin Bell	4 Mar 89	Kenilworth
	NI	51:53	Arthur Agnew	6 Aug 80	Helsinki, FIN
		51:53	G. Smyth	6 Aug 80	Helsinki, FIN
20 km	E	1:22:03	Ian McCombie	23 Sep 88	Seoul, SKO
	W	1:22:51	Steve Barry	26 Feb 83	Douglas
	S	1:25:42	Martin Bell	9 May 92	Lancaster
	NI	1:47:49	Arthur Agnew	4 Nov 78	Ashbourne, IRE

30 km	E	2:07:56	Ian McCombie	27 Apr 86	Edinburgh
	W	2:10:16	Steve Barry	7 Oct 82	Brisbane, AUS
	S	2:22:21	Martin Bell	8 May 94	Cardiff
50 km	E	3:51:37	Chris Maddocks	28 Oct 90	Burrator
	W	4:11:59	Bob Dobson	22 Oct 81	Lassing, AUT
	S	4:38:39	Bill Sutherland	17 Jul 71	Redditch

NATIONAL RECORDS OF THE UNITED KINGDOM (WOMEN)

100 m	E	11.10	Kathy Smallwood/Cook	5 Sep 81	Rome, ITA
	W	11.39	Sallyanne Short	12 Jul 92	Cwmbrân
	S	11.40	Helen Golden/Hogarth	20 Jul 74	London (CP)
	NI	11.91	Joan Atkinson	1 Sep 61	Sofia, BUL
200 m	E	22.10	Kathy Cook	9 Aug 84	Los Angeles, USA
	W	22.80	Michelle Scutt	12 Jun 82	Antrim
	S	22.98	Sandra Whittaker	8 Aug 84	Los Angeles, USA
	NI	23.62	Linda McCurry	8 Aug 78	Edmonton, CAN
300 m	E	35.46	Kathy Cook	18 Aug 84	London (CP)
	W	36.01	Michelle Probert/Scutt	13 Jul 80	London (CP)
	S	36.46	Linsey Macdonald	13 Jul 80	London (CP)
	NI	38.20	Linda McCurry	2 Aug 78	Edmonton, CAN
400 m	E	49.43	Kathy Cook	6 Aug 84	Los Angeles, USA
	W	50.63	Michelle Scutt	31 May 82	Cwmbrân
	S	51.16	Linsey Macdonald	15 Jun 80	London (CP)
	NI	53.75	Elaine McLaughlin	2 Jul 88	Antrim
		53.75	Elaine McLaughlin	12 Jul 88	Dublin (M), IRE
600 m	E	1:26.18	Diane Edwards/Modahl	22 Aug 87	London (CP)
	W	1:26.5	Kirsty McDermott/Wade	21 Aug 85	Zürich, SWZ
	S	1:27.4 i	Linsey Macdonald	12 Dec 81	Cosford
		1:29.88	Anne Clarkson/Purvis	25 Sep 82	Brisbane, AUS
	NI	1:29.46	Joanna Latimer	19 May 93	Birmingham
800 m	W	1:57.42	Kirsty McDermott/Wade	24 Jun 85	Belfast
	E	1:58.64	Kelly Holmes	15 Aug 93	Stuttgart, GER
	S	2:00.15	Rosemary Stirling/Wright	3 Sep 72	Munich, GER
	NI	2:03.27	Joanna Latimer	29 Jun 94	Helsinki, FIN
1000 m	W	2:33.70	Kirsty McDermott/Wade	9 Aug 85	Gateshead
	E	2:34.92	Christina Boxer/Cahill	9 Aug 85	Gateshead
	S	2:37.05	Chris Whittingham	27 Jun 86	Gateshead
	NI	2:48.59	Jane Ewing	26 Jun 90	Antrim
1500 m	E	3:59.96	Zola Budd	30 Aug 85	Brussels, BEL
	W	4:00.73	Kirsty Wade	26 Jul 87	Gateshead
	S	4:01.20	Yvonne Murray	4 Jul 87	Oslo, NOR
	NI	4:11.46	Ursula McKee/McGloin	20 Jan 90	Auckland, NZ
1 Mile	E	4:17.57	Zola Budd	21 Aug 85	Zürich, SWZ
	W	4:19.41	Kirsty McDermott/Wade	27 Jul 85	Oslo, NOR
	S	4:22.64	Yvonne Murray	22 Jul 94	Oslo, NOR
	NI	4:38.86	Ursula McKee/McGloin	7 Jan 90	Sydney, AUS
2000 m	S	5:26.93	Yvonne Murray	8 Jul 94	Edinburgh
	E	5:30.19	Zola Budd	11 Jul 86	London (CP)
	W	5:45.81 i	Kirsty Wade	13 Mar 87	Cosford
		5:50.17	Susan Tooby/Wightman	13 Jul 84	London (CP)
	NI	5:57.24	Ursula McKee/McGloin	25 Jun 90	Antrim
3000 m	E	8:28.83	Zola Budd	7 Sep 85	Rome, ITA
	S	8:29.02	Yvonne Murray	25 Sep 88	Seoul, SKO

3000 m	W	8:47.59		Angela Tooby	5 Jul 88	Stockholm, SWE
	NI	9:16.25		Ursula McKee/McGloin	7 Jun 90	Helsinki, FIN
5000 m	E	14:48.07		Zola Budd	26 Aug 85	London (CP)
	S	15:01.08		Liz Lynch/McColgan	5 Aug 87	Oslo, NOR
	W	15:13.22		Angela Tooby	5 Aug 87	Oslo, NOR
	NI	17:27.15		Angela McCullagh		
10 km	S	30:57.07		Liz McColgan	25 Jun 91	Hengelo, HOL
	E	31:07.88		Jill Hunter	30 Jun 91	Frankfurt, GER
	W	31:55.30		Angela Tooby	4 Sep 87	Rome, ITA
	NI	41:16.4		Wendy Dyer	Jun 89	Antrim
Half	S	1:07:11		Liz McColgan	26 Jan 92	Tokyo, JAP
Marathon	E	1:09:39		Andrea Wallace	21 Mar 93	Bath
	W	1:09:56		Susan Tooby/Wightman	24 Jul 88	Tyneside
	NI	1:15:57	#	Moira O'Boyle/O'Neill	23 Mar 86	Cavan, IRE
		1:16:23		Moira O'Neill	24 Sep 88	Londonderry
Marathon	E	2:25:56		Véronique Marot	23 Apr 89	London
	S	2:27:32		Liz McColgan	3 Nov 91	New York, USA
	W	2:31:33		Susan Tooby/Wightman	23 Sep 88	Seoul, SKO
	NI	2:37:06		Moira O'Neill	31 Oct 88	Dublin, IRE
100m H	E	12.82		Sally Gunnell	17 Aug 88	Zürich, SWZ
	W	12.91		Kay Morley-Brown	2 Feb 90	Auckland, NZ
	NI	13.29		Mary Peters	2 Sep 72	Munich, GER
	S	13.35		Pat Rollo	30 Jul 83	London (CP)
400m H	E	52.74		Sally Gunnell	19 Aug 93	Stuttgart, GER
	NI	55.91		Elaine McLaughlin	26 Sep 88	Seoul, SKO
	S	57.43		Liz Sutherland	6 Jul 78	Düsseldorf, GER
	W	58.16		Diane Fryar	9 Jul 83	Cwmbrân
High	E	1.95		Diana Elliott/Davies	26 Jun 82	Oslo, NOR
Jump	NI	1.92		Janet Boyle	29 Sep 88	Seoul, SKO
	S	1.91		Jayne Barnetson	7 Jul 89	Edinburgh
	W	1.84		Sarah Rowe	22 Aug 81	Utrecht, HOL
		1.84		Sarah Rowe	31 May 82	Cwmbrân
Pole	E	3.65		Kate Staples	11 Jun 94	Sheffield
Vault	S	2.40		Gail Marshall	24 Apr 93	Grangemouth
		2.40		Katie Fitzgerald	7 Aug 93	Birmingham
	W	2.20		Claudia Filce	16 Sep 89	Stoke
Long	E	6.90		Beverly Kinch	14 Aug 83	Helsinki, FIN
Jump	W	6.52		Gillian Regan	29 Aug 82	Swansea
	S	6.43		Myra Nimmo/McAskill	27 May 73	Edinburgh
	NI	6.11		Thelma Hopkins	29 Sep 56	Budapest, HUN
		6.11		Michelle Rea	11 Aug 90	Oporto, POR
Triple	E	14.22	#	Ashia Hansen	29 Aug 94	Welwyn
Jump		14.09		Ashia Hansen	17 Sep 94	Bedford
	S	12.89		Karen Hambrook/Skeggs	17 May 92	London (CP)
	W	12.10		Jane Falconer	29 Aug 93	Colchester
	NI	11.79		Michelle Rea	16 Jun 91	Grangemouth
Shot	E	19.36		Judy Oakes	14 Aug 88	Gateshead
	S	18.99		Meg Ritchie	7 May 83	Tucson, USA
	W	19.06	i	Venissa Head	7 Apr 84	St. Athan
		18.93		Venissa Head	13 May 84	Haverfordwest
	NI	16.40	i	Mary Peters	28 Feb 70	Bucharest, ROM
		16.31		Mary Peters	1 Jun 66	Belfast
Discus	S	67.48		Meg Ritchie	26 Apr 81	Walnut, USA
	W	64.68		Venissa Head	18 Jul 83	Athens, GRE
	NI	60.72		Jacqui McKernan	18 Jul 93	Buffalo, USA
	E	57.32		Lynda Whiteley/Wright	16 Jun 84	London (CP)

Hammer	E	59.92	Lorraine Shaw	2 Apr 94	London (Col)
	W	50.52	Sarah Moore	21 May 94	Istanbul
	S	49.78	Jean Clark	19 Sep 92	London (Col)
	NI	46.68	Julie Kirkpatrick	8 Aug 93	Wrexham
Javelin	E	77.44	Fatima Whitbread	28 Aug 86	Stuttgart, GER
	S	62.22	Diane Royle	18 May 85	Stretford
	W	59.40	Karen Hough	28 Aug 86	Stuttgart, GER
	NI	47.54	Alison Moffitt	4 Sep 93	Antrim
Hept.	E	6623	Judy Simpson	30 Aug 86	Stuttgart, GER
	S	5803	Jayne Barnetson	20 Aug 89	Kiyev, UKR
	W	5642	Sarah Rowe	23 Aug 81	Utrecht, HOL
	NI	5065 h	Catherine Scott	13 Sep 87	Tullamore, IRE
		4564	Wendy Phillips	18 Jul 82	Birmingham
4x100m	E	42.43	H. Oakes, K. Cook, (UK) B. Callender, S. Lannaman	1 Aug 80	Moscow, RUS
	S	45.2	A. Robb, S. Pringle, (ESH) H. Hogarth, E. Sutherland	27 Jun 70	London (CP)
		45.37	J. Booth, K. Hogg, J. Neilson, S. Whittaker	8 Jun 86	Lloret de Mar, SPA
	W	45.37	H. Miles, S. Lewis, S. Short, C. Smart	2 Aug 86	Edinburgh
	NI	46.36	K. Graham, H. Gourlay, J. Robinson, R. Gaylor	31 Aug 85	Tel Aviv, ISR
4x400m	E	3:22.01	L. Hanson, P. Smith, (UK) S. Gunnell, L. Keough	1 Sep 91	Tokyo, JAP
	S	3:32.92	S. Whittaker, A. Purvis, A. Baxter, L. Macdonald	9 Oct 82	Brisbane, AUS
	W	3:35.60	C. Smart, K. Wade, D. Fryar, M. Scutt	4 Jul 82	Dublin (M), IRE
	NI	3:43.63	S. McPeake, J. Latimer, S. McCann, R. Gaylor	2 Aug 90	Maia, POR

Track Walking

3000 m	E	12:49.16	Betty Sworowski	28 Jul 90	Wrexham
	S	13:31.32 i	Verity Larby/Snook	13 Feb 93	Birmingham
		13:31.5	Verity Larby/Snook	16 May 93	Portsmouth
	W	14:28.2	Karen Dunster	18 May 91	Portsmouth
5000 m	E	21:57.68 &	Lisa Langford	25 Jun 90	Antrim
		22:02.06	Betty Sworowski	28 Aug 89	Gateshead
	S	23:22.52	Verity Larby/Snook	18 Jun 94	Horsham
	W	24:32.92	Karen Nipper	21 Jul 84	Lyngby, DEN
10 km	E	45:53.9	Julie Drake	26 May 90	Fana, NOR
	S	47:10.07	Verity Larby/Snook	20 Jun 93	Horsham
	W	50:25.0	Lisa Simpson	1 Apr 87	Hornchurch
1 Hour	E	11,590 m	Lisa Langford	13 Sep 86	Woodford

Road Walking

5000 m	E	21:36	Vicky Lupton	18 Jul 92	Sheffield
	W	23:35	Lisa Simpson	31 Oct 87	Cardiff
	S	23:52	Verity Larby/Snook	23 Mar 91	London (BP)
10 km	E	45:28	Vicky Lupton	10 Jul 93	Livorno, ITA
	S	46:06	Verity Larby/Snook	25 Aug 94	Victoria, CAN
	W	49:33	Lisa Simpson	14 Mar 87	Ham
20 km	E	1:40:45	Irene Bateman	9 Apr 83	Basildon
50 km	E	4:50:51	Sandra Brown	13 Jul 91	Basildon

BRITISH INDOOR RECORDS
as at March 1995

MEN

50 m	5.76	Selwyn Clarke	19 Feb 83	Dortmund, GER
60 m	6.47	Linford Christie	19 Feb 95	Lieven, FRA
200 m	20.25	Linford Christie	19 Feb 95	Lieven, FRA
300 m	32.90	Ade Mafe	31 Jan 92	Karlsruhe, GER
400 m	45.56	Todd Bennett	3 Mar 85	Piraeus, GRE
800 m	1:44.91	Sebastian Coe	12 Mar 83	Cosford
1000 m	2:17.86	Matthew Yates	22 Feb 92	Birmingham
1500 m	3:34.20	Peter Elliott	27 Feb 90	Seville, SPA
1 mile	3:52.02	Peter Elliott	9 Feb 90	East Rutherford, USA
2000 m	5:05.20	John Gladwin	15 Mar 87	Cosford
3000 m	7:43.90	Rob Denmark	10 Mar 91	Seville, SPA
5000 m	13:21.27	Nick Rose	12 Feb 82	New York, USA
50 m Hurdles	6.48	Colin Jackson	14 Mar 92	Birmingham
60 m Hurdles	7.30	Colin Jackson	6 Mar 94	Sindelfingen, GER
High Jump	2.38	Steve Smith	4 Feb 94	Wuppertal, GER
Pole Vault	5.50 #	Brian Hooper	28 Feb 81	Camborne
	5.45	Brian Hooper	22 Feb 81	Grenoble, FRA
	5.45	Andy Ashurst	16 Feb 92	Birmingham
Long Jump	8.05	Barrington Williams	11 Feb 89	Cosford
	8.05	Stewart Faulkner	27 Feb 90	Seville, SPA
Triple Jump	17.31	Keith Connor	13 Mar 81	Detroit, USA
Shot	20.98	Geoff Capes	16 Jan 76	Los Angeles, USA
	20.98	Geoff Capes	14 Feb 76	Winnipeg, CAN
Heptathlon	5978	Alex Kruger	12 Mar 95	Barcelona, SPA

(7.16, 7.23, 14.79, 2.16, 8.36, 4.90, 2:48.66)

5000m Walk	19:22.29	Martin Rush	8 Feb 92	Birmingham
4 x 200m Relay	1:22.11	UK National Team	3 Mar 91	Glasgow

(Linford Christie, Darren Braithwaite, Ade Mafe, John Regis)

4 x 400m Relay	3:07.04	England	13 Mar 87	Cosford

(Kermitt Bentham, John Regis, Steve Heard, Paul Harmsworth)

WOMEN

50 m	6.21	Wendy Hoyte	22 Feb 81	Grenoble, FRA
60 m	7.13	Beverly Kinch	23 Feb 86	Madrid, SPA
200 m	23.00	Katharine Merry	12 Feb 94	Glasgow
400 m	51.72	Sally Gunnell	6 Mar 94	Sindelfingen, GER
800 m	2:01.12	Jane Colebrook/Finch	13 Mar 77	San Sebastian, SPA
1000 m	2:38.95	Kirsty Wade	1 Feb 87	Stuttgart, GER
1500 m	4:06.87	Zola Budd	25 Jan 86	Cosford
1 mile	4:23.86	Kirsty Wade	5 Feb 88	New York, USA
2000 m	5:40.86	Yvonne Murray	20 Feb 93	Birmingham
3000 m	8:34.80	Liz McColgan	4 Mar 89	Budapest, HUN
5000 m	15:03.17	Liz McColgan	22 Feb 92	Birmingham
50 m Hurdles	7.03	Yvette Wray/Luker	21 Feb 81	Grenoble, FRA
60 m Hurdles	8.01	Jacqui Agyepong	12 Mar 95	Barcelona, SPA
High Jump	1.94	Diana Elliott/Davies	7 Mar 82	Milan, ITA
	1.94	Debbie Marti	3 Feb 91	Cosford
	1.94	Jo Jennings	13 Mar 93	Toronto, CAN
Pole Vault	3.80	Kate Staples	4 Feb 95	Birmingham
Long Jump	6.70	Susan Hearnshaw/Telfer	3 Mar 84	Göteborg, SWE
Triple Jump	14.29	Ashia Hansen	25 Feb 95	Birmingham
Shot	19.06	Venissa Head	7 Apr 84	St. Athan
Pentathlon	4363	Kim Hagger	4 Feb 84	Vittel, FRA

(8.44, 1.82, 11.89, 6.31, 2:27.08)

3000m Walk	13:12.01	Julie Drake	12 Mar 93	Toronto, CAN
4 x 200m Relay	1:33.96	UK National Team	23 Feb 90	Glasgow

(Paula Dunn, Jennifer Stoute, Linda Keough, Sally Gunnell)

4 x 400m Relay	3:35.11	UK National Team	3 Mar 91	Glasgow

(Sandra Douglas, Sally Gunnell, Janet Levermore, Dawn Kitchen)

100 METRES

9.87	Linford Christie	15 Aug 93
10.09	Jason Livingston ¶	13 Jun 92
10.11	Allan Wells	24 Jul 80
10.15	Michael Rosswess	15 Sep 91
10.15	John Regis	29 May 93
10.20	Cameron Sharp	24 Aug 83
10.20	Elliot Bunney	14 Jun 86
10.21 A	Ainsley Bennett	8 Sep 79
10.21	Jamie Henderson	6 Aug 87
10.22	Mike McFarlane	20 Jun 86
10.23	Marcus Adam	26 Jul 91
10.23	Jason John	15 Jul 94
10.23	Terry Williams	22 Aug 94
10.25	Jason Gardener	21 Jul 94
10.26	Daley Thompson	27 Aug 86
10.26	Ernest Obeng	1 Aug 87
	10.21 for Ghana	11 Aug 80
10.28	Darren Braithwaite	3 Aug 90
10.29	Peter Radford (10.31?)	13 Sep 58
10.29	Colin Jackson	28 Jul 90
10.30	Clarence Callender	26 Jul 91
10.32	Buster Watson	1 Jul 83
10.32	Donovan Reid	4 Aug 84
10.32	Lincoln Asquith	11 Aug 86
10.32	Lenny Paul	29 May 93
10.33	Brian Green	15 Jul 72
10.33	Solomon Wariso	19 Jun 94
10.34	Drew McMaster	9 Jul 83
10.34	Barrington Williams	5 Aug 88
10.34	Toby Box	12 Jun 93
10.35 A	Barrie Kelly	13 Oct 68
10.35	Brian Taylor	29 May 93
10.36	David Jenkins	24 Jun 72
10.37	Micky Morris	23 Aug 87
10.37	Steve Gookey	20 Jul 91
10.37	Darren Campbell	26 Jul 91
10.39	Ray Burke	13 Jun 92
10.40	Trevor Hoyte	11 Aug 79
10.40	Jim Evans	24 Jul 82
10.42 A	Ron Jones	13 Oct 68
10.43	Steve Green	5 Jun 80
10.43	Julian Golding	20 Jul 94
10.44	Andy Carrott	25 Aug 89
10.44	Jason Fergus	16 Sep 92
10.44	Tremayne Rutherford	9 Jul 94
10.45	Martin Waldron	26 May 88

hand timing

10.1	David Jenkins	20 May 72
10.1	Brian Green	3 Jun 72
10.1	Ernest Obeng (for GHA)	2 Aug 79
10.2	McDonald Bailey	25 Aug 51
10.2	Menzies Campbell	20 May 67
10.2	Drew McMaster	29 Jun 80
10.2	Ed Cutting	19 May 84
10.2	Derek Redmond	2 May 87

wind assisted

10.02	Allan Wells	4 Oct 82
10.07	Cameron Sharp	4 Oct 82
10.07	John Regis	28 Aug 90
10.07	Toby Box	11 Jun 94
10.07	Michael Rosswess	11 Jun 94
10.08	Mike McFarlane	27 May 84
10.08	Jason John	11 Jun 94
10.10	Donovan Reid	26 Jun 83
10.11	Drew McMaster	26 Jun 83
10.12	Buster Watson	27 May 84
10.14	Ernest Obeng	20 Jun 87
10.14	Marcus Adam	28 Jan 90
10.17	Terry Williams	23 Aug 94
10.20	Lincoln Asquith	6 Jul 85
10.25	Darren Braithwaite	3 Aug 90
10.25	Lenny Paul	14 Jul 91
10.26	Peter Little	21 May 80
10.27	Barrington Williams	2 Jul 88
10.27	Clarence Callender	22 Jun 91
10.28	Darren Campbell	26 Jul 91
10.29	Trevor Cameron	11 Jun 94
10.31	Jim Evans	22 Aug 81
10.32	Brian Green	16 Jun 72
10.32	Harry King	22 Aug 81
10.33	Steve Gookey	20 Jul 91
10.34	Phil Davies	13 Jul 86
10.34	Jason Fergus	5 Jun 94
10.34	Julian Golding	17 Sep 94
10.35	Nigel Walker	26 Aug 89
10.36	Les Piggot	15 Jul 72
10.37	Earl Tulloch	22 Aug 81
10.37	Courtney Rumbolt	25 Jun 88
10.37	Allyn Condon	3 Jul 93
10.38	Don Halliday	17 Jul 70
10.38	Ian Green	17 Jul 70
10.38	Kevin Mark	3 Jul 93
10.38	Ejike Wodu	3 Jul 93
10.39	Trevor McKenzie	21 Jul 84
10.39	David Kirton	4 Jun 87
10.39	Dave Clark	3 Jun 90
10.39	Andrew Mensah	15 Jun 94
10.40	Steve Green	3 Jun 78
10.40	Gus McKenzie	25 Aug 81
10.40	Simon Baird	26 Jul 86
10.40	Danny Joyce	10 Jul 93
10.41	Vincent Jones	27 May 84
10.41	Eugene Gilkes	7 Sep 85

hand timing - wind assisted

10.0	Allan Wells	16 Jun 79
10.0	Drew McMaster	1 Jun 80
10.1	David Roberts	17 Jul 82
10.2	Brian Green	20 May 70
10.2	Les Piggot	19 Aug 72
10.2	Eugene Gilkes	7 Jul 84
10.2	Andy Carrott	5 Jul 88
10.2	Dave Clark	25 Jun 89

200 METRES (* 220 yards time less 0.1)

19.87 A	John Regis	31 Jul 94	
	19.94	20 Aug 93	
20.09	Linford Christie	28 Sep 88	
20.21	Allan Wells	28 Jul 80	
20.36	Todd Bennett	28 May 84	
20.41	Marcus Adam	13 Jun 92	
20.42 A	Ainsley Bennett	12 Sep 79	
20.43	Mike McFarlane	7 Oct 82	
20.47	Cameron Sharp	9 Sep 82	
20.50	Terry Williams	24 Aug 94	
20.51	Michael Rosswess	28 Sep 88	10
20.51	Solomon Wariso	28 May 94	
20.54	Ade Mafe	25 Aug 85	
20.60	Roger Black	4 Aug 90	
20.62	Buster Watson	5 Jun 83	
20.62	Donovan Reid	28 May 84	
20.66 A	Dick Steane	15 Oct 68	
20.66	David Jenkins	27 Aug 73	
20.67	Tony Jarrett	4 Aug 90	
20.70	Chris Monk	20 Aug 73	
20.71	Doug Walker	24 Aug 94	20
20.72	Darren Braithwaite	13 Jun 92	
20.72	Toby Box	24 Aug 94	
20.73 A	Ralph Banthorpe	15 Oct 68	
20.75	Dave Clark	20 Jan 90	
20.76	Andrew Carrott	5 Jul 88	
20.76	Clarence Callender	24 Jun 91	
20.77	Drew McMaster	9 Jul 83	
20.79	Phil Goedluck	6 Aug 94	
20.81	Mike St. Louis	21 Jun 86	
20.81	Paul McBurney	24 Aug 94	30
20.83	Martin Reynolds	22 Jul 70	
20.83	Claude Moseley	23 Aug 81	
20.84	Brian Green	4 Sep 71	
20.84	Earl Tulloch	25 May 81	
20.84	Jamie Baulch	24 Aug 94	
20.85	Richard Ashby	25 Aug 85	
20.86	Lincoln Asquith	28 Aug 83	
20.86	Roger Hunter	5 May 84	
20.86	Gus McCuaig	28 May 84	
20.86	Darren Campbell	4 Aug 93	40
20.87	Mark Smith	28 Jul 90	
20.88	Daley Thompson	18 Aug 79	
20.88	Phil Brown	28 May 84	
20.89	Mark Forsythe	12 Aug 90	
20.89	Jason John	14 Aug 92	
20.9 a *	Menzies Campbell	23 Jun 67	
20.90	Glen Cohen	14 Aug 76	
20.91	Trevor Hoyte	11 Jul 80	
20.91	Nigel Will	27 Aug 89	
20.91	Ian Mackie	23 Jul 94	50
20.92	Alan Pascoe	15 Jul 72	
20.93	George McCallum	30 Jun 84	
20.93	Mark Richardson	6 May 92	
20.95	Allyn Condon	26 Jun 93	
20.96	Du'aine Ladejo	8 May 93	
20.96	Peter Maitland	24 Aug 94	
20.98	Micky Morris	18 Jun 83	
20.98	Stewart Weathers	17 May 92	

wind assisted (* 220 yards time less 0.1)

20.10	Marcus Adam	1 Feb 90	
20.11	Allan Wells	20 Jun 80	
20.26	Ade Mafe	1 Feb 90	
20.48	Michael Rosswess	9 Sep 90	
20.51	Jason John	2 Jul 93	
20.55	Buster Watson	10 Aug 85	
20.55	Darren Campbell	2 Jul 93	
20.61	Martin Reynolds	22 Jul 70	
20.64	Drew McMaster	23 Aug 80	
20.7 a *	David Jones	20 May 61	10
20.70	Trevor Hoyte	14 Sep 79	
20.73	Julian Golding	17 Sep 94	
20.80	Owusu Dako	13 Jun 93	
20.84	Nigel Stickings	9 Jul 93	
20.85	Phil Brown	28 May 84	
20.85	Mark Smith	1 Jul 90	
20.88	Trevor Cameron	12 Jun 94	
20.89	Tim Bonsor	10 Aug 78	
20.89	David Grindley	13 Jun 93	
20.91	Peter Little	21 May 80	20
20.95	Stewart Weathers	4 Jun 86	
20.96	Simon Baird	31 Jul 86	
20.97	Michael Williams	10 Aug 85	

hand timing (* 220 yards time less 0.1)

20.3	David Jenkins	19 Aug 72
20.4 *	Peter Radford	28 May 60
20.6	Donovan Reid	1 Jul 84
20.7 *	Menzies Campbell	10 Jun 67
20.7	Martin Reynolds	2 Aug 70
20.7	Brian Green	3 Jun 72
20.7	Drew McMaster	16 Aug 80
20.7	Claude Moseley	28 Aug 81

wind assisted

20.4	Buster Watson	11 Aug 85
20.7	Earl Tulloch	15 Aug 82
20.7	Lincoln Asquith	2 Jul 83
20.7	Nigel Will	21 Jul 90

300 METRES

31.67	John Regis	17 Jul 92	
32.08	Roger Black	8 Aug 86	
32.14	Todd Bennett	18 Aug 84	
32.31	Mark Richardson	12 Jul 92	
32.32	Derek Redmond	16 Jul 88	
32.44	David Jenkins	4 Jul 75	
32.45	David Grindley	19 Jun 93	
32.59	Kriss Akabusi	14 Jul 91	
32.61	Brian Whittle	16 Jul 88	
32.73	Du'aine Ladejo	4 Sep 94	10
32.75	Ade Mafe	16 Jul 88	
32.79	Phil Brown	18 Aug 84	
32.82	Solomon Wariso	21 Jun 91	
32.9	Mark Hylton	21 Aug 94	
32.91	Nigel Will	12 Aug 90	
32.92	Buster Watson	24 Jun 85	

during 400m

32.06 +	Roger Black	29 Aug 91
32.35 +	David Grindley	26 Jun 93
32.4 +	David Jenkins	13 Aug 71

400 METRES

44.47	David Grindley	3 Aug 92
44.50	Derek Redmond	1 Sep 87
44.59	Roger Black	29 Aug 86
44.93	David Jenkins	21 Jun 75
44.93	Kriss Akabusi	7 Aug 88
44.94	Du'aine Ladejo	2 Aug 94
45.09	Mark Richardson	10 Jul 92
45.22	Brian Whittle	25 Sep 88
45.26	Phil Brown	26 May 85
45.27	Todd Bennett	7 Aug 88
45.30	Ade Mafe	23 Jul 93
45.33	Paul Sanders	15 Jun 91
45.47	David McKenzie	12 Jun 94
45.48	John Regis	17 Apr 93
45.49	Glen Cohen	21 May 78
45.64	Paul Harmsworth	7 Aug 88
45.65	Alan Bell	14 Jun 80
45.67	Roger Hunter	19 May 85
45.74	Steve Heard	26 May 85
45.75	Robbie Brightwell	19 Oct 64
45.81	Terry Whitehead	14 Jun 80
45.88	Wayne McDonald	17 Aug 91
45.91 A	Martin Winbolt-Lewis	17 Oct 68
45.92	Mark Thomas	27 Jun 87
45.97	Steve Scutt	14 Sep 79
45.98	Iwan Thomas	23 Aug 94
46.03	Peter Crampton	8 Aug 87
46.04	Alan Slack	27 Jun 85
46.08	Tim Graham	19 Oct 64
46.08	Rod Milne	15 Jun 80
46.10	Peter Gabbett	7 Sep 72
46.11	Martin Reynolds	4 Sep 72
46.11	Adrian Patrick	12 Jun 94
46.13	Guy Bullock	31 Jul 93
46.15	Ainsley Bennett	29 Aug 75
46.16	Gary Armstrong	15 Jul 72
46.16	Claude Moseley	1 Jul 83
46.18	Garry Cook	14 Jun 80
46.19	Roy Dickens	28 May 84
46.24	Mel Fowell	15 Jun 80
46.27	Richard Ashton	6 Aug 78
46.31	Neil Jackson	14 Jun 80
46.37	Gary Cadogan	27 Jun 87
46.37	Mark Hylton	22 Jul 94
46.39	Danny Laing	25 Sep 78
46.39	Alex Fugallo	12 Jun 94
46.42	Nigel Will	12 Jul 92
46.45	Jamie Baulch	22 Aug 94
46.49	Roger Jenkins	6 Sep 75
46.49	Mark Bishop	15 Jul 89
46.49	Paul McBurney	22 Aug 94
46.50	Calvin Henry	22 Aug 94

hand timing (* 440 yard time less 0.3)

45.6 *	Robbie Brightwell	14 Jul 62
45.7	Adrian Metcalfe	2 Sep 61
45.9	Colin Campbell	2 Jul 68
46.0	Garry Cook	20 May 81
46.3	John Wrighton	21 Aug 58
46.3	John Wilson	30 Jun 73

600 METRES

1:14.95	Steve Heard	14 Jul 91
1:15.0 +	Sebastian Coe	10 Jun 81
1:15.4	Garry Cook	30 Jul 84
1:15.4	Tom McKean	21 Jul 91
1:15.6	David Jenkins	3 Aug 74
1:15.94	Brian Whittle	28 Jul 92
1:16.0	Steve Ovett	15 Aug 79
1:16.0 +	Martin Steele	10 Jul 93

800 METRES (* 880 yards time less 0.7)

1:41.73"	Sebastian Coe	10 Jun 81
1:42.88	Steve Cram	21 Aug 85
1:42.97	Peter Elliott	30 May 90
1:43.84	Martin Steele	10 Jul 93
1:43.88	Tom McKean	28 Jul 89
1:43.98	David Sharpe	19 Aug 92
1:44.09	Steve Ovett	31 Aug 78
1:44.55	Garry Cook	29 Aug 84
1:44.59	Tony Morrell	2 Jul 88
1:44.65	Ikem Billy	21 Jul 84
1:44.65	Steve Heard	26 Aug 92
1:44.92	Curtis Robb	15 Aug 93
1:45.05	Matthew Yates	26 Aug 92
1:45.12	Andy Carter	14 Jul 73
1:45.14	Chris McGeorge	28 Jun 83
1:45.14	John Gladwin	22 Jul 86
1:45.31	Robert Harrison	21 Jul 84
1:45.35	Kevin McKay	16 Aug 92
1:45.44	Neil Horsfield	28 Jul 90
1:45.47	Brian Whittle	20 Jul 90
1:45.6	Graham Williamson	12 Jun 83
1:45.64	Paul Herbert	5 Jun 88
1:45.66	Paul Forbes	8 Jun 83
1:45.69	Steve Crabb	17 Aug 88
1:45.76	Frank Clement	10 Jul 76
1:45.85	David Strang	13 Jun 92
1:46.10	Gary Marlow	10 Jul 87
1:46.1	Colin Campbell	26 Jul 72
1:46.16	Gareth Brown	2 Jul 84
1:46.20	David Warren	29 Jun 80
1:46.21	Peter Browne	14 Jul 73
1:46.3 a	Chris Carter	4 Sep 66
1:46.3 a	Phil Lewis	27 Jan 74
1:46.37	Andrew Lill	28 Jun 92
1:46.5 a	John Boulter	18 Jun 66
1:46.54	Craig Winrow	15 Jul 94
1:46.6	Derek Johnson	9 Aug 57
1:46.63	Peter Hoffman	11 Jun 78
1:46.64	David Moorcroft	25 Jul 82
1:46.65	Steve Caldwell	31 May 82
1:46.70	Atle Douglas	9 Jun 88
1:46.7 a*	John Davies	3 Jun 68
1:46.72	Mal Edwards	13 Sep 87
1:46.8	Bob Adams	9 Aug 69
1:46.8	Dave Cropper	1 Jul 73
1:46.8	David McMeekin	6 Jun 74
1:46.92	Colin Szwed	7 Aug 82
1:46.94	Mark Kirk	20 Jul 87
1:47.0	Brian Hewson	13 Sep 58
1:47.0	Mike Rawson	13 Sep 58

1000 METRES

	2:12.18	Sebastian Coe	11 Jul 81
	2:12.88	Steve Cram	9 Aug 85
	2:15.91	Steve Ovett	6 Sep 79
	2:16.30	Peter Elliott	17 Jan 90
	2:16.34	Matthew Yates	6 Jul 90
	2:16.82	Graham Williamson	17 Jul 84
	2:16.99	Tony Morrell	28 Aug 88
	2:17.14	John Gladwin	6 Jul 90
	2:17.20	Robert Harrison	18 Aug 84
10	2:17.36	Neil Horsfield	9 Aug 91
	2:17.43	Gareth Brown	18 Aug 84
	2:17.45	Chris McGeorge	20 Aug 84
	2:17.63	Kevin McKay	14 Jul 89
	2:17.75	Steve Crabb	5 Aug 87
	2:17.79	David Sharp	31 Aug 92
	2:17.95	Mark Scruton	17 Jul 84
	2:17.96	Ikem Billy	14 Jul 89
	2:18.18	Malcolm Edwards	11 Jul 86
	2:18.2	John Boulter	6 Sep 69
20	2:18.28	Garry Cook	23 Aug 81

1500 METRES (+ during 1 mile)

	3:29.67	Steve Cram	16 Jul 85
	3:29.77	Sebastian Coe	7 Sep 86
	3:30.77	Steve Ovett	4 Sep 83
	3:32.69	Peter Elliott	16 Sep 90
	3:33.34	Steve Crabb	4 Jul 87
	3:33.79	Dave Moorcroft	27 Jul 82
	3:33.83	John Robson	4 Sep 79
	3·34.00	Matthew Yates	13 Sep 91
	3:34.01	Graham Williamson	28 Jun 83
10	3:34.1 +	Tony Morrell	14 Jul 90
	3:34.50	Adrian Passey	4 Jul 87
	3:34.53	Mark Rowland	27 Jul 88
	3:35.08	Neil Horsfield	10 Aug 90
	3:35.26	John Gladwin	5 Sep 86
	3:35.28	Jack Buckner	1 Jul 86
	3:35.66	Frank Clement	12 Aug 78
	3:35.74	Robert Harrison	26 May 86
	3:35.83	Gary Lough	15 Jul 94
	3:35.94	Paul Larkins	10 Jul 87
20	3:35.94	Kevin McKay	19 Jun 92
	3:36.45	John Mayock	5 Sep 93
	3:36.53	David Strang	15 Jul 94
	3:36.81	Mike Kearns	26 Jul 77
	3:37.55	Colin Reitz	27 Jun 85
	3:37.64	Brendan Foster	2 Feb 74
	3:37.88	Jason Dullforce	17 Jul 92
	3:37.97	Rod Finch	30 Jul 93
	3:38.05	Glen Grant	12 Aug 78
	3:38.06	Tim Hutchings	31 Aug 84
30	3:38.08	Tom Hanlon	28 Jun 92
	3:38.1	Jim McGuinness	1 Aug 77
	3:38.2 a	Jim Espir	11 Jul 80
	3:38.22	Peter Stewart	15 Jul 72
	3:38.31	Matt Barnes	23 Jul 93
	3:38.34	Rob Denmark	28 Jun 92
	3:38.52	Ray Smedley	15 Jul 72
	3:38.56	Curtis Robb	26 Jun 93

	3:38.64	Simon Fairbrother	17 Jun 92	
	3:38.65	Ian Stewart II	8 Aug 81	
	3:38.68	John Kirkbride	15 Jul 72	40
	3:38.7	Jim Douglas	27 Jun 72	
	3:38.78	Mark Scrutton	17 Jun 84	
	3:38.8	Paul Lawther	12 Jun 77	
	3:38.9	Ian Hamer	5 Aug 89	
	3:38.9	Brian Treacy	28 Aug 94	
	3:39.0	David Lewis	9 Aug 83	
	3:39.06	Andy Keith	5 Jun 93	
	3:39.10	Alan Simpson	15 Aug 64	
	3:39.12	Ian Stewart I	1 Sep 69	
	3:39.19	Steve Green	28 Aug 94	50

ONE MILE

	3:46.32	Steve Cram	27 Jul 85	
	3:47.33	Sebastian Coe	28 Aug 81	
	3:48.40	Steve Ovett	26 Aug 81	
	3:49.20	Peter Elliott	2 Jul 88	
	3:49.34	Dave Moorcroft	26 Jun 82	
	3:50.64	Graham Williamson	13 Jul 82	
	3:51.02	John Gladwin	19 Aug 87	
	3:51.31	Tony Morrell	14 Jul 90	
	3:51.57	Jack Buckner	29 Aug 84	
	3:51.76hc	Steve Crabb	14 Aug 87	10
	3:52.20		1 Jul 89	
	3:52.44	John Robson	11 Jul 81	
	3:52.75	Matthew Yates	10 Jul 93	
	3:52.99	Mark Rowland	10 Sep 86	
	3:53.20	Ian Stewart II	25 Aug 82	
	3:53.64	Kevin McKay	22 Jul 94	
	3:53.82	Gary Staines	12 Aug 90	
	3:53.85	Robert Harrison	15 Jul 86	
	3:54.2	Frank Clement	27 Jun 78	
	3:54.30	David Strang	22 Jul 94	
	3:54.39	Neil Horsfield	8 Jul 86	20
	3:54.53	Tim Hutchings	31 Jul 82	
	3:54.9	Adrian Passey	20 Aug 89	
	3:55.0	Jim McGuinness	11 Jul 77	
	3:55.3	Peter Stewart	10 Jun 72	
	3:55.38	Rob Denmark	12 Aug 90	
	3:55.41	Colin Reitz	31 Jul 82	
	3:55.68	Alan Simpson	30 Aug 65	
	3:55.8	Geoff Smith	15 Aug 81	
	3:55.9	Brendan Foster	10 Jun 72	
	3:55.96	David Lewis	23 Aug 83	30
	3:56.0	Jim Douglas	10 Jun 72	
	3:56.04	Mike Downes	25 Aug 82	
	3:56.1	Neill Duggan	11 Jun 66	
	3:56.19	Ian Hamer	5 Jul 91	
	3:56.29 i	Andy Keith	22 Jan 94	
	3:56.36	Steve Martin	5 Aug 86	
	3:56.38	Mike McLeod	31 Aug 79	
	3:56.5	John Kirkbride	10 Jun 72	
	3:56.5	Paul Davies-Hale	20 Aug 89	
	3:56.6	Walter Wilkinson	31 May 71	40
	3:56.65	Paul Larkins	17 Jul 87	
	3:56.7	Jim Espir	15 Aug 81	
	3:56.71	Chris McGeorge	5 Jul 88	
	3:56.8	Ian MCafferty	11 Jun 69	

	Time	Name	Date
	3:56.83	Simon Fairbrother	17 Aug 90
	3:56.89 i	John Mayock	20 Feb 93
	3:56.90		15 Sep 91
	3:55.57 i disq		14 Mar 92
	3:56.9	Ron Speirs	30 Apr 77
	3:56.95	Sean Cahill	31 Aug 79
	3:56.95	Dave Clarke	17 Jul 82
50	3:56.99	Alan Salter	9 Jul 85
	3:57.07	Neil Ovington	11 Jul 86
	3:57.15	Gary Taylor	5 Jul 88
	3:57.2	Derek Ibbotson	19 Jul 57
	3:57.3	Ian Stewart I	11 Jun 69
	3:57.42	Colin Ridding	5 Jul 88
	3:57.43	Stephen Halliday	28 Aug 89
	3:57.46	Barry Smith	8 Aug 80
	3:57.49	Nick Rose	8 Aug 80
	3:57.5	Mike Wiggs	5 Jul 65
60	3:57.5	Graeme Fell	1 Jun 83
	3:57.59	Adrian Weatherhead	29 Aug 75
	3:57.66	Geoff Turnbull	18 Jul 86
	3:57.68	John Whetton	3 Jul 65
	3:57.7	Ray Smedley	27 Apr 74
	3:57.74	Andy Green	3 Jul 65
	3:57.8	Mal Edwards	19 Sep 87
	3:57.81	Paul Lawther	13 Jul 83
	3:57.86	Mike Kearns	26 Jun 77
	3:57.88 i	Clifton Bradeley	9 Mar 85
70	3:58.01	Stan Taylor	18 Aug 62
	3:58.01 i	Johan Boakes	25 Jan 91
	3:58.05	Dave McMeekin	30 Aug 76
	3:58.23	Alan Mottershead	14 Sep 79
	3:58.28	Adrian Callan	13 Jul 86
	3:58.39	Matt Barnes	25 Jun 94
	3:58.42	Sean O'Neill	7 Jul 87
	3:58.42 i	Jason Dullforce	14 Mar 92
	3:58.48	Matthew de Freitas	5 Jun 93
	3:58.5	Bob Maplestone	25 May 73
80	3:58.6	John Boulter	24 Jul 68
	3:58.62	Steve Emson	31 Aug 79
	3:58.64	Ian Gillespie	5 Jun 93
	3:58.68	Steve Flint	26 May 80
	3:58.7	Allan Rushmer	26 Aug 67
	3:58.7	Norman Morrison	31 May 71
	3:58.77	Roger Hackney	13 Jul 86
	3:58.8	Roger Bannister	7 Aug 54
	3:58.8	Tony Settle	29 May 76
	3:58.8	Lawrie Spence	12 Sep 77
90	3:58.83	John Nuttall	14 Aug 91
	3:58.85	Chris Sly	8 Aug 80
	3:58.87	Tom Buckner	5 Jun 93
	3:58.9	Brian Hewson	3 Sep 58
	3:58.9	Ron Martin	11 May 74
	3:58.9	Simon Mugglestone	19 May 90
	3:58.95	Mark Scruton	10 Jun 84
	3:58.96	Tony Harris	3 Jul 65
	3:59.01	Nick Hopkins	12 Aug 90
	3:59.02	David Sharpe	27 May 90
100	3:59.1	Ron Macdonald	1 Sep 75
	3:59.1	Ashworth Laukam	16 Jun 85
	3:59.16	Glen Grant	19 Jun 76

	Time	Name	Date	
	3:59.17	Billy Dee	14 Jul 91	
	3:59.24	Mike Berisford	18 Aug 62	
	3:59.24	Derek Graham	20 Aug 66	
	3:59.28	Andy Geddes	17 Jul 87	
	3:59.29	Alistair Currie	2 Aug 85	
	3:59.30	Eamonn Martin	23 Aug 83	
	3:59.3	Ken Wood	19 Jul 57	
	3:59.3	Bruce Tulloch	27 Jan 62	110
	3:59.3	Andy Carter	10 Jun 72	
	3:59.3	Tim Redman	16 Jun 85	
	3:59.3	Mark Howard	2 Jul 89	
	3:59.36	David Heath	17 Jul 89	
	3:59.37	Peter McColgan	18 Jul 86	
	3:59.4	Bill McKim	22 Jul 64	
	3:59.4	Roy Young	14 Jul 71	
	3:59.43	John Keyworth	14 Jul 84	
	3:59.48	Gary Lough	4 Sep 94	
	3:59.5	Gareth Brown	25 Aug 84	120
	3:59.58 i	Colin Hume	5 Mar 83	
	3:59.60	Pat Chester	20 Jul 85	
	3:59.6	Craig Mochrie	28 Aug 89	
	3:59.6 i	Steve Green	4 Mar 94	
	3:59.61	Malcolm Plant	31 Aug 79	
	3:59.67	Mark Kirk	13 Jul 86	
	3:59.80	Maurice Benn	3 Jun 68	
	3:59.8	Chris Chataway	25 May 55	
	3:59.8	Ray Roseman	23 Jul 69	
	3:59.8	Ken Newton	12 Sep 77	130
	3:59.8	Steve James	9 Jun 84	
	3:59.84	Seamus McCann	5 Jul 88	
	3:59.90	Ken Penney	14 Jul 91	
	3:59.9	Gordon Pirie	23 Sep 60	
	3:59.9	Chris Mason	30 May 70	
	3:59.9	Davey Wilson	30 May 91	
	3:59.9	Joe Dunbar	18 Sep 91	
	3:59.92	Tony Leonard	8 Jul 79	
	3:59.94	Jon Richards	7 Jul 87	
	3:59.97 i	John Evans	26 Jan 91	140

2000 METRES

	Time	Name	Date	
	4:51.39	Steve Cram	4 Aug 85	
	4:52.82	Peter Elliott	15 Sep 87	
	4:53.06	Jack Buckner	15 Sep 87	
	4:53.69	Gary Staines	15 Sep 87	
	4:57.71	Steve Ovett	7 Jul 82	
	4:58.38	Graham Williamson	29 Aug 83	
	4:58.84	Sebastian Coe	5 Jun 82	
	4:59.57	Nick Rose	3 Jun 78	
	5:00.37	Tim Hutchings	29 Aug 83	
	5:01.09	Eamonn Martin	19 Jun 84	10
	5:01.48	Paul Larkins	5 Jun 88	
	5:02.35	Sean Cahill	4 Aug 85	
	5:02.61	Steve Martin	19 Jun 84	
	5:02.8 a	Frank Clement	10 Sep 78	
	5:02.86	David Moorcroft	19 Jul 86	
	5:02.93	Brendan Foster	4 Jul 75	
	5:02.98	Ian Stewart	4 Jul 75	
	5:03.16	David Bedford	8 Jul 72	
	5:03.8	Lawrie Spence	26 May 78	
	5:04.16	Eddie Wedderburn	15 Jul 78	20

3000 METRES (+ during 2 Miles)

7:32.79	Dave Moorcroft	17 Jul 82	
7:35.1	Brendan Foster	3 Aug 74	
7:39.55	Rob Denmark	1 Aug 93	
7:40.4	Nick Rose	27 Jun 78	
7:40.43	Jack Buckner	5 Jul 86	
7:40.94	Eamonn Martin	9 Jul 83	
7:41.3	Steve Ovett	23 Sep 77	
7:41.79	Gary Staines	14 Jul 90	
7:42.26	Graeme Fell	9 Jul 83	
7:42.47	David Lewis	9 Jul 83	10
7:42.77	Billy Dee	18 Jul 92	
7:43.03	Tim Hutchings	14 Jul 89	
7:43.1 +	Steve Cram	29 Aug 83	
7:43.90	Ian Stewart II	26 Jun 82	
7:44.40	Colin Reitz	9 Jul 83	
7:44.76	Paul Davies-Hale	20 Jul 85	
7:45.2 +	Geoff Turnbull	12 Sep 86	
7:45.29	Dennis Coates	9 Sep 77	
7:45.81	John Robson	13 Jul 84	
7:46.22 i	Mark Rowland	27 Feb 90	20

2 MILES

8:13.51	Steve Ovett	15 Sep 78
8:13.68	Brendan Foster	27 Aug 73
8:14.93	Steve Cram	29 Aug 83
8:15.53	Tim Hutchings	12 Sep 86
8:15.98	Geoff Turnbull	12 Sep 86
8:16.75	Dave Moorcroft	20 Aug 82
8:17.12	Jack Buckner	12 Sep 86
8:18.4 i	Nick Rose	17 Feb 78
8:18.98	Eamonn Martin	16 Jul 88
8:19.37	Nat Muir	27 Jun 80
8:20.28	David James	27 Jun 80
8:20.66	David Lewis	7 Sep 84
8:21.09	Barry Smith	27 Jun 80
8:21.86	David Black	14 Sep 73
8:21.97	Rob Denmark	9 Aug 91
8:22.0	Ian Stewart I	14 Aug 72

5000 METRES

13:00.41	Dave Moorcroft	7 Jul 82	
13:09.80	Ian Hamer	9 Jun 92	
13:10.15	Jack Buckner	31 Aug 86	
13:10.24	Rob Denmark	9 Jun 92	
13:11.50	Tim Hutchings	11 Aug 84	
13:14.28	Gary Staines	15 Aug 90	
13:14.6 a	Brendan Foster	29 Jan 74	
13:15.59	Julian Goater	11 Sep 81	
13:17.21	David Bedford	14 Jul 72	
13:17.84	Eamonn Martin	14 Jul 89	10
13:17.9	Nat Muir	15 Jul 80	
13:18.6	Steve Jones	10 Jun 82	
13:18.91	Nick Rose	28 Jun 84	
13:19.66	Ian McCafferty	14 Jul 72	
13:19.78	Jon Brown	2 Jul 93	
13:20.06	Steve Ovett	30 Jun 86	
13:21.13	David Lewis	4 Jul 85	
13:21.14	Barry Smith	7 Jun 81	
13:21.2	Tony Simmons	23 May 76	
13:21.60	Paul Davies-Hale	8 Jul 88	20

10,000 METRES

27:23.06	Eamonn Martin	2 Jul 88	
27:30.3	Brendan Foster	23 Jun 78	
27:30.80	David Bedford	13 Jul 73	
27:31.19	Nick Rose	9 Jul 83	
27:34.58	Julian Goater	26 Jun 82	
27:36.27	David Black	29 Aug 78	
27:39.14	Steve Jones	9 Jul 83	
27:39.76	Mike McLeod	4 Sep 79	
27:40.03	Richard Nerurkar	10 Jul 93	
27:43.03	Ian Stewart I	9 Sep 77	10
27:43.59	Tony Simmons	30 Jun 77	
27:43.74	Bernie Ford	9 Sep 77	
27:43.76	Geoff Smith	13 Jun 81	
27:47.16	Adrian Royle	10 Apr 82	
27:47.79	Paul Evans	5 Jul 93	
27:48.73	Gary Staines	6 Jul 91	
27:51.76	Jon Solly	20 Jun 86	
27:55.66	Steve Binns	9 Jul 83	
27:55.77	Dave Clarke	25 May 82	
27:57.77	Ian Hamer	13 Sep 91	20

MARATHON

2:07:13	Steve Jones	20 Oct 85	
2:08:33	Charlie Spedding	21 Apr 85	
2:09:08	Geoff Smith	23 Oct 83	
2:09:12	Ian Thompson	31 Jan 74	
2:09:16	Allister Hutton	21 Apr 85	
2:09:24	Hugh Jones	9 May 82	
2:09:28	Ron Hill	23 Jul 70	
2:09:28	John Graham	23 May 81	
2:09:43	Mike Gratton	17 Apr 83	
2:09:54	Tony Milovsorov	23 Apr 89	10
2:10:03	Richard Nerurkar	31 Oct 93	
2:10:12	Gerry Helme	17 Apr 83	
2:10:30	Dave Long	21 Apr 91	
2:10:36	Paul Evans	12 Apr 92	
2:10:39	Mike O'Reilly	5 Dec 93	
2:10:48	Bill Adcocks	8 Dec 68	
2:10:50	Eamonn Martin	18 Apr 93	
2:10:51	Bernie Ford	2 Dec 79	
2:10:52	Kevin Forster	17 Apr 88	
2:10:55	Chris Bunyan	18 Apr 83	20

2000 METRES STEEPLECHASE

5:19.86	Mark Rowland	28 Aug 88	
5:21.77	Tom Hanlon	11 Jun 92	
5:23.56	Tom Buckner	17 Jul 92	
5:23.6	Roger Hackney	10 Jun 82	
5:23.71	Colin Walker	28 Aug 88	
5:23.87	Colin Reitz	28 Jun 84	
5:24.91	Eddie Wedderburn	19 Aug 86	
5:26.24	Paul Davies-Hale	26 Aug 85	
5:26.64	Nick Peach	19 Aug 86	
5:26.82	David Lewis	12 Jun 83	10
5:30.6	Dennis Coates	23 Apr 78	
5:30.86	Tony Staynings	26 May 76	
5:31.04	John Hartigan	17 Aug 90	
5:31.09	Peter McColgan	5 Aug 86	
5:31.43	John Bicourt	26 May 76	
5:31.59	Michael Hawkins	20 Jan 90	

3000 METRES STEEPLECHASE

	8:07.96	Mark Rowland	30 Sep 88
	8:12.11	Colin Reitz	5 Sep 86
	8:12.58	Tom Hanlon	3 Aug 91
	8:15.16	Graeme Fell	17 Aug 83
	8:18.32	Eddie Wedderburn	5 Jul 88
	8:18.91	Roger Hackney	30 Jul 88
	8:18.95	Dennis Coates	25 Jul 76
	8:20.83	Paul Davies-Hale	10 Jun 84
	8:22.48	John Davies II	13 Sep 74
10	8:22.82	John Bicourt	8 Jun 76
	8:23.90	Justin Chaston	18 Jul 94
	8:25.15	Colin Walker	28 Jun 92
	8:25.50	Tom Buckner	28 Aug 92
	8:26.4	Andy Holden	15 Sep 72
	8:26.6	Gordon Rimmer	4 Jun 80
	8:27.21	Tony Staynings	15 Jun 80
	8:27.8	Steve Hollings	5 Aug 73
	8:27.93	Peter McColgan	25 Jun 91
	8:28.33	Spencer Duval	12 Jun 94
20	8:28.6	David Bedford	10 Sep 71

110 METRES HURDLES

	12.91	Colin Jackson	20 Aug 93
	13.00	Tony Jarrett	20 Aug 93
	13.29	Jon Ridgeon	15 Jul 87
	13.42	David Nelson	27 Aug 91
	13.43	Mark Holtom	4 Oct 82
	13.44	Hugh Teape	14 Aug 92
	13.51	Nigel Walker	3 Aug 90
	13.52	Andy Tulloch	11 Aug 94
	13.53	Paul Gray	22 Aug 94
10	13.60	Wilbert Greaves	21 Aug 85
	13.69	Berwyn Price	18 Aug 73
	13.72	David Hemery	1 Aug 70
	13.75	Lloyd Cowan	17 Jul 94
	13.79	Alan Pascoe	17 Jun 72
	13.80	Neil Owen	5 Jun 94
	13.86	Ken Campbell	23 Aug 94
	13.96	Steve Buckeridge	31 May 86
	14.03	Brett St Louis	27 Jun 87
	14.04	Daley Thompson	28 Aug 86
20	14.08	Paul Brice	26 Aug 83
	14.08	Brian Taylor	13 Apr 91

wind assisted

13.49	Nigel Walker	3 Jun 89
13.65	Berwyn Price	25 Aug 75
13.66	David Hemery	18 Jul 70
13.97	Brett St Louis	30 Jul 88
13.99	Bob Danville	14 Aug 76

hand timing

13.5	Berwyn Price	1 Jul 73
13.6	David Hemery	5 Jul 69
13.7	Alan Pascoe	5 Jul 69
13.7	C. J. Kirkpatrick	29 Jun 74
13.8	Martin Nicholson	25 Jun 94
13.9	Mike Parker	2 Oct 63
13.9	David Wilson	29 Jun 74
13.9	Brian Taylor	8 May 93

wind assisted

12.8	Colin Jackson	10 Jan 90
13.4	Berwyn Price	7 Jul 76

400 METRES HURDLES

	47.82	Kriss Akabusi	6 Aug 92	
	48.12 A	David Hemery	15 Oct 68	
	48.52		2 Sep 72	
	48.59	Alan Pascoe	30 Jun 75	
	48.73	Jon Ridgeon	6 Sep 92	
	49.03 A	John Sherwood	15 Oct 68	
	49.88		13 Aug 69	
	49.07	Gary Cadogan	22 Jul 94	
	49.11	Gary Oakes	26 Jul 80	
	49.25	Max Robertson	28 Aug 90	
	49.26	Peter Crampton	8 Aug 94	
	49.49	Mark Holtom	20 Jul 85	10
	49.60	Philip Beattie	28 Jul 86	
	49.65	Bill Hartley	2 Aug 75	
	49.82	Martin Gillingham	14 Aug 87	
	49.86	Martin Briggs	6 Jun 84	
	49.95	Steve Sole	24 Jul 83	
	50.01	Philip Harries	5 Jun 88	
	50.1 a	John Cooper	16 Oct 64	
	50.19	Lawrence Lynch	27 Jul 91	
	50.19	Steve Coupland	12 Jun 94	
	50.37	Bob Danville	27 Jul 82	20

hand timing

49.9	Andy Todd	9 Oct 69

HIGH JUMP

2.38 i	Steve Smith	4 Feb 94	
2.37		20 Sep 92	
2.37 i	Dalton Grant	13 Mar 94	
2.36		1 Sep 91	
2.32 i	Brendan Reilly	24 Feb 94	
2.31		17 Jul 92	
2.31	Geoff Parsons	26 Aug 94	
2.28 i	John Holman	28 Jan 89	
2.24		27 May 89	
2.25	Floyd Manderson	20 Aug 88	
2.24	Mark Naylor	28 Jun 80	
2.24	John Hill	23 Aug 85	
2.24	Phil McDonnell	26 Aug 85	
2.23	Mark Lakey	29 Aug 82	10
2.23 i	David Abrahams	12 Mar 83	
2.19		7 Oct 82	
2.21	Fayyaz Ahmed	29 Jun 86	
2.21	Steve Chapman	30 Jul 89	
2.20	Brian Burgess	11 Jun 78	
2.20	Trevor Llewelyn	15 Jul 83	
2.20	Byron Morrison	14 Jul 84	
2.20 i	Henderson Pierre	10 Jan 87	
2.18		16 Aug 86	
2.20	Alex Kruger	18 Jun 88	
2.20	Ossie Cham	21 May 89	
2.20 i	Warren Caswell	10 Mar 90	
2.18		2 Sep 90	20

POLE VAULT

	5.65	Keith Stock	7 Jul 81
	5.59	Brian Hooper	6 Sep 80
	5.52	Michael Edwards	13 May 93
	5.50	Neil Winter	9 Aug 92
	5.45 i	Andy Ashurst	16 Feb 92
	5.40		19 Jun 88
	5.41	Nick Buckfield	9 Jul 93
	5.40	Jeff Gutteridge ¶	23 Apr 80
	5.35	Matthew Belsham	26 Jun 93
	5.30 i	Ian Tullett	14 Mar 92
	5.30		7 Jun 92
10	5.26	Mark Johnson	31 Aug 91
	5.25	Mike Bull	22 Sep 73
	5.25	Allan Williams	29 Aug 77
	5.25	Daley Thompson	15 Jun 86
	5.25	Kevin Hughes	24 Aug 94
	5.22	Dean Mellor	27 May 91
	5.22	Paul Williamson	18 Jun 94
	5.21	Graham Eggleton	10 Jul 82
	5.20	Billy Davey	5 Jun 83
	5.20	Warren Siley	4 Aug 90
20	5.20	Mike Barber	25 Jun 94
	5.20	Tim Thomas	16 Jul 94

LONG JUMP

	8.23	Lynn Davies	30 Jun 68
	8.15	Stewart Faulkner	16 Jul 90
	8.14	Mark Forsythe	7 Jul 91
	8.10	Fred Salle	9 Sep 94
	8.08	Roy Mitchell	27 Sep 80
	8.05 i	Barrington Williams	11 Feb 89
	8.01		17 Jun 89
	8.01	Daley Thompson	8 Aug 84
	8.00	Derrick Brown	7 Aug 85
	7.98	Alan Lerwill	29 Jun 74
10	7.94 i	Paul Johnson	10 Mar 89
	7.85		3 Jun 89
	7.91	John King	26 Sep 87
	7.91	Steve Phillips	10 Aug 91
	7.90	Ian Simpson	3 Jun 89
	7.89	John Morbey	8 Aug 66
	7.87	Keith Fleming	7 Jun 87
	7.84	Wayne Griffith	25 Aug 89
	7.79	Geoff Hignett	31 May 71
	7.79	Don Porter	13 Jul 75
	7.77	Len Tyson	25 Jul 82
20	7.76	Carl Howard	31 Jul 93

wind assisted

8.17	Mark Forsythe	11 Jun 89
8.16	Roy Mitchell	26 Jun 76
8.15	Alan Lerwill	29 May 72
8.12	Derrick Brown	14 Jun 86
8.11	Daley Thompson	7 Aug 78
8.04	Ian Simpson	3 Jun 89
7.96	Colin Jackson	17 May 86
7.94	John Herbert	25 Jul 82
7.94	John King	20 Jun 86
7.93	David Burgess	15 Jun 86
7.91	Steve Ingram	18 jun 94
7.89	John Shepherd	20 Jun 86
7.87	Paul Johnson	15 May 88

TRIPLE JUMP

17.57 A	Keith Connor	5 Jun 82	
17.30		9 Jun 82	
17.44	Jon Edwards	16 Aug 93	
17.41	John Herbert	2 Sep 85	
17.21	Tosi Fasinro	27 Jul 93	
17.06	Julian Golley	10 Sep 94	
17.01	Eric McCalla	3 Aug 84	
16.95	Francis Agyepong	12 Jun 94	
16.87	Mike Makin	2 Aug 86	
16.86	Aston Moore	16 Aug 81	
16.75	Vernon Samuels	7 Aug 88	10
16.53	Larry Achike	24 Jul 94	
16.46	Fred Alsop	16 Oct 64	
16.30	Femi Abejide	27 Jun 85	
16.29 i	David Johnson	1 Mar 78	
16.18		22 Jun 75	
16.26	Joe Sweeney	3 Aug 91	
16.22	Derek Boosey	15 Jun 68	
16.20	Rez Cameron	5 Jun 88	
16.18	Tony Wadhams	6 Jul 69	
16.17	John Mackenzie	17 Sep 94	
16.16	Conroy Brown	19 Sep 81	20

wind assisted

17.81	Keith Connor	9 Oct 82
17.70	Jon Edwards	2 Jul 93
17.30	Tosi Fasinro	12 Jun 93
17.02	Aston Moore	14 Jun 81
17.00	Francis Agyepong	13 Jun 92
16.82	Vernon Samuels	24 Jun 89
16.67	Larry Achike	24 Jul 94
16.65	Fred Alsop	13 Aug 65
16.49	Tony Wadhams	16 Sep 69
16.38	Femi Abejide	10 Jun 89
16.38	Courtney Charles	22 Jul 90

SHOT

21.68	Geoff Capes	18 May 80	
20.43	Mike Winch	22 May 74	
20.33	Paul Edwards	9 Jul 91	
19.56	Arthur Rowe	7 Aug 61	
19.49	Matt Simson	28 Aug 94	
19.44 i	Simon Williams	28 Jan 89	
19.14		18 May 91	
19.43	Bill Tancred	18 May 74	
19.18	Jeff Teale	7 Aug 68	
19.01	Billy Cole	21 Jun 86	
18.94	Bob Dale	12 Jun 76	10
18.93	Paul Buxton	13 May 77	
18.62	Martyn Lucking	2 Oct 62	
18.59 i	Alan Carter	11 Apr 65	
18.26		1 May 65	
18.50	Mike Lindsay	2 Jul 63	
18.46	Roger Kennedy	22 May 77	
18.46 i	Simon Rodhouse	20 Feb 82	
18.20		25 Jul 82	
18.35	Peter Tancred	9 Jul 74	
18.34	Richard Slaney	3 Jul 83	
18.31	Shaun Pickering	23 May 92	
18.15	Mark Proctor	22 Jun 94	20

DISCUS

65.16	Richard Slaney	1 Jul 85
64.94	Bill Tancred	21 Jul 74
62.50	Bob Weir	23 Jun 84
62.36	Peter Tancred	8 May 80
61.86	Paul Mardle	13 Jun 84
61.62	Peter Gordon	15 Jun 91
61.14	Simon Williams	18 Apr 92
61.00	Allan Seatory	6 Oct 74
60.92	Graham Savory	10 May 86
[10] 60.42	Mike Cushion	16 Aug 75
60.08	Abi Ekoku	16 May 90
59.84	Colin Sutherland	10 Jun 78
59.78	Glen Smith	5 Jun 94
59.76	John Hillier	27 Jul 74
59.70	John Watts	14 Jul 72
59.20	Kevin Brown	19 Jun 91
58.64	Steve Casey	19 May 91
58.58	Darrin Morris	22 Jun 91
58.34	Geoff Capes	29 Sep 73
[20] 58.34	Lee Newman	9 Jun 94

HAMMER

77.54	Martin Girvan	12 May 84
77.30	Dave Smith	13 Jul 85
77.02	Matt Mileham	11 May 84
75.40	Chris Black	23 Jul 83
75.08	Bob Weir	3 Oct 82
74.02	Paul Head	30 Aug 90
73.86	Barry Williams	1 Jul 76
73.80	Jason Byrne	19 Sep 92
73.20	Paul Dickenson	22 May 76
[10] 72.10	Mike Jones	28 Aug 88
71.60	Shane Peacock	24 Jun 90
71.00	Ian Chipchase	17 Aug 74
70.88	Howard Payne	29 Jun 74
70.80	Peter Vivian	12 Jun 94
70.30	Stewart Rogerson	14 Aug 88
70.28	Paul Buxton	19 May 79
69.52	Jim Whitehead	23 Sep 79
68.64	Shaun Pickering	7 Apr 84
68.18	Ron James	2 Jun 82
[20] 67.82	Steve Whyte	15 Apr 89

JAVELIN (1992 model)

91.46	Steven Backley	25 Jan 92
86.94	Mike Hill	13 Jun 93
83.84	Roald Bradstock	2 May 87
82.60	Colin Mackenzie	1 Jun 91
81.70	Nigel Bevan	28 Jun 92
80.98	Dave Ottley	24 Sep 88
80.92	Mark Roberson	12 Jun 88
79.54	Gary Jenson	19 Jun 91
77.84	Peter Yates	21 Feb 87
[10] 76.28	Nick Neiland	9 Jul 94
76.10	Keith Beard	18 May 91
75.52	Marcus Humphries	25 Jul 87
75.28	Nigel Stainton	5 Aug 89
74.90	Darryl Brand	27 Jun 86
74.72	Chris Crutchley	13 Jul 86
74.70	Myles Cottrell	16 May 92
73.26	David Messom	25 Apr 87
72.92	Stefan Baldwin	8 May 93
71.94	Stephen Harrison	9 Jul 94
71.86	Tony Hatton	3 May 93 [20]

DECATHLON (1985 Tables)

8847	Daley Thompson	9 Aug 84
8078	Alex Kruger	29 May 94
7980	Simon Shirley	24 Aug 94
	8036 for NZ	29 Sep 88
7922 w	Brad McStravick	28 May 84
	7885 h	6 May 84
7904	David Bigham	28 Jun 92
7901 h	Peter Gabbett	22 May 72
7889	Eugene Gilkes	18 May 86
7874	Colin Boreham	23 May 82
7787	Brian Taylor	30 May 93
7748	Eric Hollingsworth	30 May 93 [10]
7740	Greg Richards	7 Jun 87
7713	James Stevenson	5 Jun 93
7708	Fidelis Obikwu	28 May 84
7663	Rafer Joseph	24 Aug 94
7656	Anthony Brannen	24 Jul 91
7643 w	Tom Leeson	8 Sep 85
	7565	11 Aug 85
7616	Barry Thomas	23 Aug 92
7610	Jamie Quarry	24 Aug 94
7596 h	Mike Corden	27 Jun 76
7594	Mark Bishop	3 Sep 89 [20]

3000 METRES TRACK WALK

11:24.4	Mark Easton	10 May 89
11:28.4	Phil Vesty	9 May 84
11:29.6 i	Tim Berrett	21 Jan 90
11:31.0	Andi Drake	22 Jul 90
11:32.2	Ian McCombie	20 Jul 88
11:39.0 i+	Martin Rush	8 Feb 92
11:39.54	Andy Penn	22 May 91
11:42.5	Steve Partington	16 Sep 92
11:44.68	Roger Mills	7 Aug 81
11:45.1	Chris Maddocks	9 Aug 87

10,000 METRES TRACK WALK

40:06.65	Ian McCombie	4 Jun 89
40:53.60	Phil Vesty	28 May 84
40:54.7	Steve Barry	19 Mar 83
	track short but walked full distance	
	41:13.62	19 Jun 82
40:55.6	Martin Rush	14 Sep 91
41:06.57	Chris Maddocks	20 Jun 87
41:14.3	Mark Easton	5 Feb 89
41:18.64	Andi Drake	5 Jun 88
41:33.0	Darrell Stone	6 Feb 93
41:35.6	Steve Partington	10 Jun 92
41:49.06	Sean Martindale	26 Jun 90 [10]
41:55.5	Phil Embleton	14 Apr 71
41:59.10	Andy Penn	27 Jul 91
42:06.35	Gordon Vale	2 Aug 81
42:07.42	Martin Bell	28 Jun 92
42:08.57	Paul Blagg	28 Aug 89
42:23.0	Mike Parker	2 Feb 86
42:28.0	Kieron Butler	22 Jun 93
42:34.6	Paul Nihill	28 May 72
42:35.6	Ken Matthews	1 Aug 60

20 KILOMETRES ROAD WALK

1:22:03	Ian McCombie	23 Sep 88
1:22:12	Chris Maddocks	3 May 92
1:22:51	Steve Barry	26 Feb 83
1:23:34	Andy Penn	29 Feb 92
1:23:34	Martin Rush	29 Feb 92
1:24:04	Mark Easton	25 Feb 89
1:24:04.0t	Andi Drake	26 May 90
1:24:07.6t	Phil Vesty	1 Dec 84
1:24:18	Steve Partington	12 Dec 90
1:24:25	Tim Berrett	21 Apr 90
1:24:50	Paul Nihill	30 Jul 72
1:25:05	Darrell Stone	6 Jun 92
1:25:42	Martin Bell	9 May 92
1:25:53.6t	Sean Martindale	28 Apr 89
1:27:00	Roger Mills	30 Jun 80
1:27:16	Les Morton	25 Feb 89
1:27:35	Olly Flynn	3 Oct 76
1:27:46	Brian Adams	11 Oct 75
1:27:59	Phil Embleton	3 Apr 71
1:28:02	Paul Blagg	27 Feb 82

50 KILOMETRES ROAD WALK

3:51:37	Chris Maddocks	28 Oct 90
3:57:48	Les Morton	30 Apr 89
3:59:55	Paul Blagg	5 Sep 87
4:03:08	Dennis Jackson	16 Mar 86
4:06:14	Barry Graham	20 Apr 85
4:07:23	Bob Dobson	21 Oct 79
4:07:57	Ian Richards	20 Apr 80
4:08:41	Adrian James	12 Apr 80
4:09:15	Don Thompson	10 Oct 65
4:09:22	Mike Smith	27 Mar 89
4:09:33	Mark Easton	11 Oct 92
4:10:23	Darrell Stone	6 May 90
4:10:42	Amos Seddon	9 Mar 80
4:11:31	Paul Nihill	18 Oct 64
4:12:00	Sean Martindale	16 Oct 93
4:12:02	Martin Rush	28 Jul 91
4:12:37	John Warhurst	27 May 72
4:12:50	Darren Thorn	6 May 90
4:13:25	Allan King	16 Apr 83
4:14:03	Tom Misson	20 Jun 59

4 x 100 METRES RELAY

37.77	UK	22 Aug 93
Jackson, Jarrett, Regis, Christie		
37.98	UK	1 Sep 90
Braithwaite, Regis, Adam, Christie		
38.05	UK	21 Aug 93
John, Jarrett, Braithwaite, Christie		
38.08	UK	8 Aug 92
Adam, Jarrett, Regis, Christie		
38.09	UK	1 Sep 91
Jarrett, Regis, Braithwaite, Christie		
38.28	UK	1 Oct 88
Bunney, Regis, McFarlane, Christie		
38.34	UK	9 Sep 89
Callender, Regis, Adam, Christie		
38.36	UK	31 Aug 91
Jarrett, Regis, Braithwaite, Christie		
38.39	UK	5 Aug 89
Jarrett, Regis, Adam, Christie		
38.46	UK	10 Sep 94
Braithwaite, Jarrett, Regis, Christie		
38.52	UK	1 Oct 88
Bunney, Regis, McFarlane, Christie		
38.53	UK	26 Jun 93
John, Jarrett, Regis, Christie		
38.62	UK	1 Aug 80
McFarlane, Wells, Sharp, McMaster		
38.64	UK	7 Aug 91
Livingston ¶, Regis, Callender, Rosswess		
38.64	UK	7 Aug 92
Jarrett, Regis, Adam, Christie		
38.64	UK	15 Jul 94
John, Braithwaite, Regis, Christie		
38.67	England	3 Feb 90
Callender, Regis, Adam, Christie		
38.68	UK	11 Aug 84
Thompson, Reid, McFarlane, Wells		
38.71	UK	31 Aug 86
Bunney, Thompson, McFarlane, Christie		
38.72	UK	25 Jun 94
John, Wariso, Regis, Christie		

4 x 400 METRES RELAY

2:57.53	UK	1 Sep 91
Black, Redmond, Regis, Akabusi		
2:58.22	UK	1 Sep 90
Sanders, Akabusi, Regis, Black		
2:58.86	UK	6 Sep 87
Redmond, Akabusi, Black, Brown		
2:59.13	UK	11 Aug 84
Akabusi, Cook, Bennett, Brown		
2:59.13	UK	14 Aug 94
McKenzie, Whittle, Black, Ladejo		
2:59.49	UK	31 Aug 91
Mafe, Redmond, Richardson, Akabusi		
2:59.73	UK	8 Aug 92
Black, Grindley, Akabusi, Regis		
2:59.84	UK	31 Aug 86
Redmond, Akabusi, Whittle, Black		
3:00.25	UK	27 Jun 93
Ladejo, Akabusi, Regis, Grindley		
3:00.46	UK	10 Sep 72
Reynolds, Pascoe, Hemery, Jenkins		
3:00.58	UK	30 Jun 91
Sanders, Akabusi, Whittle, Black		
3:00.68	UK	11 Sep 82
Jenkins, Cook, Bennett, Brown		
3:00.93	UK	19 Jun 92
Redmond, Akabusi, Ladejo, Black		
3:01.03	UK - Under 23	19 Jul 92
McKenzie, Grindley, Richardson, Ladejo		
3:01.12	UK	28 Jun 87
Harmsworth, Whittle, Bennett, Black		
3:01.20	UK	7 Aug 92
Richardson, Akabusi, Black, Ladejo		
3:01.21 A	UK	20 Oct 68
Winbolt Lewis, Campbell, Hemery, Sherwood		
3:01.26	UK	9 Sep 72
Reynolds, Pascoe, Hemery, Jenkins		
3:01.26	UK	5 Aug 86
Akabusi, Black, Bennett, Brown		

UNDER 20

100 METRES

10.21	Jamie Henderson	6 Aug 87
10.25	Jason Gardener	21 Jul 94
10.25	Jason Livingston	9 Aug 90
10.29	Peter Radford	13 Sep 58
10.32	Mike McFarlane	6 Aug 78
10.34	Lincoln Asquith	25 Aug 83
10.37	Darren Campbell	26 Jul 91
10.38	Elliot Bunney	22 Aug 85
10.39	Jason John	28 Jul 90
10.43	Julian Golding	20 Jul 94

wind assisted

10.22	Lincoln Asquith	26 Jun 83
10.28	Darren Campbell	26 Jul 91
10.29	Mike McFarlane	7 Aug 78
10.29	Elliot Bunney	27 May 84
10.29	Trevor Cameron	11 Jun 94
10.34	Darren Braithwaite	25 Jun 88
10.34	Julian Golding	17 Sep 94
10.37	Courtney Rumbolt	25 Jun 88
10.37	Allyn Condon	3 Jul 93
10.38	Jason John	9 Aug 90
10.38	Ejike Wodu	3 Jul 93
10.38	Kevin Mark	3 Jul 93

hand timing

10.3	Martin Reynolds	29 Jun 68

200 METRES

20.54	Ade Mafe	25 Aug 85
20.67	David Jenkins	4 Sep 71
20.73 A	Ralph Banthorpe	15 Oct 68
20.78	John Regis	29 Sep 85
20.80	Mike McFarlane	1 Jul 79
20.85	Richard Ashby	25 Aug 85
20.86	Lincoln Asquith	28 Aug 83
20.86	Roger Hunter	5 May 84
20.87	Donovan Reid	7 Oct 82
20.87	Mark Smith	28 Jul 90
20.87	Darren Campbell	19 Sep 92

wind assisted

20.61	Darren Campbell	11 Aug 91
20.73	Julian Golding	17 Sep 94
20.85	Mark Smith	1 Jul 90

hand timing

20.6	David Jenkins	19 Sep 71

400 METRES

45.36	Roger Black	24 Aug 85
45.41	David Grindley	10 Aug 91
45.45	David Jenkins	13 Aug 71
45.53	Mark Richardson	10 Aug 91
46.03	Peter Crampton	8 Aug 87
46.13	Guy Bullock	31 Jul 93
46.22	Wayne McDonald	17 Jun 89
46.32	Derek Redmond	9 Sep 84
46.37	Mark Hylton	22 Jul 94
46.48	Roger Hunter	20 May 84

hand timing

45.7	Adrian Metcalfe	2 Sep 61

800 METRES (* 880 yards time less 0.7)

1:45.64	David Sharpe	5 Sep 86
1:45.77	Steve Ovett	4 Sep 74
1:46.46	John Gladwin	7 Jul 82
1:46.63	Curtis Robb	6 Jul 91
1:46.7* a	John Davies I	3 Jun 68
1:47.0	Ikem Billy	12 Jun 83
1:47.02	Chris McGeorge	8 Aug 81
1:47.08	Atle Douglas	22 Aug 87
1:47.22	Kevin McKay	5 Jun 88
1:47.35	Peter Elliott	23 Aug 81

1000 METRES

2:18.98	David Sharpe	19 Aug 86
2:19.92	Graham Williamson	8 Jul 79
2:20.0	Steve Ovett	17 Aug 73
2:20.02	Darryl Taylor	18 Aug 84
2:20.37	Johan Boakes	17 Jun 84
2:21.17	Curtis Robb	16 Sep 90
2:21.41	Stuart Paton	17 Sep 82
2:21.71	Kevin Glastonbury	18 Jun 77
2:22.3	Chris McGeorge	19 Jul 81
2:22.69	Gary Staines	17 Sep 82

1500 METRES

3:36.6 +	Graham Williamson	17 Jul 79
3:40.09	Steve Cram	27 Aug 78
3:40.68	Brian Treacy	24 Jul 90
3:40.72	Gary Taylor	8 Jul 81
3:40.90	David Robertson	28 Jul 92
3:41.59	Chris Sly	22 Jul 77
3:42.2	Paul Wynn	9 Aug 83
3:42.5	Colin Reitz	8 Aug 79
3:42.67	Matthew Hibberd	28 Jul 92
3:42.7	David Sharpe	17 Oct 85

ONE MILE

3:53.15	Graham Williamson	17 Jul 79
3:57.03	Steve Cram	14 Sep 79
3:58.68	Steve Flint	26 May 80
3:59.4	Steve Ovett	17 Jul 74
4:00.31	Johan Boakes	5 Aug 86
4:00.6	Simon Mugglestone	16 Aug 87
4:00.67	Brian Treacy	22 Aug 90
4:01.0	David Sharpe	3 May 86
4:01.5	Tony Leonard	12 Sep 77
4:01.5	Gary Staines	19 Sep 82

3000 METRES

7:48.28	Jon Richards	9 Jul 83
7:51.84	Steve Binns	8 Sep 79
7:56.28	John Doherty	13 Jul 80
7:59.55	Paul Davies-Hale	8 Aug 81
8:00.1	Mick Morton	11 Jul 78
8:00.7	Graham Williamson	29 Jul 78
8:00.73	David Black	24 Jul 71
8:00.8	Steve Anders	1 Aug 78
8:00.88	Paul Taylor	12 Jun 85
8:01.2	Ian Stewart I	7 Sep 68

5000 METRES

13:27.04	Steve Binns	14 Sep 79
13:35.95	Paul Davies-Hale	11 Sep 81
13:37.4	David Black	10 Sep 71
13:43.82	Simon Mugglestone	24 May 87
13:44.64	Julian Goater	14 Jul 72
13:48.74	Jon Richards	28 May 83
13:48.84	John Doherty	8 Aug 80
13:49.1 a	Nat Muir	21 Aug 77
13:53.30	Ian Stewart I	3 Aug 68
13:53.3 a	Nick Lees	21 Aug 77

2000 METRES STEEPLECHASE

5:29.61	Colin Reitz	18 Aug 79
5:31.12	Paul Davies-Hale	22 Aug 81
5:32.84	Tom Hanlon	20 Jul 86
5:34.8 a	Michael Morris	24 Aug 75
5:38.01	Ken Baker	1 Aug 82
5:38.2	Spencer Duval	8 Jul 89
5:39.3 a	Graeme Fell	11 Jul 78
5:39.93	Eddie Wedderburn	9 Sep 79
5:40.2	Paul Campbell	31 Jul 77
5:40.2	John Hartigan	27 Jun 84

3000 METRES STEEPLECHASE

8:29.85	Paul Davies-Hale	31 Aug 81
8:42.75	Colin Reitz	6 Jun 79
8:44.68	Alastair O'Connor	12 Aug 90
8:44.91	Ken Baker	30 May 82
8:45.65	Spencer Duval	17 Jun 89
8:47.1	Tom Conlon	6 Jul 80
8:47.49	Tom Hanlon	8 Jun 86
8:48.43	Graeme Fell	16 Jul 78
8:50.14	David Long	13 Jul 73
8:51.02	Tony Staynings	14 Jul 72

110 METRES HURDLES (3'3")

13.77	Kevin Lumsdon	8 Aug 92
13.8	Jon Ridgeon	13 Jul 84
13.8	Paul Gray	16 Jul 88
14.0	Paul Brice	25 Jun 83
14.0	Colin Jackson	27 Aug 84
14.0	James Hughes	11 May 93
14.0	Neil Owen	2 Aug 92
	14.06	4 Jul 92
14.01	Jamie Quarry	13 Jul 91
14.1	Mark Holtom	19 Jun 77
14.1	Brett St Louis	3 Aug 86
14.13	Derek Wilson	25 Jun 83

wind assisted

13.6	Mark Holtom	9 Jul 77
13.8	Paul Brice	9 Jul 83
13.8	Colin Jackson	15 Jul 84
13.8	Brett St Louis	11 Jul 87

110 METRES HURDLES (3'6")

13.44	Colin Jackson	19 Jul 86
13.46	Jon Ridgeon	23 Aug 85
13.72	Tony Jarrett	24 May 87
13.91	David Nelson	21 Jun 86
13.97	Paul Gray	30 Jul 88
14.03	Brett St Louis	27 Jun 87
14.06	Mark Holtom	7 Aug 77
14.08	Paul Brice	26 Aug 83
14.14	Neil Owen	17 Sep 92
14.18	James Archampong	21 Jul 94

wind assisted

13.42	Colin Jackson	27 Jul 86
13.82	David Nelson	5 Jul 86

400 METRES HURDLES

50.22	Martin Briggs	28 Aug 83
50.70	Noel Levy	8 Jul 94
51.07	Philip Beattie	20 Aug 82
51.15 A	Andy Todd	18 Oct 67
51.31	Gary Oakes	9 Sep 77
51.48	Bob Brown	19 Jun 88
51.51	Max Robertson	24 Jul 82
51.55	Mark Whitby	26 Aug 83
51.66	Paul Goacher	2 Aug 80
51.91	Peter Campbell	19 Jun 88

HIGH JUMP

2.37	Steve Smith	20 Sep 92
2.27	Brendan Reilly	27 May 90
2.25	Geoff Parsons	9 Jul 83
2.24	John Hill	23 Aug 85
2.23	Mark Lakey	29 Aug 82
2.22	Dalton Grant	3 Jul 85
2.20	Byron Morrison	14 Jul 84
2.18	Ossie Cham	14 Jun 80
2.18	Alex Kruger	26 Jun 82
2.18	Stephen Ritchie	15 Jul 89
2.18	Hopeton Lindo	23 Jul 89

POLE VAULT

5.50	Neil Winter	9 Aug 92
5.30	Matthew Belsham	15 Sep 90
5.21	Andy Ashurst	2 Sep 84
5.20	Billy Davey	5 Jun 83
5.20	Warren Siley	4 Aug 90
5.20	Nick Buckfield	31 May 92
5.10	Brian Hooper	1 Oct 72
5.10	Michael Edwards	20 Jun 87
5.05	Ian Tullett	22 Aug 87
5.05	Dean Mellor	7 Jul 90

LONG JUMP

7.98	Stewart Faulkner	6 Aug 88
7.91	Steve Phillips	10 Aug 91
7.84	Wayne Griffith	25 Aug 89
7.76	Carl Howard	31 Jul 93
7.73	Jason Canning	20 Apr 88
7.72	Daley Thompson	21 May 77
7.70	Kevin Liddington	27 Aug 88
7.66	Barry Nevison	7 Jul 85
7.62	Colin Mitchell	11 Jul 78
7.61	Darren Gomersall	19 Jul 87

wind assisted

8.04	Stewart Faulkner	20 Aug 88
7.96	Colin Jackson	17 May 86
7.82	Kevin Liddington	25 Jun 89
7.72	John Herbert	15 Jun 80

TRIPLE JUMP

16.58	Tosi Fasinro	15 Jun 91
16.53	Larry Achike	24 Jul 94
16.24	Aston Moore	11 Jun 75
16.22	Mike Makin	17 May 81
16.13	Steven Anderson	11 Jun 83
16.03	John Herbert	23 Jun 81
15.95	Keith Connor	30 Aug 76
15.94	Vernon Samuels	27 Jun 82
15.93	Tayo Erogbogbo	17 Sep 94
15.92	Lawrence Lynch	13 Jul 85

wind assisted

16.81	Tosi Fasinro	15 Jun 91
16.67	Larry Achike	24 Jul 94
16.43	Mike Makin	14 Jun 81
16.31	Aston Moore	9 Aug 75
16.07	Vernon Samuels	14 Aug 82
16.01	Julian Golley	22 Jul 90

SHOT (7.26kg)

18.21 i	Matt Simson	3 Feb 89
18.11		27 Aug 89
17.78 i	Billy Cole	10 Mar 84
17.72		2 Jun 84
17.36 i	Chris Ellis	8 Dec 84
17.10		7 Jul 85
17.26 i	Geoff Capes	16 Nov 68
16.80		30 Jul 68
17.22	Tony Zaidman	4 Jul 81
16.61	Simon Williams	10 Aug 86
16.60	Alan Carter	11 May 63
16.48	Martyn Lucking	24 Aug 57
16.47	Paul Buxton	25 May 75
16.21	Mike Lindsay	29 Jul 57

SHOT (6.25kg)

19.47	Matt Simson	20 May 89
19.15	Billy Cole	19 May 84
18.66 i	Simon Williams	15 Nov 86
18.52		11 Jul 86
18.20 i	Chris Ellis	16 Feb 85
18.13		14 Jul 84
17.81	Tony Zaidman	16 May 81
17.58	Nigel Spratley	28 May 89
17.32	Andy Vince	15 May 77
17.31	Mitchell Smith	11 Jun 85
17.30	Jamie Cockburn	20 Sep 92
17.26	Neil Gray	19 May 84
17.26 i	Neal Brunning	9 Dec 89

DISCUS (2kg)

55.10	Glen Smith	31 Aug 91
53.42	Paul Mardle	25 Jul 81
53.40	Bob Weir	10 Aug 80
53.32	Paul Buxton	9 Aug 75
53.12	Lee Newman	2 Aug 92
53.02	Simon Williams	16 Aug 86
52.84	Jamie Murphy	14 Jun 92
52.14	Robert Russell	4 Jul 93
51.70	Richard Slaney	27 Jul 75
51.66	Neal Brunning	30 Jul 89

DISCUS (1.75kg)

60.76	Glen Smith	26 May 91
56.64	Jamie Murphy	19 May 90
56.10	Lee Newman	4 Jul 92
56.00	Simon Williams	17 May 86
55.94	Mark Davies	19 Aug 90
55.44	Neal Brunning	8 Jul 89
55.00	Robert Russell	16 May 93
54.50	Paul Mardle	27 Jun 81
53.84	Bob Weir	14 Sep 80
53.50	Colin Bastien	8 Jun 85

HAMMER (7.26kg)

67.48	Paul Head	16 Sep 84
67.10	Jason Byrne	6 Aug 89
66.14	Martin Girvan	21 Jul 79
65.86	Bob Weir	6 Sep 80
65.30	Karl Andrews	2 Jul 94
64.14	Ian Chipchase	26 Sep 71
63.84	Andrew Tolputt	7 Sep 86
63.72	Gareth Cook	10 Jul 88
62.82	Mike Jones	29 Aug 82
62.02	Peter Vivian	1 Jul 89

HAMMER (6.25kg)

74.92	Jason Byrne	17 Dec 89
73.28	Bob Weir	14 Sep 80
72.66	Paul Head	2 Sep 84
71.84	Gareth Cook	28 May 88
70.36	Andrew Tolputt	21 Sep 86
69.10	Karl Andrews	6 Aug 94
68.84	Eric Berry	Jul 73
67.80	Martin Girvan	7 Jul 79
67.52	Vaughan Cooper	19 May 84
67.48	Mike Jones	2 Jun 82

JAVELIN

79.50	Steve Backley	5 Jun 88
74.54	Gary Jenson	19 Sep 86
74.24	Mark Roberson	18 Jul 86
73.76	Nigel Bevan	29 Aug 87
71.74	Myles Cottrell	29 Jul 89
70.16	James Hurrion	19 Jul 91
69.62	Stefan Baldwin	8 Jul 89
68.74	Jon Clarke	14 Jun 86
68.38	James Drennen	12 Jul 91
68.30	Mark Lawrence	31 Jul 88

DECATHLON (1985 Tables)

8082	Daley Thompson	31 Jul 77
7488	David Bigham	9 Aug 90
7299	Eugene Gilkes	24 May 81
7274	James Stevenson	24 Jun 90
7247 h	Brian Taylor	7 May 89
7169	Barry Thomas	5 Aug 90
7126	Fidelis Obikwu	16 Sep 79
7112	Gavin Sunshine	30 Jul 93
7018	Jamie Quarry	30 Jun 91
6958	Roy Mitchell	29 Sep 74

3000 METRES TRACK WALK

11:54.23	Tim Berrett	23 Jun 84
12:01.89 i	Philip King	21 Feb 93
12:02.0		12 May 92
12:02.04	Phil Vesty	24 Jul 82
12:16.5	David Hucks	5 Aug 84
12:19.8	Gordon Vale	11 Mar 81
12:23.2	Martin Rush	18 Sep 83
12:23.53	Darrell Stone	19 Sep 87
12:24.45	Richard Dorman	5 Sep 80
12:25.8	Gareth Holloway	17 Jun 89
12:29.3	Ian Ashforth	19 May 85

10,000 METRES TRACK WALK

41:52.13	Darrell Stone	7 Aug 87
42:06.35	Gordon Vale	2 Aug 81
42:46.3	Phil Vesty	20 Mar 82
42:47.7	Philip King	2 May 92
43:04.09	Tim Berrett	25 Aug 83
43:42.75	Martin Rush	29 May 83
43:54.25	Gareth Brown	7 Aug 87
44:22.12	Gareth Holloway	5 Jun 88
44:22.38	Jon Vincent	1 Apr 89
44:30.0	Andy Penn	15 Mar 86

UNDER 17

100 METRES

10.51 o	Lincoln Asquith	4 Oct 80
10.67	Michael Nartey	28 Sep 91
10.69	Mike McFarlane	13 Aug 76
10.70	Steve Green	15 Jul 72
10.72	Peter Little	6 Aug 77
10.72	Trevor Cameron	7 Aug 93
10.73	Danny Joyce	17 Aug 91
10.75	Elliot Bunney	28 May 83
10.75	Dwain Chambers	28 May 94
10.76	Paul Ashen	1 Aug 81
10.76	Kevin Mark	15 Aug 92

wind assisted

10.38	Kevin Mark	3 Jul 93
10.56	Dwain Chambers	9 Jul 94
10.57	Trevor Cameron	3 Jul 93
10.62	Elliot Bunney	25 Jun 83
10.62	Jamie Nixon	7 Jul 85
10.65	Michael Williams	20 Jun 87
10.66	David Jackson	1 Jul 89

hand timing

10.5	Mike Powell	17 Sep 78

200 METRES

20.92	Ade Mafe	27 Aug 83
21.24	Peter Little	21 Aug 77
21.25	Mark Richardson	24 Jul 88
21.44	Roger Hunter	2 Aug 81
21.51	Darren Campbell	15 Sep 90
21.53	Steven Eden	2 Aug 81
21.56	Trevor Cameron	8 Aug 93
21.63	Richard Ashby	7 Aug 83
21.64	Elliot Bunney	7 Aug 83
21.65	Uvie Ugono	7 Aug 94

wind assisted

21.17	Mark Richardson	20 Aug 88
21.25	Trevor Cameron	25 Sep 93
21.32	Graham Beasley	9 Jul 94
21.38	Elliot Bunney	13 Aug 83

hand timing

21.5	Steve Green	6 Aug 72
21.5	Phil Brown	20 May 78
21.5	Lincoln Asquith	23 Aug 80
21.5	Jamie Nixon	12 May 85

wind assisted

21.0	Peter Little	30 Jul 77

400 METRES

46.43	Mark Richardson	28 Jul 88
46.74	Guy Bullock	17 Sep 92
47.81	Mark Hylton	17 Jul 93
48.11	Gary Thomas	18 Sep 82
48.25	Adrian Patrick	2 Sep 89
48.36	David Simpson	29 May 89
48.41	Mark Tyler	11 Aug 84
48.46	Philip Harvey	24 Jun 79
48.63	Wayne McDonald	19 Jul 86
48.64	Cephas Howard	26 Jun 93

hand timing

48.2	David Simpson	8 Jul 89
48.3	David McKenzie	21 Sep 86
48.4	Steve Ovett	20 Aug 72
48.4	Chris Thompson	1 Aug 81
48.5	Gary Patterson	14 Jul 84
48.5	Gareth Bakewell	13 Jul 85
48.5	Wayne McDonald	14 Jun 86

800 METRES

1:49.9	Mark Sesay	18 Jul 89
1:50.7	Peter Elliott	16 Sep 79
1:50.90	Craig Winrow	21 Aug 88
1:51.0	Chris McGeorge	1 Jul 78
1:51.05	Malcolm Edwards	20 Sep 74
1:51.3	Julian Spooner	3 Aug 77
1:51.4	Kevin McKay	19 Aug 85
1:51.6	Neil Horsfield	31 Aug 83
1:51.6	David Gerard	21 Jul 84
1:51.8	Paul Burgess	14 Jul 87

1500 METRES

3:47.7	Steve Cram	14 May 77
3:48.49	Johan Boakes	28 Jun 84
3:49.9	Kelvin Newton	20 Jun 79
3:51.1	Jason Lobo	30 Aug 86
3:51.4	Darren Mead	26 Jul 85
3:51.7	Martin Forder	19 Sep 86
3:51.8	Mark Sesay	22 Aug 89
3:52.0	Stuart Poore	6 Sep 89
3:52.47	Simon Young	4 Aug 90
3:52.6	Glen Stewart	9 Sep 87

ONE MILE

4:06.7	Barrie Williams	22 Apr 72
4:09.5	Colin Clarkson	29 Aug 77
4:09.6	Alistair Currie	9 Jun 81

3000 METRES

8:13.4	Barrie Moss	15 Jul 72
8:15.4	Kevin Steere	30 Aug 71
8:19.08	Darren Mead	26 Aug 85
8:19.38	Johan Boakes	24 Jun 84
8:23.6	Ian Stewart II	14 Dec 77
8:24.2	Simon Goodwin	16 Jul 80
8:24.2	Jason Lobo	13 Aug 86
8:25.2	Colin Clarkson	3 Aug 77
8:26.3	Paul Williams	10 Aug 83
8:26.6	Jon Dennis	23 Apr 86

1500 METRES STEEPLECHASE

4:11.2	Steven Evans	15 Jul 74
4:12.3	Chris Sly	15 Jul 74
4:13.1	John Crowley	15 Jul 74
4:13.2	David Lewis	1 Jul 78
4:13.2	Darren Mead	16 Oct 85
4:13.7	Danny Fleming	31 Jul 77
4:13.9	Eddie Wedderburn	31 Jul 77
4:14.0	David Robertson	8 Jul 89
4:14.4	Steven Arnold	7 Sep 85
4:15.0	David Caton	9 Jun 84
4:15.0	Spencer Duval	12 Jul 86

100 METRES HURDLES

12.68	Matthew Clements	8 Aug 93
12.90	Stephen Markham	17 Aug 91
12.97	Jon Snade	8 Aug 93
13.01	Hugh Teape	3 Aug 80
13.05	Brett St Louis	4 Aug 85
13.07	Jon Ridgeon	7 Aug 83
13.09	Damien Greaves	8 Jul 94
13.10	Ricky Glover	17 Aug 91
13.12	Ross Baillie	13 Aug 94
13.15	Perry Batchelor	4 Jul 92

wind assisted

12.47	Matthew Clements	9 Jul 94
12.70	Damien Greaves	9 Jul 94
12.88	Nick Csemiczky	13 Jul 91
12.90	Ricky Glover	13 Jul 91
12.99	Neil Owen	1 Jul 90
13.01	Berian Davies	30 Jul 89
13.06	Dominic Lewis	29 May 89

hand timing

12.8	Brett St Louis	28 Jul 85
12.8	Richard Dunn	29 Jun 91
12.9	Hugh Teape	31 Aug 80

wind assisted

12.6	Brett St Louis	20 Jul 85
12.9	Jon Ridgeon	9 Jul 83

400 METRES HURDLES (2'9")

53.06	Philip Beattie (3'0")	2 Aug 80
53.14	Martin Briggs	2 Aug 80
53.30	Mark Rowlands	31 Jul 94
53.55	Charles Robertson-Adams	31 Jul 94
53.58	Noel Levy	13 Jul 91
53.64	Dean Park	17 May 94
53.69	Max Robertson	2 Aug 80
53.69	Bob Brown	9 Aug 86
53.71	Andrew Bargh	11 Jul 92
53.82	Robert Taylor	9 Aug 86

hand timing

53.2	Philip Beattie	24 May 80

HIGH JUMP

2.23	Mark Lakey	29 Aug 82
2.15	Ossie Cham	14 Jul 79
2.15	Brendan Reilly	7 May 89
2.15	Stanley Osuide	1 Sep 91
2.12	Femi Abejide	11 Jul 81
2.11	Leroy Lucas	6 Aug 83
2.10	Dalton Grant	18 Sep 82
2.10	Tim Blakeway	29 Aug 87
2.10	James Brierley	16 May 93
2.09	Steve Smith	10 Sep 89

POLE VAULT

5.20	Neil Winter	2 Sep 90
4.90	Warren Siley	8 Sep 89
4.80	Billy Davey	14 Sep 80
4.76	Nick Buckfield	11 Jun 89
4.72	Ian Lewis	24 Aug 85
4.66	Michael Edwards	24 Aug 85
4.53	Keith Stock	5 Sep 73
4.50	Christian North	26 Aug 90
4.50	Michael Barber	15 Sep 90
4.50	Neil Young	5 Jun 93

LONG JUMP

7.32	Kevin Liddington	16 May 87
7.25	Alan Slack	12 Jun 76
7.21	Hugh Teape	17 May 80
7.20	Hugh Davidson	21 Jun 80
7.19	Onochie Onuorah	8 Jul 89
7.18	Barry Nevison	1 May 83
7.17	Hugh Whyte	15 Jul 79
7.15	Matthew John	29 Jun 86
7.14	Stewart Faulkner	17 Aug 85
7.12	4 athletes	

wind assisted

7.40	Matthew John	10 May 86
7.25	Nathan Morgan	27 Aug 94
7.23	Onochie Onuorah	26 May 90
7.22	Paul Hanson	7 Jul 78

TRIPLE JUMP

15.65	Vernon Samuels	18 Jul 81
15.50	Junior Campbell	18 May 86
15.45	Steven Anderson	2 Aug 81
15.28	Larry Achike	22 Jun 91
15.14	Marvin Bramble	8 Aug 93
14.94	Hugh Teape	17 May 80
14.93	Mark Whitehead	26 Aug 85
14.90	Lawrence Lynch	21 Jul 84
14.88	Ian Timbers	5 Oct 80
14.84	Peter Vaughan	2 May 83

wind assisted

15.25	Marvin Bramble	3 Jul 93
15.08	Lawrence Lynch	29 Apr 84
15.06	Craig Duncan	7 Aug 82
14.88	Carl Howard	13 Jul 90

SHOT (5kg)

19.22	Chris Ellis	4 Jun 82
18.90	Matt Simson	23 Aug 86
18.90	Neal Brunning	6 Sep 87
18.25	Billy Cole	1 Aug 81
17.91	Tony Zaidman	28 May 78
17.76	George Brocklebank	22 Jul 79
17.40	Osita Iwenjiora	20 Sep 89
17.39i	Emeka Udechuku	17 Dec 94
17.37 i	Guy Litherland	15 Dec 85
17.36	Piers Selby	10 Jul 92
17.30 i	Simon Williams	1 Dec 84
17.30	Jason Mulcahy	7 Jul 89
17.24	Mark Edwards	20 Aug 91

DISCUS (1.5kg)

56.14	Chris Symonds	6 Sep 87
55.94	Simon Williams	9 Sep 84
55.90	Guy Litherland	14 Sep 85
55.72	Keith Homer	27 Jun 82
55.52	Glen Smith	14 May 88
55.36	Neal Brunning	7 Jun 87
54.90	Emeka Udechuku	8 Jul 94
54.18	Matthew Symonds	21 Jul 84
53.80	Paul Mardle	19 May 79
52.76	Julian Willett	17 Jun 89
52.76	James South	1 Sep 91

HAMMER (5kg)

76.28	Andrew Tolputt	11 Aug 84
73.90	Paul Head	29 Aug 81
73.00	Nick Steinmetz	17 Jul 93
71.34	Tony Kenneally	7 Sep 80
70.82	Jason Byrne	20 Jun 87
68.62	Peter Vivian	16 May 87
67.64	Gareth Cook	22 Sep 85
67.48	Christopher Howe	24 Jun 84
66.92	Paul Murden	8 May 85
66.30	Malcolm Croad	21 Jul 90

JAVELIN (700g)

72.78	Gary Jenson (800g)	10 Sep 83
72.48		3 Jul 83
70.30	Colin Mackenzie	6 Jul 79
68.26	Ian Marsh	31 Jul 77
68.18	James Hurrion	3 Jun 90
66.88	David Messom	4 Jul 81
66.86	Michael Williams	16 Jul 79
66.52	Marcus Humphries	17 Sep 78
65.68	Tim Eldridge	18 Aug 91
65.16	Mark Wells	31 May 77
64.92	Jason Beaumont	11 Jun 83
64.92	Paul Bushnell	20 Sep 85

OCTATHLON (1985 Tables)

5531	James Stevenson	18 Sep 88
5378	Matthew Lewis	20 Sep 92
5311	Dean Macey	18 Sep 94
5304	Tom Leeson	28 Sep 80
5208	Fyn Corcoran	18 Sep 94
5194	Bryan Long	26 Sep 76
5149	Paul Hourihan	19 Sep 93
5121	Chris Hindley	20 Sep 92
5106	Jeremy Lay	29 Sep 85
5102	Matthew Douglas	22 Aug 93

3000 METRES TRACK WALK

12:04.9	Philip King	18 May 91
12:35.94	David Hucks	30 Aug 82
12:44.8	Gordon Vale	11 Oct 78
12:50.9	Jon Vincent	15 Jul 87
13:03.5	Ian Ashforth	16 Sep 84
13:05.8	Sean Maxwell	8 Aug 76
13:08.4	Ian McCombie	8 Aug 76
13:09.74	Kirk Taylor	2 Jun 84
13:10.6	Niall Troy	23 Jul 78
13:12.7	Tim Berrett	16 Aug 81

5000 METRES TRACK WALK

20:46.5	Philip King	29 Sep 91
22:17.5	Russell Hutchings	27 Sep 86
22:32.5	Gareth Holloway	27 Sep 86
22:35.0	Ian Ashforth	6 Jun 84
22:37.0	Jonathan Bott	27 Sep 86
22:42.0	Martin Young	20 Aug 88
22:42.19	Jon Vincent	6 Jun 86

UNDER 15

100 METRES

11.0	Norman Ellis	23 Jul 89
11.05	Jamie Nixon	21 Jul 84
11.10	Courage Edo	15 Aug 92
11.1	Michael Hitchen	24 Apr 77
11.1	Ray Burke	25 Aug 84
11.1	Duncan Game	11 May 86
11.1	Michael Williams	31 Aug 86
11.1	Jeffrey Anderson	3 Jul 89
11.1	Matthew Clements	23 Aug 92

wind assisted

10.9 dt	Ronald Don	20 Jun 81
11.00	Steven Wiggans	9 Jul 94
11.0	Malcolm James	24 Jun 77
11.0	Ian Strange	24 Jun 77
11.0	John Burt	6 Sep 80
11.0	Jeffrey Anderson	19 Aug 89
11.0	Matthew Clements	15 Sep 91
11.05	Ray Burke	11 Aug 84
11.06	Duncan Game	5 Jul 86
11.06	Paul Chantler	9 Jul 94

200 METRES
22.2	Michael Williams	12 Jul 86
22.30	Jamie Nixon	29 Sep 84
22.3	Anthony Cairns	12 Jul 86
22.4	Ade Mafe	11 Nov 81
22.4	Duncan Game	29 Jun 86
22.54	Matthew Clements	16 Aug 92
22.6	Stuart Lawrenson	27 Jun 76
22.69	Chris Blake	8 Aug 93

wind assisted
21.9	Anthony Cairns	21 Jun 86
22.26	Stephen Daly	9 Jul 94
22.39	André Duffus	9 Jul 94
22.46	Robert Allenby	9 Jul 94

400 METRES
49.8	Mark Tyler	25 Aug 82
49.9	David McKenzie	11 Aug 85
50.0	Simon Heaton	7 Jul 79
50.1	Ade Mafe	6 Sep 81
50.3	Malcolm James	29 Aug 77
50.5 i	Cephas Howard	14 Dec 91
50.7		19 May 91
50.9	Alan Leonard	30 Aug 78
50.9	Noel Goode	7 Jul 79
51.00	Paul Roberts	22 Jul 84
51.0	Michael Penn	76
51.0	Marc Newton	30 Jul 94

800 METRES
1:53.6	David Gerrard	9 Nov 83
1:56.1	Craig Winrow	12 Jul 86
1:56.6	Paul Burgess	13 Jul 85
1:56.9	Mark Sesay	17 Aug 87
1:57.1	Delroy Smith	12 Jul 86
1:57.12	Michael Combe	14 Aug 93
1:57.2 a	Tony Jarman	15 Sep 78
1:57.5	Noel Goode	11 Jul 79
1:57.7	Eric Kimani	15 Sep 81
1:57.87	Austin Finn	7 Jul 91

1500 METRES
4:03.0	Glen Stewart	28 Aug 85
4:03.0	Scott West	28 Aug 90
4:03.52	Mike Isherwood	17 Sep 82
4:03.56	Richard Youngs	17 Sep 82
4:03.6	Douglas Stones	7 Jul 79
4:03.7	David Gerard	31 Jul 83
4:05.7	Ben Mabon	1 Sep 85
4:05.8	Graham Green	19 Jun 79
4:06.0	Eric Kimani	29 Jul 81
4:06.5	Paul Hemmings	18 Jul 82

ONE MILE
4:21.9	Glen Stewart	11 Sep 85

3000 METRES
8:47.0	Ben Mabon	16 Jul 85
8:48.8	Dale Smith	14 Aug 85
8:51.1	Mark Slowikowski	4 Jun 80

8:54.6	Gary Taylor	14 Sep 77
8:54.6	David Bean	22 Jul 79
8:56.0	Paul Ryder	29 Aug 79
8:56.4	Stuart Bond	10 Sep 91
8:56.9	David Gerard	12 Oct 83
8:57.0	Philip Hennessy	28 Jul 82
8:57.6	Chris Taylor	16 Jul 69

80 METRES HURDLES
10.71	Matthew Clements	15 Aug 92
11.0	Austin Drysdale	22 Jun 75
11.1	Ricky Glover	2 Jul 89
11.1	Thomas Bradwell	14 Jul 90
11.20	Anthony Lashley	13 Jul 91
11.2	David Colford	13 May 84
11.2	Dominic Lewis	26 Sep 87
11.27	Ian Cawley	7 Aug 93

wind assisted
11.00	Tom Benn	9 Jul 94
11.02	Nick Dowsett	10 Jul 93
11.12	Sam Allen	10 Jul 93
11.17	Anthony Lashley	18 Aug 91
11.2	Mark Bentley	29 Jun 75

HIGH JUMP
2.04	Ross Hepburn	22 Aug 76
1.97	Andrew Lynch	29 Aug 88
1.95	Mark Lakey	14 Sep 80
1.94 i	Paul Byrne	10 Dec 77
1.93	Ewan Gittins	21 Jul 84
1.91	Mark Smith	15 Jul 89
1.91 i	Lee Broomfield	19 Dec 92
1.91	Edward Willers	9 Jul 94
1.91	Matthew Brereton	9 Jul 94

POLE VAULT
4.40 o	Neil Winter	1 Oct 88
4.30	Christian Linskey	19 Jun 94
4.18	Ian Lewis	24 May 83
4.00	Jimmy Lewis	9 Sep 79
3.90	Peter Eyre	2 Jul 89
3.90	Martin Parley	6 Jun 92
3.90	Christian Linskey	31 Jul 93
3.90	Steve Francis	11 Sep 93
3.80	Steve Fuller	11 May 80
3.80 i	Christian North	11 Dec 88
3.80	Mark Davis	9 Jul 91

LONG JUMP
6.79	Onochie Onuorah	17 Sep 88
6.77	Barry Nevison	30 Aug 81
6.72	David Gilkes	6 Apr 92
6.62	Martin Giraud	25 May 92
6.60	Courage Edo	8 Aug 92
6.59	Danny Smith	29 Aug 87
6.59 i	Marcellus Peters	11 Dec 93
6.51		18 Sep 93
6.58	Tony Allen	8 Aug 82
6.52	Julian Danquah	7 Jul 67
6.52	Ian Strange	24 Jun 77

wind assisted

7.12	Onochie Onuorah	17 Sep 88
6.54	David Conway	7 Jul 78
6.52	Andrew Booton	7 Jul 78

downhill

6.77	Eric Wood	57

TRIPLE JUMP

13.86	Jamie Quarry	10 Jul 87
13.79	Paul Dundas	11 Jun 88
13.77	Eugene Hechevarria	16 Sep 78
13.71	Larry Achike	10 Jun 89
13.69	Vernon Samuels	25 Aug 79
13.60	Steven Anderson	9 Jun 79
13.60	Steve Folkard	11 Jul 80
13.57	Errol Burrows	11 Jul 80
13.56	Delroy Ricketts	18 Jun 88
13.55	Darren Yeo	15 Jul 89
13.55	Michael Duberry	14 Jul 90

wind assisted

13.92	Eugene Hechevarria	8 Jul 78
13.87	Vernon Samuels	20 Sep 79

SHOT (4kg)

18.71	Chris Ellis	14 Jun 80
16.54	Geoff Hodgson	8 Jul 72
16.39	Peter Waterman	2 Jul 94
16.36 i	Billy Cole	1 Nov 79
16.11		7 Jul 79
16.29	Neal Brunning	11 Sep 85
16.14	Andrew Monaghan	70
16.05	John Nicholls	29 Jun 80
16.01	Ian McLaughlin	18 Sep 91
15.96	James Muirhead	14 Sep 85
15.95	Spencer English	3 Aug 86
15.94 i	Phil Adams	14 Dec 86

DISCUS (1.25kg)

53.08	Emeka Udechuku	5 Sep 93
50.80	Paul Mardle	3 Sep 77
50.32	Chris Symonds	23 Jul 85
50.04	Keith Homer	12 Jul 80
49.36	James Muirhead	12 May 85
49.32	Julian Douglas	16 Sep 79
49.22	Spencer English	1 Jun 86
48.84	Witold Leonowicz	23 Aug 80
48.78	Neville Lynch	7 Sep 80
48.76	Ben Walker	15 Aug 92

HAMMER (4kg)

70.78	Andrew Tolputt	9 Jul 82
67.24	Peter Vivian	22 Sep 85
64.28	Jason Byrne	22 Sep 85
63.68	Paul Binley	29 Sep 85
63.30	Richard Fedder	26 Aug 79
63.16	Tony Kenneally	29 May 78
62.06	Nick Steinmetz	4 Aug 91
61.08	Neil Curtis	11 Sep 88
60.52	Ian McLaughlin	21 Aug 91
59.94	Michael Rowlatt	2 Sep 90

JAVELIN (600g)

62.70	Paul Godwin	20 May 89
60.56	David Messom	6 Jul 79
60.56	Clifton Green	3 Jul 94
59.88	James Hurrion	17 Sep 88
59.52	Paul Price	19 Aug 79
58.94	Dan Carter	7 Aug 94
58.58	Justin Rubio	11 Jun 83
58.48	Andrew Ravenscroft	9 Aug 80
58.22	Michael Williams	21 Jul 77
57.84	Matthew Pedrick	12 Sep 93

PENTATHLON (1985 Tables)

3214	Onochie Onuorah	17 Sep 88
3187	Mark Newton	27 Aug 94
3163	Kevin Drury	27 Aug 94
3077 w	Cephas Howard	21 Sep 91
3031	Ricky Glover	17 Sep 89
3024	Tom Benn	17 Sep 94
2995	Marcellus Peters	19 Sep 93
2993	Sam Allen	19 Sep 93
2925	Scott Walker	20 Sep 92
2989	Ian Leaman	19 Sep 93

3000 METRES TRACK WALK

12:59.7	Philip King	10 Oct 89
13:35.0	Russell Hutchings	7 Sep 85
13:51.0	Robert Mecham	12 May 92
13:58.0	Jon Vincent	7 Sep 85
14:03.0	Neil Simpson	1 Apr 89
14:03.5	Nathan Kavanagh	20 Sep 81
14:13.0	Karl Atton	15 Mar 86
14:15.1 o	Matthew Hales	9 Oct 94
14:15.3		14 May 94

Road - *where superior to track time*

13:20	Jonathan Deakin	18 Sep 88
13:29	Robert Mecham	20 Apr 92
13:39	Neil Simpson	6 May 89
13:44 o	Matthew Hales	3 Dec 94
13:52	Ben Allkins	2 Dec 89
13:54	John Jones	18 Sep 88
13:56	Martin Young	23 Aug 86
13:58	Nathan Kavanagh	17 Oct 81
13:59	Stuart Monk	24 Sep 94

5000 METRES TRACK WALK

23:53.9	Philip King	27 Jun 89
24:22.0	Robert Mecham	14 Jul 92
25:32.4	Gareth Brown	4 Apr 82

Road - *where superior to track time*

23:15	Philip King	9 Dec 89
23:31	Martin Young	14 Sep 85
24:34	Karl Atton	6 Dec 86
24:52	David Hucks	1 Nov 80
24:55 o	Matthew Hales	10 Dec 94
24:56	Jonathan Deakin	19 Nov 88
25:04	John Murphy	19 Nov 94
25:08	Jimmy Ball	31 Dec 77
25:14	Stuart McInnes	9 Dec 89

UK ALL TIME LISTS - WOMEN

100 METRES

11.10	Kathy Cook	5 Sep 81
11.15	Paula Thomas	23 Aug 94
11.16	Andrea Lynch	11 Jun 75
11.20	Sonia Lannaman	25 Jul 80
11.20	Heather Oakes	26 Sep 80
11.22 A	Beverley Callender	8 Sep 79
11.35		26 Jul 81
11.27	Stephanie Douglas	26 Jul 91
11.29	Beverly Kinch	6 Jul 90
11.31	Wendy Hoyte	4 Oct 82
11.31	Shirley Thomas	3 Jul 83
11.31	Simmone Jacobs	24 Sep 88
11.32	Joan Baptiste	24 Aug 83
11.34	Katharine Merry	25 Jun 94
11.35	Sharon Danville	20 Aug 77
11.36 A	Della Pascoe	14 Oct 68
11.39 A	Val Peat	14 Oct 68
11.39	Sallyanne Short	12 Jul 92
11.40	Helen Golden	20 Jul 74
11.41	Jayne Christian	27 May 84
11.45	Helen Burkart	26 Aug 83
11.45	Marcia Richardson	14 Jul 93

wind assisted

10.93	Sonia Lannaman	17 Jul 77
11.01	Heather Oakes	21 May 80
11.08	Kathy Cook	24 Aug 83
11.13	Beverly Kinch	6 Jul 83
11.13	Shirley Thomas	27 May 84
11.18	Wendy Hoyte	4 Oct 82
11.19	Beverley Callender	21 May 80
11.23	Joan Baptiste	24 Aug 83
11.23	Jayne Christian	17 Jul 84
11.26	Simmone Jacobs	27 May 84
11.27	Katharine Merry	11 Jun 94
11.34	Sandra Whittaker	22 May 83
11.36	Sallyanne Short	26 Aug 89
11.37	Val Peat	17 Jul 70
11.37	Kaye Jeffrey	22 May 83
11.37	Helen Burkart	11 Sep 83
11.39	Pippa Windle	24 Jul 87
11.39	Marcia Richardson	11 Jun 94
11.40	Phylis Smith	3 Jun 90

hand timing

10.9	Andrea Lynch	28 May 77
11.1	Sonia Lannaman	29 Jun 80
11.1	Heather Oakes	29 Jun 80
11.2	Helen Golden	29 Jun 74
11.2	Sharon Danville	25 Jun 77
11.2	Beverly Kinch	14 Jul 84

wind assisted

10.8	Sonia Lannaman	22 May 76
11.1	Sharon Danville	22 May 76
11.1	Joan Baptiste	16 Jul 85
11.1	Beverly Kinch	9 May 87
11.2	Margaret Critchley	15 May 76

200 METRES

22.10	Kathy Cook	9 Aug 84
22.58	Sonia Lannaman	18 May 80
22.69	Paula Thomas	26 Aug 94
22.72	Beverley Callender	30 Jul 80
22.73	Jennifer Stoute	3 Aug 92
22.75	Donna Hartley	17 Jun 78
22.80	Michelle Scutt	12 Jun 82
22.85	Katharine Merry	12 Jun 94
22.86	Joan Baptiste	9 Aug 84
22.92	Heather Oakes	28 Aug 86
22.98	Sandra Whittaker	8 Aug 84
23.10	Diane Smith	11 Aug 90
23.12	Simmone Jacobs	15 Jun 91
23.14	Helen Golden	7 Sep 73
23.14	Helen Burkart	17 Jul 82
23.15	Andrea Lynch	25 Aug 75
23.17	Stephanie Douglas	12 Jun 94
23.18	Joslyn Hoyte-Smith	9 Jun 82
23.24	Sallyanne Short	28 Jun 92
23.29	Verona Elder	17 Jun 78
23.29	Aileen McGillivary	25 Jul 93

wind assisted

22.48	Michelle Scutt	4 Jul 82
22.69	Beverley Callender	24 Jun 81
22.90	Andrea Lynch	11 Jun 75
22.97	Helen Golden	26 Jul 74
23.00	Joslyn Hoyte-Smith	13 Jun 82
23.01	Simmone Jacobs	28 May 84
23.11	Linsey Macdonald	5 Jul 80
23.14	Shirley Thomas	28 May 84
23.15	Margaret Critchley	22 Jul 70

hand timing

22.9	Heather Oakes	3 May 80
22.9	Helen Burkart	6 Aug 83
23.0	Helen Golden	30 Jun 74
23.1	Andrea Lynch	21 May 77
23.1	Linda Keough	5 Jul 89
23.2	Dorothy Hyman	3 Oct 63
23.2	Margaret Critchley	2 Aug 70

wind assisted

23.1	Margaret Critchley	14 Jul 74
23.1	Sharon Danville	17 Sep 77
23.1	Linda McCurry	2 Jul 78

300 METRES

35.46	Kathy Cook	18 Aug 84
36.01	Michelle Scutt	13 Jul 80
36.44	Sally Gunnell	30 Jul 93
36.45	Joslyn Hoyte-Smith	5 Jul 80
36.46	Linsey Macdonald	13 Jul 80
36.65	Joan Baptiste	18 Aug 84
36.69	Helen Burkart	9 Sep 83
36.95	Jennifer Stoute	21 Jul 91
36.97	Donna Hartley	4 Jul 75
37.30	Verona Elder	26 May 76

hand timing

36.2	Donna Hartley	7 Aug 74
37.0	Linda Keough	22 Jul 89

400 METRES

49.43	Kathy Cook	6 Aug 84
50.40	Phylis Smith	3 Aug 92
50.63	Michelle Scutt	31 May 82
50.75	Joslyn Hoyte-Smith	18 Jun 82
50.93	Lorraine Hanson	26 Aug 91
50.98	Linda Keough	26 Aug 91
51.04	Sally Gunnell	20 Jul 94
51.16	Linsey Macdonald	15 Jun 80
51.28	Donna Hartley	12 Jul 75
51.41	Sandra Douglas	2 Aug 92
51.53	Jennifer Stoute	12 Aug 89
51.70	Verona Elder	10 Jun 78
51.93	Janine MacGregor	28 Aug 81
51.97	Linda Forsyth	31 May 82
52.09	Melanie Neef	23 Aug 94
52.12 A	Lillian Board	16 Oct 68
52.13	Helen Burkart	28 Jun 84
52.20	Ann Packer	17 Oct 64
52.26	Pat Beckford	14 Aug 88
52.43	Gladys Taylor	2 Sep 84

hand timing

51.2	Donna Hartley	28 Jul 78
51.4	Verona Elder	22 May 76
52.2	Liz Barnes	22 May 76

800 METRES

1:57.42	Kirsty Wade	24 Jun 85
1:58.64	Kelly Holmes	15 Aug 93
1:58.65	Diane Modahl	14 Jul 90
1:58.97	Shireen Bailey	15 Sep 87
1:59.05	Christina Cahill	4 Aug 79
1:59.67	Lorraine Baker	15 Aug 86
1:59.76	Paula Fryer	17 Jul 91
1:59.81	Ann Griffiths	10 Aug 94
2:00.15	Rosemary Wright	3 Sep 72
2:00.20	Anne Purvis	7 Jul 82
2:00.30	Cherry Hanson	25 Jul 81
2:00.39	Bev Nicholson	28 Aug 88
2:00.6	Jane Finch	9 Jul 77
2:00.80	Yvonne Murray	10 Jul 87
2:01.1 a	Ann Packer	20 Oct 64
2:01.11	Lynne MacIntyre	18 Aug 84
2:01.2	Joan Allison	1 Jul 73
2:01.2	Christine Whittingham	26 Aug 78
2:01.24	Christine Benning	28 Jul 79
2:01.35	Liz Barnes	10 Jul 76

1000 METRES

2:33.70	Kirsty Wade	9 Aug 85
2:34.92	Christina Cahill	9 Aug 85
2:35.32	Shireen Bailey	19 Jul 86
2:35.86	Diane Modahl	29 Aug 93
2:35.51	Lorraine Baker	19 Jul 86
2:37.05	Christine Whittingham	27 Jun 86
2:37.29	Kelly Holmes	29 Aug 93
2:37.29	Yvonne Murray	14 Jul 89
2:37.61	Bev Nicholson	14 Jul 89
2:37.82	Gillian Dainty	11 Sep 81
2:38.44	Evelyn McMeekin	23 Aug 78
2:38.58	Jo White	9 Sep 77

1500 METRES

3:59.96	Zola Budd	30 Aug 85
4:00.57	Christina Cahill	6 Jul 84
4:00.73	Kirsty Wade	26 Jul 87
4:01.20	Yvonne Murray	4 Jul 87
4:01.38	Liz McColgan	4 Jul 87
4:01.41	Kelly Holmes	12 Jun 94
4:01.53	Christine Benning	15 Aug 79
4:02.32	Shireen Bailey	1 Oct 88
4:03.17	Alison Wyeth	7 Aug 93
4:04.14	Wendy Sly	14 Aug 83
4:04.81	Sheila Carey	9 Sep 72
4:05.66	Bev Nicholson	20 Jul 90
4:05.75	Lynn Gibson	20 Jul 94
4:05.96	Lynne MacIntyre	20 Aug 84
4:06.0	Mary Cotton	24 Jun 78
4:06.24	Christine Whittingham	5 Jul 86
4:07.11	Janet Marlow	18 Aug 82
4:07.59	Ann Williams	9 Jun 92
4:07.69	Teena Colebrook	19 Aug 90
4:07.90	Gillian Dainty	16 Jun 84

ONE MILE

4:17.57	Zola Budd	21 Aug 85
4:19.41	Kirsty Wade	27 Jul 85
4:22.64	Christina Cahill	7 Sep 84
4:22.64	Yvonne Murray	22 Jul 94
4:24.57	Christine Benning	7 Sep 84
4:24.87	Alison Wyeth	6 Jul 91
4:26.11	Liz McColgan	10 Jul 87
4:26.16	Teena Colebrook	14 Jul 90
4:26.52	Bev Hartigan	14 Aug 92
4:27.80	Lisa York	14 Aug 92
4:28.07	Wendy Sly	18 Aug 84
4:28.8	Karen Hutcheson	20 Aug 89
4:29.15	Suzanne Morley	18 Aug 84
4:30.08	Lynne MacIntyre	7 Sep 84
4:30.29	Jane Shields	9 Sep 83
4:30.89	Ruth Partridge	18 Aug 84
4:31.17	Lynn Gibson	1 Jul 94
4:31.24 i	Jo White	5 Feb 83
4:31.45	Shireen Bailey	17 Sep 89
4:31.65	Gillian Dainty	26 Jun 82
4:31.83	Angela Davies	1 Jul 94

2000 METRES

5:26.93	Yvonne Murray	8 Jul 94
5:30.19	Zola Budd	11 Jul 86
5:33.85	Christina Cahill	13 Jul 84
5:37.00	Christine Benning	13 Jul 84
5:38.50	Alison Wyeth	29 Aug 93
5:39.20	Paula Radcliffe	29 Aug 93
5:40.24	Liz McColgan	22 Aug 87
5:42.15	Wendy Sly	17 Sep 82
5:43.24	Suzanne Morley	13 Jul 84
5:45.0 i	Bev Hartigan	20 Feb 93
5:45.15	Debbie Gunning	29 Aug 93
5:45.34	Lisa York	10 Jul 92
5:45.45	Ruth Partridge	13 Jul 84
5:45.81 i	Kirsty Wade	13 Mar 87
5:46.40	Sonia McGeorge	29 Aug 93

3000 METRES

8:28.83	Zola Budd	7 Sep 85
8:29.02	Yvonne Murray	25 Sep 88
8:34.80 i	Liz McColgan	4 Mar 89
8:38.23		15 Jul 91
8:37.06	Wendy Sly	10 Aug 83
8:38.42	Alison Wyeth	16 Aug 93
8:40.40	Paula Radcliffe	16 Aug 93
8:44.46	Christine Benning	22 Aug 84
8:45.69	Jane Shields	10 Aug 83
8:47.36	Jill Hunter	17 Aug 88
8:47.59	Angela Tooby	5 Jul 88
8:47.7	Kirsty Wade	5 Aug 87
8:47.71	Lisa York	31 Jul 92
8:48.72	Karen Hutcheson	28 Jan 90
8:48.74	Paula Fudge	29 Aug 78
8:49.89	Christina Cahill	20 Jul 85
8:50.52	Debbie Peel	7 Aug 82
8:51.33	Sonia McGeorge	29 Aug 90
8:51.40	Ruth Partridge	7 Aug 82
8:52.79	Ann Ford	28 Aug 77
8:53.52 i	Nicola Morris	4 Mar 89

5000 METRES

14:48.07	Zola Budd	26 Aug 85
15:01.08	Liz McColgan	5 Aug 87
15:09.98	Jill Hunter	18 Jul 92
15:10.38	Alison Wyeth	30 Aug 94
15:13.22	Angela Tooby	5 Aug 87
15:14.51	Paula Fudge	13 Sep 81
15:21.45	Wendy Sly	5 Aug 87
15:28.63	Andrea Wallace	2 Jul 92
15:31.78	Julie Holland	18 Jul 90
15:32.19	Susan Tooby	26 May 85
15:32.34	Jane Shields	5 Jun 88
15:34.16	Jill Clarke	26 May 85
15:38.84	Ann Ford	5 Jun 82
15:40.14	Helen Titterington	17 Jul 89
15:41.11	Angela Hulley	18 Jul 90
15:41.68	Debbie Peel	27 Jun 85
15:49.6	Kathy Binns	5 Apr 80

10,000 METRES

30:57.07	Liz McColgan	25 Jun 91
31:07.88	Jill Hunter	30 Jun 91
31:53.36	Wendy Sly	8 Oct 88
31:55.30	Angela Tooby	4 Sep 87
31:56.97	Yvonne Murray	24 Aug 94
32:20.95	Susan Tooby	2 Jul 88
32:21.61	Andrea Wallace	6 Jun 92
32:24.63	Sue Crehan	4 Jul 87
32:32.42	Vikki McPherson	15 Jul 93
32:36.09	Helen Titterington	29 Aug 89
32:41.29	Jenny Clague	20 Jun 93
32:42.0	Jane Shields	24 Aug 88
32:42.84	Angela Hulley	6 Aug 89
32:44.06	Suzanne Rigg	27 Jun 93
32:47.78	Julie Holland	31 Aug 90
32:57.17	Kathy Binns	15 Aug 80
32:58.2	Claire Lavers	20 Apr 91
33:05.43	Elspeth Turner	1 Jun 88
33:10.25	Shireen Samy	5 Jul 86
33:10.94	Marina Samy	28 Jul 86

MARATHON

2:25:56	Véronique Marot	23 Apr 89
2:26:51	Priscilla Welch	10 May 87
2:27:32	Liz McColgan	3 Nov 91
2:28:06	Sarah Rowell	21 Apr 85
2:28:38	Sally-Ann Hales	21 Apr 85
2:29:29	Sally Eastall	8 Dec 91
2:29:43	Joyce Smith	9 May 82
2:29:47	Paula Fudge	30 Oct 88
2:30:38	Ann Ford	17 Apr 88
2:30:51	Angela Hulley	23 Sep 88
2:31:33	Susan Tooby	23 Sep 88
2:31:33	Andrea Wallace	12 Apr 92
2:31:45	Lynn Harding	23 Apr 89
2:32:24	Yvonne Danson	27 Aug 94
2:32:53	Gillian Burley	2 Dec 84
2:33:04	Sheila Catford	23 Apr 89
2:33:07	Nicola McCracken	22 Apr 90
2:33:16	Karen Macleod	27 Aug 94
2:33:22	Carolyn Naisby	6 Dec 87
2:33:24	Sally Ellis	23 Apr 89

100 METRES HURDLES

12.82	Sally Gunnell	17 Aug 88
12.87	Shirley Strong	24 Aug 83
12.91	Kay Morley-Brown	2 Feb 90
12.93	Jackie Agyepong	6 Jul 94
13.03	Lesley-Ann Skeete	3 Aug 90
13.04	Clova Court	9 Aug 94
13.05	Judy Simpson	29 Aug 86
13.07	Lorna Boothe	7 Oct 82
13.08	Samantha Farquharson	4 Jul 94
13.11	Sharon Danville	22 Jun 76
13.16	Wendy Jeal	27 Aug 86
13.24	Kim Hagger	31 Aug 87
13.24	Keri Maddox	12 Jun 93
13.25	Diane Allahgreen	21 Jul 94
13.26	Michelle Edwards	3 Aug 90
13.28	Angela Thorp	29 Aug 93
13.29	Mary Peters	2 Sep 72
13.32	Sam Baker	29 Aug 93
13.34	Judy Vernon	7 Sep 73
13.35	Pat Rollo	30 Jul 83

wind assisted

12.78	Shirley Strong	8 Oct 82
12.80	Sally Gunnell	29 Jul 88
12.84 A	Kay Morley-Brown	8 Aug 90
12.90	Lorna Boothe	8 Oct 82
13.01	Lesley-Ann Skeete	1 Feb 90
13.06	Sharon Danville	14 Jul 84
13.10	Keri Maddox	94
13.11	Jackie Agyepong	21 Jun 92
13.12	Pat Rollo	27 May 84
13.22	Heather Ross	27 May 84

hand timing

13.0	Judy Vernon	29 Jun 74
13.0	Blondelle Caines	29 Jun 74

wind assisted

12.7	Kay Morley-Brown	10 Jan 90
12.9	Judy Vernon	18 May 74

400 METRES HURDLES

52.74	Sally Gunnell	19 Aug 93
54.63	Gowry Retchakan	3 Aug 92
55.91	Elaine McLaughlin	26 Sep 88
56.04	Sue Morley	10 Aug 83
56.05	Wendy Cearns	13 Aug 89
56.06	Christine Warden	28 Jul 79
56.15	Jacqui Parker	27 Jul 91
56.26	Louise Fraser	7 Jun 92
56.46	Yvette Wray	11 Jul 81
56.70	Lorraine Hanson	13 Aug 89
56.72	Gladys Taylor	6 Aug 84
57.00	Simone Laidlow	6 Aug 88
57.07	Verona Elder	15 Jul 83
57.38	Sarah Dean	27 Jul 91
57.41	Jennifer Pearson	6 Aug 88
57.43	Liz Sutherland	6 Jul 78
57.49	Maureen Prendergast	16 Jun 84
57.52	Clare Sugden	3 Jun 90
57.55	Sharon Danville	8 May 81
57.76	Aileen Mills	5 Aug 86
hand timing		
57.5	Victoria Lee	28 Jun 86

HIGH JUMP

1.95	Diana Davies	26 Jun 82
1.94	Louise Gittens	25 May 80
1.94 i	Debbie Marti	3 Feb 91
1.93		5 Sep 92
1.94 i	Jo Jennings	13 Mar 93
1.90		29 Sep 88
1.92	Barbara Simmonds	31 Jul 82
1.92	Judy Simpson	8 Aug 83
1.92	Janet Boyle	29 Sep 88
1.92 i	Julia Bennett	10 Mar 90
1.89		11 Jun 94
1.91	Ann-Marie Cording	19 Sep 81
1.91	Gillian Evans	30 Apr 83
1.91	Jayne Barnetson	7 Jul 89
1.91	Lea Haggett	2 Jun 91
1.90	Kim Hagger	17 May 86
1.90	Sharon Hutchings	1 Aug 86
1.88 i	Debbie McDowell	17 Jan 88
1.88 i	Kerry Roberts	16 Feb 92
1.88 i	Kelly Mason	16 Feb 92
1.87	Barbara Lawton	22 Sep 73
1.87	Moira Maguire	11 May 80
1.87	Louise Manning	6 May 84

POLE VAULT

3.65	Kate Staples	11 Jun 94
3.45	Paula Wilson	29 Aug 94
3.44	Clare Ridgley	7 Aug 93
3.42 i	Linda Stanton	8 Jan 94
3.40		26 Sep 93
3.30 i	Rhian Clarke	31 Dec 94
3.25		5 Jun 94
3.24	Claire Morrison	10 Sep 94
3.10	Dawn-Alice Wright	10 Jul 94
3.10	Leanne Mellor	21 Aug 94
3.10 i	Janine Whitlock	31 Dec 94

LONG JUMP

6.90	Beverly Kinch	14 Aug 83
6.88	Fiona May	18 Jul 90
6.83	Sue Telfer	6 May 84
6.76	Mary Rand	14 Oct 64
6.75	Joyce Oladapo	14 Sep 85
6.73	Sheila Sherwood	23 Jul 70
6.73	Yinka Idowu	7 Aug 93
6.70	Kim Hagger	30 Aug 86
6.69	Sue Reeve	10 Jun 79
6.63	Mary Berkeley	17 Jun 89
6.57	Joanne Wise	25 May 92
6.56	Denise Lewis	12 Jun 94
6.55	Ann Simmonds	22 Jul 70
6.52	Gillian Regan	28 Aug 82
6.52	Georgina Oladapo	16 Jun 84
6.51 i	Ruth Howell	23 Feb 74
6.49		16 Jun 72
6.45	Carol Zeniou	12 May 82
6.45	Margaret Cheetham	18 Aug 84
6.44	Sharon Danville	15 Jun 77
6.44	Barbara Clarke	13 Sep 81

wind assisted

7.00	Sue Telfer	27 May 84
6.98	Fiona May	4 Jun 89
6.93	Beverly Kinch	14 Aug 83
6.84	Sue Reeve	25 Jun 77
6.80	Joyce Oladapo	22 Jun 85
6.69	Joanne Wise	30 Jul 88
6.65	Mary Berkeley	4 Jun 89
6.57	Ann Simmonds	22 Aug 70
6.56	Judy Simpson	30 Aug 86
6.54	Ruth Howell	16 Jun 72
6.54	Myra Nimmo	19 Jun 76

TRIPLE JUMP

14.22	Ashia Hansen	29 Aug 94
14.08	Michelle Griffith	11 Jun 94
13.64	Rachel Kirby	7 Aug 94
13.56	Mary Agyepong	5 Jun 92
13.46	Evette Finikin	26 Jul 91
13.31	Connie Henry	9 Jul 94
12.94	Lorna Turner	9 Jul 94
12.89	Karen Skeggs	17 May 92
12.64	Liz Ghojefa	4 Sep 93
12.43	Shani Anderson	26 Jun 93
12.34	Nicola Barr	10 Jun 92
12.31	Caroline Miller	23 Jul 94
12.22	Mary Rand	18 Jun 59
12.22	Allison Forbes	9 Sep 89
12.22	Nicola Barr	16 Aug 92

wind assisted

12.93	Karen Hambrook	13 Jun 92
12.55	Lauraine Cameron	29 Aug 93
12.44	Shani Anderson	9 Jul 94
12.37	Jane Falconer	29 Aug 93
12.34	Nicola Barr	29 Aug 93

SHOT

19.36	Judy Oakes	14 Aug 88
19.06 i	Venissa Head	7 Apr 84
18.93		13 May 84
19.03	Myrtle Augee	2 Jun 90
18.99	Meg Ritchie	7 May 83
17.53	Angela Littlewood	24 Jul 80
17.45	Yvonne Hanson-Nortey	28 Jul 89
16.57	Maggie Lynes	20 Jul 94
16.40 i	Mary Peters	28 Feb 70
16.31		1 Jun 66
16.29	Brenda Bedford	26 May 76
16.05	Janis Kerr	15 May 76
15.80	Sharon Andrews	30 Jul 93
15.75 i	Caroline Savory	23 Feb 83
15.50		19 Jun 83
15.85 i	Alison Grey	12 Feb 94
15.69		11 Jun 94
15.60 i	Justine Buttle	27 Feb 88
15.45		25 Aug 88
15.48	Mary Anderson	8 Sep 85
15.46	Vanessa Redford	14 Jun 80
15.45	Susan King	27 Mar 83
15.41	Fatima Whitbread	29 Apr 84
15.32 i	Helen Hounsell	13 Feb 82
15.23	Judy Simpson	18 Jun 88

DISCUS

67.48	Meg Ritchie	26 Apr 81
64.68	Venissa Head	18 Jul 83
60.72	Jacqui McKernan	18 Jul 93
58.02	Rosemary Payne	3 Jun 72
57.32	Lynda Whiteley	16 Jun 84
56.24	Sharon Andrews	12 Jun 94
56.06	Kathryn Farr	27 Jun 86
55.66	Debbie Callaway	2 May 94
55.52	Jane Aucott	17 Jan 90
55.42	Lesley Bryant	12 Sep 80
55.06	Janet Kane	17 Jun 78
55.04	Lorraine Shaw	14 May 94
54.72	Karen Pugh	27 Jul 86
54.60	Shelley Drew	29 Aug 94
54.46	Ellen Mulvihill	14 May 86
54.46	Janette Picton	17 Aug 90
54.40	Tracy Axten	17 Jul 93
54.24	Nicola Talbot	15 May 93
53.96	Julia Avis	27 Apr 86
53.78	Emma Beales	30 Aug 93

HAMMER

59.92	Lorraine Shaw	1 Apr 94
56.76	Esther Augee	15 May 93
55.44	Lyn Sprules	19 Jul 94
54.02	Ann Gardner	19 May 93
53.34	Diana Holden	13 Jul 94
52.84	Fiona Whitehead	29 Jun 93
51.62	Julie Lavender	15 May 94
50.52	Sarah Moore	21 May 94
49.78	Jean Clark	19 Sep 92
47.10	Karen Brown	11 Sep 93

46.88	Janet Smith	25 Jun 94
46.82	Caroline Manning	16 Jun 93
46.68	Julie Kirkpatrick	8 Aug 93
46.14	Irene Duffin	1 Apr 94
45.48	Samantha Burns-Salmond	18 Jun 94
45.44	Angela Bonner	23 Jul 94
45.04	Suzanne Last	3 Sep 94
44.46	Kim Thompson	4 Jun 94
43.88	Helen McReadie	24 Apr 94
43.52	Helen Cowe	5 Jul 93

JAVELIN

77.44	Fatima Whitbread	28 Aug 86
73.58	Tessa Sanderson	26 Jun 83
62.32	Sharon Gibson	16 May 87
62.22	Diane Royle	18 May 85
60.10	Shelley Holroyd	17 Jul 93
60.00	Julie Abel	24 May 87
59.40	Karen Hough	28 Aug 86
59.36	Kirsty Morrison	4 Sep 93
58.60	Jeanette Rose	30 May 82
57.90	Anna Lockton	1 Jul 87
57.84	Amanda Liverton	3 Jun 90
56.96	Nicola Emblem	1 Feb 90
56.50	Caroline White	8 Jun 91
55.72	Karen Martin	25 Jul 92
55.70	Lynn Hayhoe	31 May 92
55.60	Susan Platt	15 Jun 68
55.38	Catherine Garside	19 May 84
55.36	Jackie Zaslona	30 Aug 80
55.30	Clova Court	27 Aug 91
55.04	Joanne Harding	24 May 87

HEPTATHLON (1985 Tables)

6623	Judy Simpson	30 Aug 86
6325	Denise Lewis	23 Aug 94
6259	Kim Hagger	18 May 86
6125	Tessa Sanderson	12 Jul 81
6094 h	Joanne Mulliner	7 Jun 87
6022	Clova Court	27 Aug 91
5826	Jenny Kelly	3 Jul 94
5803	Jayne Barnetson	20 Aug 89
5776	Kathy Warren	12 Jul 81
5671	Vikki Schofield	3 Jul 94
5642	Sarah Rowe	23 Aug 81
5633	Marcia Marriott	18 May 86
5632	Emma Beales	1 Aug 93
5594 h	Gillian Evans	22 May 83
5548	Val Walsh	18 May 86
5517	Shona Urquhart	21 Aug 88
5496	Yinka Idowu	3 Sep 89
5495	Charmaine Johnson	24 May 92
5493	Sally Gunnell	28 May 84
5446	Manndy Laing	7 Aug 83
5434 w	Debbie Woolgar	8 Jul 90
5424	Lisa Gibbs	1 Aug 93
5420	Pauline Richards	19 Jun 94

3000 METRES TRACK WALK

12:49.16	Betty Sworowski	28 Jul 90
13:03.4	Vicky Lupton	18 May 91
13:11.0	Lisa Langford	6 Jul 90
13:12.01 i	Julie Drake	12 Mar 93
13:16.0		11 Dec 90
13:25.2	Carol Tyson	6 Jul 79
13:27.9	Verity Snook	14 May 94
13:28.0	Helen Elleker	22 Jul 90
13:30.3	Carolyn Partington	5 Aug 94
13:37.1	Beverley Allen	16 May 87
13:42.10	Sylvia Black	23 May 90
13:44.0	Virginia Birch	19 Jun 84
13:46.3	Marion Fawkes	30 Jun 79
13:48.0	Sarah Brown	16 May 87
13:43.0	Melanie Wright	5 Jul 94
13:52.0	Lillian Millen	7 May 83
13:56.0	Irene Bateman	20 Sep 80

5000 METRES TRACK WALK

21:57.68	Lisa Langford	25 Jun 90
22:02.06	Betty Sworowski	28 Aug 89
22:12.21	Vicky Lupton	28 Jun 92
22:37.47	Julie Drake	17 Jul 93
22:51.23	Helen Elleker	25 Jun 90
23:11.2	Carol Tyson	30 Jun 79
23:15.04	Beverley Allen	25 May 87
23:19.2	Marion Fawkes	30 Jun 79
23:20.00	Virginia Birch	25 May 85
23:22.52	Verity Snook	19 Jun 94
23:34.43	Sylvia Black	5 Jul 92
23:35.54	Nicola Jackson	25 May 87
23:38.3	Irene Bateman	28 Jun 81
23:46.7	Lillian Millen	28 Jun 81
23:47.0	Melanie Wright	29 May 94
23:51.1	Jill Barrett	5 May 84

5k Road - *where superior to track time*

21:36	Vicky Lupton	18 Jul 92
21:50	Betty Sworowski	6 May 90
22:45 +	Verity Snook	25 Aug 94
22:51	Marion Fawkes	29 Sep 79
22:59	Carol Tyson	29 Sep 79
23:00	Beverley Allen	1 Sep 87
23:04	Carolyn Partington	26 May 94
23:13	Sylvia Black	13 Feb 93
23:25	Irene Bateman	29 Sep 79

10,000 METRES TRACK WALK

45:53.9	Julie Drake	26 May 90
46:23.08	Betty Sworowski	4 Aug 91
46:25.2	Helen Elleker	26 May 90
46:30.0	Vicky Lupton	14 Sep 94
47:10.07	Verity Snook	19 Jun 93
47:56.3	Virginia Birch	15 Jun 85
47:58.3	Beverley Allen	21 Jun 86
48:11.4	Marion Fawkes	8 Jul 79
48:34.0	Lisa Langford	15 May 86
48:34.5	Carol Tyson	22 Aug 81
48:52.5 sh	Irene Bateman	19 Mar 83
48:56.5	Sarah Brown	18 Apr 91

49:15.2	Melanie Brookes	22 Aug 92
49:39.0	Karen Smith	22 May 91
50:10.2	Brenda Lupton	17 Mar 84
50:11.2	Jill Barrett	19 Mar 83
50:25.0	Lisa Simpson	1 Apr 87
50:28.0	Andrea Crofts	21 Jul 92
50:43.87	Carolyn Partington	19 Jun 93
50:46.0	Judy Farr	25 Mar 78
50:50.0	Nicola Jackson	21 Jun 86

Road - *where superior to track time*

45:42	Lisa Langford	3 May 87
45:48	Vicky Lupton	25 Aug 94
45:59	Betty Sworowski	24 Aug 91
46:06	Verity Snook	25 Aug 94
47:21	Carolyn Partington	25 Aug 94
47:58	Nicola Jackson	27 Jun 87
47:59	Sylvia Black	29 Mar 92
48:18	Melanie Brookes	9 May 92
48:39	Karen Smith	16 Apr 94

4 x 100 METRES RELAY

42.43	UK	1 Aug 80
	Oakes, Cook, Callender, Lannaman	
42.66	UK	11 Sep 82
	Hoyte, Cook, Callender, S.Thomas	
42.71	UK	10 Aug 83
	Baptiste, Cook, Callender, S.Thomas	
42.72	UK	3 Sep 78
	Callender, Cook, Danville, Lannaman	
43.02	UK	26 Sep 80
	Oakes, Cook, Callender, Scutt	
43.03	UK	15 Aug 81
	Hoyte, Cook, Callender, S.Thomas	
43.06	UK	10 Aug 83
	Baptiste, Cook, Callender, S.Thomas	
43.11	UK	11 Aug 84
	Jacobs, Cook, Callender, Oakes	
43.15	England	9 Oct 82
	Hoyte, Cook, Callender, Lannaman	
43.18	UK	4 Aug 79
	Barnett, Hoyte, Cook, Oakes	
43.18	UK	20 Aug 83
	Baptiste, Cook, Callender, S.Thomas	
43.21	UK	18 Aug 82
	Hoyte, Cook, Callender, S.Thomas	
43.03	UK	15 Aug 81
	Hoyte, Cook, Callender, S.Thomas	
43.26 A	UK Students	13 Sep 79
	Luker, Cook, Patten, Callender	
43.30	UK	30 Aug 86
	P. Thomas, Cook, Baptiste, Hoyte	
43.32	UK	5 Jun 80
	Oakes, Cook, Callender, Lannaman	
43.32	UK	1 Sep 90
	Douglas, Kinch, Jacobs, P.Thomas	
43.35	UK	17 Aug 85
	Christian, Baptiste, Joseph, Oakes	
43.38	UK	8 Aug 86
	P. Thomas, Cook, Baptiste, Oakes	
43.43	UK	31 Aug 91
	Douglas, Kinch, Jacobs, P.Thomas	

4 x 400 METRES RELAY

3:22.01	UK	1 Sep 91
Hanson, Smith, Gunnell, Keough		
3:23.41	UK	22 Aug 93
Keough, Smith, Goddard, Gunnell		
3:23.89	UK	31 Aug 91
Hanson, Smith, Gunnell, Keough		
3:24.14	UK	14 Aug 94
Neef, Keough, Smith, Gunnell		
3:24.23	UK	8 Aug 92
Smith, Douglas, Stoute, Gunnell		
3:24.25	UK	30 Jun 91
Gunnell, Hanson, Stoute, Keough		
3:24.36	UK	5 Jun 93
Smith, Goddard, Stoute, Gunnell		
3:24.78	UK	1 Sep 90
Gunnell, Stoute, Beckford, Keough		
3:25.20	UK	7 Aug 92
Douglas, Smith, Stoute, Gunnell		
3:25.51	UK	11 Aug 84
Scutt, Barnett, Taylor, Hoyte-Smith		
3:25.82	UK	11 Sep 82
Cook, Macdonald, Taylor, Hoyte-Smith		
3:25.87	UK	19 Jun 82
Forsyth, Hoyte-Smith, Elder, Scutt		
3:26.54	UK	6 Aug 89
Keough, Stoute, Piggford, Gunnell		
3:26.6	UK	17 Aug 75
Roscoe, Taylor, Elder, Hartley		
3:26.89	UK	1 Oct 88
Keough, Stoute, Piggford, Gunnell		
3:27.04	UK	22 Aug 93
Keough, Smith, Goddard, Gunnell		
3:27.06	UK	27 Aug 94
Smith, Goddard, Keough, Gunnell		
3:27.09	UK	30 Jul 76
Barnes, Taylor, Elder, Hartley		
3:27.17	UK	3 Sep 78
Ford, Hoyte-Smith, Elder, Hartley		
3:27.19	England	12 Aug 78
Patten, Hoyte-Smith, Elder, Hartley		

UNDER 20

100 METRES

11.27 A	Kathy Smallwood	9 Sep 79
11.30	Beverly Kinch	5 Jul 83
11.36 A	Della James	14 Oct 68
11.43	Shirley Thomas	7 Aug 82
11.45	Sonia Lannaman	1 Sep 72
11.45	Simmone Jacobs	6 Jul 84
11.52	Katharine Merry	16 Sep 92
11.53	Marcia Richardson	21 Jul 91
11.54	Wendy Clarke	8 Jun 75
11.59	Heather Hunte	9 Sep 77
11.59	Stephanie Douglas	23 Jul 88

wind assisted

11.13	Beverly Kinch	6 Jul 83
11.25	Shirley Thomas	20 Aug 81
11.26	Simmone Jacobs	27 May 84
11.40	Katharine Merry	3 Jul 93
11.43	Dorothy Hyman	2 Sep 60
11.45	Stephanie Douglas	25 Jun 88
11.50	Rebecca Drummond	9 Jul 94
11.53	Wendy Clarke	22 Aug 75
11.53	Sharon Dolby	16 Aug 86

hand timing

11.3	Sonia Lannaman	9 Jun 74
11.3	Heather Hunte	15 Jul 78
11.5	Dorothy Hyman	2 Sep 60
11.5	Anita Neil	19 Jul 68
11.5	Jennifer Smart	1 Sep 61

wind assisted

11.2	Wendy Clarke	22 May 76
11.3	Helen Golden	30 May 70
11.3	Linsey Macdonald	3 May 80
11.4	Anita Neil	30 Jun 68
11.4	Helen Barnett	16 May 76
11.4	Jane Parry	5 Jul 80

200 METRES

22.70 A	Kathy Smallwood	12 Sep 79
23.10	Diane Smith	11 Aug 90
23.20	Katharine Merry	13 Jun 93
23.23	Sonia Lannaman	25 Aug 75
23.24	Sandra Whittaker	12 Jun 82
23.28	Simmone Jacobs	28 Aug 83
23.33	Linsey Macdonald	9 Jun 82
23.35	Donna Murray	26 May 74
23.42	Deborah Bunn	17 Jun 78
23.46	Shirley Thomas	31 May 82

wind assisted

23.01	Simmone Jacobs	28 May 84
23.11	Linsey Macdonald	5 Jul 80
23.16	Donna Murray	27 Jul 74
23.42	Helen Golden	21 Jul 70

hand timing

23.1	Sonia Lannaman	7 Jun 75
23.3	Donna Murray	9 Jun 74
23.3	Sharon Colyear	30 Jun 74
23.3	Linsey Macdonald	8 May 82
23.4	Helen Barnett	17 Jul 76

wind assisted

22.9	Donna Murray	14 Jul 74
23.2	Deborah Bunn	2 Jul 78
23.3	Angela Bridgeman	15 Aug 82

400 METRES

51.16	Linsey Macdonald	15 Jun 80
51.77	Donna Murray	30 Jul 74
52.54	Donna Fraser	10 Aug 91
52.65	Jane Parry	11 Jun 83
52.80	Sian Morris	18 Jun 83
52.98	Karen Williams	6 Aug 78
52.99	Angela Bridgeman	24 Jul 82
53.01 i	Marilyn Neufville	14 Mar 70
53.08	Loreen Hall	29 Jul 84
53.14	Michelle Probert	28 Jul 79

52.6	Marilyn Neufville	20 Jun 70
52.8	Lillian Board	8 Jul 67
52.9	Verona Bernard	15 Sep 72
53.3	Tracy Burges	5 Sep 81
53.5	Ruth Kennedy	30 Jun 74

800 METRES

2:01.11	Lynne MacDougall	18 Aug 84
2:01.66	Lorraine Baker	26 Jun 82
2:02.00	Diane Edwards	14 Sep 85
2:02.0	Jo White	13 Aug 77
2:02.18	Lynne Robinson	18 Jul 86
2:02.8 a	Lesley Kiernan	2 Sep 74
2:02.88 i	Kirsty McDermott	22 Feb 81
	2:04.01	29 Jul 81
2:03.11	Janet Prictoe	19 Aug 78
2:03.18	Paula Newnham	17 Jun 78
2:03.53	Christine McMeekin	25 Aug 75

1500 METRES

3:59.96	Zola Budd	30 Aug 85
4:05.96	Lynne MacDougall	20 Aug 84
4:11.12	Bridget Smyth	26 May 85
4:13.40	Wendy Smith	19 Aug 78
4:14.40	Janet Lawrence	20 Aug 77
4:14.50	Wendy Wright	20 Jun 87
4:14.56	Andrea Whitcombe	22 Aug 90
4:14.58	Ruth Smeeth	16 Jul 78
4:14.73	Mary Stewart	2 Feb 74
4:15.1	Yvonne Murray	18 Jul 82

3000 METRES

8:28.83	Zola Budd	7 Sep 85
8:51.78	Paula Radcliffe	20 Sep 92
9:03.35	Philippa Mason	19 Jul 86
9:04.14	Yvonne Murray	28 May 83
9:06.16	Helen Titterington	19 Jun 88
9:07.02	Carol Haigh	24 Jun 85
9:09.14	Lisa York	19 Jul 89
9:10.9	Julie Holland	7 Apr 84
9:12.28	Hayley Haining	20 Jul 91
9:12.97	Bernadette Madigan	30 Jun 79

100 METRES HURDLES

13.25	Diane Allahgreen	21 Jul 94
13.30	Sally Gunnell	16 Jun 84
13.32	Keri Maddox	21 Jul 91
13.46	Nathalie Byer	26 Aug 83
13.47	Samantha Baker	30 Jun 91
13.49	Angela Thorp	30 Jun 91
13.50	Lesley-Ann Skeete	6 Jun 86
13.56	Wendy McDonnell	3 Jun 79
13.57	Bethan Edwards	29 Aug 92
13.58	Lauraine Cameron	19 Jun 90
wind assisted		
13.24	Lesley-Ann Skeete	7 Jun 86
13.39	Lauraine Cameron	1 Jul 90
13.45	Louise Fraser	30 Jul 89
13.45	Samantha Baker	30 Jun 91
13.46	Wendy McDonnell	30 Jun 79

13.5	Christine Perera	19 Jul 68
wind assisted		
13.1	Sally Gunnell	7 Jul 84
13.3	Keri Maddox	14 Jul 90
13.4	Judy Livermore	27 May 79
13.4	Samantha Baker	14 Jul 90

400 METRES HURDLES

58.02	Vyvyan Rhodes	28 Jun 92
58.37	Alyson Evans	1 Sep 85
58.68	Kay Simpson	15 Jul 83
58.76	Simone Gandy	28 May 84
59.00	Diane Heath	19 Jul 75
59.01	Sara Elson	24 Aug 89
59.04	Allison Curbishley	31 Jul 93
59.12	Tracy Allen	29 Jul 89
59.13	Sue Morley	12 Aug 79
59.52	Deborah Church	25 Jul 81
hand timing		
58.3	Simone Gandy	14 Jul 84
58.7	Sara Elson	18 Jun 89
59.0	Tracy Allen	9 Jul 88
59.3	Michelle Cooney	13 Jul 85
59.4	Diane Wade	21 Jul 79

HIGH JUMP

1.91	Lea Haggett	2 Jun 91
1.90	Jo Jennings	29 Sep 88
1.89	Debbie Marti	2 Jun 84
1.88	Jayne Barnetson	3 Aug 85
1.87	Louise Manning	6 May 84
1.86	Barbara Simmonds	9 Sep 79
1.86	Claire Summerfield	7 Aug 82
1.86	Michele Wheeler	31 May 87
1.85	Gillian Hitchen	3 Jun 78
1.85	Sharon McPeake	22 Sep 81
1.85	Julia Bennett	15 Apr 89

LONG JUMP

6.90	Beverly Kinch	14 Aug 83
6.82	Fiona May	30 Jul 88
6.68	Sue Hearnshaw	22 Sep 79
6.63	Yinka Idowu	21 May 89
6.55	Joyce Oladapo	30 Jul 83
6.52	Georgina Oladapo	16 Jun 84
6.47	Joanne Wise	30 Jul 88
6.45	Margaret Cheetham	18 Aug 84
6.43	Moira Walls	18 Sep 70
6.43	Myra Nimmo	27 May 73
wind assisted		
6.93	Beverly Kinch	14 Aug 83
6.88	Fiona May	30 Jul 88
6.71	Yinka Idowu	15 Jun 91
6.69	Joanne Wise	30 Jul 88
6.49	Margaret Cheetham	4 Sep 83
6.48	Moira Walls	17 May 70

TRIPLE JUMP

13.05	Michelle Griffith	16 Jun 90
12.43	Shani Anderson	26 Jun 93
12.27	Lorna Turner	25 May 91
12.22	Mary Bignal	18 Jun 59
12.14	Jayne Ludlow	21 May 94
12.11	Jane Falconer	18 Sep 93
11.84	Jayne McCoy	7 Sep 91
11.79	Kelly Donnan	29 May 94
11.76	Stephanie Dobson	10 Sep 94
11.70	Katie Evans	20 Jun 92
wind assisted		
12.48	Lorna Turner	30 Jun 91
12.44	Shani Anderson	9 Jul 94
12.37	Jane Falconer	29 Aug 93
11.93	Jessie Aru	15 May 93
11.90	Katie Evans	25 May 91

SHOT

17.10	Myrtle Augee	16 Jun 84
16.24 i	Judith Oakes	26 Feb 77
16.05		26 Aug 77
15.72 i	Alison Grey	29 Feb 92
15.26		13 Jul 91
15.60 i	Justine Buttle	27 Feb 88
15.45		25 Aug 88
15.48	Mary Anderson	8 Sep 85
15.45	Susan King	27 Mar 83
14.75 i	Cynthia Gregory	12 Dec 81
14.70		29 Aug 81
14.66 i	Terri Salt	7 Jan 84
14.59	Dawn Grazette	19 May 91
14.54	Carol Cooksley	9 Jul 88
14.54 i	Jayne Berry	18 Mar 89

DISCUS

54.78	Lynda Whiteley	4 Oct 82
53.10	Kathryn Farr	19 Jul 86
52.58	Emma Merry	22 Aug 93
51.82	Catherine Bradley	20 Jul 85
51.24	Jane Aucott	11 Jun 86
51.12	Janette Picton	6 Jun 82
50.44	Karen Pugh	8 Jul 83
50.34	Angela Sellers	27 Jul 86
50.30	Julia Avis	19 Sep 82
49.74	Shelley Drew	10 May 92
downhill		
51.04	Fiona Condon	7 Jun 79

JAVELIN

60.14	Fatima Whitbread	7 May 80
59.40	Karen Hough	28 Aug 86
59.36	Kirsty Morrison	4 Sep 93
57.84	Amanda Liverton	3 Jun 90
57.82	Shelley Holroyd	9 Aug 92
57.80	Julie Abel	5 Jun 83
56.96	Nicola Emblem	1 Feb 90
55.72	Karen Martin	25 Jul 92
55.38	Catherine Garside	19 May 84
55.04	Tessa Sanderson	26 Sep 74

HEPTATHLON (1985 Tables)

5833	Joanne Mulliner	11 Aug 85
5642	Sarah Rowe	23 Aug 81
5496	Yinka Idowu	3 Sep 89
5493	Sally Gunnell	28 May 84
5484	Denise Lewis	30 Jun 91
5459	Jennifer Kelly	30 Jul 88
5391 w	Jackie Kinsella	22 Jun 86
5331		19 Jul 86
5377	Uju Efobi	18 Jul 93
5299	Emma Beales	26 Aug 90
5273 w	Debbie Marti	11 Aug 85
5246	Val Walsh	7 Aug 83

3000 METRES TRACK WALK

13:03.4	Vicky Lupton	18 May 91
13:47.0	Julie Drake	5 Jul 88
13:53.0 e+	Lisa Langford	23 Aug 85
14:04.1	Susan Ashforth	19 May 85
14:10.2	Carol Tyson	5 Sep 76
14:11.8	Carolyn Brown	18 Sep 92
14:12.0	Jill Barrett	11 Jun 83
14:12.8	Nicola Jackson	5 May 84
14:18.0	Gill Edgar	28 May 81
14:23.3	Joanne Pope	25 Jul 89

5000 METRES TRACK WALK

22:36.81	Vicky Lupton	15 Jun 91
23:31.67	Lisa Langford	23 Aug 85
23:55.27	Susan Ashforth	25 May 85
23:56.9	Julie Drake	24 May 88
24:02.15	Nicola Jackson	27 May 84
24:08.4	Jill Barrett	28 May 83
24:19.0	Victoria Lawrence	13 Jun 87
24:24.31	Andrea Crofts	4 Jun 89
24:27.73	Carolyn Brown	29 Aug 92
24:34.6	Tracey Devlin	17 Sep 89

Road - *where superior to track time*

23:05	Lisa Langford	2 Nov 85
23:18	Julie Drake	27 Feb 88
23:35	Lisa Simpson	31 Oct 87

10,000 METRES TRACK WALK

47:04.0	Vicky Lupton	30 Mar 91
48:34.0	Lisa Langford	15 Mar 86
49:48.7	Julie Drake	7 Feb 88
50:11.2 sh	Jill Barrett	19 Mar 83
50:25.0	Lisa Simpson	1 Apr 87
51:00.0	Karen Nipper	21 Feb 81
51:31.2	Helen Ringshaw	17 Mar 84
52:09.0	Elaine Cox	8 Apr 78
52:10.4	Sarah Brown	20 Mar 82
52:48.5	Kate Horwill	22 Aug 92

Road - *where superior to track time*

49:10	Victoria Lawrence	14 Mar 87
49:14	Carolyn Brown	29 Mar 92
49:26	Julie Drake	21 May 88
49:33	Lisa Simpson	14 Mar 87
49:47	Jill Barrett	24 Sep 83

Note: LJ, Hep
Although Idowu competed for UK Juniors, she was a Nigerian citizen at the time.

UNDER 17

100 METRES

11.45	Sonia Lannaman	1 Sep 72
11.59	Simmone Jacobs	25 Aug 83
11.60	Katharine Merry	28 Jul 90
11.61	Diane Smith	9 Aug 90
11.69	Jane Parry	6 Jun 81
11.70	Linsey Macdonald	24 May 80
11.73	Etta Kessebeh	20 Aug 81
11.77	Hayley Clements	26 Jul 85
11.78	Tatum Nelson	16 May 94
11.79	Janet Smith	26 Jul 85
wind assisted		
11.50	Rebecca Drummond	9 Jul 94
11.61	Linsey Macdonald	16 Jun 79
11.62	Kathleen Lithgow	25 Jun 88
11.63	Sharon Dolby	10 Aug 85
hand timing		
11.6	Denise Ramsden	19 Jul 68
11.6	Linsey Macdonald	25 May 80
11.6	Jane Parry	2 Aug 80
wind assisted		
11.3	Linsey Macdonald	3 May 80
11.4	Sonia Lannaman	3 Jun 72
11.4	Jane Parry	5 Jul 80
11.5	Sharon Dolby	20 Jul 85

200 METRES

23.10	Diane Smith	11 Aug 90
23.28	Simmone Jacobs	28 Aug 83
23.42	Deborah Bunn	17 Jun 78
23.43	Linsey Macdonald	20 Aug 80
23.50	Katharine Merry	20 Jul 91
23.60	Michelle Probert	12 Sep 76
23.66	Jane Parry	15 Jun 80
23.69	Donna Fraser	1 Jul 89
23.79	Sharon Colyear	5 Sep 71
23.90	Angela Bridgeman	20 Aug 80
wind assisted		
23.11	Linsey Macdonald	5 Jul 80
23.41	Katharine Merry	15 Jun 91
23.64	Jane Parry	5 Jul 80
23.70	Sonia Lannaman	16 Jun 72
hand timing		
23.8	Dawn Flockhart	27 Mar 83
23.8	Janet Smith	1 Jun 85
wind assisted		
23.2	Deborah Bunn	2 Jul 78
23.4	Hayley Clements	10 Aug 85

300 METRES

36.46	Linsey Macdonald	13 Jul 80
38.3	Marilyn Neufville	3 Aug 69
38.6	Fay Nixon	10 Sep 77
38.7	Katharine Merry	1 Sep 91
38.71	Lesley Owusu	30 Jul 94
39.2	Allison Curbishley	30 Aug 92
39.3	Sinead Dudgeon	13 Sep 92
39.40	Sophie Cocker	15 Aug 92
39.42	Alison Shingler	26 May 91
39.43	Lucy Chaffe	16 Jul 94

400 METRES

51.16	Linsey Macdonald	15 Jun 80
53.08	Loreen Hall	29 Jul 84
53.75	Linda Keough	8 Aug 80
54.01	Angela Bridgeman	16 Aug 80
54.25	Emma Langston	19 Jun 88
54.84	Carol Candlish	25 Jul 81
54.86	Ruth Kennedy	20 Jul 73
hand timing		
53.7	Linda Keough	2 Aug 80
54.2 o	Marilyn Neufville	9 Oct 69
54.4		23 Aug 69
54.6	Evelyn McMeekin	15 Sep 73
54.6	Ruth Kennedy	19 Sep 73
54.8	Elizabeth Beton	28 Aug 76

800 METRES

2:02.0	Jo White	13 Aug 77
2:03.66	Lesley Kiernan	26 Aug 73
2:03.72	Lorraine Baker	15 Jun 80
2:04.85	Louise Parker	28 Jul 79
2:06.5	Emma Langston	10 Aug 88
2:06.53	Lynne Robinson	6 Jul 85
2:06.8	Jayne Heathcote	31 May 87
2:07.0	Bridget Smyth	27 Jun 84
2:07.3	Amanda Alford	7 May 80
2:07.4	Mary Sonner	13 Sep 70

1500 METRES

4:15.20	Bridget Smyth	29 Jul 84
4:15.55	Sandra Arthurton	29 Jul 78
4:16.8	Jo White	30 Jul 77
4:21.88	Jeina Mitchell	20 Jul 91
4:22.25	Karen Hughes	24 May 81
4:22.25	Clare Keller	7 Jul 85
4:22.51	Elise Lyon	31 Jul 82
4:23.11	Gillian Stacey	2 Sep 89
4:23.25	Denise Kiernan	20 Aug 77
4:23.37	Dawn Hargan	14 Jun 87

3000 METRES

9:26.4 o	Jo White	7 Dec 77
9:28.9	Bridget Smyth	21 Apr 84
9:30.0	Yvonne Murray	4 Jul 81
9:32.20	Nicola Slater	28 Aug 93
9:33.1	Alison Hollington	6 Jun 81
9:34.5	Louise Watson	28 Aug 88
9:34.79	Helen Titterington	28 Jun 86
9:36.8	Karen Hughes	4 Jul 80
9:38.1	Elise Lyon	12 Sep 81
9:38.2	Amanda Alford	7 Mar 79

80 METRES HURDLES

11.07	Amanda Parker	7 Jun 86
11.10 Ao	Sue Scott	15 Oct 68
11.12	Samantha Farquharson	7 Jun 86
11.13	Claire St John	2 Jun 79
11.16	Ann Girvan	4 Jul 81
11.16	Stephanie Douglas	27 Jul 85
11.20	Ann Wilson	11 Aug 66
11.20	Louise Brunning	25 Jul 87
11.22	Lynda Playel	19 Aug 78
11.23	Rachel Rigby	25 Jul 87

wind assisted

11.03	Wendy McDonnell	20 Aug 77
11.11	Liz Fairs	9 Jul 94

hand timing

11.0	Wendy McDonnell	2 Jul 77
11.1	Ann Wilson	18 Sep 66
11.1	Angela Thorp	7 Jul 89
11.1	Liz Fairs	29 May 93

wind assisted

10.9	Ann Wilson	21 Jul 66
10.9	Wendy McDonnell	9 Jul 77
10.9	Samantha Farquharson	20 Jul 85
11.0	Stephanie Douglas	20 Jul 85

100 METRES HURDLES (2'9")

13.73	Ann Girvan	7 Aug 82
13.88	Natasha Danvers	28 Aug 93
13.98	Claire St John	11 Aug 79
14.04	Lauraine Cameron	7 Aug 88
14.24	Pamela St Ange	2 Oct 82
14.24	Angela Thorp	9 Jul 89
14.39	Michelle Stone	18 Aug 84
14.40	Vicki Jamison	22 Jun 93
14.52	Louise Brunning	26 Jun 88

wind assisted

13.67	Ann Girvan	4 Jul 82
13.76	Natasha Danvers	27 Aug 94

hand timing

13.7	Ann Girvan	29 Aug 81
14.1	Pamela St Ange	7 Aug 83
14.1	Nnenna Njoku	26 Jun 71

wind assisted

13.7	Nathalie Byer	4 Sep 82
13.9	Angela Thorp	9 Sep 89
14.1	Susan Mapstone	25 Aug 73
14.1	Heather Ross	9 Sep 89

300 METRES HURDLES

41.99	Natasha Danvers	10 Jul 93
42.67	Vicki Jamison	17 Jul 93
42.91	Allison Curbishley	18 Aug 91
43.03	Valerie Theobalds	13 Aug 89
43.06	Claire Griffiths	18 Aug 91
43.12	Keri Maddox	6 Aug 88
43.28	Denise Bolton	5 Sep 93
43.38	Dextene McIntosh	31 Jul 94
43.44	Joanne Mersh	13 Jul 91
43.53	Catherine Murphy	21 Jul 90

hand timing

42.4	Keri Maddox	8 May 88
42.5	Louise Brunning	8 May 88
42.8	Rachel Stafford	8 Jul 89
42.8	Vyvyan Rhodes	8 Jul 89
42.9	Valerie Theobalds	17 Jun 89
43.1	Patricia Byford	17 Jun 89
43.1	Charlotte Knowles	8 Jul 89
43.4	Joanne Mersh	15 Jun 91
43.5	Georgina Lee	7 Jul 89

400 METRES HURDLES

60.87	Karin Hendrickse	31 Jul 82
61.02	Claire Edwards	8 Sep 91
61.04	Allison Curbishley	26 Jul 92
61.10	Vicki Jamison	26 Jun 93
61.27	Kay Simpson	25 Jul 81
61.32	Debra Duncan	27 Jul 85
61.33	Denise Kiernan	17 Jul 77
61.59	Donna Pert	31 Jul 82
61.81	Joanna Douglas	27 Jul 85

hand timing

59.7	Keri Maddox	9 Jul 88
60.8	Jayne Puckeridge	9 Jul 88
61.5	Julie Lindsey	1 Sep 79
61.6	Louise Fraser	11 Jul 87

HIGH JUMP

1.89	Debbie Marti	2 Jun 84
1.85	Louise Manning	11 Sep 82
1.85	Jayne Barnetson	21 Jul 84
1.84	Ursula Fay	6 Aug 83
1.83	Jo Jennings	27 Jul 85
1.83	Tracey Clarke	2 Aug 87
1.82	Elaine Hickey	9 Aug 80
1.82	Kerry Roberts	16 Jul 83
1.82	Susan Jones	20 May 94
1.81	Barbara Simmonds	22 Jul 78

LONG JUMP

6.45	Margaret Cheetham	18 Aug 84
6.32	Georgina Oladapo	23 Jul 83
6.27	Fiona May	14 Jun 86
6.26	Joanne Wise	31 May 87
6.25	Sue Hearnshaw	9 Jul 77
6.23	Sue Scott	27 Jul 68
6.22	Ann Wilson	18 Sep 66
6.22	Michelle Stone	28 Apr 84
6.18	Sheila Parkin	4 Aug 62
6.14	Beverly Kinch	26 Jul 80

wind assisted

6.49	Margaret Cheetham	23 Sep 84
6.47	Fiona May	28 Jun 86
6.41	Sue Hearnshaw	9 Jul 77
6.33	Sue Scott	27 Aug 68
6.28	Beverly Kinch	6 Sep 80

TRIPLE JUMP

12.14	Jayne Ludlow	21 May 94
11.44	Donna Quirie	8 Aug 93
11.41	Shani Anderson	8 Sep 91
11.35	Kathryn MacKenzie	24 Jul 93
11.25 i	Jessica Aru	24 Mar 91
11.24	Pamela Anderson	25 Aug 93
11.18	Vikki Jamison	12 Jun 93
11.10	Catherine Barnes	23 Apr 94
11.05	Justina Cruickshank	24 Apr 94
11.05	Louise Eden	21 May 94
11.03	Helena King	5 Sep 87

wind assisted

11.50	Pamela Anderson	8 Aug 93

SHOT

15.08	Justine Buttle	16 Aug 86
14.40	Susan King	17 May 81
14.20 io	Terri Salt	10 Dec 83
13.77		17 Sep 83
14.04	Mary Anderson	6 May 84
13.94	Jennifer Bloss	13 May 67
13.89 i	Alison Grey	11 Feb 89
13.83		20 May 89
13.68 i	Philippa Roles	26 Feb 94
13.65		6 Aug 94
13.64	Gynthia Gregory	20 Aug 80
13.58 i	Natalie Hart	19 Mar 88
13.49	Lana Newton	11 Jul 75

DISCUS

51.60	Emma Merry	27 Jun 90
49.56	Jane Aucott	3 Aug 85
48.88	Philippa Roles	13 Aug 94
48.84	Karen Pugh	7 Aug 82
47.58	Catherine Bradley	14 Jul 84
47.50	Sarah Symonds	16 May 90
47.24	Amanda Barnes	3 Aug 85
46.76	Fiona Condon	6 Aug 77
46.34	Janette Picton	26 Mar 79
45.72	Sarah Winckless	1 Jul 90

JAVELIN

56.02	Amanda Liverton	11 Jun 89
53.42	Karen Hough	15 Jul 84
53.22	Kirsty Morrison	15 Aug 92
51.50	Shelley Holroyd	22 Jul 89
50.82	Nicola Emblem	19 Jun 87
50.04	Kim Lisbon	19 Feb 84

UNDER 15

100 METRES

11.67	Katharine Merry	13 May 89
11.86	Hayley Clements	2 Jul 83
11.89	Joanne Gardner	20 Aug 77
11.92	Jane Parry	20 Aug 77
11.95	Tatum Nelson	7 Aug 93
12.00	Diane Smith	15 Sep 89
12.02	Renate Chinyou	28 Aug 88
12.02	Sarah Wilhelmy	28 May 94
12.07	Margaret Cheetham	29 Jul 83
12.10	Helen Seery	25 Jul 91
12.10	Lesley Owusu	7 Aug 93

wind assisted

11.47	Katharine Merry	17 Jun 89
11.67	Tatum Nelson	10 Jul 93
11.78	Jane Parry	8 Aug 78
11.84	Janis Walsh	26 May 74
11.88	Sarah Claxton	9 Jul 94
11.97	Yvonne Anderson	16 Jun 79
11.97	Renate Chinyou	20 Aug 88
12.07	Leanne Eastwood	26 May 91

hand timing

11.7	Helen Barnett	20 Sep 72
11.8	Janis Walsh	6 Jul 74
11.8	Joanne Gardner	2 Jul 77

50.02	Angelique Pullen	31 Aug 85
49.24	Jacqueline Barclay	7 Aug 82
48.34	Fatima Whitbread	29 Aug 77
48.00	Claire Taylor	17 Jun 92

HEPTATHLON (1985 Tables) with 80mH

5037	Michelle Stone	1 Jul 84
5031	Yinka Idowu	18 Sep 88
4915	Denise Lewis	24 Jul 88
4861	Clover Wynter-Pink	26 Jun 94
4841	Rebecca Lewis	18 Sep 94
4839	Jackie Kinsella	21 Jul 85
4794	Claire Phythian	22 May 88
4742	Julie Hollman	26 Sep 93
4673	Denise Bolton	19 Sep 93
4653	Anne Hollman	6 May 90

with 100m 2'9" hurdles

5184	Claire Phythian	20 Aug 89
4815 w	Julie Hollman	2 May 93
4807		30 May 93

with 100m 2'6" hurdles

5071	Debbie Marti	5 Jun 83

5000 METRES TRACK WALK

23:55.27	Susan Ashforth	25 May 85
24:34.6	Tracey Devlin	17 Sep 89
24:45.4	Karen Eden	9 Jul 78
24:57.5	Angela Hodd	24 Jun 86
25:08.0	Julie Drake	22 Dec 85
25:13.8	Carla Jarvis	2 Jun 91
25:15.3	Vicky Lupton	3 Sep 88
25:18.5	Jill Barrett	16 Aug 80
25:25.02	Nina Howley	1 Jul 94
25:25.80	Kim Macadam	25 May 85

wind assisted

11.7	Diane Smith	30 Jul 89
11.8	Sonia Lannaman	30 May 70
11.8	Deborah Bunn	28 Jun 75
11.8	Delmena Doyley	6 Jul 79

200 METRES

23.72	Katharine Merry	17 Jun 89
23.90	Diane Smith	3 Sep 89
24.05	Jane Parry	16 Jul 78
24.39	Hayley Clements	3 Jul 83
24.51	Tatum Nelson	8 Aug 93
24.54	Sarah Wilhelmy	31 Jul 94
24.58	Simmone Jacobs	25 Jul 81
24.58	Donna Fraser	22 Aug 87
24.59	Janet Smith	30 Jul 83
24.63	Dawn Flockhart	4 Jul 81

wind assisted

23.54	Katharine Merry	30 Jul 89
23.99	Sarah Wilhelmy	9 Jul 94
24.35	Tatum Nelson	27 Jun 93

hand timing

23.8	Janis Walsh	23 Jun 74

wind assisted

23.6	Jane Parry	9 Jul 77
23.8	Diane Smith	9 Sep 89

800 METRES

2:06.5	Rachel Hughes	19 Jul	82
2:08.7	Emma Langston	12 Jul	86
2:09.58	Sally Ludlam	8 Jun	75
2:09.6	Isabel Linaker	1 Aug	90
2:09.77	Lorraine Baker	19 Aug	78
2:09.80	Hannah Curnock	15 Aug	92
2:10.1	Lesley Kiernan	9 Jul	71
2:10.3	Carol Pannell	9 Jul	71
2:10.6	Christina Boxer	10 Jul	71
2:10.6	Natalie Tait	12 Jul	86
2:10.66	Amanda Pritchard	15 Jul	94

1500 METRES

4:23.45	Isabel Linaker	7 Jul	90
4:27.9	Joanne Davis	9 Jul	88
4:29.0	Claire Allen	8 Jul	89
4:29.1	Valerie Bothams	16 Jul	89
4:29.6	Lynne MacDougall	16 Jul	79
4:29.9	Heidi Hosking	9 Jul	88
4:30.4	Claire Nicholson	18 Jun	87
4:31.12	Karen Hughes	31 Aug	79
4:31.45	Amanda Alford	22 Jul	78
4:31.6	Michelle Lavercombe	13 Jun	81

75 METRES HURDLES

10.93	Rachel Halstead-Peel	27 Jul	85
11.00	Louise Fraser	27 Jul	85
11.01	Nathalie Byer	16 Aug	80
11.08	Nicola Hall	29 May	94
11.09	Catherine Murphy	6 Aug	88
11.09	Orla Bermingham	25 Aug	90
11.13	Lydia Chadwick	7 Jun	86
11.15	Rachel Rigby	27 Jul	85
11.16	Diane Allahgreen	12 Aug	89
11.22	Lynda Playel	19 Aug	78

wind assisted

11.06	Kate Forsyth	10 Jul	93
11.17	Angela Thorp	25 Jul	87
11.18	Liz Fairs	5 Jul	92
11.18	Sarah Claxton	18 Sep	94

hand timing

11.0	Wendy McDonnell	31 Aug	75
11.0	Lydia Chadwick	12 Jul	86
11.0	Nina Thompson	4 Jul	87

wind assisted

10.7	Orla Bermingham	14 Jul	90
10.8	Nathalie Byer	12 Jul	80
10.8	Ann Girvan	12 Jul	80
10.9	Lauraine Cameron	16 Aug	86
10.9	Nina Thompson	7 Jun	87

HIGH JUMP

1.83	Ursula Fay	5 Jun	82
1.81	Debbie Marti	18 Sep	82
1.81	Lea Haggett	6 Jun	86
1.80	Jo Jennings	19 Aug	84
1.79 i	Julia Charlton	24 Feb	80
1.78		13 Jul	80
1.78	Claire Summerfield	28 Jul	79

1.75	Anne Gilson	2 Jun	73
1.75	Claire Smith (Nun)	8 Aug	82
1.75 i	Alison Purton	12 Dec	87
1.75	Jane Falconer	10 Jun	89

LONG JUMP

6.34	Margaret Cheetham	14 Aug	83
6.30	Fiona May	7 Jul	84
6.07	Georgina Oladapo	21 Jun	81
5.98	Sandy French	22 Jul	78
5.93 i	Sue Scott	19 Nov	66
5.88		11 Aug	66
5.93	Jackie Harris	10 Jul	87
5.86	Tammy McCammon	18 Aug	91
5.85	Kim Hagger	20 Aug	76
5.81	Yvonne Hallett	24 Aug	86
5.78	Pamela St Ange	15 Aug	81

wind assisted

6.49	Margaret Cheetham	4 Sep	83
6.05	Katharine Merry	18 Sep	88
6.02	Michelle Stone	10 Jul	82
5.99	Sandy French	8 Jul	78
5.85	Karen Glen	8 Jul	78

SHOT (3.25kg)

14.27	Susan King	19 May	79
13.69	Gloria Achille	21 Jun	80
13.61	Justine Buttle	6 Aug	84
13.50 i	Philippa Roles	19 Dec	92
13.45 i	Susan Coyne	28 Oct	82
13.43 i	Navdeep Dhaliwal	19 Dec	92
13.04		16 May	92
13.26	Yvonne Anekwe	29 Jun	86
13.22	Emily Steele	23 Jul	89
13.08	Ashley Morris	11 Aug	84
13.05	Tracy Page	21 Jun	86
12.97	Alison Grey	23 Aug	87

DISCUS

44.12	Philippa Roles	30 Aug	92
41.92	Catherine Garden	12 Sep	93
40.92	Sandra McDonald	24 Jun	78
40.84	Natalie Kerr	24 Jul	94
40.44	Catherine MacIntyre	12 Sep	82
40.34	Natalie Hart	23 Mar	86
40.22	Emma Merry	27 Aug	88
40.18	Kelly Mellis	24 Sep	94
40.14	Clare Tank	29 Aug	88
39.76	Alix Gallagher	6 Jun	87

JAVELIN

48.40	Amanda Liverton	31 Aug	87
46.98	Kirsty Morrison	30 Jun	90
43.16	Shelley Holroyd	27 Jun	87
43.08	Karen Hough	4 Sep	82
42.70	Emily Steele	23 Sep	89
41.50	Kelly Morgan	9 Jul	94
41.22	Maxine Worsfold	12 Jul	80
41.06	Heather Derbyshire	15 Aug	93
40.86	Julie Hawkins	20 Aug	77
40.80	Jenny Foster	16 Aug	92

PENTATHLON (with 800m & 75m hdls)

3518	Katharine Merry	18 Sep 88
3333	Jackie Harris	27 Jun 87
3296	Claire Everett	19 Sep 93
3225	Amy Nuttall	26 Jun 94
3216	Sally Gunnell	23 Aug 80
3213	Julie Hollman	22 Sep 91
3195	Julia Charlton	10 May 80
3193	Samantha Foster	26 Jun 94
3186	Lauraine Cameron	16 Aug 86
3175	Linda Wong	14 Sep 80

UNDER 13

80 METRES

10.2	Jane Riley	1 Jun 85
10.2	Helen Seery	20 May 89
10.3	Katharine Merry	6 Jun 87
10.3	Emma Ania	7 Sep 91
10.4	Tatum Nelson	1 Sep 91
10.5	Claire Ransome	1 Jun 85
10.5	Lynsey Scammens	18 Jun 89
10.5	Sarah Wilhelmy	12 Sep 92
10.5	Ayeesha Charles	12 Sep 92

100 METRES (y = 100 yards)

11.92	Jane Parry	20 Aug 77
12.1	Katharine Merry	26 Sep 87
11.1y	Sonia Lannaman	10 Aug 68
12.3	Joanne Gardner	24 Jun 75
12.3	Deborah Bunn	30 Aug 75
12.4	Lorraine Broxup	13 Jun 76
12.4	Sarah Claxton	31 Aug 92

wind assisted

11.8	Deborah Bunn	28 Jun 75
12.3	Barbara Parham	7 Jul 73
12.3	Susan Croker	17 Jun 78
12.3	Gail Hayes	7 Jul 78

150 METRES

19.1	Emma Ania	7 Sep 91
19.2	Helen Seery	19 Feb 89
19.5	Karlene Palmer	1 Aug 93
19.6	Sarah Wilhelmy	13 Sep 92
19.6	Laverne Slater	24 Jul 94
19.6	Stacy Hilling	27 Jul 94
19.6	Sarah Zawanda	11 Sep 94
19.7	Hannah Wood	17 Jul 94
19.7	Naomi Taplin	24 Jul 94

200 METRES

24.2	Jane Parry	28 May 77
25.4	Katharine Merry	21 Jun 87
25.4	Myra McShannon	8 May 88
25.6	Debbie Bunn	5 Jul 75
25.6	Joanne Gardner	24 Aug 75
25.6	Jane Riley	30 Jun 85
25.7	Jane Bradbeer	1 Aug 81
25.7	Donna Fraser	28 Sep 85
25.95	Sandy French	20 Aug 76

wind assisted

23.6	Jane Parry	9 Jul 77

3000 METRES TRACK WALK

14:56.4	Sarah Bennett	26 Sep 93
15:00.0	Susan Ashforth	19 Jun 84
15:00.6	Sally Wish	16 Jul 72
15:16.0	Helen Ringshaw	11 Nov 80
15:18.3	Victoria Lawrence	17 Jul 83
15:18.7	Sharon Tonks	19 Mar 83
15:19.0	Tracey Devlin	28 Mar 87
15:28.0	Kim Macadam	3 Sep 83
15:30.0	Nikola Ellis	1 Sep 84
15:36.0	Joanne Ashforth	11 Jun 86

600 METRES

1:37.5	Hannah Wood	17 Jul 94
1:38.5	Jennifer Meadows	4 Apr 93
1:38.9	Emma Ward	17 Jul 94
1:40.9	Amanda O'Shea	25 Jul 92
1:42.1	Alison Kerboas	26 Sep 93
1:42.5	Francesca Green	26 Jul 92
1:43.2	Jennifer Grogan	25 Jul 93
1:43.4	Donna Kellard	7 Sep 91
1:43.6	Belinda Hardweir	15 May 94

800 METRES

2:14.8	Janet Lawrence	10 Jul 71
2:15.05	Rachel Hughes	11 Sep 81
2:16.8	Angela Davies	25 Jul 83
2:17.20	Emma Langston	7 Sep 84
2:17.6	Michelle Wilkinson	22 Jun 85
2:17.9	Melissa Rooney	20 Jun 81
2:18.1	Lileath Rose	19 Jun 76
2:18.50	Jennifer Meadows	3 Jul 93
2:18.6	Jayne Heathcote	11 Jun 83
2:19.0	Michelle Cherry	6 Aug 83
2:19.0	Dawn Simpson	21 Jun 86

1500 METRES

4:35.5 o	Rachel Hughes	2 Dec 81
4:42.1	Stacy Washington	18 Jul 84
4:43.0	Julie Adkin	18 Jul 84
4:44.0	Paula Matheson	20 Jul 76
4:44.2	Clare Keller	13 Jun 81
4:44.7	Deborah Russell	18 Jul 76
4:44.9	Susan Jordan	20 Sep 81
4:46.8	Amanda Alford	11 Sep 76
4:47.1	Susan Byrom	29 Jun 85
4:47.6	Janet Lawrence	4 Sep 71

70 METRES HURDLES

11.0	Katharine Merry	20 Sep 87
11.1	Sarah Claxton	14 Jun 92
11.2	Claire Stuart	19 Jun 88
11.3	Sarah Culkin	18 Jun 89
11.3	Katie Challinor	22 Sep 91
11.3	Nicola Hall	23 Aug 92
11.3	Caroline Pearce	1 Aug 93
11.3	Naomi Dallaway	29 Aug 93

wind assisted

11.21	Sandra Gunn	4 Sep 88
11.26	Catriona Burr	4 Sep 88

75 METRES HURDLES

11.3	Katharine Merry	26 Sep 87
11.6	Jenny Vanes	26 Sep 87
11.78	Caroline Pearce	7 Aug 93
11.9	Cheryl Cox	4 Sep 71
11.9	Sharon McKinley	8 Aug 81
11.9	Adele Mesney	30 Jul 88
12.0	Julie Goldthorpe	13 Jun 70
12.0	Sandra White	11 Sep 77
12.1 o	Carole Petitjean	15 Nov 70
12.1	Beverley Cox	24 Sep 72
12.1	Elizabeth Fairs	1 Sep 90
12.1	Kelly Williamson	21 Jun 92
12.1	Sarah Claxton	1 Aug 92

wind assisted

11.6	Sarah Claxton	5 Jul 92

HIGH JUMP

1.69	Katharine Merry	26 Sep 87
1.68	Julia Charlton	6 Aug 78
1.65	Debbie Marti	20 Sep 80
1.65	Jane Falconer	20 Sep 87
1.63	Lindsey Marriott	11 Aug 79
1.63	Paula Davidge	13 Sep 81
1.62 io	Claire Summerfield	20 Nov 77
1.60	Denise Wilkinson	17 Jul 76
1.59	Julie O'Dell	28 Jul 74
1.59	Julia Cockram	18 May 80
1.59	Beverley Green	30 Aug 86

LONG JUMP

5.71	Sandy French	20 Aug 76
5.45	Sarah Wilhelmy	31 Aug 92
5.43	Margaret Cheetham	19 Sep 81
5.42	Katharine Merry	7 Jun 87
5.40	Kerrie Gray	1 Sep 84
5.38	Toyin Campbell	6 Aug 77
5.35	Deborah Bunn	7 Sep 75
5.34	Fiona May	12 Jun 82
5.33	Kathryn Dowsett	7 Sep 91
5.32	Ann Flannery	18 Sep 82

wind assisted

5.55	Katharine Merry	10 Jul 87

SHOT (2.72kg)

11.57 io	Navdeep Dhaliwal	12 Dec 90
11.04	Amy Wilson	12 Sep 93
10.91	Catherine Garden	8 Sep 91
10.60	Lucy Rann	29 Aug 93
10.48	Julie Robin	1 Jul 89
10.48	Natalie Kerr	9 Aug 92
10.46	Sandra Biddlecombe	4 Jul 90
10.41	Eleanor Garden	3 Sep 89

SHOT (3.25kg)

12.20	Susan King	3 Sep 77
10.77	Michele Morgan	19 Jun 82
10.68 o	Rebecca Hyams	21 Dec 85
10.64 io	Roxanne Blackwood	10 Nov 86
10.54	Claire Burnett	1 Sep 85
10.49	Alison Grey	3 Aug 85

DISCUS (0.75kg)

39.44	Catherine Garden	8 Sep 91
37.64	Sandra Biddlecombe	4 Jul 90
30.54	Eleanor Garden	10 Sep 89
29.76	Navdeep Dhaliwal	19 Aug 90
29.62	Helen Gates	3 Jul 93
29.48	Rebecca Roles	16 May 92
29.18	Lucille Shaw	10 Jul 94
29.00	Elizabeth Hay	12 Sep 92
28.86	Celyn Samuels	15 Sep 91
28.82	Louise Thomson	10 Sep 89

DISCUS (1kg)

34.22	Catherine Garden	25 Aug 91
33.86 o	Fiona Condon	13 Oct 73
31.34	Sandra Biddlecombe	9 Sep 90
30.02	Alison Moffitt	6 Jul 82
29.88	Iona Doyley	2 Sep 78
29.42	Eleanor Garden	27 Aug 89
29.12	Natalie Kerr	26 Jul 92
28.88	Jane Chapman	13 Sep 81
28.56	Amanda Franks	25 Aug 74
28.38	Sarah Hughes	9 Sep 84

JAVELIN (400gm)

33.46	Emma Claydon	26 Jul 92
33.32	Melanie Vaggers	27 Sep 94
31.58	Louise Telford	20 Aug 94
30.82	Gillian Stewart	13 Sep 92
30.54	Lesley Richardson	16 Aug 92
30.46	Lucy Rann	8 Aug 93
29.94	Stacey McLelland	12 Sep 93
29.70	Kelly Sloan	15 Sep 91
29.66	Aileen Paxton	1 Aug 93
29.40	Margaret Wilson	18 Sep 88

JAVELIN (600gm)

32.02	Claire Lacey	20 Sep 87
31.60	Emma Langston	2 Sep 84
31.44	Alison Moffitt	6 Jul 82
31.04	Shelley Holroyd	Jun 85
30.82	Diane Williams	10 Jun 72
30.44	Heather Derbyshire	12 Sep 91
30.32	Debra Smith	83
30.28	Emily Steele	1 Aug 87
29.84	Lucy Rann	12 Jun 93
29.64	Nicola Lycett	12 Jul 92

2500 METRES TRACK WALK

12:48.9	Claire Walker	20 Jul 85
12:49.0 o	Karen Eden	11 Oct 75
12:50.5	Victoria Lawrence	4 Jul 82
13:08.2	Joanne Ashforth	20 Jul 85
13:10.2	Stephanie Cooper	9 May 82
13:16.63	Jo Pickett	15 Jun 91
13:18.0	Alison Warren	4 Jun 78
13:18.0	Karen Bowers	14 Apr 79
13:18.8	Janette McKenzie	20 May 79
13:20.0 o	Katherine Griffin	11 Oct 75

UK CLUB RELAY RECORDS

MEN

Seniors

4 x 100m	39.49	Haringey	1 Jun 91
4 x 200m	1:23.5	Team Solent	19 Jul 87
4 x 400m	3:04.48	Team Solent	29 Jun 90
1600m Medley	3:20.8	Wolverhampton & Bilston	1 Jun 75
4 x 800m	7:24.4*	North Staffs and Stone	27 Jun 65
4 x 1500m	15:12.6	Bristol	5 Aug 75

* = 4 x 880y time less 2.8sec

Under 20

4 x 100m	41.30	Victoria Park	14 Aug 76
4 x 200m	1:27.6	Enfield	13 Jun 82
4 x 400m	3:15.3	Enfield	5 Sep 82
1600m Medley	3:31.6	Cardiff	14 Aug 71
4 x 800m	7:35.3	Liverpool H	14 Aug 90
4 x 1500m	16:04.3	Blackburn	15 Sep 79
4 x 110H	1:04.8	Oundle Sch	19 May 79

Under 17

4 x 100m	42.22	Thames V H	24 Jun 89
4 x 200m	1:31.2	Hercules-W.	12 Jul 78
4 x 400m	3:23.1	Enfield	1 Oct 80
1600m Medley	3:36.1	Thurrock	13 Jun 84
4 x 800m	7:52.1	Clydebank	29 Aug 87
4 x 1500m	16:27.0	Liverpool H	14 Sep 88

Under 15

4 x 100m	44.62	Sale	29 Aug 93
4 x 200m	1:36.9	Belgrave	19 Sep 93
4 x 400m	3:31.5	Ayr Seaforth	5 Sep 82
1600m Medley	3:48.4	Blackheath	29 Sep 86
4 x 800m	8:13.28	Clydebank	2 Sep 89
4 x 1500m	17:52.4	Stretford	22 Oct 85

Under 13

4 x 100m	50.5	Blackheath	12 Sep 93
4 x 200m	1:49.7	Braintree	29 Aug 94
4 x 400m	4:04.5	Blackheath	12 Sep 93
1600m Medley	4:13.7	Blackheath	28 Sep 86
4 x 800m	9:29.8	Sale	28 Jun 88

WOMEN

Seniors

4 x 100m	43.79	Hounslow	18 Sep 82
4 x 200m	1:35.15	Stretford	14 Jul 91
4 x 400m	3:31.62	Essex Ladies	31 May 92
1600m Medley	3:50.6	Coventry Godiva	5 May 84
3 x 800m	6:32.4	Cambridge H	29 Jun 74
4 x 800m	8:41.0	Cambridge H	26 May 75

Under 20

4 x 100m	48.07	Sale	14 Sep 91
4 x 200m	1:47.7	Edinburgh WM	12 Aug 90
4 x 400m	3:51.67	Sale	23 Sep 89
3 x 800m	7:33.2	Essex Ladies	12 Jun 94

Under 17

4 x 100m	47.52	Hounslow	2 Oct 82
4 x 200m	1:42.2	London Oly.	19 Aug 72
4 x 400m	3:52.1	City of Hull	3 Jul 82
1600m Medley	4:07.8	Warrington	14 Aug 75
3 x 800m	6:46.5	Haslemere	15 Sep 79
	6:46.5	Bromley L	1 Jul 84
4 x 800m	8:53.1	Havering	24 May 80

Under 15

4 x 100m	48.5	Haringey	15 Sep 79
4 x 200m	1:44.0	Bristol	15 Sep 79
3 x 800m	6:39.8	Havering	13 Sep 78
4 x 800m	9:21.4	Sale	5 Aug 78

Under 13

4 x 100m	51.2	Aberdeen	20 Aug 89
4 x 200m	1:52.5	Mitcham	24 Jul 82
3 x 800m	7:18.0	Mid Hants	14 Sep 83
4 x 800m	10:02.4	Warrington	16 Sep 75

GB & NI v RUS (indoors) Glasgow 29 January 1994

MEN

60 Metres
1. LINFORD CHRISTIE — 6.56
2. COLIN JACKSON — 6.57
3. MICHAEL ROSSWESS gst — 6.64
4. Aleks. Porkhomovskiy RUS — 6.67
5. Anri Grigorev RUS — 6.76
6. DARREN BRAITHWAITE gst — 6.80

200 Metres
1. SOLOMON WARISO — 21.01
2. DARREN CAMPBELL — 21.23
3. Oleg Fatun RUS — 21.56
4. Andrey Fedoriv RUS — 21.59

400 Metres
1. MARK RICHARDSON — 46.11
2. DU'AINE LADEJO — 46.61
3. Dmitriy Kosov RUS — 47.39
4. Innokentiy Zharov RUS — 47.75

800 Metres
1. TOM McKEAN — 1:47.60
2. Andrey Loginov RUS — 1:47.63
3. GARY BROWN gst — 1:47.75
4. ANDREW LILL — 1:49.18
5. Oleg Stepanov RUS — 1:51.46

1500 Metres
1. JOHN MAYOCK — 3:45.83
2. MATT DE FREITAS — 3:46.45
3. Sergey Melnikov RUS — 3:47.01
4. Vladimir Kolpakov RUS — 3:48.17
5. IAN GILLESPIE gst — 3:48.56

3000 Metres
1. PAUL LARKINS — 7:57.02
2. ROD FINCH — 7:57.47
3. Andrey Tikhonov RUS — 7:58.63
4. Vyacheslav Shabunin RUS — 8:01.16

60 Metres Hurdles
1. COLIN JACKSON — 7.59
2. Aleksandr Markin RUS — 7.74
3. HUGH TEAPE gst — 7.74
4. Andrey Dydalin RUS — 7.95
5. ANDY TULLOCH — 7.98

High Jump
1. STEVE SMITH — 2.30
2. DALTON GRANT — 2.30
3. Oleg Zhukovsky BLS/gst — 2.26
4. Sergey Malchenko RUS — 2.20
5. Konstantin Galkin RUS — 2.20

Pole Vault
1. Pyotr Bochkaryov RUS — 5.60
2. Denis Petushinsky RUS — 5.60
3. ANDY ASHURST — 5.30
nh MATT BELSHAM

Long Jump
1. Stanislav Tarasenko RUS — 8.06
2. Dmitriy Bagryanov RUS — 7.95
3. BARRINGTON WILLIAMS — 7.58
4. FRED SALLE — 7.51

Triple Jump
1. Vasiliy Sokov RUS — 16.87
2. Denis Kapustin RUS — 16.83
3. JONATHAN EDWARDS — 16.65
4. JULIAN GOLLEY — 16.40

Shot
1. Yevgeniy Palchikov RUS — 20.36
2. PAUL EDWARDS — 19.21
3. Sergey Nikolayev RUS — 18.90
4. MARK PROCTOR — 17.33

4 x 200 Metres Relay
1. Russia — 1:23.26
dnf GREAT BRITAIN & NI — 1:24.69

WOMEN

60 Metres
1. Olga Bogoslovskaya RUS — 7.30
2. Natalya Voronova RUS — 7.37
3. MARCIA RICHARDSON — 7.41
4. JACQUI AGYEPONG — 7.61

200 Metres
1. Galina Malchugina RUS — 22.97
2. BEV KINCH — 24.21
3. TRACY GODDARD — 24.65
4. Yelena Mizera RUS — 24.79

400 Metres
1. MELANIE NEEF — 52.91
2. Yelena Golesheva RUS — 52.98
3. Yelena Ruzina RUS — 53.59
4. GEORGINA HONLEY — 58.23

800 Metres
1. Yelena Afanasyeva RUS — 2:07.41
2. LYNN GIBSON — 2:08.56
3. DAWN GANDY — 2:08.75

1500 Metres
1. Yekat. Podkopayeva RUS — 4:19.47
2. Lyubov Kremlyova RUS — 4:20.38
3. SONIA MCGEORGE — 4:21.28
4. MELANIE FAHERTY — 4:27.48

3000 Metres
1. Olga Kovpotina RUS — 9:16.82
2. Natalya Betekhtina RUS — 9:18.44
3. DEBBIE GUNNING — 9:21.36
4. JAYNE SPARK — 9:28.45

60 Metres Hurdles
1. Eva Sokolova RUS — 8.04
2. CLOVA COURT — 8.19
3. JACQUI AGYEPONG — 8.27
4. Marina Azyabina RUS — 8.29

High Jump
1. Yelena Topchina RUS — 1.88
2. Yevgenia Zhdanova RUS — 1.88
3. JULIA BENNETT — 1.83
4. RHONA SCOBIE — 1.70

Long Jump
1. Yelena Sinchukova RUS — 6.44
2. Lyudmila Galkina RUS — 6.39
3. YINKA IDOWU — 6.15
4. DENISE LEWIS — 5.72

Triple Jump
1. Anna Biryukova RUS — 14.11
2. Yolanda Chen RUS — 13.58
3. RACHEL KIRBY — 13.31
4. MICHELLE GRIFFITH — 13.22

Shot
1. Larisa Peleschenko RUS — 18.79
2. Irina Khudorozhkina RUS — 17.32
3. MAGGIE LYNES — 16.45
4. ALISON GREY — 15.78

4 x 200 Metres Relay
1. Russia — 1:33.33
2. GREAT BRITAIN — 1:35.44

Match Result Men
1. GREAT BRITAIN & NI — 74
2. Russia — 63

Match Result Women
1. Russia — 75
2. GREAT BRITAIN & NI — 41

Combined Match Result
1. Russia — 138
2. GREAT BRITAIN & NI — 115

AUT v Eng v TCH (indoors) Vienna, AUT 6 February 1994

MEN

60 Metres
1.	JASON JOHN		6.68
2.	DARREN BRAITHWAITE		6.70
3.	Martin Simunek	TCH	6.85
4.	Martin Schützenauer	AUT	6.86

200 Metres race 1
1.	SOLOMON WARISO		21.15
2.	Jiri Svenek	TCH	21.78
3.	Thomas Griesser	AUT	22.12

200 Metres race 2
1.	Walter Pilch	TCH	21.22
2.	PHILIP GOEDLUCK		21.46
3.	Andreas Rechbauer	AUT	22.38

400 Metres race 1
1.	MARK MORRIS		47.98
2.	Lukas Soucek	TCH	48.19
3.	Oliver Münzer	AUT	48.22

400 Metres race 2
1.	EDDIE WILLIAMS		47.57
2.	Petr Puncochar	TCH	48.85
3.	Klaus Angerer	AUT	49.29

800 Metres
1.	CRAIG WINROW		1:50.29
2.	ANDREW LILL		1:50.29
3.	Michael Wildner	AUT	1:50.88
4.	Thomas Ebner	AUT	1:51.05

1500 Metres
1.	Michael Buchleitner	AUT	3:41.76
2.	Milan Drahonovsky	TCH	3:42.98
3.	TERRY WEST		3:43.39
6.	MATTHEW HIBBERD		3:50.37

3000 Metres
1.	PAUL LARKINS		8:10.5
2.	Jiri Klesnil	TCH	8:10.9
3.	ROD FINCH		8:11.2
4.	Csaba Kollar	HUN/gst	8:15.7

60 Metres Hurdles
1.	HUGH TEAPE		7.74
2.	ANDY TULLOCH		7.84
3.	Herwig Röttl	AUT	7.85
4.	Viktor Zbozinek	TCH	7.95

High Jump
1.	Jan Janku	TCH	2.21
2=	Niki Grundner	AUT	2.18
2=	BRENDAN REILLY		2.18
6.	FAYYAZ AHMED		2.10

Pole Vault
1.	Zoltan Farkas	HUN/gst	5.30
2.	ANDY ASHURST		5.20
3.	Martin Tischler	AUT	5.20
5.	MATTHEW BELSHAM		5.00

Long Jump
1.	Milan Gombala	TCH	7.84
2.	Bogdan Tudor	ROM/gst	7.77
3.	Roman Orlik	TCH	7.75
4.	FRED SALLE		7.57
6.	STEVE PHILLIPS		7.54

Triple Jump
1.	Karel Burian	TCH	16.09
2.	Michal Coubal	TCH	15.76
3.	Gyula Paloczi	HUN/gst	15.75
4.	DEREK BROWNE		15.72
5.	FEMI AKINSANYA		15.68

Shot
1.	PAUL EDWARDS		19.47
2.	Martin Bilek	TCH	18.95
3.	Jan Bartl	TCH	18.05
4.	MARK PROCTOR		17.64

4 x 200 Metres Relay
1.	ENGLAND	1:25.69
	(GOEDLUCK, WARISO, BRAITHWAITE, JOHN)	
2.	CzechRepublic	1:27.09
	(Pilch, Ondracek, Svevenk, Bocek)	
3.	Austria	1:27.84
	(Rechbauer, Knoll, Klocker, Trenkler)	

Match Result
1.	ENGLAND	126.5
2.	CzechRepublic	93
3.	Austria	57.5

WOMEN

60 Metres
1.	Sabine Tröger	AUT	7.33
2.	Hana Benesova	TCH	7.45
3.	Zdena Musinska	TCH	7.48
4.	DANAA MYHILL		7.55
6.	DONNA HOGGARTH		7.70

200 Metres race 1
1.	MARCIA RICHARDSON		24.01
2.	Sabine Kirchmaier	AUT	24.57
3.	Denisa Nemcova	TCH	24.60

200 Metres race 2
1.	Hana Benesova	TCH	24.08
2.	TRACY GODDARD		24.16
3.	Doris Auer	AUT	24.75

400 Metres race 1
1.	Helena Dziurova	TCH	54.60
2.	Fiona Ritchie	AUT	56.78
3.	NIKKI LAMB		57.59

400 Metres race 2
1.	Ludmila Formanova	TCH	53.54
2.	GEORGINA HONLEY		57.72
3.	Andrea Pospischek	AUT	58.03

800 Metres
1.	Liliana Salgeanu	ROM/gst	2:03.85
2.	DAWN GANDY		2:05.28
3.	ANGELA DAVIES		2:05.69

1500 Metres
1.	Ellen Kiessling	GER/gst	4:21.16
2.	UNA ENGLISH		4:21.42
3.	MICHELLE FAHERTY		4:23.33
4.	Ernestine Waldhör	AUT	4:24.53

60 Metres Hurdles
1.	SAM FARQUHARSON		8.26
2.	LESLEY-ANN SKEETE		8.32
3.	Iveta Rudova	TCH	8.42
4.	Petra Simova	TCH	8.61

High Jump
1.	Sigrid Kirchmann	AUT	1.94
2.	Sarka Novakova	TCH	1.92
3.	JULIA BENNETT		1.80
4.	Sieglinde Cadusch	SWZ/gst	1.80
8.	JULIE MAJOR		1.75

Long Jump
1.	Ljudmila Ninova	AUT	6.70
2.	JOANNE DEAR		6.21
3.	DENISE LEWIS		6.08
4.	Rita Schönenberger	SWZ/gst	6.02

Triple Jump
1.	Sarka Kaspakova	TCH	13.68
2.	ASHIA HANSEN		13.41
3.	Ksenija Predikaka	SLO/gst	13.00
4.	CONNIE HENRY		12.60

Shot
1.	MAGGIE LYNES		15.95
2.	Natasa Erjavec	SLO/gst	15.64
3.	SHARON ANDREWS		15.29
4.	Alice Matejkova	TCH	14.93

4 x 200 Metres Relay
1.	CzechRepublic	1:36.17
	(Pastuskova, Kostovalova, Nemcova, Benesova)	
2.	ENGLAND	1:36.62
	(RICHARDSON, GODDARD, SKEETE, MYHILL)	
3.	Austria	1:37.18
	(Tröger, Auer, Mayr, Kirchmaier)	

Match Result
1.	ENGLAND	96
2.	CzechRepublic	77
3.	Austria	59

GB & NI v USA (indoors)   Glasgow   12 February 1994

MEN

60 Metres
1. LINFORD CHRISTIE   6.53
2. COLIN JACKSON   6.55
3. MICHAEL ROSSWESS gst   6.66
4. Aaron Thigpen USA   6.71
5. DARREN BRAITHWAITE gst   6.78
6. Glenn Terry USA   7.13

200 Metres
1. JOHN REGIS   20.74
2. SOLOMON WARISO   21.10
3. Jason Hendrix USA   21.37
4. Brian Bridgewater USA   21.37

400 Metres
1. Antonio Pettigrew USA   46.04
2. MARK RICHARDSON   46.21
3. Darnell Hall USA   46.27
4. DU'AINE LADEJO   46.43

800 Metres
1. GARY BROWN   1:47.63
2. CRAIG WINROW gst   1:47.78
3. Mark Everet USA   1:48.87
4. Brad Sumner USA   1:49.75
5. TOM MCKEAN   2:09.92

1500 Metres
1. Mark Dailey USA   3:46.20
2. MATT DE FREITAS   3:46.23
3. MATT HIBBERD gst   3:47.44
4. TONY MORRELL gst   3:48.53
5. Terrance Herrington   3:49.67
6. MARTIN STEELE   3:56.20

3000 Metres
1. JOHN MAYOCK   7:55.31
2. ROD FINCH   7:56.03
3. Danny Lopez USA   8:07.69
4. Kurt Black USA   8:18.50

60 Metres Hurdles
1. COLIN JACKSON   7.36
2. TONY JARRETT   7.58
3. Allen Johnson USA   7.59
4. HUGH TEAPE gst   7.72
5. Glenn Terry USA   7.73
6. KEN CAMPBELL gst   7.99

High Jump
1. STEVE SMITH   2.32
2. Steve C Smith USA   2.26
3. DALTON GRANT   2.26
4. Tony Barton USA   2.26

Pole Vault
1. Mike Holloway USA   5.40
2. ANDY ASHURST   5.20
3. Greg Duplantis USA   5.20
4. DEAN MELLOR   4.60

Long Jump
1. BARRINGTON WILLIAMS   7.61
2. Alan Turner USA   7.52
3. Diatori Gildersleeve USA   7.33
4. FRED SALLE   7.27

Triple Jump
1. JULIAN GOLLEY   16.76
2. JONATHAN EDWARDS   16.71
3. Reggie Jones USA   16.26
4. Ray Kimble USA   16.08

Shot
1. Kevin Toth USA   20.62
2. C J Hunter USA   20.13
3. PAUL EDWARDS   19.38
4. MARK PROCTOR   17.17

4 x 200 Metres Relay
1. GREAT BRITAIN   1:24.13
2. USA   1:24.31

Match Result
1. GREAT BRITAIN & NI   79
2. USA   60

WOMEN

60 Metres
1. Holli Hyche USA   7.21
2. Chryste Gaines USA   7.37
3. MARCIA RICHARDSON   7.38
4. SOPHIA SMITH   7.51

200 Metres
1. KATHARINE MERRY   23.00
2. Holli Hyche USA   23.01
3. Flirtisha Harris USA   23.51
4. SOPHIA SMITH   24.77

400 Metres
1. SALLY GUNNELL   52.34
2. Crystal Irving USA   55.25
3. CLAIRE RAVEN   56.39

800 Metres
1. ANGELA DAVIES   2:08.28
2. DAWN GANDY   2:08.50
3. Debbie Marshall USA   2:08.74
4. Claudette Groenendaal USA   2:10.50

1500 Metres
1. LYNN GIBSON   4:25.32
2. KIRSTY WADE   4:26.05
3. Gina Procaccio USA   4:26.15
4. Michelle DiMuro USA   4:27.44

3000 Metres
1. SONIA MCGEORGE   9:08.90
2. Kathy Franey USA   9:09.80
3. Cathy Palacios USA   9:11.07
4. DEBBIE GUNNING   9:15.11

60 Metres Hurdles
1. CLOVA COURT   8.12
2. SAM FARQUHARSON   8.14
3. Dawn Bowles USA   8.20
4. Marsha Guialdo USA   8.36

High Jump
1. Angie Bradburn USA   1.93
2. Yolanda Henry USA   1.83
3. JO JENNINGS   1.83
4. JULIE MAJOR   1.75

Long Jump
1. YINKA IDOWU   6.51
2. Sharon Couch USA   6.22
3. Cynthia Jackson USA   5.87
4. DENISE LEWIS   5.82

Triple Jump
1. MICHELLE GRIFFITH   13.85
2. Cynthea Rhodes   13.49
3. Sheila Hudson USA   13.41
4. RACHEL KIRBY   13.14

Shot
1. Connie Price-Smith USA   18.03
2. MAGGIE LYNES   16.13
3. ALISON GREY   15.85
4. Christy Barrett USA   14.39

4 x 200 Metres Relay
1. USA   1:33.24
2. GREAT BRITAIN   1:36.23

Match Result
1. GREAT BRITAIN & NI   69
2. USA   59

AAA INDOOR JUNIOR CHAMPIONSHIPS Birmingham 12-13 February 1994

Men Under 20

60	Jason Gardener	6.77
200	Andy Walcott	21.67
400	Matthew Douglas	48.39
800	Eddie King	1:50.55
1500	Stuart Overthrow	4:02.49
3000	Andy Renfree	8:42.81
60H	James Archampong	8.01
HJ	James Brierley	2.15
PV	Ian Wilding	4.70
LJ	Chris Davidson	7.21
TJ	Larry Achike	15.48
SP	Simon Fricker	14.17

Under 17

Dwain Chambers	6.95
Ross Baillie	22.51
Dean Park	50.10
Bryan Hendry	2:02.39
Paul Draper	4:10.38
R Burke	9:27.72
Damien Greaves	7.99
Robert Holton	1.90
Martin Parley	4.00
Andrew Thornton	6.65
Matthew Thompson	13.63
Emeka Udechuku	14.89

Under 15

Steven Wiggans	7.43
Robert Allenby	23.74
Marc Newton	2:03.52
Patrick Brown	9.15
Kevin Drury	1.80
Christian Linskey	3.90
Marc Newton	6.04
Peter Waterman	13.54

Women Under 20

60	Diane Allahgreen	7.53
200	Debbie Mant	24.78
400	Allison Curbishley	54.78
800	Dorothea Lee	2:10.67
1500	Jeina Mitchell	4:32.11
3000	Charlotte Goff	10:24.70
60H	Diane Allahgreen	8.47
HJ	Lindsay Evans	1.73
PV	Dawn Wright	2.85
LJ	Joanne Dear	5.94
TJ	Kathryn Blackwood	11.28
SP	Eleanor Gatrell	11.18

Under 17

	Tatum Nelson	7.61
	Laura Seston	25.04
300	Ruth Nicholson	41.20
	Helen Parsons	2:16.12
	Caroline McNulty	4:42.43
	Catherine Boulton	1.76
	Katharine Horner	2.40
	Helen Pryer	5.50
	Jayne Ludlow	11.74
	Philippa Roles	13.26

Under 15

Sarah Wilhelmy	7.64
Sarah Wilhelmy	25.01
Sarah Mead	2:18.19
Nicola Hall	9.20
Antonia Bemrose	1.63
Kelly Williamson	5.35
Frances Reid-Hughes	11.06

English National Cross-Country Championships

MEN Temple Park,
South Shields 12 March 1994

WOMEN Witton Park,
Blackburn 13 February 1994

MEN

1.	DAVE LEWIS	42:35
2.	JOHN NUTTALL	42:51
3.	JOHN DOWNES	43:18
4.	KEITH ANDERSON	43:21
5.	GLYN TROMANS	43:25
6.	CHRIS ROBISON	43:35
7.	NOEL BERKELEY	43:37
8.	SPENCER NEWPORT	43:45
9.	MARK HUSPITH	43:46
10.	LARRY MATTHEWS	43:47

JUNIOR MEN (U20)

1.	Kaesa Tadeesa	ETH	29:54
2.	BRUNO WITCHALLS		30:07
3.	BEN SUTTON		30:11
4.	CIARAN McGUIRE		30:27
5.	ROB SCANLON		30:31

YOUTHS (U17)

1.	ALEX OLDFIELD	28:02
2.	KEVIN NASH	28:05
3.	ROBERT BROWN	28:26
4.	STUART BROWN	28:32
5.	ALLEN GRAFFIN	28:35

WOMEN

1.	PAULA RADCLIFFE	20:51
2.	ALISON WYETH	20:59
3.	LAURA ADAM	21:04
4.	ANGIE HULLEY	21:17
5.	ANDREA DUKE	21:31
6.	JENNY CLAGUE	21:33
7.	CAROL GREENWOOD	21:40
8.	SHIREEN BARBOUR	21:41
9.	SUSAN PARKER	21:42
10.	SHARON DIXON	21:45

JUNIOR WOMEN (U20)

1.	CLAIRE O'CONNOR	20:15
2.	ALICE BRAHAM	20:27
3.	HEIDI MOULDER	20:29

UNDER 17

1.	BEVERLEY GRAY	20:33
2.	JULIETTE OLDFIELD	20:52
3.	ALISON OUTRAM	20:53

UNDER 15

1.	JUSTINA HESLOP	13:40
2.	SONIA THOMAS	13:51
3.	EMMA ROUSTED	13:59

UNDER 13

1.	JODIE SWALLOW	12:04
2.	JEANETTE SHORTALL	12:25
3.	NICOLA COATES	12:30

AAA INDOOR CHAMPIONSHIPS Birmingham 18-19 February 1994

MEN

60 Metres (19 Feb)
1. MICHAEL ROSSWESS 6.56
2. LINFORD CHRISTIE 6.56
3. COLIN JACKSON 6.57
4. Thomas Leanderson SWE 6.68
5. DARREN BRAITHWAITE 6.72
6. Fernando Ramirez NOR 6.73
7. Kennet Kjensli NOR 6.73
8. JASON GARDENER 6.76

200 Metres (18 Feb)
1. PHILIP GOEDLUCK 21.16
2. DARREN BRAITHWAITE 21.17
3. Geir Moen NOR 21.26
4. ALLYN CONDON 22.30
   WAYNE MCDONALD dnf

400 Metres (18 Feb)
1. DU'AINE LADEJO 46.54
2. JAMIE BAULCH 46.75
3. IWAN THOMAS 47.25
4. MATTHEW DOUGLAS 48.55
5. PETE CLARKE 49.42
   GUY BULLOCK dnf

800 Metres (18 Feb)
1. TOM MCKEAN 1:48.46
2. MARTIN STEELE 1:48.59
3. CHRIS WINROW 1:48.72
4. Robert Kibet KEN 1:48.72
5. MIKE GUEGAN 1:50.93
6. Vincent Malakwen KEN 1:55.65

WOMEN

60 Metres (19 Feb)
1. BEV KINCH 7.35
2. MARCIA RICHARDSON 7.39
3. CLOVA COURT 7.47
4. SOPHIA SMITH 7.50
5. LORRAINE ROBINS 7.59
6. HELEN MILES 7.61

200 Metres (18 Feb)
1. Maria Staafgard SWE 23.78
2. MARCIA RICHARDSON 23.94
3. ALISON MAYFIELD 24.41
4. Marisa Smith IRE 24.41
5. ALANNA COOKE 25.39

400 Metres (19 Feb)
1. TRACY GODDARD 54.05
2. PAULINE RICHARDS 55.86
3. CLAIRE RAVEN 56.08
4. ELAINE SUTCLIFFE 56.34
5. KIM GOODWIN 56.39
6. CLARE BLEASDALE 56.62

800 Metres (19 Feb)
1. KIRSTY WADE 2:05.60
2. SONYA BOWYER 2:05.97
3. Ingunn Lindstedt SWE 2:06.50
4. CATHERINE ALLSOPP 2:11.08
5. RACHEL BOWEN 2:14.68

1500 Metres (18 Feb)
1. Atoi Boru KEN 3:42.25
2. IAN CAMPBELL 3:43.05
3. TERRY WEST 3:44.86
4. TONY MORRELL 3:44.77
5. PAUL BURGESS 3:49.27
6. NEIL WILLIAMS 3:51.73

3000 Metres (19 Feb)
1. MATT BARNES 7:56.08
2. Michael Buchleitner AUT 7:56.27
3. ROB DENMARK 7:56.60
4. Claes Nyberg SWE 7:57.73
5. TOM BUCKNER 7:58.92
6. STEFFAN WHITE 8:01.90

60 Metres Hurdles (19 Feb)
1. HUGH TEAPE 7.73
2. Thomas Kearns IRE 7.77
3. NEIL OWEN 7.86
4. PAUL GRAY 7.91
5. Sean Cahill IRE 8.02
6. Claes Albihn SWE 8.06
7. MARTIN NICHOLSON 8.08
8. MARK LAMBETH 8.08

High Jump (19 Feb)
1. BRENDAN REILLY 2.28
2. Hakon Sarnblom NOR 2.22
3. GEOFF PARSONS 2.22
4. Mark Mandy IRE 2.16
5. FAYYAZ AHMED 2.11
6. DAVID BARNETSON 2.06

1500 Metres (19 Feb)
1. LYNN GIBSON 4:17.01
2. ANGELA DAVIES 4:20.90
3. SHIRLEY GRIFFITHS 4:23.75
4. UNA ENGLISH 4:24.66
5. SUSAN PARKER 4:24.70
6. JULIE SWANN 4:26.25

3000 Metres (19 Feb)
1. Erika Konig AUS 9:25.58
2. JULIE BRIGGS 9:30.15
3. SARAH BENTLEY 9:37.17

60 Metres Hurdles (19 Feb)
1. SAM FARQUHARSON 8.19
2. Monica Grefstad NOR 8.23
3. LESLEY-ANN SKEETE 8.39
4. ANGELA THORP 8.40
5. NATASHA MIGHTY 8.49
6. DIANE ALLAHGREEN 8.52

High Jump (19 Feb)
1. Hanne Haugland NOR 1.94
2. JULIA BENNETT 1.85
3= KELLY MASON 1.80
3= JO JENNINGS 1.80
3= Sharon Foley IRE 1.80
6. JULIE MAJOR 1.75

Pole Vault (19 Feb)
1. Peter Widén SWE 5.45
2. Martin Voss DEN 5.30
3. Marten Ulvsback SWE 5.20
4. Trond Barthel NOR 5.20
5= ANDY ASHURST 5.20
5= Carl-Johan Alm SWE 5.20

Long Jump (19 Feb)
1. Mattias Sunneborn SWE 7.50
2. Peter Odlin SWE 7.41
3. FRED SALLE 7.39
4. BARRINGTON WILLIAMS 7.32
5. COURTNEY CHARLES 7.22
6. TOSI FASINRO 7.20

Triple Jump (19 Feb)
1. FRANCIS AGYEPONG 16.55
2. ONOCHIE ACHIKE 15.65
3. Lars Hedman SWE 15.61
4. FEMI AKINSANYA 15.57
5. VERNON SAMUELS 15.54
6. EZRA CLARKE 15.12
7. REZ CAMERON 14.72
8. MICHAEL MCDONALD 14.69

Shot (18 Feb)
1. PAUL EDWARDS 18.95
2. SHAUN PICKERING 17.32
3. DAVE CALLAWAY 17.12
4. Yoav Sharf ISR 17.08
5. STEVE WHYTE 16.94
6. NIGEL SPRATLEY 16.78

Pole Vault (19 Feb)
1. KATE STAPLES 3.46
2. LINDA STANTON 3.20
3. RHIAN CLARKE 3.20
4. CLAIRE MORRISON 3.10
5. PAULA WILSON 3.00

Long Jump (18 Feb)
1. DENISE LEWIS 6.07
2. HELEN GARRETT 5.86
3. Terrie Horgan IRE 5.80
4. JACQUELINE WHITE 5.75
5. DIANA BENNETT 5.72
6. LISA ARMSTRONG 5.61

Triple Jump (19 Feb)
1. RACHEL KIRBY 13.21
2. Ksenija Predikaka SLO 12.85
3. CONNIE HENRY 12.82
4. SHANI ANDERSON 11.69
5. KERRY JURY 11.29

Shot (18 Feb)
1. MAGGIE LYNES 15.82
2. ALISON GREY 15.50
3. DEBORAH CALLAWAY 14.25
4. Kelly Kane IRE 13.18
5. CHARMAINE JOHNSON 13.13

EUROPEAN INDOOR CHAMPIONSHIPS Paris, FRA 11-13 March 1994

MEN

60 Metres (11 Mar)
1. COLIN JACKSON — 6.49
2. Alexandros Terzian GRE — 6.51
3. MICHAEL ROSSWESS — 6.54
4. Aleks.Porkhomovskiy RUS — 6.59
5. Daniel Sangouma FRA — 6.65
6. Laurent Nevo FRA — 6.75

200 Metres (13 Mar)
1. Daniel Sangouma FRA — 20.68
2. Vladislav Dologodin UKR — 20.76
3. George Panagiotopoulos GRE — 20.99
4. Evgenio Papadopoulos GRE — 21.15
5. DARREN BRAITHWAITE — 21.30
6. Ioannis Nafpliotis GRE — 21.61

4s1 SOLOMON WARISO — 21.52
4h1 PHILIP GOEDLUCK — 21.31

400 Metres (13 Mar)
1. DU'AINE LADEJO — 46.53
2. Mikhail Vdovin RUS — 46.56
3. Rico Lieder GER — 46.82
4. Lutz Becker GER — 47.74
5. Andrea Nuti ITA — 50.05
   JAMIE BAULCH — dnf

4s1 MARK RICHARDSON — 46.77

800 Metres (13 Mar)
1. Andrey Loginov RUS — 1:46.38
2. Luis Javier Gonzalez SPA — 1:46.69
3. Ousmane Diarra FRA — 1:47.18
4. Nico Motchebon GER — 1:47.24
5. Torbjorn Johansson SWE — 1:47.42
6. Bruno Konczylo FRA — 2:00.33

5s2 MARTIN STEELE — 1:49.65
3h2 CRAIG WINROW — 1:49.88

1500 Metres (13 Mar)
1. DAVID STRANG — 3:44.57
2. Branko Zorko CRO — 3:44.64
3. Kader Chekhemani FRA — 3:44.65
4. Manuel Pancorbo SPA — 3:45.03
5. Vyacheslav Shabunin RUS — 3:45.37
6. Mickael Damian FRA — 3:45.54

4h1 IAN CAMPBELL — 3:51.50
7h3 MATT HIBBERD — 3:50.73

3000 Metres (13 Mar)
1. Kim Bauermeister GER — 7:52.34
2. Ovidiu Olteanu ROM — 7:52.37
3. ROD FINCH — 7:53.99
4. Anacieto Jimenez SPA — 7:55.78
5. Michael Buchleitner AUT — 7:56.47
6. Andres Martinez SPA — 7:59.70
7. Andrey Tikhonov RUS — 8:02.95
8. Gino van Geyte BEL — 8:11.02
9. Mirko Döring GER — 8:50.58

9h1 MATT BARNES — 8:10.88

60 Metres Hurdles (12 Mar)
1. COLIN JACKSON — 7.41
2. Georg Boroi ROM — 7.57
3. Mike Fenner GER — 7.58
4. Dan Philibert FRA — 7.60
5. Igor Kovac SVK — 7.61
6. Jiri Hudec TCH — 7.72

5s1 HUGH TEAPE — 7.77

High Jump (13 Mar)
1. DALTON GRANT — 2.37
2. Jean-Charles Gicquel FRA — 2.35
3. Hendrik Beyer GER — 2.33
4. Steinar Hoen NOR — 2.31
5. Leonid Pumalaynen RUS — 2.31
6. Hakon Sarnblom NOR — 2.29
7. BRENDAN REILLY — 2.26
8. Torsten Marschner GER — 2.26

Pole Vault (12 Mar)
1. Pyotr Bochkaryov RUS — 5.90
2. Jean Galfione FRA — 5.80
3. Igor Trandenkov RUS — 5.75
4. Denis Petushinskiy RUS — 5.75
5. Istvan Bagyula HUN — 5.70
6. Gianni Iapichino ITA — 5.60
7. Yevgeniy Krasnov ISR — 5.60
8. Valeriy Bukreyev EST — 5.60

Long Jump (13 Mar)
1. Dietmar Haaf GER — 8.15
2. Konstant. Koukodimos GRE — 8.09
3. Bogdan Tudor ROM — 8.07
4. Ivailo Mladenov BUL — 8.07
5. Stanislav Tarasenko RUS — 8.02
6. Dmitriy Bagryanov RUS — 8.01
7. Mattias Sunneborn SWE — 7.96
8. Georg Ackermann GER — 7.84

Triple Jump (12 Mar)
1. Leonid Voloshin RUS — 17.44
2. Denis Kapustin RUS — 17.35
3. Vasiliy Sokov RUS — 17.31
4. Serge Hélan FRA — 17.23
5. Georges Sainte-Rose FRA — 16.96
6. Maris Bruziks LAT — 16.83
7. Ralf Jaros GER — 16.78
8. Lars Hedman SWE — 16.66

13. FRANCIS AGYEPONG — 16.27
14. JULIAN GOLLEY — 16.17

Shot (11 Mar)
1. Aleksandr Bagach UKR — 20.66
2. Dragan Peric IEP — 20.55
3. Petur Gudmundsson ISL — 20.04
4. Manuel Martinez SPA — 19.85
5. Oliver-Sven Buder GER — 19.66
6. Paolo Dal Soglio ITA — 19.62
7. Yevgeniy Palchikov RUS — 19.50
8. Mika Halvari FIN — 19.48

14Q PAUL EDWARDS — 18.49

Heptathlon (12-13 Mar)
1. Christian Plaziat FRA — 6268
2. Henrik Dagárd SWE — 6119
3. Alain Blondel FRA — 6084
4. Tomás Dvorák TCH — 6061
5. Erki Nool EST — 5945
6. Sándor Munkacsi HUN — 5944
7. Indrek Kaseorg EST — 5888
8. Marcel Dost HOL — 5734

5000 Metres Walk (13 Mar)
1. Mikhail Shchennikov RUS — 18:34.32
2. Ronald Weigel GER — 18:40.32
3. Denis Langlois FRA — 18:43.20
4. Michele Didoni ITA — 19:01.03
5. Jean-Claude Corre FRA — 19:10.24
6. Pavol Blazek SVK — 19:14.00
7. Yevgeniy Misyulya BLS — 19:17.74
8. Stefan Johansson SWE — 19:21.82

WOMEN

60 Metres (12 Mar)
1. Nelli Cooman HOL — 7.16
2. Melanie Paschke GER — 7.19
3. Patricia Girard FRA — 7.19
4. Petya Pendareva BUL — 7.24
5. Desislava Dimitrova BUL — 7.25
6. Sabine Troger AUT — 7.31

200 Metres (13 Mar)
1. Galina Malchugina RUS — 22.41
2. Silke Knoll GER — 22.96
3. Jacqueline Poelman HOL — 23.43
4. Hana Benesova TCH — 23.67
5. Glada Gallina ITA — 23.79
6. Petya Pendareva BUL — 23.89

5s2 MARCIA RICHARDSON — 23.95

400 Metres (13 Mar)
1. Svetlana Goncharenko RUS — 51.62
2. Tatyana Alekseyeva RUS — 51.77
3. Viviane Dorsile FRA — 51.92
4. Ionela Tirlea ROM — 53.13
5. Magdalena Nedelcu ROM — 53.62
6. Kathrin Luthi SWZ — 54.06

800 Metres (13 Mar)
1. Natalya Dukhnova BLS 2:00.42
2. Ella Kovacs ROM 2:00.49
3. Carla Sacramento POR 2:01.12
4. Stella Jongmans HOL 2:01.82
5. Ester Goossens HOL 2:03.59
6. Yelena Storchovaya UKR 2:06.41

1500 Metres (13 Mar)
1. Yekaterina Podkopayeva RUS 4:06.46
2. Lyudmila Rogachova RUS 4:06.60
3. Malgorzata Rydz POL 4:06.98
4. Violeta Beclea ROM 4:07.06
5. Ellen Kiessling GER 4:10.68
6. Teresa Zuñiga SPA 4:10.99
7. Tudorita Chidu ROM 4:12.13
8. Fréderique Quentin FRA 4:13.44

3000 Metres (11 Mar)
1. Fernanda Ribeiro POR 8:50.47
2. Margareta Keszeg ROM 8:55.61
3. Anna Brzezinska POL 8:56.90
4. Christina Mai GER 8:57.49
5. Laurence Vivier FRA 8:59.95
6. ALISON WYETH 9:04.35
7. Renata Sobiesiak POL 9:09.09
8. SONIA McGEORGE 9:14.04

60 Metres Hurdles (13 Mar)
1. Yordanka Donkova BUL 7.85
2. Eva Sokolova RUS 7.89
3. Anne Piquereau FRA 7.91
4. Brigita Bukovec SLO 7.94
5. Carla Tuzzi ITA 7.97
6. Patricia Girard FRA 7.98

4s1 SAM FARQUHARSON 8.11
5h3 CLOVA COURT 8.24

High Jump (12 Mar)
1. Stefka Kostadinova BUL 1.98
2. Desislava Alexandrova BUL 1.96
3. Sigrid Kirchmann AUT 1.96
4. Tatyana Shevtchik BLS 1.96
5. Yelena Gulyayeva RUS 1.93
6. Hanne Haugland NOR 1.93
7. Britta Bilac SLO 1.93
8. Inna Gliznutsa MOL 1.90

Long Jump (11 Mar)
1. Heike Drechsler GER 7.06
2. Lyudmila Ninova AUT 6.78
3. Inessa Kravets UKR 6.72
4. Valentina Uccheddu ITA 6.69
5. Mirella Dulgheru ROM 6.61
6. Agata Karczmarek POL 6.60
7. Yelena Sinchukova RUS 6.50
8. Helga Radtke GER 6.45

Triple Jump (13 Mar)
1. Inna Lasovskaya RUS 14.88
2. Ana Biryukova RUS 14.72
3. Sofia Bozhanova BUL 14.52
4. Sarka Kaspárková TCH 14.46
5. Iva Prandzheva BUL 14.38
6. Inessa Kravets UKR 14.32
7. Helga Radtke GER 13.92
8. Rodica Petrescu ROM 13.90

10. MICHELLE GRIFFITH 13.55

15QRACHEL KIRBY 13.31
16QASHIA HANSEN 13.30

Shot (13 Mar)
1. Astrid Kumbernuss GER 19.44
2. Larisa Peleshenko RUS 19.16
3. Svetia Mitkova BUL 19.09
4. Anna Romanova RUS 18.80
5. Grit Hammer GER 18.58
6. Krystyna Danilczyk POL 18.57
7. Mihaela Oana ROM 18.31
8. Ines Wittich GER 17.89

Pentathlon (11 Mar)
1. Larisa Turchinskaya RUS 4801
2. Rita Ináncsi HUN 4775
3. Urszula Wlodarczyk POL 4668
4. Liliana Nastase ROM 4620
5. Lyudmila Mikhailova RUS 4616
6. Ines Krause GER 4503
7. Maria Kamrowska POL 4496
8. Petra Vaideanu ROM 4456

3000 Metres Walk (12 Mar)
1. Anna-Rita Sidoti ITA 11:54.32
2. Beate Gummelt GER 11:56.01
3. Yelena Arshintseva RUS 11:57.48
4. Yelena Nikolayeva RUS 11:57.49
5. Leonarda Yukhnevich BLS 12:04.46
6. Sari Essayah FIN 12:12.80
7. Olga Leonenko UKR 12:20.44
8. Kathrin Boyde GER 12:21.63

AAA HALF MARATHON CHAMPIONSHIPS York   27 March 1994

MEN

1. MARK HUDSPITH 1:03:37
2. MARK CROASDALE 1:04:43
3. KEITH ANDERSON 1:04:53
4. BILL FOSTER 1:05:20
5. COLIN WALKER 1:05:53
6. MARK COLPUS 1:06:16
7. ALAN GUILDER 1:06:26
8. TREVOR CLARK 1:06:48
9. PETER HAYNES 1:06:54
10. DAVE GRATTON 1:06:56

WOMEN

1. LINDA RUSHMERE 1:14:31
2. ANGIE HULLEY 1:16:01
3. SUE ENDERSBY 1:19:25
4. A MILLS 1:19:31
5. J FINNEY 1:21:34
6. A DOLAN 1:21:42
7. KATH KAISER 1:23:46
8. MARIE HART 1:23:57
9. SYLVIA WATSON 1:25:17
10. C FIDDES 1:25:24

IAAF WORLD CROSS COUNTRY CHAMPIONSHIPS
Budapest, HUN   26 March 1994

Senior Men (12,060m)

1.	William Sigei	KEN	34:29
2.	Simon Chemolywo	KEN	34:30
3.	Haile Gebresilasie	ETH	34:32
4.	Paul Tergat	KEN	34:36
5.	Khalid Skah	MAR	34:56
6.	James Songok	KEN	35:02
7.	Addis Abebe	ETH	35:11
8.	Ayele Mezgebu	ETH	35:14
9.	Shem Kororia	KEN	35:15
10.	Mathias Ntawulikura	RWA	35:19

32.	JOHN NUTTALL	36:00
54.	DAVE CLARKE	36:24
63.	MARTIN JONES	36:33
71.	DOMINIC BANNISTER	36:44
95.	EAMONN MARTIN	36:56
124.	BARRY ROYDEN	37:16
132.	DARREN MEAD	37:24
146.	STEVE TUNSTALL	37:33
dnf	ANDY BRISTOW	

Men's Teams

1.	Kenya	34
2.	Morocco	83
3.	Ethiopia	133
4.	Spain	174
5.	Portugal	210
6.	Italy	312
7.	France	319
8.	GREAT BRITAIN & NI	439
9.	Russia	448
10.	South Africa	535

Senior Women (6,220m)

1.	Helen Chepngeno	KEN	20:45
2.	Catherina McKiernan	IRE	20:52
3.	Conceicao Ferreira	POR	20:52
4.	Merima Denboba	ETH	20:57
5.	Albertina Dias	POR	20:59
6.	Elana Meyer	RSA	21:00
7.	Zola Pieterse	RSA	21:01
8.	Farida Fates	FRA	21:01
9.	Olga Churbanova	RUS	21:05
10.	Fernando Ribeiro	POR	21:05

45.	LAURA ADAM	21:44
77.	TANYA BLAKE	22:06
78.	WENDY ORE	22:07
80	VIKKI McPHERSON	22:11
119.	CAROL GREENWOOD	22:49
121.	JANE SPARK	22:53

Women's Teams

1.	Portugal	55
2.	Ethiopia	65
3.	Kenya	75
4.	Russia	84
5.	Spain	111
6.	South Africa	124
7.	Italy	127
8.	Japan	134
9.	France	138
10.	USA	165

14. GREAT BRITAIN & NI 280

Junior Men (8,140m)

1.	Philip Mosima	KEN	24:15
2.	Daniel Komen	KEN	24:17
3.	Abreham Tsige	ETH	24:46
4.	Philip Kemei	KEN	24:49
5.	Lemma Alemayehu	ETH	25:00

27.	DARRIUS BURROWS	25:53
49.	BEN NOAD	26:15
93.	NEIL CADDY	26:50
118.	SCOTT WEST	27:12
129.	MATTHEW O'DOWD	27:19
135.	KEVIN HOLLAND	27:30

Junior Men's Teams

1.	Kenya	18
2.	Ethiopia	27
3.	Morocco	78
4.	South Africa	95

16. GREAT BRITAIN & NI 287

Junior Women (4,300m)

1.	Sally Barsosio	KEN	14:04
2.	Rose Cheruiyot	KEN	14:05
3.	Elizabeth Cheptanui	KEN	14:15
4.	Gabriela Szabo	ROM	14:25
5.	Ruth Biwott	KEN	14:27

11.	NICOLA SLATER	14:49
26.	HEIDI MOULDER	15:24
40.	CATHERINE BERRY	15:41
42.	CLARE O'CONNOR	15:42
50.	SARAH SIMMONDS	15:47
78.	MICHELLE MATTHEWS	16:05

Junior Women's Teams

1.	Kenya	11
2.	Ethiopia	46
3.	Japan	60
4.	Romania	83
5.	GREAT BRITAIN & NI	119

NUTRASWEET LONDON MARATHON 17 April 1994

Men

1.	Dionicio Ceron	MEX	2:08:53
2.	Abebe Mekonnen	ETH	2:09:17
3.	German Silva	MEX	2:09:18
4.	Savatore Bettiol	ITA	2:09:40
5.	Grzegorz Gajdus	POL	2:09:46
6.	Martin Pitayo	MEX	2:10:58
7.	Tena Negere	ETH	2:10:59
8	EAMONN MARTIN		2:11:05
9.	Rolando Vera	ECU	2:11:15
10.	Carlos Patricio	POR	2:11:42
11.	MARK FLINT		2:12:07
12.	Fernando Couto	POR	2:12:15
13.	STEVE BRACE		2:12:23
14.	Tesafaye Bekele	NOR	2:12:24
15.	Artur de Fretas Castro	BRA	2:12:44

17.	MARK HUDSPITH	2:12:52
22.	PETE WHITEHEAD	2:13:40
26.	DALE RIXON	2:15:41
27.	MIKE O'REILLY	2:15:46
29.	BILL FOSTER	2:17:16
32.	MARK CROASDALE	2:18:04

Women

1.	Katrin Dörre	GER	2:32:34
2.	Lisa Ondieki	AUS	2:33:17
3.	Janet Mayal	BRA	2:34:21
4.	SALLY ELLIS		2:37:06
5.	SALLY EASTALL		2:37:08

6.	HAYLEY NASH	2:39:04
7.	ZINA MARCHANT	2:40:09
8.	JULIE COLEBY	2:40:31
9.	LINDA RUSHMERE	2:40:46
10.	SUZANNE RIGG	2:41:03
11.	SALLY LYNCH	2:41:47
12.	ANGIE HULLEY	2:42:40
13.	ALISON ROSE	2:45:55
18.	TRUDI THOMSON	2:47:31
19.	TRACY SWINDELL	2:48:09
20.	CATHERINE MIJOVIC	2:48:31
21.	LESLEY TURNER	2:48:34
22.	SUE ENDERSBY	2:49:03
23.	ZOE LOWE	2:49:58
25.	ELAINE FLATHER	2:50:41

IAAF ROAD RELAY CHAMPIONSHIPS Litochoro, GRE 17 April 1994

MEN

1. Morocco   1:57:56
(B Jabbour 13:35, L Khattabi 28:44, H El Guerouj 13:43,
S Hissou 27:57, B Boutayeb 13:53, K Skah 20:04)
2. Ethiopia   1:58:51
(W Bikila 13:30, B Kibret28:36, A Assefa14:17,
F Bayesa 28:52, C Kelele 14:09, H Gebrilasie 19:27)
3. Kenya   2:00:51
(P Ndirangu 13:40, J Kibor 28:19, C Kiprotich 14:16,
P Yego 29:56, J Kiprono 13:55, S Rono 20:45)

5. GREAT BRITAIN & NI   2:02:12
(KEITH CULLEN 14:01, DAVE CLARKE 29:41,
PAUL TAYLOR 14:07, MARTIN JONES 28:58,
COLIN MOORE 14:21, BARRY ROYDEN 21:04)

WOMEN

1. Russia   2:17:19
(T. Pentukova 16:12, N Galyamova 32:59, Y Kopytova 15:45,
N Solominskaya 33:21, Y Romanova 15:48, O Churbanova 23:14)
2. Ethiopia   2:19:09
(A Birece 16:05, D Tuku 32:26, L Aman 16:31,
G Edato 33:47, B Dagne16:13, A Gigi 24:07)
3. Romania   2:19:18
(D Bran 16:29, A Tecuta 33:17, M Chirila 16:02,
A Catuna 33:16, F Pena 16:49, I Negura 23:25)

8. GREAT BRITAIN & NI   2:21:52
(MARIAN SUTTON 16:42, VIKKI MacPHERSON 33:42,
TANYA BLAKE 16:41, JO THOMPSON 34:43,
SONIA McGEORGE 15:50, LAURA ADAM 24:14)

TUR v WAL v SCO v ISR Istanbul, TUR 21-22 May 1994

MEN

100 Metres wind 0.4 (21 May)
1. COLIN JACKSON   Wal   10.36
2. ELLIOT BUNNEY   Sco   10.47
3. KEVIN WILLIAMS   Wal/gst 10.68
4. Afir Golan   ISR   10.79
5. Ahmet Pekel   TUR   11.08

200 Metres wind 2.3 (22 May)
1. DOUG WALKER   Sco   21.42w
2. KEVIN WILLIAMS   Wal   21.45w
3. Ahmet Pekel   TUR   22.00w
4. Adi Paz   ISR   22.48w

400 Metres (21 May)
1. IWAN THOMAS   Wal   47.35
2. GREGOR McMILLAN   Sco   48.68
3. Yasar Yilmaz   TUR   49.29
4. Nuri Yoldas   TUR/gst 49.30
5. Yaniv Vaknin   ISR   49.93

800 Metres (22 May)
1. DARRELL MAYNARD   Wal   1:53.09
2. GRANT GRAHAM   Sco   1:53.42
3. Cevat Kücük   TUR   1:53.59
4. Danny Malool   ISR   1:54.89

1500 Metres (21 May)
1. GLEN STEWART   Sco   3:51.89
2. NICK COMMERFORD   Wal   3:52.82
3. Muzaffer Contimar TUR   3:54.42
4. Oron Toochmai   ISR   3:55.28

5000 Metres (22 May)
1. Fatih Cintimar   TUR   14:08.23
2. JUSTIN HOBBS   Wal   14:10.25
3. Remzi Atli   TUR/gst 14:32.88
4. CHRIS ROBISON   Sco   14:50.37
5. Yahya Dogan   TUR/gst 14:50.54

10000 Metres (21 May)
1. Nihat Yaylali   TUR   30:30.29
2. SHAUN TOBIN   Wal   30:35.03
3. Remzi Atli   TUR   30:37.82

3000 Metres Steeplechase (22 May)
1. JUSTIN CHASTON   Wal   8:38.53
2. GRAEME CROLL   Sco   8:54.50
3. Nihat Bagci   TUR   8:57.50
4. Nurettin Özyürek   TUR/gst 9:10.51
5. Nizar Gawad   ISR   9:39.24

110 Metres Hurdles wind 0.6 (22 May)
1. COLIN JACKSON   Wal/gst 13.23
2. PAUL GRAY   Wal   13.86
3. KEN CAMPBELL   Sco   14.28
4. Ruhan Isim   TUR   14.51
5. Eliav Bar-David   ISR   17.56

400 Metres Hurdles (21 May)
1. Aleksey Bazarov   ISR   51.08
2. PHIL HARRIES   Wal   51.13
3. DEREK PAISLEY   Sco   52.93
4. Fethi Bildirici   TUR/gst 54.04
5. Gürsel Özyurt   TUR   54.58

High Jump (21 May)
1. GEOFF PARSONS   Sco   2.21
2. Isik Bayraktar   TUR   2.05
3. DAFYDD EDWARDS   Wal   2.00
4. Arif Zeybek   TUR/gst 2.00
5. Avi Thierry   ISR   1.95

Pole Vault (22 May)
1. NEIL WINTER   Wal   5.20
2. Yaacov Dinar   ISR   4.90
3. TIM THOMAS   Wal/gst 4.90
4. DES FITZGERALD   Sco   4.20
   Ruhan Isim   TUR   nh

Long Jump (21 May)
1. Mark Malisov   ISR   7.52
2. STEVE INGRAM   Wal   7.38
3. Erim May   TUR   7.19
4. DARREN RITCHIE   Sco   6.94

Triple Jump (22 May)
1. Avi Thierry   ISR   15.75
2. Gökhan Gülsoy   TUR   15.59
3. NEIL MCMENEMY   Sco   14.89
4. PAUL FARMER   Wal   14.51

Shot (21 May)
1. Igor Avrunin   ISR   17.89
2. Yavuz Erkmen   TUR   16.83
3. LEE WILTSHIRE   Wal   16.71
4. GORDON SMITH   Sco   15.58

Discus (22 May)
1. Sergey Lukashok   ISR   58.72
2. DARRIN MORRIS   Sco   56.38
3. Igor Avrunin   ISR/gst 55.20
4. Hüseyin Yilmaz   TUR   52.56
5. Hamza Alakustekin TUR/gst 45.24
6. GARETH GILBERT   Wal   41.24

Hammer (22 May)
1. Igor Giller   ISR   63.76
2. STEVE WHYTE   Sco   61.60
3. ADRIAN PALMER   Wal   58.76
4. Oguz Kalkan   TUR/gst 54.96
5. Ömer Özcicek   TUR   53.50

Javelin (21 May)
1. Aleksandr Fingert ISR   76.60
2. Fikrt Özsoy   TUR   71.98
3. NIGEL BEVAN   Wal   68.04
4. RICHARD ATKINSON   Sco   64.88
5. SHANE LEWIS   Wal/gst 63.54

4 x 100 Metres Relay (21 May)
1. SCOTLAND   40.03
2. Israel   41.65
3. Turkey   42.22
   WALES   dsq

4 x 400 Metres Relay (22 May)
1. WALES   3:11.43
2. SCOTLAND   3:15.88
3. Turkey   3:16.06
4. Israel   3:16.73

Match Result
1. WALES   65
2. SCOTLAND   58
3. Israel   52
4. Turkey   50

73

WOMEN

100 Metres wind -0.5 (21 May)
1. Aksel Gürcan — TUR — 11.85
2. SALLYANNE SHORT — Wal — 11.88
3. JOAN BOOTH — Sco — 12.03
4. HELEN MILES — Wal/gst — 12.05
5. JANE FLEMMING — Sco/gst — 12.33

200 Metres wind 0.5 (22 May)
1. Aksel Gürcan — TUR — 23.76
2. MELANIE NEEF — Sco — 23.81
3. SALLYANNE SHORT — Wal — 24.10
4. Öznur Dursun — TUR/gst — 24.33
5. NATASHA BARTLETT — Wal/gst — 24.40
6. JOAN BOOTH — Sco/gst — 24.68

400 Metres (21 May)
1. MELANIE NEEF — Sco — 54.02
2. Öznur Dursun — TUR — 54.28
3. GILLIAN CASHELL — Wal — 55.15
4. Orit Kolodni — ISR — 55.35
5. WENDY STEELE — Sco/gst — 55.55
6. RACHEL NEWCOMBE — Wal/gst — 56.68

800 Metres (21 May)
1. CATHY DAWSON — Wal — 2:05.08
2. MARY ANDERSON — Sco — 2:07.51
3. Edna Lankri — ISR — 2:08.36

1500 Metres (22 May)
1. Duha Suliman — ISR — 4:26.82
2. LISA CARTHEW — Wal — 4:29.08
3. Melahat Kokalp — TUR — 4:31.75
4. CAROL SHARP — Sco — 4:36.86

5000 Metres (21 May)
1. Serap Aktas — TUR — 16:22.26
2. HAYLEY NASH — Wal — 16:47.66
3. SUSAN RIDLEY — Sco — 16:51.80
4. Nili Avramski — ISR — 17:53.49

100 Metres Hurdles wind 3.3 (22 May)
1. Filiz Türker — TUR — 13.90w
2. JOCELYN KIRBY — Sco — 13.93w
3. LISA GIBBS — Wal — 14.00w
4. Olga Dogadetsko — ISR — 15.10w

400 Metres Hurdles (21 May)
1. JANE LOW — Sco — 59.14
2. Olga Dogadetsko — ISR — 62.29
3. Nazan Kuzlu — TUR — 63.04
4. MICHELLE COOKE — Wal — 63.75

High Jump (21 May)
1. HAZEL MELVIN — Sco — 1.81
2. Gülsün Durak — TUR — 1.81
3. Cigdem Arslan — TUR — 1.78
4. AILSA WALLACE — Wal — 1.70
5. Lyudmila Marmen — ISR — 1.70

Long Jump (22 May)
1. Fatma Yüksel — TUR — 6.11
2. KAREN SKEGGS — Sco — 5.91
3. LISA ARMSTRONG — Wal — 5.60
4. Figen Karadag — TUR/gst — 5.65
5. Rona Hertzano — ISR — 5.53
6. JAYNE LUDLOW — Wal/gst — 5.30

Triple Jump (21 May)
1. Figen Karadag — TUR — 12.23
2. JANE LUDLOW — Wal — 12.14
3. Rona Hertzano — ISR — 12.11
4. FIONA WATT — Sco — 11.25

Shot (22 May)
1. ALISON GREY — Sco — 15.44
2. Sevgi Sen — TUR — 14.83
3. Gülseren Tavan — TUR/gst — 14.55
4. Tzila Asher — ISR — 14.00
5. KAREN COSTELLO — Sco/gst — 12.64
6. LISA GIBBS — Wal — 11.53

Discus (21 May)
1. Hüsniye Keskin — TUR — 49.94
2. ALISON GREY — Sco — 46.26
3. JAYNE FISHER — Wal — 43.24
4. Yael Dror — ISR — 37.74

Hammer (21 May)
1. SARAH MOORE — Wal — 50.52
2. Birsen Elma — TUR — 47.02
3. JEAN CLARK — Sco — 45.42

Javelin (21 May)
1. Billur Dulkadir — TUR — 55.02
2. Sema Korkmaz — TUR/gst — 52.70
3. KAREN COSTELLO — Sco — 51.34
4. ONYEMA AMADI — Wal — 48.64
5. Dorit Ashkenazi — ISR — 41.90

4 x 100 Metres Relay (21 May)
1. SCOTLAND — 46.28
2. Turkey — 46.74
3. WALES — 54.33

4 x 400 Metres Relay (22 May)
1. WALES — 3:41.80
2. SCOTLAND — 3:44.57
3. Turkey — 3:48.56
4. Israel — 3:56.41

10000 Metres Walk (21 May)
1. VICKY LARBY-SNOOK — Sco — 51:14.52
2. Yulia Kotler — ISR — 58:14.52
3. Emine Sahbaz — TUR — 61:06.51

Match Result
1. Turkey — 66
2. SCOTLAND — 55
3. WALES — 46
4. Israel — 28

CS v GB & NI v ITA (Combined Events) Prague, CS 28-29 May 1994

MEN - Decathlon
1. Jan Podebradsky — CS — 7737
2. Kamil Damasek — CS — 7660
3. Roman Sebrle — CS — 7105
4. ROBERT LAING — 7048
5. Luca Bonanni — ITA — 7013
6. ANDREW LEWIS — 6916
7. Riccardo Calcini — ITA — 6873
8. STEVE GUTTERIDGE — 6865

1. Czech Republic — 15,397
2. GREAT BRITAIN & NI — 15,093
3. Italy — 13,886

Juniors
1. Jiri Ryba — CS — 6946
2. Ales Honcl — CS — 6749
3. Pavel Loucka — CS/gst — 6671
4. BRETT HEATH — 6449
5. ROGER HUNTER — 6432
6. Roberto Zola — ITA — 6395
7. Ales Pastrnak — CS — 6324
8. Petr Hingar — gst — 6261

9. Daniele Airoldi — ITA — 6114
10. Andrea Donati — ITA — 6012
dnf CHRIS HINDLEY — 1153

1. Czech Republic — 13,695
2. GREAT BRITAIN & NI — 12,881
3. Italy — 12,509

WOMEN - Heptathlon
1. Giuliana Spada — ITA — 5979
2. Karin Periginelli — ITA — 5927
3. JENNIFER KELLY — 5617
4. CHARMAINE JOHNSON — 5463
5. Francesca Delon — ITA — 5420
6. VIKKY SCHOFIELD — 5396
7. Dana Jandova — CS — 5079
8. Martina Blazkova — CS — 4987
9. Petra Sebelkova — CS — 4969

1. Italy — 11,906
2. GREAT BRITAIN & NI — 11.080
3. Czech Republic — 10,066

Juniors
1. Katerina Nekolna — CS — 5160
2. Dagmar Votockova — CS — 4983
3. Vlasta Gruberova — CS — 4968
4. JULIE HOLLMAN — 4753
5. DENISE BOLTON — 4715
6. Alessandr Melchionda — ITA — 4536
7. Annalisa Meacci — ITA — 4265
8. MICHAELA GEE — 4207
9. Francesca Sicari — ITA — 4172

1. Czech Republic — 10.143
2. GREAT BRITAIN & NI — 9,468
3. Italy — 8,801

Overall
1. Czech Republic — 49,301
2. GREAT BRITAIN & NI — 47,393
3. Italy — 47,102

AAA CHAMPIONSHIPS Sheffield 11-12 June 1994

MEN

100 Metres wind 3.7 (11 Jun)
1. LINFORD CHRISTIE — 9.91w
2. TOBY BOX — 10.07w
3. MICHAEL ROSSWESS — 10.07w
4. JASON JOHN — 10.08w
5. ELLIOT BUNNEY — 10.21w
6. TREVOR CAMERON — 10.29w
7. STEPHEN GOOKEY — 10.40w
8. SOLOMON WARISO — 11.99w

200 Metres wind 3.2 (12 Jun)
1. SOLOMON WARISO — 20.67w
2. PHILIP GOEDLUCK — 20.83w
3. DOUGLAS WALKER — 20.85w
4. TRAVOR CAMERON — 20.88w
5. STEVEN MCCOURT — 21.03w
6. MICHAEL AFILAKA — 21.22w
7. OWUSU DAKO — 21.23w
8. JOHN KENNY — 21.28w

400 Metres (12 Jun)
1. ROGER BLACK — 44.94
2. DU'AINE LADEJO — 45.36
3. BRIAN WHITTLE — 45.46
4. DAVID MCKENZIE — 45.47
5. ADRIAN PATRICK — 46.11
6. ALEX FUGALLO — 46.39
7. ADE MAFE — 46.39
8. MARK SMITH — 46.76

800 Metres (12 Jun)
1. CRAIG WINROW — 1:48.45
2. Vincent Malakwen — KEN — 1:48.65
3. MARTIN STEELE — 1:48.68
4. ANDREW LILL — 1:48.75
5. MICHAEL GUEGAN — 1:48.92
6. TERRY WEST — 1:49.13
7. David Kiptoo — KEN — 1:49.35
8. JUSTIN SWIFT-SMITH — 1:49.74

1500 Metres (12 Jun)
1. KEVIN MCKAY — 3:40.59
2. DAVID STRANG — 3:40.85
3. GARY LOUGH — 3:41.71
4. ANTHONY MORRELL — 3:42.59
5. ANTHONY WHITEMAN — 3:42.68
6. JOHN MAYOCK — 3:42.89
7. ANDREW KEITH — 3:42.93
8. MATTHEW BARNES — 3:43.89
9. IAN GRIME — 3:44.03
10. MATTHEW HIBBERD — 3:46.74

5000 Metres (12 Jun)
1. DERMOT DONNELLY — 13:52.63
2. DARREN MEAD — 13:54.08
3. RICHARD FINDLOW — 13:55.75
4. Frank Bjorkli — NOR — 13:57.72
5. IAN HAMER — 13:57.99
6. MARK MORGAN — 13:59.46
7. John Liseiwicz — AUS — 14:01.24
8. DAVID MILES — 14:02.54
9. STEVEN HOPE — 14:02.75
10. JONATHAN GASCOYNE — 14:03.61

10000 Metres (11 Jun)
1. ROBERT DENMARK — 28:03.34
2. MARTIN JONES — 28:33.18
3. JUSTIN HOBBS — 28:45.86
4. BARRY ROYDEN — 28:47.17
5. CARL UDALL — 28:49.96
6. CHRIS ROBISON — 28:51.12
7. MARTIN McLOUGHLIN — 28:55.57
8. BASHIR HUSSAIN — 29:16.29
9. COLIN MOORE — 29:17.32
10. DOMINIC BANNISTER — 29:34.50

3000 Metres Steeplechase (12 Jun)
1. SPENCER DUVAL — 8:32.77
2. JUSTIN CHASTON — 8:32.79
3. DARREN MEAD — 8:39.79
4. GRAEME CROLL — 8:43.33
5. KEITH CULLEN — 8:43.72
6. DAVE LEE — 8:45.33
7. KEVIN HOWARD — 8:46.46
8. MIKE HAWKINS — 8:46.95

110 Metres Hurdles 0.8 (12 Jun)
1. ANDY TULLOCH — 13.70
2. PAUL GRAY — 13.76
3. LLOYD COWAN — 14.09
4. NEIL OWEN — 14.11
5. KEN CAMPBELL — 14.24
6. KEVIN LUMSDON — 14.52
dnf HUGH TEAPE
dnf MARTIN NICHOLSON

400 Metres Hurdles (12 Jun)
1. PETER CRAMPTON — 49.82
2. STEPHEN COUPLAND — 50.19
3. NOEL LEVY — 50.89
4. TONY WILLIAMS — 50.98
5. LAURENCE LYNCH — 51.01
6. GARY JENNINGS — 51.66
7. EDDIE BETTS — 52.27
dns PHIL HARRIES

High Jump (12 Jun)
1. BRENDAN REILLY — 2.24
2. GEOFF PARSONS — 2.20
3. Antoine Burke — IRE — 2.15
4. Mark Mandy — IRE — 2.15
5. FAYYAZ AHMED — 2.15
6. DAVID BARNETSON — 2.10
7. JAMES BRIERLEY — 2.10
8. ANDREW LYNCH — 2.05
9. DAFYDD EDWARDS — 2.05

Pole Vault (12 Jun)
1. ANDY ASHURST — 5.30
2= KEVIN HUGHES — 5.20
2= MIKE EDWARDS — 5.20
4= IAN TULLETT — 5.10
4= DEAN MELLOR — 5.10
6. MICHAEL BARBER — 5.00
7. MATT BELSHAM — 5.00
8. MARK JOHNSON — 4.90

Long Jump (11 Jun)
1. BARRINGTON WILLIAMS — 7.77
2. FRED SALLE — 7.60
3. MICHAEL MORGAN — 7.59
4. ONOCHIE ONUORAH — 7.39
5. STEVE SMITH — 7.36
6. CARL HOWARD — 7.35
7. SIMON SHIRLEY — 7.29
8. CHRIS COTTER — 7.20

Triple Jump (12 Jun)
1. JONATHAN EDWARDS — 17.39
2. JULIAN GOLLEY — 16.98
3. FRANCIS AGYEPONG — 16.95
4. TOSI FASINRO — 16.62
5. ONOCHIE ACHIKE — 16.29
6. JOHN MACKENZIE — 15.99
7. DEREK BROWNE — 15.64
8. FEMI AKINSANYA — 15.53

Shot (12 Jun)
1. PAUL EDWARDS — 18.32
2. John McNamara — AUS — 17.16
3. LEE NEWMAN — 17.02
4. NIGEL SPRATLEY — 16.98
5. DAVID CALLAWAY — 16.93
6. John Goddard — AUS — 16.82
7. LEE WILTSHIRE — 16.69
8. STEVE WHYTE — 16.48
9. MARK PROCTOR — 16.46

Discus (11 Jun)
1. KEVIN BROWN — 58.60
2. ROBERT WEIR — 57.94
3. GLEN SMITH — 56.22
4. LEE NEWMAN — 54.14
5. NEVILLE THOMPSON — 53.38
6. DARRIN MORRIS — 53.14
7. JAMIE MURPHY — 52.72
8. LEITH MARAR — 51.82
9. PAUL REED — 50.62

Hammer (12 Jun)
1. PETER VIVIAN — 70.80
2. PAUL HEAD — 69.08
3. MICHAEL JONES — 67.42
4. SHANE PEACOCK — 66.68
5. STEPHEN PEARSON — 64.76
6. KARL ANDREWS — 63.54
7. JOHN PEARSON — 62.78
8. STEVE WHYTE — 61.84
9. ROBERT EARLE — 58.10

Javelin (12 Jun)
1. MICK HILL — 84.60
2. STEVE BACKLEY — 84.24
3. COLIN MACKENZIE — 79.16
4. MYLES COTTRELL — 74.30
5. ROALD BRADSTOCK — 72.84
6. MARK ROBERSON — 72.62
7. Philip Spies — RSA — 70.74
8. NIGEL BEVAN — 70.10

WOMEN

100 Metres wind 2.9 (11 Jun)
1. KATHARINE MERRY   11.27w
2. STEPHANIE DOUGLAS   11.35w
3. SIMMONE JACOBS   11.37w
4. MARCIA RICHARDSON   11.39w
5. PAULA THOMAS   11.40w
6. GERALDINE McLEOD   11.51w
7. DANAA MYHILL   11.58w
8. DONNA HOGGARTH   11.78w

200 Metres wind 0.6 (12 Jun)
1. KATHARINE MERRY   22.85
2. STEPHANIE DOUGLAS   23.17
3. PAULA THOMAS   23.33
4. SIMMONE JACOBS   23.52
5. GERALDINE McLEOD   23.52
6. MARCIA RICHARDSON   23.55
7. PAULA COHEN   23.78
8. CATHERINE MURPHY   23.85

400 Metres (12 Jun)
1. MELANIE NEEF   52.56
2. TRACEY GODDARD   53.59
3. SANDRA DOUGLAS   53.78
4. JANET LEVERMORE   53.92
5. NICOLA CROWTHER   54.01
6. CLAIRE RAVEN   54.23
7. DONNA FRASER   54.90
8. GILLIAN CASHELL   55.23

800 Metres (12 Jun)
1. DIANE MODAHL   2:01.35
2. DAWN GANDY   2:03.75
3. SONYA BOWYER   2:03.79
4. HELEN DANIEL   2:04.32
5. MICHELLE FAHERTY   2:05.38
6. LINDA KEOUGH   2:05.44
7. LYNNE ROBINSON   2:06.57
8. JEINA MITCHELL   2:08.34

1500 Metres (12 Jun)
1. KELLY HOLMES   4:01.41
2. YVONNE MURRAY   4:01.44
3. ANN GRIFFITHS   4:08.71
4. BEV HARTIGAN   4:11.04
5. ANGELA DAVIES   4:11.27
6. Geraldine Nolan IRE 4:13.10
7. DEBBIE GUNNING   4:13.50
8. LYNN GIBSON   4:14.08

Horsham 18-19 June
MEN

10000 Metres Walk (19 Jun)
1. DARRELL STONE   43:09.28
2. MARK EASTON   44:06.93
3. Michael Casey AUS   45:24.83
4. ANDY O'RAWE   46:29.31
5. TIM WATT   47:51.21
6. DAVID TURNER   48:52.89
7. GARY WITTON   49:30.50
8. CHRIS SMITH   50:21.57

Decathlon (18-19 Jun)
1. BARRY THOMAS   7458
2. DAVID BIGHAM   7434
3. ANDREW LEWIS   7221

3000 Metres (11 Jun)
1. SONIA MCGEORGE   9:03.80
2. LAURA ADAM   9:12.16
3. WENDY ORE   9:14.72
4. ALISON WYETH   9:17.73
5. TANYA BLAKE   9:21.07
6. JOANNE SYMONDS   9:24.21
7. VIKKI MCPHERSON   9:26.05
8. ALISON BARNES   9:26.47

100 Metres Hurdles 0.5 (11 Jun)
1. CLOVA COURT   13.06
2. SALLY GUNNELL   13.09
3. LESLEY ANN SKEETE   13.43
4. KERI MADDOX   13.49
5. DENISE LEWIS   13.55
6. SAM FARQUHARSON   13.55
7. MELANIE WILKINS   13.72
8. JACQUIE AGYEPONG   14.13

400 Metres Hurdles (12 Jun)
1. GOWRY RETCHAKAN   57.08
2. JACQUI PARKER   57.31
3. STEPHANIE McCANN   58.09
4. CLARE BLEASDALE   58.62
5. JANE LOW   59.01
6. VYVYAN RHODES   59.36
7. STEPHANIE LLEWELLYN 59.39
8. HEATHER MYERS   1:02.11

High Jump (11 Jun)
1. JULIA BENNETT   1.89
2. DEBBI MARTI   1.86
3. JULIE MAJOR   1.83
4. LEA HAGGETT   1.80
5. DIANA DAVIES   1.75
6. TERESA ANDREWS   1.70
7. DIANA BENNETT   1.70
8. KELLY THIRKLE   1.70

PoleVault (11 Jun)
1. KATE STAPLES   3.65
2. PAULA WILSON   3.40
3. LINDA STANTON   3.30
4. CLARE RIDGLEY   3.30
5. RHIAN CLARKE   3.00
6. DAWN ALICE WRIGHT   2.80

Long Jump (12 Jun)
1. YINKA IDOWU   6.58
2. DENISE LEWIS   6.56

4. PAUL FIELD   7157
5. STEVE LEADER   7078
6. LIVIO SALVADOR-AYLOTT 7024
7. ROBERT LAING   6990
8. STEVE GUTTERIDGE   6972

WOMEN

5000 Metres Walk (19 Jun)
1. VERITY LARBY-SNOOK   23:22.52
2. VICTORIA LUPTON   23:34.50
3. Jane Barbour   AUS   23:43.23
4. MELANIE WRIGHT   24:06.27

3. ANN BROOKS   6.10
4. RUTH IRVING   6.07
5. ASHIA HANSEN   6.07
6. JENNIFER KELLY   6.01
7. VIKKI SCHOFIELD   6.01
8. LIZ GHOJEFA   5.84

Triple Jump (11 Jun)
1. MICHELLE GRIFFITH   14.08
2. ASHIA HANSEN   13.79
3. RACHEL KIRBY   13.29
4. EVETTE FINIKIN   12.85
5. CAROLINE STEAD   12.17
6. SHANI ANDERSON   12.10
7. DEBORAH ROWE   12.00

Shot (11 Jun)
1. JUDITH OAKES   18.38
2. MYRTLE AUGEE   17.37
3. MAGGIE LYNES   16.53
4. YVONNE HANSON-NORTEY 16.11
5. ALISON GREY   15.69
6. CAROL COOKSLEY   13.17
7. DAWN GRAZETTE   12.92

Discus (12 Jun)
1. JACQUI McKERNAN   56.94
2. SHARON ANDREWS   56.24
3. DEBBIE CALLAWAY   54.94
4. EMMA BEALES   52.94
5. LORRAINE SHAW   51.06
6. SARAH WINKLESS   50.90
7. TRACY AXTEN   49.32

Hammer (11 Jun)
1. LORRAINE SHAW   59.58
2. DIANA HOLDEN   49.12
3. SARAH MOORE   48.46
4. LYN SPRULES   47.84
5. ANN GARDNER   47.00
6. JULIE LAVENDER   46.96
7. JEAN CLARK   46.08

Javelin (11 Jun)
1. SHELLEY HOLROYD   57.08
2. SHARON GIBSON   56.90
3. KAREN COSTELLO   54.50
4. LUCY BURRELL   51.76
5. KIRSTY MORRISON   50.30
6. CAROLINE WHITE   50.20
7. KAREN MARTIN   49.96
8. NOELLE BRADSHAW   49.22

5. KAREN SMITH   24:18.79
6. Sian Spacey   AUS   24:50.09
7. SHARON TONKS   25:47.26
8. GILLIAN WATSON   26:40.25

Heptathlon (18-19 Jun)
1. VICKI SCHOFIELD   5587
2. PAULINE RICHARDS   5420
3. UJU EFOBI   5409
4. KERRY JURY   5334
5. EMMA LINDSEY   5321
6. KIM CROWTHER   5125
7. NATASHA MIGHTY   4912
8. JULIE HOLLMAN   4878

WALKS INTERNATIONAL Livorno, ITA 12 June 1994

MEN
20 Kilometres Walk
1.	Valentin Massana	SPA	1:20:54
2.	Thierry Toutain	FRA	1:21:20
3.	Giovanni Perricelli	ITA	1:21:42
4.	Michele Didoni	ITA	1:21:44
5.	Sándor Urbanik	HUN	1:21:55
6.	Daniel Plaza	SPA	1:22:00
7.	Robert Ihly	GER	1:22:18
8.	Jean-Claude Corre	FRA	1:22:24
9.	Fernando Vázquez	SPA	1:22:33
10.	Stefan Johansson	SWE	1:22:37
11.	Ronald Weigel	GER	1:23:11
12.	Nick A'Hern	AUS	1:23:18

20.	DARRELL STONE	1:26:53
22.	MARTIN BELL	1:27:18
31.	STEVE PARTINGTON	1:29:48
34.	CHRIS CHEESEMAN	1:30:37

35 Kilometres Walk
1.	Angel Garcia	SPA	2:31:06
2.	Valeriy Spitsin	RUS	2:32:01
3.	René Piller	FRA	2:32:04
4.	Arturo Di Mezza	ITA	2:33:03
5.	Stefan Malik	SVK	2:33:04
6.	Giuseppe De Gaetano	ITA	2:33:28
7.	Alain Lemercier	FRA	2:34:44
8.	Peter Tichy	SVK	2:35:37
9.	Basilio Laerador	SPA	2:35:50
10.	Miguel Rodriguez	MEX	2:36:24
11.	Gyula Dudás	HUN	2:36:33
12.	Paolo Bianchi	ITA	2:36:36

30.	GRAHAM WHITE	2:48:50
32.	LES MORTON	2:50:01
39.	KARL RITCH	2:55:38

JUNIOR MEN
10 Kilometres Walk
1.	Yevgeniy Shmalyuk	RUS	41:43
2.	Oleg Ishutkin	RUS	41:52
3.	Andreas Erm	GER	42:05
4.	Erik Kalina	SVK	42:33
5.	Peter Barto	SVK	42:33
6.	Sebastiano Catania	ITA	42:52
7.	Nikolay Ivanov	RUS	42:59
8.	Marcos Carracedo	SPA	43:03
9.	Alesandro Cambil	SPA	43:05
10.	Lorenzo Civallero	ITA	43:12
11.	Giovanni Sangiorgi	ITA	43:16
12.	Anthony Gillet	FRA	43:17

22.	SCOTT DAVIS	44:50
27.	JAMES CHAMBERLAIN	46:17

WOMEN
10 Kilometres Walk
1.	Anna Rita Sidoti	ITA	41:46
2.	Elisabetta Perrone	ITA	42:15
3.	Larissa Rohazova	RUS	42:31
4.	Berte Gummelt	GER	42:36
5.	Yulija Odzilyayeva	RUS	42:40
6.	Tamara Kovalenko	RUS	42:50
7.	Mária Rosza	HUN	42:53
8.	Cristiana Pellino	ITA	42:55
9.	Elena Arshintseva	RUS	43:07
10.	Kerry Junna-Saxby	AUS	43:09
11.	Kathrin Boyde	GER	43:41
12.	Rossella Giordano	ITA	44:20

25.	VERITY SNOOK	47:24
26.	LISA LANGFORD	47:34
28	CAROL PARTINGTON	47:46
31.	VICTORIA LUPTON	48:07
34.	MELANIE WRIGHT	49:04

JUNIOR WOMEN
5 Kilometres Walk
1.	Irina Stankina	RUS	21:30
2.	Nataliya Trofinova	RUS	21:33
3.	Tanyana Gudkova	RUS	21:53
4.	Maria Vasco	SPA	22:00
5.	Monika Pesti	HUN	22:05
6.	Olga Panferowa	RUS	22:09
7.	Jana Weidemann	GER	22:24
8.	Dana Pinkert	GER	22:29
9.	Anders Vounne	GER	22:43
10.	Eva Perez	SPA	22:48
11.	Melanie Seeber	GER	23:28
12.	Jessica Franzen	SWE	23:35

31.	LYNSEY TOZER	26:58

Combined Match Result
1.	Russia	445
2.	Spain	405
3.	Italy A	404
4.	Germany	364
5.	Slovakia	316
6.	Hungary	313
7.	France	306
8.	Italy B	192
9.	Australia	168
10	GREAT BRITAIN & NI	153

POL v GB & NI v GER v RUS (U20) Warsaw, POL 18 June 1994

MEN
100 Metres wind 1.6
1.	JASON GARDENER		10.42
2.	Marcin Krzywanski	POL	10.64
3.	Thomas Mittendrein	GER	10.71
4.	TREVOR CAMERON		10.72

200 Metres wind -0.8
1.	IAN MACKIE		21.30
2.	Marcin Krzywanski	POL	21.49
3.	Ulysses Hammelstein	GER	21.56
4.	MARLON DEVONISH		21.57

400 Metres
1.	GUY BULLOCK		47.40
2.	MARK HYLTON		47.54
3.	Ulrich Schnorrenberger	GER	47.83
4.	Jacek Bocian	POL	48.89

800 Metres
1.	EDDDIE KING		1:50.15
2.	Felix Leiter	GER	1:50.83
3.	Wojciech Kaldowski	POL	1:51.09
4.	Artriom Mastrow	RUS	1:51.83
8.	DES ROACHE		1:53.26

1500 Metres
1.	BRUNO WITCHALLS		3:49.57
2.	Grigorij Gienieralow	RUS	3:50.40
3.	Adam Zukowski	POL	3:50.70
8.	ALAN TATHAM		4:01.52

5000 Metres
1.	Walerij Kuzmin	RUS	14:16.03
2.	Dariusz Kruczkowski	POL	14:29.81
3.	Aleks. Mukasiejew	RUS	14:50.32
5.	KRISTEN BOWDITCH		15:00.54
6.	DAVID CONNELLY		15:08.29

3000 Metres Steeplechase
1.	Aleksiej Potapow	RUS	8:56.41
2.	CHRIS ELLIOTT		9:00.15
3.	Christian Knoblich	GER	9:00.33
7.	BEN REESE		9:09.24

110 Metres Hurdles wind 1.3
1.	Frank Busemann	GER	13.71
2.	Andriej Kislych	RUS	14.19
3.	Filip Bickel	GER	14.39
5.	JAMES ARCHAMPONG		14.62
6.	SIMON McAREE		14.94

400 Metres Hurdles
1.	NOEL LEVY		51.70
2.	Bartosz Gruman	POL	52.19
3.	Andriej Szczieglow	RUS	52.20
7.	ALEX HUNTE		54.48

High Jump
1.	Michal Majchrowicz	POL	2.20
2.	Roland Stark	GER/gst	2.20
3.	MICHAEL ROBBINS		2.14
5.	JAMES BRIERLEY		2.11

Pole Vault
1.	Jewgienij Smirjagin	RUS	5.40
2.	Przemyslaw Gurin	POL	5.20
3.	Adam Kolasa	POL	5.10
7.	NEIL YOUNG		4.80
8.	IAN WILDING		4.60

Long Jump
1.	Andriej Sazykin	RUS	7.85
2.	Kiril Sosunow	RUS	7.43
3.	Alexsander Kosenkow	GER	7.31
7.	LARRY ACHIKE		7.13
8.	ANTHONY MASON		7.05

Triple Jump
1. Wieczislaw Taranow RUS 16.15
2. LARRY ACHIKE 16.11
3. Pawel Zdrajkowski POL 15.93
4. TAYO EROGBOGBO 15.84

Shot
1. Christian Nehme GER 16.48
2. Gunnar Pfingsten GER 16.39
3. Dmitrij Wojkin RUS 15.79
8. SIMON FRICKER 14.25
9. WILLIAM FULLER 14.14

Discus
1. Andrzej Krawczyk POL 53.50
2. Alexander Forst GER 51.84
3. Michail Korowin RUS 50.18
7. JAMES SOUTH 45.88
8. BRUCE ROBB 42.88

Hammer
1. Szymon Ziolkowski POL 69.66
2. Dmitrii Churijew RUS 65.16
3. Konstantin Balandin RUS 63.48
5. KARL ANDREWS 62.10
7. WAYNE CLARKE 56.84

Javelin
1. Christian Nicolay GER 68.84
2. Aleksandr Kuzniecow RUS 68.76
3. Kai Kaufmann GER 65.16
6. STUART FABEN 61.78
7. SIMON CARTER 58.30

10000 Metres Walk
1. Andreas Erm GER 41:23.35
2. Lukasz Szela POL 43:23.16
3. Nikolaj Iwanow RUS 43:36.02
7. JAMES CHAMBERLAIN 47:42.90

4 x 100 Metres Relay
1. Germany 40.25
2. GREAT BRITAIN 40.38
(GARDNER, CAMERON, DEVONISH, MACKIE)
3. Poland 41.07
4. Russia 41.91

4 x 400 Metres Relay
1. GREAT BRITAIN 3:10.76
(HYLTON, LEVY, HEGGIE, DEACON)
2. Russia 3:11.98
3. Germany 3:12.13
4. Poland 3:12.70

WOMEN
100 Metres wind 1.9
1. Gabi Becker GER 11.85
2. Esther Moller GER 11.99
3. Jekatierina Struzkina RUS 12.04
4. Anna Glowacka POL 12.13
5. ELLANA RUDDOCK 12.16

200 Metres
1. SUSAN WILLIAMS 24.65
2. Marion Wagner GER 24.86
3. Shanta Gosh GER 24.87
4. Iwona Ciesla POL 24.96
8. ELLANA RUDDOCK 25.44

400 Metres
1. Larlsa Bolienok RUS 54.24
2. LOURETTA THORNE 54.37
3. Claudia Angerhausen GER 54.44
4. Susanne Merkel GER 55.37
5. JOANNE SLOANE 55.83

800 Metres
1. Jekatierina Fiedotowa RUS 2:04.42
2. Ludmila Woroniczewa RUS 2:05.44
3. Grazyna Penc POL 2:05.65
4. Yvonne Teichmann GER 2:06.24
5. JEINA MITCHELL 2:06.57
6. DOROTHEA LEE 2:06.92

1500 Metres
1. Lidia Chojecka POL 4:24.28
2. Christiane Soeder GER 4:25.19
3. Marzena Michalska POL 4:27.65
4. AMANDA TREMBLE 4:29.08
8. SARAH SIMMONS 4:47.15

3000 Metres
1. Natalia Polikarpowa RUS 9:31.40
2. ALICE BRAHAM 9:31.64
3. Katarzyna Somkowska POL 9:35.39
4. Tatiana Tomaszowa RUS 9:37.08
7. CLAIRE O'CONNOR 9:46.44

100 Metres Hurdles wind -0.8
1. Kirsten Bolm GER 13.58
2. DIANE ALLAHGREEN 13.85
3. Aurelia Trywianska POL 13.92
4. Claudia Ruge GER 14.13
5. ORLA BERMINGHAM 14.42

400 Metres Hurdles
1. ALLISON CURBISHLEY 59.59
2. VICKI JAMISON 60.07
3. Polina Starowierowa RUS 60.54

High Jump
1. Julia Liachowa RUS 1.84
2. Katarzyna Majchrzak POL/gst 1.84
3. JULIE CRANE 1.80
11. SUSAN JONES 1.60

Pole Vault (non scoring)
1. Janet Zach GER 3.70
2. Julia Cygankowa RUS 3.30
3. Karin Hecht GER 3.30
4. RHIAN CLARKE 3.20
5. DAWN ALICE WRIGHT 3.00

Long Jump
1. Kirsten Bolm GER 6.38
2. Anna Mironowa RUS 6.36
3. Oksana Kosiaczenko RUS 6.21
6. JOANNE DEAR 6.06
9. ADELE FORESTER 5.67

Triple Jump
1. Irina Mielnikowa RUS 12.99
2. Cornelia Eigenherr GER 12.98
3. Julia Lomakina RUS 12.56
4. SHANI ANDERSON 12.39
8. JAYNE LUDLOW 11.54

Shot
1. Nadine Kleinert GER 16.90
2. Claudia Mues GER 16.34
3. Krystyna Zakowicz POL 15.31
7. PHILLIPA ROLES 12.94
8. CHRISTINA BENNETT 12.59

Discus
1. Sabine Sievers GER 53.86
2. Claudia Mues GER 53.80
3. Oksana Jesiepczuk RUS 50.00
7. PHILIPPA ROLES 45.66
9. JULIE ROBIN 41.90

Hammer (non scoring)
1. Weronika Uszakowa RUS 56.78
2. Kirsten Münchow GER 55.78
3. Tina Schäfer GER 53.72
5. LYN SPRULES 49.00
6. JULIE LAVENDER 42.30

Javelin
1. Dorthe Patzschke GER 52.46
2. Nancy Rahmsdorf GER 50.02
3. Jelena Sawostianowa RUS 49.30
4. JOANNE BURTON 48.40
6. LUCY BURRELL 46.06

5000 Metres Walk
1. Tatiana Gudkowa RUS 22:05.76
2. Jelena Aleksiejewa RUS 22:48.50
3. Jana Weidemann GER 22:50.81
7. KATHERINE HORWILL 25:25.96
8. NIKKI HUCKERBY 27:25.38

4 x 100 Metres Relay
1. Germany 45.26
2. Poland 45.96
3. GREAT BRITAIN 46.49
(ALLAHGREEN, RUDDOCK,
BERMINGHAM, WILLIAMS)
4. Russia 46.54

4 x 400 Metres Relay
1. GREAT BRITAIN 3:40.12
(THORNE, SLOANE,
CURBISHLEY, EUSTACE)
2. Germany 3:40.51
3. Poland 3:41.71
4. Russia 3:43.08

EUROPEAN CUP Birmingham 25-26 June 1994

MEN

100 Metres wind 0.9 (25 Jun)
1.	LINFORD CHRISTIE		10.21
2.	Marc Blume	GER	10.37
3.	Pavel Galkin	RUS	10.42
4.	Sandro Floris	ITA	10.45
5.	Vladislav Dologodin	UKR	10.46
6.	Daniel Cojocaro	ROM	10.50
7.	Eric Perrot	FRA	10.56
8.	Mikael Wenholf	SWE	10.62

200 Metres wind -0.1 (26 Jun)
1.	LINFORD CHRISTIE		20.67
2.	Sergei Osovitch	UKR	20.70
3.	Daniel Sangouma	FRA	21.04
4.	Michael Huke	GER	21.11
5.	Daniel Cojocaro	ROM	21.17
6.	Andrey Fedoriv	RUS	21.18
7.	Lars Hedner	SWE	21.23
8.	Sandro Floris	ITA	21.28

400 Metres (25 Jun)
1.	ROGER BLACK		45.08
2.	Jean-Louis Rapnouil	FRA	46.43
3.	Dmitry Golovastov	RUS	46.58
4.	Rikard Rasmusson	SWE	46.93
5.	Thomas Schoenlebe	GER	46.96
6.	Andrea Nuti	ITA	47.27
7.	Vadim Ogiy	UKR	47.59
8.	Ionica Carabas	ROM	48.46

800 Metres (26 Jun)
1.	Nico Motchebon	GER	1:48.10
2.	Davide Cadoni	ITA	1:48.42
3.	CRAIG WINROW		1:48.76
4.	Andrey Loginov	RUS	1:49.91
5.	Torbjorn Johansson	SWE	1:50.26
6.	Andrey Buzhenko	UKR	1:50.64
7.	Ian Bogde	ROM	2:05.22

1500 Metres (25 Jun)
1.	Andrey Bulkovsky	UKR	3:49.33
2.	Ruediger Stenzel	GER	3:49.38
3.	GARY LOUGH		3:49.57
4.	Samir Benfares	FRA	3:49.61
5.	Guiseppe D'Urso	ITA	3:49.98
6.	Viacheslav Shabunin	RUS	3:50.44
7.	Olteanu Ovidiu	ROM	3:50.95
8.	Peter Koskenkorva	SWE	3:52.38

5000 Metres (26 Jun)
1.	Dieter Baumann	GER	13:48.95
2.	Abdelah Behar	FRA	13:49.12
3.	Olteanu Ovidiu	ROM	13:49.43
4.	JOHN MAYOCK		13:50.58
5.	Umberto Pusteria	ITA	13:51.80
6.	Vener Kashaev	RUS	13:53.48
7.	Claes Nyberg	SWE	14:13.81
8.	Valerie Chesak	UKR	14:24.49

10000 Metres (25 Jun)
1.	Francesco Panetta	ITA	28:38.45
2.	Stephane Franke	GER	28:38.99
3.	Oleg Strizhakov	RUS	29:03.55
4.	Jonny Danielson	SWE	29:10.85
5.	GARY STAINES		29:57.27
6.	Francois Barreau	FRA	30:02.33
7.	Ion Avramescu	ROM	30:04.50
8.	Igor Sorla	UKR	31:02.87

3000 Metres Steeplechase (26 Jun)
1.	Alles. Lambruschini	ITA	8:24.98
2.	Steffan Brand	GER	8:27.83
3.	JUSTIN CHASTON		8:29.99
4.	Vladimir Golyas	RUS	8:32.97
5.	Alexi Patserin	UKR	8:33.78
6.	Florin Ionescu	ROM	8:38.94
7.	Thiery Brusseau	FRA	8:40.99
8.	Magnus Bengtsson	SWE	8:58.54

110 Metres Hurdles 1.9 (26 Jun)
1.	Florian Schwarthoff	GER	13.35
2.	Vladimir Belokon	UKR	13.62
3.	ANDREW TULLOCH		13.65
4.	Laurent Ottoz	ITA	13.67
5=	George Boroi	ROM	13.68
5=	Claes Albihn	SWE	13.68
7.	Dan Philibert	FRA	13.70
8.	Vladimir Shishkin	RUS	14.04

400 Metres Hurdles (25 Jun)
1.	Sven Nylander	SWE	49.36
2.	Oleg Tverdokhleb	UKR	49.37
3.	Stephane Diagana	FRA	49.47
4.	Fabrizio Mori	ITA	49.96
5.	Edgar Itt	GER	50.08
6.	PETER CRAMPTON		50.09
7.	Ruslan Mashenko	RUS	51.23
8.	Mugur Mateescu	ROM	51.81

High Jump (25 Jun)
1.	Hendryk Beyer	GER	2.25
2.	Patrick Thavelin	SWE	2.20
3.	DALTON GRANT		2.20
4.	Leonid Pumalaynen	RUS	2.20
5.	Eugen Popescu	ROM	2.15
6.	Roberto Ferrari	ITA	2.15
7.	Joel Vincent	FRA	2.15
8.	Sergey Kolesnik	UKR	2.10

Pole Vault (26 Jun)
1.	Jean Galfione	FRA	5.70
2.	Patrik Stenlund	SWE	5.60
3.	Tim Lobinger	GER	5.60
4.	Sergei Yesipchuk	UKR	5.40
5=	MICHAEL EDWARDS		5.20
5=	Gianni Iapichino	ITA	5.20
7.	Razvan Enescu	ROM	4.40

Long Jump (25 Jun)
1.	Stanislav Tarasenko	RUS	8.02
2.	Dietmar Haaf	GER	7.84
3.	Bogdan Tudor	ROM	7.78
4.	Mattias Sunneborn	SWE	7.75
5.	Yevengeni Semenyuk	UKR	7.70
6.	BARRINGTON WILLIAMS		7.66
7.	Oliver Borderan	FRA	7.62
8.	Milko Campus	ITA	7.60

Triple Jump (26 Jun)
1.	Denis Kaspustin	RUS	17.30
2.	Tord Henriksson	SWE	16.99
3.	Serge Helan	FRA	16.92
4.	JONATHAN EDWARDS		16.88
5.	Vladimir Kravatchenko	UKR	16.16
6.	Daniele Buttiglione	ITA	16.15
7.	Karsten Richter	GER	16.12
8.	Lucien Spiea	ROM	15.91

Shot (25 Jun)
1.	Paolo Dal Soglio	ITA	19.69
2.	Roman Virastyuk	UKR	19.40
3.	Sven-Oliver Buder	GER	19.02
4.	Sergey Nicolaev	RUS	18.98
5.	Kent Larsson	SWE	18.89
6.	PAUL EDWARDS		18.10
7.	Jean-Louis Lebon	FRA	17.13
dq	Gheorghe Guset	ROM	(19.23)

Discus (26 Jun)
1.	Dimitry Shevchenko	RUS	64.74
2.	Juergen Schult	GER	64.42
3.	Vladimir Zinchenko	UKR	62.80
4.	Costel Grasu	ROM	60.62
5.	Dag Solhaug	SWE	59.72
6.	BOB WEIR		58.92
7.	Diego Fortuna	ITA	57.16
8.	Jean-Claude Retel	FRA	57.14

Hammer (26 Jun)
1.	Vasily Sidorenko	RUS	78.76
2.	Andrei Skvaryuk	UKR	78.20
3.	Christophe Epalle	FRA	78.16
4.	Heinz Weis	GER	75.02
5.	Tore Gustafsson	SWE	71.16
6.	Enrico Sgrulletti	ITA	70.72
7.	PETER VIVIAN		68.44
8.	Cosmin Sorescu	ROM	59.72

Javelin (25 Jun)
1.	Andrey Moruev	RUS	87.34
2.	Raymond Hecht	GER	85.40
3.	MIKE HILL		85.28
4.	Patrick Boden	SWE	83.82
5.	Alain Storaci	FRA	73.44
6.	Moreno Belletti	ITA	73.28
7.	Andrei Maznitchenko	UKR	70.32
8.	Dorel Greta	ROM	66.52

4 x 100 Metres Relay (25 Jun)
1.	GREAT BRITAIN & NI	38.72
	(JOHN, WARISO, REGIS, CHRISTIE)	
2.	Ukraine	38.79
	(Vaniaikine, Dologodin, Kramarenko, Osovitch)	
3.	Germany	38.81
	(Goermer, M Blume, Huke, H Blume)	
4.	Russia	39.12
	(Galkin, Fatun, Mikhailovich, Mizera)	
5.	France	39.27
	(Lomba, Perrot, Sangouma, Leconte)	
6.	Italy	39.33
7.	Sweden	39.39
8.	Romania	40.56

4 x 400 Metres Relay (26 Jun)
1.	GREAT BRITAIN	3:02.50
	(WHITTLE, PATRICK, BLACK, LADEJO)	
2.	Russia	3:03.57
	(Golovastov, Vdovin, Maschenko, Maschenko)	
3.	France	3:03.74
	(Rapnouil, Konzylo, Hilaire, Diagana)	
4.	Sweden	3:05.34
	(Rasmusson, Wallenling, Nylander, Ekman)	
5.	Italy	3:06.04
	(Vaccari, Frinolli, Aimar, Nuti)	
6.	Germany	3:06.16
7.	Romania	3:12.05

WOMEN

100 Metres wind 0.8 (25 Jun)

1.	Zhanna Tarnopolskaya	UKR	11.26
2.	KATHARINE MERRY		11.34
3.	Melanie Paschke	GER	11.37
4.	Oksana Dyachenko	RUS	11.50
5.	Sandra Myers	SPA	11.54
6.	Friederique Bangue	FRA	11.64
7.	Margarita Molchan	BLS	11.78
8.	Erica Niculae	ROM	11.89

200 Metres wind 2.9 (26 Jun)

1.	Silke Knoll	GER	23.04 w
2.	KATHARINE MERRY		23.38 w
3.	Oksana Dyachenko	RUS	23.65 w
4.	Viktoriya Formenko	UKR	23.87 w
5.	Sandra Myers	SPA	23.98 w
6.	Fabienne Ficher	FRA	24.10 w
7.	Natalyn Vinogradova	BLS	24.25 w
8.	Ionela Tirlea	ROM	24.52 w

400 Metres (25 Jun)

1.	Svetlana Goncharenko	RUS	52.08
2.	MELANIE NEEF		52.43
3.	Francine Landre	FRA	52.86
4.	Elena Nasonkina	UKR	54.16
5.	Yolanda Reyes	SPA	54.31
6.	Elena Vizitiu	ROM	55.00
7.	Natalia Ignatyuk	BLS	56.91

800 Metres (25 Jun)

1.	Patricia Djate	FRA	2:02.95
2.	Elena Zavadskaya	UKR	2:04.43
3.	Simone Weidner	GER	2:05.12
4.	Violeta Beclea	ROM	2:05.56
5.	Tamara Kuprianovich	BLS	2:05.95
6.	Elena Afanasyeva	RUS	2:06.51
7.	Dolores Rodriguez	SPA	2:08.60
dq	DIANE MODAHL		(2:02.81)

1500 Metres (26 Jun)

1.	Lyubov Kremiova	RUS	4:05.97
2.	KELLY HOLMES		4:06.48
3.	Violeta Beclea	ROM	4:09.26
4.	Ellen Keissling	GER	4:10.82
5.	Yelena Storchevaia	UKR	4:13.56
6.	Laurence Vivier	FRA	4:17.00
7.	Maria Zuniga	SPA	4:19.77

3000 Metres (25 Jun)

1.	Ludmilla Borisova	RUS	8:52.21
2.	Farida Fates	FRA	8:53.40
3.	SONIA McGEORGE		8:55.47
4.	Tatiana Byelovol	UKR	9:06.49
5.	Estela Estevez	SPA	9:08.24
6.	Elena Mazovka	BLS	9:13.76
7.	Margareta Keszeg	ROM	9:17.62
8.	Andrea Karhoff	GER	9:19.35

Match Results

10000 Metres (26 Jun)

1.	Kathrin Wesel	GER	32:26.85
2.	Rosario Murcia	FRA	32:59.80
3.	Rocio Rios	SPA	33:22.18
4.	Nadezhda Gallyamova	RUS	33:25.62
5.	Lulia Negura	ROM	33:33.40
6.	VICKI McPHERSON		34:03.07
7.	Natalia Galushko	BLS	34:55.62
8.	Natalia Vorobjeva	UKR	35:47.39

100 Metres Hurdles -1.4 (26 Jun)

1.	JAQUI AGYEPONG		13.00
2.	Yulia Graudyn	RUS	13.07
3.	Anne Piquereau	FRA	13.21
4.	Natalya Nodrova	UKR	13.22
5.	Caren Jung	GER	13.39
6.	Maria José Mardomingo	SPA	13.43
7.	Erica Niculae	ROM	13.60
8.	Irina Mylnikova	BLS	13.78

400 Metres Hurdles (25 Jun)

1.	SALLY GUNNELL		54.62
2.	Tatiana Terechtchouk	UKR	55.04
3.	Tatiana Kurochkina	BLS	56.02
4.	Vera Ordina	RUS	56.13
5.	Heike Meissner	GER	56.23
6.	Carole Nelson	FRA	57.97
7.	Ionela Tirlea	ROM	58.62
8.	Esther Lahoz	SPA	58.69

High Jump (26 Jun)

1.	Tatyana Shevchik	BLS	1.94
2.	Monica Jager	ROM	1.91
3.	Elena Gulyaova-Rodina	RUS	1.88
4.	Marion Hellman	GER	1.88
5.	Maria del Mar Martinez	SPA	1.85
6.	JULIA BENNETT		1.85
7.	Irina Mikhailchenko	UKR	1.80
8.	Maryse Maury	FRA	1.80

Long Jump (26 Jun)

1.	Heike Drechsler	GER	6.99
2.	Olga Rubleva	RUS	6.65
3.	Larisa Kuchinskaia	BLS	6.54
4.	Elena Semiraz	UKR	6.54
5.	DENISE LEWIS		6.42
6.	Mirela Dulgheru	ROM	6.39
7.	Mahob Anastasic	FRA	6.18
8.	Yolanda Rodaiguez	SPA	6.11

Triple Jump (25 Jun)

1.	Helga Radtke	GER	13.90
2.	Pedrescu Rodica	ROM	13.83
3.	Concepcion Paredes	SPA	13.81
4.	MICHELLE GRIFFITH		13.75
5.	Natalia Klimovets	BLS	13.49
6.	Victoira Vershnina	UKR	13.43
7.	Valerie Guiyoule	FRA	13.38
8.	Olga Rubleva	RUS	13.32

MEN

1.	Germany	122
2.	GREAT BRITAIN &NI	107.5
3.	Russia	102
4.	Ukraine	87
5.	Italy	84
6.	Sweden	82.5
7.	France	81
8.	Romania	50

Shot (26 Jun)

1.	Astrid Kumbernuss	GER	19.63
2.	Valentina Fedyoshina	UKR	19.30
3.	Larisa Peleshenko	RUS	18.86
4.	JUDITH OAKES		17.75
5.	Michaela Oana	ROM	17.29
6.	Natalia Gurskaya	BLS	16.82
7.	Margarita Ramos	SPA	16.59
8.	Annick Lefebvre	FRA	15.22

Discus (25 Jun)

1.	Ilke Wyludda	GER	68.36
2.	Olga Nikishina	UKR	63.48
3.	Ellina Zvereva	BLS	62.92
4.	Larisa Korotkevich	RUS	60.18
5.	Manuela Turneci	ROM	58.56
6.	JACKIE McKERNAN		55.30
7.	Angeles Barreiro	SPA	53.88
8.	Agnes Teppe	FRA	50.22

Javelin (26 Jun)

1.	Natalia Shikolenko	BLS	69.00
2.	Karen Forkel	GER	65.58
3.	Felicia Tilea	ROM	63.88
4.	Ekaterina Ivakina	RUS	63.14
5.	Nadine Auzell	FRA	58.28
6.	Irina Kostyuchenko	UKR	56.48
7.	Belen Palacios	SPA	50.10
8.	KAREN COSTELLO		49.24

4 x 100 Metres Relay (25 Jun)

1.	Ukraine	43.38
	(Sliousar, Fomenko, Tarnopolskaja, Kravtchenko)	
2.	GREAT BRITAIN & NI	43.46
	(DOUGLAS, MERRY, JACOBS, THOMAS)	
3.	Germany	44.24
	(Zipp, Lichtenhagen, Knoll, Paschke)	
4.	Russia	44.43
	(Rashupkina, Dyachenko, Zirova, Merzlyakova)	
5.	Belarus	44.64
	(Zuh, Vinogradova, Starinskaia, Molchan)	
6.	Spain	45.90
	(Blay, Garcia, Morales, Diaz)	
7.	Romania	46.19
	(Murgu, Niculae, Dulheru, Tirlea)	

4 x 400 Metres Relay (26 Jun)

1.	GREAT BRITAIN & NI	3:27.33
	(NEEF, GODDARD, SMITH, GUNNELL)	
2.	Germany	3:27.78
3.	Russia	3:28.85
4.	Ukraine	3:31.05
5.	France	3:32.00
6.	Belarus	3:33.25
7.	Romania	3:33.39
8.	Spain	3:38.20

WOMEN

1.	Germany	99
2.	Russia	96
3.	GREAT BRITAIN	89
4.	Ukraine	87
5.	Belarus	65
6.	France	61
7.	Romania	61
8.	Spain	51

EUROPEAN CUP B (Combined Events)
Bressanone, ITA 2-3 July 1994

Decathlon
1. Vitaliy Kolpakov UKR 8257
 (11.29 7.62 15.19 2.16 48.43 14.40 44.50 4.70 57.38 4:44.00)
2. Lev Lobodin UKR 8176
 (10.87 7.37 14.64 2.04 48.94 14.17 43.62 5.00 54.44 4:44.12)
3. ALEX KRUGER 7963
 (11.23 7.40 13.74 2.13 49.69 14.96 42.50 4.60 60.04 4:40.22)
4. SIMON SHIRLEY 7938
 (10.94 7.52 13.75 2.04 48.83 14.99 38.04 4.60 57.54 4:31.47)
5. Valeriy Belousov RUS 7817
 (11.28 6.98 13.61 2.04 50.40 14.45 39.44 4.90 59.38 4:38.51)
6. Aleksandr Bogdanov UKR 7771
 (10.98 7.36 13.96 2.01 48.67 14.38 39.42 4.50 50.64 4:44.37)
7. Nikolay Afanasyev RUS 7768
 (11.40 7.27 14.00 2.04 50.45 14.45 38.42 4.70 57.08 4:37.79)
8. Igor Matsanov BLR 7763
 (11.32 7.06 14.01 1.98 50.42 14.53 40.26 4.80 54.68 4:28.96)
9. Mirko Spada SWZ 7718
 (11.41 7.01 14.46 1.83 49.65 14.52 45.02 4.60 60.58 4:40.41)
10. Rolf Schlafli SWZ 7585
 (11.30 7.16 14.01 1.95 49.12 15.03 39.86 4.00 60.98 4:34.23)
11. RAFER JOSEPH 7563
 (11.17 6.86 13.14 1.83 50.33 15.06 50.66 4.40 59.92 4:47.02)
12. Yevgeniy Dudakov RUS 7551
 (11.24 7.33 13.65 2.04 51.72 15.10 46.14 4.80 38.98 4:42.78)

16. BARRY THOMAS 7350
 (11.44 7.06 13.22 2.01 52.30 14.89 37.72 4.60 56.34 4:53.59)

Team Result
1. Ukraine 24,204
2. GREAT BRITAIN & NI 23,464
3. Russia 23,136
4. Switzerland 22,830
5. Belarus 21,464
6. Poland 21,447
7. Belgium 20,406
8. Italy 19,353

EUROPEAN CUP A
Venissieux, FRA 2-3 July 1994

Heptathlon
1. Svetlana Moskalets RUS 6507
 (13.26 1.87 13.20 23.75 6.70 40.10 2:16.84)
2. Nathalie Teppe FRA 6396
 (13.76 1.81 13.41 25.84 6.15 59.78 2:15.90)
3. Peggy Beer GER 6362
 (13.40 1.78 13.56 24.87 6.21 51.26 2:15.89)
4. Larisa Teteryuk UKR 6274
 (14.38 1.87 13.93 24.76 6.08 49.20 2:16.95)
5. Urszula Wlodarczyk POL 6269
 (13.19 1.72 14.16 24.43 6.40 42.70 2:17.69)
6. Irina Tykhay RUS 6204
 (13.31 1.78 13.41 24.78 6.50 38.82 2:17.38)
7. Maria N-Kamrowska POL 6198
 (13.35 1.63 15.53 24.57 5.85 45.56 2:10.74)
8. Irina Vostrikova RUS 6165
 (13.67 1.84 14.45 25.88 6.12 43.80 2:17.96)
9. Irina Matyusheva UKR 6165
 (13.47 1.90 13.55 25.30 6.09 34.12 2:11.08)
10. Mona Steigauf GER 6114
 (13.53 1.84 12.05 24.51 6.22 38.02 2:14.76)
11. Odile Lesage FRA 6083
 (13.85 1.81 13.93 26.02 6.08 45.34 2:17.05)
12. DENISE LEWIS 6069
 (13.47 1.81 12.23 24.80 6.51 39.04 2:23.03)

19. JENNY KELLY 5826
 (14.46 1.75 14.36 24.70 6.02 39.50 2:25.62)
24. VIKKI SCHOFIELD 5671
 (14.06 1.72 11.84 25.04 6.07 38.16 2:22.83)
26. CHARMAINE JOHNSON 5486
 (14.36 1.72 13.18 25.55 5.80 34.44 2:25.31)

Team Result

1. Russia	18,876		5. Poland	18,150
2. Ukraine	18,487		6. GB & NI	17,566
3. France	18,474		7. Finland	17,354
4. Germany	18,462		8. Romania	15,482

Eng U23 v AUS U20 v NI Kings Lynn 9 July 1994

MEN

100 Metres wind 0.3
1. DANNY JOYCE 10.58
2. JASON FERGUS 10.67
3. MARK ALLEN NI 10.90
6. JOHN McADOREY NI 11.1

200 Metres race A wind -1.4
1. OWUSU DAKO 21.38
2. MARK ALLEN NI 21.50
3. AYO FALOLA gst 21.64

200 Metres race B wind -1.6
1. DOUGLAS WALKER gst 21.35
2. STEVE SIMMONS 21.59
3. JON ANDERSON NI 22.18

400 Metres
1. PAUL MCBURNEY NI 46.96
2. KENT ULYATT 47.23
3. ADRIAN PATRICK 48.07
4. MICHAEL GALLAGHER NI 48.31

800 Metres
1. Paul Byrne AUS 1:52.83
2. DAVEY WILSON NI 1:53.06
3. JUSTIN SWIFT-SMITH 1:53.37
4. PAUL WALKER 1:53.45
6. DAVID WILSON NI 1:56.66

1500 Metres
1. MATT HIBBERD 3:48.42
2. Paul Cleary AUS 3:48.59
6. STEFFAN WHITE 3:50.06
8. RICHARD BUNKELLY NI 3:51.65
9. DAVID WRIGHT NI 3:52.29

3000 Metres
1. DERMOT DONNELLY NI 8:13.03
2. JON GASCOYNE 8:15.71
3. JIM CAMPBELL NI 8:16.44
4. SPENCER BARDEN 8:17.24

110 Metres Hurdles wind -0.9
1. NEIL OWEN 14.19
2. KEVIN LUMSDON 14.30
4. CIARAN DOHERTY NI 15.16
5. GARY GALLAGHER NI 15.51

400 Metres Hurdles
1. GARY JENNINGS 51.45
2. CHRIS RAWLINSON 52.32
5. DOUGLAS THOM NI 53.95
6. TERRY PRICE NI 54.79

High Jump
1. IAN HOLLIDAY 2.05
2. ANDREW LYNCH 2.05
6. DARRAGH MURPHY NI 1.95
7. ADAM SMITH NI 1.95

Pole Vault
1. NICK BUCKFIELD 5.20
2. KEVIN HUGHES 5.10
3. NEIL YOUNG NI 4.60

Long Jump
1. STEVE PHILLIPS 7.59 w
2. Ryan Moore AUS/gst 7.45
4. JULIAN FLYNN 6.96
5. GARETH DEVLIN NI 6.86 w
7. GRAHAM McCLUSKIE NI 6.37

Triple Jump
1. Jason Wight AUS 15.71 w
2. MICHAEL McDONALD NI 15.26
3. EZRA CLARKE 15.22 w
4. JON HILTON 14.57 w
5. ADAM SMITH NI 14.33

Shot
1. PAUL EDWARDS gst 18.89
2. MATT SIMSON gst 18.80
3. LEE NEWMAN 17.33
4. GARY SOLLITT 16.56
6. JOHN HOWARD NI 12.57
7. NIGEL MONTGOMERY NI 11.69

WOMEN
100 Metres wind -3.4
1. MARCIA RICHARDSON 11.95
2. SOPHIA SMITH gst 12.17
3. DONNA HOGGARTH 12.30
4. JOYCE MADUAKA gst 12.45
6. CLAIRE O'CONNOR NI 12.80
8. SUSAN DOUGLAS NI 13.05

200 Metres wind -0.5
1. SOPHIA SMITH 23.68
2. JOYCE MADUAKA 23.96
4. CLAIRE O'CONNOR NI 24.53
5. SUSAN DOUGLAS NI 25.15

400 Metres
1. DONNA FRASER gst 54.31
2. Tamsyn Lewis AUS 54.58
3. STEPHANIE McCANN NI 54.73
4. CLARE RAVEN 55.44

800 Metres
1. JOANNE LATIMER NI 2:06.73
2. MICHELLE HARRIES 2:07.49
3. Sarah Jamieson AUS 2:08.78
4. CATHERINE ALLSOP 2:10.00
8. CATHY O'NEILL NI 2:17.36

1500 Metres
1. PAULA RADCLIFFE gst 4:23.84
2. SHARON KING 4:28.85
4. JILL BRUCE NI 4:31.83
5. PAULINE QUINN NI 4:34.00
6. JULIE SKINNER 4:42.69

3000 Metres
1. Suzie Power AUS 9:03.47
2. TANYA BLAKE 9:29.03
3. SARAH BENTLEY gst 9:35.82
4. ANDREA DUKE 9:39.41

100 Metres Hurdles wind -2.9
1. ANGELA THORP 13.32
2. KERI MADDOX 13.40
4. JANE HALE NI 14.44
5. VICKI JAMISON NI 14.77

Discus
1. GLEN SMITH 55.24
2. JAMIE MURPHY 54.44
3. JOHN MORELAND NI 47.52
6. JOHN HOWARD NI 34.46

Hammer
1. Sean Carlin AUS/gst 74.06
2. Paul Carlin AUS 67.68
3. DAVID SMITH 65.20
4. STEVE MINNIKIN 60.44
6. JOHN MORELAND NI 34.80
7. NIGEL MONTGOMERY NI 25.78

Javelin
1. NICK NIELAND 76.28
2. STEPHEN HARRISON 71.94
4. DEAN SMAHON NI 67.60
6. DAMIEN CRAWFORD NI 56.10

400 Metres Hurdles race A
1. Rebecca Campbell AUS 59.04
2. LOUISE BRUNNING gst 59.22
3. VYVYAN RHODES 59.31
4. STEPHANIE LLEWELLYN NI 60.92

400 Metres Hurdles race B
1. Lauren Poetschka gst 58.81
2. VICTORIA DAY 61.57
3. Kate Myers AUS 64.49
4. VICKI JAMISON NI 66.01

High Jump
1. Lisa Bruty AUS 1.78
2. LEA HAGGETT 1.78
3. Jane Millington AUS 1.75
4. ALISON EVANS 1.65
5. JACKIE VYFSCHAFT NI 1.65
6. ELAINE MURPHY NI 1.60

Long Jump
1. VICKI SCHOFIELD 5.92 w
2. KERENSA DENHAM 5.74 w
3. Nicole Mladens AUS 5.63 w
4. Belinda White AUS 5.08 w
5. JILL MCCARTER NI 5.04 w
6. JUDITH MCCALL NI 4.49

Triple Jump
1. CONNIE HENRY 13.31
2. LORNA TURNER 12.94
3. SHANI ANDERSON gst 12.44
5. ELIZABETH ORR NI 10.86
6. JUDITH MCCALL NI 9.85

Shot
1. Eileen Vanisi USA/gst 17.50
2. Kylie Standing AUS 14.15
4. UJU EFOBI 13.59
6. DAWN GRAZETTE 12.76
7. JACKIE McKERNAN NI 12.43
8. CAROL KANE NI 10.21

5000 Metres Walk
1. Dion Russell AUS 20:15.91
2. PHIL KING 20:49.27
4. KIERON BUTLER 22:18.53
5. MARTIN FLOOD NI 24:28.67

4 x 100 Metres Relay
1. ENGLAND B 40.99
2. ENGLAND A 41.16
3. Australia 42.11
4. NI 42.34

4 x 400 Metres Relay
1. ENGLAND 3:12.76
2. NI 3:12.83
3. Australia 3:13.95

Match Result
1. ENGLAND 188
2. Australia 108
3. NI 100

Discus
1. JACKIE McKERNAN NI 56.70
2. SHELLEY DREW 51.86
3. SHARON ANDREWS gst 51.80
4. TRACY AXTEN gst 51.64
6. SARAH WINCKLESS 50.12
8. ALISON MOFFITT NI 38.52

Hammer
1. Brenda McNaughton AUS 52.04
2. LYNN SPRULES 50.56
3. JULIE LAVENDER 49.10
5. JULIE KIRKPATRICK NI 43.20
6. SIMMONNE SHIRLOW NI 31.62

Javelin
1. Kate Farrow AUS/gst 56.32
2. KAREN MARTIN 53.20
3. JANINE KING 47.70
4. ALISON MOFFITT NI 45.88
7. KATRINA CAMPBELL NI 40.54

3000 Metres Walk
1. Natalie Saville AUS 13:12.44
2. VICKY LUPTON 13:20.23
4. CLAIRE WALKER 15:11.65

4 x 100 Metres Relay
1. ENGLAND A 45.67
2. ENGLAND B 46.83
3. NI 48.56
4. Australia DSQ

4 x 400 Metres Relay
1. NI 3:43.94
2. ENGLAND 3:44.13
3. Australia 3:45.22

Match Result
1. ENGLAND 165.5
2. Australia 122
3. NI 81.5

BEL v HOL v Wal U23 Oordegem, BEL 9 July 1994

MEN

100 Metres wind 0.5
1. TREMAYNE RUTHERFORD WAL 10.44
2. JAMIE HENTHORNE WAL 10.81

200 Metres wind 1.2
1. JAMIE BAULCH WAL 21.35
2. Patick De Clercq BEL 21.61
3. BRYN MIDDLETON WAL 21.77

400 Metres
1. EWAN THOMAS WAL 46.72
2. Olivier Melchior BEL 47.92
4. MARK PONTING WAL 48.05

800 Metres
1. CHRIS BLOUNT WAL 1:51.18
2. JOSEPH MILLS WAL 1:51.30

1500 Metres
1. CHRIS STEPHENSON WAL 3:55.46
2. Kurt Waelkens BEL 3:55.50
8. DAVID POVALL WAL 3:58.52

5000 Metres
1. MARK MORGAN WAL 14:26.19
2. Stan Rijken HOL 14:39.68
5. NATHANIEL LANE WAL 15:11.65

3000 Metres Steeplechase
1. Rene Van Dijke HOL 9:13.12
2. Miguel v d Poorten BEL 9:15.5
4. CHRIS WHITE WAL 9:46.7
8. MARK BALLINGER WAL 10:32.6

110 Metres Hurdles wind 1.1
1. Jonathan N'Senga BEL 13.87
2. Sven Pieters BEL 14.38

WOMEN

100 Metres wind 0.7
1. Cathy Lenoir BEL 11.55
2. Leen Mortimer BEL 12.02

200 Metres wind 2.5
1. Kathleen Van Hove BEL 24.29 w
2. Annemarie Kramer HOL 24.48 w
6. LOUISE SHARPE WAL 25.04 w
8. JOANNE GRONOW WAL 25.72 w

400 Metres
1. Sandra Stals BEL 55.56
2. Annick Velghe BEL 56.42
3. NICOLA DAVIES WAL 56.95
8. KAY FURSE WAL 58.68

800 Metres
1. Majelle Laman HOL 2:10.43
2. Laurence Roobaert BEL 2:10.88
6. KATHRYN BRIGHT WAL 2:11.90
7. HAYLEY PARRY WAL 2:16.41

1500 Metres
1. Veerle Dejaeghere BEL 4:26.31
2. Ine Claus BEL 4:28.81
5. CATHERINE DAVIES WAL 4:40.24
7. CLAIRE THOMAS WAL 4:41.84

3000 Metres
1. Isabelle Sluysmans BEL 9:43.15
2. Nathalie Rousseau BEL 10:14.42

3. JAMES HUGHES WAL 14.46
5. JAMES ARCHAMPONG WAL 14.57

400 Metres Hurdles
1. Jurgen Servranckx BEL 52.50
2. Marvil Chery HOL 54.32
3. DAVID GOODGER WAL 54.44
8. MATTHEW EVELEIGH WAL 57.04

High Jump
1. Rene De Belder BEL 2.09
2. Wilbert Pennings HOL 2.09
4. DAFYDD EDWARDS WAL 2.00
6. DAVID NOLAN WAL 1.95

Pole Vault
1. Rudy Senecaut BEL 4.85
2. IAN WILDING WAL 4.80
3. TIM THOMAS WAL 4.80

Long Jump
1. Niels Kruller HOL 7.32
2. Hughes Branle BEL 7.02
5. LEE EDWARDS WAL 6.86
8. PAUL ELLIS WAL 6.18

Triple Jump
1. Jan Visser Derk HOL 14.68
2. PAUL ELLIS WAL 14.16
3. RYAN ROBINSON WAL 13.89

Shot
1. Paul Aldershof HOL 16.16
2. Wim Blondeel BEL 15.70
7. GARETH MARKS WAL 12.13
8. DAVYDD FARR WAL 12.07

3. EMMA PARRY WAL 10:21.91
5. HELEDD GRUFFUDD WAL 10:35.48

100 Metres Hurdles wind 1.1
1. BETHAN EDWARDS WAL 13.80
2. Deborah Den Boer HOL 13.90
6. RACHEL KING WAL 14.37

400 Metres Hurdles
1. CLAIRE EDWARDS WAL 60.20
2. Suzanne Hameka HOL 62.90
4. EMMA DAVIES WAL 63.84

High Jump
1. Anoek Van Diessen HOL 1.82
2. TERESA ANDREWS WAL 1.79
8. AILSA WALLACE WAL 1.65

Long Jump
1. Sandrine Hennart BEL 6.09
2. Maaike Olsthoorn HOL 6.03
3. Deborah Den Boer HOL 5.95
6. EMILY STEWART WAL 5.30
8. ELINOR LAMERTON WAL 5.08

Triple Jump
1. Annmarie Hendriks HOL 12.35
2. JAYNE LUDLOW WAL 11.79
6. NICOLA JUPP WAL 10.90

Discus
1. Pieter v d Kruik HOL 53.22
2. Jo Vandaele BEL 52.56
5. GARETH MARKS WAL 41.80
6. GARETH GILBERT WAL 41.52

Hammer
1. Reginald Verschuere BEL 57.28
2. Ronald Gram HOL 56.92
3. GRAHAM HOLDER WAL 53.28
5. ROSS BLIGHT WAL 47.54

Javelin
1. Johan Kloeck BEL 68.06
2. Dirk Van Der Avert BEL 66.60
6. SHANE LEWIS WAL 54.72
7. RICHARD JONES WAL 53.92

4 x 100 Metres Relay
1. WALES 41.02
(RUTHERFORD, HENTHRONE, BAULCH, MIDDLETON)
2. Belgium 42.15
(Tahon, De Souter, Tant, De Clercq)
3. Holland 42.35
(Sedoc, Kemper, Kruller, Klarenbeek)

4 x 400 Metres Relay
1. WALES 3:10.25
(DAVIES, BAULCH, LLOYD, THOMAS)
2. WALES "B" gst 3:15.32
(PONTING, MAITLAND, BLOUNT, GOODGER)
3. Holland 3:20.73
(V D Wael, Chery, Jacobs, Ruys)

Shot
1. Corrie De Bruin HOL 17.12
2. Lieja Koeman HOL 14.58
4. PHILIPPA ROLES WAL 13.17
6. KRISSY OWEN WAL 12.64

Discus
1. Corrie De Bruin HOL 54.70
2. Veerle Blondeel BEL 49.66
4. PHILIPPA ROLES WAL 46.36
8. SARAH JOHNSON WAL 36.32

Javelin
1. Kitty Van Haperen HOL 48.16
2. ONYEMA AMADI WAL 45.96
6. HILARY DAVIES WAL 40.04

4 x 100 Metres Relay
1. Belgium 47.34
(Mortier, Bogemans, De Caluwe, Tsjomba)
2. Holland 47.81
(Asanta, Kramer, Pullens, Olsthoorn)
3. WALES 48.49
(EDWARDS, JONES, WILLIAMS, SHARPS)

4 x 400 Metres Relay
1. Belgium 3:43.88
(Velghe, Buysse, VD Plaetsen, Stals)
2. Holland 3:47.80
(Muller, Oortgiese, Hillers, Wisse)
3. WALES 3:52.06
(EDWARDS, BRIGHT, FURSE, DAVIES)

SVK v Eng v HUN v SLO v CRO   Nitra, SVK   13 July 1994

MEN

100 Metres wind -1.2
1.	JOHN JASON		10.51
2.	TERRY WILLIAMS	gst	10.56
3.	Martin Nrinarsky	SVK	10.93

200 Metres wind -0.7
1.	JOHN JASON		21.10
2.	Marian Vanderka	SVK	21.68
3.	Martin Brinarsky	SVK/gst	21.73

400 Metres
1.	DAVID McKENZIE		46.51
2.	MARK SMITH	gst	46.92
3.	Gabor Kiss	HUN	47.05

800 Metres
1.	TERRY WEST		1:48.80
2.	Slobodan Miolovic	CRO	1:48.85
3.	Stefan Balosak	SVK	1:49.00

1500 Metres
1.	Bekim Bahtiri	SLO	3:48.22
2.	TONY WHITEMAN		3:48.27
3.	Balazs Tölgyesi	HUN	3:49.25

5000 Metres
1.	Yousuf A Abdulla	QTR/gst	13:57.31
2.	DARREN MEAD		13:59.66
3.	Pesic Nebojsa	CRO	14:23.55

3000 Metres Steeplechase
1.	Milos Kovacech	SVK	8:44.10
2.	Janko Podgorsek	SLO	8:44.81
3.	Ali Saleh Ammad	QTR/gst	8:49.59
4.	MICK HAWKINS		8:53.77

WOMEN

100 Metres wind -1.6
1.	MARCIA RICHARDSON		11.86
2.	Jerneja Perc	SLO	12.00
3.	Monika Madai	HUN	12.07

200 Metres wind 0.1
1.	PAULA THOMAS		23.77
2.	Alenka Bikar	SLO	24.25
3.	Jarmila Zifcakova	SVK	24.45

400 Metres
1.	Monika Madai	HUN	53.40
2.	LINDA KEOUGH		53.40
3.	DONNA FRASER	gst	53.44
4.	NICKI CROWTHER	gst	54.70

800 Metres
1.	DAWN GANDY		2:05.35
2.	Mara Zuzul	CRO	2:05.55
3.	Krisztina Mezsaros	HUN	2:09.43

1500 Metres
1.	ANGELA DAVIES		4:18.88
2.	Aniko Javos	HUN	4:20.10
3.	Renata Polanska	SVK	4:30.06

3000 Metres
1.	DEBBIE GUNNING		9:24.93
2.	Katalin Pacz	HUN	9:35.66
3.	Tijana Stojcevic	CRO	9:38.57

110 Metres Hurdles wind 1.8
1.	ANDY TULLOCH		13.73
2.	Tibor Bedi	HUN	13.96
3.	Jaroslav Brodani	SVK	14.25

400 Metres Hurdles
1.	Jozef Kucej	SVK	50.50
2.	Dusan Kovacs	HUN	50.61
3.	Mario Somek	CRO	53.62
dns	GARY CADOGAN		

High Jump
1.	FAYYAZ AHMED		2.19
2.	Robert Ruffini	SVK	2.10
3.	Lubos Benko	SVK/gst	2.10

Pole Vault
1.	MIKE EDWARDS		5.00
2.	Jure Rovan	SLO	4.80
3.	Tine Lorenci	SLO/gst	4.80

Long Jump
1.	FRED SALLE		7.83
2.	Györgi Mako	HUN/gst	7.63
3.	Gregor Cankar	SLO	7.50

Triple Jump
1.	FEMI AKINSANYA		15.70
2.	Jan Cado	SVK/gst	15.46
3.	Janos Uzsoki	HUN	15.46

Shot
1.	Milan Haborak	SVK	18.77
2.	MATT SIMSON		18.39
3.	Mihovil Rendulic	CRO	17.50

100 Metres Hurdles wind -0.2
1.	Brigitta Bukovec	SLO	13.05
2.	SAM FARQUARSON		13.14
3.	Zita Balint	HUN	13.70

400 Metres Hurdles
1.	JACQUI PARKER		58.20
2.	Maja Gorjup	SLO	58.90
3.	Ray Szilvia	HUN	60.08

High Jump
1.	Lenka Rihakova	SVK	1.83
2.	LEA HAGGETT		1.75
3.	Nevena Lendel	CRO	1.70

Long Jump
1.	Silvija Babic	CRO	6.33
2.	Tünde Vaszi	HUN	6.22
3.	ANN BROOKS		6.03

Triple Jump
1.	ASHIA HANSEN		13.55
2.	Andrea Szirbucz	HUN	12.81
3.	Andreja Ribac	SLO	12.74

Shot
1.	JUDY OAKES		18.68
2.	Natasa Erjavec	SLO	16.78
3.	Katalin Divos	HUN	13.77

Discus
1.	Jaroslav Zitnansky	SVK	56.86
2.	Igor Primc	SLO	56.06
3.	KEVIN BROWN		55.12

Hammer
1.	Balasz Kiss	HUN	74.54
2.	PAUL HEAD		69.32
3.	Vlado Kevo	SLO	66.40

Javelin
1.	MARK ROBERSON		69.84
2.	Milan Stjepovic	SLO	69.74
3.	Lajos Varga	HUN	65.86

4 x 100 Metres Relay
1.	ENGALND	40.38
	(WILLIAMS, JOYCE, CAMBELL, JOHN)	
2.	Hungary	40.73
	(Dobos, Maklary, Bedi, Sami)	
3.	Slovakia	41.29

4 x 400 Metres Relay
1.	Hungary	3:10.78
	(Kiss, Gyulai, Szel, Nyilasi)	
2.	Croatia	3:13.79
	(Pavlovic, Marijanovic, Melad, Alebic)	
3.	Slovakia	3:16.28
dnf	ENGLAND	
	(McKENZIE, WEST, PATRICK, SMITH)	

Match Result
1.	ENGLAND	78
2.	Slovakia	59
3.	Hungary	58
4.	Slovenia	49
5.	Croatia	38

Discus
1.	LORRAINE SHAW		49.28
2.	Ivana Holubova	SVK	48.28
3.	Natasa Erjavec	SLO	47.84

Javelin
1.	Agnes Preisinger	HUN	55.72
2.	Valentina Belaic	CRO	54.84
3.	SHARON GIBSON		54.58

4 x 100 Metres Relay
1.	ENGLAND	45.12
	(FARQUARSON, RICHARDSON,	
	SMITH, THOMAS)	
2.	Hungary	46.25
	(Lörinc, Szakacs, Eisenhoffer, Madai)	
3.	Slovenia	46.29

4 x 400 Metres Relay
1.	ENGLAND	3:42.22
	(CROWTHER, KEOUGH, GANDY, FRASER)	
2.	Hungary	3:44.18
	(Doczi, Ray, Kurucz, Bori)	
3.	Slovenia	3:45.70

Match Result
1.	ENGLAND	73
2.	Hungary	54.5
3.	Slovenia	44.5
4.	Slovakia	36
5.	Croatia	31

MEN

100 Metres wind -1.0
1.	Kevin Braunskill	USA	10.43
2.	Vince Henderson	USA	10.51
3.	Tim Montgomery	USA	10.52
4.	JASON JOHN	gst	10.52
5.	TOBY BOX	gst	10.57
6.	DARREN BRAITHWAITE		10.58
7.	MICHAEL ROSSWESS		10.61
8.	DARREN CAMPBELL	gst	10.67

200 Metres wind 1.5
1.	JOHN REGIS		20.44
2.	Ron Clark	USA	20.47
3.	Marcel Carter	USA	20.55
4.	Dino Napier	USA	20.57
5.	PHILIP GOEDLUCK		20.97
6.	DOUGLAS WALKER		21.26

400 Metres
1.	Calvin Davies	USA	45.34
2.	DU'AINE LADEJO		45.61
3.	Jason Rouser	USA	45.90
4.	DAVID MCKENZIE	gst	46.35
5.	Wendell Gaskin	USA	46.39
6.	BRIAN WHITTLE		46.69
7.	IWAN THOMAS	gst	46.81
8.	ADRIAN PATRICK		47.44

800 Metres
1.	CRAIG WINROW		1:47.17
2.	Stanley Redwine	USA	1:47.40
3.	ANDREW LILL		1:47.41
4.	MARTIN STEELE		1:47.99
5.	Terril Davis	USA	1:48.73
6.	Brad Sumner	USA	1:49.15
7.	GARY BROWN	gst	1:49.78

1500 Metres
1.	KEVIN MCKAY		3:45.70
2.	Eric Nedeau	USA	3:46.32
3.	JOHN MAYOCK		3:46.66
4.	ANDREW KEITH		3:47.01
5.	Jason Pyrah	USA	3:47.24
6.	Mark Dailey	USA	3:49.76
7.	TONY MORRELL	gst	3:49.83

5000 Metres
1.	Ronnie Harris	USA	14:02.18
2.	GARY STAINES	gst	14:03.06
3.	DARREN MEAD	gst	14:05.02
4.	DAVID MILES		14:05.48
5.	JOHN SHERBAN		14:06.16
6.	DERMOT DONNELLY		14:15.57
7.	RICHARD FINDLOW	gst	14:21.39

3000 Metres Steeplechase
1.	MARK ROWLAND		8:41.45
2.	COLIN WALKER		8:44.40
3.	Dan Reese	USA	8:45.48
4.	Francis O'Neill	USA	8:46.57
5.	SPENCER DUVAL		8:47.47
6.	TOM BUCKNER	gst	8:49.16
7.	MIKE HAWKINS	gst	8:51.85
8.	Daniel Lopez	USA	8:58.49

110 Metres Hurdles wind 0.8
1.	Robert Reading	USA	13.36
2.	Allen Johnson	USA	13.43
3.	TONY JARRETT		13.45
4.	PAUL GRAY		13.65
5.	ANDY TULLOCH		13.76
6.	LLOYD COWAN	gst	14.13
dnf	Courtney Hawkins	USA	

400 Metres Hurdles
1.	Octavius Terry	USA	49.73
2.	PETER CRAMPTON		50.22
3.	Marco Morgan	USA	50.25
4.	LAWRENCE LYNCH		50.38
5.	STEVE COUPLAND		50.97
6.	GARY JENNINGS	gst	51.16
7.	TONY WILLIAMS	gst	51.38

High Jump
1.	Tony Barton	USA	2.28
2.	BRENDAN REILLY		2.28
3.	Randy Jenkins	USA	2.25
4.	DALTON GRANT		2.25
5.	GEOFF PARSONS		2.20
6.	Jeff Wylie	USA	2.20
nh	FAYYAZ AHMED	gst	

Pole Vault
1.	Kory Tarpenning	USA	5.80
2.	Bill Deering	USA	5.60
3.	Brent Burns	USA	5.60
4.	NEIL WINTER		5.40
5.	MIKE EDWARDS		5.20
6.	NICK BUCKFIELD		5.00

Long Jump
1.	Reggie Jones	USA	8.15
2.	FRED SALLE		8.10
3.	Dion Bentley	USA	8.00
4.	BARRINGTON WILLIAMS		7.90
5.	Tony Walton	USA	7.67
6.	STEVE PHILLIPS		7.56

Triple Jump
1.	JONATHAN EDWARDS		16.80
2.	FRANCIS AGYEPONG		16.77
3.	TOSI FASINRO	gst	16.55
4.	Clifton Etheridge	USA	16.33
5.	JULIAN GOLLEY		16.31

Shot
1.	Greg Tafralis	USA	20.89
2.	C. J. Hunter	USA	20.79
3.	Kevin Toth	USA	20.16
4.	PAUL EDWARDS		18.98
5.	MATTHEW SIMSON		18.58
6.	NIGEL SPRATLEY		17.55

Discus
1.	Mike Gravelle	USA	63.68
2.	Carlos Scott	USA	60.08
3.	Randy Heisler	USA	59.42
4.	ROBERT WEIR		58.72
5.	KEVIN BROWN		56.12
6.	GLEN SMITH		54.88

Hammer
1.	Lance Deal	USA	78.28
2.	PETER VIVIAN		69.62
3.	Kevin McMahon	USA	66.98
4.	Jim Driscoll	USA	66.90
5.	MICHAEL JONES		62.38
6.	PAUL HEAD		60.68

Javelin
1.	STEVE BACKLEY		84.68
2.	MICK HILL		81.98
3.	MARK ROBERSON		75.84

4 x 100 Metres Relay
1.	GREAT BRITAIN	38.91

(JOHN, BRAITHWAITE, REGIS, JARRETT)

2.	U.S.A.	39.01

(Braunskill, Carter, Henderson, Montgomery)

3.	GREAT BRITAIN U23	39.55

(RUTHERFORD, BOX, WALKER, CAMPBELL)

4 x 400 Metres Relay
1.	U.S.A.	3:01.38

(Jones, Davis, Miller, Rouser)

2.	GREAT BRITAIN	3:03.91

(McKENZIE, WHITTLE, THOMAS, LADEJO)

3.	GREAT BRITAIN U23	3:04.92

(McBURNEY, BAULCH, SLYTHE, ULYATT)

Match Result
1.	USA	206
2.	GREAT BRITAIN & NI	180

WOMEN

100 Metres wind -2.0
1.	Cheryl Taplin	USA	11.66
2.	Chryste Gaines	USA	11.72
3.	PAULA THOMAS		11.78
4.	STEPHANIE DOUGLAS		11.85
5.	Sheila Echols	USA	11.86
6.	SIMMONE JACOBS	gst	11.93
7.	MARCIA RICHARDSON		11.94

200 Metres wind -1.2
1.	Flirtisha Harris	USA	23.44
2.	Wenda Vereen	USA	23.58
3.	SIMMONE JACOBS		23.73
4.	GERALDINE McLEOD		23.81
5.	STEPHANIE DOUGLAS		23.92
6.	Shantel Twiggs	USA	24.16

400 Metres
1.	SALLY GUNNELL		51.04
2.	Michelle Collins	USA	51.19
3.	Kim Graham	USA	51.44
4.	PHYLIS SMITH		51.79
5.	MELANIE NEEF		52.23
6.	Rochelle Stevens	USA	52.38
7.	DONNA FRASER	gst	53.87
8.	JANET LEVERMORE	gst	55.90

800 Metres

1.	Nekita Beasley	USA	2:02.80
2.	SONIA BOWYER		2:03.18
3.	CATHY DAWSON	gst	2:03.39
4.	JOANNA LATIMER		2:04.05
5.	DAWN GANDY		2:04.38
6.	Tosha Woodward	USA	2:05.28
7.	Jennifer Buckley	USA	2:05.31

1500 Metres

1.	YVONNE MURRAY		4:04.19
2.	Suzy Hamilton	USA	4:04.57
3.	LYNN GIBSON		4:05.75
4.	Regina Jacobs	USA	4:06.70
5.	ANGLEA DAVIES	gst	4:09.29
6.	BEV HARTIGAN		4:12.46
7.	Julie Speights	USA	4:13.59

3000 Metres

1.	SONIA MCGEORGE		9:02.97
2.	Libbie Johnson	USA	9:03.49
3.	DEBBIE GUNNING		9:12.12
4.	Joan Nesbit	USA	9:13.34
5.	WENDY ORE		9:15.21

100 Metres Hurdles wind -2.6

1.	JACQUI AGYEPONG		13.34
2.	Lavonna Floreal	USA	13.37
3.	SAM FARQUARSON		13.77
4.	Cheryl Dickey	USA	13.85
5.	LESLEY-ANN SKEETE	gst	13.86
6.	CLOVA COURT		14.01
7.	Sherlese Taylor	USA	14.08
8.	KERI MADDOX	gst	14.17

400 Metres Hurdles

1.	Tonja Buford	USA	56.01
2.	GOWRY RETCHAKAN		56.35
3.	Connie Ellerbe	USA	57.15
4.	Trevaia Williams	USA	57.69
5.	STEPHANIE McCANN		58.09
6.	CLARE BLEASDALE		59.19
7.	JANE LOW	gst	59.80

High Jump

1.	DEBBIE MARTI		1.88
2.	Angie Bradburn	USA	1.88
3.	Karol Damon	USA	1.85
4.	JULIA BENNETT		1.80
5=	LEA HAGGETT	gst	1.80
5=	JULIE MAJOR		1.80
	Tisha Waller	USA	nh

Long Jump

1.	Cynthea Rhodes	USA	6.68
2.	Sharon Couch	USA	6.57
3.	YINKA IDOWU		6.54
4.	DENISE LEWIS		6.50
5.	Terri Hairston	USA	6.43
6.	RUTH IRVING		6.12

Triple Jump

1.	ASHIA HANSEN		14.00
2.	MICHELLE GRIFFITH		13.84
3.	RACHEL KIRBY		13.50
4.	Diana Orrange	USA	13.50
5.	Carla Shannon	USA	13.48
6.	Roshanda Glenn	USA	13.35

Shot

1.	JUDITH OAKES		18.63
2.	Dawn Dumble	USA	17.38
3.	Ramona Pagel	USA	17.36
4.	Eileen Vanisi	USA	17.22
5.	MYRTLE AUGEE		17.13
6.	MAGGIE LYNES		16.57
7.	YVONNE HANSON-NORTEY	gst	16.10

Discus

1.	Lacy Barnes-Mileham	USA	56.94
2.	Dawn Dumble	USA	56.62
3.	JACKIE McKERNAN		56.04
4.	Kristin Kuehl	USA	55.64
5.	SHARON ANDREWS		53.88
6.	DEBBIE CALLAWAY		51.92

Javelin

1.	Donna Mayhew	USA	61.50
2.	Nicole Carroll	USA	57.86
3.	SHARON GIBSON		57.56
4.	Lynda Lipson	USA	51.50
5.	JOANNA BURTON		50.00
6.	NOELLE BRADSHAW		46.78

4 x 100 Metres Relay

1.	U.S.A.	43.35
	(Twiggs, Vereen, Harris, Gaines)	
2.	GREAT BRITAIN	44.22
	(DOUGLAS, McLEOD,JACOBS, AGYEPONG)	
3.	GREAT BRITAIN U23	45.03
	(MADUAKA,RICHARDSON, SMITH, HOGGARTH)	

4 x 400 Metres Relay

1.	U.S.A.	3:26.99
	(Williams, Stevens, Malone, Kaiser-Brown)	
2.	GREAT BRITAIN	3:32.44
	(FRASER, SMITH, NEEF, CROWTHER)	

WORLD JUNIOR CHAMPIONSHIPS Lisbon, POR 20-24 July 1994

MEN

100 Metres wind 1.2 (21 Jul)

1.	Deji Aliu	NGR	10.21
2.	JASON GARDENER		10.25
3.	Deworski Odom	USA	10.25
4.	Obadele Thompson	BAR	10.29
5.	Carlton Chambers	CAN	10.30
6.	Ibrahim Meite	CIV	10.34
7.	Eric Frempong-Manso	CAN	10.37
8.	JULIAN GOLDING		10.46

200 Metres wind 1.7 (23 Jul)

1.	Anthony Wheeler	USA	20.62
2.	Deji Aliu	NGR	20.88
3.	IAN MACKIE		20.95
4.	Eric Frempong-Manso	CAN	21.01
5.	Mark Keddell	NZL	21.02
6.	Han Chaoming	CHN	21.08
7.	Ibrahim Meite	CIV	21.24
8.	Bryan Howard	USA	21.25
5s2	JULIAN GOLDING		21.21

400 Metres (22 Jul)

1.	Michael McDonald	JAM	45.83
2.	Ramon Clay	USA	46.13
3.	Shaun Farrell		46.31
4.	MARK HYLTON		46.37
5.	Desmond Johnson	USA	46.38
6.	Riaan Dempers	RSA	47.31
7=	Kunle Adejuyigbe	NGR	47.62
7=	Rohan McDonald	JAM	47.62
2h6	GUY BULLOCK		48.86

800 Metres (22 Jul)

1.	Paul Byrne	AUS	1:47.42
2.	Japhet Kimutai	KEN	1:48.22
3.	Alain Miranda	CUB	1:48.24
4.	Julius Achon	UGA	1:48.85
5.	Peter Biwott	KEN	1:49.09
6.	Abako Bekele	ETH	1:49.63
7.	David Krummenacker	USA	1:49.80
8.	Abdul. Hasan Abdulla	QAT	1:55.67
1h4	MARK GRIFFIN		1:49.27
2h3	EDWARD KING		1:51.48

1500 Metres (24 Jul)

1.	Julius Achon	UGA	3:39.78
2.	André Bucher	SWZ	3:40.46
3.	Philip Mosima	KEN	3:41.09
4.	Reyes Estévez	SPA	3:42.98
5.	Michael Power	AUS	3:43.86
6.	Paul Cleary	AUS	3:44.64
7.	Alexandru Vasile	ROM	3:44.78
8.	BRUNO WITCHALLS		3:45.11
12h2	NEIL CADDY		3:51.43

5000 Metres (24 Jul)

1.	Daniel Komen	KEN	13:45.37
2.	Regasa Habte	ETH	13:49.70
3.	Giuliano Battocletti	ITA	13:51.16
4.	Pablo Olmedo	MEX	13:55.19
5.	Kenji Takao	JPN	14:02.55
6.	Samir Moussaoui	ALG	14:03.75
7.	Benoit Zwierzchlewski	FRA	14:04.34
8.	Valery Kuzmin	RUS	14:04.50
13.	DARRIUS BURROWS		14:35.10

10000 Metres (20 Jul)

1.	Daniel Komen	KEN	28:29.74
2.	Kenji Takao	JPN	28:55.24
3.	Michitane Noda	JPN	29:00.55
4.	Regasa Habte	ETH	29:04.57
5.	Alemayehu Tekaligh	ETH	29:06.03
6.	Ko Jung-Won	KOR	29:17.23
7.	Simone Zanon	ITA	29:21.00
8.	Ivan Pérez	SPA	29:36.15

3000 Metres Steeplechase (23 Jul)

1.	Paul Chemase	KEN	8:31.51
2.	Julius Chelule	KEN	8:33.64
3.	Irba Lakhal	MAR	8:34.42
4.	Luciano Di Pardo	ITA	8:48.11
5.	Wordofa Lemma	ETH	8:48.66

6. Jose Luis Blanco — SPA — 8:49.85
7. Christian Knoblich — GER — 8:49.99
8. Cesar Perez — JPN — 8:52.45
10h2 CHRIS ELLIOTT — 9:11.95

110 Metres Hurdles 2.1 (22 Jul)
1. Frank Busemann — GER — 13.47
2. Dudley Dorival — USA — 13.65
3. Darius Pemberton — USA — 13.93
4. Sven Pieters — BEL — 14.00
5. Anier Garcia — CUB — 14.05
6. Andrey Kislykh — RUS — 14.21
7. Filip Bickel — GER — 14.23
8. Andrey Vinitskiy — UKR — 14.31
5s2 JAMES ARCHAMPONG — 14.18
5h4 SIMON MCAREE — 14.43

400 Metres Hurdles (22 Jul)
1. Gennadiy Gorbenko — UKR — 50.56
2. Miklos Roth — HUN — 50.85
3. NOEL LEVY — 50.94
4. Robert Jarábek — SVK — 50.95
5. Mohammed Al Beshi — SAU — 51.70
6. Kevin James — JAM — 51.90
7. Andrey Shcheglov — RUS — 51.99
8. Jako Jonker — RSA — 53.65
7h4 ALEX HUNTE — 54.04

High Jump (24 Jul)
1. Jagan Hames — AUS — 2.23
2. Antoine Burke — IRE — 2.20
3. Mika Polku — FIN — 2.20
4. Attila Zsivotzky — HUN — 2.20
5. Roland Stark — GER — 2.15
6. Oskari Frosen — FIN — 2.15
7= Shunichi Kobayashi — JPN — 2.10
7= Stefan Holm — SWE — 2.10
12. STUART OHRLAND — 2.05
20=Q JAMES BRIERLEY — 2.05

Pole Vault (22 Jul)
1. Viktor Chistyakov — RUS — 5.60
2. Dmitriy Markov — BLS — 5.50
3. Taoufik Lachheb — FRA — 5.30
4. Przemyslaw Gurin — POL — 5.30
5. Eric Boxley — USA — 5.30
6. Martin Lorenci — SLO — 5.20
7. Adam Kolasa — POL — 5.10
8. Jurij Rovan — SLO — 5.10

WOMEN
100 Metres wind 2.0 (21 Jul)
1. Sabrina Kelly — USA — 11.36
2. Aspen Burkett — USA — 11.40
3. Philomina Mensah — GHA — 11.43
4. Ekaterini Thanou — GRE — 11.46
5. Debbie Ferguson — BAH — 11.48
6. Kerry-Ann Richards — JAM — 11.56
7. Frédérique Bangue — FRA — 11.57
8. Daynelki Pérez — CUB — 11.58

Long Jump (21 Jul)
1. Gregor Cankar — SLO — 8.04
2. Bogdan Tarus — ROM — 8.02
3. Shigeru Tagawa — JPN — 7.85
4. Andrew Channer — CAN — 7.79
5. Darius Pemberton — USA — 7.77
6. Olivier Borderan — FRA — 7.74
7. Andrej Benda — SVK — 7.72
8. Carlos Calado — POR — 7.56

Triple Jump (24 Jul)
1. LARRY ACHIKE — 16.67
2. Leonard Cobb — USA — 16.65
3. Ronald Servius — FRA — 16.55
4. Sergey Izmaylov — UKR — 16.42
5. Cesar Javier Rizo — CUB — 16.24
6. Carlos Calado — POR — 16.14
7. Vyacheslav Taranov — RUS — 16.05
8. Jason Wight — AUS — 15.96

Shot (23 Jul)
1. Adam Nelson — USA — 18.34
2. Andreas Gustafsson — SWE — 17.95
3. Ville Tiisanoja — FIN — 17.9
4. Leif Olve Larsen — NOR — 17.75
5. Pavol Pankuch — SVK — 17.16
6. Conny Karlsson — FIN — 17.08
7. Gunnar Pfingsten — GER — 16.95
8. Christian Nehme — GER — 16.63

Discus (21 Jul)
1. Frantz Kruger — RSA — 58.22
2. Julio Peñero — ARG — 57.80
3. Timo Sinervo — FIN — 56.76
4. Andrej Krawczyk — POL — 55.68
5. Li Shaojie — CHN — 55.58
6. Robert Fazekas — HUN — 53.64
7. Doug Reynolds — USA — 53.04
8. Jason Tunks — CAN — 52.44

Hammer (23 Jul)
1. Szymon Ziolowski — POL — 70.44
2. Igor Tugay — UKR — 70.08
3. Sergey Vasilyev — RUS — 66.14
4. Tapio Kolunsarka — FIN — 65.08
5. Vadim Devyatovskiy — BLS — 64.70
6. Norbert Horvath — HUN — 63.60
7. Yosnel Montes — CUB — 62.78
8. Steve Harnapp — GER — 62.22
9. KARL ANDREWS — 62.14
dq Valdisalv Piskunov — UKR — 71.66

200 Metres wind 2.2 (23 Jul)
1. Heide Seyerling — RSA — 22.80w
2. Lakeisha Backus — USA — 22.86w
3. Tatiana Tkalich — UKR — 23.35w
4. Debbie Ferguson — BAH — 23.59w
5. Sylvianne Félix — FRA — 23.61w
6. Fabé Dia — FRA — 23.67w
7. Huang Mei — CHN — 24.11w
8s1 SUSAN WILLIAMS — 24.72
h3 SINEAD DUDGEON — dq

Javelin (24 Jul)
1. Marius Corbett — RSA — 77.98
2. Matti Narhi — FIN — 74.92
3. Isbel Luaces — CUB — 72.82
4. Segey Voynov — UZB — 72.74
5. Christian Nicolay — GER — 72.48
6. Pietari Skytta — FIN — 72.06
7. Toru Ue — JPN — 69.48
8. Kiyoshi Ishiba — JPN — 68.56
15Q STUART FABEN — 66.74

Decathlon (20-21 Jul)
1. Benjamin Jensen — NOR — 7676
2. Kalus Isekenmeier — GER — 7298
3. Glenn Linqvist — FIN — 7288
4. Alf-Gerrit Christiansen — GER — 7228
5. Thomas Tebbich — AUT — 7125
6. Gines Hidalgo — SPA — 7097
7. Arnaud Humbey — FRA — 7008
8. Tage Peterson — USA — 6973

10000 Metres Walk (21 Jul)
1. Jorge Segura — MEX — 40:26.93
2. Yevgeniy Shmalyuk — RUS — 40:32.72
3. Artur Meleskevich — BLS — 40:35.52
4. Sebastiano Catania — ITA — 40:58.46
5. Daisuke Ikeshima — JPN — 41:01.97
6. Alejandro Lopez — MEX — 41:28.14

20 Kilometres Road Race (24 Jul)
1. Clodoaldo Silva — BRA — 1:03:21
2. Carlos Garcia — SPA — 1:03:38
3. Antonello Landi — ITA — 1:03:40

4 x 100 Metres Relay (24 Jul)
1. GREAT BRITAIN &NI — 39.60
(GARDENER, GOLDING, MACKIE, CAMERON)
2. USA — 69.76
3. Canada — 39.90
4. Japan — 40.03
5. France — 40.38
6. Germany — 40.45
7. Jamaica — 40.72
8. Norway — 41.79

4 x 400 Metres Relay (24 Jul)
1. USA — 3:03.32
2. Jamaica — 3:04.12
3. GREAT BRITAIN — 3:06.59
(BULLOCK, BUDDEN, LEVY, HYLTON)
4. New Zealand — 3:07.25
5. Japan — 3:08.06
6. Germany — 3:08.77
7. Nigeria — 3:09.68
8. Cuba — 3:10.30

400 Metres (22 Jul)
1. Olabisi Afolabi — NGR — 51.97
2. Monique Hannagan — USA — 52.25
3. Hana Benesová — TCH — 52.60
4. Li Yajun — CHN — 52.62
5. Tracey Barnes — JAM — 53.46
6. Tamsyn Lewis — AUS — 53.51
7. Cicely Scott — USA — 53.57
4h3 LOURETTA THORNE — 55.06

800 Metres (22 Jul)
1. Miaoara Cosulianu ROM 2:04.96
2. Jackline Maranga KEN 2:05.05
3. Ware Kutre ETH 2:05.17
4. Grazyna Penc POL 2:05.66
5. Lyudmila Voronicheva RUS 2:06.66
6. Kumiko Okamoto JPN 2:07.09
7. Eleonora Berlanda ITA 2:07.26
8. Szilvia Csocsanszky HUN 2:10.75
7h1 JEINA MITCHELL 2:08.85
5h2 DOROTHEA LEE 2:07.68

1500 Metres (24 Jul)
1. Anita Weyermann SWZ 4:13.97
2. Marta Dominguez SPA 4:14.59
3. Atsumi Yashima JPN 4:15.84
4. Rose Cheruiyot KEN 4:17.12
5. Ware Kutre ETH 4:17.39
6. Irina Nedelenko UKR 4:18.47
7. Lidia Chojecka POL 4:18.70
8. Heather DeGeest CAN 4:19.07

3000 Metres (22 Jul)
1. Gabriela Szabo ROM 8:47.40
2. Susie Power AUS 8:56.93
3. Sally Barsosio KEN 8:59.34
4. Annemari Sandell FIN 9:04.10
5. Pamela Chepchumba KEN 9:13.33
6. Chiemi Takahashi JPN 9:14.22
7. Lu Jing CHN 9:15.98
8. Miwa Sugawara JPN 9:16.57
12. NICOLA SLATER 9:36.19
7h1 CATHERINE BERRY 9:29.48

10000 Metres (24 Jul)
1. Yoko Yamazaki JPN 32:34.11
2. Jackline Okemwa KEN 33:19.51
3. Jebiwott Keitany KEN 33:35.98
4. Maria Singeorzan ROM 33:49.19
5. Abate Birhan ETH 34:13.58
6. Lu Jing CHN 34:33.87
7. Erika Olivera CHI 34:36.96
8. Adriana Chirita ROM 34:41.87

100 Metres Hurdles 0.5 (22 Jul)
1. Kirsten Bolm GER 13.26
2. Laiasha Colander USA 13.30
3. DIANE ALLAHGREEN 13.31
4. Chen Zhenhong CHN 13.59
5. Ingvild Larsen NOR 13.66
6. Carmen Banks USA 13.72
7. Nikola Spinova TCH 13.74
2h2 ORLA BIRMINGHAM 13.87

400 Metres Hurdles (22 Jul)
1. Ionela Tirlea ROM 56.25
2. Virna De Angeli ITA 56.93
3. Emma Holmqvust SWE 57.23
4. Zhu Weiu CHN 58.10
5. Rebecca Campbell AUS 58.60
6. Kelly Oliveira BRA 59.15
7. Claudia Salvarani ITA 59.39
8. Ikiko Yamagata JPN 59.39
8h1 ALLISON CURBISHLEY (fell) 1:06.68

High Jump (23 Jul)
1. Olga Kaliturina RUS 1.88
2. Kajsa Bergqvist SWE 1.88
3= Lenka Rihakova SVK 1.88
3= Amy Acuff USA 1.88
5. Helen Sanzenbacher GER 1.85
6. Viktoriya Stepina UKR 1.85
7= Yekaterina Aleksandrova RUS 1.80
7= Dora Gyorfy HUN 1.80
7= Emelie Fardigh SWE 1.80
7= Amewu Mensah GER 1.80

Long Jump (23 Jul)
1. Yelena Lysak RUS 6.72
2. Heli Koivula FIN 6.64
3. Ingvild Larsen NOR 6.39
4. Magdalena Khristova BUL 6.39
5. Kirsten Bolm GER 6.33
6. Franziska Hofmann SWZ 6.32
7. Angela Henry USA 6.27
8. Lacena Golding JAM 6.27

Triple Jump (21 Jul)
1. Yelena Lysak RUS 14.43
2. Ren Ruiping CHN 14.36
3. Tatyana Lebedeva RUS 13.62
4. Suzette Lee JAM 13.41
5. Olga Cepero CUB 13.32
6. Cosmina Boaje ROM 13.12
7. Aneta Sadach POL 13.01
8. Daniela Bologa ROM 12.88

Shot (21 Jul)
1. Chen Xiaoyan CHN 18.76
2. Yumileidi Cumba CUB 18.09
3. Claudia Mues GER 17.07
4. Corrie De Bruin HOL 16.79
5. Shang Xiaoli CHN 16.74
6. Nadine Kleinert GER 16.70
7. Alina Pupo CUB 16.15
8. Anna Rauhala FIN 15.71

Discus (24 Jul)
1. Corrie De Bruin HOL 55.18
2. Sabine Sievers GER 54.86
3. Suzy Powell USA 52.62
4. Claudia Mues GER 52.60
5. Olga Tsander BLS 51.90
6. Yu Qingmei CHN 51.32
7. Veerle Blondeel BEL 51.28
8. Monique Nacsa AUS 50.06

Javelin (22 Jul)
1. Taina Uppa FIN 59.02
2. Maria Caridad Alvarez CUB 58.26
3. Reka Kovacs HUN 55.88
4. Odaliz Palma CUB 55.74
5. Christina Scherwin DEN 55.70
6. Wang Yang CHN 53.26
7. Angeliki Tsiolakoudi GRE 53.16
8. Mirlea Manjani ALB 52.22
13Q LUCY BURRELL 49.60
18Q KIRSTY MORRISON 47.30

Heptathlon (22-23 Jul)
1. Kathleen Gutjahr GER 5918
2. Regula Cardenas CUB 5834
3. Ding Ying CHN 5785
4. Diana Koritskaya RUS 5616
5. Deborah den Boer HOL 5604
6. Vera Inancsi HUN 5596
7. Deborah Feltrin ITA 5575
8. Annelies De Meester BEL 5521

5000 Metres Walk (23 Jul)
1. Irina Stankina RUS 21:05.41
2. Susana Feitór POR 21:12.87
3. Natalya Trofimova RUS 21:24.71
4. Mariá Vasco SPA 21:41.47
5. Song Lijuan CHN 22:03.69
6. Yuka Kamioka JPN 22:06.47
7. Evá Perez SPA 22:23.31
8. Liu Hongyu CHN 22:23.69

4 x 100 Metres Relay (24 Jul)
1. Jamaica 44.01
(Robinson, Langley, Richards, Walker)
2. Germany 44.78
(Roos, Becker, Gorigk, Moller)
3. GREAT BRITAIN &NI 45.08
(ALLAHGREEN, WILLIAMS,
DUDGEON, DRUMMOND)
4. Bulgaria 45.22
(Vassileva, Ivanova, Georgieva, Christova)
5. Italy 45.48
(Bettio, Giolli, Cuccia, Sieni)
6. New Zealand 45.57
(Miller, Wise, Hunt, Arnott)

4 x 400 Metres Relay (24 Jul)
1. USA 3:32.08
(Scott, Hennagan, Brown, McMullen)
2. Romania 3:36.59
(Mircea, Miroiu, Burlacu, Tirlea)
3. Germany 3:36.65
(Merkel, Angerhausen, Teichmann, Urbansky)
4. Russia 3:37.41
(Kotlyarova, Golovko,Voronicheva, Bolenok)
5. Finland 3:37.55
(Karkas, Niemela, Kemppainen, Suomi)
6. RSA 3:37.93
(Venter, Henning, vd Merwe, Ullrich)
7. Cuba 3:37.95
(Crespo, del Rio, Orres, Figueroa)
8. GREAT BRITAIN 3:39.80
(EUSTACE, SLOANE,
CURBISHLEY, THORNE)

MEN

100 Metres   wind -2.7 (30 Jul)
1.	TOBY BOX	10.47
2.	C Konieczny GER	10.58

200 Metres   wind -0.9 (31 Jul)
1.	E Papadopoulos GRE	21.05
2.	TOBY BOX	21.06

400 Metres   (30 Jul)
1.	A Boykov RUS	46.62
2.	T Kaehlicke GER	46.63
2.	ADRIAN PATRICK	47.09

800 Metres   (31 Jul)
1.	J Jean-Joseph FRA	1:50.34
2.	M Chiavarini ITA	1:51.13
4.	JUSTIN SWIFT-SMITH	1:51.66

1500 Metres   (30 Jul)
1.	S Vincenti ITA	3:56.50
2.	D Loeser GER	3:56.78
7.	GRANT GRAHAM	3:58.24

5000 Metres   (31 Jul)
1.	M Leone ITA	14:03.89
2.	V Kashayev RUS	14:05.62
6.	MARK MORGAN	14:49.63

3000 Metres Steeplechase   (31)
1.	S Desaulty FRA	8:46.53
2.	D Kallabis GER	8:47.11
7.	ROBERT HOUGH	9:06.13

110 Metres Hurdles   -0.4 (31 Jul)
1.	F Balzer GER	13.32
2.	NEIL OWEN	13.97

400 Metres Hurdles   (30 Jul)
1.	A Saber ITA	49.37
2.	A Belikov RUS	50.68
5.	NOEL LEVY	51.96

High Jump   (30 Jul)
1.	D Kokkotis GRE	2.24
2.	S Klyugin RUS	2.21
7.	BRENDAN REILLY	2.15

Pole Vault   (31 Jul)
1.	Gerald Baudouin FRA	5.70
2.	V Chistyakov RUS	5.65
7.	NEIL WINTER	5.20

Long Jump   (30 Jul)
1.	R Orlik TCH	7.85
2.	G Ackermann GER	7.82
7.	STEVEN PHILLIPS	7.33

Triple Jump   (31 Jul)
1.	TOSI FASINRO	16.74
2.	Igor Sautkin RUS	16.57

Shot   (30 Jul)
1.	M Martinez SPA	19.93
2.	V Kapustin RUS	18.60
5.	LEE NEWMAN	17.18

Discus   (31 Jul)
1.	N Orekhov RUS	59.56
2.	M Bilek TCH	58.60
3.	GLEN SMITH	56.50

Hammer   (31 Jul)
1.	M Kunkel GER	71.38
2.	A Papadimitriou GRE	71.54
8.	DAVID SMITH	63.94

Javelin   (30 Jul)
1.	K Gatsioudis GRE	83.82
2.	S Makarov RUS	82.54
7.	NICK NIELAND	68.26

4 x 100 Metres Relay   (30 Jul)
1.	GREAT BRITAIN	39.23
	(RUTHERFORD, BOX, WALKER, CAMPBELL)	
2.	France	39.70

4 x 400 Metres Relay   (31 Jul)
1.	Germany	3:05.48
2.	Italy	3:05.53
3.	GREAT BRITAIN	3:07.16
	(McBURNEY, BAULCH, THOMAS, PATRICK)	

Match Result
1.	Germany	103
2.	Italy	100
3.	Russia	100
4.	France	91
5.	GREAT BRITAIN &NI	85
6.	Greece	75
7.	Spain	68
8.	Czech Republic	55

WOMEN

100 Metres   wind -3.4   (30 Jul)
1.	N Anisimova RUS	11.60
2.	B Zipp GER	11.68
7.	SOPHIA SMITH	12.03

200 Metres   wind -0.3   (31 Jul)
1.	Y Leshcheva RUS	23.52
2.	I Tirlea ROM	23.62
7.	SOPHIA SMITH	24.20

400 Metres   (30 Jul)
1.	A Ruecker GER	51.42
2.	N Khrushceleva RUS	52.44
5.	DONNA FRASER	54.19

800 Metres   (30 Jul)
1.	T Grigoryeva RUS	2:01.56
2.	K Kovacs GER	2:02.??
4.	VICKY LAWRENCE	2:04.69

1500 Metres   (31 Jul)
1.	E Dedkova RUS	4:17.16
2.	G Vagnim ITA	4:19.08
5.	JEINA MITCHELL	4:22.63

3000 Metres   (30 Jul)
1.	G Szabo ROM	9:12.42
2.	L Vasilevskaya RUS	9:13.54
6.	MICHELLE HARRIES	9:59.84

100 Metres Hurdles   -1.3 (31Jul)
1.	E Nicolae ROM	13.50
2.	N Spinova TCH	13.72
3.	ANGELA THORPE	13.77

400 Metres Hurdles   (30 Jul)
1.	I Tirlea ROM	56.87
2.	E Nikishova RUS	57.36
3.	LOUISE BRUNNING	58.80

High Jump   (31 Jul)
1.	Z Kovacikova TCH	1.94
2.	V Fedorova RUS	1.92
6.	LEA HAGGETT	1.83

Long Jump   (31 Jul)
1.	L Galkina RUS	6.48
2.	C Galli ITA	6.31
5.	RUTH IRVING	6.19

Triple Jump   (30 Jul)
1.	E Dumitrascu ROM	13.79
2.	N Morandini ITA	13.77
4.	CONNIE HENRY	13.07
dq	E Lysak RUS	13.88

Shot   (31 Jul)
1.	I Korzhanenko RUS	18.36
2.	M Tuliniemi FIN	17.41
6.	ALISON GREY	15.00

Discus   (30 Jul)
1.	N Sadova RUS	60.56
2.	A Angelova BUL	59.14
5.	SHELLEY DREW	50.28

Javelin   (30 Jul)
1.	D Barby GER	57.56
2.	C Isaila ROM	56.96
6.	SHELLEY HOLROYD	52.10

4 x 100 Metres Relay   (30 Jul)
1.	Russia	44.22
2.	Germany	44.60
4.	GREAT BRITAIN	45.09
	(ALLAHGREEN, HOGGARTH, SMITH, DUDGEON)	

4 x 400 Metres Relay   (31 Jul)
1.	Germany	3:30.54
2.	Russia	3:31.46
5.	GREAT BRITAIN	3:38.18
	(FRASER, FERRIER, THORNE, MADDOX)	

Match Result
1.	Russia	100
2.	Germany	92
3.	Romania	83
4.	Czech Republic	66
5.	GREAT BRITAIN &NI	63
6.	Italy	62
7.	Finland	59
8.	Bulgaria	48

ITA v GB & NI v TCH (U20) Schio, ITA 6 August 1994

MEN

100 Metres wind 0.3
1. KEVIN MARK   10.60
2. TREVOR CAMERON   10.74

200 Metres wind 0.6
1. MARLON DEVONISH   21.28
2. TREVOR CAMERON   21.28

400 Metres
1. MARK HYLTON   46.79
2. STEPHEN McHARDY   47.48

800 Metres
1. Martin Jares   TCH   1:53.20
2. ANDREW YOUNG   1:53.88
5. CHRIS STRINGER   1:56.01

1500 Metres
1. BEN REESE   3:58.33
2. S Vrba   TCH   3:58.53
4. MARK MILES   3:59.86

5000 Metres
1. Damiaro Polti   ITA   14:38.02
2. M Brusak   TCH   14:56.87
4. DAVID CONNOLLY   15:30.15
6. MATTHEW WHITFIELD   16:32.09

3000 Metres Steeplechase
1. MATTHEW O'DOWD   9:14.22
2. A Lannelli   ITA   9:18.19
4. CRAIG WHEELER   9:31.16

110 Metres Hurdles wind 0.7
1. Michal Esterka   TCH   15.04
2. R Paris   ITA   15.05
3. JAMES ARCHAMPONG   15.18
6. DAVID COTTER   15.95

400 Metres Hurdles
1. ALEX HUNTE   52.98
2. M Marcelli   ITA   53.07
3. MATT DOUGLAS   53.34

High Jump
1. JAMES BRIERLEY   2.15
2. MIKE ROBBINS   2.10

Pole Vault
1. Andrea Giannini   ITA   5.20
2. DOMINIC SHEPHERD   4.70
5. NEIL YOUNG   4.50

Long Jump
1. Jiri Muzik   TCH   7.19
2. A Rimoldi   ITA   7.12
4. JAN IRVING   6.81
6. ANTHONY MASON   6.60

Triple Jump
1. Fabrizio Donato   ITA   14.94
2. KORI STENNETT   14.80
4. MARVIN BRAMBLE   14.38

Shot
1. Paolo Capponi   ITA   15.06
2. BILL FULLER   14.83
4. BRUCE ROBB   14.32

Discus
1. Constantino Cattaneo ITA 47.48
2. BRUCE ROBB   42.36
6. EMEKA UDECHUKU   41.54

Hammer
1. NICK STEINMETZ   56.70
2. E Marioni   ITA   56.30
6. WAYNE GIBSON   49.56

Javelin
1. Tomas Kramsey   TCH   62.32
2. MATTHEW ATKINS   58.92
6. DAMIEN HUNTINGFORD   55.84

10000 Metres Walk
1. Fabio Duccoli   ITA   46:51.19
2. I Brugnetti   ITA   47:36.50
5. STEVE HOLLIER   55:05.92

100 x 200 x 300 x 400 Metres Relay
1. GREAT BRITAIN & NI   1:56.77
(CAMERON, DEVONISH, McHARDY, HYLTON)

Match Result
1. Italy   155.5
2. GREAT BRITAIN &NI   150.5
3. Czech Republic   103

WOMEN

100 Metres wind 0.2
1. REBECCA DRUMMOND   11.96
2. M Levorato   ITA   12.17
3. LAURA SESTON   12.20

200 Metres wind -0.3
1. Bohdana Volkova   TCH   24.75
2. SINEAD DUDGEON   24.80
5. SUSAN WILLIAMS   25.35

400 Metres
1. LOURETTA THORNE   54.37
2. F Sellis   ITA   55.25
3. JOANNE SLOANE   55.30

800 Metres
1. Eleonora Berlanda ITA 2:05.57
2. DOROTHEA LEE   2:07.57
5. JENNY HARNETT   2:12.60

1500 Metres
1. Michela Allen   ITA   4:29.50
2. AMANDA TREMBLE   4:33.13
4. MICHELLE MANN   4:38.29

3000 Metres
1. ALISON OUTRAM   9:54.85
2. P de Leo   ITA   9:58.69
5. CAROLINE McNULTY   10:16.06

100 Metres Hurdles wind 0.5
1. NATASHA DANVERS   13.95
2. DENISE BOLTON   14.14

400 Metres Hurdles
1. ALLISON CURBISHLEY   60.38
2. VICKI JAMISON   61.42

High Jump
1. JULIE CRANE   1.76
2. LINDSAY EVANS   1.76

Long Jump
1. Manuela Puerari   ITA   5.94
2. D Feltrin   ITA   5.92
3. JULIE HOLLMAN   5.72
5. PAMELA ANDERSON   5.41

Triple Jump
1. Rosa Bandini   ITA   12.45
2. S Biondini   ITA   11.96
4. JAYNE LUDLOW   11.45
5. KATHRYN BLACKWOOD   11.23

Shot
1. Assunta Legnante ITA   13.89
2. PHILIPPA ROLES   gst   13.65
3. HELEN WILDING   13.17
4. CHRISTINA BENNETT   12.80

Discus
1. PHILIPPA ROLES   46.52
2. LAUREN KEIGHTLEY   44.22

Javelin
1. Vanessa Maiochi   ITA   46.04
2. R Guzdekova   TCH   44.58
3. E Nantele   ITA   42.80
4. ANGHARAD RICHARDS   41.86
5. EMMA LILLEY   41.66

5000 Metres Walk
1. Eleonora Caruso   ITA   25:28.77
2. NINA HOWLEY   25:38.51
5. NICKY HUCKERBY   26:57.66

100 x 200 x 300 x 400 Metres Relay
1. GREAT BRITAIN & NI   2:09.39
(DRUMMOND, DUDGEON, THORNE, SLOANE)

Match Result
1. GREAT BRITAIN &NI 141
2. Italy   127
3. Czech Republic   77

Combined Match Result
1. GREAT BRITAIN &NI 291.5
2. Italy   282.5
3. Czech Republic   180

EUROPEAN CHAMPIONSHIPS Helsinki, FIN 7-14 August 1994

MEN

100 Metres wind -0.5 (8 Aug)
1. LINFORD CHRISTIE 10.14
2. Geir Moen NOR 10.20
3. Aleks. Porkhomovskiy RUS 10.31
4. Oleg Kramarenko UKR 10.38
5. Daniel Cojocaru ROM 10.39
6. Marc Blume GER 10.40
7. Alexandros Terzian GRE 10.42
8. JASON JOHN 10.46
6s2 TOBY BOX 10.46

200 Metres wind -0.1 (11 Aug)
1. Geir Moen NOR 20.30
2. Vladislav Dologodin UKR 20.47
3. Patrick Stevens BEL 20.68
4. Sergey Osovich UKR 20.70
5. Jean-Charles Trouabal FRA 20.70
6. Andrey Fedoriv RUS 20.78
7. Georg Panagiotopoulos GRE 20.92
8. David Dollé SWZ 21.10
7s2 PHILIP GOEDLUCK 21.11

400 Metres (11 Aug)
1. DU'AINE LADEJO 45.09
2. ROGER BLACK 45.20
3. Matthias Rusterholz SWZ 45.96
4. Dmitriy Golovastov RUS 46.01
5. Anton Ivanov BUL 46.20
6. Mikhail Vdovin RUS 46.23
7. Stefan Balosak SVK 46.64
8. Dmitriy Kosov RUS 46.69
7s1 DAVID McKENZIE 46.65

800 Metres (14 Aug)
1. Andrea Benvenuti ITA 1:46.12
2. Vebjørn Rodal NOR 1:46.53
3. Tomás De Teresa SPA 1:46.57
4. Nico Motchebon GER 1:46.65
5. Giuseppe D'Urso ITA 1:46.90
6. CRAIG WINROW 1:47.09
7. José Cerezo SPA 1:47.58
8. Atle Douglas NOR 1:47.90
6h3 TOM McKEAN 1:49.41

1500 Metres (9 Aug)
1. Fermin Cacho SPA 3:35.27
2. Isaac Viciosa SPA 3:36.01
3. Branko Zorko CRO 3:36.88
4. Éric Dubus FRA 3:37.44
5. Andrey Bulkovskiy UKR 3:37.81
6. Manuel Pancorbo SPA 3:38.16
7. Rüdiger Stenzel GER 3:38.36
8. Abdelkader Chekhémani FRA 3:38.42
11. GARY LOUGH 3:43.09
12. DAVID STRANG 3:50.27
5h2 KEVIN MCKAY 3:40.19

5000 Metres (14 Aug)
1. Dieter Baumann GER 13:36.93
2. ROB DENMARK 13:37.50
3. Abel Antón SPA 13:38.04
4. Abdellah Béhar FRA 13:38.36

10000 Metres (7 Aug)
1. Abel Antón SPA 28:06.03
2. Vincent Rousseau BEL 28:06.63
3. Stephane Franke GER 28:07.95
4. Róbert Stefko SVK 28:08.02
5. Paulo Guerra POR 28:10.18
6. João Junqueira POR 28:10.55
7. Jan Pesava TCH 28:10.73
8. Carlos de la Torre SPA 28:10.77
15. GARY STAINES 28:25.60
22. JUSTIN HOBBS 29:28.08

Marathon (14 Aug)
1. Martin Fiz SPA 2:10:31
2. Diego Garcia SPA 2:10:46
3. Alberto Juzdado SPA 2:11:18
4. RICHARD NERURKAR 2:11:56
5. Luigi Di Lello ITA 2:12:41
6. António Rodrigues POR 2:12:43
7. Manuel Matias POR 2:12:48
8. Harri Hänninen FIN 2:13:21
27. PETER WHITEHEAD 2:16:40
31. BILL FOSTER 2:17:12
52. STEVE BRACE 2:24:21
dnf MARK FLINT, ANDY GREEN

3000 Metres Steeplechase (12 Aug)
1. Aless. Lambruschini ITA 8:22.40
2. Angelo Carosi ITA 8:23.53
3. William Van Dijck BEL 8:24.86
4. MARK ROWLAND 8:26.00
5. Vladimir Pronin RUS 8:26.33
6. Martin Strege GER 8:26.36
7. Jim Svenøy NOR 8:28.12
8. Francesco Panetta ITA 8:28.25
10. TOM HANLON 8:36.06
11. JUSTIN CHASTON 8:36.83

110 Metres Hurdles 1.1 (12 Aug)
1. COLIN JACKSON 13.08
2. Florian Schwarthoff GER 13.16
3. TONY JARRETT 13.23
4. Claude Edorh GER 13.41
5. Mike Fenner GER 13.53
6. Antti Haapakoski FIN 13.54
7. Dan Philibert FRA 13.54
8. Georg Boroi ROM 13.61
5s1 ANDREW TULLOCH 13.62

400 Metres Hurdles (10 Aug)
1. Oleg Tverdokhleb UKR 48.06
2. Sven Nylander SWE 48.22
3. Stéphane Diagana FRA 48.23
4. Pedro Rodrigues POR 48.77
5. Edgar Itt GER 49.11
6. PETER CRAMPTON 49.45
7. Vadim Zadoynov MOL 49.50

8. GARY CADOGAN 49.53
5h3 LAWRENCE LYNCH 50.24

High Jump (9 Aug)
1. Steinar Hoen NOR 2.35
2= Artur Partyka POL 2.33
2= STEVE SMITH 2.33
4. Håkan Sarnblom NOR 2.31
5= Dragutin Topic IEP 2.31
5= Jaroslaw Kotewicz POL 2.31
7. Leonid Pumalainen RUS 2.28
8. Lambros Papakostas GRE 2.28
9= DALTON GRANT 2.25
9= Jean-Charles Gicquel FRA 2.25
11. Stevan Zoric IEP 2.25
12. Ralf Sonn GER 2.25
16=Q BRENDAN REILLY 2.20

Pole Vault (11 Aug)
1. Rodion Gataullin RUS 6.00
2. Igor Trandenkov RUS 5.90
3. Jean Galfione FRA 5.85
4. Philippe Collet FRA 5.80
5. Denis Petushinskiy RUS 5.80
6. Andrej Tiwontschik GER 5.70
7. Yevgeniy Krasnov ISR 5.70
8= Gianni Iapichino ITA 5.70
8= Valeriy Bukreyev EST 5.70
24=Q MIKE EDWARDS 5.20

Long Jump (10 Aug)
1. Ivailo Mladenov BUL 8.09
2. Milan Gombala TCH 8.04
3. Konst Koukodimos GRE 8.01
4. Bogdan Tudor ROM 7.99
5. Dmitriy Bogryanov RUS 7.96
6. Stanislav Tarasenko RUS 7.93
7. Vitaliy Kirilenko UKR 7.92
8. Erik Nijs BEL 7.89
19Q BARRINGTON WILLIAMS 7.69

Triple Jump (13 Aug)
1. Denis Kapustin RUS 17.62
2. Serge Hélan FRA 17.55
3. Maris Bruzhiks LAT 17.20
4. Vasiliy Sokov RUS 16.97
5. Gennadiy Markov RUS 16.89
6. JONATHAN EDWARDS 16.85
7. Georges Sainte-Rose FRA 16.59
8. Audrius Raizgys LIT 16.59
Q FRANCIS AGYEPONG nj

Shot (13 Aug)
1. Aleksandr Klimenko UKR 20.78
2. Aleksandr Bagach UKR 20.34
3. Roman Virastyuk UKR 19.59
4. Mika Halvari FIN 19.52
5. Markus Koistinen FIN 19.51
6. Dragan Peric IEP 19.40
7. Petur Gudmundsson ISL 19.34
8. Paolo Dal Soglio ITA 19.15
13Q PAUL EDWARDS 18.54

Discus (14 Aug)
1. Vladimir Dubrovchik BLS 64.78
2. Dmitriy Shevchenko RUS 64.56
3. Jürgen Schult GER 64.18
4. Nick Sweeney IRE 63.76
5. Attila Horváth HUN 63.60
6. Vladimir Zinchenko UKR 63.60
7. Svein Inge Valvik NOR 62.02
8. Costel Grasu ROM 61.40
13Q ROBERT WEIR 57.18

Hammer (11 Aug)
1. Vasiliy Sidorenko RUS 81.10
2. Igor Astapkovich BLS 80.40
3. Heinz Weis GER 78.48
4. Igor Nikulin RUS 78.38
5. Tibor Gécsek HUN 77.62
6. Aleksey Krykun UKR 76.08
7. Christoph Epalle FRA 75.22
8. Vadim Kolesnik UKR 75.22

Javelin (8 Aug)
1. STEVE BACKLEY 85.20
2. Seppo Räty FIN 82.90
3. Jan Zelezny TCH 82.58
4. Patrik Bodén SWE 81.34
5. Raymond Hecht GER 81.18
6. MICK HILL 80.66
7. Terry McHugh IRE 80.46
8. Vladimir Sasimovich BLS 78.88
22Q COLIN MacKENZIE 74.00

WOMEN
100 Metres wind 0.6 (8 Aug)
1. Irina Privalova RUS 11.02
2. Zhanna Tarnopolskaya UKR 11.10
3. Melanie Paschke GER 11.28
4. Anelia Nuneva BUL 11.40
5. Nelli Cooman HOL 11.40
6. Petya Pendareva BUL 11.41
7. Sanna Hernesniemi FIN 11.43
8. Marina Trandenkova RUS 11.52
5s1 PAULA THOMAS 11.58
7s2 STEPHANIE DOUGLAS 11.60
7q1 MARCIA RICHARDSON 11.71

200 Metres wind 0.2 (11 Aug)
1. Irina Privalova RUS 22.32
2. Zhanna Tarnopolskaya UKR 22.77
3. Galina Malchugina RUS 22.90
4. Silke Knoll GER 22.99
5. Maya Azarashvili GEO 23.01
6. Sanna Hernesniemi FIN 23.24
7. Lucrecia Jardim POR 23.28
8. Zlatka Georgieva BUL 23.46
6s2 PAULA THOMAS 23.41
8s1 KATHARINE MERRY 23.55
6h1 SIMMONE JACOBS 23.75

400 Metres (11 Aug)
1. Marie-José Pérec FRA 50.33
2. Svetlana Goncharenko RUS 51.24
3. PHYLIS SMITH 51.30
4. Yelena Andreyeva RUS 51.65
5. Anja Rücker GER 51.85
6. MELANIE NEEF 52.10
7. Daniela Spasova BUL 52.25
8. Francine Landre FRA 52.57
6s1 LINDA KEOUGH 53.63

Decathlon (12-13 Aug)
1. Alain Blondel FRA 8453
2. Henrik Dagård SWE 8362
3. Lev Lobodin UKR 8201
4. Christian Plaziat FRA 8127
5. Stefan Schmid GER 8109
6. Sándor Munkacsi HUN 8071
7. Tomás Dvorák TCH 8065
8. Dezsõ Szábo HUN 7995

20 Kilometres Walk (8 Aug)
1. Mikhail Shchennikov RUS 1:18:45
2. Yevgeniy Misyulya BLS 1:19:22
3. Valentin Massana SPA 1:20:33
4. Giovanni De Benedictis ITA 1:20:39
5. Mikhail Orlov RUS 1:21:01
6. Giovanni Perricelli ITA 1:21:51
7. Igor Kollár SVK 1:22:23
8. Sándor Urbanik HUN 1:22:49

50 Kilometres Walk (13 Aug)
1. Valeriy Spitsyn RUS 3:41:07
2. Thierry Toutain FRA 3:43:52
3. Giovanni Perricelli ITA 3:43:55
4. Jesús Angel Garcia SPA 3:45:25
5. Robert Korzeniowski POL 3:45:57
6. German Skurygin RUS 3:46:30
7. Valentin Kononen FIN 3:47:14
8. Andrey Plotnikov RUS 3:47:43

800 Metres (10 Aug)
1. Lyubov Gurina RUS 1:58.55
2. Natalya Dukhnova BLS 1:58.55
3. Lyudmila Rogachova RUS 1:58.69
4. Malgorzata Rydz POL 1:59.12
5. ANN GRIFFITHS 1:59.81
6. Carla Sacramento POR 2:00.01
7. Patricia Djaté FRA 2:00.34
8. Anna Brzezinska POL 2:00.41
9. Irina Samorokova RUS 2:11.50
6s2 DIANE MODAHL 2:02.18

1500 Metres (14 Aug)
1. Lyudmila Rogachova RUS 4:18.93
2. KELLY HOLMES 4:19.30
3. Yekat Podkopayeva RUS 4:19.37
4. Lyubov Kremlyova RUS 4:19.77
5. Malgorzata Rydz POL 4:19.80
6. Carla Sacramento POR 4:20.62
7. Ellen Kiessling GER 4:20.79
8. Maite Zuñiga SPA 4:20.83
10h1 LYNN GIBSON 4:13.89
6h2 ANGELA DAVIES 4:12.09

3000 Metres (10 Aug)
1. Sonia O'Sullivan IRE 8:31.84
2. YVONNE MURRAY 8:36.48
3. Gabriela Szabo ROM 8:40.08
4. Olga Churbanova RUS 8:40.48
5. Lyudmila Borisova RUS 8:41.71
6. ALISON WYETH 8:45.76
7. Farida Fates FRA 8:46.04
8. Nadia Dandolo ITA 8:49.42
11. SONIA McGEORGE 8:51.55

4 x 100 Metres Relay (13 Aug)
1. France 38.57
(Lomba, Sangouma, Trouabal, Perrot)
2. Ukraine 38.98
(Osovich, Vanyaikin, Kramarenko, Dologodin)
3. Italy 38.99
(Madonia, Nettis, Marras, Floris)
4. Sweden 39.05
(Karisson, Ghansah, Hedner, Eriksson)
5. Greece 39.25
(Genovelis, Panagiotopoulos, Alexopoulos, Terzian)
6. Germany 39.36
(Blume, Görmer, Huke, Blume)
7. Finland 39.80
dq Russia
h1 GREAT BRITAIN dnf
(JOHN, JARRETT, BRAITHWAITE, CHRISTIE)

4 x 400 Metres Relay (14 Aug)
1. GREAT BRITAIN 2:59.13
(McKENZIE, WHITTLE, BLACK, LADEJO)
2. France 3:01.11
(Hilaire, Rapnouil, Farraudiére, Diagana)
3. Russia 3:03.10
(Vdovin, Kosov, Bey, Golovastov)
4. Italy 3:03.46
(Vaccari, Grossi, Sabar, Aimar)
5. Germany 3:04.15
(D Bittner, K Bittner, Becker, Itt)
6. Poland 3:04.22
7. Finland 3:04.55

10000 Metres (13 Aug)
1. Fernanda Ribeiro POR 31:08.75
2. Conceição Ferreira POR 31:32.82
3. Daria Nauer SWZ 31:35.96
4. Kathrin Wessel GER 31:38.75
5. Cristina Misaros ROM 31:41.03
6. Maria Guida ITA 31:42.14
7. Fernanda Marques POR 31:53.12
8. Klara Kashapova RUS 31:55.99
9. Claudia Lokar GER 32:08.74
10. Marleen Renders BEL 32:11.18
11. Nicole Levèque FRA 32:12.07
12. Gitte Karishøj DEN 32:26.25

Marathon (7 Aug)
1. Manuela Machado POR 2:29:54
2. Mario Curatolo ITA 2:30:33
3. Adriana Barbu ROM 2:30:55
4. Ornellia Ferrara ITA 2:31:57
5. Anuta Catuna ROM 2:32:51
6. Ritva Lemettinen FIN 2:33:05
7. Kirsi Rauta FIN 2:33:32
8. Rosanna Munerotto ITA 2:34:32
11. DANIELLE SANDERSON 2:36:26

22. MARIAN SUTTON 2:40:34
30. LESLEY TURNER 2:45:16
31. ALISON ROSE 2:45:19
32. LINDA RUSHMERE 2:45:24
35. TERESA DYER 2:50:23
16. KAREN MACLEOD 2:41:46

92

100 Metres Hurdles -1.7 (9 Aug)
1. Svetlia Dimitrova BUL 12.72
2. Yuliya Graudyn RUS 12.93
3. Yordanka Donkova BUL 12.93
4. Brigita Bukovec SLO 13.01
5. Tatyana Reshetnikova RUS 13.06
6. Julie Baumann SWZ 13.10
7. JACKIE AGYEPONG 13.17
8. Anne Piquereau FRA 13.25
5s1 CLOVA COURT 13.04
4h3 SAM FARQUHARSON 13.33

400 Metres Hurdles (12 Aug)
1. SALLY GUNNELL 53.33
2. Silvia Rieger GER 54.68
3. Anna Knoroz RUS 54.68
4. Heike Meissner GER 54.79
5. Tatyana Kurochkina BLS 55.18
6. Tatyana Tereshchuk UKR 55.53
7. Olga Nazarova RUS 55.98
8. GOWRY RETCHAKAN 56.05
7h1 JACQUI PARKER 57.83

High Jump (14 Aug)
1. Britta Bilac SLO 2.00
2. Yelena Gulyayeva RUS 1.96
3. Noele Zilinskiene LIT 1.93
4. Irina Babakova UKR 1.93
5. Hanne Haugland NOR 1.93
6. Heike Balck GER 1.93
7= Svetlana Leseva BUL 1.90
7= Yelena Topchina RUS 1.90
19=Q JULIA BENNETT 1.85
29Q DEBBI MARTI 1.85
34Q LEA HAGGETT 1.75

Long Jump (12 Aug)
1. Heike Drechsler GER 7.14
2. Inessa Kravets UKR 6.99
3. Fiona May ITA 6.90
4. Renata Nielsen DEN 6.82
5. Ljudmila Ninova AUT 6.80
6. Agata Karczmarek POL 6.67
7. Irina Mushailova RUS 6.62
8. Iva Prandzheva BUL 6.56
9. YINKA IDOWU 6.46
19Q DENISE LEWIS 6.20

Triple Jump (8 Aug)
1. Anna Biryukova RUS 14.89
2. Inna Lasovskaya RUS 14.85 w
3. Inessa Kravets UKR 14.67 w
4. Yolanda Chen RUS 14.48 w
5. Rodica Petrescu ROM 14.42
6. Sarka Kaspárková TCH 13.98
7. Ramona Molzan GER 13.82
8. Helga Radtke GER 13.77
9. Concepcion Paredes SPA 13.68
10. MICHELLE GRIFFITH 13.60
11. RACHEL KIRBY 13.45
dq Sofia Bozhanova BUL (14.58)
15Q ASHIA HANSEN 13.45

Shot (7 Aug)
1. Viktoriya Pavlysh UKR 19.61
2. Astrid Kumbernuss GER 19.49
3. Svetlia Mitkova BUL 19.49
4. Stephanie Storp GER 19.39
5. Larisa Peleshenko RUS 19.01
6. Kathrin Neimke GER 18.94
7. Valentina Fedyushina UKR 18.91
8. Anna Romanova RUS 18.40
14Q MYRTLE AUGEE 16.77
17Q MAGGIE LYNES 16.16

Discus (10 Aug)
1. Ilke Wyludda GER 68.72
2. Ellina Zvereva BLS 64.46
3. Mette Bergmann NOR 64.34
4. Nicoleta Grasu ROM 63.64
5. Olga Chernyavskaya RUS 62.54
6. Jana Lauren GER 60.44
7. Marie-Paule Geldhof BEL 59.48
8. Lyudmila Filimonova BLS 59.46
13Q JACQUI McKERNAN 57.56

Javelin (12 Aug)
1. Trine Hattestad NOR 68.00
2. Karen Forkel GER 66.10
3. Felicia Tilea ROM 64.34
4. Silke Gast GER 62.90
5. Rita Ramanauskaite LIT 61.54
6. Tanja Damaske GER 61.32
7. Kinga Zsigmond HUN 59.74
8. Antoaneta Selenska BUL 57.76
17Q SHARON GIBSON 53.82
21Q SHELLEY HOLROYD 51.26

Heptathlon (8 - 9 Aug)
1. Sabine Braun GER 6419
2. Rita Ináncsi HUN 6404
3. Urszula Wlodarczyk POL 6322
4. Larisa Turchinskaya RUS 6311
5. Svetlana Moskalets RUS 6308
6. Peggy Beer GER 6275
7. Remigija Nazaroviene LIT 6262
8. Tina Rättyä FIN 6241

10 Kilometres Walk (9 Aug)
1. Sari Essayah FIN 42:37
2. Anna-Rita Sidoti ITA 42:43
3. Yelena Nikolayeva RUS 42:43
4. Yelena Arshintseva RUS 43:23
5. Larisa Ramazanova RUS 43:25
6. Natalya Misyulya BLS 43:39
7. Elisabetta Perrone ITA 43:47
8. Susana Feitor POR 43:47
20. VICKY LUPTON 46:30
23. VERITY SNOOK 47:23
    LISA LANGFORD dq

4 x 100 Metres Relay (13 Aug)
1. Germany 42.90
   (Paschke, Zipp, Knoll, Lichtenhagen)
2. Russia 42.96
   (Anisimova, Malchugina, Trandenkova, Privalova)
3. Bulgaria 43.00
   (S Dimitrova, Nuneva, S Dimitrova, Pendareva)
4. Ukraine 43.61
   (A Slyusar, Fomenko, I Slyusar, Tarnopolskaya)
5. GREAT BRITAIN 43.63
   (DOUGLAS, MERRY, JACOBS, THOMAS)
6. Holland 43.81
   (Elissen, Poelman, de Lange, Bogaards)
7. Finland 43.96
   (Pirtimaa, Leveelahti, Hernesniemi, Salmela)
8. Italy 44.46
   (Tuzzi, Ardissone, Balzani, Gallina)

4 x 400 Metres Relay (14 Aug)
1. France 3:22.34
   (Landre, Dorsile, Elien, Pérec)
2. Russia 3:24.06
   (Khrushchelyova, Andreyeva, Zakharova, Goncharenko)
3. Germany 3:24.10
   (Janke, Rohländer, Meissner, Rücker)
4. GREAT BRITAIN 3:24.14
   (NEEF, KEOUGH, SMITH, GUNNELL)
5. Czechoslovakia 3:27.95
   (Kostoválová, Benésová, Suchovská, Formánová)
6. Switzerland 3:28.78
   (Anliker-Aebi, Lüthi, Grossenbacher, Protti)
7. Poland 3:29.75
   (Grzywocz, Warnicka, Pachut, Kilinska)
8. Finland 3:32.97
   (Haikkonen, Suomi, Jääskeläinen, Finell)

European Cup Marathon

MEN
1. Spain 8:49:54
2. Portugal 8:54:59
3. France 8:57:46
4. Germany 9:02:07
5. Poland 9:06:36
6. GREAT BRITAIN & NI 9:10:09
7. Finland 9:20:47
8. Sweden 9:25:57
9. Holland 9:28:22

WOMEN
1. Italy 10:11:48
2. Romania 10:20:48
3. France 10:39:39
4. Finland 10:43:58
5. Poland 10:45:43
6. GREAT BRITAIN & NI 10:47:38
7. Russia 11:00:19

MEN

100 Metres wind 1.9 (23 Aug)

1.	LINFORD CHRISTIE	Eng	9.91
2.	Michael Green	JAM	10.05
3.	Frank Fredericks	NAM	10.06
4.	Ato Boldon	TRI	10.07
5.	Glenroy Gilbert	CAN	10.11
6.	Olapade Adeniken	NGR	10.11
7.	Angus Nketia	NZL	10.42
dq	Horace Dove-Edwin	SLE	(10.02)
8s1	ELLIOTT BUNNEY	Sco	10.50
5s2	TERRY WILLIAMS	Eng	10.17w
5q2	JASON JOHN	Eng	10.29
6q4	JAMIE HENDERSON	Sco	10.49
5h3	PETER MAITLAND	Wal	10.55

200 Metres wind 1.5 (26 Aug)

1.	Frank Fredericks	NAM	19.97
2.	JOHN REGIS	Eng	20.25
3.	Daniel Effiong	NGR	20.40
4.	Damien Marsh	AUS	20.54
5.	TERRY WILLIAMS	Eng	20.62
6.	Oluyemi Kayode	NGR	20.64
7.	Steve Brimacombe	AUS	20.67
8.	Troy Douglas	BER	20.71
5s1	TOBY BOX	Eng	21.02
6s1	DOUG WALKER	Sco	21.08
7s1	PAUL MCBURNEY	NI	21.14
5q1	JAMIE BAULCH	Wal	20.84
6q2	PETER MAITLAND	Wal	20.96
5q3	IAN MACKIE	Sco	20.99
8q3	IWAN THOMAS	Wal	21.53

400 Metres (23 Aug)

1.	Charles Gitonga	KEN	45.00
2.	DU'AINE LADEJO	Eng	45.11
3.	Sunday Bada	NGR	45.45
4.	Paul Greene	AUS	45.50
5.	Patrick Delice	TRI	45.89
6	Eewort Coombs	STV	45.96
7.	Neil De Silva	TRI	46.27
8.	Bobang Phiri	RSA	46.35
5s1	DAVID MCKENZIE	Eng	46.18
7s2	IWAN THOMAS	Wal	45.98
5q1	BRIAN WHITTLE	Sco	47.00
5q2	PAUL MCBURNEY	NI	46.78
5q4	JAMIE BAULCH	Wal	46.45
5h1	ALEX FUGALLO	Eng	47.58

800 Metres (26 Aug)

1.	Patrick Konchellah	KEN	1:45.18
2.	Hezekiel Sepeng	RSA	1:45.76
3.	Savieri Ngidhi	ZIM	1:46.06
4.	CRAIG WINROW	Eng	1:46.91
5.	Brendan Hanigan	AUS	1:47.24
6.	William Serem	KEN	1:47.30
7.	MARTIN STEELE	Eng	1:48.04
8.	TOM McKEAN	Sco	1:50.81
5s1	ANDREW LILL	Eng	1:49.62
8s1	DAVEY WILSON	NI	1:50.43
6h1	GARY BROWN	Sco	1:49.61
7h2	MICHAEL GUEGAN	Jer	1:48.90

1500 Metres (28 Aug)

1.	Reuben Chesang	KEN	3:36.70
2.	Kevin Sullivan	CAN	3:36.78
3.	JOHN MAYOCK	Eng	3:37.22
4.	Whaddon Niewoudt	RSA	3:37.96
5.	Julius Tanui	KEN	3:38.10
6.	BRIAN TREACY	NI	3:38.93
7.	Steve Green	JAM	3:39.19
8.	KEVIN MCKAY	Eng	3:39.72
11.	GARY BROWN	Sco	3:42.66
12.	DAVID STRANG	Sco	3:48.70
6s1	ANDY KEITH	Eng	3:46.52
7s1	DAVEY WILSON	NI	3:47.11
2h2	GARY LOUGH	NI	3:44.54

5000 Metres (24 Aug)

1.	ROB DENMARK	Eng	13:23.00
2.	Philemon Hanneck	ZIM	13:23.20
3.	JOHN NUTTALL	Eng	13:23.54
4.	JON BROWN	Eng	13:23.96
5.	Philip Mosima	KEN	13:24.07
6.	Jonathan Wyatt	NZL	13:35.46
7.	Paul Sum	KEN	13:39.53
8.	JUSTIN HOBBS	Wal	13:45.53
15.	DERMOT DONNELLY	NI	14:00.00
7h1	JIM CAMPBELL	NI	14:08.41

10000 Metres (27 Aug)

1.	Lameck Aguta	KEN	28:38.22
2.	Tendai Chimusasa	ZIM	28:47.72
3.	Fackson Nkandu	JAM	28:51.72
4.	MARTIN JONES	Eng	29:08.53
5.	Peter Fonseca	CAN	29:14.85
6.	EAMONN MARTIN	Eng	29:15.81
7.	R Murusamy	MAS	29:30.19
8.	Paul Patrick	AUS	29:35.95
10.	CHRIS ROBISON	Sco	29:50.23
	JOHN SHERBAN	Sco	dnf

Marathon (28 Aug)

1.	Steve Moneghetti	AUS	2:11:49
2.	Sean Quilty	AUS	2:14:57
3.	MARK HUDSPITH	Eng	2:15:11
4.	DALE RIXON	Wal	2:16:15
5.	Pat Carroll	AUS	2:16:27
6.	Nicholas Kioko	KEN	2:16:37
7.	Carey Nelson	CAN	2:16:52
8.	COLIN MOORE	Eng	2:18:07
	DAVID BUZZA	Eng	dnf

3000 Metres Steeplechase (23 Aug)

1.	Johnstone Kipkoech	KEN	8:14.72
2.	Gideon Chirchir	KEN	8:15.25
3.	Graeme Fell	CAN	8:23.28
4.	COLIN WALKER	Eng	8:27.78
5.	TOM BUCKNER	Eng	8:29.84
6.	Joel Bourgeois	CAN	8:31.19
7.	JUSTIN CHASTON	Wal	8:32.20
8.	Paul Chemase	KEN	8:35.31
10.	SPENCER DUVAL	Eng	8:49.08

110 Metres Hurdles 1.6 (23 Aug)

1.	COLIN JACKSON	Wal	13.08
2.	TONY JARRETT	Eng	13.22
3.	PAUL GRAY	Wal	13.54
4.	ANDY TULLOCH	Eng	13.69
5.	Kyle Vander-Kuyp	AUS	13.75
6.	KEN CAMPBELL	Sco	13.86
7.	Tim Kroeker	CAN	13.93
dq	Robert Foster	JAM	(13.78)
4h1	LLOYD COWAN	Eng	13.96

400 Metres Hurdles (26 Aug)

1.	Samuel Matete	ZAM	48.67
2.	Gideon Biwott	KEN	49.43
3.	Barnabas Kinyor	KEN	49.50
4.	GARY CADOGAN	Eng	49.71
5.	Rohan Robinson	AUS	49.76
6.	Ken Harnden	ZIM	50.02
7.	PETER CRAMPTON	Eng	50.37
8.	Ian Wheatley	JAM	51.25
3h2	STEVE COUPLAND	Eng	51.34
9h3	PHIL HARRIES	Wal	59.52

High Jump (26 Aug)

1.	Tim Forsyth	AUS	2.32
2.	STEVE SMITH	Eng	2.32
3.	GEOFF PARSONS	Sco	2.31
4.	Cory Siermachesky	CAN	2.28
5.	DALTON GRANT	Eng	2.28
6.	Lochsley Thomson	AUS	2.28
7=	BRENDAN REILLY	Eng	2.25
7=	Richard Duncan	CAN	2.25

Pole Vault (27 Aug)

1.	NEIL WINTER	Wal	5.40
2.	Curtis Heywood	CAN	5.30
3.	James Miller	AUS	5.30
4.	Stefani Fotis	CYP	5.30
5.	MIKE EDWARDS	Eng	5.20
6.	ANDY ASHURST	Eng	5.20
7.	Greg Halliday	AUS	5.20
8.	NICK BUCKFIELD	Eng	5.20
	Okkert Brits RSA (5.50)		nh

Long Jump (26 Aug)

1.	Obinna Eregbu	NGR	8.05w
2.	David Culbert	AUS	8.00w
3.	Ian James	CAN	7.93w
4.	Ayodele Aladefa	NGR	7.93
5.	FRED SALLE	Eng	7.88
6.	Jai Taurima	AUS	7.87
7.	Jerome Romain	DMN	7.69w
8.	Craig Hepburn	BAH	7.65
9.	Benjamin Koech	KEN	7.62
10.	Brian Thomas	CAN	7.59
11.	Ron Chambers	JAM	7.53
12.	Andrew Owusu	GHA	7.36
13Q	BARRINGTON WILLIAMS	Eng	7.53
17Q	DUNCAN MATHIESON	Sco	7.36
	STEVE INGRAM	Wal	nm

Triple Jump (28 Aug)

1.	JULIAN GOLLEY	Eng	17.03
2.	JON EDWARDS	Eng	17.00
3.	Brian Wellman	BER	17.00
4.	Jerome Romain	DMN	16.61
5.	Edrick Floreal	CAN	16.61
6.	FRANCIS AGYEPONG	Eng	16.33
7.	Ndabazihle Mdhlongwa	ZIM	16.02
8.	James Sabulei	KEN	15.99
14Q	JOHN MacKENZIE	Sco	16.12 w
16Q	MICHAEL McDONALD	NI	15.75

Shot (28 Aug)

1.	MATT SIMSON	Eng	19.49
2.	Courtney Ireland	NZL	19.38
3.	Chima Ugwu	NGR	19.26
4.	Carel Le Roux	RSA	18.50
5.	Scott Cappos	CAN	18.35
6.	Burger Lambrechts	RSA	18.15
7.	NIGEL SPRATLEY	Eng	17.96
12.	STEVE WHYTE	Sco	16.17
14.	LEE WILTSHIRE	Wal	15.22

Discus (26 Aug)

1.	Werner Reiterer	AUS	62.76
2.	Adewale Olikoju	NGR	62.46
3.	ROBERT WEIR	Eng	60.86
4.	Martin Swart	RSA	56.42
5.	Frits Potgieter	RSA	56.10
6.	GLEN SMITH	Eng	55.84
7.	Ray Lazdins	CAN	55.60
8.	DARRIN MORRIS	Sco	54.98
10.	KEVIN BROWN	Eng	54.06

Hammer (22 Aug)

1.	Sean Carlin	AUS	73.48
2.	PAUL HEAD	Eng	70.18
3.	PETER VIVIAN	Eng	69.80
4.	MICHAEL JONES	Eng	68.42
5.	Angus Cooper	NZL	67.92
6.	Boris Stoikos	CAN	65.84
7.	John Stoikos	CAN	64.82
8.	Demetri Dionisopoulos	AUS	63.52
9.	STEVE WHYTE	Sco	63.36
11.	RUSSELL DEVINE	Sco	61.90

Javelin (28 Aug)

1.	STEVE BACKLEY	Eng	82.74
2.	MICK HILL	Eng	81.84
3.	Gavin Lovegrove	NZL	80.42
4.	NIGEL BEVAN	Wal	80.38
5.	Louis Fouche	RSA	77.00
6.	Andrew Currey	AUS	74.88
7.	MARK ROBERSON	Eng	73.78
8.	Philip Spies	RSA	72.70

Decathlon (23-24 Aug)

1.	Michael Smith	CAN	8326
2.	Peter Winter	AUS	8074
3.	SIMON SHIRLEY	Eng	7980
4.	Dean Smith	AUS	7926
5.	Douglas Pirini	NZL	7840
6.	RAFER JOSEPH	Eng	7663
7.	ALEX KRUGER	Eng	7640
8.	JAMIE QUARRY	Sco	7610

30 Kilometres Walk (25 Aug)

1.	Nick A'hern	AUS	2:07:53
2.	Tim Berrett	CAN	2:08:22
3.	Scott Nelson	NZL	2:09:10
4	DARRELL STONE	Eng	2:11:30
5.	Martin St Pierre	CAN	2:11:51
6.	Steve Baker	AUS	2:14:02
7.	STEPHEN PARTINGTON	IoM	2:14:15
8.	Craig Barrett	NZL	2:14:19
12.	CHRIS MADDOCKS	Eng	2:18:14
13.	MARK EASTON	Eng	2:20:10
14.	STEVE TAYLOR	IoM	2:21:34
	MARTIN BELL	Sco	dnf

4 x 100 Metres Relay (28 Aug)

1.	Canada	38.39
	(Bailey, Gilbert, Chambers, Surin)	
2.	Australia	38.88
	(Naylor, Jackson, Henderson, Marsh)	
3.	ENGLAND	39.39
	(JOHN, BOX, GOEDLUCK,WILLIAMS)	
4.	Jamaica	39.44
5.	SCOTLAND	39.56
6.	Ghania	39.79
7.	Gambia	41.54
8.	Botswana	41.55

4 x 400 Metres Relay (28 Aug)

1.	ENGLAND	3:02.14
	(McKENZIE, CRAMPTON, PATRICK, LADEJO)	
2.	Jamaica	3:02.32
	(Taylor, Blake, Laird, Robinson)	
3.	Trinidad & Tobago	3:02.78
	(Delice, De Silva, Stephens, I Morris)	
4.	Nigeria	3:03.06
5.	Australia	3:03.46
6.	South Africa	3:03.87
7.	WALES	3:07.80
	Kenya	dq

WOMEN

100 Metres wind -0.2 (23 Aug)

1.	Mary Onyali	NGR	11.06
2.	Christy Opara-Thompson	NGR	11.22
3.	PAULA THOMAS	Eng	11.23
4.	Melinda Gainsford	AUS	11.31
5.	Dahlia Duhaney	JAM	11.34
6.	Hermin Joseph	DMN	11.36
7.	Mary Tombiri	NGR	11.38
8.	STEPHANIE DOUGLAS	Eng	11.48
6s2	SIMMONE JACOBS	Eng	11.47
8s2	DANAA MYHILL	IoM	11.63

200 Metres wind 1.3 (26 Aug)

1.	Cathy Freeman	AUS	22.25
2.	Mary Onyali	NGR	22.35
3.	Melinda Gainsford	AUS	22.68
4.	PAULA THOMAS	Eng	22.69
5.	Pauline Davis	BAH	22.77
6.	Dahlia Duhaney	JAM	22.85
7.	Merlene Frazer	JAM	23.18
8.	GERALDINE McLEOD	Eng	23.52
5s2	STEPHANIE DOUGLAS	Eng	23.67

400 Metres (23 Aug)

1.	Cathy Freeman	AUS	50.38
2.	Fatima Yusuf	NGR	50.53
3.	Sandie Richards	JAM	50.59
4.	PHYLIS SMITH	Eng	51.46
5.	Renee Poetschka	AUS	51.51
6.	MELANIE NEEF	Sco	52.09
7.	Olabisi Afolabi	NGR	52.21
8.	Kylie Hanigan	AUS	52.55
6h1	SANDRA DOUGLAS	Eng	55.54
7h2	STEPHANIE LLEWELLYN	NI	56.97
6s2	STEPHANIE McCANN	NI	53.96
7s1	TRACY GODDARD	Eng	53.84

800 Metres (26 Aug)

1.	Inez Turner	JAM	2:01.74
2.	Charmaine Crooks	CAN	2:02.35
3.	Gladys Wamuyu	KEN	2:03.12
4.	CATHY DAWSON	Wal	2:03.17
5.	Selina Kosgei	KEN	2:03.78
6.	Lisa Lightfoot	AUS	2:03.82
7.	Melanie Collins	AUS	2:04.09
8.	Sandra Dawson	AUS	2:04.41
4h1	DAWN GANDY	Eng	2:06.52
4h2	JOANNE LATIMER	NI	2:05.19
5h3	SONYA BOWYER	Eng	2:08.14

1500 Metres (28 Aug)

1.	KELLY HOLMES	Eng	4:08.86
2.	Paula Schnurr	CAN	4:09.65
3.	Gwen Griffiths	RSA	4:10.16
4.	Leah Pells	CAN	4:10.82
5.	Margaret Leaney	AUS	4:11.48
6.	Jackline Maranga	KEN	4:12.84
7.	Robyn Meagher	CAN	4:13.91
8.	Julia Sakala	ZIM	4:18.11
9.	LYNN GIBSON	Eng	4:18.36

3000 Metres (23 Aug)

1.	Angela Chalmers	CAN	8:32.17
2.	Robyn Meagher	CAN	8:45.59
3.	ALISON WYETH	Eng	8:47.98
4.	SONIA McGEORGE	Eng	8:54.91
5.	Suzie Power	AUS	8:59.23
6.	Rose Cheruiyot	KEN	9:00.89
7.	Leah Pells	CAN	9:03.66
8.	LAURA ADAM	Sco	9:06.63

10000 Metres (24 Aug)
1. YVONNE MURRAY   Sco 31:56.97
2. Elana Meyer   RSA 32:06.02
3. Jane Omoro   KEN 32:13.01
4. SUZANNE RIGG   Eng 33:01.40
5. VIKKI McPHERSON   Sco 33:02.74
6. Ulla Marquette   CAN 33:16.29
7. Michelle Dillon   AUS 33:19.01
8. Anne Hare   NZL 33:19.66
10. ANGIE HULLEY   Eng 33:45.04
13. ZAHARA HYDE   Eng 34:43.24

Marathon (27 Aug)
1. Carole Rouillard   CAN 2:30:41
2. Lizanne Bussieres   CAN 2:31:07
3. YVONNE DANSON   Eng 2:32:24
4. KAREN MACLEOD   Sco 2:33:16
5. Nyla Carroll   NZL 2:34:03
6. Angelina Kanana   KEN 2:35:02
7. HAYLEY NASH   Wal 2:35:39
8. SALLY ELLIS   Eng 2:37:14
12. LYNN HARDING   Sco 2:40:57
13. SALLY EASTALL   Eng 2:41:32

100 Metres Hurdles -2.0 (27 Aug)
1. Michelle Freeman   JAM 13.12
2. JACQUI AGYEPONG   Eng 13.14
3. SAM FARQUHARSON   Eng 13.38
4. Dionne Rose   JAM 13.42
5. Donalda Duprey   CAN 13.75
6. Lesley Tashlin   CAN 13.85
7. Jane Flemming   AUS 13.98
   CLOVA COURT   Eng dnf

400 Metres Hurdles (26 Aug)
1. SALLY GUNNELL   Eng 54.51
2. Deon Hemmings   JAM 55.11
3. Debbie Ann Parris   JAM 55.25
4. Donaida Duprey   CAN 55.39
5. GOWRY RETCHAKAN   Eng 56.69
6. JACQUI PARKER   Eng 56.72
7. Karlene Haughton   JAM 57.00
8. Maria Usifo   NGR 59.20

5h1 JANE LOW   Sco 58.43
8h1 STEPHANIE LLEWELLYN   NI 60.41
5h2 STEPHANIE McCANN   NI 58.72

High Jump (27 Aug)
1. Alison Iinverarity   AUS 1.94
2. Charmaine Weavers   RSA 1.94
3. DEBBIE MARTI   Eng 1.91
4. Tania Dixon   NZL 1.91
5= LEA HAGGETT   Eng 1.88

5= Andrea Hughes   AUS 1.88
7. JULIA BENNETT   Eng 1.85
8. Sara McGladdery   CAN 1.85
Q HAZEL MELVIN   Sco 1.80

Long Jump (27 Aug)
1. Nicole Boegman   AUS 6.82 w
2. YINKA IDOWU   Eng 6.73
3. Christy Opara-Thompson   NGR 6.72 w
4. Jackie Edwards   BAH 6.68 w
5. Joanne Henry   NZL 6.65 w
6. Chantal Brunner   NZL 6.63
7. Dionne Rose   JAM 6.47 w
8. DENISE LEWIS   Eng 6.32 w
12. RUTH IRVING   Sco 5.90

Shot (24 Aug)
1. JUDY OAKES   Eng 18.16
2. MYRTLE AUGEE   Eng 17.64
3. Lisa-Marie Vizaniari   AUS 16.61
4. Georgette Reed   CAN 16.45
5. Christine King   NZL 16.27
6. MAGGIE LYNES   Eng 16.23
7. ALISON GREY   Sco 15.25
8. Shannon K-Kristiansen   CAN 14.98
9. Beatrice Faumuina   NZL 14.80
10. Samantha Cox   AUS 14.52
11. Erin Breaugh   CAN 14.25
12. Iammo Launa   NGU 12.71

Discus (23 Aug)
1. Danilea Costian   AUS 63.72
2. Beatrice Faumuina   NZL 57.12
3. Maria Etzebeth   RSA 55.74
4. SHARON ANDREWS   Eng 55.34
5. JACQUI McKERNAN   NI 54.86
6. Lisa-Marie Vizaniari   AUS 53.88
7. DEBBIE CALLAWAY   Eng 53.16
8. Theresa Brick   CAN 52.12
10. LORRAINE SHAW   Eng 50.50
   ALISON GREY   Sco nm

Javelin (26 Aug)
1. Louise McPaul   AUS 63.76
2. Kirsten Nabein   NZL 60.40
3. SHARON GIBSON   Eng 58.20
4. Joanna Stone   AUS 57.60
5. Valerie Tulloch   CAN 57.26
6. Kate Farrow   AUS 56.98
7. Laverne Eve   BAH 55.54
8. Kaye Nordstrom   NZL 54.90
12. KAREN COSTELLO   Sco 48.58

Heptathlon (22-23 Aug)
1. DENISE LEWIS   Eng 6325
2. Jane FLemming   AUS 6317
3. Catherine Bond-Mills   CAN 6193
4. Joanne Henry   NZL 6121
5. JENNY KELLY   Eng 5658
6. Najuma Fletcher   GUY 5611
7. Kim Vanderhoek   CAN 5467
8. Caroline Kola   KEN 5407
9. EMMA LINDSAY   Sco 5353
10. Kendall Matheson   CAN 4539
   CLOVA COURT   Eng dnf
   LISA GIBBS   Wal dnf

10 Kilometres Walk (25 Aug)
1. Kerry Junna-Saxby   AUS 44:25
2. Anne Manning   AUS 44:37
3. Janice McCaffrey   CAN 44:54
4. Holly Gerke   CAN 45:43
5. VICKY LUPTON   Eng 45:58
6. LISA LANGFORD   Eng 46:01
7. VERITY LARBY-SNOOK   Sco 46:06
9. CAROLYN PARTINGTON   IoM 47:21
11. KAREN SMITH   Eng 48:45

4 x 100 Metres Relay (28 Aug)
1. Nigeria   42.99
  (Idehen, Tombiri, O-Thompson, Onyali)
2. Australia   43.43
  (Miers, Freeman, Gainsford, Sambell)
3. ENGLAND   43.46
  (DOUGLAS, McLEOD, JACOBS, THOMAS)
4. Jamaica   43.51
5. Bahamas   44.89
6. Canada   45.15
7. Ghania   45.72

4 x 400 Metres Relay (28 Aug)
1. ENGLAND   3:27.06
  (SMITH, GODDARD, KEOUGH, GUNNELL)
2. Jamaica   3:27.63
  (R Campbell, Hemmings, Turner, Richards)
3. Canada   3:32.52
  (Yakiwchuk, Bowen, Duprey, Crooks)
4. Ghania   3:47.49
  Australia   (3:26.84)   dq
  Nigeria   (3:34.67)   dq

HUN v GB & NI v RUS v UKR (Jumps) Salótarján, HUN 12 September 1994

MEN

High Jump
1. Javier Sotomayor   CUB 2.36
2. Dragutin Topic   YUG 2.25
3. BRENDAN REILLY   2.25
18. AHMED FAYYAZ   2.05

Pole Vault
1. Konstantin Semyonov   RUS 5.61
2. Vitaliy Stepanov   RUS 5.41
3. Pál Rohánszky   HUN 5.31
4. NEIL WINTER   5.20
5= NICK BUCKFIELD   5.00

WOMEN

High Jump
1. Larisa Serebrinskaya   RUS 1.87
2. Viktoriya Fyodorova   RUS 1.87
3. Yelena Yelesina   RUS 1.87
9. JULIE MAJOR   1.70
10. LINDSAY EVANS   1.70

Match Result 1. Russia   37   2. Ukraine   26   3. Hungary   21.5   4. GREAT BRITAIN & NI   20.5

WORLD CUP London (CP) 9-11 September 1994

MEN

100 Metres wind -0.3 (9 Sep)
1. LINDFORD CHRISTIE   10.21
2. Olapade Adeniken   AFR/NGR 10.25
3. Talal Mansour   ASI/QAT 10.31
4. Aleksandr Porkhomovskiy   EUR/RUS 10.40
5. Augustine Nketia   OCE/NZL 10.42
6. Andre da Silva   AME/BRA 10.49
7. Marc Blume   GER   10.52
8. Vince Henderson   USA   10.63

200 Metres wind -1.4 (11 Sep)
1. JOHN REGIS   20.45
2. Frank Fredericks   AFR/NAM 20.55
3. Geir Moen   EUR/NOR 20.72
4. Ron Clark   USA   21.00
5. Robert Kunicki   GER   21.02
6= Ivan Garcia   AME/CUB 21.10
6= Damien Marsh   OCE/AUS 21.10
8. Huang Danwei   ASI/CHN 21.23

400 Metres (10 Sep)
1. Antonio Pettigrew   USA   45.26
2. DU'AINE LADEJO   45.44
3. Inaldo de Sena   AME/BRA 45.67
4. Ibrahim Ismail   ASI/QAT 45.74
5. Matthias Rusterholz   EUR/SWZ 45.92
6. Samson Kitur   AFR/KEN 45.98
7. Paul Greene   OCE/AUS 46.29
8. Daniel Bittner   GER   46.73

800 Metres (9 Sep)
1. Mark Everett   USA   1:46.02
2. William Tanui   AFR/KEN 1:46.84
3. CRAIG WINROW   1:47.16
4. Brendan Hanigan   OCE/AUS 1:47.41
5. Nico Motchebon   GER   1:47.67
6. Tomas de Teresa   EUR/SPA 1:48.04
7. Jose Luiz Barbosa   AME/BRA 1:48.26
8. Kim Yong-Hwan   ASI/KOR 1:51.88

1500 Metres (10 Sep)
1. Noureddine Morceli   AFR/ALG 3:34.70
2. Rudiger Stenzel   GER   3:40.04
3. Mohamed Suleiman   ASI/QAT 3:40.52
4. Jason Pyrah   USA   3:41.55
5. GARY LOUGH   3:44.10
6. Jose Valente   AME/BRA 3:44.32
7. Isaac Viciosa   EUR/SPA 3:47.22
8. Richard Potts   OCE/NZL 3:54.09

5000 Metres (11 Sep)
1. Brahim Lahlafi   AFR/MAR 13:27.96
2. JOHN NUTTALL   13:32.47
3. Martin Bremer   GER   13:33.57
4. Robbie Johnston   OCE/NZL 13:37.13
5. Bahadur Prasad   ASI/IND 13:37.20
6. Gabino Apolonio   AME/MEX 13:51.73
7. Abel Anton   EUR/SPA 13:55.02
8. Dan Mayer   USA   14:07.65

10000 Metres (9 Sep)
1. Khalid Skah   AFR/MAR 27:38.74
2. Antonio Silio   AME/ARG 28:16.54
3. ROB DENMARK   28:20.65
4. Stephane Franke   GER   28:32.07
5. Olayan A Al-Qahtani   ASI/SAU 28:41.21
6. Robert Stefko   EUR/SVK 28:45.32
7. Phillip Clode   OCE/NZL 29:19.87
8. Jim Westphal   USA   29:22.39

3000 Metres Steeplechase (10 Sep)
1. Moses Kiptanui   AFR/KEN 8:28.28
2. Sa'ed S Al-Asmari   ASI/SAU 8:35.74
3. Aless. Lambruschini   EUR/ITA 8:40.34
4. COLIN WALKER   8:41.14
5. Martin Strege   GER   8:45.18
6. Ricardo Vera   AME/URU 8:58.80
7. Dan Reese   USA   9:15.16
8. Peter Brett   OCE/AUS 9:19.11

110 Metres Hurdles -1.6 (11 Sep)
1. TONY JARRETT   13.23
2. Allen Johnson   USA   13.29
3. Emilio Valle   AME/CUB 13.45
4. Florian Schwarthoff   GER   13.47
5. Li Tong   ASI/CHN 13.59
6. Kyle Vander-Kuyp   OCE/AUS 13.71
7. Kehinde Aladefa   AFR/NGR 14.03
8. Antti Haapakosi   EUR/FIN 14.11

400 Metres Hurdles (9 Sep)
1. Samuel Matete   AFR/ZAM 48.77
2. Oleg Tverdokhleb   EUR/UKR 49.28
3. Eronildo Nd Araujo   AME/BRA 49.62
4. Olaf Hense   GER   49.97
5. Kazuhiko Yamazaki   ASI/JPN 50.22
6. GARY CADOGAN   50.48
7. Rohan Robinson   OCE/AUS 51.12
8. Marco Morgan   USA   53.58

High Jump (11 Sep)
1. Javier Sotomayor   AME/CUB 2.40
2. Tim Forsyth   OCE/AUS 2.28
3. STEVE SMITH   2.28
4. Steinar Hoen   EUR/NOR 2.25
5. Wolfgang Kreissig   GER   2.20
6. Yoshiteru Kaihoko   ASI/JPN 2.20
7. Khemraj Naiko   AFR/MRI 2.15
8. Jeff Wylie   USA   2.15

Pole Vault (10 Sep)
1. Okkert Brits   AFR/RSA 5.90
2. Jean Galfione   EUR/FRA 5.75
3= Alberto Manzano   AME/CUB 5.40
3= Andrej Tiwontschik   GER   5.40
5. Scott Huffman   USA   5.40
6. Grigoriy Yegorov   ASI/KZK 5.40
7. James Miller   OCE/AUS 5.20
  NEIL WINTER   nh (5.20)

Long Jump (9 Sep)
1. FRED SALLE   8.10
2. Douglas de Souza   AME/BRA 7.96
3. Dion Bentley   USA   7.93
4. Obinna Eregbu   AFR/NGR 7.87
5. Georg Ackermann   GER   7.84
6. Tetsuya Shida   ASI/JPN 7.72
7. David Culbert   OCE/AUS 7.59
8. Milan Gombala   EUR/TCH 7.37

Triple Jump (10 Sep)
1. Yoelvis Quesada   AME/CUB 17.61
2. JULIAN GOLLEY   17.06
3. Oleg Sakirkin   ASI/KZK 16.81
4. Lotfi Khaida   AFR/ALG 16.75w
5. Serge Helan   EUR/FRA 16.67w
6. Reggie Jones   USA   16.41w
7. Wolfgang Knabe   GER   16.07
8. Andrew Murphy   OCE/AUS 15.86w

Shot (9 Sep)
1. C J Hunter   USA   19.92
2. Aleksandr Kimenklo   EUR/UKR 19.16
3. Courtney Ireland   OCE/NZL 18.93
4. Sven Buder   GER   18.88
5. Burger Lambrechts   AFR/RSA 18.08
6. Carlos Fandino   AME/CUB 18.04
7. Bilal Saad Mubarak   ASI/QAT 17.40
8. NIGEL SPRATLEY   17.20

Discus (10 Sep)
1. Vladimir Dubrovshchik   EUR/BLS 64.54
2. Alexis Elizarde   AME/CUB 61.50
3. Adewale Olukoju   AFR/NGR 60.22
4. Werner Reiterer   OCE/AUS 60.22
5. Jürgen Schult   GER   58.88
6. Mike Gravelle   USA   56.76
7. ROBERT WEIR   55.86
  Bilal Saad Mubarak   ASI/QAT dns

Hammer (10 Sep)
1. Andrey Abduvaliyev   ASI/TJK 81.72
2. Lance Deal   USA   81.14
3. Heinz Weis   GER   80.32
4. Vasiliy Sidorenko   EUR/RUS 76.34
5. Alberto Sanchez   AME/CUB 74.72
6. Sean Carlin   OCE/AUS 74.54
7. Hakim Toumi   AFR/ALG 69.38
8. PAUL HEAD   68.38

Javelin (11 Sep)
1. STEVE BACKLEY   85.02
2. Raymond Hecht   GER   84.36
3. Gavin Lovegrove   OCE/NZL 82.28
4. Patrik Boden   EUR/SWE 80.86
5. Louis Fouche   AFR/RSA 76.98
6. Zhang Lianbiao   ASI/CHN 76.96
7. Emeterio Gonzalez   AME/CUB 76.42
8. Todd Riech   USA   70.28

4 x 100 Metres Relay (10 Sep)
1. GREAT BRITAIN & NI   38.46
(BRAITHWAITE, JARRETT, REGIS, CHRISTIE)
2. Africa   38.97
(Nwakpa, Tuffour, Kayode, Adeniken)
3. USA   39.33
(Witherspoon, McGhee, Carter, Jefferson)
4. Americas   39.39
(A da Silva, Mahorn, A Silva, R da Silva)
5. Europe/France   39.46
6. Asia/China   55.58
  Germany   dq
  Oceania   dnf

4 x 400 Metres Relay (11 Sep)
1. GREAT BRITAIN & NI   3:01.34
(McKENZIE, LADEJO, BAULCH, BLACK)
2. Africa   3:02.66
(Kemboi, Matete, Kitur, Bada)
3. Europe   3:03.26
(Rusterholz, Diagana, Vdovin, Golovastov)
4. Germany   3:04.15
(Bittner, Voelkel, Motchebon, Hense)
5. Americas   3:04.28
6. Oceania   3:05.70
7. Asia   3:12.38
  USA   dns

WOMEN

100 Metres wind -1.7 (10 Sep)
1. Irina Privalova   EUR/RUS 11.32
2. Liliana Allen   AME/CUB 11.50
3. Mary Onyali   AFR/NGR 11.52
4. Melinda Gainsford   OCE/AUS 11.55
5. Melanie Paschke   GER   11.64
6. Liu Xiaomei   ASI/CHN 11.66
7. PAULA THOMAS   11.67
8. Sheila Echols   USA   11.81

200 Metres wind -1.7 (9 Sep)
1. Merlene Ottey   AME/JAM 22.23
2. Irina Privalova   EUR/RUS 22.51
3. Cathy Freeman   OCE/AUS 22.72
4. Mary Onyali   AFR/NGR 22.82
5. Chen Zhaojing   ASI/CHN 23.20
6. PAULA THOMAS   23.22
7. Melanie Paschke   GER   23.32
8. Chryste Gaines   USA   24.21

400 Metres (11 Sep)
1. Irina Privalova   EUR/RUS 50.62
2. Fatima Yusuf   AFR/NGR 50.80
3. Jearl Miles   USA   51.24
4. PHYLIS SMITH   51.36
5. Julia Duporty   AME/CUB 52.48
6. Zhang Hangyun   ASI/CHN 52.79
7. Kylie Hanigan   OCE/AUS 53.82
8. Anja Rücker   GER   54.21

800 Metres (10 Sep)
1. Maria Mutola   AFR/MOZ 1:58.27
2. Luciana Mendes   AME/BRA 2:00.13
3. Natalya Dukhnova   EUR/BLS 2:02.81
4. Kati Kovacs   GER   2:03.32
5. Joetta Clark   USA   2:03.76
6. Lisa Lightfoot   OCE/AUS 2:03.88
7. CATHY DAWSON   2:04.13
8. Chen Xuehui   ASI/CHN 2:09.82

1500 Metres (9 Sep)
1. Hassiba Boulmerka   AFR/ALG 4:01.05
2. Angela Chalmers   AME/CAN 4:01.73
3. KELLY HOMES   4:10.81
4. Margaret Leaney   OCE/AUS 4:12.16
5. Sonia O'Sullivan   EUR/IRE 4:12.30
6. Kathy Franey   USA   4:21.48
7. Antje Beggerow   GER   4:23.65
8. Liu Jing   ASI/CHN 4:34.02

3000 Metres (11 Sep)
1. YVONNE MURRAY   8:56.81
2. Robyn Meagher   AME/CAN 9:05.81
3. Gabriela Szabo   EUR/ROM 9:15.16
4. Liu Jianying   ASI/CHN 9:15.39
5. Susie Power   OCE/AUS 9:16.01
6. Dorte Koster   GER   9:23.32
7. Cassie McWilliam   USA   9:26.50
8. Gwen Griffiths   AFR/RSA 9:31.91

10000 Metres (10 Sep)
1. Elana Meyer   AFR/RSA 30:52.51
2. Fernanda Ribeiro   EUR/POR 31:04.25
3. Wei Li   ASI/CHN 32:37.94
4. Claudia Dreher   GER   33:04.79
5. SUZANNE RIGG   33:38.14
6. Anne Cross   OCE/AUS 33:40.75
7. Laura Lamena-Coll   USA   33:43.66
8. Paola Cabrera   AME/MEX 34:41.22

100 Metres Hurdles -0.9 (10 Sep)
1. Aliuska Lopez   AME/CUB 12.91
2. Svetla Dimitrova   EUR/BUL 12.95
3. JACQUI AGYEPONG   13.02
4. Nicole Ramalalanirina AFR/MAD 13.24
5. Kristin Patzwahl   GER   13.68
6. Luo Bin   ASI/CHN 13.89
7. Sherlese Taylor   USA   14.10
8. Rachel Links   OCE/AUS 14.14

400 Metres Hurdles (9 Sep)
1. SALLY GUNNELL   54.80
2. Silvia Rieger   GER   56.14
3. Anna Knoroz   EUR/RUS 56.63
4. Donalda Duprey   AME/CAN 56.67
5. Nezha Bidouane   AFR/MAR 57.35
6. Natayla Torshina   ASI/KZK 57.60
7. Tonya Lee   USA   59.61
8. Rebecca Campbell   OCE/AUS 60.96

High Jump (9 Sep)
1. Britta Bilac   EUR/SLO 1.91
2. Charmaine Weavers   AFR/RSA 1.91
3. Silvia Costa   AME/CUB 1.91
4. Heike Balck   GER   1.88
5. Svetlana Zalevskaya ASI/KZK 1.85
6. DEBBI MARTI   1.85
7. Alison Inverarity   OCE/AUS 1.85
8. Karol Damon   USA   1.80

Long Jump (11 Sep)
1. Inessa Kravets   EUR/UKR 7.00
2. Niurka Montalvo   AME/CUB 6.70
3. Christy O-Thompson AFR/NGR 6.66
4. Yao Weili   ASI/CHN 6.60
5. Sabine Braun   GER   6.54
6. YINKA IDOWU   6.51
7. Nicole Boegman   OCE/AUS 6.45
8. Sheila Echols   USA   6.23

Triple Jump (9 Sep)
1. Anna Biryukova   EUR/RUS 14.46
2. Sheila H-Strudwick USA   14.00
3. Ren Ruiping   ASI/CHN 13.84
4. MICHELLE GRIFFITH   13.70
5. Niurka Montalvo   AME/CUB 13.64
6. Helga Radtke   GER   13.47
7. Tania Dixon   OCE/NZL 12.55
8. Hasna Atiallah   AFR/MAR 12.44

Shot (10 Sep)
1. Huang Zhihong   ASI/CHN 19.45
2. Belsy Laza   AME/CUB 19.07
3. Astrid Kumbernuss   GER   18.89
4. Viktoriya Pavlysh   EUR/UKR 18.67
5. JUDY OAKES   17.92
6. Dawn Dumble   USA   15.63
7. Fouzia Fatihi   AFR/MAR 15.48
8. Lisa-Marie Vizaniari OCE/AUS 15.23

Discus (11 Sep)
1. Ilke Wyludda   GER   65.30
2. Ellina Zvereva   EUR/BLS 63.86
3. Daniela Costian   OCE/AUS 63.38
4. Barbara Echevarria AME/CUB 62.90
5. Qui Qiaoping   ASI/CHN 57.92
6. Connie Price-Smith USA   57.04
7. JACKIE MCKERNAN   56.28
8. Lisette Etsebeth   AFR/RSA 51.54

Javelin (9 Sep)
1. Trine Hattestad   EUR/NOR 66.48
2. Isel Lopez   AME/CUB 61.40
3. Karen Forkel   GER   61.26
4. Louise McPaul   OCE/AUS 59.92
5. Zhang Li   ASI/CHN 58.82
6. SHARON GIBSON   53.32
7. Donna Mayhew   USA   51.50
8. Ronah Dwinger   AFR/RSA 49.02

4 x 100 Metres Relay (11 Sep)
1. Africa/Nigeria   42.92
(Idehen, Tombiri, O-Thompson, Onyali)
2. Germany   43.22
(Philip, Lichtenhagen, Knoll, Paschke)
3. Oceania   43.36
(Miers, Freeman, Gainsford, Seymour)
4. Asia   43.63
(C Yan, Liu Xiaomei, Chen Zhaojing, Huang Xiaoyan)
5. USA   43.79
6. Europe   43.99
7. Americas   44.26
8. GREAT BRITAIN & NI   44.45
(AGYEPONG, MCLEOD, JACOBS, THOMAS)

4 x 400 Metres Relay (9 Sep)
1. GREAT BRITAIN & NI   3:27.36
(SMITH, KEOUGH, NEEF, GUNNELL)
2. Germany   3:27.59
(Janke, Rohlander, Meissner, Rücker)
3. Americas   3:27.91
(McLeon, Richards, Bonne, Duporty)
4. Europe/France   3:29.07
(Landre, Dorsile, Elien, Perec)
5. USA   3:30.99
6. Oceania/Australia   3:31.63
7. Asia   3:40.89
dq Africa   (3:30.31)

MEN
1. Africa   116
2. GREAT BRITAIN & NI   111
3. Americas   95
4. Europe   91
5. Germany   85.5
6. USA   78
7. Asia   75
8. Oceania   62.5

WOMEN
1. Europe   111
2. Americas   98
3. Germany   79
4. Africa   78
5. GREAT BRITIAN & NI   73
6. Asia   67
7. Oceania   57
8. USA   48

Results

98

REGIONAL CHAMPIONSHIPS

	SCOTLAND Edinburgh, 24-25 June		WALES Cwmban , 18 June		NORTHERN IRELAND Antrim, 18 June	
MEN						
100	Jamie Henderson	10.37	Tremayne Rutherford	10.66	Mark Allen	11.20
200	Doug Walker	21.04	Jamie Baulch	21.85	Mark Allen	22.55
400	Paul McBurney (NI)	46.89	Iwan Thomas	47.09	Paul McBurney	47.2
	5. Hugh Kerr	48.24				
800	Tom McKean	1:48.69	Darrell Maynard	1:54.87	Davey Wilson	1:49.39
1500	Glen Stewart	3:48.41	Christian Stephenson	3:55.19	Bob Farren	3:53.43
5000	Chris Robison	14:08.52	Justin Chaston	14:01.73	Jim Campbell	14:11.85
10000	Tommy Murray	29:12.35	Mark Healey	31:13.84		
3kSt	Graeme Croll	8:53.26	David Lee	9:02.21	G Crossen	9:33.35
110H	Jamie Quarry	14.10	Paul Gray	14.38	Ciaran Doherty	15.19
400H	A Bursumato (Eng)	52.23	David Griffin	52.75	Douglas Thorn	53.80
	2. Nigel Gardner	53.00				
HJ	Geoff Parsons	2.20	David Nolan	2.06	Adam Smith	1.90
PV	Mark Johnston	5.11	Tim Thomas	4.90	M Ramsey	3.90
	3. Doug Hamilton	4.60				
LJ	John Mackenzie	7.40	Steve Ingram	7.91 w	G McCluskey	6.74
TJ	John Wiggins	13.79	Paul Farmer	14.61 w	Adam Smith	14.07
SP	J McNamara (AUS)	17.26	Lee Wiltshire	16.93	Mike Atkinson	13.75
	2. James Mason	15.45				
DT	Michael Jemi-Alade	47.80	Andrew Turner	43.28	John Moreland	50.44
HT	Russell Devine	61.72	Gareth Jones	58.74		
JT	Philip Parry (Eng)	66.04	Nigel Bevan	68.68	Damien Crawford	61.24
	5. Graham Lay	57.94				

Linwood 16-17 July   Belfast 8-9 July

Dec	Allan Leiper	6044			Ian Condron	5684

	SCOTLAND		WALES		NORTHERN IRELAND	
WOMEN						
100	Aileen McGillivary	11.56	Sallyanne Short	12.17	Stephanie McCann	12.75
200	Sinead Dudgeon	24.24	Sallyanne Short	24.75	Stephanie McCann	24.95
400	Leigh Ferrier	54.99	Gillian Cashell	54.77	Stephanie McCann	54.0
800	Mary McClung	2:09.35	Cathy Dawson	2:06.10	Jill Bruce	2:18.02
1500	Laura Adam	4:20.31	Wendy Ore	4:27.69	Jill Bruce	4:33.15
3000	Susan Ridley	9:40.32	Deborah Newhams	9:34.65		
10000	Karen McLeod	34:05.00				
100H	Sarah Richmond	14.02 w	Bethan Edwards	14.36	Elaine Faulkner	14.44
400H	Jane Low	58.66	Natasha Bartlett	59.25		
HJ	Helen Melvin	1.75	Teresa Andrews	1.70	E Murphy	1.50
PV	Pamela Murray	2.40				
LJ	Ruth Irving	6.00	Sallyanne Short	5.76 w	S Colhoun	5.16
TJ	Karen Skeggs	11.89	Nicola Jupp	10.75	E Orr	10.51
SP	Alison Grey	14.87	Krissy Owen	12.88	Alison Moffitt	11.00
DT	Alison Grey	48.86	Jayne Fisher	45.38	Alison Moffitt	40.00
HT	Julie Lavender	47.32	Sarah Moore	48.32	Julie Kirkpatrick	42.92
	2. Jean Clark	46.16				
JT	Karen Costello	50.96	Caroline White	49.24	Alison Moffitt	47.00

Linwood 16-17 July

Hep	Kim Crowther (Eng)	5051
	2. Elaine Donald	4497

AREA CHAMPIONSHIPS

	SOUTH London (CP), 25-26 June		MIDLANDS Stoke, 15-16 July		NORTH Derby, 16 July	
MEN						
100	Terry Williams	10.49	Paul White	10.61	Allyn Condon	10.70
200	Terry Williams	21.08	Paul White	21.21	Allyn Condon	21.4
400	Mark Morris	46.77	Adrian Bryan	47.58	Dave Deacon	48.10
800	Andrew Lill	1:48.18	Andy Hart	1:50.83	Mark Benson	1:53.09
1500	Paul Drake	3:53.65	Robert Whalley	3:45.55	Vince Wilson	3:48.71
5000	Spencer Newport	14:20.64	*S Hope	14:40.2	Paul Freary	14:10.76
			*Birmingham 21 May			
3kSt	Adrian Green	9:00.41	Raymond Plant	9:20.87	Mick Hawkins	8:59.44
110H	Lloyd Cowan	14.10	Paul Stubbs	14.40	Kevin Lumsdon	14.20
400H	Eddie Betts	51.15	Paul Hibbert	53.2	Tony Williams	51.50
HJ	Fayyaz Ahmed	2.11	Andrew Lynch	2.14	Rob Brocklebank	2.05
PV	Nick Buckfield	5.32	Neil Winter	5.35	Matt Belsham	4.90
LJ	Courtney Charles	7.45	Steve Phillips	7.39	Stephen Rowbotham	7.12
TJ	Francis Agyepong	16.20w	Paul Weston	15.02	Mathias Ogbeta (NIG)	15.17
					2. David Sanderson	15.14
SP	Nigel Spratley	17.25	Laine Snook	15.53	Paul Reed	16.19
DT	Neville Thompson	53.58	Kevin Brown	56.68	James Muirhead	51.82
HT	Philip Spivey	62.26	Paul Carlin (AUS)	68.76	David Smith	65.98
	2. Chris Howe	62.06	2. Steve Pearson	63.36		
JT	Colin Mackenzie	78.86	Mark Pinner	60.24	Kevin Hill	63.06
3kW	Mark Easton	12:23.80				

Sheffield 30 April/1 May

Dec	Robert Laing	6726

	SOUTH		MIDLANDS		NORTH	
WOMEN						
100	Samantha Farquharson	11.87	Clova Court	11.77	Sophia Smith	11.90
200	Simmone Jacobs	23.48	Michelle Thomas	24.71	Sophia Smith	23.9
400	Hayley Clements	54.62	Leigh Ferrier	54.88	Paula Cohen	54.02
800	Lisa Thompson	2:08.73	Alyson Layzell	2:10.97	Vickie Lawrence	2:07.05
1500	Zara Hyde	4:21.62	Maxine Newman	4:24.90	Amanda Thorpe	4:22.99
3000	Suzanne Morley	9:23.08			Kim Bennett	9:42.90
100H	Lesley-Anne Skeete	13.66	Clova Court	13.46	Diane Allahgreen	13.43
400H	Claire Bleasdale	58.86	Bonita Benjamin	61.76	Vyvyan Rhodes	58.78
HJ	Debbie Marti	1.80	Julie Crane	1.78	Kelly Thirkle	1.76
PV	Claire Ridgely	3.35	Paula Wright	3.30	Rebekah Telford	2.45
LJ	Ashia Hansen	6.27	Denise Lewis	6.38	Ann Brooks	6.00
TJ	Evette Finikin	12.65w	Katie Evans	12.01	Caroline Miller	12.02
SP	Maggie Lynes	16.37	Lorraine Shaw	14.21	Kelly Kane (IRE)	13.24
					2. Sara Allen	12.20
DT	Debbie Callaway	54.46	Lorraine Shaw	47.42	Karen Smith	44.70
HT	Lyn Sprules	53.92	Lorraine Shaw	58.96	Samantha Burns-Salmond	43.96
JT	Jo Burton	52.14	Sharon Gibson	55.20	Diane Royle	53.78
3kW	Verity Larby-Snook	13:31.78				

Sheffield, 30 April

10k	Lisa Melkevik	35:36.58

AGE CHAMPIONSHIPS

Under 20 MEN
Bedford, 2-3 July

100	Julian Golding	10.52
200	Julian Golding	21.02
400	Mark Hylton	46.94
800	Paul Bryne (AUS)	1:48.25
	2.Eddie King	1:48.93
1500	Paul Cleary (AUS)	3:49.45
	3. Neil Caddy	3:49.94
5000	Blair Martin (NZL)	14:35.77
	2. Darius Burrows	14:45.90
3kSt	Christopher Elliott	9:09.47
110H	John Whelan	14.38
400H	Matt Beckenham (AUS)	52.58
	3. Alex Hunte	53.09
HJ	Jagan Hames (AUS)	2.21
	2.Antoine Burke	2.18
PV	Neil Young	4.75
LJ	Shane Hair	7.58
	2. Chris Davidson	7.46w
TJ	Tayo Erogbogbo	15.92
SP	Justin Anlezark (AUS)	15.85
	3. William Fuller	15.08
DT	Justin Anlezark (AUS)	49.54
	2. James South	47.86
HT	Karl Andrews	65.30
JT	Shane Wylie (AUS)	69.64
	4. Stuart Faben	66.30
10kW	Dion Russell (AUS)	43:26.22
	Bimingham, 31 July	
3000	Chris Elliott	8:31.20

Under 17
Birmingham, 30-31 July

	Dwain Chambers	10.76
	Matthew Clements	21.8
	Ian Horsburgh	49.2
	Michael Combe	1:54.57
	Andrew Graffin	3:59.11
1500St	Robert Brown	4:18.20
100H	Damien Greaves	13.0
	Mark Rowlands	53.30
	Darren Joseph	1.96
	Stephen McLennan	4.20
	Nathan Morgan	6.80
	Dean Macey	14.26
	Emeka Udechuku	16.46
	Emeka Udechuku	51.26
	Matthew Bell	60.54
	Mark Francis	61.86
5kW	Jamie Costin	28:00.12
	Bedford, 3 July	
	Alan Graffin	8:51.62
	Stoke 7-8 August	
Oct	Trevor McGlynn	4545

Under 15
Birmingham, 30-31 July

	André Dufus	11.25
	André Dufus	22.7
	Marc Newton	51.0
	Lee Hughes	2:03.05
	Sam Boden	4:13.9
80H	Thomas Benn	11.41
	Jamie Dalton	1.84
	Christian Linksey	4.10
	Kevin Hibbins	6.03
	Daniel Hutchinson	13.29
	Jamie Hunt	14.85
	Carl Myerscough	39.16
	James Hawkins	57.28
3kW	Matthew Hales	14:51.12
	Bedford, 2 July	
	Simon Bentley	9:25.08
	Stoke 7-8 August	
Pen	Marc Newton	3032

Under 20 WOMEN
Bedford, 3-4 July

100	Diane Allahgreen	11.89
200	Susan Williams	24.27
400	Tamsyn Lewis (AUS)	54.52
	2. Jo Sloane	55.12
800	Jeina Mitchell	2:05.85
1500	Susie Powell (AUS)	4:19.54
	2. Catherine Berry	4:25.58
3000	Nicola Slater	9:21.20
100H	Diane Allahgreen	13.64
400H	Rebecca Campbell (AUS)	59.09
	2. Allison Curbishley	59.16
HJ	Julie Crane	1.78
PV	Clare Ridgley	3.40
LJ	Adele Forester	6.03
TJ	Nicole Mladenis (AUS)	12.46
	2. Shani Anderson	12.16
SP	Kylie Standing (AUS)	13.76
	3. Helen Wilding	12.66
DT	Monique Nacsa (AUS)	49.38
	2. Philippa Roles	44.90
HT	Lyn Sprules	54.48
JT	Kirsty Morrison	53.88
5kW	Natalie Saville (AUS)	23:12.03
	3. Katherine Horwill	25:31.47

Under 17
Birmingham, 30-31 July

	Rebecca Drummond	11.9
	Lesley Owusu	24.99
300	Lesley Owusu	38.71
	Marcia Lynch (IRE)	2:13.95
	2. Lucy Pringle	2:14.23
	Marcia Lynch (IRE)	4:37.4
	2. Dawn Adams	4:38.7
	*Caroline McNulty	10:08.96
	* Bedford 3 July	
80H	Liz Fairs	11.48
300H	Natasha Danvers	42.60
	Susan Jones	1.70
	Clare Ridgley	3.20
	Rebecca Lewis	5.69
	Jayne Ludlow	11.14
	Philippa Roles	12.82
	Philippa Roles	44.40
	Rachael Beverley	41.26
	Nicola MacKay	42.60
	Nina Howley	25:25.07

Under 15
Birmingham, 30-31 July

	Sarah Wilhelmy	12.0
	Sarah Wilhelmy	24.54
	Amanda Pritchard	2:12.2
	Emma Alberts	4:38.60
75H	Leanda Adams	11.30
	Antonia Marie Bemrose	1.70
	Jade Johnson	5.68
	Francis Reid-Hughes	11.16
	Natalie Kerr	37.12
3kW	Sarah Bennett	15:28.31
	Kelly Morgan	36.08

UK MERIT RANKINGS 1994 Compiled by Peter Matthews

This is the 27th successive year that I have compiled annual merit rankings of British athletes. As usual they are based on an assessment of form during the outdoor season. The major factors by which the rankings are determined are win-loss record, performances in the major meetings, and sequence of marks.

I endeavour to be as objective as possible, but form can often provide conflicting evidence, or perhaps an athlete may not have shown good enough results against leading rivals, or in very important competition, to justify a ranking which his or her ability might otherwise warrant.

I can only rank athletes on what they have actually achieved. Much depends on having appropriate opportunities. It is obviously harder for an athlete living in a remote part of the UK than one who is close to the major centres of competition, and it may be hard to break into the élite who get the invitations for the prestige meetings. Difficulties also arise when athletes reach peak form at different parts of the season or through injury miss significant competition.

Once again it should be pointed out that the rankings are by no means necessarily the order in which I think the athletes would have finished in an idealised contest, but simply my attempt to assess what has actually happened in 1994.

For each event the top 12 are ranked. On the first line is shown the athletes name, then their date of birth followed by the number of years ranked in the top ten (including 1994) and their ranking last year (1993), and finally, in brackets, their best mark prior to 1993. The following lines include their best six performances of the year (followed, for completeness, by significant indoor marks indicated by 'i', although indoor form, the subject of a separate assessment, is not considered in the rankings). Then follow placings at major meetings, providing a summary of the athlete's year at the event.

Abbreviations include

AAA v LC	AAA v Loughborough Students
BL	British League
CAU	Inter-Counties at Corby
CG	Commonwealth Games
Cork	Cork City Sports
Cup	Guardian Cup Final at Bedford
EC	European Championships
E.Clubs	European Clubs Cup
ECup	European Cup
E.Sch	English Schools
EU23Cp	European Under 23 Cup at Ostrava
GhG	Gateshead Games
GPF	Grand Prix Final at Paris
GWG	Goodwill Games
IA	Women's inter-area at Corby
IR	Inter-regional at Birmingham
IS	Inter-Services
JI	Junior International
	v PGR UK v Poland, Germany & Russia
	v I,C Under 19 UK v Italy & Czech Republic
K. Lynn	Under 23 international at Kings Lynn
McD	McDonald Games at Sheffield
Nitra	England v 4 nations at Nitra
SoG	Solent Games
TSB-CP	TSB Grand Prix at Crystal Palace
TDB-Ed	TSB Challenge at Edinburgh
vUSA	KP Classic at Gateshead, including UK v USA
W v Sc,IT	Wales v Scotland, Israel and Turkey at Istanbul
WCp	World Cup
WG	Welsh Games at Wrexham
WJ	World Junior Championships

BRITISH MERIT RANKINGS 1994 - MEN

100 METRES
1. **Linford Christie** 2.4.60 (12y, 1) 9.87 '93   9.91, 9.91w, 9.98, 10.01, 10.02 x 3, 10.03 x 3;
   1 CAU, 1 AAA, 1 ECp, 1 GhG, 3 Linz, 2 TSB-CP, 1 TSB-Ed, 1 EC, 1 Zürich, 1 Brussels, 1 CG, 2 Rieti, 3 Berlin, 2 GPF, 1 WCp, 1 Tokyo
2. **Jason John** 17.10.71 (5y, 2=) 10.30/10.12w '93   10.08w, 10.16w, 10.23, 10.29, 10.36, 10.37; 9.46y; 2 IR, 4 AAA, 1 Nitra, 5 TSB-CP, 5 TSB-Ed, 4 v USA, 8 EC, 5q2 CG
3. **Terry Williams** 15.11.68 (2y, -) 10.27 '92   10.17w, 10.23, 10.25, 10.31, 10.39, 10.45; 2 CAU, 5s2 AAA, 1 South, 2 Nitra, 1 Belgian, 5s2 CG, BL1: 4,2,2,-
4. **Toby Box** 9.9.72 (2y, 6) 10.34/10.25w '93   10.07w, 10.35, 10.36, 10.41, 10.46, 10.47; 3 CAU, 1 BL2 (1), 2 AAA, 5 v USA, 1 EU23Cp, 6s2 EC
5. **Michael Rosswess** 11.6.65 (6y, 4) 10.15 '91   10.07w, 10.24w, 10.25w, 10.29, 10.29, 10.37; 6 Bratislava, 1 BL1 (1), 3 AAA, 7 TSB-CP, 7 v USA
6. **Elliot Bunney** 11.12.66 (8y, -) 10.20 '86   10.20w, 10.21w, 10.34, 10.36, 10.40, 10.42; 2 Sc v W,I,T, 5 AAA, 2 Sc v W,N, 8s1 CG, BL2: 1,2,-,1
7. **Darren Braithwaite** 20.1.69 (5y, 8) 10.28/10.25w '90   10.26, 10.31w, 10.32, 10.40, 10.51, 10.58; 2 BL1 (1), 1 IR, 2 E.Clubs, 4 Bratislava, 6 v USA
8. **Jason Gardener** 18.9.75 (1y, -) 10.62/10.46w '93   10.25, 10.35, 10.40, 10.42, 10.44w, 10.48; 1 Sth J, 1 JI v PGR, 6s3 AAA, 2 AAA-J, 2 WJ
9. **John Regis** 13.10.66 (9y, 2=) 10.15 '93, 10.07w '90   10.10wA, 10.23w, 10.38, 10.55; 3 Austin, 1 BL1(3), 4 Sestriere
10. **Solomon Wariso** 11.11.66 (1y, -) 10.57 '91, 10.51w '92   10.33, 10.34, 10.37, 10.40, 10.46, 10.55; 1 BL1 (2), 8 AAA, 6dq GhG
11. **Julian Golding** 17.2.75 (0y, -) 10.58 '93   10.34w, 10.43, 10.43, 10.43, 10.45, 10.45w; 3 Sth J, 6 Middx, 4s3 AAA, 1 AJ, 8 WJ, 1 Jnr IA, 1 Cup; BL2: 2,-,-,2
12. **Jamie Henderson** 28.3.69 (3y, -) 10.21 '87   10.37w, 10.45, 10.49, 10.49, 10.49w, 10.56; 3h1 CAU, 6s2 AAA, 1 Scot, 6 TSB-Ed, 3 Sc v W.N, 6q4 CG, BL2: -,1B,-,1B

Not ranked

   Trevor Cameron 25.11.76 (0y, -) 10.72/10.7/10.57w//10.5w '93   10.29w, 10.54, 10.56, 10.57, 10.59w; 10.5; 2 Sth J, 3 Middx, 4 JI v PGR, 6 AAA, 2 JI v I,C, 3 Cup
   Colin Jackson 18.2.67 (2y, 5) 10.29 '90   10.36; 1 W v Sc,I,T
   TSB-Ed at 100 yards

Christie was for the third year the World's top 100m sprinter, although closely challenged by Dennis Mitchell, whom he beat 4-3. He now has nine successive years as the British number one, a streak bettered at any event only by the 10 years that Geoff Capes had at the head of the shot rankings 1971-80. Christie won 13 of his 16 finals and ran an extraordinary 16 times (including two wind-assisted) under 10.10. In his career he has run 38 such times and another 12 wind-assisted; Jason Livingston's 10.09 is the only other British 'legal' sub-10.10. Way behind Christie there was excellent depth in British sprinting and those ranked from 2nd to were closely matched; unfortunately injuries affected most of them. The 10th best on the 'legal' lists of 10.36 represents the best ever standard.

200 METRES
1. **John Regis** 13.10.66 (9y, 1) 19.94 '93   19.87A, 20.01, 20.17, 20.25, 20.31, 20.35; 2 Lausanne, 1B BL1 (3), 2 TSB-Ed, 1 TSB-CP, 1 v USA, 3 GWG, 1 Sestriere, 2 Monaco, 2 CG, 1 WCp, 3 Tokyo
2. **Linford Christie** 2.4.60 (10y, 2) 20.09 '88   20.67; 20.56i, 20.70i, 20.76i; 1 ECp
3. **Terry Williams** 15.11.68 (1y, -) 21.56 '92   20.50, 20.58w, 20.62, 20.84, 20.86, 21.03; Surrey, 2 Crawley, 3 CAU, 5h4 AAA, 1 South, 1 BL1 (3), 1 Belgian, 5 CG
4. **Solomon Wariso** 11.11.66 (2y, 12=) 21.14 '91   20.51, 20.60, 20.67w, 21.06, 21.12, 21.12; 21.01i, 21.01i; after drugs positive: 20.73, 20.88;   1 BL1 (1), 3 IR, 1 E Clubs, 1 AAA, after test: 2 GhG, 5 TSB-CP
5. **Phil Goedluck** 10.9.67 (1y, -) 21.21 '86, 21.15w '93   20.79, 20.89w, 20.90, 20.97, 20.99, 21.00; 1 Surrey, 1 Crawley, 2 AAA, 2 South, 5 v USA, 7s2 EC, 5 McD, BL1: 2,1B,-,1
6. **Toby Box** 9.9.72 (2y, 3=) 20.89/20.82w '93   20.72, 21.02, 21.06, 21.08, 21.08, 21.22; 1 IR, 1 BL2 (2), 8 TSB-Ed, 2 EU23Cp, 5s1 CG, 6 McD
7. **Doug Walker** 28.7.73 (1y, -) 21.51/21.3w '92   20.71, 20.85w, 21.04, 21.08, 21.14, 21.16; 2 UAU, 1 Sc v W,I,T, 1 AAA v LC, 3 AAA, 1 Scot, 6 v USA, 6s1 CG, BL3: 2,1,5,-
8. **Jason John** 17.10.71 (3y, 5) 20.89 '92, 20.51w '93   20.86, 21.02, 21.10, 21.11, 21.20, 21.34; 21.0w; 2 IR, 1 CAU, 1 BL1 (2), 1 Nitra
9. **Ian Mackie** 27.2.75 (1y, -) 21.56 '92   20.91, 20.95, 20.99, 21.00, 21.06, 21.11; 2 CAU, 5h5 AAA, 1 JI v PGR, 2 Scot, 8 GhG, 2 AAA-J, 3 WJ, 5q3 CG, 8 McD
10. **Julian Golding** 17.2.75 (1y, -) 21.59/21.4/21.48w '93   20.73w, 21.02, 21.05, 21.10, 21.19, 21.21; 3 Middx, 2 Sth J, 5s2 AAA, 1 AAA-J, 5s2 WJ, 1 Jnr IA, 1 Cup, BL2: 1,-,-,1
11. **Darren Braithwaite** 20.1.69 (1y, -) 20.72 '92   20.99, 21.04, 21.11, 21.18, 21.44; 21.1; 21.01i, 21.13i, 21.17i; 1B BL1 (1), 5 Bisl G, 4 McD
12. **Paul McBurney** 14.3.72 (0y, -) 21.75/21.73w '93   20.81, 21.14, 21.14, 21.26; 21.4; 7s1 CG

103

John Regis is number one for the seventh time in eight years, a new record for the event. He set his fourth British record and the world's fastest time of the year at the high altitude Alpine resort of Sestriere and had 11 times under 20.50, despite having to miss the Europeans through an Achilles injury. Despite his drugs ban Wariso is ranked on performances prior to 1 July when he failed the test, as I follow a policy of allowing rankings for those who get the 3-month ban. Christie only ran the distance once, and that's not usually enough to rate highly, but as he won at the European Cup he deserves a high ranking. There are five newcomers in the top ten and six in the top twelve, headed by Williams, who took over a second of his best during the year, and Goedluck, who ran consistently faster than his pre-season 'legal' pb which he had set as a junior in 1986. They were followed by a rush of good youngsters, headed by the Scots Walker and Mackie. Note also Jamie Baulch with 20.84 at the Commonwealth Games and 17 year-old Trevor Cameron, who also just missed the 100m rankings, 4th in the AAAs with 20.88w.
The 10th best standard of 20.91 has only once been bettered (20.89 in 1990).

400 METRES
1. **Du'aine Ladejo** 14.2.71 (4y, 3=) 45.25 '92, 45.2 '93   44.94, 45.00, 45.09, 45.11, 45.16, 45.21;
   2 AAA, 4 GhG, 1 TSB-Ed, 2 TSB-CP, 2 v USA, 2 GWG, 3 Monaco, 1 EC, 2 CG, 7 GPF, 2 WCp
2. **Roger Black** 31.3.66 (8y, 6) 44.59 '86   44.78, 44.94, 45.08, 45.08, 45.09, 45.10;
   1 AAA, 1 ECp, 2 GhG, 3 CP-TSB, 4 Monaco, 2 EC, 4 Zürich, 1 Rieti, 3 Berlin, 4 GPF
3. **David McKenzie** 3.9.70 (3y, 3=) 45.75 '93   45.47, 46.03, 46.18, 46.32, 46.35, 46.38;
   1 IR, 4 AAA, 1 Nitra, 7 TSB-CP, 4 v USA, 7s1 EC, 5s1 CG, 1 Cup
4. **Brian Whittle** 24.4.64 (6y, -) 45.22 '88   45.46, 46.15, 46.30, 46.50, 46.66, 46.68;
   1 BL1 (1), 3 E Clubs, 3 AAA, 6 GhG, 6 TSB-Ed, 6 v USA, 5q1 CG
5. **Iwan Thomas** 5.1.74 (1y, -) 47.37 '92   45.98, 46.34, 46.37, 46.46, 46.72, 46.81
   1 UAU, 1 W v Sc,I,T, 6s1 Welsh, 1 WG, W v Bel,Hol, 7g v USA, 7s2 CG, BL1: 2,3,-,-
6. **Ade Mafe** 12.11.66 (4y, 2) 45.30 '93   46.39, 46.64, 46.72, 46.77, 46.90, 47.00;
   1 CAU, 1 BL1 (2), 7 AAA, 8 GhG, 7 TSB-Ed
7. **Jamie Baulch** 3.5.73 (1y, -) 46.50 '93   46.45, 46.47, 46.68, 46.93, 47.23; 46.75i, 46.91i;
   2 WG, 1 W v Sc,N, 1 BL3 (4), 5q4 CG
8. **Mark Hylton** 24.9.76 (1y, -) 47.81 '93   46.37, 46.79, 46.8, 46.94, 47.09, 47.21;
   1 E.Sch, 2 CAU, JI v PGR, 1 AAA-J, 4 WJ, 1 JI v I,C, BL3: 2,1,-,-
9. **Adrian Patrick** 28.6.73 (1y, 12) 46.79 '93   46.11, 46.81, 46.88, 47.08, 47.2, 47.38;
   2 IR, 5 AAA, 3 K Lynn, 8 v USA, 3 EU23Cp
10. **Paul McBurney** 14.3.72 (1y, -) 48.26 '93   46.49, 46.78, 46.89, 46.96, 47.2, 47.92;
    2h3 CAU, 1 NI, 1 Scot, 1 K Lynn, 5q2 CG
11. **Alex Fugallo** 28.1.70 (0y, -) 47.8 '93   46.39, 46.95, 47.08, 47.09, 47.41, 47.58;
    2B IR, 2 AAA v LC, 6 AAA, 1 Belgian, 5h1 CG
12. **Mark Smith** 18.11.71 (0y, -) 47.17 '93   46.7, 46.75, 46.76, 46.92, 46.92, 46.99;
    4B IR, 4 CAU, 1 AAA v LC, 8 AAA, 3 WG, 2 Nitra, 3 Cup, BL2: -,-,1,1
    Mark Richardson 26.7.72 (5y, 10) 45.09 '92   46.11i, 46.21i, 46.69i, 46.77i; no races outdoors

No Grindley, no Redmond, no Richardson and yet still the depth of British 400m running is such that we won both European and Commonwealth titles at 4 x400m. Black's return to world-class was most heart-warming, as was Ladejo's ascent to that status. There was great friendly rivalry between them, with Ladejo winning European titles indoors and out, adding Commonwealth and World Cup second places. Such championship success give Ladejo top ranking, but Black ran faster and they ended the year 3-3. Both were in the world top ten. There was quite a gap after the big two to Mackenzie and Whittle who each ran under 45.5 at the AAAs, but no other sub-46 times. Whittle returned to the 400m rankings for the first time since 1989, when he was top! The Welsh youngsters Thomas and Baulch and Northern Irishman Paul McBurney excelled at the Commonwealth Games and they are joined in the top ten for the first time by 17 year-old Mark Hylton. In all six men are ranked for the first time.

800 METRES
1. **Craig Winrow** 22.12.71 (2y, 11) 1:47.5 '92   1:46.54, 1:46.91, 1:46.93, 1:47.06, 1:47.09, 1:47.15;
   1 AAA, 3 ECp, 2 GhG, 6 TSB-CP, 1 v USA, 6 EC, 4 CG, 9 McD, 3 WCp
2. **Martin Steele** 30.9.62 (6y, 2) 1:43.84 '93   1:46.13, 1:47.09, 1:47.39, 1:47.56, 1:47.99, 1:48.04; 1:47.78i;
   3 AAA, 3 Cork, 6 GhG, 6 TSB-Ed, 8 TSB-CP, 4 v USA, 7 CG
3. **Tom McKean** 27.10.63 (10y, 3) 1:43.88 '89   1:46.20, 1:46.28, 1:47.46, 1:47.99, 1:48.69, 1:48.71; 1:47.60i,
   1:48.46i; 9 Helsinki, 11 Lausanne, 1 Scot, 5 TSB-CP, 9 Oslo, 6h3 EC, 8 CG
4. **Andrew Lill** 9.8.71 (4y, 6) 1:46.37 '92   1:47.00, 1:47.41, 1:47.52, 1:47.55, 1:47.80, 1:48.18;
   2 Crawley, 1 IR, 4 AAA, 1 South, 3 GhG, 5 TSB-Ed, 7 TSB-CP, 3 v USA, 1 BL1 (4), 5s1 CG
5. **Michael Guegan** 19.9.66 (2y, 9) 1:47.90 '92   1:48.26, 1:48.90, 1:48.92, 1:48.95, 1:49.16, 1:49.45;
   4 Wyth, 3 Crawley, 2 CAU, 5 AAA, 2 South, 1B GhG, 1 Belgian, 7h2 CG
6. **Terry West** 19.11.68 (1y, -) 1:48.2 '92   1:48.66, 1:48.80, 1:49.13, 1:49.31, 1:49.84, 1:50.3;
   2 Wyth, 1 CAU, 6 AAA, 1 Nitra
7. **David Strang** 13.12.68 (2y, -) 1:45.85 '92   1:48.20, 1:48.25; 1:48.89i; 2 E Clubs
8. **David Wilson** 7.9.68 (1y, -) 1:48.19 '90   1:47.57, 1:49.39, 1:50.43, 1:50.50; 4h4 AAA, 1 NI, 2 K Lynn, 8s1 CG

9. **Curtis Robb** 7.6.72 (4y, 1) 1:44.92 '93   1:48.07, 1:49.56, 1:52.8; 7 TSB-Ed, 9 TSB-CP
10. **Anthony Whiteman** 13.11.71 (1y, -) ?   1:48.45, 1:49.16, 1:49.2, 1:50.4; 1 Kent, 2 Dublin, 3 South, BL4: 1,-,-,1
11. **Andrew Knight** 26.10.68 (0y, -) 1:49.3 '91   1:48.38, 1:49.21, 1:49.54, 1:50.4, 1:50.9, 1:50.94;
    2 Kent, 3B TSB-CP, 1 Solihull, 1 Lough
12. **Paul Walker** 2.12.73 (0y, 12=) 1:47.53 '93   1:48.85, 1:49.5, 1:49.72, 1:49.79, 1:50.12, 1:51.5;
    9 Wyth, 3h2 AAA, 2 Scot, 2B GhG, 4 K Lynn, 7B TSB-CP, BL2: 1,1B,1,1

Winrow, with a previous best place of 7th in 1992, reached the top, and thus fulfilled some of his junior promise. He had a fine competitive record, but he was top all too easily and it was a terrible year by the usually excellent British 800m standards. Last year I said that "the standard in depth was down considerably from our usual high levels, with the UK ranking tenth best being 1:47.59, much the worst since 1985, with the record level being 1:46.13 in 1988". Well the 10th ranking place in 1994 was 1:48.38 and that's the worst since 1980 and the best time matched that 10th best of 1988. Strang had just two races, both 1:48.2s and Guegan and West had solid seasons, but for 1:48 men to be ranked 5th to 7th shows the problems with this event, as compared to our glory days, all too clearly.

1500 METRES - 1 MILE
1. **Matthew Yates** 4.2.69 (5y, 1) 3:34.00 '91,   3:52.75M '93;35.32, 3:35.61, 3:36.47, 3:37.82, 3:39.12,
    3:39.60; 3 Lisbon, 12 Lille, dnf TSB-CP, 7 Nice, 5 Zürich, 7 Brussels, 8 Rieti, 2 Berlin, 4 GPF, 13 McD
2. **John Mayock** 26.10.70 (4y, 3) 3:36.45 '93, 3:56.90M '91   3:37.20, 3:37.22, 3:38.78, 3:39.17, 3:58.34M,
    3:42.59; 3:40.98i; 4 Seville, 6 AAA, 5 TSB-Ed, 8 TSB-CP, 3 v USA, 3 CG, 1 McD
3. **Kevin McKay** 9.2.69 (4y, 9) 3:35.94 '92, 3:54.45M '92   3:53.64M (3:38.79), 3:37.86, 3:38.08, 3:39.72; 3:40.19,
    3:40.59; 2 BL1 (1), 1 Hengelo, 1 AAA, 1 E Carr, 1 v USA, 7 Dream M, 5h2 EC, 10 Zürich, 16 Brussels, 8 CG, 15 McD
4. **Gary Lough** 6.7.70 (1y, 12=) 3:40.48 '93, 4:01.54iM/4:02.14 '92   3:35.83, 3:37.83, 3:41.71, 3:59.48M,
    4:00.00M, 3:42.7; 1 Wyth, 3 AAA, 3 ECp, 3 E Carr, 3 CP-TSB, 11 EC, dq (3)s2 CG, 5 WCp, 6 McD
5. **David Strang** 13.12.68 (1y, 10) 3:39.72/3:56.86 '93   3:36.53, 3:54.30M (3:38.55), 3:39.15, 3:39.96,
    3:40.08, 3:40.85; 3:55.43iM, 3:57.38i; 2 AAA, 4 TSB-Ed, 6 TSB-CP, 9 Dream M, 7 Hechtel, 12 EC, 12 CG
6. **Brian Treacy** 29.7.71 (1y, -) 3:40.68/4:00.67M '90   3:38.93, 3:39.65, 3:40.55, 3:40.63, 3:44.50, 3:46.34;
    3:45.46i; 3 Granada, 3h1 AAA, 6 CG
7. **Andrew Keith** 25.12.71 (1y, -) 3:39.06/3:57.7iM '93, 4:03.57 '92   3:39.44, 3:41.1, 3:58.97M, 3:42.93,
    3:45.50, 3:45.6; 3:56.29iM, 4:00.55iM; 12 NCAA, 7 AAA, 6 Cork, 6 TSB-Ed, 4 v USA, 2 Newport, 6s1 CG
8. **Tony Morrell** 3.5.62 (5y, -) 3:34.1/3:51.31M '90
    3:41.50, 3:42.45, 3:42.59, 4:01.06M, 3:43.81; 3:44.77i; 4 AAA, 3 Århus, 6 E Carr, 7 v USA
9. **Anthony Whiteman** 13.11.71 (1y, -) 3:46.1 '93, 4:08.0M '92   3:41.92, 3:42.18, 3:42.68, 3:44.56, 3:45.21,
    4:03.87M; 1 AAA v LC, 5 AAA, 1B GhG, 1 WG, 13 TSB-Ed, 2 Nitra, 2 Belgian
10. **Matt Barnes** 12.1.68 (2y, 6) 3:38.31 '93, 4:03.24M '92   3:40.47, 3:58.39M, 3:43.3, 3:43.89, 3:45.61,
    3:49.7; 3 Wyth, 8 AAA, 3 Cork, dnf E Carr, 11 TSB-Ed, BL3: 1,-,-,1
11. **David Wilson** 7.9.68 (0y, -) 3:41.8 '89, 3:59.9M '91   3:41.28, 3:43.77, 3:44.62, 3:46.86, 3:47.11;
    1 Crawley, 4 BLE, 7s1 CG
12? **Ian Gillespie** 18.5.70 (0y, -)3:40.72/3:58.64M '93   3:41.48, 3:41.65, 4:00.80M, 4:01.58M, 3:43.8, 3:44.0;
    3 BL1 (1), 5 Wyth, 2 Crawley, 4 Scot, 5 E Carr, 3 Newport, 3 Exeter, 4 Solihull, 9 McD, 11 Lough, 2 Cup
Not ranked but close
    Ian Grime 29.9.70 (0y, -) 3:44.53 '92, 4:03.7M '90   3:40.35, 3:44.03, 3:45.09, 3:45.57, 3:47.2, 3:48.87;
    3 AAA v LC, 9 AAA, 2 Tallinn, 1 Solihull, BL1: 4B,-,-,2
    Steffan White 21.12.72 (0y, -) 3:41.02, 4:00.61M, 3:43.4, 3:44.37, 3:45.03, 3:45.53;
    1B Wyth, 11 AAA, 2 AAA v LC, 4B GhG, 4 Mid, 2 Solihull, 8 McD, 3 Lough
    Matthew Hibberd 23.6.73 (0y, -) 3:42.67/4:02.45 '93   3:41.73, 3:42.5, 3:43.34, 4:02.36M, 3:45.2, 3:46.30;
    3:43.23i; 11 Wyth, 10 AAA, 1 K Lynn, 5 Solihull, 11 McD, 1 Lough, 1 Cup
    Rod Finch 5.8.67 (0y, 12=) 3:37.97/4:00.0M '93   3:38.80, 3:47.91; 3:43.80i; 2 Hengelo, 3h4 AAA

M = 1 mile time. Equivalents: 3:35.0M = 3:52.0M, 3:38.0m = 3:55.3M, 3:41.0m = 3:58.6M, 3:44.0m = 4:01.8M
(Times in brackets are 1500m times en route to 1 mile)

No one stood out so clearly as Yates did in 1993, but Mayock's Commonwealth bronze redeemed dismal performances by others in the major championships. Mayock also won at Sheffield. Yates ran twice in Britain - failing to finish at Crystal Palace and trailing in 14th in Shefield. He had produced insufficient form in the Continental races that he contested to demand selection for the Europeans; however his fine 2nd in Berlin and 4th at the Grand Prix Final, with much faster times than Mayock, was enough to keep him top of the rankings and overall he ranked ninth in the world on my merit rankings. While these two ended well, McKay's form fell away badly and Lough did not fulfill his early season promise, in which he continued to finish third in every major race (adding UK and WSG from 1993). Strang was European Indoor champion and had a solid season to the Europeans, when he ran well to make the final but then trailed in last, a feat he repeated at the Commonwealth Games. Unnoticed (indeed never even mentioned by the BBC during the 1500m races) Treacy was Britain's second best at the Commonwealth Games and he had earlier run well in several races in Spain. The last few places were difficult to determine, with conflicting race results. Rod Finch had a 3:38.80 but then only a AAA heat run and Ian Grime beat many contenders at Solihull. It is the most inexperienced group ever in this event, with five years being the longest stretch in the top ten, but therein perhaps may lie hope for the future.

3000 METRES (Not ranked this year) M = 2 miles
Rob Denmark 23.11.68 (1) 7:39.55 '93, 8:26.05M '92   7:42.62; 7:56.60i; 2 Lausanne
Mark Rowland 7.3.63 7:49.82 '89, 8:26.19M '87   7:50.30, 7:54.05; 8:02.44i, 8:09.43i;
2 Lappeenranta, 15 Köln
Gary Staines 3.7.63 7:41.79 '90, 8:23.16M '91   7:51.26, 7:53.71, 8:29.12M;
5 Lappeenranta, 2 Stockholm, 6 Göteborg
John Downes 21.7.67 7:59.50 '90   8:27.00M, 7:54.53; 3 Tampere, 2 Hechtel
Andrew Keith 25.12.71 c.8:22i/8:24   7:49.83i, 8:02.81
John Mayock 26.10.70 7:48.47i '92, 8:03.75/8:32.54M '91   7:55.31i

M = 2 mile time. Equivalents: 7:45.0m = 8:19.2M, 7:50.0m = 8:24.6M, 7:55.0m = 8:30.0M, 8:00.0m = 8:35.2M

5000 METRES
1.   **Rob Denmark** 23.11.68 (4y, 1) 13:10.24 '92   13:22.40, 13:23.00, 13:32.60, 13:37.50, 13:40.10, 13:59.80;
7 TSB-CP, 11 Oslo, 2 EC, 1 CG
2.   **John Nuttall** 11.1.67 (4y, 4) 13:24.26 '92   13:23.54, 13:25.51, 13:30.78, 13:32.47, 13:38.65, 13:39.10,
13:40.65; 10 TSB-CP, 6 Hechtel, 5 EC, 3 CG, 2 WCp
3.   **Jon Brown** 27.2.71 (4y, 2) 13:19.78 '93   13:23.96, 13:24.79, 13:34.37, 13:34.84, 13:40.62;
13 TSB-CP, 3 GWG, 8 Monaco, 4 CG
4.   **John Downes** 21.7.67 (1y, -) 13:57.56 '92   13:29.91, 13:43.07, 14:10.18; 18 AAA, 1 Gävle, 15 TSB-CP
5.   **Richard Nerurkar** 6.1.64 (5y, 5) 13:23.36 '90   13:36.89, 13:50.0, 13:53.21;
1 Oxford, 2 Rehlingen, 2 Punkulaiden
6.   **Justin Hobbs** 12.3.69 (1y, -) 14:05.7 '93   13:45.53, 13:50.72, 14:10.25; 2 W v Sc,I,T, 8 CG
7.   **Gary Staines** 3.7.63 (7y, 3) 13:14.28 '90   13:45.57, 13:56.6, 14:03.06; 2g v USA, 13 Zürich, 4 Pune
8.   **Dermot Donnelly** 23.9.70 (1y, -) 13:55.32 '93   13:47.0, 13:52.63, 13:54.80, 14:00.00, 14:15.57;
2 Crawley, 1 AAA, 6 v USA, 15 CG
9.   **David Miles** 16.11.65 (1y, -) 13:55.53 '88   13:46.66, 14:01.48, 14:02.54, 14:05.48, 14:05.87;
1 CAU, 8 AAA, 5 Cork, 4 v USA, 6 Tallinn, 1 N v Sc,W
10. **Eamonn Martin** 9.10.58 (9y, -) 13:17.84 '89   13:46.19, 13:48.61, 14:09.2+; 4 Cork, 3 Århus
11. **Paul Evans** 13.4.61 (2y, 6) 13:30.83 '92   13:46.5+, 13:47.21; 18 TSB-CP
12. **John Mayock** 26.10.70 (4y, 8) 13:26.97 '92   13:50.58; 4 ECp

Denmark, Commonwealth champion and European silver medallist, was top for the fourth successive year. Nuttall also ran brilliantly at both championships and at the World Cup, and Brown also excelled in Victoria. Ex-Irishman Downes is fourth and Nerurkar, preparing for the marathon, fifth, but then there is a huge gap to the mid-13:40s men. Mayock may deserve better for his 4th at the European Cup, but it was a slow race and his only one at the distance.

10,000 METRES
1.   **Rob Denmark** 23.11.68 (1y, -) 0   28:03.34, 28:20.65; 1 AAA, 3 WCp
2.   **Martin Jones** 21.4.67 (1y, 11) 28:57.23 '93   28:33.18, 29:08.53; 2 AAA, 4 CG
3.   **Gary Staines** 3.7.63 (6y, 3) 27:48.73 '91   28:25.60, 29:57.27; 5 ECp, 15 EC
4.   **Justin Hobbs** 12.3.69 (1y, -) 0   28:17.00, 28:45.86, 29:28.08; 3 AAA, 10 Helsinki, 22 EC, dnf CG
5.   **Eamonn Martin** 9.10.58 (6y, -) 27:23.06 '88   28:46.50, 29:15.81; 6 GWG, 6 CG
6.   **Barry Royden** 15.12.66 (1y, -) 29:20.22 '91   28:47.17, 29:38.36; 4 AAA, 4 Belgian
7.   **Carl Udall** 13.7.66 (2y, 12) 28:48.19 '92   28:49.96, 29:20.25; 5 AAA, 15 Helsinki
8.   **Chris Robison** 16.3.61 (1y, -) 28:39.35 '86   28:51.12, 29:50.23; 6 AAA, 10 CG
9.   **Richard Nerurkar** 6.1.64 (7y, 2) 27:40.03 '93   28:53.03; 4 Seville
10. **Martin McLoughlin** 23.12.58 (4y, -) 28:15.58 '86   28:55.57; 7 AAA
11. **Tommy Murray** 18.5.61 (0y, -) 29:16.42 '92   29:12.35; 1 Scot
12= **Bashir Hussain** 20.12.64 (0y, -) 30:14.16 '93   29:16.29, 29:40.30; 1 CAU, 8 AAA
12= **Andrew Pearson** 14.9.71 (1y, 8) 28:40.49 '93   29:14.91; 1 McD

Denmark said "never" again for this event after his brave World Cup run in appalling conditions, but he showed great form then and earlier to win the AAA title. He is the first man to head both 5k and 10k rankings since Nick Rose in 1980. Paul Evans and Nerurkar are our other two world-class 10k men, but the former did not finish his only track race (in Brussels), and the latter ran just one track 10k during his marathon build-up. Jones followed Denmark in the AAAs and was our best placer in Victoria, and Staines beat Hobbs, AAA 3rd placer, in Helsinki.

MARATHON
1.   **Richard Nerurkar** 6.1.64 (2y, 1) 2:10:03 '93   2:11:56 (4) EC
2.   **Eamonn Martin** 9.10.58 (2y, 2) 2:10:50 '93   2:11:05 (8) London
3.   **Mark Hudspith** 19.1.69 (1y -) 0   2:12:52 (17) London, 2:15:11 (3) CG
4.   **Dale Rixon** 8.7.66 (1y, -) 0   2:15:41 (26) London, 2:16:15 (4) CG

5. **Colin Moore** 25.11.60 (1y, -) 2:18:23 '87   2:13:35 (1) Houston, 2:18:07 (8) CG
6. **Steve Brace** 7.7.61 (7y, 9) 2:10:57 '91   2:12:23 (13) London, 2:14:43 (3) Houston, 2:17:13 (1) Dublin, 2:24:21 (52) EC
7. **Peter Whitehead** 3.12.64 (1y, -) 2:17:19 '93   2:13:40 (22) London, 2:16:40 (27) EC
8. **Mark Flint** 19.2.63 (1y, -) 2:19:04 '93   2:12:07 (11) London, dnf EC
9. **Peter Fleming** 5.1.61 (2y, 7=) 2:13:33 '93   2:14:03 (1) Naaldwijk, 2:17:33 (14) Eindhoven
10. **Robin Nash** 9.2.59 (1y, -) 2:15:12 '85   2:14:52 (17) Berlin
11. **Mike O'Reilly** 23.4.58 (4y + IRE, 3) 2:10:39 '93   2:15:46 (27) London
12. **Bill Foster** 8.8.58 (0y, -) 2:19:03 '91   2:17:12 (31) EC, 2:17:16 (29) London

Nerurkar and Martin retain their top two places. Seven of the top 12 are ranked for the first time, with most encouraging starts to their marathon career from Mark Hudspith and Dale Rixon, 3rd and 4th in Victoria.

3000 METRES STEEPLECHASE
1. **Mark Rowland** 7.3.63 (6y, -) 8:07.96 '88   8:22.20, 8:26.00, 8:29.51, 8:30.24, 8:32.65, 8:41.45; 1 Madras, 2 TSB-Ed, 1 v USA, 12 Monaco, 4 EC, 8 Berlin
2. **Colin Walker** 29.10.62 (11y, 3) 8:25.15 '92   8:27.78, 8:29.33, 8:29.65, 8:37.46, 8:41.14, 8:44.40; 1 CAU, 3 AAA, 1 TSB-Ed, 2 v USA, 4 CG, 4 WCp
3. **Justin Chaston** 4.11.68 (4y, 4) 8:32.67 '93   8:23.90, 8:28.28, 8:29.49, 8:29.99, 8:31.0, 8:31.08; 1 W v Sc,I,T, 1 AAA, 3 ECp, 9 Nice, 6 GWG, 11 EC, 7 CG
4. **Tom Hanlon** 20.5.67 (8y, 1) 8:12.58 '91   8:20.04, 8:27.74, 8:29.74, 8:31.50, 8:36.06; 3 TSB-Ed, 9 Stockholm, 9 Monaco, 10 EC
5. **Tom Buckner** 16.4.63 (4y, 2) 8:25.50 '92   8:29.84, 8:36.77, 8:38.35, 8:49.16, 8:52.84, 9:00.51; 3 CAU, 7 TSB-Ed, 1 TSB-CP, 6 v USA, 5 CG
6. **Spencer Duval** 5.1.70 (3y, 5) 8:32.77 '93   8:28.33, 8:28.63, 8:36.08, 8:46.43, 8:47.47, 8:49.08; 6 Granada, 2 AAA, 1 Århus, 5 v USA, 6 Hechtel, 10 CG
7. **Keith Cullen** 13.6.72 (3y, 8) 8:31.72 '92   8:39.71, 8:40.79, 8:42.94, 8:52.98; 2 WG, 8 TSB-Ed, 3 TSB-CP
8. **Michael Hawkins** 24.10.61 (5y, 12) 8:37.15 '89   8:38.39, 8:44.95, 8:51.85, 8:53.38, 8:53.77, 8:57.47; 2 CAU, 4 AAA, 1 North, 4 Nitra, 7 v USA, 8 Hechtel
9. **Robert Hough** 3.6.72 (2y, 9) 8:42.48 '93   8:38.80, 8:40.09, 8:49.83, 9:06.13; 5 AAA, 2 TSB-CP, 7 EU23 Cp
10. **Neil Smart** 12.5.63 (4y, -) 8:35.52 '89   8:42.44, 8:49.82, 8:52.15, 8:56,15; 1 BL1 (2), 6 AAA, 1 WG
11. **David Lee** 16.9.65 (2y, 10) 8:31.22 '92   8:45.2, 8:45.45, 8:46.23, 8:48.60, 8:50.39, 8:54.2; 1 BL2 (1), 7 AAA, 1 Welsh, 4 TSB-CP, 1 W v Sc, N, 1 Cup
12. **Graeme Croll** 1.2.66 (1y, 7) 8:41.94 '93   8:49.00, 8:50.30, 8:53.26, 8:54.50, 8:56.5, 8:59.10; 2 Sc v W,I,T, 9 AAA, 1 Scot, 11 TSB-CP

Carl Warren   8:47.00, 8:52.41, 8:53.84; 8 AAA

Rowland returns to regain the top ranking that he held each year 1988-90. Although Chaston was better for most of the year and beat him at the AAAs, Walker's brave Commonwealth 4th, despite going for broke against the Kenyans, just gives him the edge for second place to match his best ever of 1991. Hanlon also edges Chaston, by dint of a faster time and higher placing in the Europeans. Buckner beat Duval by nearly 20 seconds at the Commonwealth, so just gets ahead despite the latter's better form for most of the year. Most unusually all the top 12 had been ranked before.

110 METRES HURDLES
1. **Colin Jackson** 18.2.67 (11y, 1) 12.91 '93, 12.8 '90   12.94wA, 12.98, 12.99, 13.02, 13.03, 13.04; 1 W v Sc,I,T, 1 GhG, 1 WG, 1 TSB-Ed, 1 Oslo, 1 GWG, 1 Sestriere, 1 Monaco, 1 EC, 1 Zürich, 1 Brussels, 1 CG, 1 Berlin, 1 GPF, 1 McD, 1 Tokyo
2. **Anthony Jarrett** 13.8.68 (9y, 2) 13.00 '93   13.22, 13.23, 13.23, 13.23, 13.32, 13.32; 13.1; 1 E Clubs, dnf Lausanne, 2 TSB-Ed, 1 TSB-CP, 3 vUSA, 2 Oslo, 2 GWG, 5 Sestriere, 3 Monaco, 3 EC, dq Brussels, 2 CG, 6 Berlin, 4 McD, 3 Madrid, 1 WCp, 2 Tokyo
3. **Paul Gray** 25.5.69 (5y, 7) 13.97 '88   13.53, 13.54, 13.65, 13.76, 133.78, 13.79w; 2 W v Sc,I,T, 2 AAA, 1 Welsh, 4B GhG, 2 WG, 7= TSB-Ed, 4 v USA, 1 W v Sc,N, 3 CG, BL3: 1,1,-,1
4. **Andrew Tulloch** 1.4.67 (7y, 3) 13.59' 93   13.52, 13.62, 13.65, 13.69, 13.69w, 13.70; 2 IR, 1 BL2 (1), 1 AAA, 3 ECp, 2B GhG, 6 TSB-Ed, 1 Nitra, 6 TSB-CP. 5 v USA, 5s1EC, 4 CG, 6 McD
5. **Lloyd Cowan** 8.7.62 (5y, 9) 13.94 '90   13.75, 13.96, 14.07w, 14.08, 14.09, 14.10; 3 AAA, 3 Dublin, 1 South, 3B GhG, 3 WG, 6 v USA, 4h1 CG, 8 McD, 2 Cup, BL1: -,2,1,1
6. **Neil Owen** 18.10.73 (3y, 6) 14.01/13.99w '93   13.80, 13.93w, 13.97, 14.04, 14.10, 14.11; 1 UAU, 3 IR, 2 CAU, 4 AAA, 2 Dublin, 4 South, 6B GhG, 1 K Lynn, 2 EU23Cp, 3 Cup, BL1: 2,1,2,2
7. **Kenneth Campbell** 30.9.72 (1y, 12) 14.12 '93   13.86, 13.92, 14.12, 14.16, 14.24, 14.25; 14.2w; 2 Sc v W,I, 5 AAA, 2 Scot, 3 Sc v W,N, 6 CG, BL2: 2,3,-,1
8. **Hugh Teape** 26.12.63 (11y, 5) 13.44 '92   13.76, 14.27w, 14.78; 1 IR, fell AAA, 3h2 Belgian
9. **Martin Nicholson** 9.12.70 (1y, -) 14.29 '92   14.14, 14.18, 14.22w, 14.28, 14.33, 14.33; 13.8; 5 IR, 1 CAU, dnf AAA, 3 Cork, 7B GhG, 4 WG, 2 North, 2 Solihull, 1 Cup, BL1: 1,3,3,3

10. **Kevin Lumsdon** 3.3.74 (1y, -) 14.37/14.32w '93   14.20, 14.22, 14.26, 14.26w, 14.27w, 14.30;
    5 CAU, 1 AAA v LC, 6 AAA, 4 Cork, 5B GhG, 2 K Lynn, 1 North, 2 N v Sc,W, 1 Solihull
11= **Mark Lambeth** 3.9.72 (0y, 11) 14.24/14.20w '93   14.31, 14.39, 14.42, 14.50, 14.61, 14.67; 14.2, 14.3;
    4 IR, 3 CAU, 4h1 AAA, 2 South, 2B K Lynn, BL3: 2,2,1,-
11= **Colin Bovell** 9.3.72 (0y, -) 14.37 '92   14.17, 14.20, 14.39w, 14.46w, 14.47, 14.49; 14.1w, 14.4, 14.4;
    2 UAU, 4 CAU, 3 AAA v LC, 4h4 AAA, 5 South, 1B K Lynn, 2 Nivelles, BL3: 1B,-,1B,-
    Jamie Quarry 15.11.72 (0y, -) 14.51 '91   14.10, 14.33, 14.36, 14.38w, 14.67; 14.6; 4 BL2 (2), 1 Scot

Jackson's total of eleven sub 13.10 times (including two wind aided) is by far the best ever in the world for one season. He won all 18 finals and was a long way ahead of the rest of the world as well as being UK No. 1 for the 7th time, a record for the event. It was not a vintage season for Jarrett, ranked in the UK top two for the sixth successive year, but he still won the World Cup, and took Commonwealth silver and European bronze medals and ranked 4th in the world. Gray made a huge improvement from his best ranking of 7th in 1988 and 1993. His Commonwealth bronze to Tulloch's 4th place just gave him the edge although Tulloch beat Gray 3-2. Teape had only one one good run, but then he beat Tulloch and Owen, so he slots in at 8th. Lumsdon beat Nicholson 4-2, but Nicholson had a good record (4-5) against Owen.

400 METRES HURDLES
1. **Gary Cadogan** 8.10.66 (2y, 2) 49.25 '93   49.07, 49.21, 49.42, 49.48, 49.48A, 49.53;
   4 E Clubs, 7 Bratislava, 2 GhG, 1 TSB-Ed, dnf Nitra, 7 TSB-CP, 3 Oslo, 3 Sestriere, 8 EC, 4 CG, 3 McD, 6 WCp
2. **Peter Crampton** 4.6.69 (2y, 3) 50.34 '93   49.26, 49.45, 49.71, 49.78, 49.82, 49.90;
   5 Bratislava, 1 CAU, 1 AAA, 6 ECp, 3 GhG, 4 TSB-CP, 2 v USA, 6 EC, 7 CG, 4 McD
3. **Lawrence Lynch** 1.11.67 (6y, 4) 50.19 '91   50.24, 50.27, 50.38, 50.50, 50.73, 51.01;
   2 Middlesex, 2 IR, 5 AAA, 1 Barcelona, 6 GhG, 1 WG, 4 v USA, 5h3 EC, BL1: 2,1,2,-
4. **Steve Coupland** 15.6.65 (5y, 8) 50.63 '92   50.19, 50.97, 51.16, 51.34, 51.35, 51.5;
   2 AAA, 5 GhG, 5 v USA, 3h2 CG, BL5: -,1,1,-
5. **Noel Levy** 22.6.75 (3y, 6) 51.17 '93   50.70, 50.89, 50.91, 50.94, 51.02, 51.51;
   1 BL2 (1), 3 AAA, 1 JI v PGR, dns AAA-J, 6 TSB-Ed, 3 WJ, 5 EU23Cp, 8 McD, 1 Jnr IA
6. **Gary Jennings** 21.2.72 (1y, 11) 51.79 '93   50.60, 50.77, 50.93, 50.96, 51.16, 51.16;
   2 UAU, 2 CAU, 1 AAA v LC, 6 AAA, 3 Barcelona, 1 K Lynn, 6 v USA, 3 Belgian, BL1: 1,-,3,1
7. **Tony Williams** 1.5.72 (2y, 7) 51.3/51.39 '93   50.98, 51.27, 51.3, 51.38, 51.49, 51.50;
   1 BL5 (1), 3 IR, 2 AAA v LC, 4 AAA, 3 WG, 7 TSB-Ed, 1 North, 7 v USA
8. **Eddie Betts** 18.2.71 (1y, -) 52.36 '93   51.15, 51.50, 51.60, 51.73, 51.89, 52.03;
   1 Middlesex, 4 CAU, 3 AAA v LC, 7 AAA, 2 Dublin, 1 South, 2 WG, 1B Belgian
9= **Tim Gwynne** 20.1.71 (1y, -) 51.71 '92   51.08, 51.87, 51.88, 52.04, 52.24, 52.4;
   1 IR, 3 CAU, 7s1 AAA, BL1: 1B,2,-,-
9= **Phil Harries** 7.4.66 (6y, -) 50.01 '88   51.13, 51.63, 52.05, 52.24, 53.6; 1 UAU,
   2 W v Sc,I,T, dns AAA, 9h3 CG
9= **Gary Telfer** 10.1.65 (1y, -) 52.10 '90   51.51, 51.57, 51.7, 51.80, 51.99, 52.14;
   6s2 AAA, 1 Dublin, 2 South, 1 Cup, BL1: 2B,4,1,-
12. **Mark Bishop** 12.2.67 (2y, -) 51.28 '89   51.67, 51.91, 52.2, 52.4, 52.45, 52.8;
    5s2 AAA, 3 South, 3 Solihull, BL4: -,1,1,1

After the seven-year reign of Kriss Akabusi as top of the rankings, Cadogan succeeds to the crown, holding off the challenge of his fellow-débutant at the event in 1993, Crampton. They went 3-3 in head-to-head competition, but Cadogan ran nine times under 50 seconds to six by Crampton. Gwynne and Harries only showed form up to June, and share ninth with Telfer, even though Gwynne beat Telfer in the first two league matches. Levy is the top ranked junior at any men's track event. Slightly surprisingly the 10th best performer standard of 51.15 is the best ever.

HIGH JUMP
1. **Steve Smith** 29.3.73 (5y, 1) 2.37 '92   2.33, 2.32, 2.31, 2.28, 2.28, 2.28; 2.38i, 2.36i, 2.32i, 2.31i;
   1 BL2 (2), 2 GhG, 10 Oslo, 2= EC, 2 Brussels, 2 CG, 6 Berlin, 1 McD, 3 WCp
2. **Dalton Grant** 8.4.66 (11y, 2) 2.36 '91   2.34, 2.34, 2.30, 2.28, 2.28, 2.27; 2.37i, 2.34i, 2.33i, 2.32i;
   1 E Clubs, 3 ECp, 2 BL1 (3), 3 TSB-Ed, 4 TSB-CP, 6 Eberstadt, 4 v USA, 9= EC, 5= Zürich, 5 CG, 10 McD
3. **Brendan Reilly** 23.12.72 (5y, 3) 2.31 '92   2.28, 2.28, 2.25, 2.25, 2.25, 2.25; 2.32i, 2.28i, 2.26i, 2.26i;
   1 UAU, 1 CAU, 1 AAA v LC, 1 AAA, 3 TSB-CP, 5= Oslo, 2 v USA, 7 EU23Cp, 16= EC, 7= CG,
   6 McD, 3 Jumps Int v3N
4. **Geoff Parsons** 14.8.64 (13y, 4) 2.30i '86, 2.30 '90   2.31, 2.25, 2.24, 2.23, 2.21, 2.20; 2.22i;
   1 Sc v W,I,T, 2 AAA, 5 GhG, 2 WG, 1 Scot, 1 TSB-Ed, 3 TSB-CP, 5 v USA, 3 CG, 7=McD
5. **Fayyaz Ahmed** 10.4.66 (6y, 5) 2.21 '86   2.19, 2.18, 2.18, 2.15, 2.15, 2.12; 2.16i;
   5 AAA, 1 South, 3 WG, 6= TSB-Ed, 1 Nitra, 3 Belgian, nh v USA; 18 Jumps Int v3N, BL1: 3,3,1,-
6. **Henderson Pierre** 23.10.63 (4y, 6) 2.20i '87, 2.18 '86   2.17, 2.14, 2.14, 2.10; 2.05i;
   1 BL1 (2), 1 Belgian, 1 Eur. Police
7. **Stuart Ohrland** 6.9.75 (1y, -) 2.07 '93   2.17, 2.15, 2.14, 2.14, 2.11, 2.11; 3 IR,
   1 South-J, 8= CAU, 3 AAA-J, 6 E.Sch, 12 WJ, 1 Jnr IA

8.　**James Brierley** 31.7.77 (1y, -) 2.10 '93　2.16, 2.15, 2.15, 2.14, 2.14, 2.13; 2.15i;
　　2 World Sch, 3 CAU, 7 AAA, 1 JI v PGR, 4 AAA-J, 1 E,Sch, 20 WJ, 1 JI v I,Cs, 2 Jnr IA
9.　**Robert Brocklebank** 12.10.76 (1y, -) 2.03 '93　2.13, 2.12, 2.10, 2.10, 2.10, 2.07;
　　2 North-J, 4 Cork, 5= AAA-J, 1 North, 3 E.Sch, 1 N v W,Sc, 1 Blackpool, 4 Jnr IA
10.　**Michael Robbins** 14.3.76 (1y, -) 2.05i '92, 2.03 '93　2.14, 2.10, 2.10, 2.09, 2.08, 2.05;
　　1 North-J, 1= IR, 2 JI v PGR, 5 Cork, 5= AAA-J, 3 North, 13 E Sch, 2 Blackpool, 2 JI v I,Cs, 3 Jnr IA
11.　**David Barnetson** 1.7.71 (4y, 8) 2.19 '92　2.10, 2.10, 2.10, 2.10, 2.10, 2.10; 2.11i;
　　4= CAU, 6 AAA, 3 Scot, BL2: -,2,1=,-
12=　**Andrew Lynch** 28.6.74 (1y, 10) 2.16 '93　2.14, 2.10, 2.06, 2.05, 2.05, 2.05; 2 UAU,
　　3 IR, 7 CAU, 2= AAA v LC, 8 AAA, 4 WG, 2 K Lynn, 1 Mid
12=　**Alex Kruger** 18.11.63 (7y, 9) 2.20 '88　2.14, 2.13, 2.10, 2.10, 2.08, 2.05; 2.16i, 2.10i; 1 IR, 2 Plate
nr　**Mark Mandy** (Ireland) 19.11.72 2.24 '93　2.22, 2.17, 2.17, 2.16, 2.15, 2.15; 2.24i, 2.20i;
　　2 CAU, 4 AAA, 1 ECp B1, 6 GhG, 6= TSB-Ed, 2 Mid, 2 BLE, 9 McD, BL5: 1,1,1,-

Although held back by injury, and unable to match his indoor heights outdoors, Smith ranks as number one for the third time. Grant also was much better indoors than out, his peak performance being a splendid win at the European Indoors. The first six are the same as in 1993, the one problem being whether the great performance by Parsons at the Commonwealth Games was enough to place him ahead of Reilly, but the latter was unbeaten outdoors by a UK athlete until August and beat Parsons 4-1. Pierre was unbeaten outdoors, but only contested four meetings. The top six are followed by four juniors, all newcomers to the rankings, in places 7-10.

POLE VAULT
1.　**Neil Winter** 21.3.74 (4y, 2) 5.50 '92　5,50, 5.40, 5.40, 5.40, 5.40, 5.35, 5.30;
　　1 W v Sc,I,T, nh AAA, 1 Stoke 25/6, 5 GhG, 1 WG, 7 TSB-Ed, 1 Mid, 4 v USA, 1 W v Sc,N.
　　7 EU23Cp, 1 CG, 7 McD, nh WCp, 4 Jumps Int v3N
2.　**Michael Edwards** 19.10.68 (9y, 1) 5.52 '92　5.42, 5.30, 5.30, 5.25, 5.22, 5.20; 5.30i;
　　2= AAA, 5= ECp, nh GhG, 6 TSB-Ed, 10 TSB-CP, 1 Nitra, 5 v USA, dnq 24= EC, 5 CG, 3 Cup, BL1: -,1,2,3
3.　**Nick Buckfield** 5.6.73 (3y, 4) 5.41 '93　5.40, 5.32, 5.25, 5.20, 5.20, 5.20;
　　2 IR, 1 CAU, 7 v I,H, 1 South, 2 WG, 1 K Lynn, 3 Belgian, 6 v USA, 8 CG, nh McD, 5= Jumps Int v3N, BL1: 3,2,1,2
4.　**Andrew Ashurst** 2.1.65 (11y, 6=) 5.40 '88, 5.45i '92　5.30, 5.20, 5.20, 5.20, 5.20, 5.10; 5.30i;
　　1 IR, 1 AAA, nh GhG, 11 TSB-CP, 3 Stoke 27/7, 6 CG, 8 McD, BL1: 5,3,-,4
5.　**Kevin Hughes** 30.4.73 (2y, 8) 5.05 '93　5.25, 5.20, 5.20, 5.10, 5.10, 5.10; 1 UAU,
　　3 IR, 2= AAA, 5 Stoke 25/6, 2 K Lynn, 4 Belgian, BL1: 1,4,-,7
6.　**Michael Barber** 19.10.73 (2y, 10) 5.10 '93　5.20, 5.20, 5.20, 5.00, 5.00, 5.00; 5.10i;
　　nh IR, 6 AAA, 3 Stoke 25/6, 2 Mid, 2 Stoke 27/7, 2 Cup; BL1: 2,8,3,5
7.　**Matt Belsham** 11.10.71 (5y, 3) 5.35 '93　5.30, 5.20, 5.00, 5.00, 5.00, 5.00; 5.20i;
　　7 AAA, 2 Stoke 25/6, 1 North, 3 N v W,Sc, 1 Stoke 27/7, BL1: 4,nh,nh,nh
8.　**Ian Tullett** 15.8.69 (8y, 5) 5.30 '92　5.10, 5.00, 5.00, 5.00, 4.90, 4.90;
　　4= AAA, 3 South, 3 WG, BL1: 7,5,nh,6
9.　**Paul Williamson** 16.6.74 (1y, 11=) 5.02 '93　5.22, 5.15, 5.10, 5.00, 5.00, 5.00;
　　2 CAU, 9 AAA, 1 AAAv LC, 4 Stoke 25/6
10.　**Tim Thomas** 18.11.73 (1y, 11=) 5.00 '93　5.10, 5.10, 4.90, 4.90, 4.90, 4.80; 5.20 Exh;
　　3 W v Sc,I,T, 1 Welsh, 8 Stoke 25/6, 3 W v B,H, 2 W v Sc,N, BL3: 1,1,1,1
11.　**Dean Mellor** 25.11.71 (4y, 9) 5.22 '91　5.10, 4.90, 4.80, 4.80, 4.80, 4.80; 5.10i;
　　nh CAU, 2 AAA v LC, 4= AAA, 3 North
12.　**Mark Johnson** 7.9.64 (7y, 6=) 5.26 '91　5.11, 4.90, 4.90, 4.80, 4.80, 4.80; 8 AAA, 1 Scot, BL1: 6,6,6,9

After two years at second, Winter replaces Edwards at the top, and is only the 7th man to rank at number one since 1968; he is also the youngest. Edwards and Buckfield; were 2-2 before the Commonwealth Games, where Edwards was placed higher on count-back. Ashurst was between them on 5.20 at Victoria, but was beaten 4-1 by Edwards and was 3-3 with Buckfield. The rest of the top ten are very closely matched, with win-loss records predominantly determining the order. The top twelve cleared 5.10 or better and uniquely for this event all had ranked before. The tenth best standard of 5.10 improves upon the previous best of 5.00 each year 1991-3.

LONG JUMP
1.　**Fred Salle** 10.9.64 (8y, 1) 7.97 '86　8.10, 8.10w, 7.88, 7.85, 7.83, 7.77;
　　2 AAA, 1 AAA v LC, 1 WG, 1 Nitra, 2 v USA, 5 CG, 1 WCp
2.　**Barrington Williams** 11.9.55 (8y, 2) 8.05i/8.01 '89　7.90, 7.77, 7.69, 7.66, 7.63, 7.53; 7.65i, 7.64i;
　　2 IR, 1 CAU, 1 AAA, 6 ECp, 4 v USA, 19 dnq EC, 14 dnq CG
3.　**Michael Morgan** 30.7.66 (1y, -) 7.92/8.01w '86　7.75, 7.66, 7.59, 7.59, 7.55, 7.46;
　　3 AAA, 2 WG, 2 Cup, BL1: -,1,1,-
4.　**Steve Phillips** 17.3.72 (4y, 6) 7.91 '91　7.89w, 7.65, 7.62, 7.61, 7.59w, 7.58;
　　1 IR, 2 CAU, 1 Mid, 3 WG, 1 K Lynn, 6 v USA, 7 EU23 Cp, 3 Cup, BL1: 1,2,3,1

5.   **John Munroe** 6.1.69 (2y, 5) 7.57/7.62w '93   7.57, 7.55w, 7.50, 7.48w (7.45), 7.44, 7.30;
     4 Belgian, 1 Cup, BL1: -,-,4,2
6.   **Courtney Charles** 13.11.68 (1y, 11=) 7.45 '93   7.54, 7.45, 7.35w, 7.26, 7.14, 7.11; 7.22i;
     5 IR, 8 CAU, 1 South, 8 Belgian, BL1: 2,-,5,7
7.   **Carl Howard** 27.1.74 (3y, 4) 7.76 '93   7.45, 7.36, 7.35, 7.32, 7.21w, 7.18w; 3 CAU, 6 AAA, BL1: 3,6,-,-
8.   **Steve Ingram** 22.9.70 (1y, -) 6.91/7.13w '90   7.91w, 7.38, 7.16, 7.09, 7.07, 7.06;
     2 W v Sc,I,T, 1 Welsh, nj qual CG, BL3: 1,-,2,1
9.   **John Mackenzie** 23.8.65 (1y, -) 7.32 '93   7.41w, 7.40w (7.21), 7.36w (7.24), 7.36w (7.23), 7.23, 7.21;
     1 Scot, 3 Sc v N,W, BL1: -,3,6,3
10. **Duncan Mathieson** 8.3.69 (1y, 11=) 7.49 '93, 7.59w '91   7.60, 7.36, 7.31w, 7.28w, 7.11w, 7.08;
     2 Scot, 1 BL2 (3), 1 Sc v W,N, 17 dnq CG
11. **Ennyina Chukukere** 31.7.73 (1y, -) 7.43 '90   7.81w, 7.36, 7.24; 7.64i; 2 BL1 (3).
     Assuming British not Nigerian?
12. **Onochie Onuorah** 16.10.73 (0y, -) 7.31 '93, 7.43w '92   7.39, 7.37, 7.05; 7.03i; 4 AAA, 2 South, 6 Cup
     Alex Kruger 18,11,63 (0y, -) 7.36 '92, 7.57w '89   7.45, 7.40, 7.25, 7.18, 7.16, 7.11; 7.23i
     Simon Shirley 3.8.66 (0y, -) 7.55 '86, 7.56w '88   7.52, 7.31, 7.29, 7.11; 7 AAA

Salle retains his top ranking. He exceeded 8 metres for the first time in his long career twice with wind assistance against the USA at Gateshead. Then, having gone close to a medal in Victoria, he achieved the result of a lifetime as he won the World Cup with 8.10. Williams, who will be 40 next year, remained in second place. British long jumping was boosted by ex-Australian Michael Morgan, but remains a depressed event overall. The most amazing performance was Steve Ingram's 7.91w to win the Welsh title, but that was far superior to anything else that he did.

TRIPLE JUMP
1.   **Jonathan Edwards** 10.5.66 (8y, 1) 17.44/17.70w '93   17.39, 17.06, 17.05, 17.02w, 17.00, 16.97w;
     4 Bratislava, 5 Seville, 1 AAA, 4 ECp, 2 GhG, 1 TSB-Ed, 6 Stockholm, 3 TSB-CP, 1 v USA,
     7 GWG, 2 Monaco, 6 EC, 2 CG, 8 GPF, 7 McD
2.   **Julian Golley** 12.9.71 (5y, 3) 16.95 '92   17.06, 17.03, 16.98, 16.86, 16.82w, 16.81w;
     2 Middx, 7 Bratislava, 2 AAA, 4 TSB-Ed, 5 TSB-CP, 5 v USA,9 EC, 1 CG, 1 McD, 2 WCp, BL1: 1,2,-,-
3.   **Francis Agyepong** 16.6.65 (11y, 4) 16.88/17.00w '92   16.95, 16.95w, 16.93, 16.77, 16.57, 16.50;
     1 Middx, 1 CAU, 3 AAA, 1 South, 5 GhG, 4 TSB-CP, 2 v USA, nj EC, 6 CG, 4 McD, 1 Cup, BL1: 2,1,-,-
4.   **Tosi Fasinro** 28.3.72 (5y, 2) 17.21/17.30w '93   16.74w (16.61), 16.70, 16.68w, 16.62, 16.58, 16.56;
     1 BL4 (1), 3 Middx, 3 Bratislava, 7 Seville, 4 AAA, 4 GhG, 9 Stockholm, 8 TSB-CP, 3 v USA, 1 EU23Cp
5.   **Onochie Achike** 31.1.75 (3y, 5) 16.49 '93   16.67w (16.53), 16.52, 16.36, 16.29, 16.11, 15.95;
     1 IR, 3 BL1 (2), 5 AAA, 2 JI v P,G,R, 2 South, 5 Belgian, 1 WJ, 5 Cologne, 5 McD
6.   **John Mackenzie** 23.8.65 (2y, 8) 15.68/16.04w '93   16.17, 16.12w, 15.99, 15.43, 14.50; 16.13i; 15.18i;
     10 BL1 (2), 6 AAA, 1 Sc v N,W, dnq 14 CG, 2 Cup
7.   **Tayo Erogbogbo** 8.3.57 (1y, 0) 14.57 '92, 15.21w '93   15.93, 15.92, 15.84, 15.60, 15.56, 15.29;
     1 Mid-J, 4 IR, 4 JI v P,G,R, 12 AAA, 1 AAA-J, 8 McD, 3 Cup, BL1: 6,5,-,4
8.   **Michael McDonald** 24.8.65 (2y, -) 15.69 '91   15.78, 15.75, 15.69, 15.64w, 15.63, 15.62;
     2 UAU, 2 IR, 2 CAU, 1 AAA v LC, 2 K Lynn, 1 BLE, dnq 16 CG
9.   **Derek Browne** 28.9.66 (2y, 7) 15.95 '93   15.64, 15.50, 15.29, 15.16, 14.91; 15.72i; 15.20i;
     7 AAA, 5 South, 1 Belgian, BL1: -,5,-,4
10. **Femi Akinsanya** 29.11.69 (1y, 12) 15.74 '93   15.98, 15.70, 15.70, 15.59, 15.53, 15.53w;
     5 IR, 8 AAA, 1 Nitra, 4 Belgian, BL5: 1,1,1,1
11. **Carl Howard** 27.1.74 (0y,) 15.54 '93   15.84, 15.49, 15.26, 15.19w, 15.09; 1 UAU, BL1: 3,6,-,-
12. **Rez Cameron** 18.5.60 (5y, -) 16.20 '88, 16.32w '89   15.59w (15.49), 15.38, 15.36, 15.13, 15.10, 14.66;
     14.72i; 4 Middx, 17 AAA, 4 Cup, BL1: 5,13,3,1
     Joe Allison 16.9.59 (2y, -) 15.86 '85, 15.93w '86   15.41, 15.27, 14.98w, 14.93, 14.91, 14.90;
     15 AAA, BL1: -,8,1,-

Edwards is UK no.1 for the fifth time, although after a magnificent 17.39 at the AAAs he slipped a little from his 1993 form. He was 6-2 on win-loss against Golley, who broke through to world class with his brilliant Commonwealth gold and World Cup silver. Agyepong had some good results but disappointed in the major championships. He was 5-1 up on Fasinro, who competed well, but was most unfortunate that 4th ranking in England meant that he missed championship chances. He is followed by Achike, the World Junior champion, before a big gap to the next contenders. I included the highly promising Tayo Erogbogbo in the rankings, although the former Nigerian was unable to take up selection for the World Juniors as he had yet to receive a British passport. Allison beat Cameron 3-0, but his series of marks was much worse.

SHOT
1.   **Matthew Simson** 28.5.70 (8y, 2) 19.23 '91   19.49, 18.99, 18.97, 18.81, 18.80, 18.80; 19.17i; 18.92i;
     5 NCAA, 2 K Lynn, 2 AAA, 5 v USA, 1 CG
2.   **Nigel Spratley** 1.4.70 (5y, 4=) 17.56 '93   17.96, 17.68, 17.63, 17.62, 17.55, 17.33;
     3 Bracknell, 1 IR, 1 CAU, 4 AAA, 2 Dublin, 1 South, 2 WG, 2 Salisbury, 1 Belgian, 6 v USA, 7 CG, 8 WCp

3. **Lee Newman** 1.5.73 (2y, 10) 17.09i/16.51 '93   17.94, 17.85, 17.50, 17.46, 17.41, 17.33; 17.35i;
   2 Bracknell, 2 IR, 3 AAA, 3 WG, 3 K Lynn, 2 Belgian, 5 EU23Cp, 1 Cup, BL2: 1,-,1,1
4. **Mark Proctor** 15.1.63 (3y, 4=) 17.46 '92   18.15, 17.69, 17.38, 17.23, 17.06, 16.97; 17.79i, 17.64i, 17.33i;
   3 IR, 2 CAU, 9 AAA, 3 South, 5 WG, 1 IS, BL1: 2,3,2,-
5. **David Callaway** 4.9.63 (7y, 3) 17.55 '93   17.35, 16.94, 16.93, 16.73, 16.73, 16.68; 17.12i, 16.96i, 16.81i;
   4 Bracknell, 1 Hants, 4 IR, 7 E Clubs, 5 AAA, 2 South, 6 WG, 3 Salisbury, BL1:3,2,3,-
6. **Lee Wiltshire** 26.7.62 (3y, 8=) 17.19, 17.33, 17.03, 16.95, 16.93, 16.89;
   2 Hants, 3 W v Sc,I,T, 7 AAA, 1 Welsh, 7 WG, 14 CG
7. **Steve Whyte** 14.3.64 (7y, 8=) 17.78 '89   17.29, 16.88, 16.84, 16.75, 16.69, 16.60; 17.29i, 17.10i, 17.02i,
   16.94i; 8 AAA, 1 Sc v W,N, 12 CG
8. **Shaun Pickering** 14.11.61 (11y, 6) 18.31 '92   16.96, 16.84, 16.79, 16.48, 16.42, 16.19; 17.32i, 16.64i;
   10 AAA, 4 WG, BL1: 4,-,5,-
9. **Gary Sollitt** 13.1.72 (1y, -) 15.57 '92   16.68, 16.56, 16.41, 16.35, 16.30, 16.17;
   3 Hants, 3 CAU, 1 AAA v LC, 3 Dublin, 4 South, 4 K Lynn
10. **Paul Reed** 2.6.62 (2y, 11) 17.04 '88   16.71, 16.26, 16.19, 16.16, 16.13, 16.02; 16.56i, 16.52i, 16.28i;
    6 IR, 8 CAU, 3 Cork, 1 North, 4 Eur Police
11. **Martyn Fletcher** 21.1.69 (1y, -) 16.48 '92   16.15, 16.09, 16.08, 16.02, 15.95, 15.84; 16.35i, 16.00i;
    5 IR, 4 CAU, 2 AAA v LC, 12 AAA, 4 Cork, 4 BL1 (3), 2 North, 2 N v Sc,W, 2 Cup
12. **David Condon** 11.4.72 (0y, 12) 16.09 '93   16.41, 16.10, 16.04, 15.91, 15.87, 15.63;
    5 Bracknell, 1 Essex, 5 CAU, 13 AAA, 5 South, 3 Cup, BL1: 5,-,6,-
u **Simon Williams** 17.79; 18.00i, 17.88i; in USA

Unranked due to positive drugs test
(1) **Paul Edwards** 16.2.59 (7y, 1) 20.33 '92   19.94, 19.82, 19.44, 19.11, 19.02, 19.02; 19.47i, 19.38i, 19.27i;
     1 AAA, 7 ECp, 1 WG, 1 K Lynn, 1 Salisbury, 4 v USA, dnq 13 EC, BL1: 1,1,1,-

Simson's splendid Commonwealth gold, when he added 26 cm to his pb, assured him of top ranking after two years in second place and three in third in the previous two years. Until failing a drugs test Edwards remained Britain's best and beat Simson on the two occasions they met. There is then a big gap in class, before Sprately and Newman make the top three for the first time. Proctor had the better marks and beat Callaway 4-3, but the latter was ahead at AAA and Southern. All 12 had ranked before and the 10th best standard of 17.29 is the highest ever.

DISCUS
1. **Robert Weir** 4.2.61 (7y, 1) 62.50 '84   61.06, 60.86, 58.92, 58.72, 58.64, 57.94;
   2 AAA, 6 ECp, 4 v USA, dnq 13 EC, 3 CG, 7 WCp, 1 Cup, BL1: -, -,1,1
2. **Kevin Brown** 10.9.64 (9y, 3) 59.20 '91   58.68, 58.60, 56.78, 56.68, 56.12, 55.40;
   1 AAA, 1 Lough, 3 Nitra, 1 Mid, 5 v USA, 10 CG, BL1: 1,2,3,-
3. **Glen Smith** 21.5.72 (3y, -) 57.82 '92   59.78, 56.60, 56.52, 56.22, 55.92, 55.84;
   1 Warwicks, 3 IR, 1 CAU, 1 AAA v LC, 3 AAA, 2 Lough, 1 K Lynn, 2 Mid, 6 v USA, 3 EU23Cp, 6 CG
4. **Lee Newman** 1.5.73 (1y, -) 53.14 '93   58.34, 57.02, 56.20, 56.04, 55.90, 55.56;
   1 Bracknell, 1 IR, 2 AAA v LC, 4 AAA, 2 Dublin, 1 Belgian, 1 Rugby, 3 Cup, BL2: 1,1,1,1
5. **Darrin Morris** 28.7.67 (6y, 2) 58.58 '91   57.72, 56.38, 56.16, 55.02, 54.98, 54.76;
   2 Sc v W,I,T, 2 CAU, 6 AAA, 3 Lough, 3 Mid, 1 Sc v W,N, 8 CG, 6 Cup, BL1: 2,1,-,-
6. **Neville Thompson** 28.3.55 (28y, 4) 55.68 '93   55.40, 54.96, 54.82, 54.68, 54.62, 53.66;
   2 IR, 5 CAU, 5 AAA, 1 Dublin, 1 South, 2 Belgian, 2 Rugby, 2 Cup, BL1: 3,4,2,3
7. **Simon Williams** 17.10.67 (5y, -)61.14 '92   58.32, 57.94, 55.44, 53.80; 2 Austin
8. **Jamie Murphy** 20.3.73 (2y, 7) 55.14 '93   55.24, 54.44, 52.78, 52.72, 52.70, 52.66;
   3 AAA v LC, 7 AAA, 4 Lough, 2 K Lynn
9. **Leith Marar** 7.11.68 (2y, 6) 54.58 '93   53.52, 53.34, 53.30, 53.06, 52.50, 52.26;
   1 UAU, 3 Bracknell, 3 CAU, 8 AAA, 2 South, 4 Belgian, BL1: 5,3,5,2
10. **Gary Herrington** 31.3.61 (6y, 8) 56.02 '87   54.20, 53.56, 53.14, 52.52, 52.16, 52.14;
    2 Warwicks, 4 IR, 13 AAA, 4 Mid, 3 Rugby, 1 Eur Police
11= **Nick Woolcott** 7.4.61 (5y, 12) 55.34 '88   54.90, 54.62, 54.52, 53.28, 52.46, 51.88;
    4 CAU, 11 AAA, 3 South, BL1: 8,8,-,5
11= **Paul Reed** 2.6.62 (2y, 11) 54.26 '87   54.50, 53.44, 53.00, 52.40, 51.44, 51.40;
    5 IR, 6 CAU, 9 AAA, 2 North, 9 Eur Police
Not ranked but close
    Matt Symonds 31.7.68 (0y, -) 50.82 '90   52.16, 51.30, 51.10, 51.06, 50.60, 50.28;
    4 Bracknell, 7 CAU, 12 AAA, 4 South, 4 Cup, BL1: 7,5,7,4
    Mark Proctor 15.1.63 (1y, 5) 54.28 '93   53.40, 52.28, 50.94, 50.84, 50.60, 50.52;
    10 AAA, 5 Lough, 1 IS, BL1: 4,9,4,-

Weir retains his top ranking by a clear margin. Smith was next in the Commonwealth Games, but lost 1-4 to Brown, who also beat Morris 4-2 and reaches his highest ever ranking. Newman beat Morris 2-0. Williams had four meetings in the USA in March and April, but did not return and is difficult to rank. All 12 men have been ranked in the top 12 before.

HAMMER

1. **Paul Head** 1.7.65 (12y, 1) 74.02 '90   71.16, 70.18, 69.32, 69.14, 69.12, 69.08;
    2 CAU, 2 AAA, 1 WG, 2 Nitra, 6 v USA, 2 Kingston, 2 CG, 8 WCp, BL1: -,2,1,1
2. **Peter Vivian** 5.11.70 (4y, 6) 67.52 '93   70.80, 70.66, 70.58, 70.32, 70.14, 70.04;
    1 IR, 1 AAA, 7 ECp, 1 Belgian, 2 v USA, 1 Kingston, 3 CG, 1 Cup, BL1: 1,1,2,2
3. **Michael Jones** 23.7.63 (13y, 4) 72.10 '88   68.68, 68.42, 68.28, 68.22, 68.04, 67.42;
    1 CAU, 3 AAA, 2 WG, 5 v USA, 4 CG, 2 Cup, BL1: -,3,3,3
4. **David Smith** 2.11.74 (1y, -) 59.98 '93   67.74, 66.82, 65.98, 65.82, 65.74, 65.34;
    3 IR, 7 CAU, 1 AAA v LC, 3 WG, 3 K Lynn, 1 North, 8 EU23Cp
5. **Shane Peacock** 5.3.63 (9y, 5) 71.60 '90   66.68, 65.84, 65.70, 65.08, 64.40, 63.44;
    4 AAA, 3 Cup, BL1: 2,4,-,4
6. **Steve Pearson** 13.9.59 (2y, 12) 64.04 '93   65.24, 64.84, 64.78, 64.76, 64.48, 64.46;
    2 IR, 6 CAU, 3 AAA v LC, 5 AAA, 1 Mid, BL2: 1,1,1,1
7. **John Pearson** 30.4.66 (5y, 8) 65.20 '92   66.54, 65.36, 65.28, 64.48, 64.30, 63.92;
    1 UAU, 4 CAU, 2 AAA v LC, 7 AAA, 2 Mid
8. **Karl Andrews** 21.3.75 (1y, -) 61.60 '93   65.30, 63.56, 63.54, 63.38, 62.82, 62.70;
    5 IR, 3 CAU, 6 AAA, 5 JI v P,G,R, 1 AAA-J, 3 Mid, 10 WJ
9. **Steve Whyte** 14.3.64 (1y, -) 67.82 '89   64.02, 63.96, 63.66, 63.36, 63.10, 63.02;
    2 Sc v W,I,T, 5 CAU, 8 AAA, 1 Sc v W,N, 9 CG
10. **Russell Devine** 24.4.68 (3y, 11) 64.40 '93   65.36, 63.56, 63.32, 63.08, 62.90, 62.76;
    6 Australian, 1 Scot, 11 CG
11. **Chris Howe** 17.11.67 (6y, 10) 63.74 '90   63.06, 62.80, 62.12, 62.06, 60.86, 60.82;
    6 IR, 5 AAA v LC, 2 South, 4 Belgian, BL2: 2,2,2,2
12. **Gareth Cook** 20.2.69 (6y, 9) 67.32 '91   63.56, 63.54, 62.58, 62.40, 61.80, 61.62; 1 Surrey
nr **Jason Byrne** 9.9.70 (6y, 2) 73.80 '92   65.54 in only meeting

Vivian made excellent progress to become Britain's best in the first half of the season. Head, however, returned from injury, and his Commonwealth silver to Vivian's bronze was decisive in him just doing enough to rank as number one for the sixth successive year, although he was beaten 4-3 by Vivian. Head's six years at the top equals Chris Black's record since I started these rankings in 1968. Jones completed nine successive years in the top four, and is followed by the highest placed newcomer, David Smith, who made a huge improvement and replaces his namesake in the rankings. Whyte is in the top 12 for the 6th time since 1987, but makes the top 10 for the first time.
For the second successive year the tenth ranking mark is a new best for Britain, 65.24 this year to 64.18 in 1993.

JAVELIN

1. **Steve Backley** 12.2.69 (8y, 2) 91.46 '92   85.20, 85.02, 84.94, 84.78, 84.68, 84.66, 84.34, 84.24, 84.10;
    1/1/1 in SA, 2 AAA, 2 Helsinki, 9 GhG, 3 TSB-CP, 1 v USA, 7 Oslo, 1 EC, 2 Zürich, 1 CG, 3 McD, 1 WCp, 4 Tokyo
2. **Michael Hill** 22.10.64 (11y, 1) 86.94 '93   86.36, 85.28, 84.60, 84.44, 84.22, 83.60;
    2/2/2 in SA, 1 CAU, 1 AAA, 3 ECp, 3 Helsinki, 3 GhG, 1 TSB-Ed, 5 Stockholm, 1 TSB-CP,
    2 v USA, 4 Oslo, 6 EC, 4 Zürich, 3 Brussels, 2 CG, 7 McD
3. **Colin Mackenzie** 30.6.63 (13y, 3) 82.60 roughened tail '91, 82.38 '93   79.16, 78.86, 78.34, 78.28, 74.84,
    74.54; from dq: 80.82, 76.28; 1 IR, 2 CAU, 3 AAA, 1 South, 7 GhG, 2 WG, 5 TSB-Ed,
    10 TSB-CP, BL1: 1,2,-,-. After dq: dnq 22 EC
4. **Nigel Bevan** 3.1.68 (8y, 6) 81.70 '92   80.38, 77.94, 72.96, 72.48, 72.42, 72.06;
    3 W v Sc,I,T, 8 AAA, 1 Welsh, 3 WG, 1 W v Sc,N, 4 CG, 12 McD, 1 Cup, BL1: 2,3,2,6
5. **Mark Roberson** 13.3.67 (9y, 4) 80.92 '88   78.82, 75.84, 75.26, 74.16, 73.78, 73.70;
    2 IR, 5 E Clubs, 6 AAA, 2 South, 1 WG, 7 TSB-Ed, 1 Nitra, 3 v USA, 7 CG, BL1: 3,1,1,1
6. **Roald Bradstock** 24.4.62 (15y, 5) 83.84 '87   77.22, 76.76, 75.64, 75.54, 73.98, 72.84;
    1 BL3 (2), 5 AAA
7. **Nick Nieland** 31.1.72 (2y, 7) 74.50 '93   76.28, 73.12, 71.92, 70.74, 68.26;
    1 UAU, 1 K Lynn, 5 U23 v G,R, 7 EU23Cp, 11 McD, 2 Cup
8. **Myles Cottrell** 22.11.70 (4y, 9=) 74.70 '92   74.30, 72.22, 70.80, 70.32, 68.98, 66.72;
    6/5/- SA, 3 CAU, 4 AAA, 1 Dublin, BL1:4,6,-,-
9. **Peter Yates** 15.6.57 (17y, 11) 77.84 '87   70.54, 69.76, 69.50, 69.32, 67.80, 66.94;
    9 AAA, 4 Cup, BL2: 1,1,1,-
10. **Steve Harrison** 19.12.72 (1y, -) 64.34 '91   71.94, 69.88, 69.36, 66.92, 66.40, 65.62;
    3 IR, 2 Dublin, 3 BL2 (3), 2 K Lynn, 1 Belgian
11. **Shane Lewis** 22.8.72 (0y, -) 64.30 '93   69.68, 68.52, 67.68, 66.26, 66.12, 65.86;
    2 UAU, 5 W v Sc,I,T, 10 AAA, 2 Welsh, 4 WG, 5 K Lynn; BL3: 1,2,1,-
12. **Phil Parry** 4.10.65 (0y, -) 67.90 '92   70.00, 68.76, 66.30, 66.04, 62.96; 1 Scot, 2 Belgian; BL2: -,-,2,5

    Stefan Baldwin 26.4.70 (1y, 12) 72.92 '93   69.10, 69.02, 66.94, 66.04, 63.58, 62.74; 3 Cup: BL1: 5,4,3,8

Backley and Hill swap places at the top, with the former number one for the fifth time and with a brilliant return from injury to achieve the triple crown of European, Commonwealth and World Cup. Hill was over 80m in 19 of his 21 meetings and Backley had 15 meetings over 80m and three under. Mackenzie beat Roberson 5-2 to rank third on his performances prior to his 3-month drugs disqualification at Rovereto, where he went over 80m for the only time in 1994. Bevan added over 7 metres to his previous year's best to excel at the Commonwealth Games, and although 2-4 down to Roberson this, with another good result in the Cup, was enough to give him priority. Yates, ranking each year from 1976, equals David Ottley's all-time record of 19 years ranked.

DECATHLON

1. **Alex Kruger** 18.11.63 (9y, 1) 7986 '92   8078, 7963, 7640; 7 Götzis, 3 ECp, 7 CG
2. **Simon Shirley** 3.8.66 (2y, 2) 8036 '88   7980, 7938, 7936w; 11 Götzis, 4 ECp, 3 CG
3. **Rafer Joseph** 21.7.68 (2y, -) 7300 '91   7663, 7563, 7525; 5 Emmelshausen, 11 ECp, 6 CG
4. **Jamie Quarry** 15.11.72 (3y, -) 7018 '91   7610, 7452; 6 Emmelshausen, 8 CG
5. **Barry Thomas** 28.4.72 (4y, 8) 7616 '92   7458, 7350, 7309, 6992; 16 ECp, 1 AAA, 1 Mid, 1g Welsh
6. **David Bigham** 4.7.71 (7y, 6) 7904 '92   7434; 2 AAA
7. **Andrew Lewis** 9.3.68 (1y, -) 7094 '92   7221, 7112, 6916, 6709; 4 Azusa, 6 v Cs,It, 3 AAA, dnf Welsh, 1 Diekirch
8. **Stephen Rogers** 1.9.71 (1y, 11) 7014 '93   7203, 7064; 10 Emmelshausen, 3 Kaiserslauten
9. **Paul Field** 24.6.67 (2y, -) 7127 '92   7157; 4 AAA
10. **Steve Leader** 24.11.66 (1y, -) 6845w/6755 '93   7078; dnf North, 5 AAA
11. **Rob Laing** 30.7.66 (5y, -) 7076 '89   7048, 6990, 6726; 1 North, 4 v Cs,Ita, 7 AAA
12. **Steve Gutteridge** 5.7.71 (0y, -) 6790 '93   7047, 6972, 6865; 1B Azusa, 8 v Cs,Ita, 8 AAA

Kruger beat Shirley 2-1 to rank top for the fourth time and exceeded 8000 points at Götzis, while Shirley was most unlucky to have three scores just below that level. After two years out Joseph had by far his best ever year and improved his best by 363 points.

20 KILOMETRES WALK

1. **Darrell Stone** 2.2.68 (6y, 2=) 1:25:05 '92, 1:23:27 sh? '93   1:26:53, 1:27:02+, 1:27:24; 1 UK, 20 Livorno, dnf Douglas
2. **Martin Bell** 9.4.61 (3y, 8) 1:25:42 '92   1:26:11, 1:27:18, 1:31:08; 2 UK, 22 Livorno, 1 Douglas
3. **Steve Partington** 17.9.65 (7y, 4) 1:24:18 '90   1:24:09, 1:28:04+, 1:29:11, 1:29:48; dq UK, 2 RWA, 31 Livorno, 1 Dublin
4. **Chris Cheeseman** 11.12.58 (1y, -) 1:37:13 '91   1:29:11, 1:29:58, 1:30:37, 1:31:46; 3 UK, 1 RWA, 5 Douglas, 34 Livorno
5. **Mark Easton** 24.5.63 (8y, 6) 1:24:04 '89   1:28:06, 1:31:09+, 1:33:42; dq UK, 1 Colchester
6. **Chris Maddocks** 28.3.57 (12y, 1) 1:22:12 '92   1:28:44, 1:31:24+; dq UK, 1 Burrator
7. **Philip King** 25.11.74 (1y, -) 0   1:29:49; 3 RWA, dnf Douglas
8. **Steve Taylor** 19.3.66 (1y, -) 1:28:46 '92   1:32:34+, 1:33:52, 1:34:08, 1:36:43; 4 UK, 1 Isle of Man, 7 Douglas
9. **Graham White** 28.3.59 (2y, -) 1:31:02 '83   1:34:11; 4 RWA
10. **Karl Atton** 14.9.71 (1y, -) 1:35:38 '93   1:34:28, 1:34:43; 5 RWA, 9 Douglas

Stone won the UK title and takes his first top ranking. He went on to a great 4th at the Commonwealth 30k. Bell and Cheeseman also made good progress. Sadly it has to be said that the standard of UK walking has never been lower in world terms. The 10th best performer level is 1:34:28, exactly the same as in 1993, the worst since 1969.

30/35 KILOMETRES WALK

1. **Darrell Stone** 2.2.68 35k: 2:41:53 '90   2:11:30, 2:22:49; 3 Cardiff, 4 CG
2. **Steve Partington** 17.9.65 2:16:52 '93   2:14:15, 2:17:46; 2 Manx, 7 CG
3. **Chris Maddocks** 28.3.57 2:11:09 '85, 35k: 2:43:12 '84   2:18:14, 2:22:45; 1 Trial, 12 CG
4. **Mark Easton** 24.5.63 2:13:33 '89   2:14:16, 2:16:21, 2:20:10; 1 Manx, dq Trial, 1 Cardiff, 13 CG
5. **Steve Taylor** 19.3.66 2:24:23 '93   2:21:34; 14 CG
6. **Martin Bell** 9.4.61   2:22:21; 2 Cardiff, dnf CG
7. **Graham White** 28.3.59   2:23:52, 2:26:27; 2 Trial, 4 Cardiff. 35k: 30 Livorno 2:48:50

50 KILOMETRES WALK

1. **Les Morton** 1.7.58 (11y, 1) 3:57:48 '89   1 RWA 4:32:25
2. **Tim Watt** 19.9.66 (1y, -) 0   2 RWA 4:36:35
3. **Chris Berwick** 1.5.46 (10y, 6) 4:23:22'86   3 RWA 4:40:41
4. **Graham White** 28.3.59 (1y, -) 0   4 RWA 4:46:15

Morton is top for the 9th time in ten years, but his time when he won the RWA was 4:32:25. The event has all but died out in Britain. Super Vets Ted Shillabeer and Bob Dobson, ranked in the top ten for 26 successive years, kept the flag flying, but their best times were 4:51:44 and 4:52:35 respectively and I could not justify a ranking of more than four.

BRITISH MERIT RANKINGS 1994 - WOMEN

100 METRES
1. **Paula Thomas** 3.12.64 (9y, 3=) 11.24 '89, 11.13w '88   11.15, 11.23, 11.30, 11.37, 11.42, 11.46;
1 G.Manchester, 5 AAA, 1 WG, 3 v USA, 5s2 EC, 3 CG, 7 WCp, BL1: 2,1,-
2. **Katharine Merry** 21.9.74 (6y, 5) 11.52 '92, 11.40w '93   11.27w, 11.34, 11.34, 11.44, 11.44, 11.49;
1 BL2 (1), 1 IR, 1 IA, 1 AAA, 2 ECp
3. **Stephanie Douglas** 22.1.69 (6y, 1) 11.27 '91   11.34, 11.35w, 11.40, 11.43, 11.46, 11.48;
2 G Manchester, 2 IR, 2 AAA, 1 Dublin, 2 Helsinki, 2 WG, 4 v USA, 7s2 EC, 8 CG
4. **Simmone Jacobs** 5.9.66 (10y, 3=) 11.31 '88, 11.26w '84   11.37w, 11.47, 11.57, 11.63, 11.64, 11.65;
2 BL2 (1), 2 IA, 3 AAA, 6 Helsinki, 6 v USA, 6s2 CG
5. **Marcia Richardson** 10.2.72 (4y, 2) 11.45 '93   11.39w, 11.46, 11.49, 11.53, 11.56, 11.69; 11.6;
4 AAA, 7 Helsinki, 3 WG, 1 K Lynn, 1 Nitra, 7 v USA, 7q1 EC, BL4: 1,1,-
6. **Geraldine McLeod** 24.9.71 (3y, 6) 11.58/11.46w '93   11.51w, 11.63, 11.66, 11.70; 11.2; 6 AAA
7. **Danaa Myhill** 16.10.70 (1y, -) 11.90/11.75w '92, 11.6 '91   11.58w, 11.60, 11.63, 11.74, 11.76, 12.00; 11.6;
1 Lancs, 7 AAA, 2 Cork, 3 North, 8sq CG
8. **Aileen McGillivary** 13.8.70 (4y, 9) 11.54 '92, 11.43w '93   11.56w, 11.57w, 11.76, 11.92; 12.0;
1 Scot, 4 WG, 1 Sc v W,N
9. **Samantha Farquharson** 15.12.69 (1y, -) 11.87 '91   11.78, 11.87, 11.94, 11.96, 12.04; 11.9;
4 IR, 4 IA, 1 South, 1B Nitra
10. **Sophia Smith** 8.12.74 (1y, 11) 11.70/11.56w '93   11.82, 11.82w, 11.90, 11.93, 11.93, 11.98; 11.8;
3 IR, 1 AAA v LC, 5s2 AAA, 2 K Lynn, 2B Nitra, 1 North, 1B EU23Cp, 2 Nth IC, BL3: 1,1,-
11. **Donna Hoggarth** 14.10.73 (2y, 8) 11.61/11.55w '92   11.78w, 11.83, 11.84, 11.91, 11.97, 11.98;
2 Lancs, 3 IA, 8 AAA, 3 K Lynn, 2 North, 2 N v Sc,W, 1 Nth IC
12. **Rebecca Drummond** 18.4.78 (0y, -) 11.92 '93   11.50w, 11.81w, 11.96; 11.9;
1 Mid-I, 1 ESch-I, 1 AAA U17, 1 v It,Cz-J
Diane Allahgreen 21.2.75 (0y, -) 11.88/11.78w '93   11.89, 12.00, 12.07; 1 Nth-J, 1 AAA-J

At the beginning of the year Merry swept to the top of British sprinting, having ranked for five years at 100m as a junior. However after her brilliant 2nd place in the European Cup, she was injured and ran no more at 100m. It still seemed that she had done enough to rank number one - but then came Thomas at the Commonwealth Games, and Paula's marvellous running there is just enough for her to regain the top ranking that she held each year from 1986 to 1989. Her five years at the top is a new record for the event since 1968. Bev Kinch, number one in 1993, had only four 100m races, with bests of 11.97 and 11.8. The 10th best performance level of 11.78 is the worst since 1980.

200 METRES
1= **Katharine Merry** 21.9.74 (5y, 1) 23.20 '94   22.85, 23.00, 23.10, 23.38, 23.55, 23.73; 23.00i, 23.38i;
1 BL2 (1), 1 AAA, 2 ECp, 8s1 EC
1= **Paula Thomas** 3.12.64 (7y, -) 22.79 '88   22.69, 22.91, 23.04w, 23.09, 23.22, 23.25;
3 AAA, 1 BL1 (2), 1 WG, 1 Nitra, 6s2 EC, 4 CG, 6 WCp
3. **Stephanie Douglas** 22.1.69 (5y, 8) 23.30 '91   23.17, 23.29w, 23.30w, 23.59, 23.67w, 23.92; 23.2;
1B BL1 (1), 1 G Manchester, 2 IR, 2 AAA, 4 TSB-Ed, 5 v USA, 5s2 CG
4. **Simmone Jacobs** 5.9.66 (11y, 5) 23.12 '91, 23.01w '84   23.48, 23.52, 23.58, 23.64, 23.69, 23.73;
1 IR, 1 IA, 4 AAA, 1 South, 4 WG, 1 Belgian, 3 v USA, 6h1 EC
5. **Geraldine McLeod** 24.9.71 (3y, 12) 23.88 '92   23.47, 23.52, 23.52, 23.52, 23.52w, 23.57;
1B BL2 (1), 5 AAA, 2 WG, 6 TSB-Ed, 4 v USA, 8 CG
6. **Marcia Richardson** 10.2.72 (1y, 11) 24.07 '92, 23.4 '93   23.55, 23.62, 23.98, 24.05, 24.18, 24.21; 23.5;
6 AAA, 2 South, BL4: 1,1,-
7. **Aileen McGillivary** 13.8.70 (4y, 3) 23.29 '93   23.42w, 23.61, 23.95w, 24.69; 23.7, 24.0;
dnf IA, 3 WG, 7 TSB-Ed, 1 Sc v W,N
8. **Melanie Neef** 26.5.70 (1y, -) 24.10 '88, 23.91w '93   23.64, 23.81, 23.98, 24.10w; 24.5, 24.6w;
2 Sc v W,I,T, 1 Bruges, BL1: 3,2,-
9. **Paula Cohen** 5.2.71 (3y, 7) 23.64 '92   23.67, 23.89, 23.91, 23.98, 24.36; 24.2;
2 G Manchester, 3 IR, 7 AAA, 1 Cork, 5 WG, BL1: 4,1B,-
10. **Catherine Murphy** 21.9.75 (1y, -) 24.06/23.72w '93   23.83w, 23.85, 23.88, 24.06, 24.19w, 24.31; 24,2;
1 Sth-J, 8 AAA, 2h1 AAA-J, 2 ESch, 1 Jnr IA, 1 Cup, BL2: 2,-,1
11. **Sophia Smith** 8.12.74 (1y, 6) 23.57 '93   23.68, 23.87, 24.01, 24.14, 24.20; 23.8, 23.9w;
2 IA, 2h2 AAA, 1 BL3 (2), 2 Cork, 1 North, 1 K Lynn, 7 EU23Cp
12. **Susan Earnshaw** 13.10.70 (0y, -) 24.34/24.3/24.1w '93   23.80w, 23.94w, 24.13, 24.16; 23.5, 24.0, 24.0w;
5 IA, 4h1 AAA, 3 Cork, 2 North, 2 N v Sc,W, 1 Nth IC

The story is similar to that in the 100m, but Merry was even more brilliant in the 200m and holds on to tie for first with Thomas, who came storming through at the Commonwealth Games. Thomas had ranked first at this event in 1988 and 1989. Jacobs beat Douglas 2-1, but the latter was decisively better at the AAA and had the faster times. McLeod was close to those two, 2-2 v Douglas and 1-2 v Jacobs. Neef only ran the 200m occasionally, but edged Cohen on the one occasion that they met.

400 METRES

1. **Sally Gunnell** 29.7.66 (6y, 2) 51.11 '91   51.04, 51.92; 51.72i, 52.34i, 52.84i; 1 E Clubs, 1 v USA
2. **Phylis Smith** 29.9.65 (4y, 1) 50.40 '92   51.30, 51.36, 51.46, 51.53, 51.7, 51.79, 51.87;
    1BL1 (2), 5 GhG, 4 v USA, 3 EC, 4 WCp, 1 Cup
3. **Melanie Neef** 26.5.70 (1y, -) 54.14 '93   52.09, 52.10, 52.23, 52.43, 52.44, 52.53;
    1 AAA, 2 ECp, 7 TSB-CP, 5 v USA, 6 EC, 6 CG
4. **Linda Keough** 26.12.63 (11y, 3) 50.98 '91   52.95, 53.40, 53.4, 53.42, 53.6, 53.63; 1 Dublin, 2 Nitra, 6s1 EC
5. **Tracy Goddard** 29.11.69 (4y, 5) 53.23 '91   53.55, 53.59, 53.84, 53.93, 53.99, 54.2, 54.21; 53.72i;
    1 IR, 1 IA, 2 AAA, 7 GhG, 7s1 CG
6. **Sandra Douglas** 22.4.67 (4y, -) 51.41 '92   53.0, 53.34, 53.78, 54.38, 55.0, 55.64;
    3 AAA, 1 WG, 6h1 CG, BL1: 1,2,-
7= **Donna Fraser** 7.11.72 (2y, -) 52.54 '91   53.44, 53.75, 53.87, 54.19, 54.31, 54.47;
    2 AAA v LC, 7 AAA, 2 Dublin, 3 WG, 1 K Lynn, 3 Nitra, 7 v USA, 5 EU23 Cp
7= **Janet Levermore** 7.6.69 (1y, -) 55.39i/55.4 '91   53.53, 53.92, 54.62, 55.0, 55.24, 55.3;
    4 AAA, 2 WG, 8 v USA, 1 BL2 (3)
9. **Nicola Crowther** 15.5.70 (1y, -) 54.21 '92   53.76, 54.01, 54.4, 54.47, 54.54, 54.70;
    3 BL1 (1), 5 IA, 5 AAA, 4 WG, 4 Nitra
10. **Stephanie McCann** 23.10,65 (2y, -) 54.14 '90   53.91, 53.96, 54.0, 54.25, 54.73, 54.81;
    1 NI, 3 K Lynn, 1 BLE, 6s2 CG
11. **Claire Raven** 15.6.72 (1y, 9) 53.99 '92   54.05, 54.23, 54.28, 54.49, 54.71, 55.40;
    1 UAU, 2 IA, 1 AAA v LC, 6 AAA, dns Mid, 6 WG, 4 K Lynn
12. **Louretta Thorne** 6.5.77 (0y, -) 57.5 '93   54.27, 54.37, 54.37, 55.06, 55.8, 56.4;
    2 JI v P,G,R, 4h3 WJ, 1 JI v CS,I, 1 Jnr IA

Not ranked but close
    Susan Earnshaw 13.10.70 (0y, -) 56.4 '90   53.89, 55.2, 55.5, 56.1; 1 Plate
    Gillian Cashell 5.4.64 (0y, 12) 54.65 '93   54.35, 54.4, 54.7, 54.77, 54.80, 55.15;
    3 W v Sc,I,T, 3 IA, 8 AAA, 1 Welsh, 4 South, 2 Plate

Gunnell won all her races - two outdoors, three indoors. She ran the season's fastest time and beat Smith in the USA match. That was just enough perhaps to give her the edge over Smith, who came back from injury to gain a well deserved European medal, with 4th places in Commonwealth and World Cup. Neef leaps straight in at number three, improving her pb six times in a long, splendidly consistent season.

800 METRES

1. **Kelly Holmes** 19.4.70 (3y, 2) 1:58.64 '93   1:59.43, 1:59.92, 2:00.48, 2:00.63, 2:01.56, 2:01.80;
    2 Helsinki, 3 GhG, 1 TSB-CP, 1 McD, 2 Madrid
2. **Ann Griffiths** 20.8.65 (4y, -) 1:59.88 '91   1:59.81, 2:01.29, 2:01.67, 2:01.86, 2:02.42, 2:03.49;
    1 AAA v LC, 4 GhG, 5 TSB-CP, 5 EC
3. **Sonya Bowyer** 18.9.72 (1y, -) 2:05.85 '93   2:02.30, 2:02.92, 2:03.18, 2:03.79, 2:04.75, 2:05.92;
    1 Crawley, 2 AAA v LC, 3 AAA, 5 GhG, 7 TSB-CP, 2 v USA, 5h3 CG
4. **Catherine Dawson** 9.3.66 (2y, 10) 2:03.55 '93   2:03.17, 2:03.20, 2:03.39, 2:03.81, 2:03.83, 2:04.13;
    5 Wyth, 1 W v Sc,I,T, 1 Welsh, 2 WG, 3 v USA, 1 W v Sc,N, 4 CG, 5 McD, 7 WCp
5. **Dawn Gandy** 28.7.65 (5y, 8) 2:01.87 '88   2:03.75, 2:03.85, 2:04.38, 2:04.65, 2:05.35, 2:05.65; 2:05.28i;
    3 Wyth, 2 Crawley, 2 AAA, 6 GhG, 3 WG, 1 Nitra, 5 v USA, 4h1 CG
6. **Jo Latimer** 30.1.71 (2y, 4) 2:03.55 '93   2:03.27, 2:04.05, 2:05.19, 2:05.9, 2:06.2, 2:06.7;
    4 Wyth, 5 Crawley, 1 BL1 (2), 12 Helsinki, 1 K Lynn, 4 v USA, 4h2 CG, dnf McD
7. **Angela Davies** 21.10.70 (1y, -) 2:05.75 '93   2:03.67, 2:04.0, 2:05.21, 2:05.83, 2:06.94, 2:07.7; 2:05.69i;
    1 UAU, 1 Dublin, 2 Belgian, 1 Solihull
8. **Lynn Gibson** 6.7.69 (2y, 5) 2:02.34 '92   2:03.54, 2:06.41, 2:07.2; 2:08.56i; 3 AAA v LC, 1 WG
9. **Helen Daniel** 24.10.63 (7y, -) 2:01.86 '87   2:04.32, 2:04.63, 2:05.60, 2:05.82, 2:06.71, 2:08.5;
    3 Crawley, 4 AAA, 13 Helsinki, 6 WG
10. **Lynne Robinson** 21.6.69 (3y, -) 2:02.0 '89   2:04.7mx, 2:05.59, 2:05.60, 2:05.6, 2:06.1, 2:06.13;
    4 Crawley, 1 IA, 7 AAA, 3 Cork, 1 TSB-Ed, 2,-,2
11. **Vicki Lawrence** 9.6.73 (0y, -) 2:09.2 '93   2:04.69, 2:05.80, 2:06.12, 2:06.90, 2:07.05, 2:07.42;
    6 Stretford, 1B Wyth, 2 IA, 3h3 AAA, 2 Scot, 2 TSB-Ed, 1 North, 2 Sc v W,N, 4 EU23Cp
12. **Paula Fryer** 14.7.69 (4y, 7) 1:59.76 '91   2:05.09, 2:05.3, 2:05.43, 2:05.9, 2:06.62, 2:07.2mx;
    6 Wyth, 3 IR, 5 Cork, 5 WG, 2 North, 3 N v Sc,W, 1 Nth IC, BL1: -,1B,1

Not ranked but close
    Michelle Faherty 10.8.68 (0y, -) 2:05.57 '92   2:05.38, 2:05.4, 2:06.5, 2:07.21, 2:09.23, 2:09.4;
    2 Yorks, 2 Wyth, 5 AAA, 6 Cork, 10 Solihull
    Linda Keough 26.12.63 (1y, 3) 2:01.82 '93   2:03.69, 2:05.44, 2:06.27, 2:07.57, 2:08.08, 2:08.86;
    8 Crawley, 8 Moscow, 6 AAA, 8 GhG
nr (2) **Diane Modahl** 17.6.66 (10y, 1) 1:58.65 '90   1:59.85, 2:00.50, 2:00.50, 2:00.84, 2:01.13, 2:01.35;
    1 BL1 (1), 1 Wyth, 4 Hengelo, 1 AAA, 2 Lisbon, 1 ECp, 3 Lille, 3 TSB-CP, 4 GWG, 6s2 EC

Holmes contended for the world top ten and was unbeaten by a British athlete. She is number one for the first time, the 16th woman to top the 800m lists in the 27 years of these rankings. The unfortunate Diane Modahl, who was top six times in the previous seven years, is unranked following her drugs disqualification. She was second to Holmes on her record. Griffiths, after a lucky qualification from last place in her European Championships heat, was a great fifth in the final and Dawson ranks for the first time at number four, just behind Bowyer, who was injured when she ran at the Commonwealth Games, and ahead of a closely matched group.

1500 METRES

1. **Kelly Holmes** 19.4.70 (1y, -) 4:17.3 '93   4:01.41, 4:02.52, 4:06.48, 4:07.57, 4:07.7mx, 4:08.86, 4:09.27;
   1 AAA, 2 ECp, 4 Stockholm, 5 GWG, 2 EC, 1 CG, 3 WCp, 1 Plate
2. **Yvonne Murray** 4.10.64 (11y, 2) 4:01.20 '87, 4:23.08M '86   4:01.44, 4:22.64M (4:03.64), 4:04.19,
   4:25.2M+, 4:12.47, 4:33.4eM; 2 AAA, 1 v USA, 2 Oslo
3. **Alison Wyeth** 26.5.64 (8y, 1) 4:03.17 '93, 4:24.87M '91   4:04.19, 4:05.65, 4:08.37, 4:30.24M, 4:31.83M,
   4:14.62; 1 Crawley, 6 Granada, dns AAA, 2 Cork, 6 GhG, 7 Lausanne, 5 Nice, 8 Monaco, 2 Plate
4. **Lynn Gibson** 6.7.69 (2y, 6) 4:12.12 '93   4:05.75, 4:31.17M, 4:12.58, 4:13.89, 4:13.98, 4:14.08;
   2 Wyth, 8 AAA, 1 Dublin, 8 GhG, 3 TSB-CP, 3 v USA, 10h1 EC, 9 CG
5. **Bev Hartigan** 10.6.67 (7y, 12) 4:05.66 '90, 4:26.52M '92   4:11.04, 4:31.26M, 4:12.46, 4:13.19, 4:13.69,
   4:14.6; 1 Wyth, 3 Granada, 4 AAA, 9 GhG, 1 Wrexham, 4 TSB-CP, 6 v USA
6. **Angela Davies** 21.10.70 (1y, 11) 4:15.35 '93   4:09.29, 4:11.27, 4:31.83M, 4:12.09, 4:14.23, 4:15.1;
   3 Wyth, 2 AAA v LC, 5 AAA, 10 GhG, 2 Wrexham, 1 Nitra, 5 v USA, 6h2 EC
7. **Ann Griffiths** 20.8.65 (3y, -) 4:07.59/4:33.12M '92   4:08.71, 4:16.63, 4:18.0, 4:18.01, 4:20.2; 4:21.10i;
   1 BL1 (1), 1 IA, 3 AAA, dnf Oslo
8. **Lynne Robinson** 21.6.69 (3y, 5) 4:12.03 '93, 4:32.91M '92   4:10.32, 4:12.05, 4:13.6, 4:18.22, 4:20.1,
   4:20.18; 6 Wyth, 1 AAA v LC, dnf GhG, 1 TSB-CP, 3 Hechtel, 2 Solihull
9. **Sonia McGeorge** 2.11.64 (3y, 4) 4:10.75 '90, 4:35.7M '89   4:12.20, 4:33.12M, 4:14.80; 4:21.28i;
   2 Crawley, 11 GhG, 2 TSB-CP
10. **Debbie Gunning** 31.8.65 (3y, 9) 4:12.69 '90, 4:32.32M '91   4:13.50, 4:14.13, 4:16.50, 4:17.3;
    4 Wyth, 3 Crawley, 7 AAA
11. **Susan Parker** 24.3.70 (1y, 7) 4:12.3 '93   4:14.62, 4:15.42, 4:15.53, 4:37.82M, 4:24.3mx, 4:29.7; 4:24.70i;
    9 AAA, 5 Cork, 5 TSB-CP
12. **Michelle Faherty** 10.8.68 (1y, 10) 4:15.37/4:41.69M '93   4:16.79, 4:16.90, 4:17.27, 4:24.2, 4:24.36;
    4:23.33i; 4 Crawley, 3 Wrexham, 6 TSB-CP, 1 N v Sc,W
M = 1 mile time. Equivalents: 4:05.0m = 4:24.6M, 4:10.0m = 4:30.1M, 4:15.0m = 4:35.5M, 4:20.0m = 4:41.0M

Holmes is the first to rank first at both 800m and 1500m since Kirsty Wade in 1986. In her first major season at the event she broke into the world top ten and ranks ahead of Murray, with whom she had that great race at the AAAs, and Wyeth. Hartigan was 2-2 with Gibson, whose faster time just gave her the edge, and 4-1 with Davies, whose higher place against the USA gave her the European place. Griffiths was 3rd at the AAAs, ahead of those ranked above her, but ran the distance too infrequently to be higher.

3000 METRES

1. **Yvonne Murray** 4.10.64 (13y, 1) 8:29.02 '88   8:29.60, 8:36.48, 8:54.46, 8:56.81; 2 TSB-CP, 2 EC, 1 WCp
2. **Alison Wyeth** 26.5.64 (6y, 2) 8:38.42 '93   8:45.76, 8:46.42, 8:47.98, 8:51.34, 8:52.68, 8:54.9;
   4 AAA, 1 Dublin, 2 Helsinki, 7 TSB-CP, 6 EC, 3 CG
3. **Sonia McGeorge** 2.11.64 (7y, 4) 8:51.33 '90   8:51.55, 8:52.73, 8:54.91, 8:55.47, 8:59.55, 9:00.98;
   5 Jena, 1 AAA, 3 ECp, 5 Linz, 1 v USA, 11 EC, 4 CG
4. **Laura Adam** 28.2.65 (3y, -) 9:05.33 '92   9:02.47, 9:05.97, 9:06.63, 9:12.16, 9:15.21;
   4 E Clubs, 8 Hengelo, 2 AAA, 9 Linz, 8 CG
5. **Debbie Gunning** 31.8.65 (1y, 12=) 9:16.94 '93   9:12.12, 9:15.43, 9:23.20, 9:24.93; 9:15.11i, 9:21.36i;
   2 Dublin, 1 GhG, 1 Nitra, 3 v USA
6. **Wendy Ore** 23.5.66 (1y, -) 9:19.04 '66   9:14.72, 9:15.21; 3 AAA, 5 v USA
7. **Susan Parker** 24.3.70 (2y, 8) 9:06.2 '92   9:18.03, 9:33.18, 9:44.85; 3 IR, 2 GhG, 1 N v Sc,W
8. **Tanya Blake** 16.6.73 (1y, -) 9:17.72 '94   9:21.07, 9:25.08, 9:29.03; 5 AAA, 20 Helsinki, 2 K Lynn
9. **Sarah Bentley** 21.5.67 (1y, -) 9:33.42 '92   9:18.09, 9:25.93, 9:35.82; 9:37.17i, 9:41.74i;
   3 GhG, 3 K Lynn, 1 Solihull
10. **Jo Symonds** 19.2.68 (1y, -) 9:20.20 '93   9:24.21, 9:24.36, 9:25.44, 9:28.94, 9:41.29;
    1 BL2 (1), 6 AAA, 5 Cork, 6 GhG
11. **Amanda Wright** 14.7.68 (0y, -) 9:06.7 '92   9:19.67, 9:32.56; 4 Cork 9 GhG
12. **Angela Davies** 21.10.70 (0y, -) 9:34.8 '93   9:14.1; 1 Oxford
Not ranked but close
   Suzanne Rigg 29.11.63 (1y, 7) 9:07.3 '93   9:12.6mx, 9:24.2, 9:33.7mx, 9:34.8
   Jayne Spark 16.9.70 (1y, 5) 9:06.7mx/9:22.5 '93   9:14.3mx, 9:19.4mx, 9:26.36; 9:28.45i; 6 Cork
   Maxine Newman 15.12.70 (0y, -) 9:12.41 '90   9:26.52, 9:38.75; 1 IR, 4 GhG
   Suzanne Morley 11.10.57 (y, -) 8:56.39 '84   9:23.08, 9:24.74, 9:40.1, 9:47.47; 1 Bracknell, 1 South, 12 Belgian

nr   **Kate McCandless** USA 22.6.70 8:56.00 '93   8:59.3, 8:59.64, 9:02.24, 9:06.78, 9:09.17;
13 Rome. 1 Cork, 7 Linz, 10 Nice, 6 GWG

Murray is again top, and was the world number two to Sonia O'Sullivan in 1994. Wyeth struggled initially to recapture her 1993 form, but came through to European 6th and Commonwealth bronze and even better form at 5000m. McGeorge ran consistently well to rank third and Adam was an isolated fourth with a big gap to the rest. There was little between those ranked 7th to 12th, but all had best times that would not have seen them ranked any time in the last decade; the 10th best time of 9:17.4 is the worst since 1980. Morley's only appearance in these rankings was at 11th in 1984 when she ran 8:56.39, yet allthough her best in 1994 was over 26 secs slower she was in contention for a place.

5000 METRES (not ranked this year)
     Alison Wyeth 26.5.64 15:47.97 '91   15:10.38, 15:15.45; 1 Berlin, 3 GPF
     Suzanne Rigg 29.11.63 15:57.67 '93   15:56.83, 15:58.7, 16:28.2+, 16:47.6+; 5 Hechtel, 1 Stretford
     Carol Greenwood 15.3.66 0   15:57.29, 16:47.05+; 10 Bratislava
     Shireen Barbour 4.9.60 16:02.95 '84   16:06.49, 16:27.5; 1 AAA
     Jayne Spark 16.9.70 0   16:12.1; 2 Stretford
     Joanne Thompson 30.10.58 16:40.50 '92   16:13.43, 16:47.2+;
     Sarah Bentley 21.5.67 16:55.36 '92   16:16.82; 2 AAA
     Vikki McPherson 1.6.71 16:30+ '92   16:19.46, c.16:28.3+; 11 Hechtel
     Amanda Wright 14.7.68 16:04.51 '92   16:22.95; 3 AAA
     Angela Hulley 8.2.62 15:41.11 '90   16:25.7, 16:35.6, 16:48.4+
nr   **Katy McCandless** (USA) 22.6.70 15:34.93 '93   15:35.81, 15:41.08; 9 Stockholm, 4 GWG

Wyeth had a magnificent win in Berlin before third in the Grand Prix final.

10000 METRES
1.   **Yvonne Murray** 4.10.64 (2y, -) 33:43.80 '85   31:56.97; 1 CG
2.   **Suzanne Rigg** 29.11.63 (3y, 2) 32:44.06 '93   33:01.40, 33:38.14, 33:42.80; 3 AAA, 4 CG, 5 WCp
3.   **Vikki McPherson** 1.6.71 (3y, 1) 32:32.42 '93   33:02.74, 34:03.07; 6 ECp, 5 CG
4.   **Zahara Hyde** 12.1.63 (1y, -) 34:53.2 '89   33:23.25, 33:57.64, 34:43.24; 7 Walnut, 1 AAA, 13 CG
5.   **Karen Macleod** 24.4.58 (3y, -) 33:13.88 '89   33:34.85, 34:05.00; 11 St Denis, 1 Scot
6.   **Carol Greenwood** 15.3.66 (1y, -) 0   33:34.96; 2 AAA
7.   **Angela Hulley** 8.2.62 (4y, -) 32:42.84 '89   33:45.04, 33:49.91; 4 AAA, 10 CG
8.   **Shireen Barbour** 4.9.60 (2y, -) 33:10.25 '86   33:52.47; 5 AAA
9.   **Joanne Thompson** 30.10.58 (1y, -) 34:32.55 '90   33:56.04; 6 AAA
10.   **Alison Rose** 27.9.67 (2y, 5) 34:35.73 '93   33:57.86; 7 AAA
11.   **Daniele Sanderson** 26.10.62 (0y, -) 35:32.6 '92   34:00.46; 8 AAA
12.   **Helen Titterington** 24.10.69 (1y, -) 32:36.09 '89   34:08.00; 9 AAA

Murray's great Commonwealth run makes her a clear first, nine years after she was ranked 5th off her only previous track 10k track run in 1985. There were three Scots in the top five.

MARATHON
1.   **Yvonne Danson** 22.5.59 (2y, 4) 2:32:42 '93   2:32:24 (3) CG
2.   **Karen Macleod** 24.4.58 (3y, 2=) 2:34:30 '93   2:33:16 (4) CG
3.   **Danielle Sanderson** 26.10.62 (2y, 6) 2:37:33 '93   2:36:29 (11) EC
4.   **Hayley Nash** 30.5.63 (1y, -) 2:42:49 '93   2:35:39 (7) CG, 2:39:04 (6) London
5.   **Sally Ellis** 17.5.58 (6y, -) 2:33:24 '89   2:37:06 (4) London, 2:37:14 (8) CG
6=   **Sally Eastall** 5.1.67 (4y, -) 2:29:29 '91   2:37:08 (5) London, 2:41:32 (13) CG
6=   **Marion Sutton** 7.10.63 (4y, 2=) 2:34:38 '92   2:37:46 (16) Osaka, 2:40:34 (22) EC
8.   **Linda Rushmere** 14.11.59 (2y, -) 2:40:03 '88   2:40:17 (1) Dublin, 2:40:46 (9) London, 2:45:24 (32) EC
9.   **Zina Marchant** 30.9.50 (2y, 8) 2:39:26 '91   2:40:09 (7) London
10.   **Julie Coleby** 5.11.55 (5y, -) 2:35:53 '84   2:40:31 (8) London
11.   **Lynne Harding** 10.8.61 (3y, 5) 2:31:45 '89   2:40:57 (12) CG
12.   **Alison Rose** 27.9.67 (0y, -) 2:46:09 '93   2:45:55 (13) London, 2:45:19 (31) EC
Not ranked but close
     Teresa Dyer 29.9.59 (0y, -) 0   2:36:40 (9) Rotterdam, 2:50:23 (35) EC
     Sally Goldsmith   2:38:39 (2) Carpi
     Carolyn Hunter-Rowe 25.1.64 (0y, 11) 2:44:32 '93   2:40:28 (1) Malta, 2:53:52 (21) New York
     Suzanne Rigg 29.11.63 (0y, -) 0   2:41:03 (10) London
     Angela Hulley 8.2.62 (6y, 9) 2:30:51 '88   2:42:40 (12) London
     Lesley Turner 1.8.66 (0y, 12) 2:41:09 '93   2:45:16 (30) EC, 2:48:34 (21) London, 2:55:47 (1) Telford

Sanderson and Danson for number one? The problem is how to compare the two major championships, with the Commonwealth being run in more favourable conditions than the Europeans, or those races with London. I have gone with Danson on the basis of a medal and much faster time. It then seemed logical to put Macleod second. Rose ran well in the Europeans to just get a ranking.

100 METRES HURDLES

1. **Jackie Agyepong** 5.1.69 (7y, 2) 13.03/13.01w '93   12.93, 12.93, 12.97, 12.98w, 13.00, 13.02;
   8 AAA, 1 ECp, 2 GhG, 2 TSB-Ed, 8 TSB-CP, 5 Oslo, 1 v USA, 7 GWG, 7 EC, 3B Zürich, 2 CG,
   4 McD, 3 WCp, 1 Cup, BL2: 1,1,,-
2. **Samantha Farquharson** 15.12.69 (5y, 7) 13.28 '92   13.08, 13.09, 13.12, 13.14, 13.15, 13.21; 12.9 missed flash;
   1 BL4 (1), 2 IR, 2 IA, 6 AAA, 6 GhG, 4 TSB-Ed, 2 Nitra, 5 TSB-CP, 3 v USA, 4h3 EC, 3 CG
3. **Clova Court** 10.2.60 (3y, 3=) 13.26/13.13w '93   13.04, 13.06, 13.07, 13.21w, 13.23, 13.27;
   3 IR, 1 AAA, 1 Mid, 6 v USA, 5s1 EC, fell CG
4. **Sally Gunnell** 29.7.66 (12y, 1) 12.82/12.80w '88   13.09, 13.27w; 2 AAA
5. **Angela Thorp** 7.12.72 (4y, 5) 13.28 '93   13.32, 13.36, 13.44, 13.45, 13.56, 13.77;
   2 BL2 (1), 1 IR, 1 IA, 1 WG, 1 K Lynn, 2 North, 3 EU23Cp
6. **Lesley-Ann Skeete** 20.2.67 (10y, 10) 13.03/13.01w '90   13.42, 13.43, 13.54, 13.60, 13.66, 13.66; 13.6;
   4 IR, 3 IA, 3 AAA, 1 South, 7 GhG, 3 WG, 2 Belgian, 5 v USA, BL1: 1,2,1
7. **Diane Allahgreen** 21.2.75 (2y, 8) 13.42 '93   13.25, 13.31, 13.43, 13.48, 13.64, 13.65w;
   1 Nth-J, 7 IR, 3h1 AAA, 2 JI v P,G,R, 1 AAA-J, 1 ESch, 1 North, 3 WJ, 1 Nth IC, 8 McD
8. **Keri Maddox** 4.7.72 (5y, 3=) 13.24/13.20w '93   13.24, 13.40, 13.49, 13.52, 13.52, 13.67; 13.5, 13.5;
   5 IR, 4 IA, 4 AAA, 2 WG, 2 K Lynn, 2 Mid, 8 v USA, 1 Solihull, BL4: -,1,1
9. **Denise Lewis** 27.8.72 (1y, 12) 13.70 '92   13.47, 13.49, 13.55, 13.66, 13.80, 13.83; 13.6;
   8 IR, 5 AAA, 2 BL2 (2), 4 Mid
10. **Melanie Wilkins** 18.1.73 (1y, -) 13.67 '93   13.65w, 13.72, 13.81w, 13.86, 13.90, 13.91; 13.6;
    7 AAA, 2 South, 8 TSB-Ed, 6 Belgian, 2 Solihull, 4 Cup, BL3: -,1,1
11. **Samantha Baker** 14.4.72 (2y, 6) 13.32 '93   13.63w, 13.74w, 13.82, 13.94, 13.96, 14.00; 13.8, 13.9, 13.9;
    1 UAU, 6 IR, 2h3 AAA, 2B TSB-Ed, 5 Mid, 3 Solihull, 3 Cup, BL1: 2,1,2
12. **Natasha Danvers** 19.9.77 (0y, -) 13.88 '93   13.76w, 13.88w, 13.95, 14.03w, 14.20; 13.9w, 14.0;
    3 World Sch, 1 Sth-J, 3 South, 5 AAA-J, 1 JI v It,Cz, 1 Jnr IA

After getting close on many occasions in 1993 Agyepong broke through the 13-second barrier in Lausanne, having first run exactly that time in her splendid European Cup win, and ranks top for the first time. Farquharson made great progress, with fast times and the Commonwealth bronze to take second ranking ahead of the AAA 1-2 Court and Gunnell. Thorp, unheralded, had an excellent record, beating Farquharson 2-0 and Maddox 3-0. Allahgreen ran fast times in Lisbon for the World Junior bronze medal but lost to Skeete when they met. The overall standard was most encouraging.

400 METRES HURDLES

1. **Sally Gunnell** 29.7.66 (7y, 1) 52.74 '93   53.33, 53.51, 53.91, 54.04, 54.06, 54.51;
   1 Bratislava, 1 ECp, 1 Lausanne, 1 GhG, 1 TSB-CP, 2 Nice, 1 GWG, 1 EC, 1 CG, 1 McD, 1 WCp
2. **Gowry Retchakan** 21.6.60 (6y, 2) 54.63 '92   55.78, 56.05, 56.16, 56.35, 56.45, 56.69;
   1 AAA, 2 Lisbon, 6 GhG, 7 TSB-CP, 2 v USA, 8 EC, 5 CG
3. **Jacqui Parker** 15.10.66 (8y, 3) 56.15 '91   56.41, 56.51, 56.74, 56.72, 57.31, 57.53;
   2 Australian, 3 E Clubs, 4 Bratislava, 2 AAA, 8 TSB-CP, 1 Nitra, 7h1 EC, 6 CG, 7 McD
4. **Stephanie McCann** 26.10.65 (1y, -) 59.90 '93   58.09, 58.09, 58.66, 58.72, 58.95, 59.13;
   4 IR, 3 AAA, 7 GhG, 5 v USA, 5h2 CG
5. **Clare Bleasdale** 6.7.71 (2y, 9) 59.8 '91, 59.95 '92   58.04, 58.2, 58.5, 58.62, 58.62, 58.7;
   1 Surrey, 1 IR, 2 IA, 1 AAA v LC, 4 AAA, 1 South, 1 Belgian, 6 v USA, 1 Solihull, 1 Sth IC
6= **Jane Low** 26.8.60 (2y, 6) 59.20 '93   58.43, 58.66, 59.0, 59.01, 59.14, 59.5;
   1 Sc v W,I,T, 5 AAA, 1 Scot, 7 v USA, 5h1 CG, BL1: 1,1,-
6= **Louise Brunning** 6.3.72 (1y, -) 61.56 '93   58.07, 58.73, 58.80, 58.95, 59.22, 59.97;
   2 Surrey, 3 AAA v LC, 4h1 AAA, 2 South, 2 K Lynn, 4 Belgian, 3 EU23 Cp
8. **Vyvyan Rhodes** 5.5.73 (4y, 8) 58.02 '92   58.78, 59.3, 59.31, 59.36, 60.45, 60.8;
   6 AAA, 3 K Lynn, 1 North, BL3: -,1,1
9. **Stephanie Llewelyn** 31.12.68 (1y, 12) 59.85 '93   59.39, 59.60, 59.86, 60.41, 60.5, 60.70;
   2 BL2 (1), 2 IR, 1 IA, 7 AAA, 8h1 CG
10. **Jennifer Pearson** 3.7.62 (9y, 4) 57.41 '88   59.0, 59.4, 59.8, 59.8, 59.82, 59.9; 3 IR, 4 South, 2 Sth IC
11. **Heather Myers** 5.12.64 (0y, -) 60.05 '90   59.46, 60.51, 60.9, 60.97, 61.08, 61.1;
    8 AAA, 2 BL3 (2), 3 South, 1 Cup
12. **Allison Curbishley** 3.6.76 (1y, 5) 59.04 '93   59.16, 59.59, 59.89, 60.38, 60.94, 61.55;
    1 Nth-J, 1 JI v P,G,R, 4h3 AAA, 2 Scot, 2 AAA-J, fell h1 WJ, 1 JI v It,Cz, 2 Cup
    Kerry Maddox 4.7.72 (0y, -) 59.7 '88   59.49, 59.7, 60.2, 61.0; 1 BL4 (3), 2 Solihull

Gunnell, clearly the best in the world, completed her sweep of all major titles and now has a record seven years at no.1 in this event. She lost just one of her 11 finals, to Kim Batten (USA), whom she beat on the other four occasions that they met. Retchakan, who made both major championships finals, is second for the fifth successive year. Brunning cast aside her years of injury to begin to fulfill the promise she had shown as an intermediate at 200mh.

HIGH JUMP

1. **Debbie Marti** 14.5.68 (10y, 1) 1.93 '92, 1.94i '91   1.91, 1.89, 1.88, 1.88, 1.86, 1.86;
   2 AAA, 2 Dublin, 1 South, 1 WG, 3 TSB-Ed, 1 Belgian, 1 v USA, dnq 29 EC, 3 CG, 6 WCp, 1 Plate
2. **Julia Bennett** 26.3.70 (6y, 3) 1.86/1.92i '90   1.89, 1.88, 1.87, 1.86, 1.86, 1.85;
   1 AAA, 3 Dublin, 6 ECp, 6 TSB-Ed, 2 Belgian, 4 v USA, dnq 19= EC, 7 CG, 2 Plate
3. **Lea Haggett** 9.5.72 (4y, -) 1.91 '91   1.88, 1.86, 1.85, 1.84, 1.83, 1.80; 1.85i;
   4 AAA, 2= South, 3 WG, 2 K Lynn, 2 Nitra, 5= South, 6 EU23Cp, dnq 34 EC, 5= CG
4. **Julie Major** 19.8.70 (3y, 7) 1.83i/1.81 '90   1.85, 1.83, 1.82, 1.80, 1.75, 1.75;
   3 AAA, 2= South, 4= WG, 5 TSB-Ed, 5= v USA
5. **Hazel Melvin** 19.11.73 (3y, 9) 1.79 '93   1.81, 1.81, 1.81, 1.80, 1.79, 1.78;
   1 BL1 (1), 1 Sc v W,I,T, 1 Scot, 1 W v Sc,N, dnq 13= CG
6. **Diana Davies** 7.5.61 (16y, 6) 1.95 '82   1.82, 1.80, 1.80, 1.78, 1.75, 1.75;
   1 BL5 (1), 1 IR, 5 AAA, 1 Lough 22/6, 2 Mid, 4= WG
7. **Julie Crane** 26.9.76 (1y, -) 1.73 '93   1.81, 1.80, 1.80, 1.80, 1.79, 1.78;
   2 BL5 (1), 1 Mid-J, 2 JI, v P,G,R, 1 AAA-J, 1 Mid, 1 ESch, 2 W v Sc,N, 1 JI v I,Cz, 2 Jnr IA
8. **Jo Jennings** 20.9.69 (7y, 2) 1.94i '93, 1.90 '88   1.86, 1.80; 1.86i, 1.83i, 1.80i
9. **Lindsay Evans** 29.8.77 (1y, -) 1.75 '92   1.79, 1.78, 1.78, 1.76, 1.76, 1.76;
   1 Sth-J, 3 IR, 4 South, 3 AAA-J, 2 ESch, 1 Jnr IA
10. **Kelly Thirkle (née Mason)** 29.3.71 (5y, 5) 1.88i '92, 1.85 '91   1.76, 1.76. 1.75, 1.75, 1.74, 1.70; 1.80i, 1.80i;
    8 AAA, 2 IR, 3= Cork, 1 North, 3 N v Sc,W, 1 Cup, BL1: 2,1,1
11. **Susan Jones** 8.6.78 (0y, -) 1.75 '93   1.82, 1.76, 1.71, 1.70, 1.70, 1.70;
    2 World Sch, 2 Nth-J, 8 JI v P,G,R, 9= AAA-J, 1 ESch-I, 1 AAA U17
12. **Denise Lewis** 27.8.72 (0y, -) 1.75 '93 1.81, 1.77, 1.74, 1.73; 5 IR

Marti, who reached a peak with her Commonwealth Games bronze, is top for the fourth successive year. Bennett and Haggett, back after a year out, are second and third. Sadly, Jennings was only able to compete twice outdoors, in New Zealand in January, due to a partial rupture of her right Achilles. Davies is ranked for the 17th time, easily a record, with 15 years in the top six. She just edges Crane, whom she beat 2-1. There was a small improvement in depth, with 11 women over 1.80 in 1994, compared to the lows of nine in 1992 and eight in 1993.

POLE VAULT

1. **Kate Staples** 2.11.65 (2y, 0) 3.56 '93   3.65, 3.61, 3.40, 3.40; 3.46i, 3.45i; 1 IR, 1 IA, 1 AAA
2. **Paula Wilson** 20.11.69 (1y, -) 2.50 '93   3.45, 3.40, 3.40, 3.40, 3.40, 3.35;
   2 IR, 3 IA, 2 AAA, 1 Mid, 1 Peterborough, 1 Bedford, 1 Stoke
3. **Clare Ridgley** 11.9.77 (2y, 2) 3.30 '93   3.44, 3.41, 3.40, 3.35, 3.30, 3.20; 3.35i;
   2 IA, 4 AAA, 1 South, 1 AAA-J, 1 Salisbury, 1 AAA U17, 2 So'ton, 3 Bedford, 5 Holzminden
4. **Linda Stanton** 22.6.73 (2y, 4) 3.40 '93   3.30, 3.30, 3.20, 3.10, 3.04, 3.00; 3.42i, 3.25i, 3.20i;
   5 IR, 2 AAA v LC, 3 AAA, 1 Nth IC, 2 Bedford, ? Holzminden
5. **Rhian Clarke** 19.4.77 (2y, 3) 3.30 '93   3.25, 3.20, 3.20, 3.20, 3.20, 3.14; 3.20i;
   3= IR, 1 AAA v LC, 5 AAA, 4 JI v P,G,R, 2= South, 2 AAA-J, 2 Peterborough, 4 Bedford, ? Holzminden
6. **Claire Morrison** 30.5.69 (2y, 5) 2.90 '93   3.24, 3.20, 3.20, 3.10, 3.00, 3.00; 3.10i, 3.05i;
   3= IR, 7= AAA, 2 Mid, 3 So'ton, 5 Bedford, ? Holzminden
7. **Dawn-Alice Wright** 20.1.76 (2y, 8) 2.95 '92   3.10, 3.00, 3.00, 3.00, 3.00, 3.00;
   1 Mid-J, 6 AAA, 5 JI v P,G,R, 3 Mid, 3 AAA-J, 2 Salisbury, 1 Jnr IA, 5 So'ton, 8 Bedford, 2 Stoke
8. **Samantha Stapleton** 13.10.73 (1y, -) 2.80 '93   3.20u?, 3.00, 3.00, 2.90, 2.80; 2.85i; 2= South, 3 Salisbury
9. **Leanne Mellor** 17.3.76 (1y, -)   3.10, 3.00, 2.90, 2.80, 2.80, 2.80; 6 IR, 7= AAA, 2 Nth IC, 6 Bedford
10. **Katie Alexander** 28.4.74 (1y, -) 2.80 '93   3.00; 2.95i

Ranked for the second year, there was a good improvement in standards with 10 women clearing 3m or higher, compared to four in 1994. World class begins at 3.70, and only Staples, in her rare appearances, has yet threatened that. The biggest improvement was made by Wilson, who came in at second. Clarke beat Stanton 3-2, but the former did 3.30 twice, including at the AAAs.

LONG JUMP

1. **Yinka Idowu** 25.2.72 (6y, 2) 6.73 '93   6.73, 6.58w (6.56), 6.54, 6.51, 6.48, 6.46; 6.51i;
   7 E Clubs, 1 AAA, 1 WG, 2 TSB-Ed, 3 v USA, 9 EC, 2 CG, 6 WCp, 1 Cup
2. **Denise Lewis** 27.8.72 (3y, 4) 6.25/6.30w '93   6.56, 6.51w, 6.50w, 6.44, 6.42, 6.38;
   1 IR, 1 IA, 2 AAA, 5 ECp, 1 Mid, 4 v USA, dnq 19 EC, 8 CG, 2 Cup
3. **Ruth Irving** 20.7.74 (2y, 6) 6.17 '93, 6.22w '92   6.28, 6.27, 6.19, 6.18w, 6.13, 6.12w;
   1 UAU, 1 CU v OU, 1 AAA v LC, 4 AAA1 Scot, 6 v USA, 1 Sc v W,N, 5 EU23 Cp, 12 CG
4. **Ann Brooks** 4.5.71 (1y, -) 5.99w?/5.82 '89   6.38w, 6.14, 6.12, 6.12w, 6.10, 6.03;
   2 IR, 2 IA, 2 AAA v LC, 3 AAA, 2 Cork, 3 WG, 3 Nitra, 1 North, 1 Nth IC, BL4: 1,1,1
5. **Ashia Hansen** 5.12.71 (2y, -) 6.12 '93, 6.25w '89   6.27, 6.15, 6.14, 6.07, 6.03, 5.74;
   5 AAA, 1 South, 5 TSB-Ed, BL1: 1,1,-

6. **Liz Ghojefa** 24.2.69 (1y, 12) 6.01/6.07w '93   6.25, 6.16w (6.13), 6.13w. 6.11, 6.10w, 6.08;
   3 AAA v LC, 8 AAA, 2 South, 2 Belgian, 1 Sth IC
7. **Joanne Dear** 8.6.75 (2y, 5) 6.33 '93   6.14, 6.12w, 6.08w, 6.06w (5.99), 6.04w, 5.96; 6.21i, 6.14i;
   2 UAU, 1 Sth-J, 6 JI v P,G,R, 4 AAA-J, 6 Belgian, BL4: -,3,2
8= **Jenny Kelly** 20.6.70 (1y, -) 6.09 '93   6.02, 6.01, 6.00, 5.98, 5.97w, 5.89; 6 AAA
8= **Vikki Schofield** 29.12.72 (1y, -) 5.75/5.89w '93   6.07, 6.04w, 6.01, 6.00, 5.98, 5.92w; 7 AAA, 3 Cork
10. **Adele Forester** 27.3.76 (1y, -) 6.04 '93   6.05, 6.03, 5.98, 5.91, 5.84, 5.80;
   4 IR, 8 JI v P,G,R, 1 AAA-J, 2 E Sch
11. **Jacqui White** 12.1.71 (1y, 10=) 5.96 '92, 6.06w '93   5.98, 5.96, 5.91w, 5.88, 5.87, 5.85;
   3 UAU, 6 IR, 3 IA, 4 AAA v LC, 9 AAA, 2 Mid
12. **Rachel Kirby** 18.5.69 (0y, -) 6.00 '92   6.02, 6.01w?, 5.74; 5 IR, 2 BL4 (2)

Fiona May was British no.1 for seven successive years, 1987-93, and in 1994 rose to her highest ever world ranking of 5th - but she is now Italian. In her place Idowu steps up to the top, after three years as second. Lewis improved mightily to be a clear second. Brooks is the highest placed of five newcomers to the lists, with a splendidly consistent season, over 6m regularly. The tenth best level on the UK lists (legal jumps) was 6.05, only marginally better than 1993, which was 6.03, the lowest since 1974.

TRIPLE JUMP
1. **Michelle Griffith** 6.10.71 (5y, 1) 13.75/13.93w '93   14.08, 13.84, 13.75, 13.75w, 13.70, 13.64; 13.85i;
   7 Bratislava, 3 Budapest, 1 AAA, 4 ECp, 3 GhG, 7 Stockholm, 2 v USA, 6 GWG, 10 EC. 7 McD, 4 WCp
2. **Ashia Hansen** 5.12.71 (4y, 3) 13.31 '92, 13.48i/13.55w '93   14.22, 14.08, 14.04, 14.00, 13.79, 13.61w;
   13.86i; 2 E Clubs, 2 AAA, 4 GhG, 1 Nitra, 1 TSB-CP, 1 v USA, dnq 15 EC, 5 McD, 1 Cup, BL1: 1,1,-
3. **Rachel Kirby** 18.5.69 (4y, 2) 13.60/13.64w '93   13.64, 13.51w, 13.50w, 13.45, 13.29, 13.24; 13.31i,
   13.31i; 3 AAA, 5 GhG, 4 TSB-CP, 3 v USA, 11 EC, 8 McD
4. **Connie Henry** 15.4.72 (3y, 5) 12.77/13.03w '93   13.31, 13.10w, 13.07, 12.70, 12.67w, 12.40; 12.97i,
   12.86i, 12.82i; 1 IR, 1 K Lynn, 5 TSB-CP, 5 EU23Cp, 10 McD
5. **Evette Finikin** 25.9.63 (5y, 4) 13.46 '91   12.85, 12.82, 12.75, 12.66, 12.65w, 12.64; 12.77i, 12.76i;
   2 IR, 4 AAA, 1 South, 1 Belgian, 2 Cup, BL2: 1,1,1
6. **Lorna Turner** 11.5.72 (3y, 9) 12.53 '93   12.94, 12.49, 12.38, 12.35, 12.29, 12.05;
   2 South, 2 K Lynn, 3 Belgian, BL1: -,2,1
7= **Shani Anderson** 7.8.75 (3y, 8) 12.43 '93   12.44, 12.39, 12.26, 12.16, 12.10, 11.91;
   4 JI v P,G,R, 6 AAA, 3 South, 3 K Lynn, 2 AAA-J
7= **Karen Skeggs** 26.10.69 (5y, 6) 12.89/12.93w '92   12.45, 12.23, 12.20, 12.10, 12.04, 11.89; 1 Scot, 1 Plate
9. **Liz Ghojefa** 24.2.69 (4y, 7) 12.64 '93   12.39, 12.33, 12.29, 12.27, 12.23, 12.12; 2 Plate
10. **Caroline Miller** 16.9.72 (1y, -) 11.99 '93   12.31, 12.06, 12.05, 12.02, 11.99, 11.88;
   4 IR, 2 IA, 9 AAA, 1 North, 1 N v W,Sc, 1 Nth IC
11. **Caroline Stead** 14.9.71 (0y, -) 11.93 '93   12.17, 11.91, 11.90, 11.85; 5 AAA, 4 South
12. **Debbie Rowe** 8.9.72 (0y, -) 11.74/11.79w '93   12.00, 11.90, 11.80w, 11.77, 11.75, 11.74;
   2 BL1 (1), 3 IR, 4 IA, 7 AAA, 3 Cup

Griffith achieved the first ever 14m jump by a British woman, although she lost the record at the season's end to Hansen, who first jumped 14.22 without a wind gauge or drug testing procedures and then added a centimetre to the UK record with 14.09. Hansen ended the season with four meetings at 14m or higher, but Griffiths beat her 3-2, including at the Europeans and AAAs, to rank first for the third time. Kirby, as usual, competed at a consistently high level, and Henry joined the top three at over 13m. With the triple jump now on every other international championships programme, it was a terrible shame that it was not contested at the Commonwealth Games.

SHOT
1. **Judy Oakes** (18 y, -) 19.36 '88   18.68, 18.63, 18.51, 18.38, 18.29, 18.16;
   1 AAA, 4 ECp, 1 Nitra, 1 v USA, 1 CG, 6 McD, 5 WCp
2. **Myrtle Augee** 4.2.65 (12y, 1) 19.03 '90   17.64, 17.37, 17.13, 16.83, 16.77, 15.90;
   2 AAA, 5 GhG, 5 v USA, 14 EC, 2 CG, 7 McD
3. **Margaret Lynes** 19.2.63 (10y, 2) 16.55 '89   16.57, 16.53, 16.53, 16.39, 16.37, 16.31; 16.45i;
   1 IA, 3 AAA, 1 South, 6 GhG, 2 WG, 1 K Lynn, 1 Belgian, 6 v USA, 17 EC, 6 CG, 8 McD
4. **Yvonne Hanson-Nortey** 18.2.64 (10y, -) 17.45 '89   16.43, 16.31, 16.29, 16.28, 16.23, 16.11;
   1 IR, 4 AAA, 7 GhG, 3 WG, 7 v USA, BL3: 1,1,2
5. **Sharon Andrews** 4.7.67 (9y, 3) 15.80 '93   15.61, 15.58, 15.47, 15.43, 15.31, 15.29; 15.49i;
   1 UAU, 1 Essex, 2 IR, 4 E Clubs, 1 AAA v LC1 Cup, BL1: 1,1,1
6. **Alison Grey** 12.5.73 (5y, 4) 15.72i '92, 15.56 '93   15.69, 15.54, 15.44, 15.44, 15.30, 15.25; 15.85i, 15.78i,
   15.50i; 1 Sc v W,I,T, 2 IA, 5 AAA, 1 Scot, 1 Sc v W,N, 6 EU23Cp, 7 CG, BL1: 2,2,-
7. **Debbie Callaway** 15.7.64 (2y, 5) 14.88 '93   14.58, 14.43, 14.36, 14.35, 14.28, 14.27; 14.74i;
   2 Essex, 3 IR, 2 Cup, BL3: 2,2,3
8. **Uju Efobi** 10.10.74 (2y, 9) 14.27 '93   15.21, 14.25, 14.12, 13.83, 13.69, 13.59;
   2 AAA v LC, 4 K Lynn, 6 Belgian, 1 Sth IC

9.   **Jenny Kelly** 20.6.70 (2y, -) 14.88i '90, 14.73 '91   14.44, 14.36, 13.84, 13.62; 13.60i
10.   **Emma Beales** 7.12.71 (3y, 8) 14.53 '92   14.18, 14.13, 14.01, 13.95, 13.83, 13.76; 14.31i;
     3 IA, 3 AAA v LC, 2 South
11.   **Carol Cooksley** 22.9.69 (9y, 7) 14.71 '90, 14.76i '91   14.09, 13.90, 13.72, 13.59, 13.53, 13.52; 13.65i;
     5 IR, 4 IA, 6 AAA, 2 Mid3 Cup, BL1: -,4,2
12= **Jayne Berry** 18.7.70 (6y, 6) 14.80 '90   14.22, 13.85, 13.51; 2 W v Sc,N
12= **Lorraine Shaw** 2.4.68 (0y, -) 2.4.68   14.21, 13.72, 13.55, 13.42, 13.29, 13.11; 1 Mid

Back, after two years out, came Judy Oakes to claim her record 12th number one ranking. The closest any British athlete got to her during the year was the 52cm down that Augee was when setting her season's best at the Commonwealth Games. Lynes had her best ever set of marks and beat Hanson-Nortey on all five occasions that they met, even though the latter was over 15.90m each time. Indeed none of the top six lost to those ranked below them - remarkable consistency! The one newcomer to the rankings is Lorraine Shaw, who achieves a first with rankings at three throws events.

DISCUS
1.   **Jacqueline McKernan** 1.7.65 (10y, 1) 60.72 '93   58.56, 57.56, 57.10, 57.08, 56.94, 56.70;
     1 UAU, 1 Lough 25/5, 1 AAA v LC, 1 AAA, 1 Lough 22/6, 6 ECp, 1 K Lynn, 3 v USA, dnq 13 EC, 5 CG, 7 WCp
2.   **Sharon Andrews** 4.7.67 (8y, 3) 55.14 '93   56.24, 55.34, 54.78, 53.98, 53.88, 53.20;
     2 Essex, 2 IR, 5 E Clubs, 2 AAA v LC, 2 AAA, 3 K Lynn, 2 Belgian, 5 v USA, 4 CG, 2 Cup, BL1: 1,1,-
3.   **Debbie Callaway** 15.7.64 (9y, 2) 54.74 '93   55.66, 55.24, 54.94, 54.46, 54.32, 53.96;
     1 Essex, 1 IR, 3 AAA, 1 South, 4 Belgian, 6 v USA, 7 CG, 1 Cup, BL3: 1,1,1
4.   **Emma Beales** 7.12.71 (4y, 6) 53.78 '93   53.54, 52.98, 52.94, 52.28, 51.06, 50.96;
     3 AAA v LC, 4 AAA, 2 South
5.   **Lorraine Shaw** 2.4.68 (2y, 9=) 50.82 '93   55.04, 53.70, 53.34, 51.60, 51.28, 51.06;
     3 IR, 5 AAA, 2 Lough 22/6, 1 Mid, 1 Nitra, 10 CG
6.   **Shelley Drew** 8.8.73 (3y, 7) 51.56 '93   54.60, 53.40, 52.92, 52.56, 52.16, 51.86;
     3 UAU, 4 AAA v LC, 9 AAA, 1 Dublin, 3 Lough 22/6, 3 South, 2 K Lynn, 2g Mid, 6 EU23Cp, 1 Sth IC
7.   **Tracy Axten** 20.7.63 (5y, 4) 54.40 '93   52.28, 51.66, 51.64, 51.58, 51.36, 51.30;
     3 Lough 25/5, 7 AAA, 4 South, 4 K Lynn, BL4: 1,1,1
8.   **Sarah Winckless** 18.10.73 (2y, 9=) 51.98 '93   53.16, 52.06, 51.78, 51.50, 50.90, 50.74;
     2 UAU, 5 AAA v LC, 6 AAA, 2 Dublin, 6 South, 6 K Lynn, 2 Sth IC
9.   **Rosanne Lister** 9.5.69 (3y, -) 53.66' 91   50.64, 50.08, 49.50, 49.08, 49.06, 48.30; 3 Essex, 8 AAA, 5 South
10.   **Alison Grey** 12.5.73 (1y, 12) 48.82 '92   52.52, 51.04, 49.46, 48.86, 47.64, 47.54;
     2 Sc v W,I,T, 12 AAA, 1 Scot, 1 Sc v W.N, nt CG, BL1: 2,2,-
11= **Emma Merry** 2.7.74 (4y, 5) 52.58 '93   50.72, 49.12, 45.72; 2 Lough 25/5, 7 AAA v LC, 4 Lough 22/6
11= **Nicola Talbot** 17.2.72 (2y, 8) 54.24 '93   49.92, 47.10, 46.68, 46.04, 45.40, 45.24;
     6 AAA v LC, 10 AAA, 5 Lough 22/6, 2 Mid

McKernan was number one for the sixth time and was most unlucky to miss the European final by 2 cm. She was a little below her best at the Commonwealth Games, where Andrews finished as best UK athlete to swap places from 1993 with Callaway, whom she beat 4-3; both set pbs in 1994. Axten beat Winckless 3-1. There were no newcomers although the under-17 champion Philippa Roles only narrowly missed.

HAMMER
1.   **Lorraine Shaw** 2.4.68 (2y, 1) 56.56 '93   59.92, 59.58, 59.44, 58.96, 58.18, 58.14;
     1 Colindale 2/4, 1 Kingston, 1 IR, 1 IA, 1 AAA, 1 Horsham, 1 Mid. 1 WLHS
2.   **Lyn Sprules** 11.9.75 (2y, 7) 48.40 '93   55.44, 54.48, 54.48, 54.16, 53.92, 53.86; 2 Kingston, 1 Sth-J,
     2 IR, 4 AAA, 5 JI v P,G,R, 1 South, 1 AAA-J, 2 K Lynn, 2 WLHS, 1 Hendon, 1 Jnr IA, BL4: 1,1,-
3.   **Diana Holden** 12.2.75 (4y, 4) 52.62 '94   53.34, 51.66, 51.46, 50.74, 50.20, 50.14;
     2 Sth-J, 5 IA, 2 AAA, 2 Horsham, 2 South, 3 AAA-J, 3 WLHS, 2 Jnr IA, BL4: -,2,1
4.   **Ann Gardner** 11.10.68 (3y, 3) 54.02 '93   51.62, 49.08, 48.76, 48.20, 48.10, 47.78;
     3 Kingston, 3 IR, 4 IA, 5 AAA, 6 Horsham, 2 Mid, 2 Hendon
5.   **Sarah Moore** 15.3.73 (3y, 8) 49.40 '93   50.52, 50.08, 49.62, 49.24, 48.86, 48.46;
     2 Colindale 2/4, 5 Kingston, 1 UAU, 1 W v Sc,I,T, 3 AAA, 1 Welsh, 3 Mid, 2 W v Sc,N, 3 Hendon
6.   **Julie Lavender** 9.11.75 (3y, 9) 47.66 '93   51.62, 49.10, 48.02, 47.94, 47.06, 47.00;
     1 Nth-J, 4 IR, 6 AAA, 6 JI v P,G,R, 1 Scot, 3 AAA-J, 3 K Lynn, 1 Nth IC, 3 Jnr IA
7=   **Esther Augee** 1.1.64 (3y, 2) 56.76 '93   49.30, 49.18, 48.54, 47.86, 47.12, 46.38;
     4 Kingston, 2 IA, 9 AAA, 4 South, 4 WLHS, 6 Hendon, BL1: -,1,1
7=   **Jean Clark** 5.10.68 (4y, 6) 49.78 '92   48.98, 48.88, 47.84, 47.80, 47.64, 47.02;
     6 Kingston, 3 Sc v W,I,T, 3 IA, 7 AAA, 3 Horsham, 1 Sc v N,W, 2 Scot, 5 WLHS, 4 Hendon
9=   **Irene Duffin** 10.8.60 (1y, -) 44.82 '94   46.14, 45.22, 44.94, 44.32, 44.24, 44.24;
     3 Colindale 2/4, 8 Kingston, 6 IR, 8 AAA, 5 Horsham, 6 South, 9 Hendon, BL2: 1,1,1
9=   **Janet Smith** 7.10.74 (1y, -) 44.58 '93   46.88, 46.62, 44.82, 44.26, 44.16, 43.38;
     4 Colindale 2/4, 7 Kingston, 10 AAA, 7 Horsham, 3 South, 6 WLHS, 8 Hendon, BL4: -,5,4

11   **Fio:ia Whitehead** 31.5.70 (3y, 5) 52.84 '94   48.68, 44.84, 44.58, 44.16; nt AAA, 5 South, 5 Hendon
12=   **Samantha Burns-Salmond** 13.4.76 (0y, -) 42.62 '94   45.48, 45.30, 44.76, 44.14, 43.96, 43.68;
      2 Nth-J, 11 AAA, 4 Horsham, 6 AAA-J, 1 North, 4 N v Sc,W, 2 Nth IC, 3 Jnr IA, BL4: -,3,3
12=   **Angela Bonner** 22.11.73 (2y, -) 43.98 '93   45.44, 45.08, 44.84, 44.02, 43.86, 43.24;
      2 Welsh, 3 W v Sc,N, BL4: -,2,4

Shaw retained her top ranking and improved the British record by over 3 metres in her first competition of the year. In fact she exceeded the previous British record in all of her ten hammer competitions of 1994, in which she was unbeaten, but did not make any further improvement, so the breaking of the 60m barrier must wait another year. Sprules made the most progress to overtake another junior, Holden, who was top ranked in 1991 and 1992. Gardner beat Moore 3-1.

JAVELIN
1.   **Sharon Gibson** 31.12.61 (15y, 1) 62.32 '87   58.20, 57.56, 56.90, 55.70, 55.20, 54.82;
      2 AAA, 1 Mid, 3 v USA, dnq 17 EC, 3 CG, 6 WCp, 3 Nitra
2.   **Shelley Holroyd** 17.5.73 (6y, 2) 60.10 '93   57.08, 56.66, 55.46, 54.14, 52.44, 52.10;
      1 AAA, 1 BL1 (2), 3 GhG, dnq 21 EC, 6 EU23Cp
3.   **Diane Royle** 24.11.59 (12y, 5) 62.22 '85   55.32, 53.84 (58.84?), 53.78, 52.10; 1 BL1 (1), 1 North
4.   **Karen Costello** 21.10.68 (1y, -) 50.40 '93   54.50, 51.34, 51.30, 51.24, 50.96, 49.52;
      3 Sc v W,I,T, 3 AAA, 1 Scot, 8 ECp, 1 Sc v W,N, 12 CG, BL1: 2,2,-
5.   **Lucy Burrell** 10.3.75 (1y, -) 46.74 '93   51.76, 51.18, 50.26, 50.24, 50.02, 49.68;
      2 IR, 4 AAA, 6 JI v P,G,R, 2 AAA-J, 2 ESch, dnq 13 WJ, 1 Cup
6.   **Kirsty Morrison** 28.10.75 (4y, 3) 59.36 '93   53.88, 53.80, 53.38, 51.10, 50.60, 50.30;
      5 AAA, 1 AAA-J, 1 ESch, dnq 18 WJ, BL5: 1,-,2
7.   **Karen Martin** 24.11.74 (3y, 8) 55.72 '92   53.68, 53.20, 50.84, 50.82, 50.80, 50.62;
      7 AAA, 1 BL3 (2), 2 WG, 1 K Lynn, 1 IS, 2 N v Sc,W, 1 Nth IC
8.   **Amanda Liverton** 1.9.72 (7y, 4) 57.84 '90   53.76, 53.50, 46.68
9.   **Noelle Bradshaw** 18.12.63 (2y, 7) 52.40 '93   51.00, 51.00, 50.44, 49.52, 49.32, 49.22;
      3 IR, 8 AAA, 1 Dublin, 2 South, 4 WG, 2 Belgian, 6 v USA
10.   **Lorna Jackson** 9.1.74 (2y, 9) 52.52 '93   54.62, 51.74, 50.52, 48.68, 48.26, 47.00;
      1 Sc v W,I,T, 10 AAA, 2 Scot, 3 Cup, BL1: 5,4,2
11.   **Joanna Burton** 11.5.75 (0y, -) 50.44 '93   52.14, 50.66, 50.26, 50.00, 49.58, 48.88;
      6 BL1 (1), 1 Sth-J, 13 AAA, 4 JI v P,G,R, 1 South, 3 AAA-J, 5 v USA, 1 Jnr IA
12.   **Caroline White** 8.10.68 (7y, 6) 56.50 '91   50.58, 50.52, 50.20, 49.24, 47.70, 47.46;
      6 AAA, 1 Welsh, 5 GhG, 2 North, 1 BL1 (3)
      Denise Lewis 27.8.72 (0y, -) 47.80 '93   53.68, 48.58, 47.70, 44.80, 44.20; 2 Mid, 1 CG(Hep), 2 Cup

Gibson and Holroyd remain 1st and 2nd, the former gaining her first major championship medal of her long career with the Commonwealth bronze. The rest of the top ten were very evenly matched. Royle was undefeated, but only contested four meetings, as was Liverton on her return in three minor meetings at the end of the year.

HEPTATHLON
1.   **Denise Lewis** 27.8.72 (5y, 2) 5812 '92   6325, 6069, 5937; 2 Valladolid, 12 ECp, 1 CG
2.   **Jennifer Kelly** 20.6.70 (7y, 3) 5765 '90   5826, 5658, 5617, 5495; 1g North, 3 v It,Cs, 19 ECp, 5 CG
3.   **Vikki Schofield** 29.12.72 (4y, 9) 5268 '93   5671, 5587, 5396, 5302; 2 (1) North), 6 v It,Cs, 1 AAA, 24 ECp
4.   **Charmaine Johnson** 4.6.63 (9y, 5=) 5495 '92   5486, 5480w, 5463; 6 Valladolid, 4 v It,Cs, 26 ECp
5.   **Pauline Richards** 30.6.68 (1y, -) 5188   5420, 5201; 2 AAA, 1 Mid
6.   **Uju Efobi** 10.10.74 (2y, 8) 5377 '93   5409; 3 AAA
7.   **Emma Lindsay** 11.4.71 (1y, 11) 5190w/5163 '93   5353, 5321, 4997w; 10 Valladolid, 5 AAA, 9 CG
8.   **Claire Phythian** 7.2.73 (2y, -) 5184 '89   5372, 5291, 5177; 1 Tempe, 5 Azusa, 2 Fayetteville
9.   **Kerry Jury** 19.11.68 (3y, 10) 5335 '93   5334, 5194, 5128; 5g North, 4 AAA, 2 Mid
10.   **Diana Bennett** 14.6.74 (1y, -) 5156 '93   5212, 5071, 5070w; 4g North, dnf AAA, 1 South, 2 Welsh
11.   **Julia Bennett** 26.3.70 (1y, -) 5137 '90   5239; 3g North
12.   **Lisa Gibbs** 9.1.69 (1y, 5=) 5424 '93   5253w; dnf North, 10 Alhama, dnf CG
      Kim Crowther 19.1.66 (1y, -) 5297 '86   5125, 5079w, 5054w (5022), 5051, 5009;
      6 (2) North, 6 AAA, 1 Scot, 1 Welsh

After three years at number one, Clova Court did not finish either of her heptathlons in 1994, AAA and Commonwealth, so is out of the rankings, as Lewis, with that marvellous performance in Victoria takes over. Richards was the one newcomer, taking a splendid fifth place.

WALKS
At 3000m to 10,000m performances are on the track, unless indicated by R for road marks. All longer distances are on the road Previous personal bests are shown for track 5000m and road or track 10km.
Priority is given in these rankings to form at the standard international distance of 10 kilometres although performances at the AAA and UK distance of 5000m is also significant.

1. **Victoria Lupton** 17.4.72 (6y, 1) 22:12.21 '92, 47:04.0 '91, 46:04R '92. 45:28 sh? '94
   3km: 13:20.23, 13:50.6, 14:02.2; 2 K Lynn   5km: 23:06.0, 23:34.50; 22:45+R, 22:59+R; dq RWA, 2 AAA
   10km: 45:48R, 46:30R, 46:30t, 48:07R, 48:30R, 50:11t; 4 AAA, 2 Douglas, 31 Livorno, 20 EC, 5 CG
   20km: 1:44:48; 1 RWA
2. **Lisa Langford** 15.3.67 (10y, -) 21:57.68 '90, 45:42R '87, 48:34.0t '86   5km: 22:44.0, 22:44+R, 23:17R, 23:32R
   10km: 46:01R, 47:07R, 47:12R, 47:14R, 47:34R; 1 UK, 1 Cardiff, 26 Livorno, dq EC, 6 CG
3. **Verity Snook (née Larby)** 13.11.70 (5y, 3) 23:26.6 '93, 47:01R '93
   3km: 13:27.9, 13:31.78, 13:50.80; 13:45.64i; 1 South
   5km: 23:22.52; 22:45+R, 23:07+R, 23:11R, 23:45R, 24:26R; 1 AAA
   10km: 46:06R, 47:23R, 47:24R, 48:05t, 51:01R, 51:14.52; dnf RWA, 1 AAA, 1 Sc v W,I,T,
   25 Livorno, 23 EC, 7 CG
4. **Carolyn Partington** 27.6.66 (2y, 6) 24:38.68 '93, 50:06R/50:43.87 '93   3km: 13:30.3
   5km: 23:04R, 23:36+R, 23:48R; 8 AAA
   10km: 47:21R, 47:46R, 48:20t, 48:37R, 48:46R; 1 Manx, 3 UK, 2 AAA, 28 Livorno, 9 CG
5. **Karen Smith** 1.6.61 (4y, 8) 24:12.11 '93, 49:21R/48:56R sh? '93   3km: 14:09.0; 14:12R
   5km: 24:18.79; 24:03R, 24:11+R; 2 Mid-R, 5 AAA   10km: 48:30R , 48:45R, 48:54R; 4 UK, 2 RWA, 11 CG
6. **Melanie Wright (née Brookes)** 5.4.64 (5y, 5) 24:07.02 '93, 48:18R/49:15.2t '92, 47:40R sh?'93
   3km: 13:43.0, 13:55.3, 13:57.2, 14:04.2; 1 Warwicks
   5km: 23:57.0, 24:06.27, 24:17.0; 23:47R, 23:58R, 24:27R, 24:28R; 3 Mid-R, 1 RWA, 1 Mid-t, 4 AAA
   10km: 48:58R, 49:03R, 49:04R, 49:16t, 49:16R, 49:30R; 2 Manx, 6 UK, 3 RWA,
   3 AAA, 3 Douglas, 34 Livorno, 1 Leicester
7. **Sylvia Black** 16.4.58 (11y, 4) 23:34.43 '92, 47:59R '92   3km: 13:47.10i; 13:38R
   5km: 23:58R; 1 Mid-R   10km: 48:41R, 50:37R; 2 UK, dnf RWA
8. **Elaine Callinan** 13.9.60 (9y, 7) 24:13.4 '81, 49:28R '93, 51:51.0t '80
   3km: 14:12.9, 14:19.7; 13:52R; 2 Warwicks   5km: 24:37R
   10km: 49:17R, 49:19R, 50:00R, 51:16R, 51:22R, 51:44R; 3 Manx, 5 UK, 4 RWA, 5 Douglas, 2 Leicester
9. **Karen Kneale** 23.4.69 (1y, -) 57:04R '93   3km: 14:28.0, 14:44.0   5km: 24:50R
   10km: 51:22t, 51:24R, 51:31R, 51:41R, 52:45R, 53:05R; 4 Manx, 9 UK, 5 AAA, 6 Douglas
10. **Kim Baird** 28.2.56 (2y, 9) 26:35.0 '91, 51:46R '93
    5km: 25:05.3,25:36R; 2 RWA   20km: 1:50:21, 1:50:22; 2 RWA
11. **Siân Spacey** 13.7.64 (0y, -) 51:41R '87 5km: 24:50.09, 24:57.11; 6 AAA   10km: 50:45.0, 51:09R; 4 Douglas
12. **Nicky Jackson** 1.5.65 (6y, -) 23:35.54 '87, 50:50.0 '86   3km: 14:36.22i   5km: 25:34R, 26:12R; 4 RWA
    10km: 52:13R, 52:37t, 52:42R, 52:53R; 7 UK, 5 RWA, 6 AAA

Lupton is top for the third successive year. She started slowly, but came through to be Britain's best in Europeans and Commonwealth, and the latter race was decisive in sorting out the order of the top five. Black beat Wright twice but her season was too short to rank higher. There is a big gap after the top eight.

With thanks to Tony Miller, Alan Lindop, Ian Hodge, Tony O'Neill, John Powell and Colin Young for their comments.

27 Years of UK Merit Rankings

Summary of achievements at standard events (not including occasional rankings for such events as men's 3000m, women's 200mh, 5000m)   + indicates would have added rankings pre 1968

Leading points scorers   all events - 12 points for a first place to 1 point for 12th

Men				Women		
1.	Daley Thompson	417.5		1.	Judy Simpson	379
2.	Steve Ovett	288		2.	Sally Gunnell	302.5
3.	Mike Winch	281.5		3.	Christina Cahill	300.5
4.	David Jenkins	276		4.	Tessa Sanderson	287
5.	Sebastian Coe	262		5.	Ann Simmonds +	281
6.	Steve Cram	252.5		6.	Yvonne Murray	279.5
7.	Brendan Foster	244.5		7.	Kathy Cook	272.5
8.	Linford Christie	230		8.	Judy Oakes	258.5
9.	Alan Pascoe	225		9.	Venissa Head	243.5
10.	Peter Tancred	218		10.	Liz McColgan	241.5
11.	Bob Dobson	213		11.	Sonia Lannaman	234.5
12.	John Herbert	202		12.	Margaret Ritchie	234
				13.	Sharon Colyear	232

Ranked at most events

Men

9   Daley Thompson
100m, 200m, 400m, 110mh, 400mh, HJ, PV, LJ, Dec
5   Paul Davies-Hale
1500m, 5000m, 10,000m, Mar, 3000mSt
5   Peter Gabbet
100m, 400m, PV, LJ, Dec
5   David Lewis
1500m, 5000m, 10,000m, Mar, 3000mSt
5   Gus McKenzie
200m, 110mh, HJ, LJ, Dec

Range of distances

100m to 800m: Verona Elder
200m to 1500m: Lillian Board
800m to 10,000m: Yvonne Murray
1500m to Mar: Paul Davies-Hale
              David Lewis
              Liz McColgan
400m, 800m and Mar: Rosemary Wright

Ranked at No.1 at three events

David Bedford	5000m, 10,000m, 3000mSt	
Brendan Foster	1500m, 5000m, 10,000m	
Alan Lerwill	HJ, LJ, TJ	

Most successive years at No.1

10	Geoff Capes	SP 1971-80
9	Linford Christie	100m 1968-94
8	Mike Bull +	PV 1968-75 (1 tie)
8	David Travis	JT 1968-75

Most years at No.2
without ever reaching No.1

7	Max Robertson	400mh	1985-91
6	Wilbert Greaves	110mh	1979-85

Most perfect record

Daley Thompson	No.1 all 12 years in Decathlon	
Kriss Akabusi	No.1 all 7 years in 400mh	

Most consecutive years ranked at an event

25	Bob Dobson	50km W 1969-93
19	Keith Stock	PV 1973-91
19	Peter Yates	JT 1976-94

Women

7   Sharon Colyear
100m, 200m, 400m, 100mh, 400mh, LJ, Pen
6   Judy Vernon
100m, 200m, 100mh, HJ, LJ, Hep
6   Mary Peters
200m, 100mh, HJ, LJ, SP, Pen
6   Gladys Taylor
100m, 200m, 400m, 400mh, LJ, Hep
5   Verona Elder
100m, 200m, 400m, 800m, 400mh
5   Clova Court
200m, 100mh, SP, JT, Hep
5   Sally Gunnell
200m, 400m, 100mh, 400mh, Hep
5   Sue Reeve
100mh, HJ, LJ, SP, Pen
5   Judy Simpson
100mh, HJ, LJ, SP, Hep
5   Liz Sutherland
100m, 200m, 400m, 100mh, 400mh

Lillian Board	200m, 400m, 800m (all in '68)
Kathy Cook	100m, 200m, 400m
Liz McColgan	3000m, 10,000m, Mar
Joyce Smith	1500m, 3000m, Mar
Yvonne Murray	1500m, 3000m, 10,000m

10	Margaret Ritchie	DT 1975-84
8	Tessa Sanderson	JT 1974-81
	(also 84, 89-92)	

Most years at No.2
8   Lorna Boothe   100mh

Sally Gunnell   No.1 all 7 years in 400mh

21 Tessa Sanderson   JT 1972-92

1994 LISTS - MEN

60 METRES - Indoors

6.48	Linford Christie		2.04.60	1	Karlsruhe, GER	1	Mar
	6.52			2	Stuttgart, GER	6	Feb
	6.52			1	San Sebastian, SPA	3	Mar
	6.53			1r2	Glasgow	12	Feb
	6.53			1	Sindelfingen, GER	6	Mar
	6.56			1	Glasgow	29	Jan
	6.56			1r2	Ghent, BEL	9	Feb
	6.56			2	Birmingham	19	Feb
	6.58			1r1	Glasgow	12	Feb
	6.58			1	Birmingham	26	Feb
	6.59			1h1	San Sebastian, SPA	3	Mar
	6.60			1	Glasgow	23	Jan
	6.60			1h2	Stuttgart, GER	6	Feb
	6.64			1h2	Karlsruhe, GER	1	Mar
	6.68			2s1	Birmingham	19	Feb
	6.68			2h1	Sindelfingen, GER	6	Mar
	6.69			1s2	Glasgow	23	Jan
6.49	Colin Jackson		18.02.67	1	Paris, FRA	11	Mar
	6.55			2r2	Glasgow	12	Feb
	6.55			1s1	Paris, FRA	11	Mar
	6.57			2	Glasgow	29	Jan
	6.57			3	Birmingham	19	Feb
	6.57			1h2	Paris, FRA	11	Mar
	6.61			1s2	Birmingham	19	Feb
6.54	Michael Rosswess		11.06.65	3	Paris, FRA	11	Mar
	6.56			1	Birmingham	19	Feb
	6.59			1s2	Paris, FRA	11	Mar
	6.60			1s1	Birmingham	19	Feb
	6.63			1	Birmingham	8	Jan
	6.63			2	Glasgow	23	Jan
	6.64			3	Glasgow	29	Jan
	6.65			1h6	Birmingham	8	Jan
	6.65			1s1	Birmingham	8	Jan
	6.65			4	Birmingham	26	Feb
	6.66			2r1	Glasgow	12	Feb
	6.66			3r1	Glasgow	12	Feb
	6.67			1h1	Paris, FRA	11	Mar
	6.67			1	Birmingham	31	Dec
	6.69			1s1	Glasgow	23	Jan
6.60	Jason John		17.10.71	2r1	Vienna, AUT	6	Feb
	6.68			1r2	Vienna, AUT	6	Feb
6.70	Darren Braithwaite		20.01.69	2	Birmingham	8	Jan
	6.70			2r2	Vienna, AUT	6	Feb
	6.70			1s3	Birmingham	19	Feb
6.70	Darren Campbell	U23	12.09.73	2s2	Glasgow	23	Jan
	6.70			3	Glasgow	23	Jan
	46 performances to 6.70 by 7 athletes						
6.71	*Josephus Thomas*		*11.07.68*	*2*	*Birmingham*	*31*	*Dec*
6.72	#Solomon Wariso		11.11.66	3	Birmingham	31	Dec
6.72	Jason Fergus	U23	11.10.73	4	Birmingham	31	Dec
6.73	Jason Gardener	U20	18.09.75	2s2	Birmingham	19	Feb
6.78	*Haroun Korjie*	*U23*	*17.02.72*	*1s2*	*Birmingham*	*31*	*Dec*
6.80	Andrew Mensah		30.11.71	1s3	Birmingham	31	Dec
	(10)						
6.81	*Joslyn Thomas*		*11.07.71*	*3s3*	*Birmingham*	*31*	*Dec*
6.82	Ray Burke		11.11.69	2h6	Birmingham	8	Jan
6.82	Phil Goedluck		10.09.67	4	Glasgow	12	Feb

6.82	Mark Walcott	U23	24.11.73	1r2	Birmingham	26 Feb
6.85	Ewan Clark		4.04.69	5	Glasgow	23 Jan
6.85	Hugh Teape		26.12.63	4s3	Birmingham	19 Feb
6.86	Kevin Williams		15.12.71	1r1	Birmingham	26 Feb
6.87	Ayo Falola		29.07.68	6	Birmingham	8 Jan
6.87	Owusu Dako	U23	23.05.73	3s1	Birmingham	31 Dec
6.88	Michael Nartey	U20	12.06.75	2	Birmingham	13 Feb
6.89	Norman Ellis	U20	17.01.75	3	Birmingham	13 Feb
	(20)					
6.89	Ejike Wodu	U23	15.12.74	4s2	Birmingham	31 Dec
6.91	Roddy Slater	U23	25.12.72	1h9	Birmingham	8 Jan
6.91	Kevin Mark	U20	15.09.76	4	Birmingham	13 Feb
6.91	Peter Maitland	U23	21.01.73	2r2	Birmingham	26 Feb
6.92	Paul White	U23	1.09.74	5s3	Birmingham	31 Dec
6.93	Andrew Bull		26.06.69	3	Sheffield	19 Jan
6.93	Trevor Cameron	U20	25.11.76	1h8	Birmingham	31 Dec
6.94	Richard Rubenis	U23	10.11.73	2h2	Birmingham	8 Jan
6.95	Jonathan Edwards		10.05.66	7	Glasgow	12 Feb
6.95	Steve Phillips	U23	17.03.72	3r1	Birmingham	26 Feb
	(30)					
6.96	Terence Stamp		18.02.70	2h5	Birmingham	8 Jan
6.97	Brian Taylor		13.08.70	2h10	Birmingham	8 Jan
6.97	Marlon Devonish	U20	1.06.76	5	Birmingham	13 Feb
6.98	Mark Lambeth	U23	3.09.72	4s2	Birmingham	8 Jan
6.98	Tremayne Rutherford	U23	19.06.72	1h7	Birmingham	31 Dec
6.98	Danny Joyce	U23	9.09.74	5s2	Birmingham	31 Dec
6.99	Ed White	U23	16.11.73	6s3	Birmingham	31 Dec

Hand Timing

6.8	Mark Williams		25.04.68	1	London (CP)	27 Feb
6.9	Lewis Samuel		12.02.66	1	Sheffield	19 Jan
6.9	Darren Tingle		20.09.65	2	Sheffield	19 Jan
6.9	Lloyd Chandler		14.04.69	1q1	London (CP)	30 Jan
6.9	Kevin Mark	U20	(6.91i)	1	London (CP)	30 Jan
6.9	Mclean Okotie		31.07.69	1q2	London (CP)	30 Jan
6.9	Terence Stamp		(6.96i)	1q2	London (CP)	30 Jan
6.9	Jamie Paul		17.07.70	2	London (CP)	24 Feb
6.9	Martin Giraud	U17	16.11.77	1	London (CP)	14 Dec

100 YARDS

9.30	1.6	Linford Christie		2.04.60	1	Edinburgh	8 Jul
9.46	1.6	Jason John		17.10.71	5	Edinburgh	8 Jul
9.72	1.6	Jamie Henderson		28.03.69	6	Edinburgh	8 Jul
9.74	*1.6*	*Sanusi Turay*		*14.04.68*	*7*	*Edinburgh*	*8 Jul*

100 METRES

9.91	1.9	Linford Christie		2.04.60	1	Victoria, CAN	23 Aug
		9.98	1.8		1s1	Victoria, CAN	23 Aug
		10.01	0.2		1h1	Linz, AUT	4 Jul
		10.02	0.2		1q1	Victoria, CAN	22 Aug
		10.02	1.0		3r2	Berlin, GER	30 Aug
		10.02	0.8		1	Tokyo, JAP	15 Sep
		10.03	0.2		3	Linz, AUT	4 Jul
		10.03	-0.1		1	Brussels, BEL	19 Aug
		10.03	1.7		1r1	Berlin, GER	30 Aug
		10.05	-1.4		1	Zurich, SWZ	17 Aug
		10.06	1.5		2	Rieti, ITA	28 Aug
		10.07	1.2		2	London (CP)	15 Jul
		10.08	0.7		1q1	Helsinki, FIN	7 Aug
		10.09	0.1		1	Nuremberg, GER	10 Jun

126

Mark	Wind	Name	Cat	DOB	Pos	Venue	Date
(Christie)							
10.13	-1.7				1h1	Zurich, SWZ	17 Aug
10.13	-0.6				2	Paris, FRA	3 Sep
10.14	-0.5				1	Helsinki, FIN	8 Aug
10.19	-0.7				1s1	Helsinki, FIN	8 Aug
10.21	0.9				1	Birmingham	25 Jun
10.21	-0.3				1	London (CP)	9 Sep
10.24	0.0				1h2	Nuremberg, GER	10 Jun
10.31	-2.0				1	Seville, SPA	5 Jun
10.35	1.5				1h1	Sheffield	11 Jun
10.39	0.3				1h3	Helsinki, FIN	7 Aug
10.39	1.8				1h1	Victoria, CAN	22 Aug
10.46	-2.0				1	Gateshead	1 Jul
10.23	1.2	Jason John		17.10.71	5	London (CP)	15 Jul
10.29	0.4				5q2	Victoria, CAN	22 Aug
10.36	1.0				2	Birmingham	21 May
10.37	-0.3				3q2	Helsinki, FIN	7 Aug
10.39	-0.7				2s1	Helsinki, FIN	8 Aug
10.41	-0.4				2h5	Helsinki, FIN	7 Aug
10.45	-0.6				2	Wellington, NZ	19 Jan
10.46	-0.5				8	Helsinki, FIN	8 Aug
10.46	0.0				3	Madrid, SPA	6 Sep
10.47	-0.1				1h5	Sheffield	11 Jun
10.23	1.1	Terry Williams		15.11.68	3q4	Victoria, CAN	22 Aug
10.25	1.2				1h1	Brussels, BEL	16 Jul
10.31	1.3				4h5	Victoria, CAN	22 Aug
10.39	-1.2				1s1	London (CP)	25 Jun
10.45	-1.0				1	Brussels, BEL	17 Jul
10.46	0.9				2r1	London (He)	5 Jun
10.49	-2.0				1	London (CP)	25 Jun
10.25	1.2	Jason Gardener	U20	18.09.75	2	Lisbon, POR	21 Jul
10.35	0.8				2s2	Lisbon, POR	21 Jul
10.40	1.6				2q2	Lisbon, POR	20 Jul
10.42	1.6				1	Warsaw, POL	18 Jun
10.48	0.1				1h1	Lisbon, POR	20 Jul
10.26	1.4	Darren Braithwaite		20.01.69	4	Bratislava, SVK	1 Jun
10.32	1.0				1	Birmingham	21 May
10.40	-0.2				2	Malaga, SPA	28 May
10.28	*2.0*	*Sanusi Turay*		*14.04.68*	*2h7*	*Victoria, CAN*	*22 Aug*
10.29	1.4	Michael Rosswess		11.06.65	6	Bratislava, SVK	1 Jun
10.29	-0.2				1s1	Sheffield	11 Jun
10.37	0.3				1h3	Budapest, HUN	3 Jun
10.42	1.2				7	London (CP)	15 Jul
10.33	-2.3	#Solomon Wariso		11.11.66	1	Geneva, SWZ	19 Jun
10.34	0.9				1r1	London (He)	5 Jun
10.37	1.3				4h1	Geneva, SWZ	19 Jun
10.40	1.9				2s3	Sheffield	11 Jun
10.46	-0.2				1	Malaga, SPA	29 May
10.34	1.8	Elliot Bunney		11.12.66	4q3	Victoria, CAN	22 Aug
10.36	2.0				1h8	Sheffield	11 Jun
10.40	1.9				3s3	Sheffield	11 Jun
10.42	0.6				3h3	Victoria, CAN	22 Aug
10.47	0.4				2	Istanbul, TUR	21 May
10.50	1.8				8s1	Victoria, CAN	23 Aug
10.35	1.4	Toby Box	U23	9.09.72	2q4	Helsinki, FIN	7 Aug
10.36	1.9				1s3	Sheffield	11 Jun
10.41	1.0				1h7	Sheffield	11 Jun
10.46	1.7				6s2	Helsinki, FIN	8 Aug
10.47	-2.7				1	Ostrava, CS	30 Jul
10.36	0.4	Colin Jackson		18.02.67	1	Istanbul, TUR	21 May

(10)

127

10.38	0.1	John Regis		13.10.66	2	Eagle Rock, USA	14	May
10.43	1.5	Julian Golding	U20	17.02.75	1h5	Lisbon, POR	20	Jul
	10.43	1.3			1q4	Lisbon, POR	20	Jul
	10.43	1.1			3s1	Lisbon, POR	21	Jul
	10.45	0.3			1s2	Bedford	2	Jul
	10.46	1.2			8	Lisbon, POR	21	Jul
	10.48	1.9			4s3	Sheffield	11	Jun
10.44	0.5	Tremayne Rutherford	U23	19.06.72	1	Oordegem, BEL	9	Jul
10.45	-0.2	Tony Jarrett		13.08.68	1	Westwood, USA	9	Apr
10.45	1.8	Jamie Henderson		28.03.69	2h1	Victoria, CAN	22	Aug
	10.49	1.4			1s1	Edinburgh	25	Jun
	10.49	1.1			6q4	Victoria, CAN	22	Aug
10.46	*-1.2*	*Haroun Korjie*	*U23*	*17.02.72*	*2s1*	*London (CP)*	*25*	*Jun*
10.48	-0.5	Danny Joyce	U23	9.09.74	1r3	Ostrava, CS	30	Jul
	10.49	2.0			2h8	Sheffield	11	Jun
10.48	0.8	Phil Goedluck		10.09.67	1r2	Crawley	6	Aug
	10.49	1.9			5s3	Sheffield	11	Jun
10.49	1.7	Andrew Mensah		30.11.71	1h3	Brussels, BEL	16	Jul
10.50		Ian Mackie	U20	27.02.75	5	Prince George, CAN	13	Aug
		90 performances to 10.50 by 19 athletes						
10.54	0.2	Trevor Cameron	U20	25.11.76	1r2	Birmingham	21	May
	(20)							
10.54	1.9	Jason Fergus	U23	11.10.73	1h9	Sheffield	11	Jun
10.54	*-1.3*	*Joslyn Thomas*		*11.07.71*	*1s2*	*London (CP)*	*25*	*Jun*
10.54	1.1	Darren Campbell	U23	12.09.73	2r1	Nitra, SVK	13	Jul
10.55	0.6	Peter Maitland	U23	21.01.73	5h3	Victoria, CAN	22	Aug
10.57	1.0	Marlon Devonish	U20	1.06.76	3	Birmingham	21	May
10.57	-0.2	Lenny Paul		25.05.58	3s1	Sheffield	11	Jun
10.59		Brian Taylor		13.08.70	1D	Azusa, USA	13	Apr
10.59	1.0	Steve Gookey		21.04.71	4	Birmingham	21	May
10.60	1.6	Owusu Dako	U23	23.05.73	h	London (CP)	30	Apr
10.60	2.0	Mclean Okotie		31.07.69	3h8	Sheffield	11	Jun
10.60	*-1.2*	*Josephus Thomas*		*11.07.68*	*3s1*	*London (CP)*	*25*	*Jun*
10.60	0.3	Kevin Mark	U20	15.09.76	1	Schio, ITA	6	Aug
	(30)							
10.61	1.3	Paul White	U23	1.09.74	1	Stoke	16	Jul
10.65	0.4	Ejike Wodu	U23	15.12.74	1h4	Sheffield	11	Jun
10.66	*1.8*	*Denton Guy-Williams*	*U23*	*8.05.72*	*5h1*	*Victoria, CAN*	*22*	*Aug*
10.66	-2.5	Curtis Browne	U20	11.09.75	1	Bulle, SWZ	10	Sep
10.67	1.3	Mark Walcott	U23	24.11.73	2	Stoke	16	Jul
10.68	0.4	Kevin Williams		15.12.71	3	Istanbul, TUR	21	May
10.70		Allyn Condon	U23	24.08.74	1	Derby	16	Jul
10.72	0.0	Stewart Weathers		14.09.65	3r2	London (He)	5	Jun
10.72	0.4	Ray Burke		11.11.69	2h4	Sheffield	11	Jun
10.73		Steve Markham	U23	11.11.74	1	Gateshead	14	May
10.74	0.9	Michael Afilaka		16.11.71	5r1	London (He)	5	Jun
	(40)							
10.74	1.5	Dion Caleb		26.11.66	4h1	Sheffield	11	Jun
10.74	2.0	Mark Allen		23.09.66	4h8	Sheffield	11	Jun
10.74	-1.3	Richard Johnson		13.10.71	3r2	London (WL)	2	Jul
10.75	0.3	Keith Douglas		6.07.66	1r2	Istanbul, TUR	21	May
10.75	1.4	Dwain Chambers	U17	5.04.78	1	London (CP)	28	May
10.75	1.5	Rohan Samuel		30.01.66	5h1	Sheffield	11	Jun
10.76	0.9	Ed White	U23	16.11.73	6r1	London (He)	5	Jun
10.77	1.3	Richard Rubenis	U23	10.11.73	3	Stoke	16	Jul
10.78	0.9	James Egan	U20	12.11.75	1	Gateshead	28	May
10.78	1.0	Michael Nartey	U20	12.06.75	4h7	Sheffield	11	Jun
	(50)							
10.78	1.4	Roddy Slater	U23	25.12.72	2s1	Edinburgh	25	Jun
10.78	1.8	Jamie Henthorn	U20	20.02.77	1	Dublin (M), IRE	13	Aug
10.78	1.8	Scott Fraser	U17	31.12.77	2	Dublin (M), IRE	13	Aug

10.79	1.9	Adrian Milnes	U20	17.01.75	3h9	Sheffield	11	Jun
10.80	0.3	Dave Clark		16.02.64	2r2	Istanbul, TUR	21	May
10.80	1.9	Scott Dorset		10.04.69	8s3	Sheffield	11	Jun
10.81	-1.3	Doug Turner		2.12.66	2h2	Cwmbran	18	Jun
10.82	0.4	Steve McCourt		6.05.71	4h4	Sheffield	11	Jun
10.82	*0.4*	*Shaun Mayne*		*27.05.70*	*5h4*	*Sheffield*	*11*	*Jun*
10.82	1.0	Mike Rey		19.07.68	6h7	Sheffield	11	Jun
10.84	0.7	Steve Simmons	U23	10.11.74	5h3	Sheffield	11	Jun
	(60)							
10.84	0.7	Ayo Falola		29.07.68	6h3	Sheffield	11	Jun
10.85		Jonathan Edwards		10.05.66	2	Gateshead	14	May
10.85	0.7	John McLoughlin	U23	26.10.73	7h3	Sheffield	11	Jun
10.85	-1.7	John Kenny		17.12.70	3h3	London (CP)	25	Jun
10.85	-1.6	Matthew Clements	U17	17.09.77	2	Birmingham	31	Jul
10.86	0.9	Michael Bennett		6.02.69	7r1	London (He)	5	Jun
10.86	-0.1	Mark McIntyre		14.10.70	4h5	Sheffield	11	Jun
10.86	1.9	Craig Kerslake	U23	29.08.74	4h9	Sheffield	11	Jun
10.86	0.3	Jason Fletcher	U20	18.01.76	3s2	Bedford	2	Jul
10.86	0.8	Steve Fletcher		16.12.68	1h3	Derby	16	Jul
	(70)							
10.86	-1.6	Uvie Ugono	U17	8.03.78	3	Birmingham	31	Jul
10.86	0.8	Jamie Quarry	U23	15.11.72	3D	Victoria, CAN	23	Aug
10.87		John McAdorey	U23	16.09.74	1r1	Antrim	13	Aug
10.88	2.0	Lloyd Chandler		14.04.69	5h8	Sheffield	11	Jun
10.88	0.8	Norman Ellis	U20	17.01.75	3s1	Bedford	2	Jul
10.88	1.1	Christian Malcolm	U17	3.06.79	1	Dublin (M), IRE	13	Aug
10.89	1.0	Mark Smith		18.11.71	1r2	London (CP)	7	May
10.89	1.4	Ross Baillie	U17	26.09.77	5s1	Edinburgh	25	Jun
10.89	0.5	Andy Lewis		9.03.68	1D	Diekirch, LUX	19	Aug
10.89	0.8	Simon Shirley		3.08.66	5D	Victoria, CAN	23	Aug
	(80)							
10.90	1.4	Bryn Middleton	U20	16.02.76	1r2	Oordegem, BEL	9	Jul
10.90	1.4	Richard Moore	U23	19.01.73	1h4	Stoke	16	Jul
10.91	0.9	Daniel Money	U20	7.10.76	2	Gateshead	28	May
10.91	1.2	Clayton Archer	U20	29.05.76	2h1	London (CP)	28	May
10.91	0.3	Michael Champion	U20	3.01.75	4s2	Bedford	2	Jul
10.92	0.4	David Jackson	U23	12.05.73	6h4	Sheffield	11	Jun
10.93	1.6	Andi Knight	U23	11.11.73	5	London (CP)	1	May
10.93	1.4	Graham Beasley	U17	24.10.77	2	London (CP)	28	May
10.93	0.9	Matthew Bridle	U20	11.08.76	3	Gateshead	28	May
10.94	1.0	Mark Williams		25.04.68	2r2	London (CP)	7	May
	(90)							
10.94	0.4	Ian Craig		20.08.69	2h	Fana, NOR	26	May
10.94	0.4	Michael Tietz	U17	14.09.77	3s2	Birmingham	31	Jul
10.94	1.5	Carlo Ferri	U20	18.11.75	1r2	Edinburgh	14	Aug
10.95	-1.8	Doug Walker	U23	28.07.73	2	Edinburgh	14	May
10.95	-0.8	Larry Achike	U20	31.01.75	4s1	Bedford	2	Jul
10.96	0.9	Glenn Palmer	U23	8.11.74	8r1	London (He)	5	Jun
10.97		Anthony Wood	U23	30.03.74	3	Gateshead	14	May
10.97	0.2	Andrew Clegg	U23	8.09.73	4r2	Birmingham	21	May
10.97	1.5	Mike St.Louis		26.03.64	6h1	Sheffield	11	Jun
10.97	-1.3	Courtney Rumbolt		26.07.69	4r2	London (WL)	2	Jul
	(100)							
10.98	1.4	Tony Leigh		27.12.65	2h4	Stoke	16	Jul
10.98		Darren Scott		7.03.69	2	Stoke	11	Sep
10.99	1.3	Leon Daniels	U20	1.11.75	5	Stoke	16	Jul
10.99	1.0	Tim Barton		3.10.70	4	Bedford	18	Sep

Wind Assisted

9.91	3.7	Christie		(9.91)	1	Sheffield	11	Jun
		10.03	4.0		1s2	Sheffield	11	Jun

129

10.07	3.7	Toby Box	U23	(10.35)	2	Sheffield	11	Jun
10.07	3.7	Michael Rosswess		(10.29)	3	Sheffield	11	Jun
10.24	2.3				1h2	Sheffield	11	Jun
10.25	2.9				2	Budapest, HUN	3	Jun
10.08	3.7	Jason John		(10.23)	4	Sheffield	11	Jun
10.16	4.0				2s2	Sheffield	11	Jun
10.50	2.1				2h6	Victoria, CAN	22	Aug
10.10A	3.5	John Regis		(10.38)	4	Sestriere, ITA	31	Jul
10.23	2.9				3r2	Austin, USA	7	May
10.17	2.3	Terry Williams		(10.23)	5s2	Victoria, CAN	23	Aug
10.47	4.0				5s2	Sheffield	11	Jun
10.20		Elliot Bunney		(10.34)	1	Edinburgh	8	Jun
10.21	3.7				5	Sheffield	11	Jun
10.29	3.7	Trevor Cameron	U20	(10.54)	6	Sheffield	11	Jun
10.31	4.7	Braithwaite		(10.26)	4h1	Oslo, NOR	22	Jul
10.34	3.5	Jason Fergus	U23	(10.54)	1	Loughborough	5	Jun
10.49	4.0				7s2	Sheffield	11	Jun
10.34	3.5	Julian Golding	U20	(10.43)	1	Bedford	17	Sep
10.45	2.4				1	London (He)	27	Aug
10.37	4.0	Steve Gookey		(10.59)	3s2	Sheffield	11	Jun
10.40	3.7				7	Sheffield	11	Jun
10.37	3.7	Jamie Henderson		(10.45)	1	Edinburgh	25	Jun
10.49	4.0				6s2	Sheffield	11	Jun
10.39	2.8	Andrew Mensah		(10.49)	2	Lambertseter, NOR	15	Jun
10.48	2.2				2r1	Aartselaar, BEL	21	Jul
10.48					h	Nivelles, BEL	23	Jul
10.43	2.9	Curtis Browne	U20	(10.66)	1	Telford	9	Jul
10.44	2.9	Kevin Mark	U20	(10.60)	2	Telford	9	Jul
10.44	2.2	Gardener	U20	(10.25)	1	London (CP)	28	May
10.44	3.5	Rutherford	U23	(10.44)	2	Loughborough	5	Jun
10.47	4.0				4s2	Sheffield	11	Jun
10.48	2.3	Lenny Paul		(10.57)	2h2	Sheffield	11	Jun
10.50	2.9	Paul White	U23	(10.61)	3	Telford	9	Jul

35 performances to 10.50 by 20 athletes

10.52	2.9	Marlon Devonish	U20	(10.57)	1	Solihull	28	May
10.54		Doug Walker	U23	(10.95)	2	Edinburgh	8	Jun
10.56	2.1	Dwain Chambers	U17	(10.75)	1s1	Telford	9	Jul
10.63	3.7	Dave Clark		(10.80)	2	Edinburgh	25	Jun
10.66	4.4	Doug Turner		(10.81)	1r2	Colwyn Bay	23	Jul
10.67	3.5	Ayo Falola		(10.84)	5	Bedford	17	Sep
10.68	2.3	Scott Dorset		(10.80)	4h2	Sheffield	11	Jun
10.68	2.3	Keith Douglas		(10.75)	2h4	Edinburgh	25	Jun
10.69	2.7	Mark Allen		(10.74)	2	Fana, NOR	26	May
10.69	2.9	Andre Johnson	U20	9.01.77	4	Telford	9	Jul
10.69	3.5	Mike Rey		(10.82)	6	Bedford	17	Sep
10.70		Stephen Tucker		30.12.62	3	Edinburgh	8	Jun
10.70	3.7	Scott Fraser	U17	(10.78)	4	Edinburgh	25	Jun
10.73	2.2	Michael Nartey	U20	(10.78)	4	London (CP)	29	May
10.73	2.3	Ross Baillie	U17	(10.89)	3h4	Edinburgh	25	Jun
10.74	3.3	Joel Calliste	U17	(11.02)	2	Telford	9	Jul
10.76	2.2	Norman Ellis	U20	(10.88)	5	London (CP)	29	May
10.77	3.5	Andi Knight	U23	(10.93)	6r1	Loughborough	5	Jun
10.77	3.7	Roddy Slater	U23	(10.78)	5	Edinburgh	25	Jun
10.77	3.3	Michael Tietz	U17	(10.94)	3	Telford	9	Jul
10.78	2.9	Leon Daniels	U20	(10.99)	3	Solihull	29	May
10.78	2.9	Jason Fletcher	U20	(10.86)	4	Solihull	29	May
10.80	3.6	Bryn Middleton	U20	(10.90)	2	Newport	28	May
10.80	3.6	Neil Powell	U20	5.03.77	3	Newport	28	May

10.80	2.6	Steve McCourt		(10.82)	4r2	Loughborough	5 Jun
10.80		Alan Doris		12.03.66	4	Edinburgh	8 Jun
10.80		Andrew Howis	U23	3.07.74	5	Edinburgh	8 Jun
10.80	3.1	Andy Lewis		(10.89)	1D	Horsham	18 Jun
10.80	4.4	Andrew Clegg	U23	(10.97)	2r2	Colwyn Bay	23 Jul
10.80	4.4	Carlo Ferri	U20	(10.94)	3r2	Colwyn Bay	23 Jul
10.83	2.7	Ian Craig		(10.94)	3	Fana, NOR	26 May
10.84	3.5	Steve Shanks		3.11.69	4	London (He)	18 Aug
10.85	2.3	Richard Moore	U23	(10.90)	5h2	Sheffield	11 Jun
10.86	2.6	Courage Edo	U17	3.12.77	2s2	Telford	9 Jul
10.87	3.1	Paul Field		24.06.67	2D	Horsham	18 Jun
10.88	3.3	Mark Findlay	U17	(11.00)	4	Telford	9 Jul
10.89	2.9	Andrew Walcott	U20	11.01.75	5	Solihull	29 May
10.90	3.5	Seni Edu			7s1	Loughborough	5 Jun
10.93		Ken Campbell	U23	30.09.72	6	Edinburgh	8 Jun
10.94	3.0	Jim Stevenson		31.12.71	1D	Austin, USA	25 Mar
10.99	4.7	David Vidgen	U23	27.09.74	1D	Sheffield	30 Apr
10.99	3.0	Matthew Douglas	U20	26.11.76	1D	Sheffield	30 Apr

Hand Timing

10.4		Rosswess		(10.29)	1h1	Leamington	14 May
10.4 w		*Joslyn Thomas*		*(10.54)*	*1*	*London (WP)*	*18 Jun*
10.4 w?		Tremayne Rutherford	U23	(10.44)	1	St. Ives	17 Sep
		2 performances to 10.4 by 2 athletes including 1 wind assisted					
10.5		Roger Black		31.03.66	2r2	Canberra, AUS	25 Jan
10.5	1.3	Mclean Okotie		(10.60)	2	Enfield	15 May
10.5	1.3	Trevor Cameron	U20	(10.54)	3	Enfield	15 May
10.5 w	3.8	Richard Rubenis	U23	(10.77)	1	Loughborough	26 Jun
10.7					1	Stafford	15 Jun
10.6	1.3	Richard Johnson		(10.74)	4	Enfield	15 May
10.6		Dion Caleb		(10.74)	1r2	Carn Brea	4 Jun
10.6		Curtis Browne	U20	(10.66)	1	Birmingham	11 Jun
10.6	1.3	Paul Sanders		11.01.62	1	Salisbury	10 Jul
10.6		Rohan Samuel		(10.75)	1	Sutton Coldfield	27 Aug
10.6 w		Jamie Henthorn	U20	(10.78)	1	Carmarthen	11 Jun
10.6 w		Martin Giraud	U17	16.11.77	2r1	London (WP)	18 Jun
10.7					1	London (TB)	22 Jun
10.7		Doug Walker	U23	(10.95)	1r1	Edinburgh	24 Apr
10.7	1.4	Adrian Patrick	U23	15.06.73	1r1	Bracknell	7 May
10.7	0.8	Michael Nartey	U20	(10.78)	1h1	London (CP)	14 May
10.7	1.5	Mark Williams		(10.94)	5	London (CP)	14 May
10.7	1.4	Jason Wing		12.10.65	1r1	Kingston	4 Jun
10.7		D. Hancock			1	Aldershot	8 Jun
10.7		John McLoughlin	U23	(10.85)	1	Enfield	19 Jun
10.7		Andy Carrott		1.01.66	2	Cannock	26 Jun
10.7		Didier N'Fallo		7.10.68	1r1	Ilford	2 Jul
10.7		Lloyd Chandler		(10.88)	1r1	Dartford	2 Jul
10.7		Steve Markham	U23	(10.73)	1r1	Jarrow	2 Jul
10.7	1.9	Andre Johnson	U20	(10.69w)	1r2	Enfield	14 Aug
10.7		Cypren Edmunds		20.06.70	1	Basingstoke	21 Aug
10.7		Doug Turner		(10.81)	1	Newport	14 Sep
10.7		Graham Beasley	U17	(10.93)	1	St. Ives	17 Sep
10.7 w		Paul McBurney	U23	14.03.72	1	Belfast	23 Apr
10.7 w		Brian Ashburn		11.03.70	1	Linwood	1 May

10.7 w		Richard Moore	U23	(10.90)	2	Leamington	14 May
10.8					1	Mansfield	23 Jul
10.7 w	2.5	Norman Ellis	U20	(10.88)	1	London (CP)	15 May
10.7 w		Bryn Middleton	U20	(10.90)	1	Barry	17 May
10.7 w		John McAdorey	U23	(10.87)	1	Antrim	28 May
10.7 w		Delroy McLaren		29.01.70	2	Cannock	15 Jun
10.7 w	3.8	Tim Barton		(10.99)	2	Loughborough	26 Jun
10.7 w	3.8	Mark Dunwell		13.03.70	3	Loughborough	26 Jun
10.8					1	Nottingham	14 May
10.7 w	3.0	Lee Fairclough		23.06.70	3	Salisbury	10 Jul
10.8		Mark Smith		(10.89)	1	Crawley	17 Apr
10.8		Warren Gilder	U23	17.09.72	1	Oxford	14 May
10.8	0.8	Jamie Paul		17.07.70	2h1	London (CP)	14 May
10.8	0.1	John Kenny		(10.85)	4r1	Wolverhampton	4 Jun
10.8		C. Vincent			2	Aldershot	8 Jun
10.8		John Bowen		20.05.63	2	Cwmbran	8 Jun
10.8		Steve Simmons	U23	(10.84)	1r1	London (WF)	18 Jun
10.8		*Trevor Davis*		*26.03.63*	*1r1*	*Windsor*	*18 Jun*
10.8		Mike St.Louis		(10.97)	2	Hoo	19 Jun
10.8		Sam Kabiswa		28.10.66	1	Bromley	19 Jun
10.8		*Shaun Mayne*		*(10.82)*	*2*	*Colchester*	*19 Jun*
10.8		Darren Scott		(10.98)	1	Bebington	22 Jun
10.8		Alex Fugallo		28.01.70	2r1	London (PH)	2 Jul
10.8		Julian Thompson		28.12.66	1	Wrexham	30 Jul
10.8		Paul Bolton	U23	8.04.74	2	Wrexham	30 Jul
10.8		A. Lashore			1r2	London (TB)	13 Aug
10.8	1.6	Michael Champion	U20	(10.91)	2r1	Enfield	14 Aug
10.8 w		B. O'Donnell	U20		2	Antrim	28 May
10.8 w		Andrew Walcott	U20	(10.89w)	3	Cannock	26 Jun
10.8 w	3.0	Dan Donovan		8.10.70	4	Salisbury	10 Jul

Additional Under 20

10.9		Michael Tietz	U17	(10.94)	1	Bolton	13 Aug
10.9 w	3.4	James Craig		2.03.77	1	Grangemouth	18 Jun
10.9 w	3.4	Adam Lowles		29.01.77	2	Grangemouth	18 Jun
10.9 w		Philip Perigo	U17	25.09.78	1	Sheffield	18 Jun
11.1					1	Gateshead	22 May
10.9 w		Richard Davis	U17	(11.17)	1	Thurrock	19 Jun

Additional Under 17 (1 - 14 above)

11.00 A		Kevin Farrell		31.10.77	2	Avila, SPA	23 Jul
11.00	-1.1	Mark Findlay		20.03.78	1	Birmingham	11 Sep
11.00 w	3.7	David O'Hare		1.12.77	1	Newport	28 May
11.00 w	5.2	Steven Wiggans	U15	1.01.80	1	Telford	9 Jul
11.3					1	Blackpool	11 Jun
11.46	-1.4				2s2	Telford	8 Jul
11.0	2.0	Joel Calliste		25.04.78	1	Enfield	15 May
11.02	0.9				1s3	Birmingham	31 Jul
11.0		Andrew Row		17.10.78	1	Gateshead	5 Jun
11.03	-1.1				2	Birmingham	11 Sep
11.0		Courage Edo		(10.86w)	2	London (WL)	11 Jun
11.0		Chris Blake		8.11.78	1	Leeds	26 Jun
	(20)						
11.0		Alasdair McFarlane		13.02.78	1	Rotherham	3 Jul
11.05 w	3.3				7	Telford	9 Jul
11.03 w	3.3	Richard Webb		24.11.78	6	Telford	9 Jul

11.06 w 5.2		Paul Chantler	U15	10.09.79	2	Telford	9 Jul
11.4					1	Stoke	10 Jun
11.56	-1.4				1s1	Telford	8 Jul
11.09		Gavin Cater		16.10.77	h	London (CP)	28 May
11.09 w 2.1		Daniel Bonich		22.11.78	5s1	Telford	9 Jul
11.1					1	Hoo	1 May
11.1		Andrew Thornton		29.11.77	1	Leeds	24 Apr
11.1		G. Fearon			1	Harrow	10 May
11.1		M. Osborne			2	Harrow	10 May
11.1		C. Holland		1.09.77	1	Kings Lynn	30 May
11.1		Graham Thomas		23.09.77	1	Carmarthen	11 Jun
(30)							
11.1		Nicholas Long		1.02.79	1	Bebington	11 Jun
11.1		Jon Davis		5.03.78	1	Dublin (M), IRE	25 Jun
11.1		Nick Swaby		1.09.77	1	Cwmbran	17 Jul
11.1		John Skeete		8.09.78	1r2	Peterborough	17 Jul
11.1		Scott Walker		9.09.77	1	Deeside	17 Jul
11.12	1.1	Thomas Begen		14.04.79	2	Dublin, IRE	13 Aug
11.17	1.4	Richard Davis		3.05.78	4	London (CP)	28 May
11.17	0.3	Damien Greaves		19.09.77	1h7	Birmingham	31 Jul

Additional Under 15 (1 - 2 above)

11.20 w 5.2		Russell Johnson		14.09.80	3=	Telford	9 Jul
11.54	1.0				2h1	Birmingham	31 Jul
11.20 w 5.2		David Hobson		6.03.80	3=	Telford	9 Jul
11.25	0.5	Andre Duffus		30.10.79	1	Birmingham	31 Jul
11.25 w 5.2		Neil Akester		6.09.79	5	Telford	9 Jul
11.5					1	York	18 Jun
11.56	-1.4				2s1	Telford	8 Jul
11.3		Steven Daly		29.12.79	1	Bebington	18 Sep
11.32	0.5				2	Birmingham	31 Jul
11.3 w		Iestyn Lewis		14.04.80	1	Carmarthen	11 Jun
11.4		Soloman Povey		8.02.80	1	Kingston	17 Jul
11.52 w 2.6					1	London (He)	7 Aug
11.43 w 5.2		Antonio Matarazzo		27.03.80	6	Telford	9 Jul
11.5					1r1	Swindon	17 Jul
(10)							
11.44	-1.4	Wayne Gray		7.11.80	1s2	Telford	8 Jul
11.5		Steven Attridge		9.03.80	1	Portsmouth	26 Jun
11.5		Olisa Okwuosa			1	Kingston	1 Jul
11.5		Robert Allenby		14.10.79	2	Blackpool	14 Aug
11.5		J. Penn			3	Blackpool	14 Aug
11.52 w 5.2		Darren Burley		13.07.80	7	Telford	9 Jul
11.59 w 3.4		George Burton		22.11.79	1r1	Grangemouth	28 Aug

Under 13

12.2		Andrew Rose	U13	17.08.83	1r1	Kings Lynn	31 Jul
12.3		Tyrone Keating	U13	25.02.82	1	Colchester	29 Aug
12.4		Alexander Darlington	U13	9.09.81	2r1	Ipswich	4 Sep
12.5		Daniel Angus	U13	15.07.82	1	Carlisle	11 Sep

150 METRES

14.97	0.9	Linford Christie		2.04.60	1	Sheffield	4 Sep
15.15	0.9	John Regis		13.10.66	2	Sheffield	4 Sep
15.66	0.9	Terry Williams		15.11.68	7	Sheffield	4 Sep
15.99	0.9	Jason Gardener	U20	18.09.75	8	Sheffield	4 Sep

200 METRES

Time	Wind	Name	Cat	DOB	Pl	Venue	Date
19.87 A	1.8	John Regis		13.10.66	1	Sestriere, ITA	31 Jul
20.01	0.0				2	Monaco, MON	2 Aug
20.17	1.5				2r1	Lausanne, SWZ	6 Jul
20.25	1.5				2	Victoria, CAN	26 Aug
20.31	0.6				3	St. Petersburg, RUS	28 Jul
20.35	-0.1				2	Madrid, SPA	6 Sep
20.36	2.0				1q1	Victoria, CAN	24 Aug
20.42	-0.4				1	London (CP)	15 Jul
20.43	1.4				1	Westwood, USA	9 Apr
20.44	1.5				1	Gateshead	20 Jul
20.45	-1.4				1	London (CP)	11 Sep
20.50	0.7				2	Edinburgh	8 Jul
20.51	1.3				3	Bratislava, SVK	1 Jun
20.55	0.1				3	Tokyo, JAP	15 Sep
20.65	-0.1				1s2	Victoria, CAN	26 Aug
20.69	-1.7				1r2	London (WL)	2 Jul
20.74 i					1	Glasgow	12 Feb
20.76	-1.4				2	New York, USA	22 May
20.87 i					2r1	Stuttgart, GER	6 Feb
20.89 i					1h3	Atlanta, USA	4 Mar
20.97 i					4	Atlanta, USA	5 Mar
21.03	0.6				1h8	Victoria, CAN	24 Aug
20.50	1.6	Terry Williams		15.11.68	2q3	Victoria, CAN	24 Aug
20.62	1.5				5	Victoria, CAN	26 Aug
20.84	0.2				4s1	Victoria, CAN	26 Aug
20.86	1.2				1h3	Brussels, BEL	16 Jul
21.03	-1.5				2h1	Victoria, CAN	24 Aug
21.08	0.5				1	London (CP)	26 Jun
20.51	0.6	#Solomon Wariso		11.11.66	1r2	Malaga, SPA	29 May
20.60	1.0				1s1	Sheffield	12 Jun
21.01 i					1	Glasgow	29 Jan
21.01 i					3h4	Paris, FRA	12 Mar
21.06	0.3				1h1	Sheffield	12 Jun
21.10 i					2	Glasgow	12 Feb
20.56 i		Linford Christie		2.04.60	1	Ghent, BEL	9 Feb
20.67	-0.1				1	Birmingham	26 Jun
20.70 i					2	Birmingham	26 Feb
20.76 i					1	Sindelfingen, GER	6 Mar
20.71	2.0	Doug Walker	U23	28.07.73	3q1	Victoria, CAN	24 Aug
21.04	1.6				1	Edinburgh	24 Jun
21.08	0.2				6s1	Victoria, CAN	26 Aug
20.72	1.6	Toby Box	U23	9.09.72	3q2	Victoria, CAN	24 Aug
21.02	0.2				5s1	Victoria, CAN	26 Aug
21.06	-0.9				2	Ostrava, CS	31 Jul
21.08	-0.6				1	Birmingham	21 May
21.08	0.9				6	Sheffield	4 Sep
20.79	-0.6	Phil Goedluck		10.09.67	1r1	Crawley	6 Aug
20.90	1.0				2s1	Sheffield	12 Jun
20.97	1.5				5	Gateshead	20 Jul
20.99	0.3				4q2	Helsinki, FIN	10 Aug
21.00	0.9				5	Sheffield	4 Sep
21.01	-0.1				3h2	Helsinki, FIN	10 Aug
20.81	1.6	Paul McBurney	U23	14.03.72	4q2	Victoria, CAN	24 Aug
20.84	2.0	Jamie Baulch	U23	3.05.73	5q1	Victoria, CAN	24 Aug
20.91	1.9	Ian Mackie	U20	27.02.75	1s1	Lisbon, POR	23 Jul
20.95	1.7				3	Lisbon, POR	23 Jul
20.99	1.6				5q3	Victoria, CAN	24 Aug
21.00	1.4				1q2	Lisbon, POR	22 Jul
21.06	1.2				1h6	Lisbon, POR	22 Jul

Time	Wind	Name	Cat	DOB	Pos	Venue	Date
20.96	1.6	Peter Maitland	U23	21.01.73	6q2	Victoria, CAN	24 Aug
20.99	0.9	Darren Braithwaite		20.01.69	4	Sheffield	4 Sep
21.01 i					2s2	Paris, FRA	12 Mar
21.04	1.7				5	Oslo, NOR	22 Jul
21.02	-1.1	Jason John		17.10.71	1	Corby	30 May
21.10	-0.7				1	Nitra, SVK	13 Jul
21.02	1.7	Julian Golding	U20	17.02.75	1	Bedford	3 Jul
21.05	0.9				1s1	Bedford	3 Jul
21.10	0.9				1q4	Lisbon, POR	22 Jul
21.05	0.7	Roger Black		31.03.66	7	Edinburgh	8 Jul
21.10	1.0	Owusu Dako	U23	23.05.73	1	London (CP)	2 May

70 performances to 21.10 by 16 athletes including 11 indoors

Time	Wind	Name	Cat	DOB	Pos	Venue	Date
21.14	-0.6	Andrew Mensah		30.11.71	2r1	Crawley	6 Aug
21.17	-0.6	Stewart Weathers		14.09.65	3r1	Crawley	6 Aug
21.18	1.0	Trevor Cameron	U20	25.11.76	4s1	Sheffield	12 Jun
21.18	0.8	John Kenny		17.12.70	2s2	Sheffield	12 Jun
(20)							
21.22	0.8	Michael Afilaka		16.11.71	3s2	Sheffield	12 Jun
21.23 i		Darren Campbell	U23	12.09.73	2	Glasgow	29 Jan
21.25	1.3	Marlon Devonish	U20	1.06.76	1	Bedford	18 Sep
21.29	*1.5*	*Joslyn Thomas*		*11.07.71*	*6q4*	*Victoria, CAN*	*24 Aug*
21.30	1.8	Tremayne Rutherford	U23	19.06.72	1r2	Colwyn Bay	23 Jul
21.31	0.8	Steve McCourt		6.05.71	4s2	Sheffield	12 Jun
21.31	*-0.6*	*Haroun Korjie*	*U23*	*17.02.72*	*1r2*	*Crawley*	*6 Aug*
21.38	1.6	Mark Allen		23.09.66	3	Edinburgh	24 Jun
21.39	1.0	Steve Simmons	U23	10.11.74	5s1	Sheffield	12 Jun
21.43	1.0	Steve Gookey		21.04.71	7s1	Sheffield	12 Jun
21.45	0.9	Andrew Walcott	U20	11.01.75	4s1	Bedford	3 Jul
21.45	-0.6	Allyn Condon	U23	24.08.74	2r2	Crawley	6 Aug
(30)							
21.46 i		Wayne McDonald		5.10.70	2s2	Birmingham	7 Jan
21.50	-0.2	Brian Whittle		26.04.64	2r2	Malaga, SPA	29 May
21.50	-0.6	Alex Fugallo		28.01.70	2h2	Corby	30 May
21.50	1.8	Doug Turner		2.12.66	2r2	Colwyn Bay	23 Jul
21.53	1.6	Iwan Thomas	U23	5.01.74	8q3	Victoria, CAN	24 Aug
21.54	1.8	Curtis Browne	U20	11.09.75	2	Solihull	29 May
21.55	-1.1	Paul Sanders		11.01.62	5	Corby	30 May
21.56	-1.2	Paul White	U23	1.09.74	2	Bulle, SWZ	10 Sep
21.57	1.0	Mike Rey		19.07.68	8s1	Sheffield	12 Jun
21.58		James Egan	U20	12.11.75	1	Gateshead	29 May
(40)							
21.60 i		Mark Walcott	U23	24.11.73	2	Glasgow	23 Jan
21.61	0.5	Keith Douglas		6.07.66	1r2	Istanbul, TUR	22 May
21.62	-1.1	Richard Johnson		13.10.71	2r1	Wigan	7 May
21.62	0.2	Andi Knight	U23	11.11.73	3h3	Sheffield	12 Jun
21.64	1.5	David McKenzie		3.09.70	4r1	Crawley	28 May
21.64	-1.4	Ayo Falola		29.07.68	3r1	Kings Lynn	9 Jul
21.65	1.5	Danny Joyce	U23	9.09.74	5r1	Crawley	28 May
21.65	1.0	Uvie Ugono	U17	8.03.78	1	London (He)	7 Aug
21.66	-1.2	Steve Coupland		15.06.65	1r5	L'Alfas Del Pi, SPA	10 Apr
21.67 i		Ross Baillie	U17	26.09.77	1P	Glasgow	10 Dec
21.90	0.1				1	Edinburgh	24 Apr
(50)							
21.68		Matt Bartsch		12.12.64	h	London (CP)	1 May
21.70	-1.2	Mark Smith		18.11.71	2r1	London (CP)	7 May
21.70	0.5	Cypren Edmunds		20.06.70	4	London (CP)	26 Jun
21.70	1.8	Darren Scott		7.03.69	3r2	Colwyn Bay	23 Jul
21.71	-4.0	Dave Clark		16.02.64	3h4	Sydney, AUS	11 Mar
21.72	-0.6	Lloyd Cowan		8.07.62	6r1	Crawley	6 Aug
21.73	-2.9	Jason Gardener	U20	18.09.75	4	Bracknell	2 May
21.73	1.0	Ed White	U23	16.11.73	6	London (CP)	2 May

Time	Wind	Name	Cat	DOB	Pos	Venue	Date
21.73	*-0.6*	*Sanusi Turay*		*14.04.68*	*3r2*	*Crawley*	*6 Aug*
21.76	0.2	Gareth Davies	U23	2.10.72	6h3	Sheffield	12 Jun
21.77	1.2	Bryn Middleton	U20	16.02.76	3	Oordegem, BEL	9 Jul
	(60)						
21.78		Ade Mafe		12.11.66	5	Wellington, NZ	19 Jan
21.78 A	1.3	Kevin Farrell	U17	31.10.77	2	Avila, SPA	27 Jul
21.79	0.9	Michael Champion	U20	3.01.75	3	London (CP)	28 May
21.80	-1.9	Mike St.Louis		26.03.64	6s1	London (CP)	26 Jun
21.82		John McAdorey	U23	16.09.74	1r1	Antrim	13 Aug
21.83	1.8	Matthew Bridle	U20	11.08.76	3h5	Bedford	3 Jul
21.85	-1.7	Lewis Samuel		12.02.66	2	Sheffield	15 May
21.89	-0.6	Dalton Powell		20.08.63	5	Birmingham	21 May
21.91	1.4	Mark Hylton	U20	24.09.76	1r2	Crawley	28 May
21.91		Daniel Money	U20	7.10.76	3	Gateshead	29 May
	(70)						
21.93	0.9	Norman Ellis	U20	17.01.75	4	London (CP)	28 May
21.93	0.5	Chris Blake	U17	8.11.78	1	Gateshead	28 May
21.93	1.4	Richard Moore	U23	19.01.73	1r2	Stoke	15 Jul
21.95	1.8	Corri Henry	U20	9.12.76	3s2	Telford	9 Jul
21.95	-0.6	Scott Dorset		10.04.69	4r2	Crawley	6 Aug
21.96	1.8	Andrew Clegg	U23	8.09.73	4r2	Colwyn Bay	23 Jul
21.96	1.3	Graeme Welsh	U20	8.10.75	2	Bedford	18 Sep
22.00	0.5	Philip Perigo	U17	25.09.78	2	Gateshead	28 May
22.00	1.8	James Weston		9.01.70	5r2	Colwyn Bay	23 Jul
22.02	-1.0	Graham Beasley	U17	24.10.77	1s1	Nicosia, CYP	20 May
	(80)						
22.02	1.6	Jim Beattie	U23	22.07.73	4	Edinburgh	24 Jun
22.04		Andrew Wellens	U20	21.09.75	4	Gateshead	29 May
22.04	-2.8	John McLoughlin	U23	26.10.73	2h4	London (CP)	26 Jun
22.05	-0.4	Craig Hurst		30.12.70	3h3	Corby	30 May
22.06	0.9	Simon Bryant	U20	30.10.75	5	London (CP)	28 May
22.06	0.6	Jamie Henthorn	U20	20.02.77	2	Newport	28 May
22.06	-0.4	John Bowen		20.05.63	6h5	Sheffield	12 Jun
22.06	0.9	Kevin Mark	U20	15.09.76	7s1	Bedford	3 Jul
22.06		Kieran Gajjar	U20	25.09.76	2	Blackpool	14 Aug
22.07	1.7	Matthew Clements	U17	17.09.77	8	Bedford	3 Jul
	(90)						
22.08	1.9	Leon Daniels	U20	1.11.75	4h1	Bedford	3 Jul
22.08	0.7	Colin Derbyshire	U23	31.08.74	1h3	Derby	16 Jul
22.08	-0.6	Mark Morris		29.12.65	5r2	Crawley	6 Aug
22.08	1.0	Nick Csemiczky	U20	13.05.75	2	London (He)	7 Aug
22.09	1.4	Dwain Chambers	U17	5.04.78	2h3	London (CP)	29 May
22.13 i		Guy Bullock	U20	15.10.75	1	Birmingham	6 Feb
22.16	-0.5	Adam Lowles	U20	29.01.77	1h3	Nicosia, CYP	19 May
22.16	1.9	Larry Achike	U20	31.01.75	5h1	Bedford	3 Jul
22.18	1.0	Quincy Douglas	U20	7.09.75	1h	Lillehammer, NOR	24 Jun
22.18	-1.6	Jon Anderson	U20	10.01.75	3r2	Kings Lynn	9 Jul
	(100)						
22.20		Paul Brizzell	U20	3.10.76	1	Antrim	16 Jul

After disqualification

Time	Wind	Name	Cat	DOB	Pos	Venue	Date
20.73	-0.4	#Solomon Wariso		11.11.66	5	London (CP)	15 Jul
20.88	-1.0				2	Gateshead	1 Jul

During longer indoor race

Time		Name	Cat	DOB	Pos	Venue	Date
21.47 i+		Du'aine Ladejo		14.02.71	1m	Paris, FRA	13 Mar
21.67 i+		Mark Richardson	U23	26.07.72		Glasgow	29 Jan

136

Wind Assisted

20.58	2.6	Williams		(20.50)	1	Brussels, BEL	17	Jul
20.67	3.2	#Wariso		(20.51)	1	Sheffield	12	Jun
20.73	2.8	Julian Golding	U20	(21.02)	1	Bedford	17	Sep
20.83	3.2	Phil Goedluck		(20.79)	2	Sheffield	12	Jun
20.85	3.2	Doug Walker	U23	(20.71)	3	Sheffield	12	Jun
20.86	2.4	Jason John		(21.02)	3	Auckland, NZ	22	Jan
20.88	3.2	Trevor Cameron	U20	(21.18)	4	Sheffield	12	Jun
21.03	3.2	Steve McCourt		(21.31)	5	Sheffield	12	Jun
		8 performances to 21.10 by 8 athletes						
21.19		Dave Deacon		19.03.65	1	Gateshead	15	May
21.20	4.3	Marlon Devonish	U20	(21.25)	1	Telford	9	Jul
21.21	3.8	Paul White	U23	(21.56)	1	Stoke	15	Jul
21.28	2.5	Allyn Condon	U23	(21.45)	2r1	Colwyn Bay	23	Jul
21.30	2.8	Cypren Edmunds		(21.70)	2	Bedford	17	Sep
21.32	6.9	Graham Beasley	U17	(22.02)	1	Telford	9	Jul
21.47	2.3	Kevin Williams		15.12.71	2r1	Istanbul, TUR	22	May
21.47	2.8	Curtis Browne	U20	(21.54)	4	Bedford	17	Sep
21.49	2.8	Adrian Patrick	U23	15.06.73	5	Bedford	17	Sep
21.56	6.9	Uvie Ugono	U17	(21.65)	2	Telford	9	Jul
21.56	3.8	Ancell Maxwell		17.01.69	4	Stoke	15	Jul
21.57	3.5	Du'aine Ladejo		(21.47i+)	2r1	London (He)	5	Jun
21.57	3.8	Richard Rubenis	U23	10.11.73	5	Stoke	15	Jul
21.58		Philip Stephenson	U23	10.04.73	2	Gateshead	15	May
21.64	6.9	Chris Blake	U17	(21.93)	3	Telford	9	Jul
21.65	4.3	Michael Champion	U20	(21.79)	2	Telford	9	Jul
21.65	3.5	Philip Perigo	U17	(22.00)	1s1	Telford	9	Jul
21.72	2.2	Matthew Clements	U17	(22.07)	2h4	Bedford	3	Jul
21.75	4.3	Matthew Bridle	U20	(21.83)	3	Telford	9	Jul
21.77	3.8	Craig Hurst		(22.05)	6	Stoke	15	Jul
21.81	2.2	Daniel Money	U20	(21.91)	3h4	Bedford	3	Jul
21.90	3.1	Andrew Clegg	U23	(21.96)	4	Loughborough	5	Jun
21.91	4.3	Corri Henry	U20	(21.95)	5	Telford	9	Jul
21.91	3.8	Michael Williams		27.04.65	7	Stoke	15	Jul
21.97	2.9	Stephen Tucker		30.12.62	1	Edinburgh	14	Aug
22.02	4.5	Tony Leigh		27.12.65	3h1	Stoke	15	Jul
22.03	2.1	Simon Bryant	U20	(22.06)	1h3	London (CP)	28	May
22.03	4.3	Kieran Gajjar	U20	(22.06)	7	Telford	9	Jul
22.08		Justin Bird		3.05.71	3	Gateshead	15	May
22.08	3.1	Andy Carrott		1.01.66	5	Loughborough	5	Jun
22.09	2.9	Roddy Slater	U23	25.12.72	2	Edinburgh	14	Aug
22.10	3.3	Tony Waddington	U20	30.06.75	3h2	London (CP)	28	May
22.12	2.4	Ian Craggs	U20	6.10.76	4s1	Telford	9	Jul
22.19	6.9	Andrew Row	U17	(22.32)	6	Telford	9	Jul

Hand Timing

21.0 w	2.8	John		(21.02)	1	Kingston	31	Jul
21.1		Braithwaite		(20.99)	1	London (Nh)	15	May
21.1	-0.9	Black		(21.05)	1r1	Sheffield (W)	4	Jun
21.1 w	*2.8*	*Haroun Korjie*	*U23*	*(21.31)*	*2*	*Kingston*	*31*	*Jul*
		3 performances to 21.1 by 3 athletes incuding 1 wind assisted						
21.2		*Joslyn Thomas*		*(21.29)*	*1*	*London (WP)*	*18*	*Jun*
21.2		Paul White	U23	(21.56)	2	Peterborough	29	Aug
21.3 w		Dalton Powell		(21.89)	1	Nottingham	15	May
21.3 w		Graham Beasley	U17	(22.02)	2	Hoo	19	Jun
		21.9			1	St. Ives	17	Sep
21.4		Adrian Patrick	U23	(21.49w)	1r1	Bracknell	7	May

137

21.4		*Josephus Thomas*		*11.07.68*	*1r1*	*Basingstoke*	*4 Jun*
21.4	0.5	Allyn Condon	U23	(21.45)	1	Derby	16 Jul
21.4		Paul Sanders		(21.55)	1	Corby	31 Jul
21.4 w		Michael Champion	U20	(21.79)	1	Yate	21 Aug
21.5		Martin Blade		30.05.68	1	Aldershot	8 Jun
21.5		Nigel Will		18.10.67	1	Enfield	19 Jun
21.5		Alexis Sharp	U23	31.10.72	1	London (PH)	12 Jul
21.5	1.3	David McKenzie		(21.64)	1	Stoke	31 Jul
21.5		Curtis Browne	U20	(21.54)	2	Corby	31 Jul
21.5		Cypren Edmunds		(21.70)	1r1	London (Elt)	29 Aug
21.6		Mark Smith		(21.70)	1	Crawley	17 Apr
21.6		Kent Ulyatt	U23	10.04.72	1	Great Yarmouth	14 May
21.6		Matthew Bridle	U20	(21.83)	1	Crewe	15 May
21.6		Jason Fergus	U23	11.10.73	2	London (Nh)	15 May
21.6		*Andrew McManus*		*(21.73)*	*2r1*	*Basildon*	*4 Jun*
21.6		Nick Budden	U20	17.11.75	1	London (Col)	18 Jun
21.6	0.5	Ed White	U23	(21.73)	3	Derby	16 Jul
21.6		Richard Rubenis	U23	(21.57w)	1	Sutton Coldfield	7 Aug
21.6		Mark Hylton	U20	(21.91)	1r2	Windsor	13 Aug
21.6		Rohan Samuel		30.01.66	2	Sutton Coldfield	27 Aug
21.6 w	2.8	Kevin Mark	U20	(22.06)	1=	Enfield	14 Aug
21.7					1	Basildon	13 Aug
21.7		Andrew Clegg	U23	(21.96)	1	Liverpool	17 Apr
21.7	0.4	Craig Hurst		(22.05)	1	Stoke	14 May
21.7		Stephen Tucker		(21.97w)	1	Coatbridge	12 Jun
21.7		Graham Healy		27.04.70	2	London (PH)	12 Jul
21.7 w		Mike St.Louis		(21.80)	3	Hoo	19 Jun
21.8		Michael Williams		(21.91w)	1	High Wycombe	1 May
21.8	1.4	Norman Ellis	U20	(21.93)	1	London (CP)	14 May
21.8		Andrew Bull		26.06.69	1	Grimsby	28 May
21.8		Trevor Painter		10.08.71	1	Wigan	30 May
21.8		Phil Lewis		12.01.70	2	Coatbridge	12 Jun
21.8		Steve Markham	U23	11.11.74	1r1	Jarrow	2 Jul
21.8	-1.5	Matthew Clements	U17	(22.07)	1	Birmingham	30 Jul
21.8		Todd Bennett		6.07.62	1	London (CP)	13 Aug
21.8		*Trevor Davis*		*26.03.63*		*Windsor*	*13 Aug*
21.8 w	2.3	Ross Baillie	U17	(21.90)	1	Pitreavie	1 May
21.8 w		Paul Slythe	U23	5.09.74	4	Hoo	19 Jun
21.9		Nick Csemiczky	U20	(22.08)	1	Hayes	10 Apr
21.9		Martin Bennett		14.10.67	2	Welwyn	1 May
21.9		Mark Lambeth	U23	3.09.72	1r2	Bracknell	7 May
21.9		Ian Lonsdale		8.09.71	2r2	Cannock	7 May
21.9		Chris Bedford		28.01.70		Sheffield	7 May
21.9		Mark Dunwell		13.03.70	3	Nottingham	15 May
21.9		Corri Henry	U20	(21.95)	1	Nottingham	15 May
21.9		Richard Moore	U23	(21.93)	2	Leamington	15 May
21.9		Dave Deacon		(21.19w)	1	Gateshead	4 Jun
21.9		Adam Lowles	U20	(22.16)	1	Tweedbank	5 Jun
21.9		T. White			1r1	London (TB)	27 Jul
21.9		Ancell Maxwell		(21.56w)	5r1	Liverpool	6 Aug
21.9		Scott Dorset		(21.95)	2r3	Windsor	13 Aug
21.9		Paul Jamieson				Sutton Coldfield	27 Aug
22.0	0.4	David Gifford	U23	9.03.73	3	Stoke	14 May
22.0	-1.3	Mark Williams		25.04.68	1	London (CP)	15 May
22.0		Justin Bird		(22.08w)	1r1	Gateshead	25 May
22.0	1.8	Leon Daniels	U20	(22.08)	4	Solihull	29 May

138

22.0		C. Vincent			2	Aldershot	8	Jun
22.0		Tony Waddington	U20	(22.10w)	1r1	Reading	12	Jun
22.0		Andy Carrott		(22.08w)	4	Loughborough	22	Jun
22.0		Nick Leeland			1	Carlisle	26	Jun
22.0		David Nolan		25.07.69	3r1	Aldershot	29	Jun
22.0		Lloyd Chandler		14.04.69	1r2	Dartford	2	Jul
22.0		Colin Derbyshire	U23	(22.08)	1r1	Hull	2	Jul
22.0		Steve Shanks		3.11.69	1	Portsmouth	13	Jul
22.0		Alistair Audsley			1r1	Bolton	6	Aug
22.0		Daro Eghaghai		22.11.75	1	London (WL)	6	Aug
22.0		Paul Brizzell	U20	(22.20)	1r2	Antrim	13	Aug
22.0		Robert Alves		13.05.65	1r1	Telford	21	Aug
22.0		Jason Fletcher	U20	18.01.76	2	Telford	21	Aug
22.0		Eddie Betts		18.02.71	2	Perivale	27	Aug
22.0		Kevin Williams		(21.47w)	1	Swansea	29	Aug
22.0		Sam Kabiswa		28.10.66	1r2	London (Elt)	29	Aug
22.0		Tim Barton		3.10.70	1	Leicester	11	Sep
22.0 w		Roddy Slater	U23	(22.09w)	2	Yate	21	Aug

Doubtful Timing

20.8 w		Dave Clark		16.02.64	1	Wollongong, AUS	28	Feb

Additional Under 17 (1 - 9 above)

22.1		Dean Park		23.09.77	1	Braintree	8	May
	(10)							
22.1		Mark Findlay		20.03.78	2	Braintree	8	May
22.1		Scott Fraser		31.12.77	3	Coatbridge	12	Jun
		22.32	-1.0		4	Aberdeen	16	Jul
22.2	-0.9	Scott Walker		9.09.77	3s1	Birmingham	30	Jul
		22.24 w 6.9			7	Telford	9	Jul
22.2	-1.1	Christian Malcolm		3.06.79	3s2	Birmingham	30	Jul
		22.36	0.3		1	Colwyn Bay	2	Jul
22.26 w 6.9		John Skeete		8.09.78	8	Telford	9	Jul
		22.6	-1.1		4s2	Birmingham	30	Jul
22.26 w 5.9		Steven Daly	U15	29.12.79	1	Telford	9	Jul
		22.7			1	Bebington	11	Jun
22.3		Martin Giraud		16.11.77	1	London (TB)	22	Jun
22.3		Martin Armytage		10.03.78	1	Newport	17	Jul
22.3	-0.9	Alasdair McFarlane		13.02.78	4s1	Birmingham	30	Jul
22.32	-0.4	Andrew Row		17.10.78	2h1	Gateshead	28	May
	(20)							
22.39 w 2.6		Jonathan Moss		24.09.78	5s2	Telford	9	Jul
		22.6	0.0		2	Crewe	15	May
22.39 w 5.9		Andre Duffus	U15	30.10.79	2	Telford	9	Jul
		22.7	-0.7		1	Birmingham	30	Jul
		23.40	-1.7		1h2	Birmingham	30	Jul
22.44 w 2.6		Stephen Topliss		17.07.78	6s2	Telford	9	Jul
		22.7	-1.1		5s2	Birmingham	30	Jul
22.45 w 2.3		James Shipp		10.11.77	4	London (CP)	29	May
22.45 w 2.6		Jeremy Noon		20.09.77	7s2	Telford	9	Jul
		22.6			1	Corby	18	Jun
22.46 w 5.9		Robert Allenby	U15	14.10.79	3	Telford	9	Jul
		23.4			1	York	18	Jun
22.48 i		Andrew Lees		11.05.79	1	Birmingham	26	Feb
22.5		David O'Hare		1.12.77		Liverpool	16	Apr
22.5		Joel Calliste		25.04.78	2	Feltham	24	Jul
22.51	0.5	Andrew Thornton		29.11.77	4	Gateshead	28	May
	(30)							
22.57 w 3.5		Neil Kentish		30.09.77	5s1	Telford	9	Jul
22.63 w 3.2		Ian Horsburgh		10.01.78	1	Grangemouth	28	Aug

Additional Under 15 (1 - 3 above)

22.74 w 5.9	Luke Dart		14.09.79	4	Telford	9	Jul
23.43 -1.4				1	London (He)	7	Aug
22.88 w 5.9	Stuart Smith		20.12.79	5	Telford	9	Jul
22.9				1	Scunthorpe	29	Aug
23.0 w	Paul Chantler		10.09.79	1	Liverpool	16	Apr
23.3				2	Bebington	11	Jun
23.2 -0.7	Neil Akester		6.09.79	2	Birmingham	30	Jul
23.51 -1.7				2h2	Birmingham	30	Jul
23.29 w 3.0	Steven Attridge	U15	9.03.80	2s2	Telford	9	Jul
23.3				1r1	Rochester	18	Jun
23.7 -1.3				1	Portsmouth	11	Jun
23.30 w 5.9	Luke Davis	U15	1.01.80	6	Telford	9	Jul
23.7				1	Birmingham	11	Jun
23.30 w 5.9	Eshref Hassan	U15	7.12.79	7	Telford	9	Jul
23.59 1.2				1	London (CP)	29	May
(10)							
23.3	Kris Stewart	U15	11.04.80	1	Annan	3	Jul
23.65 1.8				1	Grangemouth	28	Aug
23.32 1.1	Michael Jones	U15	2.10.79	3	Dublin, IRE	13	Aug
23.46 w 3.0	Darren Polson	U15	29.12.79	4s2	Telford	9	Jul
23.6 -0.3				1h3	Telford	8	Jul
23.5	Antonio Matarazzo	U15	27.03.80	1	Yeovil	18	Jun
23.52 w 3.0	Anthony Spratt	U15	9.09.79	5s2	Telford	9	Jul
23.69 -0.7				h	London (He)	7	Aug
23.54 w 3.7	Chris Wadsworth	U15	9.10.79	3s3	Telford	9	Jul
23.6 -0.7	Kevin Hibbins	U15	7.11.80	3	Birmingham	30	Jul
23.6	Richard MacDonald	U15	11.01.80	1	Dundee	31	Aug
23.64 w 2.3	Jason Bale	U15	12.12.79	1	Solihull	29	May
23.7				1	Leicester	11	Jun
23.64 w 3.0	Tom Sellars	U15	7.01.80	6s2	Telford	9	Jul
(20)							
23.65 w 3.7	S. Hock	U15		4s3	Telford	9	Jul

Under 13

25.0	Tyrone Keating	U13	25.02.82	1r1	Ipswich	4	Sep
25.4	Daniel Angus	U13	15.07.82	1	Carlisle	11	Sep
25.7	Andrew Rose	U13	17.08.83	1r2	Braintree	21	Jul

300 METRES

32.45	Roger Black		31.03.66	1	Sheffield	4	Sep
32.73	Du'aine Ladejo		14.02.71	3	Sheffield	4	Sep
32.9	Mark Hylton	U20	24.09.76	1	Basingstoke	21	Aug
33.2	Paul Sanders		11.01.62	1	Salisbury	10	Jul
33.2				2	Basingstoke	21	Aug
33.6	Cypren Edmunds		20.06.70	3	Basingstoke	21	Aug
33.6	Lee Fairclough		23.06.70	4	Basingstoke	21	Aug
33.7	Dan Donovan		8.10.70	5	Basingstoke	21	Aug
33.7	Jared Deacon	U20	15.10.75	1	Gateshead	4	Sep
33.9	David Nolan		25.07.69	2	Salisbury	10	Jul
34.0	Martin Blade		30.05.68	2r2	Salisbury	30	Jul
(10)							
34.4	Nigel Will		18.10.67	1	London (Ha)	16	Apr
34.4	Simon Haynes	U23	12.08.74	6	Basingstoke	21	Aug
34.62	Brian Whittle		26.04.64	8	Sheffield	4	Sep
34.98	David Gilmour		19.03.70	1	Edinburgh	13	Jul

400 METRES

44.78	Roger Black		31.03.66	1	Rieti, ITA	28	Aug
	44.94			1	Sheffield	12	Jun
	45.08			1	Birmingham	25	Jun
	45.08			4	Monaco, MON	2	Aug
	45.09			3	Berlin, GER	30	Aug
	45.10			3	London (CP)	15	Jul
	45.17			4	Zurich, SWZ	17	Aug
	45.20			2	Helsinki, FIN	11	Aug
	45.30			2	Gateshead	1	Jul
	45.39			4	Paris, FRA	3	Sep
	45.79			1s2	Helsinki, FIN	9	Aug
	45.83			1s2	Sheffield	11	Jun
	45.88			1h1	Helsinki, FIN	8	Aug
44.94	Du'aine Ladejo		14.02.71	3	Monaco, MON	2	Aug
	45.00			2	London (CP)	15	Jul
	45.09			1	Helsinki, FIN	11	Aug
	45.11			2	Victoria, CAN	23	Aug
	45.16			1	Edinburgh	8	Jul
	45.21			2	St. Petersburg, RUS	24	Jul
	45.23			1s2	Victoria, CAN	23	Aug
	45.36			2	Sheffield	12	Jun
	45.44			2	London (CP)	10	Sep
	45.61			2	Gateshead	20	Jul
	45.70			1s1	Helsinki, FIN	9	Aug
	45.74			4	Gateshead	1	Jul
	45.80			7	Paris, FRA	3	Sep
	45.82			1s1	Sheffield	11	Jun
	45.95			1	Long Beach, USA	25	May
	45.99			1	Budapest, HUN	3	Jun
	46.26 i			1s1	Paris, FRA	12	Mar
	46.26			1q3	Victoria, CAN	22	Aug
	46.27 i			3	Birmingham	26	Feb
	46.43 i			4	Glasgow	12	Feb
	46.50			1h3	Sheffield	11	Jun
	46.50			1h2	Helsinki, FIN	8	Aug
45.46	Brian Whittle		26.04.64	3	Sheffield	12	Jun
	46.15			6	Gateshead	1	Jul
	46.30			6	Edinburgh	8	Jul
	46.50			2s1	Sheffield	11	Jun
45.47	David McKenzie		3.09.70	4	Sheffield	12	Jun
	46.03			2s2	Sheffield	11	Jun
	46.18			5s1	Victoria, CAN	23	Aug
	46.32			1	Birmingham	21	May
	46.35			4	Gateshead	20	Jul
	46.38			4q4	Victoria, CAN	22	Aug
	46.39			1h4	Victoria, CAN	22	Aug
	46.43			1	Bedford	17	Sep
45.98	Iwan Thomas	U23	5.01.74	7s2	Victoria, CAN	23	Aug
	46.34			1	Wrexham	3	Jul
	46.37			3q1	Victoria, CAN	22	Aug
	46.46			1h8	Victoria, CAN	22	Aug
46.11 i	Mark Richardson	U23	26.07.72	1	Glasgow	29	Jan
	46.21 i			2	Glasgow	12	Feb
46.11	Adrian Patrick	U23	15.06.73	5	Sheffield	12	Jun
46.37	Mark Hylton	U20	24.09.76	4	Lisbon, POR	22	Jul
46.39	Alex Fugallo		28.01.70	6	Sheffield	12	Jun
46.39	Ade Mafe		12.11.66	7	Sheffield	12	Jun

(10)

46.45	Jamie Baulch	U23	3.05.73	5q4	Victoria, CAN	22	Aug
46.47				2	Wrexham	3	Jul
46.49	Paul McBurney	U23	14.03.72	1h1	Victoria, CAN	22	Aug
60 performances to 46.5 by 12 athletes including 5 indoors							
46.7	Mark Smith		18.11.71	1	Stoke	31	Jul
46.75				3	Wrexham	3	Jul
46.77	Guy Bullock	U20	15.10.75	3	Hengelo, HOL	4	Jun
46.77	Mark Morris		29.12.65	1	London (CP)	26	Jun
46.78	Nigel Will		18.10.67	2	London (CP)	26	Jun
46.82	Kent Ulyatt	U23	10.04.72	3	London (CP)	26	Jun
46.84	Eddie Williams		1.10.70	1r1	London (WL)	2	Jul
46.85	Wayne McDonald		5.10.70	1r2	Malaga, SPA	28	May
47.01	Nick Budden	U20	17.11.75	2	Bedford	3	Jul
	(20)						
47.1	Steve Coupland		15.06.65	1	Loughborough	26	Jun
47.23	Paul Sanders		11.01.62	5s2	Sheffield	11	Jun
47.27	Paul Slythe	U23	5.09.74	2	Telford	9	Jul
47.29	Vince Rose		21.08.71	4	London (CP)	26	Jun
47.35	Dave Deacon		19.03.65	2h1	Sheffield	11	Jun
47.4	Richard Rubenis	U23	10.11.73	1r1	Cannock	11	Sep
47.76				1	Bedford	18	Sep
47.43	Tim O'Dell		29.05.70	5	London (CP)	26	Jun
47.43	Allyn Condon	U23	24.08.74	3r1	London (WL)	2	Jul
47.44	*Stephen Newman*		*26.12.70*	*1*	*Belfast*	*4*	*Jun*
47.48	Steve McHardy	U20	8.01.76	2	Verona, ITA	6	Aug
47.5	Lawrence Lynch		1.11.67	3	Geneva, SWZ	18	Jun
	(30)						
47.5	David Nolan		25.07.69	1	Aldershot	24	Jul
47.66				2h2	London (CP)	25	Jun
47.5	Jared Deacon	U20	15.10.75	1	Gateshead	3	Aug
47.53				3h1	Sheffield	11	Jun
47.5	Sam Kabiswa		28.10.66	1r1	Portsmouth	6	Aug
47.58	Adrian Bryan	U23	17.05.72	1	Stoke	16	Jul
47.58	Carl Southam	U23	11.01.74	1	Bulle, SWZ	10	Sep
47.60	Gary Cadogan		8.10.66	1	Westwood, USA	9	Apr
47.60	Mark Thomas		12.05.65	3r1	Wigan	7	May
47.60	Peter Maitland	U23	21.01.73	1r2	Oordegem, BEL	9	Jul
47.6	Martin Blade		30.05.68	1	Portsmouth	15	May
47.70				3r2	Birmingham	21	May
47.65	Lewis Samuel		12.02.66	4h1	Sheffield	11	Jun
	(40)						
47.68	Justin Bird		3.05.71	4	Edinburgh	25	Jun
47.7	Tony Williams	U23	1.05.72	2	Sheffield	14	May
47.7	Lee Fairclough		23.06.70	2r1	Croydon	2	Jul
47.73	Gareth Davies	U23	2.10.72	2r2	Oordegem, BEL	9	Jul
47.73	Stewart Weathers		14.09.65	1	Loughborough	7	Sep
47.75	*Peter Sinclair*		*6.03.67*	*3*	*Dublin (M), IRE*	*24*	*Jul*
47.8	Dan Donovan		8.10.70	3	Aldershot	24	Jul
47.87				1r1	Crawley	6	Aug
47.84	Quincy Douglas	U20	7.09.75	1	Dranner, NOR	10	Jul
47.90	Pete Clarke		9.07.65	3	Stoke	16	Jul
47.9	Martin Steele		30.09.62	1	Cleckheaton	23	Jul
47.9	Eddie Betts		18.02.71	2	London (Nh)	4	Sep
	(50)						
47.92	Alex Francis	U23	15.07.74	2	London (CP)	1	May
47.94	Mark Ponting	U20	28.04.77	2r1	Colwyn Bay	23	Jul
48.0	Darren Bernard		15.06.69	2	Croydon	14	May
48.49				4h2	London (CP)	25	Jun
48.02	Jim Stevenson		31.12.71	1D	Austin, USA	25	Mar
48.04	Trevor Painter		10.08.71	3r1	Colwyn Bay	23	Jul
48.07	Gregor McMillan		4.04.70	2h	Wrexham	3	Jul

Mark	Name	Cat	Born	Pos	Venue	Date
48.1	Gary Telfer		10.01.65	2	Enfield	15 May
48.41				2	Dublin (M), IRE	18 Jun
48.1	Simon Heggie	U20	12.01.76	1	Solihull	29 May
48.26				4	Telford	9 Jul
48.1	Dave Savage	U23	13.11.72	2	Kingston	31 Jul
48.12	Pat Strickland			1	Barn Elms	22 May
(60)						
48.16	Ben Oluoch-Olunya		25.01.70	3	London (CP)	2 May
48.2	Jon Sanders		29.10.70	3	Croydon	14 May
48.78				3	London (CP)	25 Jun
48.2	Paul Field		24.06.67	1	Welwyn	15 May
48.2	Joe Lloyd	U23	9.04.73	1	Cheltenham	21 May
48.27				3	Cwmbran	18 Jun
48.2	Chris Alderton			2	Aldershot	29 Jun
48.23	Gary Jennings	U23	21.02.72	2r2	Palafrugell, SPA	19 Jun
48.24	Hugh Kerr	U20	4.01.76	5	Edinburgh	25 Jun
48.27	Andrew Lill		9.08.71	1r2	London (He)	5 Jun
48.30	Matthew Douglas	U20	26.11.76	1h3	Bedford	2 Jul
48.3	Mark Sesay	U23	13.12.72	3	Sheffield	14 May
(70)						
48.3	Michael Gallagher		25.04.66	2r1	Wigan	2 Jul
48.31				4	Kings Lynn	9 Jul
48.3	Nick Leeland			3	Kingston	31 Jul
48.3	Mark Bishop		12.02.67	2r1	Barking	6 Aug
48.72 i				2h3	Birmingham	7 Jan
48.31	Kermitt Bentham		16.04.60	2r2	London (He)	5 Jun
48.40	Grant Purves	U23	6.04.73	4h4	Corby	30 May
48.4	Paul Roberts		24.12.69	1r2	Enfield	4 Jun
48.89				5r2	Birmingham	21 May
48.4	Simon James	U23	31.08.73	1r1	High Wycombe	30 Jul
48.4	James Weston		9.01.70	3	Enfield	31 Jul
48.48 un					Istanbul, TUR	21 May
48.4	Peter Brend	U20	2.02.77	1	Yate	21 Aug
48.50				2	London (CP)	29 May
48.47	Simon Haynes	U23	12.08.74	2h4	London (CP)	25 Jun
(80)						
48.49	Chas McCaw	U23	21.01.72	4	London (CP)	2 May
48.5	Matthew Aldwinkle	U23	23.08.74	2	Cheltenham	22 May
48.77				6h1	Sheffield	11 Jun
48.5	Wayne Martin	U20	12.08.76	1	Yate	29 Jun
48.53 i	Noel Levy	U20	22.06.75	2h2	Birmingham	18 Feb
48.53	Geoff Dearman	U20	4.08.77	4h1	Telford	8 Jul
48.53	Robert Alves		13.05.65	1s2	Stoke	16 Jul
48.57	Leroy Campbell		10.08.66	5	Stoke	16 Jul
48.6	Otis Griffiths		4.02.70	1r1	Bournemouth	7 May
48.6	Dave Griffin		5.12.63	2	Welwyn	14 May
48.6	Tom Nimmo		9.05.71	2r1	Harrow	2 Jul
48.70				1	Edinburgh	14 May
(90)						
48.6	Robert Scantlebury	U20	9.11.76	1	Reading	2 Jul
48.88				5h1	Telford	8 Jul
48.63	Stuart Cavanagh	U20	28.02.75	2	London (He)	7 Aug
48.67	Alan Murray		2.05.67	8	Edinburgh	25 Jun
48.67	Eddie King	U20	26.11.75	1	Antrim	16 Jul
48.67	Michael Champion	U20	3.01.75	1	Warsaw, POL	25 Sep
48.68	Bryan McCoy	U20		4h3	Bedford	2 Jul
48.70	Phil Goedluck		10.09.67	4	Bedford	17 Sep
48.7	Steve Kneller		9.11.71	1	Horsham	14 May
48.82				3h3	Corby	30 May

Time	Name		Date		Place		
48.7	David Gilmour		19.03.70	1r1	Coatbridge	12	Jun
48.7	Wayne Ellwood	U23	26.09.74	2	London (CP)	13	Aug
(100)							
48.76 i	Peter Crampton		4.06.69	2s2	Birmingham	31	Dec
48.8	Shane King	U23	8.02.74	1r1	Blackburn	4	Jun
48.8	Keith Palmer		19.11.64	1r1	Brighton	18	Jun
48.8	Andi Knight		26.10.68	2r1	Cardiff	2	Jul
48.93				2r1	Edinburgh	6	Aug
48.8	Justin Sleath		9.02.67	1r1	Bracknell	2	Jul
48.8	Dean Packham		9.04.67	1	Horsham	20	Aug
48.81	Joe Gowan		18.11.67	7h1	Sheffield	11	Jun
48.83	Simon Shirley		3.08.66	1D	Bressanone, ITA	2	Jul
48.86	Richard Knowles	U20	12.11.75	3h2	Telford	8	Jul
48.89	Gavin Mason	U20	6.04.77	7r1	London (WL)	2	Jul
(110)							
48.89	Michael Williams		27.04.65	2	Solihull	21	Aug
48.89	Jim Beattie	U23	22.07.73	1r2	Grangemouth	28	Aug
48.9	Clive Gilby		24.02.66	1	London (CP)	14	May
48.9	John Hammond		1.07.71	2	Cleckheaton	23	Jul
48.9	Paul Chapman	U20	10.07.76	4	Kingston	31	Jul
48.94	Anders Lustgarten	U23	9.02.74	4h6	Sheffield	11	Jun
48.98	Simon Ciaravella	U23	24.11.73	1r1	London (CP)	7	May
49.0	Simon Parsons	U23	27.10.73	1r1	London (Elt)	4	Jun
49.0	Laurence Baird	U17	10.12.77	1	Hull	11	Jun
49.0	Sandy Scott	U20	1.09.76	2r1	Coatbridge	12	Jun
(120)							
49.0	*Nigel Keogh*		*18.07.67*	*5*	*Enfield*	*31*	*Jul*
49.0	Paul Walker	U23	2.12.73	2r2	Liverpool	6	Aug

Additional Under 20 (1 - 23 above)

49.04	Adam Mole		31.08.75	6h2	Telford	8	Jul
49.15 A	Dean Park	U17	23.09.77		Avila, SPA	26	Jul
49.2	Ian Horsburgh	U17	10.01.78	1	Birmingham	30	Jul
49.35				1	Aberdeen	16	Jul
49.2	Paul Dunlop		11.02.75	1	Carlisle	6	Aug
49.30 i	Barry Middleton		10.03.75	3	Birmingham	26	Feb
49.40				1	Edinburgh	14	May
49.46	Barry O'Brien		3.07.76	4h1	Bedford	2	Jul

Additional Under 17 (1 - 3 above)

49.5	Michael Bell		23.11.77	1	Watford	31	Aug
49.6	Steve Mitchell		1.09.77	1	Croydon	15	May
49.71	Tim Slocombe		15.11.77	1	Telford	9	Jul
49.8	Stephen Payne		30.01.78	1	Enfield	14	Aug
49.88				1h3	Telford	8	Jul
49.9	Mark Rowlands		18.04.78	1	Swansea	10	Jul
49.9	James Shipp		10.11.77	1	Colchester	11	Sep
50.1	Michael Harper		20.05.78	1	London (BP)	1	May
(10)							
50.15	Adrian Christopher		16.09.77	1	London (CP)	29	May
50.15	James Hilston		25.02.79	2h2	Telford	8	Jul
50.19	Ryan Patis		4.11.77	1h2	London (CP)	28	May
50.33	Simon Robinson		13.09.77	1h1	Telford	8	Jul
50.4	Paul Harrison		11.11.77	1	Jarrow	18	Jun
50.4	Ben Harper		9.11.78	3h1	Birmingham	30	Jul
50.6	Matthew Hill		15.12.78	2h2	Birmingham	30	Jul
50.6	Graham Beasley		24.10.77	2	Peterborough	29	Aug
50.6	Kevin Farrell		31.10.77	3	Woodford	14	Sep
50.7	David Ivey		5.10.78	2	Windsor	13	Aug
(20)							

50.74	Noel Morgan	20.11.78	4h3	Telford	8	Jul
50.80	Simon Mathieson	20.01.79	2h1	Telford	8	Jul
50.8	Phillip Callow	12.05.78	2	Hoo	11	Jun
50.8	Simon Plaskett	9.04.79	1r2	Enfield	13	Aug
50.8	Robert Milner	28.12.77	1	Woking	4	Sep
50.85 i	Craig Slater	22.05.78	3	Birmingham	13	Feb
50.86	Alasdair Hempenstall	4.10.77	5s2	Telford	8	Jul
50.9	Andrew Smith	26.03.78	3h2	Birmingham	30	Jul
50.93	Neil Jennings	18.09.77	5h3	Telford	8	Jul
50.94	Nick Hamilton	13.03.79	6h3	Telford	8	Jul

Under 15

51.0	Marc Newton	15.03.80	1	Birmingham	30	Jul
51.6	Kris Stewart	11.04.80	2	Birmingham	30	Jul
52.65			1	Grangemouth	10	Jul
51.8	David Naismith	15.12.79	3	Birmingham	30	Jul
52.13	Richard McNab	22.02.80	1	Telford	9	Jul
52.2	Jay Kilshaw	19.10.79	1	Barking	11	Jun
52.91			1	London (CP)	29	May
52.3	Richard MacDonald	11.01.80	4	Birmingham	30	Jul
52.4	Jason Bale	12.12.79	5	Birmingham	30	Jul
52.57	Kristian Whitmee	1.12.79	1h4	Birmingham	30	Jul
52.59	Kerrin Young	2.09.79	1	Antrim	20	Aug
52.60	Duncan Rowley	15.04.80	1h3	Telford	8	Jul
	(10)					
52.67	Nicholas Hooper	24.09.79	2h1	Telford	8	Jul
52.69	Martin Elks	26.01.80	2h2	Telford	8	Jul
52.71	Colin Young	11.12.79	1h2	Birmingham	30	Jul
52.77	Julian Packer	2.09.79	3h3	Telford	8	Jul
52.93	Martyn Gordon	29.09.79	1	Gateshead	28	May
53.2	David Singleton	21.10.79	3	Yeovil	18	Jun
53.47	Steven Daly	29.12.79	2	Gateshead	28	May
53.56	Stephen Elswood	21.11.79	3=	London (He)	7	Aug

Under 13

60.0	David Moulton	7.09.81		London (He)	20	Jun
60.0	Philip Walsh					
60.1	Philip Nosko	29.01.82	1	Andover	30	May
60.4	Colin Joyce	21.10.81	1	Braintree	28	Jul
60.5	M. Lent		1	Basingstoke	2	Jul
60.5	Warren McKinlay	4.10.81	1r2	Braintree	7	Aug
60.5	Kerr Johnstone	3.09.82	1	Grangemouth	21	Aug

600 METRES

1:18.6	Gary Brown	21.07.67	1	Grangemouth	3	Aug
1:19.2	Paul Burgess	10.11.70	1	Wigan	17	Apr
1:19.5	Peter McDevitt	1.03.68	2	Grangemouth	3	Aug

800 METRES

Time	Name	Age/Cat	Born	Pos	Venue	Date
1:46.13	Martin Steele		30.09.62	3	Cork, IRE	25 Jun
1:47.09				6	Rome, ITA	8 Jun
1:47.39				8r1	London (CP)	15 Jul
1:47.56				3	Budapest, HUN	3 Jun
1:47.78 i				1	Birmingham	26 Feb
1:47.99				4	Gateshead	20 Jul
1:48.04				7	Victoria, CAN	26 Aug
1:48.17				4s2	Victoria, CAN	24 Aug
1:48.35				3h4	Victoria, CAN	23 Aug
1:46.20	Tom McKean		27.10.63	9	Oslo, NOR	22 Jul
1:46.28				5r1	London (CP)	15 Jul
1:47.46				3h3	Victoria, CAN	23 Aug
1:47.60 i				1	Glasgow	29 Jan
1:47.99				3s2	Victoria, CAN	24 Aug
1:48.46 i				1	Birmingham	19 Feb
1:46.54	Craig Winrow		22.12.71	6r1	London (CP)	15 Jul
1:46.91				4	Victoria, CAN	26 Aug
1:46.93				2h4	Helsinki, FIN	11 Aug
1:47.06				2h2	Victoria, CAN	23 Aug
1:47.09				6	Helsinki, FIN	14 Aug
1:47.15				2	Oslo, NOR	2 Jun
1:47.16				3	London (CP)	9 Sep
1:47.17				1	Gateshead	20 Jul
1:47.24				4s1	Helsinki, FIN	12 Aug
1:47.77				2r1	Gateshead	1 Jul
1:47.78 i				2	Glasgow	12 Feb
1:47.84				2s2	Victoria, CAN	24 Aug
1:48.00				10	Rhede, GER	29 Jul
1:48.45				1	Sheffield	12 Jun
1:47.00	Andrew Lill		9.08.71	7r1	London (CP)	15 Jul
1:47.41				3	Gateshead	20 Jul
1:47.52				2r1	Crawley	28 May
1:47.55				5	Edinburgh	8 Jul
1:47.80				3r1	Gateshead	1 Jul
1:48.18				1r1	London (CP)	26 Jun
1:48.34				5h3	Victoria, CAN	23 Aug
1:47.57	Davey Wilson		7.09.68	5h2	Victoria, CAN	23 Aug
1:47.63 i	Gary Brown		21.07.67	1	Glasgow	12 Feb
1:47.75 i				3	Glasgow	29 Jan
1:49.61				6h1	Victoria, CAN	23 Aug
1:48.07	Curtis Robb	U23	7.06.72	9r1	London (CP)	15 Jul
1:48.20	David Strang		13.12.68	2	Malaga, SPA	29 May
1:48.25				1	Chapel Hill, USA	15 May
1:48.26	Mike Guegan		19.09.66	2r1	London (CP)	26 Jun
1:48.38	Andi Knight		26.10.68	3r2	London (CP)	15 Jul
(10)						
1:48.42	Matthew Yates		4.02.69	9	Granada, SPA	1 Jun
1:48.45	Tony Whiteman		13.11.71	3r1	London (CP)	26 Jun

46 performances to 1:48.5 by 12 athletes including 6 indoors

Time	Name	Age/Cat	Born	Pos	Venue	Date
1:48.66 i	Andy Keith		25.12.71	1	Boston, USA	26 Feb
1:48.66	Terry West		19.11.68	4	Budapest, HUN	3 Jun
1:48.85	Paul Walker	U23	2.12.73	2	Edinburgh	25 Jun
1:48.93	Eddie King	U20	26.11.75	2	Bedford	3 Jul
1:49.10	Ian Grime		29.09.70	4r2	London (CP)	15 Jul
1:49.26	Tony Balogun		7.02.66	5r2	London (CP)	15 Jul
1:49.27	Mark Griffin	U20	16.02.75	1h4	Lisbon, POR	20 Jul
1:49.29	Justin Swift-Smith	U23	28.08.74	3h4	Sheffield	11 Jun
(20)						
1:49.3	Jason Lobo		18.09.69	1r1	Stretford	23 Aug

1:49.3	Ewan Calvert	U23	28.11.73	2r1	Stretford	23	Aug
1:49.42	Matt Hibberd	U23	23.06.73	3	Bulle, SWZ	10	Sep
1:49.47	Vince Wilson	U23	1.04.73	3	Edinburgh	25	Jun
1:49.48	Mark Sesay	U23	13.12.72	1	Loughborough	5	Jun
1:49.6	Grant Graham	U23	27.12.72	3r1	Stretford	23	Aug
1:49.62	Andrew Parker	U23	20.11.74	6r2	London (CP)	15	Jul
1:49.8	Andrew Hart		13.09.69	1r1	Cheltenham	20	Jul
1:49.84	Bruno Witchalls	U20	22.03.75	8r2	London (CP)	15	Jul
1:49.85	Brian Treacy		29.07.71	3	Prince George, CAN	13	Aug
(30)							
1:49.9	Matt Barnes		12.01.68	1r1	Enfield	4	Jun
1:49.94	Clive Gilby		24.02.66	2h5	Sheffield	11	Jun
1:50.06	Gary Lough		6.07.70	3	Loughborough	5	Jun
1:50.1	Ciaran Murphy		2.09.71	4r1	Stretford	23	Aug
1:50.11	Chris Blount	U20	7.06.75	4	Bedford	3	Jul
1:50.15	Tony Morrell		3.05.62	2r1	London (CP)	7	May
1:50.18	Lee Cadwallader		17.01.69	3r2	Gateshead	1	Jul
1:50.2	Tom Nimmo		9.05.71	1r1	Wolverhampton	4	Jun
1:50.25	Paul Burgess		10.11.70	5	Loughborough	5	Jun
1:50.3	Steve Cram		14.10.60	1	Jarrow	8	Jun
(40)							
1:50.49	Peter Hackley		19.02.71	4	Edinburgh	25	Jun
1:50.5	Paul Freary		3.04.68	5r1	Stretford	23	Aug
1:50.5	Ben Reese	U20	29.03.76	6r1	Stretford	23	Aug
1:50.58	Kevin McKay		9.02.69	1r1	Wigan	7	May
1:50.7	Adam Duke	U23	5.10.73	2r1	Cheltenham	20	Jul
1:50.78	Anthony Draper	U23	23.04.74	3r1	London (CP)	7	May
1:50.83	Simon Fairbrother		28.03.68	2	Casalmaggiore, ITA	24	Jun
1:50.85	Steve Green		18.02.71	3	Lawrence, USA	21	May
1:50.88	Paul Larkins		19.05.63	2r1	Wigan	7	May
1:50.9	Paul Drake		16.10.66	2r1	Bournemouth	7	May
(50)							
1:50.9	Martin Airey		28.10.70	1	Norwich	27	Jul
1:50.94	Mark Benson		21.12.63	1	Colwyn Bay	23	Jul
1:51.00	Eddie Williams		1.10.70	3r1	Wigan	7	May
1:51.0	Robert Whalley		11.02.68	3r1	Cheltenham	20	Jul
1:51.02	Peter McDevitt		1.03.68	6	Edinburgh	25	Jun
1:51.06	Paul Roberts		24.12.69	5h5	Sheffield	11	Jun
1:51.07	Dominic Hall		21.02.71	6h4	Sheffield	11	Jun
1:51.08	Des Roache	U20	5.01.76	1h4	Corby	30	May
1:51.1	Rod Finch		5.08.67	4r2	Manchester	18	May
1:51.13	Simon Brown		22.03.69	2	Stoke	16	Jul
(60)							
1:51.17	Darrell Maynard		21.08.61	7h4	Sheffield	11	Jun
1:51.2	Dale Woodman	U23	2.01.72	2r1	Enfield	4	Jun
1:51.30	Joe Mills	U23	9.07.72	2	Oordegem, BEL	9	Jul
1:51.3	Guy Amos		15.06.63	2	Norwich	27	Jul
1:51.3	Nick Bentham		7.12.70	7r1	Stretford	23	Aug
1:51.34 i	Ian Campbell		6.09.71	1	Glasgow	15	Jan
1:51.39	John MacFadyen	U23	1.08.72	8	Edinburgh	25	Jun
1:51.4	Jason Thompson		16.11.71	1r1	Bracknell	2	Jul
1:51.4	Simon Parsons	U23	27.10.73	1r1	Stretford	12	Jul
1:51.4	Neil Emberton	U23	11.09.72				
(70)							
1:51.56	Ian Mansfield	U23	27.11.74	1r2	Solihull	21	Aug
1:51.57	David Locker	U20	28.03.75	6	Bedford	3	Jul
1:51.6	Edward McLean		19.11.69	3r1	Wolverhampton	4	Jun
1:51.6	*Des English*		*6.06.67*	*2r1*	*Stoke*	*2*	*Jul*
1:51.67	Glen Stewart		7.12.70	4r1	London (CP)	7	May
1:51.7	Karl Wright	U23	29.05.74	5r1	Stretford	12	Jul
1:51.71	Ian Bowden	U20	8.02.75	4h1	Sheffield	11	Jun

1:51.72	Pat Galvin	U23	24.09.74	6r1	London (CP)	26 Jun
1:51.8	Rob Scanlon	U23	13.04.74	5r1	Cheltenham	20 Jul
1:51.8	Neil Caddy	U20	18.03.75	1	Carn Brea	27 Jul
1:51.8	Matt Kloiber		22.11.71	2	Stoke	31 Jul
(80)						
1:51.81	Larry Mangleshot		28.05.63	3r2	Solihull	21 Aug
1:51.9	Sean Price		4.01.63	3r1	Enfield	4 Jun
1:51.9	Paul Cooper	U20	30.01.75	1	Leeds	19 Jul
1:52.0	Ian Thompson		3.08.68	6r1	Cheltenham	20 Jul
1:52.05	Simon Saxby	U23	17.01.74	5h1	Sheffield	11 Jun
1:52.09	Scott Taylor	U23	16.06.74	7h5	Sheffield	11 Jun
1:52.20	Jason Dupuy		31.01.71	3h3	London (CP)	25 Jun
1:52.2	Richard White		20.01.60	7r2	Manchester	18 May
1:52.2	Neil Horsfield		7.12.66	1	Barry	27 Jul
1:52.28	Matthew De Freitas		19.09.68	4	Bracknell	2 May
(90)						
1:52.3	Chris Stringer	U20	18.02.76	4r3	Manchester	18 May
1:52.3	David Thornton	U23	27.07.73	4r4	Manchester	18 May
1:52.3	Nick Hopkins		28.08.66	6	Stretford	31 May
1:52.3	John Gercs		7.06.69	1r1	Loughborough	22 Jun
1:52.3	David Pamah		27.11.64	3	London (PH)	10 Jul
1:52.38	Ian Gillespie		18.05.70	3r1	London (He)	5 Jun
1:52.38	Alex Rosen		30.09.71	1r2	London (He)	5 Jun
1:52.4	Joel Fraser	U23	10.11.74	1	Kingston	19 Jun
1:52.4	Matthew Clarke	U20	15.11.76	1r2	Watford	27 Jul
1:52.42	Tony Bignall		17.11.71	2r2	Aartselaar, BEL	21 Jul
(100)						
1:52.46	Stephen Blake		28.12.67	5h3	Sheffield	11 Jun
1:52.46	Noel Edwards	U23	16.12.72	4	Stoke	16 Jul
1:52.50	Andrew Young	U20	20.06.77	1	Nicosia, CYP	19 May
1:52.5	Philip Healy		1.10.70	2	Antrim	30 Apr
1:52.5	Andrew Robinson		21.03.66	1	Aldershot	6 Jul
1:52.56	Steve Rees-Jones	U23	24.12.74	3h5	London (CP)	25 Jun
1:52.67	Richard Miller		29.03.67	5h5	London (CP)	25 Jun
1:52.70	Vince Rose		21.08.71	2r2	London (He)	5 Jun
1:52.7	John Wild	U23	30.08.73	3r1	Stretford	21 Jun
1:52.7	Matthew Davies		23.07.71	1r1	Reading	2 Jul
(110)						
1:52.7	Richard Ashe	U23	5.10.74	1r1	London (BP)	13 Aug
1:52.75	Mick Gooch		13.09.69	5r2	Solihull	21 Aug

Additional Under 20 (1 - 13 above)

1:52.79	Chris Woods		24.12.75	2	Telford	9 Jul
1:52.9	Richard Girvan		26.07.76	1	Coatbridge	29 May
1:53.03	Matthew Winter		31.10.75	3	Telford	9 Jul
1:53.10	Guy Clarke		22.05.75	4	Telford	9 Jul
1:53.1	Chris Elliott		29.05.75	2	Jarrow	8 Jun
1:53.33	Gavin Mason		6.04.77	7	Crawley	6 Aug
1:53.37	Alasdair Donaldson		21.06.77	3h4	Bedford	2 Jul
(20)						
1:53.38	Nick Reynolds		8.06.76	3	London (CP)	29 May
1:53.67	Alan McDougall		9.11.75	3r2	Loughborough	7 Sep
1:53.9	Alan Tatham		29.04.77	1	Derby	15 May
1:53.9	David Povall		21.07.75	3	Barry	27 Jul
1:53.97	Jan Staneke		29.11.75	4h2	Bedford	2 Jul
1:54.0	Graeme Forbes		16.02.75	2	Glasgow	16 Aug
1:54.16	Mark MacDonald		26.05.75	4h4	Bedford	2 Jul
1:54.4	Liam O'Brien		17.05.75	2	Leeds	19 Jul
1:54.51	John Dineen		10.12.75	3h5	Bedford	2 Jul
1:54.57	Michael Combe	U17	24.12.78	1	Birmingham	31 Jul
1:54.58	Sam Illidge		4.02.77	4h5	Bedford	2 Jul

Additional Under 17 (1 above)

1:54.9	Dale Canning	12.06.78	3	Stretford	2	Aug
1:54.99	Roger Morley	20.09.77	2	Birmingham	31	Jul
1:55.12	Yacin Yusuf	20.12.77	3	Birmingham	31	Jul
1:55.17	Andrew Thomas	15.05.79	4	Birmingham	31	Jul
1:55.38	Russell Cartwright	13.10.77	3	Dublin, IRE	13	Aug
1:55.6	Paul Draper	9.09.77	4r5	Manchester	18	May
1:55.7	Andrew Graffin	20.12.77	1	Basingstoke	24	Jul
1:56.0	Stewart Allen	31.08.78	2	London (CP)	29	May
1:56.5	Alasdair Cunningham	5.09.77	1	Antrim	28	May
	(10)					
1:56.77	Peter McCormick	7.02.78	5	Antrim	28	Jun
1:56.8	Stuart Bailey	6.08.78	9	Stretford	2	Aug
1:56.8	Daryl Griffin	28.01.78	4	Watford	14	Sep
1:56.9	Allen Graffin	20.12.77	2	Woking	24	Aug
1:57.09	Bryan Hendry	24.10.77	6h3	Edinburgh	24	Jun
1:57.10	Gavin McPherson	17.09.77	2	Gateshead	28	May
1:57.3	David Stanley	16.01.79		Reading	23	Aug
1:57.5	Louis Wells	6.02.78	2s2	Birmingham	30	Jul
1:57.74	Neville Johnson	3.01.78	1	Colwyn Bay	2	Jul

Under 15

2:00.88	Lee Hughes	13.09.79	1h2	Telford	8	Jul
2:01.71	Martyn Gordon	29.09.79	2h2	Telford	8	Jul
2:01.89	Matthew Crompton	2.09.79	3h2	Telford	8	Jul
2:01.91	Jonathan Salt	14.12.79	4h2	Telford	8	Jul
2:02.0	James Hand	11.06.80	6	Grangemouth	7	Sep
2:02.1	Andrew Kirk	28.09.79	1	Ipswich	15	May
2:02.3	Colin Young	11.12.79	1	Mansfield	11	Jun
2:02.6	Alan Old	1.12.79	1	Gateshead	5	Jun
2:02.6	Tom Payn	18.10.79	3	Woodford	10	Aug
2:02.9	Ross Donaldson	17.08.80	1	Blackpool	14	Aug
	(10)					
2:03.3	Gareth Roberts	22.10.79	2	Blackpool	14	Aug
2:03.4	Sam Boden	16.02.80	1	St. Ives	19	Jun
2:03.52 i	Marc Newton	15.03.80	1	Birmingham	12	Feb
	2:03.8		10r2	Stretford	31	May
2:04.27	Gareth Price	27.11.79	8	Telford	9	Jul
2:04.36	John Binfield	19.11.79	5h2	Telford	8	Jul
2:04.7	Chris Fish	22.12.79	4	Blackpool	14	Aug
2:04.8	Keith Grant	17.03.80	5	Blackpool	14	Aug
2:04.9	Wayne Cooper		1	Portsmouth	17	Jul

Doubtful Timing

2:00.6	Simon Fraser	30.11.79	1	Blackpool	17	Jul

Under 13

2:16.3	A. O'Donnell		1	Perivale	18	May
2:17.12	M. Peleszok		1	Wrexham	13	Aug
2:17.9	J. Cox		1	Leamington	14	May
2:18.3	Warren McKinlay	4.10.81	1r1	Colchester	29	Aug
2:18.4	Philip Nosko	29.01.82	1	Basingstoke	2	Jul

1000 METRES

2:19.82 A	Brian Treacy		29.07.71	2	Soria, SPA	8	Jul
	2:21.49			9	Madrid, SPA	6	Sep
2:20.05 i	Andy Keith		25.12.71	1	Boston, USA	29	Jan
	2:21.86 i			1	Syracuse, USA	20	Feb
2:20.55	Martin Steele		30.09.62	3	Victoria, CAN	19	Aug
2:20.66 i	Andrew Lill		9.08.71	2	Birmingham	26	Feb
2:21.95	Steve Green		18.02.71	6	Victoria, CAN	19	Aug
2:22.46 i	Vince Wilson	U23	1.04.73	4	Birmingham	26	Feb
2:23.55 i	Grant Graham	U23	27.12.72	6	Birmingham	26	Feb

1500 METRES

Time	Name	Born	Pos	Venue	Date
3:35.32	Matthew Yates	4.02.69	2	Berlin, GER	30 Aug
3:35.61			8	Rieti, ITA	28 Aug
3:36.47			7	Nice, FRA	18 Jul
3:37.82			7	Brussels, BEL	19 Aug
3:39.12			12	Villeneuve d'Ascq, FRA	8 Jul
3:39.60			5	Zurich, SWZ	17 Aug
3:40.55			3	Lisbon, POR	18 Jun
3:42.12			6	Rovereto, ITA	24 Jul
3:42.79			4	Paris, FRA	3 Sep
3:35.83	Gary Lough	6.07.70	3	London (CP)	15 Jul
3:37.83			4h1	Helsinki, FIN	7 Aug
3:41.71			3	Sheffield	12 Jun
3:42.7			1r1	Manchester	18 May
(3:42.98)			dq	Victoria, CAN	27 Aug
3:36.53	David Strang	13.12.68	6	London (CP)	15 Jul
3:38.55 +			7m	Oslo, NOR	22 Jul
3:39.15			4	Edinburgh	8 Jul
3:39.96			2h2	Helsinki, FIN	7 Aug
3:40.08			7	Hechtel, BEL	30 Jul
3:40.85			2	Sheffield	12 Jun
3:42.27 i			1h2	Paris, FRA	12 Mar
3:37.20	John Mayock	26.10.70	8	London (CP)	15 Jul
3:37.22			3	Victoria, CAN	28 Aug
3:38.78			4	Seville, SPA	5 Jun
3:39.17			5	Edinburgh	8 Jul
3:40.98 i			1	Seville, SPA	3 Feb
3:41.47 i			2	Stuttgart, GER	6 Feb
3:42.59			1s2	Victoria, CAN	27 Aug
3:42.89			6	Sheffield	12 Jun
3:37.86	Kevin McKay	9.02.69	3	Rhede, GER	29 Jul
3:38.08			1	Hengelo, HOL	4 Jun
3:38.79 +			9	Oslo, NOR	22 Jul
3:39.72			8	Victoria, CAN	28 Aug
3:40.19			5h2	Helsinki, FIN	7 Aug
3:40.59			1	Sheffield	12 Jun
3:42.83			16	Brussels, BEL	19 Aug
3:38.80	Rod Finch	5.08.67	2	Hengelo, HOL	4 Jun
3:38.93	Brian Treacy	29.07.71	6	Victoria, CAN	28 Aug
3:39.65			3	Cludad Real, SPA	24 Jun
3:40.55			3	Granada, SPA	1 Jun
3:40.63			2	Salamanca, SPA	22 Jul
3:39.19	Steve Green	18.02.71	7	Victoria, CAN	28 Aug
3:41.59			3	Walnut, USA	17 Apr
3:39.44	Andy Keith	25.12.71	6	Edinburgh	8 Jul
3:41.1			1	Jamaica, USA	17 May
3:42.93			7	Sheffield	12 Jun
3:40.17	Glen Stewart	7.12.70	7	Edinburgh	8 Jul
3:42.12			8	Linz, AUT	4 Jul
	(10)				
3:40.35	Ian Grime	29.09.70	1r1	Solihull	21 Aug
3:40.47	Matt Barnes	12.01.68	11	Edinburgh	8 Jul
3:41.02	Steffan White U23	21.12.72	2r1	Solihull	21 Aug
3:41.28	Davey Wilson	7.09.68	1	Belfast	4 Jun
3:41.39	*Des English*	*6.06.67*	*14*	*Rieti, ITA*	*28 Aug*
3:41.48	Ian Gillespie	18.05.70	4	Nuremberg, GER	10 Jun
3:41.65			4r1	Solihull	21 Aug
3:41.50	Tony Morrell	3.05.62	3	Arhus, DEN	7 Jul
3:42.45			5	Narbonne, FRA	19 Jun
3:42.59			4	Sheffield	12 Jun

3:41.63	Phil Mowbray	U23	19.03.73	3r1	Solihull	21	Aug
3:41.73	Matt Hibberd	U23	23.06.73	5r1	Solihull	21	Aug
3:42.5				1	Loughborough	7	Sep
3:41.92	Tony Whiteman		13.11.71	13	Edinburgh	8	Jul
3:42.18				1	Loughborough	5	Jun
3:42.68				5	Sheffield	12	Jun
3:42.50	John Wild	U23	30.08.73	1	Fayetteville, USA	23	Apr
(20)							
3:42.59	John Downes		21.07.67	2	Dublin (M), IRE	24	Jul
3:42.66	Gary Brown		21.07.67	11	Victoria, CAN	28	Aug
3:42.70	Bobby Farren		15.05.70	3	Dublin (M), IRE	24	Jul
3:42.8	Steve Cram		14.10.60	2r1	Manchester	18	May
3:42.88	Paul Larkins		19.05.63	3r1	Fayetteville, USA	9	Apr
	68 performances to 3:43.0 by 25 athletes including 3 indoors						
3:43.05 i	Ian Campbell		6.09.71	2	Birmingham	19	Feb
3:44.41				7	Barcelona, SPA	21	Jun
3:43.39 i	Terry West		19.11.68	3	Vienna, AUT	6	Feb
3:50.5				1	Cannock	11	Sep
3:43.8	Ciaran Murphy		2.09.71	4r1	Loughborough	7	Sep
3:43.90	Rob Scanlon	U23	13.04.74	6r1	Solihull	21	Aug
3:44.43	Adrian Passey		2.09.64	8	Rovereto, ITA	24	Jul
(30)							
3:44.54	Jason Boothroyd		26.11.69	4	Knoxville, USA	8	Apr
3:44.60	Simon Fairbrother		28.03.68	8	Barcelona, SPA	21	Jun
3:44.6	Spencer Barden	U23	31.03.73	6r1	Loughborough	7	Sep
3:44.7	Grant Graham	U23	27.12.72	6r1	Manchester	18	May
3:44.77	Stuart Poore	U23	30.12.72	9	Solihull	21	Aug
3:44.86	Mike Hickin		29.08.64	4h2	Sheffield	11	Jun
3:44.9	Andrew Hart		13.09.69	1	Perivale	15	Jun
3:45.05	Nick Hopkins		28.08.66	3r1	Crawley	28	May
3:45.1	Vince Wilson	U23	1.04.73	7r1	Manchester	18	May
3:45.11	Bruno Witchalls	U20	22.03.75	8	Lisbon, POR	24	Jul
(40)							
3:45.16	Jim Campbell		17.06.70	5	Dublin (M), IRE	24	Jul
3:45.3	Jason Lobo		18.09.69	2r1	Stretford	2	Aug
3:45.3	Paul Freary		3.04.68	3r1	Stretford	2	Aug
3:45.5	Robert Whalley		11.02.68	1r1	Newport	10	Aug
3:45.7	Joe Mills	U23	9.07.72	8	Loughborough	7	Sep
3:45.74	James Starling		13.08.67	4r1	Crawley	28	May
3:45.74	Darren Spawforth		1.08.69	6h2	Sheffield	11	Jun
3:46.16	Neil Caddy	U20	18.03.75	6r1	Crawley	28	May
3:46.2	Neil Ovington		26.01.63	4r1	Stretford	2	Aug
3:46.23 i	Matthew De Freitas		19.09.68	2	Glasgow	12	Feb
3:48.8				1	Portsmouth	15	May
(50)							
3:46.32	Tony Bignall		17.11.71	10	Nivelles, BEL	23	Jul
3:46.42	Spencer Duval		5.01.70	8r1	Crawley	28	May
3:46.48	Kevin Howard		7.02.66	9r1	Crawley	28	May
3:46.5	Nick Commerford		23.04.66	9	Loughborough	7	Sep
3:46.60	Glyn Tromans		17.03.69	2	Stoke	16	Jul
3:46.6	Richard Ashe	U23	5.10.74	4	Watford	10	Aug
3:46.7	Paul Drake		16.10.66	3	Salisbury	10	Jul
3:46.85	Darren Daniels		2.09.70	7h2	Sheffield	11	Jun
3:46.9	Andrew Pearson		14.09.71	5r1	Stretford	2	Aug
3:46.9	Paul Gardner		5.08.69	3r1	Cheltenham	29	Aug
(60)							
3:46.??	Mark Russell		15.03.71		Hot Springs, USA	9	Apr
3:47.0	Brad Glenton		2.11.69	5r2	Manchester	18	May
3:47.1	Steve Moseley		10.01.66	4	Salisbury	10	Jul
3:47.16	James Ellis-Smith	U23		2r2	Hot Springs, USA	9	Apr
3:47.2	Tom Buckner		16.04.63	1	Canberra, AUS	25	Jan

3:47.2	Larry Mangleshot			28.05.63	5	Watford	10 Aug
3:47.29	Neil Emberton	U23		11.09.72	3r2	Hot Springs, USA	9 Apr
3:47.3	Peter Jones			2.12.70	6r1	Stretford	2 Aug
3:47.4 un	Luke Veness	U23		5.12.73		Cal., USA	28 May
3:50.55					3h2	London (CP)	25 Jun
3:47.6	Philip Healy			1.10.70	10r1	Manchester	18 May
(70)							
3:47.6	Ian Hudspith			23.09.70	1	Milton Keynes	20 Jul
3:47.76	Kim Critchley	U23		15.07.73	2r2	Solihull	21 Aug
3:48.0	Keith Cullen	U23		13.06.72	1	London (Nh)	15 May
3:48.0	Scott West	U20		31.10.75	3	Loughborough	22 Jun
3:48.1	Bashir Hussain			20.12.64	3r1	Stretford	21 Jun
3:48.1	Justin Swift-Smith	U23		28.08.74	4r1	Cheltenham	29 Aug
3:48.27	Rob Fitzsimmons			16.08.64	11	Solihull	21 Aug
3:48.28	Chris May	U23		19.09.72	9r2	Gateshead	1 Jul
3:48.3	Richard Taylor	U23		5.12.73	4	Loughborough	22 Jun
3:48.4	Matthew Davies			23.07.71	7r1	Stretford	2 Aug
(80)							
3:48.6	Stuart Margiotta			19.11.69	5	Loughborough	22 Jun
3:48.6	Robert Hough	U23		3.06.72	1	Portsmouth	6 Aug
3:48.7	Darren Mead			4.10.68	3	Kingston	31 Jul
3:48.7	Mark Cooper			29.01.64	8r1	Stretford	2 Aug
3:48.72	Karl Keska	U23		7.05.72	1	Eugene, USA	23 Apr
3:48.9	Darius Burrows	U20		8.08.75	12	Loughborough	7 Sep
3:48.95	Frank Boyne			28.02.66	3r2	Solihull	21 Aug
3:49.0	Peter Davies			24.02.63	6	Loughborough	22 Jun
3:49.1	Spencer Newport			5.10.66	7	Loughborough	22 Jun
3:49.2	Paul Green	U23		7.04.72	4r1	Stretford	21 Jun
(90)							
3:49.27 i	Paul Burgess			10.11.70	5	Birmingham	19 Feb
3:49.3	Mike Guegan			19.09.66	2	Portsmouth	15 May
3:49.4	Craig Winrow			22.12.71	1	Stretford	26 Apr
3:49.5	Mark Fallows			8.02.62	2	Stretford	26 Apr
3:49.6	Ken Harker			25.02.71	10r1	Stretford	2 Aug
3:49.7	John MacKay			22.08.60	2	Edinburgh	24 Apr
3:49.7	Ben Reese	U20		29.03.76	6r1	Stretford	21 Jun
3:49.80	Andrew Lill			9.08.71	1	Bracknell	2 May
3:49.8	Ian Manners			25.06.64	7r1	Cheltenham	29 Aug
3:49.86	John Lucas			2.11.65	2	Derby	16 Jul
(100)							
3:50.0	Andrew Pratt			20.04.69	2	Corby	31 Jul
3:50.0	Barry Royden			15.12.66	1	Dartford	20 Aug
3:50.06	Matt Skelton	U23		8.11.72	4r2	Solihull	21 Aug
3:50.1	Martin Steele			30.09.62	1	Sheffield	14 May
3:50.4	*John Lisiewicz*			*18.07.62*	*7r1*	*Stretford*	*21 Jun*
3:50.48	Paul Hilton			21.01.68	3	Derby	16 Jul
3:50.5	Des Roache	U20		5.01.76	4h1	Edinburgh	24 Jun
3:50.6	Clive Gilby			24.02.66	2r1	Bracknell	7 May
3:50.6	Richard Bunn	U23		2.12.72	1r1	Stretford	10 May
3:50.6	Chris Nicolson	U23		19.09.73	5h1	Edinburgh	24 Jun
3:50.6	Mike Simpson			6.01.70	2r1	Stoke	2 Jul
(110)							
3:50.6	Shane Snow			31.10.66	3r2	Loughborough	7 Sep
3:50.69	Carl Leonard	U23		19.01.73		Akron, USA	23 Apr
3:50.7	Steve Edmonds			15.05.69	8	Loughborough	22 Jun
3:50.78	John O'Shea			13.04.67	1h3	London (CP)	25 Jun
3:50.80	Adam Duke	U23		5.10.73	2h3	London (CP)	25 Jun
3:50.8	Jason Dullforce			6.08.70	11r2	Manchester	18 May
3:50.85	Dave Clarke			18.06.64	3h3	London (CP)	25 Jun
3:50.85	Tony Mate	U23		15.12.74	4	Derby	16 Jul

Additional Under 20 (1 - 6 above)

3:51.2	Alan Tatham	29.04.77	3	Stretford	26	Apr
3:52.0	Eric Crowther	23.01.75	2r2	Stretford	2	Aug
3:52.0	Tom Mayo	2.05.77	3	Welwyn	29	Aug
3:52.3	Ian Mitchell	10.03.76	11	Stretford	21	Jun
(10)						
3:52.3	Stuart Overthrow	13.06.75	1r2	Stretford	2	Aug
3:52.3	Chris Elliott	29.05.75	2r2	Stretford	2	Aug
3:52.36	Ben Noad	6.05.76	5	Bedford	3	Jul
3:52.7	Andy Renfree	18.05.75	3	Stretford	2	Aug
3:52.91	Mark Miles	24.03.77	6	Bedford	3	Jul

Under 17

3:56.21	Dale Canning	12.06.78	2	Nicosia, CYP	20	May
3:59.11	Andrew Graffin	20.12.77	1	Birmingham	31	Jul
3:59.68	Allen Graffin	20.12.77	2	Birmingham	31	Jul
4:00.20	Daniel Hyde	5.10.77	1	London (CP)	29	May
4:01.3	Nick Harrison	24.09.77	1	Harrow	5	Jun
4:01.53	Yacin Yusuf	20.12.77	3	Sheffield	4	Sep
4:01.8	David Davey	8.09.77		Barry	18	Sep
4:01.94	Phil McGuinness	4.10.77	2h1	Telford	8	Jul
4:01.98	Alistair Moses	5.07.78	3h1	Telford	8	Jul
4:02.04	Edward Matthews	17.09.77	4h1	Telford	8	Jul
(10)						
4:02.04	Russell Cartwright	13.10.77	4	Sheffield	4	Sep
4:02.08	Daryl Griffin	28.01.78	2	London (CP)	29	May
4:02.10	Paul Draper	9.09.77	5h1	Telford	8	Jul
4:02.44	Tom Salmon	12.04.79	3	London (CP)	29	May
4:02.60	Michael East	20.01.78	4	London (CP)	29	May
4:03.0	Gavin Marsden	22.02.78	7	Stretford	21	Jun
4:03.15	Robert Brown	3.03.78	1	Gateshead	15	May
4:03.36	Chris Old	3.12.77	2	Gateshead	15	May
4:03.36	Paul Fisher	17.05.79	4	London (He)	17	Aug
4:05.80	Michael Combe	24.12.78	5	Sheffield	4	Sep

Under 15

4:08.81	Ross Fittall	4.09.79	1	London (CP)	15	Jul
4:11.05	Simon Lees	19.11.79	2	London (CP)	15	Jul
4:12.8	Lee Hughes	13.09.79	1	Solihull	29	May
4:12.95	Sam Boden	16.02.80	2	Telford	9	Jul
4:15.0	John Baldwin	25.10.79	2	Birmingham	30	Jul
4:15.02	Daniel Pinna	12.11.79	1h2	Telford	8	Jul
4:15.7	Oliver Laws	18.03.80	3	Solihull	29	May
4:16.2	Daniel Rowen	30.12.79	2	Birmingham	11	Jun
4:16.7	Andrew McKenna	3.01.80	1	Milton Keynes	15	Jun
4:16.9	Alan Old	1.12.79	1	Jarrow	18	Jun
(10)						
4:17.03	Daffydd Soloman	18.09.79	6	London (CP)	15	Jul
4:17.28	Louis Jones	6.11.79	5	Telford	9	Jul
4:17.74	John Mooney	23.10.79	5h2	Telford	8	Jul
4:17.90	Andrew Murphy	14.09.79	6h2	Telford	8	Jul
4:19.69	Mark Adams	31.07.80	3h2	Birmingham	30	Jul
4:20.53	Daniel Ranson	25.09.79	3h1	Birmingham	30	Jul
4:20.6	Ryan Falkner	20.11.79	1	Leicester	11	Jun
4:20.64	Daniel Hewitt	13.11.79	1	Blackpool	14	Aug
4:20.7	Ross Houston	5.12.79	2	Grangemouth	3	Aug
4:20.82	Andrew Kordowicz	20.10.79	2	Blackpool	14	Aug
4:20.86	Jody Church	3.04.80	2	London (CP)	28	May
4:20.9	Joel Ellis	2.09.79	1	Solihull	28	May

Under 13

4:35.47	Abdi Madar	25.11.81	1	Birmingham	11	Sep
4:43.0	Steven Munday	15.10.81	1		17	Jul

1 MILE

Time	Name	Cat	DOB	Pos	Venue	Date
3:53.64	Kevin McKay		9.02.69	7	Oslo, NOR	22 Jul
3:58.69				10	Zurich, SWZ	17 Aug
3:58.72				1	Gateshead	1 Jul
3:54.30	David Strang		13.12.68	9	Oslo, NOR	22 Jul
3:55.43 i				1	Boston, USA	22 Jan
3:57.38 i				1	Fairfax, USA	6 Feb
3:56.29 i	Andy Keith		25.12.71	2	Boston, USA	22 Jan
3:58.97				6	Cork, IRE	25 Jun
4:00.55 i				2	Indianapolis, USA	12 Mar
3:58.34	John Mayock		26.10.70	1	Sheffield	4 Sep
3:58.39	Matt Barnes		12.01.68	3	Cork, IRE	25 Jun
3:58.71	*Des English*		*6.06.67*	*4*	*Cork, IRE*	*25 Jun*
3:59.48	Gary Lough		6.07.70	6	Sheffield	4 Sep
4:00.00				3	Gateshead	1 Jul
3:59.6 i	Steve Green		18.02.71	1	Ames, USA	4 Mar
4:01.64 i				5	Indianapolis, USA	12 Mar
4:00.2	Bobby Farren		15.05.70	1	Antrim	10 May
4:00.61	Steffan White	U23	21.12.72	8	Sheffield	4 Sep
4:00.80	Ian Gillespie		18.05.70	5	Gateshead	1 Jul
4:01.58				9	Sheffield	4 Sep
4:01.06 [(10)]	Tony Morrell		3.05.62	6	Gateshead	1 Jul
4:01.57	John Nuttall		11.01.67	8	Gateshead	1 Jul
4:01.86				10	Sheffield	4 Sep
4:02.00	Lee Cadwallader		17.01.69	8	Cork, IRE	25 Jun

23 performances to 4:02.00 by 13 athletes including 6 indoors

Time	Name	Cat	DOB	Pos	Venue	Date
4:02.36	Matt Hibberd	U23	23.06.73	11	Sheffield	4 Sep
4:02.7	Paul Freary		3.04.68	1	Blackburn	7 Sep
4:03.3	Andrew Hart		13.09.69	1	Exeter	8 Aug
4:03.69	Darren Spawforth		1.08.69	9	Cork, IRE	25 Jun
4:03.8	Robert Whalley		11.02.68	2	Exeter	8 Aug
4:03.87	Tony Whiteman		13.11.71	1	Wrexham	3 Jul
4:03.98	Darren Daniels		2.09.70	10	Cork, IRE	25 Jun
4:05.1 [(20)]	Jason Lobo		18.09.69	2	Blackburn	7 Sep
4:05.4	Tom Buckner		16.04.63	4	Exeter	8 Aug
4:05.42	Joe Mills	U23	9.07.72	2	Wrexham	3 Jul
4:06.1	Neil Caddy	U20	18.03.75	5	Exeter	8 Aug
4:06.4	Robert Hough	U23	3.06.72	3	Southampton	4 Sep
4:06.9	Ian Manners		25.06.64	6	Exeter	8 Aug
4:07.08	Mike Proudlove		26.01.70	3	Wrexham	3 Jul
4:07.28	Rob Denmark		23.11.68	12	Sheffield	4 Sep
4:07.64	Matthew Yates		4.02.69	13	Sheffield	4 Sep
4:07.71	Stuart Margiotta		19.11.69	1	Corby	30 May
4:08.68 [(30)]	John MacKay		22.08.60	3	Corby	30 May
4:09.15	John Lucas		2.11.65	4	Corby	30 May
4:09.53	Mark Fallows		8.02.62	4	Sheffield	3 Jul
4:09.92	Glyn Tromans		17.03.69	5	Corby	30 May

Under 13

Time	Name	DOB	Pos	Venue	Date
5:15.1	Steven Munday	15.10.81	1	Jarrow	10 Aug

2000 METRES

Time	Name	DOB	Pos	Venue	Date
5:11.02	Colin Walker	29.10.62	3	Victoria, CAN	19 Aug

154

3000 METRES

7:42.62	Rob Denmark		23.11.68	2	Lausanne, SWZ	6	Jul
7:56.60 i				3	Birmingham	19	Feb
7:49.83 i	Andy Keith		25.12.71	1	Fairfax, USA	6	Feb
8:02.81				4	Stockholm, SWE	2	Aug
7:50.30	Mark Rowland		7.03.63	2	Lappeenranta, FIN	26	Jul
7:54.05				15	Cologne, GER	21	Aug
7:51.26	Gary Staines		3.07.63	5	Lappeenranta, FIN	26	Jul
7:53.71				2	Stockholm, SWE	2	Aug
7:53.99 i	Rod Finch		5.08.67	3	Paris, FRA	13	Mar
7:56.03 i				2	Glasgow	12	Feb
7:57.35 i				1h2	Paris, FRA	11	Mar
7:57.47 i				2	Glasgow	29	Jan
7:54.53	John Downes		21.07.67	3	Tampere, FIN	21	Jun
7:55.31 i	John Mayock		26.10.70	1	Glasgow	12	Feb
7:56.08 i	Matt Barnes		12.01.68	1	Birmingham	19	Feb
7:56.24	Bobby Farren		15.05.70	1	Solihull	21	Aug
7:56.39	Darren Mead		4.10.68	8	Bratislava, SVK	1	Jun
	(10)						
7:57.02 i	Paul Larkins		19.05.63	1	Glasgow	29	Jan
7:59.37 i				1	Birmingham	8	Jan
7:58.92 i	Tom Buckner		16.04.63	5	Birmingham	19	Feb
8:06.07				4	Canberra, AUS	28	Jan
7:59.97	Justin Chaston		4.11.68	6	Lublin, POL	4	Jun
	20 performances to 8:00.00 by 13 athletes including 11 indoors						
8:00.29	Spencer Barden	U23	31.03.73	2	Solihull	21	Aug
8:00.50	Mark Morgan	U23	19.08.72	3	Wrexham	3	Jul
8:01.25 i	Matthew Yates		4.02.69	7	San Sebastian, SPA	3	Mar
8:01.26	Darius Burrows	U20	8.08.75	3	Solihull	21	Aug
8:01.90 i	Steffan White	U23	21.12.72	6	Birmingham	19	Feb
8:05.30				5	Wrexham	3	Jul
8:02.03	David Miles		16.11.65	1	Edinburgh	8	Jul
8:02.07	John Sherban		30.07.64	2	Edinburgh	8	Jul
	(20)						
8:02.66 i	Steve Brooks		8.06.70	1	Oklahoma City, USA	26	Feb
8:02.87	Colin Walker		29.10.62	1	Gateshead	1	Jul
8:03.1	Ian Gillespie		18.05.70	1r1	Cheltenham	20	Jul
8:03.5	Darren Daniels		2.09.70	2r1	Cheltenham	20	Jul
8:04.07	Kim Critchley	U23	15.07.73	3	Edinburgh	8	Jul
8:04.3	Ian Robinson		21.04.69	1r1	Stretford	2	Aug
8:04.51	Spencer Newport		5.10.66	4	Edinburgh	8	Jul
8:04.92	*John Lisiewicz*		*18.07.62*	*5*	*Edinburgh*	*8*	*Jul*
8:04.?? +	Jon Brown		27.02.71	Victoria, CAN		24	Aug
8:04.?? +	John Nuttall		11.01.67	Victoria, CAN		24	Aug
8:05.06 i	Andrew Wedlake		30.11.71	3	Boston, USA	26	Feb
	(30)						
8:05.77 i	Keith Cullen	U23	13.06.72	8	Birmingham	19	Feb
8:16.27				1	Birmingham	21	May
8:05.77	Adrian Callan		28.11.62	6	Edinburgh	8	Jul
8:05.94 i	Chris Robison		16.03.61	1	Birmingham	26	Feb
8:06.48				2	Gateshead	1	Jul
8:06.60	John MacKay		22.08.60	7	Edinburgh	8	Jul
8:06.66	*David Burke*		*68*	*1*	*Tullamore, IRE*	*15*	*May*
8:06.7	Carl Udall		13.07.66	1	Loughborough	22	Jun
8:07.61 i	Steve Green		18.02.71	4	Oklahoma City, USA	26	Feb
8:08.42	*John Burke*		*18.05.70*	*6*	*Solihull*	*21*	*Aug*
8:08.43	Bashir Hussain		20.12.64	5	Sheffield	2	Jul
8:09.1	Jon Gascoyne	U23	31.03.72	1	Bracknell	2	May
8:09.25	Dominic Bannister		1.04.68	8	Edinburgh	8	Jul

8:09.29 i	Carl Warren		28.09.69	2	Ypsilanti, USA	19 Feb
(40)						
8:09.43 i	John Rollins			4	Seville, SPA	27 Feb
8:09.7 i	Peter Fleming		5.01.61	1	Glasgow	9 Mar
8:09.72 i	Robert Whalley		11.02.68	5	Birmingham	26 Feb
8:10.2	Nick Commerford		23.04.66	3r1	Cheltenham	20 Jul
8:10.21	Ian Hamer		18.04.65	3	Loughborough	5 Jun
8:10.32 i	Graeme Croll		1.02.66	2	Glasgow	23 Jan
8:10.33	Ian Hudspith		23.09.70	6	Gateshead	1 Jul
8:10.72 i	James Ellis-Smith	U23			Fayetteville, USA	21 Jan
8:11.04 i	Nick Hopkins		28.08.66	9	Birmingham	19 Feb
8:15.3				5	Bracknell	2 May
8:11.09	Chris Nicolson	U23	19.09.73	9	Edinburgh	8 Jul
(50)						
8:11.2	Barry Royden		15.12.66	1	Horsham	31 Jul
8:11.68	Stuart Margiotta		19.11.69	10	Edinburgh	8 Jul
8:12.0	Rob Birchall		14.06.70	2	Loughborough	22 Jun
8:12.04	Paul Taylor		9.01.66	7	Gateshead	1 Jul
8:12.09	Martin Jones		21.04.67	5	Loughborough	5 Jun
8:12.18	Paul Dugdale		13.05.65	11	Edinburgh	8 Jul
8:12.43	Mick Hawkins		24.10.61	8	Gateshead	1 Jul
8:13.03	Dermot Donnelly		23.09.70	1	Kings Lynn	9 Jul
8:13.1	John McMurray	U23		3	Bracknell	2 May
8:13.60	Mark Steinle	U23	27.11.74	6	Loughborough	5 Jun
(60)						
8:13.82	Ian Manners		25.06.64	8	Solihull	21 Aug
8:14.24	Robert Quinn		10.12.65	1	Edinburgh	13 Jul
8:14.37	John Hartigan		4.03.65	7	Loughborough	5 Jun
8:14.82	Glyn Tromans		17.03.69	9	Gateshead	1 Jul
8:15.3	Paul Freary		3.04.68	1	Stretford	12 Jul
8:15.7	Chris Buckley		26.07.61	6r1	Cheltenham	20 Jul
8:16.44	Jim Campbell		17.06.70	3	Kings Lynn	9 Jul
8:16.53	Steve Hope	U23	8.02.72	9	Loughborough	5 Jun
8:16.8	Geoff Hill		8.02.63	1	Woking	24 Aug
8:17.01	Dave Lee		16.09.65	9	Solihull	21 Aug
(70)						
8:17.02	Rob Fitzsimmons		16.08.64	2	Edinburgh	13 Jul
8:17.05	Tony Bignall		17.11.71	12	Gateshead	1 Jul
8:17.20	Chris Stephenson	U23	22.07.74	2	Birmingham	21 May
8:17.69 i	Richard Findlow		4.12.66	6	Birmingham	26 Feb
8:19.99				14	Gateshead	1 Jul
8:18.10 i	Tommy Murray		18.05.61	3	Glasgow	23 Jan
8:18.28	Steve Dodd		9.01.71	12	Loughborough	5 Jun
8:18.35	Paul Green	U23	7.04.72	7	Sheffield	2 Jul
8:18.47 i	Nick Smart		24.12.68	4	Glasgow	23 Jan
8:18.53	Jason Dullforce		6.08.70	12	Birmingham	19 Feb
8:18.6	Gary Gerrard ⌐		7.07.63	2	Exeter	8 Aug
(80)						
8:18.74 i	Ian Grime		29.09.70	7	Birmingham	26 Feb
8:18.8	Gary Crowther		23.09.63	9r1	Cheltenham	20 Jul
8:18.97	Mike Simpson		6.01.70	10	Solihull	21 Aug
8:19.0	John Kendall		23.09.69	2	Woking	24 Aug
8:20.17 i	Ian Johnston		4.06.64	5	Glasgow	23 Jan

Illegally Paced (runners stopping and rejoining)

8:18.9	William Coyle		3.10.62	2	Glasgow	16 Aug
8:20.0	Graeme Wight		3.06.65	3	Glasgow	16 Aug
8:20.3	Alan Puckrin		2.04.64	4	Glasgow	16 Aug

Additional Under 20 (1 above)

8:25.0	Ben Noad	6.05.76	12	Cheltenham	20	Jul
8:27.06	Matthew Young	17.03.76	2	Telford	9	Jul
8:28.0	Robert Holladay	10.01.75	1	Leeds	19	Jul
8:28.6	Kevin Nash	6.02.77	3	Aldershot	29	Jun
8:28.7	Eric Crowther	23.01.75	6	Stretford	23	Aug
8:29.00	Johnathan Prowse	15.11.75	3	Telford	9	Jul

Under 17

8:37.12	Allen Graffin	20.12.77	1	Aberdeen	16	Jul
8:45.7	Dale Canning	12.06.78	13	Stretford	23	Aug
8:47.3	Steven Simpson	18.01.78	1	Blackpool	14	Aug
8:47.33	Andrew Graffin	20.12.77	2	Aberdeen	16	Jul
8:47.4	Yacin Yusuf	20.12.77	6	London (TB)	17	Aug
8:50.09	Robert Brown	3.03.78	1	Gateshead	29	May
8:50.6	Paul Fisher	17.05.79	1	Watford	10	Aug
8:53.10	David Rose	26.06.78	2	Gateshead	29	May
8:56.9	Tim Boyle	4.07.78	1	Telford	11	Jun
8:58.13	James Hunter	19.11.77	2	Bedford	3	Jul
(10)						
8:59.62	Chris O'Neill	19.09.77	3	Bedford	3	Jul

Under 15

9:16.0	Simon Lees	19.11.79	1	Coventry	17	Jul
9:18.2	Andrew McKenna	3.01.80	1	Watford	19	Jul
9:18.5	Sam Boden	16.02.80	1	Watford	14	Sep
9:23.3	Oliver Laws	18.03.80	1	Warley	17	Jul
9:25.08	Simon Bentley	29.10.79	1	Bedford	2	Jul
9:25.7	C. Whitehouse		1	Corby	22	May
9:26.0	Matthew Watson	23.02.80	1	Cleckheaton	17	Jul
9:27.3	Daniel Rowen	30.12.79	1	Coventry	17	Jul
9:27.6	Joel Ellis	2.09.79	1	Warley	22	May
9:31.3	Keith Grant	17.03.80	1	Wigan	17	Jul
(10)						
9:31.6	Andrew Murphy	14.09.79	1	London (He)	26	Jun
9:32.90	Gareth Melvin	11.12.80	1	Gateshead	29	May
9:33.7	Mark Adams	31.07.80	1	Hull	17	Jul
9:33.7	Louis Jones	6.11.79	1	Brighton	10	Aug
9:37.09	Gavin Tomlinson	2.02.80	2	Gateshead	29	May
9:38.00	Lloyd Stewart	23.09.79	2	Bedford	2	Jul

Under 13

10:16.2	Michael Steward	20.02.82	1	Watford	10	Aug
10:17.4	Steven Munday	15.10.81	6	Jarrow	13	Jul
10:24.6	Michael Clack		1	Portsmouth	14	May
10:34.1	Nicholas Murray		2	Portsmouth	14	May

2 MILES

8:27.00	John Downes	21.07.67	2	Hechtel, BEL	30	Jul
8:29.12	Gary Staines	3.07.63	6	Gothenberg, SWE	24	Aug

5000 METRES

13:22.40	Rob Denmark	23.11.68	7	London (CP)	15	Jul
13:23.00			1	Victoria, CAN	24	Aug
13:32.60			11	Oslo, NOR	22	Jul
13:37.50			2	Helsinki, FIN	14	Aug
13:40.10			3h1	Helsinki, FIN	11	Aug
13:59.80			5h1	Victoria, CAN	22	Aug

Time	Name		Birth	Pos	Venue	Date	
13:23.54	John Nuttall		11.01.67	3	Victoria, CAN	24	Aug
13:25.51				10	London (CP)	15	Jul
13:30.78				3h2	Helsinki, FIN	11	Aug
13:32.47				2	London (CP)	11	Sep
13:38.65				5	Helsinki, FIN	14	Aug
13:39.10				6	Hechtel, BEL	30	Jul
13:40.65				5h2	Victoria, CAN	22	Aug
13:23.96	Jon Brown		27.02.71	4	Victoria, CAN	24	Aug
13:24.79				3	St. Petersburg, RUS	26	Jul
13:34.37				8	Monaco, MON	2	Aug
13:34.84				13	London (CP)	15	Jul
13:40.62				4h2	Victoria, CAN	22	Aug
13:29.91	John Downes		21.07.67	1	Gavle, SWE	4	Jul
13:43.07				15	London (CP)	15	Jul
13:36.89	Richard Nerurkar		6.01.64	2	Rehlingen, GER	23	May
13:50.0				1	Oxford	8	May
13:53.21				2	Punkolardin, FIN	29	May
13:45.53	Justin Hobbs		12.03.69	8	Victoria, CAN	24	Aug
13:50.72				6h2	Victoria, CAN	22	Aug
13:45.57	Gary Staines		3.07.63	13	Zurich, SWZ	17	Aug
13:56.6				4	Pune, IND	13	Sep
13:46.19	Eamonn Martin		9.10.58	4	Cork, IRE	25	Jun
13:48.61				3	Arhus, DEN	7	Jul
13:46.4	John Sherban		30.07.64	1	Crawley	28	May
13:46.5 +e	Paul Evans		13.04.61	12	Brussels, BEL	19	Aug
13:47.21				18	London (CP)	15	Jul
(10)							
13:46.66	David Miles		16.11.65	5	Cork, IRE	25	Jun
13:47.0	Dermot Donnelly		23.09.70	2	Crawley	28	May
13:52.63				1	Sheffield	12	Jun
13:54.80				8h2	Victoria, CAN	22	Aug
14:00.00				15	Victoria, CAN	24	Aug
13:47.92	Bobby Farren		15.05.70	7	Cork, IRE	25	Jun
13:56.70				19	London (CP)	15	Jul
13:48.9	Jim Campbell		17.06.70	3	Crawley	28	May
13:49.16	Richard Findlow		4.12.66	8	Cork, IRE	25	Jun
13:55.75				3	Sheffield	12	Jun
13:50.58	John Mayock		26.10.70	4	Birmingham	26	Jun
13:50.7	Darren Mead		4.10.68	3	Croydon	29	Jun
13:50.86				9	Cork, IRE	25	Jun
13:54.08				2	Sheffield	12	Jun
13:59.66				2	Nitra, SVK	13	Jul
13:52.54	Steve Brooks		8.06.70	4	Madison, USA	7	May
13:54.5	Barry Royden		15.12.66	1	Brighton	10	Aug
13:56.3				1	London (Elt)	29	Aug
13:55.7	Chris Robison		16.03.61	1	Grangemouth	3	Aug
(20)							
13:56.47	Spencer Duval		5.01.70	10	Cork, IRE	25	Jun
13:57.99	Ian Hamer		18.04.65	5	Sheffield	12	Jun
13:58.59	Toby Tanser		21.07.68	9	Gavle, SWE	4	Jul
13:59.07	Steve Hope	U23	8.02.72	13	Cork, IRE	25	Jun
13:59.39	Justin Chaston		4.11.68	2	Austin, USA	7	Apr
13:59.46	Mark Morgan	U23	19.08.72	6	Sheffield	12	Jun
	57 performances to 14:00.00 by 26 athletes						
14:00.16	Karl Keska	U23	7.05.72	3	Eugene, USA	16	Apr
14:00.4	Paul Davies-Hale		21.06.62	1	Portsmouth	6	Aug
14:01.24	*John Lisiewicz*		*18.07.62*	*7*	*Sheffield*	*12*	*Jun*
14:02.93	Tom Buckner		16.04.63	3	Brisbane, AUS	5	Feb
14:03.61	Jon Gascoyne	U23	31.03.72	10	Sheffield	12	Jun
(30)							
14:03.76	Keith Cullen	U23	13.06.72	3	Corby	30	May

14:03.82	Mark Steinle	U23	27.11.74	11	Sheffield	12	Jun
14:04.18	Chris Stephenson	U23	22.07.74	5	Chiba, JAP	23	Nov
14:04.5	Spencer Newport		5.10.66	2	Brighton	10	Aug
14:04.8	Andy Bristow		2.09.61	1	London (Elt)	30	Jul
14:05.05	Peter Haynes		18.09.64	14	Cork, IRE	25	Jun
14:06.56	Martin Hula		2.01.66	14	Sheffield	12	Jun
14:07.13	Paul Dugdale		13.05.65	15	Sheffield	12	Jun
14:08.03	Ian Robinson		21.04.69	8	Madison, USA	7	May
14:08.31	Ian Grime		29.09.70	2	Loughborough	7	Sep
(40)							
14:09.00	Keith Anderson		10.08.57	1	Sheffield	15	May
14:09.49	David Tune		29.10.70	16	Sheffield	12	Jun
14:09.6	Geoff Hill		8.02.63	3	Brighton	10	Aug
14:10.04	Kim Critchley	U23	15.07.73	17	Sheffield	12	Jun
14:10.76	Paul Freary		3.04.68	1	Derby	16	Jul
14:11.27	Darius Burrows	U20	8.08.75	19	Sheffield	12	Jun
14:11.27	Bashir Hussain		20.12.64	2	Derby	16	Jul
14:11.37	Andrew Wedlake		30.11.71		Philadelphia, USA	28	Apr
14:14.16	Carl Udall		13.07.66	5	Corby	30	May
14:15.00	Dave Buzza		6.12.62	1	Dublin (M), IRE	18	Jun
(50)							
14:15.12	Paul Roden		18.04.65	1	Crawley	6	Aug
14:15.2	Gary Gerrard		7.07.63	6	Crawley	28	May
14:15.42	Paul Taylor		9.01.66	20	Sheffield	12	Jun
14:15.7	Nick Rose	V40	30.12.51	2	Portsmouth	6	Aug
14:16.0	Brian Rushworth		14.12.62	1	Gateshead	25	May
14:16.1	Rob Birchall		14.06.70	3	Portsmouth	6	Aug
14:16.38	John Rollins			2	Alfaz Del Pi, SPA	9	Apr
14:17.15	Alan Puckrin		2.04.64	6	Corby	30	May
14:17.2	Stephen Green		28.07.70	1	Stretford	30	May
14:17.70	*Kassa Tadesse*	*U23*	*21.08.74*	*2*	*Crawley*	*6*	*Aug*
14:17.8	Colin Moore		25.11.60	2	Stretford	30	May
(60)							
14:17.96	Adrian Callan		28.11.62	4	Edinburgh	25	Jun
14:18.1	Mark Hudspith		19.01.69	1	Rotherham	7	May
14:18.1	Ian Hudspith		23.09.70	2	Rotherham	7	May
14:18.2	Graeme Wight		3.06.65	1	Cannock	11	Sep
14:18.31	Philip Hogston	U23	25.04.73	7	Corby	30	May
14:18.71	Gary Crowther		23.09.63	5	Derby	16	Jul
14:19.6	Mike Simpson		6.01.70	1	Kingston	4	Jun
14:20.0	Darrell Smith		10.04.67	5	Brighton	10	Aug
14:20.45	Steve Knight		17.10.63	3	Cwmbran	18	Jun
14:20.9	Spencer Barden	U23	31.03.73	1	Enfield	31	Jul
(70)							
14:20.9	Kevin Howard		7.02.66	6	Brighton	10	Aug
14:21.67	Carl Leonard	U23	19.01.73		Philadelphia, USA	28	Apr
14:21.74	Dominic Bannister		1.04.68	3	Sheffield	15	May
14:22.6	John MacKay		22.08.60	1	Glasgow	24	Aug
14:23.8	Dave Swanston		30.11.61	1	Carlisle	28	May
14:23.9	Nigel Gemmell		30.09.63	7	Brighton	10	Aug
14:24.24	David Cowan		23.08.66	2	London (CP)	25	Jun
14:24.32	Colin Walker		29.10.62	1	Bedford	18	Sep
14:24.5	Peter Wilson		28.06.62	8	Brighton	10	Aug
14:25.68	Colin Reitz		6.04.60	3	Crawley	6	Aug
(80)							
14:25.7	Stephen Wylie		12.11.71	1	Linwood	1	May
14:25.84	Adrian Mussett	U23	14.04.72	4	London (CP)	25	Jun
14:25.86	*Dave Taylor*		*9.01.64*	*5*	*London (CP)*	*25*	*Jun*
14:26.01	Paul Green	U23	7.04.72	9	Corby	30	May
14:26.5	*Jamie Harrison*		*21.12.63*	*2*	*Enfield*	*31*	*Jul*
14:26.5	Peter Tootell		12.03.63	2	Cannock	11	Sep

14:27.02	Ian Hamilton		8.03.65	6	London (CP)	25	Jun
14:27.49	Nigel Gates	V40	18.05.53	7	London (CP)	25	Jun
14:28.1	Julian Moorhouse		13.11.71	2	Kingston	4	Jun
14:28.3	Adrian Green		30.05.68	10	Brighton	10	Aug
14:28.4	Dale Laughlin		28.12.66	1	London (TB)	30	Jul
14:28.9	Kevin Goddard		18.11.64	7	Crawley	28	May
(90)							
14:28.9	Dave Knight		7.12.64	11	Brighton	10	Aug
14:30.04	Neil Panchen		30.10.69	2	Wigan	7	May
14:31.13	Gary Bishop		3.08.63	11	Corby	30	May
14:31.56	*Mark Goddard*		*12.01.64*	*4*	*Crawley*	*6*	*Aug*
14:32.5	Kevin Blake		29.05.67	3	Bracknell	7	May
14:33.3	Ben Noad	U20	6.05.76	3	Cannock	7	May
14:33.59	Ian Campbell		6.09.71	3	London (WL)	2	Jul
14:34.05	Mike Quinn		21.01.63	4	London (WL)	2	Jul
14:34.72	David Farrell		29.06.64	12	Corby	30	May
14:34.8	Nick Commerford		23.04.66	4	Enfield	31	Jul
14:35.22	*Ian Harpur*		*24.04.67*	*22*	*Sheffield*	*12*	*Jun*
14:35.26	Wayne Oxborough		10.11.66	10	London (CP)	25	Jun
(100)							
14:35.27	Roger Alsop		16.01.65	11	London (CP)	25	Jun
14:35.5	William Coyle		3.10.62	4	Grangemouth	3	Aug
14:35.71	N. Braithwaite			13	Corby	30	May

Additional Under 20 (1 - 2 above)

14:40.4	Kris Bowditch		14.01.75	3	Bournemouth	7	May
14:42.6	David Connelly		6.02.76	3	Glasgow	24	Aug
14:59.3	Matthew Young		17.03.76	1	Oxford	4	Jun
15:01.2	Michael Green		12.10.76		Carlisle	6	Aug
15:05.00	Ian Pierce		13.11.75	24	Sheffield	12	Jun
15:06.1	William Levett		6.09.75	1	London (TB)	20	Jul
15:09.0	David Simpson		25.04.75	2	Antrim	30	Apr
15:09.6	Matt O'Dowd		13.04.76	1	Carn Brea	13	Aug
(10)							
15:11.65	Andres Jones		3.02.77	5	Oordegem, BEL	9	Jul
15:13.2	John Pike			1	Lincoln	22	May
15:16.88	Kevin Holland		11.09.75	7	Bedford	3	Jul

10000 METRES

28:03.34	Rob Denmark		23.11.68	1	Sheffield	11	Jun
	28:20.65			3	London (CP)	9	Sep
28:17.00	Justin Hobbs		12.03.69	10	Helsinki, FIN	29	Jun
	28:45.86			3	Sheffield	11	Jun
28:25.60	Gary Staines		3.07.63	15	Helsinki, FIN	7	Aug
28:33.18	Martin Jones		21.04.67	2	Sheffield	11	Jun
	29:08.53			4	Victoria, CAN	27	Aug
28:46.50	Eamonn Martin		9.10.58	6	St. Petersburg, RUS	24	Jul
	29:15.81			6	Victoria, CAN	27	Aug
28:47.17	Barry Royden		15.12.66	4	Sheffield	11	Jun
28:49.96	Carl Udall		13.07.66	5	Sheffield	11	Jun
28:51.12	Chris Robison		16.03.61	6	Sheffield	11	Jun
28:53.03	Richard Nerurkar		6.01.64	4	Seville, SPA	5	Jun
28:55.57	Martin McLoughlin		23.12.58	7	Sheffield	11	Jun
(10)							
29:12.35	Tommy Murray		18.05.61	1	Edinburgh	24	Jun
29:14.91	Andrew Pearson		14.09.71	1	Sheffield	4	Sep
29:15.11	Paul Roden		18.04.65	2	Sheffield	4	Sep
29:16.29	Bashir Hussain		20.12.64	8	Sheffield	11	Jun
29:17.32	Colin Moore		25.11.60	9	Sheffield	11	Jun

19 performances to 29:20.0 by 15 athletes

29:30.84	*Jamie Harrison*		*21.12.63*		*Sydney, AUS*	*10 Mar*
29:32.29	Alan Puckrin		2.04.64	2	Edinburgh	24 Jun
29:34.50	Dominic Bannister		1.04.68	10	Sheffield	11 Jun
29:35.57	Mark Hudspith		19.01.69	11	Sheffield	11 Jun
29:37.75	Steve Brooks		8.06.70	1	Lawrence, USA	20 May
29:43.20	Mark Croasdale		10.01.60	2	Corby	30 May
(20)						
29:46.24	Toby Tanser		21.07.68	1	Stockholm, SWE	24 Sep
29:49.2	*John Lisiewicz*		*18.07.62*	*1*	*Oxford*	*17 Sep*
29:49.63	*Ian Harpur*		*24.04.67*	*3*	*Corby*	*30 May*
29:52.06	Simon Kinson		1.01.71	4	Corby	30 May
29:52.5	Steve Knight		17.10.63	1	Enfield	31 Jul
30:06.53	Ian Robinson		21.04.69	3	Lawrence, USA	20 May
30:11.0	*Amin Koikai*	U23	*74*	*1*	*Ilford*	*13 Sep*
30:12.91	Stephen Green		28.07.70	14	Sheffield	11 Jun
30:19.61	Wayne Oxborough		10.11.66	5	Corby	30 May
30:25.03	Alan Robson		14.11.59	3	Edinburgh	24 Jun
30:26.74	Peter Dymoke		30.10.61	4	Edinburgh	24 Jun
30:27.13	David Miles		16.11.65	1	Bedford	18 Sep
30:28.59	Steve Murdoch		16.04.61	2	Bedford	18 Sep
(30)						
30:29.3	William Coyle		3.10.62	1	Coatbridge	12 Jun
30:32.14	Julian Gentry		19.05.69	6	Corby	30 May
30:33.62	Ray Smedley	V40	30.09.51	7	Corby	30 May
30:35.03	Shaun Tobin		13.10.62	2	Istanbul, TUR	21 May
30:37.1	Dave Gratton		25.10.55	1	Hull	30 Apr
30:37.33	Gary Gerrard		7.07.63	15	Sheffield	11 Jun
30:40.8	Nick Francis		29.08.71	1	London (CP)	27 Apr
30:41.3	Gareth Deacon		8.08.66	1	Leicester	16 Aug
30:42.9	Nick McCaffrey		26.06.68	2	Leicester	16 Aug
30:48.3	Derek Green		13.06.58	1	Oxford	8 Jun
(40)						
30:49.70	Trevor Clark		29.04.56	8	Corby	30 May
30:49.72	Andrew Little		1.01.64	5	Edinburgh	24 Jun
30:51.7	Mark Smith		30.10.63	1	Blackburn	1 May
30:52.9	Donal Gallagher	U23	5.12.72	1	Belfast	19 Aug
30:53.8	John Matthews		29.12.64	2	London (CP)	27 Apr
30:53.91	Alaister Russell		17.06.68	1	Edinburgh	22 May
30:56.4	Colin Reitz		6.04.60	1	Kingston	31 Jul
30:58.92	Martin Ferguson		17.09.64	6	Edinburgh	24 Jun
30:59.6	Andi Drake		6.02.65	2	Kingston	31 Jul
31:02.01	Graeme Wight		3.06.65	1	Edinburgh	24 Apr
(50)						
31:02.44	Charlie Thomson		17.06.65	1	Edinburgh	14 Aug
31:04.8	Alan Reid		19.04.66	1	Inverness	17 Sep
31:05.6	Wayne Speake		11.02.64	1	Yeovil	7 May
31:05.9	Nick Peach		18.10.59	1	Liverpool	3 Sep
31:07.0	Jerry Weightman		28.01.63	3	London (CP)	27 Apr
31:07.6	Eamon Grimes		11.01.64	4	London (CP)	27 Apr
31:07.9	Gary Bishop		3.08.63	1	Corby	31 Jul
31:08.0	Chris Smales		10.10.63	3	Leeds	21 Jun
31:09.6	Darren Reilly		19.09.65	1	Liverpool	24 Aug
31:09.85	Paul Cadwallader		23.10.62	9	Corby	30 May
(60)						
31:09.96	Ken Penney		26.01.63	8	Malaga, SPA	29 May
31:10.3	Ken Conley		24.12.61	2	Corby	31 Jul
31:10.4	*Adri Hartveld*		*7.10.59*	*1*	*Stoke*	*31 Jul*
31:10.8	Ashley Long		11.04.62	3	Leicester	16 Aug
31:10.8	G. Longley			4	Leicester	16 Aug

10 KILOMETRES Road

Time	Name		DOB	Pos	Venue	Date
28:23	Paul Evans		13.04.61	1	Cardiff	31 Jul
28:45				3	Coventry	16 Oct
28:24	Martin Jones		21.04.67	4	Leipzig, GER	8 Oct
28:25	Richard Nerurkar		6.01.64	2	Cardiff	31 Jul
28:27	Jon Brown		27.02.71	5	New Orleans, USA	16 Apr
28:41				9	Mobile, USA	26 Mar
28:55				2	Marietta, USA	5 Sep
28:32	Paul Taylor		9.01.66	2	Bangor	17 Sep
28:54				5	Barnsley	6 Nov
28:38	Mark Flint		19.02.63	4	Cardiff	31 Jul
28:40	Gary Staines		3.07.63	1	Coventry	16 Oct
28:41	David Lewis		15.10.61	2	Coventry	16 Oct
28:56				1	Edinburgh	2 Oct
28:44	Andrew Pearson		14.09.71	2	Barnsley	6 Nov
28:59				4	Swansea	11 Sep
28:46	John Sherban		30.07.64	1	Grangemouth	20 Feb
(10)						
28:49	Martin McLoughlin		23.12.58	5	Cardiff	31 Jul
28:54	Carl Udall		13.07.66	2	Swansea	11 Sep
28:54	Keith Cullen	U23	13.06.72	4	Barnsley	6 Nov
29:05	*Kassa Tadesse*	U23	*21.08.74*	*3*	*Edinburgh*	*2 Oct*
29:06	Keith Anderson		10.08.57	7	Barnsley	6 Nov
29:07	*David Burke*		*68*	*1*	*Eastleigh*	*20 Mar*
29:07	Justin Hobbs		12.03.69	1	Brighton	20 Nov
29:11	Barry Royden		15.12.66	7	Coventry	16 Oct
29:13	Adrian Passey		2.09.64	8	Coventry	16 Oct
29:14	Mark Hudspith		19.01.69	7	Cardiff	31 Jul
29:14	Peter Whitehead		3.12.64	9	Barnsley	6 Nov
29:16	Glyn Tromans		17.03.69	9	Coventry	16 Oct
(20)						
29:19	Ian Hamer		18.04.65	8	Cardiff	31 Jul
29:27	Spencer Duval		5.01.70	4	Belfast	9 Apr
29:27	Dale Laughlin		28.12.66	3	Redditch	20 Aug
29:27	Bashir Hussain		20.12.64	3	Bangor	17 Sep
29:29	Tommy Murray		18.05.61	1	Greenock	2 Aug
29:30	Alan Jackson			2	Llanrwst	14 Aug
29:31	Darren Mead		4.10.68	4	Redditch	20 Aug
29:31	John Ferrin		20.02.67	4	Bangor	17 Sep
29:32	Colin Reitz		6.04.60	5	Redditch	20 Aug
29:32	Dermot Donnelly		23.09.70	1		3 Dec
(30)						
29:33	Rob Birchall		14.06.70	6	Redditch	20 Aug
29:34	Andy Green		14.12.62	1	Loughborough	27 Feb
29:34	Mike Simpson		6.01.70	1	Aylesbury	10 Aug
29:35	Jim Campbell		17.06.70	2		3 Dec
29:36	Eamonn Martin		9.10.58	1	Southend	16 Oct
29:37	Larry Matthews		11.08.65	2	Eastleigh	20 Mar
29:37	Dave Swanston		30.11.61	1	South Shields	17 Apr
29:38	Simon Rayner		28.02.64		Pontoise, FRA	13 Nov
29:39	Tom Buckner		16.04.63	13	Coventry	16 Oct
29:40	Dave Knight		7.12.64	3	Eastleigh	20 Mar
(40)						
29:41	Dave Buzza		6.12.62	9	Cardiff	31 Jul
29:42	Peter McColgan		20.02.63	14	Coventry	16 Oct
29:43	Dave Payne		19.06.66	7	Redditch	20 Aug
29:43	David Miles		16.11.65	16	Barnsley	6 Nov
29:43	*Jamie Harrison*		*21.12.63*	*2*	*Brighton*	*20 Nov*
29:44	John MacKay		22.08.60	1	Leeds	4 Dec
29:45	Dave Clarke		1.01.58	15	Coventry	16 Oct
29:46	Richard Findlow		4.12.66	17	Barnsley	6 Nov

10 MILES Road

47:00	Gary Staines		3.07.63	1	Portsmouth	9	Oct
47:52	Martin McLoughlin		23.12.58	4	Amsterdam, HOL	18	Sep
47:56	Carl Udall		13.07.66	3	Erewash	4	Sep
48:07	Tom Buckner		16.04.63	5	Portsmouth	9	Oct
48:09	Chris Buckley		26.07.61	1	Woking	6	Mar
48:09	*Jamie Lewis*		*8.03.69*	*4*	*Erewash*	*4*	*Sep*
48:19	Paul Davies-Hale		21.06.62	6	Erewash	4	Sep
48:22	Peter Whitehead		3.12.64	6	Portsmouth	9	Oct
48:27	Steve Brace		7.07.61	7	Portsmouth	9	Oct
48:27	Dave Clarke		1.01.58	8	Portsmouth	9	Oct
48:30	Paul Roden		18.04.65	1	Clitheroe	13	Mar
	(10)						
48:31	John Edwards		12.06.65	2	Woking	6	Mar
48:31	Paul Evans		13.04.61	1	Maidenhead	1	Apr
48:35	Peter Tootell		12.03.63	1	Stockport	4	Dec
48:37	Mark Flint		19.02.63	1	Stoke	5	Jun
48:37	Paul Freary		3.04.68	2	Stockport	4	Dec
48:45	*Kassa Tadesse*	U23	*21.08.74*	*7*	*Erewash*	*4*	*Sep*
48:49	Gareth Davies		25.08.62	3	Woking	6	Mar
48:54	Alan Jackson			2	Chelmsley Wood	2	Oct
48:57	Larry Matthews		11.08.65	4	Woking	6	Mar
48:59	Dave Payne		19.06.66	8	Erewash	4	Sep
48:59	Steve Harris		17.11.61	1	Worthing	4	Dec
	(20)						
49:04	Mark Croasdale		10.01.60	1	Newbury	11	Sep
49:06	Terry Booth		19.10.66	5	Woking	6	Mar
49:07	*Jamie Harrison*		*21.12.63*	*9*	*Portsmouth*	*9*	*Oct*
49:09	Darren Mead		4.10.68	10	Erewash	4	Sep
49:15	Mike Simpson		6.01.70	10	Portsmouth	9	Oct
49:24	Geoff Hill		8.02.63	11	Erewash	4	Sep
49:26	Colin Reitz		6.04.60	2	Newbury	11	Sep
49:31	Greg Newhams		27.07.58	6	Woking	6	Mar
49:31	Dave Knight		7.12.64	3	Newbury	11	Sep
49:31	Tony O'Brien		14.11.70	1	Carlisle	19	Nov
49:32	Gary Nagel		4.06.62	12	Erewash	4	Sep
	(30)						
49:34	Dave Hill	V40	31.12.50	13	Erewash	4	Sep
49:34	Robin Nash		9.02.59	14	Erewash	4	Sep
49:37	Alan Guilder		10.12.61	4	Newbury	11	Sep
49:38	*Mark Goddard*		*12.01.64*	*15*	*Erewash*	*4*	*Sep*
49:39	David Tune		29.10.70	1	Ferriby	6	Feb

Downhill

48:15	Tommy Murray		18.05.61	1	Motherwell	10	Apr
48:39	Brian Kirkwood	V40	20.09.52	2	Motherwell	10	Apr
49:31	William Coyle		3.10.62	3	Motherwell	10	Apr

HALF MARATHON

1:01:30	Paul Evans	13.04.61	4	South Shields	18	Sep
1:02:25	Barry Royden	15.12.66	5	South Shields	18	Sep
1:02:37	Rob Denmark	23.11.68	6	South Shields	18	Sep
1:02:45	Martin McLoughlin	23.12.58	29	Oslo, NOR	24	Sep
1:03:03	David Lewis	15.10.61	5	The Hague, HOL	27	Mar
1:03:03	Peter Whitehead	3.12.64	7	Honolulu, USA	10	Dec
1:03:05	Martin Jones	21.04.67	10	South Shields	18	Sep
1:03:26	John Edwards	12.06.65	1	Malta	20	Feb
1:03:33	Colin Moore	25.11.60	10	The Hague, HOL	27	Mar
1:03:36	Carl Udall	13.07.66	47	Oslo, NOR	24	Sep
	(10)					

1:03:37	Mark Hudspith		19.01.69	1	York	27	Mar
1:03:44	Chris Buckley		26.07.61	1	Bath	20	Mar
1:03:50	Peter Fleming		5.01.61	6	Philadelphia, USA	18	Sep
1:03:54	*Kassa Tadesse*	*U23*	*21.08.74*	*3*	*St. Neots*	*29*	*May*
1:03:54	Eamonn Martin		9.10.58	11	South Shields	18	Sep
1:03:56	Steve Jones		4.08.55	20	Lisbon, POR	13	Mar
1:04:08	Steve Brace		7.07.61	2	Bath	20	Mar
1:04:11	*Jamie Lewis*		*8.03.69*	*5*	*Porto, POR*	*2*	*Oct*
1:04:19	Dale Rixon		8.07.66	2	Malta	20	Feb
1:04:26	Andy Green		14.12.62	1	Londonderry	24	Sep
1:04:30	Andrew Pearson		14.09.71	60	Oslo, NOR	24	Sep
1:04:31	Ian Archbold		10.06.65	1	Worcester	20	Mar
	(20)						
1:04:38	John Ferrin		20.02.67	2	Londonderry	24	Sep
1:04:41	Mark Croasdale		10.01.60	61	Oslo, NOR	24	Sep
1:04:44	Paul Rowan		20.03.66	3	Londonderry	24	Sep
1:04:47	Colin Walker		29.10.62	1	Newcastle	1	Jan
1:04:48	Tony Graham			14	South Shields	18	Sep
1:04:50	Paul Roden		18.04.65	1	Liverpool	21	Aug
1:04:53	Keith Anderson		10.08.57	3	York	27	Mar
1:04:57	Mark Flint		19.02.63	5	Hastings	13	Mar
1:05:18	Maurice Cowman		21.09.59	18	South Shields	18	Sep
1:05:20	Bill Foster		9.08.58	4	York	27	Mar
	(30)						
1:05:25	Paul Davies-Hale		21.06.62	2	Liverpool	21	Aug
1:05:28	*Amin Koikai*	*U23*	*74*	*19*	*South Shields*	*18*	*Sep*
1:05:38	Tommy Murray		18.05.61	9	Glasgow	21	Aug
1:05:41	*Jamie Harrison*		*21.12.63*	*1*	*Nottingham*	*25*	*Sep*
1:05:43	Tim Rudd		27.05.61	2	Lake Vyrnwy	25	Sep

MARATHON

2:11:05	Eamonn Martin		9.10.58	8	London	17	Apr
2:11:56	Richard Nerurkar		6.01.64	4	Helsinki, FIN	14	Aug
2:12:07	Mark Flint		19.02.63	11	London	17	Apr
2:12:23	Steve Brace		7.07.61	13	London	17	Apr
2:14:43				3	Houston, USA	16	Jan
2:17:13				1	Dublin, IRE	31	Oct
2:12:52	Mark Hudspith		19.01.69	17	London	17	Apr
2:15:11				3	Victoria, CAN	28	Aug
2:13:34	Colin Moore		25.11.60	1	Houston, USA	16	Jan
2:18:07				8	Victoria, CAN	28	Aug
2:13:40	Peter Whitehead		3.12.64	22	London	17	Apr
2:16:40				27	Helsinki, FIN	16	Aug
2:14:03	Peter Fleming		5.01.61	1	Naaldwijk, HOL	19	Mar
2:17:33				14	Eindhoven, HOL	9	Oct
2:14:52	Robin Nash		9.02.59	17	Berlin, GER	25	Sep
2:15:41	Dale Rixon		8.07.66	26	London	17	Apr
2:16:15				4	Victoria, CAN	28	Aug
	(10)						
2:15:46	Mike O'Reilly		23.04.58	27	London	17	Apr
2:17:48				26	Fukuoka, JAP	4	Dec
2:16:48	Paul Davies-Hale		21.06.62	20	Berlin, GER	25	Sep
2:16:55	Andy Green		14.12.62	3	Honolulu, USA	11	Dec
2:17:12	Bill Foster		9.08.58	31	Helsinki, FIN	14	Aug
2:17:16				29	London	17	Apr
2:17:40	Steve Jones		4.08.55	32	Boston, USA	18	Apr
2:17:42	Ian Bloomfield	V40	23.11.52	33	Boston, USA	18	Apr
2:17:59	Hugh Jones		1.11.55	2	Graz, AUT	23	Oct
2:18:20				7	Stockholm, SWE	5	Jun
2:19:06				6	Orlando, USA	16	Jan

2:18:04	Mark Croasdale		10.01.60	32	London	17 Apr
2:18:42	Trevor Clark		29.04.56	36	London	17 Apr
2:19:34	Wayne Buxton		16.04.62	8	Seville, SPA	27 Feb
	(20)					
2:19:38	Greg Newhams		27.07.58	39	London	17 Apr
2:19:46	Gareth Davies		25.08.62	40	London	17 Apr
2:19:52	Paul Roden		18.04.65	29	Berlin, GER	25 Sep
	34 performances to 2:20:0 by 23 athletes					
2:20:24	John Edwards		12.06.65	41	London	17 Apr
2:20:24	Terry Mitchell		23.08.59	1	Belfast	2 May
2:21:06	Tim Rudd		27.05.61	44	London	17 Apr
2:21:07	John Ferrin		20.02.67	45	London	17 Apr
2:21:10	Nick Rose	V40	30.12.51	46	London	17 Apr
2:21:19	Geoff Wightman		19.11.60	25	Minneapolis/St Paul, USA	20 Oct
2:21:40	Mike Greally		18.06.60	2	Florence, ITA	4 Dec
	(30)					
2:21:43	Dan Rathbone		9.04.69	51	Boston, USA	18 Apr
2:21:57	Chris Buckley		26.07.61	1	Chiswick	25 Sep
2:22:18	Paul Froud		6.04.66	48	London	17 Apr
2:22:23	Dave Mansbridge		4.06.64	4	Calvia, SPA	4 Dec
2:22:28	Charlie Thomson		17.06.65	50	London	17 Apr
2:22:49	Mark Cooper			2	Belfast	2 May
2:22:51	Mark King		16.09.62	16	Caen, FRA	12 Jun
2:22:51	Dave Grover		11.04.65	5	Dublin, IRE	31 Oct
2:22:56	*Adri Hartveld*		*7.10.59*	*2*	*Chiswick*	*25 Sep*
2:23:06	Gregor Booth	U23	31.08.72	9	Las Vegas, USA	5 Feb
2:23:08	Fraser Clyne		23.08.55	1	Loch Rannoch	19 Jun
	(40)					
2:23:12	*Eddie Hyland*		*23.07.60*	*6*	*Dublin, IRE*	*31 Oct*
2:23:14	Shaun Tobin		13.10.62	17	Caen, FRA	12 Jun
2:23:25	Mark Hargreaves		26.08.60	52	London	17 Apr
2:23:32	Mark Roberts		12.02.59	1	Stoke	19 Jun
2:23:37	John Stephens		13.02.58	55	London	17 Apr
2:23:40	Geoff Jerwood		1.10.58	56	London	17 Apr
2:23:49	Paul Simons		4.04.64	1	Harrow	5 Nov
2:23:57	Gary Spring		20.08.63	57	London	17 Apr
2:24:07	Paul Smith	V40	12.08.54	60	London	17 Apr
2:24:09	Peter Dymoke		30.10.61	8	Dublin, IRE	31 Oct
2:24:25	Alan Guilder		10.12.61	61	London	17 Apr
	(50)					
2:24:26	Alan Chilton		16.04.71	62	London	17 Apr
2:24:30	Robbie Bryson		14.04.62	4	Belfast	2 May
2:24:38	John Wieczorek		22.11.66	64	London	17 Apr
2:24:49	Gary McIlroy		6.04.67	65	London	17 Apr
2:24:50	Stephen Stafford		6.03.59	66	London	17 Apr
2:25:00	Basil Brown		19.02.58	2	Harrow	6 Nov
2:25:06	Bob Rollins		18.05.61	2	Nottingham	25 Sep
2:25:06	Russell Phillips		2.09.58	6	Florence, ITA	4 Dec
2:25:08	Brian Bewick		1.11.65	67	London	17 Apr
2:25:09	Tony Barden		15.10.60	68	London	17 Apr
	(60)					
2:25:09	Bill Gristwood		20.03.59	69	London	17 Apr
2:25:16	Sam Doherty		10.11.59	35	Belgrade, YUG	23 Apr
2:25:17	Martin Armstrong		14.03.66	36	Belgrade, YUG	23 Apr
2:25:22	Jim Estall		9.08.54	70	London	17 Apr
2:25:31	Malcolm Fowler		30.01.63	7	Florence, ITA	4 Dec
2:25:47	Andy Magnall		1.03.62	72	London	17 Apr
2:26:04	Kevin O'Connor		20.04.67	73	London	17 Apr
2:26:07	Paul Bettridge		27.02.57	75	London	17 Apr
2:26:10	Ken Penney		26.01.63	76	London	17 Apr
2:26:14	Phillip Smith		26.05.64	3	Nottingham	25 Sep

2:26:22	Ieuan Ellis		11.05.60	1	Leeds	17	Jul
2:26:28	Tony Robinson		15.06.59	79	London	17	Apr
2:26:38	David Robertson		11.09.61	81	London	17	Apr
2:26:45	Ian Higginbottom		19.08.63	82	London	17	Apr
2:26:49	Bill Speake		24.01.71	83	London	17	Apr
2:26:51	Peter Probin	V45	15.07.47	84	London	17	Apr
2:26:56	Duncan Hurdwell		24.04.62	85	London	17	Apr
2:26:59	Steve Wheeler		3.04.61	86	London	17	Apr
2:27:06	Vince Clisham			4	Nottingham	25	Sep
2:27:11	Dave Lancaster		12.03.57	46	Rotterdam, HOL	18	Apr
	(80)						
2:27:12	Mike McGeoch		15.08.55	89	London	17	Apr
2:27:23	Andy Wetherill		6.12.57	90	London	17	Apr
2:27:25	John Boyes		9.05.58	91	London	17	Apr
2:27:29	Billy Nixon		9.02.68	13	Dublin, IRE	31	Oct
2:27:30	John Parker		31.10.54	92	London	17	Apr
2:27:33	Phil Lowery		4.08.63	93	London	17	Apr
2:27:36	Mike Girvan	V40	16.03.54	94	London	17	Apr
2:27:37	Mark Cursons		10.03.62	95	London	27	Apr
2:27:38	Martin Ferguson		17.09.64	96	London	17	Apr
2:27:39	Simon Lund		22.12.65	97	London	17	Apr
	(90)						
2:27:40	Steve Robinson		9.10.57	3	Chiswick	25	Sep
2:27:45	Eric Williams		6.05.56	3	Stoke	19	Jun
2:27:50	John Redmond		15.10.57	99	London	17	Apr
2:27:55	Bernard Gaffney		8.06.61	102	London	17	Apr
2:28:05	Peter Embleton	V40	16.04.54	103	London	17	Apr
2:28:09	James Bennett		12.11.57	104	London	17	Apr
2:28:12	Greg Dell		20.11.64	105	London	17	Apr
2:28:13	Pat Howdle		25.04.60	106	London	17	Apr
2:28:15	Richard Beaumont		2.05.71	107	London	17	Apr
2:28:21	Chris Webb		3.08.63	109	London	17	Apr
	(100)						
2:28:22	Derek Green		13.06.58	1	Abingdon	23	Oct
2:28:27	Aidan Roberts		25.08.56	110	London	17	Apr
2:28:28	Neil Moore		1.04.61	111	London	17	Apr

100 KILOMETRES (Road)

6:53:06	Erik Seedhouse		19.06.64		L'Aunis, FRA	12	Mar
7:11:29	Greg Dell		20.11.64		Saroma, JAP	26	Jun
7:13:37	Patrick Macke		18.06.55		Winschoten, HOL	3	Sep
7:18:46	Steve Moore	V45	17.12.47		Winschoten, HOL	3	Sep
7:29:46	Don Ritchie	V50	6.07.44		Victoria, CAN	31	Aug
7:35:03	Paul Taylor			1	Greenwich	8	May
7:40:47	Robin Gardner			2	Greenwich	8	May
7:56:18	Mick Francis		18.09.58		North Otago, NZL	31	Dec

24 HOURS (Track)

236.861	Don Ritchie	V50	6.07.44	London (TB)	22	Oct
226.179	James Zarei	V50	12.01.44	Guangzhou, CHN	7	May
222.720	Geoff Oliver			Doncaster	28	May
218.000	Bob Littlewood			London (TB)	22	Oct
217.718	Stephen Till			Hull	16	Jul
205.012	Mike Aris			Doncaster	28	May

24 HOURS (Road)

243.340	James Zarei	V50	12.01.44		Szeged	21	May
210.922	Brian Bosher			1	Bury	18	Sep
210.735	Mick Francis		18.09.58		Szeged	21	May

166

1500 METRES STEEPLECHASE - Under 17

4:18.20	Robert Brown		3.03.78	1	Birmingham	31	Jul
4:23.5	James Calvert		5.11.77	1	London (CP)	15	May
4:23.9	Mark Anderson		1.02.78	1	Stretford	15	May
4:24.2	Gavin Conway		1.09.77	1	Enfield	14	Aug
4:24.62	Stuart Bailey		6.08.78	2	Blackpool	14	Aug
4:25.20	Tim Davis		25.01.78	2	Telford	9	Jul
4:25.5	David Anderson		2.10.77	1r1	Whitley Bay	17	Jul
4:26.0	James Hunter		19.11.77	1	Yate	22	May
4:26.0	Michael East		20.01.78	1	Portsmouth	11	Jun
4:28.13	Paul Martin		10.07.78	3	Birmingham	31	Jul
	(10)						
4:29.3	Daniel Barron		17.01.78	1r1	Hull	1	May
4:29.7	Gavin Maley		19.05.78	1r1	London (He)	26	Jun
4:30.12	Shane Jay		12.01.78	3	Telford	9	Jul
4:30.98	Mark Wheeler		9.05.78	5	Telford	9	Jul
4:31.2	Simon Marwood		6.04.78	1r1	Manchester	1	May
4:31.69	Adrian Boyle		27.09.77	3	Aberdeen	16	Jul
4:34.42	Luke Hunt		8.10.77	4	London (CP)	28	May
4:34.6	Simon Type		1.02.78	1	Colwyn Bay	2	Jul
4:34.7	David Moore		25.04.79	1	Bebington	11	Jun
4:34.95	David Mitchenson		4.09.78	7	Telford	9	Jul
	(20)						
4:35.3	Tom Green		11.12.77	1	Coventry	17	Jul
4:35.45	Tom Cairns		20.02.78	4	Aberdeen	16	Jul
4:35.7	Jim Cook			2	Colwyn Bay	27	Jul
4:37.05	Jamie Muir		30.04.78	2	Gateshead	28	May
4:37.9	Mark Land			4h1	Birmingham	30	Jul

2000 METRES STEEPLECHASE

5:42.92	Keith Cullen	U23	13.06.72	1	Loughborough	5	Jun
5:45.11	Spencer Newport		5.10.66	2	Loughborough	5	Jun
5:45.40	Steve Wright		12.02.71	3	Loughborough	5	Jun
5:49.3	Nicholas Overton		18.12.61	1	Sheffield	15	Jun
5:49.96	Ben Reese	U20	29.03.76	1	Telford	9	Jul
5:51.00	Chris Elliott	U20	29.05.75	4	Loughborough	5	Jun
5:51.4	Dave Lee		16.09.65	1	Loughborough	27	Apr
5:51.5	Mike Jubb		20.06.70	2	Sheffield	15	Jun
5:52.7	Lee Hurst	U23	29.07.72	1	Stretford	12	Jul
5:53.5	Stuart Stokes	U20	15.12.76	1	Manchester	11	Jun
	(10)						
5:53.5	Craig Wheeler	U20	14.06.76	2	Manchester	11	Jun
5:54.07	Jon Sear		3.04.64	1	Bracknell	2	May
5:54.16	Stuart Overthrow	U20	13.06.75	2	Telford	9	Jul
5:54.93	Peter Haynes		18.09.64	2	Bracknell	2	May

Additional Under 20 (1 - 5 above)

5:55.89	Matt O'Dowd		13.04.76	6	Loughborough	5	Jun
5:56.42	Andy Fooks		26.04.75	7	Loughborough	5	Jun
5:56.9	David Connelly		6.02.76	1	Exeter	20	Aug
6:00.0	Mark McGarry		16.02.77	1r1	Derby	18	Sep
6:00.97	Kevin Nash		6.02.77	2	London (CP)	28	May
	(10)						
6:04.1	Simon Lewis		31.08.75	1	Nottingham	15	May
6:04.3	Andrew Blackmore		12.07.76	1	Telford	11	Jun

2 Barriers Short

5:53.73	Stuart Overthrow	U20	13.06.75	1	Solihull	29	May
6:00.61	Simon Lewis	U20	31.08.75	2	Solihull	29	May

3000 METRES STEEPLECHASE

8:20.04	Tom Hanlon		20.05.67	9	Monaco, MON	2	Aug
8:27.74				9	Stockholm, SWE	12	Jul
8:29.74				3	Edinburgh	8	Jul
8:31.50				5h1	Helsinki, FIN	9	Aug
8:36.06				10	Helsinki, FIN	12	Aug
8:22.20	Mark Rowland		7.03.63	8	Berlin, GER	30	Aug
8:26.00				4	Helsinki, FIN	12	Aug
8:29.51				2	Edinburgh	8	Jul
8:30.24				3h1	Helsinki, FIN	9	Aug
8:32.65				12	Monaco, MON	2	Aug
8:41.45				1	Gateshead	20	Jul
8:47.58				1	Madras, IND	5	Feb
8:23.90	Justin Chaston		4.11.68	9	Nice, FRA	18	Jul
8:28.28				1	Sheffield	12	Jun
8:29.49				6	St. Petersburg, RUS	25	Jul
8:29.99				3	Birmingham	26	Jun
8:31.0				1	Walnut, USA	16	Apr
8:31.08				7h2	Helsinki, FIN	9	Aug
8:32.20				7	Victoria, CAN	23	Aug
8:36.83				11	Helsinki, FIN	12	Aug
8:38.53				1	Istanbul, TUR	22	May
8:46.99				1h1	Sheffield	11	Jun
8:27.78	Colin Walker		29.10.62	4	Victoria, CAN	23	Aug
8:29.33				1	Edinburgh	8	Jul
8:29.65				3	Sheffield	12	Jun
8:37.46				1	Corby	30	May
8:41.14				4	London (CP)	10	Sep
8:44.40				2	Gateshead	20	Jul
8:47.81				1	Gateshead	15	May
8:28.33	Spencer Duval		5.01.70	2	Sheffield	12	Jun
8:28.63				1	Arhus, DEN	7	Jul
8:36.08				6	Hechtel, BEL	30	Jul
8:46.43				6	Granada, SPA	1	Jun
8:47.47				5	Gateshead	20	Jul
8:49.08				10	Victoria, CAN	23	Aug
8:29.84	Tom Buckner		16.04.63	5	Victoria, CAN	23	Aug
8:36.77				1	London (CP)	15	Jul
8:38.35				7	Edinburgh	8	Jul
8:49.16				6	Gateshead	20	Jul
8:38.39	Mick Hawkins		24.10.61	4	Sheffield	12	Jun
8:44.95				2	Corby	30	May
8:38.80	Robert Hough	U23	3.06.72	2	London (CP)	15	Jul
8:40.09				5	Sheffield	12	Jun
8:49.83				2h1	Sheffield	11	Jun
8:39.71	Keith Cullen	U23	13.06.72	3	London (CP)	15	Jul
8:40.79				1	Vasteras, SWE	30	Jun
8:42.94				8	Edinburgh	8	Jul
8:42.44	Neil Smart		12.05.63	6	Sheffield	12	Jun
8:49.82				1h2	Sheffield	11	Jun
(10)							
8:45.2	Dave Lee		16.09.65	5	Walnut, USA	16	Apr
8:45.45				4	London (CP)	15	Jul
8:46.23				7	Sheffield	12	Jun
8:48.60				1	London (CP)	7	May
8:47.00	Carl Warren		28.09.69	8	Sheffield	12	Jun
8:49.00	Graeme Croll		1.02.66	9	Sheffield	12	Jun
8:49.26	Ken Stirrat		1.03.70	10	Sheffield	12	Jun
8:49.4	Spencer Newport		5.10.66	1	Enfield	31	Jul
8:49.6				1	Liverpool	6	Aug
8:49.76	Darren Mead		4.10.68	1	Crawley	6	Aug

59 performances to 8:50.0 by 16 athletes

8:51.04	Kevin Howard			7.02.66	4h2	Sheffield	11 Jun
8:51.57	Adrian Green			30.05.68	2	Brussels, BEL	17 Jul
8:52.50	Steve Wright			12.02.71	5h1	Sheffield	11 Jun
8:54.88	Duncan Storey			17.09.68	2	Edinburgh	25 Jun
(20)							
8:57.4	Hugh Brasher			28.09.64	1	Bournemouth	7 May
8:57.8	Wayne Aylesbury			24.03.64	1	Barking	6 Aug
8:58.87	Jon Sear			3.04.64	2	Bedford	17 Sep
8:59.55	George Mathison			4.10.61	4	Edinburgh	25 Jun
8:59.57	Chris Elliott	U20		29.05.75	7h1	Sheffield	11 Jun
8:59.6	Matthew De Freitas			19.09.68	1	Aldershot	24 Jul
9:00.2	Simon Bell			26.12.66	2	Aldershot	24 Jul
9:00.2	Darren Preston	U23		19.12.74	3	Enfield	31 Jul
9:00.8	Billy Jenkins			13.07.71	1	Glasgow	14 Aug
9:01.44	Chris Stephenson	U23		22.07.74	1	Edinburgh	6 Aug
(30)							
9:02.2	Pat Miller			21.02.67	1	Stretford	10 May
9:02.40	Ben Rieper	U23		20.12.73	5	London (CP)	15 Jul
9:02.4	Phil Cook			7.05.69	2	Colwyn Bay	23 Jul
9:03.0	Barry Royden			15.12.66	3	Aldershot	24 Jul
9:03.61	Mike Jubb			20.06.70	2	Derby	16 Jul
9:04.2	Dan Duke			23.12.68	1	Yate	21 Aug
9:04.6	Sam Stevenson			20.12.63	1	Telford	20 Aug
9:04. ??	Steve Cairns			3.11.67	4	Aldershot	24 Jun
9:05.2	Tony O'Brien			14.11.70	3	Liverpool	6 Aug
9:05.32	James Austin			9.08.65	1	Edinburgh	14 Aug
(40)							
9:05.4	Darren Reilly			19.09.65	1	Kirkby	6 Aug
9:05.67	Peter Haynes			18.09.64	5	Corby	30 May
9:06.1	Martin Roscoe			19.09.64	2h1	Corby	29 May
9:06.5	Paul Northrop			15.01.70	1	Enfield	4 Jun
9:06.74	Michael Hutchinson			5.10.65	1	Birmingham	21 May
9:07.2	Sean Fenwick				2	Watford	14 Sep
9:07.27	Frank Boyne			28.02.66	1	Edinburgh	14 May
9:07.5	Kevin Usher			3.11.65	1	Kingston	4 Jun
9:07.60	Jason Humm			11.01.71	3	London (CP)	26 Jun
9:07.64	Lee Hurst	U23		29.07.72	8h1	Sheffield	11 Jun
(50)							
9:08.2	David Farrell			29.06.64	1	Wigan	2 Jul
9:08.7	Gerard Hargreaves				2	Kirkby	6 Aug
9:09.1	Ray Plant			13.05.68	1	Loughborough	20 Aug
9:09.24	Ben Reese	U20		29.03.76	7	Warsaw, POL	18 Jun
9:10.45	John Sherban			30.07.64	3	Bedford	17 Sep
9:10.50	Craig Wheeler	U20		14.06.76	2	Bedford	3 Jul
9:10.83	Matt O'Dowd	U20		13.04.76	3	Bedford	3 Jul
9:11.2	Graham Sunners	U23		26.03.73	2	Aldershot	6 Jul
9:11.6	Paddy Brice			8.02.69	1	Harrow	2 Jul
9:11.7	Jon Pavis			4.10.66	3	Wigan	2 Jul
(60)							
9:12.4	John Steel			27.02.63	1	Coatbridge	12 Jun
9:12.6	Graeme Saker			12.09.61	2	Bournemouth	7 May
9:12.70	Kerry Hayes			22.01.63	4	London (CP)	26 Jun
9:12.86	Quentin D'Arcy			5.06.67	3	Crawley	6 Aug
9:12.90	Mark Hirsch			12.04.68	5	Birmingham	21 May
9:13.3	Adam Clarke	U23		16.01.73	4	Bournemouth	7 May
9:13.46	Nicholas Overton			18.12.61	4h1	London (CP)	25 Jun
9:14.06	Ian Hobdell			30.07.68	5h1	London (CP)	25 Jun
9:14.32	Donald Lennon-Jones			9.05.68	2	Wigan	7 May
9:14.50	Phil LLewellyn			2.09.61	6	Wrexham	3 Jul
(70)							
9:14.5	Mike Hoey			29.04.69	2	Stoke	2 Jul
9:14.9	Tim Artus	U23		19.04.72	1	Loughborough	22 Jun
9:14.94	Paul Stelfox	U23		12.11.72	3	Wigan	7 May

9:15.0	Stephen Parr		18.03.59	3	Rotherham	7	May
9:15.16	Tim Hyde	U23	22.02.72	3	Edinburgh	6	Aug
9:16.49	Alex Moss	U23	21.09.72	4	Crawley	6	Aug
9:17.51	Kevin Downie		7.07.69	2	Edinburgh	14	Aug
9:17.53	David Connelly	U20	6.02.76	5	Bedford	3	Jul
9:17.58	Vince Garner		2.07.66	6h1	London (CP)	25	Jun
9:17.80	Kevin Nash	U20	6.02.77	6	Bedford	3	Jul
	(80)						
9:19.3	Peter Carpenter		15.09.64	7h1	Corby	29	May
9:19.4	Karl Palmer		5.02.66	3	Bracknell	7	May
9:19.4	Peter Banks		9.12.60	1	Carlisle	6	Aug
9:19.7	Andrew Morgan-Lee		1.03.69	2	Portsmouth	15	May
9:20.44	Paul Rowe		20.02.68	4	Wigan	7	May
9:20.61	Andy Fooks	U20	26.04.75	7h1	London (CP)	25	Jun
9:21.0	Michael Shackcloth			1	Blackburn	6	Aug
9:21.68	Martin Ferguson		17.09.64	5	Edinburgh	14	Aug
9:21.69	Cameron Watson		16.12.71	6	Edinburgh	14	Aug
9:21.8	Donald Naylor		5.09.71	3	Enfield	4	Jun
	(90)						
9:21.9	Mike Peters		1.10.60	1	Portsmouth	13	Aug
9:21.98	Kevin Tobin		14.07.59	4	Edinburgh	6	Aug
9:22.0	Darren Varker	U23	4.10.72	1	Plymouth	30	Jul
9:22.12	*John Lisiewicz*		*18.07.62*	*2*	*Gateshead*	*15*	*May*
9:22.6	Michael Cherrington		30.06.66	1	Kirkby	6	Aug
9:23.00	Jerry Weightman		28.01.63	6	Wigan	7	May
9:23.1	Eddie Broome	U23	3.09.72	1	Douglas, IOM	2	Jul
9:23.2	Martin Amor		22.09.68	1	Liverpool	7	May
9:23.21	Harvey Cossell	U23	1.12.74	7	London (CP)	2	May
9:24.2	Eddie Tonner	U23	3.02.73	3	Yate	21	Aug
9:24.4	Martin Gibbs		13.04.64	1	St. Ives	13	Aug
	(100)						
9:24.46	Andy Eynon		1.09.63	5	Edinburgh	6	Aug
9:25.1	Anthony Algeo	U23	22.01.73	4	Yate	21	Aug
9:25.72	Andy Coleman	U23	29.09.74	6	Edinburgh	6	Aug
9:25.8	Graeme Riley		11.01.60	1	Portsmouth (RN)	7	May
9:25.82	Lewis Jackson		12.02.71	10h2	Sheffield	11	Jun

Additional Under 20 (1 - 7 above)

9:29.62	Stuart Overthrow		13.06.75	6	Birmingham	21	May
9:32.56	Stuart Brown		16.09.76	8	Bedford	3	Jul
9:36.96	Conor Curran		15.02.75	1	Antrim	31	Jul
	(10)						
9:41.5	Steven Gay		6.01.77	1	Salisbury	7	May
9:43.89	Simon Lewis		31.08.75	6h1	Bedford	3	Jul
9:46.73	Iain Robertson		23.06.75	7h1	Bedford	2	Jul
9:49.88	Ian Westgate		24.10.76	7h2	Bedford	2	Jul

60 METRES HURDLES - Indoor

7.30	Colin Jackson	18.02.67	1	Sindelfingen, GER	6	Mar
7.36			1	Glasgow	12	Feb
7.38			1	Ghent, BEL	9	Feb
7.38			1h2	Birmingham	26	Feb
7.38			1	Birmingham	26	Feb
7.39			1s2	Paris, FRA	12	Mar
7.41			1	Paris, FRA	12	Mar
7.42			1	Stuttgart, GER	6	Feb
7.42			1	Stockholm, SWE	8	Mar
7.43			1h1	Ghent, BEL	9	Feb
7.46			1	San Sebastian, SPA	3	Mar
7.46			1h1	Sindelfingen, GER	6	Mar
7.48			1h4	Paris, FRA	12	Mar
7.54			1h2	San Sebastian, SPA	3	Mar
7.59			1	Glasgow	29	Jan

7.58	Tony Jarrett		13.08.68	2	Glasgow	12	Feb
7.61				4	Atlanta, USA	3	Mar
7.63				1h3	Atlanta, USA	3	Mar
7.69	Hugh Teape		26.12.63	3r1	Vienna, AUT	6	Feb
7.72				4	Glasgow	12	Feb
7.72				2h3	Paris, FRA	12	Mar
7.73				1	Birmingham	19	Feb
7.74				3	Glasgow	29	Jan
7.74				1r2	Vienna, AUT	6	Feb
7.75				1h1	Birmingham	19	Feb
7.76				3h2	Birmingham	26	Feb
7.77				5s1	Paris, FRA	12	Mar
	27 performances to 7.80 by 3 athletes						
7.84	Andy Tulloch		1.04.67	2r2	Vienna, AUT	6	Feb
7.86	Neil Owen	U23	18.10.73	3	Birmingham	19	Feb
7.91	Paul Gray		25.05.69	4	Birmingham	19	Feb
7.99	Ken Campbell	U23	30.09.72	6	Glasgow	12	Feb
8.01	James Archampong	U20	14.03.76	1	Birmingham	13	Feb
8.02	Mark Lambeth	U23	3.09.72	2h3	Birmingham	19	Feb
8.05	Martin Nicholson		9.12.70	1=	Glasgow	23	Jan
	(10)						
8.12	Brian Taylor		13.08.70	3	Birmingham	8	Jan
8.14	Colin Bovell	U23	9.03.72	4	Birmingham	8	Jan
8.15	Jamie Quarry	U23	15.11.72	1H	Glasgow	6	Mar
8.18	James Hughes	U23	8.11.74	2r2	Birmingham	26	Feb
8.22	Nick Csemiczky	U20	13.05.75	2h2	Birmingham	13	Feb
8.24	Rafer Joseph		21.07.68	2H	Glasgow	5	Mar
8.26	Nick Dakin		13.11.63	3	Glasgow	23	Jan
8.28	David Bigham		4.07.71	3H	Glasgow	6	Mar
8.33	Perry Batchelor	U20	11.12.75	1r2	Birmingham	6	Feb
8.34	Simon McAree	U20	28.12.75	5	Birmingham	13	Feb
	(20)						
8.38	*Pascal Renaud*		*20.04.70*	*3h3*	*Birmingham*	*19*	*Feb*
8.39	Paul Stubbs	U23	26.03.74	3r2	Birmingham	26	Feb
8.41	Kevin Lumsdon	U23	3.03.74	4r2	Birmingham	26	Feb

Hand Timing

7.8	Teape		(7.69)	1h1	London (Ha)	15	Jan
8.1	Jamie Quarry	U23	(8.15)	2r3	London (CP)	12	Feb
8.2	Nick Csemiczky	U20	(8.22)	h	London (CP)	30	Jan
8.3	Ererton Harrison		8.04.66	1	London (CP)	15	Jan
8.3	*Pascal Renaud*		*(8.38)*	*1r2*	*London (CP)*	*15*	*Jan*
8.3	Adrian Carter		7.02.68	1r2	London (CP)	17	Dec
8.3	Kirk Harries	U23	7.08.74	2	London (CP)	17	Dec
8.4	Des Wilkinson		7.01.63	6	London (CP)	30	Jan
8.4	Andy Lewis		9.03.68	1	London (Ha)	26	Feb
8.4	Keith Bunce		5.04.66	3	London (CP)	17	Dec
8.4	Clarence Allen		1.04.64	4	London (CP)	17	Dec

60 METRES HURDLES - Under 20 (3'3")

8.15	Simon McAree		28.12.75	1	Glasgow	6	Feb
8.19	David Cotter		23.02.77	2	Glasgow	6	Feb
8.2	Perry Batchelor		11.12.75	1	Birmingham	6	Feb
8.24	Grant Adams		16.10.75	3	Glasgow	6	Feb

60 METRES HURDLES - Under 17 (3'0")

7.9 i	Damien Greaves		19.09.77	1	London (CP)	30	Jan
7.9 i	Matthew Clements		17.09.77	2	London (CP)	30	Jan
8.16 i	Ross Baillie		26.09.77	2	Birmingham	12	Feb
8.3 i	Adrian Harris		21.01.78	3	London (CP)	30	Jan
8.49 i	Josef Bailey		2.12.77	1	Birmingham	6	Feb

70 METRES HURDLES - Under 13 (2'3")

11.6	L. White		1	Birmingham	2 Jul
11.7	J. Kennedy		2	Birmingham	2 Jul
11.7	M. Brady		3	Birmingham	2 Jul

75 METRES HURDLES - Under 13 (2'3")

12.1	Chris Jenkins	2.03.82	1P	Kirkby	23 Jul
12.1	Martin Taylor	31.01.82	1h1	Glasgow	11 Sep
	12.48		1P	Linwood	17 Jul
12.2	M. Scrage		1	Leicester	11 Jun
12.3	Niko Algieri		1	Carmarthen	11 Jun
12.5	T. Jefferson		1	Exeter	24 Jul

80 METRES HURDLES - Under 15 (2'9")

11.00 w 5.6	Tom Benn	20.04.80	1	Telford	9 Jul
11.30 -0.6			1s1	Telford	8 Jul
11.37 w 5.6	Patrick Brown	2.09.79	2	Telford	9 Jul
11.56 0.5			2s2	Telford	8 Jul
11.40 w 2.8	Kevin Drury	30.09.79	1P	Wrexham	27 Aug
11.50 w 5.6	Sam Hartley	27.11.79	3	Telford	9 Jul
11.66 1.4			1h5	Telford	8 Jul
11.58 w 5.6	Dominic DeCannes	11.04.80	4	Telford	9 Jul
11.7			1	Harrow	17 Jul
11.80 -0.6			4s1	Telford	9 Jul
11.58 w 2.4	Marc Newton	15.03.80	3P	Birmingham	17 Sep
11.61	Tom Bridgeman	7.11.79	1	Solihull	28 May
11.63 -0.6	David O'Leary	3.08.80	2s1	Telford	8 Jul
11.67 0.8	Chris Low	24.04.80	1	Grangemouth	28 Aug
11.7 1.9	Steve Surety	18.02.80	1	London (CP)	29 May
11.80 -2.1			2	Birmingham	30 Jul
(10)					
11.7	Steven Attridge	9.03.80	1	Kingston	17 Jul
11.7 w	Nashim Hanif	16.09.79	1	Antrim	28 May
11.75 -0.6	Sam Stephenson	15.05.80	3s1	Telford	8 Jul
11.78 0.8	Richard Poskett	6.09.79	2h1	Telford	8 Jul
11.80	Barron Mendellsohn	1.09.79	2	Sheffield	2 Jul
11.80 0.8	Martin Kennedy	12.10.79	2h3	Telford	8 Jul
11.8	Glyn Bough	20.05.80	1	York	18 Jun
11.94 1.4			4h5	Telford	8 Jul
11.8	Nicholas Hooper	24.09.79	1	Swindon	17 Jul
11.83 w 2.4			4P	Birmingham	16 Sep
11.8 w	Aaron Hughes		2	Antrim	28 May
11.81	D. Cromwell		3	Sheffield	2 Jul
(20)					
11.82 1.4	Dan Brewer	10.08.80	2h5	Telford	8 Jul
11.82 0.8	Jody Murfett	3.12.79	3h1	Telford	8 Jul
11.86 0.8	Timothy Old	29.09.79	5h1	Telford	8 Jul
11.87 -0.6	Jonathan Heggie	8.12.79	6s1	Telford	8 Jul

100 METRES HURDLES - Under 17 (3'0")

12.47 w 3.4	Matthew Clements	17.09.77	1	Telford	9 Jul
13.00 -1.5			1	Aberdeen	16 Jul
12.70 w 3.4	Damien Greaves	19.09.77	2	Telford	9 Jul
13.0 -0.7			1h2	Birmingham	30 Jul
13.09 -2.3			1s1	Telford	8 Jul
13.1 -0.7	Ross Baillie	26.09.77	2h2	Birmingham	30 Jul
13.12 1.6			1	Dublin, IRE	13 Aug
13.27 w 3.4	Richard Churchill	29.09.77	3	Telford	9 Jul
13.8 -0.1			2	Sheffield	26 Jun
13.88 -2.3			3a1	Telford	9 Jul

Perf		Name		DOB	Pos	Venue	Date	
13.33 w	3.4	Josef Bailey		2.12.77	4	Telford	9	Jul
13.7					1	Stoke	11	Jun
13.75	-1.1				1s2	Telford	9	Jul
13.37 w	2.8	Andrew Gill		19.09.77	1	Gateshead	29	May
13.6					1	Sheffield	18	Jun
13.89	1.8				1h1	Telford	8	Jul
13.4 w		Trevor McGlynn		6.06.78	1	Antrim	28	May
13.6					1	Antrim	11	Jun
13.82					3	Dublin, IRE	13	Aug
13.52 w	3.8	Jamie Sheffield		26.06.78	1O	Wrexham	27	Aug
13.7					1P	Cardiff	17	Sep
13.80					1	Colwyn Bay	2	Jul
13.62	-2.9	Ben Gritz		21.11.77	1	Birmingham	11	Sep
13.72 w	3.4	Nick Dowsett		24.11.78	5	Telford	9	Jul
14.0	0.0				1P	London (He)	24	Jul
14.05	-1.1				3s2	Telford	9	Jul
(10)								
13.75 w	3.4	Liam Collins		23.10.78	6	Telford	9	Jul
13.9					1	Gateshead	11	Jun
13.94	-1.1				2s2	Telford	9	Jul
13.8		Tim Dalton		18.01.79	1	Harrow	10	May
13.90 w	3.4				8	Telford	9	Jul
14.18	-1.8				2h1	Telford	8	Jul
13.86 w	3.4	Sean Jeremiah		21.11.77	7	Telford	9	Jul
13.9					2	Peterborough	17	Jul
13.87 w	2.1	Garry Turner		21.12.78	1	Solihull	29	May
14.1	-0.8				1h1	Birmingham	30	Jul
13.9	0.5	Adrian Harris		21.01.78	1	London (CP)	14	May
13.9		Ian Cawley		21.11.78	1	Portsmouth	26	Jun
13.93 w	3.2				4	London (CP)	29	May
14.10	-1.1				4s2	Telford	9	Jul
13.9		Ben Warmington		20.03.79	1	Jarrow	14	Aug
13.98					1	Gateshead	14	May
13.92 w	2.1	Mark Anderson		5.11.77	2	Solihull	29	May
14.0		Rob Collins		17.09.77	1	Gateshead	5	Jun
14.03					2	Gateshead	14	May
14.0		Peter Broom		6.12.77	1	Carmarthen	11	Jun
14.12					3	Colwyn Bay	2	Jul
(20)								
14.0		Charles Robertson-Adams		5.12.77	1	Cardiff	26	Jun
14.07	-0.3				1	Birmingham	10	Sep
14.0 w		John Reynolds		14.01.79	3	Antrim	28	May
14.0 w		Paul Watts		2.07.78	2	Antrim	28	May
14.05	-1.5	Mark Rowlands		18.04.78	4	Aberdeen	16	Jul
14.06 w	3.8	Paul Jones		11.04.78	2O	Wrexham	27	Aug
14.09	-2.4	Paul Mitchell		18.07.78	1	Edinburgh	14	May
14.1		Duncan Malins		12.06.78	1	Horsham	15	May
14.1		Christian Bird		19.09.78	1	Bracknell	11	Jun
14.1		Fyn Corcoran		17.03.78	1	Swindon	17	Jul
14.2		Chris Hargrave		27.02.79	1	Corby	11	Jun
(30)								
14.2		Remi Edu		14.12.78	2	Welwyn	11	Jun

Doubtful Timing

Perf		Name		DOB	Pos	Venue	Date	
13.3		Mark Rowlands		18.04.78	1	Barry	15	May

110 METRES HURDLES - Under 17 (3'0")

Perf		Name		DOB	Pos	Venue	Date	
13.71	0.9	Matthew Clements		17.09.77	2	Nicosia, CYP	19	May
14.19	0.9	Ross Baillie		26.09.77	4	Nicosia, CYP	19	May
14.38	0.9	Jon Snade	U20	31.03.77	7	Nicosia, CYP	19	May

110 METRES HURDLES - Under 20 (3'3")

13.92 w 2.6	Matthew Clements	U17	17.09.77	1	London (He)	27	Aug
14.10 w 4.1	Simon McAree		28.12.75	1	Telford	9	Jul
14.52				2	Gateshead	28	May
14.13 w 2.6	Mike Robbins		14.03.76	2	London (He)	27	Aug
14.44				1	Gateshead	28	May
14.17 w 4.1	Perry Batchelor		11.12.75	2	Telford	9	Jul
14.66 -1.8				1h1	Telford	8	Jul
14.23 w 4.1	Nick Csemiczky		13.05.75	3	Telford	9	Jul
14.43 -0.7				1	London (CP)	28	May
14.26 w 3.2	James Archampong		14.03.76	1	Newport	28	May
14.50 w 4.1	Jon Snade		31.03.77	4	Telford	9	Jul
15.08 -1.8				3h1	Telford	8	Jul
14.61 w 2.6	Damien Greaves	U17	19.09.77	4	London (He)	27	Aug
14.64 w 4.1	Mark Bushell		22.10.76	5	Telford	9	Jul
14.95 0.9				1D	Birmingham	18	Sep
14.65 w 2.8	Mark Bailey		23.07.75	2	Solihull	28	May
(10)							
14.67 w 4.1	Paul Gripton		9.11.76	6	Telford	9	Jul
14.91 0.3				h	Solihull	28	May
14.77 w 4.1	Dominic Bradley		22.12.76	7	Telford	9	Jul
14.86 w 2.8	Chris Pember		2.10.75	4	Solihull	28	May
15.24 0.3				h	Solihull	28	May
14.88 w 2.8	James Allard		11.05.77	5	Solihull	28	May
14.93 w 2.8	Robert Mason		13.09.75	6	Solihull	28	May
15.33 -2.3				5h2	Telford	8	Jul
15.10	Guy Walker		23.02.76	4	Gateshead	28	May
15.10 w 3.2	Stephen Edwards		13.06.77	2	Newport	28	May
15.13	Martyn Hendry		10.04.75	1	Grangemouth	28	Aug
15.15 -0.7	Simon Rush		23.06.76	2	London (CP)	28	May
15.30 w 2.8	Andrew Judge		24.05.75	7	Solihull	28	May
(20)							
15.40 -1.8	James Storey		26.11.76	5h1	Telford	8	Jul

Hand Timing

14.3		Nick Csemiczky		(14.43)	1	Bracknell	11	Jun
14.5		James Archampong		(14.26w)	1	Carmarthen	11	Jun
14.7 w 5.7		Grant Adams		16.10.75	1r2	Grangemouth	11	May
14.8 -2.0		Stephen Edwards		(15.10w)	1	Barry	19	Jul
14.8 w 3.0		David Cotter		23.02.77	1	Grangemouth	11	May
15.1					1	Inverness	14	May
14.9 -2.0		Martyn Hendry		(15.13)	2	Barry	19	Jul
14.9		Jon Snade		(15.08)	1	Telford	24	Jul
15.0		Dominic Bradley		(14.77w)	1	Leeds	2	May
15.07					3	Gateshead	28	May
15.0		Andrew Gill	U17	19.09.77	1	Crewe	28	Aug
15.0		Mark Bailey		(14.65w)	1	Leicester	10	Sep
(10)							
15.1		Robert Mason		(15.33)	1	Swindon	17	Apr
15.2		Lee Thompson		21.10.76	1	Grantham	14	May
15.2		James Storey		(15.40)	1	Welwyn	11	Jul
15.2		James Allard		(14.88w)	2	Telford	24	Jul
15.2		Paul Hourihan		7.11.76	1	Blackpool	14	Aug
15.2		Alex Hunte		13.07.77	1	Enfield	14	Aug
15.2 w 2.2		Steven Rae		20.07.75	1r1	Exeter	20	Aug
15.3		Tom Bradwell		4.09.75	2	Swindon	17	Apr
15.3 w 2.2		Simon Rush		(15.15)	2r1	Exeter	20	Aug
15.5 w 3.0		Steve Timmins		8.05.75	1r2	Exeter	20	Aug
(20)							
15.6 -3.9		Stuart Pope		21.02.76	1	Stoke	14	May

174

110 METRES HURDLES

Time	Wind	Name	DOB	Pos	Venue	Date
12.98	0.2	Colin Jackson	18.02.67	1	Tokyo, JAP	15 Sep
12.99	-0.3			1	Madrid, SPA	6 Sep
13.02	0.9			1	Berlin, GER	30 Aug
13.03	1.3			1	Sheffield	4 Sep
13.04	1.0			1s1	Helsinki, FIN	12 Aug
13.07	1.2			1	Rieti, ITA	28 Aug
13.08	1.1			1	Helsinki, FIN	12 Aug
13.08	1.6			1	Victoria, CAN	23 Aug
13.08	-0.8			1	Paris, FRA	3 Sep
13.16	1.5			1h2	Helsinki, FIN	11 Aug
13.19	-0.7			1	Zurich, SWZ	17 Aug
13.20	1.3			1h1	Oslo, NOR	22 Jul
13.22	-0.3			1	Oslo, NOR	22 Jul
13.22	0.0			1	Brussels, BEL	19 Aug
13.23	0.6			1	Istanbul, TUR	22 May
13.26	0.6			1	Monaco, MON	2 Aug
13.29	-1.9			1	St. Petersburg, RUS	28 Jul
13.35	-1.1			1	Wrexham	3 Jul
13.51	-2.8			1r2	Gateshead	1 Jul
13.51	1.4			1h1	Victoria, CAN	22 Aug
13.22	1.6	Tony Jarrett	13.08.68	2	Victoria, CAN	23 Aug
13.23	1.1			3	Helsinki, FIN	12 Aug
13.23	-0.3			3	Madrid, SPA	6 Sep
13.23	-1.6			1	London (CP)	11 Sep
13.32	-0.6			1	London (CP)	15 Jul
13.32	0.1			1s2	Helsinki, FIN	12 Aug
13.32	1.3			4	Sheffield	4 Sep
13.33	-1.9			2	St. Petersburg, RUS	28 Jul
13.33	0.6			3	Monaco, MON	2 Aug
13.34	0.9			6	Berlin, GER	30 Aug
13.35	-0.3			2	Oslo, NOR	22 Jul
13.40	0.7			1	Bratislava, SVK	1 Jun
13.42	0.2			2	Tokyo, JAP	15 Sep
13.43	-0.1			1h4	Helsinki, FIN	11 Aug
13.45	0.8			3	Gateshead	20 Jul
13.52	-0.7			1h2	Oslo, NOR	22 Jul
13.52	1.8			1h2	Victoria, CAN	22 Aug
13.53	-1.9			1	Malaga, SPA	28 May
13.58	0.9			1r2	Austin, USA	7 May
13.52	1.3	Andy Tulloch	1.04.67	2h3	Helsinki, FIN	11 Aug
13.62	1.0			5s1	Helsinki, FIN	12 Aug
13.65	1.9			3	Birmingham	26 Jun
13.69	1.6			4	Victoria, CAN	23 Aug
13.70	0.8			1	Sheffield	12 Jun
13.73	1.8			1	Nitra, SVK	13 Jul
13.76	0.8			5	Gateshead	20 Jul
13.76	1.3			6	Sheffield	4 Sep
13.78	-0.6			6	London (CP)	15 Jul
13.83	0.7			6	Bratislava, SVK	1 Jun
13.87	0.4			1h3	Sheffield	12 Jun
13.87	1.8			4h2	Victoria, CAN	22 Aug
13.98	-0.8			2	Birmingham	21 May
13.53	1.8	Paul Gray	25.05.69	2h2	Victoria, CAN	22 Aug
13.54	1.6			3	Victoria, CAN	23 Aug
13.65	0.8			4	Gateshead	20 Jul
13.76	0.8			2	Sheffield	12 Jun
13.78	1.3			1	Colwyn Bay	23 Jul
13.86	0.6			2	Istanbul, TUR	22 May

13.75	0.5	Lloyd Cowan			8.07.62	2h3	Brussels, BEL	17 Jul
		13.96	1.4			4h1	Victoria, CAN	22 Aug
13.76	-0.8	Hugh Teape			26.12.63	1	Birmingham	21 May
13.80		Neil Owen	U23	18.10.73	1r1	London (He)	5 Jun
		13.97	0.4			2	Ostrava, CS	31 Jul
13.86	1.6	Ken Campbell	U23	30.09.72	6	Victoria, CAN	23 Aug
		13.92	1.8			5h2	Victoria, CAN	22 Aug

65 performances to 13.99 by 8 athletes

14.10	1.2	Jamie Quarry	U23	15.11.72	1	Edinburgh	25 Jun
14.14	0.4	Martin Nicholson		9.12.70	2h3	Sheffield	12 Jun
	(10)						
14.17	1.1	Colin Bovell	U23	9.03.72	2r1	Nivelles, BEL	23 Jul
14.18	-0.8	Brian Taylor		13.08.70	1r1	London (CP)	7 May
14.18	1.9	James Archampong	U20	14.03.76	5s1	Lisbon, POR	21 Jul
14.20	1.7	Kevin Lumsdon	U23	3.03.74	1	Derby	16 Jul
14.31	-2.2	Mark Lambeth	U23	3.09.72	2	London (CP)	26 Jun
14.36	*-3.0*	*Paul Edmiston*	*U23*	*16.02.72*	*4*	*Sydney, AUS*	*12 Mar*
14.39	0.7	James Hughes	U23	8.11.74	3h4	Sheffield	12 Jun
14.40	0.7	Paul Stubbs	U23	26.03.74	1	Stoke	16 Jul
14.42		Greg Dunson		2.12.63	1r2	London (He)	5 Jun
14.43	1.7	Simon McAree	U20	28.12.75	5h4	Lisbon, POR	21 Jul
14.60	1.0	Ererton Harrison		8.04.66	3r1	Wigan	7 May
	(20)						
14.71	1.7	Chris Dorgu		11.12.69	4	Derby	16 Jul
14.74		*Pascal Renaud*		*20.04.70*	*5r1*	*London (He)*	*5 Jun*
14.75		Nick Csemiczky	U20	13.05.75	2r2	London (He)	5 Jun
14.82	-2.2	Clarence Allen		1.04.64	6	London (CP)	26 Jun
14.82	-1.5	Simon Shirley		3.08.66	2r2	Crawley	6 Aug
14.83	0.7	Adrian Caines	U23	13.11.74	2	Stoke	16 Jul
14.83	0.9	David Bigham		4.07.71	3	London (He)	18 Aug
14.84	0.7	Nick Dakin		13.11.63	4r1	Aartselaar, BEL	21 Jul
14.85	-1.0	Tim Gwynne		20.01.71	1r2	Birmingham	21 May
14.88	0.0	Andy Lewis		9.03.68	1D	Diekirch, LUX	20 Aug
14.89		Paul Field		24.06.67	7	Corby	30 May
	(30)						
14.89	0.5	Barry Thomas	U23	28.04.72	3D	Bressanone, ITA	3 Jul
14.90	1.1	Andrew David		9.09.69	2h1	London (CP)	26 Jun
14.93	1.8	Graeme Smith		20.10.71	2h2	Edinburgh	24 Jun
14.93	-0.6	Max Robertson		27.12.63	1r2	London (WL)	2 Jul
14.95		Gavin Sunshine	U23	19.02.74	3r2	London (He)	5 Jun
14.96	1.2	Alex Kruger		18.11.63	3D	Bressanone, ITA	3 Jul
14.97		David Humphreys		10.10.69	4	Solihull	21 Aug
14.98	1.3	Mike Robbins	U20	14.03.76	4	Colwyn Bay	23 Jul
14.99		William Wyllie	U23	12.07.73	4r2	London (He)	5 Jun
15.00	-0.1	Tim Tomkinson		31.10.68	4r1	London (WL)	2 Jul
	(40)						
15.04	1.2	Paul Warrillow		8.07.70	7	Edinburgh	25 Jun
15.04	1.7	Rob Laing		30.07.66	5	Derby	16 Jul
15.06		Adrian Ferrand		5.02.68	s	London (CP)	1 May
15.06	1.0	Rafer Joseph		21.07.68	3D	Bressanone, ITA	3 Jul
15.06	1.7	Chris Rawlinson	U23	19.05.72	6	Derby	16 Jul
15.08		Kirk Harries	U23	7.08.74	2	Loughborough	7 Sep
15.10		Perry Batchelor	U20	11.12.75	5	Solihull	21 Aug
15.11	-0.6	Gary Smith		20.02.71	2r2	London (WL)	2 Jul
15.12	1.2	Fraser McGlynn		2.09.63	8	Edinburgh	25 Jun
15.15		Gavin Streather		14.04.71	1	Stoke	11 Sep
	(50)						
15.16	1.1	Adrian Carter		7.02.68	4h1	London (CP)	26 Jun
15.16	-0.9	Ciaran Doherty	U20	14.01.75	4r2	Kings Lynn	9 Jul
15.20		Terry Fidler		13.10.71	5r2	London (He)	5 Jun
15.20	-0.3	Sebastian Rosato	U23	19.11.72	6h2	Sheffield	12 Jun

15.23	0.1	Steve Gutteridge		5.07.71	2D	Diekirch, LUX	20 Aug
15.25	0.8	Tony Williams	U23	1.05.72	3h2	Corby	30 May
15.29	1.4	Tony Southward		31.01.71	1D	Stoke	26 Jun
15.31	0.4	Gareth Hughes	U23	22.10.73	3h4	Corby	30 May
15.33	0.7	Gary Gallagher		7.06.71	4	Stoke	16 Jul
15.35		Les Antoine		16.12.65	6r2	London (He)	5 Jun
	(60)						
15.37	1.7	Bill McDonagh	U23	11.07.72	7	Derby	16 Jul
15.43		Neal Petley		21.05.68	7r2	London (He)	5 Jun
15.43	1.8	David Cotter	U20	23.02.77	4h2	Edinburgh	25 Jun
15.43		Gary Myles		3.02.63	7	Solihull	21 Aug
15.46	-0.4	Steve Leader		24.11.66	1D	Horsham	19 Jun
15.49	1.8	Martyn Hendry	U20	10.04.75	5h2	Edinburgh	25 Jun
15.52		Philip McIlfatrick	V40	5.02.54	h	Athens, GRE	3 Jun
15.57		Dave Savage	U23	13.11.72	7r1	London (He)	5 Jun
15.60	1.6	Ian Wells		18.02.62	4r2	Wigan	7 May
15.60	1.8	David Barnetson		1.07.71	1	Edinburgh	14 Aug
	(70)						
15.60	-0.5	Mark Perman		6.01.68	1D	London (He)	21 Aug
15.61	0.4	Mark Bailey	U20	23.07.75	3h1	Bedford	3 Jul
15.62		Elsworth Wray		14.10.70	8r1	London (He)	5 Jun
15.64	0.2	Matthew Douglas	U20	26.11.76	1D	Sheffield	1 May
15.67		Keith Bunce		5.04.66	2	Stoke	11 Sep

Wind Assisted

12.94A	2.8	Jackson		(12.98)	1	Sestriere, ITA	31 Jul
	13.05	2.5			1	Edinburgh	8 Jul
13.37	2.5	Jarrett		(13.22)	2	Edinburgh	8 Jul
	13.46A	2.8			5	Sestriere, ITA	31 Jul
13.69	2.5	Tulloch		(13.52)	6	Edinburgh	8 Jul
13.79	2.5	Gray		(13.53)	7=	Edinburgh	8 Jul
13.93	3.6	Owen	U23	(13.80)	1	London (CP)	2 May
		7 performances to 13.99 by 5 athletes					
14.36	2.1	Ererton Harrison		(14.60)	3h1	Sheffield	12 Jun
14.61	2.5	Paul Field		(14.89)	1D	Horsham	19 Jun
14.67	2.5	Andy Lewis		(14.88)	2D	Horsham	19 Jun
14.77	4.3	David Bigham		(14.83)	5	Bedford	17 Sep
14.81	2.4	Perry Batchelor	U20	(15.10)	4h2	Bedford	3 Jul
14.84	3.6	Tony Southward		(15.29)	3	London (CP)	2 May
14.88	2.6	Rob Laing		(15.04)	1D	Horsham	19 Jun
14.92	3.7	Chris Rawlinson	U23	(15.06)	2	Bedford	18 Sep
15.02	3.6	Jeremy Thompson	U23	11.06.73	4	London (CP)	2 May
15.03	2.6	Rafer Joseph		(15.06)	3D	Emmelshausen, GER	29 May
15.16	2.5	Steve Gutteridge		(15.23)	4D	Horsham	18 Jun
15.43	2.1	David Brooking		22.10.68	6h1	Sheffield	12 Jun
15.45	3.7	Richard Leggate	U23	20.07.74	3	Bedford	18 Sep
15.47	3.1	Stephen Rogers		1.09.71	2D	Emmelshausen, GER	29 May
15.62	4.3	Steve Timmins	U20	8.05.75	6	Bedford	17 Sep
15.66	4.3	Nathan Hart	U23	1.07.73	7	Bedford	17 Sep

Hand Timing

13.1	0.1	Tony Jarrett		(13.22)	1r1	Austin, USA	7 May
13.8		Martin Nicholson		(14.14)	3	Cork, IRE	25 Jun
13.8	1.9	Gray		(13.53)	1	Enfield	31 Jul
	14.0	1.1			1r1	Bracknell	7 May
14.0	-0.1	Tulloch		(13.52)	1r1	Wolverhampton	4 Jun
		5 performances to 14.0 by 4 athletes					
14.1		Colin Bovell	U23	(14.17)	1	Exeter	17 Jul
14.2	1.5	Mark Lambeth	U23	(14.31)	1r1	Cardiff	2 Jul
14.2	1.5	James Hughes	U23	(14.39)	2r1	Cardiff	2 Jul

14.2 w		Paul Edmiston	U23	(14.36)	1	Perth, AUS	12	Nov
14.3 w	2.2	Paul Stubbs	U23	(14.40)	2	Stoke	31	Jul
14.7		David Bigham		(14.83)	1	Woodford	23	Apr
14.7		Tim Tomkinson		(15.00)	1	Aldershot	8	Jun
14.7		Adrian Caines	U23	(14.83)	3	Loughborough	22	Jun
14.7	0.3	Simon Shirley		(14.82)	3	Kingston	31	Jul
14.7	1.9	Chris Dorgu		(14.71)	3	Enfield	31	Jul
14.7		Rafer Joseph		(15.06)	2r1	Liverpool	6	Aug
14.7		Pascal Renaud		(14.74)	1	London (TB)	20	Aug
14.7 w		Perry Batchelor	U20	(15.10)	1	Cannock	26	Jun
		14.9			1	Telford	20	Aug
14.8		Sebastian Rosato	U23	(15.20)	1	Oxford	14	May
14.8		Tim Gwynne		(14.85)	1	Leamington	15	May
14.8		Graham Richardson		15.11.64	1	Aldershot	8	Jun
14.8		Andrew Smailes		22.04.68	2	Cosford	15	Jun
14.8		Clarence Allen		(14.82)	1	London (Col)	18	Jun
14.8		Andy Lewis		(14.88)	2	Cannock	11	Sep
14.9	1.1	Steve Ingram		22.09.70	3r1	Bracknell	7	May
14.9		Andy Hodge		18.12.68	2	Oxford	14	May
14.9		Chris Rawlinson	U23	(15.06)	2	Kirkby	6	Aug
14.9		Kirk Harries	U23	(15.08)	3	London (TB)	20	Aug
15.0		Jeremy Thompson	U23	(15.02w)	1	Portsmouth	15	May
15.0		David Brooking		(15.43w)	1	Carn Brea	4	Jun
15.0		Paul Warrillow		(15.04)	2	Aldershot	29	Jun
15.0	0.0	Gary Gallagher		(15.33)	1	Dublin (B), IRE	17	Jul
15.1		Tony Southward		(15.29)	2	Stoke	23	Apr
15.1		Mark Bailey	U20	(15.61)	1	Mansfield	10	May
15.1		Paul Gripton	U20	9.11.76	1	Warley	14	May
15.1	1.5	Neil Fraser		8.06.63	1r2	Wolverhampton	4	Jun
15.1		Anthony Brannen		16.09.68	1r1	Kingston	4	Jun
15.1		Charles Edsall	U23	2.05.74	1	Windsor	18	Jun
15.1		Jonathon Tullett	U23	11.02.73	1	Basingstoke	18	Jun
15.1		Gavin Streather		(15.15)	4r1	Liverpool	6	Aug
15.2		Eric Hollingsworth		6.12.62		Melbourne, AUS	12	Feb
15.2		Tony Williams	U23	(15.25)	1r1	Cannock	7	May
15.2		Des Wilkinson		7.01.63	1	Portsmouth (RN)	7	May
15.2		Les Antoine		(15.35)	3	Leamington	15	May
15.2	1.5	Gareth Hughes	U23	(15.31)	2r2	Wolverhampton	4	Jun
15.2		Stuart Caudery		19.11.66	2	Carn Brea	4	Jun
15.2		Kevin Furlong		19.05.70	1	Wigan	4	Jun
15.2		Neal Killen		10.04.59	2	Aldershot	8	Jun
15.2		Mark Perman		(15.60)	1	London (WF)	18	Jun
15.2		Andrew Haines	U23	15.10.72	1	Yate	29	Jun
15.2		Neil Cox	U20	26.04.76	2	Yate	29	Jun
15.2		Eddie Betts		18.02.71	1	Crawley	13	Aug
15.2		Stephen Booth		21.10.71	1	London (BP)	13	Aug
15.3	-0.1	Andy Gill		19.02.70	2r2	Bournemouth	7	May
15.3	0.0	Peter Linder		26.05.67	1r2	Coventry	7	May
15.3		Richard Leggate	U23	(15.45w)	5	Gateshead	4	Jun
15.4		Andrew Kennard		2.01.66	1	Bromley	1	May
15.4		Scott McPherson	U23	24.03.73	3	Oxford	14	May
15.4	-1.8	Colin Anderson		18.02.59	1r2	Sheffield (W)	4	Jun
15.4	1.5	Nathan Hart	U23	(15.66w)	4r1	Cardiff	2	Jul
15.4		David Vidgen	U23	27.09.74	2	Perivale	30	Jul
15.4		Mark Burbridge	U23	17.11.73	1	London (CP)	13	Aug
15.4		Kris Focke		28.03.69	2	London (WP)	13	Aug
15.4		Matthew Johnson	U23	2.05.74	1	London (Elt)	13	Aug

15.4	John Hadler		18.08.69	2	London (Elt)	13 Aug
15.5	Fraser Dean	U23	12.11.73	1D	Colorado Springs, USA	15 Apr
15.5	B. Marsden			1	High Wycombe	14 May
15.5	Dominic Bradley	U20	22.12.76	1	Stretford	2 Jul
15.5	Martin Swingler		11.05.63	1	St. Ives	2 Jul
15.5	Andy Douglas		19.07.62	2r1	Liverpool	6 Aug
15.5	Matthew Douglas	U20	(15.64)	1	Southampton	13 Aug
15.5	Dominic Lewis	U23	14.09.72	1	St. Ives	13 Aug

400 METRES HURDLES

49.07	Gary Cadogan		8.10.66	3	Oslo, NOR	22 Jul
	49.21			1	Edinburgh	8 Jul
	49.42			4s1	Helsinki, FIN	8 Aug
	49.48 A			3	Sestriere, ITA	31 Jul
	49.48			5	Madrid, SPA	6 Sep
	49.53			8	Helsinki, FIN	10 Aug
	49.55			2h2	Helsinki, FIN	7 Aug
	49.71			4	Victoria, CAN	26 Aug
	49.74			3	Sheffield	4 Sep
	50.18			1h1	Victoria, CAN	24 Aug
	50.48			6	London (CP)	9 Sep
	50.50			2	Gateshead	1 Jul
	50.93			2	Budapest, HUN	3 Jun
	51.32			7	Bratislava, SVK	1 Jun
49.26	Peter Crampton		4.06.69	3s2	Helsinki, FIN	8 Aug
	49.45			6	Helsinki, FIN	10 Aug
	49.71			3h1	Helsinki, FIN	7 Aug
	49.78			4	London (CP)	15 Jul
	49.82			1	Sheffield	12 Jun
	49.90			1	Corby	30 May
	50.09			6	Birmingham	25 Jun
	50.22			2	Gateshead	20 Jul
	50.27			5	Bratislava, SVK	1 Jun
	50.37			7	Victoria, CAN	26 Aug
	50.49			4	Sheffield	4 Sep
	50.51			3	Gateshead	1 Jul
	50.92			3h3	Victoria, CAN	24 Aug
	51.03			1s2	Sheffield	11 Jun
50.19	Steve Coupland		15.06.65	2	Sheffield	12 Jun
	50.97			5	Gateshead	20 Jul
	51.16			5	Gateshead	1 Jul
	51.34			3h2	Victoria, CAN	24 Aug
	51.35			3s1	Sheffield	11 Jun
	51.5			1r1	Sheffield (W)	4 Jun
50.24	Lawrence Lynch		1.11.67	5h3	Helsinki, FIN	7 Aug
	50.27			1	Wrexham	3 Jul
	50.38			4	Gateshead	20 Jul
	50.50			1	Celle Ligure, ITA	24 Jun
	50.73			1	Barcelona, SPA	21 Jun
	51.01			5	Sheffield	12 Jun
	51.05			2s1	Sheffield	11 Jun
	51.30			1r1	London (He)	5 Jun
	51.40			6	Gateshead	1 Jul
50.60	Gary Jennings	U23	21.02.72	2r1	Aartselaar, BEL	21 Jul
	50.77			3	Brussels, BEL	16 Jul
	50.93			2r1	Nivelles, BEL	23 Jul
	50.96			2	Corby	30 May
	51.16			3	Barcelona, SPA	21 Jun
	51.16			6	Gateshead	20 Jul
	51.19			1r2	Loughborough	5 Jun
	51.44			1r1	Wigan	7 May
	51.45			1	Kings Lynn	9 Jul

50.70	Noel Levy	U20	22.06.75	6	Edinburgh	8	Jul
50.89				3	Sheffield	12	Jun
50.91				2s2	Lisbon, POR	21	Jul
50.94				3	Lisbon, POR	22	Jul
51.02				1s1	Sheffield	11	Jun
50.98	Tony Williams	U23	1.05.72	4	Sheffield	12	Jun
51.27				2r2	Loughborough	5	Jun
51.3				1	Cannock	7	May
51.38				7	Gateshead	20	Jul
51.49				7	Edinburgh	8	Jul
51.50				1	Derby	16	Jul
51.08	Tim Gwynne		20.01.71	3	Corby	30	May
51.13	Phil Harries		7.04.66	2	Istanbul, TUR	21	May
51.15	Eddie Betts		18.02.71	1	London (CP)	26	Jun
51.50				2	Wrexham	3	Jul
	67 performances to 51.50 by 10 athletes						
51.51	Gary Telfer		10.01.65	1r1	London (WL)	2	Jul
51.67	Mark Bishop		12.02.67	3	London (CP)	26	Jun
51.80	Paul Hibbert		31.03.65	3h2	Sheffield	11	Jun
51.83	Anthony Borsumato	U23	13.12.73	2	Derby	16	Jul
51.87	Dave Savage	U23	13.11.72	1	Solihull	21	Aug
52.0	Chris Rawlinson	U23	19.05.72	1	Wigan	2	Jul
52.32				2	Kings Lynn	9	Jul
52.20	Craig White		4.04.71	2	Colwyn Bay	23	Jul
52.39	Paul Thompson	U23	22.03.72	2	Eugene, USA	16	Apr
52.66	Dave Griffin		5.12.63	1h3	London (CP)	25	Jun
52.70	Mark Davidson		15.11.68	1	Edinburgh	24	Apr
	(20)						
52.81	Greg Dunson		2.12.63	3h5	Sheffield	11	Jun
52.81	Paul Beaumont		27.03.63	4	London (CP)	26	Jun
52.83	Derek Paisley	U23	1.12.73	3	Istanbul, TUR	21	May
52.84	Colin Anderson		18.02.59	5	London (CP)	26	Jun
52.9	Chris Cashell		11.05.66	1	Salisbury	10	Jul
53.22				3h3	London (CP)	25	Jun
52.98	Alex Hunte	U20	13.07.77	1	Schio, ITA	6	Aug
53.00	Nigel Gardner	U23	15.04.72	2	Edinburgh	25	Jun
53.1	*Chris Martin*		*12.09.69*	*5*	*Kingston*	*31*	*Jul*
53.47				*2r2*	*London (He)*	*5*	*Jun*
53.15	Adam Hartley		27.02.69	4	Derby	16	Jul
53.2	Bob Brown		3.10.69	2	Sheffield	14	May
53.2	Gavin Streather		14.04.71	1	London (Nh)	15	May
53.25				2	Bedford	17	Sep
	(30)						
53.3	Andy Gill		19.02.70	3r1	Barking	6	Aug
53.31	*Nigel Keogh*		*18.07.67*	*2*	*Dublin, IRE*	*24*	*Jul*
53.34	Matthew Douglas	U20	26.11.76	3	Schio, ITA	6	Aug
53.34	David Gifford	U23	9.03.73	5	Solihull	21	Aug
53.35	Simon Wassell		7.04.69	5h1	Sheffield	11	Jun
53.47	Douglas Thom		13.04.68	3	Edinburgh	25	Jun
53.5	Martin Briggs		4.01.64	2	Loughborough	7	Sep
53.53	Barry Middleton	U20	10.03.75	2	Edinburgh	14	Aug
53.55	Steve Lamb	U20	10.10.75	2h1	Bedford	2	Jul
53.6	Richard Holt		28.11.71	2	Enfield	31	Jul
53.69				3h3	Derby	16	Jul
53.7	Andy Edwards		15.09.69	2	London (Elt)	29	Aug
	(40)						
53.71	Ian Wells		18.02.62	4	Bedford	17	Sep
53.78	John Bell	U23	10.09.73	4h3	Derby	16	Jul
53.8	Henrik Hartmann	U23	7.09.72	4	Enfield	31	Jul
53.99				6h2	Sheffield	11	Jun
53.83	Chris Martin	U23		h	London (CP)	30	Apr

180

53.87	Jason Toal	U23	8.11.74	5h2	Sheffield	11	Jun
53.89	John McIlwham	U23	29.02.72	3h4	Corby	30	May
54.0	Darren Gallagher		7.06.71	2	Stoke	14	May
54.45				3	Belfast	18	Jun
54.0	Jason Davenhill		3.10.69	2	Aldershot	6	Jul
54.02	Howard Moscrop		16.12.57	5r1	Crawley	6	Aug
54.03	Marvin Gray		18.12.71	3	Cwmbran	18	Jun
	(50)						
54.05	Colin Bovell	U23	9.03.72	4r1	Aartselaar, BEL	21	Jul
54.1	Chris Scott		31.08.68	6	Enfield	31	Jul
54.20	Terry Price		26.07.57	2r2	London (WL)	2	Jul
54.2	Andrew Kennard		2.01.66	3	Enfield	15	May
54.21	Carl Foster	U20	24.10.75	3h1	Bedford	2	Jul
54.3	Glenn Gray		21.04.68	1	Watford	30	Jul
54.33	Simon Rush	U20	23.06.76	2	London (CP)	29	May
54.4	Steve Freeman		8.09.67	2	Rotherham	7	May
54.4	Stephen Pratt		6.02.71	3	London (PH)	10	Jul
54.42	Mark Purser	U23	18.04.72	2h1	London (CP)	25	Jun
	(60)						
54.42	Ian Neely	U23	29.12.74	5	Dublin (M), IRE	24	Jul
54.44	David Goodger	U20	19.09.75	3	Oordegem, BEL	9	Jul
54.45	Chris Cholerton		13.02.63	3h2	Derby	16	Jul
54.48	Richard Scott	U23	14.09.73	3h1	London (CP)	25	Jun
54.5	Andrew Bargh	U20	21.08.76	2	Southampton	4	Sep
54.92				3h3	Bedford	2	Jul
54.51	Steve Timmins	U20	8.05.75	2h3	Bedford	2	Jul
54.52	Andy Douglas		19.07.62	7	Edinburgh	25	Jun
54.6	Graham Richardson		15.11.64	3	Aldershot	6	Jul
54.6	Tim Chambers		6.07.71	2	Cleckheaton	23	Jul
54.82				4h2	Derby	16	Jul
54.7	Mark Green		28.06.71	4r1	Bournemouth	7	May
	(70)						
54.7	Duncan Harbour		17.10.66	1	Bracknell	14	May
54.7	Chris Morrison		27.12.70	1	Stretford	14	May
54.7	*Kerry Kirkham*		*5.03.69*	*1*	*Loughborough*	*25*	*May*
54.75				*h*	*Dublin, IRE*	*23*	*Jul*
54.77	Lloyd Cowan		8.07.62	5r2	London (He)	5	Jun
54.8	Simon Clifford	U20	22.03.75	4	Salisbury	10	Jul
54.8	Keith Newton		12.12.68	1	Reading	13	Aug
55.23				4h1	London (CP)	25	Jun
54.8	Darran Bruce		23.04.70	1r2	London (Elt)	29	Aug
54.9	Jon Lawford	U20	30.06.76	2	Cannock	26	Jun
55.19				1	London (He)	7	Aug
54.91	Andy Colver		8.01.70	6h5	Sheffield	11	Jun
54.94	Rey Guevara	U20	12.08.77	1h1	Telford	8	Jul
54.98	Paul Martin	U20	19.05.76	2	Gateshead	29	May
	(80)						
55.01	Danny Hodge		8.03.63	3r1	Edinburgh	6	Aug
55.03	Jon Goodwin	U20	22.09.76	2h2	Bedford	2	Jul
55.1	Sean Campbell	U20	19.12.75	1	Kingston	18	May
55.1	Andrew Judge	U20	24.05.75	3	Loughborough	22	Jun
55.51				6h1	Bedford	2	Jul
55.1	Matt Allison	U23	26.02.73	1r2	Barking	6	Aug
55.1	Chris Dorgu		11.12.69	1	Perivale	17	Aug
55.2	James Melville-Jackson	U23	24.01.74	2	Loughborough	25	May
55.35				3r2	Loughborough	5	Jun
55.2	Dale Daborn		14.11.66	3	Cosford	15	Jun
55.2	Mark Newman		5.06.71	1	Stretford	23	Aug
55.3	Martin Holgate		2.11.65	1	Woodford	14	Sep
	(90)						
55.32	Darren Cooper		1.02.66	4	London (He)	18	Aug

55.34	Martin Maynard		4.09.71	3r2	London (WL)	2	Jul
55.39	Lee Thompson	U20	21.10.76	3h2	Telford	8	Jul
55.47	Les Antoine		16.12.65	6	Birmingham	21	May
55.5	E. Cole			1	Hoo	19	Jun
55.5	Neil Flanagan		21.02.66	3	Wigan	2	Jul
55.6	Charles Robertson-Adams	U17	5.12.77	1r2	Loughborough	23	Jul
55.6	Matthew Leslie	U20	17.06.76	2	Stretford	23	Aug
	55.67			3h2	Bedford	2	Jul
55.74	Andrew Blackmore	U20	12.07.76	6	Bulle, SWZ	10	Sep
55.8	Nick Green	U23	5.09.74	3	Loughborough	25	May

Additional Under 20 (1 - 20 above)

56.0	Jeremy Bridger		23.09.75	1	Yate	21	Aug
	56.37			4h3	Telford	8	Jul
56.5	Ian Pease		28.09.76	2	London (WP)	18	Jun
56.8	Andrew Ramsay		19.09.76	2	Barry	19	Jul
57.0	Stephen Robertson		9.07.75	1	Grangemouth	7	Sep
57.04	Matthew Eveleigh		7.01.76	8	Oordegem, BEL	9	Jul

400 METRES HURDLES - Under 17

53.30	Mark Rowlands		18.04.78	1	Birmingham	31	Jul
53.55	Charles Robertson-Adams		5.12.77	2	Birmingham	31	Jul
53.64	Dean Park		23.09.77	3	Nicosia, CYP	17	May
55.3	Steve Mitchell		1.09.77	1	Kingston	11	Jun
55.61	Mark Anderson		5.11.77	2	Solihull	29	May
55.9	Fyn Corcoran		17.03.78	1	Yeovil	18	Jun
	56.47			4	Telford	9	Jul
55.94	Jamie Sheffield		26.06.78	2	Colwyn Bay	2	Jul
56.08	James Hillier		3.04.78	3	Colwyn Bay	2	Jul
56.33	Russell Quelch		9.09.78	4	Birmingham	31	Jul
56.45	David Keoghan		9.10.78	3s2	Telford	9	Jul
	(10)						
56.54	Adrian Harris		21.01.78	4s1	Telford	9	Jul
56.56	Darren Walsham		12.01.78	3h1	Telford	8	Jul
56.67	David Head-Rapson		26.05.78	2h3	Telford	8	Jul
56.70	Robert Milner		28.12.77	3h3	Telford	8	Jul
56.74	James Hesketh		18.10.77	1	Gateshead	28	May
56.74	William Eason		13.07.79	4s2	Telford	9	Jul
56.85	Ruben Tabares		22.10.78	6s1	Telford	9	Jul
57.20	Alastair Newmarch		28.11.78	7s1	Telford	9	Jul
57.3	Steven Evans			1	Colwyn Bay	11	Jun
57.3	Paul Caulfield		12.05.78	1	Leeds	26	Jun
	(20)						
57.39	Nick James		9.04.78	2	Birmingham	11	Sep
57.4	Wayne Carnell		2.09.77	1r2	Cwmbran	17	Jul
57.7	Garry Turner		21.12.78	1	Nottingham	26	Jun
	57.84			2	Birmingham	10	Sep
57.72	Aaron Hardy		17.03.78	3	Gateshead	28	May
57.73	George Holmes		21.08.78	5h3	Telford	8	Jul
57.75	Paul Mitchell		18.07.78	1	Grangemouth	9	Jul
57.8	Nick Harrison		24.09.77	1	Welwyn	11	Jul
57.81	John Colaco		3.02.78	4h4	Telford	8	Jul
57.86	Ben Gritz		21.11.77	3	Birmingham	11	Sep
57.9	Graham Thomas		23.09.77	1	Carmarthen	11	Jun
	(30)						
57.92	Gavin Hodgson		1.02.78	4h2	Telford	8	Jul
57.96	Stefan Laffley		10.09.77	5h1	Birmingham	31	Jul
58.0	Michael Nesbeth			2	Enfield	14	Aug

HIGH JUMP

2.38 i	Steve Smith	U23	29.03.73	2	Wuppertal, GER	4	Feb
	2.36 i			2	Liverpool	24	Feb
	2.33			2=	Helsinki, FIN	9	Aug
	2.32 i			1	Glasgow	12	Feb
	2.32			2	Victoria, CAN	26	Aug
	2.31 i			2	Frankfurt, GER	9	Feb
	2.31			2	Brussels, BEL	19	Aug
	2.30 i			1	Glasgow	29	Jan
	2.30 i			5=	Berlin, GER	4	Mar
	2.28			2	Gateshead	1	Jul
	2.28			1	Zurich, SWZ	17	Aug
	2.28			3	London (CP)	11	Sep
	2.25			6	Berlin, GER	30	Aug
	2.24			1	Sheffield	4	Sep
	2.23			Q	Helsinki, FIN	7	Aug
2.37 i	Dalton Grant		8.04.66	1	Paris, FRA	13	Mar
	2.34 i			3	Liverpool	24	Feb
	2.34			1	Jena, GER	3	Jun
	2.33 i			3	Weinhelm, GER	18	Mar
	2.32 i			1	Banska Bystrica, SVK	26	Jan
	2.30 i			2	Glasgow	29	Jan
	2.30 i			2	Birmingham	26	Feb
	2.30			6	Eberstadt, GER	10	Jul
	2.30			2=	Halle, GER	31	Jul
	2.28			6=	Nice, FRA	18	Jul
	2.28			5	Victoria, CAN	26	Aug
	2.27 i			2	Gundelsheim, GER	6	Mar
	2.27			1	Malaga, SPA	28	May
	2.26 i			3	Glasgow	12	Feb
	2.26			Q	Helsinki, FIN	7	Aug
	2.25 i			2	Madrid, SPA	11	Feb
	2.25			4	London (CP)	15	Jul
	2.25			4	Gateshead	20	Jul
	2.25			3	Salamanca, SPA	22	Jul
	2.25			9=	Helsinki, FIN	9	Aug
	2.23 i			Q	Paris, FRA	12	Mar
	2.21			4	Dulsburg, GER	12	Jun
	2.20			5=	Zurich, SWZ	17	Aug
2.32 i	Brendan Reilly	U23	23.12.72	4	Liverpool	24	Feb
	2.28 i			1	Birmingham	19	Feb
	2.28			1	Loughborough	5	Jun
	2.28			2	Gateshead	20	Jul
	2.26 i			Q	Paris, FRA	12	Mar
	2.26 i			7	Paris, FRA	13	Mar
	2.26 i			3	Salgotarjan, HUN	12	Sep
	2.25 i			7	Birmingham	26	Feb
	2.25			1	London (CP)	30	Apr
	2.25			1	Corby	30	May
	2.25			3	Lisbon, POR	18	Jun
	2.25			3	London (CP)	15	Jul
	2.25			7=	Victoria, CAN	26	Aug
	2.24 i			2	Birmingham	8	Jan
	2.24			1	Sheffield	12	Jun
	2.23			1	Reduit, MAU	2	Oct
2.31	Geoff Parsons		14.08.64	3	Victoria, CAN	26	Aug
	2.25			1	Edinburgh	8	Jul
	2.24			2	Wrexham	3	Jul
	2.23			1	Nairobi, KEN	18	Jun
	2.22 i			3	Birmingham	19	Feb
	2.21			1	Istanbul, TUR	21	May

2.24 i	*Mark Mandy*	*U23*	*19.11.72*	*1*	*Birmingham*	*8*	*Jan*
	2.22			1	Dublin (M), IRE	18	Jun
	60 performances to 2.20 by 4 athletes including 24 indoors						
2.19	Fayyaz Ahmed		10.04.66	1	Nitra, SVK	13	Jul
2.17	Henderson Pierre		29.10.63	1	Brussels, BEL	16	Jul
2.17	Stuart Ohrland	U20	6.09.75	1	London (He)	27	Aug
2.16 i	Alex Kruger		18.11.63	1H	Berlin, GER	18	Feb
	2.14			1D	Gotzis, AUT	28	May
2.16	James Brierley	U20	31.07.77	1	Telford	20	Aug
2.14	Mike Robbins	U20	14.03.76	3	Warsaw, POL	18	Jun
(10)							
2.14	Andrew Lynch	U23	28.06.74	1	Stoke	16	Jul
2.13	Rob Brocklebank	U20	12.10.76	1	Blackpool	14	Aug
2.12	Damon Rutland	U20	10.07.75	1	Exeter	20	Aug
2.11 i	David Barnetson		1.07.71	5	Stange, NOR	30	Jan
	2.10			1	Inverness	15	May
2.11	Marlon Huggins		11.02.71	2	London (He)	5	Jun
2.11	Stuart Smith	U20	2.08.76	3	Stoke	16	Jul
2.11	Mark Latham	U20	13.01.76	1	Barking	6	Aug
2.11	Ian Holliday	U23	9.12.73	1	Bedford	18	Sep
2.10 i	Dafydd Edwards	U23	19.09.74	1	London (CP)	15	Jan
	2.05			9	Sheffield	12	Jun
2.10	Nathan Hart	U23	1.07.73	3	London (CP)	30	Apr
(20)							
2.10	Fred Salle		10.09.64	1	Crawley	6	Aug
2.10	Andrew Skelding		8.11.71	1	Brierley Hill	20	Aug
2.09	Colin Bent		12.04.70	1	Aldershot	6	Jul
2.08	Mark Roach		11.04.65		Lisbon, POR	17	Sep
2.07	Richard Laws	U20	8.10.75	5	Telford	9	Jul
2.06	Paul Dovell	U20	5.05.77	1	Bournemouth	11	Jun
2.06	Andrew Lowe	U20	6.03.76	1	Stretford	11	Jun
2.06	David Nolan	U20	16.05.75	1	Cwmbran	18	Jun
2.06	Ben Challenger	U17	7.03.78	1	Telford	9	Jul
2.06	Chris Hindley	U20	21.01.76	1D	Wrexham	27	Aug
(30)							
2.05 i	Darren Otter	U23	6.03.74	9	Birmingham	8	Jan
	2.05			1	Sheffield	14	May
2.05	William Wyllie	U23	12.07.73	4=	London (CP)	30	Apr
2.05	Gary Jones	U23	15.07.72	2	Blackburn	1	May
2.05	Stanley Osuide	U23	30.11.74	1	Bracknell	2	May
2.05	John Wallace		9.10.68	2	Rotherham	7	May
2.05	Darragh Murphy	U23	20.01.74	1	Hayes	11	May
2.05	Steve Ingram		22.09.70	1	Barry	15	May
2.05	Simon Shirley		3.08.66	4=D	Gotzis, AUT	28	May
2.05	Andrew Weston	U23	4.12.73	2=	Loughborough	5	Jun
2.05	Ian Gidley		13.11.70	5	London (WL)	2	Jul
(40)							
2.05	Tony Gilhooly	U20	26.03.76	7=	Bedford	3	Jul
2.05	Steve Chapman		28.01.66	1	Watford	30	Jul
2.05	Paul Burraway		30.11.68	2	Barking	6	Aug
2.04	Ian Massey	U20	9.09.76	8	Telford	9	Jul
2.03 i	Jason Allan	U23	17.09.72	1	Glasgow	16	Jan
	2.00			1	Linwood	1	May
2.03	Simon Kett	U20	9.10.75	3	Bournemouth	11	Jun
2.03	James Leaver	U20	15.09.75	2	Bournemouth	11	Jun
2.03	Stuart Brown	U23	27.11.72		Newport	14	Aug
2.02	Paul Hourihan	U20	7.11.76	1D	Kirkby	23	Jul
2.01	Paul Gilding	U20	2.01.75	1	Brighton	24	May
(50)							
2.01	Matthew Newman		13.10.67	1	Ealing	4	Jun
2.01	Barry Thomas	U23	28.04.72	13D	Bressanone, ITA	2	Jul
2.01	Billy Jewers		27.09.62	1	Ilford	2	Jul

Height	Name	Cat	DOB	Pos	Venue	Date	
2.01	Matthew Cordy	U20	29.09.75	9	Telford	9	Jul
2.01	Brad Knowles	U20	17.11.76	10	Telford	9	Jul
2.00 i	Jason Dronfield		5.07.70	12	Birmingham	8	Jan
2.00 i	David Bigham		4.07.71	2	London (Ha)	15	Jan
2.00 i	Martin Pate	U20	16.03.77	3	Glasgow	16	Jan
2.00 i	Alan Scobie		11.10.63	2	Glasgow	16	Jan
	2.00			1	Glasgow	15	May
2.00 i	Barry Saunders	U23	24.07.73	2	London (Ha)	29	Jan
	(60)						
2.00 i	Richard Aspden	U20	15.10.76	2	Birmingham	6	Feb
	2.00			1	Horsham	10	Apr
2.00 i	Jamie Quarry	U23	15.11.72	1H	Glasgow	5	Mar
	1.97			4=D	Emmelshausen, GER	28	May
2.00	*Olu Robincocker*	*U20*	*27.11.75*	*2*	*Hull*	*24*	*Apr*
2.00	Dean Macey	U17	12.12.77	1	Luton	1	May
2.00	Dominic Norriss		29.12.71	2	Bournemouth	7	May
2.00	Anthony Brannen		16.09.68	3	Bournemouth	7	May
2.00	Shaka Bunsie	U20	22.05.75	5	Wigan	7	May
2.00	Andy Hodge		18.12.68	1	Oxford	14	May
2.00	Kerry Bigham	U23	25.07.72	1	Leamington	15	May
2.00	Mark Smith	U23	14.09.74	3	Wolverhampton	4	Jun
2.00	Michael Toone	U20	25.09.76	1	Crewe	11	Jun
	(70)						
2.00	Mike Wright	U17	15.09.77	1	York	18	Jun
2.00	Andy Holbrook		24.11.70	2	Yate	29	Jun
2.00	Michael Morgan		30.07.66	6	London (WL)	2	Jul
2.00	Andrew Penk	U17	19.09.78	1	Colwyn Bay	2	Jul
2.00	Matthew Webb	U23	72	2	Reading	2	Jul
2.00	Darren Joseph	U17	4.04.78	2	Telford	9	Jul
2.00	Canisus Alcindor		27.04.63	4	Corby	31	Jul
2.00	Gary Blandford		17.12.63	1	Portsmouth	6	Aug
2.00	Dominic Savory	U20	16.12.75	3	Blackpool	14	Aug
2.00	Rupert Charles		25.10.60	22=Q	Victoria, CAN	18	Aug
	(80)						
2.00	Scott Hill	U23	8.05.72	1	Yate	21	Aug
2.00	Matthew Feldwick			2	Peterborough	29	Aug
2.00	Stuart Judge	U23	29.11.73	3	Peterborough	29	Aug
2.00	Roger Brehaut		1.06.65	1	Guernsey	24	Sep
1.98 i	Jim Stevenson		31.12.71	3P	Princeton, USA	5	Mar
	1.98			5=D	Austin, USA	25	Mar
1.98	Kieran Derbyshire	U20	18.01.77	1	Cleckheaton	4	Jun
1.98	Darren Clark	U20	15.03.76	1	Portsmouth	11	Jun
1.98	Deiniol Evans	U23	16.02.73	2	Cardiff	17	Jul
1.98	Unuakpor Esegbona		16.04.68	2=D	Stoke	6	Aug
1.98	Keith Mainstone	U23	15.03.74	1	Basingstoke	13	Aug
	(90)						
1.98	Keith Oag	U17	11.11.77	2	Dublin (M), IRE	13	Aug
1.98	Adam Smith	U20	20.02.77	1	Dublin (M), IRE	13	Aug
1.97 i	Rafer Joseph		21.07.68	4H	Glasgow	5	Mar

Additional Under 20 (1 - 34 above)

1.96	Craig Noble		21.06.75	1	Banff	16	Jun

Additional Under 17 (1 - 6 above)

1.95	James Pursglove		24.09.77	1	Derby	15	May
1.95	Matt Perry		15.02.78	5	Cwmbran	18	Jun
1.95	James Lees		3.07.78	2=	Yate	21	Aug
1.95	Clint Nicholls		16.02.79	1	Braintree	18	Sep
	(10)						
1.94 i	Robert Holton		8.09.78	1	Birmingham	10	Feb
	1.90			1	Nottingham	15	May
1.91	David Franks		21.09.78	1	Stretford	11	Jun

1.91	Steven McWhan		2.03.78	1	Dumfries	14	Jun
1.91	Lee Broomfield		5.12.77	Q	Telford	8	Jul
1.91	Robert Creese		1.12.77	Q	Telford	8	Jul
1.91	Simon Lewis		26.09.77	Q	Telford	8	Jul
1.91	Richard Sear		21.08.79	5	Telford	9	Jul
1.91	Edward Willers	U15	18.09.79	1	Telford	9	Jul
1.91	Matthew Brereton	U15	16.04.80	2	Telford	9	Jul
1.90	Glen Thurgood		6.10.77	2	Birmingham	24	Apr
	(20)						
1.90	Matt Deasy		30.07.78	1	Exeter	15	May
1.90	Trevor McGlynn		6.06.78	1	Antrim	11	Jun
1.90	Jay Hancock		12.07.78	3	Colwyn Bay	2	Jul
1.90	James Vincent-Smith		28.06.78	1	Exeter	24	Jul
1.90	Simon Critchley		18.03.78	1	Blackpool	14	Aug

Additional Under 15 (1 - 2 above)

1.87	Kevin Drury		30.09.79	1P	Wrexham	27	Aug
1.85	Andrew Smith		10.01.80	1	London (He)	7	Aug
1.85	Jamie Dalton		20.09.79	1	Swansea	21	Aug
1.84	Marc Newton		15.03.80	1	Tamworth	21	Aug
1.83	Martin Lloyd		18.06.80		London (Elt)	24	Sep
1.81	Dan Reardon		14.04.80	1	Solihull	18	Sep
1.80	Gary Neblett		27.12.79	2	Basildon	10	Jul
1.80	Robert Toms		7.08.80	2	London (He)	7	Aug
	(10)						
1.80	Lewis Erdman		29.11.79	1	London (TB)	20	Aug
1.80	Ian Wilson		7.10.79	1	Sutton Coldfield	28	Aug
1.80	Neil Dixon			1	Gateshead	3	Sep
1.78	Andrew Cresswell		4.04.80	1	Redditch	11	Jun
1.78	Andrew Chaddock		13.03.80	1	Corby	18	Jun
1.78	Nick Martin		4.03.80	1	Peterborough	17	Jul
1.78	Wayne Gray		7.11.80	1	Birmingham	11	Sep
1.77	Jason McDade		3.04.80	1	Ipswich	15	May
1.77	Richard MacDonald		11.01.80	1	Glasgow	14	Aug
1.76	Rasheed Banda		18.03.80	1	Brighton	11	Jun
	(20)						
1.76	James Sedge		19.10.79	Q	Telford	8	Jul
1.76	James Blackmore		8.10.79	Q	Telford	8	Jul
1.76	John-Paul Shepherd		29.02.80	1	Middlesbrough	17	Jul

Under 13

1.65	David Mayo		26.04.82	1	Grimsby	25	Sep
1.57	J. Moore			1	London (TB)	14	Aug
1.57	D. May			1	Lincoln	10	Sep
1.55	Marcus Donavan		14.09.81	1	London (WF)	7	Aug

POLE VAULT

5.50	Neil Winter	U23	21.03.74	1	Crawley	6	Aug
5.40				4	Gateshead	20	Jul
5.40				1	Colwyn Bay	23	Jul
5.40				1	Victoria, CAN	27	Aug
5.40				1	Bedford	17	Sep
5.35				1	Stoke	16	Jul
5.30				1	Swansea	15	Jun
5.30				1	Stoke	25	Jun
5.30				1	Wrexham	3	Jul
5.20				1	Istanbul, TUR	22	May
5.20				7	Edinburgh	8	Jul
5.20				7	Ostrava, CS	31	Jul
5.20				7	Sheffield	4	Sep
5.20				4	Salgotarjan, HUN	12	Sep

5.42	Mike Edwards		19.10.68	4	Abilene, USA	12	May
	5.30 i			1	Fargo, USA	12	Mar
	5.30			1	London (He)	5	Jun
	5.30			6	Edinburgh	8	Jul
	5.25			3	Crawley	6	Aug
	5.22			10	Walnut, USA	17	Apr
	5.20			6=	Philadelphia, USA	30	Apr
	5.20			2=	Sheffield	12	Jun
	5.20			5=	Birmingham	26	Jun
	5.20			10	London (CP)	15	Jul
	5.20			5	Gateshead	20	Jul
	5.20			5=	Hechtel, BEL	30	Jul
	5.20			24=Q	Helsinki, FIN	9	Aug
	5.20			5	Victoria, CAN	27	Aug
5.40	Nick Buckfield	U23	5.06.73	2	Crawley	6	Aug
	5.32			1	London (CP)	25	Jun
	5.25			1	Stoke	31	Jul
	5.20			2	London (He)	5	Jun
	5.20			1	Kingston	19	Jun
	5.20			1	London (WL)	2	Jul
	5.20			1	Kings Lynn	9	Jul
	5.20			3	Brussels, BEL	17	Jul
	5.20			8	Victoria, CAN	27	Aug
5.30 i	Andy Ashurst		2.01.65	3	Glasgow	29	Jan
	5.30			1	Sheffield	12	Jun
	5.20 i			2	Vienna, AUT	6	Feb
	5.20 i			2	Glasgow	12	Feb
	5.20 i			5=	Birmingham	19	Feb
	5.20 i			5	Birmingham	26	Feb
	5.20			3	London (He)	5	Jun
	5.20			11	London (CP)	15	Jul
	5.20			6	Victoria, CAN	27	Aug
5.30	Matt Belsham		11.10.71	8	Sheffield	4	Sep
	5.20 i			1	Stoke	27	Jul
	5.20			1	Birmingham	8	Jan
5.25	Kevin Hughes	U23	30.04.73	2	Stoke	25	Jun
	5.20			1	Corby	24	Aug
	5.20			2=	Sheffield	12	Jun
5.22	Paul Williamson	U23	16.06.74	1	Enfield	31	Jul
5.20	Mike Barber	U23	19.10.73	1	Grimsby	18	Jun
	5.20			3	Stoke	25	Jun
	5.20			2	Stoke	16	Jul
5.20 ns	Tim Thomas	U23	18.11.73	1	Dilbeek, BEL	13	Aug
	5.10			1	Wells	16	Jul
				2	Colwyn Bay	23	Jul

56 performances to 5.20 by 9 athletes including 7 indoors

5.11	Mark Johnson		7.09.64	1	Edinburgh	25	Jun
	(10)						
5.10 i	Dean Mellor		25.11.71	3	Birmingham	8	Jan
	5.10			4=	Sheffield	12	Jun
5.10	Ian Tullett		15.08.69	4=	Sheffield	12	Jun
5.06	Mark Grant		17.05.71	2	Corby	24	Aug
5.02	Bob Kingman	U23	21.02.73	2	Peterborough	29	Aug
5.01	Brian Hooper	V40	18.05.53	2	Wrexham	13	Aug
5.00	Warren Siley	U23	16.01.73	2	Wigan	2	Jul
5.00	Mark Hodgkinson	U23	20.07.72	3	Stoke	16	Jul
5.00 ns	Ian Wilding	U20	3.03.75	2	Wells	16	Jul
	4.85			1	Stoke	30	May
4.90	Matt Weaver	U23	14.11.73	1	Oxford	14	May
4.90	Dominic Shepherd	U20	11.12.76	1	Stoke	11	Sep

4.81	Rafer Joseph		21.07.68	1	Liverpool	6	Aug
4.80	Alex Kruger		18.11.63	8D	Gotzis, AUT	29	May
4.80	Neil Young	U20	20.02.77	7	Warsaw, POL	18	Jun
4.80	Barry Thomas	U23	28.04.72	1D	Horsham	19	Jun
4.80 ns	Paul Beswick		5.12.68	3	Wells	16	Jul
4.60 i				4=	Birmingham	26	Feb
4.60				3=	Corby	30	May
4.80	Geoff Gregory	U23	8.06.74	4	Wrexham	13	Aug
4.80	Dan Gilby		9.07.70	1	London (Elt)	29	Aug
4.75	Steve Gutteridge		5.07.71	1D	Azusa, USA	14	Apr
4.75	Dave Gordon		20.03.68	3	Corby	24	Aug
4.70 i	Keith Stock		18.03.57	8	Birmingham	8	Jan
(30)							
4.70	Steve Leader		24.11.66	2D	Horsham	19	Jun
4.65	Gary Jackson		28.04.68	1		28	Apr
4.65	Doug Hamilton		19.05.61	1	Pitreavie	20	Aug
4.60	Gavin Sunshine	U23	19.02.74	9	Wigan	7	May
4.60	Mark Davis	U20	1.03.77	6	Nicosia, CYP	17	May
4.60	Simon Shirley		3.08.66	18D	Gotzis, AUT	29	May
4.60	Duncan Pearce		21.10.70	8	London (WL)	2	Jul
4.60	David Bigham		4.07.71	5	Bedford	17	Sep
4.60	Warren Jousiffe	U20	27.05.77	1	Feltham	18	Sep
4.50 i	Kevin Treen	U20	1.02.76	3	Birmingham	6	Feb
4.40				1	Portsmouth	2	Apr
(40)							
4.50	Des Fitzgerald	U23	26.11.72	1	Pitreavie	8	May
4.50	Egryn Jones		1.11.71	2	Cwmbran	18	Jun
4.50	Livio Salvador-Aylott	U23	18.07.73	4D	Horsham	19	Jun
4.50	Rob Laing		30.07.66	5D	Horsham	19	Jun
4.50	Robin Hill	U20	23.02.77	3	Telford	9	Jul
4.50	Andy Buchanan		12.09.70	1	Southampton	13	Aug
4.50	Jon Yapp	U20	1.02.75	2	Telford	20	Aug
4.50	Damon Cooper	U23	5.07.74	3	Stoke	11	Sep
4.45	Robert Thickpenny	U20	17.07.76	1	Solihull	18	Sep
4.40 i	Stephen Lloyd	U23	2.03.72	3H	Birmingham	3	Jan
4.20				1	Oxford	15	May
(50)							
4.40 i	Paul Pentland		9.09.69	2	Glasgow	23	Jan
4.40 i	Neil Young	U23	27.09.73	4	Birmingham	6	Feb
4.20				5	Stoke	14	May
4.40	Matthew Buck	U23	5.04.74	5	London (CP)	1	May
4.40	Tim Anstiss		17.11.61	3	Bournemouth	7	May
4.40	Stephen Rogers		1.09.71	8=D	Emmelshausen, GER	29	May
4.40	Neil Turner	U20	17.05.77	1	Reading	2	Jul
4.40	Glyn Price		12.09.65	2	Swansea	20	Jul
4.40	Billy Davey		25.01.64	1	London (He)	30	Jul
4.40	*Alan Burke*		*23.05.65*	*2*	*London (Ha)*	*30*	*Jul*
4.40	Justin Richards		25.01.71	1	London (WP)	13	Aug
4.40	Wayne Weimann		2.05.66	1	Welwyn	13	Aug
(60)							
4.35	Garry Chiles		15.05.66	1	London (BP)	13	Aug
4.35	Matthew Evans	U20	19.11.75	1	Telford	17	Sep
4.30 i	James Robinson	U20	27.08.76	1H	Birmingham	2	Jan
4.30				1	Brierley Hill	1	May
4.30	David Griffiths	U23	22.12.74		Loughborough	27	Apr
4.30	David McLeod		26.03.63	2	Gateshead	15	May
4.30	Simon Rush	U20	23.06.76	1	Kingston	18	May
4.30	Christian Linskey	U15	14.06.80	1	Sheffield	18	Jun
4.30	Terry Fidler		13.10.71	6D	Horsham	19	Jun
4.30	Jamie Quarry	U23	15.11.72	9D	Victoria, CAN	24	Aug
4.25	Tony Matthews		17.12.62	2	Newcastle	25	Jun

4.25	Brian Hughes		6.01.70	2	Telford	17	Sep
4.21	Dean Robinson		25.06.70	1	Warley	14	May
4.20 i	Chris Wills	U20	18.05.76	5	Birmingham	12	Feb
4.20				1	Harrow	24	Apr
4.20 i	Paul Howard		19.10.66	2	London (Ha)	26	Feb
4.20				3	Wolverhampton	4	Jun
4.20 i	John Taylor		13.05.57	5	Wakefield	5	Mar
4.20				1	Stretford	15	May
4.20	Brett Heath	U20	6.01.75	1	Crawley	17	Apr
4.20	Richard Ramsey	U23	6.10.72	1	Loughborough	27	Apr
4.20	Simon Eastwood		18.04.65	1	Luton	1	May
4.20	Greg Conlon	U23	18.12.74	6	London (CP)	1	May
4.20	Alan Hardy		4.09.58	4	London (CP)	7	May
	(80)						
4.20	Gavin Showell	U23	29.09.72	4	Stoke	14	May
4.20	Peter Holt	U20	12.02.77	2	Gateshead	28	May
4.20	Mike Nicholl		29.07.61	10	Corby	30	May
4.20	Paul Field		24.06.67	1	Oxford	4	Jun
4.20	Paul Wray		16.02.66	10	London (He)	5	Jun
4.20	Ian Noble	U20	2.04.77	1	Wakefield	12	Jun
4.20	Brett Armstrong	U20	9.09.76		Stoke	18	Jun
4.20	Allan Leiper		23.07.60	8	Edinburgh	25	Jun
4.20	Tony Southward		31.01.71	2D	Stoke	26	Jun
4.20	Adam Davis	U23	19.11.72	1D	Stoke	26	Jun
	(90)						
4.20	Martin Parley	U17	26.07.78	1	Aberdeen	16	Jul
4.20	Peter Darbyshire		3.11.65	1	Liverpool	23	Jul
4.20	Steve McLennan	U17	17.11.78	1	Birmingham	31	Jul
4.20	Nick Pritchard	U23	5.12.72	3	Enfield	31	Jul
4.20	Owen Chaplin	U17	2.12.77	2	Birmingham	31	Jul
4.20	Stephen Gascoigne		20.12.66		London (Elt)	13	Aug
4.20	Ben Flint	U17	16.09.78		Oordegem, BEL	18	Aug
4.20	Dylan MacDermott		1.12.70	2	London (Elt)	29	Aug
4.15	William Wyllie	U23	12.07.73	7=	Stoke	16	Jul
4.15	Craig Guite	U20	19.08.77	1	Blackpool	14	Aug
	(100)						
4.15	James Skelton	U20		3	Yate	21	Aug
4.12	Chris Bennett	U20			Vancouver, CAN	14	May
4.11	Paul Jones	U17	11.04.78	1	Wrexham	21	Aug
4.10 i	Trevor Sloman		21.03.68	4=H	Birmingham	3	Jan
4.10 i	Mark Perman		6.01.68	4=H	Birmingham	3	Jan
4.10	Jeremy Hames		17.11.70	1	Loughborough	17	Apr
4.10	Eric Scott	U23	20.01.72	3	Edinburgh	24	Apr
4.10	Richard Sutton	U23	1.04.73	1	Welwyn	15	May
4.10	Steve Francis	U17	31.01.79	1	Colwyn Bay	2	Jul
4.10	Steve Plint		13.01.63	1	Croydon	2	Jul
	(110)						
4.10	Donald Darroch		30.05.65	2	Liverpool	23	Jul
4.10	Neil Fairlamb	U20	13.03.76	2	Yate	23	Jul
4.10	Andy Lewis		9.03.68	1	Reading	13	Aug
4.10	Stephen Bradley	U23	24.02.74	1	Cannock	17	Aug

Additional Under 17 (1 - 7 above)

4.05	Gavin Card		11.05.78	1	Jarrow	18	Jun
4.00	Robert Bell		17.12.77	1	London (CP)	28	May
4.00	Andrew Penk		19.09.78	2	Colwyn Bay	2	Jul
	(10)						
4.00	Edward Richards		19.09.77		Oostend, BEL	16	Aug
3.90	Rufus Cooper		24.02.79	3	Kingston	18	May
3.90	Rob Collins		17.09.77	5	Birmingham	31	Jul
3.90	Ian Holdsworth		12.01.78	1	Birmingham	11	Sep

3.85	Adam Pengilly		14.10.77	1	Stoke	11 Sep
3.81	Darren Beddows		4.05.78	1	Swansea	10 Jul
3.80	Steven Robinson		1.09.77	3	Milton Keynes	7 May
3.80	Neal Davis		11.10.77	2	Basildon	22 May
3.80	Richard Hulse		22.09.78	3	Gateshead	29 May
3.80	Thomas Richards		13.11.78	1	Harrow	5 Jun
	(20)					
3.80	Ben Johnston		8.11.78	1	Sheffield	2 Jul
3.70	James Palmer		21.04.78	8	Birmingham	31 Jul
3.70	Richard Smith	U15	17.01.81	1	Peterborough	29 Aug

Additional Under 15 (1 above)

3.60	Stephen Smith		13.02.80	1	Peterborough	11 Jun
3.60	Jon Parry		13.04.80	1	Swansea	20 Jul
3.40	Ben West					
3.40 i	Tom Benn		20.04.80	1	London (CP)	29 Jan
3.35	Adam Walker		16.11.79	3	Telford	8 Jul
3.31	Charles Rule		22.05.80	1	Pitreavie	20 Aug
3.30	David Ingram		19.01.80	1	Barking	22 May
3.30	Darren Neport		4.09.79	1	Hoo	26 Jun
3.20	John Gullaksen		24.02.80	2	Middlesbrough	17 Jul
	(10)					
3.20	Chris Boundy		25.12.79	2	Birmingham	11 Sep
3.15	Alex Thomas		31.12.79	1	Stoke	18 Jun
3.15	Neil Cook		23.11.79	7	Telford	8 Jul
3.15	Matthew O'Riley		13.11.79	8	Telford	8 Jul
3.10	Paul Miles		14.09.80	1	Cardiff	26 Jun
3.10	P. Harrison			1	Woodford	11 Jul
3.00	S. Gill		1.09.79	1	Bebington	5 Jun
3.00	David Raw		1.02.81	1	Jarrow	18 Jun
3.00	J. Baker			1	Cardiff	26 Jun
3.00	Simon Ayres		5.10.79	10	Telford	8 Jul
	(20)					
3.00	Martyn Dunbar		25.05.80	1	Middlesbrough	11 Jul
3.00	David Allistair			2	Stoke	11 Sep

Under 13

3.00	Ollive	U13		1	Sutton	18 Sep
2.90 ns	Philip Wade	U13	24.05.82	1	Wells	15 Jul
2.50	Iain Clarke	U13	19.01.82	1	Corby	16 Jun
2.30	L. Checkley	U13		1	Harrow	5 Jul

Note: Performances marked ns were set in a town centre (not in a stadium) but are considered valid.

LONG JUMP

8.10	-0.2	Fred Salle	10.09.64	1	London (CP)	9 Sep
		8.10 w 4.7		2	Gateshead	20 Jul
		7.88 1.9		5	Victoria, CAN	26 Aug
		7.85 1.3		Q	Victoria, CAN	24 Aug
		7.83 1.1		1	Nitra, SVK	13 Jul
		7.77 0.9		1	Bracknell	2 May
		7.68 1.5		1	Wrexham	3 Jul
		7.61 1.1		1	Loughborough	5 Jun
		7.60 0.2		2	Sheffield	11 Jun
		7.57 i		4	Vienna, AUT	6 Feb
		7.51 i		4	Glasgow	29 Jan
7.91 w	4.6	Steve Ingram	22.09.70	1	Cwmbran	18 Jun
		7.38		2	Istanbul, TUR	21 May

Mark	Wind	Name	Cat	DOB	Pos	Venue	Day	Mon
7.90	1.7	Barrington Williams		11.09.55	4	Gateshead	20	Jul
7.77	0.9				1	Sheffield	11	Jun
7.69	1.1				19Q	Helsinki, FIN	9	Aug
7.66	0.8				6	Birmingham	25	Jun
7.65 i					1	Birmingham	26	Feb
7.64 i					1	Birmingham	8	Jan
7.63	1.3				1	Corby	30	May
7.61 i					1	Glasgow	12	Feb
7.58 i					3	Glasgow	29	Jan
7.53	0.7				14Q	Victoria, CAN	24	Aug
7.89 w		Steve Phillips	U23	17.03.72	1	Warley	4	May
7.65					1	Wigan	17	Apr
7.62					1	Leamington	15	May
7.61	0.4				1	Bulle, SWZ	10	Sep
7.59 w	2.5				1	Kings Lynn	9	Jul
7.58	0.9				2	Corby	30	May
7.58	0.6				1	Crawley	6	Aug
7.57					1	Peterborough	27	Mar
7.57	0.7				1	Loughborough	22	Jun
7.56	-0.4				1	Wigan	7	May
7.56 w	5.3				6	Gateshead	20	Jul
7.54 i					6	Vienna, AUT	6	Feb
7.53					1	Welwyn	2	May
7.51	1.1				*	Gateshead	20	Jul
7.81 w		*Enyinna Chukukere*	*U23*	*31.07.73*	*4*	*Knoxville, USA*	*9*	*Apr*
7.64 i					*1*	*Princeton, USA*	*6*	*Mar*
7.36	*0.2*				*2*	*London (WL)*	*2*	*Jul*
7.75	0.5	Michael Morgan		30.07.66	4	Hechtel, BEL	30	Jul
7.66	1.7				2	Wrexham	3	Jul
7.59	2.0				1	London (He)	5	Jun
7.59	0.8				3	Sheffield	11	Jun
7.55	-0.7				1	London (WL)	2	Jul
7.62		Gareth Davies		11.05.71	1	Oxford	14	May
7.60	1.4	Duncan Mathieson		8.03.69	1	Stoke	31	Jul
7.57	0.8	John Munroe		6.01.69	4	Brussels, BEL	17	Jul
7.55 w					1	Kingston	31	Jul
7.50					1	Enfield	20	Jul
7.54	-1.4	Courtney Charles		13.11.68	2	Wigan	7	May
7.53 w		Andy Lewis		9.03.68	1D	Wrexham	27	Aug
7.39					1	Cannock	11	Sep
		(10)						
7.52	0.3	Simon Shirley		3.08.66	2D	Bressanone, ITA	2	Jul

49 performances to 7.50 by 11 athletes including 7 indoors and 7 wind assisted

Mark	Wind	Name	Cat	DOB	Pos	Venue	Day	Mon
7.48		Stewart Faulkner		19.02.69	1	London (CP)	27	Apr
7.46 w	3.2	Chris Davidson	U20	4.12.75	2	Bedford	3	Jul
7.21 i					1	Birmingham	12	Feb
7.10					7	London (CP)	25	Jun
7.45		Carl Howard	U23	27.01.74	1	Hayes	11	May
7.45	2.0	Alex Kruger		18.11.63	7D	Gotzis, AUT	28	May
7.44 w		Julian Flynn	U23	3.07.72	2	Wigan	17	Apr
7.25 i					1	Wakefield	13	Feb
7.18					1	Corby	4	Jun
7.42 w		Gary Jones	U23	15.07.72	1	Blackburn	1	May
7.12					2	Rotherham	7	May
7.41 w		John Mackenzie		23.08.65	2	Kingston	31	Jul
7.24	1.7				*	Crawley	6	Aug
7.40	0.3	Garry Slade		10.10.68	3	Corby	30	May
7.39	0.8	Onochie Onuorah	U23	16.10.73	4	Sheffield	11	Jun
		(20)						
7.36	1.5	Steve Smith	U23	29.03.73	5	Sheffield	11	Jun

Mark		Wind	Name	Cat	DOB	Pos	Venue		Date
7.36			A. Walker			1	Aldershot	6	Jul
7.36	w	3.9	Jamie Quarry	U23	15.11.72	1	Enfield	31	Jul
7.17		1.3				*	Loughborough	5	Jun
7.32		-0.9	Larry Achike	U20	31.01.75	5	London (He)	5	Jun
7.32	w	3.5	Chris Cotter	U23	3.02.72	4	London (He)	5	Jun
7.28						2	Bracknell	2	May
7.30			Gary Smith		20.02.71	1	London (He)	29	Jun
7.30	w		Anthony Wood	U23	30.03.74	1	Middlesbrough	2	Apr
7.29		0.0				2	Cork, IRE	25	Jun
7.27		1.7	Jim Stevenson		31.12.71	1D	Austin, USA	25	Mar
7.27			Jonathan Edwards		10.05.66	1	Gateshead	15	May
7.27			John Shepherd		23.12.61	3	London (CP)	25	Jun
		(30)							
7.26			Dean Cocks		18.01.67	1	Woodford	10	Aug
7.25			Glyn Chidlow		21.10.71	2	Oxford	14	May
7.25	w		Nathan Morgan	U17	30.06.78	1	London (He)	27	Aug
6.81						1	Leicester	11	Jun
7.25	w		William Wyllie	U23	12.07.73	2D	Wrexham	27	Aug
7.11		1.0				1D	Stoke	25	Jun
7.24			Tony Mason	U20	8.03.76	1	Ipswich	15	May
7.23		1.0	Tosi Fasinro	U23	28.03.72	7	Malaga, SPA	28	May
7.23	w	2.1	Rob Laing		30.07.66	4D	Prague, CS	28	May
7.11		1.4				3D	Horsham	18	Jun
7.22			Joe Sweeney		17.07.65	1	Cardiff	2	Jul
7.22			Mike Swift	U23	27.08.72	1	Liverpool	23	Jul
7.21			Gavin Sunshine	U23	19.02.74	6D	Emmelshausen, GER	28	May
		(40)							
7.20			John Herbert		20.04.62	3	Bracknell	2	May
7.19		1.4	Paul Field		24.06.67	2D	Horsham	18	Jun
7.18			Stefan Rose	U20	7.04.75	1	Basingstoke	21	Aug
7.17			James Clawley	U20	15.10.75	1	Sheffield (W)	4	Jun
7.17	w	3.3	Mark Bignell		17.09.68	8	London (He)	5	Jun
7.06		0.9				*	London (He)	5	Jun
7.17	w		Warren Siley	U23	16.01.73	3	Kingston	31	Jul
7.16	w		Marcellas Peters	U17	20.11.78	1	Croydon	18	Jun
7.08						1O	Birmingham	17	Sep
7.15	w	3.4	Darren Ritchie	U20	14.02.75	6	Corby	30	May
6.97						1	Edinburgh	14	May
7.13			Mark Findlay	U17	20.03.78	2	Warsaw, POL	24	Sep
7.13	w		Mark Bushell	U20	22.10.76	1D	Birmingham	17	Sep
		(50)							
7.12			Stephen Rowbotham		6.03.68	1	Derby	16	Jul
7.12	w	2.1	Paul Johnson		8.03.68	4	Birmingham	21	May
7.00		1.1				*	Birmingham	21	May
7.11			Mark Lawrence		26.01.71	4	Loughborough	5	Jun
7.10			Matthew Bridle	U20	11.08.76	3	Rotherham	7	May
7.09			Matthew Birchall		11.01.71	1	Blackburn	11	May
7.09			*Mathias Ogbeta*		*19.06.68*	*1*	*Carlisle*	*6*	*Aug*
7.08			Paul Williamson	U23	16.06.74	1	Derby	29	Apr
7.08		1.9	Trevor Sinclair		6.08.61	6	Crawley	6	Aug
7.08		0.5	Gary Munroe		12.04.69	1	Peterborough	6	Aug
7.07	i		Dinkar Sabnis	U23	23.09.73	2	Glasgow	23	Jan
7.02						2	Glasgow	22	May
7.07			Barry Thomas	U23	28.04.72	3D	Wrexham	27	Aug
		(60)							
7.06	w	4.1	Anthony Brannen		16.09.68	2	Barking	6	Aug
6.89						2	Stoke	2	Jul
7.05	w	4.1	Bassey Essien	U23	17.11.73	5	Bedford	17	Sep
6.97						3	Liverpool	6	Aug
7.04			Paul Ralph		16.12.67	1	Hoo	19	Jun
7.03			Junior Campbell		13.02.70	2	London (Nh)	15	May

7.03 w	5.2	Jan Irving	U20	4.03.77	3	Telford	9 Jul
		7.02			1	Bebington	11 Jun
7.02 i		Dalton Grant		8.04.66	11	Birmingham	19 Feb
7.02	1.0	Brian Downer	U20	1.12.75	1	London (CP)	29 May
7.02		Andrew Slaughter	U20	22.10.75	1	Peterborough	2 Jul
7.02		David Bigham		4.07.71	2	Liverpool	6 Aug
7.01		Femi Akinsanya		29.11.69	2	Croydon	2 Jul
	(70)						
7.01 w		Paul Dundas	U23	14.01.74	2	Warley	4 May
7.00		Nigel Bourne	U23	18.04.72		Enfield	15 May
7.00		Mark Swales	U20	29.01.75	1	Colchester	19 Jun
7.00		William Stark	U20	11.03.77	1	Barry	19 Jul
6.99 i		Brian Ashburn		11.03.70	3	Glasgow	23 Jan
6.99		David Gardner		14.12.68	1	Newcastle	27 Apr
6.99 w	4.4	Ian Roberts		15.06.68	3	Cwmbran	18 Jun
6.96		Dave Reeve	U23	25.05.73	2	Oxford	20 Feb
6.96		Colin Rattigan		20.11.60	7	Wigan	7 May
6.96		Greg Richards		25.04.56	2	Reading	14 Aug
	(80)						
6.95		R. Turner			1	Oxford	15 May
6.95		Francis Adams		19.10.69	3	London (Nh)	15 May
6.95		Stuart Gibbs		4.03.62	1	London (WF)	19 Jun
6.95		Matt Allison	U23	26.02.73	1D	Wakefield	24 Sep
6.95 w	3.2	Steve Gutteridge		5.07.71	4D	Horsham	18 Jun
		6.90 1.2			3D	Azusa, USA	13 Apr
6.94		D. Finch			1	Portsmouth	23 Mar
6.94		Nick Hubbard	U20	17.04.76	1	Yate	23 Jul
6.93		Julian Rifat		23.03.69	1	Basildon	30 Jul
6.93		Lee Edwards	U20	14.09.75	3	Edinburgh	6 Aug
6.93 w	2.6	Stuart Clarke	U20	16.10.75	4	Telford	9 Jul
	(90)						
6.92		Neil McMenemy		6.04.67	2	Edinburgh	14 May
6.92	1.0	Martin Giraud	U17	16.11.77	Q	Nicosia, CYP	17 May
6.92	1.5	Andrew Weston	U23	4.12.73	2D	Stoke	25 Jun
6.92		C. Buchanan			3	Aldershot	6 Jul
6.92 w	3.0	Anthony Malcolm	U20	15.02.76	1	Exeter	20 Aug
6.91		Jason Wing		12.10.65	2	Perivale	18 May
6.91		*Nicholas Warchalowski*		*10.11.71*	*3*	*Glasgow*	*22 May*
6.91		Nicky Gordon	U20	7.01.77	2	Gateshead	28 May
6.91		Ezra Clarke	U23	9.12.74	2	Yate	21 Aug
6.90		James Robinson	U20	27.08.76	1D	Birmingham	23 Apr
6.90		Todd Bennett		6.07.62	4	Sheffield (W)	4 Jun
	(100)						
6.90		Ruddy Farquharson		26.03.61	1	Cosford	15 Jun
6.90	1.2	Morris Philipson	U23	26.02.73	5	Derby	16 Jul
6.90 w	5.3	Marlon Franklin	U20	9.03.75	6	Telford	9 Jul

Additional Under 17 (1 - 4 above)

6.87 w		Andrew Thornton		29.11.77	1	Gateshead	15 May
		6.62			4	Telford	9 Jul
6.85		David Clerihew		11.09.77	1	Coatbridge	24 Apr
6.73		Andrew Roberts		19.09.77	1	Bury	22 May
6.73		Scott Walker		9.09.77	2O	Birmingham	17 Sep
6.73 i		Ross Baillie		26.09.77	1P	Glasgow	10 Dec
6.73 w	2.1	Peter Zdanowski		3.01.78	2	Birmingham	30 Jul
		6.64 2.0			1	London (CP)	29 May
	(10)						
6.68		Neil Brown		6.04.78	1	Cardiff	26 Jun
6.65		James Peacock		29.09.77	1	London (Nh)	14 May

6.65		Dean Macey		12.12.77	1	Enfield	14	Aug
6.60 w		Nick Dowsett		24.11.78	3O	Birmingham	17	Sep
6.50	1.7	Matt Perry		15.02.78	4	Birmingham	30	Jul
6.40		Stephen Tang		10.11.77				

Under 15

6.36 w	3.6	Marc Newton		15.03.80	1P	Wrexham	27	Aug
6.26					1P	Birmingham	17	Sep
6.18		Mark Faulkner		14.11.79	1	Portsmouth	11	Jun
6.16	-2.1	Ola Omomo		6.03.80	1	Telford	8	Jul
6.16		Tom Benn		20.04.80	3P	Birmingham	17	Sep
6.16		Andrew Squire		30.09.79	2P	Birmingham	17	Sep
6.13		Jason McDade		3.04.80	1	Colchester	29	Aug
6.10		Kevin Hibbins		7.11.80	1	Peterborough	29	Aug
6.09		Lewis Erdman		29.11.79	1	London (BP)	28	May
6.09		Terry Poole		20.11.79	1	Brighton	11	Jun
6.06 w		James Morris		2.12.79	1	Brecon	19	Jun
	(10)							
6.05		Daniel Hutchinson		25.12.79	1	Peterborough	28	Aug
6.04		Mike Harris		30.01.80	1	Portsmouth	17	Jul
6.04		Ray Saunders		26.04.80	1	Cwmbran	17	Jul
6.03		Mike Stuart		7.05.80	1	Yeovil	18	Jun
6.02		John Pilling		3.02.80	1	Blackpool	11	Jun
6.01		Neil Akester		6.09.79	1	Lincoln	24	Jul
6.00		Chris Low		24.04.80	1	Dundee	17	Apr
5.95		Ronan George		10.01.80	1	London (He)	11	Jun
5.95		Sleniba Alla		19.10.79	1	Milton Keynes	26	Jun
5.94		Matthew Dobson		20.01.80	4P	Birmingham	17	Sep
	(20)							
5.92		Sean Walker		11.06.80	1	Yate	11	Jul
5.90 w	2.1	Kevin Drury		30.09.79	2P	Wrexham	27	Aug

Under 13

5.45		Martin Taylor		31.01.82	1	Glasgow	2	Jun
5.24		Dwayne Grant			1	London (CP)	5	Jun
5.14		Chris Jenkins	U13	2.03.82	1	Bebington	14	May

TRIPLE JUMP

17.39	1.9	Jonathan Edwards		10.05.66	1	Sheffield	12	Jun
17.06	0.0				3	Monaco, MON	2	Aug
17.05	1.2				2	Gateshead	1	Jul
17.02 w	3.9				4	Bratislava, SVK	1	Jun
17.00	1.6				2	Victoria, CAN	28	Aug
16.97 w	5.6				5	Seville, SPA	5	Jun
16.88	0.8				4	Birmingham	26	Jun
16.88	0.5				1	Edinburgh	8	Jul
16.85	0.5				6	Helsinki, FIN	13	Aug
16.83 i					*	Stuttgart, GER	6	Feb
16.80	-0.1				1	Gateshead	20	Jul
16.73	2.0				*	Seville, SPA	5	Jun
16.73 w	2.6				6	Stockholm, SWE	12	Jul
16.72	0.1				Q	Helsinki, FIN	11	Aug
16.71 i					2	Glasgow	12	Feb
16.71	0.5				3	London (CP)	15	Jul
16.65 i					3	Glasgow	29	Jan
16.57					7	St. Petersburg, RUS	29	Jul
16.52	0.9				Q	Victoria, CAN	27	Aug

Perf	Wind	Name	Cat	DOB	Pos	Venue	Date
17.06	0.9	Julian Golley		12.09.71	2	London (CP)	10 Sep
17.03	0.9				1	Victoria, CAN	28 Aug
16.98	0.6				2	Sheffield	12 Jun
16.86	1.5				Q	Victoria, CAN	27 Aug
16.82 w	3.9				2	London (He)	5 Jun
16.81 w	2.7				2	Enfield	15 May
16.76 i					1	Glasgow	12 Feb
16.75 w	2.1				1	Sheffield	4 Sep
16.66	1.9				*	Enfield	15 May
16.59					1	Kingston	31 Jul
16.57 i					4	Birmingham	26 Feb
16.55	1.4				*	London (He)	5 Jun
16.54	0.6				5	London (CP)	15 Jul
16.51 w	2.7				7	Bratislava, SVK	1 Jun
16.50	1.0				*	Sheffield	4 Sep
16.41	0.6				Q	Helsinki, FIN	11 Aug
16.40 i					4	Glasgow	29 Jan
16.36	1.2				1	Wigan	7 May
16.35	0.6				9	Helsinki, FIN	11 Aug
16.31	0.3				5	Gateshead	20 Jul
16.95	1.3	Francis Agyepong		16.06.65	3	Sheffield	12 Jun
16.95 w	2.6				1	London (He)	5 Jun
16.93	1.0				1	Enfield	15 May
16.77	0.5				2	Gateshead	20 Jul
16.73 i					2	Birmingham	26 Feb
16.57	0.3				4	London (CP)	15 Jul
16.55 i					1	Birmingham	19 Feb
16.50	0.9				1	Corby	30 May
16.42 w	2.4				4	Sheffield	4 Sep
16.33	1.3				6	Victoria, CAN	28 Aug
16.30	1.9				Q	Victoria, CAN	27 Aug
16.74 w	2.5	Tosi Fasinro	U23	28.03.72	1	Ostrava, CS	31 Jul
16.70	-1.0				4	Gateshead	1 Jul
16.68 w	2.5				3	Bad Cannstatt, GER	10 Jul
16.62	0.6				4	Sheffield	12 Jun
16.61	0.3				*	Ostrava, CS	31 Jul
16.58	1.5				5	Bratislava, SVK	1 Jun
16.56	1.1				3	Enfield	15 May
16.55	1.7				3	Gateshead	20 Jul
16.43 w	4.5				7	Seville, SPA	5 Jun
16.35 w	3.2				9	Stockholm, SWE	12 Jul
16.31	0.3				8	London (CP)	15 Jul
16.67 w	2.4	Larry Achike	U20	31.01.75	1	Lisbon, POR	24 Jul
16.53	0.7				*	Lisbon, POR	24 Jul
16.52	-0.7				5	Cologne, GER	21 Aug
16.36	1.8				5	Sheffield	4 Sep

65 performances to 16.30 by 5 athletes including 8 indoors and 14 wind assisted

Perf	Wind	Name	Cat	DOB	Pos	Venue	Date
16.17	1.2	John Mackenzie		23.08.65	2	Bedford	17 Sep
15.98		Femi Akinsanya		29.11.69	1	Croydon	2 Jul
15.93	1.2	Tayo Erogbogbo	U20	8.03.75	3	Bedford	17 Sep
15.84		Carl Howard	U23	27.01.74	1	London (CP)	30 Apr
15.78		Michael McDonald		24.08.65	1	Corby	31 Jul
	(10)						
15.72 i		Derek Browne		28.09.66	4	Vienna, AUT	6 Feb
15.64	1.1				7	Sheffield	12 Jun
15.59 w	2.4	Rez Cameron		18.05.60	4	Bedford	17 Sep
15.49	1.7				*	Bedford	17 Sep
15.55 i		Joe Sweeney		17.07.65	3	Lievin, FRA	6 Jan
15.43					3	Corby	31 Jul
15.54 i		Vernon Samuels		15.10.64	5	Birmingham	19 Feb
15.34	1.4				3	Birmingham	21 May
15.46		Ezra Clarke	U23	9.12.74	2	Bracknell	2 May

15.41		Joe Allison		16.09.59	1	Cannock	26	Jun
15.71		*Akin Oyediran*		*27.11.59*	*3*	*Fayetteville, USA*	*16*	*Apr*
15.36		Paul Ralph		16.12.67	1	Stoke	2	Jul
15.28		Dave Sanderson		6.05.71	1	Manchester	10	Jul
15.24	0.6	Michael Brown		6.05.62	3	London (CP)	26	Jun
15.18	-1.0	Marvin Bramble	U20	10.06.77	2	Nicosia, CYP	19	May
(20)								
15.18		Ruddy Farquharson		26.03.61	1	Aldershot	6	Jul
15.17	*1.2*	*Mathias Ogbeta*		*19.06.68*	*1*	*Derby*	*16*	*Jul*
15.13	0.9	Neil McMenemy		6.04.67	4	Corby	30	May
15.06	0.8	Jon Hilton	U23	11.01.74	11	Sheffield	12	Jun
15.05		Eugene Hechevarria		30.12.63	1	Mansfield	23	Jul
15.02	-0.7	Paul Weston		6.10.67	1	Stoke	16	Jul
15.02		Kori Stennett	U20	2.09.76	1	London (He)	27	Aug
14.99	-0.6	Keith Ible		9.11.68	3	Crawley	6	Aug
14.98	-0.9	Steve Phillips	U23	17.03.72	1	Bulle, SWZ	10	Sep
14.93	-0.9	Julian Flynn	U23	3.07.72	2	Bulle, SWZ	10	Sep
14.87		Mike Swift	U23	27.08.72	3	London (CP)	30	Apr
(30)								
14.84		Mark Richards		1.07.70	1	London (TB)	16	Jun
14.80		A. Walker			1	Aldershot	8	Jun
14.80		Stuart Richmond		11.04.69	3	London (Elt)	29	Aug
14.75		Dave Reeve	U23	25.05.73	1	Loughborough	27	Apr
14.75		Chris Cotter	U23	3.02.72	1	Exeter	15	May
14.73		Gareth Davies		11.05.71	1	Oxford	14	May
14.63		Andy Hodge		18.12.68	2	Oxford	14	May
14.61		Martin Rossiter		4.09.69	1	Welwyn	14	Aug
14.61 w 3.7		Paul Farmer		17.11.69	1	Cwmbran	18	Jun
14.51					4	Istanbul, TUR	22	May
14.60		Simon Gee	U20	23.04.75	1	Liverpool	6	Aug
(40)								
14.56 w 2.7		James Leaver	U20	15.09.75	2	Telford	9	Jul
14.40					2	London (He)	27	Aug
14.53	0.4	Anthony Brannen		16.09.68	1	Newport	26	Jun
14.53 w		Dean Macey	U17	12.12.77	1	Luton	1	May
14.26	-1.0				1	Birmingham	30	Jul
14.52 w		Michael Morgan		30.07.66	4	Kingston	31	Jul
14.47 w		M. Louisy			2	Luton	1	May
14.47 w 3.0		Sam Bobb	U20	29.08.75	3	Telford	9	Jul
14.23					1	Bromley	19	Jun
14.47 w 2.6		Mel Fowler		7.07.66	3	London (He)	18	Aug
14.35	1.2				*	London (He)	18	Aug
14.46		Matthew Randall		28.04.70	3	London (Elt)	29	Aug
14.45	1.8	Ray Smith		24.12.67	7	Corby	30	May
14.43		Michael Dockery		29.07.71	3	Stoke	2	Jul
(50)								
14.42		Martin Goodall		2.10.64	1	Portsmouth	14	May
14.41		Nigel Bourne	U23	18.04.72	1	Crawley	14	Aug
14.40 w 2.2		Dean Goulding	U20	14.06.75	4	Bedford	2	Jul
14.17					1	Sheffield	18	Jun
14.38 w 3.8		Abu Garba	U20	6.05.76	4	Telford	9	Jul
14.25					1	Brighton	11	Jun
14.33	1.1	Adam Smith	U20	20.02.77	5	Kings Lynn	9	Jul
14.33		Amofa Osei	U23	15.12.73	6	Kings Lynn	9	Jul
14.31	-2.2	Paul Hibbert		31.03.65	7	London (WL)	2	Jul
14.30		Junior Lewis		19.03.66	1	Perivale	30	Jul
14.29 w 3.5		Andrew Slaughter	U20	22.10.75	5	Telford	9	Jul
14.26					1	Peterborough	2	Jul
14.27		Mark Lawrence		26.01.71	4	London (CP)	30	Apr
(60)								
14.27		Stephen Haunch		6.04.70	1	Warley	14	May
14.24	1.1	Junior Campbell		13.02.70	5	Bedford	17	Sep
14.21	0.9	Albert Earle		10.01.58	3	Stoke	16	Jul

14.16	0.6	Paul Ellis	U20	2.11.75	2	Oordegem, BEL	9	Jul
14.16		Mike McKernan	U17	28.11.78	3	London (He)	27	Aug
14.15		Jonathan Bridge		19.11.67	2	Blackburn	4	Jun
14.14	*0.4*	*Manny Nsudoh*	*U23*	*8.04.72*	*2*	*Croydon*	*15*	*May*
14.14		John Wiggins		1.07.71	2	Blackpool	15	May
14.14 w	4.0	Rob Weston	U20	16.03.77	6	Telford	9	Jul
14.12	1.2	Iwobi Onoura	U23	21.05.74	12	London (He)	5	Jun
14.11		Wyn Morris		25.02.61	2	London (He)	7	May
	(70)							
14.10		*Olu Robincocker*	*U20*	*27.11.75*	*2*	*Cannock*	*11*	*Sep*
14.07	0.5	James Peacock	U17	29.09.77	1	Telford	8	Jul
14.06		Dinkar Sabnis	U23	23.09.73	1	Glasgow	22	May
14.00		J. Mason	U20		1	Blackpool	14	Aug
13.99		Denis Costello		3.12.61	1	Great Yarmouth	14	May
13.99		Stefan Rose	U20	7.04.75	4	London (Elt)	29	May
13.97 i		William Stark	U20	11.03.77	3	Glasgow	23	Jan
13.97					3	Exeter	20	Aug
13.97	-1.0	John Naylor	U17	19.04.78	3	Birmingham	30	Jul
13.94		John Booth		3.02.68	2	Bromley	19	Jun
13.94		Bassey Essien	U23	17.11.73	2	Harrow	2	Jul
13.93 i		Garry Slade		10.10.68	9	Birmingham	26	Feb
	(80)							
13.92		David Dixon		2.03.60	1	Carlisle	26	Jun
13.92	0.9	Adrian Browne	U17	14.07.78	3	Telford	8	Jul
13.90		Elphinston Hinds		15.07.60	2	Watford	30	Jul

Additional Under 17 (1 - 5 above)

13.84		Charles Robertson-Adams		5.12.77	1	Telford	14	May
13.81		Marc Grover		25.02.78	1	Bracknell	11	Jun
13.77 i		Matthew Thompson		7.01.78	2	Birmingham	10	Feb
13.68	-1.0				5	Birmingham	30	Jul
13.77	1.3	Adrian Jefferies		12.04.79	5	Telford	8	Jul
13.75		Peter Wilkinson		7.08.78	1	Middlesbrough	17	Jul
	(10)							
13.73		Charles Cole			3	Aberdeen	16	Jul
13.65		Stuart Wells		26.07.79	2	Barking	12	Jun
13.60		Leke Ilo			1	Kingston	11	Jun
13.58		Vince Martorana		18.10.77	1	London (He)	26	Jun

Under 15

13.29		Daniel Hutchinson	25.12.79	1	Birmingham	31	Jul
13.19		Richard MacDonald	11.01.80	1	Grangemouth	28	Aug
12.68	-1.3	Syful Ahmed	25.10.79	2	Telford	8	Jul
12.59	0.2	Ray Saunders	26.04.80	3	Telford	8	Jul
12.54		Alastair Gudgeon	26.10.79	1	Peterborough	11	Jun
12.43	-2.8	Nicholas Myers	25.03.80	4	Telford	8	Jul
12.40		Michael Sleet	6.06.80	1	Andover	4	Sep
12.37		John Burke	25.11.79	1	Jarrow	18	Jun
12.30		Sahr Foday	6.11.79	1	London (He)	11	Jun
12.22	-1.8	Saverio Marasa	19.09.79	7	Telford	8	Jul
	(10)						
12.21		Kevin Drury	30.09.79		Shrewsbury	14	Jul
12.16		Jonathon Miller	10.06.81	1	Birmingham	11	Jun
12.14		Olisa Okwuosa		1	London (He)	7	Aug
12.12		Peter Francis	28.08.80	1	Havering	11	Jun
12.06		S. Lewis		1	Exeter	24	Jul
12.05		J. Warman		1	Yate	11	Jun
12.04		Michael Allen		1	Antrim	23	Jul
12.03		Karl Evans	9.07.80		Brecon	19	Jun

Under 13

10.68	E. Efoyini		1	Birmingham	2	Jul
10.65	S. Coghlan		2	Birmingham	2	Jul
10.36	Richard Oparka	28.07.82	1	Aberdeen	5	Jun

SHOT

19.94	¶Paul Edwards		16.02.59	1	College Station, USA	21	May
19.82				1	Walton	11	May
19.47 i				1	Vienna, AUT	6	Feb
19.44				1	College Station, USA	25	May
19.38 i				3	Glasgow	12	Feb
19.27 i				1	London (CP)	15	Jan
19.21 i				2	Glasgow	29	Jan
19.11				1	Southampton	10	May
19.02				1	London (He)	5	Jun
19.02				1	Wrexham	3	Jul
18.98				1	Roehampton	6	Jul
18.98 i				4	Gateshead	20	Jul
18.95 i				1	Birmingham	18	Feb
18.89				1	Kings Lynn	9	Jul
18.84				1	London (WL)	2	Jul
18.78				1	Vancouver, CAN	29	May
18.77 i				1	Horsham	8	Jan
18.72 i				1	Horsham	19	Feb
18.65				1	Horsham	8	May
18.56				1	Bournemouth	23	Jul
18.55				1	Salisbury	10	Jul
18.54				13Q	Helsinki, FIN	12	Aug
18.53				9	San Jose, USA	28	May
18.49 i				14Q	Paris, FRA	11	Mar
18.36				1	Wigan	7	May
18.32				1	Sheffield	12	Jun
18.10				7	Birmingham	25	Jun
19.49	Matt Simson		28.05.70	1	Victoria, CAN	28	Aug
19.17 i				2	Gainesville, USA	26	Feb
18.99				1	Gainesville, USA	26	Mar
18.97				3	Victoria, CAN	19	Aug
18.92 i				4	Indianapolis, USA	11	Mar
18.81				1	Fayetteville, USA	14	May
18.80				5	Boise, USA	4	Jun
18.80				2	Kings Lynn	9	Jul
18.64				1	Gainesville, USA	30	Apr
18.58				5	Gateshead	20	Jul
18.58				1	Guildford	13	Aug
18.42 i				1	Gainesville, USA	21	Jan
18.41				1	Gainesville, USA	16	Apr
18.39				2	Nitra, SVK	13	Jul
18.06				1	Luton	2	Jul
17.78 i				1	Gainesville, USA	8	Jan
18.15	Mark Proctor		15.01.63	1	Loughborough	22	Jun
17.79 i				2	Horsham	8	Jan
17.69				2	London (WL)	2	Jul
17.64 i				4	Vienna, AUT	6	Feb
18.00 i	Simon Williams		17.10.67	1	Lubbock, USA	29	Jan
17.88 i				1	Flagstaff, USA	19	Feb
17.79					Irvine, USA	23	Apr
17.96	Nigel Spratley		1.04.70	7	Victoria, CAN	28	Aug
17.68				1	Brussels, BEL	16	Jul
17.64				7	Victoria, CAN	19	Aug
17.63				2	Wrexham	3	Jul
17.62				2	Salisbury	10	Jul
17.55				6	Gateshead	20	Jul
17.94	Lee Newman	U23	1.05.73	1	Bournemouth		Apr
17.85				1	Tenerife, SPA	13	Apr
17.50				1	Yate	21	Aug

59 performances to 17.50 by 6 athletes including 16 indoors

17.41	Lee Wiltshire		26.07.62	1	Swindon	1	May
17.35	Dave Callaway		4.09.63	1	Portsmouth	15	May
17.32 i	Shaun Pickering		14.11.61	2	Birmingham	18	Feb
16.96				1	Amsterdam, HOL	20	May
17.29 i	Steve Whyte		14.03.64	1	Birmingham	8	Jan
17.29				1	Luton	30	Jul
(10)							
16.71	Paul Reed		2.06.62	4	London (He)	18	Aug
16.68	Gary Sollitt	U23	13.01.72	3	Portsmouth	15	May
16.41	David Condon	U23	11.04.72	1	London (Nh)	15	May
16.35 i	Martyn Fletcher		21.01.69	4	Birmingham	26	Feb
16.15				2	Loughborough	5	Jun
16.29	Gordon Smith		10.10.68	1	Banchory	1	May
16.18	Jamie Cockburn	U23	30.01.73	4	London (He)	5	Jun
16.12 i	Jim Mason	U23	22.03.72	1	London (CP)	17	Dec
15.94				3	Derby	16	Jul
16.11	Simon Armstrong		29.05.62	1	Bournemouth	14	May
16.10	Denzil McDonald		11.10.65	1	London (Nh)	4	Sep
15.95	James Muirhead		26.01.71	2	Leeds	13	Aug
(20)							
15.90	Antony Zaidman		18.03.62	1	London (WL)	20	Jul
15.79	Peter Weir		2.09.63	5	London (He)	5	Jun
15.75	Mark Edwards	U23	2.12.74	2	Bulle, SWZ	10	Sep
15.74	Stephan Hayward	U23	30.07.74	1	Bearsden	11	Jun
15.59	Matt Symonds		31.07.68	2	Kingston	31	Jul
15.53	Laine Snook		2.07.68	1	Stoke	16	Jul
15.39	Jason Mulcahy	U23	26.05.73	1	Stoke	31	Jul
15.27	Daley Thompson		30.07.58	2	Barn Elms	22	May
15.24	Greg Richards		25.04.56	1	Hayes	30	Jul
15.14	Mark Davies		10.01.71	1	Kingston	2	Jul
(30)							
15.08	Bill Fuller	U20	19.10.76	3	Bedford	2	Jul
15.04	Jamie Murphy	U23	20.03.73	1	Loughborough	26	Jun
14.99	Bryan Kelly	U23	29.12.73	2	Liverpool	17	Apr
14.92	Matthew Twigg		18.07.69	9	Corby	30	May
14.91	Abi Ekoku		13.04.66	3	Kingston	31	Jul
14.88 i	Graeme Stark		12.10.63	1	Worksop	30	Jan
13.83				8	Edinburgh	24	Jun
14.84	Bruce Robb	U20	27.07.77	1	Edinburgh	8	Jun
14.84	Neville Thompson		28.03.55	2	Stoke	31	Jul
14.83 i	Brian Redman		25.10.68	1	London (Ha)	15	Jan
14.72				3	Stoke	31	Jul
14.82	*Terry McHugh*		*22.08.63*	*1*	*Bracknell*	*4*	*Jun*
14.81	Simon Matthews		21.05.71	1	Stretford	21	Jun
(40)							
14.76	Morris Fox		30.04.63	10	Corby	30	May
14.76	Alex Kruger		18.11.63	4	Bedford	18	Sep
14.75	Chris Symonds		15.11.70	1	Kingston	19	Jun
14.74	Andy Turner		29.08.63	2	Bournemouth	14	May
14.74	Leith Marar		7.11.68	1	Enfield	20	Jul
14.73	Scott Hayes	U23	4.01.73	1	Kingston	16	Apr
14.68 i	Rafer Joseph		21.07.68	1P	London (CP)	23	Jan
14.66	Wiseman			2	Aldershot	6	Jul
14.62	Jeff Clare		21.03.65	1	Kirkby	11	Sep
14.58	Dave Eastlake		2.07.63	1	Jarrow	23	Jul
(50)							
14.51	John Nicholls		1.09.65	1	Wigan	4	Jun
14.50	Gareth Cook		20.02.69	1	Thurrock	18	Jun
14.49	Eric Hollingsworth		6.12.62	1	Melbourne, AUS	8	Feb
14.48	Guy Marshall		24.09.71	1	Hull	24	Aug

14.45	Rob Smith		3.11.66	11	Corby	30 May
14.36	Scott Wedderburn		28.04.65	1	St. Ives	2 Jul
14.32	Jason Young			2	Bearsden	11 Jun
14.32	Emeka Udechuku	U17	10.07.79	5	Verona, ITA	6 Aug
14.29	Peter Beaton	U23	5.04.72	3	Kingston	19 Jun
14.29	Simon Fricker	U20	14.07.75	5	Bedford	2 Jul
(60)						
14.27 i	Steve Bergin		17.06.66	2	Gateshead	13 Feb
14.10				2	Gateshead	15 May
14.27	Steve Casey		26.02.66	4	London (CP)	7 May
14.27	Guy Perryman		2.11.58	2	Bracknell	2 Jul
14.24	Robert Russell	U23	5.08.74	1	Cleckheaton	23 Jul
14.23	*George Antonatos*	*U23*	*30.09.74*	*1*	*Grantham*	*14 May*
14.23	Steve Head		21.10.58	3	London (Nh)	15 May
14.22	Neal Killen		10.04.59	2	Aldershot	8 Jun
14.22	Kevin Brown		10.09.64	2	Loughborough	7 Aug
14.19	Brian Taylor		13.08.70	1D	Azusa, USA	13 Apr
14.17	Barry Nash		4.09.71	2	Kingston	2 Jul
14.16 i	Piers Selby	U20	3.11.75	2	Birmingham	13 Feb
14.02				1	Basingstoke	18 Jun
(70)						
14.16	Simon Shirley		3.08.66	3D	Victoria, CAN	23 Aug
14.13	Julian Rifat		23.03.69	2	Basildon	30 Jul
14.12	Mike Oliver	V40	23.03.53	1	Crawley	26 Mar
14.12	Alun Thomas		16.03.57	3	Cwmbran	18 Jun
14.11 i	David Burnett	U20	27.01.76	3	Birmingham	13 Feb
14.04				6	Bedford	2 Jul
14.09 i	Andy Lewis		9.03.68	1	London (Ha)	26 Feb
13.62				2	London (PH)	2 Jul
14.08	John Tyler	U23	6.03.74	3	Hayes	11 May
14.06	Colin Smith		11.09.57	3	Bracknell	2 Jul
14.03	Glen Smith	U23	21.05.72	2	Loughborough	22 Jun
13.98	Ian Lindley		3.12.55	1	Middlesbrough	4 Jun
(80)						
13.98	Clayton Turner		9.01.68	1	London (BP)	30 Jul
13.97	Neil Mason		10.02.71	3	Bearsden	11 Jun
13.96 i	Neil Elliott		10.04.71	5	Glasgow	23 Jan
13.95	Jeremy Hames		17.11.70	2	Loughborough	23 Jul
13.94	*John Farrelly*		*4.12.67*	*5*	*Dublin (M), IRE*	*18 Jun*
13.90	Darrin Morris		28.07.67	3	Edinburgh	24 Apr
13.90	Paul Allan		21.06.70	3	Glasgow	22 May
13.88	Rory Birbeck	U23	24.09.73	2	Blackburn	11 May
13.87	¶John Painter		12.06.58	1	London (TB)	10 Sep
13.85	*Kengo Kubota*		*26.06.68*	*1*	*Glasgow*	*15 May*
13.85	Bruce Shepherd		20.03.67	4	Glasgow	22 May
13.85	Mike Atkinson		6.03.58	1	Antrim	18 Jun
(90)						
13.84	A. Wain			1	Peterborough	29 Aug
13.84	Michael Morgan		30.07.66	6	Bedford	17 Sep
13.83 i	Ewart Hulse		21.01.62	9	Birmingham	26 Feb
13.64				1	Newport	26 Jun
13.82	Bill Fuller	V45	5.02.48	3	Croydon	15 May
13.80	Phil Adams		3.11.71	9	Wigan	7 May
13.78 i	Matt Bundock	U20	18.11.76	4	Birmingham	13 Feb
13.33				6	Warsaw, POL	24 Sep
13.77	Howard Lamb		13.03.69	4	Harrow	2 Jul
13.73	Ian Taylor		2.07.67	1	Telford	14 May
13.71	Julian Hislop		9.01.60	4	Bedford	7 May
13.71	George Baker	U20	14.08.76	1	London (BP)	13 Aug
(100)						

13.69	Malcolm Croad	U23	27.10.73	3	London (CP)	1	May
13.69	James South	U20	4.01.75	10	Wigan	7	May
13.68	Dave Sharp				Leamington	15	May
13.59	Philip Davies		12.10.60		Crewe	7	May

Additional Under 20 (1 - 8 above)

13.47	Simon James		21.01.77	4	Cannock	11	Sep
13.36	Tony Soalla-Bell		3.10.76	4	London (TB)	30	Jul
	(10)						
13.26	Simon Keller		10.11.76	1	Mansfield	10	Apr
13.25 i	Liam McIntyre		22.09.76	2	Glasgow	16	Feb
13.06				6	Liverpool	6	Aug
13.20	Andrew Squires		27.02.75	2	Exeter	17	Jul
13.10 i	Karl Andrews		21.03.75	6	Birmingham	13	Feb

Professional

13.72	Steve Aitken		8.07.66	2	Nethybridge	21	Aug

SHOT - Under 20 - 6.25kg

16.34	Bill Fuller		19.10.76	1	Telford	9	Jul
15.95	James South		4.01.75	1	Luton	12	Jun
15.70	Simon Fricker		14.07.75	1	Bournemouth	11	Jun
15.50	George Baker		14.08.76	3	Telford	9	Jul
15.45	Bruce Robb		27.07.77	1	Pitreavie	14	Jun
15.42	Andrew Squires		27.02.75	1	Exeter	20	Aug
15.29	Dinos Alexopoulos		2.12.76	4	Telford	9	Jul
15.25	Liam McIntyre		22.09.76	1	Grangemouth	3	Aug
15.18	David Burnett		27.01.76	1	Ipswich	17	Apr
15.15	Piers Selby		3.11.75	1	Aldershot	12	Jun
	(10)						
15.09	Tony Soalla-Bell		3.10.76	2	Kingston	11	Jun
14.95	Matt Bundock		18.11.76	1	Middlesbrough	28	Aug
14.70	Robert Snow		1.09.75	2	London (WP)	8	May
14.62 i	Karl Andrews		21.03.75	1	Birmingham	6	Feb
14.28	Daniel Brunt		23.04.76	1	Hull	24	Jul
14.27	Simon James		21.01.77	1	Telford	14	May
14.20	Simon Keller		10.11.76	1	Redditch	28	Aug
14.20	Craig Rogers		14.02.76	1	Colwyn Bay	3	Sep
14.12	John Howard		16.09.75	1	Antrim	16	Jul
13.97	Brian McEvilly		27.12.75	1	Ashton-U-Lyne	12	Jun
	(20)						
13.83 i	Sudip Burman-Roy	U17	15.01.78	2	London (CP)	17	Dec
13.69	Segun Akinjiola		1.10.75	7	Telford	9	Jul
13.67	Karl Kaiser		26.02.75	1D	Middlesbrough	9	Apr
13.65	A. Robinson			1	Colwyn Bay	11	Jun
13.61	Graham Lloyd-Bennett		26.10.76	1	Hoo	11	Jun
13.60	David McGrath		8.09.75	1	Ashton-U-Lyne	12	Jun

Over Age

16.53	Mark Edwards	U23	2.12.74	1	Telford	9	Jul

SHOT - Under 17 - 5kg

17.39 i	Emeka Udechuku		10.07.79	1	London (CP)	17	Dec
16.46				1	Birmingham	31	Jul
15.57	Sudip Burman-Roy		15.01.78	2	London (CP)	29	May
15.46	Ian McMullan		15.06.78	1	Antrim	23	Jul
15.12	Dave Irwin		18.12.78	2	Antrim	23	Jul
14.93 i	Dean Macey		12.12.77	1P	Glasgow	10	Dec

14.83	Ben Walker		8.06.78	1	Crawley	26	Mar
14.82	Alan Rudkin		5.11.78	1	Grantham	24	Apr
14.78	Matthew Pilkington		19.12.77	1	Corby	18	Jun
14.66	James Bull		12.02.79	3	Birmingham	31	Jul
14.66	Paul Williams		21.09.77	1	Loughborough	7	Aug
	(10)						
14.57	Nick Barber		22.11.78	1	Scunthorpe	29	Aug
14.48	Tim King		10.12.77	2	London (He)	17	Jul
14.42	Stephen Birse		8.10.77	1	Middlesbrough	11	Jun
14.26 i	Ben Barnes		28.10.78	5	Birmingham	13	Feb
14.26	Peter Waterman	U15	12.09.79	1	Sheffield	2	Jul
14.19	D. Smith			2	Corby	18	Jun
14.13	Gareth Trott		1.05.78	2	Enfield	14	Aug
14.08	Matthew Phillips		22.09.77	1	Cardiff	26	Jun
14.06	Paul Carroll		25.01.78	1	Hull	1	May
13.87	Martin Mortley		8.09.78	5	Telford	8	Jul
	(20)						
13.79	John Urquhart		14.11.77	1	Glasgow	14	May
13.71	Alex Gibson		3.11.77				
13.49	Steve Thomas		4.04.78	1	Newport	28	May

Over Age

17.11 o	Bruce Robb	U20	27.07.77	1	Dublin, IRE	13	Aug

SHOT - Under 15 - 4kg

16.39	Peter Waterman		12.09.79	1	London (Col)	2	Jul
15.27	Jamie Hunt		29.11.79	1	Norwich	27	Jul
15.19	Andy Castle		8.12.79	1	Yeovil	11	Jun
15.03	Carl Myerscough		21.10.79	1	Blackpool	25	Sep
14.54	Martin Wilson		28.09.79	1	Colchester	29	Aug
14.46	William Kirkpatrick		28.02.80	1	Belfast	21	Aug
14.23	David Daniels		16.11.79	1	Enfield	11	Jul
14.18	Peter Stephen		10.09.79	1	Aberdeen	24	Jul
14.11	Ian Bleasdale		29.05.80	2	Blackpool	14	Aug
14.04	Zak Rickall		6.03.80	1	Hull	11	Jun
	(10)						
14.03	Jimmy Khafas		27.11.79	2	Enfield	11	Jul
13.92	James Hawkins		14.12.79	1	Peterborough	17	Jul
13.81	Andrew Sheridan		1.11.79	1	London (He)	26	Jun
13.78	Mike Roberts		30.09.79	1	Woodford	11	Jul
13.64	Warren Woad		16.03.80	6	Telford	8	Jul
13.61	Dean Knighton		16.03.80	1	Solihull	18	Sep
13.60	David Readle		10.02.80	1	Kirkby	11	Sep
13.57	Darren Formosa		27.10.79	1	Jarrow	18	Jun
13.48	Andrew Westwood		18.04.80	1	Redditch	11	Jun
13.40	Graeme Allan		24.09.80	1	Inverness	17	Sep
	(20)						
13.35	Kriss Stafford		11.09.79	1	Barking	11	Jun
13.23	Andrew Waters		11.10.79	3	Braintree	18	Sep

SHOT - Under 13 - 3.25kg

12.61	A. Magan			1	Birmingham	2	Jul
12.16	Liam Walsh			1	Colwyn Bay	3	Sep
12.10	John Barnes		6.05.82	1	Lincoln	10	Sep
11.84	T. Freed			2	Birmingham	2	Jul

DISCUS

61.06	Robert Weir			4.02.61	1	Corby	31	Jul
	60.86				3	Victoria, CAN	26	Aug
	58.92				6	Birmingham	26	Jun
	58.72				4	Gateshead	20	Jul
	58.64				1	London (WL)	2	Jul
	57.94				2	Sheffield	11	Jun
	57.40				1	Bedford	17	Sep
	57.18				13Q	Helsinki, FIN	12	Aug
	57.10				7	Modesto, USA	14	May
	55.86				7	London (CP)	10	Sep
59.78	Glen Smith	U23		21.05.72	1	Loughborough	5	Jun
	56.60				3	Ostrava, CS	31	Jul
	56.52				1	Corby	29	May
	56.22				3	Sheffield	11	Jun
	56.22				2	Stoke	15	Jul
	55.92				1	Loughborough	25	May
	55.84				6	Victoria, CAN	26	Aug
	55.54				2	Loughborough	22	Jun
	55.24				1	Kings Lynn	9	Jul
58.68	Kevin Brown			10.09.64	2	Victoria, CAN	19	Aug
	58.60				1	Sheffield	11	Jun
	56.78				1	Loughborough	22	Jun
	56.68				1	Stoke	15	Jul
	56.12				5	Gateshead	20	Jul
	55.40				1	Loughborough	7	Aug
	55.12				3	Nitra, SVK	13	Jul
58.34	Lee Newman	U23		1.05.73	1	Bromley	9	Jun
	57.02				2	Loughborough	5	Jun
	56.20				1	Birmingham	21	May
	56.04				1	Rugby	10	Aug
	55.90				1	Wolverhampton	4	Jun
	55.56				1	London (CP)	7	May
	55.36				1	London (Elt)	29	Aug
	55.16				1	Bracknell	2	May
58.32	Simon Williams			17.10.67	2	Austin, USA	9	Apr
	57.94				1	El Paso, USA	16	Apr
	55.44				1	Tempe, USA	26	Mar
57.72	Darrin Morris			28.07.67	1	Hayes	11	May
	56.38				2	Istanbul, TUR	22	May
	56.16				1	Loughborough	27	Apr
	55.02				1	Edinburgh	24	Apr
55.40	Neville Thompson			28.03.55	2	Rugby	10	Aug
55.24	Jamie Murphy	U23		20.03.73	1	Loughborough	26	Jun
	43 performances to 55.00 by 8 athletes							
54.62	Nick Woolcott			7.04.61	2	Lisbon, POR	17	Sep
54.50	Paul Reed			2.06.62	1	Portsmouth	13	Jul
	(10)							
54.32	Jeff Clare			21.03.65	1	Kirkby	11	Sep
54.20	Gary Herrington			31.03.61	1	London (He)	17	Aug
53.80	Perris Wilkins			12.11.68	1	Yate	23	Jul
53.52	Leith Marar			7.11.68	2	Loughborough	7	Aug
53.40	Mark Proctor			15.01.63	1	Cosford	15	Jun
53.16	Abi Ekoku			13.04.66	1	London (TB)	20	Aug
52.46	Steve Casey			26.02.66	2	Bracknell	2	May
52.16	Matt Symonds			31.07.68	4	Bedford	17	Sep
51.82	James Muirhead			26.01.71	1	Derby	16	Jul
51.32	Scott Hayes	U23		4.01.73	1	London (Nh)	15	May
	(20)							
50.88	John Menton			2.05.70	3	Dublin, IRE	18	Jun
50.80	John Moreland			13.09.58	5	Stoke	15	Jul

50.66	Rafer Joseph		21.07.68	1D	Bressanone, ITA	3	Jul
50.56	Mark Davies		10.01.71	1	Dartford	20	Aug
50.50	Robert Russell	U23	5.08.74	1	Leeds	13	Aug
50.40	Steve Whyte		14.03.64	1	Luton	30	Jul
49.76	Michael Jemi-Alade		13.10.64	6	Stoke	15	Jul
49.18	*James Highland*		*2.06.65*	*1*	*Peterborough*	*2*	*Jul*
49.08	Geoff Tyler	V45	30.09.48	9	Sydney, AUS	13	Nov
48.82	Gareth Cook		20.02.69	1	Thurrock	18	Jun
48.68	Matthew Twigg		18.07.69	1	Sheffield (W)	4	Jun
48.56	Denzil McDonald		11.10.65	10	Wigan	7	May
(30)							
48.46	¶Paul Edwards		16.02.59	1	Salisbury	10	Jul
48.36	Shaun Pickering		14.11.61	8	London (WL)	2	Jul
48.32	James South	U20	4.01.75	2	London (Nh)	15	May
48.28	Chris Symonds		15.11.70	3	Hayes	11	May
48.02	Andrew Kruszewski		7.04.59	1	Cardiff	2	Jul
47.82	Neil Sougrin		14.05.71	1	Enfield	19	Jun
47.76	Stephan Hayward	U23	30.07.74	2	Edinburgh	24	Jun
47.54	Simon Armstrong		29.05.62	1	Exeter	17	Jul
47.46	Greg Richards		25.04.56	1	London (Nh)	2	Jul
47.22	David Sweeney		9.02.62	2	Helsingborg, SWE	3	Aug
(40)							
47.20	Peter Weir		2.09.63	11	London (He)	5	Jun
47.14	Nigel Spratley		1.04.70	1	Bedford	7	May
46.28	Tony Satchwell	V40	3.02.53		Jersey	23	Jun
45.76	Ian Taylor		2.07.67	1	Telford	20	Aug
45.70	Bruce Robb	U20	27.07.77	3	Colwyn Bay	23	Jul
45.62	Eugene Gilkes		5.03.62	2	Bedford	7	May
45.58	*Garry Power*		*1.09.62*	*2*	*Dartford*	*13*	*Aug*
45.34	Matt Simson		28.05.70	1	Guildford	13	Aug
45.12	Rob Earle		15.09.60	1	Braintree	18	Sep
45.02	Andy Turner		29.08.63	2	Bournemouth	7	May
45.00	Stephen Ayre		20.10.67	2	Gateshead	4	Jun
(50)							
44.94	Neil Elliott		10.04.71	3	Glasgow	22	May
44.74	*Kengo Kubota*		*26.06.68*	*4*	*Edinburgh*	*24*	*Jun*
44.60	Emeka Udechuku	U17	10.07.79		Reading	30	Aug
44.56	Andrew Squires	U20	27.02.75	2	Exeter	17	Jul
44.54	Morris Fox		30.04.63	2	Stoke	2	Jul
44.36	Simon Jones		23.02.65	1		23	Jul
44.30	Simon Fricker	U20	14.07.75	5	Bedford	3	Jul
44.24	Ian McMullan	U23	3.05.74	1	London (Col)	18	Jun
44.24	Guy Litherland		13.11.68	2	Telford	20	Aug
44.08	*John Farrelly*		*4.12.67*	*1*	*Tullamore, IRE*	*15*	*May*
43.94	Steven Lloyd	U23	20.03.74	2	Kirkby	6	Aug
43.82	Matt Bundock	U20	18.11.76	5	Liverpool	6	Aug
(60)							
43.80	Jeremy Hames		17.11.70	1D	Stoke	25	Jun
43.78	Bryan Kelly	U23	29.12.73	1	Liverpool	17	Apr
43.48	Neil Griffin	V45	28.05.48	10	London (CP)	25	Jun
43.46	Simon Matthews		21.05.71		Stretford	21	Jun
43.44	Alex Kruger		18.11.63	15D	Gotzis, AUT	29	May
43.38	Lee Broadhead	U20	11.05.75	4	Loughborough	5	Jun
43.18	Ashley Ward		1.08.64	2	Carshalton	4	Jun
43.06	Jan Brzezinski		4.06.62	2	Thurrock	18	Jun
42.78	Jon Gillo		10.12.70	1	Salisbury	15	May
42.62	Ivan Washington		18.11.56	1	Portsmouth	6	Aug
(70)							
42.58	N. Dixon	U23	73	1	Basildon	30	Jul
42.50	Liam McIntyre	U20	22.09.76	6	Liverpool	6	Aug
42.46	Neal Killen		10.04.59		Rotherham	7	May
42.42	Chris Howe		17.11.67		Loughborough	1	Jun

42.38	Brian Taylor		13.08.70	4	London (CP)	7	May
42.32	Ewart Hulse		21.01.62	1	Wrexham	15	May
42.30	Gareth Gilbert	U23	24.08.72	5	Derby	16	Jul
42.24	Mark Tout		24.01.61	2	Kingston	4	Jun
42.18	Mark Quigley	U23	6.11.74	1	Liverpool	7	May
42.06	Iain Park	U23	16.07.74	3	Edinburgh	24	Apr
	(80)						
42.02	Peter Roberts		19.09.71		Oxford	23	Apr
42.00	Greg Madigan		28.10.57	3	Kingston	19	Jun
41.94	Nick Tabor		17.12.54	1	Southampton	13	Aug
41.82	Michael Conerney	U23	30.10.72	1	Cambridge	22	Oct
41.80	Gareth Marks	U20	31.05.77	5	Oordegem, BEL	9	Jul
41.78	Justin Bryan		16.08.69	2	Cwmbran	18	Jun
41.78	Dave Eastlake		2.07.63	2	Carlisle	10	Jul
41.78	Clayton Turner		9.01.68	1	Horsham	21	Aug
41.68	¶John Painter		12.06.58	2	Norwich	30	Jul
41.62	Simon Shirley		3.08.66	19D	Gotzis, AUT	29	May
	(90)						
41.60	Glen Townsend		23.04.64	1	Lancaster	7	May
41.54	Chris Franks		19.01.66	3	Oxford	14	May
41.46	Mark Line		3.09.62	1	Bebington	14	May
41.38	Jamie Quarry	U23	15.11.72	5	Glasgow	22	May
41.36	John Little	V40	14.04.53		Rotherham	7	May
41.34	Gary Parsons			1	Kings Lynn	10	Apr
41.30	David Abernethy		5.09.55	1	Carlisle	14	May
41.14	Malcolm Croad	U23	27.10.73	1	Oxford	27	Apr
41.12	Mark Edwards	U23	2.12.74	4	Telford	20	Aug
41.00	B. Lambert			1	Oxford	8	May
	(100)						
40.98	Wiseman			2	Aldershot	6	Jul
40.90	Ben Walker	U17	8.06.78	1	Watford	30	Jul
40.86	Jan Drzewiecki		29.11.57	1	Perivale	1	May
40.74	Elliott Cole	U23	19.09.73	6	Derby	16	Jul
40.72	Paul Howard		19.10.66	1D	Horsham	19	Jun
40.70	Michael Reiss		17.06.63	3	Norwich	30	Jul
40.64	Bruce Shepherd		20.03.67	4	Coatbridge	12	Jun
40.44	Alun Williams			6	Loughborough	22	Jun
40.08	Pete Lowe		4.07.65	3	Portsmouth	6	Aug

Downhill

44.72	Simon Jones		23.02.65	1	Bury St Edmonds	31	Jul

DISCUS - Under 20 - 1.75kg

52.76	Emeka Udechuku	U17	10.07.79	1	Middlesbrough	28	Aug
51.70	James South		4.01.75	1	Ipswich	17	Apr
48.70	Lee Broadhead		11.05.75	1	Stoke	14	May
48.38	Simon Fricker		14.07.75	1	London (CP)	29	May
48.02	Matt Bundock		18.11.76	1	Stretford	12	Jun
47.68	Andrew Squires		27.02.75	1	London (He)	7	Aug
47.42	Bruce Robb		27.07.77	1	Grangemouth	1	Jun
46.06	Liam McIntyre		22.09.76	1	Glasgow	15	May
45.94	Gareth Marks		31.05.77	1	Colwyn Bay	2	Jul
44.70	Ray McKenna		14.09.75	1	Ipswich	23	Jul
	(10)						
44.30	Andrew Rutland		13.01.76	3	London (He)	27	Aug
43.00	Daniel Brunt		23.04.76	1	Hull	24	Jul
42.52	Scott Barker		22.07.77	1	Corby	12	Jun
42.50	James Kindon		18.06.76	4	Telford	9	Jul
42.10	Louis Hodgson		29.12.76	1	Wakefield	18	Sep
42.04	David Burnett		27.01.76	1	Braintree	18	Sep
41.96	Richard Lyman		15.11.75	2	Solihull	17	Apr
41.84	Adam Tear		12.08.75		Hull		
41.66	Craig Munden		24.12.76	1	Southampton	11	Sep

41.50	Dean Daniels		1.02.76	1	Birmingham	11 Jun
	(20)					
41.36	Matthew Pilkington	U17	19.12.77	4	London (He)	27 Aug
41.30	James Robinson		3.11.76	1	Brighton	12 Jun

Over Age

| 46.96 | Mark Edwards | U23 | 2.12.74 | 1 | Leicester | 11 Jun |

DISCUS - Under 17 - 1.5kg

54.90	Emeka Udechuku		10.07.79	1	Telford	8 Jul
51.72	Ben Walker		8.06.78	1	Watford	29 Aug
47.78	Hector Lawrence		1.11.77	3	Telford	8 Jul
47.36	Alan Rudkin		5.11.78	1	Grantham	24 Apr
46.98	Matthew Pilkington		19.12.77	4	Telford	8 Jul
45.98	*Nigel Travers*		*22.10.77*	*3*	*Birmingham*	*31 Jul*
45.16	Andrew Rollins		20.03.78	1	Kirkby	11 Sep
44.40	Steve Thomas		4.04.78	1	Colwyn Bay	2 Jul
44.16	Ben Cordingley		19.05.78	1	Peterborough	17 Jul
44.10	John Urquhart		14.11.77	1	Glasgow	14 May
43.04	Sudip Burman-Roy		15.01.78	4	London (CP)	29 May
	(10)					
42.66	Andrew Elder		28.12.77	1	Woking	4 Sep
42.20	S. Thompson			1	Yeovil	11 Sep
42.14	David Lovett		13.09.78	1	Portsmouth	7 Aug
42.00	David Black		9.10.78	1	Nottingham	26 Jun
41.46	Peter Fraser		28.01.78	6	Aberdeen	16 Jul
41.38	Andrew Benn		2.09.77	1	Bedford	26 Jun
41.20	Steven Freestone		5.08.78	8	Telford	8 Jul
41.06	Eddie Birchall		28.11.77	1	Enfield	1 May
41.04	Tim King		10.12.77	2	Grantham	14 May
40.94	Dave Irwin		18.12.78	1	Antrim	24 Jul
	(20)					

DISCUS - Under 15 - 1.25kg

44.56	Peter Waterman		12.09.79	1	Crawley	2 Jun
43.34	Carl Myerscough		21.10.79	1	Blackpool	25 Sep
42.26	Andrew Waters		11.10.79	1	Perivale	18 May
42.26	George Skevis		12.10.79	1	Crawley	20 Jul
41.14	Ian Bleasdale		29.05.80	2	Birmingham	11 Sep
40.10	Steven Stanford		9.12.79	2	Blackpool	25 Sep
39.94	S. Hodgson			1	Hull	17 Jul
39.84	William Kirkpatrick		28.02.80		Tullamore, IRE	17 Jul
39.54	Darren Formosa		27.10.79	1	Gateshead	15 May
39.18	Anthony Allport		30.09.79	1	Birmingham	11 Jun
	(10)					
39.02	Nathan Jones		10.03.80	1	Sandown	25 Sep
38.78	Richard Morton			2	Stockport	26 Jun
38.68	Richard Hughes		3.10.79	3	Birmingham	11 Sep
38.62	Ben Gilbert		21.09.79	3	Telford	8 Jul
38.56	Graeme Allan		24.09.80	3	Dublin, IRE	13 Aug
38.26	Andy Castle		8.12.79	1	Yeovil	15 May
38.04	Adrian Cluskey		30.12.80	4	Birmingham	11 Sep
37.70	Chris Aherne		21.12.79	1	Swansea	29 Aug
37.54	Warren Woad		16.03.80	4	Birmingham	11 Sep
37.48	Zak Rickall		6.03.80	1	Hull	11 Jun
	(20)					
37.20	Jonathan Rackham		29.11.79	1	Lincoln	10 Sep

DISCUS - Under 13 - 1kg

| 38.30 | Liam Walsh | | | 1 | Wrexham | 13 Aug |
| 33.66 | A. Magan | | | 1 | Birmingham | 2 Jul |

HAMMER

					Pos	Venue	Date
71.16	Paul Head		1.07.65		1	Crawley	6 Aug
	70.18				2	Victoria, CAN	22 Aug
	69.32				2	Nitra, SVK	13 Jul
	69.14				1	London (WL)	2 Jul
	69.12				2	Kingston	31 Jul
	69.08				2	Sheffield	12 Jun
	68.38				8	London (CP)	10 Sep
	68.28				1	Wrexham	3 Jul
	67.54				Q	Corby	30 May
	67.08				2	London (He)	5 Jun
	66.78				2	Corby	30 May
	65.60				1	Grendon Hall	15 Oct
70.80	Peter Vivian		5.11.70		1	Sheffield	12 Jun
	70.66				2	London (Col)	3 Aug
	70.58				1	Kingston	31 Jul
	70.32				1	London (Col)	1 Apr
	70.14				1	Birmingham	21 May
	70.04				1	Kingston	16 Apr
	69.92				1	London (Col)	17 Apr
	69.88				2	Crawley	6 Aug
	69.80				3	Victoria, CAN	22 Aug
	69.62				2	Gateshead	20 Jul
	69.44				1	Wigan	7 May
	69.32				1	London (He)	5 Jun
	68.78				2	London (WL)	2 Jul
	68.56				1	Brussels, BEL	15 Jul
	68.44				7	Birmingham	26 Jun
	67.78				1	Bedford	17 Sep
	66.36				1	Enfield	14 May
68.68	Michael Jones		23.07.63		3	London (WL)	2 Jul
	68.42				4	Victoria, CAN	22 Aug
	68.28				1	Corby	30 May
	68.22				Q	Corby	30 May
	68.04				1	Horsham	14 May
	67.42				3	Sheffield	12 Jun
	67.08				3	Crawley	6 Aug
	66.84				2	Wrexham	3 Jul
	66.34				2	Bedford	17 Sep
	65.90				3	London (He)	5 Jun
67.74	David Smith	U23	2.11.74		1	Hull	26 Jun
	66.82				3	Wrexham	3 Jul
	65.98				1	Derby	16 Jul
	65.82				1	Wakefield	13 Apr
	65.74				1	Loughborough	5 Jun
	65.34				1	Wakefield	20 Aug
	65.20				3	Kings Lynn	9 Jul
66.68	Shane Peacock		5.03.63		4	Sheffield	12 Jun
	65.84				4	Crawley	6 Aug
	65.70				2	Wigan	7 May
	65.08				3	Bedford	17 Sep
66.54	John Pearson		30.04.66		1	Loughborough	14 May
	65.36				2	Loughborough	5 Jun
	65.28				1	Hayes	11 May
65.54	Jason Byrne		9.09.70		1	Brierley Hill	7 May
65.36	Russell Devine		24.04.68		1	Melbourne, AUS	23 Apr
65.30	Karl Andrews	U20	21.03.75		1	Bedford	2 Jul
65.24	Stephen Pearson		13.09.59		1	Burton	19 Jul

57 performances to 65.00 by 10 athletes

64.02	Steve Whyte		14.03.64	1	Perivale	15 Jun
63.56	Gareth Cook		20.02.69	1	Thurrock	18 Jun
63.06	Chris Howe		17.11.67	4	Brussels, BEL	15 Jul
62.70	David Smith		21.06.62	2	Derby	16 Jul
62.70	*Phil Spivey*		*15.05.61*	*5*	*Crawley*	*6 Aug*
62.56	Adrian Palmer		10.08.69	1	Edinburgh	6 Aug
61.68	Robert Weir		4.02.61	5	London (WL)	2 Jul
61.68	Rob Earle		15.09.60	6	Crawley	6 Aug
61.52	Stewart Rogerson		4.02.62	1	Stretford	14 May
60.60	Steve Minnikin	U23	4.01.72	1	Leeds	19 Jul
60.34	Paul Barnard	U23	27.07.72	1	Middlesbrough	30 Jul
	(20)					
60.06	William Beauchamp		9.09.70	2	Perivale	4 Jun
59.84	Dave Allan		17.10.70	1	Inverness	15 May
59.40	Gareth Jones		14.12.68	1	Cwmbran	11 May
58.76	Craig Ellams	U23	24.11.72	1	Stoke	2 Jul
58.72	Malcolm Fenton		12.02.56	1	Kings Lynn	27 May
57.96	Malcolm Croad	U23	27.10.73	1	Oxford	14 May
57.66	Alan McNicholas	U23	10.12.74	1	Bedford	18 Sep
57.58	Shaun Pickering		14.11.61	7	Malaga, SPA	28 May
57.40	Graham Holder	U23	16.01.72	2	London (Elt)	30 Jul
57.24	Wayne Clarke	U20	24.12.75	1	Grantham	14 May
	(30)					
57.04	Lawrie Nisbet		18.06.61	1	Glasgow	22 May
56.82	Simon Bown	U23	21.11.74	2	Colchester	19 Jun
56.74	Paul Dickenson	V40	4.12.49	2	Athens, GRE	3 Jun
56.70	Nick Steinmetz	U20	9.12.76	1	Verona, ITA	6 Aug
56.60	Stuart Spratley	U23	18.07.72	5	Wigan	7 May
56.38	Steve Sammut		3.05.67	1	Haselmere	19 Jul
56.18	John Nevis		24.12.69	2	Hull	14 May
56.16	Glen Kerr	U23	27.10.74	2	Luton	15 May
55.92	*Ed Healey*	*V40*	*54*	*1*	*London (Col)*	*18 Jun*
	56.96 un					
55.62	Neil Curtis	U23	30.07.74	1	Corby	15 May
55.46	Steve McEvoy		23.05.63	1	Enfield	19 Jun
	(40)					
55.26	Steve Angell		8.04.70	1	Harrow	4 Sep
55.02	Anthony Swain	U20	17.01.75	1	Hull	30 Apr
54.64	Russell Tolputt		17.09.64	4	Cardiff	2 Jul
54.58	Iain Park	U23	16.07.74	2	London (Col)	1 Apr
54.38	Dave Gisbey		2.05.60	1	Edinburgh	13 Jul
54.22	Scott Thompson	U23	29.09.74	2	Gateshead	15 May
54.20	Michael Madden		13.09.65	1	Windsor	25 Jun
54.16	Mark Miller		10.11.71	3	Enfield	19 Jun
54.16	Eric Kerr		9.12.64	4	Dublin, IRE	23 Jul
54.12	Matt Spicer		18.05.71	2	Stoke	31 Jul
	(50)					
53.32	Graham Middleton		17.09.60	1	Cannock	26 Jun
53.18	Mark Broughton		23.10.63	4	London (Col)	18 Jun
53.12	Neil Williams	U23	31.10.72	1	Cannock	11 Sep
52.82	Mark Sheridan		17.06.70	1	Kingston	19 Jun
52.80	Maurice Hicks		1.01.70	1	Haselmere	16 Aug
52.44	Rob Careless	U23	7.09.74	3	Bulle, SWZ	10 Sep
52.42	Mike Floyd	U20	26.09.76	2	Stoke	9 Oct
52.38	Geoff Bush		20.03.56	8	Derby	16 Jul
52.30	Bruce Shepherd		20.03.67	2	Glasgow	22 May
51.88	Simon Jones		23.02.65	1	Newquay	16 Jun
	(60)					
51.76	John Owen		28.10.64	4	Edinburgh	6 Aug
51.32	James Goss	U23	11.09.73	3	Enfield	14 May
51.26	Ewart Hulse		21.01.62	1	Cardiff	17 Jul

Time	Name		DOB		Venue	Date	
51.02	Sean Jones		21.03.69	1	Aldershot	6	Jul
50.94	Tony Irving	U20	30.04.75	6	Bedford	2	Jul
50.94	Mark Proctor		15.01.63	2	Aldershot	6	Jul
50.78	Bill Fuller	U20	19.10.76	1	Barn Elms	22	May
50.60	Michael Reiss		17.06.63	3	London (PH)	2	Jul
50.22	Wayne Gibson	U20	25.02.76	7	Bedford	2	Jul
50.20	Callum Bruce	U20	28.02.75	1	Grangemouth	4	May
	(70)						
50.10	Andy Charij			2	Kingston	19	Jun
50.04	Douglas Read		15.04.67	16	Corby	30	May
49.90	Andy Turner		29.08.63	2	Barking	6	Aug
49.68	Jason Dibble		15.02.71	4	Portsmouth	6	Aug
49.60	Chris Edgar	U23	11.06.73	2	Stretford	14	May
49.24	Greg Bastille	U23	25.04.73	3	Haselmere	19	Jul
49.18	Russell Payne-Dwyer		11.09.60	9	Wigan	7	May
49.10	Ian McLaughlin	U20	4.01.77	8	Cardiff	2	Jul
48.96	James Johnson	U20	8.06.77	1	Stoke	4	Jun
48.90	Andrew Moore			2	Rotherham	7	May
	(80)						
48.88	Wesley Clarke		31.12.63	1	Brighton	18	Jun
48.80	David Nicholl		16.09.69	1	Antrim	18	Jun
48.76	Chris Mallon	U23	4.08.72	1	Barn Elms	21	Aug
48.60	Carl Gregory	U20	17.08.77	3	Feltham		
48.48	Mark Gulliver	U23	11.02.72	4	Stoke	2	Jul
48.46	Chris O'Connell		17.01.59	4	Barking	6	Aug
48.26	Rupert Spencer-Smith		25.07.68	1	London (Ha)	30	Jul
48.24	Anthony Doran	U23	22.10.72	2	Cardiff	17	Jul
48.18	Alan Woods	V40	27.03.51	3	Telford	20	Aug
47.88	Chris Smale		11.08.65	3	Thurrock	18	Jun
	(90)						
47.88	Mark Roberson	U20	21.03.75	2	Perivale	30	Jul
47.82	Douglas Aitchison		31.12.66	1	Glasgow	14	Aug
47.74	Martin Roberts		1.03.60	3	Stoke	23	Apr
47.66	Simon Armstrong		29.05.62	2	Exeter	17	Jul
47.64	Simon Blackwell		6.02.63	1	Colchester	11	Sep
47.62	Ross Blight	U20	28.05.77	3	Cardiff	24	Jun
47.58	Mark Roy		30.03.64	5	Barking	6	Aug
47.52	Matthew Blows	U23	21.06.74	3	Woodford	23	Apr
47.30	Matthew Bell	U17	2.06.78	3	Loughborough	23	Jul
47.16	Luigi Antoniazzi		13.09.62	3	Bournemouth	23	Jul
	(100)						
47.12	Keith Robinson	V40	9.02.52	4	Bournemouth	7	May
47.12	Douglas Spikes	U20	1.07.76	4	Perivale	4	Jun
47.08	Phil Tyler			2	Welwyn	13	Aug
47.04	Lachie Carter		25.11.70	3	Coatbridge	12	Jun
46.98	Gary Curtis		21.11.61	1	London (Nh)	2	Jul
46.96	*G. Kollias*			2	*Birmingham*		*May*
46.92	Richard Breffitt	U20	23.11.75	4	Loughborough	26	Jun
46.82	Matthew Hammond			3	Middlesbrough	14	Aug
46.66	Nick Woolcott		7.04.61	2	Kingston	18	Jun
46.62	Barry Williams	V45	5.03.47	3	Blackburn	17	Aug
46.58	Neville Thompson		28.03.55	9	Crawley	6	Aug
	(110)						
46.56	Greg Carroll		7.07.71	1	Crawley	30	Jul
46.42	Neil Townsend		3.05.63	2	London (Nh)	2	Jul
46.36	Matt Symonds		31.07.68	2	London (Elt)	29	Aug
46.34	Simon Bowman		11.09.71	2	St. Albans	18	Jun
46.34	Robert Snow	U20	1.09.75	1	London (BP)	30	Jul

HAMMER - Under 20 - 6.25kg

69.10	Karl Andrews		21.03.75	1	Warley	1	Aug
62.60	Nick Steinmetz		9.12.76	2	Telford	9	Jul
62.60	Wayne Clarke		24.12.75	1	Guildford	24	Jul
62.12	Anthony Swain		17.01.75	1	Wakefield	20	Aug
58.32	Tony Irving		30.04.75	1	Carlisle	10	Jul
58.14	Wayne Gibson		25.02.76	1	Middlesbrough	20	Jun
57.90	Mike Floyd		26.09.76	3	Manchester	4	Sep
54.68	Bill Fuller		19.10.76	1	London (CP)	27	Apr
54.18	Ross Blight		28.05.77	1	Colwyn Bay	2	Jul
53.16	Robert Snow		1.09.75	1	Haselmere	5	Jul
	(10)						
52.56	Alex Beattie		19.04.76	1	Kingston	11	Jun
52.12	Andrew Benn	U17	2.09.77	1	Braintree	18	Sep
51.52	Ian McLaughlin		4.01.77	6	Telford	9	Jul
51.36	Mark Roberson		21.03.75	1	Milton Keynes	11	Jun
50.64	Douglas Spikes		1.07.76	1	Hounslow	24	Jul
50.62	Callum Bruce		28.02.75	2	Grangemouth	11	May
50.60	David Shenton	U17	20.10.77	5	Manchester	4	Sep
50.50	Carl Gregory		17.08.77	1	Luton	10	Apr
49.72	Matthew Bell	U17	2.06.78	3	London (He)	27	Aug
49.58	Leyton Rutherford		2.06.76	1	Great Yarmouth	14	May
	(20)						
48.64	Adam Devonshire	U17	2.03.79	7	Wakefield	20	Aug
48.64	David Robinson	U17	12.01.78	6	Manchester	4	Sep
47.46	Shannon Cocker		15.03.76	1	Carlisle	15	May
47.44	Neil Jones		1.08.77	1	Wrexham	14	May
47.26	Kevin Davies	U17	11.01.78	2	Exeter	20	Aug
47.10	Brett Marsh		20.01.76	2	Redditch	28	Aug

HAMMER - Under 17 - 5kg

63.24	Matthew Bell		2.06.78	1	Rugby	17	Jul
59.50	Damien Slater		14.10.77	1	Thurrock	5	Jun
59.22	Andrew Benn		2.09.77	1	London (Nh)	28	Aug
57.60	Dean Hughes		22.09.78	1	Croydon	17	Jul
56.70	Kevin Davies		11.01.78	1	Telford	8	Jul
56.68	Robin Walker		8.02.78	1	Scunthorpe	1	May
56.60	Adam Devonshire		2.03.79	2	Telford	8	Jul
	56.76 un						
56.24	David Shenton		20.10.77	1	Gateshead	11	Jun
56.20	David Robinson		12.01.78	1	Manchester	4	Sep
55.68	Mark Elliott		3.04.78	1	Telford	17	Sep
	(10)						
55.20	Paul Gorham		7.08.78	5	Telford	8	Jul
54.50	John Urquhart		14.11.77	1	Grangemouth	6	Jul
53.28	Neil Bulman		7.09.77	1	Middlesbrough	11	Jun
52.72	Tim Wurr		1.03.79	2	Telford	17	Sep
52.16	Mark Lattimer		21.02.78	2	Corby	15	May
51.06	James Hawkins	U15	14.12.79	2	Enfield	14	Aug
50.90	Sudip Burman-Roy		15.01.78	1	Birmingham	11	Sep
49.24	Paul McNamara		3.10.78	9	Telford	8	Jul
49.02	Paul Stewart		5.10.77	1	Exeter	11	Jun
48.54	John Parkin		23.02.79	3	Telford	11	Sep
	(20)						
47.70	Mark Clinch		23.10.78	2	Leeds	26	Jun

HAMMER - Under 15 - 4kg

57.52	James Hawkins	14.12.79	1	Telford	9	Jul
57.30	James Punch	19.12.79	1	Corby	13	Sep
54.14	Chris Aherne	21.12.79	1	Swansea	29	Aug
52.02	Peter Waterman	12.09.79	1	London (Col)	26	Jun
50.76	Andy Castle	8.12.79	1	Yeovil	11	Jun
49.60	Jack Harker	14.09.79	1	Birmingham (Un)	1	May
47.40	Andrew Carter	18.10.79	2	Solihull	29	May
46.42	James Ball	17.04.80	3	Telford	9	Jul
46.38	Ian Bleasdale	29.05.80	1	Bebington	11	Jun
45.22	Andrew Gibson	11.05.80	1	Manchester	4	Sep
(10)
44.38	Gregory Pannell	24.07.80	4	Telford	9	Jul
44.14	Andrew Waters	11.10.79	3	Braintree	18	Sep
43.82	Thomas Cunnane	14.08.80	2	Manchester	4	Sep
43.38	Matthew Bray	3.10.79	1	Milton Keynes	26	Jun
42.94	Jason Stone	15.10.80	1	Haselmere	19	Jun
42.56	Gareth Nottingham	20.12.79	5	Telford	9	Jul
42.50	Matthew Sannigar	31.03.80	1	Stoke	11	Jun
42.06	Victor Dickinson	23.11.79	7	Telford	9	Jul
41.80	David Daniels	16.11.79	3	London (He)	7	Aug
41.44	Tom Dewey	31.01.80	1	London (WP)	7	May

HAMMER - Under 13 - 3.25kg

| 44.38 | Ross Thomson | 7.12.81 | 1 | Manchester | 4 | Sep |
| 34.06 | M. Tinwell | | 2 | Manchester | 4 | Sep |

JAVELIN

86.36	Mick Hill	22.10.64	1	Lahti, FIN	5	Jun
	85.28		3	Birmingham	25	Jun
	84.60		1	Sheffield	12	Jun
	84.44		Q	Helsinki, FIN	7	Aug
	84.22		1	London (CP)	15	Jul
	83.60		1	Corby	30	May
	83.40		1	Edinburgh	8	Jul
	83.30		3	Helsinki, FIN	29	Jun
	83.18		2	Port Elizabeth, RSA	3	Apr
	83.16		3	Brussels, BEL	19	Aug
	82.56		3	Gateshead	1	Jul
	81.98		2	Gateshead	20	Jul
	81.92		2	Pietersburg, RSA	18	Mar
	81.84		2	Victoria, CAN	28	Aug
	81.62		4	Oslo, NOR	22	Jul
	81.40		2	Madrid, SPA	6	Sep
	81.26		5	Stockholm, SWE	12	Jul
	81.14		2	Cape Town, RSA	5	Apr
	80.66		6	Helsinki, FIN	8	Aug
	80.28		4	Zurich, SWZ	17	Aug
	78.80		7	Sheffield	4	Sep
	77.18		8	Berlin, GER	30	Aug
85.20	Steve Backley	12.02.69	1	Helsinki, FIN	8	Aug
	85.02		1	London (CP)	11	Sep
	84.94		1	Khania, GRE	5	Jun
	84.78		3	Sheffield	4	Sep
	84.68		1	Gateshead	20	Jul
	84.66		2	Helsinki, FIN	29	Jun
	84.34		1	Pietersburg, RSA	18	Mar
	84.24		2	Sheffield	12	Jun
	84.10		1	Port Elizabeth, RSA	3	Apr

(Backley)	83.82		1	Kuortane, FIN	25 Jun
	83.24		1	Cape Town, RSA	5 Apr
	82.74		1	Victoria, CAN	28 Aug
	82.28		5	Berlin, GER	30 Aug
	81.58		Q	Helsinki, FIN	7 Aug
	81.16		2	Zurich, SWZ	17 Aug
	80.98		7	Oslo, NOR	22 Jul
	79.94		4	Tokyo, JAP	15 Sep
	79.64		3	London (CP)	15 Jul
82.14	*Terry McHugh*	*22.08.63*	*Q*	*Helsinki, FIN*	*7 Aug*
80.38	Nigel Bevan	3.01.68	4	Victoria, CAN	28 Aug
	77.94		1	Bedford	17 Sep
79.16	#Colin Mackenzie	30.06.63	3	Sheffield	12 Jun
	78.86		1	London (CP)	26 Jun
	78.34		1	Belfast	4 Jun
	78.28		7	Gateshead	1 Jul
	(80.82) after postive drug test		(1)	Rovereto, ITA	24 Jul
78.82	Mark Roberson	13.03.67	2	London (CP)	26 Jun
77.22	Roald Bradstock	24.04.62	1	Westwood, USA	9 Apr
	48 performances to 77.00 by 6 athletes				
76.28	Nick Nieland	U23	31.01.72	1	Kings Lynn	9 Jul
74.30	Myles Cottrell		22.11.70	4	Sheffield	12 Jun
71.94	Steve Harrison	U23	19.12.72	2	Kings Lynn	9 Jul
70.54	Peter Yates		15.06.57	1	Harrow	2 Jul
	(10)				
70.00	Phil Parry		4.10.65	2	Harrow	2 Jul
69.68	Shane Lewis	U23	22.08.72	1	Oxford	23 Apr
69.20	Keith Beard		8.11.61	3	Assen, HOL	16 Jul
69.10	Stefan Baldwin		26.04.70	4	London (He)	5 Jun
67.64	Tony Smith		17.05.58	4	London (WL)	2 Jul
67.60	Dean Smahon		8.12.61	4	Kings Lynn	9 Jul
66.74	Stuart Faben	U20	28.02.75	15Q	Lisbon, POR	22 Jul
66.62	Tony Hatton		18.06.70	5	London (He)	5 Jun
66.60	Kevin Hill	U23	17.06.73	1	Stretford	23 Aug
65.82	Demetrio Barros		29.06.71	1	Bournemouth	7 May
	(20)				
65.82	James Drennen	U23	16.08.72	1	Newport	26 Jun
65.80	David Bigham		4.07.71	2	Wolverhampton	4 Jun
65.08	Alan Holloway		22.06.60	1	Loughborough	27 Apr
64.88	Richard Atkinson	U23	9.10.74	4	Istanbul, TUR	21 May
64.46	Duncan MacDonald	U23	30.03.74	1	Sheffield (W)	4 Jun
64.10	Gary Jenson		14.02.67	5	London (WL)	2 Jul
64.06	*James Highland*		*2.06.65*	*1*	*Peterborough*	*2 Jul*
63.80	Simon Shirley		3.08.66	2D	Victoria, CAN	24 Aug
63.78	Robert Mullen		8.08.64	1	Aldershot	6 Jul
63.50	Andrew Whiting	U23	7.03.74	1	Bedford	18 Sep
63.14	Graham Lay	U20	13.11.75	1	Telford	8 Jul
	(30)				
63.06	Mark Pinner		12.05.64	1	Cannock	26 Jun
63.04	James Hurrion	U23	11.11.73	1	Oxford	20 Feb
62.44	Dwayne Marsden	U23	25.10.73		Derby	2 Jul
62.02	Richard Hooper		29.03.58	1	Bebington	15 May
61.96	Dave Bailey	U23	19.10.73	1	Cannock	11 Sep
61.92	Rob Laing		30.07.66	2	Derby	16 Jul
61.76	Simon Bennett	U23	16.10.72	1	Yate	29 Jun
61.72	Damien Crawford		22.08.68	3	Dublin (M), IRE	24 Jul
61.62	Michael Morgan		30.07.66	4	Crawley	6 Aug
61.60	Nigel Stainton		19.08.59	1	Croydon	2 Jul
	(40)				
61.54	Stewart Maxwell		29.06.58	1	Crewe	7 May
61.48	Jon Clarke		20.11.67	3	Cwmbran	18 Jun

61.38	Jon Wilkinson		17.02.62	1D	Sheffield	1	May
61.26	Simon Carter	U20	5.03.75	1	London (CP)	29	May
60.70	David Wilson		5.09.70	1	Kettering	20	Aug
60.60	Ken Rehill		4.11.68	1	London (BP)	9	Apr
60.48	David Hanna	U20	13.12.75	1	Belfast	23	Apr
60.42	Peter Johnson	U20	25.09.75	3	Telford	8	Jul
60.36	Lyndon Medcroft	U23	20.10.72	1	Cheltenham	15	May
60.34	Steve Langdon		1.01.58	1	Norwich	30	Jul
	(50)						
60.04	Alex Kruger		18.11.63	4D	Bressanone, ITA	3	Jul
60.00	Paul Bushnell		12.11.68	1	London (PH)	7	May
59.92	Rafer Joseph		21.07.68	5D	Bressanone, ITA	3	Jul
59.90	Sean Evans	U20	3.10.76	1	Exeter	20	Aug
59.86	Dean Johnson	U20	31.12.75	1	Gateshead	29	May
59.80	Matt Atkins	U20	23.06.77	6	Bedford	3	Jul
59.78	Anthony Norman		5.07.63	1	Guildford	13	Aug
59.68	David Bradley	U23	30.04.72	2	Loughborough	27	Apr
59.66	Andrew Hayward	U23	26.10.74	1	Liverpool	3	Sep
59.58	Alistair Gidley	U23	5.09.72	5	Harrow	5	Jul
	(60)						
59.52	*Cyrus Doomasia*	*U23*	*31.03.73*	*6*	*London (CP)*	*26*	*Jun*
59.50	Chris Smith	U20	27.11.75	1	Edinburgh	6	Aug
59.38	Tim Eldridge	U20	15.03.76	1	Barking	11	Jun
59.28	Trevor Ratcliffe		9.03.64	2	St. Ives	1	May
59.28	Steve Greening		15.02.68	1	High Wycombe	22	Jun
59.18	Damian Huntingford	U20	11.06.77	7	Bedford	3	Jul
59.14	Stuart Bartlett		20.10.64	3	Edinburgh	25	Jun
59.06	Richard Jones	U20	26.06.75	1	Swansea	3	Apr
58.92	David Pescod	U23	15.04.73	1	Jarrow	23	Jul
58.90	Kevin Murch		11.11.58	1	Brierley Hill	7	May
58.56	Andrew Quixley		8.11.64	2	Aldershot	6	Jul
	(70)						
58.54	Stephen Rogers		1.09.71	5D	Emmelshausen, GER	29	May
58.46	Stuart Loughran	U20	19.02.76	1	Carmarthen	14	May
58.46	Matthew Bamford		19.09.58	1	Hayes	30	Jul
58.30	John Trower		6.02.56	4	Loughborough	5	Jun
58.30	Simon Achurch	U23	27.12.74	3	Kingston	31	Jul
58.20	Greg Hayward		28.01.64	1	Oxford	27	Apr
58.18	Gary Jepp		23.06.66	1	Aldershot	29	Jun
58.18	Sean O'Hanlon	U20	3.09.76	5	Telford	8	Jul
58.12	Pawlo Ostapowycz	V40	1.07.52	1	Telford	1	May
58.02	Barry Thomas	U23	28.04.72	1D	Stoke	7	Aug
	(80)						
57.78	Paul Verheyden	U23	22.09.72	1	Braintree	18	Sep
57.68	Scott MacHardie		26.06.69	2	Cardiff	2	Jul
57.68	David Odwar	U20	23.12.76	1	London (BP)	13	Aug
57.66	Dominic Collins	U20	2.10.76	2	Exeter	20	Aug
57.66	Stephen Savill		10.03.67	2	Braintree	18	Sep
57.60	Tim Newenham		1.04.60	1	Norwich	27	Jul
57.46	David Sketchley	U20	25.02.76	1	Colchester	15	Jun
57.24	Buster Watson		19.11.57	5	Enfield	31	Jul
57.16	Ken Hayford		10.03.63	2	Bromley	19	Jun
57.06	James Worland	U23	3.02.72	1	Brighton	18	Jun
	(90)						
57.02	James Scott		21.09.71	4	London (SP)	29	Aug
56.80	Jamie Wilkinson	U23	21.04.74	2	Leeds	13	Aug
56.64	Wayne Powell		27.07.71	1	Yate	21	Aug
56.58	Seth Kirkham	U20	9.09.75	1	Harrow	24	Apr
56.58	Stephen Birse	U17	8.10.77	1	Middlesbrough	11	Jun
56.40	Zhina Fuat	U20	27.03.76	2	Bournemouth	23	Jul
56.38	Andy Clarke		10.08.70		Stretford	15	May

56.30	Jeremy Goldsmith	U23	6.12.73	2	Sheffield (W)	4	Jun
56.22	Landley Darlington	U20	19.01.77	4	Gateshead	29	May
56.18	Jeremy Hames		17.11.70	3	Coventry	7	May
	(100)						
56.18	Paul Cooper	U20	4.12.76	2	Barking	11	Jun
56.12	Mark Welch	U23	9.11.74	9	Corby	30	May
56.06	Paul Gore	U23	4.12.72	1	Leeds	13	Aug
56.02	Stephen Rowbotham		6.03.68	3	Loughborough	26	Jun
55.84	David Evans	U20	23.01.76	8	Telford	8	Jul
55.82	Paul Barbour	U23	5.12.73	3	Belfast	4	Jun
55.76	Mark Sheridan		17.06.70	1	Kingston	19	Jun
55.68	M. Stone	U20		1	Portsmouth	11	Jun
55.66	Luigi Antoniazzi		13.09.62	5	Cwmbran	18	Jun
55.56	Ciaran Doherty	U20	14.01.75	4	Antrim	18	Jun
	(110)						
55.52	Livon Houslin		2.11.60	12	London (He)	5	Jun
55.48	Peter Jones	U23	8.10.72	8	Wigan	7	May
55.36	Paul Howard		19.10.66	7	Liverpool	6	Aug

Additional Under 20 (1 - 25 above)

54.78	Fraser Keith		1.08.75	1	Hull	11	Jun
54.72	Sandy Henderson		7.07.75	2	Edinburgh	14	May
54.68	Simon Forster	U17	15.10.77	1	Stretford	31	Jul
54.44	Roger Hunter		10.03.76	1D	Birmingham	18	Sep
54.44	Simon Pavitt		12.07.76				
	(30)						
54.42	Dean Macey	U17	12.12.77	1O	London (He)	21	Aug
54.24	Adam Spratt			1	Derby	29	Apr
53.68	Mark Francis	U17	23.09.77	3	Southampton	13	Aug
53.64	Josh Harrison		14.08.75	1	Middlesbrough	28	Aug
53.50	Andrew Aylward		31.08.77	1	Brighton	11	Jun
53.44	Graeme Leeson		27.03.75	1	Grantham	18	Jun
53.32	J. Haigh			2	Oxford	11	Jun
53.24	Keith Lavelle		13.05.77	1	Telford	11	Jun
52.84	Paul Bale		20.12.76	1	Leamington	11	Jun
52.54	David Matthews		7.07.76	1	Redditch	11	Jun

JAVELIN - Under 17 - 700g

62.86	Mark Francis		23.09.77	1	Telford	8	Jul
61.36	Andrew Benn		2.09.77	1	Braintree	18	Sep
60.20	Jason Oakes		29.09.77	2	Telford	8	Jul
58.80	Ian Burns		20.09.77	1	Carlisle	4	Sep
58.76	Paul Startin		22.11.77	3	Telford	8	Jul
58.76	Dan Carter	U15	15.04.80	1	Colchester	29	Aug
58.36	Peter Fraser		28.01.78	2	Birmingham	30	Jul
57.60	Stephen Birse		8.10.77	5	Telford	8	Jul
56.84	Richard Salt		28.10.77	1	Blackpool	14	Aug
56.80	Ben Cascoe		26.12.77	3	London (CP)	29	May
	(10)						
56.76	Matthew Phillips		22.09.77	1	Leamington	15	May
55.64	Stuart Walker		22.09.78	7	Telford	8	Jul
54.94	Alex Gibson		3.11.77	1	Barking	11	Jun
54.94	Simon Forster		15.10.77	1	Stretford	23	Aug
54.86	Robert Charlesworth		25.03.79	1	Peterborough	29	Aug
54.72	Chris Gaffon			1	London (TB)	17	Jul
54.64	Lee Hammond		13.11.77	1	Redditch	29	Aug
54.62	Christopher Jack		17.11.77	1	Ipswich	11	Jun
54.60	B. Donald			1		11	Jun
54.58	David Parker	U15	28.02.80	1	Grimsby	25	Sep
	(20)						
54.48	Julian Saint			1	Bedford	26	Jun

54.38	Matthew Davies	16.09.78	1	Colwyn Bay	2	Jul
54.34	Ben Cotton	10.03.78	1	St. Ives	14	May
54.20	Jordan James	24.05.78	4	Birmingham	30	Jul
53.86	Bryn Samuel	11.10.77	1	Colwyn Bay	11	Jun
53.56	Jeremy Smyth	11.08.78	1	Kirkwall	21	Aug
53.34	Nick Morley	15.04.78	6	Birmingham	30	Jul

JAVELIN - Under 15 - 600g

60.56	Clifton Green	10.10.79	1	Hoo	3	Jul
58.94	Dan Carter	15.04.80	2	London (He)	7	Aug
55.96	David Parker	28.02.80	1	Gateshead	29	May
54.16	Tony Rigby	22.02.80	1	Ipswich	4	Sep
52.42	Robert Southward	24.03.80	1	Oldham	21	Aug
50.20	Tim Kitney	26.04.80	1	Andover	4	Sep
48.44	Michael Allen		1	Antrim	20	Aug
47.72	Tim Pamphlett	18.02.81	1	Hoo	11	Jun
47.70	Ben Poynter		1	London (BP)	24	Jul
47.50	Paul Foster	20.10.79	1	Yate	7	Aug
(10)						
47.48	Thomas Platt	3.03.80	2	Hoo	11	Jun
47.46	Andrew Squire	30.09.79	1	Stoke	18	Jun
47.08	Jamie Dalton	20.09.79	1	Swansea	29	Aug
46.94	Marcus Graham	11.09.79	6	Telford	8	Jul
46.88	Paul Robinson		1	Windsor	5	Jun
46.72	Nikki Flowers	15.02.80	1	Newport	5	Jun
46.64	Chris Thomas		1	Colwyn Bay	2	Jul
46.56	Max Shale	20.01.81	1	Oxford	11	Jun
46.14	Russell Oram	14.08.80	7	Telford	8	Jul
46.02	Neil Oxley	7.12.79	1	Nottingham	14	May
(20)						
45.78	Ben King-Smith	30.09.79	8	Telford	8	Jul
45.64	Peter Maguire	24.01.80	1	Leicester	11	Jun
45.32	Paul Kelly	22.12.79	2	Oxford	11	Jun
45.22	Tommy Black	26.11.79	2	Barking	11	Jun
45.12	Mark Colebourn	5.12.79	1	Derby	11	Jun

Under 13

| 38.44 | Jonathan Lundman | 7.12.81 | 5 | Braintree | 18 | Sep |

JAVELIN - Under 13 - 400g

40.58	Jonathan Lundman	7.12.81	1	Colchester	28	Aug
39.84	M. Patience		1	Swindon	18	Jun
38.74	Daniel Britton	25.09.81	1	Bournemouth	28	Aug
36.82	Martin Waters	20.01.82	1	Sandown	14	Jun
35.96	Keith Simpson	19.10.81	1	Inverness	11	Sep
32.96	Matthews		1	Luton	14	May
32.94	E. Mathers		3	Birmingham	2	Jul

DECATHLON

Mark	Name	100	LJ	SP	HJ	400	110H	DT	PV	JT	1500	DOB	Rk	Place	Date
8078	Alex Kruger											18.11.63	7	Gotzis, AUT	29 May
		11.22	7.45	14.63	2.14	50.05	15.09	43.44	4.80	57.08	4:34.86				
7963													3	Bressanone, ITA	3 Jul
		11.23	7.40	13.74	2.13	49.69	14.96	42.50	4.60	60.04	4:40.22				
7640													7	Victoria, CAN	24 Aug
		11.28	7.18	14.07	2.10	50.14	15.10	41.58	4.50	58.08	5:02.80				
1 Hour 6926													2	Salzburg, AUT	24 Sep
		11.42	6.99	14.29	2.10	59.92	15.82	42.02	4.20	56.20	5:15.30				
7980	Simon Shirley											3.08.66	3	Victoria, CAN	24 Aug
		10.89	7.11	14.16	2.04	48.90	14.87	38.38	4.60	63.80	4:32.34				
7938													4	Bressanone, ITA	3 Jul
		10.94	7.52	13.75	2.04	48.83	14.99	38.04	4.60	57.54	4:31.47				
7936 w													11	Gotzis, AUT	29 May
		10.92W	7.31	12.89	2.05	49.24	15.37	41.62	4.60	61.12	4:27.45				
7663	Rafer Joseph											21.07.68	6	Victoria, CAN	24 Aug
		11.06	6.80	13.04	1.95	50.50	15.08	48.30	4.70	54.64	4:40.48				
7563													11	Bressanone, ITA	3 Jul
		11.17	6.86	13.14	1.83	50.33	15.06	50.66	4.40	59.92	4:47.02				
7525													5	Emmelshausen, GER	29 May
		11.21	6.55	13.45	1.94	51.82	15.03w	48.68	4.80	57.72	4:56.93				
7610	Jamie Quarry											U23 15.11.72	8	Victoria, CAN	24 Aug
		10.86	6.89	13.44	1.95	49.76	14.36	41.08	4.30	51.54	4:33.24				
7452													6	Emmelshausen, GER	29 May
		10.96	7.15	12.93	1.97	49.38	14.67	38.62	4.20	48.12	4:38.57				
7458	Barry Thomas											U23 28.04.72	1	Horsham	19 Jun
		11.34w	6.94 12.88		1.95	52.55	15.06w	39.90	4.80	56.24	4:33.98				
7350													16	Bressanone, ITA	3 Jul
		11.44	7.06	13.22	2.01	52.30	14.89	37.72	4.60	56.34	4:53.59				
7309													1	Wrexham	28 Aug
		11.22	7.07	13.33	1.94	52.20	15.00w	38.66	4.40	56.82	4:51.90				
6992													1	Stoke	7 Aug
		11.3	6.80	12.37	1.98	51.07	16.6	39.18	4.40	58.02	4:57.79				
7434	David Bigham											4.07.71	2	Horsham	19 Jun
		11.19w	6.77	12.87	1.95	49.75	14.83w	37.10	4.20	59.70	4:32.25				
7221	Andy Lewis											9.03.68	3	Horsham	19 Jun
		10.80w	7.29w	13.44	1.89	50.37	14.67w	32.90	4.00	50.00	4:50.30				
7112													1	Diekirch, LUX	20 Aug
		10.89	7.28	12.66	1.90	49.90	14.88	31.46	4.00	52.08	4:57.66				
6916													6	Prague, CS	29 May
		11.02	7.26	13.31	1.86	50.24	15.30	32.08	3.90	48.90	5:04.77				
6709													4	Azusa, USA	14 Apr
		10.84w	7.05w	12.79	1.82	51.68	15.11	33.08	3.45	50.52	5:06.4				
7203	Stephen Rogers											1.09.71	10	Emmelshausen, GER	29 May
		11.68	6.80	12.23	1.94	50.32	15.47w	37.10	4.40	58.54	4:36.05				
7064													2	Kaiser-Lautern, GER	10 Jul
		11.62	6.79	12.85	1.94	50.74	15.75	38.16	4.40	55.44	4:53.82				
7157	Paul Field											24.06.67	4	Horsham	19 Jun
		10.87w	7.19	12.38	1.89	49.59	14.61w	33.52	3.80	45.28	4:32.58				
7078	Steve Leader											24.11.66	5	Horsham	19 Jun
		11.25w	6.57w	12.12	1.86	50.51	15.46	36.56	4.70	46.20	4:31.81				
(10) 7048	Rob Laing											30.07.66	3	Prague, CS	29 May
		11.56	7.23w	12.14	1.83	52.11	15.25	39.38	4.40	59.90	5:08.44				
6990													7	Horsham	19 Jun
		11.67	7.11	12.25	1.83	52.95	14.88w	38.80	4.50	56.46	5:06.17				
6726													1	Sheffield	1 May
		11.57w	6.96	11.92	1.86	52.92	15.68	35.70	4.20	56.24	5:07.47				

7047	Steve Gutteridge				5.07.71	1	Azusa, USA			14 Apr
	11.50w	6.90	12.49	1.92	52.50	15.42	38.80	4.75	48.86	4:54.92
6972						8	Horsham			19 Jun
	11.60w	6.95w	12.48	1.92	52.83	15.16w	39.84	4.60	47.32	5:01.33
6865						8	Prague, CS			29 May
	11.63	6.91w	12.68	1.86	52.11	15.24	35.64	4.60	47.42	4:59.62
7024	Livio Salvador-Aylott		U23	18.07.73		6	Horsham			19 Jun
	11.05w	6.76w	12.13	1.86	50.64	15.76	32.04	4.50	53.08	4:40.12
6791						3	Azusa, USA			14 Apr
	11.18w	6.49w	11.51	1.82	50.94	15.74w	36.06	4.17	54.46	4:50.61
6883	Tony Southward				31.01.71	1	Stoke			26 Jun
	11.54	6.57	12.57	1.92	51.76	15.29	36.98	4.20	48.86	4:43.92
6792	Stephen Rowbotham				6.03.68	9	Horsham			19 Jun
	11.41	6.77w	13.10	1.80	51.93	15.71w	38.88	3.80	53.92	4:50.40
6697						2	Sheffield			1 May
	11.40w	6.89	12.32	1.83	51.81	15.93	37.68	3.80	52.96	4:58.33
6719	William Wyllie		U23	12.07.73		2	Wrexham			28 Aug
	11.04	7.25	10.73	1.97	51.68	15.22w	30.62	4.00	44.04	5:05.20
6645						2	Stoke			26 Jun
	11.22	7.11	9.75	1.92	51.98	15.45	33.14	4.10	47.46	5:02.37
6673	Matt Allison		U23	26.02.73		1	Wakefield			25 Sep
	11.3	6.95	11.84	1.78	49.9	15.9	37.86	3.50	50.28	4:37.8
6671	Terry Fidler				13.10.71	10	Horsham			19 Jun
	11.54w	6.68w	11.27	1.80	52.58	15.25w	33.72	4.30	49.00	4:42.42
6579	Brett Heath		U20	6.01.75		1	Sheffield			1 May
	11.83w	6.41	11.65	1.88	52.04	15.88	36.80	4.20	39.78	4:28.37
6569	Terry Gyorffy				28.01.65	3	Wrexham			28 Aug
	11.50	6.56	11.85	1.85	53.30	15.76w	37.80	3.90	53.16	4:59.24

(20)

6565 w	Roger Hunter		U20	10.03.76		2	Sheffield			1 May
	11.64w	6.55W	10.59	1.94	50.27	16.25	32.24	3.50	53.46	4:33.05
6563				*	Sheffield	1	May			
	6.54w									
6548	Adrian Ferrand				5.02.68	11	Horsham			19 Jun
	11.47w	6.27w	12.14	1.95	52.77	15.30w	35.40	3.80	43.42	4:46.58
6519 w	Paul Howard				19.10.66	12	Horsham			19 Jun
	12.17	6.41W	13.19	1.95	55.75	16.02w	40.72	4.10	54.44	5:09.07
6450						*	Horsham			19 Jun
	6.10									
6514	Chris Hindley		U20	21.01.76		3	Sheffield			1 May
	11.87w	6.31	11.69	2.00	53.37	16.30	38.94	3.60	43.88	4:25.28

46 performances to 6500 by 24 athletes

6414	Mark Perman				6.01.68	1	Watford			24 Jul
	11.6	6.62	11.33	1.84	51.9	15.6	35.68	4.00	43.92	4:51.1
6411	William Gilles		U23	15.02.73		3	Stoke			26 Jun
	11.87	6.76w	9.36	1.92	52.27	15.94w	28.38	3.80	52.94	4:33.94
6411	Jeremy Goldsmith		U23	6.12.73		4	Wrexham			28 Aug
	11.50w	6.58	11.48	1.76	52.22	16.06w	33.56	3.60	54.06	4:46.52
6359	Matthew Douglas		U20	26.11.76		4	Sheffield			1 May
	10.99w	6.64	11.00	1.91	48.71	15.64	24.48	2.50	45.84	4:33.32
6359	Paul Hourihan		U20	7.11.76		1	Kirkby			24 Jul
	11.6	6.75	10.91	2.02	52.6	16.2	32.78	3.50	45.26	4:42.9
6317	Michael Brown				4.06.69	4	Stoke			26 Jun
	11.56w	6.41	11.45	1.80	52.64	16.44w	36.68	3.60	50.26	4:49.62

(30)

6286	Anthony Brannen				16.09.68	1	Middlesbrough			10 Apr
	11.6	6.71	13.02	1.96	55.9	15.6	35.98	3.00	47.80	4:50.3
6277 w	David Vidgen		U23	27.09.74		4	Sheffield			1 May
	10.99W	6.73	12.84	1.77	51.54	15.86	29.78	3.40	44.26	5:12.50

6259	Jon Wilkinson				17.02.62	5	Sheffield			1 May
	12.05w	5.80	12.39	1.77	54.39	16.14	39.60	3.60	61.38	4:57.07
6256	Andrew Weston			U23	4.12.73	5	Stoke			26 Jun
	11.88	6.92	10.04	2.01	53.47	16.50	31.62	4.00	38.26	4:50.50
6244	Duncan Gauden				11.02.68	6	Stoke			26 Jun
	11.53	6.52w	11.04	1.83	53.14	16.68	36.66	3.50	45.60	4:43.63
6158	Fraser Dean			U23	12.11.73	2	Alamosa, USA			13 May
	11.1	6.37	9.99	1.82	51.9	15.7	29.20	3.80	41.50	4:46.9
6121	Unuakpor Esegbona				16.04.68	4	Stoke			7 Aug
	11.5	6.66	10.89	1.98	52.20	1.63	32.88	3.60	40.94	5:13.43
6095	Martin Holgate				2.11.65	14	Horsham			19 Jun
	11.25w	6.21w	10.19	1.77	51.36	16.46w	29.92	3.80	38.92	4:41.38
6094	James Courtney				9.12.71	3	London (He)			21 Aug
	11.53	6.30	11.36	1.66	50.62	16.40	34.96	3.70	36.58	4:44.63
6044	Allan Leiper				23.07.60	1	Linwood			17 Jul
	11.89	6.29	11.52	1.79	53.17	16.45	31.32	4.10	42.56	5:00.92
(40)										
6005	Richard Czernik			U23	12.07.72	5	Wrexham			28 Aug
	11.58w	6.31	11.34	1.82	52.06	17.36	35.16	3.20	44.76	4:51.20
5911	Simon Wassell				7.04.69	5	Stoke			7 Aug
	11.4	5.87	10.09	1.74	50.29	16.6	35.72	2.80	45.28	4:34.94
5899	Daniel Honneyman			U20	13.10.75	6	Sheffield			1 May
	11.60w	6.11	9.15	1.76	52.59	16.45	31.82	3.30	47.40	4:42.28
5850	David Ralson			U20	22.02.77	2	London (He)			21 Aug
	11.64	6.15	9.74	1.75	52.66	16.77	28.76	3.70	48.22	4:57.93
5845	John McIlwham			U23	29.02.72	7	Stoke			26 Jun
	11.74	5.88w	8.74	1.71	51.71	16.11w	26.94	3.80	36.88	4:22.01
5841	Geoff Ingram				31.01.68	2	Aldershot			2 Aug
	11.4	6.79	9.80	1.66	52.0	17.6	29.22	3.50	43.64	4:39.5
5816	Brian Hughes				6.01.70	6	Wrexham			28 Aug
	11.98	6.29	9.20	1.85	55.64	16.20w	31.08	4.10	47.14	5:21.42
5805	Robert Treu				1.12.69	7	Wrexham			28 Aug
	11.88	6.19	11.34	1.70	54.30	16.54w	36.94	3.60	45.06	5:17.26
5784	Dale Daborn				14.11.66	3	Aldershot			2 Aug
	11.2	5.72	9.41	1.78	50.8	16.3	31.30	2.80	43.68	4:38.2
5783	*Ian Condron*				*7.10.59*	*1*	*Waterford, IRE*			*6 Jun*
	11.58	*6.51*	*11.36*	*1.70*	*53.88*	*18.26*	*35.96*	*3.70*	*44.28*	*5:16.34*
5752	Chris Lawniczak			U23	24.03.72	1	Peterborough			25 Sep
	12.0	6.54	10.70	1.87	54.7	16.2	27.00	4.00	34.88	5:02.5
(50)										
5716	Kenneth Pearson			U23	9.07.72	2	Linwood			17 Jul
	12.26	6.09w	9.10	1.82	53.36	17.01	29.02	3.50	44.68	4:35.81
5695	Matthew Gillard			U20	11.07.75	2	Wakefield			25 Sep
	11.6	6.13	11.65	1.69	51.7	18.1	32.90	3.50	35.02	4:40.3
5674	Ciaran Doherty			U20	14.01.75	8	Stoke			7 Aug
	11.6	6.22w	9.94	1.77	54.05	15.8	25.50	3.10	54.18	5:11.15
5648	Dean Macey			U17	12.12.77	1	Braintree			25 Sep
	11.9w	6.25	10.66	1.92	55.7	17.2	29.88	3.10	49.12	4:59.3
5647	Mark Atkin			U20	30.12.75	7	Sheffield			1 May
	11.49w	6.19	10.10	1.82	52.60	17.33	31.24	2.80	36.26	4:44.32
5588	Garry Smith				2.01.66	1	Aldershot			17 Jun
	11.9	6.13	11.02	1.84	56.3	17.7	34.20	3.60	43.76	5:08.0
5545	Jamie Malcolm				5.10.69	9	Stoke			26 Jun
	12.31	6.06	11.51	1.86	57.98	17.02w	36.46	3.00	49.80	5:18.78
5451	Neal Killen				10.04.59	2	Aldershot			17 Jun
	11.4	6.13	13.19	1.69	52.4	16.5	37.34	3.60	38.80	dnf
5436	Jody Rodger			U23	29.11.73	11	Stoke			26 Jun
	12.06	5.95	9.16	1.77	53.27	17.02w	30.28	3.10	43.18	5:01.13
5395	Mark Crompton				31.12.63	7	Sheffield			1 May
	12.20w	5.93	8.93	1.86	57.23	17.41	31.12	3.60	42.90	5:04.00
(60)										

5388   Steve Bartliff   30.12.67 4   Aldershot   2 Aug
        11.7   6.37   9.31   1.63   53.2   17.7   30.52   3.20   40.90   4:54.4
5386   Wayne Gadd   21.05.71 4   London (He)   21 Aug
        12.80   5.42   9.94   1.78   54.74   17.34   30.00   3.30   47.40   4:39.44
5265   Jon Gregory   U23   3.10.72 12   Stoke   26 Jun
        11.69w   5.67w   9.13   1.77   52.74   16.08   24.72   2.80   39.76   5:15.66
5261   Adam Young   2.09.68   2   Peterborough   25 Sep
        12.0   6.41   9.97   1.90   57.0   16.1   25.94   3.00   47.16   5:55.8
5248   Howard Crane   U23   12.10.73   1   Blackpool   24 Apr
        12.4   5.85   10.53   1.76   54.8   17.5   27.68   3.20   41.94   4:51.9
5235 w John Culshaw   20.11.62   9   Wrexham   28 Aug
        12.28W   5.89   9.89   1.73   53.4   18.20w   26.02   2.90   40.92   4:38.84
5234   Michael Bull   6.06.70 10   Stoke   7 Aug
        11.5   6.07   11.31   1.68   54.18   17.5   30.18   3.10   29.32   5:07.70
5219   Dean Mellor   25.11.71 11   Stoke   7 Aug
        11.2   5.67   7.39   1.74   54.76   20.9   25.64   4.90   36.06   5:08.13
5173   Adam Davis   U23   19.11.72 13   Stoke   26 Jun
        11.96   5.86   10.80   1.65   56.57   18.05   29.46   4.20   31.52   5:26.75
5172 w Gareth Hughes   U23   22.10.73   8   Sheffield   1 May
        11.40W   5.97   9.04   1.83   53.43   16.14   23.52   2.80   26.98   5:19.62
        (70)
5136   Matthew Randall   28.04.70   3   Crawley   18 Sep
        12.2   6.57   9.80   1.76   56.6   16.7   27.02   2.30   48.34   5:18.5
5120   Mark Pendlebury   U23   3.10.74   9   Sheffield   1 May
        11.90w   6.13   10.41   1.83   55.07   20.32   28.56   2.60   40.84   4:53.54
5117   Nicholas Walker   24.02.64 12   Stoke   7 Aug
        11.9   6.12   9.69   1.59   53.55   19.6   33.28   3.60   37.92   5:13.13
5102   Thomas Molloy   U23   25.03.73   3   Aldershot   17 Jun
        12.0   6.10   8.88   1.87   54.8   18.4   27.24   2.50   38.70   4:46.0
5099   Ian Hunt   2.12.64   5   Aldershot   2 Aug
        11.8   5.90   11.20   1.72   55.9   20.6   32.72   2.80   50.64   5:09.9
5055   Nick Sargeant   U23   8.05.73 15   Stoke   26 Jun
        11.70w   5.96   9.66   1.71   54.93   20.33   29.74   2.80   48.04   5:11.56
5030   John Smith   7.07.71   6   Aldershot   2 Aug
        12.1   5.70   7.86   1.72   51.5   20.6   23.22   2.70   42.68   4:10.7
5019   William Paine   30.03.64   1   Hoo   18 Sep
        12.5   5.57   11.90   1.64   54.6   16.8   37.36   nhc   46.56   5:04.1
5004   Chris Cummings   8.11.67   2   Belfast   9 Jul
        12.4   5.43   10.52   1.76   55.8   17.0   27.56   3.20   35.88   5:05.4

DECATHLON - Under 20 with Under 20 Implements

6958 w Roger Hunter   10.03.76   1   Birmingham   18 Sep
        11.47w   6.69   12.79   1.92   51.13   15.88   38.24   3.90   54.44   4:38.44
        6705   1   York   26 Jun
        11.9   6.42   13.23   1.95   50.8   15.6   39.28   3.60   52.02   4:43.0
6622   Mark Bushell   22.10.76   2   Birmingham   18 Sep
        11.15w   7.13   11.47   1.89   54.00   14.95   35.00   3.90   42.66   5:03.46
6211 w David Ralson   22.02.77   3   Birmingham   18 Sep
        11.46W   6.37   11.17   1.80   52.39   16.20   32.14   3.40   48.90   4:45.67
        5852   2   Oxford   26 Jun
        11.9   6.41   11.08   1.82   52.7   16.2   33.14   3.20   45.92   5:06.5
6181   Mark Atkin   30.12.75   4   Birmingham   18 Sep
        11.23w   6.53   12.03   1.80   52.72   16.59   40.10   2.70   39.28   4:39.21
6108   Chris Hindley   21.01.76   1   Oxford   26 Jun
        12.2   6.10   12.60   2.00   53.8   16.2   38.12   3.60   44.18   5:06.5
6040   Scott McDermott   2.12.75   1   Linwood   17 Jul
        11.84w   6.37   11.46   1.85   53.18   16.56w   32.04   3.40   46.76   4:53.66
5934   Steve Benton   26.09.76   5   Birmingham   18 Sep
        11.34w   6.65   10.28   1.83   57.68   16.49   32.78   3.70   45.26   5:08.06

5856	James Robinson			27.08.76	1	Birmingham		24 Apr
	11.89	6.90	11.24	1.76	57.9	16.16	36.28	4.10	41.22	5:40.53
5757	Mike Robbins			14.03.76	1	Wakefield		25 Sep
	11.7	6.04	11.11	1.99	53.1	15.0	24.70	2.70	37.08	4:50.9
5749	Karl Kaiser			26.02.75	2	Middlesbrough		10 Apr
	11.4	5.58	13.67	1.72	52.4	15.6	38.16	2.80	32.58	5:04.2
	(10)								
5748	Rob Weston			16.03.77	6	Birmingham		18 Sep
	11.59w	6.35	10.63	1.77	52.32	16.07	28.70	2.70	37.52	4:43.68
5731	Simon Parley			6.04.76	1	Exeter		26 Jun
	11.7	6.02	9.62	1.81	54.8	16.1	30.56	3.70	38.08	4:43.5
5715 w	Jon Goodwin			22.09.76	7	Birmingham		18 Sep
	11.77W	5.75	9.68	1.77	52.32	16.10	30.20	3.00	39.98	4:34.21
5076					1	Exeter		8 May
	11.9	5.37	9.57	1.81	52.1	16.7	28.76	nhc	36.82	4:33.8
5712	Edward Galbraith			3.10.75	8	Birmingham		18 Sep
	11.69	6.52	9.67	1.86	55.05	15.62	31.46	3.30	32.36	5:06.74
5653	Steven Rae			20.07.75	5	Dilbeek, BEL		7 Aug
	11.82	6.15	12.33	1.70	53.62	16.23	37.48	2.62	41.00	5:15.07
5464	David Bullock			1.12.76	9	Birmingham		18 Sep
	11.80	6.34	9.41	1.68	52.67	16.87	27.32	2.70	37.80	4:38.19
5417	Mark Dobbie			5.03.77	3	Linwood		17 Jul
	12.08	6.21	10.57	1.61	54.04	15.77w	30.36	2.90	38.88	5:05.28
5412	Kevin Ricketts			29.06.76	2	Wrexham		28 Aug
	12.32w	6.32	9.89	1.88	56.9	17.56	29.92	3.00	42.42	4:51.84
5368	Adam Carswell			8.01.76	10	Birmingham		18 Sep
	12.37	6.17	10.69	1.86	57.20	15.91	27.70	2.60	51.82	5:29.20
5334	Arron Bonning			9.11.75	2	Basildon		26 Jun
	12.2	5.94	10.80	1.66	55.6	16.9	31.22	3.40	41.84	5:01.0
	(20)								
5312	Matthew Gillard			11.07.75	9	Sheffield		1 May
	11.36w	5.94w	10.59	1.70	51.99	16.64	28.20	2.50	27.96	4:59.60
5290	Brett Marsh			20.01.76	3	Exeter		26 Jun
	12.2	5.88	12.60	1.72	54.0	19.2	35.52	2.90	43.24	5:04.6
5172	Craig Holgate			21.09.76	12	Birmingham		18 Sep
	12.08w	5.56	9.60	1.65	53.88	17.62	24.86	3.20	31.18	4:23.94
5170	Lee Rudd			15.09.76	3	Blackpool		26 Jun
	11.7	6.07	9.19	1.74	52.2	17.9	22.02	2.80	41.00	4:54.2
5149	Lee Parkes			23.12.76	3	Wakefield		25 Sep
	12.5	5.64	12.48	1.81	56.9	18.3	30.86	3.00	44.46	5:07.7
5137	Michael Leonard			28.05.77	13	Birmingham		18 Sep
	12.14	5.66	12.07	1.68	58.45	18.94	42.06	2.70	43.66	5:16.74
5133	Ben Watson-Jones			24.11.75	14	Birmingham		18 Sep
	11.96	6.13	9.41	1.86	56.33	18.05	28.80	3.60	35.00	5:41.28
5133	Stuart Ohrland			6.09.75	2	Braintree		25 Sep
	12.1w	6.27	9.80	2.07	56.7	16.3	27.04	1.70	32.22	5:04.3
5128	Edward Cox			30.12.76	4	Oxford		26 Jun
	11.7	6.36	9.99	1.76	53.1	18.8	30.94	2.10	40.42	5:05.0
5077	George Baker			14.08.76	5	Oxford		26 Jun
	11.8	5.91	15.46	1.55	58.5	17.7	35.86	2.40	44.86	5:47.4
	(30)								
5027	Matt Lethbridge			22.01.77	1	Crawley		18 Sep
	11.8	6.26	9.15	1.70	54.0	15.9	24.36	2.10	33.90	5:03.1

Over Age

5522	Mark Pendlebury		U23	3.10.74	1	Blackpool		26 Jun
	12.4	5.95	11.68	1.83	54.7	17.7	40.00	2.65	45.10	4:55.9
5495	Julian Clare		U23	13.09.74	2	Blackpool		26 Jun
	12.0	6.12	11.52	1.74	5.63	17.2	35.04	3.70	43.62	5:28.3
5266	Darren Watts		U23	15.11.74	1	Millfield		8 May
	12.0	5.70	10.96	1.93	53.8	16.9	33.34	NHC	43.58	4:56.8

OCTATHLON - Under 17

5311	Dean Macey				12.12.77	1	Birmingham	18	Sep
	14.79w	6.45	49.56	53.58	1.95	38.58	12.87 4:49.84	(a)	
5208	Fyn Corcoran				17.03.78	2	Birmingham	18	Sep
	14.27w	6.18	46.90	52.94	1.74	38.82	12.63 4:33.40	(a)	
5051	Scott Walker				9.09.77	3	Birmingham	18	Sep
	14.37w	6.73	39.02	51.41	1.83	31.56	11.66 4:48.24	(a)	
5026	Ben Walker				8.06.78	4	Birmingham	18	Sep
	15.54	5.74	47.62	54.15	1.77	44.08	13.23 4:46.07	(a)	
4867	Alan Rudkin				5.11.78	5	Birmingham	18	Sep
	15.22w	5.81	46.88	56.86	1.68	46.60	13.66 5:02.10	(a)	
4858	Marcellas Peters				20.11.78	6	Birmingham	18	Sep
	14.47w	7.08	29.82	51.67	1.80	34.44	9.38 4:50.76	(a)	
4696	James Hodson				28.09.78	7	Birmingham	18	Sep
	16.00w	5.47	41.78	52.65	1.74	35.52	11.49 4:30.51	(a)	
4640	Adam Pengilly				14.10.77	8	Birmingham	18	Sep
	14.38w	6.13	41.78	55.68	1.68	33.18	11.21 4:50.96	(a)	
4576	Scott Exley				9.02.78	9	Birmingham	18	Sep
	14.16w	6.02	33.46	53.50	1.80	30.60	10.34 4:55.66	(a)	
4545	Trevor McGlynn				6.06.78	1	Stoke	7	Aug
	13.7	6.04	33.12	54.38	1.86	29.44	10.49 5:05.46	(a)	
(10)									
4526	Peter Carr				10.09.77	10	Birmingham	18	Sep
	14.45w	6.08	36.48	55.48	1.65	30.24	10.92 4:38.99	(a)	
4521	Jamie Sheffield				26.06.78	1	Wrexham	28	Aug
	13.52w	6.49	33.90	54.10	23.38	1.72	10.10 4:54.22	(d)	
4517	Nick Dowsett				24.11.78	1	Braintree	25	Sep
	14.0	35.08	6.48	55.8	1.71	10.20	35.64 5:12.4	(c)	
4495	Sam Oteng				12.04.78	12	Birmingham	18	Sep
	15.53	5.75	45.88	55.57	1.65	37.44	12.13 5:12.23	(a)	
4485	Gurmukh Sahans				8.10.78	2	London (He)	21	Aug
	15.16	41.70	6.01	55.68	1.67	10.68	34.42 4:55.88	(c)	
4484	Gerry Murray				13.02.78	1	Linwood	17	Jul
	12.14	5.13	1.65	52.43	14.81	28.00	39.84 4:42.17	(b)	
4469	Sam Allen				26.10.78	13	Birmingham	18	Sep
	14.77w	6.08	35.92	53.30	1.68	31.04	10.80 5:01.69	(a)	
4445	Paul Carroll				25.01.78	3	Blackpool	26	Jun
	15.6	5.25	37.34	55.6	1.74	34.94	14.02 4:58.7	(a)	
4419	Kevin Davies				11.01.78	4	Exeter	26	Jun
	15.4	5.22	29.06	54.5	1.62	37.50	12.63 4:32.1	(a)	
4407	Alex Gibson				3.11.77	2	Braintree	25	Sep
	16.5	48.60	6.00w	57.6	1.62	12.54	37.36 5:08.7	(c)	
(20)									
4402	David Cuthill				18.01.78	2	Linwood	17	Jul
	12.00	5.95	1.71	54.28	16.34	27.00	36.22 4:44.46	(b)	
4385	Leo Barker				26.12.78	4	London (He)	21	Aug
	15.52	42.20	6.17	59.81	1.76	11.16	33.24 5:01.42	(c)	
4356	Erik Toemen				1.07.78	1	Oxford	26	Jun
	15.5	56.0	40.62	55.5	1.84	26.82	9.57 4:38.1	(a)	
4337	Jason Plumb				9.11.77	14	Birmingham	18	Sep
	15.21w	5.65	40.86	54.12	1.59	32.10	9.97 4:49.93	(a)	
4301	Andrew Young				15.02.78	17	Birmingham	18	Sep
	14.46w	5.99	30.88	56.53	1.65	34.10	11.21 5:09.15	(a)	
4248	Aleks Stanojevic				18.01.78	3	Oxford	26	Jun
	16.3	6.20	40.98	55.3	1.72	26.36	8.70 4:39.5	(a)	
4234	Ben Motherwell				28.02.78	18	Birmingham	18	Sep
	14.74	5.71	37.06	56.08	1.59	26.14	9.72 4:33.88	(a)	
4227	Alex Gore				25.03.78	4	Basildon	26	Jun
	17.1	52.9	37.04	52.1	15.5	39.02	11.78 5:02.3	(a)	

4225	Paul Jones				11.04.78	2	Wrexham	28 Aug
	14.06w	6.27	43.78	58.10	26.12	16.6	10.86 5:36.06	(d)
4224	Sion Owen				6.03.79	20	Birmingham	18 Sep
	15.52w	5.30	32.90	52.95	1.71	22.30	9.88 4:25.06	(a)
(30)								
4207	Daniel Spooner				5.01.78	21	Birmingham	18 Sep
	15.67	6.08	34.50	55.85	1.80	25.58	9.74 4:56.79	(a)

Order of Events
a)   100mH, LJ, JT, 400m, HJ, DT, SP, 1500m
b)   100m, LJ, HJ, 400m, 100mH, DT, JT, 1500m
c)   100mH, JT, LJ, 400m, HJ, SP, DT, 1500m
a)   100mH, LJ, JT, 400m, DT, HJ, SP, 1500m

PENTATHLON - BOYS

3187	Marc Newton			15.03.80	1	Wrexham	27 Aug
	12.56w	1.81	6.36w	12.50	2:09.98	(b)	
3163	Kevin Drury			30.09.79	2	Wrexham	27 Aug
	11.40w	1.87	5.90w	12.46	2:16.30	(b)	
3024	Tom Benn			20.04.80	2	Birmingham	17 Sep
	11.09w	12.20	6.16	1.62	2:16.89	(a)	
2880	Peter Stephen			10.09.79	1	Linwood	17 Jul
	1.74	12.24	14.12	5.35w	2:21.18	(c)	
2758	Andrew Squire			30.09.79	3	Birmingham	17 Sep
	12.58w	12.37	6.16	1.47	2:16.87	(a)	
2739	Nicholas Hooper			24.09.79	4	Birmingham	17 Sep
	11.83w	10.34	5.85	1.50	2:12.29	(a)	
2680 w	Matthew Dobson			20.01.80	5	Birmingham	17 Sep
	12.89W	10.10	5.94	1.71	2:20.18	(a)	
2662	Sam Hartley			27.11.79	3	Wrexham	27 Aug
	11.84w	1.54	5.32w	10.79	2:13.84	(b)	
2655	James Leech			16.10.79	6	Birmingham	17 Sep
	11.74w	10.24	5.84	1.68	2:28.51	(a)	
2649	Ben Graham			22.01.80	7	Birmingham	17 Sep
	12.23	9.73	5.64	1.65	2:16.96	(a)	
(10)							
2623	Darren Wright			7.09.79	5	Wrexham	27 Aug
	12.48w	1.72	5.80w	10.48	2:27.88	(b)	
2619	Jason McDade			3.04.80	8	Birmingham	17 Sep
	12.35w	10.65	5.90	1.77	2:35.68	(a)	
2591	Tony Blann			10.09.79	9	Birmingham	17 Sep
	12.26w	11.69	5.56	1.53	2:22.40	(a)	
2568	Ryan Motley			27.10.79	10	Birmingham	17 Sep
	12.52w	11.86	5.51	1.53	2:21.92	(a)	
2567	Chris Low			24.04.80	2	Linwood	17 Jul
	1.68	12.04	10.34	5.25	2:23.82	(c)	
2550	Gary Hall			25.07.80	11	Birmingham	17 Sep
	12.79w	9.28	5.56	1.74	2:22.89	(a)	
2519	Michael Sleet			6.06.80	12	Birmingham	17 Sep
	12.56w	10.97	5.31	1.65	2:25.25	(a)	
2513	Tom Payn			18.10.79	2	Basildon	26 Jun
	13.5	8.45	5.47	1.56	2:05.1	(a)	
2511	Matthew Crompton			2.09.79	13	Birmingham	17 Sep
	13.57	10.37	5.17	1.59	2:11.01	(a)	
2510	Edward Morris			3.03.80	14	Birmingham	17 Sep
	12.00	10.48	4.98	1.53	2:16.67	(a)	
(20)							
2480	Anthony Murray			12.10.79	3	Linwood	17 Jul
	1.53	13.17	9.75	4.94	2:07.45	(c)	

2468	Richard Brown				22.12.79	2	London (WL)	25 Jun
	12.5	10.08	5.00	1.59	2:15.9 (a)			
2466	Tony Rigby				22.02.80	4	Basildon	26 Jun
	12.5	11.24	5.37	1.53	2:23.0 (a)			
2444	Edward Coats				14.06.80	15	Birmingham	17 Sep
	12.85w	9.61	5.56	1.50	2:17.87 (a)			
2432	Daniel Dyer				17.12.79	3	London (He)	24 Jul
2429	Chris Roberts				7.02.80	1	Cardiff	17 Sep
	1.57	13.1	5.53	10.60	2:23.0 (d)			

Order of Events
a)   80mH, SP, LJ, HJ, 800m   b)   80mH, HJ, LJ, SP, 800m
c)   HJ, 100m, SP, LJ, 800m   d)   HJ, 100m, LJ, SP, 800m

Non Standard Events - 80mH, SP, 200m, LJ, 1500m

2792	Peter Stephen				10.09.79	3	Grangemouth	11 Jun
	12.3	11.77	24.7	5.18	5:06.5 (sc)			
2814	Anthony Murray				12.10.79	1	Grangemouth	11 Jun
	12.8	9.84	24.7	4.94	4:28.0 (sc)			
2804	Chris Low				24.04.80	2	Grangemouth	11 Jun
	12.0	10.60	24.8	5.45	5:05.7 (sc)			
2696	Paul Armstrong				20.10.79	4	Grangemouth	11 Jun
	12.1	8.27	24.9	4.75	4:34.6 (sc)			
2804	Chris Low				24.04.80	2	Grangemouth	11 Jun
	12.0	10.60	24.8	5.45	5:05.7 (sc)			
2814	Anthony Murray				12.10.79	1	Grangemouth	11 Jun
	12.8	9.84	24.7	4.94	4:28.0 (sc)			

2000 Metres Walk - Track - Under 13

10:57.0	Nathan Adams		14.04.82	1	Bolton	7 May
10:58.6	Alan Hogg		3.06.83	1	Brierley Hill	9 Oct
11:08.0	Graham Murney		20.09.81	4	Leicester	18 May
11:10.5 o	Paul Steer		14.01.82	2	Brierley Hill	9 Oct
11:54.0				6	Leamington	6 Aug
11:11.0	Daniel King		30.05.83	3	Bolton	7 May
11:13.4	Liam Grange		18.08.83	3	Brierley Hill	9 Oct
11:16.2 o	Philip Hollin		14.11.81	4	Brierley Hill	9 Oct
11:48.0				5	Leamington	6 Aug
11:49.0	Dominic King		30.05.83	4	Bolton	7 May
11:52.0	Ashleigh Fern		8.04.82	5	Bolton	7 May
11:52.6	Andrew Ball		13.05.83	5	Brierley Hill	9 Oct
(10)						
11:53.0	Paul Miles			6	Leicester	22 Nov
11:53.0	Simeon Adamsn		1.07.84	7	Leicester	22 Nov

3000 Metres Walk - Track

11:52.2	Steve Partington		17.09.65	1	Douglas, IOM	5 Aug
12:03.33	Philip King	U23	25.11.74	1	Bracknell	2 May
12:04.78	Mark Easton		24.05.63	2	Bracknell	2 May
12:23.50	Martin Bell		9.04.61	1	Corby	30 May
12:27.3	Steve Brennan		4.11.65	2	Douglas, IOM	5 Aug
12:28.5	Steve Taylor		19.03.66	1	Douglas, IOM	15 Dec
12:32.4	Jimmy Ball		17.02.63	1	Portsmouth	14 May
12:42.3	Karl Atton		14.09.71	1	Loughborough	15 May
12:52.8	Andy O'Rawe		8.09.63	1	Canvey Island	7 Jun
12:53.7	Jamie O'Rawe	U23	3.02.73	1	Canvey Island	20 Aug
(10)						
12:55.02	Bob Care	V45	8.04.47	1	Bedford	16 Jul
12:59.63	Gary Witton	U23	25.08.73	2	Corby	30 May
13:01.88	Scott Davis	U20	3.04.75	3	Corby	30 May

13:03.01	Derek Cross	V45	30.04.49	2	Bedford	16 Jul
13:10.2	James Chamberlain	U20	31.07.75	2	Loughborough	15 May
13:10.6	Graham White		28.03.59	1	London (WL)	20 Jul
13:10.73	Brian Adams	V45	13.03.49	1	Sheffield	21 Sep
13:14.13	Noel Carmody		24.12.56	3	London (CP)	26 Jun
13:14.3	Chris Smith		23.12.58	4	Corby	30 May
13:15.2	David Keown	U23	18.07.74	3	Douglas, IOM	5 Aug
13:21.1 [(20)]	Stuart Phillips		15.04.63	2	London (Nh)	15 May
13:23.7	Karl Orchard		6.01.70	5	Loughborough	15 May
13:24.2	Allan Callow	V45	4.09.45	2	Douglas, IOM	15 Dec
13:25.07	Dave Turner		20.10.57	1	Sheffield	15 May
13:30.4	Allan King		3.12.56	6	Loughborough	15 May
13:31.0	Darren Thorn		17.07.62	1	Coventry	5 Jul
13:36.0	John Hall	V45	18.01.49	1	London (BP)	5 Sep
13:45.44	Les Morton		1.07.58	2	Sheffield	21 Sep

Additional Juniors

14:15.1 o	Matthew Hales	U15	6.10.79	1	Brierley Hill	9 Oct
14:15.3				1	Horsham	14 May
14:31.2	Stuart Monk	U17	23.03.79	1	Woodford	13 Jul
14:31.2	John Murphy	U15	6.03.81	2	Brierley Hill	9 Oct
14:44.0	Thomas Taylor	U15	30.01.81	2	Bolton	7 May
15:15.0	Michael Kemp	U15	23.12.79	3	Leicester	25 May
15:28.4	David Crane	U17	18.12.77	7	Woodford	14 Sep
15:28.7	Scott Taylor	U17	28.07.78	9	Loughborough	15 May
15:40.0	Stephen Crane	U15	24.02.80	4	Bolton	7 May
15:52.0	Robert Warren	U15	17.07.81	2	Brighton	10 May
16:26.0	Paul Spilane	U15	27.09.79	7	Bolton	7 May
16:26.97	Anthony Round	U15	11.01.80	6	Birmingham	17 Sep

3000 Metres Walk - Road - Juniors

13:44 o	Matthew Hales	U15	6.10.79	1	Calne	3 Dec
13:59	Stuart Monk	U17	23.03.79	2	Dublin, IRE	24 Sep
14:35	Robert Mecham	U17	14.09.77	1	Steyning	4 Apr
15:21	Scott Taylor	U17	28.07.78	5	Dublin, IRE	24 Sep
15:34	Robert Warren	U15	17.07.81	2	Steyning	5 Nov
15:39	Stephen Crane	U15	24.02.80	4	Holmewood	30 Apr
15:52	Alan Hogg	U13	3.06.83	2	Calne	3 Dec

5000 Metres Walk - Track - Juniors

20:49.27	Philip King	U23	25.11.74	2	Kings Lynn	9 Jul
22:18.33	Kieron Butler	U23	16.07.72	4	Kings Lynn	9 Jul
22:51.1	Martin Young	U23	11.07.72	3	Leamington	6 Aug
23:46.2	Stuart Monk	U17	23.03.79	2	Brierley Hill	9 Oct
26:08.0	David Crane	U17	18.12.77	1	Bolton	7 May
26:19.36	Steve Hollier	U20	27.02.76	1	Birmingham	17 Sep
26:20.0	Michael Kemp	U15	23.12.79	1	Leicester	16 Aug

Road

23:06	Stuart Monk	U17	23.03.79	1	Bexley	10 Dec
23:49	James Chamberlain	U20	31.07.75	1	Dublin, IRE	26 Mar
24:55	Matthew Hales	U15	6.10.79	2	Bexley	10 Dec
25:04	John Murphy	U15	6.03.81	1	Birmingham	19 Nov
25:16	Guy Bailey	U20	16.09.76	5	Coventry	29 Jan
25:45	Michael Kemp	U15	23.12.79	2	Birmingham	19 Nov

10000 Metres Walk - Track

42:23.0	Steve Partington		17.09.65	1	Douglas, IOM	13	Apr
42:32.3	Martin Bell		9.04.61	1	Corby	29	May
42:57.0	Mark Easton		24.05.63	1	Brighton	29	Jan
43:09.28	Darrell Stone		2.02.68	1	Horsham	19	Jun
43:19.3				1	Brighton	21	Jul
43:41.5	Philip King	U23	25.11.74	1	Bolton	7	May
44:18.3	Chris Cheeseman		11.12.58	1	London (BP)	4	May
45:28.2	Steve Taylor		19.03.66	2	Bolton	7	May
45:35.8	Karl Atton		14.09.71	3	Bolton	7	May
45:50.3	Kieron Butler	U23	16.07.72	2	Corby	29	May
46:29.31	Andy O'Rawe		8.09.63	4	Horsham	19	Jun
(10)							
46:33.6	Derek Cross	V45	30.04.49	2	London (BP)	4	May
46:34.0	Allan King		3.12.56	1	Leicester	25	Oct
46:41.0	Brian Adams	V45	13.03.49	1	Sheffield	14	Sep
47:07.1	Scott Davis	U20	3.04.75	4	Bolton	7	May
47:22.0	Bob Care	V45	8.04.47	1	Solihull	14	Aug
47:42.90	James Chamberlain	U20	31.07.75	7	Warsaw, POL	18	Jun
47:47.0	Chris Smith		23.12.58	3	Leicester	25	Oct
47:51.21	Tim Watt		19.09.66	5	Horsham	19	Jun
48:02.5	Allan Callow	V45	4.09.45	6	Bolton	7	May
48:10.1	Gary Witton	U23	25.08.73	2	Brighton	21	Jul
(20)							
48:11.6	Dave Turner		20.10.57	7	Bolton	7	May
48:21.0	Noel Carmody		24.12.56	1	Hoo	17	Sep
48:40.9	Karl Orchard		6.01.70	1	Solihull	29	May
48:48.3	Colin Bradley		2.02.56	1	Newport	28	May
48:52.1	John Hall	V45	18.01.49	5	Corby	29	May
52:45.4	Guy Bailey	U20	16.09.76	11	Bolton	7	May

10000 Metres Walk - Road - Juniors

44:50	Scott Davis	U20	3.04.75	22	Livorno, ITA	12	Jun
46:17	James Chamberlain	U20	31.07.75	27	Livorno, ITA	12	Jun
47:38	Steve Hollier	U20	27.02.76	4	Solihull	29	Oct
50:20	Stuart Monk	U17	23.03.79	3	Chigwell Row	17	Dec
52:44	Guy Bailey	U20	16.09.76	4	Holmewood	30	Apr
52:46	Robert Mecham	U17	14.09.77	5	Steyning	5	Nov

20 Kilometres Walk

1:26:11	Martin Bell		9.04.61	1	Douglas, IOM	25	Jun
1:27:18				22	Livorno, ITA	12	Jun
1:26:53	Darrell Stone		2.02.68	20	Livorno, ITA	12	Jun
1:27:02 +				4m	Victoria, CAN	25	Aug
1:27:24				1	Stoneleigh	19	Mar
1:28:04 +	Steve Partington		17.09.65	5m	Victoria, CAN	25	Aug
1:29:11				2	Birmingham	21	May
1:29:48				31	Livorno, ITA	12	Jun
1:28:06	Mark Easton		24.05.63	1	Colchester	29	May
1:28:44	Chris Maddocks		28.03.57	1	Burrator	1	May
1:29:11	Chris Cheeseman		11.12.58	1	Birmingham	21	May
1:29:58				5	Douglas, IOM	25	Jun
1:29:49	Philip King	U23	25.11.74	3	Birmingham	21	May
1:32:34 +	Steve Taylor		19.03.66	8m	Victoria, CAN	25	Aug
1:34:11	Graham White		28.03.59	4	Birmingham	21	May
1:34:28	Karl Atton		14.09.71	5	Birmingham	21	May
(10)							

Time	Name	Cat	DOB	Pos	Venue	Date
1:35:24	Andy O'Rawe		8.09.63	2	Colchester	29 May
1:35:40	Gareth Holloway		2.02.70	11	Douglas, IOM	25 Jun
1:35:49	Allan Callow	V45	4.09.45	2	Douglas, IOM	26 May
1:36:12	Noel Carmody		24.12.56	6	Birmingham	21 May
1:36:39	Steve Brennan		4.11.65	12	Douglas, IOM	25 Jun
1:36:59	Tim Watt		19.09.66	7	Birmingham	21 May
1:37:10	Scott Davis	U20	3.04.75	8	Birmingham	21 May
1:37:32	Allan King		3.12.56	1	Leicester	22 Oct
1:39:49	David Keown	U23	18.07.74	3	Douglas, IOM	26 May

Short course

Time	Name	Cat	DOB	Pos	Venue	Date
1:24:09	Steve Partington		17.09.65	1	Dublin, IRE	24 Sep

30 Kilometres Walk

Time	Name	Cat	DOB	Pos	Venue	Date
2:11:30	Darrell Stone		2.02.68	4	Victoria, CAN	25 Aug
2:14:15	Steve Partington		17.09.65	7	Victoria, CAN	25 Aug
2:17:46				2	Douglas, IOM	26 Feb
2:14:16	Mark Easton		24.05.63	1	Douglas, IOM	26 Feb
2:16:21				1	Cardiff	8 May
2:20:10				13	Victoria, CAN	25 Aug
2:18:14	Chris Maddocks		28.03.57	12	Victoria, CAN	25 Aug
2:21:34	Steve Taylor		19.03.66	14	Victoria, CAN	25 Aug
2:22:21	Martin Bell		9.04.61	2	Cardiff	8 May
2:23:52	Graham White		28.03.59	4	Cardiff	8 May
2:27:11	Chris Cheeseman		11.12.58	3	Horsham	16 Apr
2:30:57	Kevin Walmsley		6.09.67	3	Douglas, IOM	26 Feb
2:33:08	Karl Atton		14.09.71	4	Horsham	16 Apr
2:33:08 (10)	Philip King	U23	25.11.74	5	Horsham	16 Apr

35 Kilometres Walk

Time	Name	Cat	DOB	Pos	Venue	Date
2:48:50	Graham White		28.03.59	30	Livorno, ITA	12 Jun
2:50:01	Les Morton		1.07.58	32	Livorno, ITA	12 Jun
2:55:38	Karl Atton		14.09.71	39	Livorno, ITA	12 Jun

50 Kilometres Walk

Time	Name	Cat	DOB	Pos	Venue	Date
4:32:25	Les Morton		1.07.58	1	Holmewood	3 Sep
4:36:35	Tim Watt		19.09.66	2	Holmewood	3 Sep
4:40:41	Chris Berwick	V45	1.05.46	3	Holmewood	3 Sep
4:46:15	Graham White		28.03.59	4	Holmewood	3 Sep
4:47:12	Dave Turner		20.10.57	1	Bradford	30 May
4:48:32	Steve Brennan		4.11.65	5	Holmewood	3 Sep
4:51:44	Ed Shillabeer	V50	2.08.39	20	Podebrady, TCH	23 Apr
4:52:35	Bob Dobson	V50	4.11.42	18	Seran, FRA	25 Sep
4:59:07	Colin Bradley		2.02.56	1	Basildon	13 Aug

100 Miles Walk

Time	Name	Cat	DOB	Pos	Venue	Date
18:39:42	Richard Brown	V45	18.11.46	1	Hungarton	30 Jul
20:31:54	Brian Ashwell	V60	18.07.32	2	Hungarton	30 Jul
20:56:19	Tony Collins	V50	1.10.42	3	Hungarton	30 Jul

4 x 100 METRES

38.46	National Team (D Braithwaite, T Jarrett, J Regis, L Christie)	1	London (CP)	10	Sep
38.64	National Team (J John, D Braithwaite, J Regis, L Christie)	1	London (CP)	15	Jul
38.72	National Team (J John, S Wariso, J Regis, L Christie)	1	Birmingham	25	Jun
38.91	National Team (J John, D Braithwiate, J Regis, T Jarrett)	1	Gateshead	20	Jul
39.23	National Under 23 Team (T Rutherford, T Box, D Walker, D Campbell)	1	Ostrava, TCH	30	Jul
39.39	England (J John, T Box, P Goedluck, T Williams)	3	Victoria, CAN	28	Aug
39.51	England (M Smith, T Box, P Goedluck, T Williams)	2h2	Victoria, CAN	27	Aug
39.55	National Under 23 Team (T Rutherford, T Box, D Walker, D Campbell)	3	Gateshead	20	Jul
39.56	Scotland (E Bunney, I Mackie, J Henderson, D Walker)	5	Victoria, CAN	28	Aug
39.60	National Junior Team U20 (J Gardener, J Golding, I Mackie, T Cameron)	1	Lisbon, POR	24	Jul
39.67	Scottish Selection (E Bunney, D Clark, J Henderson, D Walker)	1	Dublin, IRE	18	Jun
39.77	Haringey AC (S Adepegba, A Mensah, D Braithwaite, S Wariso)	2	Malaga, SPA	28	May
39.92	National Junior Team U20 (J Gardener, J Golding, I Mackie, T Cameron)	1h3	Lisbon, POR	23	Jul
40.03	Scotland (E Bunney, D Clark, J Henderson, D Walker)	1	Istanbul, TUR	21	May
40.11	National Junior Team U20 (J Gardener, J Golding, I Mackie, T Cameron)	3	London (CP)	15	Jul
40.14	National 'B' Team (J Fergus, S Wariso, P Goedluck, D Joyce)	4	London (CP)	15	Jul
40.16	Scotland (D Mathieson, I Mackie, J Henderson, D Walker)	4h2	Victoria, CAN	27	Aug
40.34	Haringey AC (A Mensah, T Jarrett, C Callender, S Wariso)	1	London (WL)	2	Jul
40.38	National Junior Team U20 (J Gardener, T Cameron, M Devonish, I Mackie)	2	Warsaw, POL	18	Jun
40.38	England (T Williams, D Joyce, D Campbell, J John)	1	Nitra, SVK	13	Jul
40.50	Belgrave Harriers (L Paul, H Korjie(SLE), J Regis, N Owen)	2	London (WL)	2	Jul

Additional National Teams

40.52	Wales (K Williams, P Maitland, T Rutherford, P Gray)	1	Colwyn Bay	23	Jul
42.34	Northern Ireland (J McAdorey, J Anderson, Gallagher, M Allen)	4	Kings Lynn	9	Jul

Additonal Club Teams (1 - 2 above)

40.79	Edinburgh Southern	1	London (CP)	7	May
40.8	Cardiff	2	Enfield	31	Jul
41.0	North London/SLE	1	Hayes	30	Jul
41.0	Newham & Essex Beagles	2	Kingston	31	Jul
41.07	Sale	3	London (WL)	2	Jul

41.15	Thames Valley		4	London (WL)	2	Jul
41.4	Bedford & County		3	Kingston	31	Jul
41.6	Blackheath		3	Enfield	31	Jul
41.7	Team Solent		1	Corby	31	Jul
41.78	Windsor Slough & Eton		3	Bedford	17	Sep
41.79	Shaftesbury Barnet		4	Bedford	17	Sep
41.8	Loughborough Students		1=	Loughborough	22	Jun
41.90	West London Institute		1	London (CP)	2	May
42.0	Woodford Green		2	Stoke-on-Trent	31	Jul
42.03	Birchfield		5	Bedford	17	Sep
42.12	Ballymena & Antrim		1	Antrim	13	Aug
42.14	Salford University		2	London (CP)	2	May
42.15	Shaftesbury Barnet	U20	1	Chatillon, FRA	24	Sep
42.27	Old Gaytonians		2	London (CP)	7	May

Additional Under 20 Teams (1 - 5 above)

40.99	National Junior Team		2	Loughborough	5	Jun
41.29	National Junior 'B' Team		3	Loughborough	5	Jun
41.52	West Midland Schools		1	Telford	9	Jul
41.89	Scotland Schools		3	Nicosia, CYP	20	May
41.90	South of England		1	London (He)	27	Aug
42.14	North		3	Colwyn Bay	23	Jul

Additional Under 20 Club Teams (1 above)

42.3	Blackheath		1	Middlesbrough	28	Aug
43.6	Ballyclare HS		2	Antrim	28	May
43.8	Blackheath	U17	1	Dartford	4	Sep
43.83	Sale	U17	1	Birmingham	11	Sep
43.9	Gateshead		1	Jarrow	12	Jun
44.0	Telford		2	Stretford	12	Jun
44.2	Campbell College		3	Antrim	28	May
44.2	Belgrave	U17	2	Peterborough	17	Jul
44.3	Birchfield		2	Middlesbrough	28	Aug

Additional Under 17 Teams

41.91	Scotland Schools		1	Aberdeen	16	Jul
42.37	England Schools		2	Aberdeen	16	Jul
42.58	Essex Schools		1	Telford	9	Jul
42.60	Bedfordshire Schools		2	Telford	9	Jul

Additional Under 17 Club Teams (1 - 3 above)

44.97	Shettleston		1	Edinburgh	25	Jun
45.17	Gateshead		2	Birmingham	11	Sep
45.2	Edinburgh Southern		1h1	Edinburgh	21	Aug
45.3	Birchfield		1	Cwmbran	17	Jul
45.3	Cannock & Stafford		1	Cwmbran	17	Jul
45.3	Ayr Seaforth		1	Edinburgh	21	Aug
45.3	Bedford & County		1	Ipswich	4	Sep

Under 15 Teams

45.13	Wiltshire Schools		1h4	Telford	9	Jul
45.34	Wales		1	Dublin, IRE	13	Aug
45.49	Essex Schools		1	Telford	9	Jul
45.51	Blackheath		1	Birmingham	11	Sep
45.67	London Schools		2h4	Telford	9	Jul
45.73	Lancashire Schools		3h4	Telford	9	Jul
45.74	Humberside Schools		2	Telford	9	Jul
45.83	Hampshire Schools		4	Telford	9	Jul

Additional Under 15 Club Teams (1 above)

46.2	Wakefield	1	Sheffield (W)	26	Jun
46.8	Basildon	1	Barking	12	Jul
46.83	Sale	2	Birmingham	11	Sep
47.11	Gateshead	3	Birmingham	11	Sep
47.19	Liverpool Harriers	4	Birmingham	11	Sep
47.2	Old Gaytonians	1	Hoo	26	Jun
47.5	Hutchesons' GS	1	Grangemouth	11	Jun
47.5	Borough of Hounslow	2	Hoo	26	Jun
47.75	Cannock & Stafford	5	Birmingham	11	Sep

Under 13 Teams

51.5	Braintree & District	1	Ipswich	4	Sep
51.7	Blackheath	1	Hoo	2	Jul
51.9	Mandale	1	Middlesbrough	17	Jul
52.43	Borough of Enfield	2	Birmingham	11	Sep
52.7	Annadale Striders	1	Antrim	25	Jun
52.9 X	Belfast RA	sf	Antrim	28	May
53.0 X	Omagh Academy	1	Antrim	28	May
53.3 X	Belfast GS	1	Belfast	17	May
53.42	Liverpool Harriers	3	Birmingham	11	Sep
53.52	Gateshead	4	Birmingham	11	Sep

4 x 200 METRES

1:24.13 i	National Team	1	Glasgow	12	Feb
	(T Jarrett, D Campbell, S Wariso, P Goedluck)				
1:25.69 i	England	1	Vienna, AUT	6	Feb
	(P Goedluck, S Wariso, D Braithwaite, J John)				
1:27.2 i	AA of Wales	1	Birmingham	26	Feb
1:27.4 i	Midland Counties AA	2	Birmingham	26	Feb
	(D Powell, A Walcott, M Devonshire, M Walcott)				
1:27.6 i	South of England	3	Birmingham	26	Feb
1:28.3 i	North of England	4	Birmingham	26	Feb
1:29.7 i	Scotland	5	Birmingham	26	Feb
1:30.3	Hercules Wimbledon	1	Sutton	13	Jul
1:30.5	Thames Valley	1	Perivale	27	Aug
1:30.9	Queens Park	2	Perivale	27	Aug

Additional Club Teams (1 - 3 above)

1:31.4	Oxford University		1	Oxford	27	Feb
1:31.6	Croydon		2	London (TB)	16	Jun
1:31.6	Kingston & Poly		1	Kingston	27	Jul
1:32.5	Belgrave			London (TB)	27	Jul
1:32.6	Aberdeen		1	Aberdeen	24	Jul
1:32.7	Herne Hill		3	London (TB)	16	Jun
1:33.7	Oundle School	U20	1	Oxford	7	May

Additional Under 20 Teams (1 above)

1:33.78 X	Lagan Valley	U17	1	Antrim	20	Aug
1:34.6	Belgrave		1	Carshalton	11	Sep
1:34.8	King's School Canterbury		2	Oxford	7	May
1:35.0	Belgrave	U17	1	London (TB)	22	Jun
1:36.0	Wimbledon College	U17	2	London (TB)	22	Jun
1:36.2	Shettleston	U17	1	Wishaw	29	Jun
1:36.8	Kent College, Canterbury		3h2	Oxford	7	May
1:36.8	Bedford & County	U17	1	Corby	8	May
1:37.5	Abingdon School		1h1	Oxford	7	May
1:37.70 X	North Down	U17	2	Antrim	20	Aug

Under 17 Teams

1:31.80 i	England Schools		1	Birmingham	27 Feb
1:32.89 i	Scottish Schools		2	Birmingham	27 Feb
1:34.6 i	Nottinghamshire Schools		1	Birmingham	8 Feb
1:35.70 i	Wales Schools		3	Birmingham	27 Feb

Additional Under 17 Club Teams (1 - 6 above)

1:37.9	Ealing Southall & Middlesex		1	Perivale	27 Aug
1:38.0	Epsom College		1	Oxford	7 May
1:38.0 X	Ballymena & Antrim		1	Belfast	28 Jul
1:38.1	Hercules Wimbledon		1	Carshalton	11 Sep

Under 15 Teams

1:41.7	Brighton & Hove		1	Horsham	10 Jul
1:41.73 X	Annadale Striders		1	Antrim	20 Aug
1:41.8	Sutton & District		1	Carshalton	11 Sep
1:41.8	Herne Hill		2	Carshalton	11 Sep
1:42.3 i	Staffordshire Schools		1	Birmingham	8 Feb
1:42.4 i	West Midland Schools		2	Birmingham	8 Feb
1:43.1	Hercules Wimbledon		3	Carshalton	11 Sep
1:44.07 i	Royal Sutton Coldfield		1	Birmingham	8 Jan
1:44.15 X	Ballymena & Antrim		2	Antrim	20 Aug
1:44.2	Highgate School		1	London (He)	25 Jun
1:44.3	Croydon		1	Croydon	31 Jul
1:44.4	Epsom College		1	London (He)	25 Jun

Under 13 Teams

1:49.7	Braintree & District		1	Colchester	29 Aug
1:50.9	Croydon	U11	1	Walton-on-Thames	19 Sep
1:50.9 X	Annadale Striders		1	Antrim	20 Aug
1:54.9	Guildford & Godalming	U11	2	Walton-on-Thames	19 Sep
1:55.0	Sutton & District	U11	3	Walton-on-Thames	19 Sep
1:56.0	Aldershot F & D		1	Kingston	9 Jul

4 x 400 METRES

2:59.13	National Team		1	Helsinki, FIN	14 Aug
	(D McKenzie, B Whittle, R Black, D Ladejo)				
3:01.34	National Team		1	London (CP)	11 Sep
	(D McKenzie, D Ladejo, J Baulch, R Black)				
3:02.14	England		1	Victoria, CAN	28 Aug
	(D McKenzie, P Crampton, A Patrick, D Ladejo)				
3:02.50	National Team		1	Birmingham	26 Jun
	(D Ladejo, A Patrick, B Whittle, R Black)				
3:03.68	Wales		4h1	Victoria, CAN	27 Aug
	(P Maitland, J Baulch, P Gray, I Thomas)				
3:03.91	National Team		2	Gateshead	20 Jul
	(D McKenzie, B Whittle, I Thomas, D Ladejo)				
3:04.92	National Under 23 Team		3	Gateshead	20 Jul
	(P McBurney, J Baulch, P Slythe, K Ulyatt)				
3:06.59	National Junior Team	U20	3	Lisbon, POR	24 Jul
	(G Bullock, N Budden, N Levy, M Hylton)				
3:06.89	Haringey		1	Malaga, SPA	29 May
	(W McDonald, L Lynch, S Wariso, B Whittle)				
3:07.12	England		3h2	Victoria, CAN	27 Aug
	(M Smith, A Fugallo, A Patrick, D McKenzie)				
3:07.16	National Under 23 Team		3	Ostrava, TCH	31 Jul
	(P McBurney, J Baulch, I Thomas, A Patrick)				
3:07.80	Wales		7	Victoria, CAN	28 Aug
	(P Maitland, J Baulch, P Gray, I Thomas)				

3:10.11	Thames Valley		1	London (WL)	2	Jul
	(G Telfer, K Bentham, E Williams, V Rose)					
3:10.13	England		1	Wrexham	3	Jul
	(M Smith, A Williams, L Lynch, M Morris)					
3:10.25	Wales		2	Wrexham	3	Jul
	(I Thomas, J Baulch, G Davies, J Lloyd)					
3:10.25	Wales		1	Oordegem, BEL	9	Jul
	(G Davies, J Baulch, J Lloyd, I Thomas)					
3:10.6	Team Solent		1	Sheffield (W)	4	Jun
	(R Black, L Fairclough, M Blade, P Sanders)					
3:10.76	National Junior Team	U20	1	Warsaw, POL	18	Jun
	(S Heggie, J Deacon, N Levy, M Hylton)					
3:10.96	National Junior Team	U20	1h1	Lisbon, POR	23	Jul
	(J Deacon, N Budden, N Levy, M Hylton)					
3:11.43	Wales		1	Istanbul, TUR	22	May
	(I Thomas, P Harries, J Weston, D Maynard)					
3:11.98	Cardiff		1	Edinburgh	6	Aug
	(M Ponting, J Weston, P Gray, J Baulch)					

Additional National Teams

3:12.83	Northern Ireland	2	Kings Lynn	9	Jul
	(D Thom, M Gallagher, B McCoy, P McBurney)				
3:15.88	Scotland	2	Istanbul, TUR	22	May

Additional Club Teams (1 - 4 above)

3:12.38	Newham & Essex Beagles	1	Wigan	7	May
3:13.64	Loughborough Students	1	London (CP)	2	May
3:13.9	Belgrave	1	Kingston	31	Jul
3:14.06	West London Institute	2	London (CP)	2	May
3:14.3	Woodford Green	1	Stoke-on-Trent	31	Jul
3:15.0	Shaftesbury Barnet	2	Stoke-on-Trent	31	Jul
3:15.0	Blackheath	3	Enfield	31	Jul
3:15.41	Sale	2	London (He)	5	Jun
3:15.8	Windsor Slough & Eton	2	Corby	31	Jul
3:16.03	Crawley	2	Crawley	6	Aug
3:16.1	Borough of Enfield	4	Enfield	31	Jul
3:16.4	Sheffield	1	Loughborough	26	Jun
3:16.6	Trafford	1	Kirkby	6	Aug
3:16.7	City of Stoke	3	Stoke-on-Trent	31	Jul
3:16.79	Birchfield	2	Bedford	17	Sep
3:16.8	GEC Avionics	1	Dartford	4	Sep

Additional Under 20 Teams (1 - 3 above)

3:17.76	Wales	4	Colwyn Bay	23	Jul
3:19.5	Scotland Schools	1	Barry	19	Jul
3:19.5	Scotland	1	Exeter	20	Aug
3:20.2	Wales	2	Barrry	19	Jul
3:20.42	Midlands	1	London (He)	27	Aug
3:20.64	South of England	2	London (He)	27	Aug
3:21.36	England Schools	4	Nicosia, CYP	20	May

Under 20 Club Teams

3:24.62	Blackheath	5	Warsaw, POL	24	Sep
3:26.3	Braintree	1	Barking	12	Jul
3:27.3	Havering Mayesbrook	2	Barking	12	Jul
3:28.3	Middlesbrough & Cleveland	1	Stretford	12	Jun
3:28.6	Reading	1	Derby	18	Sep
3:28.9	Belgrave	1	Hounslow	24	Jul
3:30.1	Peterborough	2	Derby	18	Sep
3:30.2	Crawley	1	Horsham	10	Jul
3:30.2	Telford	1	Telford	24	Jul

3:30.3	Newport	1	Swansea	17 Apr
3:30.5	Birchfield	1	Harrow	24 Apr
3:30.5	Felsted School	1h1	Oxford	7 May

Under 17 Teams

3:21.68	England Schools	1	Aberdeen	16 Jul
3:23.49	Scotland Schools	2	Aberdeen	16 Jul
3:29.0 X	Ulster Schools	1	Dublin	25 Jun
3:29.82	Wales Schools	3	Aberdeen	16 Jul
3:30.8	Sale	1	Blackpool	17 Jul
3:31.25	Blackheath	1	Birmingham	11 Sep
3:31.9	Braintree	1	Barking	12 Jul
3:31.9	Havering Mayesbrook	2	Barking	12 Jul
3:32.3	Liverpool Pembroke	2	Blackpool	17 Jul
3:32.5	Coventry Godiva	1	Nottingham	26 Jun

Additional Under 17 Club Teams (1 - 6 above)

3:32.9	Lagan Valley	1	Belfast	18 Aug
3:32.91	Old Gaytonians	3	Birmingham	11 Sep
3:33.4	Birchfield	1	Cwmbran	17 Jul
3:33.6	Ayr Seaforth	1	Dumfries	7 Aug

Under 15 Teams

3:40.6	Medway	1	Dartford	4 Sep
3:44.07	Blackheath	1	Birmingham	11 Sep
3:44.98	Liverpool Harriers	2	Birmingham	11 Sep
3:46.80	Gateshead	3	Birmingham	11 Sep
3:47.1	Haringey	1	Woodford	17 Jul
3:49.1	Derby & County	1	Coventry	17 Jul
3:49.2	Telford	1	Cwmbran	17 Jul
3:49.94	Sale	4	Birmingham	11 Sep
3:50.1	Shaftesbury Barnet	1	Croydon	17 Jul
3:50.3	Sutton & District	1	Carshalton	11 Sep

Under 13 Teams

4:11.5	Blackheath	1	Dartford	4 Sep
4:33.0	Pitreavie	1	Pitreavie	3 Jul
4:34.3	Bexley Boro	2h2	Dartford	4 Sep
4:35.6	Arbroath	1	Arbroath	21 Aug
4:35.8	Aberdeen	1	Glasgow	31 Jul

1000 METRES MEDLEY

1:56.12	National Police Team	5	London (He)	18 Aug
	(D Bigham, P Field, S Shanks, D Deacon)			
1:56.77	National Junior Team U18	1	Schio, ITA	6 Aug
	(T Cameron, M Devonish, S McArdy, M Hylton)			
1:57.27	National Junior 'B' Team U18	2	Schio, ITA	6 Aug
	(K Mark, J Archampong, A Hunte, M Douglas)			

1600 METRES MEDLEY

3:27.98 i	South of England	1	Birmingham	26 Feb
3:28.31 i	North of England	2	Birmingham	26 Feb
3:31.04 i	Midland Counties	3	Birmingham	26 Feb
3:34.3	Blackheath	1	Dartford	4 Sep

Under 20 Teams

3:36.9	St Edmunds College	1	London (He)	25 Jun
3:41.1	Forest School	2	London (He)	25 Jun
3:48.8	Highgate School	3	London (He)	25 Jun

Under 17 Teams

3:50.7	Highgate School	U16	1	London (He)	25	Jun
3:52.0	St Ignatius School	U16	2	London (He)	25	Jun
3:52.3	Tayside		1	Dundee	29	May
3:52.5	Bedford School	U16	3	London (He)	25	Jun
3:53.7	Lord Wandsworth College	U16	4	London (He)	25	Jun

Under 15 Teams

3:59.3	Southend High School	1	London (He)	25	Jun
4:01.6	Forest School	2	London (He)	25	Jun
4:01.8	Bedford School	3	London (He)	25	Jun

Under 13 Teams

4:32.1	St Ignatius School	1	London (He)	25	Jun
4:41.6	Highgate School	2	London (He)	25	Jun
4:45.0	Lord Wandsworth College	3	London (He)	25	Jun

4 x 800 METRES

7:37.5	BMC England		1	Oxford	17 Sep
	(N Williams, M Barrow, K Wright, M Gooch)				
7:37.7	BMC Juniors	U20	2	Oxford	17 Sep
	(B Reese, A McDougall, I Bowden, C Blount)				
7:44.7	BMC Wales		3	Oxford	17 Sep
	(S Mosley, M Kinnane, T Cordy, M Jones)				
7:52.1	Gateshead		1	Gateshead	3 Aug
7:56.9	Wallsend		2	Gateshead	3 Aug
8:01.4	Cambridge University		1	Oxford	27 Feb

Additional Under 20 Teams

8:07.0	Cramlington		4	Gateshead	3 Aug
8:19.4	Trinity School		1	Oxford	7 May
8:19.4	Annadale Striders	U17	1	Belfast	16 Jun

Additional Under 17 Teams (1 above)

8:20.1	Gateshead	1	Gateshead	3	Aug
8:24.0	Wirral	1	Warrington	12	Jul
8:26.7	Epsom College	1	Oxford	7	May
8:31.3	Warrington	2	Warrington	12	Jul

Under 15 Teams

8:55.0 X	Annadale Striders	1	Belfast	16	Jun
9:00.3	Wirral	1	Warrington	12	Jul

Under 13 Teams

10:08.6 X	Willowfield	1	Belfast	16	Jun
10:16.5	Wirral	1	Crewe	28	Jun

4 x 1500 METRES

16:56.9	Cambridge University	1	Oxford	27 Feb
17:08.4	Oxford University	2	Oxford	27 Feb

4 x 1 MILE

16:37.1	British Milers Club	1	Oxford	17 Sep
	(N Caddy, T Buckner, S Barden, I Grime)			
17:10.5	BMC Wales	2	Oxford	17 Sep
	(N Comerford, S Mosley, M Davies, S Snow)			
17:42.2	BMC South	3	Oxford	17 Sep
	(A Renfree, D Rankin, M Roberts, J Brooks)			

X as Northern Ireland age groups and therefore possibly including older athletes.

1994 LISTS - WOMEN

50 METRES - Indoors

6.2	Bev Kinch		14.01.64	1	Horsham	17 Feb
6.4				1	Horsham	13 Jan

60 METRES - Indoors

7.34	Katharine Merry	U23	21.09.74	1	Glasgow	23 Jan
7.38				2mx	Birmingham	6 Feb
7.41				1h2	Glasgow	23 Jan
7.35	Bev Kinch		14.01.64	1	Birmingham	19 Feb
7.38				1h1	Birmingham	19 Feb
7.38	Marcia Richardson	U23	10.02.72	3	Glasgow	12 Feb
7.39				2	Birmingham	19 Feb
7.41				3	Glasgow	29 Jan
7.43				1	Birmingham	26 Feb
7.49				1h2	Birmingham	19 Feb
7.51				h	Lievin, FRA	6 Jan
7.40	Stephanie Douglas		22.01.69	1	Birmingham	31 Dec
7.44				1	Birmingham	8 Jan
7.47				1h1	Birmingham	8 Jan
7.50				1h3	Birmingham	31 Dec
7.46	Phylis Smith		29.09.65	2	Birmingham	8 Jan
7.48				1s2	Birmingham	8 Jan
7.51				1h2	Birmingham	8 Jan
7.47	Clova Court		10.02.60	3	Birmingham	19 Feb
7.55				2h2	Birmingham	19 Feb
7.55				2	Birmingham	31 Dec
7.51	Sophia Smith	U23	8.12.74	4	Glasgow	12 Feb
7.51	Diane Allahgreen	U20	21.02.75	1h1	Birmingham	13 Feb
7.53				1	Birmingham	13 Feb
7.52	Danaa Myhill		16.10.70	3	Birmingham	8 Jan
7.55				1h3	Birmingham	8 Jan
7.55				4	Vienna, AUT	6 Feb
7.52	Lorraine Robins		13.05.70	1	Birmingham	6 Feb
	(10)					
7.55	Tatum Nelson	U17	17.12.78	1	Birmingham	26 Feb
7.56	Sam Farquharson		15.12.69	3	Birmingham	31 Dec
7.57	Melanie Neef		26.05.70	2	Glasgow	23 Jan
7.57	Angela Thorp	U23	7.12.72	2	Birmingham	26 Feb
7.60	Donna Hoggarth	U23	14.10.73	2h4	Birmingham	8 Jan
7.60	Rebecca Drummond	U17	18.04.78	1s2	Birmingham	12 Feb
7.61	Jacqui Agyepong		5.01.69	4	Glasgow	29 Jan
7.61	Helen Miles		2.03.67	6	Birmingham	19 Feb
7.62	Laura Seston	U17	9.02.79	2s2	Birmingham	12 Feb
7.64	Sarah Wilhelmy	U15	2.02.80	1	Birmingham	12 Feb
	(20)					
7.64	Sue Earnshaw		13.10.70	4	Birmingham	26 Feb
7.65	Sarah Chesney	U23	3.03.73	7	Birmingham	19 Feb
7.68	Sarah Oxley	U23	3.07.73	2h2	Birmingham	31 Dec
7.69	Malgorzata Rostek	U20	25.03.77	1	Glasgow	6 Feb
7.69	Fiona Hutchison	U20	18.01.77	1	Glasgow	10 Feb
7.69	Wooday Sidibe	U17	14.11.78	2s1	Birmingham	12 Feb
7.69	Joanne Dear	U20	8.06.75	1h3	Birmingham	13 Feb
7.70	Bev Christopher	U20	14.01.75	2	Birmingham	13 Feb
7.70	Donna Fraser	U23	7.11.72	8	Birmingham	19 Feb
7.71	Ann Brooks		4.05.71	2h1	Birmingham	31 Dec
	(30)					
7.72	Tracy Goddard		29.11.69	3h4	Birmingham	8 Jan

29 performances to 7.55 by 11 athletes

7.72	Gillian Hegney	U17	4.11.77	1	Glasgow	12 Feb
7.72	Dawn Rose	U17	25.01.79	1h2	Birmingham	31 Dec
7.73	Ayeesha Charles	U15	4.09.79	2	Birmingham	12 Feb
7.73	Christine Bloomfield		12.02.68	3h1	Birmingham	31 Dec
7.74	Alison Mayfield		12.05.69	4r1	Birmingham	3 Jan
7.74	Claire Haslam		18.12.63	5s2	Birmingham	8 Jan
7.77	Fiona Boswell		10.02.68	2	Glasgow	15 Jan
7.77	Debbie Mant	U20	11.10.75	3	Birmingham	6 Feb
7.77	Janet Levermore		7.06.69	4	Birmingham	6 Feb
	(40)					
7.78	Alanna Cooke		11.01.70	1r3	Birmingham	2 Jan
7.78	Natalie Hynd	U17	30.01.78	2	Glasgow	12 Feb
7.78	Keeley Butler	U20	24.03.75	4h2	Birmingham	19 Feb
7.79	Theresa Crosbie	U20	17.07.75	3	Glasgow	6 Feb
7.80	Sharon Tunaley		2.09.68	7	Birmingham	31 Dec

Additional Under 17 (1 - 7 above)

7.87	Kirsty Payne		22.10.77	1h2	Birmingham	9 Jan
7.88	Sarah Hunter		19.05.78	2h3	Birmingham	12 Feb
7.88	Joanne Colegate		24.11.77	3	Glasgow	12 Feb
	(10)					
7.89	Joanne Beavan		23.06.78	2	Birmingham	3 Jan
7.89	Lesley Owusu		21.12.78	4	Glasgow	12 Feb
7.89	Stacey Rodd		19.05.78	6r2	Birmingham	26 Feb
7.90	Hannah Paines		6.04.79	3	Birmingham	27 Feb
7.92	Jennifer Impett		18.11.77	4h3	Birmingham	12 Feb
7.93	Melanie Roberts		2.03.78	4h1	Birmingham	9 Jan
7.94	Gahlie Davis		3.05.79	4s1	Birmingham	12 Feb
7.94	Gael Davies		5.02.79	1h3	Birmingham	31 Dec
7.98	Alison Stewart		19.01.78	3	Glasgow	6 Feb
7.98	Emma Rowicki		29.11.77	5	Glasgow	12 Feb
	(20)					
7.99	Natalie Howarth		1.04.78	5h3	Birmingham	12 Feb

Additional Under 15 (1 - 2 above)

7.95	Maria Bolsover		5.06.80	3	Birmingham	12 Feb
7.97	Claire Weston		26.07.80	1	Birmingham	6 Feb
7.97	Karlene Palmer		23.10.80	3	Birmingham	12 Feb
7.99	Natalie Smart		23.08.80	5	Birmingham	12 Feb

Hand Timing

7.4	Richardson	U23	(7.38)	1	London (CP)	30 Jan
	7.5			1s1	London (CP)	30 Jan
7.5	Sophia Smith	U23	(7.51)	1h1	Sheffield	19 Jan
	3 performances to 7.5 by 2 athletes					
7.6	Ashia Hansen		5.12.71	1s2	London (CP)	30 Jan
7.7	Christine Bloomfield		(7.73)	1	London (CP)	14 Dec

75 METRES - Under 13

10.1	Leah Tribe		3.09.81	1	Croydon	26 Jun
10.1	Rebecca Bates		16.05.82	1r1	Solihull	17 Jul
10.1	Laverne Slater		26.01.82	1	Bromley	24 Jul
10.1	Stacy Hilling		11.09.81	1	Carn Brea	17 Aug
10.2	Rachel Redmond		7.12.81	1r2	Stoke	5 Jun
10.2	Stefanie Oates		19.11.81	1r1	Ashton-U-Lyne	5 Jun
10.2	Naomi Taplin		18.12.81	1r1	Yeovil	24 Jul
10.3	K. Blackman			1	London (Nh)	15 May
10.3	Faye Pickering		13.06.82	1r1	Kirkby	5 Jun
10.3	Jenny McCarthy		22.02.82	2r1	Ashton-U-Lyne	5 Jun
	(10)					
10.3	Jenny Ward			1r2	Kirkby	5 Jun
10.3	Leanne Foxall		1.10.81	2r2	Solihull	17 Jul
10.37	Vicky Hyland		27.10.81	1r1	Birmingham	11 Sep

80 METRES - Under 13

10.6		Sarah Zawada		9.04.82	1	Guildford	11 Sep
10.7		Stacy Hilling		11.09.81	1r3	Kirkby	24 Jul
10.9		Stefanie Oates		19.11.81	h	Stretford	15 May
10.9		Naomi Taplin		18.12.81	1	Oxford	15 May
10.9		Jenny McCarthy		22.02.82	2r3	Kirkby	24 Jul
11.00	0.5	Fiona Harrison		30.11.81	1	Sheffield	15 May
11.0		Sam St John			1	Crawley	26 Mar
11.0		Cheryl Gibbons		21.09.81	1	Wigan	17 Apr
11.0		Clare Russell		11.11.81	1	Stretford	15 May
11.0		Emma Brown		15.10.81	1r1	Windsor	3 Jul
	(10)						
11.0		Crystal Kagbo		23.06.82	1	Reading	3 Jul
11.0		Melissa Anderson		30.03.82	1	Jarrow	16 Jul
11.0		Sandra Owusu		30.09.81	2	Basingstoke	7 Aug

100 METRES

11.15	1.5	Paula Thomas		3.12.64	2s2	Victoria, CAN	23 Aug
		11.23	-0.2		3	Victoria, CAN	23 Aug
		11.30	0.2		2h4	Victoria, CAN	22 Aug
		11.37	0.4		1h3	Helsinki, FIN	7 Aug
		11.42	0.3		3q3	Helsinki, FIN	7 Aug
		11.46	1.2		1h3	Sheffield	11 Jun
		11.48	-0.3		2s1	Sheffield	11 Jun
		11.48	0.8		1	Reduit, MAU	2 Oct
		11.53	-1.1		1	Wrexham	3 Jul
		11.58	0.5		5s1	Helsinki, FIN	8 Aug
11.34	0.8	Katharine Merry	U23	21.09.74	2	Birmingham	25 Jun
		11.38	0.7		1s2	Sheffield	11 Jun
		11.44	-0.6		1	Birmingham	21 May
		11.44	1.9		1h1	Sheffield	11 Jun
		11.49	-0.1		1	Birmingham	8 May
		11.61	-1.2		1	Corby	30 May
11.34	1.2	Stephanie Douglas		22.01.69	3s1	Victoria, CAN	23 Aug
		11.40	0.9		5q2	Helsinki, FIN	7 Aug
		11.43	-0.3		1s1	Sheffield	11 Jun
		11.46	-0.1		2	Helsinki, FIN	29 Jun
		11.48	-0.2		8	Victoria, CAN	23 Aug
		11.49	0.5		2h3	Victoria, CAN	22 Aug
		11.58	-1.1		2	Wrexham	3 Jul
		11.60	0.2		4h5	Helsinki, FIN	7 Aug
		11.60	1.0		7s2	Helsinki, FIN	8 Aug
		11.63	-0.2		1h4	Sheffield	11 Jun
		11.64	-0.6		2	Birmingham	21 May
11.46	1.2	Marcia Richardson	U23	10.02.72	2h3	Sheffield	11 Jun
		11.49	0.7		2h1	Budapest, HUN	3 Jun
		11.53	0.7		2s2	Sheffield	11 Jun
		11.56	-1.0		3	Budapest, HUN	3 Jun
11.47	1.5	Simmone Jacobs		5.09.66	6s2	Victoria, CAN	23 Aug
		11.57	-0.3		3s1	Sheffield	11 Jun
		11.63	-0.1		6	Helsinki, FIN	29 Jun
		11.64	-0.2		2h4	Sheffield	11 Jun
		11.65			1s2	Reykjavik, ICE	18 Jun
		11.65	0.9		3h2	Victoria, CAN	22 Aug
11.60	0.5	Danaa Myhill		16.10.70	5h3	Victoria, CAN	22 Aug
		11.63	1.5		8s2	Victoria, CAN	23 Aug
	39 performances to 11.65 by 6 athletes						
11.66	0.7	Geraldine McLeod		24.09.71	3s2	Sheffield	11 Jun
11.76	2.0	Aileen McGillivary		13.08.70	1	Colwyn Bay	23 Jul

236

11.77	0.1	Clova Court		10.02.60	1	Stoke	16	Jul
11.78	0.9	Tatum Nelson	U17	17.12.78	1h	Nicosia, CYP	16	May
	(10)							
11.78	1.6	Sam Farquharson		15.12.69	1r2	Nitra, SVK	13	Jul
11.81	0.7	Tracy Goddard		29.11.69	2r1	Victoria, CAN	19	Aug
11.82	0.7	Sophia Smith	U23	8.12.74	5s2	Sheffield	11	Jun
11.83	-0.3	Donna Hoggarth	U23	14.10.73	4s1	Sheffield	11	Jun
11.88	0.5	Sallyanne Short		6.03.68	3	Istanbul, TUR	21	May
11.88		Alison Thompson	U23	11.02.74	2h2	Edinburgh	24	Jun
		11.86 (doubtful timing)			1	Carlisle	4	Sep
11.88	1.7	Laura Seston	U17	9.02.79	1h3	Bedford	2	Jul
11.88		Jacqui Parker		15.10.66		Perth, AUS	12	Dec
11.89	-1.7	Diane Allahgreen	U20	21.02.75	1	Bedford	2	Jul
11.89	1.3	Sue Earnshaw		13.10.70	1	Bedford	18	Sep
	(20)							
11.90	1.2	Joan Booth		18.12.68	3h3	Sheffield	11	Jun
11.92	-0.3	Annabel Soper		18.11.71	1h2	London (CP)	25	Jun
11.93	1.9	Alison Davies		6.04.61	3h1	Sheffield	11	Jun
11.94	1.9	Jayne Mitchell		29.03.63	4h1	Sheffield	11	Jun
11.94	1.2	Christine Bloomfield		12.02.68	4h3	Sheffield	11	Jun
11.94	1.3	Donna Fraser	U23	7.11.72	4	Victoria, CAN	19	Aug
11.96	1.4	Lorraine Robins		13.05.70	1h2	Brussels, BEL	16	Jul
11.96	0.2	Rebecca Drummond	U17	18.04.78	1	Schio, ITA	6	Aug
11.97	-0.6	Bev Kinch		14.01.64	5	Birmingham	21	May
11.99	0.5	Ellana Ruddock	U20	23.02.76	1h2	Bedford	2	Jul
	(30)							
12.00	0.3	Catherine Murphy	U20	21.09.75	1	London (CP)	29	May
12.00	-0.2	Joice Maduaka	U23	30.09.73	5h4	Sheffield	11	Jun
12.00	1.4	Jane Fleming	U23	6.10.72	1h1	Edinburgh	25	Jun
12.02	-1.0	Angela Thorp	U23	7.12.72	3	Birmingham	8	May
12.02	1.1	Sarah Wilhelmy	U15	2.02.80	1	London (CP)	28	May
12.02	*0.3*	*Evadne McKenzie*	*U20*	*19.05.75*	*1h1*	*Telford*	*8*	*Jul*
12.04	1.4	Morag Baxter		22.08.69	2h1	Edinburgh	25	Jun
12.04	1.7	Fiona Hutchison	U20	18.01.77	2h3	Bedford	2	Jul
12.04	0.1	Sarah Oxley	U23	3.07.73	2	Stoke	16	Jul
12.04		Elaine Wyard/Sutcliffe		6.04.70	1	Wrexham	30	Jul
12.05	0.5	Helen Miles		2.03.67	4	Istanbul, TUR	21	May
	(40)							
12.06	1.4	Dawn Flockhart		16.05.67	3h1	Edinburgh	25	Jun
12.07	-0.6	Georgina Oladapo		15.05.67	2s1	London (CP)	25	Jun
12.07	0.5	Bev Christopher	U20	14.01.75	3h1	Bedford	2	Jul
12.07	1.7	Joanne Dear	U20	8.06.75	4h3	Bedford	2	Jul
12.07	0.3	Leanne Eastwood	U20	23.11.76	2h1	Telford	8	Jul
12.07	0.5	Debbie Mant	U20	11.10.75	4h2	Bedford	2	Jul
12.10	1.9	Ann Inniss		28.08.63	6h1	Sheffield	11	Jun
12.10	-0.1	Natalie Hynd	U17	30.01.78	1	Edinburgh	8	Jul
12.13		Victoria Shipman	U20	31.03.77	2	Loughborough	5	Jun
12.14	1.7	Shani Anderson	U20	7.08.75	5h3	Bedford	2	Jul
	(50)							
12.14	0.4	Sinead Dudgeon	U20	9.07.76	1	Grangemouth	9	Jul
12.16		Louise Sharps	U20	9.07.77	1	Dublin, IRE		Sep
12.18	0.4	Louise Fraser		10.10.70	2r2	Colwyn Bay	23	Jul
12.19		Janet Levermore		7.06.69	3	Loughborough	5	Jun
12.19	-1.5	Dawn Cousins		16.03.68	3s2	London (CP)	25	Jun
12.19	1.1	Sarah Claxton	U15	23.09.79	1s2	Telford	9	Jul
12.21	0.3	Jannette Niccolls	U20	7.09.76	1h3	Telford	8	Jul
12.21	-1.9	Ann Brooks		4.05.71	3h1	Derby	16	Jul
12.22	-0.6	Claire Haslam		18.12.63	4s1	London (CP)	25	Jun
12.24		Louretta Thorne	U20	6.05.77	5	London (CP)	29	May
	(60)							
12.24	-1.2	Alison Mayfield		12.05.69	6	Corby	30	May

12.24	*-1.0*	*Jean Oyeyemi*	*U15*	*24.08.81*	*1s1*	*Telford*	*9*	*Jul*
12.25	-0.6	Michelle Thomas		16.10.71	8	Birmingham	21	May
12.26	-0.6	Lorraine Crossley	U23	4.01.72	6s1	London (CP)	25	Jun
12.27	1.9	Jackie Evans	U23	5.04.74	7h1	Sheffield	11	Jun
12.27	1.2	Donna Bannister	U23	27.12.72	7h3	Sheffield	11	Jun
12.27	-0.3	Julie Howard		24.09.66	4h2	London (CP)	25	Jun
12.28	-0.3	Yvonne Cole		18.11.65	5h2	London (CP)	25	Jun
12.28	-1.0	Gillian Hegney	U17	4.11.77	1	Grangemouth	9	Jul
12.29	0.1	Julie Rolfe	U23	22.05.73	5	Stoke	16	Jul

Additional Under 17 (1 - 5 above)

12.31	-0.2	Dawn Rose		25.01.79	1h2	Birmingham	30	Jul
12.33	-1.6	Evette Williams		23.03.78	1	Birmingham	10	Sep
12.36	1.5	Hannah Paines		6.04.79	1	Colwyn Bay	2	Jul
12.38	0.2	Gahlie Davis		3.05.79	3	London (CP)	29	May
12.38	-1.0	Lesley Owusu		21.12.78	1	Birmingham	11	Sep
	(10)							
12.40	1.9	Delyth Jones		12.03.79	1	Newport	28	May
12.40	0.6	Susan Mary Douglas		3.11.77	1	Antrim	11	Jun
12.42	1.9	Gael Davies		5.02.79	2	Newport	28	May
12.43	0.2	Emma Dengate		26.10.77	4	London (CP)	29	May
12.44	-0.1	Nicola Hutchison		1.02.79	3=	Edinburgh	8	Jul
12.48	1.9	Angharad James		7.04.79	3	Newport	28	May
12.48	-0.9	Jennifer Impett		18.11.77	2h4	Telford	8	Jul
12.48	-1.0	Lucy Chaffe		25.03.79	2	Birmingham	11	Sep
12.51	0.5	Amanda Forrester		29.09.78	1h1	Telford	8	Jul
12.51	0.7	Susan Christie		7.03.79	3	Dublin, IRE	13	Aug
	(20)							
12.53		Helen Plumb		18.03.78	1	Gateshead	28	May
12.55	-1.6	Amanda Waite		1.02.78	3	Birmingham	10	Sep
12.58	1.9	Lucy Parsons		10.02.79	5	Newport	28	May
12.60	0.2	Sarah Beadle		16.05.79	5	London (CP)	29	May

Wind Assisted

11.27	2.9	Katharine Merry	U23	(11.34)	1	Sheffield	11	Jun
11.37	2.9	Simmone Jacobs		(11.47)	3	Sheffield	11	Jun
11.35	2.9	Douglas		(11.34)	2	Sheffield	11	Jun
11.39	2.9	Marcia Richardson	U23	(11.46)	4	Sheffield	11	Jun
11.40	2.9	Thomas		(11.15)	5	Sheffield	11	Jun
11.50	4.1	Rebecca Drummond	U17	(11.96)	1	Telford	9	Jul
11.51	2.9	Geraldine McLeod		(11.66)	6	Sheffield	11	Jun
11.56	3.3	Aileen McGillivary		(11.76)	1	Edinburgh	25	Jun
		11.57 3.5			1h2	Edinburgh	25	Jun
11.58	2.9	Danaa Myhill		(11.60)	7	Sheffield	11	Jun
11.63	6.4	Catherine Murphy	U20	(12.00)	1	London (He)	27	Aug
		11 performances to 11.65 by 10 athletes						
11.78	2.9	Donna Hoggarth	U23	(11.83)	8	Sheffield	11	Jun
11.81		Melanie Neef		26.05.70	1	Edinburgh	8	Jun
11.81	2.1	Ashia Hansen		5.12.71	1	Bedford	17	Sep
11.84	4.1	Laura Seston	U17	(11.88)	2	Telford	9	Jul
11.84	*6.4*	*Evadne McKenzie*	*U20*	*(12.02)*	*2*	*London (He)*	*27*	*Aug*
11.86	*4.0*	*Jean Oyeyemi*	*U15*	*(12.24)*	*1*	*Telford*	*9*	*Jul*
11.88	4.0	Sarah Claxton	U15	(12.19)	2	Telford	9	Jul
11.89	3.1	Ellana Ruddock	U20	(11.99)	2	Telford	9	Jul
11.90	3.3	Dawn Flockhart		(12.06)	2	Edinburgh	25	Jun
11.92	3.5	Sinead Dudgeon	U20	(12.14)	3h2	Edinburgh	25	Jun
11.93	3.3	Morag Baxter		(12.04)	4	Edinburgh	25	Jun
11.93	4.1	Dawn Rose	U17	(12.31)	3	Telford	9	Jul
11.94	2.5	Joice Maduaka	U23	(12.00)	2	Loughborough	5	Jun
11.95	3.1	Leanne Eastwood	U20	(12.07)	3	Telford	9	Jul

238

11.97	2.1	Victoria Shipman	U20	(12.13)	2	Solihull	28	May
11.99	3.3	Jane Fleming	U23	(12.00)	6	Edinburgh	25	Jun
12.07	3.1	Jannette Niccolls	U20	(12.21)	4	Telford	9	Jul
12.13	4.1	Amanda Forrester	U17	(12.51)	4	Telford	9	Jul
12.14	4.1	Jennifer Impett	U17	(12.48)	5	Telford	9	Jul
12.15	4.1	Emma Dengate	U17	(12.43)	6	Telford	9	Jul
12.19	2.6	Lee McConnell	U17	9.10.78	1	Edinburgh	4	Sep
12.19	2.1	Joanna Clark	U23	11.02.73	7	Bedford	17	Sep
12.21	2.7	Kim Whittaker	U17	12.11.77	3s1	Telford	8	Jul
12.22	w?	Keeley Butler	U20	24.03.75	1s	London (CP)	30	Apr
12.24	4.0	Lisa Thomas	U15	22.06.80	3	Telford	9	Jul
12.24	3.1	Hayley Upson	U20	16.04.77	5	Telford	9	Jul
12.26	3.1	Adele Foster	U20	16.11.76	6	Telford	9	Jul
12.28	4.1	Delyth Jones	U17	(12.40)	1h1	Newport	28	May
12.28	4.0	Kelli Bailey	U15	(12.55)	4	Telford	9	Jul
12.29	3.4	Gahlie Davis	U17	(12.38)	2h2	London (CP)	29	May

Additional Under 17

12.30	6.4	Kirsty Payne		22.10.77	5	London (He)	27	Aug
12.34	4.1	Gael Davies		(12.42)	2h1	Newport	28	May
12.35	2.6	Helen Plumb		(12.53)	5s2	Telford	8	Jul
12.42	3.2	Melanie Purkiss		11.03.79	1h3	London (CP)	29	May
12.42	2.6	Elizabeth Hall		16.10.78	6s2	Telford	8	Jul
12.44	3.2	Tracy Bishop		1.05.79	2h3	London (CP)	29	May
12.47	2.7	Sarah Miles		14.12.78	5s1	Telford	8	Jul
12.48	3.4	Sarah Beadle		(12.60)	3h2	London (CP)	29	May
12.58	2.7	Melanie Roberts		2.03.78	7s1	Telford	8	Jul

Hand Timing

11.2		Geraldine McLeod		(11.66)	1	Los Angeles, USA	21	May
11.5		Thomas		(11.15)	1	Stretford	14	May
11.5		Douglas		(11.34)	2	Stretford	14	May
		11.5	0.9		1	Kingston	31	Jul
11.6	1.7	Richardson	U23	(11.46)	1	Bracknell	14	May
		11.6			1	Corby	31	Jul
11.6		Myhill		(11.60)	2	Cork, IRE	25	Jun
11.6		Paula Cohen		5.02.71	4	Cork, IRE	25	Jun
		8 performances to 11.6 by 6 athletes						
11.7		Jacqui Agyepong		5.01.69	1	Bournemouth	19	Jun
11.7		Diane Allahgreen	U20	(11.89)	1	Bebington	22	Jun
11.8		Lorraine Robins		(11.96)	1	High Wycombe	21	May
11.8		Sinead Dudgeon	U20	(12.14)	1	Aberdeen	12	Jun
11.8		Sophia Smith	U23	(11.82)	1	Sheffield	19	Jun
11.8		Alison Mayfield		(12.24)	1	Leicester	20	Jun
11.8		Dawn Flockhart		(12.06)	2	Aberdeen	23	Jun
11.8		Sue Earnshaw		(11.89)	5	Cork, IRE	25	Jun
11.8	*0.9*	*Evadne McKenzie*	*U20*	*(12.02)*	*2*	*Kingston*	*31*	*Jul*
11.8		Bev Kinch		(11.97)	1	Feltham	13	Aug
11.8 w	4.0	Fiona Hutchison	U20	(12.04)	2	Glasgow	18	Jun
11.8 w		Ann Brooks		(12.21)	1	Hull	7	Aug
11.9		Jayne Mitchell		(11.94)	1	Bebington	27	Mar
11.9	2.0	Phylis Smith		29.09.65	1r2	Grangemouth	7	May
11.9		Ann Inniss		(12.10)	2	Leicester	19	Jun
11.9		Ellana Ruddock	U20	(11.99)	1	Cannock	26	Jun
11.9	0.2	Rebecca Drummond	U17	(11.96)	1	Birmingham	30	Jul
11.9 w		Victoria Shipman	U20	(12.13)	2	Nottingham	14	May
		12.1			1	Loughborough	22	Jun
11.9 w		Alison Davies		(11.93)	1	Croydon	15	May

12.0		Lorraine Crossley	U23	(12.26)	2	Enfield	4 May
12.0		Morag Baxter		(12.04)	3	Aberdeen	12 Jun
12.0		Melanie Neef		(11.81w)	2r1	Stretford	18 Jun
12.0		Claire Haslam		(12.22)	1r2	Bournemouth	19 Jun
12.0	0.9	Sarah Wilhelmy	U15	(12.02)	1	Birmingham	30 Jul
12.0		Dawn Cousins		(12.19)	1	Basildon	13 Aug
12.0 w		Susan Williams	U20	2.06.77	2	Aldershot	4 Jun
12.1		Samantha Barr		14.08.70	1	Horsham	8 May
12.1		Ashia Hansen		(11.81w)	1	London (Nh)	15 May
12.1		Rebecca Kilgour	U20	18.10.75	1	Yeovil	18 Jun
12.1		Hayley Clements		17.09.68	2	Hoo	19 Jun
12.1		Janet Levermore		(12.19)	2	Bournemouth	19 Jun
12.1		Julie Rolfe	U23	(12.29)	2	Loughborough	22 Jun
12.1		Sharon Williams		20.05.70	1	Salisbury	10 Jul
12.1		Hayley Upson	U20	(12.24w)	1	Norwich	16 Jul
12.1	0.9	Louise Fraser		(12.18)	3	Kingston	31 Jul
12.1		Julie Howard		(12.27)	1	Exeter	8 Aug
12.1		Sam Baker	U23	14.04.72	1	Wyndley	27 Aug
12.1 w		Louretta Thorne	U20	(12.24)	1	High Wycombe	14 May
12.1 w		Sharon Tunaley		2.09.68	3	Nottingham	14 May
12.1 w	5.3	Susan Christie	U17	(12.51)	2	Glasgow	18 Jun
12.1 w	4.0	Malgorzata Rostek	U20	25.03.77	3	Glasgow	18 Jun
12.1 w	4.0	Kathryn Gray	U20	4.06.76	4	Glasgow	18 Jun
12.1 w	3.2	Louise Sharps	U20	(12.16)	1	Swansea	29 Aug

Additional Under 17

12.2		Kirsty Payne		(12.30w)	1	Telford	28 Apr
12.2		Melanie Roberts		(12.58w)	1	Bebington	11 Jun
12.2		Lucy Chaffe		(12.48)	1	London (WF)	26 Jun
12.2	0.2	Dawn Rose		(12.31)	3	Birmingham	30 Jul
12.2		Elizabeth Hall		(12.42w)	1	Sutton Coldfield	27 Aug
12.2 w	5.3	Gillian Hegney		(12.28)	3	Glasgow	18 Jun
12.3		Helen Plumb		(12.53)	1	Hull	1 May
12.3		Sharon Hollett		26.12.78	1	Glasgow	21 May
12.3		Amanda Forrester		(12.51)	1r2	Stoke	5 Jun
12.3		Amanda Waite		(12.55)	1	Thurrock	19 Jun
12.3		Melanie Purkiss		(12.42w)	1	Southampton	9 Aug
12.3		Evette Williams		(12.33)	1	Dartford	13 Aug
12.3		Natasha Danvers		19.09.77	3	London (Elt)	29 Aug
12.3 w	8.7	Nicola Hutchison		(12.44)	1h3	Glasgow	18 Jun
12.4					1	Kirkby	5 Jun
12.4		Wooday Sidibe		14.11.78	1	London (CP)	9 Apr
12.4		Jane Murphy		17.12.77	1	Oldham	9 Apr
12.4		Stacey Rodd		19.05.78	1	Barry	27 Apr
12.4		Tracy Bishop		(12.44w)	1	Harrow	10 May
12.4		Liz Fairs		1.12.77	2	Hull	24 Jul
12.4		Shelley-Anne Bowen		12.05.79	1	Reading	11 Sep

Additional Under 15 (1 - 3 above)

12.2		Ayeesha Charles		4.09.79	1	Kingston	23 Apr
		12.49 -0.4			2h3	Birmingham	30 Jul
12.2		Kelli Bailey		8.09.79	1	Brierley Hill	24 Jul
		12.55 1.1			2s2	Telford	9 Jul
12.2 w		Vicky Brackstone		10.04.80	1	Crewe	15 May
12.36 w 4.0		Sonya Green		6.03.80	5	Telford	9 Jul
12.36 w 4.0		Amanda Freeman		16.10.79	6	Telford	9 Jul
12.4					1	Thurrock	19 Jun
12.4		Rachael Kay		8.09.80	1	Ashton-U-Lyne	6 Jun
12.4		Elizabeth Lloyd		1.12.79	1	Stoke	11 Jun

12.4		Debbie Sinnott	28.03.80	1	Bebington	11	Jun
12.4		Eve Miller	1.12.79	1	Norwich	16	Jul
12.41 w 2.1		Karlene Palmer	23.10.80	2h1	London (CP)	28	May
12.46	1.1			3	London (CP)	28	May
12.47	-0.4	Maria Bolsover	5.06.80	1h3	Birmingham	30	Jul

Under 13

12.8		Stacy Hilling	11.09.81	2r1	Carn Brea	4	Jun
12.9		Stefanie Oates	19.11.81	1	Oldham	10	Jul
13.0		Naomi Taplin	18.12.81		Andover	8	May
13.0		Andrea Lang	6.03.82	1	Ayr	17	May
13.0	5.9	Wendy Thomson	28.06.82	1s2	Glasgow	18	Jun
13.35				2	Grangemouth	10	Jul
13.0	5.9	Charlotte Todd	7.12.81	2s2	Glasgow	18	Jun
13.1		Fiona Harrison	30.11.81	1	Sheffield	18	Jun
13.1		Cheryl Gibbons	21.09.81	2	Oldham	10	Jul
13.2		Rachel Redmond	7.12.81	1	Stafford		Jun
13.2		Rebecca Bates	16.05.82	2	Stafford		Jun
	(10)						
13.2		Serena Woodhouse	20.10.81	1	Stoke	24	Jul
13.2		Hannah Wood	17.11.81	1	Sutton Coldfield	27	Aug
13.2		Sarah Zawada	9.04.82	1r1	Guildford	27	Aug
13.2		Sophie Carvill	16.02.82	1	Bournemouth	29	Aug

Doubtful Timing

12.8		Anna McGovern	4.11.81	1	Carmarthen	11	Jun
13.2		Nerys Gealy		2	Carmarthen	11	Jun

150 METRES - Under 13

19.6		Laverne Slater	26.01.82	1	Bromley	24	Jul
19.6		Stacy Hilling	11.09.81	1	Carn Brea	27	Jul
19.6		Sarah Zawada	9.04.82	1	Guildford	11	Sep
19.7		Hannah Wood	17.11.81	1r1	Solihull	17	Jul
19.7		Naomi Taplin	18.12.81	1r1	Yeovil	24	Jul
19.8		Jenny McCarthy	22.02.82	1r1	Ashton-U-Lyne	5	Jun
19.8		Rachel Redmond	7.12.81	1r2	Solihull	17	Jul
19.9		Lynsey McDonnell	19.11.81	1r2	Ashton-U-Lyne	5	Jun
19.9		Gemma Morris	27.01.82	2r1	Solihull	17	Jul
19.9		Rebecca Bates	16.05.82	3r1	Solihull	17	Jul
	(10)						
20.0		Stefanie Oates	19.11.81	2r1	Ashton-U-Lyne	5	Jun
20.1		Elizabeth Lem		2r2	Solihull	17	Jul
20.2		Elaine Inglis	8.04.82	3r1	Ashton-U-Lyne	5	Jun
20.3		Leah Tribe	3.09.81	1r1	Croydon	26	Jun

200 METRES

22.69	1.3	Paula Thomas	3.12.64	4	Victoria, CAN	26	Aug
22.91	1.4			3s1	Victoria, CAN	26	Aug
23.09	1.2			3	Sheffield	4	Sep
23.22	-1.7			6	London (CP)	9	Sep
23.25	0.0			1	Wrexham	3	Jul
23.33	0.6			3	Sheffield	12	Jun
23.39	-0.3			4h3	Helsinki, FIN	10	Aug
23.41˙	1.4			6s2	Helsinki, FIN	11	Aug
23.57	0.9			1h4	Sheffield	12	Jun
23.77	0.1			1	Nitra, SVK	13	Jul

22.85	0.6	Katharine Merry	U23	21.09.74	1	Sheffield	12	Jun
23.00 i					1	Glasgow	12	Feb
23.00	1.7				1	Birmingham	8	May
23.10	1.6				1h1	Sheffield	12	Jun
23.38 i					1mx	Birmingham	6	Feb
23.55	0.3				8s1	Helsinki, FIN	11	Aug
23.73	0.3				3h2	Helsinki, FIN	10	Aug
23.17	0.6	Stephanie Douglas		22.01.69	2	Sheffield	12	Jun
23.59	-0.5				1h3	Sheffield	12	Jun
23.47	1.2	Geraldine McLeod		24.09.71	4h1	Victoria, CAN	24	Aug
23.52	0.6				5	Sheffield	12	Jun
23.52	0.0				2	Wrexham	3	Jul
23.52	1.3				8	Victoria, CAN	26	Aug
23.57	0.9				2h4	Sheffield	12	Jun
23.48	0.8	Simmone Jacobs		5.09.66	1	London (CP)	26	Jun
23.52	0.6				4	Sheffield	12	Jun
23.58	-0.4				1	Brussels, BEL	17	Jul
23.64	0.1				1	Corby	30	May
23.69	1.1				1h2	Brussels, BEL	16	Jul
23.73	-1.2				3	Gateshead	20	Jul
23.75	-2.1				6h1	Helsinki, FIN	10	Aug
23.76	-2.4				1h2	Sheffield	12	Jun
23.55	0.6	Marcia Richardson	U23	10.02.72	6	Sheffield	12	Jun
23.62	-0.5				2h3	Sheffield	12	Jun
23.61	0.0	Aileen McGillivary		13.08.70	3	Wrexham	3	Jul
23.64	0.7	Melanie Neef		26.05.70	1	Brugge, BEL	3	Jul
23.67		Paula Cohen		5.02.71	1	Cork, IRE	25	Jun
23.78	0.6				7	Sheffield	12	Jun
23.68	-0.5	Sophia Smith	U23	8.12.74	1	Kings Lynn	9	Jul
	(10)							
23.80	1.2	Clova Court		10.02.60	1H	Horsham	18	Jun
		40 performances to 23.80 by 11 athletes including 2 indoors						
23.85	0.6	Catherine Murphy	U20	21.09.75	8	Sheffield	12	Jun
23.91	0.9	Alison Davies		6.04.61	3h4	Sheffield	12	Jun
23.96	-0.5	Joice Maduaka	U23	30.09.73	2	Kings Lynn	9	Jul
24.10 i		Bev Kinch		14.01.64	3	Birmingham	26	Feb
24.10	0.5	Sallyanne Short		6.03.68	3	Istanbul, TUR	22	May
24.13		Sue Earnshaw		13.10.70	3	Cork, IRE	25	Jun
24.16 i		Tracy Goddard		29.11.69	2r2	Vienna, AUT	6	Feb
24.16	-0.8	Donna Fraser	U23	7.11.72	4	London (CP)	26	Jun
24.18	1.2	Emma Lindsay		11.04.71	2H	Horsham	18	Jun
	(20)							
24.18	0.0	Dawn Flockhart		16.05.67	6	Wrexham	3	Jul
24.18	0.5	Sue Briggs		26.03.67	1h1	Hull	21	Aug
24.21	-2.4	Alison Mayfield		12.05.69	3h2	Sheffield	12	Jun
24.22	-0.6	Sinead Dudgeon	U20	9.07.76	1h2	Edinburgh	24	Jun
24.27	-0.5	Jacqui Agyepong		5.01.69	3h3	Sheffield	12	Jun
24.27	1.1	Susan Williams	U20	2.06.77	1	Bedford	3	Jul
24.28	0.7	Alanna Cooke		11.01.70	1H	Sheffield	30	Apr
24.36	0.3	Debbie Mant	U20	11.10.75	1h2	Bedford	3	Jul
24.39	1.1	Louretta Thorne	U20	6.05.77	1h3	Telford	8	Jul
24.40	0.5	Natasha Bartlett	U23	19.01.74	5	Istanbul, TUR	22	May
	(30)							
24.45	1.6	Michelle Thomas		16.10.71	5h1	Sheffield	12	Jun
24.48	0.9	Donna Bannister	U23	27.12.72	5h4	Sheffield	12	Jun
24.48		Elaine Wyard/Sutcliffe		6.04.70	1	Wrexham	30	Jul
24.53	-0.5	Claire O'Connor	U23	24.09.74	4	Kings Lynn	9	Jul
24.54	-0.5	Sarah Wilhelmy	U15	2.02.80	1	Birmingham	31	Jul
24.56	-2.4	Hayley Clements		17.09.68	4h2	Sheffield	12	Jun
24.57	0.7	Kerry Jury		19.11.68	2H	Sheffield	30	Apr
24.57	-3.0	Annabel Soper		18.11.71	2s1	London (CP)	26	Jun

24.58		Stephanie McCann		26.10.65	7	Prince George, CAN	13	Aug
24.65		Sarah Oxley	U23	3.07.73	2	Solihull	21	Aug
	(40)							
24.68	0.5	Joan Booth		18.12.68	6	Istanbul, TUR	22	May
24.69	0.8	Fiona Hutchison	U20	18.01.77	1h1	Nicosia, CYP	19	May
24.70	-0.3	Jenny Kelly		20.06.70	3H	Venissieux, FRA	2	Jul
24.70	1.4	Rebecca Kilgour	U20	18.10.75	4	Telford	9	Jul
24.76	1.1	Victoria Shipman	U20	31.03.77	3h3	Telford	8	Jul
24.78	1.2	Pauline Richards		30.06.68	4H	Horsham	18	Jun
24.80	-2.6	Denise Lewis	U23	27.08.72	3H	Venissieux, FRA	2	Jul
24.81		Diane Allahgreen	U20	21.02.75	1	Gateshead	28	May
24.82	1.1	Lesley Owusu	U17	21.12.78	1	London (CP)	28	May
24.82	-2.7	Leigh Ferrier	U23	15.08.72	4	Bulle, SWZ	10	Sep
	(50)							
24.83	0.9	Maria Bolsover	U15	5.06.80	1h5	Telford	8	Jul
24.87		Michelle Griffith		6.10.71	4	Solihull	21	Aug
24.88		Janet Levermore		7.06.69	1r2	Birmingham	24	Apr
24.90	0.6	Helen Miles		2.03.67	2	Cardiff	8	May
24.90		Leanne Eastwood	U20	23.11.76	2	Gateshead	28	May
24.91 i		Jo Sloane	U20	2.12.76	1	Birmingham	6	Feb
24.94	0.7	Natasha Mighty		21.12.70	2H	Sheffield	30	Apr
24.94		Claire Phythian	U23	7.02.73	1H	Fayetteville, USA	12	May
24.94	-1.0	Lee McConnell	U17	9.10.78	1	Aberdeen	16	Jul
24.95	0.5	Alison Thompson	U23	11.02.74	2h2	Derby	16	Jul
	(60)							
24.97	-3.0	Claire Haslam		18.12.63	4s1	London (CP)	26	Jun
24.97		Jackie White		12.01.71	6	Solihull	21	Aug
24.99	-0.5	Lorraine Bell	U20	21.06.77	3h1	Edinburgh	24	Jun
25.00	0.9	Denise Bolton	U20	1.02.77	1H	Sheffield	30	Apr
25.01	0.2	Bev Christopher	U20	14.01.75	4	London (CP)	28	May
25.01	0.9	Elaine Viney		20.12.71	6h4	Sheffield	12	Jun
25.02	-0.5	Louise Whitehead	U20	26.03.75	2h1	Hull	21	Aug
25.02	-1.8	Donna Hoggarth	U23	14.10.73	1h2	Hull	21	Aug
25.04 i		Laura Seston	U17	9.02.79	1	Birmingham	13	Feb
		25.34	1.6		2h2	London (CP)	28	May
25.04	-1.1	Vikki Schofield	U23	29.12.72	3H	Venissieux, FRA	2	Jul
	(70)							
25.04	0.6	Elizabeth Hall	U17	16.10.78	1h3	Birmingham	31	Jul
25.05 i		Danaa Myhill		16.10.70	1h2	Birmingham	7	Jan
25.09	0.3	Rachael Kay	U15	8.09.80	2	Gateshead	29	May
25.09	1.7	Amanda Waite	U17	1.02.78	1h3	Telford	8	Jul
25.09	1.4	Kate Teasdale	U20	27.12.75	7	Telford	9	Jul
25.10	0.6	Kim Goodwin		16.05.70	3	Cardiff	8	May
25.10	0.9	Patricia Weiss	U17	24.12.77	1s2	Telford	9	Jul
25.11	-0.9	Emily Feltham	U20	17.08.77	4h1	Telford	8	Jul
25.13	0.9	Evette Williams	U17	23.03.78	2s2	Telford	9	Jul
25.14		Helen Seery	U20	6.09.76	3	Gateshead	28	May
	(80)							
25.15	-0.5	Susan Mary Douglas	U17	3.11.77	5	Kings Lynn	9	Jul
25.17	1.0	Sally Evans	U20	14.05.75	4h1	Stoke	16	Jul
25.18	-1.0	Louise Stuart		18.05.67	2h1	Derby	16	Jul
25.19		Vyvyan Rhodes	U23	5.05.73	7	Solihull	21	Aug
25.20	0.2	Keeley Butler	U20	24.03.75	2h2	Stoke	16	Jul
25.26	0.6	Sarah Still	U20	24.09.75	1H	Linwood	16	Jul
25.27	-0.4	Wendy Young	U23	3.02.74	4	Edinburgh	24	Jun
25.29 i		Tatum Nelson	U17	17.12.78	1h1	Birmingham	13	Feb
25.29 i		Wooday Sidibe	U17	14.11.78	2	Birmingham	13	Feb
		25.39	0.9		3s2	Telford	9	Jul

During longer indoor race

24.62 i+		Sally Gunnell		29.07.66	1	Birmingham	26	Feb

Additional Under 17 (1 - 10 above)

25.30		Amanda Gray		22.03.79	1	Derby	11	Jun
25.31	1.1	Sarah Hunter		19.05.78	3	London (CP)	28	May
25.43	1.9	Kirsty Payne		22.10.77	1h2	Telford	8	Jul
25.45	1.7	Michelle Murray		22.11.78	3h3	Telford	8	Jul
25.45	1.0	Natalie Hynd		30.01.78	4	Birmingham	31	Jul
25.51 i		Gael Davies		5.02.79	1h1	Birmingham	31	Dec
25.53	0.9	Melanie Clarke		25.02.78	4s2	Telford	9	Jul
25.54	0.2	Angharad James		7.04.79	1	Newport	28	May
25.55	0.9	Lucy Carter		7.03.78	5s2	Telford	9	Jul
25.57	1.1	Helen Pryer		21.01.79	5	London (CP)	28	May
	(20)							
25.57	1.8	Rebecca Clark		15.09.78	2h1	Telford	8	Jul

Wind Assisted

23.04	2.2	Thomas		(22.69)	2h3	Victoria, CAN	24	Aug
23.29	2.6	Douglas		(23.17)	2h2	Victoria, CAN	24	Aug
		23.30	2.3		4	Edinburgh	8	Jul
		23.67	2.7		5s2	Victoria, CAN	26	Aug
23.38	2.9	Merry	U23	(22.85)	2	Birmingham	26	Jun
23.42	3.0	Aileen McGillivary		(23.61)	1	Colwyn Bay	23	Jul
23.52	2.3	McLeod		(23.47)	6	Edinburgh	8	Jul
		23.58	2.7		4s2	Victoria, CAN	26	Aug
23.80	2.7	Sue Earnshaw		(24.13)	1	Hull	21	Aug

9 performances to 23.80 by 6 athletes

23.83	3.5	Catherine Murphy	U20	(23.85)	1	Bedford	17	Sep
23.99	3.4	Sarah Wilhelmy	U15	(24.54)	1	Telford	9	Jul
24.06	2.7	Donna Hoggarth	U23	(25.02)	2	Hull	21	Aug
24.11	2.1	Susan Williams	U20	(24.27)	3q1	Lisbon, POR	22	Jul
24.13	3.5	Sarah Oxley	U23	(24.65)	2	Bedford	17	Sep
24.16	3.6	Dawn Flockhart		(24.18)	1	Edinburgh	4	Sep
24.47	3.5	Melanie Wilkins	U23	18.01.73	4	Bedford	17	Sep
24.50	3.5	Christine Bloomfield		12.02.68	5	Bedford	17	Sep
24.54	2.1	Louise Whitehead	U20	(25.02)	1	Wrexham	30	Jul
24.58	3.4	Maria Bolsover	U15	(24.83)	2	Telford	9	Jul
24.64	3.5	Louise Stuart		(25.18)	6	Bedford	17	Sep
24.68	3.0	Fiona Hutchison	U20	(24.69)	4	Colwyn Bay	23	Jul
24.69	4.8	Kirsty Payne	U17	(25.43)	1	Telford	9	Jul
24.70	4.8	Amanda Waite	U17	(25.09)	2	Telford	9	Jul
24.85	2.1	Bev Christopher	U20	(25.01)	2h3	London (CP)	28	May
24.88	4.8	Patricia Weiss	U17	(25.10)	3	Telford	9	Jul
24.89	4.0	Lee McConnell	U17	(24.94)	1	Edinburgh	4	Sep
24.90	3.4	Rachael Kay	U15	(25.09)	3	Telford	9	Jul
24.90	3.4	Ayeesha Charles	U15	4.09.79	4	Telford	9	Jul
24.98	3.0	Louise Sharps	U20	9.07.77	5	Colwyn Bay	23	Jul
24.99	2.6	Fiona Calder		4.05.71	1r2	Edinburgh	4	Sep
25.08	2.6	Karlene Palmer	U15	23.10.80	1s2	Telford	9	Jul
25.14	2.1	Ruth Watson	U15	(25.58)	2s3	Telford	9	Jul
25.14	5.0	Kim Crowther-Price		19.01.66	1H	Wrexham	27	Aug
25.20	2.7	Helen Roscoe	U15	(25.52)	2s1	Telford	9	Jul
25.20	2.7	Lois Cresswell	U15	(25.62)	4s1	Telford	9	Jul

Additional Under 17

25.41 w	4.8	Melanie Clarke		(25.53)	5	Telford	9	Jul
25.46 w	4.8	Lucy Carter		(25.55)	6	Telford	9	Jul

Hand Timing

23.2	1.7	Douglas		(23.17)	1	Kingston	31 Jul
23.5		Marcia Richardson	U23	(23.55)	1	Corby	31 Jul
23.5		Sue Earnshaw		(24.13)	1r1	Derby	11 Sep
23.7	0.8	McGillivary		(23.61)	1	Stoke	31 Jul
		4 performances to 23.7 by 4 athletes					
23.9 w	4.0	Sinead Dudgeon	U20	(24.22)	1	Glasgow	18 Jun
24.0		Alison Mayfield		(24.21)	1	Corby	24 Apr
24.0	1.8	Dawn Flockhart		(24.18)	2	Coatbridge	22 May
24.0 w	5.5	Lee McConnell	U17	(24.94)	1	Coatbridge	22 May
24.9					1	Glasgow	17 Apr
24.2		Phylis Smith		29.09.65	1r1	Grangemouth	7 May
24.2		Donna Hoggarth	U23	(25.02)	1	Blackpool	14 May
24.2		Danaa Myhill		(25.05i)	2	Blackpool	14 May
24.2		Michelle Thomas		(24.45)	1	Leamington	14 May
24.2		Tracy Goddard		(24.16i)	1	Barking	4 Jun
24.1 un						, CAN	7 Aug
24.2 w?		Christine Bloomfield		(24.50w)	1	Windsor	13 Aug
24.4					1	London (TB)	20 Aug
24.2 w		Leanne Eastwood	U20	(24.90)	1	Liverpool	3 Sep
24.8					1	Carlisle	26 Jun
24.3 w	4.0	Fiona Hutchison	U20	(24.69)	2	Glasgow	18 Jun
24.4		Donna Bannister	U23	(24.48)	2	London (CP)	14 May
24.4		Marcia Walker		27.05.70	1	Bournemouth	19 Jun
24.4		Joanna Clark	U23	11.02.73	2	Sheffield	19 Jun
24.4 w		Kim Goodwin		(25.10)	1	Hull	7 Aug
24.7					3	Blackpool	14 May
24.4 w?		Sharon Tunaley		2.09.68	1	Yate	13 Aug
25.0	1.4				4	Enfield	31 Jul
24.5		Alison Thompson	U23	(24.95)	1	Carlisle	10 Jul
24.5		Annabel Soper		(24.57)	1	Aldershot	7 Aug
24.5	1.6	Rebecca Kilgour	U20	(24.70)	1	Exeter	20 Aug
24.6		Jennifer Stoute		16.04.65	2r1	Grangemouth	7 May
24.6		Janet Levermore		(24.88)	2	Bournemouth	19 Jun
24.6		Victoria Shipman	U20	(24.76)	3	Sheffield	19 Jun
24.6		Sarah Oxley	U23	(24.65)	1	Sutton Coldfield	27 Aug
24.7	-0.9	Leigh Ferrier	U23	(24.82)	1	Stoke	14 May
24.7		Lorraine Robins		13.05.70	2	High Wycombe	21 May
24.7		Kate Teasdale	U20	(25.09)		Bebington	11 Jun
24.7		Melanie Wilkins	U23	(24.47w)	3	Corby	31 Jul
24.7		Louise Whitehead	U20	(25.02)	2	Cleckheaton	7 Aug
24.7		Evette Williams	U17	(25.13)	1	Crawley	13 Aug
24.8		Amanda Waite	U17	(25.09)	1	Braintree	8 May
24.8		Vicky Day	U23	19.06.72	1	London (Nh)	15 May
24.8		Gillian Archard/Cashell		5.04.64		Southampton	4 Jun
24.8		Claire Haslam		(24.97)	1r2	Bournemouth	19 Jun
24.8		Jennie Sprott		24.07.68	2	Aldershot	16 Jul
24.8		Julie Howard		24.09.66	1	Exeter	8 Aug
24.8 w?		Debbie Marti		14.05.68	2	Enfield	9 Apr
24.8 w		Sally Evans	U20	(25.17)	1	Warley	14 May
24.8 w	2.3	Morag Baxter		22.08.69	2	Aberdeen	24 Jul
24.9		Jayne Mitchell		29.03.63	1	Bebington	14 May
24.9		Helen Seery	U20	(25.14)	2	Carlisle	26 Jun
24.9		Samantha Barr		14.08.70	1	Portsmouth	13 Jul
24.9		Elaine Viney		(25.01)	1	St. Ives	13 Aug
24.9		Natalie Hynd	U17	(25.45)	2	Coatbridge	28 Aug
24.9 w?		Sarah Chesney	U23	3.03.73	1	Hayes	10 Apr
25.1					3	Aldershot	16 Jul

Mark	Wind	Name	Cat	DOB/Mark	Pos	Venue	Date
24.9 w?		Emily Feltham	U20	(25.11)	3	Yeovil	18 Jun
25.0		Lucy Chaffe	U17	25.03.79	2	Braintree	8 May
25.0		Rebecca Lewis	U17	31.12.77	1	Crewe	14 May
25.0		Ellana Ruddock	U20	23.02.76	4	Leamington	14 May
25.0		Keeley Butler	U20	(25.20)	5	Leamington	14 May
25.0		Kate Bullen		12.02.71	6	Leamington	14 May
25.0	1.8	Lisa Vannet	U23	8.11.74	3	Coatbridge	22 May
25.0		Emma Symonds	U20	5.06.77	1	Norfolk	16 Jul
25.0		Nicola Crowther		15.05.70	1r2	Stoke	24 Jul
25.0		Clare Bleasdale		6.07.71	1	Guildford	13 Aug
25.0		Ruth Nicholson	U17	23.09.77	1	Bromley	21 Aug
25.0		Natasha Danvers	U17	19.09.77	1r2	Windsor	3 Sep
25.0 w		Claire Raven	U23	15.06.72	2	Loughborough	27 Apr
25.1					1	Cannock	26 Jun
25.0 w		Stephanie McPeake/Llewellyn		31.12.68	1	Watford	30 Jul
25.1	-0.5	Wooday Sidibe	U17	(25.39)	1	Croydon	15 May
25.1		Katharine Reeves	U23	2.03.73	2	Bromley	19 Jun
25.1		Helena Fuller	U23	27.08.72	5	Bournemouth	19 Jun
25.1		Hayley Upson	U20	16.04.77	1r2	Norfolk	16 Jul
25.1		Samantha Jones	U20	9.08.76	1r2	Aldershot	16 Jul
25.1		Louise Sharps	U20	(24.98w)	1	Swansea	29 Aug
25.1 w		Vicki Jamison	U20	19.05.77	1	Antrim	30 Apr
25.1 w		Rachel Newcombe		25.02.67	4	Bournemouth	19 Jun
25.1 w	2.3	Jane Low		26.08.60	3	Aberdeen	24 Jul

Additional Under 17

Mark	Wind	Name	DOB/Mark	Pos	Venue	Date
25.3		Sarah Cootes	3.11.78	3	Braintree	8 May
25.3		Laura Seston	(25.34)	1	Ipswich	14 May
25.3		Rosalind Baker	10.04.78	1	Horsham	15 May
25.3		Sharon Hollett	26.12.78	2	Glasgow	4 Sep
25.3 w	5.5	Alison Stewart	19.01.78	3r2	Coatbridge	22 May
25.4		Susan Christie	7.03.79	1	Grangemouth	21 May
25.4		Jennifer Impett	18.11.77	1H	Exeter	25 Jun
25.5		Jane Murphy	17.12.77	1	Bebington	11 Jun
25.5		Julie Pratt	20.03.79	2	London (WF)	26 Jun
25.5		Joanne Colegate	24.11.77	1	Stoke	24 Jul
25.5		Claire Spurway	4.04.78	1	Yate	14 Aug
25.5		Syrena Pinel	13.01.79	2	Yate	14 Aug

Additional Under 15 (1 - 8 above)

Mark	Wind	Name	DOB/Mark	Pos	Venue	Date
25.37 w	2.1	Lindsay Impett	4.01.80	3s2	Telford	9 Jul
25.40 w	2.1	Lindsay Fleet	1.06.81	4s3	Telford	9 Jul
(10)						
25.4		Ayeesha Charles	(24.90w)	1	Kingston	23 Apr
25.42 w		Karen Gear	30.09.79	2	London (CP)	29 May
25.63	-0.4			1h3	Telford	8 Jul
25.46 w	2.6	Tracy Martin	4.04.80	3s2	Telford	9 Jul
25.63	1.7			2	Solihull	29 May
25.52	-0.1	Helen Roscoe	4.12.79	1h4	Birmingham	31 Jul
25.52	1.9	Jennifer Meadows	17.04.81	1h3	Hull	21 Aug
25.57 w	2.6	Dominique Coldwell	6.09.79	5s2	Telford	9 Jul
25.58	-0.4	Ruth Watson	29.11.79	1h6	Telford	8 Jul
25.62	1.7	Lois Cresswell	12.01.81	1	Solihull	29 May
25.63	-0.4	Karen Gear	30.09.79	1h3	Telford	8 Jul
25.63 w	2.7	Elizabeth Alder	20.11.80	5s1	Telford	9 Jul

Under 13

26.5		Naomi Taplin		18.12.81	1	Southampton	29	May
26.5		Stefanie Oates		19.11.81	1	Oldham	10	Jul
26.6		Serena Woodhouse		20.10.81	1	Mansfield	4	Sep
26.7	2.0	Sarah Zawada		9.04.82	3	Portsmouth	11	Jun
26.8		Cheryl Gibbons		21.09.81	2	Oldham	10	Jul
26.8		Nicola Lapczuk		18.11.82	1	Sutton Coldfield	27	Aug
26.8		Andrea Lang		6.03.82	1	Livingston	4	Sep
27.1		Stacy Hilling		11.09.81	2r1	Carn Brea	4	Jun
27.1		Hannah Wood		17.11.81	2	Sutton Coldfield	27	Aug
27.2	2.9	Wendy Thomson		28.06.82	1	Glasgow	18	Jun
		27.46 1.7			2	Grangemouth	10	Jul
	(10)							
27.4		Allie Lindsay			1	Birmingham	2	Jul
27.5	1.9	Lynn Davidson		13.12.81	2h1	Glasgow	18	Jun
27.5	2.8	Gemma Hair		3.11.81	1	Inverness	7	Aug
27.6		Isla Ross		26.12.81	2	Livingston	12	Jun
27.6		Rebecca Bates		16.05.82	1	Stoke	Jul	

300 METRES

37.06	Sally Gunnell		29.07.66	3	Edinburgh	8	Jul
37.33	Melanie Neef		26.05.70	5	Edinburgh	8	Jul
37.47	Phylis Smith		29.09.65	7	Edinburgh	8	Jul
38.42	Tracy Goddard		29.11.69	8	Edinburgh	8	Jul
38.7	Elaine Wyard/Sutcliffe		6.04.70	1	Gateshead	3	Sep
38.71	Lesley Owusu	U17	21.12.78	1	Birmingham	30	Jul
38.9	Gillian Archard/Cashell		5.04.64	1	Basingstoke	21	Aug
39.17 i	Geraldine McLeod		24.09.71	1	Birmingham	2	Jan
39.43	Lucy Chaffe	U17	25.03.79	2	Aberdeen	16	Jul
39.57	Suzanne McGowan	U17	13.04.78	3	Aberdeen	16	Jul

Additional Under 17 (1 - 3 above)

40.10	Sharon Hollett		26.12.78	4	Aberdeen	16	Jul
40.10	Elizabeth Walker		30.05.79	3	Birmingham	30	Jul
40.4	Sarah Cootes		3.11.78	3	London (CP)	29	May
	40.58			5	Birmingham	30	Jul
40.55	Rosalind Baker		10.04.78	1h1	London (CP)	28	May
40.56	Nina Rogers		19.09.78	3	Telford	9	Jul
40.70	Nicola Youden		2.11.77	6	Birmingham	30	Jul
40.8	Vicky Pincott		27.05.78	2	Horsham	14	May
	(10)						
40.8	Simone Harrison		2.09.77	1	Hoo	18	Jun
	40.94			7	Birmingham	30	Jul
40.86	Lucy Parsons		10.02.79	1	Colwyn Bay	2	Jul
41.0	Joanne Colegate		24.11.77	1r2	Leicester	16	Jul
41.0	Michelle John		13.04.78	1	Yeovil	24	Jul
	41.02			7	Aberdeen	16	Jul
41.02	Nicola Aitken		18.12.78	3h2	London (CP)	28	May
41.1	Emma Hall		10.08.78	1	Yeovil	18	Jun
41.1	Lorna Rice		10.01.79	1	Sutton Coldfield	27	Aug
41.20 i	Ruth Nicholson		23.09.77	1	Birmingham	13	Feb
41.2	Kelly Patterson		19.12.78	2	Hoo	18	Jun
41.27	Claire Everett		25.06.79	5s2	Birmingham	30	Jul
	(20)						
41.28	Susan Mary Douglas		3.11.77	1	Belfast	21	Aug
41.4	Patricia Weiss		24.12.77	1	Cleckheaton	7	Aug
41.43	Lisa Potrac		1.02.79	5s2	Telford	8	Jul
41.45	Rebecca Forster		2.10.77	5s1	Telford	8	Jul
41.5	Emily Grennan		8.06.78	1	Warley	15	May
41.5	Andrea Bullock		1.03.78	4h2	Telford	8	Jul
41.5	Leigh Newton		13.01.78	2	Bolton	17	Jul
41.5	Lucy Carter		7.03.78	1	Peterborough	31	Jul
41.51	Claire Phillips		2.04.78	6s1	Telford	8	Jul

400 METRES

51.04	Sally Gunnell		29.07.66	1	Gateshead	20 Jul
	51.72 i			1	Sindelfingen, GER	6 Mar
	51.92			1r3	Schwechat, AUT	29 May
	52.34 i			1	Glasgow	12 Feb
	52.84 i			1	Birmingham	26 Feb
	Note also 3 hurdle times would qualify as leading performances !					
51.30	Phylis Smith		29.09.65	3	Helsinki, FIN	11 Aug
	51.36			4	London (CP)	11 Sep
	51.46			4	Victoria, CAN	23 Aug
	51.53			7	Lausanne, SWZ	6 Jul
	51.7			1r1	Stretford	18 Jun
	51.79			4	Gateshead	20 Jul
	51.87			1h1	Helsinki, FIN	8 Aug
	51.90			3s2	Helsinki, FIN	9 Aug
	52.09			6	Sheffield	4 Sep
	52.31			2s2	Victoria, CAN	22 Aug
	52.83			1h3	Victoria, CAN	22 Aug
	52.90			5	Gateshead	1 Jul
	52.90			1	Bedford	17 Sep
52.09	Melanie Neef		26.05.70	6	Victoria, CAN	23 Aug
	52.10			6	Helsinki, FIN	11 Aug
	52.23			5	Gateshead	20 Jul
	52.43			2	Birmingham	25 Jun
	52.44			3h2	Helsinki, FIN	8 Aug
	52.53			7	London (CP)	15 Jul
	52.55			4s1	Helsinki, FIN	9 Aug
	52.56			1	Sheffield	12 Jun
	52.75			3s1	Victoria, CAN	22 Aug
	52.91 i			1	Glasgow	29 Jan
	53.21			3h4	Victoria, CAN	22 Aug
	53.85 i			1	Glasgow	15 Jan
	53.96			1h3	Sheffield	11 Jun
	53.98 i			1	Glasgow	23 Jan
52.95	Linda Keough		26.12.63	6h3	Helsinki, FIN	8 Aug
	53.40			2	Nitra, SVK	13 Jul
	53.4			1mx	Horsham	31 Jul
	53.42			1	Victoria, CAN	19 Aug
	53.6			1	London (WL)	20 Jul
	53.63			6s1	Helsinki, FIN	9 Aug
	53.7			1	Salisbury	10 Jul
53.0	Sandra Douglas		22.04.67	2r1	Stretford	18 Jun
	53.34			1	Wrexham	3 Jul
	53.78			3	Sheffield	12 Jun
53.44	Donna Fraser	U23	7.11.72	3	Nitra, SVK	13 Jul
	53.75			3	Wrexham	3 Jul
	53.87			7	Gateshead	20 Jul
53.53	Janet Levermore		7.06.69	2	Wrexham	3 Jul
	53.92			4	Sheffield	12 Jun
53.55	Tracy Goddard		29.11.69	4h4	Victoria, CAN	22 Aug
	53.59			2	Sheffield	12 Jun
	53.72 i			3	Birmingham	26 Feb
	53.84			7s1	Victoria, CAN	22 Aug
	53.93			1	Corby	30 May
	53.99			1h1	Sheffield	11 Jun
53.76	Nicola Crowther		15.05.70	4	Wrexham	3 Jul
53.9	Georgina Oladapo		15.05.67	1	Feltham	13 Aug
	(10)					
53.91	Stephanie McCann		26.10.65	4h3	Victoria, CAN	22 Aug
	53.96			6s2	Victoria, CAN	22 Aug
	54.0			1	Antrim	18 Jun

248

53.98	Sue Earnshaw		13.10.70	1	Bedford	18 Sep
54.0	Katharine Merry	U23	21.09.74	1	Leamington	14 May

60 performances to 54.0 by 13 athletes including 7 indoors

54.02	Paula Cohen		5.02.71	1	Derby	16 Jul
54.05	Claire Raven	U23	15.06.72	1	London (CP)	2 May
54.15	Sonya Bowyer	U23	18.09.72	2	London (CP)	2 May
54.27	Louretta Thorne	U20	6.05.77	1	London (He)	27 Aug
54.35	Gillian Archard/Cashell		5.04.64	3	Corby	30 May
54.49	Alanna Cooke		11.01.70	4	Corby	30 May
54.62	Hayley Clements		17.09.68	1	London (CP)	26 Jun
(20)						
54.70	Dawn Gandy		28.07.65	1h1	London (CP)	25 Jun
54.7	Kelly Holmes		19.04.70	1	Bracknell	19 Jun
54.76	Leigh Ferrier	U23	15.08.72	2	Bulle, SWZ	10 Sep
54.77	Stephanie McPeake/Llewellyn		31.12.68	1	Crawley	28 May
54.78 i	Allison Curbishley	U20	3.06.76	1	Birmingham	13 Feb
55.93				1h2	Telford	8 Jul
54.81	Karen Mills	U23	24.10.73	2	Dublin, IRE	23 Jul
55.0	Clare Bleasdale		6.07.71	2mx	Horsham	31 Jul
55.44				2	Bracknell	2 May
55.02	Elaine Wyard/Sutcliffe		6.04.70	2	Derby	16 Jul
55.11	Vicky Day	U23	19.06.72	2h1	London (CP)	25 Jun
55.12	Jo Sloane	U20	2.12.76	2	Bedford	3 Jul
(30)						
55.30	Rachel Newcombe		25.02.67	5	Wrexham	3 Jul
55.3	Sandra Leigh		26.02.66	1	Harrow	21 Aug
55.57				1h2	London (CP)	25 Jun
55.33	Alison Thorne	U23	25.09.72	3	London (CP)	2 May
55.34	Paula Fryer		14.07.69	1	Sheffield	14 May
55.4	Denise Facey		8.02.69	1	Croydon	8 May
55.42				2	Sheffield	14 May
55.4	Geraldine McLeod		24.09.71	1r1	Bournemouth	19 Jun
55.88 i				1h2	Birmingham	7 Jan
55.43	Wendy Steele		7.01.66	2	Edinburgh	14 May
55.46	Tanya Blake		16.01.71	1	Hot Springs, USA	7 Apr
55.50	Veronica Boden	V35	23.12.58	4	Derby	16 Jul
55.5	Joanna Latimer		30.01.71	1r2	Stretford	18 Jun
(40)						
55.53	Kim Goodwin		16.05.70	5	Derby	16 Jul
55.55	¶Diane Modahl		17.06.66	2	Birmingham	21 May
55.56	Pauline Richards		30.06.68	2	Stoke	16 Jul
55.6	Dawn Flockhart		16.05.67	1	Stoke	31 Jul
55.6	Michelle Pierre	U23	30.09.73	1	Corby	31 Jul
55.61				4	London (CP)	2 May
55.68	Stacey Jacques	U20	24.06.77	2	Hull	21 Aug
55.74	Joanna Clark	U23	11.02.73	4h1	Sheffield	11 Jun
55.78	Julie Forester		4.05.69	7h2	Sheffield	11 Jun
55.8	Dyanna Clarke	V35	27.02.58	2	Hoo	19 Jun
56.39				1h3	London (CP)	25 Jun
55.81	Katharine Reeves	U23	2.03.73	3h1	London (CP)	25 Jun
(50)						
55.83	Michelle Thomas		16.10.71	2	Bedford	17 Sep
55.89	Emma Langston/Clapson		22.11.71	3	Bedford	18 Sep
55.96	Susan Hendry	U20	30.06.76	2h1	Bedford	2 Jul
56.0	Gowry Retchakan		21.06.60	2	Croydon	8 May
56.0	Pat Divine		21.10.67	2r2	Stretford	18 Jun
56.0	Suzanne Stanton		3.02.62	1	London (CP)	13 Aug
56.03	Edwina Gates		26.06.66	3	Bracknell	2 May
56.1	Katharine Eustace	U20	16.04.75	3	Salisbury	10 Jul
56.14				1	Birmingham	24 Apr
56.11	Lisa Vannet	U23	8.11.74	2	Edinburgh	24 Jun

56.13 i	Natasha Bartlett	U23	19.01.74	2	Birmingham	26	Feb
(60)							
56.20	Lorraine Bell	U20	21.06.77	1	Grangemouth	9	Jul
56.2	Alyson Evans/Layzell		16.12.66	1	Rugby	14	Aug
56.3	Sarah Stevenson	U23	31.12.73	1	Nottingham	14	May
56.3	Nikki Lamb		15.02.69	2	Croydon	14	May
56.3	Jennie Sprott		24.07.68	2	London (Elt)	29	Aug
56.72				2h3	London (CP)	25	Jun
56.39	Elizabeth Williams	U20	2.06.77	2h2	Bedford	2	Jul
56.4	Cathy White/Dawson		9.03.66	2	Enfield	14	May
56.4	Elaine Viney		20.12.71	3	Wigan	7	Aug
56.69				4h1	London (CP)	25	Jun
56.4	Louise Brunning	U23	6.03.72	3	London (Elt)	29	Aug
56.5	Jenny Pearson		3.07.62	3	Hoo	19	Jun
(70)							
56.5	Jillian Reynolds		17.12.70	1	Aldershot	24	Jul
56.5	Louise Whitehead	U20	26.03.75	1	Bolton	13	Aug
57.36 i				2h3	Birmingham	31	Dec
56.6	Lucy Chaffe	U17	25.03.79	1	Telford	24	Jul
56.70 i	Maureen Barnes		21.04.63	2h2	Birmingham	31	Dec
57.2				1	Brighton	4	Jun
56.7	Julie Moore	U23	5.12.73	1	Douglas, IOM	5	Sep
57.21				1	London (CP)	30	Apr
56.79	Gillian McIntyre		6.11.64	1	Glasgow	14	May
56.8	Clare Hill	U20	14.12.76	1	Antrim	28	May
57.16				4h2	Bedford	2	Jul
56.8	Lynne Robinson		21.06.69	1	Leicester	3	Sep
56.9	Marcia Richardson	U23	10.02.72	2	Bracknell	19	Jun
56.94	Rosie Bagwell/Thorner		7.08.67	3h2	Stoke	16	Jul
(80)							
56.95	Nicola Davies	U20	25.11.75	3	Oordegem, BEL	9	Jul
57.0	Helen Parsons	U17	6.01.78	1	Reading	7	May
57.0	Vickie Lawrence	U23	9.06.73	1	Blackpool	19	Jun
57.0	Heather Myers		5.12.64	1r2	Aldershot	7	Aug
57.0	Kate Bullen		12.02.71	1	Wyndley	27	Aug
57.42 i				3h1	Birmingham	31	Dec
57.04	Kathryn Saunders	U20	21.08.77	1	London (CP)	29	May
57.14 i	Vyvyan Rhodes	U23	5.05.73	1h1	Birmingham	7	Jan
57.14	Sharon Tunaley		2.09.68	3h1	Stoke	16	Jul
57.20 i	Kelly Woods	U20	28.05.75	3	Birmingham	13	Feb
57.2	Jeina Mitchell	U20	21.01.75	1	London (CP)	2	Jun
(90)							
57.2	Mary Kitson		2.04.63	1	Luton	3	Sep
57.2	Julie Swann		15.07.62	3r1	Derby	11	Sep
57.25 i	Georgina Honley		12.01.67	2h2	Birmingham	7	Jan
57.30 i	Mary Anderson		2.09.67	2	Glasgow	15	Jan
57.4				2r2	Grangemouth	7	May
57.3	Judy Thomas		20.01.63	h	Leamington	14	May
57.3	Sue Briggs		26.03.67	4	Kingston	31	Jul
57.37	Ruth Nicholson	U17	23.09.77	7	Nicosia, CYP	17	May
57.39	Jayne Mallows		6.07.70	1	Loughborough	7	Sep
57.4	Helen Daniel		24.10.63	2	London (Elt)	1	May
57.4	Jayne Puckeridge		23.10.71	1	Swansea	8	May
(100)							
57.4	Katherine Morris	U20	5.09.75	2	Cleckheaton	7	Aug
57.4	Claire Haslam		18.12.63	1	London (Nh)	4	Sep
57.54				6	Bedford	17	Sep
57.43	Coral Davis		15.05.61	4	Bracknell	2	May
57.5	Karen Manuel	U20	2.11.75	4r1	Bournemouth	19	Jun

After drugs disqualification

53.52	¶Diane Modahl	17.06.66	2	Victoria, CAN	19 Aug

Additional Under 17 (1 - 3 above)

57.62	Vicky Pincott	27.05.78	2	London (He)	7 Aug
57.7	Suzanne McGowan	13.04.78	1	Grangemouth	1 Jun
57.9	Lesley Owusu	21.12.78	1	Windsor	3 Sep
58.4	Zoe Peatfield	8.12.77	1	Stretford	10 May
58.51	Lorna Scott	27.07.78	2	Antrim	28 Jun
58.64 i	Nicola Youden	2.11.77	2	Glasgow	23 Jan
58.8	Cecily Hall	12.10.78	2	Ilford	4 Jun
(10)					
58.8	Rebecca Lovett	11.05.78	1r2	Kingston	13 Aug
58.86	Jaclyn Anderson	23.03.79	2	Edinburgh	4 Sep
58.9	Emma Davies	9.10.78	1	Peterborough	23 Apr
58.9	Lisa Potrac	1.02.79	1	Stretford	12 Jun
59.0	Nicola Aitken	18.12.78	2	Bedford	21 May

600 METRES

1:28.9 e+	Ann Griffiths	20.08.65	4m	Helsinki, FIN	10 Aug
1:30.7	Alyson Evans/Layzell	16.12.66	1	Cheltenham	6 Jul
1:33.5	Paula Fryer	14.07.69	1	Sheffield	20 Mar
Under 13					
1:37.5	Hannah Wood	17.11.81	1	Solihull	17 Jul
1:38.9	Emma Ward	2.01.82	2	Solihull	17 Jul
1:43.6	Belinda Hardweir	22.10.81	1	London (Nh)	15 May
1:44.0	Hazel Connell	8.02.82	1r1	Liverpool	1 May
1:44.1	Catherine Riley	4.06.82	1	Gateshead	3 Sep
1:44.6	Cheryl Gibbons	21.09.81	2r1	Kirkby	5 Jun
1:44.7	Ellen Fowler	5.10.81	1r2	Solihull	17 Jul
1:44.8	Gemma Fensome	9.02.82	1	London (He)	1 May
1:45.06	Louise Whittaker	29.11.82	2r1	Birmingham	11 Sep
1:45.08	Maria Hardiman	16.11.81	3r1	Birmingham	11 Sep
(10)					
1:45.5	Ellie Yavari	15.09.81	1r1	Wakefield	17 Jul
1:45.5	Lorna King	22.01.83	1	Wrexham	30 Jul
1:45.53	Danielle Hock	18.02.82	4r1	Birmingham	11 Sep
1:45.66	Rebecca Heathcote		5r1	Birmingham	11 Sep
1:45.7	Nikki Daniels	25.08.82	1r2	Stoke	4 Jun
1:46.0	Clare Booker	12.12.81	2r2	Solihull	17 Jul
1:46.3	Rebecca Williams	13.02.82	1	London (Elt)	19 Jun
1:46.5	Kate Elder	4.04.82	1r1	Carlisle	17 Jul

800 METRES

1:59.43	Kelly Holmes	19.04.70	1	London (CP)	15 Jul
	1:59.92		2	Madrid, SPA	6 Sep
	2:00.48		2	Helsinki, FIN	29 Jun
	2:00.63		1	Khania, GRE	5 Jun
	2:01.56		1	Sheffield	4 Sep
	2:01.80		3	Gateshead	1 Jul
	2:03.3		1	Enfield	14 May
1:59.81	Ann Griffiths	20.08.65	5	Helsinki, FIN	10 Aug
	2:01.29		3s1	Helsinki, FIN	8 Aug
	2:01.67		5	London (CP)	15 Jul
	2:01.86		4	Gateshead	1 Jul
	2:02.42		7h2	Helsinki, FIN	7 Aug
	2:03.49		1	Loughborough	5 Jun
2:01.13	¶Diane Modahl	17.06.66	4	Hengelo, HOL	4 Jun
	2:01.35		1	Sheffield	12 Jun
	2:02.62 i		3	Stockholm, SWE	8 Mar
	2:03.7		1r1	Manchester	18 May

2:02.30	Sonya Bowyer	U23	18.09.72	5	Gateshead	1	Jul
2:02.92				7	London (CP)	15	Jul
2:03.18				2	Gateshead	20	Jul
2:03.79				3	Sheffield	12	Jun
2:03.17	Cathy White/Dawson		9.03.66	4	Victoria, CAN	26	Aug
2:03.20				5	Sheffield	4	Sep
2:03.39				3	Gateshead	20	Jul
2:03.81				3h3	Victoria, CAN	24	Aug
2:03.83				2	Seville, SPA	5	Jun
2:03.27	Joanna Latimer		30.01.71	12	Helsinki, FIN	29	Jun
2:03.54	Lynn Gibson		6.07.69	1	Wrexham	3	Jul
2:03.67	Angela Davies		21.10.70	1	Solihull	21	Aug
2:04.0				1	Loughborough	22	Jun
2:03.69	Linda Keough		26.12.63	8	Moscow,RUS	5	Jun
2:03.75	Dawn Gandy		28.07.65	2	Sheffield	12	Jun
2:03.85				4	Narbonne, FRA	19	Jun
	(10)						
2:03.78	Tanya Blake		16.01.71	4	Walnut, USA	17	Apr
34 performances to 2:04.0 by 11 athletes including 1 indoors							
2:04.32	Helen Daniel		24.10.63	4	Sheffield	12	Jun
2:04.50	Abigail Hunte		12.05.71	2	Fairfax, USA	22	May
2:04.69	Vickie Lawrence	U23	9.06.73	4	Ostrava, CS	30	Jul
2:04.7 mx	Lynne Robinson		21.06.69	1	Solihull	6	Jul
2:05.59				1	Corby	30	May
2:04.84	Alyson Evans/Layzell		16.12.66	4	Wrexham	3	Jul
2:05.0	Bev Hartigan		10.06.67	2	Cork, IRE	25	Jun
2:05.09	Paula Fryer		14.07.69	5	Wrexham	3	Jul
2:05.38	Michelle Faherty		10.08.68	5	Sheffield	12	Jun
2:05.60 i	Kirsty Wade		6.08.62	1	Birmingham	19	Feb
	(20)						
2:05.69	Mary McClung		19.02.71	2	Tuscaloosa, USA	23	Apr
2:05.85	Jeina Mitchell	U20	21.01.75	1	Bedford	3	Jul
2:06.0	Mary Kitson		2.04.63	1	Loughborough	7	Sep
2:06.17	Natalie Tait	U23	24.08.72	3	Solihull	21	Aug
2:06.5	Sue Parker		24.03.70	4	Loughborough	5	Jun
2:06.67	Dorothea Lee	U20	28.07.77	4	Solihull	21	Aug
2:06.7	Jillian Jones		23.12.69	1	Southampton	12	Jul
2:06.9 mx	Lisa Thompson		12.07.62	2	Barn Elms	13	Jul
2:07.38				8	Solihull	21	Aug
2:07.02	Michelle Harries	U23	4.01.72	5	Solihull	21	Aug
2:07.26	Alison Wyeth		26.05.64	2	Bedford	18	Sep
	(30)						
2:07.3	Mary Anderson		2.09.67	2r1	Stretford	18	Jun
2:07.3	Maxine Newman		15.12.70	2	Cheltenham	20	Jul
2:07.43	Sandra Leigh		26.02.66	3	Corby	30	May
2:07.45	Lynn Taylor		5.08.67	5	Brussels, BEL	17	Jul
2:07.6	Catherine Allsopp	U23	30.11.73	8	Cork, IRE	25	Jun
2:07.94	Julie Swann		15.07.62	4	Corby	30	May
2:08.1	Debbie Gunning		31.08.65	1	Salisbury	15	May
2:08.14	Sue Bevan		15.12.59	8r2	Vienna, AUT	29	May
2:08.39	Lesley Mallows	U23	27.04.73	9	Solihull	21	Aug
2:08.5	Phylis Smith		29.09.65	2	Stretford	26	Apr
	(40)						
2:08.54	Jayne Spark		16.09.70	6	Corby	30	May
2:08.6	Caroline Slimin		27.08.65	2	Salisbury	10	Jul
2:08.6	Michelle Wilkinson	U23	1.01.73	4	Loughborough	7	Sep
2:08.7	Catherine Gowland/Rawnsley-Pemberton	V35	22.08.59	5	Loughborough	7	Sep
2:08.79	Alison Parry		19.06.66	4	Istanbul, TUR	21	May
2:08.9	Jacqui Parker		15.10.66	1	Perth, AUS	16	Jan
2:09.14	Tanya Baker	U23	23.11.74	1	Columbia, USA	8	May
2:09.36	Wendy Williams		9.02.68	4	Bracknell	2	May

2:09.5	Amanda Thorpe		21.07.71	2	Stretford	31	May
2:09.5 mx	Sue Morley	V35	11.10.57		Brighton	10	Aug
(50)							
2:09.68	Gillian Archard/Cashell		5.04.64	3	Bedford	18	Sep
2:09.7	Lisa Carthew		6.04.71		Cardiff	3	Aug
2:09.8	Laura Adam		28.02.65	2	Bromley	19	Jun
2:09.87	Carol-Ann Gray		7.04.64	3	Edinburgh	8	Jul
2:10.0	Janet Holt	V35	10.10.56	3r1	Stretford	18	Jun
2:10.2	Sarah Bentley		21.05.67	2	Stoke	24	Jul
2:10.3	Suzanne Stanton		3.02.62	1	Wigan	7	Aug
2:10.4	Veronica Boden	V35	23.12.58	2r2	Stretford	18	Jun
2:10.5	Rhonda MacPhee	U20	30.04.76	2	Hoo	16	Jul
2:10.54	Rachel Jordan	U23	29.01.72	5	Bulle, SWZ	10	Sep
(60)							
2:10.66	Amanda Pritchard	U15	18.03.80	1	London (CP)	15	Jul
2:10.9	Lorraine Baker/Strain		9.04.64	2r2	Manchester	18	May
2:10.9	Angela Coates		2.04.67	1	Stretford	21	Jun
2:11.05	Sheila Gollan		18.07.64	3	London (He)	18	Aug
2:11.1	Sarah Bull	U20	4.06.75	1	Sheffield	19	Jun
2:11.19	Karen Johns	U15	18.08.80	2	London (CP)	15	Jul
2:11.2 mx	Jane Groves	U20	17.05.77	1	Stretford	2	Aug
2:11.22	Sharon King	U23	27.01.72	2h2	Derby	16	Jul
2:11.4	Sarah Salmon	U23	9.09.74	3	Exeter	8	Aug
2:11.5	Alison Potts	U23	15.10.74	4r1	Stretford	18	Jun
(70)							
2:11.51	Sally Entwistle	U23	27.09.73	8	Loughborough	5	Jun
2:11.59	Jenny Harnett	U20	11.03.76	5	Bedford	3	Jul
2:11.6	Julie Skinner	U23	6.08.72	1	London (Nh)	15	May
2:11.7	Wendy Farrow		25.12.71	4	Stoke	24	Jul
2:11.7	Jo Davis	U23	20.09.73	4	Exeter	8	Aug
2:11.84	Corinne Munt		25.07.63	4h3	London (CP)	25	Jun
2:11.90	Kathryn Bright	U20	27.03.76	6	Oordegem, BEL	9	Jul
2:11.9	Jane Ewing		22.10.69	4	London (WF)	6	Aug
2:11.94 i	Amanda Crowe	U23	21.10.73	1r2	Birmingham	26	Feb
2:12.0	Sarah Simmons	U20	12.01.75	2	Swansea	8	May
(80)							
2:12.10	Hayley Parkinson	U20	5.12.75	6	Bedford	3	Jul
2:12.2	Helen Parsons	U17	6.01.78	1	Horsham	15	May
2:12.2	Tanya Blake	U23	16.06.73	3	Bromley	19	Jun
2:12.2	Julie Stacey	U23	15.11.72	1	London (WF)	3	Sep
2:12.27	Jayne Puckeridge		23.10.71	6	London (CP)	26	Jun
2:12.3	Sarah Wells		11.08.69	2	Horsham	15	May
2:12.37	Julie Hitchmough	U23	1.06.74	4	London (CP)	2	May
2:12.37	Clare Duncan	U17	22.08.79	1	Gateshead	29	May
2:12.38	Vicki Andrews		31.08.69	4	London (He)	18	Aug
2:12.4	Helen Pattinson	U23	2.01.74	2	Blackpool	14	May
(90)							
2:12.45	Charlotte Goff	U20	6.07.77	2	Telford	9	Jul
2:12.5	Elizabeth Garraghan		25.01.67	2	London (Nh)	15	May
2:12.5	Amanda Tremble	U20	2.11.76	1	Jarrow	12	Jun

After drugs disqualification

1:59.85	¶Diane Modahl		17.06.66	4	St. Petersburg, RUS	28	Jul
2:00.50				dq(2)	Lisbon, POR	18	Jun
2:00.50				3	London (CP)	15	Jul
2:00.84				3	Lille, FRA	8	Jul
2:02.18				6s2	Helsinki, FIN	8	Aug
2:02.81				1	Birmingham	25	Jun

Additional Under 17 (1 - 2 above)

2:12.57	Jade Himsworth	4.08.79	1	Aberdeen	16	Jul
2:12.6	Ellen O'Hare	4.02.78	1	Cheltenham	13	Jul
2:13.04	Hannah Curnock	16.04.78	5	Nicosia, CYP	20	May
2:13.36	Rachael Ogden	23.07.79	1	Telford	9	Jul
2:13.6	Philippa McCrea	1.03.78	2	Jarrow	13	Jul
2:13.65	Jennifer Ward	22.09.78	1	Dublin, IRE	13	Aug
2:14.23	Lucy Pringle	3.08.78	2	Birmingham	31	Jul
2:14.26	Rebecca Lovett	11.05.78	2	London (CP)	29	May
	(10)					
2:14.91	Emma Davies	9.10.78	1	Solihull	21	Aug
2:16.10	Kate Doherty	23.07.79	2	Solihull	29	May
2:16.12	Olivia Hills	7.03.79	1	Sheffield	2	Jul
2:16.13	Hayley Whitehead	14.05.79	3h1	Birmingham	31	Jul
2:16.21	Lois Joslin	1.03.79	4	London (CP)	29	May

Under 15 (1 - 2 above)

2:13.32	Laura McCabe	24.01.80	3	London (CP)	15	Jul
2:14.64	Emma Alberts	22.11.79	4	London (CP)	15	Jul
2:16.0	Georgie Salmon	1.11.79	6	Cheltenham	24	Jul
2:16.28	Emily Hathaway	22.12.79	3	Telford	9	Jul
2:16.5	Simone Hardy	9.11.79	2	Solihull	29	May
2:16.59	Carean Vernon	2.06.80	5	London (CP)	15	Jul
2:16.61	Sarah Fensome	28.09.79	2h1	Birmingham	30	Jul
2:16.70	Amanda O'Shea	8.09.79	1	London (CP)	29	May
	(10)					
2:16.7	Jessica Woolley	26.01.80	4	Birmingham	30	Jul
2:16.79	Becky Williams	1.10.80	4	Telford	9	Jul
2:16.80	Jennifer Meadows	17.04.81	2h1	Telford	8	Jul
2:17.0	Laura Hale	21.01.80	4	Solihull	29	May
2:17.30 i	Sarah Mead	16.10.79	3	Birmingham	27	Feb
2:18.01			7	Aberdeen	16	Jul

Under 13

2:22.9	Hannah Wood	17.11.81	1	Yate	14	Aug
2:23.4	Suzanne Hasler	7.04.82		Sutton Coldfield	24	Jul
2:23.7	Amanda Child	28.11.81	1	Watford	27	Jul
2:23.9	Emma Ward	2.01.82	1	Stoke	14	May
2:24.7	Belinda Hardweir	22.10.81	1r1	Aldershot	16	Jul
2:24.7	Nikki Daniels	25.08.82	1r2	Coventry	14	Aug
2:25.7	Gemma Mounsey	17.07.82	1	Carmarthen	7	Aug
2:25.8	Isla Ross	26.12.81	1	Inverness	5	Jun
2:26.1	Nicola Sallis	4.12.81	1	Brighton		May
2:26.5	Debbie Hadfield	14.07.82	1	Carlisle	10	Jul
	(10)					
2:26.9	Eva Kennerley	15.10.81	1	Gateshead	9	Jul
2:27.7	Rebecca Conway	4.11.81		London (WF)	15	Jun
2:27.8	Joanne Green		1	Leicester	11	Jun
2:28.01	Claire Couper	29.04.82	1	Grangemouth	10	Jul

1500 METRES

4:01.41	Kelly Holmes	19.04.70	1	Sheffield	12	Jun
	4:02.52		4	Stockholm, SWE	12	Jul
	4:06.48		2	Birmingham	26	Jun
	4:07.57		5	St. Petersburg, RUS	25	Jul
	4:07.7 mx		1	Aldershot	8	Jun
	4:08.86		1	Victoria, CAN	28	Aug
	4:09.27		3h2	Helsinki, FIN	12	Aug
	4:10.2		1	Enfield	15	May
	4:10.81		3	London (CP)	9	Sep
	4:12.51		2h1	Sheffield	11	Jun

4:01.44	Yvonne Murray		4.10.64	2	Sheffield	12	Jun
	4:03.64 +			2m	Oslo, NOR	22	Jul
	4:04.19			1	Gateshead	20	Jul
	4:12.47			1h1	Sheffield	11	Jun
4:04.19	Alison Wyeth		26.05.64	5	Nice, FRA	18	Jul
	4:05.65			8	Monaco, MON	2	Aug
	4:08.37			7	Lausanne, SWZ	6	Jul
	4:14.62			1	Crawley	28	May
	4:15.98			4	Granada, SPA	1	Jun
4:05.75	Lynn Gibson		6.07.69	3	Gateshead	20	Jul
	4:12.58			3	London (CP)	15	Jul
	4:13.89			10h1	Helsinki, FIN	12	Aug
	4:13.98			3h1	Sheffield	11	Jun
	4:14.08			8	Sheffield	12	Jun
	4:14.9			2r1	Manchester	18	May
4:08.71	Ann Griffiths		20.08.65	3	Sheffield	12	Jun
4:09.29	Angela Davies		21.10.70	5	Gateshead	20	Jul
	4:11.27			5	Sheffield	12	Jun
	4:12.09			6h2	Helsinki, FIN	12	Aug
	4:14.23			2	Wrexham	3	Jul
	4:15.1			3r1	Manchester	18	May
4:10.32	Lynne Robinson		21.06.69	3	Hechtel, BEL	30	Jul
	4:12.05			1	London (CP)	15	Jul
	4:13.6			1	Cheltenham	20	Jul
4:11.04	Bev Hartigan		10.06.67	4	Sheffield	12	Jun
	4:12.46			6	Gateshead	20	Jul
	4:13.19			4	London (CP)	15	Jul
	4:13.69			1	Wrexham	3	Jul
	4:14.6			1r1	Manchester	18	May
	4:15.71			1h2	Sheffield	11	Jun
	4:15.97			3	Granada, SPA	1	Jun
4:12.20	Sonia McGeorge		2.11.64	2	London (CP)	15	Jul
	4:14.80			2	Crawley	28	May
4:13.50	Debbie Gunning		31.08.65	7	Sheffield	12	Jun
	4:14.13			4h1	Sheffield	11	Jun
(10)							
4:14.62	Sue Parker		24.03.70	9	Sheffield	12	Jun
	4:15.42			5h1	Sheffield	11	Jun
	4:15.53			5	London (CP)	15	Jul
	48 performances to 4:16.0 by 11 athletes						
4:16.70	Maxine Newman		15.12.70	6h1	Sheffield	11	Jun
4:16.79	Michelle Faherty		10.08.68	6	London (CP)	15	Jul
4:18.61	Caroline Slimin		27.08.65	1	Solihull	21	Aug
4:19.70	Jayne Spark		16.09.70	6h2	Sheffield	11	Jun
4:19.7 mx	Amanda Thorpe		21.07.71		Stretford	21	Jun
	4:22.69			4	Corby	30	May
4:20.31	Laura Adam		28.02.65	1	Edinburgh	25	Jun
4:20.60	Wendy Ore		23.05.66	3	Solihull	21	Aug
4:21.36	Wendy Williams		9.02.68	6	Crawley	28	May
4:21.42 i	Una English		14.08.70	2	Vienna, AUT	6	Feb
(20)							
4:21.5	Sue Morley	V35	11.10.57	1	Crawley	20	Jul
4:21.62	Zahara Hyde		12.01.63	1	London (CP)	25	Jun
4:22.07	Jillian Jones		23.12.69	2	Corby	30	May
4:22.09	Joanne Symonds		19.02.68	7	Crawley	28	May
4:22.3	Sonya Bowyer	U23	18.09.72	1	Loughborough	22	Jun
4:22.32	Michelle Harries	U23	4.01.72	8h1	Sheffield	11	Jun
4:22.63	Jeina Mitchell	U20	21.01.75	5	Ostrava, CS	31	Jul
4:22.9	Sarah Bentley		21.05.67	2	Stretford	23	Aug
4:23.07	Lisa Carthew		6.04.71	4	Solihull	21	Aug
4:23.10	Elaine Foster		21.07.63	3	Loughborough	5	Jun

4:23.2	Sharon King	U23	27.01.72	8r1	Manchester	18 May
4:23.36	Jo Davis	U23	20.09.73	5	Solihull	21 Aug
4:23.5	Andrea Whitcombe		8.06.71	1	Enfield	31 Jul
4:23.75 i	Shirley Griffiths	U23	23.06.72	3	Birmingham	19 Feb
4:23.84	Paula Radcliffe	U23	17.12.73	1	Kings Lynn	9 Jul
4:24.2	Bronwyn Cardy-Wise	V40	26.01.52	1	Redditch	5 May
4:24.28	Helen Daniel		24.10.63	2	London (CP)	25 Jun
4:24.5	Sue Bevan		15.12.59	2	Enfield	31 Jul
4:24.6	Claire Forbes		25.03.71	2	Loughborough	22 Jun
4:24.62	Anna Moutrie/Wittekind		7.12.64	3	London (CP)	25 Jun
(40)						
4:24.71	Julie Skinner	U23	6.08.72	1	Bracknell	2 May
4:24.76	Teena Colebrook	V35	18.12.56	4	Walnut, USA	16 Apr
4:24.86	*Teresa Duffy*		*6.07.69*	*1*	*Belfast*	*4 Jun*
4:24.92	Carol-Ann Gray		7.04.64	6	Corby	30 May
4:25.13	Mary McClung		19.02.71	3	Atlanta, USA	21 May
4:25.30	Alison Barnes		6.11.69	10	Crawley	28 May
4:25.32	Liz Talbot	U23	5.12.74	4	Loughborough	7 Sep
4:25.38	Tanya Blake	U23	16.06.73	6	Loughborough	5 Jun
4:25.58	Catherine Berry	U20	8.10.75	2	Bedford	2 Jul
4:25.82	Wendy Farrow		25.12.71	7	Solihull	21 Aug
4:25.9	Diane Brockley		5.02.67	2	Stretford	10 May
(50)						
4:26.05 i	Kirsty Wade		6.08.62	2	Glasgow	12 Feb
4:26.07 i	Julie Swann		15.07.62	4	Birmingham	26 Feb
	4:28.38			7	Loughborough	7 Sep
4:26.07	Sarah Simmons	U20	12.01.75	9h2	Sheffield	11 Jun
4:26.5	Penny Thackray	U23	18.08.74	1	Sheffield	20 Jul
4:27.21	Mary Kitson		2.04.63	10	London (CP)	15 Jul
4:27.31	Nicky Slater	U20	11.01.77	2	Telford	9 Jul
4:27.46	Jill Bruce	U23	25.07.73	2	Belfast	4 Jun
4:27.5	Amanda Wright		14.07.68	2	Cheltenham	20 Jul
4:27.53	*Nnenna Lynch*		*3.07.71*	*1*	*London (CP)*	*2 May*
4:27.59	Tanya Blake		16.01.71	1	Fayetteville, USA	23 Apr
4:27.91	Amanda Tremble	U20	2.11.76	3	Bedford	2 Jul
(60)						
4:28.12	Janet Holt	V35	10.10.56	2	Derby	16 Jul
4:28.41	Sarah Salmon	U23	9.09.74	9	Solihull	21 Aug
4:28.5	Lisa Hollick		1.01.70	1	Watford	13 Jul
4:28.62 i	Esther Evans	U23	22.12.73	7	Birmingham	19 Feb
	4:31.92			2	London (CP)	2 May
4:29.74	Lorraine Baker/Strain		9.04.64	1	Birmingham	21 May
4:30.3	*Kate McCandless*		*22.06.70*	*3*	*Enfield*	*14 May*
4:30.34	Pauline Quinn		2.08.70	8	Dublin, IRE	23 Jul
4:30.4	Sarah Wallace	U23	31.05.73	4	Loughborough	25 May
4:30.52	Andrea Duke	U23	6.07.73	4	Derby	16 Jul
4:30.68	Sharon Dixon		22.04.68	9	Loughborough	5 Jun
4:31.0	Sally Young	V35	29.09.55	2	Hoo	4 Jun
(70)						
4:31.0	Clare Pauzers		2.08.62			
4:31.05	Dawn Adams	U17	19.10.78	1	Gateshead	28 May
4:31.1	Chaanah Fothergill	U23	22.02.72	2	Sheffield	20 Jul
4:31.2	Joanne Holden		20.02.65	1	Colchester	19 Jun
4:31.5	Julie Stacey	U23	15.11.72	1	Yate	21 Aug
4:31.5	Gabrielle Collison		10.02.66	1	Sutton	18 Sep
4:31.9	Ann Terek		22.09.64	1	Antrim	3 Sep
4:32.0	Alice Braham	U20	17.01.76	1	Yeovil	11 Jun
4:32.04	Catherine Gowland/Rawnsley-Pemberton		22.08.59	1r2	Hull	21 Aug
4:32.24	Mara Myers	U23	13.08.73	4	London (CP)	25 Jun
(80)						
4:32.6	Elinor Doubell		27.09.71	3	Croydon	8 May

LINFORD CHRISTIE. Rated number 1 in the world by those who know!

JOHN REGIS. The world's fastest time for 200m this year (at altitude).

ROGER BLACK. Is back!

DU'AINE LADEJO. A great rival for Roger and won the European Championship.

RICHARD NERURKAR. Britain's best Marathon runner who concentrates on championship races.

ROB DENMARK. Had an excellent season and ranks number 1 in both 5000m and 10000m in Britain.

TONY JARRETT. Still number 2 in Britain!

STEVE BACKLEY. Returned from injury to win the European and Commonwealth titles.

STEVE SMITH. Injury held back his outdoor season after a brilliant indoor start.

FRED SALLE. At last a long jumper worthy of mention.

PAULA THOMAS. Returned to her very best form. She is second on the left with her relay friends.

MELANIE NEEF. Six personal bests this year to move into the top three in Britain.

KELLY HOLMES. Top ranked in the U.K. for 800m and 1500m.

YVONNE MURRAY. Set a series of performances ending with Commonwealth gold at 10000m.

SALLY GUNNELL. Lost only once and won all the major titles.

KATE STAPLES. Another batch of British records in the Pole Vault.

ASHIA HANSEN. Set official and unofficial Triple Jump records.

DENISE LEWIS. A marvellous breakthrough to win Commonwealth gold in the
Heptathlon.

4:32.6	Jo Thompson	V35	30.10.58	2	Yate	29 Jun
4:32.67	Juliette Oldfield	U20	14.04.77	7	Nicosia, CYP	19 May
4:32.9	Susan Harrison		6.08.71	2	Leamington	14 May
4:32.9	Sheila Gollan		18.07.64	1	Stoke	31 Jul
4:33.1	Hayley Parkinson	U20	5.12.75	1	Inverness	5 Jun
4:33.14	Helen Pattinson	U23	2.01.74	2r2	Hull	21 Aug
4:33.64	Claire Swift	U20	17.10.76	2	Gateshead	29 May
4:33.68	Liz Francis		22.12.63	11	Solihull	21 Aug
4:33.8	Jane Ewing		22.10.69	2	Stretford	18 Jun

Additional Under 17 (1 above)

4:34.8	Caroline McNulty		3.12.77	3	Oxford	8 May
4:35.24	Justina Heslop		3.03.79	2	Gateshead	28 May
4:35.7	Hannah Curnock		16.04.78	6	Oxford	8 May
4:36.3 mx	Karen Montador		14.05.79	5	Grangemouth	1 Jun
4:42.67				2	Edinburgh	14 May
4:36.81	Ellen O'Hare		4.02.78	3	Telford	9 Jul
4:38.26	Jennifer Ward		22.09.78	1	Edinburgh	14 May
4:38.3	Clare Duncan		22.08.79	1	Liverpool	1 May
4:40.6	Andrea Kershaw		22.03.78	4	Stretford	21 Jun
4:40.69	Clare Thomas		26.08.79	4	Aberdeen	16 Jul
(10)						
4:41.12	Sheila Fairweather		24.11.77	5	Aberdeen	16 Jul
4:41.31	Carolyn Smith		3.10.77	3	Gateshead	28 May
4:41.7	Karen Nicol		1.11.77	2	Stretford	23 Aug
4:41.78	Vicky Robinson		17.10.77	1	Hull	21 Aug
4:42.02	Claire Demaine		6.09.78	5	Gateshead	28 May
4:42.1	Sonia Thomas		16.05.79	1	Gateshead	11 Jun
4:42.94	Anne Connolly		18.02.78	4	Telford	9 Jul
4:43.41	Carol Vettraino		16.10.77	3	Edinburgh	14 May
4:43.43	Katie Wallace		19.09.78	1	London (He)	7 Aug
4:43.6	Paula Whitney		21.03.79	6	Stretford	2 Aug
(10)						
4:44.1	Susan Pendrich		29.09.78	1	Hoo	11 Jun
4:44.88	Stacey Wallace		8.10.78	1	London (CP)	29 May
4:45.0	Jennifer Gibson		21.06.78	3	Stretford	10 May
4:45.04	Heather Carson		18.07.79	3	Hull	21 Aug
4:45.1	Lucy Hale		8.04.78	3	Cannock	26 Jun
4:45.1	Louise Rowe		8.11.78	3	Hornchurch	16 Jul
4:45.1	Rebecca McKenna		6.01.78	4	Birmingham	30 Jul
4:45.98	Kirsty Macaulay		26.04.78	2	London (He)	7 Aug

Under 15

4:36.4	Emma Alberts		22.11.79	1	Jarrow	11 Jun
4:40.75	Emma Deakin		3.03.80	2	Gateshead	29 May
4:41.40	Georgie Salmon		1.11.79	2	Birmingham	31 Jul
4:42.35	Michelle Whalley		1.10.80	2	Hull	21 Aug
4:43.30	Tommy Kemp		5.03.80	2	Telford	9 Jul
4:43.76	Katie Dennison		8.06.80	3	Birmingham	31 Jul
4:43.91	Carean Vernon		2.06.80	3	Telford	9 Jul
4:43.94	Caroline Walsh		29.04.80	4	Telford	9 Jul
4:44.0	Caroline Bell		14.07.80	1	Cannock	Apr
4:45.0	Amanda Pritchard		18.03.80		Swansea	20 Jul
(10)						
4:45.30	Jodie Swallow		23.06.81	6	Telford	9 Jul
4:45.3	Laura Hale		21.01.80	1	Cheltenham	11 Jun
4:45.6	Keri Myton		26.10.79	1	London (CP)	27 May
4:45.64	Kate Grimshaw		26.10.79	2h2	Telford	8 Jul
4:45.9	Jessica Woolley		26.01.80	9	Warley	3 Aug
4:46.8	Claire Kennedy		29.01.80	3	London (CP)	27 May

Under 13

4:56.3	Lisa Williams	29.12.81	2	Aldershot	16	Jul
5:01.2	Amanda Child	28.11.81	1	Watford	31	Aug
5:01.7	Emma Morris	6.11.81	1	Andover	30	May
5:01.9	Katie Brooks	17.02.82	1	St. Albans	19	Jun
5:01.9	Nicola Sallis	4.12.81	1	London (TB)	14	Aug
5:02.2	Emma Ward	2.01.82	1	Stoke	11	Sep
5:03.5	Sam Hunt	26.02.82	1	Exeter	24	Jul
5:03.8	Ellie Yavari	15.09.81	1	Bebington	17	May
5:05.0	Gemma Mounsey	17.07.82	1	Swansea	20	Jul
5:05.4	Harriet Dean	2.02.82		London (TB)	14	Aug
	(10)					
5:06.0	N. Grime		1	Oldham	10	Jul
5:06.0	Lorna King	22.01.83	1	Cheltenham	21	Aug
5:06.2	Elizabeth Wheeler	31.10.81	1	Solihull	18	Sep
5:06.3	Kate Elder	4.04.82		York	7	Aug
5:06.4	Ruth Gross		1	Stretford	15	May
5:06.4	Emma Rutland	9.10.81	1	Blackpool	11	Jun
5:06.7	Nichola Coates	24.03.82	1	Carlisle	28	May
5:07.0	Laura Tucker	11.05.82	1	Solihull	11	Sep
5:07.5	Louise Whittaker	29.11.82	1	Warrington	25	Jun
5:08.1	Gemma Viney	7.01.83	1	Crawley	20	Jul

1 MILE

4:22.64	Yvonne Murray	4.10.64	2	Oslo, NOR	22	Jul
	4:25.2 +		2	Edinburgh	8	Jul
	4:33.4 +e		1m	Helsinki, FIN	10	Aug
4:30.24	Alison Wyeth	26.05.64	6	Gateshead	1	Jul
	4:31.83		2	Cork, IRE	25	Jun
4:31.17	Lynn Gibson	6.07.69	8	Gateshead	1	Jul
4:31.26	Bev Hartigan	10.06.67	9	Gateshead	1	Jul
4:31.83	Angela Davies	21.10.70	10	Gateshead	1	Jul
4:33.12	Sonia McGeorge	2.11.64	11	Gateshead	1	Jul
4:37.67	Maxine Newman	15.12.70	4	Cork, IRE	25	Jun
4:37.82	Sue Parker	24.03.70	5	Cork, IRE	25	Jun
4:44.94	Amanda Thorpe	21.07.71	6	Cork, IRE	25	Jun
4:50.4	Wendy Farrow	25.12.71	1	Oxford	17	Sep

2000 METRES

5:26.93	Yvonne Murray	4.10.64	2	Edinburgh	8	Jul
	5:37.7 +		2m	London (CP)	15	Jul
	5:38.33		2	Sheffield	4	Sep
	5:41.57 +		1m	Helsinki, FIN	10	Aug
5:43.13	Alison Wyeth	26.05.64	3	Sheffield	4	Sep
	5:49.5 +		5m	London (CP)	15	Jul
5:54.72	Zahara Hyde	12.01.63	2	Victoria, CAN	19	Aug

3000 METRES

8:29.60	Yvonne Murray	4.10.64	2	London (CP)	15	Jul
	8:36.48		2	Helsinki, FIN	10	Aug
	8:54.46		1h2	Helsinki, FIN	7	Aug
	8:56.81		1	London (CP)	11	Sep
8:45.76	Alison Wyeth	26.05.64	6	Helsinki, FIN	10	Aug
	8:46.42		2	Helsinki, FIN	29	Jun
	8:47.98		3	Victoria, CAN	23	Aug
	8:51.34		7	London (CP)	15	Jul
	8:52.68		3h1	Helsinki, FIN	7	Aug
	8:54.9		1	Watford	14	Sep
	9:04.35 i		6	Paris, FRA	11	Mar
	9:06.80 i		1	Birmingham	26	Feb
	9:09.24 +		2	Berlin, GER	30	Aug

8:51.55	Sonia McGeorge		2.11.64	11	Helsinki, FIN	10 Aug
8:52.73				4h1	Helsinki, FIN	7 Aug
8:54.91				4	Victoria, CAN	23 Aug
8:55.47				3	Birmingham	25 Jun
8:59.55				5	Linz, AUT	4 Jul
9:00.98				5	Jena, GER	3 Jun
9:02.97				1	Gateshead	20 Jul
9:03.80				1	Sheffield	11 Jun
9:08.90 i				1	Glasgow	12 Feb
9:14.04 i				8	Paris, FRA	11 Mar
8:59.30	*Kate McCandless*		*22.06.70*	*13*	*Rome, ITA*	*8 Jun*
9:02.47	Laura Adam		28.02.65	8	Hengelo, HOL	4 Jun
9:05.97				9	Linz, AUT	4 Jul
9:06.63				8	Victoria, CAN	23 Aug
9:12.16				2	Sheffield	11 Jun
9:15.21				4	Vienna, AUT	29 May
9:12.12	Debbie Gunning		31.08.65	3	Gateshead	20 Jul
9:15.11 i				4	Glasgow	12 Feb
9:15.43				1	Gateshead	1 Jul
9:12.6 mx	Suzanne Rigg		29.11.63		Stretford	2 Aug
9:24.2				1	Windsor	20 Jul
9:14.1	Angela Davies		21.10.70	1	Oxford	8 May
9:14.3 mx	Jayne Spark		16.09.70	6	Stretford	23 Aug
9:26.36				6	Cork, IRE	25 Jun
9:14.72	Wendy Ore		23.05.66	3	Sheffield	11 Jun
9:15.21				5	Gateshead	20 Jul
	36 performances to 9:16.0 by 9 athletes including 5 indoors					
9:17.4 mx	Amanda Thorpe		21.07.71	1	Stretford	23 Aug
9:40.17				2	Birmingham	21 May
(10)						
9:17.6 mx	Carol Greenwood		15.03.66	8	Stretford	10 May
9:26.1				1	Sheffield	25 May
9:17.70 i	Alice Braham	U20	17.01.76	1	Norman, USA	3 Dec
9:26.31				3	Bedford	3 Jul
9:18.03	Sue Parker		24.03.70	2	Gateshead	1 Jul
9:18.09	Sarah Bentley		21.05.67	3	Gateshead	1 Jul
9:18.4 mx	Zahara Hyde		12.01.63		Brighton	10 Aug
9:28.64				3	Bracknell	10 Aug
9:19.0	Alison Barnes		6.11.69	1	Crawley	1 Jun
9:19.67	Amanda Wright		14.07.68	4	Cork, IRE	25 Jun
9:21.07	Tanya Blake	U23	16.06.73	5	Sheffield	11 Jun
9:21.20	Nicky Slater	U20	11.01.77	1	Bedford	3 Jul
9:23.08	Sue Morley	V35	11.10.57	1	London (CP)	26 Jun
(20)						
9:24.21	Joanne Symonds		19.02.68	6	Sheffield	11 Jun
9:25.5	Susan Harrison		6.08.71	1	Solihull	29 May
9:25.86	Catherine Berry	U20	8.10.75	2	Bedford	3 Jul
9:26.05	Vikki McPherson		1.06.71	7	Sheffield	11 Jun
9:26.52	Maxine Newman		15.12.70	4	Gateshead	1 Jul
9:27.0	Elaine Foster		21.07.63	2	Solihull	29 May
9:27.3	Andrea Whitcombe		8.06.71	1	Watford	10 Aug
9:27.44	Shireen Barbour		4.09.60	5	Gateshead	1 Jul
9:30.15 i	Julie Briggs		13.03.69	2	Birmingham	19 Feb
9:47.3				1	Horsham	21 Aug
9:30.67	Caroline Slimin		27.08.65	3	London (CP)	26 Jun
(30)						
9:31.91	Wendy Farrow		25.12.71	8	Gateshead	1 Jul
9:32.8	Sue Ridley		25.10.65	1	Grangemouth	7 May
9:33.47	*Edwige Pitel*		*4.06.67*	*4*	*London (CP)*	*26 Jun*
9:33.9 mx	Janet Holt	V35	10.10.56	20	Stretford	26 Apr
9:42.6				2	Grangemouth	7 May

9:34.47	Sally Young	V35	29.09.55	5	London (CP)	26	Jun
9:34.5 mx	Jo Thompson	V35	30.10.58	6	Cheltenham	22	Jun
9:38.41				14	Gateshead	1	Jul
9:34.65	Deborah Newhams		18.01.62	1	Cwmbran	18	Jun
9:34.7	Bev Hartigan		10.06.67	3	Wigan	7	Aug
9:35.60	*Teresa Duffy*		*6.07.69*	*11*	*Sheffield*	*11*	*Jun*
9:35.76	Penny Thackray	U23	18.08.74	11	Gateshead	1	Jul
9:37.01	Andrea Duke	U23	6.07.73	13	Gateshead	1	Jul
9:37.10	Kim Bennett		16.05.69	1	Hull	21	Aug
(40)							
9:37.41	*Nnenna Lynch*		*3.07.71*	*1*	*London (CP)*	*2*	*May*
9:37.42	Sharon Dixon		22.04.68	2	London (CP)	2	May
9:37.55	Hayley Nash		30.05.63	2	Cwmbran	18	Jun
9:37.9	Ann Terek		22.09.64	2	Tullamore, IRE		
9:37.95	Joanne Holden		20.02.65	6	London (CP)	26	Jun
9:38.7 mx	Chaanah Fothergill	U23	22.02.72	26	Stretford	2	Aug
9:48.65				2	Derby	16	Jul
9:38.87	Alison Outram	U20	14.06.77	2	Telford	8	Jul
9:39.8	Gabrielle Collison		10.02.66	2	London (Elt)	29	Aug
9:40.15	Mara Myers	U23	13.08.73	15	Sheffield	11	Jun
9:41.14	Lisa Hollick		1.01.70	2	Solihull	21	Aug
9:42.1	Annette Bell		5.09.64	2	Sheffield	25	May
(50)							
9:42.1	Angie Hulley		8.02.62	3	Sheffield	25	May
9:42.55	*Wendy Sutherland*		*30.05.63*	*3*	*Solihull*	*21*	*Aug*
9:42.66	Louise Watson		13.12.71	22	Walnut, USA	16	Apr
9:43.2	Anna Moutrie/Wittekind		7.12.64	1	Enfield	31	Jul
9:43.36 i	Sharon King	U23	27.01.72	5	Birmingham	26	Feb
9:44.36	Lisa Melkevick-Mawer		22.05.68	15	Gateshead	1	Jul
9:45.22	Karen Cornwall		26.08.66	2	Hull	21	Aug
9:45.7	Liz Talbot	U23	5.12.74	1	London (He)	3	Sep
9:45.8	Deborah Percival	V35	22.04.58	3	London (Elt)	29	Aug
9:45.89	Margaret Boleman	V35	7.03.59	3	Bedford	17	Sep
9:45.9 mx	Claire O'Connor	U20	5.06.75	23	Stretford	26	Apr
9:46.44				7	Warsaw, POL	18	Jun
(60)							
9:46.38	Hayley Yelling	U23	3.01.74	7	London (CP)	26	Jun
9:48.7	Caroline Horne	V35	7.11.56	3	London (Elt)	29	Aug
9:48.96	Joan Lasenby		26.04.60	4	Bedford	17	Sep
9:49.73 i	Kirsten Scobie		13.11.67	7	Birmingham	26	Feb
9:50.36	Sarah Simmons	U20	12.01.75	5	Birmingham	21	May
9:51.3 mx	Hayley Ward	U20	3.03.77	3	Stretford	2	Aug
9:52.17	Hayley Parkinson	U20	5.12.75	7	Edinburgh	13	Jul
9:53.09	Karen Harvey/Edmondson		17.03.62	2	Birmingham	8	May
9:53.4	Paula Fudge	V40	30.03.52	1	High Wycombe	21	May
9:53.5	Beverley Gray	U20	24.04.77	1	Hull	11	Jun
(70)							
9:53.8	Fiona Phillips		8.03.60	1	Yate	21	Aug
9:53.9	Lorraine Jenner		29.12.71	1	Aldershot	7	Aug
9:54.1	Sarah Wallace	U23	31.05.73	1	Grantham	14	May
9:54.42	Nicola Brown	U23	17.03.74	17	Gateshead	1	Jul
9:54.86 i	Shirley Griffiths	U23	23.06.72	2	Birmingham	31	Dec
9:54.95	Claire Forbes		25.03.71	18	Gateshead	1	Jul
9:55.0 mx	Jackie Newton		28.08.64	8	Stretford	23	Aug
9:55.09	Claire Swift	U20	17.10.76	2	Sheffield	30	Apr
9:55.1	Marina Steadman		4.09.60	1	Bracknell	4	Jun
9:55.12	Debbie Sullivan	U23	24.01.72	10	London (CP)	26	Jun
(80)							
9:55.2	Sally Baines		2.03.70	1	Redditch	24	Apr
9:56.3	Amanda Tremble	U20	2.11.76	1	Jarrow	8	Jun
9:56.46	Laura Woffenden		14.08.70	5	Hull	21	Aug
9:56.57	Jessica Turnbull	U20	4.07.75	4	London (CP)	2	May
9:56.72	Elaine MacKay		26.01.65	4	Edinburgh	25	Jun

260

9:57.1	Danielle Sanderson		26.10.62	1	London (PH)	21	May
9:57.3	Carolina Weatherill		13.05.68	1	Portsmouth	16	Jul
9:57.8	S. Brown			2	Aldershot	7	Aug
9:58.0	Amanda Larby		13.11.70	1	Croydon	8	May
9:58.4	*Fatmagul Bosnak*			*1*	*Guildford*	*13*	*Aug*
9:58.6	Kath Bailey		25.03.68	2	Aldershot	29	Jun
	(90)						
9:58.8	Lucy Taylor		8.11.63	4	Grangemouth	7	May
9:59.26	Jill Bruce	U23	25.07.73	1	Antrim	7	May
9:59.84	Michelle Harries	U23	4.01.72	6	Ostrava, CS	6	Aug
9:59.94	Debbie Kilner		2.11.61	5	Edinburgh	25	Jun

Under 17

10:04.0	Clare Duncan		22.08.79	1	Kirkby	5	Jun
10:08.7	Heather Carson		18.07.79	8	Stretford	23	Aug
10:08.8	Dawn Adams		19.10.78	1	Liverpool	1	May
10:08.87	Caroline McNulty		3.12.77	1	Aberdeen	16	Jul
10:09.14	Vicky Robinson		17.10.77	2	Aberdeen	16	Jul
10:10.8	Katie Wallace		19.09.78	2	Southampton	4	Jun
10:13.3	Andrea Kershaw		22.03.78	23	Stretford	12	Jul
10:13.39	Jennifer Gibson		21.06.78	4	Telford	8	Jul
10:13.7	Jennifer Heath		22.12.77	27	Stretford	10	May
10:16.3	Pamela Crawley		20.02.78	1	Coatbridge	19	Jun
	(10)						
10:16.34	Kirsty Macaulay		26.04.78	5	Telford	8	Jul
10:20.19	Caroline Wood		5.01.79	6	Telford	8	Jul
10:20.38	Carol Vettraino		16.10.77	4	Aberdeen	16	Jul
10:20.56	Natalie Armiger		19.10.77	1	Gateshead	28	May
10:21.0	Claire Demaine		6.09.78	1	Carlisle	17	Jul
10:22.70mx	Jane Moss		23.08.79	15	Barn Elms	4	Jun
10:23.21	Paula Gowing		31.05.78	1	Stoke	16	Jul
10:24.14	Rebecca McKenna		6.01.78	1	London (He)	20	Aug
10:24.3	Jo Winterbourne		11.01.78	1	Bracknell	27	Jul
10:27.2	Sheila Fairweather		24.11.77	2	Kirkby	5	Jun
	(20)						
10:28.11 i	Heledd Gruffudd		16.11.78	2	Birmingham	13	Feb
10:28.84				6	Aberdeen	16	Jul
10:28.9	Carly Scott		19.07.79	2	Ilford	4	Jun
10:32.5	Emma Brooker		26.10.78	2	Salisbury	21	May
10:33.4	Stacey Wallace		8.10.78	1	Woking	24	Aug
10:33.6	Gabby Hawson		3.02.79	2	Salisbury	4	Jun
10:33.8	Jennifer Ward		22.09.78	1	Pitreavie	10	Apr

5000 METRES

15:10.38	Alison Wyeth		26.05.64	1	Berlin, GER	30	Aug
15:15.45				3	Paris, FRA	3	Sep
15:35.81	*Kate McCandless*		*22.06.70*	*4*	*St. Petersburg, RUS*	*29*	*Jul*
15:56.83	Suzanne Rigg		29.11.63	6	Hechtel, BEL	30	Jul
15:58.7				1	Stretford	14	Aug
16:28.2 +					Victoria, CAN	24	Aug
15:57.29	Carol Greenwood		15.03.66	10	Bratislava, SVK	1	Jun
16:06.49	Shireen Barbour		4.09.60	1	Birmingham	30	Jul
16:27.5				1	Bournemouth	19	Jun
16:12.1	Jayne Spark		16.09.70	2	Stretford	14	Aug
16:13.43	Jo Thompson	V35	30.10.58	1	Crawley	28	May
16:16.86	Sarah Bentley		21.05.67	2	Birmingham	30	Jul
16:19.46	Vikki McPherson		1.06.71	11	Hechtel, BEL	30	Jul
16:28.3 +					Victoria, CAN	24	Aug
16:22.95	Amanda Wright		14.07.68	3	Birmingham	30	Jul
16:23.85 i	Louise Watson		13.12.71		,USA		
16:39.79				2	Westwood, USA	30	Apr
	(10)						
16:25.7 mx	Angie Hulley		8.02.62	1	Stretford	29	May
16:35.6				1	Leeds	21	Jun

16:27.5 +	Yvonne Murray		4.10.64		Victoria, CAN	24	Aug
16:28.18	*Wendy Sutherland*		*30.05.63*	*4*	*Birmingham*	*30*	*Jul*
16:36.0	Zahara Hyde		12.01.63	1	London (CP)	27	Apr
16:38.3	Susan Harrison		6.08.71	2	Leeds	21	Jun
16:39.57	Sharon Dixon		22.04.68	2	Crawley	28	May
16:44.44	Elaine Foster		21.07.63	1	Stoke	7	Aug
16:44.5	Danielle Sanderson		26.10.62	1	Watford	27	Jul
16:44.58	Gabrielle Collison		10.02.66	3	Crawley	28	May
16:46.13	Alison Barnes		6.11.69	5	Birmingham	30	Jul
16:47.4 +e	Andrea Wallace		22.11.66	3	Sheffield	12	Jun
(20)							
16:47.66	Hayley Nash		30.05.63	2	Istanbul, TUR	21	May
16:48.0 +e	Heather Heasman		27.09.63	6	Sheffield	12	Jun
16:48.2 +e	Helen Titterington		24.10.69	7	Sheffield	12	Jun
16:48.77	Joanne Holden		20.02.65	6	Birmingham	30	Jul
16:48.8	Sally Young		29.09.55	2	London (CP)	27	Apr
16:51.80	Sue Ridley		25.10.65	3	Istanbul, TUR	21	May
16:56.1	Loretta Sollars		29.10.63	3	Leeds	21	Jun
17:02.84	Lisa Melkevick-Mawer		22.05.68	8	Birmingham	30	Jul
17:05.6	Lucy Wright		17.11.69	4	Leeds	21	Jun
17:11.0	Janet Holt	V35	10.10.56	1	London (WF)	6	Aug
(30)							
17:11.4	Anne Ridley		7.05.65	2	Bournemouth	19	Jun
17:12.30	Marion Eldridge	V40	27.03.54	2	Athens, GRE	Jun	
17:16.8	Catherine Mijovic		11.04.61	3	Bournemouth	19	Jun
17:20.77	Angela Joiner		14.02.69	5	Crawley	28	May
17:22.69	Maureen Woolridge	V35	25.11.58	6	Crawley	28	May
17:29.03	Kathleen Atkin		30.04.64	3	Loughborough	7	Sep
17:30.1	Devina Manship		12.12.69	1	Leicester	19	Jun
17:30.2	Hayley Yelling	U23	3.01.74	1	Hounslow	10	Jul

10000 METRES

31:56.97	Yvonne Murray		4.10.64	1	Victoria, CAN	24	Aug
33:01.40	Suzanne Rigg		29.11.63	4	Victoria, CAN	24	Aug
33:38.14				5	London (CP)	10	Sep
33:42.80				3	Sheffield	12	Jun
33:02.74	Vikki McPherson		1.06.71	5	Victoria, CAN	24	Aug
34:03.07				6	Birmingham	26	Jun
33:23.25	Zahara Hyde		12.01.63	1	Sheffield	12	Jun
33:57.64				7	Walnut, USA	16	Apr
33:34.85	Karen Macleod	V35	24.04.58	11	St. Denis, FRA	10	Jun
34:05.00				1	Edinburgh	25	Jun
33:34.96	Carol Greenwood		15.03.66	2	Sheffield	12	Jun
33:45.04	Angie Hulley		8.02.62	10	Victoria, CAN	24	Aug
33:49.91				4	Sheffield	12	Jun
33:52.47	Shireen Barbour		4.09.60	5	Sheffield	12	Jun
33:56.04	Jo Thompson	V35	30.10.58	6	Sheffield	12	Jun
33:57.86	Alison Rose		27.09.67	7	Sheffield	12	Jun
(10)							
34:00.46	Danielle Sanderson		26.10.62	8	Sheffield	12	Jun
34:08.00	Helen Titterington		24.10.69	9	Sheffield	12	Jun
34:12.98	Heather Heasman		27.09.63	10	Sheffield	12	Jun
34:19.51	Amanda Wright		14.07.68	11	Sheffield	12	Jun
34:36.83	Louise Watson		13.12.71	3	Boise, USA	1	Jun
35:00.49	Lisa Melkevick-Mawer		22.05.68	12	Sheffield	12	Jun
35:08.23	Sharon Dixon		22.04.68	13	Sheffield	12	Jun
35:11.74	Clare Pauzers		2.08.62	14	Sheffield	12	Jun
35:37.57	Lisa Hollick		1.01.70	15	Sheffield	12	Jun
35:47.76	Sally Lynch		6.11.64	16	Sheffield	12	Jun
(20)							
36:05.78	Lucy Wright		17.11.69	2	Sheffield	30	Apr
36:24.13	Meryl Whitley		12.04.69	3	Sheffield	30	Apr

10 KILOMETRES ROAD

Time	Name	Cat	DOB	Pos	Venue	Date
32:31	Heather Heasman		27.09.63	2	Barnsley	6 Nov
32:47				2	Coventry	16 Oct
32:38	Liz McColgan		24.05.64	1	Coventry	16 Oct
32:55	Marian Sutton		7.10.63	1	Cardiff	31 Jul
33:50				1	Bangor	17 Sep
32:56	Alison Wyeth		26.05.64	1	Eastleigh	20 Mar
33:09	Andrea Wallace		22.11.66	1	Belfast	9 Apr
33:15	Wendy Ore		23.05.66	2	Cardiff	31 Jul
33:41				1	Stoke	7 Aug
33:21	*Lesley Morton*		*25.12.63*	*4*	*Cardiff*	*31 Jul*
33:21	Angie Hulley		8.02.62	1	Llanrwst	14 Aug
33:51				4	Coventry	16 Oct
33:23	Hayley Nash		30.05.63	5	Cardiff	31 Jul
33:28	Jill Hunter		14.10.66	3	Barnsley	6 Nov
33:38	Teresa Dyer		29.09.59	1	Loughborough	27 Feb
(10)						
33:38	Catherine Mijovic		11.04.61	1	Swansea	11 Sep
33:44	Kath Bailey		25.03.68	2	Eastleigh	20 Mar
33:49	Lynne Robinson		21.06.69	2	Belfast	9 Apr
33:54				2	Loughborough	27 Feb
33:54	Shireen Barbour		4.09.60	5	Coventry	16 Oct
33:54	Amanda Wright		14.07.68	6	Coventry	16 Oct
33:58	Louise Watson		13.12.71		Oakland, USA	
34:02	Danielle Sanderson		26.10.62	1	Teddington	5 Jun
34:02	Suzanne Rigg		29.11.63	2	London	10 Jul
34:02	*Cathy Shum*		*30.05.61*	*3*	*Stoke*	*7 Aug*
34:03	Alison Rose		27.09.67	1	Leeds	4 Dec
34:09	Caroline Horne	V35	7.11.56	1	Ewell	6 Feb
(20)						
34:18	Deborah Percival	V35	22.04.58	2	Ewell	6 Feb
34:19	Joanne Symonds		19.02.68	3	Loughborough	27 Feb
34:21	Deborah Newhams		18.01.62	6	Cardiff	31 Jul
34:27	Caroline Slimin		27.08.65	3	Eastleigh	20 Mar
34:27	Andrea Duke	U23	6.07.73	7	Barnsley	6 Nov
34:28	Fiona Phillips		8.03.60	7	Cardiff	31 Jul
34:29	Karen Cornwall		26.08.66		Doncaster	16 Oct
34:31	Zina Marchant	V40	30.09.50	4	Liverpool	22 May
34:32	Lucy Wright		17.11.69	2	Leeds	4 Dec
34:34	Lucy Elliott		9.03.66	1	Clitheroe	27 Dec
(30)						
34:35	Julie Coleby	V35	5.11.55	1	Wallsend	10 Apr
34:35	Lisa Hollick		1.01.70	2	Brighton	20 Nov
34:36	Sally Ellis	V35	17.05.58	1	Preston	1 Mar
34:36	Sandra Bentley	V35	17.02.58	3	Glasgow	29 May
34:36	Helen Titterington		24.10.69	8	Barnsley	6 Nov
34:40				1	Warrington	21 Aug
34:41	Linda Rushmere		14.11.59	5	Liverpool	22 May
34:43	Joanne Holden		20.02.65	2	Llanrwst	14 Aug
34:47	Sue Morley	V35	11.10.57	4	Eastleigh	20 Mar
34:47	*Wendy Sutherland*		*30.05.63*	*3*	*Llanrwst*	*14 Aug*
34:48	Jane Shields		23.08.60	4	Glasgow	29 May
34:48	*Edwige Pitel*		*4.06.67*	*1*	*Basingstoke*	*27 Nov*
34:51	Chaanah Fothergill	U23	22.02.72	4	Loughborough	27 Feb
(40)						
34:51	Carol Holmes		13.12.63	1	Eynsham	27 Nov
34:52	Lynn Harding		10.08.61	1	Newcastle	6 Nov
34:53	*Teresa Duffy*		*6.07.69*	*7*	*Liverpool*	*22 May*
34:57	Elaine Foster		21.07.63	1	Rugby	10 Apr
34:59	Lisa Melkevick-Mawer		22.05.68	1	Cleethorpes	1 Jan
34:59	Kim Bennett		16.05.69	2	Doncaster	16 Oct

10 MILES ROAD

Time	Name	Cat	DOB	Pos	Venue	Date
54:07 +	Andrea Wallace		22.11.66	1	South Shields	18 Sep
54:41	Angie Hulley		8.02.62	1	Erewash	4 Sep
54:44	Karen Macleod	V35	24.04.58	2	The Hague, HOL	18 Dec
55:41				5	New York, USA	16 Apr
55:47				1	Ostestry	31 Jul
55:10	Wendy Ore		23.05.66	2	Erewash	4 Sep
55:20	Jo Thompson	V35	30.10.58	1	Woking	6 Mar
55:32	Hayley Nash		30.05.63	1	Newport	2 Apr
55:36	*Lesley Morton*		*25.12.63*	*3*	*Erewash*	*4 Sep*
55:38	Suzanne Rigg		29.11.63	3	Portsmouth	9 Oct
55:42	Danielle Sanderson		26.10.62	4	Erewash	4 Sep
55:58				2	Woking	6 Mar
56:04	Kath Bailey		25.03.68	3	Woking	5 Mar
56:06	Lynn Harding		10.08.61	1	Tynemouth	6 Mar
	(10)					
56:11	Zahara Hyde		12.01.63	1	Hayling Island	27 Nov
56:36	Paula Fudge	V40	30.03.52	4	Woking	5 Mar
56:41	Alison Rose		27.09.67	5	Woking	5 Mar
56:41	Jill Hunter		14.10.66	4	Portsmouth	9 Oct
56:41	Caroline Horne	V35	7.11.56	1	Twickenham	16 Oct
57:24	Sally Lynch		6.11.64	7	Woking	5 Mar
57:30	*Wendy Sutherland*		*30.05.63*	*2*	*Twickenham*	*16 Oct*
57:34	Marian Sutton		7.10.63	1	St Eval	24 Jul
57:42	Nikala Jones			8	Woking	5 Mar
57:42	Heather Heasman		27.09.63	1	Newbury	11 Sep
57:47	Linda Rushmere		14.11.59	1	Nottingham	3 Jun
	(20)					
57:47	Elaine Foster		21.07.63	1	Chelmsley Wood	2 Oct
57:56	Deborah Percival	V35	22.04.58	1	Canterbury	30 Jan
57:59	Deborah Newhams		18.01.62	3	Newport	2 Apr
58:11	Julie Coleby	V35	5.11.55	2	Carlisle	19 Nov
58:16	Elaine McBrinn		19.12.63	1	Motherwell	10 Apr
58:18	Kim Bennett		16.05.69	1	Hull	6 Feb
58:36	Sue Endersby	V35	12.10.57	1	Blackpool	7 Aug
58:38	Jackie Newton		28.08.64	8	Erewash	4 Sep
58:49	Diane Underwood	V40	20.12.52	9	Erewash	4 Sep
58:50	Joanne Symonds		19.02.68	1	Tipton	20 Nov
	(30)					
58:53	Kim Osment		3.04.63	1	Witney	18 Sep
58:58	Catherine Mijovic		11.04.61	1	Heckington	31 Jul
58:59	*Teresa Tuohy*	*V35*	*1.06.59*	*3*	*Twickenham*	*16 Oct*
59:00	Carol Holmes		13.12.63	4	Newbury	11 Sep

HALF MARATHON

Time	Name	Cat	DOB	Pos	Venue	Date
1:11:34	Andrea Wallace		22.11.66	2	South Shields	18 Sep
1:12:48	*Cathy Shum*		*30.05.61*	*1*	*Killeraule, IRE*	*28 Aug*
1:13:11	Danielle Sanderson		26.10.62	1	St. Neots	29 May
1:13:13				29	Oslo, NOR	24 Sep
1:14:00				2	Bath	20 Mar
1:13:16	Hayley Nash		30.05.63	1	Bath	20 Mar
1:13:19	Angie Hulley		8.02.62	31	Oslo, NOR	24 Sep
1:13:34	Marian Sutton		7.10.63	3	St. Neots	29 May
1:13:47	Suzanne Rigg		29.11.63	4	South Shields	18 Sep
1:13:52	Karen Macleod	V35	24.04.58	1	Stroud	23 Oct
1:13:57	*Lesley Morton*		*25.12.63*	*2*	*Glasgow*	*21 Aug*
1:14:05	Teresa Dyer		29.09.59	1	Fleet	20 Mar
1:14:06	Heather Heasman		27.09.63	46	Oslo, NOR	24 Sep
1:14:15	Catherine Mijovic		11.04.61	47	Oslo, NOR	24 Sep
	(10)					

1:14:31	Linda Rushmere		14.11.59	1	York	27	Mar
1:14:43	Sue Dilnot		14.01.62	4	Glasgow	21	Aug
1:14:55	Caroline Horne	V35	7.11.56	7	South Shields	18	Sep
1:14:56	Sally Ellis	V35	17.05.58	3	Bath	20	Mar
1:15:15	Amanda Wright		14.07.68	2	Liverpool	21	Aug
1:15:26	Alison Rose		27.09.67	4	Bath	20	Mar
1:15:28	Lynn Harding		10.08.61	1	Helensburgh	24	Jul
1:15:35	Kath Bailey		25.03.68		Glasgow	21	Aug
1:16:25	Karen Cornwall		26.08.66	6	Bath	20	Mar
1:16:31	Zina Marchant	V40	30.09.50	7	Bath	20	Mar
(20)							
1:16:40	Lesley Turner		1.08.66	1	Brighton	27	Feb
1:16:42	Brenda Walker	V35	24.08.56	1	Isle of Man	26	Feb
1:16:47	Sue Endersby	V35	12.10.57	1	Benidorm, SPA	27	Nov
1:16:48	Deborah Newhams		18.01.62	2	Wilmslow	27	Mar
1:16:48	Jayne Spark		16.09.70	9	South Shields	18	Sep
1:16:49	Sally Lynch		6.11.64	8	Bath	20	Mar
1:17:01	*Wendy Sutherland*		*30.05.63*	*1*	*London (WP)*	*18*	*Sep*
1:17:07	Janice Moorekite	V35	1.05.57	1	Lake Vyrnwy	25	Sep
1:17:11	Paula Fudge	V40	30.03.52	2	Stroud	23	Oct
1:17:25	Trudi Thomson	V35	18.01.59	1	Bridge of Allan	7	Aug
1:17:38	Bronwyn Cardy-Wise	V40	26.01.52	1	Worcester	20	Mar
(30)							
1:17:42	Elaine McBrinn		19.12.63	1	Coatbridge	7	Aug
1:17:56	Elaine MacKay		26.01.65	2	Helensburgh	24	Jul
1:18:07	Julie Coleby	V35	5.11.55	1	Langbaurgh	20	Mar
1:18:19	Heather Jennings		10.07.60		Keswick	15	May
1:18:22	Sally Eastall		5.01.63	1	Great Yarmouth	24	Jul
1:18:37	Jane Shields		23.08.60	1	Bridlington	23	Oct
1:18:58	Annette Bell		5.09.64	2	Worcester	20	Mar
1:19:00	Sandra Branney	V40	30.04.54	2	Nottingham	25	Sep
1:19:06	Jan Rashleigh			3	Worcester	20	Mar
1:19:08	Yvonne Hill		13.08.63	4	Worcester	20	Mar
(40)							
1:19:14	Andrea Duke	U23	6.07.73	13	Gateshead	18	Sep
1:19:16	L. Williams			4	Lake Vyrnwy	25	Sep
1:19:17	Marina Steadman		4.09.60	1	Bracknell	8	May
1:19:20	Carolyn Hunter-Rowe		25.01.64	1	York	23	Jan

MARATHON

2:32:24	Yvonne Danson	V35	22.05.59	3	Victoria, CAN	27	Aug
2:33:16	Karen Macleod	V35	24.04.58	4	Victoria, CAN	27	Aug
2:35:39	Hayley Nash		30.05.63	7	Victoria, CAN	27	Aug
	2:39:04			6	London	17	Apr
2:36:29	Danielle Sanderson		26.10.62	11	Helsinki, FIN	7	Aug
2:36:40	Teresa Dyer		29.09.59	9	Rotterdam, HOL	17	Apr
2:37:06	Sally Ellis	V35	17.05.58	4	London	17	Apr
	2:37:14			8	Victoria, CAN	27	Aug
2:37:08	Sally Eastall		5.01.63	5	London	17	Apr
	2:41:32			13	Victoria, CAN	27	Aug
2:37:46	Marian Sutton		7.10.63	16	Osaka, JAP	30	Jan
	2:40:34			22	Helsinki, FIN	7	Aug
2:38:39	Sally Goldsmith			2	Carpi, ITA	23	Oct
2:40:09	Zina Marchant	V40	30.09.50	7	London	17	Apr
(10)							
2:40:17	Linda Rushmere		14.11.59	1	Dublin, IRE	31	Oct
	2:40:46			9	London	17	Apr
	2:45:24			32	Helsinki, FIN	7	Aug
2:40:28	Carolyn Hunter-Rowe		25.01.64	1	Malta	20	Feb
2:40:31	Julie Coleby	V35	5.11.55	8	London	17	Apr
2:40:57	Lynn Harding		10.08.61	12	Victoria, CAN	27	Aug

2:41:03	Suzanne Rigg		29.11.63	10	London	17 Apr
2:41:47	Sally Lynch		6.11.64	11	London	17 Apr
2:42:40	Angie Hulley		8.02.62	12	London	17 Apr
2:42:47	*Cathy Shum*		*30.05.61*	*2*	*Dublin, IRE*	*31 Oct*
2:43:18	Trudi Thomson	V35	18.01.59	3	Dublin, IRE	31 Oct
	2:47:31			18	London	17 Apr
2:44:48	Caroline Horne	V35	7.11.56	4	Dublin, IRE	31 Oct
2:45:16	Lesley Turner		1.08.66	30	Helsinki, FIN	7 Aug
	2:48:34			21	London	17 Apr
(20)						
2:45:19	Alison Rose		27.09.67	31	Helsinki, FIN	7 Aug
	2:45:55			13	London	17 Apr
2:45:46	Gillian Horovitz	V35	7.06.55	14	Minneapolis/St Paul, USA	20 Oct
	2:48:24			14	New York, USA	6 Nov
2:48:09	Tracy Swindell		8.11.66	19	London	17 Apr
2:48:10	Janice Moorekite	V35	1.05.57	7	Dublin, IRE	31 Oct
2:48:31	Catherine Mijovic		11.04.61	20	London	17 Apr
2:49:03	Sue Endersby	V35	12.10.57	22	London	17 Apr
2:49:25	Sandra Bentley	V35	17.02.58	16	Rotterdam, HOL	17 Apr
2:49:58	Zoe Lowe		7.07.65	23	London	17 Apr
2:50:41	Elaine Flather		2.02.66	25	London	17 Apr
2:51:21 dh	Judith Burnett	V35	14.10.58	1	Valle Nalon, SPA	6 Nov
	2:55:18			37	London	17 Apr
(30)						
2:51:31	*Christina Scobey*		*1.06.66*	*16*	*New York, USA*	*6 Nov*
2:51:33	Susan Abbiss		20.10.59	26	London	17 Apr
2:51:59	Jane Gardner	V40		18	Rotterdam, HOL	17 Apr
2:52:11	Beccy Richardson/Cameron		17.07.60	19	Rotterdam, HOL	17 Apr
2:52:56	Dianne Hepplewhite	V40	2.11.51	27	London	17 Apr
2:53:40	Eleanor Hill		8.08.62	2	Belfast	2 May
2:54:09	Bonny Appleby	V40	15.02.53	30	London	17 Apr
2:54:42	Janette Picton		4.03.63	32	London	17 Apr
2:54:57	Judith Morris	V35	23.06.58	33	London	17 Apr
2:55:03	Kath Kaiser	V40	24.08.51	34	London	17 Apr
2:55:15	Denise Hodgesteger	V40	18.08.53	35	London	17 Apr
(40)						
2:55:20	Janice Gjelseth		16.09.60	38	London	17 Apr
2:55:25	Eryl Davies		30.11.60	40	London	17 Apr
2:55:44	Vanessa Aisthorpe	V35	19.09.58	43	London	17 Apr
2:55:49	Denise Wakefield	V40	29.03.54	44	London	17 Apr
2:55:50	Janice Needham	V40	9.11.52	45	London	17 Apr
2:55:56	Libby Jones		25.04.61	46	London	17 Apr
2:56:14	Jane Siegert		6.02.69	47	London	17 Apr
2:56:23	Beverley Brown		9.05.65	48	London	17 Apr
2:56:48	Amanda Yorwerth		18.05.67	49	London	17 Apr
2:56:56	Yvonne Hill		13.08.63	50	London	17 Apr
(50)						
2:57:18	M. Burke			3	Belfast	2 May
2:57:35	Barbara Parker	V35	29.04.58	51	London	17 Apr
2:57:53	Ann Cartwright	V35	22.09.54	52	London	17 Apr
2:58:20	Julia Gilbert		14.09.61	53	London	17 Apr
2:58:40	Sylvia Watson	V45	29.09.47	54	London	17 Apr
2:59:09	Sarah Springman	V35	26.12.56	55	London	17 Apr
2:59:18	Julia Gates	V35	12.05.59	13	Liberte, FRA	12 Jun
2:59:21	Lorraine Branch		9.11.59	56	London	17 Apr
2:59:35	Claire Mee		24.04.64	57	London	17 Apr
2:59:36	Joan Daily	V35	2.06.54	58	London	17 Apr
(60)						
2:59:53	Marilyn Gradden		26.01.61	60	London	17 Apr
3:00:06	Maggie Sinclair	V40	2.04.54	61	London	17 Apr
3:00:16	Margaret Thompson	V40	8.07.54	1	Stoke	19 Jun

3:00:19	Celia Duncan	V40	4.06.53	62	London	17	Apr
3:00:59	Leslie Watson	V45	4.02.45	1	Isle of Wight	21	May
3:01:21	Lynne Quigley		19.02.69	64	London	17	Apr
3:01:36	Catherine McCarthy	V40	21.08.53	65	London	17	Apr
3:01:43	Julia Harvey		18.01.60	66	London	17	Apr
3:02:27	Barbara Boylan	V35	27.02.58	67	London	17	Apr
3:02:38	Karen Nisbet	V35	28.04.57	69	London	17	Apr
(70)							
3:02:43	June Cowper	V40	21.07.50	70	London	17	Apr
3:02:46	Caroline Hipkin		18.03.71	71	London	17	Apr
3:02:54	Denise Johnson	V35	12.03.59	72	London	17	Apr
3:03:32	Tracy Owen		29.04.64	75	London	17	Apr
3:03:47	Susan Neal	V40	31.10.50	77	London	17	Apr
3:03:48	Barbara Stevens	V35	2.05.56	2	Nottingham	25	Sep
3:04:19	Anne Smith	V40	7.06.49	78	London	17	Apr
3:04:29	Elizabeth Craig		7.07.60	79	London	17	Apr
3:04:41	Frances Cooke	V35	8.12.56	80	London	17	Apr
3:04:47	Jennifer Morris		11.04.61	82	London	17	Apr
(80)							
3:05:06	Paula Bongers	V40	17.12.51	84	London	17	Apr
3:05:22	Jayne Gregory		26.01.66	85	London	17	Apr
3:05:31	Marion Potter	V35	16.02.57	86	London	17	Apr
3:05:32	Julie Grice		28.10.66	87	London	17	Apr
3:05:41	Hilary Walker	V40	9.11.53	3	Windsor	25	Sep
3:05:43	Sheryl Reason		9.06.69	88	London	17	Apr
3:05:51	Sheila Greener	V40	21.03.50	89	London	17	Apr
3:06:15	Yvonne Thomas	V35	31.03.57	91	London	17	Apr
3:06:16	Anne-Marie Hughes		8.05.62	3	Nottingham	25	Sep
3:06:19	Andrea Dennison		22.04.63	92	London	17	Apr
(90)							
3:06:26	Liz Clarke	V35	14.02.57	93	London	17	Apr
3:06:36	Rita Banks	V50	26.12.43	2	Stoke	19	Jun
3:06:37	Caroline Armstrong	V40	30.09.53	94	London	17	Apr
3:06:41	Tina Hissey		13.05.67	95	London	17	Apr
3:06:44	Louise Forrest		14.11.61	96	London	17	Apr
3:06:49	Mary Picksley	V40	7.01.52	97	London	17	Apr
3:07:01	Jane Boulton	V35	2.04.56	98	London	17	Apr
3:07:05	Vanessa Hamlet		14.09.69	99	London	17	Apr
3:07:14	Jackie Coulson		10.08.61	100	London	17	Apr
3:07:24	Lynne Duance	V45	28.12.46	101	London	17	Apr
(100)							
3:07:27	Lorraine McArthy		30.12.63	102	London	17	Apr
3:07:29	Karen Barlow		15.11.67	103	London	17	Apr
3:07:32	Jan Thomson			2	Loch Rannoch	19	Jun
3:07:44	Yvonne Shashoua		16.03.62	104	London	17	Apr

100 KILOMETRES - Track

| 9:17:23 | Sharon Gayter | | | | London (TB) | 22 | Oct |
| 9:46:29 | Marianne Savage | V45 | 26.01.49 | | London (TB) | 22 | Oct |

100 KILOMETRES - Road

7:42:17	Trudi Thomson	V35	18.01.59	2	Saroma, JAP	26	Jun
8:05:20	Carolyn Hunter-Rowe		25.01.64	10	Saroma, JAP	26	Jun
8:24:30	Sylvia Watson	V45	29.09.47	16	Saroma, JAP	26	Jun
9:10:32					Winschoten, HOL	3	Sep
8:28:59	Sharon Gayter				Winschoten, HOL	3	Sep
8:40:41				1	Greenwich	8	May
8:44:59	Hilary Walker	V40	9.11.53		Winschoten, HOL	3	Sep
9:18:33	Sue Ashley	V40	10.10.52		Victoria, CAN	31	Aug
9:22:48	Ruth Fletcher	V35		1	Edinburgh	31	Jul

267

24 HOURS - Track

204.674	Sharon Gayter			London (TB)	22	Oct
200.925	Marianne Savage	V45	26.01.49	London (TB)	22	Oct
170.912	Hilary Walker	V40	9.11.53	London (TB)	22	Oct
165.601	Brenda Barnett			Hull	16	Jul

24 HOURS - Road

188.103	Sandra Brown	V45	1.04.49	Szeged	21	May
186.390	Eleanor Robinson	V45	20.11.47	Szeged	21	May
172.485	Marianne Savage	V45	26.01.49	Szeged	21	May

1500 METRES STEEPLECHASE

5:18.2 mx	Sally Young	V35	29.09.55		Crawley	5	Jul
5:43.8	Lisa Baillie	U20	25.05.77	1	Grangemouth	1	Jun
5:49.6	Allison Higgins	U23	8.04.72	2	Grangemouth	1	Jun

2000 METRES STEEPLECHASE (2' 6" Barriers)

6:53.7	Sharon Dixon		22.04.68	1	Horsham	8	May
7:00.7	Sally Young	V35	29.09.55	2	Horsham	8	May

2000 METRES STEEPLECHASE

7:05.76	Veronica Boden	V35	23.12.58	1	Bedford	16	Jul
7:09.9 mx					Stretford	2	Aug
7:22.34	Sally Young	V35	29.09.55	2	Bedford	16	Jul
8:27.4 mx	Michelle Evans	U20		5	Stretford	2	Aug

60 METRES HURDLES - Indoors

8.11	Sam Farquharson		15.12.69	4s1	Paris, FRA	13	Mar
	8.14			2	Glasgow	12	Feb
	8.17			4h1	Paris, FRA	11	Mar
	8.19			1	Birmingham	19	Feb
	8.20			2r2	Vienna, AUT	6	Feb
	8.22			5	Birmingham	26	Feb
	8.26			1r1	Vienna, AUT	6	Feb
	8.33			1h3	Birmingham	19	Feb
8.12	Clova Court		10.02.60	1	Glasgow	12	Feb
	8.19			2	Glasgow	29	Jan
	8.19			3	Birmingham	26	Feb
	8.24			5h3	Paris, FRA	11	Mar
	8.33			1	Birmingham	8	Jan
	8.37			1h2	Birmingham	8	Jan
8.14	Jacqui Agyepong		5.01.69	2	Birmingham	26	Feb
	8.27			3	Glasgow	29	Jan
	8.31			1h1	Birmingham	19	Feb
8.29	Lesley-Ann Skeete		20.02.67	1	Glasgow	23	Jan
	8.32			2r1	Vienna, AUT	6	Feb
	8.37			3r2	Vienna, AUT	6	Feb
	8.39			2	Birmingham	8	Jan
	8.39			3	Birmingham	19	Feb
	8.41			1h2	Glasgow	23	Jan
	8.44			8	Birmingham	26	Feb
8.39	Angela Thorp	U23	7.12.72	2h1	Birmingham	19	Feb
	8.40			4	Birmingham	19	Feb
	8.50			1r1	Birmingham	26	Feb
8.45	Diane Allahgreen	U20	21.02.75	2h2	Birmingham	19	Feb
	8.47			1	Birmingham	13	Feb
8.49	Natasha Mighty		21.12.70	5	Birmingham	19	Feb
8.50	Keri Maddox	U23	4.07.72	2	Glasgow	23	Jan

31 performances to 8.50 by 8 athletes

8.55	Orla Bermingham	U20	7.10.75	2	Birmingham	13 Feb
8.55	Melanie Wilkins	U23	18.01.73	7	Birmingham	19 Feb
(10)						
8.56	Sam Baker	U23	14.04.72	2h3	Birmingham	8 Jan
8.61	Jocelyn Kirby	V35	21.11.57	1h1	Glasgow	23 Jan
8.63	Lisa Gibbs		9.01.69	3r1	Birmingham	26 Feb
8.73	Theresa Crosbie	U20	17.07.75	1	Glasgow	6 Feb
8.73	Uju Efobi	U23	10.10.74	2r2	Birmingham	26 Feb
8.77	Jane Hale	U23	4.01.74	5h1	Birmingham	19 Feb
8.80	Vicki Jamison	U20	19.05.77	2	Glasgow	6 Feb
8.82	Sarah Richmond	U23	6.01.73	2h3	Glasgow	23 Jan
8.83	Clare Mackintosh		2.04.71	3h3	Glasgow	23 Jan
8.87	Kate Forsyth	U17	5.06.79	1	Birmingham	27 Feb
(20)						
8.89	Louise Colledge	U17	12.10.77	1	Birmingham	12 Feb
8.90	Paula Woodland	U17	21.12.78	2	Birmingham	12 Feb
8.94	Gail Murchie/Walker		7.12.71	1	Glasgow	15 Jan
8.99	Teresa Springate		8.03.69	3h1	Birmingham	8 Jan
8.99	Alison Purton	U23	25.11.72	2h2	Glasgow	23 Jan
8.99	Lorraine Brackstone	U17	15.02.78	2	Birmingham	6 Feb
8.99	Sharon Price	U20	10.12.75	2h1	Birmingham	13 Feb

Additional Under 17 (1 - 4 above)

9.02	Nicola Sharp		29.10.77	4	Birmingham	12 Feb
9.03	Rachael Kennedy		15.06.78	5	Birmingham	12 Feb
9.05	Amanda Batt		9.11.77	6	Birmingham	12 Feb
9.13	Stacey Moxey		6.10.77	1	Glasgow	10 Feb
9.13	Rebecca Lewis		31.12.77	P	Glasgow	10 Dec
9.20	Claire Pearson		23.09.78	3	Birmingham	6 Feb
(10)						
9.20	Jackie Tindal		21.01.79	P	Glasgow	10 Dec
9.21	Hazel Clarke		17.03.79	1P	Glasgow	5 Mar
9.22	Clover Wynter-Pink		29.11.77	P	Glasgow	10 Dec
9.22	Angie Nyhan		13.04.78	P	Glasgow	10 Dec
9.24	Katie Challoner		18.09.78	4	Birmingham	6 Feb

Hand Timing

8.3	Angela Thorp	U23	(8.39i)	1	Sheffield	19 Jan
8.4	Agyepong		(8.14)	1r1	London (CP)	15 Jan
	8.5			1r2	London (CP)	15 Jan
	3 performances to 8.5 by 2 athletes					
8.7	Natasha Danvers	U17	19.09.77	2	London (CP)	30 Jan
8.7	Uju Efobi	U23	(8.73i)	1r2	London (CP)	12 Feb
8.8	Gowry Retchakan		21.06.60	2r1	London (CP)	12 Feb
8.9	Diana Bennett	U23	14.06.74	3r2	London (CP)	15 Jan
8.9	Jenny Kelly		20.06.70	3r3	London (CP)	15 Jan
8.9	Charmaine Johnson		4.06.63	1P	London (CP)	23 Jan

Additional Under 17

9.1	Emma Blunt		26.10.77	1	London (CP)	30 Jan
9.1	Emma Brown		7.11.78	1r1	London (CP)	17 Dec
9.2	Virginia Dodd		30.06.79	4	London (CP)	30 Jan
9.2	Kirsty Mayhead		17.02.78	1	London (CP)	27 Feb

Under 15

9.09	Julie Davis		16.11.79	3	Birmingham	27 Feb
9.1	Nicola Hall		14.12.79	1	London (CP)	30 Jan
9.1	Clare O'Sullivan		8.05.80	1r2	London (CP)	17 Dec
9.19	Clare Anning			P	Glasgow	10 Dec
9.2	Eve Miller		1.12.79	2	London (CP)	30 Jan

70 METRES HURDLES - Under 13

11.5		Kate Churchman	2.11.81	1	Thurrock	19	Jun
11.6		Seonaid Ferry	19.11.81	1	Coatbridge	22	May
11.6		Lucy Michie	4.09.81	1	Livingston	4	Sep
11.66	1.3	Gemma Hair	3.11.81	1	Edinburgh	4	Sep
11.7		Kate Thorner	13.01.82	1	Millfield	8	Jun
11.7	3.1	Stacie King	19.01.82	1h2	Brecon	19	Jun
11.79	1.3	Charlotte Todd	7.12.81	2	Edinburgh	4	Sep
11.8		Gemma Cross	22.10.81	1	Leamington	15	May
11.8		Alexis Carter	23.10.81	2	Leamington	15	May
11.8		K. Bridge		1	Yate	3	Jul
	(10)						
11.8		Cheryl Gibbons	21.09.81	1	Warrington	27	Aug

75 METRES HURDLES - Under 15

11.08		Nicola Hall	14.12.79	1	London (CP)	29	May
11.18	0.6	Sarah Claxton	23.09.79	1P	Birmingham	18	Sep
11.2		Kelly Williamson	4.12.79	1	Sheffield	22	Jun
11.35	-0.6			2	Birmingham	31	Jul
11.21 w 4.0		Leanda Adams	7.12.79	2	Telford	9	Jul
11.30	-0.6			1	Birmingham	31	Jul
11.24	1.1	Lynn Fairweather	15.01.80	1	Dublin, IRE	13	Aug
11.24 w 4.0		Cheryl Kennedy	10.02.80	3	Telford	9	Jul
11.36	0.5			1	Gateshead	29	May
11.3		Amy Bergiers	19.09.79	1P	Swansea	9	Jul
11.51	0.6			5	Birmingham	31	Jul
11.36 w 4.0		Katy Lestrange	17.09.79	4	Telford	9	Jul
11.53	-0.6			2s1	Telford	8	Jul
11.4		Rachael Kay	8.09.80	1	Ashton-U-Lyne	5	Jun
11.41 w 4.0		Eve Miller	1.12.79	5	Telford	9	Jul
11.5				2	Norwich	16	Jul
11.58	0.4			2h1	Birmingham	31	Jul
	(10)						
11.5 un		Amy Nuttell	6.02.80				
11.5		Lesley McGoldrick	12.09.79	1P	York	26	Jun
11.52	0.4	Naomi Hodge-Dallaway	1.06.81	1h1	Birmingham	31	Jul
11.52	-0.6	Katherine Livesey	15.12.79	6	Birmingham	31	Jul
11.53 w 4.0		Laura Haylock	20.02.80	6	Telford	9	Jul
11.6		Leanne Dennis	30.12.79	2	Brecon	19	Jun

Under 13

12.6		Kate Churchman	2.11.81	3	Barking	11	Jun
12.8		Sarah Zawada	9.04.82	1r1	Basingstoke	7	Aug

80 METRES HURDLES - Under 17

11.11 w 5.6		Liz Fairs	1.12.77	1	Telford	9	Jul
11.48	0.9			1h2	Telford	8	Jul
11.27 w 5.6		Julie Pratt	20.03.79	2	Telford	9	Jul
11.55	1.4			1	London (CP)	29	May
11.39 w 5.6		Louise Colledge	12.10.77	3	Telford	9	Jul
11.58	0.9			2h2	Telford	8	Jul
11.40 w 5.6		Kate Forsyth	5.06.79	4	Telford	9	Jul
11.66	0.9			3h2	Telford	8	Jul
11.52	1.7	Lorraine Brackstone	15.02.78	1h4	Telford	8	Jul
11.64 w 5.6		Paula Woodland	21.12.78	6	Telford	9	Jul
11.68	0.9			4h2	Telford	8	Jul
11.67	1.4	Amanda Batt	9.11.77	2	London (CP)	29	May
11.72		Kathryn Williams	10.11.77	2	Dublin, IRE	13	Aug
11.72 w 2.8		Rebecca Lewis	31.12.77	1H	Birmingham	17	Sep
12.10	-1.7			2	Birmingham	11	Sep

11.74 w 5.6	Rachael Kennedy		15.06.78	7	Telford	9 Jul
11.82 -1.0				4s1	Telford	8 Jul
(10)						
11.75 w 5.6	Abigail Ashby		23.11.77	8	Telford	9 Jul
11.94 1.7				4h4	Telford	8 Jul
11.86 w 2.2	Emma Anderson		19.06.79	1h3	Telford	8 Jul
11.88 1.7	Katherine Oakes		24.11.77	2h4	Telford	8 Jul
11.94 w 2.2	Claire Pearson		23.09.78	3h3	Telford	8 Jul
11.99				2	Stoke	11 Sep
11.96 w 2.1	Emma Blunt		26.10.77	2h3	London (CP)	29 May
12.05 1.4				4	London (CP)	29 May
12.04 -0.6	Jackie Tindal		21.01.79	1	Grangemouth	9 Jul
12.04 w 2.2	Vicky Styles		8.12.77	4h3	Telford	8 Jul
12.04 w 2.2	Virginia Dodd		30.06.79	5h3	Telford	8 Jul
12.06 0.2	Victoria Henson		9.01.79	1h1	Telford	8 Jul
12.06 w 2.2	Lucy Baden		21.10.77	6h3	Telford	8 Jul
(20)						
12.07 w	Stacey Moxey		6.10.77	1	Edinburgh	1 Jun

Hand Timing

11.4		Liz Fairs		(11.48)	1	Sheffield	22 Jun
11.5		Julie Pratt		(11.55)	1	Barking	4 Jun
11.7		Claire Pearson		(11.99)	1	Carshalton	18 Sep
11.8		Katherine Oakes		(11.88)	1	Hoo	18 Jun
11.9		Emma Blunt		(12.05)	1	Kingston	23 Apr
11.9	0.6	Kirsty Mayhead		17.02.78	2	Croydon	15 May
11.9		Victoria Henson		(12.06)	1	Peterborough	11 Jun
11.9		Emma Anderson		(11.86w)	1	Stoke	11 Jun
11.9		Clover Wynter-Pink		29.11.77	1H	London (WL)	25 Jun
11.9		Julie Davis	U15	16.11.79	1	Dublin (B), IRE	25 Jun
11.9 w 5.4		Jackie Tindal		(12.04)	1	Glasgow	18 Jun
12.0		Nicola Sharp		29.10.77	2	Bracknell	26 Mar
12.0		Amanda Humble		15.08.79	1H	Jarrow	21 May
12.0		Vicky Styles		(12.04w)	1	Bebington	11 Jun
12.0		Rebecca Lewis		(12.10)	1H	Blackpool	25 Jun
12.0		Emma Brown		7.11.78	2	Carshalton	25 Jun
12.0		Jackie Capp		31.03.78	1	Norwich	16 Jul
12.0		Virginia Dodd		(12.04w)	2	Norwich	16 Jul
12.0 w 5.4		Stacey Moxey		(12.07w)	2	Glasgow	18 Jun

100 METRES HURDLES

12.93 1.4	Jacqui Agyepong	5.01.69	2r2	Lausanne, SWZ	6 Jul
12.93 1.3			2	Edinburgh	8 Jul
12.97 1.1			1h1	Helsinki, FIN	8 Aug
13.00 -1.4			1	Birmingham	26 Jun
13.02 -0.9			3	London (CP)	10 Sep
13.11 1.8			4	Sheffield	4 Sep
13.12 -0.7			5	Oslo, NOR	22 Jul
13.14 0.9			1h2	Sheffield	11 Jun
13.14 -2.0			2	Victoria, CAN	27 Aug
13.17 -1.1			1	Budapest, HUN	3 Jun
13.17 -1.7			7	Helsinki, FIN	9 Aug
13.19 -1.2			3r2	Zurich, SWZ	17 Aug
13.27 0.4			1h1	Budapest, HUN	3 Jun
13.28 -1.9			4s2	Helsinki, FIN	9 Aug
13.29 -0.4			8	London (CP)	15 Jul
13.34 -4.7			2	Gateshead	1 Jul
13.34 -2.6			1	Gateshead	20 Jul
13.41 -1.7			1	Birmingham	8 May

13.04	-0.4	Clova Court		10.02.60	5s1	Helsinki, FIN	9 Aug
13.06	0.5				1	Sheffield	11 Jun
13.07	1.5				1H2	Victoria, CAN	22 Aug
13.23	0.2				5h4	Helsinki, FIN	8 Aug
13.27	1.0				3h1	Victoria, CAN	26 Aug
13.43	-0.3				1h4	Sheffield	11 Jun
13.46	-2.1				1	Stoke	16 Jul
13.49	-0.7				3	Birmingham	21 May
13.08	0.4	Sam Farquharson		15.12.69	1r2	Linz, AUT	4 Jul
13.09	1.0				2h1	Victoria, CAN	26 Aug
13.12	1.3				4	Edinburgh	8 Jul
13.14	-0.2				2	Nitra, SVK	13 Jul
13.15	-0.4				5	London (CP)	15 Jul
13.21	0.9				2h2	Sheffield	11 Jun
13.33	-0.6				4h3	Helsinki, FIN	8 Aug
13.38	-2.0				3	Victoria, CAN	27 Aug
13.48	-0.7				2	Birmingham	21 May
13.09	0.5	Sally Gunnell		29.07.66	2	Sheffield	11 Jun
13.24	1.9	Keri Maddox	U23	4.07.72	1h2	Stoke	16 Jul
13.40	-2.9				2r1	Kings Lynn	9 Jul
13.49	0.5				4	Sheffield	11 Jun
13.25	1.1	Diane Allahgreen	U20	21.02.75	1s2	Lisbon, POR	21 Jul
13.31	0.5				3	Lisbon, POR	22 Jul
13.43	0.6				1	Derby	16 Jul
13.48	0.5				2h1	Lisbon, POR	21 Jul
13.32	-2.9	Angela Thorp	U23	7.12.72	1r1	Kings Lynn	9 Jul
13.36	-1.0				1	Wrexham	3 Jul
13.44	-0.6				1	Corby	30 May
13.45	-0.7				1	Birmingham	21 May
13.42	0.6	Lesley-Ann Skeete		20.02.67	2	Brussels, BEL	17 Jul
13.43	0.5				3	Sheffield	11 Jun
13.47	1.5	Denise Lewis	U23	27.08.72	3H	Venissieux, FRA	2 Jul
13.49	1.9				3h2	Stoke	16 Jul

51 performances to 13.50 by 9 athletes

13.72	0.5	Melanie Wilkins	U23	18.01.73	7	Sheffield	11 Jun
	(10)						
13.80	1.1	Bethan Edwards	U23	2.05.73	1	Oordegem, BEL	9 Jul
13.82	-0.6	Sam Baker	U23	14.04.72	1	London (CP)	2 May
13.84	1.5	Louise Fraser		10.10.70	1	Colwyn Bay	23 Jul
13.95	0.5	Natasha Danvers	U17	19.09.77	1	Schio, ITA	6 Aug
13.97	-0.3	Natasha Mighty		21.12.70	3h4	Sheffield	11 Jun
14.01	0.3	Orla Bermingham	U20	7.10.75	1r2	Vienna, AUT	29 May
14.06	1.8	Vikki Schofield	U23	29.12.72	6H	Venissieux, FRA	2 Jul
14.14	0.5	Denise Bolton	U20	1.02.77	2	Schio, ITA	6 Aug
14.16	0.6	Jane Hale	U23	4.01.74	2	London (CP)	2 May
14.19	-0.3	Jocelyn Kirby	V35	21.11.57	4h4	Sheffield	11 Jun
	(20)						
14.26	0.5	Vicki Jamison	U20	19.05.77	2	Belfast	4 Jun
14.29	-0.3	Sarah Richmond	U23	6.01.73	5h4	Sheffield	11 Jun
14.30		Claire Phythian	U23	7.02.73	1H	Fayetteville, USA	12 May
14.32	1.8	Kim Crowther-Price		19.01.66	H	Horsham	18 Jun
14.32	-0.1	Kerry Jury		19.11.68	1H	Stoke	6 Aug
14.36	0.7	Clare Mackintosh		2.04.71	1h2	Edinburgh	25 Jun
14.36	1.7	Charmaine Johnson		4.06.63	7H	Venissieux, FRA	2 Jul
14.37	0.9	Teresa Springate		8.03.69	4h2	Sheffield	11 Jun
14.37	1.1	Rachel King	U20	11.05.76	6	Oordegem, BEL	9 Jul
14.43		Jenny Kelly		20.06.70	3H1	Victoria, CAN	22 Aug
	(30)						
14.47	1.8	Diana Bennett	U23	14.06.74	2H	Horsham	18 Jun
14.51	1.7	Susan Jones	U17	8.06.78	1h2	Gateshead	29 May
14.54	0.9	Katy Bartlett	U23	6.05.73	6h2	Sheffield	11 Jun

14.54	0.7	Katy Sketchley	U23	9.07.73	2h2	Edinburgh	25	Jun
14.57		Jo MacDonald	U20	3.09.75	3h2	Telford	8	Jul
14.58	1.5	Megan Jones	U20	10.07.76	6	Colwyn Bay	23	Jul
14.59	0.7	Lorna Silver	U23	10.01.74	1	Edinburgh	4	Sep
14.66	-0.6	Alison Purton	U23	25.11.72	5	London (CP)	2	May
14.66	0.2	Sharon Price	U20	10.12.75	1	Solihull	28	May
14.70	0.7	Gail Murchie/Walker		7.12.71	3h2	Edinburgh	25	Jun
	(40)							
14.72	-0.1	Pauline Richards		30.06.68	2H	Stoke	6	Aug
14.74	-2.2	Anne Hollman	U23	18.02.74	H	London (He)	20	Aug
14.78	-0.3	Patricia Naughton	U20	17.04.75	7	Bedford	3	Jul
14.81	1.0	Samantha Male	U20	11.04.76	1	London (He)	7	Aug
14.85	0.9	Joanne Suddes	U20	27.01.77	3h1	Telford	8	Jul
14.86	1.4	Natasha Bartlett	U23	19.01.74	2h1	Hull	21	Aug
14.88	0.4	Theresa Crosbie	U20	17.07.75	2	Glasgow	14	May
14.88		Leah Lackenby	U23	18.09.74	2	Gateshead	14	May
14.88	1.8	Eleanor Cave	U23	23.01.73	3H	Horsham	18	Jun
14.88	1.0	Hannah Jenkin	U20	30.09.76	2	London (He)	7	Aug
	(50)							
14.90	0.6	Janine Whitlock	U23	11.08.73	4	Derby	16	Jul
14.91	1.8	Rebecca Foster		14.04.71	4H	Horsham	18	Jun
14.96	1.6	Emma Lindsay		11.04.71	6H	Victoria, CAN	22	Aug
14.99	1.4	Katie Budd	U20	3.01.76	2h1	London (CP)	29	May
14.99	1.8	Sarah Damm		12.09.70	5H	Horsham	18	Jun
15.06	1.0	Bianca Liston	U17	28.05.78	3	London (He)	7	Aug
15.07	1.0	Kelly Sotherton	U20	13.11.76	4	London (He)	7	Aug
15.08	0.9	Sally Sager	U20	28.03.77	5h1	Telford	8	Jul
15.09	2.0	Elizabeth Gibbens	U20	5.04.77	1H	Birmingham	17	Sep
15.14		Lorna McCulloch		10.03.71	1	Edinburgh	8	Jun
	(60)							
15.14		Stephanie Nicholson	U20	28.06.76	1h3	Telford	8	Jul
15.14	-0.1	Jacqueline Cooke	U20	20.06.76	1H	Stoke	6	Aug
15.16	-1.2	Julie Major		19.08.70	6	London (CP)	26	Jun

Additional Under 17 (1 - 3 above)

15.37	-1.0	Amanda Batt		9.11.77	5	London (He)	7	Aug

Wind Assisted

12.98	2.1	Agyepong		(12.93)	1h2	Victoria, CAN	26	Aug
	13.13	3.8			7	St. Petersburg, RUS	26	Jul
	13.22	4.4			1	Bedford	17	Sep
13.21	3.1	Court		(13.04)	1H	Horsham	18	Jun
13.27	2.3	Gunnell		(13.09)	1h1	Sheffield	11	Jun

5 performances to 13.50 by 3 athletes

13.62	4.4	Yinka Idowu	U23	25.02.72	2	Bedford	17	Sep
13.63	4.4	Sam Baker	U23	(13.82)	3	Bedford	17	Sep
13.65	4.4	Melanie Wilkins	U23	(13.72)	4	Bedford	17	Sep
13.68	2.8	Michelle Campbell		24.02.69	4	Azusa, USA	23	Apr
13.74	3.8	Natasha Mighty		(13.97)	1H	Sheffield	30	Apr
13.76	3.4	Natasha Danvers	U17	(13.95)	1	London (He)	27	Aug
13.80	3.8	Lisa Gibbs		9.01.69	2H	Sheffield	30	Apr
13.87	2.2	Orla Bermingham	U20	(14.01)	2h2	Lisbon, POR	21	Jul
13.93	3.3	Jocelyn Kirby	V35	(14.19)	2	Istanbul, TUR	22	May
14.02	2.1	Sarah Richmond	U23	(14.29)	1	Edinburgh	25	Jun
14.04	3.6	Denise Bolton	U20	(14.14)	2	Telford	9	Jul
14.05	3.1	Uju Efobi	U23	10.10.74	3H	Horsham	18	Jun
14.06	4.6	Patricia Naughton	U20	(14.78)	3h1	Bedford	3	Jul
14.16	2.1	Clare Mackintosh		(14.36)	2	Edinburgh	25	Jun
14.19	4.0	Kerry Jury		(14.32)	3h1	Stoke	16	Jul
14.22	3.8	Kim Crowther-Price		(14.32)	1H	Wrexham	27	Aug
14.24	2.2	Jo MacDonald	U20	(14.57)	2	London (CP)	29	May

14.41	2.1	Clare Bushby	U20	7.09.76	4	Edinburgh	25	Jun
14.47	2.1	Katy Sketchley	U23	(14.54)	5	Edinburgh	25	Jun
14.53	3.6	Hannah Jenkin	U20	(14.88)	5	Telford	9	Jul
14.60 w	3.7	Pauline Richards		(14.72)	1H	Horsham	18	Jun
14.64	2.3	Janine Whitlock	U23	(14.90)	7h1	Sheffield	11	Jun
14.69	2.2	Samantha Male	U20	(14.81)	3	London (CP)	29	May
14.72	3.1	Kelly Sotherton	U20	(15.07)	H	Birmingham	17	Sep
14.74	2.7	Rebecca Foster		(14.91)	4H	Sheffield	30	Apr
14.75	2.7	Julie Major		(15.16)	5H	Sheffield	30	Apr
14.80	2.2	Katie Budd	U20	(14.99)	5	London (CP)	29	May
14.96	3.6	Stephanie Nicholson	U20	(15.14)	7	Telford	9	Jul
14.99	3.0	Jenny Pearson		3.07.62	3	Bedford	18	Sep
15.01	3.7	Julie Hollman	U20	16.02.77	2H	Horsham	18	Jun
15.03	4.6	Jacqueline Cooke	U20	(15.14)	8h1	Bedford	3	Jul
15.04	2.2	Debbie Nicklin	U20	9.12.75	7	London (CP)	29	May
15.04	4.0	Jane Saxelby	U23	14.01.72	5h1	Stoke	16	Jul
15.09	2.5	Emma Green		25.01.64	1H	Sheffield	30	Apr
15.14	4.0	Claire Morrison		30.05.69	6h1	Stoke	16	Jul
15.16	2.7	Julia Bennett		26.03.70	6H	Sheffield	30	Apr
15.16	2.8	Teresa Andrews	U20	4.01.77	3	Newport	28	May

Hand Timing

13.2		Agyepong		(12.93)	1	Bournemouth	19	Jun
13.3	-1.0	Farquharson		(13.08)	1	Enfield	31	Jul
13.5		Maddox	U23	(13.24)	1	Loughborough	22	Jun

3 performances to 13.5 by 3 athletes

13.6		Melanie Wilkins	U23	(13.72)	1	Corby	31	Jul
13.7		Bethan Edwards	U23	(13.80)	1	Brecon	5	Jun
13.8	1.7	Sam Baker	U23	(13.82)	2	Kingston	31	Jul
14.0		Vicki Jamison	U20	(14.26)	1	Antrim	30	Apr
14.0		Jocelyn Kirby	V35	(14.19)	1r1	Leicester	19	Jun
14.1		Yinka Idowu	U23	(13.62w)	1	London (WF)	3	Sep
14.2		Sarah Richmond	U23	(14.29)	1	Grangemouth	12	Jun
14.3		Leah Lackenby	U23	(14.88)	1H	Jarrow	21	May
14.3	0.2	Megan Jones	U20	(14.58)	1	Newport	26	Jun
14.3		Teresa Springate		(14.37)	1	Windsor	13	Aug
14.3 w		Susan Jones	U17	(14.51)	1	Wigan	17	Apr
		14.4			1	Leeds	2	May
14.4		Jo MacDonald	U20	(14.57)	1	Kingston	19	Jun
14.4	-0.5	Uju Efobi	U23	(14.05w)	1	Yate	21	Aug
14.4		Natasha Turner	U23	8.11.74	4	London (Elt)	29	Aug
14.5	1.1	Hannah Jenkin	U20	(14.88)	2	London (Nh)	14	May
14.5		Katy Sketchley	U23	(14.54)	1	Colchester	19	Jun
14.5		Pauline Richards		(14.72)	2	Corby	31	Jul
14.6		Hayley Jones		20.09.71	1	Leamington	14	May
14.6	1.1	Marie Major	U23	4.05.74	3	London (Nh)	14	May
14.6	1.1	Julie Major		(15.16)	4	London (Nh)	14	May
14.6		*Olive Burke*		*12.09.66*	*2*	*Sheffield*	*19*	*Jun*
14.7	0.2	Helen Blanchard	U23	11.07.72	3	Newport	26	Jun
14.7	1.7	Jenny Pearson		(14.99w)	4	Kingston	31	Jul
14.7		Anne Hollman	U23	(14.74)	1	St. Ives	13	Aug
14.8	-3.1	Stephanie McCann		26.10.65	1	Antrim	7	May
14.8		Janine Whitlock	U23	(14.90)	3	Carlisle	26	Jun
14.8	0.2	Claire Morrison		(15.14w)	4	Newport	26	Jun
14.9		Sarah Damm		(14.99)	2	Stoke	9	Apr
14.9		Gowry Retchakan		21.06.60	1	Croydon	8	May
14.9		Clare Wise		22.08.69	1r2	Aldershot	7	Aug
14.9		Stephanie Law	U23	21.04.72	1	London (WF)	13	Aug

274

15.0		Emma Beales		7.12.71	5	Corby	31	Jul
15.0 w	3.4	Paula Wilkin	U23	28.03.74	2	Hull	14	May
15.1		Julia Bennett		(15.16w)	2	London (BP)	10	Apr
15.1		Julie Pratt	U17	20.03.79	2	Stretford	12	Jun
15.1		Naomi Siddall	U20	2.04.75	1	Rotherham	19	Jun
15.1		Heather Myers		5.12.64	3	Aldershot	24	Jul
15.2		Debbie Robson	U20	12.07.76	3	Stoke	31	Jul
15.2		Liz Fairs	U17	1.12.77	1	Crewe	28	Aug

Additional Under 17

15.3	Louise Colledge	12.10.77	2	Stretford	24	Jul
15.4	Emma Blunt	26.10.77	1r2	Hornchurch	16	Jul

Timekeepers missed flash

12.9	Sam Farquharson	15.12.69	1	Barry	18	May

300 METRES HURDLES - Under 17

42.20	Natasha Danvers		19.09.77	1h1	Birmingham	31	Jul
43.38	Dextene McIntosh		27.08.78	2	Birmingham	31	Jul
44.1	Pamela Johnstone		16.03.79	1	Wakefield	17	Jul
	45.10			1	Grangemouth	9	Jul
44.2	Liz Fairs		1.12.77	1	Lincoln	7	Aug
	45.74			4	Birmingham	31	Jul
44.25	Kathryn Williams		10.11.77	3	Birmingham	31	Jul
44.28	Vicki Jamison	U20	19.05.77	1	Dublin, IRE	13	Aug
44.44	Cecily Hall		12.10.78	2	Telford	9	Jul
44.60	Kate Moody		7.04.79	2	Birmingham	11	Sep
44.6	Gael Davies		5.02.79	1	Solihull	29	May
	45.08			3h1	Birmingham	31	Jul
44.78	Leah Brock		15.03.79	3	Telford	9	Jul
	(10)						
44.8	Kirsty Mayhead		17.02.78	1	Kingston	11	Jun
44.92	Alice Wright		31.12.78	5	Telford	9	Jul
44.92	Leanne Buxton		27.05.78	2h1	Birmingham	31	Jul
45.0	Emma Brown		7.11.78	2	Kingston	11	Jun
45.36	Amanda Humble		15.08.79	3	Gateshead	29	May
45.46	Susan Jones		8.06.78	3	Birmingham	11	Sep
45.5	Eleanor Chamberlain		17.04.79	2	Solihull	29	May
45.53	Michelle John		13.04.78	6	Aberdeen	16	Jul
45.58	Jodi Hallett		8.11.78	7	Telford	9	Jul
45.6	Amanda Gray		22.03.79	1	Stoke	24	Jul
	46.72			4h3	Birmingham	31	Jul
	(20)						
45.7	Gayle Stanway		29.10.77	2	Coatbridge	28	Aug
	47.04			2	Grangemouth	9	Jul
45.71	Dominique Hardy		26.01.78	2h2	Telford	8	Jul
46.1	Caroline Cox		23.11.77	1	Cannock	1	May
46.1	Theresa Pugh		28.07.78	3	Solihull	29	May
46.21	Kim-Anne Taylor		10.02.78	2	London (CP)	29	May
46.37	Linda Crocker		2.04.79	3	London (CP)	29	May
46.4	Louise Dixon		29.11.77	1	Bebington	14	May
46.6	Sarah Griffiths		24.04.78	1	Milton Keynes	11	Jun
46.6	Niki Pocock		9.05.79	1	Guildford	11	Sep
46.8	Louise Clowes		19.07.78	2	Birmingham	1	May
	(30)						
46.8	Paula Woodland		21.12.78	1	Oxford	11	Jun
46.88	Lyndsey Devlin		14.03.79	5h1	Birmingham	31	Jul
46.9	Katie Treble		21.11.78	1	Carn Brea	12	Jun
46.9	Vicky Styles		8.12.77	1	Bolton	17	Jul
46.9	Amy Baden		30.05.79	1	Exeter	24	Jul
46.96	Rebecca Wright		20.12.77	4	Birmingham	11	Sep
46.99	Tracey Hilton		9.03.78	5h2	Telford	8	Jul

400 METRES HURDLES

53.33	Sally Gunnell		29.07.66	1	Helsinki, FIN	12	Aug
53.51				1	St. Petersburg, RUS	24	Jul
53.91				2	Nice, FRA	18	Jul
54.04				1	London (CP)	15	Jul
54.06				1	Lausanne, SWZ	6	Jul
54.51				1	Victoria, CAN	26	Aug
54.60				1s2	Helsinki, FIN	10	Aug
54.62				1	Birmingham	25	Jun
54.69				1	Gateshead	1	Jul
54.74				1	Bratislava, SVK	1	Jun
54.80				1	London (CP)	9	Sep
55.17				1h2	Helsinki, FIN	9	Aug
55.24				1	Sheffield	4	Sep
55.25				1h1	Victoria, CAN	24	Aug
55.78	Gowry Retchakan		21.06.60	3s1	Helsinki, FIN	10	Aug
56.05				8	Helsinki, FIN	12	Aug
56.16				2	Lisbon, POR	18	Jun
56.35				2	Gateshead	20	Jul
56.45				4h3	Helsinki, FIN	9	Aug
56.69				5	Victoria, CAN	26	Aug
56.74				7	London (CP)	15	Jul
56.76				2h1	Victoria, CAN	24	Aug
56.9				1	Horsham	31	Jul
57.08				1	Sheffield	12	Jun
57.1				1	Peterborough	10	Jul
57.29				6	Gateshead	1	Jul
58.07				1h1	Sheffield	11	Jun
56.41	Jacqui Parker		15.10.66	4	Bratislava, SVK	1	Jun
56.51				2	Sydney, AUS	13	Mar
56.72				6	Victoria, CAN	26	Aug
56.74				6	Jena, GER	3	Jun
57.31				2	Sheffield	12	Jun
57.53				4h2	Victoria, CAN	24	Aug
57.59				1	Perth, AUS	27	Feb
57.78				3	Padua, ITA	10	Jul
57.81				3r3	Schwechat, AUT	29	May
57.83				7h1	Helsinki, FIN	9	Aug
57.95				1h1	Sydney, AUS	11	Mar
58.04				3	Walnut, USA	17	Apr
58.13				7	Sheffield	4	Sep
58.20				1	Nitra, SVK	13	Jul
58.04	Clare Bleasdale		6.07.71	1	Brussels, BEL	16	Jul
58.2				1	Guildford	13	Aug
58.07	Louise Brunning	U23	6.03.72	1	Aartselaar, BEL	21	Jul
58.09	Stephanie McCann		26.10.65	3	Sheffield	12	Jun
58.09				5	Gateshead	20	Jul
	46 performances to 58.2 by 6 athletes						
58.43	Jane Low		26.08.60	5h1	Victoria, CAN	24	Aug
58.78	Vyvyan Rhodes	U23	5.05.73	1	Derby	16	Jul
59.0	Jenny Pearson		3.07.62	1	Kingston	31	Jul
59.82				4	London (CP)	26	Jun
59.16	Allison Curbishley	U20	3.06.76	2	Bedford	3	Jul
	(10)						
59.25	Natasha Bartlett	U23	19.01.74	1	Cwmbran	18	Jun
59.39	Stephanie McPeake/Llewellyn		31.12.68	7	Sheffield	12	Jun
59.46	Heather Myers		5.12.64	3	London (CP)	26	Jun
59.49	Keri Maddox	U23	4.07.72	2	Solihull	21	Aug
59.72	Vicky Day	U23	19.06.72	2	Loughborough	5	Jun

276

59.9	Lorna Silver	U23	10.01.74	1	Yate	21 Aug
60.58				1	Colwyn Bay	23 Jul
60.0	Veronica Boden	V35	23.12.58	1	London (WF)	6 Aug
60.49				3r1	Corby	30 May
60.07	Vicki Jamison	U20	19.05.77	2	Warsaw, POL	18 Jun
60.20	Claire Edwards	U23	20.10.74	1	Oordegem, BEL	9 Jul
60.7	Barbara Brittain		24.10.66	2	Bracknell	2 May
61.39				1	Birmingham	8 May
(20)						
60.9	Debbie Duncan		13.02.69	2r1	Stretford	18 Jun
61.29				3h2	London (CP)	25 Jun
61.4	Denise Bolton	U20	1.02.77	1	Stretford	12 Jun
62.73				3h1	Bedford	2 Jul
61.5	Rachel Halstead-Peel		15.09.70	2	Sheffield	14 May
62.62				6h3	Sheffield	11 Jun
61.54	Katy Bartlett	U23	6.05.73	3	Derby	16 Jul
61.68	Julia Sykes	U20	27.05.75	5h1	Sheffield	11 Jun
61.7	Karen Spackman		20.08.69	1	Hoo	16 Jul
63.14				5h2	London (CP)	25 Jun
61.76	Bonita Benjamin		1.06.67	1	Stoke	16 Jul
61.84	Clare Wise		22.08.69	1r2	Corby	30 May
61.90	Joanne Mahony	U20	22.10.76	1	Telford	9 Jul
61.9	Joanna Cadman		1.06.68	3r1	Grangemouth	7 May
63.19				8h2	Sheffield	11 Jun
(30)						
61.9	Natasha Turner	U23	8.11.74	3	London (Elt)	29 Aug
66.43				8	London (CP)	26 Jun
61.96	Denise Facey		8.02.69	2	Hull	21 Aug
62.0	Cathy White/Dawson		9.03.66	1	St. Ives	1 May
62.19	*Olive Burke*		*12.09.66*	*1*	*Tullamore, IRE*	*15 May*
62.2	Julie Harkin	U23	8.08.74	1	Loughborough	26 Jun
63.07				7h2	Sheffield	11 Jun
62.2	Julia Bennett		26.03.70	1r2	Exeter	3 Sep
62.23	Claire Griffiths	U20	1.01.76	2	Gateshead	28 May
62.33	Julia Carter		28.03.71	2	Stoke	16 Jul
62.40	Carol Dawkins		8.12.60	4h2	London (CP)	25 Jun
62.47	Sarah Veysey	U20	4.03.75	3	Stoke	16 Jul
62.55	Kathy Thurston	U20	2.01.76	2h1	Bedford	2 Jul
(40)						
62.6	Alison Currie/Mahindru		15.07.68	1r2	Stretford	18 Jun
63.72				3r2	Corby	30 May
62.6	Katie Jones	U20	4.01.77	2r2	Stretford	18 Jun
62.6	Sandra Leigh		26.02.66	1	Woking	16 Jul
62.70	Sarah Ditchfield	U20	26.03.75	3	Hull	21 Aug
62.8	Kate Norman	U20	1.01.76	1	Bromley	19 Jun
63.20				6	Bedford	3 Jul
62.8	Vikki Schofield	U23	29.12.72	1	Cleckheaton	7 Aug
62.9	Dyanna Clarke	V35	27.02.58	1	Hoo	19 Jun
62.9	Sarah Baigent		22.12.71	1	Aldershot	16 Jul
62.92				2	London (CP)	1 May
62.9	Anne Hollman	U23	18.02.74	1	Wigan	7 Aug
62.95	Carolyn Smith		6.10.61	2r2	Edinburgh	4 Sep
(50)						
63.0	Alanna Cooke		11.01.70	1r1	Derby	11 Sep
63.14	Orla Bermingham	U20	7.10.75	1	Chatilon, FRA	24 Sep
63.3	Alyson Evans/Layzell		16.12.66	1	Cheltenham	1 May
63.3	Michelle Cooke		28.11.64	1	Swansea	8 May
63.75				4	Istanbul, TUR	21 May
63.4	Ruth World	U23	19.03.74	2	Bromley	19 Jun
63.46	Linda Gabriel		27.07.64	4	Stoke	16 Jul

63.5	Elaine Donald	U23	30.04.74	4	Inverness	5 Jun
64.28				5	London (CP)	1 May
63.5	Isobel Donaldson		24.01.64	2	Aldershot	16 Jul
63.6	Rachel Briars	U20	29.01.76	1	Bebington	11 Jun
63.6	Emma Davies	U20	14.03.75	1	Barry	19 Jul
63.84				4	Oordegem, BEL	9 Jul
(60)						
63.66	Elizabeth Waters	U20	19.02.77	4	Telford	9 Jul
63.67	Celia Brown	U20	22.01.77	5	Telford	9 Jul
63.7	Hilary Moore		23.09.60	2	Portsmouth	16 Jul
63.71	Julie Rogers		15.01.64	2r2	Birmingham	8 May
63.72	Naomi Ward	U23	19.10.74	4	London (CP)	1 May
63.78	Jane Lapido		24.08.69	6h2	London (CP)	25 Jun
63.80	Jane Fuller	U20	21.04.76	6	Telford	9 Jul
63.8	Paula Cohen		5.02.71	5r1	Stretford	18 Jun
63.9	Charlotte Cutler	U23	16.10.72	1	Oxford	14 May
64.86				8	London (CP)	1 May
64.00	Angela Warburton		24.01.64	5	Derby	16 Jul
(70)						
64.0	Rosie Bagwell/Thorner		7.08.67	1	Bristol	4 Jun
64.1	Alison Hesketh		29.04.63	1	Stretford	14 May
64.1	Teresa Springate		8.03.69	3	Basildon	3 Sep
64.15	Tania Sexton		7.08.63	1	Birmingham	24 Apr
64.4	Claire Entwistle	U20	9.12.76	3	Telford	24 Jul
64.4	Alison Brown	V35	7.10.58	5	London (WF)	6 Aug
64.49	Sarah Burke	U23	11.07.73	7h2	London (CP)	25 Jun
64.5	Alison McDonnell	U23	28.06.72	2	Bristol	4 Jun
64.5	Cecily Hall	U17	12.10.78	2	Colchester	19 Jun
64.5	Natasha Mighty		21.12.70	2	Woking	16 Jul
(80)						
64.56	Anna Roze	U23	6.11.74	6	London (CP)	1 May
64.6	Moira McBeath		30.04.62	2	Aberdeen	12 Jun
64.70	Cathy Yarwood		17.06.69	6	Derby	16 Jul
64.7	Julie Price		18.12.70	4	Croydon	14 May
64.7	Tanya Wilkinson		1.04.70	2	Coventry	14 Aug
64.76	Anya Hutchinson	U20	16.07.77	2	Solihull	28 May
64.8	Anne Carr	U20	1.05.76	1	Exeter	20 Aug
64.86	Judy Thomas		20.01.63	2	Birmingham	24 Apr
64.9	Hannah Jenkin	U20	30.09.76	1	Bedford	21 May
64.9	Viginia Mitchell		29.01.63	3	Woking	16 Jul
(90)						
64.9	Andrea Askey	U23	9.11.74	2	Wigan	7 Aug
65.0	Sharon Trafford	U23	10.08.73	3	London (CP)	14 May
65.63				8h2	London (CP)	25 Jun
65.0	Leanne Buxton	U17	27.05.78	3	Aldershot	16 Jul
65.1	Leah Brock	U17	15.03.79	4	Telford	24 Jul
65.12	Maureen Barnes		21.04.63	2	Bedford	18 Sep
65.2	Kate Haywood	U23	23.12.74	1	Warley	14 May
65.39				5	Stoke	16 Jul
65.2	Alison Fenwick		6.02.63	2	Plymouth	21 May
65.3	Rachel Smith	U20	3.03.76	1	Oxford	5 Jun
65.3	Stephanie North		16.01.71	2r1	Bournemouth	19 Jun
65.59				6	Bedford	17 Sep
65.35	Charlotte Knowles	U23	11.10.72	1r2	Cardiff	8 May
(100)						
65.4	Margaret Still		9.05.65	1	Hull	30 Apr
65.4	Carolyn May	U23	15.10.74	1	Horsham	16 Jul
65.4	Dextene McIntosh	U17	27.08.78	1r2	Windsor	13 Aug
65.45	Louise Gregory	U23	11.05.74	5	Bedford	17 Sep
65.5	Lorna Turner	U23	11.05.72	3r2	Stretford	18 Jun
65.52	Elaine Faulkner		11.01.68	3	Antrim	7 May

65.55	Rachel Newcombe		25.02.67	3r2	Birmingham	8	May
65.6	Suzanne Barrington		3.08.71	2	Oxford	14	May
65.7	Sally Sager	U20	28.03.77	1	Mansfield	8	May
65.9	Tracy Brunger		8.06.70	1r2	Harrow	23	Apr
	(110)						
65.9	Caroline Whitehurst		3.07.59	2	Hull	30	Apr
66.0	Sarah Dean		10.12.63	1r2	Enfield	21	May

Additional Under 17 (1 - 4 above)

66.2	Amanda Humble		15.08.79	1	Jarrow	12	Jun
67.2	Theresa Pugh		28.07.78	1	Brierley Hill	24	Apr
67.5	Sarah Griffiths		24.04.78	5	Corby	31	Jul
67.7	Sally Youden		2.11.77	1	Grangemouth	4	Sep
67.8	Emma Brown		7.11.78	1	Carshalton	4	Jun

HIGH JUMP

1.91	Debbie Marti		14.05.68	3	Victoria, CAN	27	Aug
	1.89			1	Brussels, BEL	17	Jul
	1.88			3	Edinburgh	8	Jul
	1.88			1	Gateshead	20	Jul
	1.86			2	Sheffield	11	Jun
	1.86			1	Wrexham	3	Jul
	1.85			1	Stoke	31	Jul
	1.85			29Q	Helsinki, FIN	12	Aug
	1.85			Q	Victoria, CAN	23	Aug
	1.85			6	London (CP)	9	Sep
	1.83			1	Horsham	8	May
	1.83			2	Dublin (M), IRE	18	Jun
1.89	Julia Bennett		26.03.70	1	Sheffield	11	Jun
	1.88			1	Aldershot	24	Jul
	1.87			2	Brussels, BEL	17	Jul
	1.86			1H	Sheffield	30	Apr
	1.86			1	Croydon	15	May
	1.85 i			1	Birmingham	8	Jan
	1.85 i			2	Birmingham	19	Feb
	1.85			6	Birmingham	26	Jun
	1.85			6	Edinburgh	8	Jul
	1.85			19=Q	Helsinki, FIN	12	Aug
	1.85			Q	Victoria, CAN	23	Aug
	1.85			7	Victoria, CAN	27	Aug
	1.84 i			1P	London (CP)	23	Jan
	1.84			1	Kingston	23	Apr
	1.83 i			1P	Birmingham	3	Jan
	1.83 i			3	Glasgow	29	Jan
	1.83			1T	London (CP)	27	Apr
1.88	Lea Haggett	U23	9.05.72	5=	Victoria, CAN	27	Aug
	1.86			1	Portsmouth	16	Jul
	1.85			Q	Victoria, CAN	23	Aug
	1.85 i			1	London (CP)	17	Dec
	1.84			3	Wrexham	3	Jul
	1.83			6	Ostrava, CS	30	Jul
1.86	Jo Jennings		20.09.69	1	Auckland, NZ	22	Jan
	1.86 i			1	Birmingham	26	Feb
	1.83 i			3	Glasgow	12	Feb
1.85	Julie Major		19.08.70	5	Edinburgh	8	Jul
	1.83			3	Sheffield	11	Jun
	40 performances to 1.83 by 5 athletes including 8 indoors						
1.82	Susan Jones	U17	8.06.78	2	Nicosia, CYP	20	May
1.82	Diana Davies		7.05.61	4=	Wrexham	3	Jul
1.81	Hazel Melvin	U23	19.11.73	1	Istanbul, TUR	21	May

1.81	Denise Lewis	U23	27.08.72	8=H	Venissieux, FRA	2	Jul
1.81	Julie Crane	U20	26.09.76	1	Telford	9	Jul
(10)							
1.80 i	Kelly Mason/Thirkle		29.03.71	3=	Birmingham	19	Feb
1.76				1	Derby	16	Jul
1.79	Teresa Andrews	U20	4.01.77	2	Oordegem, BEL	9	Jul
1.79	Lindsay Evans	U20	29.08.77	1	London (He)	27	Aug
1.78	Lee McConnell	U17	9.10.78	1	Grangemouth	9	Jul
1.77	Michelle Dunkley	U17	26.01.78	1	Peterborough	29	Aug
1.76 i	Nicola Baker	U23	8.10.74	1	Gateshead	13	Feb
1.76 i	Cathy Boulton	U17	2.11.77	1	Birmingham	13	Feb
1.76				3	Telford	9	Jul
1.76	Claire Phythian	U23	7.02.73	H	Tempe, USA	24	Mar
1.76	Rachael Forrest	U17	25.12.77	2	Telford	9	Jul
1.75	Gemma Samphire	U23	5.10.73	1	Bournemouth	15	May
(20)							
1.75	Alison Evans	U23	13.12.73	1	Hull	26	Jun
1.75	Jenny Kelly		20.06.70	18=H	Venissieux, FRA	2	Jul
1.75	Lisa Brown	U20	16.03.76	6	Bedford	2	Jul
1.75	Leone Dickinson	U20	5.11.75	3	Telford	8	Jul
1.75	Gill Howard		14.04.69	2	Peterborough	10	Jul
1.74 i	Claire Everett	U17	25.06.79	1	Birmingham	27	Feb
1.70				5	Telford	9	Jul
1.74	Emma Lindsay		11.04.71	1H	Linwood	16	Jul
1.73 i	Ailsa Wallace	U20	12.03.77	2	Birmingham	13	Feb
1.70				4	Istanbul, TUR	21	May
1.73	Alison Purton	U23	25.11.72	1	Birmingham	8	May
1.73	Fiona McPhail		23.06.71	2	Birmingham	8	May
(30)							
1.73	Eleanor Cave	U23	23.01.73	1	Oxford	14	May
1.73	Debra Harvey	U20	13.11.75	1	Portsmouth	11	Jun
1.73	Vikki Schofield	U23	29.12.72	3	Derby	16	Jul
1.72	Uju Efobi	U23	10.10.74	1H	Horsham	18	Jun
1.72	Kerry Jury		19.11.68	3H	Horsham	18	Jun
1.72	Jenny Brown	V35	21.05.59	1	Athens, GRE		Jun
1.72	Charmaine Johnson		4.06.63	20=H	Venissieux, FRA	2	Jul
1.71 i	Diana Bennett	U23	14.06.74	3=P	Birmingham	3	Jan
1.71				2H	Sheffield	30	Apr
1.71 i	Emma Beales		7.12.71	3=P	Birmingham	3	Jan
1.71	Jennifer Farrell		8.04.65	1	Annan	3	Jul
(40)							
1.71	Elizabeth Gibbens	U20	5.04.77	H	Birmingham	17	Sep
1.71	Leah Lackenby	U23	18.09.74	H	Birmingham	17	Sep
1.70 i	Rhona Scobie		18.10.62	1	Glasgow	16	Jan
1.70				3	Grangemouth	7	May
1.70 i	Claire Howard	U20	9.07.75		London (CP)	22	Feb
1.70				2	London (CP)	1	May
1.70 i	Beverley Howarth	U20	4.09.76	7	Birmingham	26	Feb
1.70				1	Blackburn	1	May
1.70	Debbie McIlroy	U17	18.12.77	1	York	10	Apr
1.70	*L. Buetner*			*3*	*London (CP)*	*1*	*May*
1.70	Alanna Dearden	U20	2.07.77	1	Croydon	14	May
1.70	Krissy Owen	U20	14.12.75	1	Hereford	22	May
1.70	Lisa Gibbs		9.01.69	10H	Alhama, SPA	5	Jun
1.70	Clare Watton	U17	23.12.77	1	Redditch	11	Jun
(50)							
1.70	Sharon Woolrich	U20	1.05.76	2	Portsmouth	11	Jun
1.70	Kerry Saunders	U20	28.03.77	2	Sheffield	19	Jun
1.70	Julie Hollman	U20	16.02.77	3	Peterborough	10	Jul
1.70	Antonia Bemrose	U15	3.09.79	1	Birmingham	30	Jul
1.70	Michelle Smith	U17	1.01.78	1	London (He)	7	Aug

1.70	Sara Veevers	U23	26.04.74	1	Bolton	7	Aug
1.70	Michele Wheeler/Marsella		10.01.68	1	Coventry	14	Aug
1.69	Kelly Sotherton	U20	13.11.76	1H	London (WL)	25	Jun
1.69	Hayley Young	U15	26.09.79	2	Telford	9	Jul
1.68 i	Michala Gee	U20	8.12.75	5P	Birmingham	3	Jan
	1.67			4=	Derby	16	Jul
(60)							
1.68	Lisa Flynn		26.01.71	1	Basingstoke	23	Apr
1.68	Dextene McIntosh	U17	27.08.78	2	Harrow	24	Apr
1.68	Val Adams		30.09.66	1	Gateshead	14	May
1.68	Rachel Martin	U17	9.09.78	1	Whitehaven	11	Jun
1.68	Natasha Mighty		21.12.70	4H	London (He)	20	Aug
1.68	Anne Hollman	U23	18.02.74	3H	London (He)	20	Aug
1.67	Hazel Clarke	U17	17.03.79	1	Wrexham	8	May
1.67	Nicole Smallwood	U17	9.10.77	1	Birmingham	11	Jun
1.67	Rebecca Wallbank	U17	17.06.78	1	Welwyn	22	Jun
1.67	Louise Gentle	U17	4.09.78	9	Telford	9	Jul
(70)							
1.67	Danielle Hinchliffe	U17	18.12.78	1	Oldham	10	Jul
1.67	Keira Stout	U15	6.03.80	1	Crawley	3	Sep
1.66 i	Catherine Parsons	U23	9.05.73	5P	London (CP)	23	Jan
	1.65			4=	Bracknell	2	May
1.66	Nadia Brewer	U15	14.04.80	1	Hoo	11	Jun
1.66	Elizabeth Mather	U20	28.05.76	1	Manchester	11	Jun
1.66	Anne Carr	U20	1.05.76	1	Stoke	18	Jun
1.66	Carrie Donnelly	U17	18.06.78	1	Belfast	3	Jul
1.66	Kate Hawker	U20	22.01.77	4	Telford	8	Jul
1.66	Samantha Foster	U15	9.09.79	4	Telford	9	Jul
1.66	Joanna Morris	U17	16.10.77	1	Swindon	13	Aug
(80)							
1.65 i	Kay Fletcher		14.10.67	5=	Birmingham	8	Jan
1.65 i	Fiona Lapka		17.12.66	8	Birmingham	8	Jan
	1.65			7=	London (CP)	25	Jun
1.65 i	Natasha Turner	U23	8.11.74	4	London (Ha)	30	Jan
1.65 i	Jackie Tindal	U17	21.01.79	2	Glasgow	10	Feb
1.65 i	Emma Kerr	U17	15.10.77	1	Glasgow	10	Feb
	1.65			2	Glasgow	14	May
1.65 i	Gail Taylor	U20	2.06.76	10	Birmingham	13	Feb
1.65	Kelly Trowers	U17	12.07.79	1	Birmingham	1	May
1.65	Justina Cruickshank	U17	27.09.77	1	Bebington	1	May
1.65	E. Bauer			7	London (CP)	1	May
1.65	Kerry Roberts		15.09.67	6	London (CP)	1	May
(90)							
1.65	Jenny Walker		28.01.69	3=	Birmingham	8	May
1.65	Emma Hanson	U20	28.10.75	1	Cardiff	8	May
1.65	Wendy MacDonald	U23	25.12.72	1	Hayes	11	May
1.65	Samantha Stapleton	U23	13.10.73	1	Bracknell	14	May
1.65	Sarah Potter	U20	28.10.75	2	Portsmouth	14	May
1.65	Susan Noble	U23	3.01.74	2	Gateshead	14	May
1.65	Victoria Wiseman	U20	14.11.76	1	London (Nh)	15	May
1.65	Claudia Filce	U23	11.11.72	3	Cwmbran	18	Jun
1.65	Lesley Lavers		6.08.68	2	Bromley	19	Jun
1.65	Lucy Webb	U17	28.07.79	1	Blackpool	19	Jun
(100)							
1.65	Paula Reed	U17	26.03.78	1	Gateshead	19	Jun
1.65	Carolyn May	U23	15.10.74	2	Oxford	28	Jun
1.65	Jackie Vyfschaft		15.12.64	5	Kings Lynn	9	Jul
1.65	Aneska Binks			4	Peterborough	10	Jul
1.65	Katie Evans	U23	4.02.74	6=	Stoke	16	Jul
1.65	Sarah Still	U20	24.09.75	1H	Linwood	16	Jul
1.65	Kerensa Denham	U23	8.03.74	1	Crawley	16	Jul

1.65	Adele Jones	U17	23.09.77	1	Solihull	17	Jul
1.65	Stephanie Paul		13.09.66	1	London (WL)	20	Jul
1.65	Hannah Wise	U23	8.10.74	3	Corby	31	Jul
(110)							
1.65	Rachel Hems		10.12.69	3	London (WF)	6	Aug
1.65	Lorna Turner	U23	11.05.72	4	London (WF)	6	Aug
1.65	Jane Cain		24.10.67	2	Peterborough	29	Aug
1.65	Jane Lilford		28.11.70	2	London (Elt)	29	Aug
1.65	Natasha Danvers	U17	19.09.77	1	London (Nh)	4	Sep
1.65	Iona Frazer	U15	28.10.79	1	London (WL)	11	Sep

Additional Under 17 (1 - 26 above)

1.64	Kelly Vine		26.07.78	1	Cleckheaton	11	Jun
1.64	Catherine Ledger		6.02.79	1	St. Ives	19	Jun

Additional Under 15 (1 - 5 above)

1.63 i	Katherine Livesey		15.12.79	1P	Birmingham	3	Jan
1.63				6	Telford	9	Jul
1.63	Anna Biscoe		13.09.79	5	Telford	9	Jul
1.63	Nicola McGovern		26.11.79	1	Carlisle	7	Aug
1.61	Kate Franklin		16.07.80	1	Bristol	15	Jul
1.60	Justina Gordon		10.05.80	2	London (CP)	29	May
(10)							
1.60	Chloe Cozens		9.04.80	1	Luton	11	Jun
1.60	Vicky Awanah		3.09.79	1	London (BP)	2	Jul
1.60	Denise Gayle		11.09.79	8	Telford	9	Jul
1.60	Judith Payne		7.07.80	10	Telford	9	Jul
1.60	Hannah Jones			1	Newport	31	Jul
1.60	Gillian Stewart		21.01.80	1	Dublin, IRE	13	Aug
1.60	Julie Hynan		23.05.80	2	Birmingham	11	Sep
1.60	Gemma Ashton		26.01.81	1	Solihull	18	Sep
1.60	Anna Ledger		13.06.80	2	Colchester	18	Sep

Under 13

1.52	Sophie McQueen		3.12.81	1	Wakefield	18	Sep
1.48	Danielle Parkinson		2.09.81	1	Warrington	30	May
1.48	Fiona Harrison		30.11.81	T	Cleckheaton	20	Jul
1.48	Katie Bell		1.02.82	2	Wakefield	18	Sep
1.48	Rebecca Kenshole		21.10.81	1	Exeter	27	Sep
1.47	Claire Lidster		26.10.81	1	London (TB)	14	Aug
1.46	Crystal Kagbo		23.06.82		Woking	16	Jul
1.45	Melanie Vaggers		16.06.82	1	Exeter	29	May
1.45	Katie Cowlard		17.09.81	1	Windsor	3	Jul
1.45	Kate Churchman		2.11.81	1	Ipswich	3	Jul
(10)							
1.45	Samantha Rose		18.02.82	1	Peterborough	31	Jul
1.45	Belinda Patrick		9.04.82	1	Glasgow	7	Aug
1.45	Eleanor Lucas		29.11.81		South Woodham	12	Aug
1.45	Donna Chatfield		15.09.81	1	Guildford	11	Sep
1.45	Rebecca Miles		22.12.81	1	Tonbridge	11	Sep
1.45	Alexis Carter		23.10.81	1	Solihull	18	Sep
1.43	Kara Dunckley		19.03.82		Exeter	3	Sep

Over Age

1.50 i	Rebecca Kenshole		21.10.81	1	Swansea	30	Dec

POLE VAULT

3.65	Kate Staples		2.11.65	1	Sheffield	11	Jun
3.61				1	Corby	29	May
3.46 i				1	Birmingham	19	Feb
3.45 i				8	Zwelbrucken, GER	29	Jan
3.40				1	Birmingham	21	May
3.40				1	Barn Elms	22	May

3.45	Paula Wilson		20.11.69	1	Peterborough	29	Aug
3.40				1	Stoke	14	May
3.40				2	Sheffield	11	Jun
3.40				1	Norwich	27	Jul
3.40				1	Bedford	17	Sep
3.40 i				1	Birmingham	31	Dec
3.35 i				1	Birmingham	26	Feb
3.35				1	Wrexham	13	Aug
3.30				2	Birmingham	21	May
3.30				1	Stoke	16	Jul
3.20				3	Corby	29	May
3.20				1	Stoke	11	Sep
3.20 i				1	Stoke	10	Dec
3.44	Clare Ridgley	U17	11.09.77	5	Holzminden, GER	10	Sep
3.41				1	Salisbury	10	Jul
3.40				1	Bedford	2	Jul
3.35 i				3	Lievin, FRA	12	Feb
3.35				1	London (CP)	26	Jun
3.30				4	Sheffield	11	Jun
3.30 i				2	Birmingham	31	Dec
3.20 i				1	Ewell	27	Mar
3.20				1	Portsmouth	14	May
3.20				2	Corby	29	May
3.20				1	Birmingham	30	Jul
3.20				1	London (He)	7	Aug
3.20				2	Southampton	4	Sep
3.20				3	Bedford	17	Sep
3.10 i				1	Horsham	8	Jan
3.10 i				1	London (CP)	17	Dec
3.42 i	Linda Stanton	U23	22.06.73	1	Birmingham	8	Jan
3.30				3	Sheffield	11	Jun
3.30				2	Bedford	17	Sep
3.25 i				2	Birmingham	26	Feb
3.20 i				2	Birmingham	19	Feb
3.20				1	Sheffield	15	May
3.10				1	Hull	21	Aug
3.30 i	Rhian Clarke	U20	19.04.77	3	Birmingham	31	Dec
3.25				1	Loughborough	5	Jun
3.20 i				3	Birmingham	19	Feb
3.20				3=	Birmingham	21	May
3.20				4	Warsaw, POL	18	Jun
3.20				2	Bedford	2	Jul
3.20				2	Peterborough	29	Aug
3.10 i				1	Kings Lynn	5	Mar
3.10				1	Barn Elms	22	May
3.10				4	Bedford	17	Sep
3.24	Claire Morrison		30.05.69		Holzminden, GER	10	Sep
3.20				3=	Birmingham	21	May
3.20				2	Stoke	16	Jul
3.10 i				4	Birmingham	19	Feb
3.10				1	Yate	15	May
3.20 un	Samantha Stapleton	U23	13.10.73				
3.00				2=	London (CP)	26	Jun
3.10	Dawn-Alice Wright	U20	20.01.76	2	Salisbury	10	Jul
3.10	Leanne Mellor	U20	17.03.76	2	Hull	21	Aug
3.10 i	Janine Whitlock	U23	11.08.73	4	Birmingham	31	Dec

61 performances to 3.10 by10 athletes including 18 indoors

3.00	Katie Alexander	U23	28.04.74	1	Basingstoke	21	Aug
2.90	Sue Drummie		19.06.71	1	Croydon	15	May
2.80	Julia Cockram		1.01.68	1	London (BP)	10	Jul

2.80	Stacey Dicker	U23	19.12.73	7	Bedford	17 Sep
2.80 i	Fiona Peake	U20	31.05.77	6	Birmingham	31 Dec
2.70				4	Barn Elms	22 May
2.70 i	Lisa Caryl	U20	21.11.75	2	Wakefield	5 Mar
2.70	Katharine Horner	U17	6.01.78	1	London (CP)	27 Apr
2.70	Gail Marshall		1.04.71	1	London (CP)	30 Apr
2.65	Suzanne Lever		2.10.67	4	Stoke	16 Jul
2.65 io	Joanna Whitfield	U17	5.01.78	1	Bath	4 Dec
2.40 i				1	Birmingham	6 Feb
2.40				1	Stoke	11 Sep
	(20)					
2.60	Maria Newton		22.07.66	2	London (CP)	27 Apr
2.60	Claudia Filce	U23	11.11.72	1	Wrexham	30 Jul
2.60	Rebekah Telford	U20	4.11.76	3	Hull	21 Aug
2.60 i	Susan Crossland	U20	3.03.77	2	Stoke	19 Nov
2.40				1	Stretford	14 May
2.55	Fiona Allan	U20	6.11.75	1	Grantham	12 Jun
2.50	Tracy Bloomfield	U15	13.09.79	1	Horsham	31 Jul
2.50	Alison Ronald		20.01.67	4	Stoke	2 Aug
2.50	Emma Hornby	U23	12.12.73	1	Warley	3 Aug
2.50 i	Pamela Murray		13.01.67		Stoke	3 Aug
2.40				1	Edinburgh	24 Jun
2.50	Rosalind Jevon-Powell	U17	29.07.78	1	Grimsby	25 Sep
	(30)					
2.45	Helen Beddow		10.09.67	2	Derby	16 Jul
2.35 i	Katie Fitzgerald	U17	18.11.77	1	Glasgow	23 Jan
2.30				1	Edinburgh	15 May
2.35	Danielle Codd	U17	17.02.79	3	Derby	16 Jul
2.30	Beverley Howarth	U20	4.09.76	1	Blackburn	15 Jun
2.30	Lynsay Perides	U17	24.05.79	2	London (He)	7 Aug
2.20	Elizabeth Beckingsale	U15	20.03.80	1	Norwich	27 Jul

LONG JUMP

6.73	1.6	Yinka Idowu	U23	25.02.72		2	Victoria, CAN	27 Aug
	6.58 w	2.3				1	Sheffield	12 Jun
	6.56	1.9				*	Sheffield	12 Jun
	6.54	1.3				3	Gateshead	20 Jul
	6.51 i					1	Glasgow	12 Feb
	6.51	1.4				6	London (CP)	11 Sep
	6.48	0.8				Q	Helsinki, FIN	11 Aug
	6.46	1.6				2	Edinburgh	8 Jul
	6.46	1.5				9	Helsinki, FIN	12 Aug
	6.40	0.9				Q	Victoria, CAN	26 Aug
	6.32	2.0				1	Bedford	17 Sep
	6.31	-1.2				1	Wrexham	3 Jul
	6.18	0.4				10	Oslo, NOR	22 Jul
	6.15 i					3	Glasgow	29 Jan
6.56	1.7	Denise Lewis	U23	27.08.72		2	Sheffield	12 Jun
	6.51 w	2.2				2H	Venissieux, FRA	3 Jul
	6.50 w	3.5				4	Gateshead	20 Jul
	6.44	2.0				2H	Victoria, CAN	23 Aug
	6.42	-0.5				5	Birmingham	26 Jun
	6.38	1.0				1	Stoke	16 Jul
	6.37	1.1				*	Gateshead	20 Jul
	6.32	-0.3				1	Corby	30 May
	6.32 w				2.4	8	Victoria, CAN	27 Aug
	6.30	1.0				1H	Valladolid, SPA	8 May
	6.28	1.6				2	Bedford	17 Sep
	6.23	2.0				1	Stoke	15 May
	6.20	-1.9				19Q	Helsinki, FIN	11 Aug
	6.14	1.0				Q	Victoria, CAN	26 Aug

Mark	Wind	Name	Cat	DOB	Pos	Venue	Day	Mon
6.38 w		Ann Brooks		4.05.71	1	Hull	7	Aug
6.14					1	Hounslow	10	Jul
6.10	1.6				3	Sheffield	12	Jun
6.32 w	2.1	Liz Ghojefa		24.02.69	2	Brussels, BEL	16	Jul
6.13	1.4				*	Brussels, BEL	16	Jul
6.28		Ruth Irving	U23	20.07.74	1	Oxford	14	May
6.27					1	Loughborough	27	Apr
6.19	-1.4				5	Ostrava, CS	31	Jul
6.18 w	6.1				1	Loughborough	5	Jun
6.27	1.9	Ashia Hansen		5.12.71	1	London (CP)	26	Jun
6.15	0.8				5	Edinburgh	8	Jul
6.21 i		Joanne Dear	U20	8.06.75	2	Vienna, AUT	6	Feb
6.14	1.3				1	London (CP)	28	May
6.12		Julia Bennett		26.03.70	2	Kingston	23	Apr

42 performances to 6.10 by 8 athletes including 3 indoors and 7 wind assisted

Mark	Wind	Name	Cat	DOB	Pos	Venue	Day	Mon
6.07	1.6	Vikki Schofield	U23	29.12.72	15=H	Venissieux, FRA	3	Jul
6.05		Adele Forester	U20	27.03.76	1	Jarrow	12	Jun
(10)								
6.04		Kim Hagger		2.12.61	1	London (WF)	6	Aug
6.02	-0.2	Jenny Kelly		20.06.70	9H	Venissieux, FRA	3	Jul
6.02		Rachel Kirby		18.05.69	2	Feltham	10	Jul
5.99	-0.1	Julie Hollman	U20	16.02.77	1	Telford	8	Jul
5.94		Eleanor Cave	U23	23.01.73	2	Oxford	14	May
5.93 i		Helen Garrett		26.11.64	2	Birmingham	26	Feb
5.93	1.3	Joyce Hepher		11.02.64	2	London (CP)	15	May
5.93 w		Sarah Damm		12.09.70	1	Telford	14	May
5.68					1H	Birmingham	24	Apr
5.91 w		Karen Skeggs		26.10.69	2	Istanbul, TUR	22	May
5.88					1	Kingston	31	Jul
5.89		Charmaine Johnson		4.06.63	1	Bracknell	19	Jun
(20)								
5.89		Kerensa Denham	U23	8.03.74	1	Croydon	13	Aug
5.89 w		Connie Henry	U23	15.04.72	2	Enfield	14	May
5.81	1.0				3	Birmingham	21	May
5.89 w	2.8	Emma Lindsay		11.04.71	2H	Horsham	19	Jun
5.70	-0.2				7H	Victoria, CAN	23	Aug
5.88		Lisa Gibbs		9.01.69	1	Croydon	11	May
5.88		Sallyanne Short		6.03.68	1	Cwmbran	15	May
5.87 w		Lorraine Lynch		5.10.68	3	Enfield	14	May
5.70					2	Enfield	21	May
5.87 w	3.7	Rebecca Lewis	U17	31.12.77	2	Kingston	31	Jul
5.73	1.6				1	Telford	8	Jul
5.86		Lynne Draper		10.05.67	1	Horsham	15	May
5.85 w?		Debbie Marti		14.05.68	2	Bedford	18	Sep
5.83		Claire Phythian	U23	7.02.73	H	Azusa, USA	15	Apr
(30)								
5.83 w		Caroline Black	U23	19.05.72	1	Glasgow	24	Apr
5.74	1.6				1	Stoke	31	Jul
5.83 w		Stephanie Dobson	U20	4.03.75	3	Hull	7	Aug
5.81	1.5				2	Bulle, SWZ	10	Sep
5.82		Michelle Griffith		6.10.71	1	Bedford	21	May
5.81 w	2.7	Uju Efobi	U23	10.10.74	3H	Horsham	19	Jun
5.54	1.7				*	Horsham	19	Jun
5.81		Sarah Ramminger	U20	1.10.75	1	Aberdeen	24	Jul
5.80		Diana Bennett	U23	14.06.74	3	Croydon	14	May
5.80		Linda Davidson		29.05.70	2	Stretford	18	Jun
5.80 w	3.2	Pauline Richards		30.06.68	4H	Horsham	19	Jun
5.67					2H	Stoke	7	Aug
5.80 w?		Jayne Molyneux		21.10.68	1	Carlisle	26	Jun
5.56					1	Aldershot	7	Aug
5.79	1.6	Sandra Cull	U20	10.12.75	1H	Kirkby	24	Jul

Mark		Name	Cat	Date	Pos	Venue		Date
5.78 i		Mandy Bell		5.12.65	2	London (Ha)	29	Jan
5.78		Emma Beales		7.12.71	1	Ilford	4	Jun
5.56					1	Colchester	19	Jun
5.77		Hayley Martin	U20	25.05.76	3	Oxford	14	May
5.77		Kim Crowther-Price		19.01.66	1H	Wrexham	28	Aug
5.77		Nicola Barr		26.04.70	1	Aberdeen	12	Jun
5.76		Tammy McCammon	U20	17.10.76	1	Hayes	23	Apr
5.75		Angela Willis		22.07.69	1	Southampton	23	Apr
5.74		Caroline Miller	U23	16.09.72	1	Mansfield	8	May
5.74	1.0	Tina Malcolm		8.09.67	3	London (CP)	14	May
5.74		Pamela Anderson	U20	16.10.76	1	Glasgow	15	May
(50)								
5.74 w		Louretta Thorne	U20	6.05.77	1	Carn Brea	4	Jun
5.74		Sarah Still	U20	24.09.75	2	Aberdeen	12	Jun
5.73 i		Sarah Wilhelmy	U15	2.02.80	1	London (CP)	30	Jan
5.55	1.6				4	Birmingham	31	Jul
5.73		Louise Eden	U17	11.12.77	1	Harrow	24	Apr
5.73		Sarah Hanson	U23	25.11.72	1	Birmingham	24	Apr
5.73		Kathryn Blackwood	U20	31.03.76				
5.71		Paula Thomas		3.12.64	2	Grangemouth	7	May
5.71	0.2	Evette Finikin		25.09.63	9	Brussels, BEL	16	Jul
5.71 w	2.7	Isobel Donaldson		24.01.64	4	Bedford	17	Sep
5.56					1H	Aldershot	2	Aug
5.70 i		Natasha Mighty		21.12.70	2P	London (CP)	23	Jan
5.54	1.4				7H	Sheffield	1	May
(60)								
5.70		Donna King	U20	26.01.76	1	Swansea	8	May
5.70		Katie Gibb	U20	19.12.75	1	Blackpool	14	May
5.70		Allison Forbes		15.08.62	3	Stretford	18	Jun
5.70 w?		Mhairi Livingstone		1.09.69	1	Carlisle	28	May
5.69		Kerry Jury		19.11.68	1	Warley	14	May
5.69		Caroline Stead		14.09.71	1	Bromley	19	Jun
5.69	0.4	Nicola Turner	U20	26.09.75	3	Telford	8	Jul
5.69		Rebecca Folds	U20	28.01.75	1	Carn Brea	23	Jul
5.69		Denise Bolton	U20	1.02.77		Middlesbrough	29	Aug
5.68		Hayley Jones		20.09.71	1	Leamington	24	May
(70)								
5.68	1.4	Jade Johnson	U15	7.06.80	1	Birmingham	31	Jul
5.68		Sarah Claxton	U15	23.09.79	1	Milton Keynes	6	Sep
5.67		Kelly Sotherton	U20	13.11.76	1	Portsmouth	11	Jun
5.67 w		Clova Court		10.02.60	2	Birmingham	8	May
5.48	1.2				*	Horsham	19	Jun
5.66		Nikki Gilding	U23	16.05.72	1	Harrow	23	Apr
5.66		Gemma Holt	U23	20.12.72	2	Oxford	4	Jun
5.66 w	2.2	Kelly Williamson	U15	4.12.79	1	Birmingham	31	Jul
5.48	0.8				1	Telford	9	Jul
5.65		Lorna Turner	U23	11.05.72	4	Kingston	23	Apr
5.65		Debbie Woolgar		10.03.65	3	London (Elt)	29	Aug
5.64 i		Rebecca Foster		14.04.71	3	Wakefield	5	Mar
5.64					2	Loughborough	27	Apr
5.55 w	3.4				5H	Sheffield	1	May
(80)								
5.64	1.6	Jo Willoughby		30.11.63	2	Cwmbran	18	Jun
5.62		Debbie Rowe	U23	8.09.72	1	Mansfield	11	Jun
5.62		Fiona Allan	U20	6.11.75	1	Mansfield	11	Jun
5.61 i		Lisa Armstrong	U23	5.11.73	6	Birmingham	18	Feb
5.60					3	Istanbul, TUR	22	May
5.61		Amy Logan	U20	21.01.75	2	Blackburn	1	May
5.61		Teresa Springate		8.03.69	3	Windsor	13	Aug
5.59		Sharon Wright	U20	6.10.76	1	Grantham	18	Jun
5.59		Nicola Clarke	U20	14.04.77	1	Jarrow	19	Jun

286

5.58		Catherine Burrows	U20	11.02.76	1	Bebington	14	May
5.58		Kathryn MacKenzie	U20	5.03.77	2	Portsmouth	11	Jun
(90)								
5.58 w		Nicola Hutchison	U17	1.02.79	1	Glasgow	18	Jun
5.56					1	Glasgow	23	Apr
5.57 w	2.2	Belinda Samuels	U17	29.11.78	2	Birmingham	30	Jul
5.55	1.0				*	Birmingham	30	Jul
5.56 w	2.2	Debbie Harrison	U17	13.11.78	2	Telford	8	Jul
5.40	-0.9				1	Solihull	29	May
5.55 i		Helen Pryer	U17	21.01.79	1	London (CP)	26	Feb
5.55		Lisa Vincent	U23	23.09.74	1	Woking	23	Apr
5.53		Ade Rawcliffe	U23	27.12.72	3	Loughborough	27	Apr
5.51		Trisha Roche		15.06.68	3	Birmingham	24	Apr
5.51		Banke Olofinjana	U23	14.05.72	4	Enfield	14	May
5.51		Natalie Butler	U17	25.11.78	1	Oxford	15	May
5.51		Catriona Slater	U20	27.01.77	2	Colchester	19	Jun
(100)								
5.51	-0.3	Sally Evans	U20	14.05.75	9	Bedford	2	Jul
5.51		Hilary Moore		23.09.60	2	Exeter	3	Sep

Additional Under 17 (1 - 7 above)

5.50	Adele Bailey	9.09.77	1	Derby	10	May
5.49 w	Fiona Paul	5.09.78	2	Glasgow	18	Jun
5.44 i			1	Glasgow	15	Jan
5.48	Michelle Dunkley	26.01.78	1	Bedford	11	Sep
(10)						
5.48	Kathryn Dowsett	24.11.78	1	Chatilon, FRA	24	Sep
5.47	Syrena Pinel	13.01.79	1	Mansfield	5	Jun
5.46	Davenia John	29.12.77	1	Oxford	4	Jun
5.46	Bianca Liston	28.05.78	1	London (WF)	26	Jun
5.45	Faithlyn Edwards	26.11.78	2	Harrow	24	Apr
5.44	Claire Everett	25.06.79	2	Thurrock	3	Sep
5.43	Angie Nyhan	13.04.78	1	York	10	Apr
5.41	Donna Conroy	21.09.77	1	Liverpool	17	Apr
5.41	Louise Dixon	29.11.77	1	Bebington	24	Apr
5.40	Liz Fairs	1.12.77	2	Hull	24	Jul
5.40	Abigail Ashby	23.11.77	3H	Birmingham	18	Sep

Additional Under 15 (1 - 4 above)

5.39	1.3	Helen Redfern	26.04.80	2	Gateshead	29	May
5.38		Gemma Salmon	13.01.80	1	Mansfield	5	Jun
5.38	1.3	Alex Ward	11.03.80	5	Birmingham	31	Jul
5.37 io		Katherine Livesey	15.12.79	P	Glasgow	10	Dec
5.32				1	Blackpool	11	Sep
5.35		Lucy Atunumuo	4.11.80	1	Welwyn	3	Sep
5.33 io		Amy Nuttell	6.02.80	P	Glasgow	10	Dec
5.25				3	Hull	21	Aug
(10)							
5.32		Cherone Fearon	4.03.80	2	Coventry	14	Aug
5.30		Rebecca White	5.06.80	1	Wakefield	18	Sep
5.29		Emma Hughes	15.09.80	1	Colchester	23	Apr
5.28		Ayeesha Charles	4.09.79	1	Oxford	15	May
5.28		Danielle Freeman	11.02.80	2Q	Telford	8	Jul
5.25		Suzanne Batty	29.04.80	1	Liverpool	10	Apr
5.25		Suzanne Whitehead	13.05.80	1	Barnsley	10	Jul

Under 13

4.88		Fiona Harrison	30.11.81	1	Lincoln	10	Sep
4.84		Sally Drew	23.11.82	1	Plymouth	13	Jul
4.82	0.9	Aimee Cutler	7.10.81	1	Brecon	19	Jun
4.82		Helen Reeks	25.03.82	1	London (TB)	14	Aug

287

4.81		Katrina Buccierri	24.06.83	1	Rotherham	3	Jul
4.77		Rebecca Bates	16.05.82	4	Coventry	14	Aug
4.77		Joanne Owbridge	19.01.82	1	Lincoln	10	Sep
4.76		Cheryl Gibbons	21.09.81	1	Kirkby	11	Sep
4.74		Sarah Whitehall	9.10.81	1	Swansea	28	Aug
4.73		C. Gray		1	Scunthorpe	29	Aug
	(10)						
4.72		Kirsty Roach	8.12.81	2	Kirkby	11	Sep
4.69		Rowena Mackay	4.02.82	2	London (TB)	14	Aug

TRIPLE JUMP

14.22		Ashia Hansen	5.12.71	1	Welwyn	29	Aug
	14.09	0.8		1	Bedford	17	Sep
	14.04	1.3		1	London (CP)	15	Jul
	14.00	1.2		1	Gateshead	20	Jul
	13.86 i			1	London (Ha)	30	Jan
	13.79	0.9		2	Sheffield	11	Jun
	13.61 w	2.1		4	Gateshead	1	Jul
	13.60	0.6		5	Sheffield	4	Sep
	13.58	-0.5		2	Schwechat, AUT	29	May
	13.55	-0.2		1	Nitra, SVK	13	Jul
	13.45	0.8		15Q	Helsinki, FIN	7	Aug
	13.41 i			2	Vienna, AUT	6	Feb
	13.30 i			16Q	Paris, FRA	12	Mar
	13.03			1	Stretford	18	Jun
	13.02			1	London (Nh)	14	May
14.08	0.7	Michelle Griffith	6.10.71	1	Sheffield	11	Jun
	13.85 i			1	Glasgow	12	Feb
	13.84	1.5		2	Gateshead	20	Jul
	13.75	0.3		4	Birmingham	25	Jun
	13.75 w	5.1		3	Gateshead	1	Jul
	13.74 i			1	Birmingham	26	Feb
	13.70	1.0		4	London (CP)	9	Sep
	13.64	-0.1		Q	Helsinki, FIN	7	Aug
	13.62 w	2.3		3	Budapest, HUN	3	Jun
	13.60	0.9		10	Helsinki, FIN	8	Aug
	13.55 i			10	Paris, FRA	13	Mar
	13.55 w	2.2		7	Sheffield	4	Sep
	13.54 i			4	San Sebastian, SPA	3	Mar
	13.49	0.0		6	St. Petersburg, RUS	24	Jul
	13.48			*	Budapest, HUN	3	Jun
	13.47	1.4		1	Bracknell	15	Mar
	13.42	0.2		7	Bratislava, SVK	1	Jun
	13.41 i			Q	Paris, FRA	12	Mar
	13.38	1.1		*	Sheffield	4	Sep
	13.35	0.9		*	Sheffield	4	Sep
	13.22 i			4	Glasgow	29	Jan
	13.16	1.1		*	Gateshead	1	Jul
	13.10 i			1	Birmingham	26	Feb
	13.04	1.5		7	Stockholm, SWE	12	Jul
13.64	1.1	Rachel Kirby	18.05.69	Q	Helsinki, FIN	7	Aug
	13.51 w	2.8		5	Gateshead	1	Jul
	13.50 w	2.3		3	Gateshead	20	Jul
	13.45	0.7		11	Helsinki, FIN	8	Aug
	13.31 i			3	Glasgow	29	Jan
	13.31 i			3	Birmingham	26	Feb
	13.31 i			15Q	Paris, FRA	12	Mar
	13.29	0.8		3	Sheffield	11	Jun
	13.24	0.2		4	London (CP)	15	Jul

13.21 i					1	Birmingham	19 Feb
13.14 i					4	Glasgow	12 Feb
13.14	0.7				8	Sheffield	4 Sep
13.31	1.5	Connie Henry	U23	15.04.72	1	Kings Lynn	9 Jul
13.10 w					1	Enfield	14 May
13.07	0.5				5	Ostrava, CS	30 Jul

54 performances to 13.00 by 4 athletes including 15 indoors and 7 wind assisted

12.94	1.0	Lorna Turner	U23	11.05.72	2	Kings Lynn	9 Jul
12.85	0.9	Evette Finikin		25.09.63	4	Sheffield	11 Jun
12.45		Karen Skeggs		26.10.69	1	Bedford	18 Sep
12.44 w 3.5		Shani Anderson	U20	7.08.75	3	Kings Lynn	9 Jul
12.39	-0.7				4	Warsaw, POL	18 Jun
12.39	-0.6	Liz Ghojefa		24.02.69	1	Enfield	31 Jul
12.31		Caroline Miller	U23	16.09.72	1	Colwyn Bay	23 Jul
	(10)						
12.17	0.6	Caroline Stead		14.09.71	5	Sheffield	11 Jun
12.14	0.5	Jayne Ludlow	U17	7.01.79	2	Istanbul, TUR	21 May
12.07	-1.1	Nicola Barr		26.04.70	1	Corby	29 May
12.01	1.1	Katie Evans	U23	4.02.74	1	Stoke	16 Jul
12.00	0.8	Debbie Rowe	U23	8.09.72	7	Sheffield	11 Jun
11.97	1.1	Kerensa Denham	U23	8.03.74	8	Sheffield	11 Jun
11.85		Lauraine Cameron	U23	21.03.72	1	Horsham	16 Jul
11.82		Rachel Atkinson	U23	26.05.73	2	Kingston	31 Jul
11.79		Kelly Donnan	U20	14.04.77	3	Corby	29 May
11.76	*0.5*	*Jarmila Bubikova*	*U20*	*8.01.77*	*3*	*Bedford*	*3 Jul*
11.76	0.3	Stephanie Dobson	U20	4.03.75	4	Bulle, SWZ	10 Sep
	(20)						
11.71	1.9	Marcia Richardson	U23	10.02.72	1	Bracknell	19 Jun
11.69	2.0	Kathryn Blackwood	U20	31.03.76	1	Telford	9 Jul
11.65 w 3.3		Elizabeth Gibbens	U20	5.04.77	2	Telford	9 Jul
11.35	0.9				4	Bedford	3 Jul
11.63		Jane Falconer	U23	20.09.74	1	Oxford	14 May
11.63		Fiona Watt	U23	29.01.73	1	Edinburgh	4 Sep
11.62		Eleanor Cave	U23	23.01.73	2	Oxford	14 May
11.61 w 2.8		Kelly Sotherton	U20	13.11.76	3	Telford	9 Jul
11.56					1	Portsmouth	11 Jun
11.58 i		Jennifer Charles		1.06.68	4	London (Ha)	29 Jan
11.43	0.4				10	Sheffield	11 Jun
11.56 i		Kerry Jury		19.11.68	3	Birmingham	26 Feb
11.35	1.1				5	Birmingham	21 May
11.51		Nicola Clarke	U20	14.04.77	1	Derby	24 Apr
	(30)						
11.47		Christine Bloomfield		12.02.68	2	Windsor	13 Aug
11.47 w 3.3		Sarah Ramminger	U20	1.10.75	1	Exeter	20 Aug
11.23	0.3				7	Bedford	3 Jul
11.46		Linda Davidson		29.05.70	4	Grangemouth	7 May
11.46		Gill Howard		14.04.69	1	Aldershot	7 Aug
11.44	1.9	Fiona Allan	U20	6.11.75	4	Telford	9 Jul
11.44		Joanne Nicklin		12.07.67	1	Colchester	29 Aug
11.43		Debbie Woolgar		10.03.65	1	Perivale	16 Jul
11.43		Pamela Anderson	U20	16.10.76	1	Glasgow	15 May
11.40		Kathryn MacKenzie	U20	5.03.77	2	Portsmouth	11 Jun
11.40		Joanne Scott	U20	31.12.76	1	Jarrow	19 Jun
	(40)						
11.39 i		Mhairi Livingstone		1.09.69	5	Birmingham	26 Feb
11.36		Jenny Brown	V35	21.05.59	1	London (Elt)	29 Aug
11.33		Lisa Vincent	U23	23.09.74	1	Woking	23 Apr
11.30		Clare Mackintosh		2.04.71	1	Coatbridge	22 May
11.30 w 2.9		Catherine Burrows	U20	11.02.76	5	Telford	9 Jul
11.10					4	Kingston	31 Jul
11.27		Caroline Black	U23	19.05.72	2	Edinburgh	4 Sep

11.25		Nicola Venton	U20	26.11.75	1	Ipswich	23	Apr
11.21		Stacy McGivern	U20	14.12.76	1	St. Ives	14	May
11.20		Nikki Gilding	U23	16.05.72	1	Horsham	14	May
11.20		Isobel Donaldson		24.01.64	2	Aldershot	7	Aug
	(50)							
11.16		Susan Harries		9.09.70	1	Basildon	3	Sep
11.12		Ruth Irving	U23	20.07.74	3	Oxford	14	May
11.12		Jodie Hurst	U20	21.06.77	1	Wolverhampton	28	Aug
11.10		Catherine Barnes	U17	28.09.77	1	London (CP)	23	Apr
11.08		Amy Molner	U23	19.03.73	1	Colchester	23	Apr
11.08		Stephanie Aneto	U20	23.08.77	2	London (WF)	3	Sep
11.08		Danielle Rasbuary	U23	15.01.74	1	Liverpool	3	Sep
11.07		Sophia Thorpe		3.01.70	1	London (Elt)	23	Apr
11.07		Emily Stewart	U23	2.08.74	1	Hull	26	Jun
11.06		Adele Forester	U20	27.03.76	1	Hull	24	Apr
	(60)							
11.05		Justina Cruickshank	U17	27.09.77	1	Harrow	24	Apr
11.05		Louise Eden	U17	11.12.77		Birmingham	21	May
11.05	0.1	Trisha Roche		15.06.68	1	Newport	26	Jun
11.04	1.6	Kerry Saunders	U20	28.03.77	9	Telford	9	Jul
11.03		Anna Roze	U23	6.11.74	5	London (CP)	2	May
11.02		Kate Rogers	U17	14.02.79	1	Solihull	29	May
11.02		Clare Ridgley	U17	11.09.77	1	Kingston	19	Jun
11.02		Stephanie Law	U23	21.04.72	2	London (WF)	13	Aug
11.01 i		Rebecca Foster		14.04.71	1	Dewsbury	6	Mar
11.00		Sarah Richmond	U23	6.01.73	2	Kingston	19	Jun
	(70)							

Additional Under 17 (1 - 6 above)

10.92		Lucy Clements		20.07.78	2	Hull	26	Jun
10.84		Joanne Bright		4.10.77	3	Dartford	16	Jul
10.74		Emma Graves		18.05.79	2	Colchester	19	Jun
10.69 w	2.3	Natalie Butler		25.11.78	13	Bedford	3	Jul
10.57					1	Hoo	16	Jul
	(10)							
10.62 i		Louise Clowes		19.07.78	1	Birmingham	8	Feb
10.26					1	Stoke	30	May
10.59		Emily Tugwell		26.05.78	1	Carn Brea	12	Jun
10.59		Rebecca Maycock		13.02.78	3	Colchester	19	Jun
10.58		Mairi Donald		6.05.79	1	Grangemouth	22	Jun
10.57		Kelly Smith		29.10.78	1	Welwyn	11	Jun
10.54		Gemma Robinson		30.12.78	5	Birmingham	31	Jul
10.54 i		Hannah Moody		26.07.79	1	Birmingham	31	Dec
10.50		Joanna Payne		11.10.78	3	Solihull	29	May
10.44		Fiona Hunter		14.09.78	1	Edinburgh	15	May
10.44		Joanne Tomlinson		5.11.77	2	Blackpool	7	Aug
	(20)							
10.43		Leigh Hubbard		30.09.77	1	Cheltenham	28	Aug
10.42	0.7	Paula Reed		26.03.78	3	Remiremont, FRA	24	Sep
10.38		Rosie Collyer		19.02.78	4	Solihull	29	May
10.38		Suzanne Sheppard		24.09.78	1	Antrim	29	Jun
10.38 i		Julia Johnson		21.09.79	1	London (CP)	17	Dec
10.36		Anna Armishaw		11.02.78	1	Walton	16	Jul
10.36		Gahlie Davis		3.05.79	1	London (BP)	3	Sep
10.33		Andrea Hoskins		6.10.77	3	Yate	21	Aug
10.32		Eve Webster		7.10.77	2	Horsham	16	Jul

SHOT

18.68	Judy Oakes	V35	14.02.58	1	Nitra, SVK	13	Jul
	18.63			1	Gateshead	20	Jul
	18.51			1	Corby	31	Jul
	18.38			1	Sheffield	11	Jun
	18.29			1	London (TB)	4	Jun
	18.16			1	Victoria, CAN	24	Aug
	18.06			1	Aldershot	7	Aug
	17.92			5	London (CP)	10	Sep
	17.75			4	Birmingham	26	Jun
	17.65 i			1	London (CP)	17	Dec
	17.61			6	Sheffield	4	Sep
	17.51			1	Worthing	30	May
	17.45			1	London (CP)	1	Jun
	16.43			1	Croydon	21	May
17.64	Myrtle Augee		4.02.65	2	Victoria, CAN	24	Aug
	17.37			2	Sheffield	11	Jun
	17.13			5	Gateshead	20	Jul
	16.83			5	Gateshead	1	Jul
	16.77			14Q	Helsinki, FIN	7	Aug
	15.90			7	Sheffield	4	Sep
	15.51			1	Stoke	31	Jul
16.57	Maggie Lynes		19.02.63	6	Gateshead	20	Jul
	16.53			1	Tenerife, SPA	13	Apr
	16.53			3	Sheffield	11	Jun
	16.45 i			3	Glasgow	29	Jan
	16.39			2	Wrexham	3	Jul
	16.37			1	London (CP)	26	Jun
	16.31			6	Gateshead	1	Jul
	16.27			1	Barking	4	Jun
	16.23			6	Victoria, CAN	24	Aug
	16.20			1	Kings Lynn	21	May
	16.16			17Q	Helsinki, FIN	7	Aug
	16.15			1	Brussels, BEL	17	Jul
	16.14			1	Corby	30	May
	16.13 i			2	Glasgow	12	Feb
	16.10			1	Exeter	14	May
	15.95 i			1	Vienna, AUT	6	Feb
	15.82 i			1	Birmingham	18	Feb
	15.65 i			1	London (CP)	15	Jan
16.43	Yvonne Hanson-Nortey		18.02.64	1	Sheffield	19	Jun
	16.31			1	Sheffield	14	May
	16.29			3	Wrexham	3	Jul
	16.28			7	Gateshead	1	Jul
	16.23			1	Birmingham	21	May
	16.11			4	Sheffield	11	Jun
	16.10			1	Croydon	8	May
	16.10			7	Gateshead	20	Jul
	15.91			2	Tenerife, SPA	13	Apr
15.85 i	Alison Grey	U23	12.05.73	3	Glasgow	12	Feb
	15.78 i			4	Glasgow	29	Jan
	15.69			5	Sheffield	11	Jun
	15.54			2	Stretford	18	Jun
	15.50 i			2	Birmingham	18	Feb
15.61	Sharon Andrews		4.07.67	1	Stretford	18	Jun
	15.58			1	Enfield	31	Jul
	55 performances to 15.50 by 6 athletes including 9 indoors						
15.21	Uju Efobi	U23	10.10.74	1	Bromley	23	Apr
14.74 i	Debbie Callaway		15.07.64	1	London (Ha)	29	Jan
	14.58			3	Aldershot	7	Aug

14.44	Jenny Kelly		20.06.70	1H	Prague, CS	28	May
14.31 i	Emma Beales		7.12.71	1P	London (CP)	23	Jan
	14.18			1	Ilford	4	Jun
(10)							
14.22	Jayne Berry		18.07.70	2	Colwyn Bay	23	Jul
14.21	Lorraine Shaw		2.04.68	1	Stoke	16	Jul
14.15	Tracy Axten		20.07.63	1	London (He)	18	Aug
14.09	Carol Cooksley		22.09.69	1	Loughborough	22	Jun
13.90 i	Charmaine Johnson		4.06.63	2P	London (CP)	23	Jan
	13.60			3H	Prague, CS	28	May
13.88	Clova Court		10.02.60	1	Birmingham	8	May
13.68 i	Philippa Roles	U17	1.03.78	4	Birmingham	26	Feb
	13.65			2	Verona, ITA	6	Aug
13.68	*Kelly Kane*	*U23*	*28.10.74*	*1*	*Dublin, IRE*	*24*	*Jul*
13.66 i	Helen Cowe		7.09.66	5	Birmingham	26	Feb
	13.63			1	Aberdeen	24	Jul
13.48 i	Joanne Duncan		27.12.66	4	Birmingham	8	Jan
	13.46			5	Stretford	18	Jun
13.22	Denise Lewis	U23	27.08.72	6H	Victoria, CAN	22	Aug
(20)							
13.19	Irene Duffin		10.08.60	1	London (CP)	15	May
13.19	Vickie Foster		1.04.71	1	Aldershot	16	Jul
13.17	Helen Wilding	U20	25.10.76	3	Schio, ITA	6	Aug
13.12	Christina Bennett	U17	27.02.78	1	Kingston	11	Jun
13.12	Debbie Woolgar		10.03.65	1	Brighton	23	Jun
13.01 i	Emma Merry	U23	2.07.74	7	Birmingham	26	Feb
13.01	Fay Champion		27.09.66	6	Birmingham	21	May
12.92	Dawn Grazette	U23	26.09.72	7	Sheffield	11	Jun
12.88	Krissy Owen	U20	14.12.75	1	Cwmbran	18	Jun
12.80	Eleanor Gatrell	U20	5.10.76	1	London (CP)	28	May
(30)							
12.75	Angela Lambourn		9.04.66	1	Loughborough	26	Jun
12.75	Jane Aucott		10.10.68	2	Kingston	31	Jul
12.64	Karen Costello		21.10.68	5	Istanbul, TUR	22	May
12.62	Natasha Smith	U20	6.06.77	1	Barn Elms	22	May
12.54	Lisa Gibbs		9.01.69	4	Wrexham	3	Jul
12.52	Navdeep Dhaliwal	U17	30.11.77	1	Glasgow	24	Apr
12.52	Michaela Woodland-Nascimento	U23	19.11.73	1	Jarrow	14	Aug
12.48	Lorraine Henry		16.09.67	2	Jarrow	14	Aug
12.45	Bronwin Carter	V40	25.04.51	1	Brighton	21	May
12.43	Jacqui McKernan		1.07.65	7	Kings Lynn	9	Jul
(40)							
12.41	Pauline Shirt	U17	21.05.78	1	Cleckheaton	12	Jun
12.29 i	Julie Robin	U20	16.01.77	3	Glasgow	23	Jan
	12.02			1	Glasgow	17	Apr
12.28	Gillian Burns		12.07.64	3	Sheffield	19	Jun
12.24	Tracy Shorts	U23	4.11.72	1	Newtonmore	6	Aug
12.21	Anna-Lisa Howard	U17	18.04.78	1	Norwich	16	Jul
12.20	Sara Allen		7.12.70	2	Derby	16	Jul
12.16	Karen Smith	U23	10.02.74	1	Crewe	14	May
12.16	Helen Arnold	U17	5.10.78	1b	Brighton	21	May
12.15	Kim Crowther-Price		19.01.66	1H	Linwood	16	Jul
12.11	Sarah Damm		12.09.70	1	Telford	14	May
(50)							
12.06	Lynne Barnett	U23	12.08.74	5	Edinburgh	25	Jun
12.04 i	Sharon Nash	U23	5.05.74	1	London (CP)	23	Feb
	11.93			2	London (CP)	15	May
12.01	Jackie Gordon		22.12.67	1	London (CP)	10	Aug
11.99 i	Alison Dutch		25.05.65	4	Glasgow	23	Jan
11.99	Karen Skeggs		26.10.69	1	Hoo	19	Jun
11.98	Karen Martin	U23	24.11.74	1	Aldershot	6	Jul

11.98	Pauline Richards		30.06.68	2H	Stoke	6	Aug
11.91	Claire Burnett	U23	17.10.72	2	Reading	13	Aug
11.89	Jacquie Burke	U20	12.09.76	1H	Birmingham	17	Sep
11.88	Irene Timmis		28.03.65	3	Salisbury	21	May
	(60)						
11.88	Louise Batho	U20	27.11.76	3	Telford	9	Jul
11.87	Sharon Gibson		31.12.61	1	Nottingham	14	May
11.87	Vikki Heath	U20	27.12.76	1	Barking	11	Jun
11.84	Mary Anderson		2.09.67	4	Grangemouth	7	May
11.84	Vikki Schofield	U23	29.12.72	28H	Venissieux, FRA	2	Jul
11.83	Lesley Brannan	U20	13.09.76	1	Wrexham	29	May
11.81	Jackie Barclay		17.01.66	2	Peterborough	10	Jul
11.78	Sharon Hutchings		11.12.70	1	Exeter	4	Jun
11.73	Esther Augee		1.01.64	5	London (CP)	26	Jun
11.72	Heather Seager		4.04.68	1	Yeovil	14	May
	(70)						
11.72	Claire McKenzie	U20	5.05.75	2	Swansea	29	Aug
11.71	Nicola Talbot	U23	17.02.72	1	Telford	1	May
11.69	Alyson Hourihan		17.10.60	1	Cardiff	17	Jul
11.67	Alison Moffitt		6.10.69	1	Antrim	10	Sep
11.66	Catherine Garden	U17	4.09.78	1	Coatbridge	28	Aug
11.64	Tracee Capps	U23	29.11.73	2	Corby	1	May
11.63	Clover Wynter-Pink	U17	29.11.77	1H	London (WP)	7	May
11.60	Carol Bennett	U20	11.01.77	1	Jarrow	19	Jun
11.59	Kathleen Cartmell	U17	31.05.78	1	Jarrow	18	Jun
11.58	Emma Jones	U20	9.07.77	3	London (CP)	28	May
	(80)						
11.55	Jennifer Elphick		24.11.66	2	Portsmouth	14	May
11.52	Lorna Jackson	U23	9.01.74	6	Bedford	17	Sep
11.51	V. Duffy	V35			London (BP)	25	Apr
11.47	Natasha Huggins	U20	20.10.76	1	St. Ives	13	Aug
11.44	Rachel Hopgood	U17	2.06.78	1	Gateshead	28	May
11.43	Jo Evans		3.10.68	4	Cwmbran	18	Jun
11.43	Donna Williams	U17	7.10.78	3	Remiremont, FRA	24	Sep
11.41	Sara Birkinshaw	U23	19.11.72	1	Gateshead	19	Jun
11.40	Ann Gardner		11.10.68	3	Corby	14	May
11.39	Anne-Marie Cartmel	U23	18.11.73	1	Carlisle	10	Apr
	(90)						
11.38	Glenys Morton		17.06.60	1	Leicester	19	Jun
11.37	Gaynor Haskell	U20	11.08.76	1	Portsmouth	11	Jun
11.37	Tracy Rea	U17	19.01.79	1	Corby	18	Jun
11.33 i	Susan Atack/Armitage		10.05.68	1	Worksop	30	Jan
	11.04			5	Hull	21	Aug
11.31	Michelle Cornick	U20	21.09.76	1	Bournemouth	11	Jun
11.31	Alison George		11.12.62	2	Cannock	26	Jun
11.30	Louise Dixon	U17	29.11.77	1	Bebington	14	May
11.29	Joanne Essex		16.04.63	2	Bournemouth	16	Jul
11.27	Lauraine Cameron	U23	21.03.72	1	Horsham	16	Jul
11.26	Helen Thackeray		26.06.71	1	Hull	14	May
	(100)						
11.25 i	Natasha Mighty		21.12.70	3P	Birmingham	3	Jan
11.25	Cheryl Done		25.09.70	1	Cosford	15	Jun
11.24	Noelle Bradshaw		18.12.63	3	Portsmouth	14	May
11.23	Eleanor Garden	U20	20.11.76	1	Pitreavie	1	May
11.23	Tracey Quartey		16.12.71	2	Enfield	14	May
11.18	Sarah Moore	U23	15.03.73	5	Cwmbran	18	Jun
11.16	Cathy-Ann Hill	U20	4.05.77	1	Swindon	1	May
11.09	Sarah Owen	V35	18.03.55	6	Cwmbran	18	Jun
11.08	Lindsey Oliver	U17	12.03.78	1	Bebington	11	Jun
11.07	Nicola Gautier		21.03.78	2	Sheffield	10	Apr

Additional Under 17 (1 - 14 above)

11.06	Caroline Wallhead	13.12.78	1	Grimsby	19	Jun
11.02	Lisa Munden	13.03.78	1	Bournemouth	14	May
11.01	Michelle Harrison	29.09.78	2	Corby	18	Jun
10.96	Rachel Johnstone	22.01.78	1	Leicester	11	Jun
10.96	Emma Clarence	2.12.78	2	Sheffield	2	Jul
10.86	Fiona Hunter	14.09.78	1P	Grangemouth	11	Jun
	(20)					
10.84	Lynsey Herrington	31.05.79	2	Carshalton	25	Jun
10.84	Michelle Askham	2.08.78	2	Hull	21	Aug
10.83	Joanne Roberts	7.03.79	6	Telford	9	Jul
10.81 i	Victoria Shepherd	26.01.80	1	Wakefield	18	Dec
10.79	Gemma Johnson	21.07.78	1	Cannock	1	May
10.75	Angie Nyhan	13.04.78	1H	York	26	Jun
10.62	Melanie Walker	29.04.79	1	Bracknell	14	May
10.55	Lauren Keightley	2.08.79	1	Horsham	10	Apr
10.53	Sally Baines	4.12.78	1	St. Ives	29	May
10.52	Vicky Brown	22.02.78	1	Exeter	24	Jul
	(30)					
10.48	Natalie Clarke	5.09.77	1	London (He)	11	Jun

SHOT - Under 15 - 3.25kg

12.84	Victoria Shepherd	26.01.80	1	Gateshead	4	Sep
12.05	Frances Reid-Hughes	18.03.80	1	Portsmouth	13	Aug
12.02 un	Julie McCorry	7.11.79	1	Dublin, IRE		
11.84			2	Tullamore, IRE	4	Jun
11.99	Rebecca Chamberlain	7.09.79	1	Swansea	26	Jun
11.96	Amy Wilson	31.12.80	1	Colchester	4	Sep
11.90	Tuvola Akiwumu	15.10.79	1	London (CP)	11	Jun
11.84	Lucy Rann	5.09.80	1	Basingstoke	2	Jul
11.74	Natalie Kerr	17.11.79	1	Leicester	4	Jul
11.71	Michelle Woods	2.08.80	1	Birmingham	11	Sep
11.26	Debbie Spokes	7.08.80	1	Sheffield	2	Jul
	(10)					
11.22	Elizabeth Richards	9.11.79	2	Telford	9	Jul
11.14	Sadie Buckland	11.03.80	1	Colchester	18	Sep
10.87	Jenny Hopgood	22.06.80	1	Bournemouth	9	Apr
10.85	Lorraine Hewitt	8.01.80	1	Bromley	24	Jul
10.81	Julie Dunkley		3	Birmingham	11	Sep

Under 13

8.99	Kim Cannon	27.07.82	2	Basildon	13	Aug
8.89	Chidinma Nwanokwu	27.10.81	1	London (TB)	3	Sep
8.59	Anna Smith	6.10.81		Rugby	14	Aug

SHOT - Under 13 - 2.72kg

10.36	Elizabeth Bowyer	8.09.81	1	Bebington	22	Jun
10.07	Seonaid Ferry	19.11.81	1	Coatbridge	22	May
10.06	Kelly Ridgway	21.11.81	1	Birmingham	23	Apr
9.89	Ruth Hughes	12.09.81	1	Dartford	20	Aug
9.86	Lesley Ann Roy	3.01.82	1	Glasgow	4	Sep
9.66	Donna Medlock	26.10.81	1	Bromley	24	Jul
9.66	Kim Cannon	27.07.82	1	Basildon	7	Aug
9.66	Dawn Hutley	26.09.81	1	Braintree	21	Aug
9.53	Laura Crockford	14.10.81	2	Grangemouth	10	Jul
9.32	Ellen Falconer	9.12.81	1	Inverness	21	Aug
	(10)					
9.29	Kirsty Robb	14.10.81	1A	Birmingham	11	Sep
9.28	Anna Smith	6.10.81	1	Cheltenham	29	Aug
9.23	Emma Sutherland	10.01.82	2B	Birmingham	11	Sep
9.19	N. Buckland		1	Colchester	11	Sep
9.16	Lydia Agnew		1	Antrim	20	Aug
9.14	Chidinma Nwanokwu	27.10.81	1	London (TB)	14	Aug
9.08	Lucille Shaw	2.06.82	1	Reading	10	Jul

DISCUS

58.56	Jacqui McKernan		1.07.65	1	Loughborough	22	Jun
	57.56			13Q	Helsinki, FIN	9	Aug
	57.10			1	Loughborough	5	Jun
	57.08			1	Stoke	31	Jul
	56.94			1	Sheffield	12	Jun
	56.70			1	Kings Lynn	9	Jul
	56.50			1	London (CP)	1	May
	56.28			7	London (CP)	11	Sep
	56.04			3	Gateshead	20	Jul
	55.36			1	Dublin, IRE	3	Jul
	55.30			6	Birmingham	25	Jun
	54.88			1	Loughborough	25	May
	54.86			5	Victoria, CAN	23	Aug
56.24	Sharon Andrews		4.07.67	2	Sheffield	12	Jun
	55.34			4	Victoria, CAN	23	Aug
	54.78			2	Bedford	17	Sep
	53.98			2	Loughborough	5	Jun
	53.88			5	Gateshead	20	Jul
	53.20			1	Enfield	25	May
	53.06			2	Brussels, BEL	17	Jul
	52.70			1	Stretford	18	Jun
	52.68			1	Enfield	31	Jul
	52.44			1	London (Nh)	4	Sep
55.66	Debbie Callaway		15.07.64	1	Bracknell	2	May
	55.24			1	Bedford	17	Sep
	54.94			3	Sheffield	12	Jun
	54.46			1	London (CP)	25	Jun
	54.32			1	Sheffield	19	Jun
	53.96			1	Corby	31	Jul
	53.16			7	Victoria, CAN	23	Aug
	53.04			1	Southampton	10	May
	52.98			1	Basildon	3	Sep
	52.64			1	London (Nh)	14	May
	52.32			1	Aldershot	7	Aug
	52.30			1	Oxford	4	Jun
	52.16			1	Bromley	23	Apr
	52.16			1	Braintree	18	Sep
	52.06			1	Southampton	4	Sep
55.04	Lorraine Shaw		2.04.68	1	Cheltenham	14	May
	53.70			1	Stoke	16	Jul
	53.34			2	Loughborough	22	Jun
54.60	Shelley Drew	U23	8.08.73	1	London (Elt)	29	Aug
	53.40			1	Dublin (M), IRE	18	Jun
	52.92			3	Loughborough	22	Jun
	52.56			1	St. Ives	13	Aug
	52.16			3	London (CP)	26	Jun
53.54	Emma Beales		7.12.71	3	Loughborough	5	Jun
	52.98			2	London (CP)	26	Jun
	52.94			4	Sheffield	12	Jun
	52.28			2	Bournemouth	16	Jul
53.16	Sarah Winckless	U23	18.10.73	2	Dublin (M), IRE	18	Jun
	52.06			1	Oxford	28	Jun
52.52	Alison Grey	U23	12.05.73	2	Stretford	18	Jun
52.28	Tracy Axten		20.07.63	1	Bournemouth	16	Jul
	54 performances to 52.00 by 9 athletes						
50.72	Emma Merry	U23	2.07.74	4	Loughborough	22	Jun
	(10)						
50.64	Rosanne Lister		9.05.69	2	Luton	1	May
49.92	Nicola Talbot	U23	17.02.72	1	Telford	14	May
48.88	Philippa Roles	U17	1.03.78	1	Dublin (M), IRE	13	Aug

48.64	Helen Cowe		7.09.66	3	Bedford	17 Sep
48.12	Sarah Henton	U23	4.05.73	4	London (CP)	1 May
47.82	Judy Oakes	V35	14.02.58	2	Aldershot	7 Aug
47.76	Uju Efobi	U23	10.10.74	2	Bedford	18 Sep
46.70	Susan Freebairn		22.08.65	1	Glasgow	14 May
46.54	Karen Smith	U23	10.02.74	1	Birmingham	24 Apr
46.50	Jane Aucott		10.10.68	3	Stretford	18 Jun
	(20)					
45.38	Jayne Fisher		2.11.70	1	Cwmbran	18 Jun
45.20	Joanne Essex		16.04.63	1	Welwyn	29 Aug
45.10	Julie Robin	U20	16.01.77	2	Glasgow	17 Apr
44.92	Lauren Keightley	U17	2.08.79	1	Telford	8 Jul
44.80	Myrtle Augee		4.02.65	1	London (CP)	15 May
44.68	Tasha Saint-Smith	U20	20.12.75	1	Enfield	14 May
44.44	Sarah Symonds	U23	28.12.73	3	Exeter	3 Sep
44.18	Lucy Capes	U20	1.12.75	2	Sheffield	19 Jun
43.58	Helen McCreadie	U20	10.05.75	1	Glasgow	24 Apr
43.28	Rachel Hopgood	U17	2.06.78	1	York	18 Jun
	(30)					
43.18	Fay Champion		27.09.66	2	Southampton	4 Sep
43.02	Alyson Hourihan		17.10.60	1	Brecon	5 Jun
42.72	Catherine Garden	U17	4.09.78	1	Pitreavie	1 May
42.60	Sharon Nash	U23	5.05.74	1	Windsor	3 Sep
42.56	Jackie Wright	V40	8.10.53		Horsham	21 Aug
42.26	Helen Wilding	U20	25.10.76	1	Carlisle	26 Jun
41.88	Vickie Foster		1.04.71	1	Thurrock	3 Sep
41.74	Michelle Wright	U23	26.04.74	1	Yate	14 Aug
41.68	Rebecca Hardy		11.11.68	3	Birmingham	3 May
41.68	Claire Cameron	V35	3.10.58	4	Glasgow	14 May
	(40)					
41.28	Leanne Grey	U17	6.02.78	1	Leamington	14 May
41.26	Michelle Wallace	U23	1.11.72	4	Stoke	16 Jul
41.20	Lorraine Charlton/McCalla		20.09.60	4	Corby	31 Jul
41.18	Joanna Wood	U23	2.10.72	1	Birmingham	8 May
40.98	Michaela Woodland-Nascimento	U23	19.11.73	1	Norwich	27 Jul
40.84	Natalie Kerr	U15	17.11.79	1	Sutton Coldfield	24 Jul
40.72	Debbie Woolgar		10.03.65			
40.70	Jenny Hope		1.09.62	3	Birmingham	24 Apr
40.66	Alison Moffitt		6.10.69	1	Antrim	10 Sep
40.44	Jenny Hopkins	U20	9.08.75	6	London (CP)	30 Apr
	(50)					
40.24	Eleanor Garden	U20	20.11.76	1	Barry	19 Jul
40.22	Christina Bennett	U17	27.02.78	1	Carshalton	25 Jun
40.18	Kelly Mellis	U15	4.12.79	1	Telford	24 Sep
40.08	Navdeep Dhaliwal	U17	30.11.77	3	Aberdeen	16 Jul
40.08	Lyn Sprules	U20	11.09.75	2	Luton	3 Sep
40.04	Irene Duffin		10.08.60	3	London (CP)	14 May
40.04	Rebecca West	U23	9.09.74	1	Dartford	16 Jul
39.94	Tracy Shorts	U23	4.11.72	6	Edinburgh	25 Jun
39.94	Jo Evans		3.10.68	6	Bedford	17 Sep
39.68	Sara Allen		7.12.70	4	Derby	16 Jul
	(60)					
39.36	Tracey Quartey		16.12.71	2	Enfield	25 May
39.02	Lynsey Braddock	U17	14.10.77	5	Perivale	6 Aug
38.94	Elizabeth Whittle	U20	23.06.75		Middlesbrough	29 Aug
38.86	Tammy Nicholls	U17	21.07.78	1	Hornchurch	11 Jun
38.84	Sarah Moore	U23	15.03.73	1	High Wycombe	29 Aug
38.82	Julie Kirkpatrick	U23	14.07.72	2	Antrim	18 Jun
38.82	Heather Eden	U20	13.04.77	1	Bury St Edmonds	31 Jul
38.68	Liz Ellis		24.01.66		Derby	15 May
38.46	Yvonne Hanson-Nortey		18.02.64	3	Aldershot	7 Aug
38.40	Carol Cooksley		22.09.69	4	Coventry	14 Aug
	(70)					

38.38	Michelle Cornick	U20	21.09.76	3	Telford	8	Jul
38.38	Lynsey Herrington	U17	31.05.79	8	London (Elt)	29	Aug
37.88	Claire Phillips	U20	13.03.75	1	Hastings	30	May
37.86	Hannah Middlemiss	U20	5.03.76	1	Jarrow	19	Jun
37.84	Tracee Capps	U23	29.11.73	1	Corby	14	May
37.84	Donna Williams	U17	7.10.78	1	Middlesbrough	5	Jun
37.82	Lorraine Henry		16.09.67	1	Ipswich	23	Jul
37.74	Rachel Morris		20.09.70	3	Wigan	7	Aug
37.60	Zoe Tristram		15.11.69	1	Grantham	14	May
37.54	Samantha Burns-Salmond	U20	13.04.76	6	Enfield	31	Jul
	(80)						
37.54	Kate Semus		18.01.70	7	Enfield	31	Jul
37.40	Bronwin Carter	V40	25.04.51	2	Portsmouth	16	Jul
37.36	Charlotte Davies	U20	21.04.76	1	St. Ives	17	Sep
37.34	Kirsty Perrett	U20	17.03.76	1	Gateshead	14	May
37.02	Heather MacLeod	U23	12.03.72	4	Inverness	5	Jun
37.02	Joanna Bradley	U17	23.08.79	1	Guildford	13	Aug
36.96	Joanne Coote		10.02.68	5	Derby	16	Jul
36.88	Sarah Johnson	U20	24.08.77	1	Barry	14	May
36.80	Maria Merrigan	U20	24.10.75	1	Loughborough	7	Aug
36.78	Ann Gardner		11.10.68	2	Corby	14	May
	(90)						
36.78	Sandra Terry		28.04.69	2	Aldershot	29	Jun
36.62	Laura Perry	U20	4.06.75	1	Birmingham	11	Jun
36.58	Alison Faben	U20	7.02.77	6	Telford	8	Jul
36.48	Catherine Lane	U20	18.11.76	1	Welwyn	11	Jun
36.34	J. Cavergen			4	Loughborough	27	Apr
36.26	*Pamela Thomson*	*U17*	*29.03.78*	*2*	*Grangemouth*	*9*	*Jul*
36.06	Angela Mitchell		17.08.65	11	London (CP)	26	Jun

Additional Under 17 (1 - 12 above)

35.94	Katie Hopkins		6.11.77	2	Bracknell	11	Jun
35.86	Marcelle Edwards		9.01.78	3	Stretford	12	Jun
35.80	Nicola Edley		30.08.78	2	Rotherham	2	May
35.50	Debra Monds		25.02.78	1	Blackpool	25	Sep
35.08	Claire Sugden		16.09.78	2	Cleckheaton	12	Jun
34.80	Sara Manning		12.07.78	1	St. Albans	19	Jun
34.54	Susan Backhouse		6.12.78	1	Cleckheaton	11	Jun
34.52	Amanda Emery		1.12.77	1	Solihull	17	Apr
	(20)						
34.46	Shelley Williams		4.10.77	1	Welwyn	11	Jun
34.32	Helen Arnold		5.10.78	1	Crawley	28	Aug
34.28	Laura Wood		31.10.78	1	Stretford	11	Jun
34.14	Michelle Bowden		5.09.78	1	Dingwall	7	Jun
33.94	Zoe Campbell		9.01.78	1	Sheffield	22	Jun
33.78	Donna McEwan		17.01.78	1	Leamington	11	Jun
33.52	Kelly Kirkham		2.03.79	11	Telford	8	Jul
33.44	Julie Pinfold		18.07.79	1	Leicester	3	Sep
33.40	Lisa Stapley		2.04.78	2	Peterborough	2	May
33.40	Leanne Sullivan		27.03.79	1	London (WL)	11	Jun
	(20)						
33.40	Fiona Linton-Forrest		23.01.78	1	Hoo	11	Jun
33.20	Melanie McLean		17.01.78	1	Jarrow	18	Jun
33.14	Lisa Medlycott		9.12.77	13	Telford	8	Jul

Additional Under 15 (1 - 2 above)

34.70	Rebecca Roles		14.12.79	1	Brecon	19	Jun
33.56	Joan MacPherson		18.09.80	1	Guildford	11	Sep
33.46	Maria Hood		20.12.79	1	Bournemouth	12	Jun
33.06	Alex Hajipavlis		3.10.80	1	Sandwell	24	Jul
33.00	Clara Thompson			3	Birmingham	30	Jul
32.96	Elizabeth Hay		1.11.79	1	Welwyn	11	Jun

32.52	Michelle Woods			2.08.80	1	Ipswich	4	Sep
32.30	Louise Munro			8.07.80	1	Horsham	21	Aug
	(10)							
31.66	Lindsey Dixon			31.08.80	1	Jarrow	18	Jun
31.46	Sarah Strickleton			10.05.80	1	Cannock	4	Sep
31.28	Julie Wyatt			30.11.79	1	Grangemouth	4	Sep
31.26	Abigail Weston			8.03.80	1	Bracknell	11	Jun
30.88	Carly Burton			14.10.80	1	Bromley	21	Aug
30.88	Rachel Cox			27.06.80	1	Telford	17	Sep

Under 13

26.16	Lucille Shaw			2.06.82		Mansfield	5	Jun
23.98	Chidinma Nwanokwu			27.10.81	1	Braintree	13	Aug
23.68	Emma Morris			25.01.82		Blackpool	24	Sep

DISCUS - Under 13 - 0.75kg

29.18	Lucille Shaw			2.06.82	1	Reading	10	Jul
28.42	Emma Childs			13.02.82	1	Guildford	27	Aug
27.74	Lesley Ann Roy			3.01.82	1	Coatbridge	28	Aug
26.54	Laura Crockford			14.10.81	1	Aberdeen	3	Aug
24.98	Rebecca Hawkins			4.01.82	1	Bracknell	29	Jun
24.90	C. Mulcahy				1	Telford	15	May
24.64	Natalie Jones			21.02.82	1	Sandown	25	Sep
23.86	K. Phillips				1	Solihull	18	Sep
23.42	Jenna Brooker			23.10.81	2	Guildford	11	Sep
23.24	Jessica Robinson			19.02.82	1	Bromley	10	Jul
	(10)							
22.98	Nicola Mead			20.06.82	1	Cwmbran	3	Sep

HAMMER

59.92	Lorraine Shaw		2.04.68	1	London (Col)	1	Apr
	59.58			1	Sheffield	11	Jun
	59.44			1	Birmingham	21	May
	58.96			1	Stoke	15	Jul
	58.18			1	Corby	29	May
	58.14			1	London (Col)	17	Apr
	58.06			1	Cheltenham	14	May
	57.98			1	Kingston	16	Apr
	57.96			1	London (Col)	3	Aug
	57.66			1	Horsham	18	Jun
55.44	Lyn Sprules	U20	11.09.75	1	Haslemere	19	Jul
	54.48			1	Bedford	2	Jul
	54.48			1	London (He)	7	Aug
	54.16			1	Feltham	13	Jul
	53.92			1	London (CP)	25	Jun
	53.86			2	London (Col)	3	Aug
	53.38			1	Perivale	21	Aug
	53.10			2	Feltham	13	Aug
	52.82			1	London (He)	18	Aug
	52.70			1	Feltham	10	Jul
	52.22			1	Guildford	18	May
	52.20			1	Luton	3	Sep
	52.18			1	Braintree	18	Sep
	52.02			1	London (WL)	4	May
	52.02			1	High Wycombe	27	Jul
	51.80			1	Cardiff	8	May
	51.78			1	Ipswich	23	Apr
	51.72			1	London (He)	27	Aug
	51.60			1	Enfield	14	May
	51.54			2	Birmingham	21	May
	51.42			1B	Enfield	14	May

(Sprules)	51.40				1	Braintree	18	Sep
	50.64				1	London (CP)	29	May
	50.56				2	Kings Lynn	9	Jul
	50.26				1	Bournemouth	16	Jul
	50.20				2	Kingston	16	Apr
53.34	Diana Holden	U20	12.02.75		1	Feltham	13	Aug
	51.66				2	London (He)	27	Aug
	51.46				2	Luton	3	Sep
	50.74				2	Haslemere	19	Jul
	50.20				3	London (Col)	3	Aug
	50.14				2	Bedford	2	Jul
	50.00				2	London (CP)	29	May
51.62	Ann Gardner		11.10.68		1	Corby	14	May
51.62	Julie Lavender	U20	9.11.75		1	Gateshead	15	May
50.52	Sarah Moore	U23	15.03.73		1	Istanbul, TUR	21	May
	50.08				2	London (Col)	1	Apr
	47 performances to 50.00 by 6 athletes							
49.30	Esther Augee		1.01.64		1	London (CP)	14	May
48.98	Jean Clark		5.10.68		2	Bournemouth	16	Jul
48.68	Fiona Whitehead		31.05.70		1	Haselmere	5	Jul
46.88	Janet Smith		7.10.64		3	London (CP)	25	Jun
	(10)							
46.14	Irene Duffin		10.08.60		3	London (Col)	1	Apr
45.74	Julie Kirkpatrick	U23	14.07.72		1	Belfast	3	Aug
45.48	Samantha Burns-Salmond	U20	13.04.76		4	Horsham	18	Jun
45.44	Angela Bonner	U23	22.11.73		3	Colwyn Bay	23	Jul
45.04	Suzanne Last		11.01.70		1	Basildon	3	Sep
44.46	Kim Thompson	U23	5.01.73			Sunderland	4	Jun
43.88	Helen McCreadie	U20	10.05.75		1	Glasgow	24	Apr
43.56	Karen Brown		31.08.68		5	Birmingham	21	May
43.56	Caroline Manning	U23	5.03.73		1	Basildon	13	Aug
43.24	Myrtle Augee		4.02.65		2	Brighton	4	Jun
	(20)							
43.08	Rachael Beverley	U17	23.07.79		1	Middlesbrough	12	Jul
42.96	Helen Cowe		7.09.66		1	Elgin	16	Jul
42.44	Catherine Garden	U17	4.09.78		1	Grangemouth	9	Jul
42.14	Louise Kay	U17	1.12.77		1	Bolton	22	Jul
42.12	Helen Arnold	U17	5.10.78		1	Southampton	11	Sep
41.94	Sharon Nash	U23	5.05.74		2	Windsor	3	Sep
41.72	Jennifer Cunnane	V35	23.02.57		1	Wakefield	10	Jul
41.32	Linda Low		20.01.71		1	Edinburgh	15	May
41.32	Allison Wood	U23	30.12.72		3	Haslemere	19	Jul
41.12	Leanne Jones	U23	13.05.74			Swansea	25	Jun
	(30)							
40.66	Samantha Smith	U23	31.10.74		2	High Wycombe	21	May
40.62	Imogen Martin	U23	13.02.74		1	Colchester	23	Apr
40.52	Cheryl Cunnane	U20	8.02.77		1	Leeds	26	Apr
40.30	Annette O'Conor		20.08.71		2	Woking	23	Apr
39.82	Diane Smith		15.11.60		2	Leeds	13	Aug
39.82 un	Emma Jones	U20	9.07.77		1	Bournemouth		
	38.56				1	Hayes	21	May
39.46	Vickie Foster		1.04.71		1	Thurrock	3	Sep
39.34	Rachel Hall	U23	23.12.74		1	Middlesbrough	20	Jun
39.06	Joanne Coote		10.02.68		1	Wakefield	7	Aug
38.82	Noelle Bradshaw		18.12.63		2	Bracknell	4	Jun
	(40)							
38.72	Joanne Eley	U23	12.01.74		3	Hull	21	Aug
38.08	Rachel Elliott	U20	6.09.75		1	Stoke	30	May
38.06	Helen Wilding	U20	25.10.76		1	Sheffield	19	Jun
37.96	Elizabeth Whittle	U20	23.06.75			Middlesbrough	29	Aug
37.72	Esther Sneddon	U23	30.06.74		1	Antrim	29	Jun

37.36	Evaun Williams	V55	19.02.37	2	Kingston	23	Apr
37.28	Sarah Winckless	U23	18.10.73	6	London (Elt)	29	Aug
37.14	Claire Burnett	U23	17.10.72	3	Windsor	3	Sep
36.96	Sarah Head		31.07.65	1	London (Elt)	23	Apr
36.88	Natasha Smith	U20	6.06.77	1	Guildford	18	May
	(50)						
36.82	Rosemary Redmond	U17	3.10.78	1	Barn Elms	22	May
36.80	Tracy Axten		20.07.63	5	Hull	7	Aug
36.76	Claire McKenzie	U20	5.05.75	1	Brecon	5	Jun
36.62	Sarah Hughes	U20	14.03.75	1	Cardiff	17	Jul
36.60	Rosanne Lister		9.05.69	2	Basildon	3	Sep
36.56	Susan Freebairn		22.08.65	5	London (WF)	6	Aug
36.52	Marcelle Edwards	U17	9.01.78	1	Stretford	12	Jun
36.48	Anna Town	U20	22.04.75	2	Welwyn	4	Apr
36.46	Lucy Mills	U23	24.11.72	2	London (He)	3	Sep
36.24	Sheena Parry	U17	16.11.77	5	Birmingham	30	Jul
	(60)						
36.12	Christina Bennett	U17	27.02.78	3	Kingston	13	Aug
36.08	Jenny Clarke	V40	19.10.52		Grantham	19	Jun
36.06	Siobhan Hart	U20	15.06.75	4	Luton	3	Sep
35.94	Philippa Roles	U17	1.03.78	1	Swansea	15	Jun
35.94	Rachel Fraser	U23	30.09.74	1	Aldershot	7	Aug
35.76	Carice Allen	U17	25.09.77	5	London (He)	27	Aug
35.68	Sarah Harrison	U17	1.03.79	1	London (Elt)	19	Jun
35.56	Lindsey Jones	U17	8.09.77	2	Leeds	24	Apr
35.42	Aline Cross	U23	20.09.73	1	Aberdeen	23	Apr
35.18	Andrea Jenkins	U20	4.10.75	5	London (He)	7	Aug
	(70)						
35.08	Uju Efobi	U23	10.10.74	5	London (WF)	3	Sep
34.24	Lorraine Henry		16.09.67	2	London (He)	3	Sep
34.00	Lesley Brannan	U20	13.09.76	2	Derby	11	Sep

Additional Under 17 (1 - 12 above)

33.00	Rachel Johnstone		22.01.78	2	Solihull	17	Apr
32.54	Emma Welbourn		14.02.79	9	Derby	16	Jul
32.14	Lindsay Ross		27.12.77	3	Grangemouth	9	Jul
32.06	Rachael Dunn		4.03.79	3	Solihull	29	May
31.58	Marian Simpson		2.11.77	11	Birmingham	30	Jul
31.40	Louise Campbell		22.02.79	1	Carlisle	4	Sep
30.76	Karen Smith		12.12.77	1b	Leamington	30	May

JAVELIN

58.20	Sharon Gibson		31.12.61	3	Victoria, CAN	26	Aug
	57.56			3	Gateshead	20	Jul
	56.90			2	Sheffield	11	Jun
	55.70			1	Enfield	31	Jul
	55.20			1	Stoke	16	Jul
	54.82			1	Middlesbrough	7	Aug
	54.58			3	Nitra, SVK	13	Jul
	54.44			1	Nottingham	14	May
	53.82			17Q	Helsinki, FIN	11	Aug
	53.32			6	London (CP)	9	Sep
	52.76			1	Leicester	22	May
57.08	Shelley Holroyd	U23	17.05.73	1	Sheffield	11	Jun
	56.66			3	Gateshead	1	Jul
	55.46			2	Budapest, HUN	3	Jun
	54.14			6	Bratislava, SVK	1	Jun
	52.42			1	Stretford	18	Jun
	52.10			6	Ostrava, CS	30	Jul

55.32	Diane Royle		24.11.59	1	Grangemouth	7	May
53.78				1	Derby	16	Jul
52.84				1	Stretford	31	May
52.10				1	Kingston	31	Jul
54.62	Lorna Jackson	U23	9.01.74	1	Edinburgh	4	Sep
54.50	Karen Costello		21.10.68	3	Sheffield	11	Jun
53.88	Kirsty Morrison	U20	28.10.75	1	Bedford	2	Jul
53.80				1	Harrow	23	Apr
53.38				1	Telford	9	Jul
53.76	Mandy Liverton	U23	1.09.72	1	Reading	13	Aug
53.50				1	Yate	21	Aug
53.68	Karen Martin	U23	24.11.74	1	Colorado Springs, USA	7	May
53.20				2	Kings Lynn	9	Jul
53.68	Denise Lewis	U23	27.08.72	1H	Victoria, CAN	23	Aug
52.14	Jo Burton	U20	11.05.75	1	London (CP)	25	Jun
	32 performances to 52.00 by10 athletes						
51.76	Lucy Burrell	U20	10.03.75	4	Sheffield	11	Jun
51.00	Noelle Bradshaw		18.12.63	1	Woking	4	Apr
50.86	Nicola Emblem		27.03.71	3	Stretford	18	Jun
50.58	Caroline White		8.10.68	5	Gateshead	1	Jul
49.86 un	Katie Granger	U20	31.03.75	3	Exeter	2	Aug
48.14				4	Bedford	2	Jul
49.50	Janine King	U23	18.02.73	1	Birmingham	21	May
49.04	Onyema Amadi	U23	28.06.73	2	Cwmbran	18	Jun
48.88	Clova Court		10.02.60	1	Stoke	24	Jul
47.32	Lucy Stevenson	U23	30.01.73	1	Peterborough	29	Aug
47.00	Alison Moffitt		6.10.69	1	Antrim	18	Jun
(20)							
46.60	Michelle Fields	U23	15.05.73	1	Grantham	14	May
45.96	Angharad Richards	U20	9.12.76	3	Cwmbran	18	Jun
45.68	Linda Gray		23.03.71	1	Grimsby	28	May
45.58	Lucy Cook	U20	11.09.75	2	Sheffield	19	Jun
44.94	Lynn Hayhoe		20.03.63	1	Welwyn	14	May
44.62	Mari-Anne Daykin	U23	16.02.73	2	Aldershot	24	Jul
44.28	Katrina Campbell	U23	8.03.72	1	Antrim	10	Sep
44.06	Joanne Walker	U17	2.03.78	1	Aberdeen	16	Jul
44.02	Hilary Davies	U20	9.02.75	5	Wrexham	3	Jul
43.90	Teri Oboh	U23	7.10.73	1	Crawley	16	Jul
(30)							
43.86	Jackie Barclay		17.01.66	1	Glasgow	17	Apr
43.68	Emma Lilley	U20	2.05.76	1	York	11	Jun
43.52	Claire Taylor	U20	6.08.76	1	Telford	14	May
43.46	Siona Kelly	U23	19.04.74	1	Carlisle	14	May
43.20	Krissy Owen	U20	14.12.75	1	Colwyn Bay	11	Jun
43.06	Emily Steele	U23	10.09.74	2	Birmingham	8	May
43.04	Clover Wynter-Pink	U17	29.11.77	1H	London (WL)	26	Jun
43.02	Helen Potter	U23	25.06.74	2	Stretford	26	Apr
42.88	Rebecca Foster		14.04.71	1	Loughborough	27	Apr
42.60	Nicola Mackay	U17	26.08.78	1	Birmingham	30	Jul
(40)							
42.54	Janell Currie/Kelly		8.12.67	1	Glasgow	15	May
42.22	Sian Lax	U17	4.08.79	2	Birmingham	30	Jul
42.16	Sara Fry		19.01.62	1	Portsmouth	13	Jul
42.14	Katie Amos	U17	13.11.78	1	Thurrock	5	Jul
41.80	Julie Nightingale	U20	28.04.75	1	Eastbourne	13	Aug
41.54	Emma Beales		7.12.71	1	Colchester	19	Jun
41.50	Kelly Morgan	U15	17.06.80	1	Telford	9	Jul
41.48	Charmaine Johnson		4.06.63	2	London (CP)	1	May
41.36	Paula Blank	U17	13.12.77	1	Portsmouth	13	Aug
41.32	Tammie Francis	U17	14.11.78	2	Yeovil	4	Sep
(50)							

41.04	Melissa Spackman		19.10.71	1	Gateshead	14 May
40.94	Liz Pidgeon	U20	27.04.77	1	Barking	11 Jun
40.86	Tammy Carless	U20	10.01.77	2	Eastbourne	13 Aug
40.82	Wendy Newman		31.08.71	1	London (Nh)	15 May
40.76	Helen Thackeray		26.06.71	1	Hull	14 May
40.72	Jenna Allen	U17	2.05.79	2	Telford	9 Jul
40.68	Sylveen Monaghan	U23	25.08.72	3	Birmingham	8 May
40.64	Laura Kaluza	U20	19.07.77	1	Blackpool	11 Jun
40.64	Katherine Evans	U17	19.11.77	1	Coventry	14 Aug
40.62	Hayley Martin	U20	25.05.76	2	Woking	4 Apr
	(60)					
40.60	Sarah Simmans	U17	29.11.78	1	Stretford	11 Jun
40.54	Isobel Donaldson		24.01.64	1H	Aldershot	2 Aug
40.54	Emma Rich	U20	14.05.77	1	London (TB)	13 Aug
40.48	Karen Miller		4.02.64	1	Norfolk	16 Jul
40.48	*Schola Mujawamaria*		*12.07.65*	*1*	*Perivale*	*16 Jul*
40.32	Louise Smith	U20	11.07.77	1	Ipswich	15 May
40.30	Natalie Duff		30.12.71	2	Loughborough	27 Apr
40.22	Heather Derbyshire	U17	12.09.78	1	Harrow	24 Apr
40.22	Denise Alleyne		31.10.70	1	Hayes	11 May
40.18	Jenny Kelly		20.06.70	4H	Prague, CS	29 May
40.12	Karen Moody		20.07.67	2	Cardiff	8 May
	(70)					
40.12	Debbie Rice		26.03.70	2	Hull	14 May
40.12	Esther Sneddon	U23	30.06.74	2	Inverness	5 Jun
40.02	Jacqueline Cotton		29.12.69	2	Wigan	7 Aug
39.96	Nicola Jupp	U20	26.10.75		Bracknell	15 May
39.96	Adele Turner	U20	10.08.76	1	Gateshead	28 May
39.92	Donna Loveland	U17	28.06.78	1	Braintree	18 Sep
39.90	Melanie Burrows	U20	7.08.76	1	Yeovil	18 Jun
39.78	Andrea Cundy	U17	13.07.78	2	Peterborough	29 Aug
39.76	Lindsay Evans	U20	29.08.77		Derby	18 Sep
39.72	Yvette Bennett		2.07.65	1	Leicester	19 Jun
	(80)					
39.72	Lesley Lavers		6.08.68	2	Ealing	6 Aug
39.68	Jenny Foster	U17	6.09.77	1	Carlisle	17 Jul
39.66	Anne-Marie Stirling	U23	24.07.73	1	Warley	14 May
39.66	Nicky Rolfe		19.08.69	1	Bracknell	14 May
39.64	Nicola Cox			1	Rotherham	8 May
39.56	Linda Low		20.01.71	5	London (CP)	1 May
39.50	Leila Gould	U23	22.03.74	1	Perivale	3 Sep
39.42	Victoria Storey	U17	21.11.77	1	Stoke	19 Jun
39.34	Karen Slaughter		2.12.70	1	Enfield	21 May
39.28	Gemma Johnson	U17	21.07.78	5	Telford	9 Jul
	(90)					
39.22	S. Muzekovra			1	Bracknell	19 Jun
39.08	Caroline Hatton		14.06.63	1	Worthing	23 Apr
39.08	Sue Lawrence		25.11.70	2	London (Nh)	15 May
39.02	Claire Phythian	U23	7.02.73	H	Fayetteville, USA	13 May
39.00	Nicola Connell		17.12.68	1	Blackpool	6 Aug
38.94	Louise Hepplethwaite	U17	3.02.79	1	Stretford	14 May
38.90	Julie Moore		6.08.70	1	St. Ives	3 Sep
38.88	Claire Archer	U20	30.09.76	1	Yeovil	14 May
38.86	Joanne Mersh	U23	19.10.74	2	Dagenham	4 Jun
38.82	Judy Oakes	V35	14.02.58	3	Aldershot	7 Aug
	(100)					
38.80	Lynsay Munro	U20	1.02.77	2	Edinburgh	4 Sep
38.72	Amanda Brown	U20	11.05.75	1	Portsmouth	3 Sep
38.70	Donna Lepkowski	U23	7.11.74	3	Aldershot	29 Jun
38.66	Sally Green	U20	11.05.76	1	Watford	16 Jul
38.62	Anna-Lisa Howard	U17	18.04.78	2	London (CP)	28 May
38.50	Cheryl Done		25.09.70	2H	Aldershot	2 Aug

38.44	Pauline Richards		30.06.68	2H	Horsham	19	Jun
38.36	Sarah Damm		12.09.70	1H	Birmingham	24	Apr
38.32	Catherine Possamai	U20	11.04.75	2	Loughborough	25	May
38.18	Manndy Laing		7.11.59	3	Bournemouth	19	Jun
	(110)						
38.16	Anne-Marie Cartmel	U23	18.11.73	2	Croydon	8	May
38.16	Vikki Schofield	U23	29.12.72	25H	Venissieux, FRA	3	Jul
38.14	H. Hunt			6	Aldershot	24	Jul
38.10	Cheryl Quinn	U23	29.04.74	2	York	10	Apr
38.02	Debbie Marti		14.05.68	1	Bedford	18	Sep
38.00	Joanna Parry	U17	5.03.78	1	Portsmouth	15	May
38.00	Diana Bennett	U23	14.06.74	2	Bedford	18	Sep

Additional Under 17 (1 - 19 above)

37.86	Amanda Humble		15.08.79	2	Gateshead	29	May
	(20)						
36.72	Melissa Rogers		26.11.78	1	Croydon	25	Jun
36.12	Kate Hardy		26.12.78	3	Stretford	12	Jun
36.12	Leanne Morrall		7.07.79	1	Redditch	28	Aug
36.02	Helen Cookersole		14.03.78	1	Hoo	11	Jun
35.92	Claire Fawkes		24.10.77	2	Braintree	18	Sep
35.82	Claire Turnbull		17.12.77	1	Brighton	11	Jun
35.78	Emily Dougall		15.03.78	1	Aberdeen	29	May
35.62	Beverley MacPhee		20.03.79	1	Tonbridge	14	Jun
35.44	Nicola Gautier		21.03.78	1	Sheffield	14	May
35.32	Christina Bennett		27.02.78	1	Croydon	15	May

Additional Under 15 (1 above)

37.86	Alison Neall		8.11.79	1	Braintree	18	Sep
37.20	Nicola Lycett		10.03.80	2	Telford	9	Jul
36.72	Clare Lockwood		7.10.79	1	Colwyn Bay	2	Jul
36.36	Lucy Rann		5.09.80	1	Portsmouth	15	May
36.22	Christine Head		18.12.79	1	Ipswich	10	Jul
35.74	Lisa Porter		2.11.79	1	Corby	24	Apr
35.60	Lesley Richardson		6.10.79	1	Dublin, IRE	13	Aug
34.48	Emma Claydon		1.06.80	2	London (He)	7	Aug
33.96	Rehanne Skinner		13.11.79	1	York	11	Jun
	(20)						
33.48	Eleanor Ford		16.01.80	1	Bournemouth	11	Jun
33.38	Samantha Fox		30.04.80	1	Sutton	26	Jun
33.24	Claire Simms		17.10.79	1	Coventry	14	Aug
32.88	Michelle Stone		7.01.80	1	Portsmouth	16	Jul
31.58	Vicki Halligan		1.11.79	1	Inverness	5	Jun

Under 13

| 24.70 | Clare Warrington | | 28.07.82 | 2 | Wigan | 13 | Jun |
| 22.20 | Melanie Vaggers | | 16.06.82 | 14 | London (He) | 7 | Aug |

JAVELIN - Under 13 - 400 gram

33.32	Melanie Vaggers		16.06.82	1	Exeter	27	Sep
31.58	Louise Telford		7.01.82	1	Pitreavie	20	Aug
27.14	Clare Warrington		28.07.82	1	Warrington	16	Jul
26.94	Natasha Campbell		6.08.82	1	Bromley	21	Aug
26.94	Faye Bowring		22.10.81	1	Bournemouth	28	Aug
26.64	Eve Russell		27.09.82	1	Plymouth	2	Jul
26.10	Alison Eardley		11.11.81	1	Colwyn Bay	3	Sep
25.80	K. Sayers			3	Birmingham	3	Jul
25.16	L. Briggs			1	Telford	17	Jul
24.44	Jemma Spellacy		27.11.82	1	Clacton	14	Aug
	(10)						
24.40	Rebecca Schaufler		30.10.81	1	Guildford	27	Aug
23.70	Samantha Askin		6.01.82	1	Scunthorpe	29	Aug

HEPTATHLON

6325	Denise Lewis			U23	27.08.72	1	Victoria, CAN		23	Aug
	13.66	1.74	13.22	25.11		6.44	53.68	2:17.60		
	6069					12	Venissieux, FRA		3	Jul
	13.47	1.81	12.23	24.80		6.51w	39.04	2:23.03		
	5937					2	Valladolid,SPA		8	May
	14.03	1.77	11.96	25.01w		6.30	44.80	2:23.60		
5826	Jenny Kelly				20.06.70	19	Venissieux, FRA		3	Jul
	14.46	1.75	14.36	24.70		6.02	39.50	2:25.62		
	5658					5	Victoria, CAN		23	Aug
	14.43	1.68	13.62	25.43		6.00	38.90	2:21.96		
	5617					3	Prague, CS		29	May
	14.70	1.69	14.44	25.87		5.89	40.18	2:23.72		
	5495					1	Sheffield		1	May
	14.57w	1.62	13.84	25.15		5.79w	37.48	2:23.58		
5671	Vikki Schofield			U23	29.12.72	24	Venissieux, FRA		3	Jul
	14.06	1.72	11.84	25.04		6.07	38.16	2:22.83		
	5587					1	Horsham		19	Jun
	14.12w	1.69	11.26	25.29w		6.04w	37.38	2:19.29		
	5396					6	Prague, CS		29	May
	14.63	1.69	11.06	25.74		5.98	36.34	2:21.45		
	5302					2	Sheffield		1	May
	14.30w	1.68	10.72	25.53		5.65	35.64	2:22.31		
5486	Charmaine Johnson				4.06.63	26	Venissieux, FRA		3	Jul
	14.36	1.72	13.18	25.55		5.80	34.44	2:25.31		
	5480 w					6	Valladolid,SPA		8	May
	14.61	1.71	13.50	26.15W		5.82	39.06	2:27.10		
	5463					4	Prague, CS		29	May
	14.73	1.69	13.60	25.76		5.78	35.12	2:21.65		
5420	Pauline Richards				30.06.68	2	Horsham		19	Jun
	14.60w	1.60	11.25	24.78		5.80w	38.44	2:18.51		
	5201					1	Stoke		7	Aug
	14.72	1.58	11.98	24.99		5.67	33.84	2:24.6		
5409	Uju Efobi			U23	10.10.74	3	Horsham		19	Jun
	14.05w	1.72	13.26	25.89w		5.81w	35.58	2:34.96		
5372	Claire Phythian			U23	7.02.73	2	Fayetteville, USA		13	May
	14.30	1.70	11.03	24.94		5.46	39.02	2:25.12		
	5291					5	Azusa, USA		15	Apr
	14.61	1.70	9.79	25.21		5.83	35.14	2:22.81		
	5177					1	Tempe, USA		25	Mar
	14.71	1.76	10.30	25.58		5.69	36.28	2:34.82		
5353	Emma Lindsay				11.04.71	9	Victoria, CAN		23	Aug
	14.96	1.74	9.61	24.61		5.70	34.74	2:18.03		
	5321					5	Horsham		19	Jun
	15.78w	1.72	10.08	24.18		5.89w	33.98	2:19.14		
5334	Kerry Jury				19.11.68	4	Horsham		19	Jun
	14.21w	1.72	10.00	24.75		5.66	31.56	2:20.68		
	5194					5	Sheffield		1	May
	14.39w	1.68	10.81	24.57		5.21	31.56	2:21.20		
	5128					2	Stoke		7	Aug
	14.32	1.64	10.27	24.83		5.68	32.10	2:30.0		
5253 w	Lisa Gibbs				9.01.69	10	Alhama, SPA		6	Jun
	13.98W	1.70	11.98	25.99		5.72w	36.44	2:38.11		
(10)										
5239	Julia Bennett				26.03.70	3	Sheffield		1	May
	15.16w	1.86	9.84	25.58		5.72	26.48	2:19.06		
5212	Diana Bennett			U23	14.06.74	4	Sheffield		1	May
	14.67w	1.71	9.99	26.02		5.75w	29.50	2:14.92		
	5071					1	London (He)		21	Aug
	15.13	1.68	10.69	27.06		5.53	34.20	2:16.67		

(Bennett) 5070 w   2   Wrexham   28 Aug
  14.68w 1.68   10.19   26.64W   5.70   32.38   2:22.40
5125 Kim Crowther-Price   19.01.66 6   Horsham   19 Jun
  14.32   1.54   11.65   25.47w   5.72w   31.96   2:24.43
  5079 w   1   Wrexham   28 Aug
  14.22w 1.53   11.98   25.14W   5.77   26.86   2:25.84
  5054 w   6   Sheffield   1 May
  14.43w 1.53   11.98   25.83   5.52W   32.56   2:23.39
  5051   1   Linwood   17 Jul
  14.43   1.59   12.15   25.65   5.55   29.68   2:27.54
  5022   *   Sheffield   1 May
                                     5.41w
  5009   1   Middlesbrough 10 Apr
  14.5   1.52   12.07   26.0   5.72   34.44   2:27.8
5112 Sarah Damm   12.09.70 1   Birmingham   24 Apr
  15.53   1.60   11.11   25.75   5.68   38.36   2:22.27
5036 Natasha Mighty   21.12.70 7   Sheffield   1 May
  13.74w 1.59   10.02   24.94   5.54   34.24   2:37.20
37 performances to 5000 by 15 athletes
4962 Rebecca Foster   14.04.71 8   Sheffield   1 May
  14.74w 1.56   10.71   26.36   5.55w   38.64   2:29.54
4878 Julie Hollman   U20 16.02.77 8   Horsham   19 Jun
  15.01w 1.69   9.39   25.77   5.57w   28.40   2:27.64
4839 Eleanor Cave   U23 23.01.73 9   Horsham   19 Jun
  14.88   1.66   10.39   26.32w   5.31w   29.22   2:26.01
4823 Kelly Sotherton   U20 13.11.76 1   Birmingham   18 Sep
  14.72w 1.65   10.06   26.11   5.54   29.54   2:33.66
4783 Debbie Woolgar   10.03.65 1   Crawley   18 Sep
  15.4   1.60   12.94   27.8   5.41   35.92   2:31.5
      (20)
4750 Denise Bolton   U20   1.02.77 9   Sheffield   1 May
  14.34w 1.56   9.42   25.00   5.06   25.80   2:23.41
4738 w Jenny Brown   21.05.59 10   Horsham   19 Jun
  16.20w 1.69   9.57   27.21w   5.26W   36.06   2:22.67
  4727   *   Horsham   19 Jun
                                     5.22w
4643 Sarah Still   U20 24.09.75 1   Linwood   17 Jul
  15.65   1.65   9.43   25.26   5.54   21.70   2:29.29
4625 Michala Gee   U20   8.12.75 10   Sheffield   1 May
  15.48w 1.65   8.64   26.06   5.17   28.64   2:24.71
4620 Orla Bermingham   U20   7.10.75 4   Sheffield   1 May
  14.14w 1.56   8.53   25.56   4.87   26.22   2:23.74
4586 Elizabeth Gibbens   U20   5.04.77 3   Birmingham   18 Sep
  15.09   1.71   9.99   26.48   5.01   29.24   2:39.34
4546 Julie Major   19.08.70 11   Sheffield   1 May
  14.75w 1.68   9.76   26.99   5.27   24.96   2:37.85
4546 Isobel Donaldson   24.01.64 1   Aldershot   2 Aug
  16.1   1.51   8.30   27.9   5.56   40.54   2:21.2
4536 Cheryl Done   25.09.70 2   Aldershot   2 Aug
  16.0   1.54   11.12   28.1   5.20   38.50   2:27.5
4517 Sarah Ramminger   U20   1.10.75 2   Linwood   17 Jul
  15.68   1.62   9.86   26.09   5.49   24.44   2:35.48
      (30)
4514 Anne Carr   U20   1.05.76 2   Blackpool   26 Jun
  15.9   1.64   8.72   26.4   5.09   29.40   2:22.0
4497 Elaine Donald   U23 30.04.74 2   Linwood   17 Jul
  15.42   1.50   8.77   26.24   5.24   29.38   2:23.74
4478 w Leah Lackenby   U23 18.09.74 6   Birmingham   18 Sep
  15.29w 1.71   9.53   26.62W   5.10   30.94   2:48.17
  4384   1   Jarrow   22 May
  14.3   1.61   9.02   26.6   5.44   27.92   2:53.9

4465	Claire Everett	U17	25.06.79	2	London (He)	21 Aug
	15.68 1.59 8.75	26.52 5.18			25.98 2:23.47	
4456 w	Teresa Andrews	U20	4.01.77	1	Wrexham	28 Aug
	15.82w 1.71 10.55	26.54W 5.43			19.64 2:39.94	
4449	Emma Green		25.01.64	13	Sheffield	1 May
	15.09w 1.56 9.29	27.11 5.23			36.14 2:43.95	
4369	Louise Batho	U20	27.11.76	7	Birmingham	18 Sep
	15.68w 1.53 11.09	27.89 5.02			31.86 2:34.12	
4360	Sandra Cull	U20	10.12.75	1	Kirkby	24 Jul
	16.4 1.64 9.64	27.2 5.79			25.96 2:40.2	
4328	Katie Budd	U20	3.01.76	7	Sheffield	1 May
	15.17w 1.56 9.07	27.88 5.22			27.84 2:33.04	
4324	Alanna Cooke		11.01.70	14	Sheffield	1 May
	15.82 1.29 9.09 24.28	4.87w 23.38			2:15.29	

(40)

4313	Jacquie Burke	U20	12.09.76	8	Birmingham	18 Sep
	16.14w 1.53 11.89	27.08 4.71			31.22 2:35.98	
4302	Amanda Wale		14.10.70	3	Wrexham	28 Aug
	16.02w 1.59 8.88	27.60w 5.19			34.06 2:39.26	
4290 w	Esther Sneddon	U23	30.06.74	3	Linwood	17 Jul
	16.04W 1.53 9.52	27.86 4.65			39.72 2:32.81	
4277	Fay Champion		27.09.66	3	Stoke	7 Aug
	16.35 1.61 12.37	27.96 4.64			30.18 2:38.2	
4260 w	Fiona Allan	U20	6.11.75	9	Birmingham	18 Sep
	15.66 1.56 9.51	27.15W 5.41			25.80 2:42.21	
4172				3	Oxford	26 Jun
	15.9 1.49 8.98	27.0 5.49			27.38 2:38.9	
4242	Rachel Smith	U20	3.03.76	2	Oxford	26 Jun
	15.5 1.58 9.24	26.9 5.18			18.14 2:26.2	
4206	Stephanie Nicholson	U20	28.06.76	3	York	26 Jun
	15.7 1.50 9.50	26.7 5.21			22.34 2:29.4	
4182	Charlotte Lewis	U20	10.05.75	8	Sheffield	1 May
	16.08w 1.62 8.24	27.80 5.25w			22.64 2:30.14	
4168 w	Samantha Male	U20	11.04.76	10	Birmingham	18 Sep
	14.74w 1.50 7.88	26.32W 5.22			28.88 2:52.80	
4162				3	London (WL)	26 Jun
4144	Sarah Ditchfield	U20	26.03.75	11	Birmingham	18 Sep
	15.55w 1.50 7.95	28.18 4.94			28.06 2:24.96	

(50)

4124 w	Katy Sketchley	U23	9.07.73	1	Braintree	25 Sep
	14.8 1.50 9.54	26.2W 5.10			24.86 2:52.1	
4082	Sarah Godbeer	U20	10.06.77	1	Exeter	26 Jun
	16.6 1.51 9.15	25.6 5.00			27.80 2:41.5	
4058	Sharon Wright	U20	6.10.76	1	Lincoln	8 May
	15.7 1.46 8.78	27.3 5.30			28.08 2:41.3	
4057	Paula Blank	U17	13.12.77	9	Sheffield	1 May
	16.73 1.50 9.98	27.37 4.33			37.68 2:38.43	
4026	Leone Dickinson	U20	5.11.75	15	Sheffield	1 May
	16.30 1.62 9.20	27.62 4.95			23.86 2:42.59	
3982	Jacqueline Cooke	U20	20.06.76	4	Stoke	7 Aug
	15.14 1.52 6.37	26.99 4.81			21.88 2:31.4	
3969	Ruth Calvert	U20	22.10.75	4	York	26 Jun
	17.3 1.56 9.12	25.9 5.13			25.16 2:46.0	
3957	*Jarmila Bubikova*	*U20*	*8.01.77*	*3*	*Basildon*	*26 Jun*
	17.1 1.49 8.74	*27.4 5.16*			*33.70 2:43.6*	
3957	Kate Haywood	U23	23.12.74	15	Birmingham	18 Sep
	15.34 1.41 7.77	27.43 5.00			24.64 2:34.22	
3914	Anya Hutchinson	U20	16.07.77	4	Oxford	26 Jun
	16.4 1.40 7.77	27.9 4.68			29.64 2:20.6	
3889	Lesley Irvine	U20	1.01.77	4	Basildon	26 Jun
	15.8 1.40 7.96	27.5 5.17			29.80 2:42.8	

	Name	Cat	DOB	Pos	Venue	Date
3889	Michele Gillham	U23	8.10.74	1	Hoo	18 Sep
	15.6 1.54 8.12	26.8	4.69		25.72 2:46.5	
3886	Elaine Wyard/Sutcliffe		6.04.70	1	Wakefield	25 Sep
	19.4 1.40 8.33	25.4	4.91		28.24 2:20.8	
3872	Catherine Wemyss	U20	19.05.77	2	Exeter	26 Jun
	17.1 1.57 8.82	28.4	5.13		32.86 2:51.0	
3865	Jane O'Malley	U20	18.07.77	5	York	26 Jun
	16.1 1.56 8.34	26.9	4.76		17.38 2:33.7	
3856	Nicola Gautier	U17	21.03.78	1	Sheffield	25 Sep
	16.9 1.42 10.16	28.0	4.78		31.02 2:38.3	
3832	Karen Sanders	U20	13.11.76	17	Birmingham	18 Sep
	17.05w 1.56 9.25	27.77	4.70		24.54 2:40.22	

HEPTATHLON - Under 17

	Name	DOB	Pos	Venue	Date
4861	Clover Wynter-Pink	29.11.77	1	London (WL)	26 Jun
	11.9 1.60 11.63	26.1 4.99		43.04 2:35.6	
4841	Rebecca Lewis	31.12.77	1	Birmingham	18 Sep
	11.72w 1.56 10.18	25.66 5.54		32.82 2:29.10	
4503	Angie Nyhan	13.04.78	3	Birmingham	18 Sep
	12.34 1.56 10.14	27.39w 5.28		32.90 2:31.65	
4489	Claire Everett	25.06.79	4	Birmingham	18 Sep
	12.59 1.56 9.23	26.19 5.44		25.94 2:26.75	
4475	Amanda Humble	15.08.79	1	Jarrow	22 May
	12.0 1.58 9.56	26.2 5.03		33.72 2:38.5	
4431	Louise Dixon	29.11.77	1	Sheffield	1 May
	12.81 1.59 10.85	25.94 5.18		24.40 2:34.03	
4406	Abigail Ashby	23.11.77	5	Birmingham	18 Sep
	11.94w 1.53 9.25	26.88w 5.40		26.70 2:32.87	
4303	Nicola Gautier	21.03.78	2	Stoke	7 Aug
	12.62w 1.35 10.15	26.58 5.12		34.78 2:31.2	
4302	Jennifer Impett	18.11.77	1	Exeter	26 Jun
	12.2 1.51 7.88	25.4 5.10		24.44 2:28.1	
4293	Amanda Gray	22.03.79	1	Oxford	26 Jun
	12.3 1.48 7.22	25.5 5.03		27.04 2:23.5	
(10)					
4265	Paula Blank	13.12.77	1	Peterborough	25 Sep
	12.9 1.54 9.68	27.5 4.65		37.80 2:32.5	
4203	Hazel Clarke	17.03.79	2	Blackpool	26 Jun
	12.3 1.66 8.72	27.1 5.06		27.22 2:42.4	
4064	Cathy Boulton	2.11.77	2	Oxford	26 Jun
	12.7 1.69 6.96	26.9 5.33		14.70 2:34.5	
4051	Jodi Hallett	8.11.78	2	Exeter	26 Jun
	12.6 1.60 8.34	27.2 4.57		22.86 2:28.8	
4023	Jackie Tindal	21.01.79	4	Stoke	7 Aug
	12.17w 1.56 9.42	26.02 4.85		18.72 2:47.8	
4003	Emma Blunt	26.10.77	2	London (WF)	8 May
	12.2 1.51 8.69	27.5 5.13		20.58 2:37.0	
3974	Amy Baden	30.05.79	3	Exeter	26 Jun
	12.1 1.45 8.62	26.9 5.08		23.04 2:41.6	
3971	Kate Rogers	14.02.79	5	Stoke	7 Aug
	12.78w 1.50 7.23	26.41 5.28		18.40 2:34.1	
3957	Donna Conroy	21.09.77	1	Kirkby	24 Jul
	13.0 1.49 10.29	26.8 5.06		20.14 2:42.1	
3954	Joanna Morris	16.10.77	1	London (He)	21 Aug
	12.50 1.65 8.76	28.86 4.84		21.20 2:39.01	
(20)					
3922	Debbie Harrison	13.11.78	12	Birmingham	18 Sep
	12.51 1.47 7.47	26.77w 5.33		20.52 2:41.61	
3917	Natalie Butler	25.11.78	4	Oxford	26 Jun
	12.5 1.54 7.97	27.4 5.16		26.46 2:51.5	

3867	Hannah Stares		13.11.78	4	Exeter	26 Jun
	12.5	1.57	7.73	26.7	4.74	22.52 2:45.9	
3864	Fionna McWhinnie		25.04.78	3	London (WL)	26 Jun
	13.3	1.57	8.55	29.4	4.82	27.32 2:34.1	
3864	Bianca Liston		28.05.78	1	Hoo	25 Sep
	12.4	1.48	6.94	26.9	5.17	19.70 2:37.8	
3851	Kathryn Dowsett		24.11.78	13	Birmingham	18 Sep
	12.84	1.56	7.68	26.84w	5.04	26.00 2:56.91	
3833	Patricia Taylor		14.03.79	14	Birmingham	18 Sep
	12.42	1.50	7.63	27.65w	5.07	22.42 2:44.51	
3816	Leanne Buxton		27.05.78	16	Birmingham	18 Sep
	12.31	1.38	8.14	26.26w	4.91	17.20 2:36.64	
3809	Amanda Edwards		11.09.77	7	Sheffield	1 May
	13.37w	1.38	8.44	27.59	4.63	30.90 2:34.48	
3800	Stephanie Phillips		25.10.78	1	Crawley	18 Sep
	12.7	1.51	7.72	28.5	5.13	24.16 2:42.8	

PENTATHLON - Under 15

3225	Amy Nuttell		6.02.80	1	Basildon	26 Jun
	11.9	9.09	5.15	1.59	2:26.0		
3193	Samantha Foster		9.09.79	2	Basildon	26 Jun
	11.8	9.39	5.20	1.65	2:38.0		
3142	Katherine Livesey		15.12.79	1	Stoke	7 Aug
	5.15	11.6	8.36	1.63	2:35.56		
2996	Hayley Warrilow		10.04.80	3	Stoke	7 Aug
	5.05	12.2	8.84	1.57	2:36.27		
2970	Sarah Claxton		23.09.79	3	Basildon	26 Jun
	11.6	10.58	5.33	1.56	3:02.6		
2930	Hayley Young		26.09.79	4	Basildon	26 Jun
	12.4	7.44	4.90	1.65	2:36.8		
2912	Lindsay Impett		4.01.80	1	Exeter	26 Jun
	12.0	8.80	1.49	4.85	2:32.9		
2908	Alison Kerboas		21.05.81	4	Birmingham	18 Sep
	12.31	8.55	1.56	4.78	2:33.97		
2862	Laura White		5.09.79	6	Birmingham	18 Sep
	11.83	8.87	1.50	5.05	2:44.97		
2861	Kelly Williamson		4.12.79	1	Oxford	26 Jun
	11.6	9.37	1.42	5.22	2:46.8		
(10)							
2826	Eve Miller		1.12.79	10	Birmingham	18 Sep
	11.74	10.09	1.44	4.76	2:43.27		
2822	Chloe Cozens		9.04.80	5	Exeter	26 Jun
	12.9	9.25	4.84	1.53	2:38.3		
2760	Danielle Freeman		11.02.80	1	Wakefield	25 Sep
	13.8	7.27	1.54	5.13	2:33.5		
2757	Caroline Pearce		1.09.80	6	Basildon	26 Jun
	12.1	8.28	4.85	1.41	2:34.7		
2757 w	Kelly Moreton		18.09.79	2	Wrexham	27 Aug
	4.58	11.90W	7.50	1.56	2:40.50		
2655				1	Cardiff	17 Sep
	4.49	12.2	7.22	1.53	2:40.0		
2741	Lesley McGoldrick		12.09.79	1	York	26 Jun
	11.5	8.88	1.45	4.67	2:45.3		
2736	Gillian Stewart		21.01.80	1	Linwood	17 Jul
	4.59	12.17	1.57	8.73	2:48.38		
2732	Elizabeth Sherman		15.09.79	13	Birmingham	18 Sep
	12.35	7.87	1.56	4.76	2:44.58		
2730	Julia Johnson		21.09.79	1	Hoo	18 Sep
	5.07	12.7	9.85	1.48	2:52.9		
2718	Maria Grantham		14.12.79	1	Kirkby	24 Jul
	4.62	12.3	7.59	1.39	2:26.1		

```
2711   Joanne Hyslop                    13.03.80  14   Birmingham      18  Sep
       12.44      8.09    1.56   4.41    2:39.98
2687   Victoria Reynolds                22.04.80   4   Blackpool       26  Jun
       13.0       9.23    4.87   1.50    2:47.0
2674   Kay Goodman                      17.11.80   1   Peterborough    25  Sep
       4.89       12.6    7.45   1.51    2:43.0
2671   Fran Yearsley                    24.03.80   5   Stoke            7  Aug
       4.63       13.1    6.76   1.51    2:29.45
2636   Lisa Thompson                    25.04.81   3   Wrexham         27  Aug
       4.73       12.70w  6.73   1.53    2:39.64
2625   Jane Cuddy                       25.08.81   7   Blackpool       26  Jun
       12.2       8.06    5.04   1.35    2:42.9
2617   Catherine Ryan                    4.02.80   4   Wrexham         27  Aug
       4.75       12.74w  8.34   1.56    2:54.22
2594   Carmilla Carmichael               1.12.79   2   Exeter          26  Jun
       13.1       7.10    1.58   4.41    2:39.6
2578   Christine Head                   18.12.79   2   Woking           7  Aug
       4.77       13.0    8.79   1.48    2:50.2
2562   Antonia Bemrose                   3.09.79   3   London (He)     24  Jul
       4.76       13.4    7.21   1.64    2:55.7
     (30)
2560   Denise Sullivan                  27.12.79   2   Watford         23  Jul
       4.71       12.4    7.16   1.49    2:47.2
2559   Louise Gauld                     24.08.80   2   Linwood         17  Jul
       4.21       13.27w  1.48   7.55    2:30.17
2557   Lisa Whigham                     14.08.80   2   Grangemouth     11  Jun
       12.7       1.34    7.09   4.52    2:26.7
2552   Elena Dundjerovic                13.09.79   2   London (WL)     26  Jun
       12.7       6.97    1.42   4.88    2:41.2
2539   Helen Redfern                    26.04.80   9   Blackpool       26  Jun
       12.1       6.40    5.17   1.41    2:51.3
2538   Julie McCorry                     7.11.79   1   Antrim          26  Jun
       13.8       1.46   11.45   4.75    3:11.4
2538   Laura Redmond                    19.04.81   3   Linwood         17  Jul
       4.54       13.24w  1.51   7.47    2:41.34
2536   Maria Pringle                    18.12.80  10   Blackpool       26  Jun
       12.8       8.30    4.52   1.50    2:48.9
2535   Emma March                       15.11.79   2   York            26  Jun
       12.3       7.68    1.45   4.46    2:43.7
2527   Stephanie Hamilton               27.06.80   4   Grangemouth     11  Jun
       13.1       1.55    9.17   4.45    2:56.3
```

Under 13
```
2074   Lindsey Maguire                  15.01.82       Grangemouth     11  Jun
```

PENTATHLON - Under 13
```
2451   Seonaid Ferry                    19.11.81   1   Linwood         17  Jul
       4.45       11.78   9.30   1.40    2:51.41
2419   Donna Medlock                    26.10.81   1   Woking           7  Aug
       4.64       12.3    9.00   1.33    2:45.4
2373   Tina Thirlwell                    5.09.81   1   Kirkby          24  Jul
       4.61       12.5    6.69   1.36    2:36.7
2337   Cheryl Gibbons                   21.09.81   2   Kirkby          24  Jul
       4.40       11.9    5.96   1.36    2:36.2
2269   Gemma Hair                        3.11.81   1   Inverness       18  Sep
       11.8       8.08    1.40
2265 * Suzanne Hasler                    7.04.82   1   Much Wenlock    10  Jul
       4.49       14.2    6.37   1.34    2:34.9
                                                      Scored off 75m Hurdles
2177   Gaby Howell                      25.01.82   1   Crawley         18  Sep
       4.07       12.4    5.89   1.38    2:40.4
```

2145	Vicky Hyland				27.10.81	3	Kirkby	24	Jul
	4.54	13.3	6.33	1.24	2:36.7				
2125 *	Melanie Vaggers				16.06.82	1	Exeter	8	May
	3.79	13.5	8.06	1.39	2:52.5		Scored off 75m Hurdles		
2103	Cathy Young					2	Woking	7	Aug
	4.22	14.1	6.07	1.42	2:42.6				
(10)									
2089	Julia Peters				6.09.81	4	Kirkby	24	Jul
	4.46	12.2	6.36	1.30	2:54.4				
2074	Rebecca Conway				4.11.81	1	London (Ha)	7	Aug
	3.98	13.3	6.50	1.27	2:34.7				
2064	Rachel Peacock				18.05.82	1	Bournemouth	22	May
	4.24	12.0	6.48	1.28	2:52.2				
2049	Danielle Parkinson				2.09.81	5	Kirkby	24	Jul
	4.34	12.6	6.48	1.36	2:59.1				
2042	Stephanie Little				5.11.81	2	Wrexham	28	Aug
	3.90	12.30w	6.91	1.33	2:51.36				
2022	Lesley Alderman-Foord				13.01.82	3	Woking	7	Aug
	4.18	13.3	6.43	1.30	2:45.6				

2000 METRES WALK - Track - Under 13

10:41.0	Amy Hales		16.03.82	1	Bolton	7	May
11:02.4	Louise Richmond		15.12.81	2	Leamington	6	Aug
11:19.2	Katie Ford		21.10.81	3	Leamington	6	Aug
11:38.8	Vanessa Caines		17.04.83	2	Horsham	14	May

2500 METRES WALK - Road - Under 15

13:24	Amy Hales		16.03.82	1	Bexley	12	Dec
13:55	Louise Richmond	U13	15.12.81	1	Leicester	26	Mar
13:55	Kirsty Coleman		17.11.80	2	Bexley	10	Dec

3000 METRES WALK - Track

13:20.23	Vicky Lupton	U23	17.04.72	2	Kings Lynn	9	Jul
13:50.6				1	Sheffield	14	May
14:02.2				1	Brierley Hill	9	Oct
13:27.9	Verity Larby/Snook		13.11.70	1	Portsmouth	14	May
13:31.78				1	London (CP)	26	Jun
13:45.64 i				1	Birmingham	26	Feb
13:50.8				1	Bracknell	2	May
13:30.3	Carolyn Partington		27.06.66	1	Douglas, IOM	5	Aug
13:43.0	Melanie Brookes/Wright		5.04.64	1	Coventry	5	Jul
13:55.3				1	Rugby	31	Aug
13:57.2				1	Leamington	6	Aug
14:04.2				1	Leamington	14	May
13:47.10 i	Sylvia Black	V35	16.04.58	2	Birmingham	26	Feb
14:09.0	Karen Smith		1.06.61	2	Coventry	5	Jul
14:12.9	Elaine Callanin		13.09.60	2	Brierley Hill	9	Oct
14:26.0	Karen Kneale		23.04.69	1	Douglas, IOM	15	Dec
14:36.22 i	Nicky Jackson		1.05.65	3	Birmingham	26	Feb
14:44.8	Sarah Brown		28.09.64	1	Horsham	14	May
(10)							
14:45.8	Claire Walker/Childs	U23	8.10.72	2	Leamington	6	Aug
14:47.9	Kim Baird	V35	28.02.56	1	Warley	14	May
14:59.0	Sarah Bennett	U15	27.07.80	1	Bolton	7	May
15:01.2	Kath Horwill	U20	26.01.75	3	Leamington	6	Aug
15:03.45	Julie Drake		21.05.69	2	Bracknell	2	May
15:05.0	Helen Sharratt	U23	18.12.72	1	Southend	9	Jan
15:05.7	Gill Watson		26.05.64	2	Sheffield	14	May
15:07.0	Sharon Tonks		18.04.70	2	Warley	14	May
15:13.22	Joanne Pope		17.01.71	3	Bracknell	2	May
15:15.3	Nikki Huckerby	U20	27.02.78	4	Brierley Hill	9	Oct
15:18.90		U17		1	Birmingham	17	Sep

15:15.5	Claire Whitehouse	U17	11.04.79	1	Bournemouth	14 May
15:20.7	Lynsey Tozer	U20	6.12.75	5	Brierley Hill	9 Oct
15:26.56	Nina Howley	U17	22.01.78	2	Birmingham	17 Sep
15:32.45	Catherine Charnock	U20	3.05.75	2	London (CP)	2 May
15:38.3	Sandra Brown	V45	1.04.49	1	London (CP)	10 Aug
15:38.77	Cath Reader	V40	19.10.54	1	Bedford	16 Jul
15:47.89 i	Brenda Lupton	V40	5.10.52	5	Birmingham	26 Feb
15:58.9	Clare Ellis	U17	27.04.78	5	Leamington	6 Aug
16:04.88	Sally Warren	U17	29.01.78	3	Birmingham	17 Sep
16:15.5	Samantha Vines	U20	28.02.77	2	Bournemouth	14 May
(30)						
16:19.17	Ann Lewis	V45	29.12.47	2	London (CP)	26 Jun
16:21.0	Amy Hales	U15	16.03.82	1	Brighton	18 Dec
16:36.0		U15		3	Brighton	8 Feb
16:26.2	Carla Jarvis	U20	5.08.75	3	Warley	14 May

Road - Junior

15:27	Nikki Huckerby	U17	27.02.78	1	Dublin, IRE	24 Sep
15:27	Amy Hales	U13	16.03.82	1	Calne	3 Dec
15:34	Clare Ellis	U17	27.04.78	2	Dublin, IRE	24 Sep
15:52	Kelly Bartlett	U15	13.10.79	2	Holmewood	30 Apr
15:55	Kirsty Coleman	U15	17.11.80	2	Calne	3 Dec

5000 METRES WALK - Track

22:40.0	Lisa Langford		15.03.67	1	Coventry	19 Jul
23:06.0	Vicky Lupton	U23	17.04.72	1	Sheffield	14 Sep
23:34.50				2	Horsham	19 Jun
23:22.52	Verity Larby/Snook		13.11.70	1	Horsham	19 Jun
23:47.0	Melanie Brookes/Wright		5.04.64	1	Solihull	29 May
23:57.0				1	Coventry	26 Jul
24:06.27				4	Horsham	19 Jun
24:18.79	Karen Smith		1.06.61	5	Horsham	19 Jun
24:50.09	*Sian Spacey*		*13.07.64*	*6*	*Horsham*	*19 Jun*
25:05.3	Kim Baird	V35	28.02.56	1	Solihull	26 Jun
25:06.0	Sarah Brown		28.09.64	1	Brighton	9 Aug
25:21.0	Julie Drake		21.05.69	2	Brighton	10 May
25:25.02	Nina Howley	U17	22.01.78	1	Birmingham	31 Jul
25:25.96	Kath Horwill	U20	26.01.75	7	Warsaw, POL	18 Jun
(10)						
25:43.0	Claire Walker/Childs	U23	8.10.72	2	Coventry	26 Jul
25:47.26	Sharon Tonks		18.04.70	7	Horsham	19 Jun
25:54.0	Gill Watson		26.05.64	2	Sheffield	14 Sep
26:11.0	Catherine Charnock	U20	3.05.75	2	Bolton	7 May
26:13.0	Joanne Pope		17.01.71	2	Brighton	9 Aug
26:14.09	Lynsey Tozer	U20	6.12.75	1	Birmingham	17 Sep
26:19.78	Clare Ellis	U17	27.04.78	2	Birmingham	31 Jul
26:28.74	Nikki Huckerby	U17	27.02.78	3	Birmingham	31 Jul
26:40.0	Carla Jarvis	U20	5.08.75	4	Bolton	7 May
26:48.92	Brenda Lupton	V40	5.10.52	2	Sheffield	21 Sep
(20)						
26:50.98	Cath Reader	V40	19.10.54	1	Bedford	17 Jul
27:27.43	Theresa Ashman	U23	16.06.73	10	Horsham	19 Jun
27:40.35	Ann Lewis	V45	29.12.47	2	London (He)	21 Aug
27:49.0	Claire Whitehouse	U17	11.04.79	4	Bolton	7 May

Road

22:44 +	Lisa Langford		15.03.67	4=m	Victoria, CAN	25 Aug
23:14				1	Coventry	29 Jan
23:17				1	Solihull	29 Oct
23:32				1	Worcester	26 Feb
22:45 +	Vicky Lupton	U23	17.04.72	6=m	Victoria, CAN	25 Aug
22:59 +				m	Helsinki, FIN	9 Aug

22:45 +	Verity Larby/Snook		13.11.70	6=m	Victoria, CAN	25 Aug
23:07 +				m	Helsinki, FIN	9 Aug
23:11				1	Bexley	12 Mar
23:45				1	Bexley	12 Feb
23:04	Carolyn Partington		27.06.66	1	Douglas, IOM	26 May
23:36 +				8m	Victoria, CAN	25 Aug
23:48				1	Douglas, IOM	6 Feb
23:58	Sylvia Black	V35	16.04.58	1	Sutton Coldfield	12 Feb
23:58	Melanie Brookes/Wright		5.04.64	1	Holmewood	10 Apr
24:03	Karen Smith		1.06.61	2	Sutton Coldfield	12 Feb
24:37	Elaine Callanin		13.09.60	2	Holmewood	10 Apr
24:50	Karen Kneale		23.04.69	2	Douglas, IOM	26 May
25:10	Sarah Brown		28.09.64	1	Brighton	19 Nov
(10)						
25:27	Sharon Tonks		18.04.70	1	Tamworth	3 Dec
25:33	Helen Sharratt	U23	18.12.72	2	Bexley	12 Dec
25:34	Nicky Jackson		1.05.65	3	Holmewood	10 Apr
25:36	Kim Baird	V35	28.02.56	2	Birmingham	21 May
25:38	Kath Horwill	U20	26.01.75	3	Birmingham	21 May
25:49	Nina Howley	U17	22.01.78	5	Holmewood	10 Apr
25:49	Lynsey Tozer	U20	6.12.75	1	Birmingham	19 Nov
26:07 o	Nikki Huckerby	U17	27.02.78	3	Tamworth	3 Dec
26:45				3	Worcester	26 Feb
26:15	Gill Watson		26.05.64	5	Holmewood	10 Apr
26:18	Catherine Charnock	U20	3.05.75	5	Birmingham	21 May
(20)						
26:27	Sandra Brown	V45	1.04.49	3	London (CP)	5 Feb
26:27	Liz Corran	V35	23.09.55	1	Douglas, IOM	13 Nov
26:28	Claire Walker/Childs	U23	8.10.72	6	Birmingham	21 May
26:43	Brenda Lupton	V40	5.10.52	8	Holmewood	10 Apr
26:47	Clare Ellis	U17	27.04.78	9	Holmewood	10 Apr

10000 METRES WALK - Track

46:30.0	Vicky Lupton	U23	17.04.72	1	Sheffield	14 Sep
50:11.0				4	Bolton	7 May
48:05.0	Verity Larby/Snook		13.11.70	1	Bolton	7 May
48:20.0	Carolyn Partington		27.06.66	2	Bolton	7 May
49:16.0	Melanie Brookes/Wright		5.04.64	3	Bolton	7 May
51:22.0	Karen Kneale		23.04.69	5	Bolton	7 May
51:24.0	Liz Corran	V35	23.09.55	2	Douglas, IOM	13 Apr
52:37.0	Nicky Jackson		1.05.65	6	Bolton	7 May
53:20.5	Sarah Brown		28.09.64	1	Brighton	21 Jul
53:44.0	Gill Watson		26.05.64	8	Bolton	7 May
54:00.7	Sandra Brown	V45	1.04.49	1	London (BP)	4 May
(10)						
54:19.0	Cath Reader	V40	19.10.54	9	Bolton	7 May
55:35.0	Brenda Lupton	V40	5.10.52	3	Sheffield	14 Sep
58:26.0	Sally Hall		14.02.71	10	Bolton	7 May
58:56.4	Ann Lewis	V45	29.12.47	1	Solihull	14 Aug
58:58.0	Helena Battle		5.04.62	11	Bolton	7 May

10000 METRES WALK - Road

45:48	Vicky Lupton	U23	17.04.72	5	Victoria, CAN	25 Aug
46:30				20	Helsinki, FIN	9 Aug
48:07				31	Livorno, ITA	12 Jun
48:30				2	Douglas, IOM	25 Jun
46:01	Lisa Langford		15.03.67	6	Victoria, CAN	25 Aug
47:07				1	Stoneleigh	19 Mar
47:12				1	Cardiff	8 May
47:14				1	Tamworth	3 Dec
47:34				26	Livorno, ITA	12 Jun

46:06	Verity Larby/Snook			13.11.70	7	Victoria, CAN	25	Aug
47:23					23	Helsinki, FIN	9	Aug
47:24					25	Livorno, ITA	12	Jun
47:21	Carolyn Partington			27.06.66	9	Victoria, CAN	25	Aug
47:46					28	Livorno, ITA	12	Jun
48:37					1	Douglas, IOM	26	Feb
48:46					3	Stoneleigh	19	Mar
48:30	Karen Smith			1.06.61	2	Horsham	16	Apr
48:45					11	Victoria, CAN	25	Aug
48:54					4	Stoneleigh	19	Mar
48:41	Sylvia Black	V35		16.04.58	2	Stoneleigh	19	Mar
50:37					1	Birmingham	17	Dec
48:58	Melanie Brookes/Wright			5.04.64	1	Leicester	11	Sep
49:03					3	Horsham	16	Apr
49:04					34	Livorno, ITA	12	Jun
49:16					2	Douglas, IOM	26	Feb
49:30					6	Stoneleigh	19	Mar
49:59					3	Douglas, IOM	25	Jun
49:17	Elaine Callanin			13.09.60	5	Stoneleigh	19	Mar
49:19					3	Douglas, IOM	26	Feb
50:00					2	Tamworth	3	Dec
51:09	Sian Spacey			13.07.64	4	Douglas, IOM	25	Jun
CAN								
51:31	Karen Kneale			23.04.69	6	Douglas, IOM	25	Jun
51:50	Sarah Brown			28.09.64	1	Brighton	19	Nov
(10)								
52:13	Nicky Jackson			1.05.65	7	Stoneleigh	19	Mar
52:39	Sharon Tonks			18.04.70	1	Birmingham	19	Nov
53:08	Kath Horwill	U20		26.01.75	10	Stoneleigh	19	Mar
53:25	Sandra Brown	V45		1.04.49	7	Horsham	16	Apr
53:28	Lynsey Tozer	U20		6.12.75	2	Birmingham	17	Dec
53:48	Claire Walker/Childs	U23		8.10.72	11	Stoneleigh	19	Mar
53:58	Nikki Huckerby	U20		27.02.78	3	Birmingham	17	Dec
55:35		U17			15	Stoneleigh	19	Mar
54:41	Liz Corran	V35		23.09.55	12	Stoneleigh	19	Mar
54:45	Brenda Lupton	V40		5.10.52	13	Stoneleigh	19	Mar
54:46	Nina Howley	U17		22.01.78	14	Stoneleigh	19	Mar
(20)								
55:10	Gill Watson			26.05.64	10	Horsham	16	Apr
56:55	Catherine Charnock	U20		3.05.75	16	Stoneleigh	19	Mar
57:15	Julie Bellfield			1.11.68	1	Coventry	3	Mar
57:22	Helen Sharratt	U23		18.12.72	1	Ilford	26	Jul
57:40	Maureen Cox	V40		7.09.50	18	Stoneleigh	19	Mar
58:23	Mary Wallen	V40		9.06.52	19	Stoneleigh	19	Mar
58:37	Suzanne Ford-Dunn	U23		25.04.73	2	Steyning	5	Nov

20 KILOMETRES WALK

1:44:48	Vicky Lupton	U23		17.04.72	1	Holmewood	3	Sep
1:50:21	Kim Baird	V35		28.02.56	2	Holmewood	3	Sep
1:51:38	Sarah Brown			28.09.64	3	Holmewood	3	Sep
1:52:04	Sandra Brown	V45		1.04.49	4	Holmewood	3	Sep
1:54:46	Cath Reader	V35		19.10.54	1	Colchester	29	May

50 KILOMETRES WALK

4:56:27	Sandra Brown	V45		1.04.49	1	Basildon	13	Aug
5:56:25	Kath Crilley	V45		8.09.47	1	Burrator	1	May

100 MILES WALK

19:09:17	Sandra Brown	V45		1.04.49	1	Hungarton	30	Jul

4 x 100 METRES

43.46	National Team	2	Birmingham	25	Jun
	(S Douglas, K Merry, S Jacobs, P Thomas)				
43.46	England	3	Victoria, CAN	28	Aug
	(S Douglas, G McLeod, S Jacobs, P Thomas)				
43.63	National Team	5	Helsinki, FIN	13	Aug
	(S Douglas, K Merry, S Jacobs, P Thomas)				
44.03	National Team	2h2	Helsinki, FIN	13	Aug
	(S Douglas, K Merry, S Jacobs, P Thomas)				
44.12	National Team	1	Helsinki, FIN	29	Jun
	(S Jacobs, G McLeod, M Richardson, S Douglas)				
44.22	National Team	2	Gateshead	20	Jul
	(S Douglas, G McLeod, S Jacobs, J Agyepong)				
44.45	National Team	8	London (CP)	11	Sep
	(J Agyepong, G McLeod, S Jacobs, P Thomas)				
45.03	National Under 23 Team	3	Gateshead	20	Jul
	(J Maduaka, M Richardson, S Smith, D Hoggarth)				
45.08	National Junior Team U20	3	Lisbon, POR	24	Jul
	(D Allahgreen, S Williams, S Dudgeon, R Drummond)				
45.09	National Under 23 Team	4	Ostrava, TCH	30	Jul
	(D Allahgreen, D Hoggarth, S Smith, S Dudgeon)				
45.12	England	1	Nitra, SVK	13	Jul
	(S Farquharson, M Richardson, S Smith, P Thomas)				
45.36	England	1	Wrexham	3	Jul
	(G McLeod, M Richardson, S Jacobs, P Thomas)				
45.67	England Under 23 Team	1	Kings Lynn	9	Jul
	(S Smith, M Richardson, J Maduaka, D Hoggarth)				
45.71	North	1	Corby	30	May
45.75	Shaftesbury Barnet	1	Birmingham	8	May
	(C Haslam, S Jacobs, C Murphy, J Agyepong)				
45.84	AAA	1	Loughborough	5	Jun
	(L Robbins, D Fraser, S Smith, J Maduaka)				
45.99	England Schools U17	1	Nicosia, CYP	20	May
	(N Danvers, L Owusu, R Drummond, T Nelson)				
46.02	Scotland	2	Corby	30	May
46.06	Shaftesbury Barnet	1	Bedford	17	Sep
	(C Murphy, M Walker, C Haslam, J Agyepong)				
46.17	Sale	2	Bedford	17	Sep
	(S. Baker, P Smith, L Stuart, A Thompson)				
46.28	Scotland	1	Istanbul, TUR	21	May
	(M Baxter, J Booth, J Fleming, M Neef)				

Additional National Teams

48.49	Wales	3	Oordegem, BEL	9	Jul
	(Edwards, Jones, Williams, L Sharpe)				
48.56	Northern Ireland	3	Kings Lynn	9	Jul
	(J Hale, C O'Connor, S Douglas, S McCann)				

Additional Club Teams (1 - 2 above)

46.4	Edinburgh Woollen Mill	1	Stoke-on-Trent	31	Jul
46.70	Essex Ladies	3	Bedford	17	Sep
46.8	Trafford	2	Grangemouth	7	May
47.1	Windsor Slough & Eton	1	Corby	31	Jul
47.4	Rotherham	1	Loughborough	26	Jun
47.5	City of Glasgow	3	Stretford	18	Jun
47.5	Basildon	1	Havering	7	Sep
47.6	Bromley Ladies	2	Stoke-on-Trent	31	Jul
47.92	Cardiff	1	Cardiff	8	May
48.02	Team Solent	1	Bedford	18	Sep
48.1	Borough of Hounslow	1	Hoo	19	Jun

48.1	Birchfield		2	Bournemouth	19 Jun
48.1	City of Hull		1	Leeds	13 Aug
48.13	Aldershot Farnham & District		5	Bedford	17 Sep
48.2	Spenborough		1	Sheffield	14 May
48.2	Ealing Southall & Middlesex		2	Bracknell	19 Jun
48.2	Essex Ladies	U17	1	Barking	12 Jul
48.3	Croydon		1	Croydon	8 May
48.4	Coventry Godiva		1	Coventry	14 Aug

Additional Under 20 Teams (1 - 2 above)

46.49	National Team		3	Warsaw, POL	18 Jun
46.71	National Team		2h3	Lisbon, POR	23 Jul
46.73	England Schools		h	Nicosia, CYP	19 May
47.01	South of England		1	London (He)	27 Aug
47.38	North		1	Colwyn Bay	23 Jul

Additional National Teams

| 47.82 | Scotland | | 2 | Colwyn Bay | 23 Jul |
| 48.71 | Wales | | 3 | Dublin | 13 Aug |

Additional Under 20 Club Teams (1 above)

49.1	Walton		1	Carshalton	11 Sep
49.16	Cannock & Stafford	U17	2	Birmingham	11 Sep
49.17	City of Stoke		1	Stoke-on-Trent	30 May
49.2	St George's School		1	Grangemouth	11 Jun
49.3	City of Glasgow	U17	1	Kirkby	5 Jun
49.5	Team Solent	U15	1	Southampton	23 Apr
49.7	Wigan & District		1	Harrow	24 Apr
49.77	Sale		1	Remiremont, FRA	24 Sep
49.8	Ipswich	U17	1	St Ives	19 Jun

Additional Under 17 Teams (1 above)

47.55	England Schools		1	Aberdeen	16 Jul
48.01	Kent Schools		1h4	Telford	9 Jul
48.02	Scotland Schools		2	Aberdeen	16 Jul
48.21	Essex Schools		1	Telford	9 Jul
48.47	Surrey Schools		2	Telford	9 Jul
48.55	Staffordshire Schools		3	Telford	9 Jul

Additional Under 17 Club Teams (1 - 5 above)

49.8	Crawley		1	Horsham	10 Jul
50.0	Windsor Slough & Eton		1	Croydon	26 Jun
50.1	Dartford		2	Croydon	26 Jun
50.15	Peterborough (Cambs Schools)		4h3	Telford	9 Jul
50.2	City of Stoke		1	Birmingham	1 May
50.2	Derby		1	Leicester	17 Jul

Additional Under 15 Teams (1 above)

48.80	Essex Schools		1	Telford	9 Jul
49.38	Hampshire Schools		2	Telford	9 Jul
49.55	Derbyshire Schools		3	Telford	9 Jul
49.57	Hampshire Schools		1h2	Telford	9 Jul
49.60	Staffordshire Schools		1h1	Telford	9 Jul

Additional Under 15 Club Teams (1 above)

50.38	Coventry Godiva		1	Birmingham	11 Sep
50.9	Blackpool & Fylde		1	Blackpool	19 Jun
50.99	Essex Ladies		2	Birmingham	11 Sep
51.0	Ipswich		1	Ipswich	10 Jul
51.08	Liverpool Harriers		3	Birmingham	11 Sep
51.1	Tower Hamlets		1	Eastbourne	13 Aug
51.2	Telford		1	Telford	8 May
51.20	Cannock & Stafford		4	Birmingham	11 Sep

Under 13 Teams

53.52	Ayr Seaforth	1	Linwood	17	Jul
53.6	Braintree	1	Barking	12	Jul
53.90	Sale	1	Birmingham	11	Sep
54.5	City of Stoke	1	Solihull	17	Jul
54.5	Sussex AA	1	London (TB)	14	Aug
54.5	Liverpool Pembroke	1	Kirkby	11	Sep

4 x 200 METRES

1:35.44 i	National Team	2	Glasgow	29	Jan
	(B Kinch, M Richardson, T Goddard, C Court)				
1:36.23 i	National Team	2	Glasgow	12	Feb
	(K Merry, M Richardson, D Lewis, C Court)				
1:36.62 i	England	2	Vienna, AUT	6	Feb
	(M Richardson, T Goddard, LA Skeete, D Myhill)				
1:38.27 i	North of England	1	Birmingham	26	Feb
1:39.17 i	South of England	2	Birmingham	26	Feb
1:40.47 i	Midland Counties	3	Birmingham	26	Feb
	(K Jury, R Drummond, K Maddox, A Mayfield)				
1:40.55 i	England Schools	U17 1	Birmingham	27	Feb
	(A Charles, L Owusu, S Wilhelmy, T Nelson)				
1:43.16 i	Scotland	4	Birmingham	26	Feb
1:43.4	Epsom & Ewell	1	Carshalton	11	Sep
	E Koseoglu, L Ghojefa, J Bennett, D Bennett)				
1:43.70 i	Scotland Schools	U17 2	Birmingham	27	Feb
	(P Thomson, M McEwan, L Sinclair, J Tindall)				

Additional Club Teams (1 above)

1:45.3	Bromley Ladies	1	Dartford	4	Sep
1:45.6	Ashford	2	Dartford	4	Sep
1:45.8	Medway	3	Dartford	4	Sep
1:47.9	Arbroath	1	Aberdeen	22	May

Under 17 Club Teams

1:48.0	Hercules Wimbledon	U15 1	Carshalton	11	Sep
1:48.05 i	Victoria Park AAC	1	Glasgow	30	Jan
1:49.2	Bromley Ladies	1	Bromley	10	Jul
1:49.8	GEC Avionics	1	Dartford	4	Sep

Additional Under 15 Teams (1 above)

1:50.1	Bromley Ladies	1	Dartford	4	Sep
1:50.4	Medway	1h2	Dartford	4	Sep
1:51.70 i	Coventry Godiva	1	Birmingham	8	Jan
1:52.4	Blackheath	3	Dartford	4	Sep
1:52.4	Motherwell	1	Edinburgh	21	Aug
1:52.5	Kingston & Poly	2	Carshalton	11	Sep

Under 13 Teams

1:57.7	Ayr Seaforth	1	Edinburgh	21	Aug
1:58.1	Edinburgh Woollen Mill	2	Edinburgh	21	Aug
1:59.1	Great Yarmouth	1	Norwich	27	Jul
1:59.6	Dundee Hawkhill	1	Dundee	29	May

1000 METRES MEDLEY

2:09.39	National Junior Team	U18 1	Schio, ITA	6	Aug
	(R Drummond, S Dudgeon, L Thorne, J Sloane)				
2:12.78	National Junior "B" Team	U18 3	Schio, ITA	6	Aug
	(L Seston, S Williams, V Jamison, A Curbishley)				

Under 17 Teams

2:21.3	Sutton & District	1	Carshalton	11	Sep
2:23.4	Croydon	2	Carshalton	11	Sep

4 x 400 METRES

Time	Team		Pos	Venue	Date
3:24.14	National Team		4	Helsinki, FIN	14 Aug
	(M Neef, L Keough, P Smith, S Gunnell)				
3:27.06	England		1	Victoria, CAN	28 Aug
	(P Smith, T Goddard, L Keough, S Gunnell)				
3:27.25	National Team		1h1	Helsinki, FIN	13 Aug
	(M Neef, L Keough, P Smith, S Gunnell)				
3:27.33	National Team		1	Birmingham	26 Jun
	(M Neef, T Goddard, P Smith, S Gunnell)				
3:27.36	National Team		1	London (CP)	9 Sep
	(P Smith, L Keough, M Neef, S Gunnell)				
3:32.44	National Team		2	Gateshead	20 Jul
	(D Fraser, P Smith, M Neef, N Crowther)				
3:38.18	National Under 23 Team		5	Ostrava, TCH	31 Jul
	(D Fraser, L Ferrier, L Thorne, K Maddox)				
3:38.70	National Junior Team	U20	4h2	Lisbon, POR	23 Jul
	(K Eustace, J Sloane, A Curbishley, L Thorne)				
3:39.32	Essex Ladies		1r2	Schwechat, AUT	29 May
	(V Day, J Parker, S Bevan, S Gunnell)				
3:39.80	National Junior Team	U20	8	Lisbon, POR	24 Jul
	(K Eustace, J Sloane, A Curbishley, L Thorne)				
3:40.12	National Junior Team	U20	1	Warsaw, POL	18 Jun
	(L Thorne, J Sloane, A Curbishley, K Eustace)				
3:40.7	Sale		1	Stretford	18 Jun
	(J Latimer, B Benjamin, P Smith, P Fryer)				
3:41.80	Wales		1	Istanbul, TUR	22 May
	(N Bartlett, G Cashell, C Dawson, R Newcombe)				
3:42.22	England		1	Nitra, SVK	13 Jul
	(N Crowther, L Keough, D Gandy, D Fraser)				
3:43.22	Birchfield		1	Birmingham	8 May
	(K Merry, J Levermore, R Jordan, G McLeod)				
3:43.56	AAA		1	Loughborough	5 Jun
	(J Levermore, C Bleasdale, V Day, E Sutcliffe)				
3:43.94	Northern Ireland		1	Kings Lynn	9 Jul
	(J Latimer, C Hill, S Llewelyn, S McCann)				
3:44.00	England		1	Wrexham	3 Jul
	(N Crowther, J Levermore, C Raven, D Gandy)				
3:44.13	England Under 23 Team		2	Kings Lynn	9 Jul
	(V Day, V Rhodes, D Fraser, S Bowyer)				
3:44.2	Trafford		2	Stretford	18 Jun
	(K Jones, V Boden, P Cohen, S Douglas)				

Additional National Team

Time	Team	Pos	Venue	Date
3:44.57	Scotland	2	Istanbul, TUR	22 May

Additional Club Teams (1 - 4 above)

Time	Team		Pos	Venue	Date
3:46.5	City of Glasgow		2	Grangemouth	7 May
3:48.1	Team Solent		1	Corby	31 Jul
3:48.8	Aldershot F & D		2	Corby	31 Jul
3:48.98	Loughborough University		1	London (CP)	2 May
3:49.21	Shaftesbury Barnet		2	Bedford	17 Sep
3:49.25	Coventry Godiva		3	Bedford	17 Sep
3:49.9	Edinburgh Woollen Mill		1	Stoke-on-Trent	31 Jul
3:51.0	Hallamshire		1	Sheffield	19 Jun
3:51.24	West London Institute		2	London (CP)	2 May
3:52.06	Bromley Ladies		2	Bedford	18 Sep
3:52.4	Borough of Hounslow		1	Enfield	31 Jul
3:53.7	Croydon		1	Aldershot	7 Aug
3:54.7	Windsor Slough & Eton		1	Bracknell	19 Jun
3:54.8	Walton	U20	1	Carshalton	11 Sep

3:54.8	Epsom & Ewell		2	Carshalton	11 Sep
3:55.0	Ashford		1	Hoo	19 Jun

Additional Under 20 Teams (1 - 4 above)

3:47.53	English Schools		1	Aberdeen	16 Jul
3:52.0	South of England		1	London (He)	27 Aug
3:53.0	Midlands		2	London (He)	27 Aug
3:56.3	Crawley	U17	1	Horsham	10 Jul
3:57.0	Scotland		1	Exeter	20 Aug
3:59.9	North of England		3	London (He)	27 Aug
4:00.5	Wigan & District		1	Stretford	12 Jun
4:00.9	Welsh Schools		1	Barry	19 Jul

Additional Under 20 Club Teams (1 - 2 above)

4:02.4	Essex Ladies		1	Telford	24 Jul
4:03.2	Trafford		2	Stretford	12 Jun
4:03.37	Sale		1	Remiremont, FRA	24 Sep
4:06.6	Aberdeen		2	Inverness	7 Aug
4:06.8	City of Stoke		1	Solihull	17 Apr
4:07.0	Hallamshire		1	Hull	24 Jul
4:07.1	Coventry Godiva		1	Stoke-on-Trent	30 May
4:07.9	Peterborough		1	Guildford	24 Jul

Additional Under 17 Teams (1 above)

4:22.1	Newquay & Par		1	Carn Brea	25 May

1600 METRES MEDLEY

3:59.37 i	North of England		1	Birmingham	26 Feb
4:02.28 i	Midland Counties		2	Birmingham	26 Feb
4:06.37 i	AA of Wales		3	Birmingham	26 Feb
4:08.11 i	Scotland		4	Birmingham	26 Feb

3 x 800 METRES

6:55.2	Brighton & Hove		1	Horsham	10 Jul
6:57.2	Croydon		1	Carshalton	11 Sep
7:01.3	Crawley	U17	1	Horsham	10 Jul
7:03.3	Lisburn		1	Antrim	10 Sep
7:15.1	Vale Royal	U15	1	Warrington	12 Jul
7:16.7	Oxford University		1	Oxford	27 Feb
7:20.9	Warrington		1	Warrington	12 Jul
7:23.5	Southend	U17	1	Barking	12 Jul

Additional Under 15 Teams (1 above)

7:26.5	Basildon		1	Barking	12 Jul
7:27.9	Medway		1	Dartford	4 Sep
7:28.0	Havering Mayesbrook		2	Barking	12 Jul
7:32.7	Hercules Wimbledon		1	Carshalton	11 Sep
7:32.9	Corby		1	Corby	23 Jun
7:33.8	Crawley		1	Horsham	10 Jul
7:34.4	Sutton & District		2	Carshalton	11 Sep
7:37.7	Kettering Town		2	Corby	23 Jun

Under 13 Teams

7:46.18	Dundee Hawkhill		1	Linwood	16 Jul
7:51.9	Chelmsford		1	Barking	12 Jul
7:53.7	Phoenix		1	Horsham	10 Jul
7:56.7	Essex Ladies		2	Barking	12 Jul
7:59.5	Stockport		1	Stockport	21 Jun
8:03.2	Wirral		1	Crewe	28 Jun

Leading Women Veterans

100 Metres

12.3	Jocelyn Kirby	W35 (Midd & C)	Leicester	19	Jun
12.6	Angela Mullinger	W35 (Bournem'th)	Athens, GRE	12	Jun
12.9	Amanda Day	W35(Bromley V)	Swindon	29	May
13.0	Helen Godsell	W40 (Bromley V)	London (Col)	4	Sep
13.13	Joylyn Saunders	W40 (Steve & H)	Athens, GRE	12	Jun
13.3	Irene Morrison	W40 (Larkhall)	Coatbridge	13	Aug
13.30	Brenda Elliott	W40 (Cramlington)	Bedford	16	Jul
13.1	Maureen Lewington	W45 (Birchfield H)	Solihull	31	Jul
13.12	Valerie Parsons	W45 (Woking)	Athens, GRE	12	Jun
13.5	Yvonne Priestman	W45 (Broms & R)	Warley	15	May
14.0	Marjorie Hocknell	W50 (Riddings)	Grimsby	19	Jun
14.2	Elizabeth Stagg	W50 (Salisbury)	Exeter	19	Jun
14.20	Una Gore	W55 (City of Bath)	Edmonton, CAN	7	Aug
14.7	Barbara Colwell	W55 (A F&D)	Swindon	29	May
16.1	Eileen Kear	W60 (Radley L)	London (Col)	4	Sep
16.39	Betty Steedman	W60 (Musselb)	Bedford	16	Jul
17.29	Mary Wixey	W70 (MVAC)	Eugene, USA	13	Aug
23.09	Mavis Williams	W80 (Worthing)	Athens, GRE	12	Jun

200 Metres

25.2	Jocelyn Kirby	W35 (Midd & C)	Leicester	19	Jun
25.9	Dyanna Clarke	W35 (TVH)	London (WL)	6	Jul
26.12	Alison Brown	W35 (EWM)	Athens, GRE	12	Jun
26.65	Joylyn Saunders	W40 (Steve & H)	Athens, GRE	12	Jun
27.2	Helen Godsell	W40 (Bromley V)	London (Col)	4	Sep
27.22	Brenda Elliott	W40 (Cramlington)	Athens, GRE	12	Jun
27.07	Valerie Parsons	W45 (Woking)	Athens, GRE	12	Jun
27.5	Yvonne Priestman	W45 (Broms & R)	Warley	15	May
27.54	Maureen Lewington	W45 (Birchfield H)	Athens, GRE	12	Jun
28.63	Majorie Hocknell	W50 (Riddings)	Athens, GRE	12	Jun
29.1	Elizabeth Stagg	W50 (Salisbury)	Exeter	19	Jun
30.25	Una Gore	W55 (City of Bath)	Edmonton, CAN	7	Aug
30.3	Barbara Colwell	W55 (A F&D)	Swindon	29	May
30.4	Jean Hulls	W55 (Bromley V)	London (Col)	4	Sep
34.44	Betty Steedman	W60 (Mussel)	Bedford	16	Jul
35.5	Eileen Kear	W60 (Radley L)	London (Col)	4	Sep
32.53i	Jo Ogden	W65 (Thurrock H)	Glasgow	20	Mar
36.39	Mary Wixey	W70 (MVAC)	Eugene, USA	14	Aug

400 Metres

55.50	Veronica Boden	W35 (Trafford)	Derby	16	Jul
55.8	Dyanna Clarke	W35 (TVH)	Hoo	19	Jun
57.27	Alison Brown	W35 (EWM)	Edinburgh	24	Jun
59.79	Joylyn Saunders	W40 (Steve & H)	Bedford	16	Jul
60.58	Caroline Marler	W40 (Ottley)	Bedford	16	Jul
60.9	Jackie Walpole	W40 (Exeter)	Exeter	3	Sep
66.8	Lynda Robson	W45 (Leamington)	Leamington	29	Jun
67.4	Yvonne Priestman	W45 (Broms & R)	Redditch	5	May
65.19	Marjorie Hocknell	W50 (Riddings)	Athens, GRE	5	Jun
69.74	Josie Kimber	W50 (Medway)	Bedford	16	Jul
66.6	Jean Hulls	W55 (Bromley V)	London (CP)	15	May
75.6	Joyce Smith	W55 (Shaftes B)	Ilford	27	Jun
76.82	Mary Holmes	W55 (Camb & C)	Bedford	16	Jul
88.2	Barbara Robson	W60 (Metros)	Richmond	26	Jun
89.19	Brenda Green	W60 (Serp RC)	Athens, GRE	12	Jun
79.02	Monica Stone	W65 (Altrincham)	Athens, GRE	12	Jun
96.55	Josie Waller	W70 (Teignbridge)	Bedford	16	Jul

800 Metres

2:08.7	Catherine Rawnsley-Pemberton	W35	(Spen)	Loughborough	7 Sep
2:09.5	Suzanne Morley	W35	(Brighton)	Brighton	10 Aug
2:10.4	Veronica Boden	W35	(Trafford)	Stretford	18 Jun
2:18.72	Marian Eldridge	W40	(Fleet & C)	Athens, GRE	12 Jun
2:19.72	Caroline Marler	W40	(Ottley)	Athens, GRE	12 Jun
2:20.0	Diane Marsh	W40	(Norfolk O)	Norwich	16 Jul
2:20.9	Pat Gallagher	W45	(Westbury)	Yate	15 May
(2:19.47i				Birmingham	2 Jan)
2:36.23	Josie Kimber	W50	(Medway)	Bedford	16 Jul
2:39.09	Jean Hulls	W55	(Bromley V)	Athens, GRE	12 Jun
2:45.4	Joyce Smith	W55	(Shaftes B)	Enfield	16 May
3:11.4	Toni Borthwick	W60	(Trent Part)	Watford	25 Jul
3:16.6	Barbara Robson	W60	(Metros)	Reading	25 Jul
3:08.1	Joselyn Ross	W65	(Garden C J)	Watford	24 Jul
3:36.14	Jose Waller	W70	(Teignbridge)	Bedford	16 Jul

1500 Metres

4:21.5	Suzanne Morley	W35	(Brighton)	Crawley	21 Jul
4:28.12	Janet Holt	W35	(Trafford)	Derby	16 Jul
4:31.0	Sally Young	W35	(Parkside)	Hoo	4 Jun
4:42.9	Marian Eldridge	W40	(Fleet & C)	Reading	8 May
4:43.6	Paula Fudge	W40	(Hounslow)	Feltham	13 Aug
4:46.2	Pat Gallagher	W45	(Westbury)	Yate	15 May
(4:45.55i				Birmingham	9 Jan)
5:07.1	Elaine Statham	W50	(Stoke)	Stoke	29 Jun
5:25.2	Joyce Smith	W55	(Shaftes B)	Ilford	27 Jun
5:33.62	Joan Manners	W55	(Clevedon)	Bedford	16 Jul
6:38.3	Barbara Robson	W60	(Metros)	Richmond	26 Jun
6:41.1	Betty Smith	W60	(Kettering)	Kettering	22 Jun
6:10.3	Joselyn Ross	W65	(Garden C J)	Watford	24 Jul
6:54.73	Jose Waller	W70	(Teignbridge)	Bedford	16 Jul

3000 Metres

9:23.08	Suzanne Morley	W35	(Brighton)	London (CP)	26 Jun
9:33.9	Janet Holt	W35	(Trafford)	Stretford	26 Apr
9:34.2	Joanne Thompson	W35	(City of Bath)	Cheltenham	22 Jun
9:53.4	Paula Fudge	W40	(Hounslow)	Wycombe	21 May
10:02.0	Bronwen Cardy-Wise	W40	(Broms & R)	Redditch	17 Apr
10:11.4	Pat Gallagher	W45	(Westbury H)	Swindon	1 May
10:22.55	Jane Davies	W45	(Epsom & E)	Bedford	18 Sep
10:53.0	Elaine Statham	W50	(Stoke)	Stoke	24 Jul
11:40.6	Joyce Smith	W55	(Shaftesbury B)		
14:08.3	Mary Steggles	W60	(Fleet & C)	Woking	16 May
13:09.42i	Joselyn Ross	W65	(Garden C J)	Glasgow	20 Mar

5000 Metres

16:13.43	Joanne Thompson	W35	(City of Bath)	Crawley	29 May
16:48.8	Sally Young	W35	(Parkside)	London (CP)	27 Apr
17:11.0	Janet Holt	W35	(Trafford)	Waltham Forest	6 Aug
17:12.30	Marian Eldridge	W40	(Fleet & C)	Athens, GRE	12 Jun
17:46.9	Paula Fudge	W40	(Hounslow)	Hounslow	10 Jul
17:53.32	Denise Hoogesteger	W40	(Wells City)	Bedford	16 Jul
18:28.7	Felicity Garland	W45	(Redhill RR)	Grantham	19 Jun
18:34.5	Elaine Statham	W50	(Stoke)	Solihull	26 Jun
20:14.99	Joan Manners	W55	(Clevedon)	Bedford	16 Jul
20:29.8	Joyce Smith	W55	(Shaftes B)	Watford	25 Jul
21:18.?	D Adam	W60	(Fife)	Fife	12 Oct
24:12.7	Mary Steggles	W60	(Fleet & C)	Portsmouth	25 Jul
22:23.63	Joselyn Ross	W65	(Garden C J)	Eugene, USA	12 Aug
25:07.42	Jose Waller	W70	(Teignbridge)	Bedford	16 Jul

10000 Metres

33:34.85	Karen MacLeod	W35	(Edinburgh)	St Denis, FRA	10 Jun
33:56.04	Joanne Thompson	W35	(City of Bath)	Sheffield	12 Jun
39:49.5	Diana Braverman	W40	(Camb & C)	Bedford	8 Jun
38:15.?	Elizabeth Gilchrist	W45	(Scottish V)	Turku, FIN	3 Jul
38:21.5	Jane Davies	W45	(Epsom & E)	London (WP)	8 May
39:18.0	Elaine Statham	W50	(Stoke)	Solihull	14 Aug
41:25.6	Ann Nally	W50	(Altrincham)	London (BP)	7 Sep
42:06.6	Joan Manners	W55	(Clevedon)	Solihull	14 Aug

80 Metres Hurdles

12.65	Jean Wills	W40	(Bournem'th)	Athens, GRE	12 Jun
14.5	Sue Dodson	W40	(Chelmsford)	Sheffield	25 Sep
14.6	Gwen Cunningham	W40	(Bexley)	Hoo	18 Sep
14.0	Jean Wills	W45	(Bournem'th)	Sheffield	25 Sep
14.5*	Pat Oakes	W45	(Dartford H)	London (Col)	4 Sep
13.94	Marjorie Hocknell	W50	(Riddings)	Athens, GRE	12 Jun
15.0	Nanette Cross	W50	(Bromley V)	Hoo	18 Sep
16.3	Carina Graham	W55	(Woking)	Swindon	29 May
18.3	Betty Steedman	W60	(Mussel)	Sheffield	25 Sep

100 Metres Hurdles

14.0	Jocelyn Kirby	W35	(Middlesbro)	Leicester	19 Jun
(13.93w				Istanbul, TUR	22 May)
15.9	Debbie Keenleyside	W35	(Dacorum)	Bournemouth	3 Sep
16.0	Jennifer Brown	W35	(Ashford)	Dartford	16 Jul
16.1	Jean Wills	W40	(Bournem'th)	Hayes	21 May
22.0	Marilyn Scrivener	W45	(Horsham BS)		
19.4	Marjorie Hocknell	W50	(Riddings)	Grimsby	19 Jun

300 Metres Hurdles

51.6	Jane Thwaites	W35	(Horsham BS)		
58.1	Pat Oakes	W45	(Dartford H)	Hoo	14 Aug
48.43	Marjorie Hocknell	W50	(Riddings)	Athens, GRE	12 Jun
55.97	Jean Hulls	W55	(Bromley V)	Athens, GRE	12 Jun

400 Metres Hurdles

60.0	Veronica Boden	W35	(Trafford)	Waltham Forest	6 Aug
62.9	Dyanna Clarke	W35	(Thames VH)	Hoo	19 Jun
64.4	Alison Brown	W35	(EWM)	London (WF)	6 Aug
66.9	Jean Wills	W40	(Bournem'th)	Exeter	24 Jul
68.3	Jackie Walpole	W40	(Exeter)	Exeter	15 May
72.05	Lynda Robson	W45	(Leamington)	Bedford	16 Jul
72.1	Marjorie Hocknell	W50	(Riddings)	Grimsby	19 Jun

1500 Metres Steeplechase

5:18.2	Sally Young	W35	(Parkside)	Crawley	5 Jul
6:14.0	Di Leakey	W35	(Woking)	Crawley	5 Jul
7:44.6	Marilyn Scrivener	W45	(Horsham)	Crawley	5 Jul

2000 Metres Steeplechase

7:05.76	Veronica Boden	W35	(Trafford)	Bedford	16 Jul
7:22.34	Sally Young	W35	(Parkside)	Bedford	16 Jul

3000 Metres Steeplechase (2'6")

15:26.7	Marilyn Scrivener	W45	(Horsham)	Horsham	26 Jul

High Jump

1.72	Jennifer Brown	W35	(Ashford)	Athens, GRE	12 Jun
1.60	Veronica Boden	W35	(Trafford)	Bolton	13 Aug
1.45	Gwen Cunningham	W40	(Bexley)	London (Elt)	23 Apr
1.43	Pam Garvey	W40	(Corby)	Solihull	31 Jul

1.37	Maria Williams	W45 (Rowntrees)	Leeds	24 Jul
1.36	Jean Wills	W45 (Bournem'th)	Sheffield	25 Sep
1.35	Joanne Smallwood	W50 (Halesowen)	Bedford	16 Jul
1.25	Jean Hulls	W55 (Bromley V)	London (Col)	4 Sep
1.15	Barbara Colwell	W55 (A F&D)	London (Col)	4 Sep
1.00	Betty Steedman	W60 (Mussel)	Sheffield	25 Sep
0.96	Mary Wixey	W70 (MVAC)	Athens, GRE	12 Jun

Pole Vault

2.20	Bridget Wood	W35 (Ryston R)	Kings Lynn	22 Jun
2.10i	G Hevingham	W40 (N Devon)	Bath	4 Dec
2.00	Carol Eames	W45 (Bournem'th)	Reading	2 Oct
2.10	Dorothy McLennan	W55 (Walton)	Crawley	17 Apr

Long Jump

5.35w	Jennifer Brown	W35 (Ashford)	Sheffield	25 Sep
5.26	Veronica Boden	W35 (Trafford)	Waltham Forest	6 Aug
5.20	Carol Filer	W35 (Wymond J)	Bedford	27 Aug
5.02	Gwen Cunningham	W40 (Bexley)	London (Elt)	23 Apr
4.99	Jean Wills	W40 (Bournem'th)	Athens, GRE	12 Jun
(5.02i			Glasgow	20 Mar)
4.75	Jean Wills	W45 (Bournem'th)	Sheffield	25 Sep
4.48i	Sylvia Wood	W45 (Linlithgow)	Glasgow	20 Mar
4.43	Averil Green	W50 (Eastbourne)	Horsham	30 May
4.40	Sylvia Wood	W50 (Linlithgow)	Coatbridge	13 Aug
3.98	Carina Graham	W55 (Woking)	Woking	16 May
3.87	Betty Steedman	W60 (Mussel)	Bedford	16 Jul
3.30	Mary Wixey	W70 (MVAC)	Athens, GRE	12 Jun

Triple Jump

11.36	Jennifer Brown	W35 (Ashford)	London (Elt)	29 Aug
10.34w	Danea Herron	W35 (Finn Valley)	Bedford	16 Jul
10.13	Jean Wills	W40 (Bournem'th)	Guildford	13 Aug
10.18	Pat Oakes	W45 (Dartford H)	Dartford	20 Aug
9.03	Christine Terry	W50 (Worthing)	Horsham	14 May
8.80	Sylvia Wood	W50 (Linlithgow)	Coatbridge	13 Aug
8.21	Carina Graham	W55 (Woking)	Swindon	29 May
7.12	Barbara Colwell	W55 (A F&D)	Guildford	27 Jun
8.17w	Betty Steedman	W60 (Mussel)	Bedford	16 Jul
(7.41			Bedford	16 Jul)
6.39	Mary Wixey	W70 (MVAC)	Bedford	16 Jul

Shot

18.68	Judith Oakes	W35 (Croydon H)	, SLO	13 Jul
11.51	V Duffy	W35 (Met Police)	London (BP)	25 Apr
11.09	Sarah Owen	W35 (Newport H)	Cwmbran	18 Jun
12.45	Bronwin Carter	W40 (Portsmouth)	Brighton	21 May
10.46	Jacqueline Wright	W40 (Bracknell)	Bracknell	19 Jun
9.97	Barbara Terry	W45 (Bromley V)	Dartford	25 Jul
8.73	Joyce Rammell	W45 (Dumfries)	Coatbridge	13 Aug
(9.10i			Glasgow	20 Mar)
8.53	Liz Sissons	W45 (Epsom & E)	Croydon	15 May
9.47	Liz Sissons	W50 (Epsom & E)	London (Col)	4 Sep
9.33	Jean Atack	W50 (Wakefield H)	Leeds	24 Jul
(9.41i			Worksop	30 Jan)
9.09	Averil Green	W50 (Eastbourne)	Brighton	25 Jul
12.45	Evaun Williams	W55 (Essex L)	Athens, GRE	12 Jun
7.54	Angela Moore	W60 (Rugby)	Cannock	2 Oct
7.32	Marie Grant-Stevens	W60 (Brighton)	London (WL)	28 Aug
8.93	Jo Ogden	W65 (Thurrock H)	London (WL)	28 Aug
(9.11i			Glasgow	20 Mar)
5.09	Mary Wixey	W70 (MVAC)	Bedford	16 Jul
4.70	Mavis Williams	W80 (Worthing)	Athens, GRE	12 Jun

Discus

47.82	Judith Oakes	W35 (Croydon H)	Aldershot	7	Aug
41.68	Claire Cameron	W35 (Glasgow)	Glasgow	15	May
35.86	V Duffy	W35 (Met Police)	London (BP)	17	May
42.56	Jacqueline Wright	W40 (Bracknell)	Horsham	21	Aug
37.40	Bronwin Carter	W40 (Portsmouth)	Portsmouth	16	Jul
26.90	Val Bovell	W45 (Yeovil)	Watford	16	Jul
26.74	Joyce Rammell	W45 (Dumfries)	Ayr	11	Jun
26.34	Marlene Simmonds	W45 (Ryston R)	Grantham	19	Jun
24.42	Sylvia Weeks	W50 (Eastbourne)	Brighton	25	Jul
24.30	Liz Sissons	W50 (Epsom & E)	Hornchurch	16	Jul
29.54	Evaun Williams	W55 (Essex L)	Bedford	16	Jul
19.04	Marie Grant-Stevens	W60 (Brighton)	London	9	Jul
16.88	Jo Ogden	W65 (Thurrock H)	Cannock	2	Oct
13.16	Mary Wixey	W70 (MVAC)	Solihull	26	Jun

Hammer

41.72	Jennifer Cunnane	W35 (Wakefield H)	Wakefield	10	Jul
33.42	Elaine Le Claire	W35 (Jersey Sp)	Bedford	16	Jul
31.60	Angela Morgan	W35 (Eastbourne)	Eastbourne	13	Aug
36.08	Jennifer Clarke	W40 (Peterbro)	Grantham	19	Jun
33.30	Annabella Smith	W45 (Hounslow)	Haslemere	19	Jul
45.00	Pat McNab	W50 (Shaftes B)	London (WL)	9	Jul
36.40	Christine Terry	W50 (Worthing)	Eastbourne	27	Jun
45.02	Evaun Williams	W55 (Essex L)	Athens, GRE	12	Jun
33.02	Carole Derrien	W55 (Jersey Sp)	Jersey	31	Jul
17.48	Angela Moore	W60 (Rugby)	Cannock	2	Oct
28.30	Jo Ogden	W65 (Thurrock H)	London (WL)	28	Aug

Javelin

38.82	Judith Oakes	W35 (Croydon H)	Aldershot	7	Aug
37.60	Jennifer Brown	W35 (Ashford)	Bedford	18	Sep
34.82	Jean Lintern	W40 (Crawley)	Bromley	21	May
28.12	Vilma Thompson	W40 (Bromley V)	London (Col)	4	Sep
27.42	Stella Bacon	W45 (Reading)	Windsor	17	May
31.20	Carole Morris	W50 (Birchfield H)	Solihull	26	Jun
29.08	Averil Green	W50 (Eastbourne)	Eastbounre	27	Jun
37.78	Evaun Williams	W55 (Essex L)	Athens, GRE	12	Jun
31.62	Carina Graham	W55 (Woking)	Woking	16	May
19.80	Mary E Smith	W60 (Wells C H)	Exeter	19	Jun
19.78	Ann Sissons	W60 (Epsom & E)	Kingston	27	Jun
19.38	Brenda Atkinson	W60 (Shaftes B)	Watford	24	Jul
28.30	Jo Ogden	W65 (Thurrock H)	London (WL)	28	Aug
13.80	Mary Wixey	W70 (MVAC)	Tamworth	24	Apr
10.80	Mavis Williams	W80 (Worthing)	Eastbourne	27	Jun

Pentathlon

3782	Jennifer Brown	W35 (Ashford)	Athens, GRE	12	Jun
3046	Hazel Barker	W35 (Leeds City)	Solihull	14	Aug
3493i	Jean Wills	W40 (Bournem'th)	Bedford	26	Mar
2918i	Emily McMahon	W40 (Enfield)	Bedford	26	Mar
2775i	Pat Oakes	W45 (Dartford H)	Bedford	26	Mar
2643i	Marlene Simmonds	W45 (Ryston R)	Bedford	26	Mar
2929i	Jackie Charles	W50 (White H)	Bedford	26	Mar

Heptathlon

5117	Jennifer Brown	W35 (Ashford)	Sheffield	25	Sep
(4738w	not age adjusted		Horsham	19	Jun)
4103	Sarah Owen	W35 (Newport H)	Sheffield	25	Sep
4082	Hazel Barker	W35 (Leeds City)	Sheffield	25	Sep
3568	Sue Dodson	W40 (Chelmsford)	Sheffield	25	Sep
4696	Jean Wills	W45 (Bournem'th)	Sheffield	25	Sep
3342	Betty Steedman	W60 (Mussle)	Sheffield	25	Sep

MENS INDEX

ABERNETHY David J. 5.09.55, Barrow & F :
DT - 41.30 (46.70-85)
ACHIKE Onochie 'Larry' U20 31.01.75, Craw:
100 - 10.95, 200 - 22.16, LJ - 7.32 (7.46-93),
TJ - 16.67w/16.53
ACHURCH Simon U23 27.12.74, Peterbro :
JT - 58.30
ADAMS Brian V45 13.03.49, Leics WC :
3kW - 13:10.73 (12:02.2-76),
10kW - 46:41.0 (42:40.0-75)
ADAMS Francis 19.10.69, Thames Valley :
LJ - 6.95 (6.95-93)
ADAMS Grant U20 16.10.75, Ayr Seaforth :
60HJ - 8.24i,
110HJ - 14.7w (14.72w/14.8-93)
ADAMS Mark U15 31.07.80, City of Hull :
1500 - 4:19.69, 3k - 9:33.7
ADAMS Nathan U13 14.04.82, Sheffield RWC :
2kW - 10:57.0
ADAMS Philip 3.11.71, Sale :
SP - 13.80 (15.58-92)
ADAMSN Simeon U13 1.07.84, Sheff RWC :
2kW - 11:53.0
AFILAKA Michael 16.11.71, N& EB/Salf Un :
100 - 10.74, 200 - 21.22 (21.09w-93)
AGYEPONG Francis K. 16.06.65, Shaftesbury B :
TJ - 16.95 (17.00w-92)
AHERNE Christopher U15 21.12.79, Cardiff :
DTB - 37.70, HTB - 54.14
AHMED Fayyaz 10.04.66, Shaftesbury Barnet :
HJ - 2.19 (2.21-86)
AHMED Syful U15 25.10.79, London Schools :
TJ - 12.68
AIREY Martin 28.10.70, Brighton :
800 - 1:50.9
AITCHISON Douglas 31.12.66, Perth :
HT - 47.82 (49.90-90)
AITKEN Steven 8.07.66, Dundee HH :
SP - 13.72 (14.91-90)
AKESTER Neil U15 6.09.79, City of Hull :
100 - 11.25w/11.5/11.56,
200 - 23.2/23.51, LJ - 6.01
AKINJIOLA Olusegun U20 1.10.75, Blackheath :
SPJ - 13.69
AKINSANYA Oluwafemi 29.11.69, Peterbro :
LJ - 7.01 (7.22-91), TJ - 15.98
ALCINDOR Canisus 27.04.63, Birchfield :
HJ - 2.00 (2.15-85)
ALDERTON Chris, Army/Team Solent :
400 - 48.2
ALDWINKLE Matthew U23 23.08.74, Notts :
400 - 48.5/48.77
ALEXOPOULOS Dinos U20 2.12.76,
Yeovil Oly/Millfield Sch : SPJ - 15.29
ALGEO Anthony U23 22.01.73, Blackheath :
3kSt - 9:25.1
ALGIERI Niko U13, Preseli :
75HC - 12.3
ALLA Sleniba U15 19.10.79, Milton Keynes :
LJ - 5.95
ALLAN David Neil 17.10.70, Edinb SH/Inv :
HT - 59.84
ALLAN Graeme U15 24.09.80, Elgin :
SPB - 13.40, DTB - 38.56
ALLAN Jason U23 17.09.72, Clydesdale :
HJ - 2.03i/2.00 (2.05-93)

ALLAN Paul J. 21.06.70, Aberdeen :
SP - 13.90 (14.42-93)
ALLARD James U20 11.05.77, Birchfield :
110HJ - 14.88w/15.2
ALLEN Clarence 1.04.64, Herne Hill :
60H - 8.4i, 110H - 14.8/14.82 (14.8-92)
ALLEN Mark 23.09.66, Border :
100 - 10.69w/10.74 (10.6-92/10.63w-93),
200 - 21.38
ALLEN Michael U15, Ballymena & Antrim :
TJ - 12.04, JTB - 48.44
ALLEN Sam U17 26.10.78, Rowntrees :
OctY - 4469
ALLEN Stewart U17 31.08.78, Thurrock :
800 - 1:56.0,
ALLENBY Robert U15 14.10.79, Cleethorpes :
100 - 11.5, 200 - 22.46w/23.4 (23.65-93)
ALLISON Joseph 16.09.59, Newham & EB :
TJ - 15.41 (15.93w-86/15.86-85)
ALLISON Matthew U23 26.02.73, Leeds :
400H - 55.1, LJ - 6.95, Dec - 6673
ALLISTAIR David U15, Wirral :
PV - 3.00
ALLPORT Anthony U15 30.09.79, Birchfield :
DTB - 39.18
ALSOP Roger 16.01.65, Belgrave :
5k - 14:35.27
ALVES Robert 13.05.65, Sandwell :
200 - 22.0 (22.0-89), 400 - 48.53 (48.14-92)
AMOR Martin 22.09.68, Copeland :
3kSt - 9:23.2 (9:11.1-92)
AMOS Guy 15.06.63, Norfolk :
800 - 1:51.3
ANDERSON Colin Lloyd 18.02.59, Team S/Army :
110H - 15.4 (14.64-87),
400H - 52.84 (51.85-90)
ANDERSON David U17 2.10.77, Elswick :
1.5kSt - 4:25.5
ANDERSON Jonathon U20 10.01.75, Anna Str :
200 - 22.18 (21.45w-92/21.71-93)
ANDERSON Keith 10.08.57, Bingley :
5k - 14:09.00, 10kR - 29:06, HMar - 1:04:53
ANDERSON Mark U17 1.02.78, Bolton :
1.5kSt - 4:23.9
ANDERSON Mark U17 5.11.77, City of Stoke :
100HY - 13.92w (13.9-93), 400HY - 55.61
ANDREWS Karl Kristian U20 21.03.75, Westb :
SP - 13.10i (13.81-92),
SPJ - 14.62i (14.27-93),
HT - 65.30, HTJ - 69.10
ANGELL Steven 8.04.70, Old Gaytonians :
HT - 55.26
ANGUS Daniel U13 15.07.82, Mandale :
100 - 12.5, 200 - 25.4
ANSTISS Timothy J. 17.11.61, Hounslow :
PV - 4.40 (4.90-80)
ANTOINE Leslie 16.12.65, Belgrave :
110H - 15.2/15.35 (14.97w-87/15.05-89),
400H - 55.47 (51.38-88)
ANTONATOS George U23 30.09.74, Holb/GRE :
SP - 14.23 (14.45-93)
ANTONIAZZI Luigi 13.09.62, Bournemouth :
HT - 47.16, JT - 55.66 (57.72-93)
ARCHAMPONG James Quarshie U20 14.03.76,
Carmarthen : 60H - 8.01i,
110HJ - 14.26w/14.5 (14.24-93), 110H - 14.18

ARCHBOLD Ian 10.06.65, Morpeth :
HMar - 1:04:31
ARCHER Clayton U20 29.05.76, Thames VH :
100 - 10.91
ARIS Mike, :
24HrT - 205.012
ARMSTRONG Brett U20 9.09.76, Sandwell :
PV - 4.20
ARMSTRONG J. Simon 29.05.62, Bournem'th :
SP - 16.11 (16.52-90),
DT - 47.54 (50.22-92), HT - 47.66
ARMSTRONG Martin 14.03.66, Valli :
Mar - 2:25:17
ARMSTRONG Paul U15 20.10.79, Pitreavie :
PenB - 2696
ARMYTAGE Martin U17 10.03.78, Yate :
200 - 22.3
ARTUS Tim U23 19.04.72, Westbury :
3kSt - 9:14.9
ASHBURN Brian A. 11.03.70, Cambuslang :
100 - 10.7w/11.23
    (10.5w-90/10.52w/10.7/10.73-89)
LJ - 6.99i (7.55wdh-90/7.38-92)
ASHE Richard U23 5.10.74, Hillingdon :
800 - 1:52.7, 1500 - 3:46.6
ASHURST Andrew John 2.01.65, Sale :
PV - 5.30i/5.30 (5.45i-92/5.40-88)
ASHWELL Brian V60 18.07.32, Leics WC :
100MW - 20:31:54
ASPDEN Richard U20 15.10.76, Epsom & E :
HJ - 2.00i/2.00 (2.05-93)
ATKIN Mark A. U20 30.12.75, Sheffield :
Dec - 5647, DecJ - 6181
ATKINS Matthew U20 23.06.77, Derby & Co :
JT - 59.80
ATKINSON Michael A. 6.03.58, Annadale Str :
SP - 13.85 (16.35-81)
ATKINSON Richard U23 9.10.74, Wakefield :
JT - 64.88 (67.22-93)
ATTON Karl R. 14.09.71, Leics WC :
3kW - 12:42.3, 10kW - 45:35.8 (45:14.7-92),
20kW - 1:34:28,
30kW - 2:33:08 (2:29:11-93),
35kW - 2:55:38
ATTRIDGE Steven U15 9.03.80, Bas & MH :
100 - 11.5/11.63, 200 - 23.29w/23.3/23.7,
80HB - 11.7
AUDSLEY Alistair, Manx :
200 - 22.0
AUSTIN James 9.08.65, Clydesdale :
3kSt - 9:05.32
AYLESBURY Wayne Paul 24.03.64, Leeds :
3kSt - 8:57.8 (8:38.81-92)
AYLWARD Andrew U20 31.08.77, Brighton :
JT - 53.50
AYRE Stephen C. 20.10.67, Morpeth :
DT - 45.00 (48.12-86)
AYRES Simon U15 5.10.79, Ipswich :
PV - 3.00

B ACKLEY Stephen James 12.02.69, Camb H :
    JT - 85.20 (91.46-92)
BAILEY David U23 19.10.73, Telford :
JT - 61.96
BAILEY Guy U20 16.09.76, Coventry RWC :
5kWR - 25:16 (24:30-92),
10kW - 52:45.4, 10kWR - 52:44

BAILEY Josef U17 2.12.77, City of Stoke :
60HY - 8.49i, 100HY - 13.33w/13.7/13.75,
BAILEY Mark U20 23.07.75, Birchfield :
110HJ - 14.65w/15.0 (14.64w/14.99-92),
110H - 15.1/15.61
BAILEY Stuart U17 6.08.78, Wigan :
800 - 1:56.8, 1.5kSt - 4:24.62
BAILLIE Ross U17 26.09.77, Victoria P AAC :
100 - 10.73w/10.89,
200 - 21.67i/21.8w/21.90, 60HY - 8.16i,
100HY - 13.1/13.12, 110HY - 14.19,
LJ - 6.73i
BAIRD Laurence U17 10.12.77, Cleethorpes :
400 - 49.0
BAKER George U20 14.08.76, Oxford City :
SP - 13.71, SPJ - 15.50,
DecJ - 5077 (5552-93)
BAKER J. U15, R Sutton Coldfield :
PV - 3.00
BALDWIN John U15 25.10.79, Ealing,S & Mx :
1500 - 4:15.0
BALDWIN Stefan M. 26.04.70, Thames Valley :
JT - 69.10 (72.92-93)
BALE Jason U15 12.12.79, Leics Cor :
200 - 23.64w/23.7, 400 - 52.4
BALE Paul U20 20.12.76, Warwicks Sch :
JT - 52.84
BALL Andrew U13 13.05.83, Birchfield :
2kW - 11:52.6
BALL James R. 17.02.63, Steyning :
3kW - 12:32.4 (12:20.0-87)
BALL James U15 17.04.80, Bedford & County :
HTB - 46.42
BALOGUN Anthony 7.02.66, Woodford Green :
800 - 1:49.26 (1:49.2-91)
BAMFORD Matthew 19.09.58, Hillingdon :
JT - 58.46 (59.24-91)
BANDA Rasheed U15 18.03.80, Eastb'rne Coll :
HJ - 1.76
BANKS Peter G. 9.12.60, Blackburn :
3kSt - 9:19.4 (9:03.7-85)
BANNISTER Dominic 1.04.68, Shaftesbury B :
3k - 8:09.25, 5k - 14:21.74 (14:12.27-93),
10k - 29:34.50
BARBER Michael W. U23 19.10.73, Birchfield :
PV - 5.20
BARBER Nick U17 22.11.78, Hallamshire :
SPY - 14.57
BARBOUR Paul U23 5.12.73, Annadale Str :
JT - 55.82 (59.62-93)
BARDEN Anthony J. 15.10.60, Basildon :
Mar - 2:25:09
BARDEN Spencer Christian U23 31.03.73, GEC :
1500 - 3:44.6, 3k - 8:00.29 (7:58.08-93),
5k - 14:20.9 (14:02.9-93)
BARGH Andrew U20 21.08.76, Team Solent :
400H - 54.5/54.92
BARKER Leo U17 26.12.78, Diss :
OctY - 4385
BARKER Scott U20 22.07.77, Kettering :
DTJ - 42.52
BARNARD Paul U23 27.07.72, Edin/Middlesbro :
HT - 60.34
BARNES Ben U17 28.10.78, Blackheath :
SPY - 14.26i
BARNES John U13 6.05.82, Hull Springhead :
SPC - 12.10

325

BARNES Matthew John 12.01.68, Enfield :
  800 - 1:49.9 (1:48.8-89),
  1500 - 3:40.47 (3:38.31-93),
  1M - 3:58.39, 3k - 7:56.08i
BARNETSON David 1.07.71, ESH/Inverness :
  110H - 15.60 (15.4-91),
  HJ - 2.11i/2.10 (2.19-92)
BARRON Daniel U17 17.01.78, Gateshead :
  1.5kSt - 4:29.3
BARROS Demetrio 29.06.71, Hounslow :
  JT - 65.82 (66.92-93)
BARTLETT Stuart G. 20.10.64, Old Gaytonians :
  JT - 59.14
BARTLIFF Steve 30.12.67, Army :
  Dec - 5388
BARTON Tim 3.10.70, Charnwood :
  100 - 10.7w/10.99, 200 - 22.0
BARTSCH Matthew 12.12.64, Crawley :
  200 - 21.68 (21.5-92/21.56w-93)
BASTILLE Gregory U23 25.04.73, Hounslow :
  HT - 49.24
BATCHELOR Perry U20 11.12.75, Cov G :
  60HJ - 8.2, 110HJ - 14.17w/14.66 (14.4-93),
  60H - 8.33i, 110H - 14.7w/14.81w/14.9/15.10
BAULCH James Steven U23 3.05.73, Cardiff :
  200 - 20.84, 400 - 46.45
BEARD Keith 8.11.61, Leiden :
  JT - 69.20 (76.10-91)
BEASLEY Graham U17 24.10.77, Luton :
  100 - 10.7/10.93,
  200 - 21.3w/21.32w/21.9/22.02, 400 - 50.6
BEATON Peter U23 5.04.72, Pitreavie :
  SP - 14.29
BEATTIE Alex U20 19.04.76, Guildford & G :
  HTJ - 52.56
BEATTIE Jim U23 22.07.73, Lochgelly :
  200 - 22.02, 400 - 48.89
BEAUCHAMP William 9.09.70, Ealing,S & Mx :
  HT - 60.06 (60.98-93)
BEAUMONT Paul 27.03.63, Belgrave/Army :
  400H - 52.81 (51.23-89)
BEAUMONT Richard 2.05.71, Bicester RR :
  Mar - 2:28:15
BEDDOWS Darren U17 4.05.78, Swansea :
  PV - 3.81
BEDFORD Christopher 28.01.70, Wakefield :
  200 - 21.9 (21.9-91/22.15w-90)
BEGEN Thomas U17 14.04.79, Shettleston :
  100 - 11.12
BELL John U23 10.09.73, North Shields Poly :
  400H - 53.78 (53.70-92)
BELL Martin 9.04.61, Annan/Splott C :
  3kW - 12:23.50 (11:54.96i-93/12:04.6-88),
  10kW - 42:32.3 (42:07.42-92),
  20kW - 1:26:11 (1:25:42-92), 30kW - 2:22:21
BELL Matthew U17 2.06.78, Corby :
  HT - 47.30, HTJ - 49.72, HTY - 63.24
BELL Michael U17 23.11.77, Coventry Godiva :
  400 - 49.5
BELL Robert U17 17.12.77, Thurrock :
  PV - 4.00
BELL Simon 26.12.66, Cambridge Harriers :
  3kSt - 9:00.2 (8:59.79-93)
BELSHAM Matthew 11.10.71, Sale :
  PV - 5.30 (5.35-93)
BENN Andrew U17 2.09.77, S London :
  DTY - 41.38, HTJ - 52.12,
  HTY - 59.22, JTY - 61.36

BENN Thomas U15 20.04.80, Woodford Grn :
  80HB - 11.00w/11.30, PV - 3.40i,
  LJ - 6.16, PenB - 3024
BENNETT Chris U20, :
  PV - 4.12
BENNETT James A. 12.11.57, Greenock Glen :
  Mar - 2:28:09
BENNETT Martin 14.10.67, Old Gaytonians :
  200 - 21.9 (21.7-93),
BENNETT Michael 6.02.69, Birchfield :
  100 - 10.86 (10.5w-87/10.7-92/10.72w-88/10.79-91)
BENNETT Simon U23 16.10.72, N Devon :
  JT - 61.76
BENNETT Todd Anthony 6.07.62, Team Sol :
  200 - 21.8 (20.36-84), LJ - 6.90 (7.01-82)
BENSON Mark 21.12.63, Leeds :
  800 - 1:50.94 (1:48.78-93)
BENT Colin 12.04.70, Shaftesbury B/RAF :
  HJ - 2.09
BENTHAM Kermitt E. 16.04.60, Thames VH :
  400 - 48.31 (46.57-87)
BENTHAM Nicolas Peter 7.12.70, Doncaster :
  800 - 1:51.3 (1:49.4-92)
BENTLEY Simon U15 29.10.79, Solihull & SH :
  3k - 9:25.08
BENTON Steven U20 26.09.76, Thurrock :
  DecJ - 5934
BERGIN Steven 17.06.66, B&A/W&B/Qu Univ :
  SP - 14.27i/14.10 (16.09-89)
BERNARD Darren 15.06.69, Herne Hill :
  400 - 48.0/48.49 (46.65-88)
BERWICK Christopher V45 1.05.46, Leics WC :
  50kW - 4:40:41 (4:23:22-86)
BESWICK Paul A. 5.12.68, GEC :
  PV - 4.80ex/4.60i/4.60 (4.75-93)
BETTRIDGE Paul J. 27.02.57, Havering :
  Mar - 2:26:07 (2:21:15-92)
BETTS Edward G. 18.02.71, Queens Park :
  200 - 22.0, 400 - 47.9,
  110H - 15.2, 400H - 51.15
BEVAN Nigel Charles 3.01.68, Belgrave :
  JT - 80.38 (81.70-92)
BEWICK Brian 1.11.65, Sunderland :
  Mar - 2:25:08
BIGHAM David Bryce 4.07.71, Woodford Grn :
  60H - 8.28i (8.21i-92),
  110H - 14.7/14.77w/14.83 (14.5w-91/14.59-92),
  HJ - 2.00i/1.95 (2.02-89),
  PV - 4.60 (4.60-90), LJ - 7.02 (7.26-92),
  JT - 65.80, Dec - 7434 (7904-92)
BIGHAM Kerry U23 25.07.72, Coventry G :
  HJ - 2.00 (2.05i-93/2.04-92)
BIGNALL Anthony 17.11.71, Haringey/Boxhill :
  800 - 1:52.42 (1:51.02-93),
  1500 - 3:46.32 (3:44.58-92), 3k - 8:17.05
BIGNELL Mark J. 17.09.68, Crawley :
  LJ - 7.17w/7.06 (7.16-90)
BINFIELD John U15 19.11.79, Solihull & SH :
  800 - 2:04.36
BIRBECK Rory U23 24.09.73, Hyndburn :
  SP - 13.88
BIRCHALL Edward U17 28.11.77, Enfield :
  DTY - 41.06
BIRCHALL Matthew 11.01.71, Blackburn :
  LJ - 7.09
BIRCHALL Rob 14.06.70, Peterborough :
  3k - 8:12.0, 5k - 14:16.1,
  10kR - 29:33

BIRD Christian U17 19.09.78, Reading :
100HY - 14.1
BIRD Justin Paul 3.05.71, Morpeth :
200 - 22.0/22.08w (22.0-91), 400 - 47.68
BIRSE Stephen U17 8.10.77, Middlesbro & C :
SPY - 14.42, JT - 56.58, JTY - 57.60
BISHOP Gary 3.08.63, Croydon :
5k - 14:31.13, 10k - 31:07.9 (31:07.4-91)
BISHOP Mark Andrew Paul 12.02.67, Havering :
400 - 48.3/48.72i (46.49-89),
400H - 51.67 (51.28-89)
BLACK David James U17 9.10.78, Cann & St :
DTY - 42.00
BLACK Roger Anthony 31.03.66, Team Sol :
100 - 10.5 (10.4-87/10.57-91),
200 - 21.05 (20.60-90),
300 - 32.45 (32.06+-91/32.08-86),
400 - 44.78 (44.59-86)
BLACK Tom U15 26.11.79, Essex Sch :
JTB - 45.22
BLACKMORE Andrew U20 12.07.76, Telford :
2kSt - 6:04.3 (5:55.65-93), 400H - 55.74
BLACKMORE James U15 8.10.79, Wells :
HJ - 1.76
BLACKWELL Simon 6.02.63, Camb & Col :
HT - 47.64 (49.26-91)
BLADE Martin 30.05.68, Team Solent :
200 - 21.5, 300 - 34.0, 400 - 47.6/47.70
BLAKE Chris U17 8.11.78, Sale :
100 - 11.0, 200 - 21.64w/21.93
BLAKE Kevin 29.05.67, Cardiff :
5k - 14:32.5
BLAKE Stephen 28.12.67, Windsor S & E :
800 - 1:52.46 (1:52.2-93)
BLANDFORD Gary 17.12.63, Team Solent :
HJ - 2.00 (2.12-84)
BLANN Anthony U15 10.09.79, Hamps Sch :
PenB - 2591
BLEASDALE Ian U15 29.05.80, Liverpool H :
SPB - 14.11, DTB - 41.14, HTB - 46.38
BLIGHT Ross U20 28.05.77, Cardiff :
HT - 47.62, HTJ - 54.18
BLOOMFIELD Ian V40 23.11.52, Chester Le S :
Mar - 2:17:42 (2:17:14-93)
BLOUNT Christopher U20 7.06.75, Newport :
800 - 1:50.11
BLOWS Matthew U23 21.06.74, Woodford Grn :
HT - 47.52 (50.12-93)
BOBB Samuel U20 29.08.75, Blackheath :
TJ - 14.47w/14.23
BODEN Sam U15 16.02.80, Camb & Colr'dge :
800 - 2:03.4, 1500 - 4:12.95, 3k - 9:18.5
BOLTON Paul U23 8.04.74, Wigan :
100 - 10.8 (10.57w/10.7/10.76-93)
BONICH Daniel M. U17 22.11.78, Bexley :
100 - 11.09w/11.1
BONNING Arron U20 9.11.75, Havering :
DecJ - 5334
BOOTH Gregor U23 31.08.72, Stranraer :
Mar - 2:23:06
BOOTH John 3.02.68, Belgrave :
TJ - 13.94
BOOTH Stephen R. 21.10.71, Oxford Univ :
110H - 15.2 (15.38H/15.53-93)
BOOTH Terry 19.10.66, Woking :
10MR - 49:06
BOOTHROYD Jason 26.11.69, Sale :
1500 - 3:44.54 (3:44.2-91)

BORSUMATO Anthony U23 13.12.73,
City of Stoke/Staffs Univ : 400H - 51.83
BOSHER Brian, Darlington :
100kR - 8:30:00, 24Hr - 210.922
BOUGH Glyn U15 20.05.80, Berry-H Mansfield :
80HB - 11.8/11.94
BOUNDY Christohpher U15 25.12.79, Gate :
PV - 3.20
BOURNE Nigel U23 18.04.72, Queens Park :
LJ - 7.00, TJ - 14.41
BOVELL Colin U23 9.03.72, Cardiff :
60H - 8.14i, 110H - 14.1/14.17, 400H - 54.05
BOWDEN Ian U20 8.02.75, Skyrac :
800 - 1:51.71 (1:50.8-93)
BOWDITCH Kristen U20 14.01.75, C of Stoke :
5k - 14:40.4
BOWEN Martin John P. 20.05.63, Cardiff :
100 - 10.8, 200 - 22.06 (21.65-91)
BOWMAN Simon 11.09.71, Diss :
HT - 46.34 (49.68-93)
BOWN Simon Paul U23 21.11.74, Haringey :
HT - 56.82
BOX Toby U23 9.09.72, Wolverhampton & B :
100 - 10.07w/10.35 (10.34-93), 200 - 20.72
BOYES John A. 9.05.58, Bournemouth :
Mar - 2:27:25 (2:13:20-85)
BOYLE Adrian U17 27.09.77, :
1.5kSt - 4:31.69
BOYLE Tim U17 4.07.78, Shropshire Sch :
3k - 8:56.9
BOYNE Frank 28.02.66, Aberdeen :
1500 - 3:48.95, 3kSt - 9:07.27 (9:06.3-93)
BRACE Steven 7.07.61, Bridgend :
10MR - 48:27 (47:38-93),
HMar - 1:04:08 (1:02:29-90),
Mar - 2:12:23 (2:10:57-91)
BRADLEY Colin 2.02.56, Trowbridge :
10kW - 48:48.3 (46:00.3-87),
50kW - 4:59:07 (4:33:42-87)
BRADLEY David U23 30.04.72, Lough St :
JT - 59.68
BRADLEY Dominic U20 22.12.76, Stockport :
110HJ - 14.77w/15.0/15.07, 110H - 15.5
BRADLEY Stephen U23 24.02.74, Wolves & B :
PV - 4.10 (4.30-93)
BRADSTOCK Arne Roald 24.04.62, Enfield :
JT - 77.22 (83.84-87)
BRADWELL Thomas U20 4.09.75, Derby & Co :
110HJ - 15.3
BRADY M. U13, :
70HC - 11.7
BRAITHWAITE Darren 20.01.69, Haringey :
60 - 6.70i (6.64i-91),
100 - 10.26 (10.25w-90),
200 - 20.99 (20.72-92)
BRAITHWAITE N., :
5k - 14:35.71
BRAMBLE Marvin U20 10.06.77, Blackheath :
TJ - 15.18 (15.25w-93)
BRANNEN Anthony 16.09.68, City of Stoke :
110H - 15.1 (14.3-92/14.35-89),
HJ - 2.00 (2.10i-93/2.07-88),
LJ - 7.06w/6.89 (7.29w-93/7.21-91),
TJ - 14.53, Dec - 6286 (7656-91)
BRASHER Hugh 28.09.64, Hounslow :
3kSt - 8:57.4
BRAY Matthew U15 3.10.79, Milton Keynes :
HTB - 43.38

327

BREFFITT Richard U20 23.11.75, Notts :
HT - 46.92 (52.74-93)
BREHAUT Roger 1.06.65, Guernsey :
HJ - 2.00 (2.00-87)
BREND Peter A. U20 2.02.77, N Devon :
400 - 48.4/48.50
BRENNAN Steve 4.11.65, Manx H :
3kW - 12:27.3, 20kW - 1:36:39 (1:35:38-93),
50kW - 4:48:32
BRERETON Matthew U15 16.04.80, Mers Sch:
HJ - 1.91
BREWER Daniel U15 10.08.80, Blackheath :
80HB - 11.82
BRICE Patrick 8.02.69, Blackheath/CUAC :
3kSt - 9:11.6 (8:54.03-93)
BRIDGE Jonathan D. 19.11.67, Blackburn :
TJ - 14.15 (14.64-91)
BRIDGEMAN Tom U15 7.11.79, Yate :
80HB - 11.61
BRIDGER Jeremy U20 23.09.75, Yeovil Oly :
400H - 56.0/56.37 (55.6/55.71-93)
BRIDLE Matthew U20 11.08.76, Trafford :
100 - 10.93 (10.9-93),
200 - 21.6/21.75w/21.83 (21.41w-93),
LJ - 7.10
BRIERLEY James U20 31.07.77, Telford :
HJ - 2.16
BRIGGS Martin Christopher 4.01.64,
C of Stoke/Birm Un : 400H - 53.5 (49.86-84)
BRISTOW Andrew D.J. 2.09.61, Brighton :
5k - 14:04.8 (13:34.60-92)
BRITTON Daniel U13 25.09.81, Bournemouth :
JTC - 38.74
BRIZZELL Paul U20 3.10.76, Ballymena & A :
200 - 22.0/22.20
BROADHEAD Lee U20 11.05.75, Cann & St :
DT - 43.38, DTJ - 48.70
BROCKLEBANK Robert J. U20 12.10.76,
Blackburn : HJ - 2.13
BROOKING David 22.10.68, City of Plymouth :
110H - 15.0/15.43w (15.55-93)
BROOKS Stephen 8.06.70, Bing/Iowa St Univ :
3k - 8:02.66i (8:15.90-91),
5k - 13:52.54, 10k - 29:37.75
BROOM Peter U17 6.12.77, Carmarthen :
100HY - 14.0/14.12
BROOME Edward U23 3.09.72, Blackp'l/OUAC :
3kSt - 9:23.1 (9:16.3-93)
BROOMFIELD Lee U17 5.12.77, Kingston & P :
HJ - 1.91 (1.91i-92)
BROUGHTON Mark A. 23.10.63, Met. Police :
HT - 53.18 (54.28-93)
BROWN Basil 19.02.58, Herne Hill :
Mar - 2:25:00 (2:22:06-86)
BROWN Gareth 21.07.67, Cabersport/Edinb :
600 - 1:18.6 (1:16.83-92),
800 - 1:47.63i/1:49.61 (1:47.15-93),
1500 - 3:42.66
BROWN Jonathan M. 27.02.71, Sheffield :
3k - 8:04.??+ (7:51.72-93),
5k - 13:23.96 (13:19.78-93),
10kR - 28:27 (28:05-93)
BROWN Kevin 10.09.64, Birchfield :
SP - 14.22, DT - 58.68 (59.20-91)
BROWN Michael 6.05.62, Haringey :
TJ - 15.24 (16.15-89)
BROWN Michael J. 4.06.69, Norfolk/Staffs Un :
Dec - 6317

BROWN Neil U17 6.04.78, Birchfield :
LJ - 6.68
BROWN Patrick U15 2.09.79, Gateshead :
80HB - 11.37w/11.56
BROWN Richard U15 22.12.79, Waverley :
PenB - 2468
BROWN Richard V45 18.11.46, Surrey WC :
100MW - 18:39:42 (16:50:28-93)
BROWN Robert 3.10.69, Leeds :
400H - 53.2 (51.3/51.33-89)
BROWN Robert U17 3.03.78, Elswick :
1500 - 4:03.15, 3k - 8:50.09,
1.5kSt - 4:18.20
BROWN Simon James 22.03.69, C of Stoke :
800 - 1:51.13 (1:49.84-88)
BROWN Stuart U23 27.11.72, Deeside :
HJ - 2.03
BROWN Stuart U20 16.09.76, Skyrac :
3kSt - 9:32.56
BROWNE Adrian U17 14.07.78, W S & E :
TJ - 13.92
BROWNE Curtis U20 11.09.75, Birchfield :
100 - 10.43w/10.6/10.66,
200 - 21.47w/21.5/21.54
BROWNE Derek 28.09.66, Belgrave :
TJ - 15.72i/15.64 (15.95-93)
BRUCE Callum U20 28.02.75, Pitreavie :
HT - 50.20, HTJ - 50.62
BRUCE Darran D. 23.04.70, GEC :
400H - 54.8 (54.64-89)
BRUNT Daniel U20 23.04.76, Chesterfield :
SPJ - 14.28, DTJ - 43.00
BRYAN Adrian U23 17.05.72, Birchfield :
400 - 47.58
BRYAN Justin 16.08.69, Torfaen :
DT - 41.78
BRYANT Simon U20 30.10.75, Colchester & T :
200 - 22.03w/22.06 (22.0w-93)
BRYSON Robin 14.04.62, Newcastle :
Mar - 2:24:30
BRZEZINSKI Jan 4.06.62, Ealing,S & Mx :
DT - 43.06
BUCHANAN Andrew I. 12.09.70, AF&D :
PV - 4.50
BUCHANAN C., Army :
LJ - 6.92
BUCK Matthew U23 5.04.74, Thurrock :
PV - 4.40 (4.50-93)
BUCKFIELD Nicholas U23 5.06.73, Crawley :
PV - 5.40 (5.41-93)
BUCKLEY Christopher T.P. 26.07.61, Westb :
3k - 8:15.7 (8:11.6-89), 10MR - 48:09,
HMar - 1:03:44 (1:03:05-88),
Mar - 2:21:57 (2:15:48-91)
BUCKNER Thomas Christopher 16.04.63,
Havant : 1500 - 3:47.2 (3:42.85-92),
1M - 4:05.4 (3:58.87-93),
3k - 7:58.92i/8:06.07 (7:50.90-92),
5k - 14:02.93, 10kR - 29:39, 10MR - 48:07,
3kSt - 8:29.84 (8:25.50-92)
BUDDEN Nicholas U20 17.11.75, Norfolk :
200 - 21.6 (21.5w-93),
400 - 47.01 (46.89-93)
BULL Andrew 26.06.69, Sheffield :
60 - 6.93i, 200 - 21.8 (21.61w-93/21.78-92)
BULL James U17 12.02.79, Ipswich :
SPY - 14.66
BULL Michael P. 6.06.70, Notts : Dec - 5234

BULLOCK David U20 1.12.76, Stourport Sch :
DecJ - 5464
BULLOCK Guy Ross U20 15.10.75, Liv Pem :
200 - 22.13i (21.80w/21.8/21.82-93),
400 - 46.77 (46.13-93)
BULMAN Neil Andrew U17 7.09.77, Mand/NESH :
HTY - 53.28
BUNCE Keith St.John 5.04.66, Notts :
60H - 8.4i (8.1i/8.14i-88),
110H - 15.67 (14.3w/14.46w/14.48-88)
BUNDOCK Matthew U20 18.11.76, Blackheath :
SP - 13.78i/13.33, SPJ - 14.95,
DT - 43.82, DTJ - 48.02
BUNN Richard U23 2.12.72, Lincoln City :
1500 - 3:50.6 (3:47.78-93)
BUNNEY Elliot John 11.12.66, Edinburgh SH :
100 - 10.20w/10.34 (10.20-86)
BUNSIE Shaka U20 22.05.75, Shaftesbury B :
HJ - 2.00 (2.00-93)
BURBRIDGE Mark U23 17.11.73, Peterbro :
110H - 15.4 (15.3-93)
BURGESS Paul William 10.11.70, Wigan :
600 - 1:19.2 (1:18.43-90),
800 - 1:50.25 (1:47.80-91),
1500 - 3:49.27i (3:46.83-89)
BURKE Alan P. 23.05.65, Hounslow/IRE :
PV - 4.40 (5.00-89)
BURKE David   68, London Irish/IRE :
3k - 8:06.66, 10kR - 29:07
BURKE John 18.05.70, London Irish/IRE :
3k - 8:08.42
BURKE John U15 25.11.79, North S Poly :
TJ - 12.37
BURKE Raymond Nicholas 11.11.69, SB :
60 - 6.82i (6.71i-92), 100 - 10.72 (10.39-92)
BURLEY Darren U15 13.07.80, Blackheath :
100 - 11.52w/11.7
BURMAN-ROY Sudip U17 15.01.78, Blackh'th :
SPJ - 13.83i, SPY - 15.57,
DTY - 43.04, HTY - 50.90
BURNETT David U20 27.01.76, Shaftesbury B :
SP - 14.11i/14.04, SPJ - 15.18,
DTJ - 42.04 (42.88-93)
BURNS Ian T. U17 20.09.77, Durham Sch :
JTY - 58.80
BURRAWAY Paul 30.11.68, Hounslow :
HJ - 2.05 (2.10-93)
BURROWS Darius U20 8.08.75, Birchfield :
1500 - 3:48.9, 3k - 8:01.26, 5k - 14:11.27
BURTON George U15 22.11.79, Dundee HH :
100 - 11.59w
BUSH Geoffrey 20.03.56, Sheffield/RAF :
HT - 52.38
BUSHELL Mark U20 22.10.76, Rotherham :
110HJ - 14.64w/14.95, LJ - 7.13w,
DecJ - 6622
BUSHNELL Paul R. 12.11.68, Chelmsford :
JT - 60.00 (70.00-90)
BUTLER Kieron U23 16.07.72, Somer :
5kW - 22:18.33 (22:06.6-91),
10kW - 45:50.3 (42:28.0-93)
BUXTON Wayne 16.04.62, Bristol :
Mar - 2:19:34 (2:16:38-91)
BUZZA David 6.12.62, Cornwall AC :
5k - 14:15.00,(13:50.20-88),
10kR - 29:41 (29:10-84)
BYRNE Jason 9.09.70, Berry-Hill Mans/WLHS :
HT - 65.54 (73.80-92)

CADDY Neil U20 18.03.75, Newquay & P :
800 - 1:51.8, 1500 - 3:46.16,
1M - 4:06.1 (4:04.9-93)
CADOGAN Gary A. 8.10.66, Haringey :
400 - 47.60 (46.37-87), 400H - 49.07
CADWALLADER Lee 17.01.69, Liverpool H :
800 - 1:50.18 (1:47.43-93), 1M - 4:02.00
CADWALLADER Paul 23.10.62, Sefton :
10k - 31:09.85 (30:55.4-91)
CAINES Adrian U23 13.11.74, Sparkhill :
110H - 14.7/14.83 (14.85-93)
CAIRNS Steven 3.11.67, Peterborough/Army :
3kSt - 9:04.??
CAIRNS Tom U17 20.02.78, Carmarthen :
1.5kSt - 4:35.45
CALEB Dion 26.11.66, Haringey/Army :
100 - 10.6/10.74 (10.70-93)
CALLAN Adrian 28.11.62, Wolves & B/Springb :
3k - 8:05.77, 5k - 14:17.96 (13:58.93-88)
CALLAWAY David J. 4.09.63, Haringey :
SP - 17.35 (17.55-93)
CALLISTE Joel U17 25.04.78, Ealing,S & Mx :
100 - 10.74w/11.0/11.02, 200 - 22.5
CALLOW J. Allan V45 4.09.45, Manx H :
3kW - 13:24.2 (13:06.0-72),
10kW - 48:02.5 (46:44.0-73),
20kW - 1:35:49 (1:34:14-73)
CALLOW Phillip U17 12.05.78, Kent Sch :
400 - 50.8
CALVERT Ewan U23 28.11.73, TVH/Aberd'n :
800 - 1:49.3
CALVERT James U17 5.11.77, Tunbridge W :
1.5kSt - 4:23.5
CAMPBELL Sean U20 19.12.75, Walton :
400H - 55.1
CAMERON Rezlimond 18.05.60, Thames VH :
TJ - 15.59w/15.49 (16.32w-89/16.20-88)
CAMERON Trevor U20 25.11.76, Shaftes B :
60 - 6.93i, 100 - 10.29w/10.5/10.54,
200 - 20.88w/21.18
CAMPBELL Darren A. U23 12.09.73, Sale :
60 - 6.70i (6.70i-93),
100 - 10.54 (10.28w/10.37-91),
200 - 21.23i (20.55w/20.86-93)
CAMPBELL Ian 6.09.71, Har/Dundee HH :
800 - 1:51.34i (1:49.95-93),
1500 - 3:43.05i/3:44.41 (3:43.64-93),
5k - 14:33.59 (14:27.90-93)
CAMPBELL James 17.06.70, Annadale Str :
1500 - 3:45.16,
3k - 8:16.44 (7:57.66-93), 5k - 13:48.9,
10kR - 29:35 (29:33-92)
CAMPBELL Kenneth William U23 30.09.72,
Edinburgh SH : 100 - 10.93w,
60H - 7.99i, 110H - 13.86
CAMPBELL Leroy 10.08.66, Leics Cor :
400 - 48.57
CAMPBELL P. I. Junior 13.02.70, Woodford Gr :
LJ - 7.03 (7.49w-88/7.36-89),
TJ - 14.24 (15.81w-89/15.50-86)
CANNING Dale U17 12.06.78, Stockport :
800 - 1:54.9, 1500 - 3:56.21,
3k - 8:45.7 (8:47.7-93)
CARD Gavin U17 11.05.78, Morpeth :
PV - 4.05
CARE Robert V45 8.04.47, Sandwell :
3kW - 12:55.02 (12:46.03-90),
10kW - 47:22.0

CARELESS Robert U23 7.09.74, Telford :
HT - 52.44
CARMODY Noel 24.12.56, Cambridge H :
3kW - 13:14.13 (12:26.49-91),
10kW - 48:21.0 (44:45.63-91),
20kW - 1:36:12 (1:34:38-90)
CARNELL Wayne U17 2.09.77, Exeter :
400HY - 57.4
CARPENTER Peter 15.09.64, Bedford & Co :
3kSt - 9:19.3 (9:15.3-91)
CARR Peter U17 10.09.77, Penzance :
OctY - 4526
CARROLL Gregory 7.07.71, Thurrock :
HT - 46.56 (53.14-92)
CARROLL Paul U17 25.01.78, Liverpool Pem:
SPY - 14.06, OctY - 4445
CARROTT Andrew James 1.01.66, N & EB :
100 - 10.7 (10.2w-88/10.44-89),
200 - 22.0/22.08w (20.76-88)
CARSWELL Adam U20 8.01.76, Exeter :
DecJ - 5368
CARTER Adrian R. 7.02.68, Thames Valley :
60H - 8.3i (8.2i-90/8.32i-91),
110H - 15.16 (14.72w/14.75-90)
CARTER Andrew U15 18.10.79, Cannock & St :
HTB - 47.40
CARTER Daniel U15 15.04.80, Harlow :
JTY - 58.76, JTB - 58.94
CARTER Lachlan 25.11.70, Clydesd/Glas Un:
HT - 47.04 (50.76-92)
CARTER Simon U20 5.03.75, GEC :
JT - 61.26 (61.54-93)
CARTWRIGHT Russell U17 13.10.77, Cov G :
800 - 1:55.38, 1500 - 4:02.04
CASCOE Benjamin U17 26.12.77, Belgrave :
JTY - 56.80
CASEY Stephen 26.02.66, Woodford Green :
SP - 14.27 (16.15-91), DT - 52.46 (58.64-91)
CASHELL Christopher 11.05.66, Team Solent :
400H - 52.9/53.22 (51.89-91)
CASTLE Andrew U15 8.12.79, Yeovil Oly :
SPB - 15.19, DTB - 38.26, HTB - 50.76
CATER Gavin U17 16.10.77, Portsmouth :
100 - 11.09,
CAUDERY Stuart 19.11.66, Cornwall AC :
110H - 15.2
CAULFIELD Paul U17 12.05.78, Liverpool H :
400HY - 57.3
CAVANAGH Stuart U20 28.02.75, Bas & MH :
400 - 48.63
CAWLEY Ian U17 21.11.78, Bournemouth :
100HY - 13.9/13.93w/14.10
CHADDOCK Andrew U15 13.03.80, Stockport :
HJ - 1.78
CHALLENGER Ben U17 7.03.78, Charnwood :
HJ - 2.06
CHAMBERLAIN James U20 31.07.75, Leics WC :
3kW - 13:10.2 (12:50.7-93), 5kWR - 23:49,
10kW - 47:42.90 (46:37.0-93),
10kWR - 46:17 (45:30-93)
CHAMBERS Dwain U17 5.04.78, Haringey :
100 - 10.56w/10.75, 200 - 22.09
CHAMBERS Timothy 6.07.71, Leeds :
400H - 54.6/54.82 (54.51-90)
CHAMPION Michael U20 3.01.75, Blackheath :
100 - 10.8/10.91, 200 - 21.4w/21.65w/21.79,
400 - 48.67

CHANDLER Lloyd 14.04.69, Thames Valley :
60 - 6.9i (6.9i-90),
100 - 10.7/10.88 (10.60w-88/10.66-91),
200 - 22.0 (21.5-88/21.87-91)
CHANTLER Paul U15 10.09.79, Liverpool H :
100 - 11.06w/11.4/11.56,
200 - 23.0w/23.3/23.83
CHAPLIN Owen U17 2.12.77, Telford :
PV - 4.20
CHAPMAN Paul U20 10.07.76, Coventry G :
400 - 48.9
CHAPMAN Steven 28.01.66, Thames Valley :
HJ - 2.05 (2.21-89)
CHARIJ Andrij, Basingstoke & MH :
HT - 50.10 (52.72-93)
CHARLES Courtney 13.11.68, Thames Valley :
LJ - 7.54
CHARLES Rupert C. 25.10.60, Queens Park :
HJ - 2.00 (2.18-82)
CHARLESWORTH Robert U17 25.03.79, Corby :
JTY - 54.86
CHASTON Justin 4.11.68, Belgrave :·
3k - 7:59.97, 5k - 13:59.39, 3kSt - 8:23.90
CHECKLEY L. U13, :
PV - 2.30
CHEESEMAN Christopher 11.12.58,
Surrey WC/Crawley/Thames H & H :
10kW - 44:18.3 (43:05.11-93),
20kW - 1:29:11, 30kW - 2:27:11
CHERRINGTON Michael 30.06.66, Mandale :
3kSt - 9:22.6
CHIDLOW Glyn 21.10.71, Oxford Univ :
LJ - 7.25
CHILES Garry 15.05.66, Norfolk/RAF/Lough :
PV - 4.35
CHILTON Alan 16.04.71, Handy Cross Jog:
Mar - 2:24:26
CHOLERTON Christopher James 13.02.63,
Derby & Co : 400H - 54.45 (52.70-92)
CHRISTIE Linford 2.04.60, Thames Valley :
60 - 6.48i (6.43+-91), 100Y - 9.30,
100 - 9.91 (9.87-93), 150 - 14.97,
200 - 20.56i/20.67 (20.09-88)
CHRISTOPHER Adrian U17 16.09.77, Reading :
400 - 50.15
CHUKUKERE Enyinna U23 31.07.73, SB/NIG :
LJ - 7.81w/7.64i/7.36
CHURCH Jody U15 3.04.80, Southend :
1500 - 4:20.86
CHURCHILL Richard U17 29.09.77, Stainforth :
100HY - 13.27w/13.8/13.88
CIARAVELLA Simon U23 24.11.73, Woodf'd Gr :
400 - 48.98 (47.33-93)
CLACK Michael U13, Portsmouth :
3k - 10:24.6
CLARE Jeffrey M. 21.03.65, Haringey :
SP - 14.62 (15.76-87), DT - 54.32 (55.60-88)
CLARE Julian U23 13.09.74, Trafford :
DecJ - 5495oa (5802-93)
CLARK Darren U20 15.03.76, AF&D :
HJ - 1.98 (2.00-93)
CLARK David James 16.02.64, Edinburgh SH :
100 - 10.63w/10.80
(10.2w-89/10.39w-90/10.48i-89/10.60-90)
200 - 20.8wdb/21.71 (20.75-90)
CLARK Ewan 4.04.69, Edinburgh/Pitreavie :
60 - 6.85i

CLARK Trevor 29.04.56, Poole :
10k - 30:49.70 (30:40.2-92), Mar - 2:18:42
CLARKE Adam U23 16.01.73,
C of Stoke/Staffs Univ : 3kSt - 9:13.3
CLARKE Andrew 10.08.70, Wigan :
JT - 56.38 (59.88-93)
CLARKE David 18.06.64, Newham & Essex B :
1500 - 3:50.85
CLARKE David R. 1.01.58, Hercules Wimb :
10kR - 29:45 (28:10-85),
10MR - 48:27 (47:25-88)
CLARKE Guy U20 22.05.75, Lanc & Morc :
800 - 1:53.10 (1:52.1-93)
CLARKE Iain U13 19.01.82, Corby :
PV - 2.50 (2.50-93)
CLARKE Jonathan 20.11.67, Swansea :
JT - 61.48 (68.74-86)
CLARKE Matthew U20 15.11.76, Daventry :
800 - 1:52.4
CLARKE Peter 9.07.65, Coventry Godiva :
400 - 47.90 (48.29-91)
CLARKE S. Ezra U23 9.12.74, Shaftesbury B :
LJ - 6.91, TJ - 15.46
CLARKE Stuart U20 16.10.75, Bournemouth :
LJ - 6.93w
CLARKE Wayne A. R. U20 24.12.75, Peterbro :
HT - 57.24, HTJ - 62.60
CLARKE Wesley 31.12.63, Ilford :
HT - 48.88
CLAWLEY James U20 15.10.75, Cannock & St :
LJ - 7.17
CLEGG Andrew U23 8.09.73, Liverpool H :
100 - 10.80w/10.97 (10.8-93),
200 - 21.7/21.90w/21.96
CLEMENTS Matthew U17 17.09.77, Camb & C :
100 - 10.85 (10.7w/10.8-93),
200 - 21.72w/21.8/22.07 (21.8-93),
60HY - 7.9i (8.13i-93),
100HY - 12.47w/13.00 (12.68-93),
110HY - 13.71, 110HJ - 13.92w
CLERIHEW David U17 11.09.77, Corstorphine :
LJ - 6.85
CLIFFORD Simon U20 22.03.75, Team Sol :
400H - 54.8
CLINCH Mark U17 23.10.78, East Cheshire :
HTY - 47.70
CLISHAM Vince, Coventry Godiva :
Mar - 2:27:06
CLUSKEY Adrian U15 30.12.80, Blackheath :
DTB - 38.04
CLYNE Fraser J. 23.08.55, Aberdeen :
Mar - 2:23:08 (2:11:50-84)
COATS Edward U15 14.06.80, Guildford & G :
PenB - 2444
COCKBURN James P. U23 30.01.73, Haringey :
SP - 16.18
COCKER Shannon U20 15.03.76, Cumbria Co :
HTJ - 47.46
COCKS Dean 18.01.67, Woodford Green :
LJ - 7.26 (7.41-90)
COGHLAN S. U13, :
TJ - 10.65
COLACO Jonathan U17 3.02.78, Hillingdon :
400HY - 57.81
COLE Charles U17, Carmarthen :
TJ - 13.73
COLE E., North London :
400H - 55.5 (54.8-92)

COLE Elliott U23 19.09.73, Sale :
DT - 40.74 (42.40-93)
COLEBOURN Mark U15 5.12.79, Derby & Co :
JTB - 45.12
COLEMAN Andy U23 29.09.74, Enfield :
3kSt - 9:25.72
COLLINS Dominic U20 2.10.76, Cornwall AC :
JT - 57.66
COLLINS Liam U17 23.10.78, Gateshead :
100HY - 13.75w/13.9/13.94
COLLINS Robert U17 17.09.77, Gateshead :
100HY - 14.0/14.03, PV - 3.90
COLLINS Tony V50 1.10.42, Birchfield :
100MW - 20:56:19 (20:13:28-92)
COLVER Andrew 8.01.70, Charnwood :
400H - 54.91 (54.1/54.14-92)
COMBE Michael U17 24.12.78, Scottish Bord :
800 - 1:54.57, 1500 - 4:05.80
COMMERFORD Nick 23.04.66, Cardiff :
1500 - 3:46.5, 3k - 8:10.2, 5k - 14:34.8
CONDON Allyn U23 24.08.74, Sale :
100 - 10.70 (10.37w-93/10.62-92),
200 - 21.28w/21.4/21.45 (20.95-93),
400 - 47.43
CONDON David U23 11.04.72, Shaftesbury B :
SP - 16.41 (16.09-93)
CONDRON Ian W. 7.10.59, Lisburn/IRE :
Dec - 5783 (6343-89)
CONERNEY Michael U23 30.10.72, Brain/CUAC :
DT - 41.82 (44.28-93)
CONLEY Kenneth 24.12.61, Border :
10k - 31:10.3 (30:25.75-92)
CONLON Greg U23 18.12.74, Bristol :
PV - 4.20 (4.20-92)
CONNELLY David U20 6.02.76, Shettleston :
5k - 14:42.6, 2kSt - 5:56.9, 3kSt - 9:17.53
CONWAY Gavin U17 1.09.77, Newham & EB :
1.5kSt - 4:24.2
COOK Austin James Gareth 20.02.69,
Sutton & Dist/WLHS : SP - 14.50 (14.59-90),
DT - 48.82 (49.20-90), HT - 63.56 (67.32-91)
COOK Jim U17, Gwent Sch :
1.5kSt - 4:35.7
COOK Neil U15 23.11.79, City of Hull :
PV - 3.15
COOK Philip 7.05.69, Barry :
3kSt - 9:02.4 (8:55.6-93)
COOPER Damon U23 5.07.74, Thurrock :
PV - 4.50 (4.50-93)
COOPER Darren 1.02.66, Peterborough :
400H - 55.32 (54.3-90)
COOPER Mark, Southampton City :
Mar - 2:22:49
COOPER Mark 29.01.64, Wolverhampton & B :
1500 - 3:48.7
COOPER Paul U20 30.01.75, City of Hull :
800 - 1:51.9
COOPER Paul U20 4.12.76, Braintree :
JT - 58.46
COOPER Rufus U17 24.02.79, Kingston & P :
PV - 3.90
COOPER Wayne U15, Reading :
800 - 2:04.9
CORCORAN Fyn U17 17.03.78, Cornwall AC :
100HY - 14.1, 400HY - 55.9/56.47,
OctY - 5208
CORDINGLEY Ben U17 19.05.78, Blackheath :
DTY - 44.16

CORDY Matthew U20 29.09.75, Portsmouth :
HJ - 2.01 (2.03-93)
COSSELL Harvey U23 1.12.74, Invicta :
3kSt - 9:23.21
COSTELLO Denis M. 3.12.61, Belgrave :
TJ - 13.99 (15.66-83)
COTTER Christopher U23 3.02.72, SB :
LJ - 7.32w/7.28 (7.67w/7.47-93),
TJ - 14.75 (15.19-93)
COTTER David U20 23.02.77, Nairn :
60HJ - 8.19, 110HJ - 14.8w/15.1,
110H - 15.43
COTTON Ben U17 10.03.78, March :
JTY - 54.34
COTTRELL Myles R.M. 22.11.70, Belgrave :
JT - 74.30 (74.70-92)
COUPLAND Steven C. 15.06.65, Sheffield :
200 - 21.66 (21.14-93),
400 - 47.1 (47.92-91), 400H - 50.19
COURTNEY James 9.12.71, Brentwood :
Dec - 6094
COWAN David 23.08.66, Hercules Wimb :
5k - 14:24.24
COWAN Lloyd 8.07.62, Shaftesbury Barnet :
200 - 21.72 (21.3w-93/21.48w/21.7-86/21.71-93),
110H - 13.75, 400H - 54.77 (51.22-84)
COWMAN Maurice 21.09.59, Westbury :
HMar - 1:05:18 (1:04:35-90)
COX Edward U20 30.12.76, Here & Worcs Sch :
DecJ - 5128
COX J. U13, Leamington :
800 - 2:17.9
COX Neil U20 26.04.76, Swindon :
110H - 15.2,
COYLE William 3.10.62, Shettleston :
3k - 8:18.9il (8:06.3-92),
5k - 14:35.5 (14:18.2-90),
10k - 30:29.3, 10MR - 49:31dh
CRAGGS Ian U20 6.10.76, Gateshead :
200 - 22.12w
CRAIG Ian 20.08.69, Annadale Striders :
100 - 10.83w/10.94 (10.4wdb/10.65w/10.83-93)
CRAIG James U20 2.03.77, Cambuslang :
100 - 10.9w/11.14
CRAM Stephen 14.10.60, Jarrow & Hebburn :
800 - 1:50.3 (1:42.88-85),
1500 - 3:42.8 (3:29.67-85)
CRAMPTON Peter 4.06.69, Spenborough :
400 - 48.76i (46.03-87), 400H - 49.26
CRANE David U17 18.12.77, Surrey WC :
3kW - 15:28.4, 5kW - 26:08.0
CRANE Howard U23 12.10.73, Rossendale :
Dec - 5248
CRANE Stephen U15 24.02.80, Surrey WC :
3kW - 15:40.0, 3kWR - 15:39
CRAWFORD Damien 22.08.68, L Irish/Sparta :
JT - 61.72 (70.34-91)
CREESE Robert U17 1.12.77, Thames Valley :
HJ - 1.91
CRESSWELL Andrew U15 4.04.80, H & W Sch :
HJ - 1.78
CRITCHLEY Kim U23 15.07.73, Rowntrees :
1500 - 3:47.76, 3k - 8:04.07, 5k - 14:10.04
CRITCHLEY Simon U17 18.03.78, G. Man Sch :
HJ - 1.90
CROAD Malcolm U23 27.10.73,
Old Gaytonians/OUAC/WLHS : SP - 13.69,
DT - 41.14 (42.46-92), HT - 57.96 (61.22-92)

CROASDALE Mark 10.01.60, Lanc & Morc :
10k - 29:43.20, 10MR - 49:04 (49:21-92),
HMar - 1:04:41 (1:03:47-93),
Mar - 2:18:04 (2:17:45-93)
CROLL Graeme 1.02.66, Cambuslang :
3k - 8:10.32i (8:07.6-90),
3kSt - 8:49.00 (8:41.94-93)
CROMPTON Mark T. 31.12.63, Blackpool :
Dec - 5395 (5571-89)
CROMPTON Matthew U15 2.09.79, Jarrow & H :
800 - 2:01.89, PenB - 2511
CROMWELL D. U15, :
80HB - 11.81
CROSS Derek V45 30.04.49, Verlea :
3kW - 13:03.01, 10kW - 46:33.6
CROWTHER Eric U20 23.01.75, Sale :
1500 - 3:52.0, 3k - 8:28.7
CROWTHER Gary Michael 23.09.63, Salford :
3k - 8:18.8 (8:05.4-88),
5k - 14:18.71 (13:52.72-87)
CSEMICZKY Nicholas U20 13.05.75, TVH :
200 - 21.9/22.08, 60H - 8.2i/8.22i,
110HJ - 14.23w/14.3/14.43 (14.28-92),
110H - 14.75
CULLEN Keith John U23 13.06.72, Chelm :
1500 - 3:48.0 (3:43.12-92),
3k - 8:05.77i/8:16.27 (8:00.87-92),
5k - 14:03.76 (13:54.52-91),
10kR - 28:54 (28:36-92), 2kSt - 5:42.92,
3kSt - 8:39.71 (8:31.72-92)
CULSHAW John 20.11.62, Tamworth :
Dec - 5235w (5314-92)
CUMMINGS Christopher 8.11.67, Lisburn :
Dec - 5004 (5261-89)
CUNNANE Thomas U15 14.08.80, Wakefield :
HTB - 43.82
CUNNINGHAM Alasdair U17 5.09.77, Belf Oly :
800 - 1:56.5 (1:55.99-93)
CURRAN Conor U20 15.02.75, Annadale Str :
3kSt - 9:36.96
CURSONS Mark D. 10.03.62, Old Gaytonians :
Mar - 2:27:37
CURTIS Gary 21.11.61, Haringey :
HT - 46.98 (52.60-88)
CURTIS Neil U23 30.07.74, Corby :
HT - 55.62
CUTHILL David U17 18.01.78, Kilbarchan :
OctY - 4402
CZERNIK Richard U23 12.07.72, Dudley & St :
Dec - 6005

D'ARCY Quentin 5.06.67, N&EB/RAF :
3kSt - 9:12.86 (9:11.9-92)
DABORN Dale K.R. 14.11.66, Highgate/RAF :
400H - 55.2 (54.0-92/54.03-89),
Dec - 5784 (5811-91)
DAKIN Nicholas 13.11.63, N&EB/Loughro :
60H - 8.26i (8.20i-88),
110H - 14.84 (14.28-93)
DAKO Owusu U23 23.05.73, Sale :
60 - 6.87i, 200 - 21.10 (20.80w-93)
100 - 10.60 (10.5w-93/10.59w-92/10.60-93)
DALTON Jamie U15 20.09.79, Preseli :
HJ - 1.85, JTB - 47.08
DALTON Timothy U17 18.01.79, Old Gayton'ns :
100HY - 13.8/13.90w/14.18
DALY Steven U15 29.12.79, Elan Valley :
100 - 11.3/11.32, 200 - 22.26w/22.7, 400 - 53.47

DANIELS Darren 2.09.70, Birchfield :
  1500 - 3:46.85, 1M - 4:03.98, 3k - 8:03.5
DANIELS David U15 16.11.79, Enfield :
  SPB - 14.23, HTB - 41.80
DANIELS Dean U20 1.02.76, Birchfield :
  DTJ - 41.50 (43.88-93)
DANIELS Leon U20 1.11.75, Solihull & S H :
  100 - 10.78w/10.99, 200 - 22.0/22.08
DARBYSHIRE Peter 3.11.65, Wigan :
  PV - 4.20
DARLINGTON Alexander U13 9.09.81, Bec ° Co :
  100 - 12.4
DARLINGTON Landley Sean U20 19.01.77,
  Stamford & Deeping : JT - 56.22
DARROCH Donald I. 30.05.65, Liverpool Pem :
  PV - 4.10 (4.30-90)
DART Luke U15 14.09.79, Frome :
  200 - 22.74w/23.43
DAVENHILL Jason C.M. 3.10.69, Exeter/RAF :
  400H - 54.0 (52.65-93)
DAVEY David U17 8.09.77, Barry :
  1500 - 4:01.8
DAVEY William 25.01.64, Hounslow :
  PV - 4.40 (5.20-83)
DAVID Andrew 9.09.69, S London :
  110H - 14.90
DAVIDSON Christopher U20 4.12.75, Dartford :
  LJ - 7.46w/7.21i/7.10
DAVIDSON Mark 15.11.68, TVH/Aberdeen :
  400H - 52.70 (50.79-89)
DAVIDSON Ritchie, Dundee HH :
  100kR - 8:36:20
DAVIES Gareth W. 25.08.62, Bridgend :
  10MR - 48:49, Mar - 2:19:46
DAVIES Gareth U23 2.10.72, Sale :
  200 - 21.76 (21.5/21.55w-93/21.65-92),
  400 - 47.73 (47.39-93)
DAVIES Gareth M. 11.05.71, Swansea/OUAC :
  LJ - 7.62, TJ - 14.73
DAVIES Kevin U17 11.01.78, Taun/Brymore Sch :
  HTJ - 47.26, HTY - 56.70, OctY - 4419
DAVIES Mark Howard 10.01.71, Tonbridge :
  SP - 15.14 (15.56-92), DT - 50.56 (53.06-92)
DAVIES Matthew 23.07.71, Cambridge & Col :
  800 - 1:52.7 (1:52.1-92),
  1500 - 3:48.4 (3:48.0-93)
DAVIES Matthew U17 16.09.78, Swansea :
  JTY - 54.38
DAVIES Peter 24.02.63, Haringey :
  1500 - 3:49.0 (3:43.96-92)
DAVIES Philip 12.10.60, Wirral :
  SP - 13.59 (14.41-87)
DAVIES-HALE Paul 21.06.62, Cannock & St :
  5k - 14:00.4 (13:21.60-88),
  10MR - 48:19 (46:58-83),
  HMar - 1:05:25 (1:01:39-91),
  Mar - 2:16:48 (2:11:25-89)
DAVIS Adam Gareth U23 19.11.72, Corby/
  Staffs Univ : PV - 4.20 (4.70-92), Dec - 5173
DAVIS Jonathon U17 5.03.78, Lagan Valley :
  100 - 11.1 (12.67-90)
DAVIS Luke U15 1.01.80, Tipton :
  200 - 23.30w/23.7
DAVIS Mark U20 1.03.77, Corby :
  PV - 4.60
DAVIS Neal U17 11.10.77, Southend :
  PV - 3.80 (4.00-93)

DAVIS Richard U17 3.05.78, Bedford & Co :
  100 - 10.9w/11.17
DAVIS Scott U20 3.04.75, Coventry RWC :
  3kW - 13:01.88 (12:55.0-93),
  10kW - 47:07.1 (45:30.02-92),
  10kWR - 44:50 (44:41-93),
  20kW - 1:37:10
DAVIS Timothy U17 25.01.78, Invicta :
  1.5kSt - 4:25.20
DAVIS Trevor 26.03.63, Windsor S & E/ANG :
  100 - 10.8 (10.4-86/10.64-90),
  200 - 21.8/22.24 (21.41-90)
DE FREITAS Matthew 19.09.68, Ports/Lough :
  800 - 1:52.28 (1:50.48-91),
  1500 - 3:46.23i/3:48.8 (3:39.66-93),
  3kSt - 8:59.6
DEACON David William 19.03.65, Morpeth :
  200 - 21.19w/21.9 (21.24-93),
  400 - 47.35 (47.10-93)
DEACON Gareth 8.08.66, Coventry Godiva :
  10k - 30:41.3
DEACON Jared Mark U20 15.10.75, Morpeth :
  300 - 33.7, 400 - 47.5/47.53
DEAN Fraser U23 12.11.73, Craw/Adams St Un :
  110H - 15.5, Dec - 6158
DEARMAN Geoffrey U20 4.08.77, Hounslow :
  400 - 48.53
DEASY Matthew U17 30.07.78, Exeter :
  HJ - 1.90
DECANNES Dominic U15 11.04.80, Thames VH :
  80HB - 11.58w/11.7/11.80
DELL Gregory J. 20.11.64, Vale of Aylesbury :
  Mar - 2:28:12 (2:28:23-93), 100kR - 7:11:29
DENMARK Robert N. 23.11.68, Basildon :
  1M - 4:07.28 (3:55.38-90),
  3k - 7:42.62 (7:39.55-93),
  5k - 13:22.40 (13:10.24-92),
  10k - 28:03.34, HMar - 1:02:37
DERBYSHIRE Colin U23 31.08.74, Doncaster :
  200 - 22.0/22.08 (21.54w/21.6/21.80-93)
DERBYSHIRE Kieran U20 18.01.77, Donc :
  HJ - 1.98 (2.00-93)
DEVINE J. Russell 24.04.68, Inverness :
  HT - 65.36
DEVONISH Marlon U20 1.06.76, Coventry G :
  60 - 6.97i, 100 - 10.52w/10.57,
  200 - 21.20w/21.25
DEVONSHIRE Adam U17 2.03.79, Bed & Co :
  HTJ - 48.64, HTY - 56.76un/56.60
DEWEY Tommy U15 31.01.80, Croydon :
  HTB - 41.44 (42.20-93)
DIBBLE Jason 15.02.71, Cannock & Stafford :
  HT - 49.68
DICKENSON Derek Paul V45 4.12.49, Dac :
  HT - 56.74 (73.20-76)
DICKINSON Victor U15 23.11.79, Ryedale :
  HTB - 42.06
DINEEN John U20 10.12.75, Bromsgrove & R :
  800 - 1:54.51
DIXON David W. 2.03.60, Border :
  TJ - 13.92 (14.11-91)
DIXON N. U23   73, Southend :
  DT - 42.58
DIXON Neil U15, Gateshead :
  HJ - 1.80
DOBBIE Mark U20 5.03.77, Aberdeen :
  DecJ - 5417

DOBSON Matthew U15 20.01.80, W Yorks Sch :
LJ - 5.94, PenB - 2680w
DOBSON Robert W. V50 4.11.42, Ilford :
50kW - 4:52:35 (4:07:23-79)
DOCKERY Michael 29.07.71, City of Stoke :
TJ - 14.43
DODD Steven 9.01.71, Blackheath :
3k - 8:18.28 (8:14.21-93)
DOHERTY Ciaran U20 14.01.75, Sparta/Bord :
110H - 15.16, JT - 55.56, Dec - 5674
DOHERTY Seamus 10.11.59, Annadale Str :
Mar - 2:25:16 (2:25:01-88)
DONALD B. U17, Scottish Sch :
JTY - 54.60
DONALDSON Alasdair U20 21.06.77, Pitr :
800 - 1:53.37
DONALDSON Ross U15 17.08.80, Ches Sch :
800 - 2:02.9
DONAVAN Marcus U13 14.09.81, Hertford & W :
HJ - 1.55
DONNELLY Dermot 23.09.70, Annadale Str :
3k - 8:13.03 (8:00.58-93), 5k - 13:47.0,
10kR - 29:32 (29:19-91)
DONOVAN Daniel 8.10.70, Crawley :
100 - 10.8w, 300 - 33.7, 400 - 47.8/47.87
DOOMASIA Cyrus U23 31.03.73, Herne H/IND :
JT - 59.52
DORAN Anthony U23 22.10.72, Llanelli :
HT - 48.24
DORGU Chris 11.12.69, Hounslow :
110H - 14.7/14.71, 400H - 55.1
DORIS Alan B. 12.03.66, Edinburgh :
100 - 10.80w (10.51w/10.57-90)
DORSET Scott 10.04.69, Newham & Essex B :
100 - 10.68w/10.80 (10.6/10.65-89),
200 - 21.9/21.95 (21.4/21.88-89)
DOUGLAS Andrew J. 19.07.62, ESH/Army :
110H - 15.5 (14.9w-91/15.20-92),
400H - 54.52 (53.5-91/53.59-92)
DOUGLAS Keith 6.07.66, Edinburgh SH :
100 - 10.68w/10.75 (10.65w/10.7-92),
200 - 21.61 (21.47w/21.56-92)
DOUGLAS Matthew U20 26.11.76, Milton K :
100 - 10.99w, 400 - 48.30,
110H - 15.5/15.64, 400H - 53.34,
Dec - 6359
DOUGLAS Quincy U20 7.09.75, :
200 - 22.18, 400 - 47.84
DOVELL Paul U20 5.05.77, Dorchester :
HJ - 2.06
DOWNER Brian U20 1.12.75, Croydon :
LJ - 7.02
DOWNES John 21.07.67, London Irish :
1500 - 3:42.59, 3k - 7:54.53,
2M - 8:27.00, 5k - 13:29.91
DOWNIE Kevin 7.07.69, East Kilbride :
3kSt - 9:17.51
DOWSETT Nicholas J.E. U17 24.11.78, Walth :
100HY - 13.72w/14.0/14.05,
LJ - 6.60w (6.22-93), OctY - 4517
DRAKE Andrew Paul 6.02.65, Coventry G :
10k - 30:59.6
DRAKE Paul 16.10.66, Bournemouth :
800 - 1:50.9 (1:50.49-92), 1500 - 3:46.7
DRAPER Anthony U23 23.04.74, Blackheath :
800 - 1:50.78
DRAPER Paul U17 9.09.77, Sale :
800 - 1:55.6, 1500 - 4:02.10

DRENNEN James U23 16.08.72, Bristol :
JT - 65.82 (68.38-91)
DRONFIELD Jason A. 5.07.70, Leics Cor :
HJ - 2.00i (2.08-90)
DRURY Kevin U15 30.09.79, Oswestry :
80HB - 11.40w, HJ - 1.87, LJ - 5.90w,
TJ - 12.21, PenB - 3163
DRZEWIECKI Jan 29.11.57, Bracknell :
DT - 40.86 (44.40-91)
DUFFUS Andre U15 30.10.79, Haringey :
100 - 11.25, 200 - 22.39w/22.7/23.40
DUGDALE William Paul 13.05.65, Horwich :
3k - 8:12.18 (8:05.74-91),
5k - 14:07.13 (13:56.74-93)
DUKE Adam U23 5.10.73, Thames Valley :
800 - 1:50.7 (1:48.8-92),
1500 - 3:50.80 (3:45.3-92)
DUKE Daniel James Maxwell 23.12.68, Bristol :
3kSt - 9:04.2 (8:49.53-88)
DULLFORCE Jason Mark 6.08.70, Enfield :
1500 - 3:50.8 (3:37.88-92), 3k - 8:18.53
DUNBAR Martyn U15 25.05.80, Mandale :
PV - 3.00
DUNDAS Paul U23 14.01.74, Wolves & B :
LJ - 7.01w (7.06w-92/6.97-91)
DUNLOP Paul U20 11.02.75, Preston :
400 - 49.2 (48.8-93/49.34-92)
DUNSON J. Gregory 2.12.63, RAF/Shaft B :
110H - 14.42 (14.23w-89/14.29-86),
400H - 52.81 (50.88-92)
DUNWELL Mark 13.03.70, Notts :
100 - 10.7w/10.8/11.10 (10.7w/10.90w-93,
200 - 21.9 (21.7w-93)
DUPUY Jason 31.01.71, Bexley :
800 - 1:52.20
DUVAL Spencer Gavin 5.01.70, C & S/Lough :
1500 - 3:46.42, 5k - 13:56.47,
10kR - 29:27, 3kSt - 8:28.33
DYER Daniel U15 17.12.79, Bexley :
PenB - 2432
DYMOKE Peter L. 30.10.61, Livingston :
10k - 30:26.74, Mar - 2:24:09

EARLE Albert St.Clair 10.01.58, W & B :
TJ - 14.21 (15.14-79)
EARLE Robert B. 15.09.60, Haringey :
DT - 45.12 (45.12-90), HT - 61.68
EASON William U17 13.07.79, Camb & Col :
400HY - 56.74
EAST Michael John U17 20.01.78, Portsmouth :
1500 - 4:02.60, 1.5kSt - 4:26.0
EASTLAKE David 2.07.63, Morpeth :
SP - 14.58 (14.60-91), DT - 41.78
EASTON Mark Jonathan 24.05.63, Surrey WC :
3kW - 12:04.78 (11:24.4-89),
10kW - 42:57.0 (41:14.3-89),
20kW - 1:28:06 (1:24:04-89),
30kW - 2:14:16 (2:13:33-89)
EASTWOOD Simon 18.04.65, Milton Keynes :
PV - 4.20
EDGAR Christopher U23 11.06.73, Sale/Falk/
NWHS : HT - 49.60 (53.50-93)
EDMISTON Paul James U23 16.02.72,
Bed & Co/AUS : 110H - 14.2w/14.36
EDMONDS Steve 15.05.69, Birchfield :
1500 - 3:50.7
EDMUNDS Cypren 20.06.70, Thames Valley :
100 - 10.7, 200 - 21.30w/21.5/21.70, 300 - 33.6

EDO Courage U17 3.12.77, Herne Hill :
 100 - 10.86w/11.0 (11.10-92)
EDSALL Charles K. U23 2.05.74, Havant :
 110H - 15.1 (15.23w/15.43-93)
EDU Remi U17 14.12.78, Herts Sch :
 100HY - 14.2
EDU Seni, Loughborough Studnts :
 100 - 10.90w (10.8-93)
EDWARDS Andrew 15.09.69, Windsor S & E :
 400H - 53.7 (52.5/53.09-93)
EDWARDS Dafydd U23 19.09.74, Cardiff :
 HJ - 2.10i/2.05 (2.05-91)
EDWARDS John S. 12.06.65, Bridgend :
 10MR - 48:31, HMar - 1:03:26, Mar - 2:20:24
EDWARDS Jonathan David 10.05.66, Gate :
 60 - 6.95i (6.77i-93),
 100 - 10.85 (10.6w-89/10.63w-90/10.7/10.80-92),
 LJ - 7.27 (7.45w/7.41-92),
 TJ - 17.39 (17.70w/17.44-93)
EDWARDS Lee U20 14.09.75, Cardiff :
 LJ - 6.93
EDWARDS Mark U23 2.12.74, Charn/Lough :
 SP - 15.75, SPJ - 16.53o (16.29-93),
 DT - 41.12 (43.02-92), DTJ - 46.96o
EDWARDS Michael 19.10.68, Belgrave :
 PV - 5.42 (5.52-93)
EDWARDS Noel U23 16.12.72, Leamington :
 800 - 1:52.46 (1:51.70-91)
¶EDWARDS Paul M. 16.02.59, Belgrave :
 SP - 19.94 (20.33-91), DT - 48.46 (57.12-88)
EDWARDS Stephen U20 13.06.77, Carm :
 110HJ - 14.8/15.10w
EFOYINI E. U13, :
 TJ - 10.68
EGAN James Nicholas U20 12.11.75, Skyrac :
 100 - 10.78, 200 - 21.58
EGMAGHA Daro U20 22.11.75, Cambridge H :
 200 - 22.0
EKOKU Abi 13.04.66, Belgrave :
 SP - 14.91 (17.45-90), DT - 53.16 (60.08-90)
ELDER Andrew U17 28.12.77, Bracknell :
 DTY - 42.66
ELDRIDGE Timothy U20 15.03.76, Shaftes B:
 JT - 59.38 (62.96-93)
ELKS Martin U15 26.01.80, City of Stoke :
 400 - 52.69
ELLAMS Craig U23 24.11.72, City of Stoke :
 HT - 58.76
ELLIOTT Christopher John U20 29.05.75,
 Portsmouth/Northumberland Un :
 800 - 1:53.1, 1500 - 3:52.3,
 2kSt - 5:51.00, 3kSt - 8:59.57
ELLIOTT Mark U17 3.04.78, Telford :
 HTY - 55.68
ELLIOTT Neil 10.04.71, Edinburgh/Helen :
 SP - 13.96i/13.27, DT - 44.94
ELLIS Ieuan T. 11.05.60, Elswick :
 Mar - 2:26:22 (2:13:21-86)
ELLIS Joel U15 2.09.79, Sparkhill :
 1500 - 4:20.9, 3k - 9:27.6
ELLIS Norman U20 17.01.75, GEC :
 60 - 6.89i,
 100 - 10.7w/10.76w/10.88 (10.7w/10.8-92)
 200 - 21.8/21.93
ELLIS Paul U20 2.11.75, Colwyn Bay :
 TJ - 14.16
ELLIS-SMITH James U23, Reigate :
 1500 - 3:47.16, 3k - 8:10.72i

ELLWOOD Wayne U23 26.09.74, Blackpool :
 400 - 48.7/49.47
ELSWOOD Stephen U15 21.11.79, Hounslow :
 400 - 53.56
EMBERTON Neil U23 11.09.72, Wrexham :
 800 - 1:51.4 (1:51.20-93), 1500 - 3:47.29
EMBLETON Peter V40 16.04.54, Durham :
 Mar - 2:28:05 (2:27:07-91)
ENGLISH Desmond 6.06.67, Havering/IRE :
 800 - 1:51.6 (1:48.4-91),
 1500 - 3:41.39, 1M - 3:58.71
ERDMAN Lewis U15 29.11.79, Herne Hill :
 HJ - 1.80, LJ - 6.09
EROGBOGBO Tayo U20 8.03.75, Birch/NIG :
 TJ - 15.93
ESEGBONA Unuakpor H. 16.04.68, C of Stoke :
 HJ - 1.98, Dec - 6121 (6274w-93)
ESSIEN Bassey U23 17.11.73, Blackheath :
 LJ - 7.05w/6.97, TJ - 13.94 (14.82-92)
ESTALL James H. V40 9.08.54, Belgrave :
 Mar - 2:25:22
EVANS David U20 23.01.76, Birchfield :
 JT - 55.84
EVANS Deiniol U23 16.02.73, Llanelli :
 HJ - 1.98 (1.98-93)
EVANS Karl U15 9.07.80, :
 TJ - 12.03
EVANS Matthew U20 19.11.75, Telford :
 PV - 4.35
EVANS Paul William 13.04.61, Belgrave :
 5k - 13:46.5+e/13:47.21 (13:30.83-92),
 10kR - 28:23, 10MR - 48:31 (47:26-91),
 HMar - 1:01:30
EVANS Sean U20 3.10.76, City of Plymouth :
 JT - 59.90
EVANS Steven U17, Colwyn Bay :
 400HY - 57.3
EVELEIGH Matthew U20 7.01.76, Carm :
 400H - 57.04
EXLEY Scott U17 9.02.78, Millfield Sch :
 OctY - 4576
EYNON Andrew 1.09.63, Swansea :
 3kSt - 9:24.46

FABEN Stuart U20 28.02.75, Hunt :
 JT - 66.74
FAIRBROTHER Simon 28.03.68, Haringey :
 800 - 1:50.83 (1:47.7-92),
 1500 - 3:44.60 (3:38.64-92)
FAIRCLOUGH Lee 23.06.70, Team Solent :
 100 - 10.7w (10.7-93), 300 - 33.6,
 400 - 47.7 (47.6-92/47.87-93)
FAIRLAMB Neil U20 13.03.76, City of Stoke :
 PV - 4.10
FALKNER Ryan U15 20.11.79, Oadby & W :
 1500 - 4:20.6
FALLOWS Mark Christopher 8.02.62, Edinb :
 1500 - 3:49.5 (3:45.96-93), 1M - 4:09.53
FALOLA Ayo 29.07.68, Woodford Green :
 60 - 6.87i (6.85i-90),
 100 - 10.67w/10.84 (10.51w-90/10.53-92),
 200 - 21.64 (21.1w-90/21.15-91)
FARMER Paul A. 17.11.69, Cardiff :
 TJ - 14.61w/14.51 (14.94w-90/14.89-89)
FARQUHARSON Ruddy A. 26.03.61, Telf/RAF :
 LJ - 6.90 (6.99-92),
 TJ - 15.18 (15.59w/15.57-85)

FARRELL David W. 29.06.64, Border :
5k - 14:34.72, 3kSt - 9:08.2 (9:02.37-93)
FARRELL Kevin U17 31.10.77, Havering :
100 - 11.00A, 200 - 21.78A, 400 - 50.6
FARRELLY John 4.12.67, London Irish/IRE :
SP - 13.94 (14.90-91), DT - 44.08 (47.52-89)
FARREN Robert 15.05.70, Sparta :
1500 - 3:42.70, 1M - 4:00.2,
3k - 7:56.24, 5k - 13:47.92
FASINRO Ibrahim 'Tosi' U23 28.03.72, Har :
LJ - 7.23,
TJ - 16.74w/16.70 (17.30w/17.21-93)
FAULKNER Mark U15 14.11.79, Team Solent :
LJ - 6.18
FAULKNER Stewart 19.02.69, Birchfield :
LJ - 7.48 (8.15-90)
FEARON G. U17, :
100 - 11.1
FELDWICK Matthew, Huntingdon :
HJ - 2.00
FENTON Malcolm L. 12.02.56, Newham & EB :
HT - 58.72 (62.42-82)
FENWICK Sean, Harborough :
3kSt - 9:07.2
FERGUS Jason R. U23 11.10.73, Brentwood :
60 - 6.72i (6.72i-93),
100 - 10.34w/10.54 (10.4-93/10.44-92),
200 - 21.6 (21.33-92)
FERGUSON Martin M. 17.09.64, Edinburgh :
10k - 30:58.92 (30:43.6-89),
Mar - 2:27:38, 3kSt - 9:21.68 (9:17.2-88)
FERN Ashleigh U13 8.04.82, Leics WC :
2kW - 11:52.0
FERRAND Adrian J. 5.02.68, N & EB/Lond Un :
110H - 15.06, Dec - 6548 (6726-93)
FERRI Carlo U20 18.11.75, Shettleston :
100 - 10.80w/10.94 (10.80w-93)
FERRIN John 20.02.67, North Belfast :
10kR - 29:31 (29:16-92),
HMar - 1:04:38 (1:03:52-92), Mar - 2:21:07
FIDLER Terrence R. 13.10.71, Crawley :
110H - 15.20 (15.1w-91),
PV - 4.30 (4.50-91), Dec - 6671 (6683-91)
FIELD Paul C. 24.06.67, Met. Police :
100 - 10.87w (10.8-91/10.90-92),
400 - 48.2/49.59 (48.37-92),
110H - 14.61w/14.89, PV - 4.20,
LJ - 7.19, Dec - 7157
FINCH D., Team Solent :
LJ - 6.94
FINCH Rodney 5.08.67, Southampton C/Army :
800 - 1:51.1,
1500 - 3:38.80 (3:37.97-93),
3k - 7:53.99i (7:59.33-93)
FINDLAY Mark U17 20.03.78, Blackheath :
100 - 10.88w/11.00, 200 - 22.1, LJ - 7.13
FINDLOW Richard David 4.12.66, Bradford :
3k - 8:17.69i/8:19.99 (7:59.09-90),
5k - 13:49.16 (13:44.58-92),
10kR - 29:46 (29:19-92)
FISH Chris U15 22.12.79, G. Manchester Sch :
800 - 2:04.7
FISHER Paul U17 17.05.79, Milton Keynes :
1500 - 4:03.36, 3k - 8:50.6
FITTALL Ross U15 4.09.79, Dursley :
1500 - 4:08.81
FITZGERALD Des U23 26.11.72, Pitreavie :
PV - 4.50

FITZSIMMONS Robert Gerald 16.08.64, Kilb :
1500 - 3:48.27 (3:42.49-92),
3k - 8:17.02 (8:06.2-90)
FLANAGAN Neil 21.02.66, Rowntrees :
400H - 55.5 (53.7-91)
FLEMING Peter Ross 5.01.61, Leslie Deans :
3k - 8:09.7i (8:08.5-90),
HMar - 1:03:50 (1:02:52-93),
Mar - 2:14:03 (2:13:33-93)
FLETCHER Jason U20 18.01.76, Corby :
100 - 10.78w/10.86 (10.7w-93),
200 - 22.0 (22.0-93)
FLETCHER Martyn 21.01.69, Birchfield :
SP - 16.35i/16.15 (16.48-92)
FLETCHER Stephen 16.12.68, Derby & Co :
100 - 10.86 (10.3db-90/10.51w/10.6/10.62-89)
FLINT Benjamin U17 16.09.78, Rotherham :
PV - 4.20
FLINT Mark A. 19.02.63, Telford/RAF :
10kR - 28:38, 10MR - 48:37 (47:16-93),
HMar - 1:04:57 (1:01:56-93), Mar - 2:12:07
FLOWERS Nikki U15 15.02.80, Cardiff :
JTB - 46.72
FLOYD Michael U20 26.09.76, Sale :
HT - 52.42, HTJ - 57.90
FLYNN Julian T. U23 3.07.72, Birchfield :
LJ - 7.44w/7.25i/7.18 (7.52-92),
TJ - 14.93 (15.32-93)
FOCKE Kris 28.03.69, Hercules Wimb/BEL :
110H - 15.4 (14.71-93)
FODAY Sahr U15 6.11.79, Middlesex Sch :
TJ - 12.30
FOOKS Andrew U20 26.04.75, Taunton :
2kSt - 5:56.42, 3kSt - 9:20.61
FORBES Graeme U20 16.02.75, Clydesdale :
800 - 1:54.0
FORMOSA Darren U15 27.10.79, Gateshead :
SPB - 13.57, DTB - 39.54
FORSTER Simon U17 15.10.77, Trafford :
JT - 54.68, JTY - 54.94
FOSTER Carl U20 24.10.75, Hallamshire :
400H - 54.21
FOSTER Paul U15 20.10.79, Yate :
JTB - 47.50
FOSTER William R.G. 9.08.58, Blackheath :
HMar - 1:05:20 (1:04:52-90),
Mar - 2:17:12
FOWLER Malcolm A. 30.01.63, Met. Police :
Mar - 2:25:31
FOWLER R. Melville 7.07.66, Inverness :
TJ - 14.47w/14.35 (14.57-85)
FOX Morris 30.04.63, City of Stoke :
SP - 14.76 (14.83i-92), DT - 44.54
FRANCIS Alex U23 15.07.74, W Suff/Lough :
400 - 47.92
FRANCIS Mark U17 23.09.77, Sutton & Dist :
JT - 53.68, JTY - 62.86
FRANCIS Michael 18.09.58, Forres :
100kR - 7:56:18, 24Hr - 210.735
FRANCIS Nick 29.08.71, Cambridge Harriers :
10k - 30:40.8
FRANCIS Peter U15 28.08.80, Essex Sch :
TJ - 12.12
FRANCIS Steven U17 31.01.79, Newport :
PV - 4.10
FRANKLIN Marlon U20 9.03.75, Birchfield :
LJ - 6.90w (6.60-91)

FRANKS Christopher 19.01.66, Oxford City :
DT - 41.54 (43.68-91)
FRANKS David U17 21.09.78, G. Man Sch :
HJ - 1.91
FRASER Joel U23 10.11.74, Crawley :
800 - 1:52.4 (1:52.3-93)
FRASER Neil W. 8.06.63, Edinburgh SH :
110H - 15.1 (14.1/14.11-87)
FRASER Peter U17 28.01.78, Aberdeen :
DTY - 41.46, JTY - 58.36
FRASER Scott U17 31.12.77, Inverness :
100 - 10.70w/10.78, 200 - 22.1/22.32
FRASER Simon U15 30.11.79, Liverpool H :
800 - 2:00.6db
FREARY Paul 3.04.68, Bolton :
800 - 1:50.5, 1500 - 3:45.3 (3:43.3-91),
1M - 4:02.7 (4:01.51-91),
3k - 8:15.3 (8:07.84-90),
5k - 14:10.76, 10MR - 48:37
FREED T. U13, :
SPC - 11.84
FREEMAN Stephen 8.09.67, Liverpool Pem :
400H - 54.4 (52.8/52.89-92)
FREESTONE Steven U17 5.08.78, Charn :
DTY - 41.20
FRICKER Simon David U20 14.07.75, Bournem'th :
SP - 14.29 (14.40-93),
SPJ - 15.70 (15.93-93),
DT - 44.30 (46.10-93), DTJ - 48.38
FROUD Paul M. 6.04.66, Brighton :
Mar - 2:22:18
FUAT Zhina U20 27.03.76, Enfield :
JT - 56.40
FUGALLO Alexander 28.01.70, Highgate :
100 - 10.8 (10.42w-90/10.5-89/10.60-92),
200 - 21.50 (21.20w-89/21.2/21.26-90),
400 - 46.39
FULLER William J. V45 5.02.48, Epsom & E :
SP - 13.82 (17.87-72)
FULLER William U20 19.10.76, Sutton & Dist :
SP - 15.08, SPJ - 16.34,
HT - 50.78, HTJ - 54.68
FURLONG Kevin 19.05.70, Manx H :
110H - 15.2 (15.2/15.29w/15.47-93)

G ADD Wayne A.H. 21.05.71, E Grinstead :
Dec - 5386
GAFFNEY Bernard P. 8.06.61, Massey F :
Mar - 2:27:55 (2:27:11-92)
GAFFON Chris U17, Eastbourne GS :
JTY - 54.72
GAJJAR Kieran U20 25.09.76, W Yorks Sch :
200 - 22.03w/22.06
GALBRAITH Edward U20 3.10.75, Bas & MH :
DecJ - 5712
GALLAGHER Darren 7.06.71, Annadale Str/GEC :
400H - 54.0/54.45 (54.23-93)
GALLAGHER Donal U23 5.12.72, Sparta :
10k - 30:52.9
GALLAGHER Gary 7.06.71, GEC/Staffs Univ :
110H - 15.0/15.33 (15.20w-93)
GALLAGHER Michael 25.04.66, Border :
400 - 48.3/48.31
GALVIN Patrick U23 24.09.74, Bideford :
800 - 1:51.72
GARBA Abu U20 6.05.76, Eastbourne GS :
TJ - 14.38w/14.25

GARDENER Jason U20 18.09.75, C of Bath :
60 - 6.73i, 100 - 10.25,
150 - 15.99, 200 - 21.73
GARDNER David 14.12.68, Morpeth :
LJ - 6.99 (7.02-93)
GARDNER Nigel U23 15.04.72, Woodford Gr :
400H - 53.00 (52.62-93)
GARDNER Paul 5.08.69, Telford/RAF :
1500 - 3:46.9
GARDNER Robin, Woodstock R :
100kR - 7:40:47
GARNER Vincent 2.07.66, AF&D :
3kSt - 9:17.58
GASCOIGNE Stephen 20.12.66, Blackheath :
PV - 4.20 (4.70-88)
GASCOYNE Jonathon J. U23 31.03.72, Enf :
3k - 8:09.1, 5k - 14:03.61
GATES Nigel V40 18.05.53, Brighton :
5k - 14:27.49 (13:50.8-78)
GAUDEN Duncan J. 11.02.68, Telford :
Dec - 6244
GAY Steven U20 6.01.77, Dorchester :
3kSt - 9:41.5
GEE Simon U20 23.04.75, Liverpool H :
TJ - 14.60
GEMMELL Nigel 30.09.63, Southampton City :
5k - 14:23.9 (14:19.5-91),
GENTRY Julian 19.05.69, Newham & E B :
10k - 30:32.14
GEORGE Ronan U15 10.01.80, Mx Sch :
LJ - 5.95
GERCS John 7.06.69, Rugby/Loughbro St :
800 - 1:52.3 (1:50.60/1:50.6-93)
GERRARD Gary 7.07.63, Wigan Phoenix/RN :
3k - 8:18.6 (8:06.4-91),
5k - 14:15.2 (14:06.40-91),
10k - 30:37.33 (29:39.2-93)
GIBBS Martin 13.04.64, Chelmsford :
3kSt - 9:24.4 (9:15.1-89)
GIBBS Stuart 4.03.62, Dacorum :
LJ - 6.95
GIBSON Alex U17 3.11.77, Brentwood :
SPY - 13.71, JTY - 54.94, OctY - 4407
GIBSON Andrew U15 11.05.80, Middlesbro/NESH :
HTB - 45.22
GIBSON Wayne U20 25.02.76, Middlesbro & C :
HT - 50.22, HTJ - 58.14
GIDLEY Alistair U23 5.09.72, Old Gaytonians :
JT - 59.58 (62.88-93)
GIDLEY Ian 13.11.70, Sale :
HJ - 2.05 (2.05-93)
GIFFORD David U23 9.03.73, Cannock & St :
200 - 22.0, 400H - 53.34
GILBERT Ben U15 21.09.79, Windsor S & E :
DTB - 38.62
GILBERT Gareth U23 24.08.72, Cardiff :
DT - 42.30 (44.62-93)
GILBY Clive Roger 24.02.66, Cambridge H:
400 - 48.9 (48.8-89),
800 - 1:49.94 (1:47.90-92),
1500 - 3:50.6 (3:46.27-92)
GILBY Daniel P. 9.07.70, Cambridge Harriers :
PV - 4.80 (5.00-91)
GILDER Warren U23 17.09.72, Enfield :
100 - 10.8/11.23 (10.7w/10.74w/10.92-92)
GILDING Paul U20 2.01.75, Brighton :
HJ - 2.01 (2.03i/2.01-93)

GILHOOLY Tony U20 26.03.76, Cambuslang :
  HJ - 2.05
GILKES Eugene Albert Emery 5.03.62, N & EB :
  DT - 45.62 (49.86-92)
GILL Andrew Robert 19.02.70, GEC :
  110H - 15.3 (14.41w-89/14.9-90/14.92-88),
  400H - 53.3 (52.78-91)
GILL Andrew U17 19.09.77, Bingley :
  100HY - 13.37w/13.6/13.89, 110HJ - 15.0
GILL S. U15 1.09.79, Preston :
  PV - 3.00
GILLARD Matthew U20 11.07.75, Wakefield :
  Dec - 5695, DecJ - 5312
GILLES William U23 15.02.73, Croydon :
  Dec - 6411
GILLESPIE Ian 18.05.70, Birchfield :
  800 - 1:52.38 (1:50.1-93),
  1500 - 3:41.48 (3:40.72-93),
  1M - 4:00.80 (3:58.64-93), 3k - 8:03.1
GILLO Jonathon 10.12.70, Southampton City :
  DT - 42.78 (49.44-91)
GILMOUR David 19.03.70, SB/East Kilbride :
  300 - 34.98, 400 - 48.7/49.04 (48.05-91)
GIRAUD Martin U17 16.11.77, Hercules Wimb:
  60 - 6.9i, 100 - 10.6w/10.7, 200 - 22.3,
  LJ - 6.92 (7.11w/6.93-93)
GIRVAN Michael V40 16.03.54, Warrington :
  Mar - 2:27:36
GIRVAN Richard U20 26.07.76, Kilbarchan/
  Annadale Striders : 800 - 1:52.9
GISBEY David Edward 2.05.60, Edinb SH :
  HT - 54.38
GLENTON Bradford 2.11.69, Southampton C :
  1500 - 3:47.0 (3:44.09-92)
GODDARD Kevin 18.11.64, Team Solent :
  5k - 14:28.9
GODDARD Mark 12.01.64, Shaftesbury B/RSA :
  5k - 14:31.56 (14:17.19-92), 10MR - 49:38
GOEDLUCK Philip Adrian Troy 10.09.67, Bel :
  60 - 6.82i, 100 - 10.48 (10.47w-87),
  200 - 20.79, 400 - 48.70
GOLDING Julian U20 17.02.75, Blackheath :
  100 - 10.34w/10.43, 200 - 20.73w/21.02
GOLDSMITH Jeremy G. U23 6.12.73, Team S :
  JT - 56.30 (57.20-93), Dec - 6411
GOLLEY Julian Quintin Patrick 12.09.71, TVH :
  TJ - 17.06
GOOCH Mick 13.09.69, Grimsby :
  800 - 1:52.75
GOODALL Martin J. 2.10.64, Team Solent :
  TJ - 14.42
GOODGER David U20 19.09.75, Newport :
  400H - 54.44
GOODWIN Jon U20 22.09.76, C of Plymouth :
  400H - 55.03, DecJ - 5715w/5076
GOOKEY Steven John 21.04.71, Rown/Notts Un:
  100 - 10.37w/10.59 (10.33w/10.37-91),
  200 - 21.43 (20.99-92)
GORDON David 20.03.68, Newham & E B :
  PV - 4.75 (5.05i-88)
GORDON Martyn U15 29.09.79, Middlesbro & C :
  400 - 52.93, 800 - 2:01.71
GORDON Nicholas 7.01.77, Bourne :
  LJ - 6.91 (7.18w/7.07-93)
GORE Alex U17 25.03.78, Basildon :
  OctY - 4227
GORE Paul U23 4.12.72, Liverpool H :
  JT - 56.06 (62.28-93)

GORHAM Paul U17 7.08.78, Thurrock :
  HTY - 55.20
GOSS James U23 11.09.73, Enfield :
  HT - 51.32
GOULDING Dean U20 14.06.75, Sheffield :
  TJ - 14.40w/14.17
GOWAN Joseph 18.11.67, Leeds :
  400 - 48.81 (48.25-92)
GRAFFIN Allen U17 20.12.77, Tonbridge :
  800 - 1:56.9, 1500 - 3:59.68, 3k - 8:37.12
GRAFFIN Andrew U17 20.12.77, Tonbridge :
  800 - 1:55.7, 1500 - 3:59.11, 3k - 8:47.33
GRAHAM Anthony, Newport :
  HMar - 1:04:48
GRAHAM Ben U15 22.01.80, Telford :
  PenB - 2649
GRAHAM Grant U23 27.12.72, Clydesdale :
  800 - 1:49.6, 1k - 2:23.55i, 1500 - 3:44.7
GRAHAM Marcus U15 11.09.79, Blackheath :
  JTB - 46.94
GRANGE Liam U13 18.08.83, Steyning :
  2kW - 11:13.4
GRANT Dalton 8.04.66, Haringey :
  HJ - 2.37i/2.34 (2.36-91),
  LJ - 7.02i (7.14w/7.00-93)
GRANT Dwayne U13, Blackheath :
  LJ - 5.24
GRANT Keith U15 17.03.80, Pendle :
  800 - 2:04.8, 3k - 9:31.3
GRANT Mark 17.05.71, Thames Valley :
  PV - 5.06
GRATTON Dave 25.10.55, Wakefield :
  10k - 30:37.1 (30:05.51-92)
GRAY Glenn 21.04.68, Herne Hill :
  400H - 54.3
GRAY Marvin 18.12.71, Cardiff :
  400H - 54.03
GRAY Paul 25.05.69, Cardiff :
  60H - 7.91i, 110H - 13.53
GRAY Wayne U15 7.11.80, Blackheath :
  100 - 11.44, HJ - 1.78
GREALLY Michael 18.06.60, Pitreavie :
  Mar - 2:21:40
GREAVES Damien David U17 19.09.77, N & EB :
  100 - 11.17, 60HY - 7.9i (8.38-93),
  100HY - 12.70w/13.0/13.09, 110HJ - 14.61w
GREEN Adrian David 30.05.68, Woodford Gr :
  5k - 14:28.3, 3kSt - 8:51.57 (8:51.1-89)
GREEN Andrew Richard 14.12.62, Warr :
  10kR - 29:34 (28:41-90),
  HMar - 1:04:26 (1:02:48-93),
  Mar - 2:16:55 (2:12:12-93)
GREEN Clifton Paul U15 10.10.79, Medway :
  JTB - 60.56
GREEN Derek 13.06.58, White Horse :
  10k - 30:48.3, Mar - 2:28:22 (2:23:45-93)
GREEN Mark 28.06.71, Hounslow :
  400H - 54.7 (54.1/54.30-93)
GREEN Michael Stephen U20 12.10.76,
  Blackburn : 5k - 15:01.2
GREEN Nicholas U23 5.09.74, Lincoln Well :
  400H - 55.8 (55.8-92/56.16-93)
GREEN Paul U23 7.04.72, East Cheshire :
  1500 - 3:49.2, 3k - 8:18.35, 5k - 14:26.01
GREEN Stephen H. 18.02.71, Trafford :
  800 - 1:50.85 (1:50.6-92), 1k - 2:21.95,
  1500 - 3:39.19, 1M - 3:59.6i (4:06.5-90),
  3k - 8:07.61i (8:11.1-90)

338

GREEN Stephen 28.07.70, Bingley :
5k - 14:17.2, 10k - 30:12.91
GREEN Tom U17 11.12.77, Solihull & SH :
1.5kSt - 4:35.3
GREENING Stephen 15.02.68, Birchfield :
JT - 59.28 (63.24-91)
GREGORY Carl U20 17.08.77, Hounslow :
HT - 48.60, HTJ - 50.50
GREGORY Geoffrey U23 8.06.74, Wolves & B :
PV - 4.80
GREGORY Jonathan U23 3.10.72, Rown/Lough :
Dec - 5265 (5271-92)
GRIFFIN Daryl U17 28.01.78, Ipswich :
800 - 1:56.8, 1500 - 4:02.08
GRIFFIN David 5.12.63, Cardiff :
400 - 48.6, 400H - 52.66
GRIFFIN Mark U20 16.02.75, Walton :
800 - 1:49.27
GRIFFIN Neil V45 28.05.48, Windsor S & E :
DT - 43.48 (51.66-80)
GRIFFITHS David U23 22.12.74, C of Stoke :
PV - 4.30
GRIFFITHS Otis 4.02.70, Havering :
400 - 48.6
GRIME Ian 29.09.70, Newham & Essex B :
800 - 1:49.10, 1500 - 3:40.35,
3k - 8:18.74i (8:12.01-93), 5k - 14:08.31
GRIMES Eamon 11.01.64, Swindon :
10k - 31:07.6 (30:37.5-92)
GRIPTON Paul U20 9.11.76, Bromsgrove & R :
110HJ - 14.67w/14.91, 110H - 15.1
GRISTWOOD William E. 20.03.59, E ,S & Mx :
Mar - 2:25:09
GRITZ Ben U17 21.11.77, Old Gaytonians :
100HY - 13.62, 400HY - 57.86
GROVER David T. 11.04.65, Sunderland :
Mar - 2:22:51 (2:22:23-92)
GROVER Marc U17 25.02.78, Windsor S & E :
TJ - 13.81
GUDGEON Alastair U15 26.10.79, Wisbech :
TJ - 12.54
GUEGAN Michael Gerald 19.09.66, Jersey :
800 - 1:48.26 (1:47.90-92), 1500 - 3:49.3
GUEVARA Reynaldo U20 12.08.77, Haringey :
400H - 54.94
GUILDER Alan J. 10.12.61, Blackheath :
10MR - 49:37 (49:05-93),
Mar - 2:24:25 (2:21:46-93)
GUITE Craig U20 19.08.77, Rotherham :
PV - 4.15
GULLAKSEN John U15 24.02.80, Hull Spart :
PV - 3.20
GULLIVER Mark U23 11.02.72, Leeds :
HT - 48.48 (49.22-91)
GUTTERIDGE Steven T. 5.07.71, Highgate :
110H - 15.16w/15.23 (15.04-93),
PV - 4.75 (4.80-93),
LJ - 6.95w/6.90 (7.06-93), Dec - 7047
GUY-WILLIAMS Denton U23 8.05.72,
North London/SLE :
100 - 10.66 (10.65w-93)
GWYNNE Timothy J. 20.01.71, Birchfield :
110H - 14.8/14.85, 400H - 51.08 (51.71-92)
GYORFFY Terry 28.01.65, Basingstoke & MH :
Dec - 6569

HACKLEY Peter 19.02.71, Border :
800 - 1:50.49 (1:47.59-93)
HADLER John 18.08.69, Cambridge Harriers :
110H - 15.4 (14.8w/14.9-89/15.61-92)
HAIGH J. U20, Oxford Sch :
JT - 53.32
HAINES Andrew U23 15.10.72, Crawley :
110H - 15.2 (15.1-92/15.13w/15.17-91)
HALES Matthew U15 6.10.79, Steyning :
3kW - 14:15.1o/14:15.3,
3kWR - 13:44o, 5kWR - 24:55
HALL Dominic 21.02.71, Highgate :
800 - 1:51.07 (1:50.9-91)
HALL Gary U15 25.07.80, Sutton & District :
PenB - 2550
HALL John D. V45 18.01.49, Belgrave :
3kW - 13:36.0 (12:53.28-82),
10kW - 48:52.1 (45:58.0-78)
HAMER Ian Martin 18.04.65, Swansea :
3k - 8:10.21 (7:46.40-90),
5k - 13:57.99 (13:09.80-92), 10kR - 29:19
HAMES Jeremy E. 17.11.70, Charnwood :
PV - 4.10, SP - 13.95, DT - 43.80, JT - 56.18
HAMILTON Douglas W. 19.05.61, Edin SH :
PV - 4.65 (4.75-87)
HAMILTON Ian 8.03.65, Invicta :
5k - 14:27.02
HAMILTON Nicholas U17 13.03.79, Blackh'th :
400 - 50.94
HAMMOND John 1.07.71, Trafford :
400 - 48.9/49.48 (47.60-93)
HAMMOND Lee U17 13.11.77, Coventry G :
JTY - 54.64
HAMMOND Matthew U23, Scunthorpe :
HT - 46.82 (49.44-93)
HANCOCK D., Army :
100 - 10.7
HANCOCK Jay U17 12.07.78, Swansea :
HJ - 1.90
HAND James U15 11.06.80, Edinburgh :
800 - 2:02.0
HANIF Nashim U15 16.09.79, Ulster Sch :
80HB - 11.7w
HANLON Thomas 20.05.67, Leslie Deans RC :
3kSt - 8:20.04 (8:12.58-91)
HANNA David U20 13.12.75, Lagan Valley :
JT - 60.48
HARBOUR Duncan 17.10.66, Peterborough :
400H - 54.7 (53.4/53.68-93)
HARDY Aaron U17 17.03.78, Mandale :
400HY - 57.72
HARDY Alan P. 4.09.58, Blackheath :
PV - 4.20 (4.50-92)
HARGRAVE Chris U17 27.02.79, Bed & Co :
100HY - 14.2
HARGREAVES Gerard, Gateshead :
3kSt - 9:08.7
HARGREAVES Mark 26.08.60, Bournemouth :
Mar - 2:23:25
HARKER Jack U15 14.09.79, Corby :
HTB - 49.60
HARKER Ken 25.02.71, Mandale :
1500 - 3:49.6
HARPER Ben U17 9.11.78, Braintree :
400 - 50.4
HARPER Michael U17 20.05.78, Braintree :
400 - 50.1,

339

HARPUR Ian 24.04.67, Southampton City/IRE :
5k - 14:35.22, 10k - 29:49.63
HARRIES Kirk U23 7.08.74, Hillingdon :
60H - 8.3i, 110H - 14.9/15.08
HARRIES Philip James Charles 7.04.66,
Derby & Co/Loughborough Studnts :
400H - 51.13 (50.01-88)
HARRIS Adrian U17 21.01.78, Blackheath :
60HY - 8.3i, 100HY - 13.9, 400HY - 56.54
HARRIS Michael U15 30.01.80, Team Solent :
LJ - 6.04
HARRIS Steven 17.11.61, Haringey :
10MR - 48:59
HARRISON Ererton W. 8.04.66, Thames VH :
60H - 8.3i (8.10i-89),
110H - 14.36w/14.60 (14.11-91)
HARRISON James 21.12.63, Blackheath/AUS :
5k - 14:26.5 (13:27.98-89), 10k - 29:30.84,
10kR - 29:43, 10MR - 49:07, HMar - 1:05:41
HARRISON Josh U20 14.08.75, Birchfield :
JT - 53.64
HARRISON Nick U17 24.09.77, Shaftesbury B :
1500 - 4:01.3, 400HY - 57.8
HARRISON P. U15, Southend :
PV - 3.10
HARRISON Paul U17 11.11.77, Durham Sch :
400 - 50.4 (52.81-92)
HARRISON Stephen U23 19.12.72, Blackh'th :
JT - 71.94
HART Andrew 13.09.69, Coventry Godiva :
800 - 1:49.8 (1:48.06-92), 1500 - 3:44.9,
1M - 4:03.3 (4:02.7-91)
HART Nathan U23 1.07.73, WS&E/Bristol Un. :
110H - 15.4/15.66w, HJ - 2.10 (2.10-93)
HARTIGAN John Patrick 4.03.65, Tipton :
3k - 8:14.37 (7:51.53-89)
HARTLEY Adam 27.02.69, Leeds :
400H - 53.15
HARTLEY Sam U15 27.11.79, Melksham :
80HB - 11.50w/11.66, PenB - 2662
HARTMANN Henrik U23 7.09.72, Enfield :
400H - 53.8/53.99
HARTVELD Adri 7.10.59, City of Stoke/HOL :
10k - 31:10.4 (30:20.01-92),
Mar - 2:22:56 (2:15.32-86)
HASSAN Eshref U15 7.12.79, Belgrave :
200 - 23.30w/23.59
HATTON Anthony 18.06.70, Haringey/Lough :
JT - 66.62 (71.86-93)
HAUNCH Stephen 6.04.70, Liverpool Pem :
TJ - 14.27
HAWKINS Christopher Michael 24.10.61, Bing :
3k - 8:12.43 (7:58.37i-88/8:04.33?/8:04.7-91),
3kSt - 8:38.39 (8:37.15-89)
HAWKINS James U15 14.12.79, Medway :
SPB - 13.92, HTY - 51.06, HTB - 57.52
HAYES Kerry D. 22.01.63, Milton Keynes :
3kSt - 9:12.70 (8:54.31-89)
HAYES Scott U23 4.01.73, Thames Valley :
SP - 14.73 (15.35-91), DT - 51.32 (51.36-93)
HAYFORD Kenneth N. 10.03.63, Cambridge H :
JT - 57.16 (69.90-87)
HAYNES Peter 18.09.64, Basildon :
5k - 14:05.05, 2kSt - 5:54.93,
3kSt - 9:05.67 (9:02.0-93)
HAYNES Simon U23 12.08.74, Windsor S & E :
300 - 34.4, 400 - 48.47

HAYWARD Andrew U23 26.10.74, Rowntrees :
JT - 59.66
HAYWARD Gregory 28.01.64, Peterbro/RAF :
JT - 58.20 (61.96-90)
HAYWARD Stephan U23 30.07.74, Edin/Sc Bord :
SP - 15.74, DT - 47.76
HEAD Paul 1.07.65, Newham & Essex B :
HT - 71.16 (74.02-90)
HEAD Stephen 21.10.58, Newham & Essex B :
SP - 14.23 (14.44-89)
HEAD-RAPSON David U17 26.05.78, Camb H :
400HY - 56.67
HEALEY Ed V40   54, London Irish/IRE :
HT - 55.92/56.96un
HEALY Graham 27.04.70, Havering :
200 - 21.7 (21.6-91/22.11-90)
HEALY Philip 1.10.70, Ballydrain :
800 - 1:52.5 (1:51.7-93),
1500 - 3:47.6 (3:43.8-93)
HEATH Brett U20 6.01.75, Havering :
PV - 4.20, Dec - 6579
HECHEVARRIA Eugene 30.12.63, Westbury :
TJ - 15.05
HEGGIE Jonathan U15 8.12.79, Trent P :
80HB - 11.87
HEGGIE Simon U20 12.01.76, Hallamshire :
400 - 48.1/48.26
HEMPENSTALL Alasdair U17 4.10.77, Tavist :
400 - 50.86
HENDERSON James Alistair 28.03.69, ESH :
100Y - 9.72, 100 - 10.37w/10.45 (10.21-87)
HENDERSON Sandy U20 7.07.75, ESH :
JT - 54.72
HENDRY Bryan U17 24.10.77, Irvine :
800 - 1:57.09
HENDRY Martyn U20 10.04.75, Edinburgh :
110HJ - 14.9/15.13 (14.81w/15.1-93),
110H - 15.49
HENRY Corri U20 9.12.76, Notts :
200 - 21.9/21.91w/21.95
HENTHORN James U20 20.02.77, Carm :
100 - 10.6w/10.78, 200 - 22.06
HERBERT John A.A. 20.04.62, Haringey :
LJ - 7.20 (7.94w-82/7.74-85)
HERRINGTON Gary 31.03.61, Rugby :
DT - 54.20 (56.02-87)
HESKETH James U17 18.10.77, Doncaster :
400HY - 56.74
HEWITT Daniel U15 13.11.79, Lincoln Well :
1500 - 4:20.64
HIBBERD Matthew J. U23 23.06.73, TVH :
800 - 1:49.42 (1:49.2-92),
1500 - 3:41.73, 1M - 4:02.36
HIBBERT Paul N. 31.03.65, Birchfield :
400H - 51.80 (51.58-93),
TJ - 14.31 (15.45w-86/15.30-85)
HIBBINS Kevin U15 7.11.80, Grantham :
200 - 23.6/24.01, LJ - 6.10
HICKIN Michael 29.08.64, Hounslow :
1500 - 3:44.86
HICKS Maurice 1.01.70, Hounslow :
HT - 52.80 (53.70-92)
HIGGINBOTTOM Ian 19.08.63, Beaumont Leys :
Mar - 2:26:45 (2:20:23-91)
HIGHLAND James 2.06.65, Diss/AUS :
DT - 49.18 (52.10-93), JT - 64.06 (67.76-93)
HILL David V40 31.12.50, Thames H & H :
10MR - 49:34

HILL Geoffrey 8.02.63, Swansea :
3k - 8:16.8 (8:02.3-88),
5k - 14:09.6 (14:01.90-88), 10MR - 49:24
HILL Kevin U23 17.06.73, Wigan :
JT - 66.60
HILL Matthew U17 15.12.78, Stainforth :
400 - 50.6 (53.13-92)
HILL Michael Christopher 22.10.64, Leeds :
JT - 86.36 (86.94-93)
HILL Robin U20 23.02.77, Hemsworth :
PV - 4.50
HILL Scott U23 8.05.72, Edinburgh :
HJ - 2.00 (2.00-89)
HILLIER James U17 3.04.78, Newport :
400HY - 56.08
HILSTON James U17 25.02.79, Belgrave :
400 - 50.15
HILTON Jon U23 11.01.74, Sale :
TJ - 15.06
HILTON Paul 21.01.68, Derby & Co :
1500 - 3:50.48
HINDLEY Christopher U20 21.01.76, Worksop :
HJ - 2.06, Dec - 6514,
DecJ - 6108 (6244-93)
HINDS Elphinston 15.07.60, Thames Valley :
TJ - 13.90 (15.20w-85/14.82-91)
HIRSCH Mark 12.04.66, Birchfield :
3kSt - 9:12.90
HISLOP Julian 9.01.60, Newham & Essex B :
SP - 13.71 (15.50-88)
HOBBS Justin 12.03.69, Cardiff :
5k - 13:45.53, 10k - 28:17.00,
10kR - 29:07 (28:45-93)
HOBDELL Ian 30.07.68, Hounslow :
3kSt - 9:14.06 (9:10.8-93)
HOBSON David U15 6.03.80, Leeds :
100 - 11.20w
HOCK S. U15, Wigan :
200 - 23.65w
HODGE Andrew J. 18.12.68, Blackh'th/CUAC :
110H - 14.9 (15.41w-92),
HJ - 2.00 (2.10-93), TJ - 14.63 (14.90w-93)
HODGE Daniel 8.03.63, Windsor S & E :
400H - 55.01 (54.1/54.23-92)
HODGKINSON Mark R. U23 20.07.72, Birch :
PV - 5.00
HODGSON Gavin U17 1.02.78, Border :
400HY - 57.92
HODGSON Louis U20 29.12.76, Wakefield :
DTJ - 42.10
HODGSON S. U15, City of Hull :
DTB - 39.94
HODSON James U17 28.09.78, Sale :
OctY - 4696
HOEY Michael 29.04.69, Bournemouth :
3kSt - 9:14.5
HOGG Alan U13 3.06.83, Steyning :
2kW - 10:58.6, 3kWR - 15:52
HOGSTON Philip U23 25.04.73, Blackheath :
5k - 14:18.31
HOLBROOK Andrew 24.11.70, Bristol :
HJ - 2.00
HOLDER Graham P. U23 16.01.72, Bexley :
HT - 57.40
HOLDSWORTH Ian U17 12.01.78, Old Gayt :
PV - 3.90
HOLGATE Craig U20 21.09.76, Barrow & F :
DecJ - 5172

HOLGATE Martin C. 2.11.65, Woodford Grn :
400H - 55.3, Dec - 6095 (6344w-93/6279-91)
HOLLADAY Robert U20 10.01.75, Rotherham :
3k - 8:28.0
HOLLAND C. U17 1.09.77, Thurrock :
100 - 11.1
HOLLAND Kevin U20 11.09.75, Crawley :
5k - 15:16.88
HOLLIDAY Ian U23 9.12.73, Gateshead :
HJ - 2.11
HOLLIER Steve U20 27.02.76, Wolves & B :
5kW - 26:19.36 (25:02.9-93), 10kWR - 47:38
HOLLIN Philip U13 14.11.81, Sheffield RWC :
2kW - 11:16.2o
HOLLINGSWORTH Eric M. 6.12.62, Old Gayt :
110H - 15.2 (14.8db-93/15.2-90/15.25w/15.26-93),
SP - 14.49 (15.27-93)
HOLLOWAY Alan J. 22.06.60, Charn/Lough :
JT - 65.08 (67.62-89)
HOLLOWAY Gareth P. 2.02.70, Splott C :
20kW - 1:35:40 (1:31:59-92)
HOLMES George U17 21.08.78, Liverpool H :
400HY - 57.73
HOLT Peter U20 12.02.77, Hemsworth :
PV - 4.20 (4.30-93)
HOLT Richard 28.11.71, Blackh'th/Sheff Univ :
400H - 53.6/53.69 (52.89-93)
HOLTON Robert U17 8.09.78, Berry H M:
HJ - 1.94i/1.90
HONNEYMAN Daniel U20 13.10.75, Chelt :
Dec - 5899
HOOPER Brian Roger Leslie V40 18.05.53,
Windsor S & E : PV - 5.01 (5.59-80)
HOOPER Nicholas U15 24.09.79, Yeovil Oly :
400 - 52.67, 80HB - 11.8/11.83w,
PenB - 2739
HOOPER Richard J.G. 29.03.58, Birchfield :
JT - 62.02 (70.10-89)
HOPE Steven U23 8.02.72, Tipton :
3k - 8:16.53, 5k - 13:59.07
HOPKINS Nicholas J. 28.08.66, Reigate :
800 - 1:52.3 (1:50.5-85),
1500 - 3:45.05 (3:43.24-85),
3k - 8:11.04i/8:15.3 (7:59.66-90)
HORSBURGH Ian Joseph U17 10.01.78, Sc Bord :
200 - 22.63w, 400 - 49.2/49.35
HORSFIELD John Neil 7.12.66, Newport :
800 - 1:52.2 (1:45.44-90)
HOUGH Robert S.D. U23 3.06.72, Sheffield :
1500 - 3:48.6 (3:46.0-92),
1M - 4:06.4 (4:05.4-92), 3kSt - 8:38.80
HOURIHAN Paul U20 7.11.76, Liverpool H :
110HJ - 15.2, HJ - 2.02, Dec - 6359
HOUSLIN Livon 2.11.60, Thames Valley :
JT - 55.52 (63.92-92)
HOUSTON Ross U15 5.12.79, Central :
1500 - 4:20.7
HOWARD Carl U23 27.01.74, Newham & E B :
LJ - 7.45 (7.76-93), TJ - 15.84
HOWARD John U20 16.09.75, Annadale Str :
SPJ - 14.12
HOWARD Kevin G. 7.02.66, Crawley :
1500 - 3:46.48 (3:45.3-89), 5k - 14:20.9,
3kSt - 8:51.04 (8:46.46-93)
HOWARD Paul 19.10.66, Woodford Green :
PV - 4.20i/4.20 (4.40-90),
DT - 40.72 (43.06-90), JT - 55.36 (65.10-91),
Dec - 6519w/6450 (7094-92)

HOWDLE Patrick 25.04.60, City of Hull :
Mar - 2:28:13 (2:26:37-92)
HOWE Christopher W. 17.11.67,
Woodford Gr/Lough :
DT - 42.42 (44.84-90), HT - 63.06 (63.74-90)
HOWIS Andrew U23 3.07.74, Edinburgh Univ :
100 - 10.80w
HUBBARD Nicholas U20 17.04.76, Banbury :
LJ - 6.94
HUDSPITH Ian 23.09.70, Morpeth :
1500 - 3:47.6, 3k - 8:10.33, 5k - 14:18.1
HUDSPITH Mark E. 19.01.69, Morpeth :
5k - 14:18.1 (13:51.73-91),
10k - 29:35.57 (29:02.38-92),
10kR - 29:14, HMar - 1:03:37, Mar - 2:12:52
HUGGINS Marlon A. 11.02.71, Thames VH :
HJ - 2.11 (2.12i-89)
HUGHES Aaron U15, Ulster Sch :
80HB - 11.8w
HUGHES Brian C. 6.01.70, R Sutton Coldfield :
PV - 4.25, Dec - 5816 (6098-93)
HUGHES Dean U17 22.09.78, Hounslow :
HTY - 57.60
HUGHES Dylan U20 27.10.75, :
2kSt - 6:20.0
HUGHES Gareth U23 22.10.73, Liverpool H :
110H - 15.2/15.31 (15.2-93), Dec - 5172w
HUGHES James U23 8.11.74, Cardiff :
60H - 8.18i, 110H - 14.2/14.39
HUGHES Kevin M. U23 30.04.73, Haringey :
PV - 5.25
HUGHES Lee U15 13.09.79, Telford :
800 - 2:00.88, 1500 - 4:12.8
HUGHES Richard U15 3.10.79, Cannock & St :
DTB - 38.68
HULA Martin 2.01.66, Shaftesbury Barnet :
5k - 14:06.56
HULSE G.Ewart W. 21.01.62, Colwyn Bay :
SP - 13.83i/13.64 (14.09-93),
DT - 42.32, HT - 51.26 (54.62-91)
HULSE Richard U17 22.09.78, Liverpool H :
PV - 3.80
HUMM Jason Alex 11.01.71, Cambridge H :
3kSt - 9:07.60
HUMPHREYS David James 10.10.69, Birch :
110H - 14.97 (14.30w-89/14.45-91)
HUNT Ian 2.12.64, RAF :
Dec - 5099
HUNT Jamie U15 29.11.79, Norfolk :
SPB - 15.27
HUNT Luke U17 8.10.77, Old Gaytonians :
1.5kSt - 4:34.42
HUNTE Alex U20 13.07.77, Haringey :
110HJ - 15.2, 400H - 52.98
HUNTER James U17 19.11.77, Westbury :
3k - 8:58.13,
1.5kSt - 4:26.0
HUNTER Roger U20 10.03.76, Skyrac :
JT - 54.44, Dec - 6565w/6563,
DecJ - 6958w/6705
HUNTINGFORD Damian U20 11.06.77, GEC :
JT - 59.18
HURDWELL Duncan L. 24.04.62, Maidenhead :
Mar - 2:26:56
HURRION James U23 11.11.73, Cov G/OUAC:
JT - 63.04 (70.16r-91)
HURST Craig 30.12.70, C of Stoke/Lough :
200 - 21.7/21.77w/22.05 (21.72w/21.81-92)

HURST Lee U23 29.07.72, East Cheshire :
2kSt - 5:52.7, 3kSt - 9:07.64
HUSSAIN Bashir 20.12.64, Stockport :
1500 - 3:48.1 (3:47.4-90),
3k - 8:08.43 (8:01.72-91),
5k - 14:11.27 (14:07.89-90),
10k - 29:16.29, 10kR - 29:27 (29:14-92)
HUTCHINSON Daniel U15 25.12.79, Bourne :
LJ - 6.05, TJ - 13.29
HUTCHINSON Michael Innes 5.10.65, Traff :
3kSt - 9:06.74 (8:50.61-92)
HYDE Daniel U17 5.10.77, Torbay :
1500 - 4:00.20
HYDE Timothy U23 22.02.72, Windsor S & E :
3kSt - 9:15.16 (9:14.5-92)
HYLAND Eamonn 23.07.60, Redhill/IRE :
Mar - 2:23:12 (2:17:58-92)
HYLTON Mark U20 24.09.76, Windsor S & E :
200 - 21.6/21.91, 300 - 32.9, 400 - 46.37

IBLE Keith 9.11.68, Shaftesbury Barnet :
TJ - 14.99
ILLIDGE Sam U20 4.02.77, Lincoln Well :
800 - 1:54.58
ILO Leke U17, Surrey Sch :
TJ - 13.60
INGRAM David U15 19.01.80, Brighton :
PV - 3.30
INGRAM Geoff 31.01.68, RAF :
Dec - 5841
INGRAM Stephen 22.09.70, Swansea :
110H - 14.9, HJ - 2.05, LJ - 7.91w/7.38
IRVING Anthony U20 30.04.75, Border :
HT - 50.94, HTJ - 58.32
IRVING Jan U20 4.03.77, Wirral :
LJ - 7.03w/7.02
IRWIN David U17 18.12.78, Annadale Str :
SPY - 15.12, DTY - 40.94
IVEY David U17 5.10.78, Windsor S & E :
400 - 50.7

JACK Christopher U17 17.11.77, Ipswich :
JTY - 54.62
JACKSON Alan, Stourport :
10kR - 29:30 (29:01-93),
10MR - 48:54 (49:23-92)
JACKSON Colin Ray 18.02.67, Brecon :
60 - 6.49i, 100 - 10.36 (10.29-90), 60H - 7.30i,
110H - 12.94wA/12.98 (12.8w-90/12.91-93)
JACKSON David U23 12.05.73, Rotherham :
100 - 10.92 (10.5wdb-89/10.53w/10.59-91)
JACKSON Gary 28.04.68, Birchfield :
PV - 4.65 (4.90-86)
JACKSON Lewis 12.02.71, Enfield :
3kSt - 9:25.82
JAMES Jordan U17 24.05.78, Tamworth :
JTY - 54.20
JAMES Nicholas U17 9.04.78, Cannock & St :
400HY - 57.39
JAMES Simon U20 21.01.77, Telford :
SP - 13.47, SPJ - 14.27
JAMES Simon R. U23 31.08.73, Wycombe :
400 - 48.4 (48.86-93)
JAMIESON Paul, Liverpool Pembroke :
200 - 21.9/22.57
JARRETT Anthony Alexander 13.08.68, Har :
100 - 10.45 (10.42w-87), 60H - 7.58i (7.50i-90),
110H - 13.1/13.22 (13.00-93)

342

JAY Shane U17 12.01.78, Luton :
1.5kSt - 4:30.12
JEFFERIES Adrian U17 12.04.79, Swindon :
TJ - 13.77
JEFFERSON T. U13, City of Plymouth :
75HC - 12.5
JEMI-ALADE Michael 13.10.64, Edin SH :
DT - 49.76 (52.38-87)
JENKINS Christopher U13 2.03.82, Liv H :
75HC - 12.1, LJ - 5.14
JENKINS William 13.07.71, Greenock Glen :
3kSt - 9:00.8 (9:00.8-93)
JENNINGS Gary U23 21.02.72, N&EB/Lough :
400 - 48.23, 400H - 50.60
JENNINGS Neil U17 18.09.77, Mandale :
400 - 50.93
JENSON Gary 14.02.67, Haringey :
JT - 64.10 (79.54-91)
JEPP Gary A. 23.06.66, AF&D :
JT - 58.18 (59.98-87)
JEREMIAH Sean U17 21.11.77, Old Gayt :
100HY - 13.86w/13.9
JERWOOD Geoffrey 1.10.58, Herne Hill :
Mar - 2:23:40 (2:17:04-89)
JEWERS William S. 27.09.62, Bas & MH :
HJ - 2.01 (2.14-86)
JOHN Jason 17.10.71, Newham & Essex B :
60 - 6.60i (6.60i-93), 100Y - 9.46,
100 - 10.08w/10.23,
200 - 20.86w/21.02 (20.51w-93/20.89-92)
JOHNSON Andre U20 9.01.77, Blackheath :
100 - 10.69w/10.7 (11.03-93)
JOHNSON Dean U20 31.12.75, Hallamshire :
JT - 59.86 (60.50-93)
JOHNSON James U20 8.06.77, Tipton :
HT - 48.96
JOHNSON Mark 7.09.64, Haringey :
PV - 5.11 (5.26-91)
JOHNSON Matthew U23 2.05.74, Hert & Ware :
110H - 15.4 (15.4/15.51-93)
JOHNSON Neville U17 3.01.78, Swansea :
800 - 1:57.74 (1:56.79-93)
JOHNSON Paul 8.03.68, Birchfield :
LJ - 7.12w/7.00 (7.94i-89/7.87w-88/7.85-89)
JOHNSON Peter U20 25.09.75, Liverpool H :
JT - 60.42
JOHNSON Richard 13.10.71, Thames Valley :
100 - 10.6/10.74, 200 - 21.62 (21.5-90)
JOHNSON Russell U15 14.09.80, Blackheath :
100 - 11.20w/11.54
JOHNSTON Ben U17 8.11.78, Wirral :
PV - 3.80
JOHNSTON Ian 4.06.64, Enfield/Falkirk :
3k - 8:20.17i (8:13.84i-91)
JOHNSTONE Kerr U13 3.09.82, Falkirk :
400 - 60.5
JONES Andres U20 3.02.77, Carmarthen :
5k - 15:11.65
JONES Egryn 1.11.71, Swansea :
PV - 4.50 (4.60-93)
JONES Gareth 14.12.68, Cardiff :
HT - 59.40
JONES Gary U23 15.07.72, Wigan :
HJ - 2.05 (2.06-91), LJ - 7.42w/7.12
JONES Louis U15 6.11.79, Phoenix :
1500 - 4:17.28, 3k - 9:33.7

JONES Martin John 21.04.67, Horwich :
3k - 8:12.09, 10k - 28:33.18,
10kR - 28:24, HMar - 1:03:05
JONES Michael U15 2.10.79, Cambuslang :
200 - 23.32
JONES Michael 23.07.63, Shaftes B/WLHS :
HT - 68.68 (72.10-88)
JONES Nathan U15 10.03.80, Sandown :
DTB - 39.02
JONES Neil U20 1.08.77, Wrexham :
HTJ - 47.44
JONES Paul U17 11.04.78, Wrexham :
100HY - 14.06w, PV - 4.11, OctY - 4225
JONES Peter 2.12.70, City of Hull :
1500 - 3:47.3
JONES Peter U23 8.10.72, Crawley :
JT - 55.48 (59.00-90)
JONES Richard W. U20 26.06.75, Neath :
JT - 59.06 (63.78-93)
JONES Robin Evans Hugh 1.11.55, Ranelagh :
Mar - 2:17:59 (2:09:24-82)
JONES Sean 21.03.69, Thames Valley/Army :
HT - 51.02 (54.88-92)
JONES Simon 23.02.65, Diss :
DT - 44.72dh/44.36 (44.44-86), HT - 51.88
JONES Stephen H. 4.08.55, Newport :
HMar - 1:03:56 (1:00:59-86),
Mar - 2:17:40 (2:07:13-85)
JOSEPH Darren U17 4.04.78, Solihull & S H :
HJ - 2.00
JOSEPH Rafer E.L. 21.07.68, Old Gaytonians :
60H - 8.24i, 110H - 14.7/15.03w/15.06,
HJ - 1.97i (1.98-91), PV - 4.81,
SP - 14.68i/13.45 (14.01-87), DT - 50.66,
JT - 59.92, Dec - 7663
JOUSIFFE Warren U20 27.05.77, Hounslow :
PV - 4.60
JOYCE Colin U13 21.10.81, Braintree :
400 - 60.4
JOYCE Daniel U23 9.09.74, Bedford & Co :
60 - 6.98i (6.88i-93),
100 - 10.48 (10.40w/10.47-93),
200 - 21.65 (21.5w/21.60w-93)
JUBB Mike 20.06.70, Derby & Co :
2kSt - 5:51.5, 3kSt - 9:03.61
JUDGE Andrew U20 24.05.75, Coventry G :
110HJ - 15.30w, 400H - 55.1/55.51
JUDGE Stuart U23 29.11.73, Coventry G :
HJ - 2.00

KABISWA Samuel 28.10.66, Croydon :
100 - 10.8, 200 - 22.0 (21.7/21.82-93),
400 - 47.5/49.19 (48.83-93)
KAISER Karl U20 26.02.75, Middlesbro & C :
SPJ - 13.67 (14.57-93), DecJ - 5749
KEATING Tyrone U13 25.02.82, Braintree :
100 - 12.3, 200 - 25.0
KEITH Andrew 25.12.71, Hereford/Prov Un :
800 - 1:48.66i (1:47.56-92), 1k - 2:20.05i,
1500 - 3:39.34 (3:39.06-93),
1M - 3:56.29i (4:03.57-92),
3k - 7:49.83i/8:02.81
KEITH Fraser U20 1.08.75, Grimsby :
JT - 54.78
KELLER Simon U20 10.11.76, Newark :
SP - 13.26, SPJ - 14.20
KELLY Bryan U23 29.12.73, Liverpool H :
SP - 14.99 (15.75-93), DT - 43.78 (46.86-93)

343

KELLY Paul U15 22.12.79, Oxford Sch :
JTB - 45.32
KEMP Michael U15 23.12.79, Leics WC :
3kW - 15:15.0, 5kW - 26:20.0, 5kWR - 25:45
KENDALL John 23.09.69, AF&D :
3k - 8:19.0 (8:09.1-91)
KENNARD Andrew 2.01.66, Walton :
110H - 15.4 (15.3-93),
400H - 54.2 (53.2/54.02-93)
KENNEDY J. U13, :
70HC - 11.7
KENNEDY Martin U15 12.10.79, Herts Sch :
80HB - 11.80
KENNY John David Patrick 17.12.70, Woodf'd Grn :
100 - 10.8/10.85 (10.4w-90/10.64-93),
200 - 21.18 (21.1-90/21.14w-89)
KENTISH Neil U17 30.09.77, Northampton :
200 - 22.57w/22.7
KEOGH Nigel 18.07.67, Blackheath/IRE :
400 - 49.0 (47.9-92/48.40-90),
400H - 53.31 (52.89-91)
KEOGHAN David U17 9.10.78, Bolton :
400HY - 56.45
KEOWN David U23 18.07.74, Manx H :
3kW - 13:15.2, 20kW - 1:39:49
KERR Eric 9.12.64, Luton :
HT - 54.16 (53.94-93)
KERR Glen U23 27.10.74, Bedford & County :
HT - 56.16
KERR Hugh U20 4.01.76, Har/Ayr Seaforth :
400 - 48.24
KERSLAKE Criag U23 29.08.74, Torfaen :
100 - 10.86
KESKA Karl U23 7.05.72, Birch/Oregon Univ. :
1500 - 3:48.72, 5k - 14:00.16
KETT Simon U20 9.10.75, Bournemouth :
HJ - 2.03 (2.03-93)
KHAFAS Jimmy U15 27.11.79, Enfield :
SPB - 14.03
KILLEN Neal A. 10.04.59, Aldershot Serv :
110H - 15.2 (14.55w/14.6/14.71-87),
SP - 14.22, DT - 42.46 (43.36-87),
Dec - 5451 (7011w-87/6944-85)
KILSHAW Jay U15 19.10.79, Thurrock :
400 - 52.2/52.91
KINDON James U20 18.06.76, Yeovil Oly :
DTJ - 42.50
KING Alistair Mark 16.09.62, Haringey :
Mar - 2:22:51
KING Allan 3.12.56, Leics WC :
3kW - 13:30.4 (12:08.8-85),
10kW - 46:34.0 (43:37.9-80),
20kW - 1:37:32 (1:28:30-85)
KING Daniel U13 30.05.83, Colchester Jog :
2kW - 11:11.0
KING Dominic U13 30.05.83, Colchester Jog :
2kW - 11:49.0
KING Edward U20 26.11.75, Ballymena & A :
400 - 48.67, 800 - 1:48.93
KING Philip U23 25.11.74, Coventry RWC :
3kW - 12:03.33 (12:01.89i-93/12:02.0-92),
5kW - 20:49.27 (20:16.40-93),
10kW - 43:41.5 (42:47.7-92),
20kW - 1:29:49, 30kW - 2:33:08
KING Shane U23 8.02.74, Kendal :
400 - 48.8/49.93
KING Tim U17 10.12.77, Holbeach :
SPY - 14.48, DTY - 41.04

KING-SMITH Ben U15 30.09.79, Somer Sch :
JTB - 45.78
KINGMAN Robert U23 21.02.73, N & EB/RAF :
PV - 5.02
KINSON Simon 1.01.71, Leamington :
10k - 29:52.06
KIRK Andrew U15 28.09.79, Ipswich :
800 - 2:02.1
KIRKHAM Kerry 5.03.69, Loughborough /IRE :
400H - 54.7/54.75 (53.69-89)
KIRKHAM Seth U20 9.09.75, Old Gaytonians :
JT - 56.58
KIRKPATRICK William U15 28.02.80, Lagan V :
SPB - 14.46, DTB - 39.84
KIRKWOOD Brian V40 20.09.52, Leslie Deans :
10MR - 48:39dh
KITNEY Timothy J. U15 26.04.80, Medway :
JTB - 50.20
KLOIBER Matthew 22.11.71, Bristol :
800 - 1:51.8
KNELLER Steven 9.11.71, Birchfield :
400 - 48.7/48.82 (48.29-93)
KNIGHT Andrew G. 26.10.68, Camb H/Lough :
400 - 48.8/48.93 (48.38-89), 800 - 1:48.38
KNIGHT Andrew U23 11.11.73, Luton/Lough :
100 - 10.77w/10.93 (10.6w/10.7/10.81-93),
200 - 21.62 (21.4-93)
KNIGHT David J. 7.12.64, Brighton :
5k - 14:28.9, 10kR - 29:40 (29:21-92),
10MR - 49:31
KNIGHT Steve 17.10.63, Cardiff :
5k - 14:20.45, 10k - 29:52.5
KNIGHTON Dean U15 16.03.80, Derby & Co :
SPB - 13.61
KNOWLES Bradley U20 17.11.76, Birchfield :
HJ - 2.01 (2.03-93)
KNOWLES Richard U20 12.11.75, Solihull & SH :
400 - 48.86
KOIKAI Amin U23   74, Ilford/KEN :
10k - 30:11.0, HMar - 1:05:28
KOLLIAS G., Oxford Univ :
HT - 46.96 (47.84-93)
KORDOWICZ Andrew U15 20.10.79, W Yorks Sch :
1500 - 4:20.82
KORJIE Haroun U23 17.02.72, Belgrave/SLE :
60 - 6.78i (6.77i-93), 100 - 10.46,
200 - 21.1w/21.31 (21.3-93)
KRUGER Alexander Eaton 18.11.63, Border :
110H - 14.96 (14.8w-89/14.9-90/14.92-93),
HJ - 2.16i/2.14 (2.20-88),
PV - 4.80 (4.80-92), LJ - 7.45 (7.57w-89),
SP - 14.76, DT - 43.44 (45.06-93),
JT - 60.04, Dec - 8078
KRUSZEWSKI Andrew P. 7.04.59, Camb H :
DT - 48.02 (51.26-92)
KUBOTA Kengo 26.06.68, Edin/Strath Un/JAP :
SP - 13.85, DT - 44.74

LADEJO Du'aine 14.02.71, Belgrave :
200 - 21.47i+/21.57w (20.96-93),
300 - 32.73, 400 - 44.94
LAFFLEY Stefan U17 10.09.77, Sale :
400HY - 57.96
LAING Robert H. 30.07.66, Liverpool H :
110H - 14.88w/15.04
(14.7w/14.8/14.82w-91/14.90-92)
PV - 4.50 (4.60-88), LJ - 7.23w/7.11,
JT - 61.92 (67.48-87), Dec - 7048 (7076-89)

LAMB Howard 13.03.69, Old Gaytonians :
SP - 13.77 (13.89-93)
LAMB Steven U20 10.10.75, City of Stoke :
400H - 53.55
LAMBERT B., Oxford Univ :
DT - 41.00 (42.34-93)
LAMBETH Mark U23 3.09.72, Enfield :
60 - 6.98i, 200 - 21.9, 60H - 8.02i,
110H - 14.2/14.31 (14.20w/14.24-93)
LANCASTER Dave 12.03.57, Rowntrees :
Mar - 2:27:11 (2:24:33-85)
LAND Mark U17, Bury :
1.5kSt - 4:37.9
LANGDON Stephen 1.01.58, Hercules Wimb :
JT - 60.34 (63.52-93)
LARKINS Paul Stephen 19.05.63, N & EB :
800 - 1:50.88 (1:47.13-84),
1500 - 3:42.88 (3:35.94-87),
3k - 7:57.02i (7:47.54-89)
LASHORE A., Serpentine :
100 - 10.8
LATHAM Mark U20 13.01.76, City of Stoke :
HJ - 2.11
LATTIMER Mark U17 21.02.78, Corby :
HTY - 52.16
LAUGHLIN Dale 28.12.66, Chelmsford :
5k - 14:28.4 (13:43.29-91),
10kR - 29:27 (28:55-93)
LAVELLE Keith U20 13.05.77, Telford :
JT - 53.24
LAWFORD Jonathon U20 30.06.76, N & EB :
400H - 54.9/55.19
LAWNICZAK Christian U23 24.03.72, Peterbro :
Dec - 5752
LAWRENCE Hector U17 1.11.77, Haringey :
DTY - 47.78
LAWRENCE Mark 26.01.71, Leeds/Notts Univ :
LJ - 7.11 (7.33-93), TJ - 14.27 (14.52-93)
LAWS Oliver U15 18.03.80, Wenlock O :
1500 - 4:15.7, 3k - 9:23.3
LAWS Richard U20 8.10.75, Morpeth :
HJ - 2.07
LAY Graham U20 13.11.75, Scarborough :
JT - 63.14
LEADER Steven 24.11.66, Enfield :
110H - 15.46 (15.2/15.50-89),
PV - 4.70 (4.90-90), Dec - 7078
LEAVER James U20 15.09.75, Bournemouth :
HJ - 2.03, TJ - 14.56w/14.40 (14.60w-93)
LEE David James 16.09.65, Blackh'th/Lough :
3k - 8:17.01 (8:09.94-88),
2kSt - 5:51.4 (5:39.39-88),
3kSt - 8:45.2 (8:31.22-92)
LEECH James U15 16.10.79, Notts Sch :
PenB - 2655
LEELAND Nick, Trafford :
200 - 22.0, 400 - 48.3
LEES Andrew U17 11.05.79, Edinburgh :
200 - 22.48i (22.88-93)
LEES James U17 3.07.78, Yate :
HJ - 1.95
LEES Simon U15 19.11.79, Solihull & SH :
1500 - 4:11.05, 3k - 9:16.0
LEESON Graeme U20 27.03.75, Verlea :
JT - 53.44 (54.10-93)
LEGGATE Richard U23 20.07.74, Gateshead :
110H - 15.3/15.45w (15.18w/15.62-93)

LEIGH Anthony 27.12.65, City of Stoke :
100 - 10.98 (10.79w/10.8-91),
200 - 22.02w (21.8-93)
LEIPER J. Allan 23.07.60, AF&D :
PV - 4.20 (4.70-87), Dec - 6044 (6441-89)
LENNON-JONES Donald 9.05.68, N & EB :
3kSt - 9:14.32 (9:06.4-89)
LENT M. U13, AF&D :
400 - 60.5
LEONARD Carl U23 19.01.73, Swansea :
1500 - 3:50.69, 5k - 14:21.67
LEONARD Michael U20 28.05.77, Thurrock :
DecJ - 5137
LESLIE Matthew U20 17.06.76, Wirral :
400H - 55.6/55.67
LETHBRIDGE Matthew U20 22.01.77, Craw :
DecJ - 5027
LEVETT William U20 6.09.75, Bridgnorth :
5k - 15:06.1
LEVY Noel U20 22.06.75, :
400 - 48.53i (47.8-92/47.82-93),
400H - 50.70
LEWIS Andrew 9.03.68, Highgate :
100 - 10.80w/10.89 (10.7-91),
60H - 8.4i (8.23i-93),
110H - 14.67w/14.8/14.88,
PV - 4.10, LJ - 7.53w/7.39,
SP - 14.09i/13.62, Dec - 7221
LEWIS Colin David 15.10.61, Rossendale :
10kR - 28:41 (28:14-86),
HMar - 1:03:03 (1:01:17-92)
LEWIS Dominic U23 14.09.72, Newham & E B :
110H - 15.5 (14.51-93)
LEWIS Iestyn U15 14.04.80, Carmarthen :
100 - 11.3w
LEWIS James 8.03.69, Swansea/IRE :
10MR - 48:09, HMar - 1:04:11
LEWIS Junior U13 03.03.66, Verlea :
TJ - 14.30 (14.11-93)
LEWIS Philip E. 12.01.70, Tonbridge/EUAC :
200 - 21.8 (21.74w-93/21.8-91)
LEWIS S. U15, Exeter :
TJ - 12.06
LEWIS Shane U23 22.08.72, Swansea :
JT - 69.68
LEWIS Simon U17 26.09.77, Oxford City :
HJ - 1.91
LEWIS Simon U20 31.08.75, Retford :
2kSt - 6:00.612bs/6:04.1 (6:02.0-93),
3kSt - 9:43.89
LILL Andrew Richard 9.08.71, Newham & EB :
400 - 48.27 (47.7-92/48.23-90),
800 - 1:47.00 (1:46.37-92),
1k - 2:20.66i (2:20.54-93), 1500 - 3:49.80
LINDER Peter 26.05.67, Coventry Godiva :
110H - 15.3
LINDLEY Ian 3.12.55, Bingley :
SP - 13.98 (17.87i/17.58-81)
LINE Mark 3.09.62, Liverpool Pembroke :
DT - 41.46 (43.72-93)
LINSKEY Christian U15 14.06.80, Barnsley :
PV - 4.30
LISIEWICZ John 18.07.62, Morpeth/AUS :
1500 - 3:50.4, 3k - 8:04.92, 5k - 14:01.24,
10k - 29:49.2, 3kSt - 9:22.12
LITHERLAND Guy 13.11.68, Birch/Lough St :
DT - 44.24 (48.34-93)

LITTLE Andrew 1.01.64, Shettleston :
10k - 30:49.72 (30:46.9-93)
LITTLE John V40 14.04.53, Border :
DT - 41.36/41.10 (43.38-89)
LITTLEWOOD Robert, Walthamstow :
100kR - 8:23:31, 24HrT - 218.000
LLEWELLYN Philip 2.09.61, Shaftesbury B :
3kSt - 9:14.50
LLOYD Joseph U23 9.04.73, Cheltenham :
400 - 48.2/48.27
LLOYD Martin U15 18.06.80, Bexley :
HJ - 1.83
LLOYD Stephen J. U23 2.03.72, Oxford City :
PV - 4.40i/4.20 (4.35-91)
LLOYD Steven J. U23 20.03.74, Border :
DT - 43.94
LLOYD-BENNETT Graham U20 26.10.76,
Tunbridge Wells : SPJ - 13.61
LOBO Jason 18.09.69, Blackburn :
800 - 1:49.3 (1:47.7-89),
1500 - 3:45.3 (3:44.14-93),
1M - 4:05.1 (4:00.39-91)
LOCKER David Alan U20 28.03.75, C of Stoke :
800 - 1:51.57
LONG Ashley D. 11.04.62, Coalville :
10k - 31:10.8,
LONG Nicholas U17 1.02.79, Mersey Schools :
100 - 11.1
LONGLEY G., Coalville :
10k - 31:10.8
LONSDALE Ian 8.09.71, Peterborough :
200 - 21.9 (21.7-91)
LOUGH Gareth 6.07.70, Annadale Str/Lough :
800 - 1:50.06 (1:49.01-93),
1500 - 3:35.83, 1M - 3:59.48
LOUGHRAN Stuart U20 19.02.76, Carm:
JT - 58.46
LOUISY M., Luton :
TJ - 14.47w
LOVETT David U17 13.09.78, Southampton C :
DTY - 42.14
LOW Chris U15 24.04.80, Arbroath :
80HB - 11.67, LJ - 6.00, PenB - 2804/2567
LOWE Andrew U20 6.03.76, Sale :
HJ - 2.06
LOWE Peter 4.07.65, Sheffield :
DT - 40.08
LOWERY Philip I. 4.08.63, Lancaster & Morc:
Mar - 2:27:33
LOWLES Adam U20 29.01.77, Scottish Bord :
100 - 10.9w/11.01 (10.86w-93),
200 - 21.9/22.16
LUCAS John Stephen 2.11.65, Wallsend :
1500 - 3:49.86 (3:46.3-84/3:46.30-90),
1M - 4:09.15
LUMSDON Kevin U23 3.03.74, Morpeth :
60H - 8.41i (8.12i-93), 110H - 14.20
LUND Simon N. 22.12.65, Wigan Phoenix :
Mar - 2:27:39
LUNDMAN Jonathan U13 7.12.81, Braintree :
JTB - 38.44, JTC - 40.58
LUSTGARTEN Anders U23 9.02.74, Ox C/OUAC :
400 - 48.94
LYMAN Richard U20 15.11.75, Halesowen :
DTJ - 41.96
LYNCH Andrew U23 28.06.74, Thames Valley :
HJ - 2.14 (2.16-93)

LYNCH Lawrence 1.11.67, Haringey :
400 - 47.5 (47.02-93),
400H - 50.24 (50.19-91)

MACDERMOTT Dylan 1.12.70, Belgrave :
PV - 4.20 (4.90i-92/4.85-90)
MACDONALD Duncan J. U23 30.03.74,
Croydon/Birmingham Univ. :
JT - 64.46 (65.70-93)
MACDONALD Mark U20 26.05.75, Bristol :
800 - 1:54.16
MACDONALD Richard U15 11.01.80, Perth :
200 - 23.6, 400 - 52.3/53.96,
HJ - 1.77, TJ - 13.19
MACEY Dean U17 12.12.77, Castle Point :
HJ - 2.00, LJ - 6.65, TJ - 14.53w/14.26,
SPY - 14.93i, JT - 54.42,
Dec - 5648, OctY - 5311
MACFADYEN John U23 1.08.72, ESH/StrathUn :
800 - 1:51.39 (1:50.46-92)
MACHARDIE Scott 26.06.69, Cambridge H :
JT - 57.68 (65.68-92)
MACKAY John C. 22.08.60, Shettleston :
1500 - 3:49.7 (3:46.79-91),
1M - 4:08.68 (4:08.67-92),
3k - 8:06.60 (8:06.2-90),
5k - 14:22.6 (14:16.4-90),
10kR - 29:44 (29:34-93)
MACKE Patrick 18.06.55, Grantham :
100kR - 7:13:37 (6:52:39-89)
#MACKENZIE Colin T. 30.06.63, Newham & EB :
JT - 80.82/79.16 (82.60-91)
MACKENZIE John 23.08.65, Bel/Dundee HH :
LJ - 7.41w/7.24 (7.32-93), TJ - 16.17
MACKIE Ian U20 27.02.75, Pitreavie :
100 - 10.50, 200 - 20.91
MADAR Abdi U13 25.11.81, Blackheath :
1500 - 4:35.47
MADDEN Michael J. 13.09.65, Newquay & P :
HT - 54.20 (55.92-93)
MADDOCKS Christopher Lloyd 28.03.57,
Plymouth City W :
20kW - 1:28:44 (1:22:12-92),
30kW - 2:18:14 (2:11:09-88)
MADIGAN Gregory 28.10.57, Team Solent :
DT - 42.00
MAFE Adeoye O. 12.11.66, Thames Valley :
200 - 21.78 (20.26w-90/20.54-85),
400 - 46.39 (45.30-93)
MAGAN A. U13, :
SPC - 12.61, DTC - 33.66
MAGNALL Andrew M. 1.03.62, Luton :
Mar - 2:25:47 (2:24:44-93)
MAGUIRE Peter U15 24.01.80, Oadby & W :
JTB - 45.64
MAINSTONE Keith U23 15.03.74, Horsham BS :
HJ - 1.98
MAITLAND Peter U23 21.01.73, Swansea :
60 - 6.91i (6.82i-92),
100 - 10.55 (10.5w-92),
200 - 20.96, 400 - 47.60
MALCOLM Anthony U20 15.02.76, Salisbury :
LJ - 6.92w (7.16-93)
MALCOLM Christian U17 3.06.79, Newport :
100 - 10.88, 200 - 22.2/22.36
MALCOLM Jamie 5.10.69, Wirral :
Dec - 5545 (5642-92)

346

MALEY Gavin U17 19.05.78, Havering :
1.5kSt - 4:29.7
MALINS Duncan U17 12.06.78, Crawley :
100HY - 14.1
MALLON Chris U23 4.08.72, Richmond & T :
HT - 48.76
*MANDY Mark U23 19.11.72, Cannock & St/IRE :
HJ - 2.24i/2.22 (2.24-93)*
MANGLESHOT Lawrence Philip 28.05.63,
Woodford Grn : 800 - 1:51.81 (1:50.4-85),
1500 - 3:47.2 (3:43.74-89)
MANNERS Ian 25.06.64, Swansea :
1500 - 3:49.8 (3:42.6-89),
1M - 4:06.9 (4:01.27-90),
3k - 8:13.82 (7:57.01-90)
MANSBRIDGE David C. 4.06.64, Telford :
Mar - 2:22:23
MANSFIELD Ian U23 27.11.74, Lincoln Well :
800 - 1:51.56
MARAR Leith 7.11.68, Belgrave :
SP - 14.74 (16.13-93), DT - 53.52 (54.58-93)
MARASA Saverio U15 19.09.79, Suffolk Sch :
TJ - 12.22
MARGIOTTA Stuart 19.11.69, GEC/Lough St :
1500 - 3:48.6 (3:44.94-92), 1M - 4:07.71,
3k - 8:11.68 (8:09.30-91)
MARK Kevin U20 15.09.76, Ealing,S & Mx :
60 - 6.9i/6.91i (6.9i/6.96i-93),
100 - 10.44w/10.60 (10.38w-93),
200 - 21.6w/21.7/22.06 (21.7-93/21.97-92)
MARKHAM Stephen U23 11.11.74, Middlesbro :
100 - 10.7/10.73, 200 - 21.8
MARKS Gareth U20 31.05.77, Swansea :
DT - 41.80, DTJ - 45.94
MARSDEN B., Wycombe :
110H - 15.5
MARSDEN Dwayne U23 25.10.73, Chesterf'ld :
JT - 62.44
MARSDEN Gavin U17 22.02.78, Wirral :
1500 - 4:03.0
MARSH Brett U20 20.01.76, Newquay & Par :
HTJ - 47.10, DecJ - 5290
MARSHALL Guy 24.09.71, Hull Springhead :
SP - 14.48
MARTIN Chris U23, Oxford City/Oxford Univ :
400H - 53.83
*MARTIN Chris 12.09.69, Newham & Essex B :
400H - 53.1/53.47*
MARTIN Eamonn Thomas 9.10.58, Basildon :
5k - 13:46.19 (13:17.84-89),
10k - 28:46.50 (27:23.06-88),
10kR - 29:36 (28:14-89),
HMar - 1:03:54 (1:02:52-93),
Mar - 2:11:05 (2:10:50-93)
MARTIN Nick U15 4.03.80, Old Gaytonians :
HJ - 1.78
MARTIN Paul U20 19.05.76, Cleethorpes :
400H - 54.98
MARTIN Paul U17 10.07.78, Tonbridge :
1.5kSt - 4:28.13
MARTIN Wayne U20 12.08.76, Trowbridge :
400 - 48.5/49.41
MARTORANA Vince U17 18.10.77, SB :
TJ - 13.58
MARWOOD Simon U17 6.04.78, Mandale :
1.5kSt - 4:31.2
MASON Anthony U20 8.03.76, Ipswich :
LJ - 7.24

MASON Gavin U20 6.04.77, Belgrave :
400 - 48.89, 800 - 1:53.33
MASON J. U20, Southampton City :
TJ - 14.00
MASON James Ryder U23 22.03.72, Cardiff :
SP - 16.12i/15.94
MASON Neil T. 10.02.71, Edinburgh :
SP - 13.97 (14.68-92)
MASON Robert U20 13.09.75, City of Stoke :
110HJ - 14.93w/15.1/15.33
MASSEY Ian U20 9.09.76, Liverpool H :
HJ - 2.04
MATARAZZO Antonio U15 27.03.80, Chelt :
100 - 11.43w/11.5, 200 - 23.5
MATE Anthony U23 15.12.74, Gateshead :
1500 - 3:50.85,
MATHERS E. U13, :
JTC - 32.94
MATHIESON Duncan Graham 8.03.69,
ESH/Aberdeen : LJ - 7.60
MATHIESON Simon U17 20.01.79, Bristol :
400 - 50.80
MATHISON George P. 4.10.61, Edinburgh SH :
3kSt - 8:59.55 (8:50.6-90)
MATTHEWS . U13, :
JTC - 32.96
MATTHEWS Anthony D. 17.12.62, Leeds :
PV - 4.25 (4.60-90)
MATTHEWS David U20 7.07.76, B & A :
JT - 52.54
MATTHEWS Edward U17 17.09.77, Hamps Sch :
1500 - 4:02.04
MATTHEWS John 29.12.64, Bracknell :
10k - 30:53.8 (30:34.3-93)
MATTHEWS Lawrence 11.08.65, Salf/OUAC :
10kR - 29:37 (29:18-92), 10MR - 48:57
MATTHEWS Simon 21.05.71, Kendal :
SP - 14.81, DT - 43.46
MAXWELL Ancell 17.01.69, Liverpool H :
200 - 21.56w/21.9/22.21 (21.8-91)
MAXWELL Stewart 29.06.58, Wirral/RAF :
JT - 61.54 (64.22-88)
MAY Christopher U23 19.09.72, Liverpool H :
1500 - 3:48.28 (3:45.06-93)
MAY D. U13, Humberside Sch :
HJ - 1.57
MAYNARD Darrell 21.08.61, Belgrave/Army :
800 - 1:51.17 (1:49.5a-88)
MAYNARD Martin 4.09.71, Birchfield :
400H - 55.34 (53.52-91)
*MAYNE Shaun 27.05.70, Bedford & Co/AUS:
100 - 10.8/10.82*
MAYO David U13 26.04.82, Hull Springhead :
HJ - 1.65
MAYO Thomas U20 2.05.77, Cannock & Staff :
1500 - 3:52.0
MAYOCK John Paul 26.10.70, Cannock & Staff :
1500 - 3:37.20 (3:36.45-93),
1M - 3:58.34 (3:55.57i-92/3:56.89i-93/3:56.90-91),
3k - 7:55.31i (7:48.47i-92/7:50.70-93),
5k - 13:50.58 (13:26.97-92)
MCADOREY John U23 16.09.74, B & A :
100 - 10.7w/10.87
(10.7w-91/10.83w-92/10.85-91),
200 - 21.82
MCAREE Simon U20 28.12.75, North S Poly :
60H - 8.34i, 60HJ - 8.15i,
110HJ - 14.10w/14.52, 110H - 14.43

347

MCBURNEY Paul U23 14.03.72, Lisburn :
100 - 10.7w (10.7dt-90/10.91-92),
200 - 20.81, 400 - 46.49
MCCAFFREY Nick Philip 26.06.68, Oadby & W :
10k - 30:42.9
MCCAW Charles U23 21.01.72, Woodford Grn/
Birm Un : 400 - 48.49 (48.3-90/48.43-92)
MCCOLGAN Peter Conor 20.02.63,
Dundee HH/Sparta : 10kR - 29:42 (29:27-91)
MCCORMICK Peter U17 7.02.78, B & A :
800 - 1:56.77
MCCOURT Steven 6.05.71, Wigan :
100 - 10.80w/10.82 (10.8-93),
200 - 21.03w/21.31
MCCOY Bryan U20, Ballymena & Antrim :
400 - 48.68
MCDADE Jason U15 3.04.80, Ipswich :
HJ - 1.77, LJ - 6.13,
PenB - 2619
MCDERMOTT Scott U20 2.12.75, E Kilbride :
DecJ - 6040
MCDEVITT Peter 1.03.68, Shettleston :
600 - 1:19.5, 800 - 1:51.02
MCDONAGH William U23 11.07.72, Leeds :
110H - 15.37
MCDONALD Denzil 11.10.65, N & EB :
SP - 16.10, DT - 48.56 (51.62-91)
MCDONALD Michael John 24.08.65,
Ballymena & Antrim/Border/Queen's Univ :
TJ - 15.78
MCDONALD Wayne Washington 5.10.70, Har :
200 - 21.46i (21.05w-89/21.10-91),
400 - 46.85 (45.88-91)
MCDOUGALL Alan U20 9.11.75, GEC :
800 - 1:53.67
MCEVILLY Brian U20 27.12.75, Southport :
SPJ - 13.97
MCEVOY Stephen 23.05.63, Met. Pol/WLHS :
HT - 55.46
MCFARLANE Alasdair U17 13.02.78, Granth :
100 - 11.0/11.05w/11.34, 200 - 22.3
MCGARRY Mark U20 16.02.77, Gateshead :
2kSt - 6:00.0
MCGEOCH Michael I. 15.08.55, Les Croupiers :
Mar - 2:27:12 (2:17:58-83)
MCGLYNN Fraser 2.09.63, Edinburgh :
110H - 15.12
MCGLYNN Trevor U17 6.06.78, Sparta :
100HY - 13.4w/13.6/13.82,
HJ - 1.90, OctY - 4545
MCGRATH David U20 8.09.75, Rowntrees :
SPJ - 13.60
MCGUINNESS Philip U17 4.10.77, Liv H :
1500 - 4:01.94
MCHARDY Stephen U20 8.01.76, Dudley & St :
400 - 47.48
MCHUGH Terrance 22.08.63, Herne Hill/IRE :
SP - 14.82 (15.07-93), JT - 82.14 (84.54-91)
MCILFATRICK Philip V40 5.02.54, Lisburn :
110H - 15.52 (14.7/14.99-84)
MCILROY Gary 6.04.67, Epsom & Ewell :
Mar - 2:24:49
MCILWHAM John U23 29.02.72, Blackpool :
400H - 53.89, Dec - 5845
MCINTYRE Liam U20 22.09.76, Edinburgh SH :
SP - 13.25i/13.06, SPJ - 15.25,
DT - 42.50, DTJ - 46.06

MCINTYRE Mark 14.10.70, Haringey :
100 - 10.86 (10.4w-90/10.60-91)
MCKAY Kevin John 9.02.69, Sale :
800 - 1:50.58 (1:45.35-92),
1500 - 3:37.86 (3:35.94-92), 1M - 3:53.64
MCKEAN Thomas 27.10.63, Haringey :
800 - 1:46.20 (1:43.88-89)
MCKENNA Andrew U15 3.01.80, Milton K :
1500 - 4:16.7, 3k - 9:18.2
MCKENNA Ray U20 14.09.75, Watford :
DTJ - 44.70
MCKENZIE David Colin 3.09.70, Shaftesbury B :
200 - 21.5/21.64 (21.54-90), 400 - 45.47
MCKERNAN Michael U17 28.11.78, Cov G :
TJ - 14.16
MCKINLAY Warren U13 4.10.81, Braintree :
400 - 60.5, 800 - 2:18.3
MCLAREN Delroy 29.01.70, Cannock & Staff :
100 - 10.7w/11.08
(10.6w-93/10.75w-89/10.78-91)
MCLAUGHLIN Ian U20 4.01.77, WS&E/WLHS :
HT - 49.10 (51.50-93), HTJ - 51.52
MCLEAN Edward 19.11.69, Wolves & B :
800 - 1:51.6
MCLENNAN Stephen U17 17.11.78, Houns :
PV - 4.20
MCLEOD David 26.03.63, Morpeth/Bella :
PV - 4.30 (4.60-93)
MCLOUGHLIN John U23 26.10.73, Enfield :
100 - 10.7/10.85 (10.6w-93/10.67w/10.68-92),
200 - 22.04 (21.44-93)
MCLOUGHLIN Martin 23.12.58, Liv Pem :
10k - 28:55.57 (28:15.58-86),
10kR - 28:49 (28:45-88),
10MR - 47:52 (46:26un-87/47:02-93),
HMar - 1:02:45 (1:02:50un-89/1:02:57-88)
MCMENEMY Neil 6.04.67, N&EB/Central :
LJ - 6.92, TJ - 15.13
MCMILLAN Gregor William 4.04.70, Haringey :
400 - 48.07 (47.41-92)
MCMULLAN Ian U17 15.06.78, Lisburn :
SPY - 15.46
MCMULLAN Ian U23 3.05.74, Met. Police :
DT - 44.24 (47.10-91)
MCMURRAY John U23, Devon Sch :
3k - 8:13.1
MCNAB Richard U15 22.02.80, Rotherham :
400 - 52.13
MCNAMARA Paul U17 3.10.78, Luton :
HTY - 49.24
MCNICHOLAS Alan U23 10.12.74, Bed & Co :
HT - 57.66
MCPHERSON Gavin U17 17.09.77, Barrow & F :
800 - 1:57.10
MCPHERSON Scott U23 24.03.73, Soton C/OUAC :
110H - 15.4
MCWHAN Steven U17 2.03.78, Nithsdale :
HJ - 1.91
MEAD Darren 4.10.68, Belgrave :
1500 - 3:48.7 (3:45.8-86), 3k - 7:56.39,
5k - 13:50.7, 10kR - 29:31,
10MR - 49:09 (48:45-89),
3kSt - 8:49.76 (8:37.68-93)
MECHAM Robert U17 14.09.77, Steyning :
3kWR - 14:35 (13:29-92), 10kWR - 52:46
MEDCROFT Lyndon U23 20.10.72, Sale :
JT - 60.36 (64.46-91)

MELLOR Dean 25.11.71, Rotherham :
PV - 5.10i/5.10 (5.22-91), Dec - 5219
MELVILLE-JACKSON James U23 24.01.74,
Windsor S & E/Loughborough Studnts :
400H - 55.2/55.35
MELVIN Gareth U15 11.12.80, Border :
3k - 9:32.90
MENDELLSOHN Barron U15 1.09.79, Herc W :
80HB - 11.80
MENSAH Andrew Peter 30.11.71, Haringey :
60 - 6.80i, 100 - 10.39w/10.49, 200 - 21.14
MENTON John 2.05.70, London Irish/IRE :
DT - 50.88 (52.96-93)
MIDDLETON Barry U20 10.03.75, Aberdeen :
400 - 49.30i/49.40, 400H - 53.53
MIDDLETON Bryn U20 16.02.76, Cardiff :
100 - 10.7w/10.80w/10.90, 200 - 21.77
MIDDLETON Graham 17.09.60, Cannock & St :
HT - 53.32 (55.00-82)
MILES David 16.11.65, Gateshead :
3k - 8:02.03, 5k - 13:46.66,
10k - 30:27.13, 10kR - 29:43
MILES Mark U20 24.03.77, Solihull & S Heath :
1500 - 3:52.91
MILES Paul U15 14.09.80, Birchfield :
PV - 3.10
MILES Paul U13, :
2kW - 11:53.0
MILLER Jonathon U15 10.06.81, W Mid Sch :
TJ - 12.16
MILLER Mark 10.11.71, Enfield :
HT - 54.16 (56.12-93)
MILLER Pat 21.02.67, Barrow & Furness :
3kSt - 9:02.2 (9:06.67-92)
MILLER Richard 29.03.67, Shaftesbury Barnet :
800 - 1:52.67 (1:51.8-89)
MILLS Joseph U23 9.07.72, Chelmsford :
800 - 1:51.30, 1500 - 3:45.7, 1M - 4:05.42
MILNER Robert U17 28.12.77, Belgrave :
400 - 50.8, 400HY - 56.70
MILNES Adrian U20 17.01.75, Harborough :
100 - 10.79
MINNIKIN Steve U23 4.01.72, Doncaster :
HT - 60.60 (61.76-93)
MITCHELL Ian U20 10.03.76, Skyrac :
1500 - 3:52.3
MITCHELL Paul U17 18.07.78, Edinburgh SH :
100HY - 14.09, 400HY - 57.75
MITCHELL Stephen U17 1.09.77, Epsom & E :
400 - 49.6, 400HY - 55.3
MITCHELL Terrence 23.08.59, Fife :
Mar - 2:20:24 (2:17:56-92)
MITCHENSON David U17 4.09.78, Swindon :
1.5kSt - 4:34.95
MOLE Adam U20 31.08.75, Northampton :
400 - 49.04 (47.84-93)
MOLLOY Thomas U23 25.03.73, Army :
Dec - 5102
MONEY Daniel U20 7.10.76, Sale :
100 - 10.91, 200 - 21.81w/21.91
MONK Stuart U17 23.03.79, Loughton :
3kW - 14:31.2, 3kWR - 13:59, 5kW - 23:46.2,
5kWR - 23:06, 10kWR - 50:20
MOONEY John U15 23.10.79, Morpeth :
1500 - 4:17.74
MOORE Andrew, Rotherham :
HT - 48.90 (49.78-92)

MOORE Colin 25.11.60, Bingley :
5k - 14:17.8 (13:33.95-90),
10k - 29:17.32 (28:13.13-90),
HMar - 1:03:33 (1:02:22-85), Mar - 2:13:34
MOORE David U17 25.04.79, Liverpool H :
1.5kSt - 4:34.7
MOORE J. U13, Poole :
HJ - 1.57
MOORE Neil 1.04.61, Barnsley :
Mar - 2:28:28
MOORE Richard U23 19.01.73, Birchfield :
100 - 10.7w/10.85w/10.90,
200 - 21.9/21.93 (21.88w-92)
MOORE Stephen R. V45 17.12.47, Herts & W :
100kR - 7:18:46
MOORHOUSE Julian 13.11.71, Leeds :
5k - 14:28.1
MORELAND John R. 13.09.58, Rugby :
DT - 50.80
MORGAN Mark U23 19.08.72, Cardiff :
3k - 8:00.50, 5k - 13:59.46
MORGAN Michael 30.07.66, Belgrave :
HJ - 2.00,
LJ - 7.75 (8.01wAUS/7.92AUS-86),
TJ - 14.52w, SP - 13.84, JT - 61.62
MORGAN Nathan U17 30.06.78, Leics Cor :
LJ - 7.25w/6.81
MORGAN Noel U17 20.11.78, Trowbridge :
400 - 50.74
MORGAN-LEE Andrew 1.03.69, Soton City :
3kSt - 9:19.7 (9:14.00-93)
MORLEY Nick U17 15.04.78, Colchester & T :
JTY - 53.34
MORLEY Roger U17 20.09.77, Lincoln Well :
800 - 1:54.99
MORRELL Anthony 3.05.62, Morpeth :
800 - 1:50.15 (1:44.59-88),
1500 - 3:41.50 (3:34.1+-90/3:35.60-89),
1M - 4:01.06 (3:51.31-90)
MORRIS Darrin L. 28.07.67, Belgrave/Pitr :
SP - 13.90 (14.92i/14.85-89),
DT - 57.72 (58.58-91)
MORRIS Edward U15 3.03.80, Stourport :
PenB - 2510
MORRIS James U15 2.12.79, Swansea :
LJ - 6.06w
MORRIS Mark 29.12.65, Shaftesbury Barnet :
200 - 22.08 (21.7/21.78-89), 400 - 46.77
MORRIS Wyn 25.02.61, Shaftesbury Barnet :
TJ - 14.11 (15.28w-85/15.19-89)
MORRISON Christopher 27.12.70, Trafford :
400H - 54.7 (52.6-91/54.24-88)
MORTLEY Martin Trevor U17 8.09.78, Medway :
SPY - 13.87
MORTON Leslie 1.07.58, Sheffield RWC :
3kW - 13:45.44 (12:24.0-85),
35kW - 2:50:01 (2:37:27-91),
50kW - 4:32:25 (3:57:48-89)
MORTON Richard U15, Stockport :
DTB - 38.78
MOSCROP Howard W. 16.12.57, Crawley :
400H - 54.02 (51.4-84/52.66-93)
MOSELEY Stephen J. 10.01.66, Cardiff :
1500 - 3:47.1
MOSES Alistair U17 5.07.78, Reigate :
1500 - 4:01.98
MOSS Alex U23 21.09.72, Thames Valley :
3kSt - 9:16.49

349

MOSS Jonathan U17 24.09.78, Sale :
200 - 22.39w/22.6
MOTHERWELL Ben U17 28.02.78, Camb & C :
OctY - 4234
MOTLEY Ryan U15 27.10.79, Lincs Sch :
PenB - 2568
MOULTON David U13 7.09.81, S London :
400 - 60.0
MOWBRAY Philip U23 19.03.73, EUAC/Hunter's BT :
1500 - 3:41.63,
MUIR James U17 30.04.78, Normandy Park :
1.5kSt - 4:37.05
MUIRHEAD James Cameron 26.01.71,
Liverpool H/Loughborough Studnts :
SP - 15.95 (16.14-93), DT - 51.82
MULCAHY Jason U23 26.05.73, Blackheath :
SP - 15.39 (15.98-93)
MULLEN Robert 8.08.64, Army :
JT - 63.78 (64.90-87)
MUNDAY Steven U13 15.10.81, Morpeth :
1500 - 4:43.0, 1M - 5:15.1, 3k - 10:17.4
MUNDEN Craig U20 24.12.76, Bournemouth :
DTJ - 41.66
MUNROE Gary 12.04.69, Newham & Essex B :
LJ - 7.08
MUNROE John 6.01.69, Thames Valley/RAF :
LJ - 7.57 (7.62w/7.57-93)
MURCH Kevin 11.11.58, Rugby :
JT - 58.90 (69.02-89)
MURDOCH Steven 16.04.61, Border :
10k - 30:28.59
MURFETT Jody U15 3.12.79, West Norfolk :
80HB - 11.82
MURNEY Graham U13 20.09.81, Leics WC :
2kW - 11:08.0 (11:08.0-93)
MURPHY Andrew U15 14.09.79, Shaftes B:
1500 - 4:17.90, 3k - 9:31.6
MURPHY Ciaran 2.09.71, Sale :
800 - 1:50.1, 1500 - 3:43.8 (3:43.5-92)
MURPHY Darragh U23 20.01.74, L Irish/Lough :
HJ - 2.05 (2.11-91)
MURPHY James U23 20.03.73, Corby :
SP - 15.04, DT - 55.24
MURPHY John U15 6.03.81, Leics WC :
3kW - 14:31.2, 5kWR - 25:04
MURRAY Alan 2.05.67, Kilmarnock/Edinb :
400 - 48.67 (48.1-93/48.34-87)
MURRAY Anthony U15 12.10.79, Airdrie :
PenB - 2814/2480
MURRAY Gerard U17 13.02.78, Airdrie :
OctY - 4484
MURRAY Nicholas U13, AF&D :
3k - 10:34.1
MURRAY Thomas 18.05.61, Spango Valley :
3k - 8:18.10i (8:11.46i-92),
10k - 29:12.35, 10kR - 29:29 (29:18-88),
10MR - 48:15dh,
HMar - 1:05:38 (1:05:34-92)
MUSSETT Adrian U23 14.04.72, Chelmsford :
5k - 14:25.84
MYERS Nicholas U15 25.03.80, Birchfield :
TJ - 12.43
MYERSCOUGH Carl Andrew U15 21.10.79,
Blackpool : SPB - 15.03, DTB - 43.34
MYLES Gary 3.02.63, Cannock & Stafford :
110H - 15.43 (14.55-83)

N'FALLO Didier 7.10.68, Ilford :
100 - 10.7
NAGEL Gary Roderick 4.06.62, Valli :
10MR - 49:32 (48:21+-90)
NAISMITH David U15 15.12.79, Derby & Co :
400 - 51.8
NARTEY Michael U20 12.06.75, Blackheath :
60 - 6.88i,
100 - 10.7/10.73w/10.78 (10.5w-92/10.67-91)
NASH Barry 4.09.71, Milton Keynes :
SP - 14.17
NASH Kevin U20 6.02.77, AF&D :
3k - 8:28.6, 2kSt - 6:00.97, 3kSt - 9:17.80
NASH Robin 9.02.59, Westbury :
10MR - 49:34, Mar - 2:14:52
NAYLOR Donald 5.09.71, Swansea/CUAC :
3kSt - 9:21.8
NAYLOR Jonathan U17 19.04.78, Chester & E :
TJ - 13.97
NEBLETT Gary U15 27.12.79, Enfield :
HJ - 1.80
NEELY Ian U23 29.12.74, Ballymena & A :
400H - 54.42
NEPORT Darren U15 4.09.79, Enfield :
PV - 3.30
NERURKAR Richard David 6.01.64, Bingley :
5k - 13:36.89 (13:23.36-90),
10k - 28:53.03 (27:40.03-93),
10kR - 28:25, Mar - 2:11:56 (2:10:03-93)
NESBETH Michael U17, Croydon :
400HY - 58.0
NEVIS John 24.12.69, City of Hull :
HT - 56.18 (56.10-93)
NEWENHAM Timothy O. 1.04.60, Card/Lough :
JT - 57.60 (70.30-89)
NEWHAMS Gregory 27.07.58, Bridgend :
10MR - 49:31 (48:21+-90),
Mar - 2:19:38 (2:17:20-90)
NEWMAN Lee Jon U23 1.05.73, Blackheath :
SP - 17.94, DT - 58.34,
NEWMAN Mark 5.06.71, Trafford :
400H - 55.2
NEWMAN Matthew 13.10.67, Old Gaytonians :
HJ - 2.01 (2.05-87)
NEWMAN Stephen 26.12.70, London Irish/IRE:
400 - 47.44
NEWMARCH Alastair U17 28.11.78, Lincs Sch :
400HY - 57.20
NEWPORT Spencer John 5.10.66, Blackh'th :
1500 - 3:49.1 (3:43.46-87),
3k - 8:04.51 (8:02.34-90),
5k - 14:04.5 (13:56.82-92),
2kSt - 5:45.11 (5:37.74-90),
3kSt - 8:49.4 (8:40.87-92)
NEWTON Keith 12.12.68, Woodford Green :
400H - 54.8/55.23 (54.6/55.03-93)
NEWTON Marc D. U15 15.03.80, Tamworth :
400 - 51.0, 800 - 2:03.52i/2:03.8,
80HB - 11.58w, HJ - 1.84,
LJ - 6.36w/6.26, PenB - 3187
NICHOLL David 16.09.69, Ballymena & A :
HT - 48.80 (49.16-93)
NICHOLL Michael 29.07.61, R S Coldfield :
PV - 4.20 (4.60-93)
NICHOLLS Clinton U17 16.02.79, Basildon :
HJ - 1.95
NICHOLLS John S. 1.09.65, Sale :
SP - 14.51 (15.31-88)

NICHOLSON Martin 9.12.70, Birchfield :
  60H - 8.05i (8.01i-93), 110H - 13.8/14.14
NICOLSON Christian U23 19.09.73, EUAC :
  1500 - 3:50.6, 3k - 8:11.09
NIELAND Nicholas U23 31.01.72, SB/Bris Un :
  JT - 76.28
NIMMO Thomas 9.05.71, Edinburgh SH :
  400 - 48.6/48.70 (47.99-92),
  800 - 1:50.2 (1:49.0-92)
NISBET Clive Lawrence 18.06.61, ESH :
  HT - 57.04 (62.40-86)
NIXON William 9.02.68, Bournemouth :
  Mar - 2:27:29
NOAD Ben U20 6.05.76, Bristol :
  1500 - 3:52.36, 3k - 8:25.0, 5k - 14:33.3
NOBLE Craig U20 21.06.75, Fraserburgh :
  HJ - 1.96
NOBLE Ian U20 2.04.77, Leeds :
  PV - 4.20
NOLAN David 25.07.69, Soton City/Army :
  200 - 22.0, 300 - 33.9, 400 - 47.5/47.66
NOLAN David U20 16.05.75, Swansea :
  HJ - 2.06
NOON Jeremy U17 20.09.77, Coventry G :
  200 - 22.45w/22.6
NORMAN Anthony 5.07.63, Woking :
  JT - 59.78
NORRISS Dominic 29.12.71, Hounslow :
  HJ - 2.00 (2.00i/2.00-89)
NORTHROP Paul 15.01.70, Enf/London Univ. :
  3kSt - 9:06.5 (8:51.25-90)
NOSKO Philip U13 29.01.82, Andover :
  400 - 60.1, 800 - 2:18.4
NOTTINGHAM Gareth U15 20.12.79, Bucks Sch :
  HTB - 42.56
NSUDOH Immanuel U23 8.04.72, Croy/NIG :
  TJ - 14.14 (14.40-93)
NUTTALL John Barry 11.01.67, Preston :
  1M - 4:01.57 (3:58.83-91),
  3k - 8:04.??+ (7:51.58-93), 5k - 13:23.54

O'BRIEN Anthony 14.11.70, Liverpool H :
  10MR - 49:31, 3kSt - 9:05.2
O'BRIEN Barry U20 3.07.76, Middlesbro & C :
  400 - 49.46
O'BRIEN Liam U20 17.05.75, Skyrac :
  800 - 1:54.4,
O'CONNELL Christopher A. 17.01.59, Leeds :
  HT - 48.46 (52.98-87)
O'CONNOR Kevin 20.04.67, Cornwall AC :
  Mar - 2:26:04
O'DELL Timothy 29.05.70, Woodford Green :
  400 - 47.43 (47.37-90)
O'DONNELL A. U13, Ealing,Southall & Mx :
  800 - 2:16.3
O'DONNELL B. U20, :
  100 - 10.8w
O'DOWD Matthew U20 13.04.76, Swindon :
  5k - 15:09.6, 2kSt - 5:55.89,
  3kSt - 9:10.83
O'HANLON Sean U20 3.09.76, Dacorum :
  JT - 58.18
O'HARE David U17 1.12.77, Deeside :
  100 - 11.00w, 200 - 22.5
O'LEARY David U15 3.08.80, Liverpool H :
  80HB - 11.63
O'NEILL Christopher U17 19.09.77, Oadby & W :
  3k - 8:59.62

O'RAWE Andy 8.09.63, Southend :
  3kW - 12:52.8, 10kW - 46:29.31,
  20kW - 1:35:24
O'RAWE Jamie U23 3.02.73, Southend :
  3kW - 12:53.7 (12:46.7-92)
O'REILLY Michael 23.04.58, Highgate :
  Mar - 2:15:46 (2:10:39-93)
O'RILEY Matthew U15 13.11.79, Wirral :
  PV - 3.15
O'SHEA John 13.04.67, Hounslow :
  1500 - 3:50.78 (3:47.5-90)
OAG Keith U17 11.11.77, Elgin :
  HJ - 1.98
OAKES Jason U17 29.09.77, Gateshead :
  JTY - 60.20
ODWAR David U20 23.12.76, Oxford City :
  JT - 57.68
OGBETA Mathias 19.06.68, Preston/NIG :
  LJ - 7.09, TJ - 15.17
OHRLAND Stuart U20 6.09.75, Chelmsford :
  HJ - 2.17, DecJ - 5133
OKOTIE Mclean 31.07.69, Serpentine :
  60 - 6.9i, 100 - 10.5/10.60
OKWUOSA Olisa U15, Middlesex Sch :
  100 - 11.5, TJ - 12.14
OLD Alan U15 1.12.79, Gateshead :
  800 - 2:02.6, 1500 - 4:16.9
OLD Christopher U17 3.12.77, Houghton-le-Sp :
  1500 - 4:03.36
OLD Timothy U15 29.09.79, Millfield Sch :
  80HB - 11.86
OLIVER Geoff, :
  24HrT - 222.720
OLIVER Michael J. V40 23.03.53, Brighton :
  SP - 14.12 (15.67-91)
OLLIVE . U13, Crawley :
  PV - 3.00
OLUOCH-OLUNYA Ben 25.01.70, Milton K :
  400 - 48.16
OMOMO Ola U15 6.03.80, Dartford :
  LJ - 6.16
ONOURA Iwobi U23 21.05.74, Haringey :
  TJ - 14.12 (14.70-93)
ONUORAH Onochie C. U23 16.10.73, SB :
  LJ - 7.39 (7.43w-92)
OPARKA Richard U13 28.07.82, Tayside :
  TJ - 10.36
ORAM Russell U15 14.08.80, Bas & MH :
  JTB - 46.14
ORCHARD Karl 6.01.70, Leics WC :
  3kW - 13:23.7 (13:12.0-93),
  10kW - 48:40.9 (46:27.0-93)
OSBORNE M. U17, :
  100 - 11.1
OSEI Amofa U23 15.12.73, Ipswich/OUAC :
  TJ - 14.33
OSTAPOWYCZ Pawlo H. V40 1.07.52, Traff :
  JT - 58.12 (60.38-93)
OSUIDE Stanley U23 30.11.74, Belgrave :
  HJ - 2.05 (2.15-91)
OTENG Samuel U17 12.04.78, Shaftesbury B :
  OctY - 4495
OTTER Darren U23 6.03.74, Doncaster :
  HJ - 2.05i/2.05 (2.07-93)
OVERTHROW Stuart U20 13.06.75, Glous :
  1500 - 3:52.3, 2kSt - 5:53.732bs/5:54.16,
  3kSt - 9:29.62

OVERTON Nicholas A. 18.12.61, Nene Vall H :
2kSt - 5:49.3, 3kSt - 9:13.46
OVINGTON Neil J. 26.01.63, Thames Valley :
1500 - 3:46.2 (3:43.2-86)
OWEN John N. 28.10.64, Swansea :
HT - 51.76 (52.74-88)
OWEN Neil U23 18.10.73, Belgrave :
60H - 7.86i, 110H - 13.80
OWEN Sion U17 6.03.79, Crewe & Nantwich :
OctY - 4224
OXBOROUGH Wayne 10.11.66, Thames H&H :
5k - 14:35.26, 10k - 30:19.61
OXLEY Neil U15 7.12.79, Newark :
JTB - 46.02
OYEDIRAN Ademola 27.11.59, Herne H/NIG :
TJ - 15.71 (15.91i/15.78-84)

PACKER Julian U15 2.09.79, Exeter :
400 - 52.77
PACKHAM Dean Conrad 9.04.67, Crawley :
400 - 48.8/49.14 (48.0-89/48.61-86)
PAINE William N. 30.03.64, Ashford :
Dec - 5019 (5928-91)
¶PAINTER John J. T. 12.06.58, Norfolk :
SP - 13.87 (16.32i/16.09-89),
DT - 41.68 (50.36-88)
PAINTER Trevor 10.08.71, Wigan :
200 - 21.8, 400 - 48.04
PAISLEY Derek U23 1.12.73, Pitreavie/EUAC :
400H - 52.83
PALMER Adrian M. 10.08.69, Cardiff :
HT - 62.56
PALMER Glenn U23 8.11.74, Crawley :
100 - 10.96,
PALMER James U17 21.04.78, Norfolk :
PV - 3.70
PALMER Karl 5.02.66, Swansea :
3kSt - 9:19.4 (9:00.8-92)
PALMER Keith A. 19.11.64, Southend :
400 - 48.8/50.85 (48.8-93/48.92-92)
PAMAH David 27.11.64, Highgate :
800 - 1:52.3 (1:50.44-93)
PAMPHLETT Tim U15 18.02.81, GEC :
JTB - 47.72
PANCHEN Neil 30.10.69, Thames Valley/
Cambridge University :
5k - 14:30.04 (14:13.3-93)
PANNELL Gregory U15 24.07.80,
City of Plymouth :
HTB - 44.38
PARK Dean U17 23.09.77, Newham & E B :
200 - 22.1, 400 - 49.15A (50.6-93/52.17-92),
400HY - 53.64
PARK Iain U23 16.07.74, Hillingdon/Falkirk :
DT - 42.06 (42.26-93), HT - 54.58
PARKER Andrew Jamie U23 20.11.74, SB :
800 - 1:49.62
PARKER David U15 28.02.80, Scarborough :
JTY - 54.58, JTB - 55.96
PARKER John W. V40 31.10.54, Tipton :
Mar - 2:27:30 (2:23:26-92)
PARKES Lee U20 23.12.76, Rotherham :
DecJ - 5149
PARKIN John U17 23.02.79, Colwyn Bay :
HTY - 48.54
PARLEY Martin U17 26.07.78, Bristol :
PV - 4.20

PARLEY Simon M. U20 6.04.76, Bristol :
DecJ - 5731
PARR Stephen 18.03.59, Gateshead :
3kSt - 9:15.0 (8:52.8-90)
PARRY Jonathan U15 13.04.80, Swansea :
PV - 3.60
PARRY Philip John 4.10.65, Old Gaytonians :
JT - 70.00
PARSONS Gary, Cambridge & Colr'dge :
DT - 41.34 (42.08-93)
PARSONS Geoffrey Peter 14.08.64,
London AC/Blue Circle : HJ - 2.31,
PARSONS Simon U23 27.10.73, Huntingdon :
400 - 49.0, 800 - 1:51.4
PARTINGTON Stephen W. 17.09.65, Manx H :
3kW - 11:52.2 (11:42.5-92),
10kW - 42:23.0 (41:35.6-92),
20kW - 1:28:04+ (1:24:18-90),
30kW - 2:14:15
PASSEY Adrian 2.09.64, Bromsgrove & R :
1500 - 3:44.43 (3:34.50-87), 10kR - 29:13
PATE Martin U20 16.03.77, Victoria Pk AAC :
HJ - 2.00i (2.01-93)
PATIENCE M U13, Winchester :
JTC - 39.84
PATIS Ryan U17 4.11.77, Medway :
400 - 50.19
PATRICK Adrian Leroy John U23 15.06.73,
Windsor S & E : 100 - 10.7 (10.7-91),
200 - 21.4/21.49w (22.08-91), 400 - 46.11
PAUL Jamie 17.07.70, Cambridge Harriers :
60 - 6.9i, 100 - 10.8,
PAUL Lenox 25.05.58, Belgrave/Army :
100 - 10.48w/10.57 (10.25w-91/10.32-93)
PAVIS Jon 4.10.66, Rowntrees :
3kSt - 9:11.7 (9:04.78-90)
PAVITT Simon U20 12.07.76, Braintree :
JT - 54.44
PAYN Tom U15 18.10.79, Colchester & T :
800 - 2:02.6, PenB - 2513
PAYNE Dave 19.06.66, Tipton :
10kR - 29:43, 10MR - 48:59 (47:09-92)
PAYNE Stephen U17 30.01.78, Andover :
400 - 49.8/49.88
PAYNE-DWYER Russell H. 11.09.60, Birch :
HT - 49.18 (56.62-86)
PEACH Nick 18.10.59, Sale :
10k - 31:05.9 (30:50.11-87)
PEACOCK James U17 29.09.77, Thurrock :
LJ - 6.65, TJ - 14.07
PEACOCK Shane 5.03.63, Birchfield :
HT - 66.68 (71.60-90)
PEARCE Duncan James 21.10.70, Sale :
PV - 4.60 (4.80-92)
PEARSON Andrew 14.09.71, Longwood :
1500 - 3:46.9 (3:42.2-91),
10k - 29:14.91 (28:40.49-93),
10kR - 28:44 (28:42-93),
HMar - 1:04:30 (1:04:21-93)
PEARSON John T. 30.04.66, Yeovil Oly/WLHS :
HT - 66.54
PEARSON Kenneth W.G. U23 9.07.72,
Cent/St Andrews Un : Dec - 5716 (5745-93)
PEARSON Stephen G. 13.09.59, W & B/NWHS :
HT - 65.24
PEASE Ian U20 28.09.76, Hercules Wimbledon :
400H - 56.5

PELESZOK M. U13, Shrewsbury :
800 - 2:17.12
PEMBER Christopher U20 2.10.75, Hereford :
110HJ - 14.86w/15.24 (14.67w-93)
PENDLEBURY Mark U23 3.10.74, Leigh :
Dec - 5120, DecJ - 5522oa (5310-93)
PENGILLY Adam U17 14.10.77, Taunton :
PV - 3.85, OctY - 4640
PENK Andrew U17 19.09.78, Wrexham :
HJ - 2.00, PV - 4.00
PENN J. U15, Frodsham :
100 - 11.5
PENNEY Kenneth Anthony 26.01.63, Haringey :
10k - 31:09.96 (30:30.0-88), Mar - 2:26:10
PENTLAND Paul 9.09.69, Edinburgh :
PV - 4.40i (4.40-92)
PERIGO Philip U17 25.09.78, Stainforth :
100 - 10.9w/11.1 (11.30w-93),
200 - 21.65w/22.00
PERMAN Mark R. 6.01.68, Walthamstow :
110H - 15.2/15.60 (15.06w-93/15.2-89/15.24-92),
PV - 4.10i (4.30-93), Dec - 6414 (6606-93)
PERRY Matthew Robin U17 15.02.78, Cardiff :
HJ - 1.95, LJ - 6.50
PERRYMAN Guy St.D.M. 2.11.58, Bracknell :
SP - 14.27 (16.58-89)
PESCOD David U23 15.04.73, Sunderland :
JT - 58.92
PETERS Marcellas U17 20.11.78, Derby & Co :
LJ - 7.16w/7.08, OctY - 4858
PETERS Mike 1.10.60, Havant :
3kSt - 9:21.9
PETLEY Neal Stewart 21.05.68, Sale :
110H - 15.43 (14.92w-86/15.0-85/15.09-86)
PHILIPSON Morris U23 26.02.73, East Ches :
LJ - 6.90 (6.98-90)
PHILLIPS Matthew U17 22.09.77, Birchfield :
SPY - 14.08, JTY - 56.76
PHILLIPS Russell K. 2.09.58, Met. Police :
Mar - 2:25:06
PHILLIPS Steven U23 17.03.72, Birchfield :
60 - 6.95i, LJ - 7.89w/7.61 (7.91-91),
TJ - 14.98 (15.04-91)
PHILLIPS Stuart 15.04.63, Ilford :
3kW - 13:21.1 (12:17.6-91)
PICKERING Shaun Desforges 14.11.61,
Haringey/ACC Amsterdam :
SP - 17.32i/16.96 (18.31-92),
DT - 48.36 (54.38-89), HT - 57.58 (68.64-84)
PIERCE Robert Ian U20 13.11.75, Wrexham :
5k - 15:05.00
PIERRE Henderson 29.10.63, Haringey :
HJ - 2.17 (2.20i-87/2.18-86)
PIKE John U20, Holbeach :
5k - 15:13.2
PILKINGTON Matthew John U17 19.12.77, Charn :
SPY - 14.78, DTJ - 41.36, DTY - 46.98
PILLING John U15 3.02.80, Preston :
LJ - 6.02
PINNA Daniel D. U15 12.11.79, Milton Keynes :
1500 - 4:15.02
PINNER Mark 12.05.64, Wolverhampton & B :
JT - 63.06 (65.74-93)
PLANT Raymond 13.05.68, Newcastle :
3kSt - 9:09.1
PLASKETT Simon U17 9.04.79, Wycombe :
400 - 50.8

PLATT Thomas U15 3.03.80, Dartford :
JTB - 47.48
PLINT Steven 13.01.63, Sheffield :
PV - 4.10
PLUMB Jason U17 9.11.77, Burnley :
OctY - 4337
POLSON Darren U15 29.12.79, Herne Hill :
200 - 23.46w/23.6
PONTING Mark U20 28.04.77, Cardiff :
400 - 47.94
POOLE Terry U15 20.11.79, Brighton :
LJ - 6.09
POORE Stuart U23 30.12.72, Team Solent :
1500 - 3:44.77
POPE Stuart U20 21.02.76, City of Stoke :
110HJ - 15.6
POSKETT Richard U15 6.09.79, Humberside Sch :
80HB - 11.78
POVALL David U20 21.07.75, Newport :
800 - 1:53.9
POVEY Soloman U15 8.02.80, Blackheath :
100 - 11.4/11.52w
POWELL Dalton 20.08.63, Belgrave :
200 - 21.3w/21.89 (21.1db/21.24w/21.26-92)
POWELL Neil U20 5.03.77, Cardiff :
100 - 10.80w,
POWELL Wayne 27.07.71, Stroud :
JT - 56.64 (59.36-93)
POWER Garry 1.09.62, Herne Hill/IRE :
DT - 45.58 (48.98-86)
POYNTER Benedict U15, Croydon :
JTB - 47.70
PRATT Andrew 20.04.69, Windsor S & E :
1500 - 3:50.0
PRATT Stephen 6.02.71, Queens Park :
400H - 54.4 (54.15-91)
PRESTON Darren U23 19.12.74, Enfield/
Brunel Univ :
3kSt - 9:00.2
PRICE Gareth U15 27.11.79, Sutton & Dist :
800 - 2:04.27
PRICE Glyn A. 12.09.65, Swansea :
PV - 4.40 (4.80-90)
PRICE Sean Myrion 4.01.63, Cardiff :
800 - 1:51.9 (1:49.67-86)
PRICE Terence P. 26.07.57, N&EB/Royal Navy :
400H - 54.20 (52.39-93)
PRITCHARD Nicholas U23 5.12.72, Cardiff :
PV - 4.20 (4.40-91)
PROBIN Peter M. V45 15.07.47, Met. Police :
Mar - 2:26:51
PROCTOR Mark A. 15.01.63, N& EB/RAF :
SP - 18.15, DT - 53.40 (54.28-93),
HT - 50.94 (53.70-93)
PROUDLOVE Michael 26.01.70, Crewe & N :
1M - 4:07.08
PROWSE Johnathan U20 15.11.75, Blackpool :
3k - 8:29.00
PUCKRIN Alan 2.04.64, Greenock Glenpark :
3k - 8:20.3il (8:00.49i-89),
5k - 14:17.15 (13:57.22-89), 10k - 29:32.29
PUNCH James U15 19.12.79, Corby :
HTB - 57.30
PURSER Mark U23 18.04.72, Croydon :
400H - 54.42 (52.26-93)
PURSGLOVE James U17 24.09.77, Derby & Co :
HJ - 1.95

PURVES Grant U23 6.04.73, Edinburgh SH :
400 - 48.40

Q UARRY James S. U23 15.11.72,
Blackheath/Falkirk :
100 - 10.86, 60H - 8.1i/8.15i,
110H - 14.10, HJ - 2.00i/1.97 (1.99-91),
PV - 4.30, LJ - 7.36w/7.17,
DT - 41.38, Dec - 7610
QUELCH Russell U17 9.09.78, AF&D :
400HY - 56.33
QUIGLEY Mark U23 6.11.74, Copeland :
DT - 42.18 (45.92-93)
QUINN Michael R. 21.01.63, Highgate :
5k - 14:34.05 (14:17.9-91)
QUINN Robert 10.12.65, Kilbarchan :
3k - 8:14.24 (8:05.7-85)
QUIXLEY Andrew 8.11.64, Royal Navy :
JT - 58.56 (63.94-92)

R ACKHAM Jonathan U15 29.11.79,
Humberside Sch : DTB - 37.20
RAE Steven U20 20.07.75, Annan :
110HJ - 15.2w, DecJ - 5653
RALPH Paul 16.12.67, GEC :
LJ - 7.04, TJ - 15.36 (15.54-93)
RALSON David U20 22.02.77, Oxford City :
Dec - 5850, DecJ - 6211w/5852
RAMSAY Andrew U20 19.09.76, Black Isle :
400H - 56.8
RAMSEY Richard U23 6.10.72, Annadale Str/
Loughborough Studnts : PV - 4.20 (4.60-92)
RANDALL Matthew 28.04.70, Hastings :
TJ - 14.46 (14.48-93), Dec - 5136
RANSON Daniel U15 25.09.79, Notts :
1500 - 4:20.53
RATCLIFFE Trevor 9.03.64, Dacorum :
JT - 59.28 (64.38-88)
RATHBONE Daniel 9.04.69, Brighton :
Mar - 2:21:43 (2:18:35-93)
RATTIGAN Colin E. 20.11.60, Haringey :
LJ - 6.96 (7.60-88)
RAW David U15 1.02.81, Chester Le Street :
PV - 3.00
RAWLINSON Christopher U23 19.05.72, Traff :
110H - 14.9/14.92w/15.06, 400H - 52.0/52.32
RAYNER Simon 28.02.64, Hercules Wimb :
10kR - 29:38 (29:33-90)
READ Douglas 15.04.67, Milton Keynes :
HT - 50.04 (55.54-88)
READLE David U15 10.02.80, Liverpool Pem :
SPB - 13.60
REARDON Daniel U15 14.04.80, RS Coldfield :
HJ - 1.81
REDMAN Brian 25.10.68, Woodford Green :
SP - 14.83i/14.72 (15.20i-92/14.92-90)
REDMOND John 15.10.57, City of Hull :
Mar - 2:27:50
REED Paul 2.06.62, Morpeth :
SP - 16.71 (17.04-88), DT - 54.50
REES-JONES Steve U23 24.12.74, Brighton :
800 - 1:52.56
REESE Ben U20 29.03.76, Wirral :
800 - 1:50.5, 1500 - 3:49.7, 2kSt - 5:49.96,
3kSt - 9:09.24
REEVE David U23 25.05.73, Bristol/CUAC :
LJ - 6.96 (7.22-91),
TJ - 14.75 (15.38w/15.21-90)

REGIS John Paul Lyndon 13.10.66, Belgrave :
100 - 10.10wA/10.38 (10.07w-90/10.15-93),
150 - 15.15, 200 - 19.87A
REHILL Ken 4.11.68, Newham & Essex B :
JT - 60.60
REID Alan 19.04.66, Peterhead :
10k - 31:04.8
REILLY Brendan Anthony John U23 23.12.72,
Corby/Loughborough Studnts :
HJ - 2.32i/2.28 (2.31-92)
REILLY Darren 19.09.65, Liverpool Pembroke :
10k - 31:09.6, 3kSt - 9:05.4 (9:04.3-89)
REISS Michael 17.06.63, Highgate :
DT - 40.70 (43.18-88), HT - 50.60
REITZ Colin Robert 6.04.60, Newham & E B :
5k - 14:25.68 (13:37.31-87),
10k - 30:56.4 (30:34.82-92),
10kR - 29:32 (28:07-84), 10MR - 49:26
RENAUD Pascal 20.04.70, Crawley/FRA :
60H - 8.3i/8.38i,
110H - 14.7/14.74 (14.58-92)
RENFREE Andrew U20 18.05.75, Newquay & P :
1500 - 3:52.7
REY David 19.07.68, Windsor S & E :
100 - 10.69w/10.82 (10.58-89),
200 - 21.57 (21.2w-91/21.23-90)
REYNOLDS John U17 14.01.79, Annadale
Striders :
100HY - 14.0w
REYNOLDS Nick U20 8.06.76, Basildon :
800 - 1:53.38
RICHARDS Edward U17 19.09.77, Oxford C :
PV - 4.00
RICHARDS Gregory Roy 25.04.56, N London :
LJ - 6.96 (7.65w/7.33-87), SP - 15.24,
DT - 47.46 (50.66-91)
RICHARDS Justin L. 25.01.71, Worthing :
PV - 4.40 (4.90-91)
RICHARDS Mark 1.07.70, Belgrave :
TJ - 14.84
RICHARDS Thomas U17 13.11.78, Oxford C :
PV - 3.80
RICHARDSON Graham 15.11.64, Army :
110H - 14.8, 400H - 54.6 (53.4-93)
RICHARDSON Mark Austin U23 26.07.72, WS &E :
200 - 21.67i+ (20.93-92),
400 - 46.11i (45.09-92)
RICHMOND Stuart Anthony 11.04.69, GEC :
TJ - 14.80
RICKALL Zak U15 6.03.80, Normandy Park :
SPB - 14.04, DTB - 37.48
RICKETTS Kevin U20 29.06.76, Deeside :
DecJ - 5412
RIEPER Benjamin U23 20.12.73, Leigh :
3kSt - 9:02.40
RIFAT Julian 23.03.69, Shaftesbury Barnet :
LJ - 6.93 (7.20-91), SP - 14.13
RIGBY Tony U15 22.02.80, Bedford & County :
JTB - 54.16, PenB - 2466
RILEY Graeme 11.01.60, Royal Navy :
3kSt - 9:25.8 (9:00.1-83)
RITCHIE Darren U20 14.02.75, Edinb/Sc Bord :
LJ - 7.15w/6.97 (7.00-93)
RITCHIE Don V50 6.07.44, Forres :
100kR - 7:29:46 (6:51:14-89),
24HrT - 236.861
RIXON Dale 8.07.66, Cardiff :
HMar - 1:04:19, Mar - 2:15:41

354

ROACH Mark 11.04.65, Old Gaytonians :
HJ - 2.08 (2.10-85)
ROACHE Desmond U20 5.01.76, Clydesdale :
800 - 1:51.08, 1500 - 3:50.5
ROBB Bruce U20 27.07.77, Pitreavie :
SP - 14.84, SPJ - 15.45,
SPY - 17.11o (15.73-93),
DT - 45.70, DTJ - 47.42
ROBB Curtis U23 7.06.72, Liv H/Sheff Un:
800 - 1:48.07 (1:44.92-93)
ROBBINS Michael U20 14.03.76, Rotherham :
110HJ - 14.13w/14.44, 110H - 14.98,
HJ - 2.14, DecJ - 5757
ROBERSON Mark W. U20 21.03.75, Milton K :
HT - 47.88, HTJ - 51.36 (51.36-93)
ROBERSON Mark 13.03.67, Haringey :
JT - 78.82 (80.92-88)
ROBERTS Aidan 25.08.56, Bolton :
Mar - 2:28:27
ROBERTS Andrew U17 19.09.77, Wigan :
LJ - 6.73
ROBERTS Chris U15 7.02.80, Powys Sch :
PenB - 2429
ROBERTS Gareth U15 22.10.79, Keswick :
800 - 2:03.3
ROBERTS Ian 15.06.68, Shaftesbury Barnet :
LJ - 6.99w (7.19w-92)
ROBERTS Mark S. 12.02.59, Potteries Mar :
Mar - 2:23:32 (2:19:19-92)
ROBERTS Martin 1.03.60, Cannock & Staff :
HT - 47.74
ROBERTS Michael U15 30.09.79, Invicta :
SPB - 13.78
ROBERTS Paul 24.12.69, Cardiff/Loughro :
400 - 48.4/48.89 (48.0-89/48.20-88),
800 - 1:51.06 (1:49.48-93)
ROBERTS Peter 19.09.71, Swansea :
DT - 42.02 (44.52-90)
ROBERTSON David T. 11.09.61, Saltwell :
Mar - 2:26:38
ROBERTSON Iain U20 23.06.75, Norfolk :
3kSt - 9:46.73
ROBERTSON Maximillian 27.12.63, Belgrave :
110H - 14.93 (14.14-86)
ROBERTSON Stephen U20 9.07.75, Falkirk :
400H - 57.0
ROBERTSON-ADAMS Charles U17 5.12.77,
Telford : 100HY - 14.0/14.07, 400H - 55.6,
400HY - 53.55, TJ - 13.84
ROBINCOCKER Olu U20 27.11.75, Traff/NIG :
HJ - 2.00 (2.00-93), TJ - 14.10 (14.15-93)
ROBINSON Andrew 21.03.66, Haringey :
800 - 1:52.5
ROBINSON A. U20, Gwynedd Sch :
SPJ - 13.65
ROBINSON Anthony 15.06.59, Valli :
Mar - 2:26:28
ROBINSON David U17 12.01.78, Sund/NESH :
HTJ - 48.64, HTY - 56.20
ROBINSON Dean 25.06.70, Tipton :
PV - 4.21 (4.30-90)
ROBINSON Ian 21.04.69, Prest/Iowa St Univ :
3k - 8:04.3 (8:01.12i-92),
5k - 14:08.03 (14:03.93-92),
10k - 30:06.53 (29:32.92-92)
ROBINSON James U20 3.11.76, Brighton :
DTJ - 41.30

ROBINSON James U20 27.08.76, Tipton :
PV - 4.30i/4.30, LJ - 6.90, DecJ - 5856
ROBINSON Keith V40 9.02.52, Havering :
HT - 47.12 (53.38-81)
ROBINSON Paul U15, Stamford & Deeping :
JTB - 46.88
ROBINSON Ronald Steve 9.10.57, Chelt :
Mar - 2:27:40
ROBINSON Simon U17 13.09.77, Border :
400 - 50.33
ROBINSON Steven U17 1.09.77, Milton K :
PV - 3.80
ROBISON Christopher 16.03.61, Spango Val :
3k - 8:05.94i/8:06.48,
5k - 13:55.7 (13:54.66-84),
10k - 28:51.12 (28:39.35-86)
ROBSON Alan 14.11.59, Leslie Deans RC :
10k - 30:25.03 (29:42.2-89)
RODEN Paul Anthony 18.04.65, Sale :
5k - 14:15.12 (13:52.4-86),
10k - 29:15.11 (29:03.07-92),
10MR - 48:30 (47:36-93),
HMar - 1:04:50 (1:03:19-93), Mar - 2:19:52
RODGER Jody U23 29.11.73, W London IHE :
Dec - 5436
ROGERS Craig U20 14.02.76, Birchfield :
SPJ - 14.20
ROGERS Stephen A. 1.09.71, Liverpool Pem :
110H - 15.47w, PV - 4.40 (4.50-93),
JT - 58.54, Dec - 7203
ROGERSON Stewart 4.02.62, Sale :
HT - 61.52 (70.30-88)
ROLLINS Andrew U17 20.03.78, Wigan :
DTY - 45.16
ROLLINS John, :
3k - 8:09.43i, 5k - 14:16.38
ROLLINS Robert 18.05.61, Bridgend/RAF :
Mar - 2:25:06 (2:21:41-90)
ROSATO Sebastian 23 19.11.72, GEC/CUAC :
110H - 14.8/15.20 (14.8db-93)
ROSCOE Martin Peter 19.09.64, Leeds :
3kSt - 9:06.1 (8:53.2-89)
ROSE Andrew U13 17.08.83, Braintree :
100 - 12.2, 200 - 25.7
ROSE David U17 26.06.78, Border :
3k - 8:53.10
ROSE Nicholas H. V40 30.12.51, Bristol :
5k - 14:15.7, Mar - 2:21:10
ROSE Stefan U20 7.04.75, Team Solent :
LJ - 7.18, TJ - 13.99
ROSE Vincent 21.08.71, Thames Valley :
400 - 47.29, 800 - 1:52.70 (1:51.35-93)
ROSEN Alexander 30.09.71, Haringey :
800 - 1:52.38 (1:50.89-92)
ROSSITER Martin R. 4.09.69, Huntingdon/
Reading University : TJ - 14.61
ROSSWESS Michael 11.06.65, Birchfield :
60 - 6.54i/6.56i,
100 - 10.07w/10.29 (10.15-91)
ROUND Anthony U15 11.01.80, Chorley :
3kW - 16:26.97
ROW Andrew U17 17.10.78, Gateshead :
100 - 11.0/11.03, 200 - 22.19w/22.32
ROWAN Paul 20.03.66, Willowfield :
HMar - 1:04:44
ROWBOTHAM Stephen 6.03.68, Rotherham :
LJ - 7.12, JT - 56.02, Dec - 6792

ROWE Paul 20.02.68, Birchfield :
3kSt - 9:20.44 (9:10.71-93)
ROWEN Daniel U15 30.12.79, Solihull & S H :
1500 - 4:16.2, 3k - 9:27.3
ROWLAND Mark Robert 7.03.63, Phoenix :
3k - 7:50.30 (7:46.22i-90/7:49.82-89),
3kSt - 8:22.20 (8:07.96-88)
ROWLANDS Mark Stuart U17 18.04.78, Swan :
400 - 49.9, 100HY - 13.3dbt/14.05,
400HY - 53.30
ROWLEY Duncan U15 15.04.80, Newbury :
400 - 52.60
ROY Mark 30.03.64, GEC :
HT - 47.58 (48.98-93)
ROYDEN Barry Mark 15.12.66, Medway :
1500 - 3:50.0 (3:45.7-92),
3k - 8:11.2 (8:05.56-91),
5k - 13:54.5 (13:54.03-91),
10k - 28:47.17, 10kR - 29:11,
HMar - 1:02:25, 3kSt - 9:03.0
RUBENIS Richard U23 10.11.73, Telford :
60 - 6.94i (6.92i-93), 100 - 10.5w/10.7/10.77,
200 - 21.57w/21.6, 400 - 47.4/47.76
RUDD Lee U20 15.09.76, Cumbrian Sch :
DecJ - 5170
RUDD Timothy J. 27.05.61, Stourport :
HMar - 1:05:43, Mar - 2:21:06 (2:20:34-93)
RUDKIN Alan U17 5.11.78, Holbeach :
SPY - 14.82, DTY - 47.36, OctY - 4867
RULE Charles U15 22.05.80, Edinburgh :
PV - 3.31
RUMBOLT Courtney Orville 26.07.69, SB :
100 - 10.97 (10.37w-88/10.48-90)
RUSH Simon U20 23.06.76, Woking :
110HJ - 15.15/15.3w (15.2-93),
400H - 54.33, PV - 4.30
RUSHWORTH Brian 14.12.62, Sunderland :
5k - 14:16.0 (13:50.6-86)
RUSSELL Alaister 17.06.68, Law & Dist :
10k - 30:53.91 (30:20.07-92)
RUSSELL Mark D. 15.03.71, Rotherham :
1500 - 3:46.?? (3:46.68-93)
RUSSELL Robert U23 5.08.74, Scarborough :
SP - 14.24, DT - 50.50 (52.14-93)
RUTHERFORD Leyton U20 2.06.76, Norfolk :
HTJ - 49.58
RUTHERFORD Tremayne U23 19.06.72, Card :
60 - 6.98i (6.86iun/6.96i-93),
100 - 10.4w?/10.44, 200 - 21.30 (21.20-93)
RUTLAND Andrew U20 13.01.76, Sunderland :
DTJ - 44.30
RUTLAND Damon U20 10.07.75, Newquay & P :
HJ - 2.12

SABNIS Dinkar U23 23.09.73, Aberdeen :
LJ - 7.07i/7.02 (7.06-93),
TJ - 14.06 (14.09-91)
SAHANS Gurmukh U17 8.10.78, Hounslow :
OctY - 4485
SAINT Julian U17, Bedford & County :
JTY - 54.48
SAKER Graeme 12.09.61, GEC :
3kSt - 9:12.6 (8:57.4-92)
SALLE Frederick Ebong 10.09.64, Belgrave :
HJ - 2.10 (2.14i-86/2.13-85), LJ - 8.10
SALMON Thomas U17 12.04.79, GrYarmouth :
1500 - 4:02.44

SALT Jonathan U15 14.12.79, Leics Cor :
800 - 2:01.91
SALT Richard U17 28.10.77, Lanc & Morc:
JTY - 56.84
SALVADOR-AYLOTT Livio U23 18.07.73, Old G :
PV - 4.50, Dec - 7024
SAMMUT Steven 3.05.67, Team Solent :
HT - 56.38 (57.22-93)
SAMUEL Bryn U17 11.10.77, Colwyn Bay :
JTY - 53.86
SAMUEL Lewis John Derek 12.02.66, Bel :
60 - 6.9i, 200 - 21.85 (21.1w?-91/21.48-90),
400 - 47.65 (46.53-90)
SAMUEL Rohan 30.01.66, Old Gaytonians :
100 - 10.6/10.75
(10.5w-89/10.58w-92/10.6/10.73-89)
200 - 21.6/22.27 (21.86-93)
SAMUELS Vernon George 15.10.64, W & B :
TJ - 15.54i/15.34 (16.82w-89/16.75-88)
SANDERS Jon 29.10.70, Kingston & Poly :
400 - 48.2/48.78
SANDERS Paul David 11.01.62, Team Solent :
100 - 10.6 (10.4w-92/10.66w-90/10.78-91),
200 - 21.4/21.55 (20.8w-92/21.04-89),
300 - 33.2 (33.34-91), 400 - 47.23 (45.33-91)
SANDERSON David 6.05.71, Sale :
TJ - 15.28 (15.72w-93/15.29-92)
SANNIGAR Matthew U15 31.03.80, C of Stoke :
HTB - 42.50
SARGEANT Nicholas U23 8.05.73,
RAF/WLIHE/Grantham : Dec - 5055
SATCHWELL Anthony W. V40 3.02.53, Jers :
DT - 46.28 (53.54-73)
SAUNDERS Barry U23 24.07.73, Thurrock :
HJ - 2.00i (2.03-92)
SAUNDERS Raymond U15 26.04.80, Birch :
LJ - 6.04, TJ - 12.59
SAVAGE David U23 13.11.72, Sale :
400 - 48.1 (48.72-93),
110H - 15.57 (15.4-93/15.50w-92),
400H - 51.87
SAVILL Stephen 10.03.67, Havering :
JT - 57.66 (61.08-89)
SAVORY Dominic U20 16.12.75, Holbeach :
HJ - 2.00
SAXBY Simon U23 17.01.74, City of Hull :
800 - 1:52.05 (1:50.6-93)
SCANLON Robert U23 13.04.74, Coventry G :
800 - 1:51.8, 1500 - 3:43.90
SCANTLEBURY Robert U20 9.11.76, Herc W :
400 - 48.6/48.88
SCOBIE Alan P. 11.10.63, Edinburgh :
HJ - 2.00i/2.00 (2.08-89)
SCOTT Chris 31.08.68, City of Hull :
400H - 54.1 (54.1-93)
SCOTT Darren 7.03.69, Frodsham :
100 - 10.8/10.98, 200 - 21.70
SCOTT Eric U23 20.01.72, Shettleston :
PV - 4.10,
SCOTT James 21.09.71, Crawley :
JT - 57.02
SCOTT Richard U23 14.09.73, Exeter :
400H - 54.48
SCOTT Sandy U20 1.09.76, Moray RR :
400 - 49.0 (50.16-93)
SCRAGE M. U13, Leics Sch :
75HC - 12.2

SEAR Jonathon 3.04.64, Woodford Green :
  2kSt - 5:54.07, 3kSt - 8:58.87 (8:58.25-93)
SEAR Richard U17 21.08.79, Oxford City :
  HJ - 1.91
SEDGE James U15 19.10.79, Avonside :
  HJ - 1.76
SEEDHOUSE Erik L. 19.06.64, City of Hull :
  100kR - 6:53:06
SELBY Piers U20 3.11.75, Basingstoke & MH :
  SP - 14.16i/14.02 (14.18-93),
  SPJ - 15.15 (15.20-93)
SELLARS Tom U15 7.01.80, Southend :
  200 - 23.64w
SESAY Mark Gavin U23 13.12.72, Leeds :
  400 - 48.3 (48.19-90),
  800 - 1:49.48 (1:48.30-90)
SHACKCLOTH Michael, Salford :
  3kSt - 9:21.0
SHALE Max U15 20.01.81, Oxford City :
  JTB - 46.56
SHANKS R. Stephen 3.11.69, Border :
  100 - 10.84w (10.7/10.80w-90/10.85-89),
  200 - 22.0/22.30 (21.6/21.66w/21.91-91)
SHARP Alexis U23 31.10.72, Blackheath :
  200 - 21.5
SHARP Dave, Coventry Godiva :
  SP - 13.68
SHEFFIELD Jamie U17 26.06.78, Wrexham :
  100HY - 13.52w/13.7/13.80,
  400HY - 55.94, OctY - 4521
SHENTON David U17 20.10.77, Gate/NESH :
  HTJ - 50.60, HTY - 56.24
SHEPHERD Bruce David 20.03.67, Aberd/Elg :
  SP - 13.85 (14.50-93),
  DT - 40.64 (42.76-91), HT - 52.30
SHEPHERD Dominic U20 11.12.76, C of Stoke :
  PV - 4.90
SHEPHERD John S. 23.12.61, Enfield :
  LJ - 7.27 (7.89w-86/7.66-88)
SHEPHERD John-Paul U15 29.02.80, Mand :
  HJ - 1.76
SHERBAN John Ian 30.07.64, SB/Falkirk :
  3k - 8:02.07 (7:58.47-91),
  5k - 13:46.4 (13:39.43-91),
  10kR - 28:46 (28:43-89),
  3kSt - 9:10.45 (8:48.92-92)
SHERIDAN Andrew U15 1.11.79, Blackheath :
  SPB - 13.81
SHERIDAN Mark D. 17.06.70, Crawley :
  HT - 52.82 (56.02-91), JT - 55.76 (57.66-91)
SHILLABEER Edmund H. V55 2.08.39,
  Plymouth City W :
  50kW - 4:51:44 (4:28:06-86)
SHIPP James U17 10.11.77, Great Yarmouth :
  200 - 22.45w (23.12-92), 400 - 49.9
SHIRLEY Simon 3.08.66, Belgrave :
  100 - 10.89, 400 - 48.83 (48.0/48.32-88),
  110HY - 14.7/14.82, HJ - 2.05 (2.09-85),
  PV - 4.60 (4.70-88),
  LJ - 7.52 (7.56w-88/7.55-86),
  SP - 14.16 (14.29-89),
  DT - 41.62 (44.68-91),
  JT - 63.80 (65.00-93),
  Dec - 7980 (8036AUS-88)
SHOWELL Gavin U23 29.09.72, Tamworth :
  PV - 4.20 (4.30-91)
SILEY Warren Gladstone U23 16.01.73, Traff :
  PV - 5.00 (5.20-90), LJ - 7.17w

SIMMONS Steven U23 10.11.74, Walth :
  100 - 10.8/10.84, 200 - 21.39
SIMONS Paul 4.04.64, Shaftesbury Barnet :
  Mar - 2:23:49
SIMPSON David U20 25.04.75, Willowfield :
  5k - 15:09.0
SIMPSON Keith U13 19.10.81, Aberdeen :
  JTC - 35.96
SIMPSON Michael 6.01.70, Hounslow :
  1500 - 3:50.6, 3k - 8:18.97 (8:15.5-93),
  5k - 14:19.6, 10kR - 29:34, 10MR - 49:15
SIMPSON Steven Thomas U17 18.01.78,
  Blackpool : 3k - 8:47.3
SIMSON Matthew 28.05.70, Thurrock :
  SP - 19.49, DT - 45.34 (46.54-92)
SINCLAIR Peter David 6.03.67, L Irish/IRE :
  400 - 47.75 (47.20-91)
SINCLAIR Trevor 6.08.61, Birchfield :
  LJ - 7.08 (7.56w/7.50i/7.47-84)
SINGLETON David U15 21.10.79, Swindon :
  400 - 53.2
SKEETE John U17 8.09.78, Blackheath :
  100 - 11.1/11.25, 200 - 22.26w/22.6
SKELDING Andrew J. 8.11.71, Dudley & St :
  HJ - 2.10
SKELTON James U20, Worthing :
  PV - 4.15
SKELTON Matthew U23 8.11.72, Tonbridge :
  1500 - 3:50.06
SKETCHLEY David U20 25.02.76, Colch & T :
  JT - 57.46
SKEVIS George U15 12.10.79, Crawley :
  DTB - 42.26
SLADE Garry 10.10.68, Leeds :
  LJ - 7.40 (7.69w-88/7.68-92),
  TJ - 13.93i (14.50-91)
SLATER Craig U17 22.05.78, Milton Keynes :
  400 - 50.85i (50.3-93/52.03-92)
SLATER Damien U17 14.10.77, Bed & Co/WLHS :
  HTY - 59.50
SLATER Roderick U23 25.12.72, TVH/Falkirk :
  60 - 6.91i (6.87i-93),
  100 - 10.77w/10.78 (10.62w/10.69-93),
  200 - 22.0w/22.09w (21.63-93)
SLAUGHTER Andrew U20 22.10.75, Epsom & E :
  LJ - 7.02, TJ - 14.29w/14.26
SLEATH Justin E. 9.02.67, Bracknell :
  400 - 48.8 (46.99-91)
SLEET Michael U15 6.06.80, Invicta :
  TJ - 12.40, PenB - 2519
SLOCOMBE Tim U17 15.11.77, Wimborne :
  400 - 49.71
SLOMAN Trevor 21.03.68, Walthamstow :
  PV - 4.10i (4.50-91)
SLYTHE Paul J. U23 5.09.74, GEC :
  200 - 21.8w, 400 - 47.27
SMAHON Dean Carey 8.12.61, Lisburn/RUC :
  JT - 67.60
SMAILES Andrew David 22.04.68, W & B/RAF :
  110H - 14.8 (14.6w-90/14.7/14.74-87)
SMALE Christopher 11.08.65, Sutton & Dist :
  HT - 47.88 (54.52-89)
SMALES Chris 10.10.63, Longwood :
  10k - 31:08.0 (30:38.3-93)
SMART Neil Sidney 12.05.63, Sale :
  3kSt - 8:42.44 (8:35.52-89)
SMART Nicholas 24.12.68, Westbury :
  3k - 8:18.47i (8:07.53-92)

SMEDLEY Raymond J. V40 30.09.51, Gate :
  10k - 30:33.62 (28:24.15-75)
SMITH Adam U20 20.02.77, Annadale Str :
  HJ - 1.98, TJ - 14.33
SMITH Andrew U17 26.03.78, Mandale :
  400 - 50.9
SMITH Andrew U15 10.01.80, Southampton C :
  HJ - 1.85
SMITH C. Anthony 17.05.58, Shaftesbury B :
  JT - 67.64 (69.94-91)
SMITH Christopher James U20 27.11.75,
  Edinburgh/Arbroath : JT - 59.50
SMITH Christopher J. 23.12.58, Leics WC :
  3kW - 13:14.3 (12.05.0-87),
  10kW - 47:47.0 (43:15.0-87)
SMITH Colin P. 11.09.57, Portsmouth :
  SP - 14.06 (15.54-89)
SMITH D. U17, Derby & Co :
  SPY - 14.19
SMITH Darrell Luke 10.04.67, Blackheath :
  5k - 14:20.0 (13:58.62-92)
SMITH David 21.06.62, City of Hull/NESH :
  HT - 62.70 (77.30-85)
SMITH David U23 2.11.74, City of Hull/NWHS :
  HT - 67.74
SMITH Garry 2.01.66, Peterborough :
  Dec - 5588 (5735-86)
SMITH Gary 20.02.71, Shaftesbury Barnet :
  110H - 15.11 (14.87w/15.00-91),
  LJ - 7.30 (7.35-93)
SMITH Glen E. U23 21.05.72, Solihull & SH :
  SP - 14.03, DT - 59.78
SMITH Gordon Campbell 10.10.68, Aberdeen :
  SP - 16.29
SMITH Graeme 20.10.71, Edinburgh/Heriot W :
  110H - 14.93 (14.78w/14.8-92)
SMITH John 7.07.71, Army :
  Dec - 5030 (5409-91)
SMITH Mark 30.10.63, Gateshead :
  10k - 30:51.7 (30:17.58-93)
SMITH Mark U23 14.09.74, Old Gaytonians :
  HJ - 2.00 (2.07-91)
SMITH Mark Richard 18.11.71, Woodford Grn :
  100 - 10.8/10.89 (10.4w/10.6-90/10.68-92),
  200 - 21.6/21.70 (20.85w/20.87-90),
  400 - 46.7/46.75
SMITH Paul W. V40 12.08.54, Brecon :
  Mar - 2:24:07 (2:21:24-91)
SMITH Phillip 26.05.64, Bridgend/Forres :
  Mar - 2:26:14
SMITH Raymond L. 24.12.67, Old Gaytonians :
  TJ - 14.45 (15.26-91)
SMITH Richard U15 17.01.81, Peterborough :
  PV - 3.70
SMITH Robert Mark 3.11.66, Edinburgh SH :
  SP - 14.45 (15.14i-90/15.06-91)
SMITH Stephen U15 13.02.80, Peterborough :
  PV - 3.60
SMITH Steven U23 29.03.73, Liverpool H :
  HJ - 2.38i/2.33 (2.37-93),
  LJ - 7.36 (7.65w-93/7.51-92)
SMITH Stuart U20 2.08.76, Coventry Godiva :
  HJ - 2.11
SMITH Stuart U15 20.12.79, Grimsby :
  200 - 22.88w/22.9
SMYTH Jeremy U17 11.08.78, Stromness :
  JTY - 53.56

SNADE Jonathan U20 31.03.77, Telford :
  110HY - 14.38,
  110HJ - 14.50w/14.9/15.08
SNOOK Laine 2.07.68, Exeter :
  SP - 15.53
SNOW Robert U20 1.09.75, Guildf& G/Junction 10 :
  SPJ - 14.70, HT - 46.34, HTJ - 53.16
SNOW Shane 31.10.66, Highgate :
  1500 - 3:50.6
SOALLA-BELL Anthony U20 3.10.76, Herne H :
  SP - 13.36, SPJ - 15.09
SOLLITT Gary U23 13.01.72, Southampton C :
  SP - 16.68
SOLOMAN Daffydd U15 18.09.79, Cardiff :
  1500 - 4:17.03
SOUGRIN Neil 14.05.71, Enfield :
  DT - 47.82
SOUTH James U20 4.01.75, Shaftesbury B :
  SP - 13.69, SPJ - 15.95,
  DT - 48.32, DTJ - 51.70
SOUTHAM Carl U23 11.01.74, Charnwood :
  400 - 47.58 (46.59-92)
SOUTHWARD Anthony 31.01.71, C of Stoke :
  110H - 14.84w/15.1/15.29,
  PV - 4.20 (4.20-93), Dec - 6883
SOUTHWARD Robert U15 24.03.80, Wirral :
  JTB - 52.42
SPAWFORTH Darren 1.08.69, Wakefield :
  1500 - 3:45.74 (3:40.48-92), 1M - 4:03.69
SPEAKE Wayne 11.02.64, Wells :
  10k - 31:05.6
SPEAKE William J. 24.01.71, Bilderston B :
  Mar - 2:26:49
SPENCER-SMITH Rupert 25.07.68, Haringey :
  HT - 48.26 (54.16-90)
SPICER Matthew William 18.05.71, Bristol :
  HT - 54.12 (58.42-89)
SPIKES Douglas U20 1.07.76, Ealing,S & Mx :
  HT - 47.12, HTJ - 50.64
SPILANE Paul U15 27.09.79, Leics WC :
  3kW - 16:26.0 (16:00.6-93)
SPIVEY Philip 15.05.61, Belgrave/AUS :
  HT - 62.70 (70.94-86)
SPOONER Daniel U17 5.01.78, Bingley :
  OctY - 4207
SPRATLEY Nigel 1.04.70, Reading :
  SP - 17.96, DT - 47.14
SPRATLEY Stuart J. U23 18.07.72, SB :
  HT - 56.60 (60.96-92)
SPRATT Adam U20, Hull Spartan :
  JT - 54.24
SPRATT Anthony U15 9.09.79, Croydon :
  200 - 23.52w/23.69
SPRING Gareth M. 20.08.63, Bedford & Co :
  Mar - 2:23:57 (2:14:27-92)
SQUIRE Andrew U15 30.09.79, Cannock & St:
  LJ - 6.16, JTB - 47.46, PenB - 2758
SQUIRES Andrew U20 27.02.75, N Devon :
  SP - 13.20, SPJ - 15.42,
  DT - 44.56, DTJ - 47.68
ST.LOUIS Michael Antony 26.03.64, Herne H :
  100 - 10.8/10.97 (10.4w-85/10.52-87),
  200 - 21.7w/21.80 (20.81-86)
STAFFORD Kriss U15 11.09.79, Canvey Isl :
  SPB - 13.35
STAFFORD Stephen J. 6.03.59, Barnsley :
  Mar - 2:24:50

STAINES Gary Martin 3.07.63, Belgrave :
3k - 7:51.26 (7:41.79-90),
2M - 8:29.12 (8:23.16-91),
5k - 13:45.57 (13:14.28-90),
10k - 28:25.60 (27:48.73-91),
10kR - 28:40 (28:28-87),
10MR - 47:00 (46:11-93)
STAINTON Nigel 19.08.59, Bristol :
JT - 61.60 (75.28-89)
STAMP Terence 18.02.70, Southampton City :
60 - 6.9i/6.96i (6.84i-93)
STANEKE Jan U20 29.11.75, Wirral :
800 - 1:53.97
STANFORD Steven U15 9.12.79, Liverpool H :
DTB - 40.10
STANLEY David U17 16.01.79, Bas & MH :
800 - 1:57.3
STANOJEVIC Aleks U17 18.01.78, Warw Sch :
OctY - 4248
STARK Graeme 12.10.63, Rotherham :
SP - 14.88i/13.83 (14.70-85)
STARK William U20 11.03.77, Aberdeen :
LJ - 7.00, TJ - 13.97i/13.97
STARLING James Mark 13.08.67, Soton City :
1500 - 3:45.74 (3:44.77-91)
STARTIN Paul U17 22.11.77, Leics Cor :
JTY - 58.76
STEEL John A. 27.02.63, Edinburgh SH :
3kSt - 9:12.4 (8:54.86-88)
STEELE Martin Douglas 30.09.62, Longwood :
400 - 47.9 (47.4-90/48.65-93),
800 - 1:46.13 (1:43.84-93),
1k - 2:20.55 (2:19.50i-91),
1500 - 3:50.1 (3:42.8-92)
STEER Paul U13 14.01.82, Leics WC :
2kW - 11:10.5o
STEINLE Mark U23 27.11.74, Blackheath :
3k - 8:13.60, 5k - 14:03.82
STEINMETZ Rolf Nicholas U20 9.12.76, Bed & Co :
HT - 56.70, HTJ - 62.60
STELFOX Paul U23 12.11.72, Sale :
3kSt - 9:14.94
STENNETT Kori U20 2.09.76, Cheltenham :
TJ - 15.02
STEPHEN Peter U15 10.09.79, Cumbernauld :
SPB - 14.18, PenB - 2880
STEPHENS John M. 13.02.58, Sunderland :
Mar - 2:23:37 (2:21:12-86)
STEPHENSON Christian U23 22.07.74, Card :
3k - 8:17.20, 5k - 14:04.18,
3kSt - 9:01.44
STEPHENSON Philip U23 10.04.73, Sund :
200 - 21.58w/22.24
STEPHENSON Sam U15 15.05.80, London Sch :
80HB - 11.75
STEVENSON James M. 31.12.71, Sheffield :
100 - 10.94w (10.90-90),
400 - 48.02 (47.16-90),
HJ - 1.98i/1.98 (2.03-93), LJ - 7.27 (7.32-93)
STEVENSON Samuel 20.12.63, Telford :
3kSt - 9:04.6
STEWARD Michael U13 20.02.82, Bed & Co:
3k - 10:16.2
STEWART Glen 7.12.70, Edinburgh SH :
800 - 1:51.67 (1:49.9-91), 1500 - 3:40.17
STEWART Kris U15 11.04.80, Scottish Bord :
200 - 23.3/23.65, 400 - 51.6/52.65

STEWART Lloyd U15 23.09.79, Corby :
3k - 9:38.00
STEWART Paul U17 5.10.77, C of Plymouth :
HTY - 49.02
STIRRAT Kenneth A. 1.03.70, Halifax/Birm Un :
3kSt - 8:49.26
STOCK Keith Frank 18.03.57, Haringey :
PV - 4.70i (5.65-81)
STOKES Stuart U20 15.12.76, Bolton :
2kSt - 5:53.5
STONE Darrell Richard 2.02.68, Steyning :
10kW - 43:09.28 (41:33.0-93),
20kW - 1:26:53 (1:25.05-92/1:23:27sh-93),
30kW - 2:11:30
STONE Jason U15 15.10.80, Hounslow :
HTB - 42.94
STONE M. U20, Hamps Sch :
JT - 55.68
STOREY Duncan 17.09.68, Dundee/TVH :
3kSt - 8:54.88
STOREY James U20 26.11.76, Enfield :
110HJ - 15.2/15.40
STRANG David Maxwell 13.12.68, Haringey :
800 - 1:48.20 (1:45.85-92),
1500 - 3:36.53, 1M - 3:54.30
STREATHER Gavin Blair 14.04.71,
Woodford Green/Loughborough Studnts :
110H - 15.1/15.15,
400H - 53.2/53.25 (53.18-91)
STRICKLAND Pat, :
400 - 48.12
STRINGER Christpher U20 18.02.76, Sale :
800 - 1:52.3
STUART Michael U15 7.05.80, Exeter :
LJ - 6.03
STUBBS Paul U23 26.03.74, City of Stoke :
60H - 8.39i, 110H - 14.3w/14.40
SUNNERS Graham U23 26.03.73, Liv Pem/RAF :
3kSt - 9:11.2 (9:09.53-92)
SUNSHINE Gavin S. U23 19.02.74, N & EB :
110H - 14.95 (14.94-93),
PV - 4.60 (4.70-92), LJ - 7.21
SURETY Steven U15 18.02.80, Basildon :
80HB - 11.7/11.80
SUTTON Richard U23 1.04.73, Enfield :
PV - 4.10
SWABY Nick U17 1.09.77, Birchfield :
100 - 11.1
SWAIN Anthony Michael U20 17.01.75,
Wakefield/Eastern Region HS :
HT - 55.02 (56.28-93), HTJ - 62.12
SWALES Mark U20 29.01.75, Old Gaytonians :
LJ - 7.00
SWANSTON David 30.11.61, Copeland :
5k - 14:23.8 (14:10.98-90),
10kR - 29:37 (29:08-90/28:41un-93)
SWEENEY David 9.02.62, Sparta :
DT - 47.22
SWEENEY Joseph L. 17.07.65, Windsor S & E :
LJ - 7.22 (7.41-87),
TJ - 15.55i/15.43 (16.26-91)
SWIFT Michael U23 27.08.72, Blackpool/
London Univ : LJ - 7.22, TJ - 14.87
SWIFT-SMITH Justin U23 28.08.74, SB :
800 - 1:49.29, 1500 - 3:48.1 (3:45.40-93)
SWINGLER Martin 11.05.63, Airedale :
110H - 15.5 (15.2w-88/15.34-87)

SYMONDS Christopher M. 15.11.70, Crawl/WLIHE :
SP - 14.75 (15.37-91), DT - 48.28 (50.46-92)
SYMONDS Matthew John 31.07.68, TVH :
SP - 15.59, DT - 52.16, HT - 46.36

TABARES Ruben U17 22.10.78, Blackh'th :
400HY - 56.85
TABOR Nicholas E. V40 17.12.54, Soton City :
DT - 41.94 (53.02-80)
TADESSE Kassa U23 21.08.74, Bel/ETH :
5k - 14:17.70, 10kR - 29:05,
10MR - 48:45 (47:43-93), HMar - 1:03:54
TANG Stephen U17 10.11.77, :
LJ - 6.40
TANSER Toby 21.07.68, Sparvagens :
5k - 13:58.59, 10k - 29:46.24
TATHAM Alan U20 29.04.77, Derby & Co :
800 - 1:53.9, 1500 - 3:51.2
TAYLOR Brian P.J.P. 13.08.70, Old Gayt :
60 - 6.97i (6.78i-93),
100 - 10.59 (10.35-93),
60H - 8.12i (7.83i-93),
110H - 14.18 (13.7db/13.9-93/14.08-91),
SP - 14.19 (14.63-93), DT - 42.38
TAYLOR David 9.01.64, Blackheath/RSA :
5k - 14:25.86,
TAYLOR Ian J. 2.07.67, Telford :
SP - 13.73, DT - 45.76 (49.44-93)
TAYLOR John 13.05.57, Leigh :
PV - 4.20i/4.20 (4.20-91)
TAYLOR Martin U13 31.01.82, Victoria Pk AAC :
75HC - 12.1/12.48, LJ - 5.45
TAYLOR Paul Thomas 9.01.66, Border :
3k - 8:12.04 (7:53.38-93),
5k - 14:15.42 (13:45.31-89), 10kR - 28:32
TAYLOR Paul, Woodstock R :
100kR - 7:35:03
TAYLOR Richard U23 5.12.73, Coventry G :
1500 - 3:48.3
TAYLOR Scott U17 28.07.78, Leics WC :
3kW - 15:28.7, 3kWR - 15:21
TAYLOR Scott U23 16.06.74, Pitreavie :
800 - 1:52.09
TAYLOR Steve 19.03.66, Manx H :
3kW - 12:28.5, 10kW - 45:28.2 (44:38.2-92),
20kW - 1:32:34+ (1:28:46-92),
30kW - 2:21:34
TAYLOR Thomas U15 30.01.81, Leics WC :
3kW - 14:44.0,
TEAPE Hugh D. 26.12.63, Enfield :
60 - 6.85i, 60H - 7.69i (7.69i-92),
110H - 13.76 (13.44-92)
TEAR Adam U20 12.08.75, Grimsby :
DTJ - 41.84
TELFER Gary 10.01.65, Thames Valley :
400 - 48.1/48.41, 400H - 51.51
THICKPENNY Robert U20 17.07.76, Peterbro :
PV - 4.45 (4.50-93)
THOM Douglas 13.04.68, B&A/Scottish Bord :
400H - 53.47
THOMAS Alex U15 31.12.79, Sandwell :
PV - 3.15
THOMAS Alun 16.03.57, Met. Police :
SP - 14.12
THOMAS Andrew U17 15.05.79, Liverpool H :
800 - 1:55.17

THOMAS Barry V.S. U23 28.04.72, Sheff/BUAC :
110H - 14.89 (14.81-92), HJ - 2.01 (2.05-92),
PV - 4.80 (5.00-92), LJ - 7.07 (7.44-92),
JT - 58.02 (59.14-93), Dec - 7458 (7616-92)
THOMAS Chris U15, Gwent Sch :
JTB - 46.64
THOMAS Graham U17 23.09.77, Carmarthen :
100 - 11.1, 400HY - 57.9 (55.29-93)
THOMAS Iwan U23 5.01.74, Newham & EB :
200 - 21.53, 400 - 45.98
THOMAS Josephus 11.07.68, N London/SLE :
60 - 6.71i, 100 - 10.60 (10.43w/10.47-92),
200 - 21.4 (21.3/21.40-92)
THOMAS Joslyn 11.07.71, N London/SLE :
60 - 6.81i, 100 - 10.4w/10.54,
200 - 21.2/21.29
THOMAS Mark 12.05.65, Birchfield :
400 - 47.60 (45.92-87)
THOMAS Stephen U17 4.04.78, Swansea :
SPY - 13.49, DTY - 44.40
THOMAS Timothy U23 18.11.73, Swansea :
PV - 5.20ex/5.10
THOMPSON Francis Morgan 'Daley' 30.07.58,
Newham & Essex B : SP - 15.27 (16.10-84)
THOMPSON Ian 3.08.68, Shaftesbury Barnet :
800 - 1:52.0
THOMPSON Jason 16.11.71, Dartford :
800 - 1:51.4
THOMPSON Jeremy U23 11.06.73,
Portsm/Warwick Univ. : 110H - 15.0/15.02w
THOMPSON Julian A. 28.12.66, Newham & EB :
100 - 10.8 (10.90-87)
THOMPSON Lee U20 21.10.76, Middlesbro :
110HJ - 15.2, 400H - 55.39
THOMPSON Matthew U17 7.01.78, C of Stoke :
TJ - 13.77i/13.68 (13.82-93)
THOMPSON Neville L. 28.03.55, SB :
SP - 14.84 (15.26i-88/15.15-87),
DT - 55.40 (55.68-93), HT - 46.58 (49.46-84)
THOMPSON Paul U23 22.03.72, Cannock & S :
400H - 52.39
THOMPSON S. U17, Wells :
DTY - 42.20
THOMPSON Scott U23 29.09.74, Birchfield :
HT - 54.22
THOMSON Charles 17.06.65, Cambuslang :
10k - 31:02.44 (30:29.6-91), Mar - 2:22:28
THOMSON Ross U13 7.12.81, North East SH :
HTC - 44.38
THORN Darren M.M. 17.07.62, Cov RWC :
3kW - 13:31.0 (12:15.0-89)
THORNTON Andrew U17 29.11.77, Elswick :
100 - 11.1 (11.50-92), 200 - 22.51,
LJ - 6.87w/6.62 (6.70i-93)
THORNTON David U23 27.07.73, Hyndburn :
800 - 1:52.3
THURGOOD Glen U17 6.10.77, Lowestoft :
HJ - 1.90
TIETZ Michael U17 14.09.77, Derby & Co :
100 - 10.77w/10.9/10.94
TILL Stephen, Basingstoke & MH :
24HrT - 217.718
TIMMINS Stephen U20 8.05.75, Blackheath :
110HJ - 15.5w, 110H - 15.62w, 400H - 54.51
TINGLE Darren P.S. 20.09.65, Sheffield :
60 - 6.9i
TINWELL M. U13, Sale/North West HS :
HTC - 34.06

360

TOAL Jason U23 8.11.74, Shaftesbury Barnet :
400H - 53.87 (53.43-93)
TOBIN Kevin 14.07.59, Swansea :
3kSt - 9:21.98 (9:15.3-93)
TOBIN Shaun 13.10.62, Swansea :
10k - 30:35.03 (30:31.27-92), Mar - 2:23:14
TOEMEN Erik U17 1.07.78, Berry-Hill Mansf :
OctY - 4356
TOLPUTT Russell 17.09.64, W S & E/WLHS :
HT - 54.64 (60.38-92)
TOMKINSON Tim 31.10.68, Sale/Army :
110H - 14.7/15.00 (14.5-92/14.74w-93)
TOMLINSON Gavin U15 2.02.80, Crewe & N :
3k - 9:37.09
TOMS Robert U15 7.08.80, Reading :
HJ - 1.80
TONNER Edward U23 3.02.73, Kilmarnock :
3kSt - 9:24.2
TOONE Michael U20 25.09.76, Liverpool H :
HJ - 2.00
TOOTELL Peter 12.03.63, Trafford :
5k - 14:26.5 (13:41.02-89),
10MR - 48:35 (47:43-87)
TOPLISS Stephen U17 17.07.78, Lincoln Well :
200 - 22.44w/22.7
TOUT Mark J. 24.01.61, Hounslow :
DT - 42.24 (44.94-90)
TOWNSEND Glen 23.04.64, Western (I.O.M.) :
DT - 41.60 (44.24-90)
TOWNSEND Neil 3.05.63, Herne Hill :
HT - 46.42 (47.30-93)
TRAVERS Nigel U17 22.10.77, Belvedere/IRE :
DTY - 45.98
TREACY Brian Francis 29.07.71, Annadale Str :
800 - 1:49.85 (1:49.39-90), 1k - 2:19.82A,
1500 - 3:38.93
TREEN Kevin U20 1.02.76, Birchfield :
PV - 4.50i/4.40 (4.40-93)
TREU Robert 1.12.69, Guildford & G :
Dec - 5805
TROMANS Glyn 17.03.69, Coventry G/Lough :
1500 - 3:46.60 (3:43.2-92),
1M - 4:09.92 (4:05.6-90),
3k - 8:14.82, 10kR - 29:16
TROTT Gareth U17 1.05.78, Portsmouth :
SPY - 14.13
TROWER John 6.02.56, Telford :
JT - 58.30 (63.82-89)
TUCKER Stephen 30.12.62, Shettleston :
100 - 10.70w (10.6w-88/10.8/10.82-92),
200 - 21.7/21.97w (21.5w-87/22.07-92)
TULLETT Ian Roger 15.08.69, Belgrave :
PV - 5.10 (5.30i/5.30-92)
TULLETT Jonathon U23 11.02.73, Blackheath :
110H - 15.1
TULLOCH Andrew George 1.04.67, W & B :
60H - 7.84i (7.76i-93), 110H - 13.52
TUNE David 29.10.70, Rotherham :
5k - 14:09.49, 10MR - 49:39
TURAY Sanusi 14.04.68, Thames Valley/SLE :
100Y - 9.74, 100 - 10.28,
200 - 21.73 (21.04A-92/21.56-91)
TURNER Andrew 29.08.63, Bournemouth :
SP - 14.74, DT - 45.02 (46.90-90),
HT - 49.90 (50.42-90)
TURNER Clayton S. 9.01.68, Horsham BS :
SP - 13.98 (15.52-91), DT - 41.78 (45.26-91)

TURNER David 20.10.57, Yorkshire RWC :
3kW - 13:25.07, 10kW - 48:11.6,
50kW - 4:47:12 (4:45:56-91)
TURNER Douglas 2.12.66, Cardiff :
100 - 10.66w/10.7/10.81 (10.7-91),
200 - 21.50
TURNER Garry U17 21.12.78, Notts :
100HY - 13.87w/14.1, 400HY - 57.7/57.84
TURNER Neil U20 17.05.77, Oxford City :
PV - 4.40 (4.40-93)
TURNER R., Oxford City :
LJ - 6.95
TWIGG Matthew 18.07.69, Peterbro/Lough :
SP - 14.92, DT - 48.68 (49.42-91)
TYLER Geoffrey A. V45 30.09.48, Sale :
DT - 49.08 (55.42-80)
TYLER John U23 6.03.74, C of Stoke/Lough :
SP - 14.08 (15.38-93/15.12-92)
TYLER Phil, Tonbridge :
HT - 47.08
TYPE Simon U17 1.02.78, Cardiff :
1.5kSt - 4:34.6

U DALL Carl 13.07.66, Burton/Omega :
3k - 8:06.7 (8:01.5-91),
5k - 14:14.16 (13:50.19-91),
10k - 28:49.96 (28:48.19-92),
10kR - 28:54, 10MR - 47:56, HMar - 1:03:36
UDECHUKU Emeka U17 10.07.79, Blackh'th :
SP - 14.32, SPY - 17.39i/16.46,
DT - 44.60, DTJ - 52.76, DTY - 54.90,
100 - 10.86, 200 - 21.56w/21.65
UGONO Uvie U17 8.03.78, Southwark :
100 - 10.8, 200 - 22.0
ULYATT Kent U23 10.04.72, Norfolk :
200 - 21.6 (21.84-92), 400 - 46.82
URQUHART Ronald John U17 14.11.77,
Helensburgh : SPY - 13.79,
DTY - 44.10, HTY - 54.50
USHER Kevin 3.11.65, Hounslow :
3kSt - 9:07.5 (9:03.3-90)

V ARKER Darren U23 4.10.72, Newq & P :
3kSt - 9:22.0
VENESS Luke U23 5.12.73, Hastings :
1500 - 3:47.4un/3:50.55
VERHEYDEN Paul U23 22.09.72, Blackheath :
JT - 57.78
VIDGEN David U23 27.09.74, Milton Keynes :
100 - 10.99w (10.92w-93),
110H - 15.4, Dec - 6277w (6214-93)
VINCENT C., Army :
100 - 10.8, 200 - 22.0
VINCENT-SMITH James U17 28.06.78, Taunt :
HJ - 1.90
VIVIAN Peter J.P. 5.11.70, TVH/WLHS :
HT - 70.80

W ADDINGTON Anthony U20 30.06.75, Read :
200 - 22.0/22.10w/22.24
WADE Philip U13 24.05.82, City of Bath :
PV - 2.90ex
WADSWORTH Christopher U15 9.10.79, Basil :
200 - 23.54w
WAIN A., Nene Vallley H/CUAC :
SP - 13.84
WALCOTT Andrew U20 11.01.75, Wolves & B :
100 - 10.8w/10.89w (10.8-92), 200 - 21.45

WALCOTT Mark U23 24.11.73, Wolves & B :
60 - 6.82i, 100 - 10.67 (10.6w-92),
200 - 21.60i (21.5/21.60-93)
WALKER A., Army :
LJ - 7.36, TJ - 14.80
WALKER Adam U15 16.11.79, Crawley :
PV - 3.35
WALKER Ben T. U17 8.06.78, Tring :
SPY - 14.83, DT - 40.90,
DTY - 51.72, OctY - 5026
WALKER Colin Frederick 29.10.62, Gate :
2k - 5:11.02,
3k - 8:02.87 (7:57.83i-89/7:59.90-88),
5k - 14:24.32 (13:50.93-91),
HMar - 1:04:47 (1:03:59-92),
3kSt - 8:27.78 (8:25.15-92)
WALKER Douglas U23 28.07.73, Edinburgh :
100 - 10.54w/10.7/10.95 (10.69-91),
200 - 20.71
WALKER Guy U20 23.02.76, Scunthorpe :
110HJ - 15.10
WALKER Nicholas O. 24.02.64, Gloucester :
Dec - 5117 (5510-92)
WALKER Paul U23 2.12.73, Liv H/EUAC :
400 - 49.0 (49.0i/49.0-93/49.12i-92),
800 - 1:48.85 (1:47.53-93)
WALKER Robin U17 8.02.78, Scunthorpe :
HTY - 56.68
WALKER Scott U17 9.09.77, Crewe & Nant :
100 - 11.1/11.47, 200 - 22.2/22.24w,
LJ - 6.73, OctY - 5051
WALKER Sean U15 11.06.80, City of Bath :
LJ - 5.92
WALKER Stuart U17 22.09.78, Derby & Co :
JTY - 55.64
WALLACE John 9.10.68, Morpeth :
HJ - 2.05 (2.16-90)
WALMSLEY Kevin 6.09.67, Manx H :
30kW - 2:30:57
WALSH Liam U13, Derby & Co :
SPC - 12.16, DTC - 38.30
WALSH Philip U13, Ryde :
400 - 60.0
WALSHAM Darren U17 12.01.78, Bexley :
400HY - 56.56
WARCHALOWSKI Nicholas 10.11.71, ESH/SWE :
LJ - 6.91
WARD Ashley K. 1.08.64, Crawley :
DT - 43.18 (47.70-82)
#WARISO Solomon Christopher 11.11.66, Har :
60 - 6.72i, 100 - 10.33, 200 - 20.51
WARMAN J. U15, AVON S :
TJ - 12.05
WARMINGTON Ben U17 20.03.79, North SP :
100HY - 13.9/13.98
WARREN Carl 28.09.69, Cann & S/E Mich Un :
3k - 8:09.29i, 3kSt - 8:47.00
WARREN Robert U15 17.07.81, Steyning :
3kW - 15:52.0, 3kWR - 15:34
WARRILLOW Paul 8.07.70, ESH/Team Solent :
110H - 15.0/15.04 (14.9w/14.95w-90/15.0-93/15.04-91)
WASHINGTON Ivan 18.11.56, Sheffield :
DT - 42.62 (46.06-88)
WASSELL Simon 7.04.69, Rotherham :
400H - 53.35 (52.92-93), Dec - 5911
WATERMAN Peter U15 12.09.79, Blackheath :
SPY - 14.26, SPB - 16.39,
DTB - 44.56, HTB - 52.02

WATERS Andrew U15 11.10.79, Oxford City :
SPB - 13.23, DTB - 42.26, HTB - 44.14
WATERS Martin U13 20.01.82, Isle :
JTC - 36.82
WATSON Cameron 16.12.71, Pitreavie :
3kSt - 9:21.69
WATSON Graeme Lynton George 'Buster'
19.11.57, Blackheath : JT - 57.24 (59.74-87)
WATSON Matthew U15 23.02.80, Bingley :
3k - 9:26.0
WATSON-JONES Benjamin U20 24.11.75, Gate :
DecJ - 5133
WATT Tim 19.09.66, Steyning :
10kW - 47:51.21, 20kW - 1:36:59,
50kW - 4:36:35
WATTS Darren U23 15.11.74, Yeovil Oly :
DecJ - 5266oa (5607-93)
WATTS Paul U17 2.07.78, Annadale Striders :
100HY - 14.0w
WEATHERS Stewart Kennedy 14.09.65, TVH :
100 - 10.72 (10.5-85/10.64-89),
200 - 21.17 (20.95w-86/20.98-92),
400 - 47.73
WEAVER Matthew U23 14.11.73, Old G/OUAC :
PV - 4.90
WEBB Christopher P. 3.08.63, Harborough :
Mar - 2:28:21
WEBB Matthew U23   72, Oxford City :
HJ - 2.00
WEBB Richard U17 24.11.78, Derby & Co :
100 - 11.03w
WEDDERBURN Scott 28.04.65, Huntingdon :
SP - 14.36
WEDLAKE Andrew 30.11.71, Bournem'th/Prov Un :
3k - 8:05.06i (8:17.9-92), 5k - 14:11.37
WEIGHTMAN Jeremy 28.01.63, Haringey :
10k - 31:07.0 (30:59.2-91),
3kSt - 9:23.00 (9:15.2-92)
WEIMANN Wayne 2.05.66, Huntingdon :
PV - 4.40
WEIR Peter 2.09.63, Birchfield :
SP - 15.79 (16.00-88), DT - 47.20
WEIR Robert B. 4.02.61, Birchfield :
DT - 61.06 (62.50-84), HT - 61.68 (75.08-82)
WELCH Mark U23 9.11.74, Army/Kettering :
JT - 56.12 (58.94-92)
WELLENS Andrew U20 21.09.75, Harrogate :
200 - 22.04
WELLS Ian 18.02.62, Belgrave :
110H - 15.60 (15.04-91),
400H - 53.71 (53.3-91/53.54-92)
WELLS Louis U17 6.02.78, Enfield :
800 - 1:57.5
WELLS Stuart U17 26.07.79, Havering :
TJ - 13.65
WELSH Graeme U20 8.10.75, Border :
200 - 21.96
WEST Ben U15, :
PV - 3.40
WEST Scott U20 31.10.75, Birchfield :
1500 - 3:48.0
WEST Terence 19.11.68, Morpeth :
800 - 1:48.66 (1:48.2-92),
1500 - 3:43.39i/3:50.5 (3:47.1-92)
WESTGATE Ian U20 24.10.76, Norfolk :
3kSt - 9:49.88
WESTON Andrew D. U23 4.12.73, Read/Lough :
HJ - 2.05 (2.11-92), LJ - 6.92, Dec - 6256

WESTON James 9.01.70, Cardiff :
200 - 22.00, 400 - 48.4/48.48un
WESTON Paul 6.10.67, Bristol :
TJ - 15.02 (15.46-92)
WESTON Robert U20 16.03.77, Devon Sch :
TJ - 14.14w, DecJ - 5748
WESTWOOD Andrew U15 18.04.80, Hereford :
SPB - 13.48
WETHERILL Andrew 6.12.57, Sutton-in-A:
Mar - 2:27:23
WHALLEY Robert 11.02.68, C of Stoke/Staffs Un :
800 - 1:51.0, 1500 - 3:45.5 (3:42.0-92),
1M - 4:03.8 (4:02.1-92), 3k - 8:09.72i
WHEELER Craig U20 14.06.76, Trafford :
2kSt - 5:53.5, 3kSt - 9:10.50
WHEELER Mark U17 9.05.78, Trafford :
1.5kSt - 4:30.98
WHEELER Stephen K. 3.04.61, Bourton RR :
Mar - 2:26:59 (2:24:36-92)
WHITE Craig Elliot 4.04.71, Sale :
400H - 52.20
WHITE Edward U23 16.11.73, Sale :
60 - 6.99i, 100 - 10.76, 200 - 21.6/21.73
WHITE Graham 28.03.59, Brighton :
3kW - 13:10.6 (12:26.1-88),
20kW - 1:34:11 (1:31:02-83),
30kW - 2:23:52, 35kW - 2:48:50,
50kW - 4:46:15
WHITE L. U13, :
70HC - 11.6
WHITE Paul Adrian U23 1.09.74, TVH :
60 - 6.92i, 100 - 10.50w/10.61,
200 - 21.2/21.21w/21.56
WHITE Richard J. 20.01.60, N & EB :
800 - 1:52.2 (1:49.00-89)
WHITE Steffan U23 21.12.72, Coventry G :
1500 - 3:41.02, 1M - 4:00.61,
3k - 8:01.90i/8:05.30 (8:04.53-92)
WHITE T., Herne Hill :
200 - 21.9
WHITEHEAD Peter Kenneth 3.12.64, Skyrac :
10kR - 29:14, 10MR - 48:22 (47:51-93),
HMar - 1:03:03 (1:02:34-93), Mar - 2:13:40
WHITEHOUSE C. U15, Tipton :
3k - 9:25.7
WHITEMAN Anthony 13.11.71, GEC :
800 - 1:48.45, 1500 - 3:41.92, 1M - 4:03.87
WHITING Andrew U23 7.03.74, Reading :
JT - 63.50
WHITMEE Kristian U15 1.12.79, Chorley H :
400 - 52.57
WHITTLE Brian 26.04.64, Har/Ayr Seaforth :
200 - 21.50 (21.0w/21.34-86),
300 - 34.62 (32.61-88),
400 - 45.46 (45.22-88)
WHYTE Stephen A. 14.03.64, Luton :
SP - 17.29i/17.29 (17.78-89),
DT - 50.40, HT - 64.02 (67.82-89)
WIECZOREK John 22.11.66, Accrington :
Mar - 2:24:38
WIGGANS Steven U15 1.01.80, Preston :
100 - 11.00w/11.3/11.46
WIGGINS John 1.07.71, Blackburn :
TJ - 14.14 (14.34w-91/14.21-93)
WIGHT Graeme 3.06.65, Shettleston :
3k - 8:20.0il, 5k - 14:18.2, 10k - 31:02.01
WIGHTMAN Geoffrey 19.11.60, Dartford :
Mar - 2:21:19 (2:13:17-91)

WILD Jonathon U23 30.08.73, Sale/Okla St Un :
800 - 1:52.7, 1500 - 3:42.50
WILDING Ian U20 3.03.75, City of Stoke :
PV - 5.00ex/4.85
WILKINS Perris 12.11.68, Banbury :
DT - 53.80
WILKINSON Desmond F. 7.01.63, Luton :
60H - 8.4i (8.38i-90),
110H - 15.2/15.82 (14.3-86/14.35w-84/14.49-86)
WILKINSON James Gareth U23 21.04.74, Telf :
JT - 56.80 (58.60-92)
WILKINSON Jonathon 17.02.62, Spen :
JT - 61.38, Dec - 6259
WILKINSON Peter U17 7.08.78, Middlesbro :
TJ - 13.75
WILL Nigel Simon 18.10.67, Enfield :
200 - 21.5 (20.7w-90/20.91-89),
300 - 34.4 (32.91-90), 400 - 46.78 (46.42-92)
WILLERS Edward U15 18.09.79, Braintree :
HJ - 1.91
WILLIAMS Alun, Torfaen/RAF :
DT - 40.44 (41.72-92)
WILLIAMS Anthony Richard U23 1.05.72, Sheff :
400 - 47.7 (47.65-93),
110H - 15.2/15.25 (15.13w/15.16-93),
400H - 50.98
WILLIAMS Barrington Chester 11.09.55, C & S :
LJ - 7.90 (8.05i/8.01-89)
WILLIAMS Barry V45 5.03.47, Trafford :
HT - 46.62 (73.86-76)
WILLIAMS Edward 1.10.70, Thames Valley :
400 - 46.84, 800 - 1:51.00
WILLIAMS Eric J.H. 6.05.56, Stockport :
Mar - 2:27:45 (2:16:56-84)
WILLIAMS Kevin 15.12.71, Cardiff :
60 - 6.86i (6.78i-93),
100 - 10.68 (10.56-93), 200 - 21.47w/22.0
WILLIAMS Mark R. 25.04.68, Blackheath :
60 - 6.8i (6.89i-93),
100 - 10.7/10.94 (10.5w/10.60w/10.6/10.70-92),
200 - 22.0 (21.5-90/21.57w/21.73-93)
WILLIAMS Michael Andrew 27.04.65, Leics C :
200 - 21.8/21.91w (20.97w-85/21.35-84),
400 - 48.89
WILLIAMS Neil U23 31.10.72, Colwyn B/NWHS :
HT - 53.12 (55.02-91)
WILLIAMS Paul U17 21.09.77, Charnwood :
SPY - 14.66
WILLIAMS Simon Alexander 17.10.67, Enfield :
SP - 18.00i/17.79 (19.44i-89/19.17-91),
DT - 58.32 (61.14-92)
WILLIAMS Terry 15.11.68, Shaftesbury B :
100 - 10.17w/10.23, 150 - 15.66, 200 - 20.50
WILLIAMSON Paul U23 16.06.74, Grimsby :
PV - 5.22, LJ - 7.08
WILLS Chris U20 18.05.76, Birchfield :
PV - 4.20i/4.20 (4.40-93)
WILSON David 7.09.68, Annadale Striders :
800 - 1:47.57, 1500 - 3:41.28
WILSON David 5.09.70, Tipton :
JT - 60.70 (64.86-88)
WILSON Ian U15 7.10.79, Coventry Godiva :
HJ - 1.80
WILSON Martin U15 28.09.79, Lowestoft :
SPB - 14.54
WILSON Peter 28.06.62, White Horse :
5k - 14:24.5

WILSON Vincent U23 1.04.73, Jarrow & H :
800 - 1:49.47, 1k - 2:22.46i (2:23.84-93),
1500 - 3:45.1
WILTSHIRE Lee 26.07.62, Portsmouth :
SP - 17.41
WING Jason 12.10.65, Hounslow :
100 - 10.7 (10.7-93),
LJ - 6.91 (7.22w/7.21-86)
WINROW Craig Nicholas 22.12.71, Wigan :
800 - 1:46.54, 1500 - 3:49.4
WINTER Matthew U20 31.10.75, Blackpool :
800 - 1:53.03
WINTER Neil Stephen U23 21.03.74, SB :
PV - 5.50 (5.50-92)
WISEMAN ., Army :
SP - 14.66, DT - 40.98
WITCHALLS Bruno U20 22.03.75, Mole V :
800 - 1:49.84, 1500 - 3:45.11
WITTON Gary U23 25.08.73, Brighton :
3kW - 12:59.63 (12:45.92-93),
10kW - 48:10.1
WOAD Warren U15 16.03.80, Old Gaytonians :
SPB - 13.64, DTB - 37.54
WODU Ejike U23 15.12.74, Blackheath :
60 - 6.89i, 100 - 10.65 (10.38w/10.55-93)
WOOD Anthony U23 30.03.74, Middlesbro :
100 - 10.97, LJ - 7.30w/7.29 (7.40w-93)
WOODMAN Dale U23 2.01.72, Cardiff/RAF :
800 - 1:51.2
WOODS Alan P. V40 27.03.51, Birchfield :
HT - 48.18 (57.24-78)
WOODS Christopher U20 24.12.75, Cleve :
800 - 1:52.79
WOOLCOTT Nicholas D. 7.04.61, Haringey :
DT - 54.62 (55.34-88), HT - 46.66 (49.14-81)
WORLAND James U23 3.02.72, Southend :
JT - 57.06
WRAY Elsworth 14.10.70, Haringey :
110H - 15.62 (15.11w-89/15.18-90)
WRAY Paul K. 16.02.66, Shaftesbury Barnet :
PV - 4.20 (5.00-91)
WRIGHT Darren U15 7.09.79, Wrexham :
PenB - 2623
WRIGHT Karl U23 29.05.74, Leigh :
800 - 1:51.7
WRIGHT Michael U17 15.09.77, Scarborough :
HJ - 2.00

WRIGHT Steven 12.02.71, Gate/Newc Univ :
2kSt - 5:45.40, 3kSt - 8:52.50
WURR Timothy U17 1.03.79, Leamington :
HTY - 52.72
WYLIE Stephen 12.11.71, Cambuslang :
5k - 14:25.7
WYLLIE William U23 12.07.73, Birch/BUAC :
110H - 14.99 (14.91-92), HJ - 2.05 (2.11-91),
PV - 4.15 (4.20-91),
LJ - 7.25w/7.11 (7.33w-92), Dec - 6719

YAPP Jonathan U20 1.02.75, Telford :
PV - 4.50
YATES Matthew Stewart 4.02.69, N & EB :
800 - 1:48.42 (1:45.05-92),
1500 - 3:35.32 (3:34.00-91),
1M - 4:07.64 (3:52.75-93),
3k - 8:01.25i (7:50.82i-93)
YATES Peter Derek 15.06.57, Blackheath :
JT - 70.54 (77.84-87)
YOUNG Adam 2.09.68, Peterborough :
Dec - 5261 (5886-92)
YOUNG Andrew U17 15.02.78, Warwicks Sch :
OctY - 4301
YOUNG Andrew U20 20.06.77, Victoria Prk H :
800 - 1:52.50,
YOUNG Colin U15 11.12.79, Berry-Hill Mans :
400 - 52.71, 800 - 2:02.3
YOUNG Jason, Irvine :
SP - 14.32
YOUNG Kerrin U15 2.09.79, North Down :
400 - 52.59
YOUNG Martin U23 11.07.72, Roadhogs :
5kW - 22:51.1 (22:35.0-89)
YOUNG Matthew Stewart U20 17.03.76, Ox C :
3k - 8:27.06, 5k - 14:59.3
YOUNG Neil U23 27.09.73, City of Stoke :
PV - 4.40i (4.40-91)
YOUNG Neil U20 20.02.77, Lisburn :
PV - 4.80
YUSUF Yacin U17 20.12.77, Croydon :
800 - 1:55.12, 1500 - 4:01.53, 3k - 8:47.4
ZAIDMAN Antony Adam 18.03.62, Haringey :
SP - 15.90 (17.87i-83/17.22-81)
ZAREI James V50 12.01.44, Croydon :
24HrT - 226.179 (254.819km-89),
24Hr - 243.340 (243.564km-89)
ZDANOWSKI Peter U17 3.01.78, Wycombe :
LJ - 6.73w/6.64

With the change of age group descriptions it is obvious that changes must be made to the names of the events. Whilst this is easy to organanize in the main lists, it is much more difficult with the index where a concise code is required. I have, therefore, decided to keep the previous descriptions of the events. This should not cause any confusion since the age group of each athlete is clearly shown in the new form eg U15 but some examples will clarify this.

A **J** after an event is used to designate an Under 20 event
eg 110HJ - 110 metres hurdles with 3'3" hurdles

A **Y** or an **I** is an Under 17 event (men and women)
eg 100HJ - 100 metres hurdles with 3' 0" hurdles Heptl - Heptathlon with Under 17 implements

A **B** or a **G** is an Under 15 event (men and women)
eg JTB - 600 gram Javelin SPG - 3.25kg Shot

A **C** or an **M** is an Under 13 event (men and women)
eg SPC - 3.25kg Shot SPM - 2.72kg Shot

WOMENS INDEX

ABBISS Susan V35 20.10.59, Valli :
Mar - 2:51:33
ADAM Laura Margaret 28.02.65, Parkside :
800 - 2:09.8 (2:07.7-89),
1500 - 4:20.31 (4:17.66-89), 3k - 9:02.47
ADAMS Dawn U17 19.10.78, Liverpool H :
1500 - 4:31.05, 3k - 10:08.8
ADAMS Leanda U15 7.12.79, City of Stoke :
75HG - 11.21w
ADAMS Valerie 30.09.66, Darlington :
HJ - 1.68 (1.77-85)
AGNEW Lydia U13, Lisburn :
SPM - 9.16
AGYEPONG Jacqueline 5.01.69, Shaft Barnet :
60 - 7.61i (7.41i-89),
100 - 11.7 (11.72w-88/11.81-93),
200 - 24.27 (24.1w-93/24.18-90),
60H - 8.14i (8.12i-90), 100H - 12.93
AISTHORPE Vanessa V35 19.09.58, Cleeth :
Mar - 2:55:44
AITKEN Nicola U17 18.12.78, Windsor S & E :
300 - 41.02, 400 - 59.0
AKIWUMU Tuvola U15 15.10.79, Hercules W :
SPG - 11.90 (11.02-93)
ALBERTS Emma U15 22.11.79, Gateshead :
800 - 2:14.64, 1500 - 4:36.4
ALDER Elizabeth U15 20.11.80, Gloucester L :
200 - 25.63w
ALDERMAN-FOORD Lesley U13 13.01.82, And :
PenM - 2022
ALEXANDER Katie U23 28.04.74, Camb H :
PV - 3.00
ALLAHGREEN Diane U20 21.02.75, Liv H :
60 - 7.51i,
100 - 11.7/11.89 (11.78w/11.88-93),
200 - 24.81 (24.39w-93),
60H - 8.45i (8.43i-93), 100H - 13.25
ALLAN Fiona U20 6.11.75, Notts :
PV - 2.55, LJ - 5.62 (5.81-91), TJ - 11.44,
Hep - 4260w/4172 (4215-93)
ALLEN Carice U17 25.09.77, Telford :
HT - 35.76
ALLEN Jenna U17 2.05.79, Charnwood :
JT - 40.72
ALLEN Sara 7.12.70, Sale :
SP - 12.20 (12.39-89), DT - 39.68 (42.06-89)
ALLEYNE Denise 31.10.70, Hounslow/WLIHE :
JT - 40.22 (46.14-93)
ALLSOPP Catherine U23 30.11.73, Lough S :
800 - 2:07.6
AMADI Onyema U23 28.06.73, Cardiff :
JT - 49.04
AMOS Katie U17 13.11.78, Thurrock :
JT - 42.14
ANDERSON Emma U17 19.06.79, Stoke :
80HI - 11.86w/11.9
ANDERSON Jaclyn U17 23.03.79, Aberdeen :
400 - 58.86
ANDERSON Mary Caroline 2.09.67, Edin WM :
400 - 57.30i/57.4 (53.68-87),
800 - 2:07.3 (2:05.41-89),
SP - 11.84 (15.48-85)
ANDERSON Melissa U13 30.03.82, Cram :
80 - 11.0
ANDERSON Pamela U20 16.10.76, Glasgow :
LJ - 5.74, TJ - 11.43 (11.50w-93)

ANDERSON Shani U20 7.08.75, Bromley :
100 - 12.14, TJ - 12.44w/12.39 (12.43-93)
ANDREWS Sharon Nivan 4.07.67, Essex L :
SP - 15.61 (15.80-93), DT - 56.24
ANDREWS Teresa U20 4.01.77, Preseli :
100H - 15.16w/15.49, HJ - 1.79,
Hep - 4456w (3886-92)
ANDREWS Vicki 31.08.69, Wolves & B :
800 - 2:12.38 (2:10.3-93)
ANETO Stephanie U20 23.08.77, Essex L :
TJ - 11.08
ANNING Clare U15, Cardiff :
60H - 9.19i
APPLEBY Bonny E. V40 15.02.53, Invicta :
Mar - 2:54:09
ARCHARD Gillian 5.04.64, Team Solent :
see CASHELL
ARCHER Claire U20 30.09.76, Mandale :
JT - 38.88
ARMIGER Natalie U17 19.10.77, Border :
3k - 10:20.56
ARMISHAW Anna U17 11.02.78, N Devon :
TJ - 10.36
ARMITAGE Susan 10.05.68, Wakefld (nee ATACK) :
SP - 11.33i/11.04 (12.81-85)
ARMSTRONG Caroline A. V40 30.09.53,
South West RR : Mar - 3:06:37
ARMSTRONG Lisa Marie U23 5.11.73, Card :
LJ - 5.61i/5.60 (6.25-92)
ARNOLD Helen U17 5.10.78, Portsmouth :
SP - 12.16, DT - 34.32, HT - 42.12
ASHBY Abigail U17 23.11.77, Rowntrees :
80HI - 11.75w/11.94, LJ - 5.40, Hepl - 4406
ASHLEY Susan E. V40 10.10.52, Epsom & E :
100kR - 9:18:33 (8:29:22-93)
ASHMAN Theresa Jane U23 16.06.73, Birch :
5kW - 27:27.43 (25:21.00-91)
ASHTON Gemma U15 26.01.81, Whitby H :
HJ - 1.60,
ASKEY Andrea U23 9.11.74, Wigan :
400H - 64.9 (64.8-93)
ASKHAM Michelle U17 2.08.78, Hallamshire :
SP - 10.84
ASKIN Samantha U13 6.01.82, Stainforth :
JTM - 23.70
ATACK Susan 10.05.68, Wakefield :
see ARMITAGE
ATKIN Kathleen 30.04.64, Charnwood :
5k - 17:29.03
ATKINSON Rachel U23 26.05.73,
Sale/Leeds Univ : TJ - 11.82
ATUNUMUO Lucy U15 4.11.80, Hercules Wim :
LJ - 5.35
AUCOTT Jane Christine 10.10.68, Cov G :
SP - 12.75 (12.99i-86/12.89-93),
DT - 46.50 (55.52-90)
AUGEE Esther 1.01.64, Essex L :
SP - 11.73, HT - 49.30 (56.76-93)
AUGEE Myrtle Sharon Mary 4.02.65, Bromley :
SP - 17.64 (19.03-90),
DT - 44.80 (46.64-92), HT - 43.24
AWANAH Vicky U15 3.09.79, Herne Hill :
HJ - 1.60
AXTEN Tracy 20.07.63, Hounslow :
SP - 14.15, DT - 52.28 (54.40-93),
HT - 36.80 (40.56-93)

BACKHOUSE Susan U17 6.12.78, Leeds :
DT - 34.54
BADEN Amy U17 30.05.79, Exeter :
300H - 46.9, Hepl - 3974
BADEN Lucy U17 21.10.77, Exeter :
80HI - 12.06w
BAGWELL Rosie 7.08.67, Bristol :
see THORNER
BAIGENT Sarah 22.12.71, Reading :
400H - 62.9/62.92 (62.5-90)
BAILEY Adele U17 9.09.77, Derby LAC :
LJ - 5.50
BAILEY Kathryn 25.03.68, New Forest :
3k - 9:58.6 (9:52.0-93), 10kR - 33:44 (33:37-93),
10MR - 56:04 (55:48-93), HMar - 1:15:35
BAILEY Kelli U15 8.09.79, Telford :
100 - 12.2/12.28w/12.55
BAILLIE Lisa U20 25.05.77, Avonside :
1.5kSt - 5:43.8
BAINES Sally I. U17 4.12.78, Steve & NH :
SP - 10.53
BAINES Sally Ann 2.03.70, Tipton :
3k - 9:55.2 (9:31.49-90)
BAIRD Kim V35 28.02.56, Dudley & Stourb :
3kW - 14:47.9 (14:34.8-93), 5kW - 25:05.3,
5kWR - 25:36 (24:35-93), 20kW - 1:50:21
BAKER Lorraine 9.04.64, Coventry Godiva :
see STRAIN
BAKER Nicola U23 8.10.74, Gateshead :
HJ - 1.76i (1.76-93)
BAKER Rosalind U17 10.04.78, Crawley :
200 - 25.3, 300 - 40.55 (40.4-93)
BAKER Samantha U23 14.04.72, Sale :
100 - 12.1/12.36 (11.9w-90/12.08-93/12.1-92),
60H - 8.56i (8.42i-91), 100H - 13.63w/13.8/13.82
(13.32dt-93/13.4w-90/13.43-93)
BAKER Tanya U23 23.11.74, Andover :
800 - 2:09.14 (2:13.5-90)
BANKS Rita V50 26.12.43, Stone MM :
Mar - 3:06:36 (3:04:45-91)
BANNISTER Donna U23 27.12.72, Bromley :
100 - 12.27 (12.19-93), 200 - 24.4/24.48
BARBOUR Shireen 4.09.60, Birchfield :
3k - 9:27.44 (9:08.4-84), 5k - 16:06.49,
10k - 33:52.47, 10kR - 33:54
BARCLAY Jaqueline 17.01.66, Glasgow :
SP - 11.81 (12.58-86), JT - 43.86 (50.38-84)
BARLOW Karen L. 15.11.67, Herne Hill :
Mar - 3:07:29
BARNES Alison 6.11.69, Bournemouth :
1500 - 4:25.30, 3k - 9:19.0 (9:09.1-92),
5k - 16:46.13 (16:12.73-93)
BARNES Catherine U17 28.09.77, Winch :
TJ - 11.10
BARNES Maureen A. 21.04.63, Bromley :
400 - 56.70i/57.2/57.51 (54.5-84),
400H - 65.12 (59.3/60.19-84)
BARNETT Brenda, Buxton :
24HrT - 165.601
BARNETT Lynne U23 12.08.74, Perth :
SP - 12.06 (12.83-93)
BARR Nicola 26.04.70, Edinburgh WM :
LJ - 5.77 (5.77-91), TJ - 12.07 (12.34-92)
BARR Samantha 14.08.70, Basildon :
100 - 12.1/12.37 (12.0-91), 200 - 24.9
BARRINGTON Suzanne 3.08.71,
CUAC/City of Stoke : 400H - 65.6

BARTLETT Katherine U23 6.05.73, C of Hull :
100H - 14.54, 400H - 61.54
BARTLETT Kelly U15 13.10.79, Dudley & St :
2.5kW - 13:51.8, 3kWR - 15:52
BARTLETT Natasha U23 19.01.74, Cardiff :
200 - 24.40 (24.3w-91),
400 - 56.13i (55.79-93),
100H - 14.86, 400H - 59.25
BATES Rebecca U13 16.05.82, City of Stoke :
75 - 10.1, 100 - 13.2, 150 - 19.9,
200 - 27.6, LJ - 4.77
BATHO Louise U20 27.11.76, Thurrock :
SP - 11.88, Hep - 4369
BATT Amanda U17 9.11.77, Enfield :
60H - 9.05i, 80HI - 11.67 (11.53w-93),
100H - 15.37 (15.1w-93)
BATTLE Helena 5.04.62, Bolton :
10kW - 58:58.0
BATTY Suzanne U15 29.04.80, Wirral :
LJ - 5.25
BAUER E., Edinburgh Univ :
HJ - 1.65
BAXTER Morag 22.08.69, Glasgow :
100 - 11.93w/12.0/12.04 (11.78w/11.97-93),
200 - 24.8w (24.7w-89/24.71-93)
BEADLE Sarah U17 16.05.79, GEC :
100 - 12.48w/12.60
BEALES Emma Jay 7.12.71, Milton Keynes :
100H - 15.0 (14.50w-93/14.68-92),
HJ - 1.71i (1.76-92),
LJ - 5.78/5.56 (6.20w?/5.99-92),
SP - 14.31i/14.18 (14.53-92),
DT - 53.54 (53.78-93), JT - 41.54 (42.48-93)
BEAVAN Joanne U17 23.06.78, Broms & R :
60 - 7.89i (7.84i-93)
BECKINGSALE Elizabeth U15 20.03.80,
Gresham : PV - 2.20
BEDDOW Helen 10.09.67, Rotherham :
PV - 2.45
BELL Annette 5.09.64, Lincoln Well :
3k - 9:42.1 (9:14.6-92),
HMar - 1:18:58 (1:14:07-91)
BELL Caroline U15 14.07.80, Cannock & Staff :
1500 - 4:44.0
BELL Katie U13 1.02.82, Cleethorpes :
HJ - 1.48
BELL Lorraine U20 21.06.77, Leominster :
200 - 24.99, 400 - 56.20
BELL Mandy 5.12.65, Queens Park :
LJ - 5.78i (6.25-92)
BELLFIELD Julie 1.11.68, Dudley & Stourb :
10kWR - 57:15 (54:11-92)
BEMROSE Antonia Marie U15 3.09.79, AF&D :
HJ - 1.70, PenG - 2562
BENJAMIN Bonita 1.06.67, Sale :
400H - 61.76 (60.2/60.54-93)
BENNETT Carol U20 11.01.77, Hull Spring :
SP - 11.60
BENNETT Christina Jayne U17 27.02.78,
Epsom & Ewell : SP - 13.12, DT - 40.22,
HT - 36.12, JT - 35.32
BENNETT Diana Faye U23 14.06.74, Eps & E :
60H - 8.9i, 100H - 14.47, HJ - 1.71i/1.71 (1.75-92),
LJ - 5.80 (5.85-93), JT - 38.00, Hep - 5212
BENNETT Julia Margaret 26.03.70, Eps & E :
100H - 15.1/15.16w (14.8-92/15.01-90),
400H - 62.2, HJ - 1.89 (1.92i-90),
LJ - 6.12, Hep - 5239

BENNETT Kim 16.05.69, Rotherham :
3k - 9:37.10 (9:31.08-91),
10kR - 34:59 (34:32-92),
10MR - 58:18 (57:22-92)
BENNETT Sarah U15 27.07.80, Birchfield :
2.5kW - 12:24.6, 3kW - 14:59.0 (14:56.4-93)
BENNETT Yvette 2.07.65, Medway :
JT - 39.72 (42.64-91)
BENTLEY Sandra V35 17.02.58, Tipton :
10kR - 34:36, Mar - 2:49:25 (2:42:54-91)
BENTLEY Sarah 21.05.67, City of Stoke :
800 - 2:10.2, 1500 - 4:22.9,
3k - 9:18.09, 5k - 16:16.86
BERGIERS Amy U15 19.09.79, Carmarthen :
75HG - 11.3/11.51
BERMINGHAM Orla U20 7.10.75, Essex L :
60H - 8.55i, 100H - 13.87w/14.01,
400H - 63.14, Hep - 4620
BERRY Catherine U20 8.10.75, Kingston & P :
1500 - 4:25.58, 3k - 9:25.86
BERRY Jayne N. 18.07.70, Cardiff :
SP - 14.22 (14.80-90)
BEVAN Susan F. V35 15.12.59, Essex L :
800 - 2:08.14 (2:01.93-91),
1500 - 4:24.5 (4:18.75-91)
BEVERLEY Rachael U17 23.07.79, Mandale :
HT - 43.08
BINKS Aneska, Leics Cor :
HJ - 1.65
BIRKINSHAW Sara Jayne U23 19.11.72,
Rockingham : SP - 11.41 (11.78-92)
BISCOE Anna U15 13.09.79, Southend :
HJ - 1.63
BISHOP Tracy U17 1.05.79, Parkside :
100 - 12.4/12.44w
BLACK Caroline E. U23 19.05.72, Edin WM :
LJ - 5.83w/5.74 (6.03w-91/6.00-92),
TJ - 11.27
BLACK Sylvia V35 16.04.58, Birchfield :
3kW - 13:47.10i (13:42.10-90),
5kWR - 23:58 (23:13-93),
10kWR - 48:41 (47:59-92)
BLACKMAN K. U13, Barking Sch :
75 - 10.3
BLACKWOOD Kathryn U20 31.03.76, Dart :
LJ - 5.73 (5.77-92), TJ - 11.69 (11.80w-93)
BLAKE Tanya U23 16.06.73, Blackheath :
800 - 2:12.2 (2:11.6-92),
1500 - 4:25.38 (4:22.04-93),
3k - 9:21.07 (9:17.72-93)
BLAKE Tanya-Gee 16.01.71, City of Hull/Ark :
400 - 55.46 (54.9-89), 800 - 2:03.78,
1500 - 4:27.59
BLANCHARD Helen U23 11.07.72, C of Stoke :
100H - 14.7/15.24 (15.11w/15.15-90)
BLANK Paula U17 13.12.77, Verlea :
JT - 41.36, Hep - 4057, Hepl - 4265
BLEASDALE Clare H. 6.07.71, Guildford & G :
200 - 25.0 (25.0-91),
400 - 55.0/55.44, 400H - 58.04
BLOOMFIELD Christine 12.02.68, Essex L :
60 - 7.7i/7.73i (7.67i-93),
100 - 11.94 (11.59-93/11.72-91),
200 - 24.2w?/24.4/24.50w/25.34
(23.70-93/23.7mx), TJ - 11.47
BLOOMFIELD Tracy U15 13.09.79, Guild & G :
PV - 2.50

BLUNT Emma U17 26.10.77, Epsom & Ewell :
60H - 9.1i, 80HI - 11.9/11.96w/12.05,
100H - 15.4, Hepl - 4003
BODEN Veronica V. V35 23.12.58, Trafford :
400 - 55.50 (55.1-87), 800 - 2:10.4,
2kSt - 7:05.76,
400H - 60.0/60.49 (58.8-87/59.53-78)
BOLEMAN Margaret V35 7.03.59, Sale :
3k - 9:45.89 (9:44.84-93)
BOLSOVER Maria Teresa U15 5.06.80, Hallam :
60 - 7.95i, 100 - 12.47, 200 - 24.58w/24.83
BOLTON Denise U20 1.02.77, Wigan :
200 - 25.00, 100H - 14.04w/14.14,
400H - 61.4/62.73, LJ - 5.69 (5.81-93),
Hep - 4750
BONGERS Paula V40 17.12.51, Holland Sp :
Mar - 3:05:06
BONNER Angela U23 22.11.73, Cardiff :
HT - 45.44
BOOKER Clare U13 12.12.81, City of Stoke :
600 - 1:46.0
BOOTH Joan 18.12.68, Edinburgh WM :
100 - 11.90 (11.70w-93),
200 - 24.68 (24.13w-93)
BOSNAK Fatmagul, Walton/TUR :
3k - 9:58.4
BOSWELL Fiona 10.02.68, Edinburgh WM :
60 - 7.77i (7.7i-91)
BOULTON Catherine U17 2.11.77, Radley :
HJ - 1.76i/1.76, Hepl - 4064
BOULTON Jane V35 2.04.56, Crowborough :
Mar - 3:07:01
BOWDEN Michelle U17 5.09.78, Black Isle :
DT - 34.14
BOWEN Shelley-Anne U17 12.05.79, Reading :
100 - 12.4 (12.31-93)
BOWRING Faye U13 22.10.81, Bournemouth :
JTM - 26.94
BOWYER Elizabeth U13 8.09.81, Wirral :
SPM - 10.36
BOWYER Sonya U23 18.09.72, Sale/Lough :
400 - 54.15, 800 - 2:02.30, 1500 - 4:22.3
BOYLAN Barbara V35 27.02.58, Cardiff :
Mar - 3:02:27
BRACKSTONE Lorraine U17 15.02.78, Stoke :
60H - 8.99i, 80HI - 11.52
BRACKSTONE Victoria U15 10.04.80, Stoke :
100 - 12.2w/12.84,
BRADDOCK Lynsey U17 14.10.77, Bracknell :
DT - 39.02
BRADLEY Joanna U17 23.08.79, Ashford :
DT - 37.02
BRADSHAW Noelle E. 18.12.63, Portsm Far :
SP - 11.24 (12.06-92), HT - 38.82,
JT - 51.00 (52.40-93)
BRAHAM Alice U20 17.01.76,
Parkside/Oklahoma St Un :
1500 - 4:32.0, 3k - 9:17.70i/9:26.31
BRANCH Lorraine V35 9.11.59, Chelmsford :
Mar - 2:59:21 (2:58:21-92)
BRANNAN Lesley U20 13.09.76, Wrexham :
SP - 11.83, HT - 34.00
BRANNEY Sandra V40 30.04.54, Glasgow :
HMar - 1:19:00 (1:12:22-86)
BREWER Nadia U15 14.04.80, Blackheath :
HJ - 1.66
BRIARS Rachel U20 29.01.76, Wirral :
400H - 63.6

BRIDGE K. U13, Bath :
70HM - 11.8
BRIGGS Julie 13.03.69, Crawley :
3k - 9:30.15i/9:47.3 (9:17.3-92)
BRIGGS L. U13, Telford :
JTM - 25.16
BRIGGS Susan 26.03.67, Trafford :
200 - 24.18 (24.02i-92/24.1/24.17w-89),
400 - 57.3 (56.4-92)
BRIGHT Joanne U17 4.10.77, Dartford :
TJ - 10.84
BRIGHT Kathryn U20 27.03.76, Newport :
800 - 2:11.90 (2:10.80-93)
BRITTAIN Barbara 24.10.66, Peterborough :
400H - 60.7/61.39 (59.69-93)
BROCK Leah U17 15.03.79, Trafford :
300H - 44.78, 400H - 65.1
BROCKLEY Diane 5.02.67, Trafford :
1500 - 4:25.9 (4:22.71-92)
BROOKER Emma U17 26.10.78, Ipswich :
3k - 10:32.5
BROOKER Jenna U13 23.10.81, AF&D :
DTM - 23.42
BROOKES Melanie 5.04.64, Nuneaton :
see WRIGHT
BROOKS Ann 4.05.71, City of Hull :
60 - 7.71i, 100 - 11.8w/12.21,
LJ - 6.38w/6.14
BROOKS Katie U13 17.02.82, St Albans :
1500 - 5:01.9
BROWN Alison J. V35 7.10.58, Edin WM :
400H - 64.4 (60.41-87)
BROWN Amanda U20 11.05.75, Kingston & P :
JT - 38.72
BROWN Beverley A. 9.05.65, Stubbington :
Mar - 2:56:23 (3:00:23-89)
BROWN Celia U20 22.01.77, Chelmsford :
400H - 63.67
BROWN Emma U13 15.10.81, Haslemere :
80 - 11.0
BROWN Emma U17 7.11.78, Sutton :
60H - 9.1i, 80HI - 12.0,
300H - 45.0, 400H - 67.8
BROWN Jennifer A. V35 21.05.59, Ashford :
HJ - 1.72 (1.73-89), TJ - 11.36,
Hep - 4738w/4727 (4803w-89)
BROWN Karen Louise 31.08.68, Sale :
HT - 43.56 (47.10-93)
BROWN Lisa U20 16.03.76, Lochgelly :
HJ - 1.75 (1.76-93)
BROWN Nicola U23 17.03.74, Tynedale :
3k - 9:54.42
BROWN S., Hallamshire :
3k - 9:57.8
BROWN Sandra V45 1.04.49, Surrey WC :
24Hr - 188.103, 3kW - 15:38.3,
5kWR - 26:27 (25:02-92),
10kW - 54:00.7 (52:43.71-93),
10kWR - 53:25 (52:15-93),
20kW - 1:52:04 (1:48:29-91), 50kW - 4:56:27,
100MW - 19:09:17 (18:50:29-92)
BROWN Sarah A. 28.09.64, Steyning :
3kW - 14:44.8 (13:48.0-87),
5kW - 25:06.0 (24:00.0-91),
5kWR - 25:10 (23:57-87),
10kW - 53:20.5 (48:56.5-91),
10kWR - 51:50 (49:22-89),
20kW - 1:51:38

BROWN Vicky U17 22.02.78, Newquay & Par :
SP - 10.52
BRUCE Jill U23 25.07.73, Dromore :
1500 - 4:27.46, 3k - 9:59.26
BRUNGER Tracy 8.06.70, Medway :
400H - 65.9 (65.0-90)
BRUNNING Louise U23 6.03.72,
Sutton & District/Loughborough Studnts :
400 - 56.4, 400H - 58.07
BUBIKOVA Jarmila U20 8.01.77, Essex L/CS :
TJ - 11.76, Hep - 3957
BUCCIERRI Katrina U13 24.06.83, Hallam :
LJ - 4.81
BUCKLAND N. U13, Braintree :
SPM - 9.19
BUCKLAND Sadie U15 11.03.80, Braintree :
SPG - 11.14
BUDD Katie J. U20 3.01.76, Shaftesbury B :
100H - 14.80/14.99, Hep - 4328 (4414-93)
BUETNER L., Cardiff :
HJ - 1.70
BULL Sarah U20 4.06.75, Derby LAC :
800 - 2:11.1
BULLEN Kate 12.02.71, Birchfield :
200 - 25.0 (25.0-92),
400 - 57.0/57.42i/57.97
BULLOCK Andrea U17 1.03.78, Cannock & S :
300 - 41.5
BURKE Jacquie U20 12.09.76, Hull Spring :
SP - 11.89, Hep - 4313
BURKE M., Perth :
Mar - 2:57:18
BURKE Olive C. 12.09.66, Croydon/IRE :
100H - 14.6, 400H - 62.19 (60.61-93)
BURKE Sarah U23 11.07.73, Bracknell :
400H - 64.49 (62.52-93)
BURNETT Claire U23 17.10.72, C of Plymouth :
SP - 11.91, HT - 37.14
BURNETT Judith A. V35 14.10.58, C of Bath :
Mar - 2:51:21dh/2:55:18 (2:51:33-91)
BURNS Gillian 12.07.64, Wirral :
SP - 12.28 (12.96-90)
BURNS-SALMOND Samantha U20 13.04.76,
City of Hull : DT - 37.54, HT - 45.48
BURRELL Lucy U20 10.03.75, Coventry G :
JT - 51.76
BURROWS Catherine U20 11.02.76, Wigan :
LJ - 5.58 (5.60w-93), TJ - 11.30w/11.10
BURROWS Melanie U20 7.08.76, C of Plym :
JT - 39.90
BURTON Carly U15 14.10.80, Ashford :
DT - 30.88 (24.44-93)
BURTON Joanna U20 11.05.75, Dorchester :
JT - 52.14
BUSHBY Clare U20 7.09.76, North Shields P :
100H - 14.41w (15.6-92)
BUTLER Keeley U20 24.03.75, Coventry G :
60 - 7.78i (7.74i-93),
100 - 12.22w? (12.1/12.22w-93/12.57-90),
200 - 25.0/25.20 (24.4w/24.45-93)
BUTLER Natalie U17 25.11.78, Oxford City :
LJ - 5.51, TJ - 10.69w/10.57,
Hepl - 3917
BUXTON Leanne U17 27.05.78, Brighton :
300H - 44.92, 400H - 65.0,
Hepl - 3816

368

CADMAN Joanna 1.06.68, Edinburgh WM :
400H - 61.9/63.19 (60.7/61.06-93)
CAIN Jane C. 24.10.67, Bedford & County :
HJ - 1.65 (1.80-86)
CAINES Vanessa U13 17.04.83, Steyning :
2kW - 11:38.8
CALDER Fiona 4.05.71, Glasgow :
200 - 24.99w (25.0-92)
CALLANIN Elaine 13.09.60, Solihull & S H :
3kW - 14:12.9, 5kWR - 24:37,
10kWR - 49:17 (49:12-81)
CALLAWAY Deborah A. 15.07.64, AF&D :
SP - 14.74i/14.58 (14.88-93), DT - 55.66
CALVERT Ruth U20 22.10.75, Bingley :
Hep - 3969 (4068-93)
CAMERON Claire V35 3.10.58, Glasgow :
DT - 41.68 (46.34-85)
CAMERON Lauraine S. U23 21.03.72, Walth:
TJ - 11.85 (12.55w-93), SP - 11.27
CAMERON Rebecca 17.07.60, Bridgend
(nee RICHARDSON) :
Mar - 2:52:11 (2:50:56-89)
CAMPBELL Katrina U23 8.03.72, Lisburn :
JT - 44.28
CAMPBELL Louise U17 22.02.79, Lagan V :
HT - 31.40
CAMPBELL Michelle 24.02.69, Essex L :
100H - 13.68w (13.26-90)
CAMPBELL Natasha U13 6.08.82, Medway :
JTM - 26.94
CAMPBELL Zoe U17 9.01.78, Notts :
DT - 33.94
CANNON Kim U13 27.07.82, Basildon :
SPG - 8.99, SPM - 9.66
CAPES Lucy U20 1.12.75, Hallamshire :
DT - 44.18
CAPP Jackie U17 31.03.78, Luton :
80HI - 12.0
CAPPS Tracee U23 29.11.73, Corby :
SP - 11.64 (12.74-93), DT - 37.84 (38.58-93)
CARDY-WISE Bronwyn G. V40 26.01.52, B & R :
1500 - 4:24.2, HMar - 1:17:38 (1:14:06-86)
CARLESS Tammy U20 10.01.77, Tower H :
JT - 40.86
CARMICHAEL Carmilla U15 1.12.79, Glos Sch :
PenG - 2594
CARR Anne U20 1.05.76, City of Stoke :
400H - 64.8, HJ - 1.66, Hep - 4514 (4525-93)
CARSON Heather U17 18.07.79, East Ches:
1500 - 4:45.04, 3k - 10:08.7
CARTER Alexis U13 23.10.81, Broms & R :
70HM - 11.8, HJ - 1.45
CARTER Bronwin A. V40 25.04.51, Ports Far :
SP - 12.45 (13.89-84), DT - 37.40 (41.08-84)
CARTER Julia 28.03.71, Notts :
400H - 62.33
CARTER Lucy U17 7.03.78, Bedford & Co :
200 - 25.46w/25.55, 300 - 41.5
CARTHEW Lisa Jane 6.04.71, Swansea :
800 - 2:09.7, 1500 - 4:23.07 (4:22.42-93)
CARTMEL Anne-Marie U23 18.11.73, Hallam :
SP - 11.39 (11.44-93), JT - 38.16 (40.14-93)
CARTMELL Kathleen U17 31.05.78, Cope :
SP - 11.59 (11.81-93)
CARTWRIGHT Ann V40 22.09.54, Wrexham :
Mar - 2:57:53 (2:54:22-93)
CARVILL Sophie U13 16.02.82, Yeovil Oly :
100 - 13.2

CARYL Lisa U20 21.11.75, Liverpool H :
PV - 2.70i (2.70-93)
CASHELL Gillian 5.04.64, Team S (nee ARCHARD) :
200 - 24.8 (24.5/25.28-93),
300 - 38.9, 400 - 54.35, 800 - 2:09.68
CAVE Eleanor U23 23.01.73, Parkside/OUAC :
100H - 14.88 (14.7-91/14.80-90),
HJ - 1.73 (1.78-90), LJ - 5.94,
TJ - 11.62, Hep - 4839 (4932-91)
CAVERGEN J., Cambridge University :
DT - 36.34
CHAFFE Lucy U17 25.03.79, Essex L :
100 - 12.2/12.48 (12.47-93),
200 - 25.0 (25.26w-93), 300 - 39.43,
400 - 56.6
CHALLONER Katie U17 18.09.78, Shrews :
60H - 9.24i (9.23i-93)
CHAMBERLAIN Eleanor U17 17.04.79, Birch:
300H - 45.5
CHAMBERLAIN Rebecca U15 7.09.79,
Bournemouth : SPG - 11.99
CHAMPION Fay 27.09.66, Yate :
SP - 13.01, DT - 43.18,
Hep - 4277 (4306-93)
CHARLES Ayeesha U15 4.09.79, Oxford City :
60 - 7.73i, 100 - 12.2/12.49,
200 - 24.90w/25.4, LJ - 5.28
CHARLES Jennifer 1.06.68, Herne Hill :
TJ - 11.58i/11.43
CHARLTON Lorraine 20.09.60, Birchfield :
see MCCALLA
CHARNOCK Catherine U20 3.05.75, Barr & F :
3kW - 15:32.45, 5kW - 26:11.0,
5kWR - 26:18, 10kWR - 56:55
CHATFIELD Donna U13 15.09.81, Guild & G :
HJ - 1.45
CHESNEY Sarah U23 3.03.73, Essex L :
60 - 7.65i,
200 - 24.9w?/25.1/25.51 (25.1-90/25.26w-93)
CHILD Amanda U13 28.11.81, Milton Keynes :
800 - 2:23.7, 1500 - 5:01.2
CHILDS Clare U23 8.10.72,Cov RWC
(nee WALKER) : 3kW - 14:45.8,
5kW - 25:43.0, 5kWR - 26:28, 10kWR - 53:48
CHILDS Emma U13 13.02.82, Guildford & G :
DTM - 28.42
CHRISTIE Susan U17 7.03.79, Motherwell :
100 - 12.1w/12.51 (12.38w-93), 200 - 25.4
CHRISTOPHER Beverley U20 14.01.75, Cov G :
60 - 7.70i, 100 - 12.07 (11.78w/12.0-93),
200 - 24.85w/25.01 (24.28w/24.73-93)
CHURCHMAN Kate U13 2.11.81, Braintree :
70HM - 11.5, 75HG - 12.6, HJ - 1.45
LANGSTON/CLAPSON Emma 22.11.71, Brom :
400 - 55.89 (54.25-88)
CLARENCE Emma Jane U17 2.12.78, Sale :
SP - 10.96
CLARK Jean 5.10.68, Milton Keynes :
HT - 48.98 (49.78-92)
CLARK Joanna U23 11.02.73, AF&D :
100 - 12.19w, 200 - 24.4, 400 - 55.74
CLARKE Nicola U20 14.04.77, Hull Spring :
LJ - 5.59, TJ - 11.51
CLARK Rebecca U17 15.09.78, Coventry G :
200 - 25.57
CLARKE Dyanna V35 27.02.58, TVH :
400 - 55.8/56.39, 400H - 62.9

CLARKE Elizabeth M. V35 14.02.57, Les Croup :
Mar - 3:06:26 (2:53:29-91)
CLARKE Hazel U17 17.03.79, Copeland :
60H - 9.21i, HJ - 1.67, Hepl - 4203
CLARKE Jenny V40 19.10.52, Peterborough :
HT - 36.08
CLARKE Melanie U17 25.02.78, Westbury :
200 - 25.41w/25.53
CLARKE Natalie U17 5.09.77, Middlesex Sch :
SP - 10.48
CLARKE Rhian U20 19.04.77, Ipswich :
PV - 3.30i/3.25 (3.30-93)
CLAXTON Sarah U15 23.09.79, Colch & T :
100 - 11.88w/12.19, 75HG - 11.18,
LJ - 5.68, PenG - 2970
CLAYDON Emma Jayne U15 1.06.80, Medway :
JT - 34.48
CLEMENTS Hayley D. 17.09.68, Dartford :
100 - 12.1/12.35 (12.05w/12.1-93),
200 - 24.56 (23.4w-85/23.8/23.90-86),
400 - 54.62
CLEMENTS Lucy U17 20.07.78, Solihull & SH :
TJ - 10.92
CLOWES Louise U17 19.07.78, Stoke :
300H - 46.8, TJ - 10.62i/10.26
COATES Angela 2.04.67, Bingley :
800 - 2:10.9 (2:06.9-88)
COATES Nichola U13 24.03.82, Cramlington :
1500 - 5:06.7
COCKRAM Julia 1.01.68, Belgrave :
PV - 2.80
CODD Danielle U17 17.02.79, Trafford :
PV - 2.35
COHEN Paula 5.02.71, Trafford :
100 - 11.6 (11.63-93), 200 - 23.67 (23.64-92),
400 - 54.02, 400H - 63.8 (62.9-92)
COLDWELL Dominique U15 6.09.79, Hull Ach :
200 - 25.57w
COLE Yvonne 18.11.65, Croydon :
100 - 12.28 (12.18-93)
COLEBROOK Christine 'Teena' V35 18.12.56,
Peterborough : 1500 - 4:24.76 (4:07.69-90)
COLEBY Julie V35 5.11.55, Durham :
10kR - 34:35, 10MR - 58:11 (55:57-82),
HMar - 1:18:07 (1:18:01-93), Mar - 2:40:31
COLEGATE Joanne U17 24.11.77, Derby L :
60 - 7.88i, 200 - 25.5 (24.75-93), 300 - 41.0
COLEMAN Kirsty U15 17.11.80, Steyning :
2.5kWR - 13:55, 3kWR - 15:55
COLLEDGE Louise U17 12.10.77, Leics Cor :
60HI - 8.89i,
80HI - 11.39w/11.58 (11.3/11.52-93),
100H - 15.3 (15.1/15.29-93)
COLLISON Gabrielle 10.02.66, Belgrave :
1500 - 4:31.5, 3k - 9:39.8, 5k - 16:44.58
COLLYER Rosie U17 19.02.78, Telford :
TJ - 10.38
CONNELL Hazel U13 8.02.82, Glasgow :
600 - 1:44.0
CONNELL Nicola 17.12.68, Scunthorpe :
JT - 39.00 (42.12-88)
CONNOLLY Anne U17 18.02.78, Skyrac :
1500 - 4:42.94
CONROY Donna U17 21.09.77, Liv Pem :
LJ - 5.41 (5.46-93), Hepl - 3957
CONWAY Rebecca U13 4.11.81, Harlow :
800 - 2:27.7, PenM - 2074

COOK Lucy U20 11.09.75, Croydon :
JT - 45.58
COOKE Alanna Jane 11.01.70, Rotherham :
60 - 7.78i, 200 - 24.28, 400 - 54.49,
400H - 63.0, Hep - 4324
COOKE Frances V35 8.12.56, Thorney :
Mar - 3:04:41
COOKE Jacqueline U20 20.06.76, Bed & Co :
100H - 15.03w/15.14 (14.96w-93/15.0-92),
Hep - 3982
COOKE T. Michelle 28.11.64, Swansea :
400H - 63.3/63.75 (59.9/59.95-88)
COOKERSOLE Helen U17 14.03.78, GEC :
JT - 36.02
COOKSLEY Carol Ann 22.09.69, Coventry G :
SP - 14.09 (14.76i-91/14.71-90),
DT - 38.40 (44.70-89)
COOTE Joanne 10.02.68, Rowntrees :
DT - 36.96 (38.66-92), HT - 39.06
COOTES Sarah U17 3.11.78, Basildon :
200 - 25.3/26.16, 300 - 40.4/40.58
CORNICK Michelle U20 21.09.76, Dorchester :
SP - 11.31, DT - 38.38
CORNWALL Karen 26.08.66, Valli :
3k - 9:45.22, 10kR - 34:29,
HMar - 1:16:25 (1:15:24-92)
CORRAN Elizabeth V35 23.09.55, Manx H :
5kWR - 26:27, 10kW - 51:24.0,
10kWR - 54:41
COSTELLO Karen 21.10.68, Glas/Heriot Watt :
SP - 12.64, JT - 54.50
COTTON Jacqueline 29.12.69, Wigan :
JT - 40.02 (41.50-85)
COULSON Jackie D. 10.08.61, :
Mar - 3:07:14
COUPER Claire U13 29.04.82, Falkirk :
800 - 2:28.01
COURT Clova 10.02.60, Birchfield :
60 - 7.47i, 100 - 11.77 (11.5w-90/11.6-87),
200 - 23.80 (23.57-90), 60H - 8.12i,
100H - 13.04, LJ - 5.67w/5.48 (6.10-92),
SP - 13.88 (14.23-93), JT - 48.88 (55.30-91)
COUSINS Dawn 16.03.68, Basildon :
100 - 12.0/12.19 (11.9-89/12.00-90)
COWE Helen 7.09.66, Sale/Aberdeen :
SP - 13.66i/13.63 (14.24-93),
DT - 48.64, HT - 42.96 (43.52-93)
COWLARD Katie U13 17.09.81, Guild & G :
HJ - 1.45
COWPER June V40 21.07.50, Imperial :
Mar - 3:02:43 (2:47:32-88)
COX Caroline U17 23.11.77, Leics Cor :
300H - 46.1
COX Maureen V40 7.09.50, Manx H :
10kWR - 57:40
COX Nicola U23, Rotherham :
JT - 39.64
COX Rachel U15 27.06.80, Birchfield :
DT - 30.88
COZENS Chloe U15 9.04.80, Beds Sch :
HJ - 1.60, PenG - 2822
CRAIG Elizabeth F. 7.07.60, Serpentine :
Mar - 3:04:29
CRANE Julie U20 26.09.76, Notts :
HJ - 1.81
CRAWLEY Pamela A. U17 20.02.78, Glasgow :
3k - 10:16.3 (10:16.96-93)

CRESSWELL Lois U15 12.01.81, RS Coldfield :
200 - 25.20w/25.62
CRILLEY Kath V45 8.09.47, Surrey WC :
50kW - 5:56:25 (5:53:41-93)
CROCKER Linda U17 2.04.79, Huntingdon :
300H - 46.37
CROCKFORD Laura U13 14.10.81, Aberdeen :
SPM - 9.53, DTM - 26.54
CROSBIE Theresa U20 17.07.75, Glasgow :
60 - 7.79i, 60H - 8.73i (8.60i-93),
100H - 14.88 (13.9w/14.01w/14.34-92)
CROSS Aline U23 20.09.73, Orkney Isl/EUAC :
HT - 35.42 (38.92-91)
CROSS Gemma U13 22.10.81, Rugby :
70HM - 11.8
CROSSLAND Susan U20 3.03.77, Wigan :
PV - 2.60i/2.40
CROSSLEY Lorraine U23 4.01.72, ES & Mx :
100 - 12.0/12.26
CROWE Amanda U23 21.10.73, Stoke :
800 - 2:11.94i (2:06.35-93)
CROWTHER Nicola Jane 15.05.70, Cov G :
200 - 25.0 (24.69-93), 400 - 53.76
CROWTHER-PRICE Kimberley 19.01.66,
Middlesbro & C : 200 - 25.14w,
100H - 14.22w/14.32, LJ - 5.77 (5.95w/5.79-88),
SP - 12.15, Hep - 5125 (5297-86)
CRUICKSHANK Justina U17 27.09.77, Traff :
HJ - 1.65 (1.71-93), TJ - 11.05
CUDDY Jane U15 25.08.81, Liverpool H :
PenG - 2625
CULL Sandra U20 10.12.75, Whitby Heath :
LJ - 5.79, Hep - 4360
CUNDY Andrea U17 13.07.78, Peterborough :
JT - 39.78
CUNNANE Cheryl U20 8.02.77, Wakefield :
HT - 40.52
CUNNANE Jennifer V35 23.02.57, Wakefield :
HT - 41.72
CURBISHLEY Allison U20 3.06.76, Edin WM :
400 - 54.78i/55.93 (55.7-93),
400H - 59.16 (59.04-93)
CURNOCK Hannah L. U17 16.04.78, Westbury :
800 - 2:13.04 (2:09.80-92),
1500 - 4:35.7 (4:33.9-93)
CURRIE Alison 15.07.68, Glasgow :
see MAHINDRU
CURRIE Janell H. 8.12.67, Glasgow :
see KELLY
CUTLER Aimee L. U13 7.10.81, Torfaen :
LJ - 4.82
CUTLER Charlotte U23 16.10.72, S'end/CUAC :
400H - 63.9/64.86 (63.6-93)

DAILY Joan W. V40 2.06.54, Stockport :
Mar - 2:59:36
DAMM Sarah 12.09.70, Stoke :
100H - 14.9/14.99 (14.7w-89),
LJ - 5.93w/5.68 (5.84-88),
SP - 12.11 (12.43i/12.28-90),
JT - 38.36, Hep - 5112
DANIEL Helen J. 24.10.63, Cambridge H :
400 - 57.4 (55.0-87),
800 - 2:04.32 (2:01.86-87), 1500 - 4:24.28
DANIELS Nikki U13 25.08.82, City of Stoke :
600 - 1:45.7, 800 - 2:24.7
DANSON Yvonne V35 22.05.59, Formby :
Mar - 2:32:24

DANVERS Natasha U17 19.09.77, Croydon :
100 - 12.3, 200 - 25.0, 60H - 8.7i (8.62i-93),
100H - 13.76w/13.95 (13.88-93),
300H - 42.20 (41.99-93), HJ - 1.65 (1.65-93)
DAVIDSON Linda 29.05.70, Glasgow :
LJ - 5.80 (5.95-92), TJ - 11.46 (11.81-93)
DAVIDSON Lynn U13 13.12.81, Giffnock :
200 - 27.5
DAVIES Alison 6.04.61, Woking :
100 - 11.9w/11.93 (11.88w/11.9-93),
200 - 23.91 (23.87-93)
DAVIES Angela 21.10.70, Basingstoke & MH/
Loughborough Studnts :
800 - 2:03.67, 1500 - 4:09.29,
1M - 4:31.83, 3k - 9:14.1
DAVIES Charlotte U20 21.04.76, Bracknell :
DT - 37.36 (39.92-92)
DAVIES Diana Clare 7.05.61, Leics Cor :
HJ - 1.82 (1.95-82)
DAVIES Emma U17 9.10.78, Andover :
400 - 58.9, 800 - 2:14.91
DAVIES Emma U20 14.03.75, Barry :
400H - 63.6/63.84 (62.7/63.10-93)
DAVIES Eryl V. 30.11.60, Bridgend :
Mar - 2:55:25 (2:43:26-87)
DAVIES Gael U17 5.02.79, Gloucester L :
60 - 7.94i, 100 - 12.34w/12.42,
200 - 25.51i, 300H - 44.6/45.08
DAVIES Hilary U20 9.02.75, Brecon :
JT - 44.02 (44.66-93)
DAVIES Nicola U20 25.11.75, Wrexham :
400 - 56.95
DAVIS Coral 15.05.61, Croydon :
400 - 57.43 (56.7-93)
DAVIS Gahlie U17 3.05.79, Wimborne :
60 - 7.94i, 100 - 12.29w/12.38, TJ - 10.36
DAVIS Joanne U23 20.09.73, Exeter :
800 - 2:11.7 (2:09.68-90), 1500 - 4:23.36
DAVIS Julie U15 16.11.79, Lagan Valley :
60H - 9.09i, 80HI - 11.9
DAWKINS Carol A. 8.12.60, Team Solent :
400H - 62.40 (58.28-85)
DAWSON Catherine 9.03.66, Highgate
(nee WHITE) : 400 - 56.4 (54.77-92),
800 - 2:03.17, 400H - 62.0 (59.46-93)
DAY Victoria U23 19.06.72, Essex L :
200 - 24.8 (24.8-93), 400 - 55.11 (54.92-93),
400H - 59.72
DAYKIN Mari-Anne L. U23 16.02.73, Tonbridge :
JT - 44.62 (46.08-93)
DEAKIN Emma U15 3.03.80, Preston :
1500 - 4:40.75
DEAN Harriet U13 2.02.82, Radley :
1500 - 5:05.4
DEAN Sarah G. 10.12.63, Essex L :
400H - 66.0 (57.38-91)
DEAR Joanne M. U20 8.06.75, Windsor S & E :
60 - 7.69i (7.66i-93),
100 - 12.07 (11.81w/12.0-93),
LJ - 6.21i/6.14 (6.33-93)
DEARDEN Alanna U20 2.07.77, Kingston & P :
HJ - 1.70
DEMAINE Claire U17 6.09.78, Sale :
1500 - 4:42.02, 3k - 10:21.0
DENGATE Emma U17 26.10.77, Guild & G :
100 - 12.15w/12.43
DENHAM Kerensa U23 8.03.74, Blackheath :
HJ - 1.65 (1.68-92), LJ - 5.89, TJ - 11.97

371

DENNIS Leanne U15 30.12.79, Swansea :
75HG - 11.6/11.88
DENNISON Andrea M. 22.04.63, Bradford :
Mar - 3:06:19
DENNISON Katie U15 8.06.80, City of Hull :
1500 - 4:43.76
DERBYSHIRE Heather U17 12.09.78, Traff :
JT - 40.22 (41.06-93)
DEVLIN Lyndsey U17 14.03.79, Barnsley :
300H - 46.88
DHALIWAL Navdeep U17 30.11.77, Glasgow :
SP - 12.52, DT - 40.08
DICKER Stacey U23 19.12.73, :
PV - 2.80
DICKINSON Leone U20 5.11.75, Bingley :
HJ - 1.75, Hep - 4026
DILNOT Susan Mary 14.01.62, Lordshill :
HMar - 1:14:43 (1:12:41sh-89)
DITCHFIELD Sarah U20 26.03.75, Preston :
400H - 62.70 (60.92-93), Hep - 4144
DIVINE Patricia 21.10.67, Edinburgh WM :
400 - 56.0 (54.64-90)
DIXON Lindsey U15 31.08.80, Sunderland :
DT - 31.66
DIXON Louise U17 29.11.77, Wigan :
300H - 46.4, LJ - 5.41,
SP - 11.30, Hepl - 4431
DIXON Sharon Jane 22.04.68, Parkside :
1500 - 4:30.68 (4:24.15-92),
3k - 9:37.42 (9:21.90-93),
5k - 16:39.57 (16:24.83-91),
10k - 35:08.23, 2KSTW - 6:53.7
DOBSON Stephanie U20 4.03.75, Cann & St :
LJ - 5.83w/5.81 (5.97-93), TJ - 11.76
DODD Virginia U17 30.06.79, Norfolk :
60H - 9.2i, 80HI - 12.0/12.04w
DOHERTY Kate U17 23.07.79, Cheltenham :
800 - 2:16.10
DONALD Elaine U23 30.04.74, Helensburgh :
400H - 63.5/64.28, Hep - 4497
DONALD Mairi U17 6.05.79, Helensburgh :
TJ - 10.58
DONALDSON Isobel 24.01.64, AF&D/WRAF :
400H - 63.5 (62.9-93),
LJ - 5.71w/5.56 (5.76w/5.72-93),
TJ - 11.20, JT - 40.54 (42.78-85),
Hep - 4546 (5038-93)
DONE Cheryl 25.09.70, Western/WRAF :
SP - 11.25, JT - 38.50 (38.80-93),
Hep - 4536 (4670-92)
DONNAN Kelly U20 14.04.77, Seaton :
TJ - 11.79
DONNELLY Carrie U17 18.06.78, Lisburn :
HJ - 1.66
DOUBELL Elinor 27.09.71, AF&D :
1500 - 4:32.6 (4:27.16-90)
DOUGALL Emily U17 15.03.78, Aberdeen :
JT - 35.78
DOUGLAS L. Stephanie 22.01.69, Sale :
60 - 7.40i (7.25i-91), 100 - 11.34 (11.27-91),
200 - 23.17
DOUGLAS Sandra M. 22.04.67, Trafford :
400 - 53.0/53.34 (51.41-92)
DOUGLAS Susan Mary U17 3.11.77, Lisburn :
100 - 12.40, 200 - 25.15,
300 - 41.28 (41.15-93)
DOWSETT Kathryn U17 24.11.78, Essex L :
LJ - 5.48 (5.50-92), Hepl - 3851

DRAKE Julie Elizabeth 21.05.69, Brighton :
3kW - 15:03.45 (13:12.01i-93/13:16.0-90),
5kW - 25:21.0 (22:37.47-93)
DRAPER Lynne 10.05.67, Croydon :
LJ - 5.86
DREW Sally U13 23.11.82, City of Plymouth :
LJ - 4.84
DREW Shelley Jean U23 8.08.73,
Sutton & D/Bir Univ. : DT - 54.60
DRUMMIE Susan 19.06.71, Belgrave :
PV - 2.90 (2.95-93)
DRUMMOND Rebecca Louise U17 18.04.78,
Stoke : 100 - 11.50w/11.9/11.96 (11.92-93)
DUANCE Lynne J. V45 28.12.46, Burnham :
Mar - 3:07:24
DUDGEON Sinead U20 9.07.76, Edinburgh :
100 - 11.8/11.92w/12.14 (11.88w/12.06-93),
200 - 23.9w/24.22
DUFF Natalie 30.12.71, Lisburn/Lough St :
JT - 40.30 (41.84-93)
DUFFIN Irene M. 10.08.60, Shaftesbury B :
SP - 13.19 (14.44-90),
DT - 40.04 (44.90-87), HT - 46.14
DUFFY Teresa 6.07.69, Beechmount/IRE :
1500 - 4:24.86 (4:21.59-91),
3k - 9:35.60 (9:12.87-91), 10kR - 34:53 (34:07-93)
DUFFY V. V35, Met. Police :
SP - 11.51
DUKE Andrea U23 6.07.73, Mandale :
1500 - 4:30.52, 3k - 9:37.01 (9:32.37-91),
10kR - 34:27, HMar - 1:19:14
DUNCAN Celia G. V40 4.06.53, AF&D :
Mar - 3:00:19 (2:42:56-85)
DUNCAN Clare U17 22.08.79, Liverpool H :
800 - 2:12.37, 1500 - 4:38.3 (4:36.6-93),
3k - 10:04.0
DUNCAN Debra A. 13.02.69, Essex L :
400H - 60.9/61.29 (59.65-87)
DUNCAN Joanne 27.12.66, Essex L :
SP - 13.48i/13.46 (14.17-93)
DUNCKLEY Kara U13 19.03.82, Radley :
HJ - 1.43
DUNDJEROVIC Elena U15 13.09.79, St Albans :
PenG - 2552
DUNKLEY Julie U15, Dartford :
SPG - 10.81
DUNKLEY Michelle U17 26.01.78, Kettering :
HJ - 1.77, LJ - 5.48
DUNN Rachael U17 4.03.79, Gloucester L :
HT - 32.06
DUTCH Alison 25.05.65, Edinburgh WM :
SP - 11.99i (12.48-91)
DYER Teresa E. V35 29.09.59, Peterborough :
10kR - 33:38 (32:43-93),
HMar - 1:14:05 (1:13:26-93), Mar - 2:36:40

EARDLEY Alison U13 11.11.81, Colwyn B :
JTM - 26.10
EARNSHAW Susan 13.10.70, Roth/Leeds P :
60 - 7.64i, 100 - 11.8/11.89,
200 - 23.5/23.80w/24.13, 400 - 53.98
EASTALL Sally R. 5.01.63, St Edmunds Pac :
HMar - 1:18:22 (1:14:33-91),
Mar - 2:37:08 (2:29:29-91)
EASTWOOD Leanne U20 23.11.76, Wigan :
100 - 11.95w/12.07 (11.86w/11.9/12.00-93),
200 - 24.2w/24.8/24.90 (24.26-93)

EDEN Heather U20 13.04.77, Ipswich :
DT - 38.82
EDEN Louise U17 11.12.77, Trafford :
LJ - 5.73, TJ - 11.05
EDLEY Nicola U17 30.08.78, Rotherham :
DT - 35.80
EDMONDSON Karen 17.03.62, Bournemouth
(nee HARVEY) : 3k - 9:53.09 (9:27.72-82)
EDWARDS Amanda U17 11.09.77, Stockport :
Hepl - 3809
EDWARDS Bethan U23 2.05.73, Cardiff :
100H - 13.7/13.80 (13.57-92)
EDWARDS Claire U23 20.10.74, Wrexham :
400H - 60.20
EDWARDS Faithlyn U17 26.11.78, Essex L :
LJ - 5.45 (5.60-93)
EDWARDS Marcelle U17 9.01.78, Essex L :
DT - 35.86, HT - 36.52
EFOBI Uju Eugenie U23 10.10.74, Bromley :
60H - 8.7i/8.73i,
100H - 14.05w/14.4 (14.17-93),
HJ - 1.72 (1.72-93),
LJ - 5.81w/5.54 (5.92w-93/5.84-92),
SP - 15.21, DT - 47.76, HT - 35.08,
Hep - 5409
ELDER Kate U13 4.04.82, Hull Springhead :
600 - 1:46.5, 1500 - 5:06.3
ELDRIDGE Marion V40 27.03.54, Fleet & Cr :
5k - 17:12.30
ELEY Joanne U23 12.01.74, Derby LAC :
HT - 38.72
ELLIOTT Lucy 9.03.66, Liverpool H :
10kR - 34:34
ELLIOTT Rachel U20 6.09.75, Telford :
HT - 38.08 (40.32-93)
ELLIS Clare U17 27.04.78, Solihull & S Heath :
3kW - 15:58.9 (15:20.86-93), 3kWR - 15:34,
5kW - 26:19.78, 5kWR - 26:47 (26:12-93)
ELLIS Liz 24.01.66, Derby LAC :
DT - 38.68
ELLIS Sally V35 17.05.58, Birchfield :
10kR - 34:36 (34:08-90),
HMar - 1:14:56 (1:11:38-88),
Mar - 2:37:06 (2:33:24-89)
ELPHICK Jennifer 24.11.66, Southampton C :
SP - 11.55 (14.01-90)
EMBLEM Nicola 27.03.71, Edinburgh WM :
JT - 50.86 (56.96-90)
EMERY Amanda U17 1.12.77, Stoke :
DT - 34.52
ENDERSBY Susan V35 12.10.57, Barnsley :
10MR - 58:36, HMar - 1:16:47, Mar - 2:49:03
ENGLISH Una Marie Clare 14.08.70, Havering/
Manr Univ : 1500 - 4:21.42i (4:11.82-92)
ENTWISTLE Claire U20 9.12.76, Wigan :
400H - 64.4
ENTWISTLE Sally U23 27.09.73, Rossendale :
800 - 2:11.51
ESSEX Joanne E. 16.04.63, Harlow :
SP - 11.29 (12.02-87), DT - 45.20 (50.06-89)
EUSTACE Katharine U20 16.04.75, Bristol :
400 - 56.1/56.14 (55.33-93)
EVANS Alison C. U23 13.12.73, Solihull & SH :
HJ - 1.75
EVANS Alyson 16.12.66, Cheltenham :
see LAYZELL
EVANS Esther U23 22.12.73, Vale of Ayles:
1500 - 4:28.62i/4:31.92

EVANS Jacqueline U23 5.04.74, Basildon :
100 - 12.27 (12.15w-93)
EVANS Joanne 3.10.68, Cardiff :
SP - 11.43, DT - 39.94
EVANS Katherine V. U23 4.02.74, Birchfield :
HJ - 1.65 (1.78-90), TJ - 12.01
EVANS Katherine U17 19.11.77, Coventry G :
JT - 40.64
EVANS Lindsay U20 29.08.77, Ipswich :
HJ - 1.79, JT - 39.76
EVANS Michelle U20, Newcastle :
2kSt - 8:27.4mx
EVANS Sally U20 14.05.75, Tipton :
200 - 24.8w/25.17, LJ - 5.51 (5.52-92)
EVERETT Claire U17 25.06.79, Norfolk :
300 - 41.27, HJ - 1.74i/1.70 (1.71-93),
LJ - 5.44, Hep - 4465, Hepl - 4489
EWING Jane 22.10.69, Edinburgh WM :
800 - 2:11.9 (2:06.8-89),
1500 - 4:33.8 (4:20.04-90)

F ABEN Alison U20 7.02.77, Hunt :
DT - 36.58
FACEY Denise 8.02.69, Hallamshire :
400 - 55.4/55.42 (55.30-92),
400H - 61.96 (61.1-91)
FAHERTY Michelle M. 10.08.68, Skyrac :
800 - 2:05.38, 1500 - 4:16.79 (4:15.37-93)
FAIRS Elizabeth U17 1.12.77, Chesterfield :
100 - 12.4,
80HI - 11.11w/11.4/11.48 (11.1/11.26-93),
100H - 15.2, 300H - 44.2/45.74 (44.93-93),
LJ - 5.40
FAIRWEATHER Lynn U15 15.01.80, Lasswade :
75HG - 11.24
FAIRWEATHER Sheila U17 24.11.77, Glasgow :
1500 - 4:41.12, 3k - 10:27.2
FALCONER Ellen U13 9.12.81, Caithness :
SPM - 9.32
FALCONER Jane Olivia U23 20.09.74,
Essex L/Cambridge University :
TJ - 11.63 (12.37w/12.10-93)
FARQUHARSON Samantha 15.12.69, Cardiff :
60 - 7.56i, 100 - 11.78,
60H - 8.11i, 100H - 12.9mf/13.08
FARRELL Jennifer 8.04.65, Border :
HJ - 1.71 (1.86-86)
FARROW Wendy 25.12.71, Derby LAC :
800 - 2:11.7 (2:11.1-92),
1500 - 4:25.82 (4:23.47-92),
1M - 4:50.4 (4:42.91-92), 3k - 9:31.91
FAULKNER Elaine 11.01.68, Lisburn :
400H - 65.52
FAWKES Claire U17 24.10.77, Braintree :
JT - 35.92
FEARON Cherone U15 4.03.80, Bristol :
LJ - 5.32
FELTHAM Emily U20 17.08.77, Salisbury :
200 - 24.9w?/25.11 (24.71w-93)
FENSOME Gemma U13 9.02.82, Shaftes B :
600 - 1:44.8
FENSOME Sarah U15 28.09.79, Shaftes B :
800 - 2:16.61,
FENWICK Alison E. 6.02.63, Shaftes B :
400H - 65.2 (62.84-92)
FERRIER Leigh U23 15.08.72, Sale :
200 - 24.7/24.82 (24.68-93), 400 - 54.76

FERRY Seonaid U13 19.11.81, Lochgelly :
70HM - 11.6/11.90, SPM - 10.07,
PenM - 2451
FIELDS Michelle U23 15.05.73, Peterborough :
JT - 46.60 (50.48-93)
FILCE Claudia Dawn U23 11.11.72, Wrexham :
HJ - 1.65 (1.67-93), PV - 2.60
FINIKIN Evette 25.09.63, Shaftesbury Barnet :
LJ - 5.71 (6.29w/6.25i/6.14-89),
TJ - 12.85 (13.46-91)
FISHER Jayne 2.11.70, Swansea :
DT - 45.38 (45.46-93)
FITZGERALD Katie U17 18.11.77, Pitreavie :
PV - 2.35i/2.30 (2.40-93)
FLATHER Elaine F. 2.02.66, Southampton RR :
Mar - 2:50:41
FLEET Lindsay U15 1.06.81, Bromley :
200 - 25.40w/26.28
FLEMING Jane U23 6.10.72, GUAC/Glasgow :
100 - 11.99w/12.00
FLETCHER Kay 14.10.67, Dudley & Stourb :
HJ - 1.65i (1.83-89)
FLETCHER Ruth V35, Tynedale :
100kR - 9:22:48
FLOCKHART Dawn 16.05.67, Edinburgh WM :
100 - 11.8/11.90w/12.06 (11.7w-84/11.80-85),
200 - 24.0/24.16w/24.18 (23.71-84),
400 - 55.6 (55.1-89)
FLYNN Lisa 26.01.71, Stevenage & NH :
HJ - 1.68 (1.71-93)
FOLDS Rebecca U20 28.01.75, Exeter :
LJ - 5.69 (5.73-93)
FORBES Allison T. 15.08.62, Trafford :
LJ - 5.70 (6.09w-91/6.07-90)
FORBES Claire 25.03.71, Jersey/Lough St :
1500 - 4:24.6 (4:18.52-90),
3k - 9:54.95 (9:13.75-92)
FORD Eleanor U15 16.01.80, Dorset Sch :
JT - 33.48
FORD Katie U13 21.10.81, Sheffield RWC :
2kW - 11:19.2
FORD-DUNN Suzanne U23 25.04.73, Steyn :
10kWR - 58:37
FORESTER Adele U20 27.03.76, Sunderland :
LJ - 6.05, TJ - 11.06 (11.45w-93)
FORESTER Julie 4.05.69, Shaftesbury Barnet :
400 - 55.78,
FORREST Louise 14.11.61, Garden City :
Mar - 3:06:44
FORREST Rachael U17 25.12.77, Wenlock O :
HJ - 1.76
FORRESTER Amanda U17 29.09.78, Stoke :
100 - 12.13w/12.3/12.51
FORSTER Rebecca U17 2.10.77, Bournem'th :
300 - 41.45
FORSYTH Kate U17 5.06.79, North Shields P :
60H - 8.87i,
80HI - 11.40w/11.66
FOSTER Adele U20 16.11.76, Hull Spring :
100 - 12.26w/12.45 (12.2-93)
FOSTER Elaine C. 21.07.63, Charn/Lough St :
1500 - 4:23.10 (4:19.7-92),
3k - 9:27.0 (9:21.18-92),
5k - 16:44.44 (16:09.83-92),
10kR - 34:57, 10MR - 57:47
FOSTER Jenny U17 6.09.77, Sale :
JT - 39.68 (41.32-93)

FOSTER Rebecca 14.04.71, Wigan :
100H - 14.74w/14.91
(14.26w-93/14.8-89/14.96-93),
LJ - 5.64i/5.64 (5.66i-91), TJ - 11.01i,
JT - 42.88 (43.26-89),
Hep - 4962 (5165-93)
FOSTER Samantha U15 9.09.79, Basildon :
HJ - 1.66, PenG - 3193
FOSTER Vickie 1.04.71, Salisbury :
SP - 13.19 (13.61-93),
DT - 41.88 (48.62-93), HT - 39.46
FOTHERGILL Chaanah U23 22.02.72,
Hallamshire/Cambridge University :
1500 - 4:31.1 (4:29.1-93),
3k - 9:38.7mx/9:48.65 (9:32.0-92),
10kR - 34:51
FOWLER Ellen U13 5.10.81, Solihull & SH :
600 - 1:44.7
FOX Samantha U15 30.04.80, Bracknell :
JT - 33.38
FOXALL Leanne U13 1.10.81, Birchfield :
75 - 10.3
FRANCIS Elizabeth 22.12.63, Cardiff :
1500 - 4:33.68
FRANCIS Tammie U17 14.11.78, Bournem'th :
JT - 41.32
FRANKLIN Kate U15 16.07.80, Bristol :
HJ - 1.61
FRASER Donna Karen U23 7.11.72, Croydon :
60 - 7.70i (7.69i-93),
100 - 11.94 (11.77w-91/11.88-93),
200 - 24.16 (23.69-89),
400 - 53.44 (52.54-91)
FRASER Louise 10.10.70, Trafford :
100 - 12.1/12.18 (11.6/11.68w-90/11.88-89),
100H - 13.84 (13.36-91)
FRASER Rachel U23 30.09.74, AF&D :
HT - 35.94
FRAZER Iona U15 28.10.79, Thames Valley :
HJ - 1.65
FREEBAIRN Susan 22.08.65, Glasgow :
DT - 46.70, HT - 36.56
FREEMAN Amanda U15 16.10.79, Bed& Co :
100 - 12.36w/12.4
FREEMAN Danielle U15 11.02.80, Leeds :
LJ - 5.28, PenG - 2760
FRY Sara 19.01.62, Met. Police/Lincoln Well :
JT - 42.16 (47.70-78)
FRYER Paula Tracy 14.07.69, Sale :
400 - 55.34 (54.7-92),
600 - 1:33.5 (1:29.62+-91),
800 - 2:05.09 (1:59.76-91)
FUDGE Paula V40 30.03.52, Hounslow :
3k - 9:53.4 (8:48.74-78),
10MR - 56:36 (53:44-88),
HMar - 1:17:11 (1:11:37-88)
FULLER Helena U23 27.08.72, Peterborough :
200 - 25.1 (25.0-90)
FULLER Jane K. U20 21.04.76, Parkside :
400H - 63.80

G ABRIEL Linda 27.07.64, Coventry G :
    400H - 63.46
GANDY Dawn Suzanne 28.07.65, Team Sol :
400 - 54.70 (53.8/53.98-87),
800 - 2:03.75 (2:01.87-88)

374

GARDEN Catherine U17 4.09.78, Pitreavie :
SP - 11.66, DT - 42.72, HT - 42.44
GARDEN Eleanor U20 20.11.76, Pitreavie :
SP - 11.23 (11.30-93), DT - 40.24
GARDNER Ann 11.10.68, Corby :
SP - 11.40 (12.84-87), DT - 36.78,
HT - 51.62 (54.02-93)
GARDNER Jane V40, Arena :
Mar - 2:51:59
GARRAGHAN Elizabeth 25.01.67, Enfield :
800 - 2:12.5
GARRETT Helen J. 26.11.64, Cambridge H :
LJ - 5.93i (6.32-87)
GATES Edwina C. 26.06.66, Team Solent :
400 - 56.03 (54.1-93/54.30-89)
GATES Julia H. V35 12.05.59, Brighton :
Mar - 2:59:18 (2:36:31-86)
GATRELL Eleanor U20 5.10.76, Woking :
SP - 12.80
GAULD Louise U15 24.08.80, Edinburgh :
PenG - 2559
GAUTIER Nicola U17 21.03.78, Hallamshire :
SP - 11.07, JT - 35.44,
Hep - 3856, HepI - 4303
GAYLE Denise U15 11.09.79, Barnet :
HJ - 1.60
GAYTER Sharon, Mandale :
100kT - 9:17:23, 100kR - 8:28:59,
24HrT - 204.674
GEALY Nerys U13, Carmarthen :
100 - 13.2dt
GEAR Karen U15 30.09.79, Exeter :
200 - 25.42w/25.63 (26.8-92)
GEE Michala U20 8.12.75, Rotherham :
HJ - 1.68i/1.67, Hep - 4625
GENTLE Louise U17 4.09.78, Bedford & Co :
HJ - 1.67
GEORGE Alison 11.12.62, Cannock & Staff :
SP - 11.31 (11.56-93)
GHOJEFA Elizabeth 24.02.69, Epsom & E :
LJ - 6.32w/6.13, TJ - 12.39 (12.64-93)
GIBB Katie U20 19.12.75, Pendle :
LJ - 5.70
GIBBENS Elizabeth U20 5.04.77, Invicta :
100H - 15.09, HJ - 1.71,
TJ - 11.65w/11.35, Hep - 4586
GIBBONS Cheryl U13 21.09.81, Liverpool Pem :
80 - 11.0, 100 - 13.1, 200 - 26.8,
600 - 1:44.6, 70HM - 11.8,
LJ - 4.76, PenM - 2337
GIBBS Lisa 9.01.69, Torfaen :
60H - 8.63i, 100H - 13.80w (13.9/13.93-93),
HJ - 1.70 (1.74-93), LJ - 5.88 (5.96-93),
SP - 12.54, Hep - 5253w (5424-93)
GIBSON Jennifer U17 21.06.78, Oldham & R :
1500 - 4:45.0, 3k - 10:13.39
GIBSON Lynn M. 6.07.69, Oxford City/WLIHE :
800 - 2:03.54 (2:02.34-92),
1500 - 4:05.75, 1M - 4:31.17
GIBSON Sharon Angela 31.12.61, Notts :
SP - 11.87 (13.50-82),
JT - 58.20 (62.32-87)
GILBERT Julia A. 14.09.61, Thames H & H :
Mar - 2:58:20
GILDING Nicola U23 16.05.72, Brighton :
LJ - 5.66 (5.84-89), TJ - 11.20
GILLHAM Michele U23 8.10.74, Tonbridge :
Hep - 3889 (4048-93)

GJELSETH Janice 16.09.60, Shettleston :
Mar - 2:55:20
GODBEER Sarah U20 10.06.77, Exeter :
Hep - 4082
GODDARD Tracy Carol 29.11.69, Bas & MH :
60 - 7.72i (7.42i-89),
100 - 11.81 (11.8-87),
200 - 24.1un/24.16i/24.2
(23.64w-93/23.9w-92/24.1-89, 24.26-91)
300 - 38.42 (37.48-93),
400 - 53.55 (53.23-91)
GOFF Charlotte U20 6.07.77, Colchester & T :
800 - 2:12.45
GOLDSMITH Sally, Edinburgh WM :
Mar - 2:38:39
GOLLAN Sheila 18.07.64, Edinburgh WM :
800 - 2:11.05 (2:10.36-90),
1500 - 4:32.9 (4:28.89-92)
GOODMAN Kay U15 17.11.80, Peterborough :
PenG - 2674
GOODWIN Kim 16.05.70, City of Hull :
200 - 24.4w/24.7/25.10, 400 - 55.53
GORDON Jackie 22.12.67, Birchfield :
SP - 12.01 (13.12-92)
GORDON Justina U15 10.05.80, Andover :
HJ - 1.60
GOULD Leila U23 22.03.74, Havant :
JT - 39.50 (42.72-89)
GOWING Paula U17 31.05.78, Bristol :
3k - 10:23.21
GOWLAND Catherine E. V35 22.08.59, Spen :
see RAWNSLEY-PEMBERTON
GRADDEN Marilyn J. 26.01.61, Epsom & Ewell :
Mar - 2:59:53
GRANGER Katie U20 31.03.75, Exeter :
JT - 49.86un/48.14 (50.32-93)
GRANTHAM Maria U15 14.12.79, East Ches:
PenG - 2718
GRAVES Emma U17 18.05.79, Norfolk :
TJ - 10.74
GRAY Amanda U17 22.03.79, Derby LAC :
200 - 25.30, 300H - 45.6/46.72, HepI - 4293
GRAY Beverley U20 24.04.77, Riddings :
3k - 9:53.5
GRAY C. U13, Mandale :
LJ - 4.73
GRAY Carol-Ann 7.04.64, Edinburgh :
800 - 2:09.87, 1500 - 4:24.92
GRAY Kathryn U20 4.06.76, Glasgow :
100 - 12.1w/12.44 (12.4-90/12.42w-91)
GRAY Linda 23.03.71, Lincoln Well :
JT - 45.68
GRAZETTE Dawn Amanda U23 26.09.72, Croy :
SP - 12.92 (14.59-91)
GREEN Emma 25.01.64, Hallamshire :
100H - 15.09w (14.2/14.29w-87/14.58-91),
Hep - 4449 (4877-87)
GREEN Joanne U13, Leics Cor :
800 - 2:27.8
GREEN Sally U20 11.05.76, Dacorum :
JT - 38.66
GREEN Sonya U15 6.03.80, Seaton :
100 - 12.36w
GREENER Sheila V40 21.03.50, Blyth RC :
Mar - 3:05:51
GREENWOOD Carol 15.03.66, Bingley :
3k - 9:17.6mx/9:26.1,
5k - 15:57.29, 10k - 33:34.96

GREGORY Jayne L. 26.01.66, Gainsborough :
  Mar - 3:05:22
GREGORY Louise U23 11.05.74, Sale :
  400H - 65.45 (64.16-92)
GRENNAN Emily U17 8.06.78, Solihull & SH :
  300 - 41.5
GREY Alison Helen U23 12.05.73, Glasgow :
  SP - 15.85i/15.69, DT - 52.52
GREY Leanne U17 6.02.78, Birchfield :
  DT - 41.28
GRICE Julie E. 28.10.66, Hull Springhead :
  Mar - 3:05:32
GRIFFITH Michelle Amanda 6.10.71, WS & E :
  200 - 24.87, LJ - 5.82 (6.12w/6.05-90),
  TJ - 14.08
GRIFFITHS Ann Margaret 20.08.65, Sale :
  600 - 1:28.9e+ (1:26.7-90), 800 - 1:59.81,
  1500 - 4:08.71 (4:07.59-92)
GRIFFITHS Claire U20 1.01.76, Sale :
  400H - 62.23 (61.74-93)
GRIFFITHS Sarah B. U17 24.04.78, WS & E :
  300H - 46.6, 400H - 67.5
GRIFFITHS Shirley U23 23.06.72, Gateshead :
  1500 - 4:23.75i (4:26.7-93),
  3k - 9:54.86i (9:23.8-93)
GRIME N. U13, Salford :
  1500 - 5:06.0
GRIMSHAW Kate U15 26.10.79, North SP :
  1500 - 4:45.64
GROSS Ruth U13, East Cheshire :
  1500 - 5:06.4
GROVES Jane U20 17.05.77, Vale Park :
  800 - 2:11.2mx (2:14.7-92)
GRUFFUDD Heledd U17 16.11.78, Carm :
  3k - 10:28.11i/10:28.84
GUNNELL Sally Jane Janet 29.07.66, Essex L :
  200 - 24.62i+ (23.30-93),
  300 - 37.06 (36.44-93), 400 - 51.04,
  100H - 13.09 (12.80w/12.82-88),
  400H - 53.33 (52.74-93)
GUNNING Deborah 31.08.65, Andover :
  800 - 2:08.1 (2:05.65-93),
  1500 - 4:13.50 (4:12.69-90), 3k - 9:12.12

HADFIELD Debbie U13 14.07.82, Mand :
  800 - 2:26.5
HAGGER Kim 2.12.61, Essex L :
  LJ - 6.04 (6.70-86)
HAGGETT Lea M. U23 9.05.72, Croydon :
  HJ - 1.88 (1.91-91)
HAIR Gemma U13 3.11.81, Aberdeen :
  200 - 27.5, 70HM - 11.66,
  PenM - 2269
HAJIPAVLIS Alexandra U15 3.10.80, Sandwell :
  DT - 33.06
HALE Jane U23 4.01.74, Lagan Valley :
  60H - 8.77i (8.57i-93),
  100H - 14.16 (13.85-93)
HALE Laura U15 21.01.80, Gloucester L :
  800 - 2:17.0, 1500 - 4:45.3 (5:05.8-92)
HALE Lucy U17 8.04.78, Cannock & Stafford :
  1500 - 4:45.1
HALES Amy U13 16.03.82, Steyning :
  2kW - 10:41.0, 2.5kW - 13:38.26,
  2.5kWR - 13:24o, 3kW - 16:21.0o,
  3kWR - 15:27
HALL Cecily U17 12.10.78, Norfolk :
  400 - 58.8, 300H - 44.44, 400H - 64.5

HALL Elizabeth U17 16.10.78, Solihull & SH :
  100 - 12.2/12.42w/12.65, 200 - 25.04
HALL Emma U17 10.08.78, Swindon :
  300 - 41.1
HALL Nicola U15 14.12.79, Ipswich :
  60H - 9.1i, 75HG - 11.08
HALL Rachel U23 23.12.74, Middlesbro & C :
  HT - 39.34
HALL Sally 14.02.71, Birchfield :
  10kW - 58:26.0
HALLETT Jodi U17 8.11.78, Bristol :
  300H - 45.58, Hepl - 4051
HALLIGAN Vicki U15 1.11.79, Falkirk :
  JT - 31.58
HALSTEAD-PEEL Rachel J. 15.09.70, C of Hull :
  400H - 61.5/62.62
HAMILTON Stephanie U15 27.06.80, Edinb WM :
  PenG - 2527
HAMLET Vanessa C. 14.09.69, Rossendale :
  Mar - 3:07:05
HANSEN Ashia 5.12.71, Essex L :
  60 - 7.6i, 100 - 11.81w/12.1,
  LJ - 6.27, TJ - 14.22
HANSON Emma U20 28.10.75, Cardiff :
  HJ - 1.65 (1.68-93)
HANSON Sarah U23 25.11.72, Birchfield :
  LJ - 5.73
HANSON-NORTEY Yvonne W. 18.02.64, Hallam :
  SP - 16.43 (17.45-89), DT - 38.46 (48.06-89)
HARDIMAN Maria U13 16.11.81, Liverpool H :
  600 - 1:45.08
HARDING Lynn 10.08.61, Houghton-le-Spring :
  10kR - 34:52 (33:26-89),
  10MR - 56:06 (56:03-89),
  HMar - 1:15:28 (1:13.09-89),
  Mar - 2:40:57 (2:31:45-89)
HARDWEIR Belinda U13 22.10.81, Essex L :
  600 - 1:43.6, 800 - 2:24.7
HARDY Dominique U17 26.01.78, Kettering :
  300H - 45.71
HARDY Kate U17 26.12.78, Bromley :
  JT - 36.12
HARDY Rebecca J. 11.11.68, Highgate :
  DT - 41.68 (44.00-86)
HARDY Simone U15 9.11.79, Kettering :
  800 - 2:16.5
HARKIN Julie U23 8.08.74, Rotherham :
  400H - 62.2/63.07
HARNETT Jenny U20 11.03.76, Medway :
  800 - 2:11.59
HARRIES Michelle U23 4.01.72, Parkside :
  800 - 2:07.02 (2:05.88-91),
  1500 - 4:22.32 (4:19.9-93), 3k - 9:59.84
HARRIES Susan 9.09.70, Havering :
  TJ - 11.16 (11.32-93)
HARRISON Debbie U17 13.11.78, RS Coldfield :
  LJ - 5.56w/5.40, Hepl - 3922
HARRISON Fiona U13 30.11.81, Barnsley :
  80 - 11.00, 100 - 13.1, HJ - 1.48, LJ - 4.88
HARRISON Michelle U17 29.09.78, Derby L :
  SP - 11.01
HARRISON Sarah U17 1.03.79, Cambridge H :
  HT - 35.68
HARRISON Simone U17 2.09.77, Croydon :
  300 - 40.8/40.94
HARRISON Susan 6.08.71, Leam/Leeds Poly :
  1500 - 4:32.9 (4:28.6-91), 3k - 9:25.5,
  5k - 16:38.3

HART Siobhan U20 15.06.75, Guildford & G :
  HT - 36.06
HARTIGAN Beverley Marie 10.06.67, Birch:
  800 - 2:05.0 (2:00.39-88),
  1500 - 4:11.04 (4:05.66-90),
  1M - 4:31.26 (4:26.52-92),
  3k - 9:34.7 (9:03.88i-90/9:10.4-92)
HARVEY Debra Jayne U20 13.11.75, Soton C:
  HJ - 1.73
HARVEY Julia P. 18.01.60, Shettleston :
  Mar - 3:01:43
HARVEYSON Karen 17.03.62, Bournemouth :
  see EDMONDSON
HASKELL Gaynor U20 11.08.76, AF&D :
  SP - 11.37
HASLAM Claire M. 18.12.63, Shaftesbury B :
  60 - 7.74i,
  100 - 12.0/12.22 (12.0-91/12.10-92),
  200 - 24.8/24.97 (24.4-91/24.79-92),
  400 - 57.4/57.54
HASLER Suzanne U13 7.04.82, R S Coldfield :
  800 - 2:23.4, PenM - 2265*
HATHAWAY Emily U15 22.12.79, R S Coldfield :
  800 - 2:16.28
HATTON Caroline J. 14.06.63, Worthing :
  JT - 39.08 (50.48-89)
HAWKER Kate U20 22.01.77, Yeovil Oly :
  HJ - 1.66
HAWKINS Rebecca U13 4.01.82, Easthampst'd :
  DTM - 24.98
HAWSON Gabby U17 3.02.79, Jersey :
  3k - 10:33.6
HAY Elizabeth U15 1.11.79, Verlea :
  DT - 32.96 (33.12-93)
HAYHOE Lynn M. 20.03.63, Shaftesbury B :
  JT - 44.94 (55.70-92)
HAYLOCK Laura U15 20.02.80, Camb & Col :
  75HG - 11.53w
HAYWOOD Katherine U23 23.12.74, Stourport :
  400H - 65.2/65.39 (63.72-93), Hep - 3957
HEAD Christine U15 18.12.79, Norfolk :
  JT - 36.22, PenG - 2578
HEAD Sarah 31.07.65, Newham & Essex B :
  HT - 36.96
HEASMAN Heather 27.09.63, Invicta :
  5k - 16:48.0+e (16:19.4-93),
  10k - 34:12.98 (33:19.48-92), 10kR - 32:31,
  10MR - 57:42 (57:15-93), HMar - 1:14:06
HEATH Jennifer U17 22.12.77, Sale :
  3k - 10:13.7
HEATH Vikki U20 27.12.76, Basildon :
  SP - 11.87 (12.08-93)
HEATHCOTE Rebecca U13, Cannock & St :
  600 - 1:45.66
HEGNEY Gillian U17 4.11.77, Glasgow :
  60 - 7.72i, 100 - 12.2w/12.28 (11.99w-93)
HEMS Rachel J. 10.12.69, Coventry Godiva :
  HJ - 1.65 (1.76-85)
HENDRY Susan U20 30.06.76, Aberdeen :
  400 - 55.96
HENRY Corinne U23 15.04.72, Shaftesbury B :
  LJ - 5.89w/5.81 (6.12w-93/6.05-91),
  TJ - 13.31
HENRY Lorraine 16.09.67, Shaftesbury B :
  SP - 12.48 (12.80-93),
  DT - 37.82 (43.88-90), HT - 34.24
HENSON Victoria U17 9.01.79, Peterborough :
  80HI - 11.9/12.06

HENTON Sarah U23 4.05.73, Horsh/BUAC. :
  DT - 48.12
HEPHER Joyce Elena 11.02.64, Bromley :
  LJ - 5.93 (6.80w/6.75-85)
HEPPLETHWAITE Louise U17 3.02.79, Traff :
  JT - 38.94
HEPPLEWHITE Dianne A. V40 2.11.51, Arena :
  Mar - 2:52:56
HERRINGTON Lynsey U17 31.05.79, AF&D :
  SP - 10.84, DT - 38.38
HESKETH Alison 29.04.63, Stockport :
  400H - 64.1
HESLOP Justina Sara U17 3.03.79, Elswick :
  1500 - 4:35.24
HEWITT Lorraine U15 8.01.80, Medway :
  SPG - 10.85 (8.43-92)
HIGGINS Allison U23 8.04.72, Loudon :
  1.5kSt - 5:49.6
HILL Cathy-Ann U20 4.05.77, Swindon :
  SP - 11.16 (11.60-92)
HILL Clare U20 14.12.76, Sparta :
  400 - 56.8/57.16
HILL Eleanor 8.08.62, :
  Mar - 2:53:40 (2:49:09-93)
HILL Yvonne A. 13.08.63, Birchfield :
  HMar - 1:19:08, Mar - 2:56:56 (2:55:56-92)
HILLING Stacy U13 11.09.81, Cornwall AC :
  75 - 10.1, 80 - 10.7, 100 - 12.8,
  150 - 19.6, 200 - 27.1
HILLS Olivia U17 7.03.79, Millfield Sch :
  800 - 2:16.12
HILTON Tracey U17 9.03.78, Wombwell :
  300H - 46.99
HIMSWORTH Jade U17 4.08.79, Holbeach :
  800 - 2:12.57
HINCHLIFFE Danielle U17 18.12.78, Old & R :
  HJ - 1.67
HIPKIN Caroline W. 18.03.71, Ryston :
  Mar - 3:02:46
HISSEY Tina J. 13.05.67, Sevenoaks :
  Mar - 3:06:41
HITCHMOUGH Julie U23 1.06.74, Dudley & St :
  800 - 2:12.37
HOCK Danielle U13 18.02.82, Wigan :
  600 - 1:45.53
HODGE-DALLAWAY Naomi U15 1.06.81, Tower H :
  75HG - 11.52
HODGESTEGER Denise V40 18.08.53, Wells :
  Mar - 2:55:15
HOGGARTH Donna U23 14.10.73, Preston :
  60 - 7.60i (7.54i-93),
  100 - 11.78w/11.83 (11.55w/11.61-92),
  200 - 24.06w/24.2/25.02 (24.15-93)
HOLDEN Diana U20 12.02.75, Hounslow :
  HT - 53.34
HOLDEN Joanne 20.02.65, Shaftesbury B :
  1500 - 4:31.2, 3k - 9:37.95,
  5k - 16:48.77, 10kR - 34:43
HOLLETT Sharon U17 26.12.78, Helensburgh :
  100 - 12.3, 200 - 25.3, 300 - 40.10
HOLLICK Lisa 1.01.70, Shaftesbury Barnet :
  1500 - 4:28.5,
  3k - 9:41.14 (9:27.67-91),
  10k - 35:37.57 (34:11.2-91),
  10kR - 34:35 (33:24-93)
HOLLMAN Anne Marie U23 18.02.74, Peterbro :
  100H - 14.7/14.74 (14.1w/14.3/14.43w/14.51-92),
  400H - 62.9/67.51 (61.56-93), HJ - 1.68 (1.69-91)

HOLLMAN Julie U20 16.02.77, Peterborough :
  100H - 15.01w/15.45, HJ - 1.70 (1.70-93),
  LJ - 5.99, Hep - 4878
HOLMES Carol 13.12.63, Longwood :
  10kR - 34:51, 10MR - 59:00
HOLMES Kelly 19.04.70, Ealing S & Mx/Army :
  400 - 54.7, 800 - 1:59.43 (1:58.64-93),
  1500 - 4:01.41
HOLROYD Shelley U23 17.05.73, Sale :
  JT - 57.08 (60.10-93)
HOLT Gemma U23 20.12.72, AF&D :
  LJ - 5.66 (5.86w/5.81-91)
HOLT Janet M. V35 10.10.56, Trafford :
  800 - 2:10.0 (2:05.9-89),
  1500 - 4:28.12 (4:16.9-89),
  3k - 9:33.9mx/9:42.6 (9:27.5-93),
  5k - 17:11.0
HONLEY Georgina 12.01.67, Shaftesbury B :
  400 - 57.25i (53.63-89)
HOOD Maria U15 20.12.79, Bournemouth :
  DT - 33.46
HOPE Jennifer 1.09.62, Wolverhampton & B :
  DT - 40.70 (43.94-90)
HOPGOOD Jenny U15 22.06.80, Portsm Fare :
  SPG - 10.87 (7.89-92)
HOPGOOD Rachel U17 2.06.78, Hallamshire :
  SP - 11.44, DT - 43.28
HOPKINS Jennifer U20 9.08.75, Reading :
  DT - 40.44 (41.34-93)
HOPKINS Kathryn U17 6.11.77, Reading :
  DT - 35.94
HORNBY Emma U23 12.12.73, Stourport :
  PV - 2.50
HORNE Caroline A. V35 7.11.56, Crawley :
  3k - 9:48.7 (9:32.6-84),
  10kR - 34:09 (33:08-85),
  10MR - 56:41 (55:58-85),
  HMar - 1:14:55 (1:13:43-84),
  Mar - 2:44:48 (2:37:26-85)
HORNER Katharine U17 6.01.78, Dorking :
  PV - 2.70
HOROVITZ Gillian P. V35 7.06.55, AF&D :
  Mar - 2:45:46 (2:36:52-92)
HORWILL Katherine U20 26.01.75, Dudley & St :
  3kW - 15:01.2 (14:41.0-93),
  5kW - 25:25.96, 5kWR - 25:38 (25:05-91),
  10kWR - 53:08
HOSKINS Andrea U17 6.10.77, N Devon :
  TJ - 10.33
HOURIHAN Alyson J. 17.10.60, Cardiff :
  SP - 11.69 (12.41-92), DT - 43.02 (43.58-92)
HOWARD Anna-Lisa U17 18.04.78, Norfolk :
  SP - 12.21, JT - 38.62
HOWARD Claire U20 9.07.75, Leics Cor :
  HJ - 1.70i/1.70 (1.73-93)
HOWARD Gillian 14.04.69, Derby LAC/CUAC :
  HJ - 1.75 (1.81i-92/1.80-90), TJ - 11.46
HOWARD Julie 24.09.66, City of Plymouth :
  100 - 12.1/12.27 (11.7w/11.9-88/12.00-93),
  200 - 24.8/25.34
    (24.2w?-93/24.7-88/24.77w-93/24.87-90)
HOWARTH Beverley U20 4.09.76, Blackburn :
  HJ - 1.70i/1.70 (1.73-93), PV - 2.30
HOWARTH Natalie U17 1.04.78, Leeds :
  60 - 7.99i
HOWELL Gaby U13 25.01.82, Brighton :
  PenM - 2177

HOWLEY Nina U17 22.01.78, Sheffield RWC :
  3kW - 15:26.56 (15:13.0-93),
  5kW - 25:25.02,
  5kWR - 25:49, 10kWR - 54:46
HUBBARD Leigh M. U17 30.09.77, Banbury :
  TJ - 10.43
HUCKERBY Nikki U17 27.02.78, Birchfield :
  3kW - 15:15.3o, 3kWR - 15:27,
  5kW - 26:28.74, 5kWR - 26:07o,
  10kWR - 53:58
HUGGINS Natasha U20 20.10.76, Hercules W :
  SP - 11.47 (11.47-93)
HUGHES Anne-Marie 8.05.62, Shettleston :
  Mar - 3:06:16 (3:07:48-91)
HUGHES Emma L. U15 15.09.80, Luton :
  LJ - 5.29
HUGHES Ruth U13 12.09.81, Thurrock :
  SPM - 9.89
HUGHES Sarah U20 14.03.75, Wrexham :
  HT - 36.62
HULLEY Angela J. 8.02.62, Leeds :
  3k - 9:42.1 (9:17.05-90),
  5k - 16:25.7mx/16:35.6 (15:41.11-90),
  10k - 33:45.04 (32:42.84-89),
  10kR - 33:21, 10MR - 54:41,
  HMar - 1:13:19 (1:12:25-90),
  Mar - 2:42:40 (2:30:51-88)
HUMBLE Amanda U17 15.08.79, North S P :
  80HI - 12.0, 300H - 45.36, 400H - 66.2,
  JT - 37.86, HepI - 4475
HUNT H., :
  JT - 38.14
HUNT Sam U13 26.02.82, City of Plymouth :
  1500 - 5:03.5
HUNTE Abigail 12.05.71, Villanova Univ :
  800 - 2:04.50
HUNTER Fiona U17 14.09.78, Arbroath :
  TJ - 10.44, SP - 10.86
HUNTER Jill 14.10.66, Valli :
  10kR - 33:28 (31:42-89),
  10MR - 56:41 (51:41-91)
HUNTER Sarah U17 19.05.78, Shaftesbury B :
  60 - 7.88i, 200 - 25.31
HUNTER-ROWE Carolyn 25.01.64, Pudsey & B :
  HMar - 1:19:20 (1:17:39-93), Mar - 2:40:28,
  100kR - 8:05:20 (7:27:19-93)
HURST Jodie U20 21.06.77, City of Stoke :
  TJ - 11.12
HUTCHINGS Sharon L. 11.12.70, Newbury :
  SP - 11.78 (12.24-93)
HUTCHINSON Anya U20 16.07.77, Notts :
  400H - 64.76, Hep - 3914
HUTCHISON Fiona U20 18.01.77, Glasgow :
  60 - 7.69i, 100 - 11.8w/12.04,
  200 - 24.3w/24.68w/24.69
HUTCHISON Nicola U17 1.02.79, Glasgow :
  100 - 12.3w/12.4/12.44, LJ - 5.58w/5.56
HUTLEY Dawn U13 26.09.81, Chelmsford :
  SPM - 9.66
HYDE Zahara 12.01.63, Woking :
  1500 - 4:21.62 (4:19.36-93), 2k - 5:54.72,
  3k - 9:18.4mx/9:28.64 (9:05.49-91),
  5k - 16:36.0, 10k - 33:23.25,
  10MR - 56:11
HYLAND Vicky U13 27.10.81, Sale :
  75 - 10.37, PenM - 2145
HYNAN Julie U15 23.05.80, Liverpool H :
  HJ - 1.60

HYND Natalie U17 30.01.78, Pitreavie :
60 - 7.78i, 100 - 12.10 (12.01w-93),
200 - 24.9/25.45 (25.41-93)
HYSLOP Joanne U15 13.03.80, Coventry G :
PenG - 2711

I DOWU Oluyinka U23 25.02.72, Ex L :
100H - 13.62w/14.1 (13.70-92),
LJ - 6.73 (6.73-93)
IMPETT Jennifer U17 18.11.77, Wimborne :
60 - 7.92i,
100 - 12.14w/12.48 (12.09w/12.2-93),
200 - 25.4 (24.8-93), Hepl - 4302
IMPETT Lindsay U15 4.01.80, Wimborne :
200 - 25.37w (27.2-92), PenG - 2912
INGLIS Elaine U13 8.04.82, Edinburgh WM :
150 - 20.2
INNISS Antoinette S. 28.08.63, Leics Cor :
100 - 11.9/12.10 (11.6w-83/11.7-85/11.82-88),
IRVINE Lesley U20 1.01.77, Corby :
Hep - 3889
IRVING Ruth U23 20.07.74, Wirral :
LJ - 6.28, TJ - 11.12

J ACKSON Lorna U23 9.01.74, Edinb WM :
SP - 11.52 (11.90-93), JT - 54.62
JACKSON Nicola S. 1.05.65, Trowbridge :
3kW - 14:36.22i (14:02.8+-87),
5kWR - 25:34,
10kW - 52:37.0 (50:50.0-86),
10kWR - 52:13 (47:58-87)
JACOBS Kim Simmone Geraldine 5.09.66, SB :
100 - 11.37w/11.47 (11.26w-84/11.31-88),
200 - 23.48 (23.01w-84/23.12-91)
JACQUES Stacey U20 24.06.77, Hallamshire :
400 - 55.68
JAMES Angharad U17 7.04.79, Swansea :
100 - 12.48, 200 - 25.54
JAMISON Victoria U20 19.05.77, Lagan V :
200 - 25.1w (25.1-93), 60H - 8.80i,
100H - 14.0/14.26 (13.8dt-93),
300H - 44.28 (42.67-93), 400H - 60.07
JARVIS Carla U20 5.08.75, Bromsgrove & R :
3kW - 16:26.2 (14:36.39-91),
5kW - 26:40.0 (25:13.8-91)
JENKIN Hannah U20 30.09.76, Basildon :
100H - 14.5/14.53w/14.88, 400H - 64.9
JENKINS Andrea U20 4.10.75, Bedford & Co :
HT - 35.18
JENNER Lorraine 29.12.71, AF&D :
3k - 9:53.9
JENNINGS Heather 10.07.60, Beaumont Leys :
HMar - 1:18:19 (1:15:54-90)
JENNINGS Joanne 20.09.69, Essex L :
HJ - 1.86 (1.94i-93/1.90-88)
JEVON-POWELL Rosalind U17 29.07.78, Notts :
PV - 2.50
JOHN Davenia U17 29.12.77, Windsor S & E :
LJ - 5.46
JOHN Michelle U17 13.04.78, Swansea :
300 - 41.0/41.02, 300H - 45.53
JOHNS Karen U15 18.08.80, Shildon :
800 - 2:11.19
JOHNSON Charmaine R. 4.06.63, W S & E :
60H - 8.9i (8.88i-93), 100H - 14.36,
HJ - 1.72 (1.72-89), LJ - 5.89 (6.00w-90/5.92-92),
SP - 13.90i/13.60 (14.29-93),
JT - 41.48, Hep - 5486 (5495-92)

JOHNSON Denise V35 12.03.59, Spen:
Mar - 3:02:54
JOHNSON Gemma Lynne U17 21.07.78, BHM :
SP - 10.79, JT - 39.28
JOHNSON Jade U15 7.06.80, Herne Hill :
LJ - 5.68
JOHNSON Julia U15 21.09.79, Invicta :
TJ - 10.38i, PenG - 2730
JOHNSON Sarah U20 24.08.77, Swansea :
DT - 36.88 (36.88-92)
JOHNSTONE Pamela U17 16.03.79, Edinb WM :
300H - 44.1/45.10
JOHNSTONE Rachel U17 22.01.78, Leics C :
SP - 10.96 (11.19-93), HT - 33.00
JOINER Angela 14.02.69, Charnwood :
5k - 17:20.77
JONES Adele U17 23.09.77, Solihull & SH :
HJ - 1.65 (1.72-93)
JONES Delyth U17 12.03.79, Crewe & Nant :
100 - 12.28w/12.40
JONES Elizabeth 25.04.61, Hailsham :
Mar - 2:55:56
JONES Emma W. U20 9.07.77, Bournemouth :
SP - 11.58, HT - 39.82un/38.56
JONES Hannah U15, Torfaen :
HJ - 1.60
JONES Hayley 20.09.71, R Sutton Coldfield :
100H - 14.6 (14.2-93/14.36w-90/14.37-93),
LJ - 5.68
JONES Jillian 23.12.69, Southampton City :
800 - 2:06.7 (2:04.97-93),
1500 - 4:22.07 (4:16.0-93)
JONES Katie U20 4.01.77, Trafford :
400H - 62.6
JONES Leanne U23 13.05.74, Rhondda :
HT - 41.12
JONES Lindsey U17 8.09.77, Wakefield :
HT - 35.56
JONES Megan U20 10.07.76, Newport :
100H - 14.3/14.58 (14.44w-93)
JONES Natalie U13 21.02.82, Ryde :
DTM - 24.64
JONES Nikala, Poole Runners :
10MR - 57:42
JONES Samantha U20 9.08.76, Reading :
200 - 25.1 (25.12-92)
JONES Susan Eva U17 8.06.78, Wigan :
100H - 14.3w/14.4/14.51, 300H - 45.46,
HJ - 1.82
JORDAN Rachel U23 29.01.72, Birchfield :
800 - 2:10.54
JOSLIN Lois U17 1.03.79, Enfield :
800 - 2:16.21
JUPP Nicola U20 26.10.75, Reading :
JT - 39.96
JURY Kerry 19.11.68, Wigan :
200 - 24.57, 100H - 14.19w/14.32,
HJ - 1.72 (1.73-90), LJ - 5.69 (5.74-90),
TJ - 11.56i/11.35 (11.72w-91/11.71-92),
Hep - 5334 (5335-93)

K AGBO Crystal U13 23.06.82, Woking :
80 - 11.0, HJ - 1.46
KAISER Kath M. V40 24.08.51, Valley Str :
Mar - 2:55:03
KALUZA Laura U20 19.07.77, Sale :
JT - 40.64 (42.24-93)

KANE *Kelly U23 28.10.74, Blackpool/IRE :*
  SP - 13.68 (13.70-93)
KAY Louise U17 1.12.77, Bolton :
  HT - 42.14
KAY Rachael U15 8.09.80, Wigan :
  100 - 12.4, 200 - 24.90w/25.09,
  75HG - 11.4
KEIGHTLEY Lauren U17 2.08.79, Bracknell :
  SP - 10.55, DT - 44.92
KELLY Janell H. 8.12.67, Glas (nee CURRIE) :
  JT - 42.54 (46.64-91)
KELLY Jennifer A. 20.06.70, Bromley :
  200 - 24.70, 60H - 8.9i (8.9-90),
  100H - 14.43 (14.35-90),
  HJ - 1.75 (1.75-89), LJ - 6.02 (6.09-93),
  SP - 14.44 (14.88i-90/14.73-91),
  JT - 40.18 (42.44-92), Hep - 5826
KELLY Siona U23 19.04.74, Sale :
  JT - 43.46
KEMP Tommy U15 5.03.80, Burton :
  1500 - 4:43.30
KENNEDY Cheryl U15 10.02.80, Jarrow & H :
  75HG - 11.24w
KENNEDY Claire L. U15 29.01.80, Milton K :
  1500 - 4:46.8
KENNEDY Rachael U17 15.06.78, Hull Spring :
  60H - 9.03i, 80HI - 11.74w/11.82
KENNERLEY Eva U13 15.10.81, Elswick :
  800 - 2:26.9
KENSHOLE Rebecca U13 21.10.81, Exeter :
  HJ - 1.50o/1.48
KEOUGH Linda 26.12.63, Basingstoke & MH :
  400 - 52.95 (50.98-91),
  800 - 2:03.69 (2:01.82-93)
KERBOAS Alison U15 21.05.81, Wigan :
  PenG - 2908
KERR Emma U17 15.10.77, Ayr Seaforth :
  HJ - 1.65i/1.65 (1.65-93)
KERR Natalie V.S. U15 17.11.79, R Sutton
Coldfield :
  SPG - 11.74, DT - 40.84
KERSHAW Andrea U17 22.03.78, Oldham & R :
  1500 - 4:40.6, 3k - 10:13.3
KILGOUR Rebecca U20 18.10.75, Newton A :
  100 - 12.1, 200 - 24.5/24.70
KILNER Debbie 2.11.61, Aberdeen :
  3k - 9:59.94,
KINCH Beverly 14.01.64, Trafford :
  50 - 6.2i, 60 - 7.35i (7.13i-86),
  100 - 11.8/11.97
    (11.1w-87/11.13w-83/11.2-84/11.29-90),
  200 - 24.10i (23.57-93)
KING Donna Marie U20 26.01.76, Leics Cor :
  LJ - 5.70 (5.97-93)
KING Janine U23 18.02.73, Trafford :
  JT - 49.50
KING Lorna U13 22.01.83, Banbury :
  600 - 1:45.5, 1500 - 5:06.0
KING Rachel U20 11.05.76, Cardiff :
  100H - 14.37
KING Sharon Marie U23 27.01.72, Sale :
  800 - 2:11.22 (2:10.8-93),
  1500 - 4:23.2 (4:21.18-92), 3k - 9:43.36i
KING Stacie U13 19.01.82, Barry :
  70HM - 11.7
KIRBY Jocelyn A. V35 21.11.57, Middlesbro :
  60H - 8.61i (8.52i-91),
  100H - 13.93w/14.0/14.19 (13.79-89)

KIRBY Rachel 18.05.69, Blackheath :
  LJ - 6.02, TJ - 13.64
KIRKHAM Kelly U17 2.03.79, Hereford :
  DT - 33.52 (36.98-93)
KIRKPATRICK Julie U23 14.07.72, Lisburn :
  DT - 38.82 (44.18-92), HT - 45.74 (46.68-93)
KITSON Mary J. 2.04.63, Hounslow :
  400 - 57.2 (55.19-88),
  800 - 2:06.0 (2:02.83-91),
  1500 - 4:27.21 (4:15.57i-92/4:24.19-90)
KNEALE Karen 23.04.69, Manx H :
  3kW - 14:26.0, 5kWR - 24:50,
  10kW - 51:22.0, 10kWR - 51:31
KNOWLES Charlotte U23 11.10.72, Hounslow :
  400H - 65.35 (63.9-89)

LACKENBY Leah J. U23 18.09.74, Gate :
  100H - 14.3/14.88, HJ - 1.71,
  Hep - 4478w/4384
LAING Manndy J. V35 7.11.59, Liverpool H :
  JT - 38.18 (38.98-84)
LAMB Nicola 15.02.69, Croydon :
  400 - 56.3/57.59i/57.66 (55.0-85)
LAMBOURN Angela J. 9.04.66, Northampton :
  SP - 12.75 (13.75-91)
LANE Catherine U20 18.11.76, Tring :
  DT - 36.48
LANG Andrea U13 6.03.82, Ayr Seaforth :
  100 - 13.0, 200 - 26.8
LANGFORD Lisa Martine 15.03.67, Wolves & B :
  5kW - 22:40.0 (21:57.68-90),
  5kWR - 22:44+ (22:01-89),
  10kWR - 46:01 (45:42-87)
LAPCZUK Nicola U13 18.11.82, Derby LAC :
  200 - 26.8
LAPIDO Jane 24.08.69, :
  400H - 63.78
LAPKA Fiona 17.12.66, Exeter :
  HJ - 1.65i/1.65 (1.74-84)
LARBY Amanda 13.11.70, AF&D :
  3k - 9:58.0 (9:50.0-93)
LARBY Verity A. 13.11.70, AF&D :
  see SNOOK
LASENBY Joan 26.04.60, Essex L :
  3k - 9:48.96 (9:42.1-93)
LAST Suzanne F. 11.01.70, Medway :
  HT - 45.04
LATIMER Joanna M. 30.01.71, Sale/OUAC :
  400 - 55.5 (55.59-93), 800 - 2:03.27
LAVENDER Julie U20 9.11.75, Sunderland :
  HT - 51.62
LAVERS Lesley 6.08.68, Parkside :
  HJ - 1.65, JT - 39.72 (40.18-90)
LAW Stephanie U23 21.04.72, Nene Valley H :
  100H - 14.9 (14.8-93/15.26-91), TJ - 11.02
LAWRENCE Susan 25.11.70, Thurrock :
  JT - 39.08 (39.50-92)
LAWRENCE Victoria U23 9.06.73, Blackpool :
  400 - 57.0, 800 - 2:04.69,
LAX Sian U17 4.08.79, Wenlock O :
  JT - 42.22
LAYZELL Alyson 16.12.66, Chelt (nee EVANS) :
  400 - 56.2, 600 - 1:30.7, 800 - 2:04.84,
  400H - 63.3
LEDGER Anna U15 13.06.80, Ipswich :
  HJ - 1.60
LEDGER Catherine U17 6.02.79, Ipswich :
  HJ - 1.64

LEE Dorothea U20 28.07.77, Yeovil Oly :
800 - 2:06.67
LEIGH Sandra C. 26.02.66, Stevenage & NH :
400 - 55.3/55.57 (52.75-91), 800 - 2:07.43,
400H - 62.6 (61.8-93)
LEM Elizabeth U13, Shrewsbury :
150 - 20.1
LEPKOWSKI Donna U23 7.11.74, AF&D :
JT - 38.70
LESTRANGE Katy U15 17.09.79, Warrington :
75HG - 11.36w
LEVER Suzanne 2.10.67, Milton Keynes :
PV - 2.65 (2.65i-93)
LEVERMORE Janet 7.06.69, Birchfield :
60 - 7.77i, 100 - 12.1/12.19,
200 - 24.6/24.88 (24.2w?-86/24.6-89),
400 - 53.53
LEWIS Ann V45 29.12.47, AF&D :
3kW - 16:19.17, 5kW - 27:40.35,
10kW - 58:56.4
LEWIS Charlotte U20 10.05.75, Brighton :
Hep - 4182 (4341-93)
LEWIS Denise U23 27.08.72, Birchfield :
200 - 24.80, 100H - 13.47, HJ - 1.81,
LJ - 6.56, SP - 13.22, JT - 53.68, Hep - 6325
LEWIS Rebecca U17 31.12.77, Sale :
200 - 25.0, 60H - 9.13i,
80HI - 11.72w/12.0/12.10,
LJ - 5.87w/5.73, HepI - 4841
LIDSTER Claire U13 26.10.81, Jersey :
HJ - 1.47
LILFORD Jane 28.11.70, Sale/Warwick Univ. :
HJ - 1.65 (1.78-89)
LILLEY Emma U20 2.05.76, Bingley :
JT - 43.68
LINDSAY Allie U13, Crawley :
200 - 27.4
LINDSAY Emma 11.04.71, Edinburgh WM/Lisb :
200 - 24.18, 100H - 14.96,
HJ - 1.74 (1.75-88),
LJ - 5.89w/5.70 (5.90i-93/5.72-89),
Hep - 5353
LINTON-FORREST Fiona U17 23.01.78, Ashf'd :
DT - 33.40
LISTER Rosanne 9.05.69, Havering :
DT - 50.64 (53.66-91), HT - 36.60
LISTON Bianca U17 28.05.78, Bromley :
100H - 15.06, LJ - 5.46, HepI - 3864
LITTLE Stephanie U13 5.11.81, Newport :
PenM - 2042
LIVERTON Amanda Jayne U23 1.09.72, Exeter :
JT - 53.76 (57.84-90)
LIVESEY Katherine U15 15.12.79, Blackpool :
75HG - 11.52, HJ - 1.63i/1.63,
LJ - 5.37io/5.32, PenG - 3142
LIVINGSTONE Mhairi 1.09.69, Stewartry :
LJ - 5.70w? (5.63-92), TJ - 11.39i (11.09-91)
LLEWELLYN Stephanie 31.12.68,
Shaftesbury Barnet (nee MCPEAKE) :
200 - 25.0w, 400 - 54.77, 400H - 59.39
LLOYD Elizabeth U15 1.12.79, Cannock & St :
100 - 12.4
LOCKWOOD Clare U15 7.10.79, Colwyn Bay :
JT - 36.72
LOGAN Amy U20 21.01.75, Gateshead :
LJ - 5.61 (5.83w?/5.70-93)
LOVELAND Donna U17 28.06.78, Southend :
JT - 39.92

LOVETT Rebecca U17 11.05.78, GEC :
400 - 58.8, 800 - 2:14.26 (2:13.42-93)
LOW Jane Kathryn 26.08.60, Glasgow :
200 - 25.1w, 400H - 58.43
LOW Linda 20.01.71, Edinburgh :
HT - 41.32, JT - 39.56 (41.08-93)
LOWE Zoe A. 7.07.65, St Albans :
Mar - 2:49:58
LUCAS Eleanor U13 29.11.81, :
HJ - 1.45
LUDLOW Jayne U17 7.01.79, Cardiff :
TJ - 12.14
LUPTON Brenda V40 5.10.52, Sheffield RWC :
3kW - 15:47.89i (14:42.9-91),
5kW - 26:48.92 (24:18.6-84),
5kWR - 26:43 (24:05-82),
10kW - 55:35.0 (50:10.2-84),
10kWR - 54:45 (50:22-83)
LUPTON Victoria Anne U23 17.04.72, Sheff RWC :
3kW - 13:20.23 (13:03.4-91),
5kW - 23:06.0 (22:12.21-92),
5kWR - 22:45+ (21:36-92),
10kW - 46:30.0,
10kWR - 45:48 (45:28sh-93), 20kW - 1:44:48
LYCETT Nicola U15 10.03.80, Newcastle :
JT - 37.20
LYNCH Lorraine A. 5.10.68, Essex L/Lough St :
LJ - 5.87w/5.70 (6.27w-90/6.14i-92/6.12-90)
LYNCH Nnenna 3.07.71, Oxford Univ/USA :
1500 - 4:27.53 (4:13.25-91),
3k - 9:37.41 (9:09.46-92)
LYNCH Sally A. 6.11.64, Newport :
10k - 35:47.76 (34:24.21-91),
10MR - 57:24 (56:48-90),
HMar - 1:16:49 (1:16:28-91), Mar - 2:41:47
LYNES Margaret Tracey 19.02.63, Croydon :
SP - 16.57

M ACAULAY Kirsty U17 26.04.78, Rich& T :
1500 - 4:45.98, 3k - 10:16.34
MACDONALD Joanne U20 3.09.75, Epsom & E :
100H - 14.24w/14.4/14.57 (14.21w-93)
MACDONALD Wendy Anne U23 25.12.72,
Cambridge Harriers/WLIHE :
HJ - 1.65 (1.80i-90/1.76-89)
MACKAY Elaine 26.01.65, Edinburgh :
3k - 9:56.72, HMar - 1:17:56
MACKAY Nicola U17 26.08.78, Kettering :
JT - 42.60
MACKAY Rowena U13 4.02.82, Guernsey :
LJ - 4.69
MACKENZIE Kathryn U20 5.03.77, Portsm :
LJ - 5.58 (5.59w-93), TJ - 11.40
MACKINTOSH Clare 2.04.71, Glasgow :
60H - 8.83i,
100H - 14.16w/14.36 (14.0w?-93), TJ - 11.30
MACLEOD Heather U23 12.03.72, Inverness :
DT - 37.02 (38.42-91)
MACLEOD Karen M. A. V35 24.04.58, Edinb :
10k - 33:34.85 (33:17.88-89),
10MR - 54:44/55:41 (53:42dh-93/54:34-92),
HMar - 1:13:52 (1:11:45-92), Mar - 2:33:16
MACPHEE Beverley U17 20.03.79, GEC :
JT - 35.62
MACPHEE Rhonda U20 30.04.76, GEC :
800 - 2:10.5
MACPHERSON Joan U15 18.09.80, Bas & MH :
DT - 33.56

MADDOX Keri U23 4.07.72,
Cannock & Stafford/Staffs Univ :
60H - 8.50i (8.47i-92),
100H - 13.24 (13.20w/13.24-93), 400H - 59.49
MADUAKA Joice U23 30.09.73, Bromley :
100 - 11.94w/12.00 (11.81w/11.87-93),
200 - 23.96
MAGUIRE Lindsey U13 15.01.82, Edinb WM :
PenG - 2074
MAHINDRU Alison 15.07.68, Glas (nee CURRIE) :
400H - 62.6/63.72
MAHONY Joanne U20 22.10.76, Wirral :
400H - 61.90
MAJOR Julie 19.08.70, Basildon :
100H - 14.6/14.75w/15.16 (14.6-90/15.06-93),
HJ - 1.85, Hep - 4546 (4879-90)
MAJOR Marie Ann U23 4.05.74, Basildon :
100H - 14.6 (14.39w/14.4/14.72-93)
MALCOLM Tina J. 8.09.67, Birchfield :
LJ - 5.74 (6.19-87)
MALE Samantha U20 11.04.76, AF&D :
100H - 14.69w/14.81, Hep - 4168w/4162
MALLOWS Jayne 6.07.70, Coventry Godiva :
400 - 57.39 (56.1-92/56.32-91)
MALLOWS Lesley U23 27.04.73, Coventry G :
800 - 2:08.39 (2:07.90-91)
MANNING Caroline Louise U23 5.03.73, Wok :
HT - 43.56 (46.82-93)
MANNING Sara U17 12.07.78, St Albans :
DT - 34.80
MANSHIP Devina 12.12.69, Leics C/Texas Un :
5k - 17:30.1 (16:17.49-92)
MANT Deborah U20 11.10.75, Bournemouth :
60 - 7.77i,
100 - 12.07 (11.7w?/11.75w/11.88-93),
200 - 24.36 (23.96w/24.08-93)
MANUEL Karen U20 2.11.75, Bournemouth :
400 - 57.5
MARCH Emma U15 15.11.79, Rowntrees :
PenG - 2535
MARCHANT Zina D. V40 30.09.50, C of Bath :
10kR - 34:31, HMar - 1:16:31 (1:13:38-90),
Mar - 2:40:09 (2:39:26-91)
MARSELLA Michele Dawn 10.01.68,
Coventry Godiva (nee WHEELER) :
HJ - 1.70 (1.86-87)
MARSHALL Gail 1.04.71, Glasgow Univ :
PV - 2.70
MARTI Debora Jane 14.05.68, Bromley :
200 - 24.8w?, HJ - 1.91 (1.94i-91/1.93-92),
LJ - 5.85w? (6.22w-85/6.19-92),
JT - 38.02 (41.26-86)
MARTIN Hayley U20 25.05.76, Camb H/OUAC :
LJ - 5.77, JT - 40.62
MARTIN Imogen Dee U23 13.02.74, Luton :
HT - 40.62
MARTIN Karen Lesley U23 24.11.74, Derby L/RAF :
SP - 11.98, JT - 53.68 (55.72-92)
MARTIN Rachel U17 9.09.78, West Coast :
HJ - 1.68
MARTIN Tracy U15 4.04.80, Coventry Godiva :
200 - 25.46w/25.63
MASON Kelly Michelle 29.03.71, Sale :
see THIRKLE
MATHER Elizabeth U20 28.05.76, Sale :
HJ - 1.66
MAY Carolyn U23 15.10.74, Guildford & G :
400H - 65.4, HJ - 1.65 (1.76-91)

MAYCOCK Rebecca U17 13.02.78, Milton K :
TJ - 10.59
MAYFIELD Alison 12.05.69, Notts :
60 - 7.74i,
100 - 11.8/12.24 (11.8-91/11.94-93),
200 - 24.0/24.21 (23.7-91/24.11-93)
MAYHEAD Kirsty U17 17.02.78, Epsom & E :
60H - 9.2i, 80HI - 11.9, 300H - 44.8
MCARTHY Lorraine P. 30.12.63, Blaydon :
Mar - 3:07:27
MCBEATH Moira 30.04.62, Caithness :
400H - 64.6 (59.96-86)
MCBRINN Elaine 19.12.63, Shettleston :
10MR - 58:16, HMar - 1:17:42
MCCABE Laura U15 24.01.80, Vale Park :
800 - 2:13.32
MCCALLA Lorraine 20.09.60, Bir (nee CHARLTON) :
DT - 41.20 (47.26-93)
MCCAMMON Tammy U20 17.10.76, Hillingdon :
LJ - 5.76 (5.86-91)
MCCANDLESS Kate 22.06.70, Parkside/USA :
1500 - 4:30.3 (4:25.94-93),
3k - 8:59.30 (8:56.00-93),
5k - 15:35.81 (15:34.93-93)
MCCANN Stephanie A. 26.10.65, Lisburn :
200 - 24.58 (24.03w/24.35-90), 400 - 53.91,
100H - 14.8 (14.69-87), 400H - 58.09
MCCARTHY Catherine A. V40 21.08.53, C of Bath :
Mar - 3:01:36 (2:58:51-90)
MCCARTHY Jenny U13 22.02.82, Warrington :
75 - 10.3, 80 - 10.9, 150 - 19.8
MCCLUNG Mary 19.02.71, Kilmarnock :
800 - 2:05.69, 1500 - 4:25.13
MCCOLGAN Elizabeth 24.05.64, Dundee HH :
10kR - 32:38 (30:38-89)
MCCONNELL Lee U17 9.10.78, Glasgow :
100 - 12.19w,
200 - 24.0w/24.89w/24.9/24.94, HJ - 1.78
MCCORRY Julie U15 7.11.79, Ballymena & A :
SPG - 12.02un/11.84, PenG - 2538
MCCREA Philippa U17 1.03.78, Carlisle :
800 - 2:13.6 (2:13.4-93)
MCCREADIE Helen U20 10.05.75, EdinbWM :
DT - 43.58, HT - 43.88
MCCULLOCH Lorna 10.03.71, Edinburgh WM :
100H - 15.14 (14.28-91)
MCDONNELL Alison U23 28.06.72, Tring :
400H - 64.5
MCDONNELL Lynsey U13 19.11.81, Warr :
150 - 19.9
MCEWAN Donna U17 17.01.78, Nuneaton :
DT - 33.78
MCGEORGE Sonia Marian 2.11.64,
Brighton/Loughborough Studnts :
1500 - 4:12.20 (4:10.75-90),
1M - 4:33.12, 3k - 8:51.55 (8:51.33-90)
MCGILLIVARY Aileen 13.08.70, Edinb WM :
100 - 11.56w/11.76 (11.43w-93/11.54-92),
200 - 23.42w/23.61 (23.29-93)
MCGIVERN Stacy U20 14.12.76, Camb & Col :
TJ - 11.21
MCGOLDRICK Lesley U15 12.09.79, Gate :
75HG - 11.5 (11.57-93), PenG - 2741
MCGOVERN Anna U13 4.11.81, Preseli :
100 - 12.8dt
MCGOVERN Nicola U15 26.11.79, Liverpool H :
HJ - 1.63

MCGOWAN Suzanne U17 13.04.78, Motherwell :
  300 - 39.57 (39.48-93), 400 - 57.7
MCILROY Debra U17 18.12.77, Richmond & Z :
  HJ - 1.70 (1.70-93)
MCINTOSH Dextene U17 27.08.78, Essex L :
  300H - 43.38, 400H - 65.4, HJ - 1.68
MCINTYRE Gillian 6.11.64, Glasgow :
  400 - 56.79 (53.76-92)
MCKENNA Rebecca U17 6.01.78, Bournem'th :
  1500 - 4:45.1 (4:39.0-93), 3k - 10:24.14
MCKENZIE Claire U20 5.05.75, Barry :
  SP - 11.72, HT - 36.76
MCKENZIE Evadne U20 19.05.75, ES & Mx/JAM :
  100 - 11.8/11.84w/12.02,
MCKERNAN Jacqueline Lena 1.07.65, Lisburn/
  Loughbro : SP - 12.43 (13.31i-91/13.20-92),
  DT - 58.56 (60.72-93)
MCLEAN Melanie U17 17.01.78, Gateshead :
  DT - 33.20
MCLEOD Geraldine Ann 24.09.71, Birchfield :
  100 - 11.2/11.51w/11.66 (11.58-93),
  200 - 23.47 (23.4-93),
  300 - 39.17i, 400 - 55.4/55.88i
MCNULTY Caroline U17 3.12.77, Yate :
  1500 - 4:34.8, 3k - 10:08.87
MCPEAKE Stephanie 31.12.68, Shaftesbury B :
  see LLEWELLYN
MCPHAIL Fiona 23.06.71, Wigan/WRAF :
  HJ - 1.73
MCPHERSON Vikki 1.06.71, Glas/Glas Univ :
  3k - 9:26.05 (9:10.1-92), 5k - 16:19.46,
  10k - 33:02.74 (32:32.42-93)
MCQUEEN Sophie U13 3.12.81, Cleethorpes :
  HJ - 1.52
MCWHINNIE Fionna U17 25.04.78, Bas & MH :
  Hepl - 3864
MEAD Nicola U13 20.06.82, Torfaen :
  DTM - 22.98
MEAD Sarah U15 16.10.79, Torfaen :
  800 - 2:17.30i/2:18.01,
MEADOWS Jennifer U15 17.04.81, Wigan :
  200 - 25.52 (26.49-93), 800 - 2:16.80
MEDLOCK Donna U13 26.10.81, Thurrock :
  SPM - 9.66, PenM - 2419
MEDLYCOTT Lisa U17 9.12.77, Swindon :
  DT - 33.14
MEE Claire E. 24.04.64, Vale of Aylesbury :
  Mar - 2:59:35
MELKEVICK-MAWER Lisa 22.05.68, Clee :
  3k - 9:44.36, 5k - 17:02.84, 10k - 35:00.49,
  10kR - 34:59 (34:45-92)
MELLIS Kelly U15 4.12.79, Banbury :
  DT - 40.18
MELLOR Leanne U20 17.03.76, Rotherham :
  PV - 3.10
MELVIN Hazel U23 19.11.73, Glasgow :
  HJ - 1.81
MERRIGAN Maria U20 24.10.75, Coventry G :
  DT - 36.80 (38.28-93)
MERRY Emma Louise U23 2.07.74, Cov G :
  SP - 13.01i (13.62-93), DT - 50.72 (52.58-93)
MERRY Katharine U23 21.09.74, Birchfield :
  60 - 7.34i, 100 - 11.27w/11.34,
  200 - 22.85, 400 - 54.0
MERSH Joanne U23 19.10.74, Essex L :
  JT - 38.86 (39.14-93)
MICHIE Lucy U13 4.09.81, Ayr Seaforth :
  70HM - 11.6

MIDDLEMISS Hannah U20 5.03.76, Mandale :
  DT - 37.86 (40.42-93)
MIGHTY A. D. Natasha 21.12.70, Radley :
  200 - 24.94, 60H - 8.49i,
  100H - 13.74w/13.97 (13.90-93),
  400H - 64.5, HJ - 1.68,
  LJ - 5.70i/5.54 (5.64w-93/5.59-92),
  SP - 11.25i (11.46-92), Hep - 5036
MIJOVIC Catherine H. 11.04.61, Birchfield :
  5k - 17:16.8, 10kR - 33:38,
  10MR - 58:58 (57:24-92),
  HMar - 1:14:15, Mar - 2:48:31
MILES Helen Louise 2.03.67, Cardiff :
  60 - 7.61i (7.46i-91),
  100 - 12.05 (11.4/11.41w/11.50-88),
  200 - 24.90 (23.7w-88/23.81w/23.89-91)
MILES Rebecca U13 22.12.81, Tonbridge :
  HJ - 1.45
MILES Sarah U17 14.12.78, Newbury :
  100 - 12.47w/12.61 (12.10w/12.3-93)
MILLER Caroline U23 16.09.72, Preston :
  LJ - 5.74 (6.03w/5.85-93), TJ - 12.31
MILLER Eve U15 1.12.79, Hertford & Ware :
  100 - 12.4, 60H - 9.2i,
  75HG - 11.41w/11.5/11.58, PenG - 2826
MILLER Karen A. 4.02.64, Crawley :
  JT - 40.48 (50.12-87)
MILLS Karen U23 24.10.73, Lagan Valley :
  400 - 54.81
MILLS Lucy U23 24.11.72, Bedford & County :
  HT - 36.46 (42.46-91)
MITCHELL Angela 17.08.65, Parkside :
  DT - 36.06
MITCHELL Jayne Amanda 29.03.63, Wirral :
  100 - 11.9/11.94 (11.23w/11.41-84),
  200 - 24.9 (23.6-85/23.84-84)
MITCHELL Jeina Sophia U20 21.01.75, Croy :
  400 - 57.2, 800 - 2:05.85,
  1500 - 4:22.63 (4:19.09-92)
MITCHELL Viginia 29.01.63, Woking :
  400H - 64.9
¶MODAHL Diane Dolores 17.06.66, Sale :
  400 - 53.52/55.55 (53.28A-92/53.38-93),
  800 - 1:59.85dq/2:01.13 (1:58.65-90)
MOFFITT Alison J. 6.10.69, North Down :
  SP - 11.67, DT - 40.66 (47.22-91),
  JT - 47.00 (47.54-93)
MOLNER Amy U23 19.03.73, Colchester & T :
  TJ - 11.08
MOLYNEUX Jayne 21.10.68, Wirral :
  LJ - 5.80w?/5.56
MONAGHAN Sylveen U23 25.08.72, Sale :
  JT - 40.68 (46.46-91)
MONDS Debra U17 25.02.78, Wigan :
  DT - 35.50
MONTADOR Karen U17 14.05.79, Central :
  1500 - 4:36.3mx/4:42.67
MOODY Hannah U17 26.07.79, Skyrac :
  TJ - 10.54i
MOODY Karen 20.07.67, Cannock & Stafford :
  JT - 40.12 (44.96un-87/44.66-84)
MOODY Kate U17 7.04.79, Cannock & Staff:
  300H - 44.60
MOORE Hilary J. 23.09.60, Exeter :
  400H - 63.7 (63.1-85),
  LJ - 5.51 (5.60-91)
MOORE Julie 6.08.70, Holland Sports :
  JT - 38.90 (42.22-92)

MOORE Julie U23 5.12.73, Manx/Lough St:
400 - 56.7/57.21
MOORE Sarah Louise U23 15.03.73, Bristol :
SP - 11.18 (11.99-91), DT - 38.84,
HT - 50.52
MOOREKITE Janice V35 1.05.57, Invicta :
HMar - 1:17:07, Mar - 2:48:10
MORETON Kelly U15 18.09.79, Newport :
PenG - 2757w/2655
MORGAN Kelly U15 17.06.80, Salisbury :
JT - 41.50
MORLEY Suzanne V35 11.10.57, Brighton :
800 - 2:09.5mx (2:02.79-85),
1500 - 4:21.5 (4:11.00-85),
3k - 9:23.08 (8:56.39-84),
10kR - 34:47 (34:37-92)
MORRALL Leanne U17 7.07.79, Solihull & SH :
JT - 36.12
MORRIS Emma U13 25.01.82, Burnley :
DT - 23.68
MORRIS Emma U13 6.11.81, Frome :
1500 - 5:01.7
MORRIS Gemma U13 27.01.82, Birchfield :
150 - 19.9
MORRIS Jennifer D. 11.04.61, Spectrum S :
Mar - 3:04:47
MORRIS Joanna U17 16.10.77, Newbury :
HJ - 1.66 (1.67-93), HepI - 3954
MORRIS Judith A. V35 23.06.58, Bromley :
Mar - 2:54:57
MORRIS Katherine U20 5.09.75, Sale :
400 - 57.4
MORRIS Rachel 20.09.70, Shaftesbury B :
DT - 37.74 (43.58-91)
MORRISON Claire 30.05.69, Bristol :
100H - 14.8/15.14w, PV - 3.24
MORRISON Kirsty U20 28.10.75, Medway :
JT - 53.88 (59.36-93)
MORTON Glenys 17.06.60, Leics Cor :
SP - 11.38 (11.84-84)
MORTON Lesley 25.12.63, Westbury/NZ :
10kR - 33:21 (33:08-91), 10MR - 55:36,
HMar - 1:13:57 (1:13:49-91)
MOSS Jane U17 23.08.79, West Norfolk :
3k - 10:22.70mx
MOUNSEY Gemma U13 17.07.82, Carm :
800 - 2:25.7, 1500 - 5:05.0
MOUTRIE Anna L. 7.12.64, Parkside
(nee WITTEKIND) : 1500 - 4:24.62,
3k - 9:43.2 (9:19.11-88)
MOXEY Stacey U17 6.10.77, Edinburgh WM :
60H - 9.13i, 80HI - 12.0w/12.07w/12.14
MUJAWAMARIA Scholastica 12.07.65, H W/UGA :
JT - 40.48 (52.06-89)
MULCAHY C. U13, :
DTM - 24.90
MUNDEN Lisa U17 13.03.78, Bournemouth :
SP - 11.02
MUNRO Louise U15 8.07.80, Southampton C :
DT - 32.30
MUNRO Lynsay U20 1.02.77, Edinburgh WM :
JT - 38.80
MUNT Corinne 25.07.63, Essex L :
800 - 2:11.84
MURCHIE Gail 7.12.71, Aberdeen :
see WALKER
MURPHY Catherine Ann U20 21.09.75, SB :
100 - 11.63w/12.00, 200 - 23.83w/23.85 (23.72w-93)

MURPHY Jane U17 17.12.77, Elan Valley :
100 - 12.4, 200 - 25.5
MURRAY Michelle U17 22.11.78, Sutton :
200 - 25.45
MURRAY Pamela 13.01.67, Glasgow :
PV - 2.50i/2.40
MURRAY Yvonne Carole Grace 4.10.64, Motherwell :
1500 - 4:01.44 (4:01.20-87),
1M - 4:22.64, 2k - 5:26.93,
3k - 8:29.60 (8:29.02-88), 5k - 16:27.5+,
10k - 31:56.97
MUZEKOVRA S., Wycombe :
JT - 39.22
MYERS Heather R. 5.12.64, AF&D :
400 - 57.0 (56.6-82),
100H - 15.1 (14.6-91), 400H - 59.46
MYERS Mara U23 13.08.73, Oxford Univ :
1500 - 4:32.24, 3k - 9:40.15
MYHILL Danaa L. 16.10.70, Western (I.O.M.) :
60 - 7.52i, 100 - 11.58w/11.60,
200 - 24.2/25.05i (24.86-92)
MYTON Keri U15 26.10.79, Medway :
1500 - 4:45.6

NASH Hayley L. 30.05.63, Cardiff :
3k - 9:37.55 (9:13.65-92),
5k - 16:47.66 (16:25.7-92),
10kR - 33:23 (33:10-89),
10MR - 55:32, HMar - 1:13:16, Mar - 2:35:39
NASH Sharon U23 5.05.74, GEC :
SP - 12.04i/11.93 (12.67-93),
DT - 42.60 (44.32-93), HT - 41.94
NAUGHTON Patricia U20 17.04.75, Nenagh :
100H - 14.06w/14.78
NEAL Susan V40 31.10.50, Les Croupiers :
Mar - 3:03:47 (2:50.18-89)
NEALL Alison U15 8.11.79, Croydon :
JT - 37.86
NEEDHAM Janice E. V40 9.11.52, Rochdale :
Mar - 2:55:50 (2:55:33-93)
NEEF Melanie 26.05.70, Glasgow :
60 - 7.57i,
100 - 11.81w/12.0 (11.69w-88/11.88-91),
200 - 23.64, 300 - 37.33, 400 - 52.09
NELSON Tatum U17 17.12.78, Tunbridge W :
60 - 7.55i, 100 - 11.78 (11.67w-93),
200 - 25.29i (24.35w/24.51-93)
NEWCOMBE Rachel 25.02.67, Liverpool H :
200 - 25.1w, 400 - 55.30 (55.19-92),
400H - 65.55
NEWHAMS Deborah 18.01.62, Bridgend :
3k - 9:34.65, 10kR - 34:21,
10MR - 57:59, HMar - 1:16:48
NEWMAN Maxine Claire 15.12.70, Coventry G :
800 - 2:07.3 (2:06.16-92),
1500 - 4:16.70 (4:10.07-92),
1M - 4:37.67, 3k - 9:26.52 (9:12.41-90)
NEWMAN Wendy 31.08.71, Essex L :
JT - 40.82 (44.20-93)
NEWTON Jackie 28.08.64, Stockport :
3k - 9:55.0mx, 10MR - 58:38
NEWTON Leigh U17 13.01.78, Blackpool :
300 - 41.5 (41.4-93)
NEWTON Maria Angela 22.07.66, Ashford :
PV - 2.60 (2.70-93)
NICCOLLS Jannette U20 7.09.76, Hercules W :
100 - 12.07w/12.21 (12.2-92)

NICHOLLS Tammy U17 21.07.78, Basildon :
DT - 38.86
NICHOLSON Ruth U17 23.09.77, Tunbridge W :
200 - 25.0 (25.77-92),
300 - 41.20i (40.59-93),
400 - 57.37 (56.3mx-93)
NICHOLSON Stephanie U20 28.06.76, C of Hull :
100H - 14.96w/15.14, Hep - 4206
NICKLIN Debra U20 9.12.75, Colchester & T :
100H - 15.04w (14.8/14.84w-93)
NICKLIN Joanne 12.07.67, Colchester & T :
TJ - 11.44
NICOL Karen U17 1.11.77, Preston :
1500 - 4:41.7
NIGHTINGALE Julie U20 28.04.75, Eastb'rne GS :
JT - 41.80 (42.44-93)
NISBET Karen L. V35 28.04.57, Red Rose :
Mar - 3:02:38 (3:00:57-93)
NOBLE Susan U23 3.01.74, Middlesbro & C :
HJ - 1.65 (1.73-92)
NORMAN Katrina U20 1.01.76, Walton :
400H - 62.8/63.20
NORTH Stephanie 16.01.71, Shaftesbury B :
400H - 65.3/65.59 (63.8-91)
NUTTELL Amy U15 6.02.80, Holbeach :
75HG - 11.5un, LJ - 5.33io/5.25 (5.45-93),
PenG - 3225
NWANOKWU Chidinma U13 27.10.81, Herne H :
SPG - 8.89, SPM - 9.14, DT - 23.98
NYHAN Angela U17 13.04.78, Rowntrees :
60H - 9.22i, LJ - 5.43, SP - 10.75,
HepI - 4503

O'CONNOR Claire U23 24.09.74, E Down :
200 - 24.53
O'CONNOR Claire U20 5.06.75, Oldham & R :
3k - 9:45.9mx/9:46.44 (9:43.8mx-93)
O'CONOR Annette 20.08.71, Bracknell :
HT - 40.30 (42.32-90)
O'HARE Ellen U17 4.02.78, Cirencester :
800 - 2:12.6, 1500 - 4:36.81
O'MALLEY Jane U20 18.07.77, Hull Achilles :
Hep - 3865
O'SHEA Amanda U15 8.09.79, Hercules Wim :
800 - 2:16.70 (2:15.05-93)
O'SULLIVAN Clare U15 8.05.80, Sutton & D :
60H - 9.1i
OAKES Judith Miriam V35 14.02.58, Croydon :
SP - 18.68 (19.36-88),
DT - 47.82 (53.44-88),
JT - 38.82 (46.66-86)
OAKES Katherine U17 24.11.77, AF&D :
80HI - 11.8/11.88
OATES Stefanie U13 19.11.81, East Cheshire :
75 - 10.2, 80 - 10.9, 100 - 12.9,
150 - 20.0, 200 - 26.5
OBOH Oteri U23 7.10.73, Herne Hill :
JT - 43.90 (48.30-92)
OGDEN Rachael U17 23.07.79, Rowntrees :
800 - 2:13.36
OLADAPO Georgina 15.05.67, Hounslow :
100 - 12.07 (11.61w/11.64-85), 400 - 53.9
OLDFIELD Juliette U20 14.04.77, Kettering :
1500 - 4:32.67. (4:32.25-93)
OLIVER Lindsey U17 12.03.78, Liverpool H :
SP - 11.08
OLOFINJANA Banke U23 14.05.72, Tower H :
LJ - 5.51

ORE Wendy E. 23.05.66, Cardiff :
1500 - 4:20.60, 3k - 9:14.72,
10kR - 33:15, 10MR - 55:10
OSMENT Kim 3.04.63, Witney :
10MR - 58:53
OUTRAM Alison U20 14.06.77, Parkside :
3k - 9:38.87
OWBRIDGE Joanne U13 19.01.82, Hull Spring :
LJ - 4.77
OWEN Krissy U20 14.12.75, Eryri :
HJ - 1.70, SP - 12.88, JT - 43.20 (41.78-93)
OWEN Sarah J. V35 18.03.55, Newport :
SP - 11.09 (13.32-81)
OWEN Tracy A. 29.04.64, Arena :
Mar - 3:03:32
OWUSU Lesley U17 21.12.78, Windsor S & E :
60 - 7.89i, 100 - 12.38 (12.10-93),
200 - 24.82 (24.41w-93), 300 - 38.71,
400 - 57.9
OWUSU Sandra U13 30.09.81, W S & E :
80 - 11.0
OXLEY Sarah U23 3.07.73, Birchfield :
60 - 7.68i, 100 - 12.04,
200 - 24.13w/24.6/24.65
OYEYEMI Jean U15 24.08.81, Herts Sch/NIG :
100 - 11.86w/12.24

PAINES Hannah U17 6.04.79, Cardiff :
60 - 7.90i, 100 - 12.36,
PALMER Karlene J. U15 23.10.80, W S & E :
60 - 7.97i, 100 - 12.41w/12.46,
200 - 25.08w
PARKER Barbara A. V35 29.04.58, Jersey :
Mar - 2:57:35
PARKER Jacqueline T. 15.10.66, Essex L :
100 - 11.88, 800 - 2:08.9 (2:03.78i-93),
400H - 56.41 (56.15-91)
PARKER Susan 24.03.70, Sale :
800 - 2:06.5 (2:05.50-93),
1500 - 4:14.62 (4:12.3-93), 1M - 4:37.82,
3k - 9:18.03 (9:06.2-92)
PARKINSON Danielle U13 2.09.81, Rochdale :
HJ - 1.48, PenM - 2049
PARKINSON Hayley U20 5.12.75, EUAC :
800 - 2:12.10, 1500 - 4:33.1, 3k - 9:52.17
PARRY Alison 19.06.66, Croydon :
800 - 2:08.79 (2:03.88-91)
PARRY Joanna U17 5.03.78, Southampton C :
JT - 38.00
PARRY Sheena U17 16.11.77, Rhondda :
HT - 36.24
PARSONS Catherine U23 9.05.73, Hounslow :
HJ - 1.66i/1.65 (1.70-90)
PARSONS Helen U17 6.01.78, Crawley :
400 - 57.0, 800 - 2:12.2
PARSONS Lucy U17 10.02.79, Cardiff :
100 - 12.58, 300 - 40.86
PARTINGTON Carolyn 27.06.66, Manx :
3kW - 13:30.3, 5kWR - 23:04,
10kW - 48:20.0, 10kWR - 47:21
PATRICK Belinda U13 9.04.82, Nithsdale :
HJ - 1.45
PATTERSON Kelly Anne U17 19.12.78, And :
300 - 41.2/42.07
PATTINSON Helen U23 2.01.74, Preston :
800 - 2:12.4, 1500 - 4:33.14
PAUL Fiona U17 5.09.78, Edinburgh WM :
LJ - 5.49w/5.44i (5.32-93)

PAUL Stephanie 13.09.66, Ealing S & M/Army :
HJ - 1.65 (1.70-91)
PAUZERS Clare 2.08.62, Herne H/London RR :
1500 - 4:31.0, 10k - 35:11.74
PAYNE Joanna U17 11.10.78, Stourport :
TJ - 10.50
PAYNE Judith U15 7.07.80, Wakefield :
HJ - 1.60
PAYNE Kirsty U17 22.10.77, Shrewsbury :
60 - 7.87i, 100 - 12.2/12.30w (12.44-92),
200 - 24.69w/25.43 (25.20-93)
PEACOCK Rachel U13 18.05.82, Wimborne :
PenM - 2064
PEAKE Fiona U20 31.05.77, Woking :
PV - 2.80i/2.70
PEARCE Caroline U15 1.09.80, Huntingdon :
PenG - 2757 (2391-93)
PEARSON Claire U17 23.09.78, Leics Cor :
60H - 9.20i, 80HI - 11.7/11.94w/11.99
PEARSON Jennifer Ann 3.07.62, Ashford :
400 - 56.5 (54.6-88),
100H - 14.7/14.99w (14.5-92/14.78-91),
400H - 59.0/59.82 (57.41-88)
PEATFIELD Zoe U17 8.12.77, Stockport :
400 - 58.4
PENDRICH Susan U17 29.09.78, Dartford :
1500 - 4:44.1 (4:37.76-93)
PERCIVAL Deborah V35 22.04.58, GEC :
3k - 9:45.8 (9:45.5-90), 10kR - 34:18,
10MR - 57:56 (57:44-93)
PERIDES Lynsay U17 24.05.79, Bedford & Co :
PV - 2.30
PERRETT Kirsty U20 17.03.76, Middlesbro :
DT - 37.34
PERRY Laura Helen Susan U20 4.06.75,
Dudley & Stourbridge :
DT - 36.62 (39.56-91)
PETERS Julia U13 6.09.81, Wigan :
PenM - 2089
PHILLIPS Claire U17 2.04.78, Sutton :
300 - 41.51
PHILLIPS Claire U20 13.03.75, Hastings :
DT - 37.88
PHILLIPS Fiona 8.03.60, City of Bath :
3k - 9:53.8, 10kR - 34:28
PHILLIPS K. U13, Eckington :
DTM - 23.86
PHILLIPS Stephanie U17 25.10.78, Hastings :
Hepl - 3800
PHYTHIAN Claire U23 7.02.73, Wigan :
200 - 24.94 (24.91w-90/25.03-89),
100H - 14.30, HJ - 1.76 (1.78-89),
LJ - 5.83 (5.88w-91/5.78-90),
JT - 39.02, Hep - 5372
PICKERING Faye U13 13.06.82, Preston :
75 - 10.3
PICKSLEY Mary L. V40 7.01.52, Steel City :
Mar - 3:06:49 (3:06:18-92)
PICTON Janette 4.03.63, Burnham :
Mar - 2:54:42
PIDGEON Elizabeth U20 27.04.77, Chelm :
JT - 40.94
PIERRE Michelle U23 30.09.73, Croydon :
400 - 55.6/55.61 (54.9/55.39-92)
PINCOTT Vicky U17 27.05.78, Crawley :
300 - 40.8, 400 - 57.62
PINEL Syrena U17 13.01.79, Leics Cor :
200 - 25.5, LJ - 5.47

PINFOLD Julie U17 18.07.79, Birchfield :
DT - 33.44
PITEL Edwige 4.06.67, Shaftesbury B/FRA :
3k - 9:33.47, 10kR - 34:48
PLUMB Helen U17 18.03.78, Wakefield :
100 - 12.3/12.35w/12.53
POCOCK Niki U17 9.05.79, AF&D :
300H - 46.6
POPE Joanne 17.01.71, Brighton :
3kW - 15:13.22 (14:15.0-93),
5kW - 26:13.0 (24:35.0-90)
PORTER Lisa U15 2.11.79, Northampton :
JT - 35.74
POSSAMAI Catherine U20 11.04.75, Chelm :
JT - 38.32 (40.74-92)
POTRAC Lisa U17 1.02.79, Bromley :
300 - 41.43, 400 - 58.9
POTTER Helen U23 25.06.74, Trafford :
JT - 43.02 (45.06-93)
POTTER Marion J. V35 16.02.57, Norwich RR :
Mar - 3:05:31
POTTER Sarah U20 28.10.75, Portsmouth :
HJ - 1.65
POTTS Alison U23 15.10.74, Glas/Strath Un :
800 - 2:11.5 (2:10.53-92)
PRATT Julie U17 20.03.79, Essex L :
200 - 25.5, 80HI - 11.27w/11.5/11.55,
100H - 15.1
PRICE Julie 18.12.70, Epsom & Ewell :
400H - 64.7
PRICE Sharon U20 10.12.75, R SColdfield :
60H - 8.99i, 100H - 14.66 (14.43w-93)
PRINGLE Lucy U17 3.08.78, Northampton :
800 - 2:14.23
PRINGLE Maria U15 18.12.80, Copeland :
PenG - 2536
PRITCHARD Amanda U15 18.03.80, Cardiff :
800 - 2:10.66, 1500 - 4:45.0,
PRYER Helen U17 21.01.79, Camberley :
200 - 25.57, LJ - 5.55i (5.48-93)
PUCKERIDGE Jayne 23.10.71,
Medway/Loughborough Studnts :
400 - 57.4 (56.1-89/56.13-93), 800 - 2:12.27
PUGH Theresa U17 28.07.78, R S Coldfield :
300H - 46.1, 400H - 67.2
PURKISS Melanie U17 11.03.79, Team Sol :
100 - 12.3/12.42w
PURTON Alison U23 25.11.72, Bir/Birm Univ. :
60H - 8.99i (8.94i-93),
100H - 14.66 (14.40-92), HJ - 1.73 (1.76-89)

QUARTEY Tracey 16.12.71, Tower H :
SP - 11.23 (12.60-91),
DT - 39.36 (46.74dh/45.16-90)
QUIGLEY Lynne 19.02.69, Red Rose :
Mar - 3:01:21
QUINN Cheryl U23 29.04.74, Gateshead :
JT - 38.10 (38.68-90)
QUINN Pauline 2.08.70, Ballymena & Antrim :
1500 - 4:30.34 (4:27.37-90)

RADCLIFFE Paula J. U23 17.12.73,
Bedford & County :
1500 - 4:23.84 (4:11.6-93)
RAMMINGER Sarah Jane U20 1.10.75, Arb :
LJ - 5.81, TJ - 11.47w/11.23, Hep - 4517
RANN Lucy U15 5.09.80, Ryde :
SPG - 11.84, JT - 36.36

RASBUARY Danielle U23 15.01.74, Hull Ach :
TJ - 11.08
RASHLEIGH Jan, Bolton :
HMar - 1:19:06
RAVEN Claire Heather U23 15.06.72,
Coventry Godiva/Loughborough Studnts :
200 - 25.0w/25.1 (24.52w?/24.8-93),
400 - 54.05 (53.99-92)
RAWCLIFFE Adedigba U23 27.12.72, C of Stoke :
LJ - 5.53 (5.65-89)
RAWNSLEY-PEMBERTON Catherine E. V35
22.08.59, Spenborough (nee GOWLAND) :
800 - 2:08.7, 1500 - 4:32.04 (4:22.15-92)
REA Tracy U17 19.01.79, Coventry Godiva :
SP - 11.37
READER Catherine V40 19.10.54, Colch Jog:
3kW - 15:38.77 (15:07.1-91),
5kW - 26:50.98 (25:52.5-92),
10kW - 54:19.0 (52:43.3-92),
20kW - 1:54:46 (1:48:22-92)
REASON Sheryl J. 9.06.69, Stockport :
Mar - 3:05:43
REDFERN Helen U15 26.04.80, Liverpool H :
LJ - 5.39, PenG - 2539
REDMOND Laura A. U15 19.04.81, Edinburgh :
PenG - 2538
REDMOND Rachel U13 7.12.81, City of Stoke :
75 - 10.2, 100 - 13.2, 150 - 19.8
REDMOND Rosemary U17 3.10.78, E,S & M :
HT - 36.82
REED Paula U17 26.03.78, Sale :
HJ - 1.65 (1.65-93), TJ - 10.42
REEKS Helen U13 25.03.82, Wimborne :
LJ - 4.82
REEVES Katharine U23 2.03.73, Tonbridge :
200 - 25.1 (24.9-92), 400 - 55.15 (55.15-92)
REID-HUGHES Frances U15 18.03.80, Tonbr:
SPG - 12.05
RETCHAKAN Gowry P. 21.06.60, Thurrock :
400 - 56.0 (54.63Hur-92/55.1-91),
60H - 8.8i (8.7i-92/8.94i-89),
100H - 14.9 (14.0-92/14.52w-89),
400H - 55.78 (54.63-92)
REYNOLDS Jillian 17.12.70, Havering :
400 - 55.6 (54.9-93/55.65-87)
REYNOLDS Victoria U15 22.04.80, Blackpool :
PenG - 2687
RHODES Vyvyan Anne U23 5.05.73, Hallam :
200 - 25.19, 400 - 57.14i (55.99i-93),
400H - 58.78 (58.02-92)
RICE Deborah 26.03.70, City of Hull :
JT - 40.12 (46.30-91)
RICE Lorna U17 10.01.79, Coventry Godiva :
300 - 41.1
RICH Emma U20 14.05.77, Yeovil Olympiads :
JT - 40.54
RICHARDS Angharad U20 9.12.76, Guild & G :
JT - 45.96 (46.20-93)
RICHARDS Elizabeth U15 9.11.79, E,Sl & M :
SPG - 11.22
RICHARDS Pauline 30.06.68, Birchfield :
200 - 24.78 (24.76-93),
400 - 55.56 (55.33-93),
100H - 14.5/14.60w/14.72 (14.69-93),
LJ - 5.80w/5.67, SP - 11.98, JT - 38.44,
Hep - 5420
RICHARDSON Lesley J. U15 6.10.79, Nith :
JT - 35.60

RICHARDSON Marcia M. U23 10.02.72,
Windsor S & E/W London IHE :
60 - 7.38i (7.36i-93),
100 - 11.39w/11.46 (11.45-93),
200 - 23.5/23.55 (23.4-93),
400 - 56.9 (56.9-92),
TJ - 11.71 (11.83-93)
RICHARDSON Rebecca 17.07.60, Bridgend :
See CAMERON
RICHMOND Louise U13 15.12.81, Sol & S H :
2kW - 11:02.4, 2.5kWR - 13:55
RICHMOND Sarah U23 6.01.73, Pitr/Glas Un :
60H - 8.82i (8.7i-93/8.79i-91),
100H - 14.02w/14.2/14.29, TJ - 11.00
RIDGLEY Clare Louise U17 11.09.77, Team S :
PV - 3.44, TJ - 11.02
RIDGWAY Kelly U13 21.11.81, Swansea :
SPM - 10.06
RIDLEY Susan 'Anne' 7.05.65, Shaftesbury B:
5k - 17:11.4
RIDLEY Susan 25.10.65, Edinburgh WM :
3k - 9:32.8 (9:27.94-93),
5k - 16:51.80
RIGG Suzanne 29.11.63, Warrington :
3k - 9:12.6mx/9:24.2 (9:07.3-93),
5k - 15:56.83,
10k - 33:01.40 (32:44.06-93),
10kR - 34:02 (32:35-92),
10MR - 55:38 (53:42-93),
HMar - 1:13:47 (1:12:07-93), Mar - 2:41:03
RILEY Catherine U13 4.06.82, Parkside :
600 - 1:44.1
ROACH Kirsty U13 8.12.81, Liverpool Pem :
LJ - 4.72
ROBB Kirsty U13 14.10.81, Sale :
SPM - 9.29
ROBERTS Joanne U17 7.03.79, Braintree :
SP - 10.83
ROBERTS Kerry Jane 15.09.67, Brighton :
HJ - 1.65 (1.88i/1.86-92)
ROBERTS Melanie U17 2.03.78, Wigan :
60 - 7.93i (7.90i-93),
100 - 12.2/12.58w (12.48-93)
ROBIN Julie U20 16.01.77, Glasgow :
SP - 12.29i/12.02 (12.61-92), DT - 45.10
ROBINS Lorraine A. 13.05.70, Hounslow :
60 - 7.52i (7.5i-93), 100 - 11.8/11.96,
200 - 24.7
ROBINSON Eleanor V45 20.11.47, Border :
24Hr - 186.390 (240.169km-89)
ROBINSON Gemma U17 30.12.78, Dartford :
TJ - 10.54
ROBINSON Jessica U13 19.02.82, Dartford :
DTM - 23.24
ROBINSON Lynne Elizabeth 21.06.69, Cov G :
400 - 56.8 (54.6-86),
800 - 2:04.7mx/2:05.59 (2:02.0-89/2:02.50-92),
1500 - 4:10.32, 10kR - 33:49
ROBINSON Victoria U17 17.10.77, Stoke :
1500 - 4:41.78 (4:39.96-93), 3k - 10:09.14
ROBSON Debbie U20 12.07.76, Cannock & St:
100H - 15.2
ROCHE Patricia 15.06.68, Cardiff :
LJ - 5.51 (5.62-93), TJ - 11.05
RODD Stacey U17 19.05.78, Barry :
60 - 7.89i, 100 - 12.4 (12.31-93)
ROGERS Julie A. 15.01.64, Birchfield :
400H - 63.71 (60.92-93)

ROGERS Kate U17 14.02.79, Newark :
  TJ - 11.02, HepI - 3971
ROGERS Melissa U17 26.11.78, AF&D :
  JT - 36.72
ROGERS Nina U17 19.09.78, Derby LAC :
  300 - 40.56
ROLES Philippa U17 1.03.78, Swansea :
  SP - 13.68i/13.65, DT - 48.88, HT - 35.94
ROLES Rebecca U15 14.12.79, Swansea :
  DT - 34.70,
ROLFE Julie U23 22.05.73, Northampton :
  100 - 12.1/12.29 (12.0/12.09w-93/12.15-92)
ROLFE Nicola 19.08.69, Newbury :
  JT - 39.66 (42.24-90)
RONALD Alison 20.01.67, Falkirk :
  PV - 2.50
ROSCOE Helen U15 4.12.79, Liverpool H :
  200 - 25.20w/25.52
ROSE Alison 27.09.67, Edinburgh WM :
  10k - 33:57.86 (34:35.73-93),
  10kR - 34:03, 10MR - 56:41,
  HMar - 1:15:26, Mar - 2:45:19
ROSE Dawn U17 25.01.79, Leamington :
  60 - 7.72i, 100 - 11.93w/12.2/12.31
ROSE Samantha U13 18.02.82, Kettering :
  HJ - 1.45
ROSS Isla U13 26.12.81, Black Isle :
  200 - 27.6, 800 - 2:25.8
ROSS Lindsay U17 27.12.77, Nithsdale :
  HT - 32.14
ROSTEK Malgorzata U20 25.03.77, Glasgow :
  60 - 7.69i, 100 - 12.1w (12.26-93)
ROWE Deborah U23 8.09.72, Coventry G :
  LJ - 5.62 (5.81w?-92/5.78-93), TJ - 12.00
ROWE Louise U17 8.11.78, Enfield :
  1500 - 4:45.1
ROWICKI Emma U17 29.11.77, Blackpool :
  60 - 7.98i
ROY Lesley Ann U13 3.01.82, Pitreavie :
  SPM - 9.86, DTM - 27.74
ROYLE Diane V35 24.11.59, Sale :
  JT - 55.32 (62.22-85)
ROZE Anna U23 6.11.74, Shaftesbury Barnet :
  400H - 64.56 (62.9/63.72-93),
  TJ - 11.03
RUDDOCK Ellana U20 23.02.76, Coventry G :
  100 - 11.89w/11.9/11.99,
  200 - 25.0/25.44 (24.9w-93)
RUSHMERE Linda V35 14.11.59, Redhill :
  10kR - 34:41, 10MR - 57:47,
  HMar - 1:14:31, Mar - 2:40:17 (2:40:03-88)
RUSSELL Clare U13 11.11.81, Oldham & Roy :
  80 - 11.0
RUSSELL Eve U13 27.09.82, Tavistock :
  JTM - 26.64
RUTLAND Emma U13 9.10.81, Blackpool :
  1500 - 5:06.4
RYAN Catherine U15 4.02.80, Shrewsbury :
  PenG - 2617

S AGER Sally U20 28.03.77, Barnsley :
  100H - 15.08, 400H - 65.7
SAINT-SMITH Tasha U20 20.12.75, Enfield :
  DT - 44.68
SALLIS Nicola U13 4.12.81, Brighton :
  800 - 2:26.1, 1500 - 5:01.9
SALMON Gemma U15 13.01.80, Leics Cor :
  LJ - 5.38

SALMON Georgina U15 1.11.79, Bristol :
  800 - 2:16.0, 1500 - 4:41.40 (4:43.6-93)
SALMON Sarah U23 9.09.74, Newquay & Par :
  800 - 2:11.4, 1500 - 4:28.41
SAMPHIRE Gemma U23 5.10.73, Dorchester :
  HJ - 1.75 (1.78-92)
SAMUELS Belinda U17 29.11.78, Birchfield :
  LJ - 5.57w/5.55
SANDERS Karen U20 13.11.76, Colch & T :
  Hep - 3832
SANDERSON Danielle 26.10.62, Watford :
  3k - 9:57.1 (9:45.0-92), 5k - 16:44.5,
  10k - 34:00.46, 10kR - 34:02 (33:57-93),
  10MR - 55:42, HMar - 1:13:11, Mar - 2:36:29
SAUNDERS Kathryn U20 21.08.77, Bracknell :
  400 - 57.04
SAUNDERS Kerry U20 28.03.77, Derby LAC :
  HJ - 1.70, TJ - 11.04
SAVAGE Marianne V45 26.01.49, Centurian :
  100kT - 9:46:29, 24HrT - 200.925,
  24Hr - 172.485 (209.214km-89)
SAXELBY Jane U23 14.01.72, Notts :
  100H - 15.04w/15.3
SAYERS K. U13, King's Sch :
  JTM - 25.80
SCHAUFLER Rebecca U13 30.10.81, Brack :
  JTM - 24.40
SCHOFIELD Victoria U23 29.12.72, Roth :
  200 - 25.04, 100H - 14.06, 400H - 62.8,
  HJ - 1.73, LJ - 6.07, SP - 11.84,
  JT - 38.16, Hep - 5671
SCOBEY Christina L. 1.06.66, Lond Oly/USA :
  Mar - 2:51:31
SCOBIE Kirsten 13.11.67, Leeds :
  3k - 9:49.73i (9:29.72-93)
SCOBIE Rhona 18.10.62, Glasgow :
  HJ - 1.70i/1.70 (1.83-85)
SCOTT Carly U17 19.07.79, Milton Keynes :
  3k - 10:28.9
SCOTT Joanne U20 31.12.76, Elswick :
  TJ - 11.40
SCOTT Lorna U17 27.07.78, Glasgow :
  400 - 58.51,
SEAGER Heather 4.04.68, Yeovil Olympiads :
  SP - 11.72
SEERY Helen Marie U20 6.09.76, Spen :
  200 - 24.9/25.14 (24.5w/24.63-93)
SEMUS Kate 18.01.70, Parkside :
  DT - 37.54 (39.10-90)
SESTON Laura U17 9.02.79, Ipswich :
  60 - 7.62i, 100 - 11.84w/11.88,
  200 - 25.04i/25.3/25.34
SEXTON Tania 7.08.63, Cardiff :
  400H - 64.15 (63.74-93)
SHARP Nicola U17 29.10.77, Bournemouth :
  60H - 9.02i,
  80HI - 12.0 (11.5/11.57w/12.09-93)
SHARPS Louise U20 9.07.77, Deeside :
  100 - 12.1w/12.16,
  200 - 24.98w/25.1/25.58 (25.50-93)
SHARRATT Helen U23 18.12.72, Southend :
  3kW - 15:05.0 (15:05.0-92), 5kWR - 25:33,
  10kWR - 57:22 (56:08-92)
SHASHOUA Yvonne R. 16.03.62, E London :
  Mar - 3:07:44
SHAW Lorraine A. 2.04.68, Gloucester L :
  SP - 14.21, DT - 55.04, HT - 59.92

388

SHAW Lucille U13 2.06.82, Gloucester L :
  SPM - 9.08, DT - 26.16, DTM - 29.18
SHEPHERD Victoria U15 26.01.80, Wakefield :
  SP - 10.81i, SPG - 12.84
SHEPPARD Suzanne U17 24.09.78, Lisburn :
  TJ - 10.38
SHERMAN Elizabeth U15 15.09.79, Thurrock :
  PenG - 2732
SHIELDS Jane Elizabeth 23.08.60, Sheffield :
  10kR - 34:48, HMar - 1:18:37
SHIPMAN Victoria U20 31.03.77, Derby LAC :
  100 - 11.9w/11.97w/12.1/12.13,
  200 - 24.6/24.76
SHIRT Pauline U17 21.05.78, Hallamshire :
  SP - 12.41
SHORT Sallyanne 6.03.68, Torfaen :
  100 - 11.88 (11.36w-89/11.39-92),
  200 - 24.10 (23.19w-90/23.24-92), LJ - 5.88
SHORTS Tracy U23 4.11.72, Edinburgh/Kilb :
  SP - 12.24, DT - 39.94
SHUM Cathy 30.05.61, Cannock & Staff/IRE :
  10kR - 34:02 (33:30-93),
  HMar - 1:12:48, Mar - 2:42:47 (2:38:14-93)
SIDDALL Naomi U20 2.04.75, Barnsley :
  100H - 15.1/15.22 (14.95w/15.03-93)
SIDIBE Wooday U17 14.11.78, Croydon :
  60 - 7.69i, 100 - 12.4 (12.1-93),
  200 - 25.1/25.29i/25.39
SIEGERT Jane E. 6.02.69, Great Yarmouth :
  Mar - 2:56:14
SILVER Lorna U23 10.01.74, Dundee HH :
  100H - 14.59, 400H - 59.9/60.58
SIMMANS Sarah U17 29.11.78, Oldham & R :
  JT - 40.60
SIMMONS Sarah U20 12.01.75, Medway :
  800 - 2:12.0, 1500 - 4:26.07, 3k - 9:50.36
SIMMS Claire U15 17.10.79, City of Stoke :
  JT - 33.24
SIMPSON Marian U17 2.11.77, Aberdeen :
  HT - 31.58
SINCLAIR Maggie V40 2.04.54, Glasgow :
  Mar - 3:00:06
SINNOTT Debbie U15 28.03.80, Liverpool H :
  100 - 12.4/12.90
SKEETE Lesley-Ann 20.02.67, Trafford :
  60H - 8.29i (8.06i-87),
  100H - 13.42 (13.01w/13.03-90)
SKEGGS Karen 26.10.69, Ashford :
  LJ - 5.91w/5.88 (6.29w/6.09-89),
  TJ - 12.45 (12.93w/12.89-92), SP - 11.99
SKETCHLEY Katy U23 9.07.73, Colch & T :
  100H - 14.47w/14.5/14.54 (14.15-92),
  Hep - 4124w (4509-92)
SKINNER Julie U23 6.08.72, Thurrock :
  800 - 2:11.6 (2:11.1-92), 1500 - 4:24.71
SKINNER Rehanne U15 13.11.79, Scar :
  JT - 33.96
SLATER Catriona U20 27.01.77, Chelmsford :
  LJ - 5.51 (5.59-92)
SLATER Laverne U13 26.01.82, Wycombe :
  75 - 10.1, 150 - 19.6
SLATER Nicola Simone U20 11.01.77, Radley :
  1500 - 4:27.31, 3k - 9:21.20
SLAUGHTER Karen 2.12.70, Essex L :
  JT - 39.34 (51.08-91)
SLIMIN Caroline 27.08.65, Basingstoke & MH :
  800 - 2:08.6, 1500 - 4:18.61, 3k - 9:30.67,
  10kR - 34:27

SLOANE Joanne U20 2.12.76, Stourport :
  200 - 24.91i (24.49w-92/24.50-93),
  400 - 55.12
SMALLWOOD Nicole U17 9.10.77, Halesowen :
  HJ - 1.67
SMART Natalie U15 23.08.80, Reading :
  60 - 7.99i
SMITH Anna U13 6.10.81, Hereford :
  SPG - 8.59, SPM - 9.28
SMITH Anne V45 7.06.49, Chiltern :
  Mar - 3:04:19
SMITH Carolyn 6.10.61, Dundee HH :
  400H - 62.95
SMITH Carolyn U17 3.10.77, Liverpool H :
  1500 - 4:41.31
SMITH Diane 15.11.60, Hull Spartan :
  HT - 39.82
SMITH Janet 7.10.64, Windsor S & E :
  HT - 46.88
SMITH Karen U23 10.02.74, City of Stoke :
  SP - 12.16, DT - 46.54 (46.64-93)
SMITH Karen 1.06.61, Coventry RWC :
  3kW - 14:09.0 (14:02.29-93),
  5kW - 24:18.79 (24:12.11-93),
  5kWR - 24:03, 10kWR - 48:30
SMITH Karen U17 12.12.77, Gloucester L :
  HT - 30.76
SMITH Kelly U17 29.10.78, Herts Sch :
  TJ - 10.57
SMITH Louise U20 11.07.77, Ipswich :
  JT - 40.32
SMITH Michelle Louise U17 1.01.78, Salisbury :
  HJ - 1.70
SMITH Natasha U20 6.06.77, Hounslow :
  SP - 12.62, HT - 36.88 (37.28-92)
SMITH Phylis 29.09.65, Sale :
  60 - 7.46i (7.39i-90),
  100 - 11.9 (11.40w-90/11.60-87),
  200 - 24.2 (23.40-92),
  300 - 37.47 (37.37-91),
  400 - 51.30 (50.40-92), 800 - 2:08.5
SMITH Rachel U20 3.03.76, Oxford City :
  400H - 65.3, Hep - 4242
SMITH Samantha U23 31.10.74, Hounslow :
  HT - 40.66
SMITH Sophia U23 8.12.74, Hallamshire :
  60 - 7.5i/7.51i,
  100 - 11.82 (11.56w/11.70-93),
  200 - 23.68 (23.57-93)
SNEDDON Esther U23 30.06.74, Central :
  HT - 37.72, JT - 40.12, Hep - 4290w
SNOOK Verity A. 13.11.70, AF&D (nee LARBY) :
  3kW - 13:27.9, 5kW - 23:22.52,
  5kWR - 22:45+,
  10kW - 48:05.0 (47:10.07-93),
  10kWR - 46:06
SOLLARS Loretta 29.10.63, Leeds :
  5k - 16:56.1
SOPER Annabel 18.11.71, Croydon :
  100 - 11.92 (11.5w/11.7/11.82-90),
  200 - 24.5/24.57 (24.28w/24.5-87)
SOTHERTON Kelly Jade U20 13.11.76, Ports :
  100H - 14.72w/15.07, HJ - 1.69,
  LJ - 5.67 (5.77-92),
  TJ - 11.61w/11.56, Hep - 4823
SPACEY Sian 13.07.64, Belgrave/CAN :
  5kW - 24:50.09, 10kWR - 51:09

389

SPACKMAN Karen 20.08.69, Bromley :
400H - 61.7/63.14 (63.10-93)
SPACKMAN Melissa 19.10.71, Notts :
JT - 41.04 (46.56-92)
SPARK Jayne Clare 16.09.70, Altrincham :
800 - 2:08.54 (2:06.24-93),
1500 - 4:19.70 (4:13.62-93),
3k - 9:14.3mx/9:26.36 (9:06.7mx/9:22.5-93),
5k - 16:12.1, HMar - 1:16:48
SPELLACY Jemma U13 27.11.82, Castle Pt :
JTM - 24.44
SPOKES Debbie U15 7.08.80, Bournemouth :
SPG - 11.26
SPRINGMAN Sarah M. V35 26.12.56, CUAC :
Mar - 2:59:09
SPRINGATE Teresa Jayne 8.03.69, Medway :
60H - 8.99i (8.88i-91),
100H - 14.3/14.37 (14.03-93),
400H - 64.1/66.28 (61.92-93),
LJ - 5.61 (5.96-90)
SPROTT Jennie 24.07.68, Reading :
200 - 24.8, 400 - 56.3/56.72
SPRULES Lyn U20 11.09.75, Hounslow :
DT - 40.08 (40.72-93), HT - 55.44
SPURWAY Claire U17 4.04.78, Cannock & St :
200 - 25.5/25.98 (25.16-93)
STACEY Julie U23 15.11.72, Bromley :
800 - 2:12.2 (2:10.2-92),
1500 - 4:31.5 (4:21.70-91)
STANTON Linda Mary U23 22.06.73, Roth :
PV - 3.42i/3.30 (3.40-93)
STANTON Suzanne 3.02.62, Birchfield :
400 - 56.0 (53.40-86),
800 - 2:10.3 (2:05.87-91)
STANWAY Gayle U17 29.10.77, Glasgow :
300H - 45.7/47.04
STAPLES Katharine 2.11.65, Essex L :
PV - 3.65
STAPLETON Samantha U23 13.10.73, Brack :
HJ - 1.65 (1.66-93), PV - 3.20un/3.00
STAPLEY Lisa U17 2.04.78, Horsham BS :
DT - 33.40
STARES Hannah U17 13.11.78, Yate :
Hepl - 3867
STEAD Caroline 14.09.71, Parkside :
LJ - 5.69, TJ - 12.17
STEADMAN Marina 4.09.60, Bracknell :
3k - 9:55.1 (9:16.8-84),
HMar - 1:19:17 (1:13:29sh-87/1:13:43-89)
STEELE Emily U23 10.09.74, Birchfield :
JT - 43.06 (45.80-92)
STEELE Wendy E. 7.01.66, Edinburgh WM :
400 - 55.43 (54.84-92)
STEVENS Barbara V35 2.05.56, Redhill :
Mar - 3:03:48
STEVENSON Lucy U23 30.01.73, Sale :
JT - 47.32 (52.00-92)
STEVENSON Sarah Anne Louise U23 31.12.73,
Notts : 400 - 56.3 (56.66-93)
STEWART Alison U17 19.01.78, Victoria Pk AAC :
60 - 7.98i, 200 - 25.3w
STEWART Emily U23 2.08.74, Hallam/Sheff Un :
TJ - 11.07 (11.23w/11.08-92)
STEWART Gillian U15 21.01.80, Edinburgh :
HJ - 1.60, PenG - 2736
STILL Margaret 9.05.65, Wakefield :
400H - 65.4 (58.44-88)

STILL Sarah U20 24.09.75, Aberdeen :
200 - 25.26, HJ - 1.65,
LJ - 5.74, Hep - 4643
STIRLING Anne-Marie U23 24.07.73, Dudley & S :
JT - 39.66
ST JOHN Sam U13, Tunbridge Wells :
80 - 11.0
STONE Michelle U15 7.01.80, Exeter :
JT - 32.88
STOREY Victoria U17 21.11.77, Sale :
JT - 39.42
STOUT Keira U15 6.03.80, Braintree :
HJ - 1.67
STOUTE Jennifer Elaine 16.04.65, Essex L :
200 - 24.6 (22.73-92)
STRAIN Lorraine 9.04.64, Cov G (nee BAKER) :
800 - 2:10.9 (1:59.67-86),
1500 - 4:29.74 (4:11.94-90)
STRICKLETON Sarah U15 10.05.80, Wigan :
DT - 31.46
STUART Katherine Louise 18.05.67, Sale :
200 - 24.64w/25.18 (23.3-91/23.32w-89/23.36-90)
STYLES Vicky U17 8.12.77, Liverpool H :
80HI - 12.0/12.04w, 300H - 46.9
SUDDES Joanne U20 27.01.77, North S Poly :
100H - 14.85
SUGDEN Claire U17 16.09.78, Bingley :
DT - 35.08
SULLIVAN Deborah U23 24.01.72, Havering :
3k - 9:55.12
SULLIVAN Denise U15 27.12.79, Enfield :
PenG - 2560
SULLIVAN Leanne U17 27.03.79, Tower H :
DT - 33.40
SUTCLIFFE Elaine 6.04.70, Wakefield
(nee WYARD):
100 - 12.04 (11.8/11.94w/12.03-90),
200 - 24.48 (24.4-93), 300 - 38.7,
400 - 55.02, Hep - 3886
SUTHERLAND Emma U13 10.01.82, Edin WM :
SPM - 9.23
SUTHERLAND Wendy 30.05.63, Serp/NZ :
3k - 9:42.55, 5k - 16:28.18,
10kR - 34:47, 10MR - 57:30,
HMar - 1:17:01
SUTTON Marian 7.10.63, Tipton :
10kR - 32:55, 10MR - 57:34 (54:17-93),
HMar - 1:13:34 (1:11:42-93),
Mar - 2:37:46 (2:34:38-92)
SWALLOW Jodie U15 23.06.81, Brentwood :
1500 - 4:45.30
SWANN Julie 15.07.62, Wolverhampton & B :
400 - 57.2 (56.6-85/57.10-91), 800 - 2:07.94,
1500 - 4:26.07i/4:28.38 (4:27.0-93)
SWIFT Claire U17 17.10.76, Liverpool H :
1500 - 4:33.64, 3k - 9:55.09
SWINDELL Tracy 8.11.66, Thurrock :
Mar - 2:48:09
SYKES Julia U20 27.05.75, Spenborough :
400H - 61.68
SYMONDS Emma U20 5.06.77, Norfolk :
200 - 25.0 (25.57w-93)
SYMONDS Joanne 19.02.68, Birchfield :
1500 - 4:22.09 (4:25.2-93),
3k - 9:24.21 (9:20.20-93), 10kR - 34:19,
10MR - 58:50
SYMONDS Sarah Louise U23 28.12.73, Radley :
DT - 44.44 (47.50-90)

TAIT Natalie J. U23 24.08.72, Hounslow :
800 - 2:06.17 (2:05.1-89)
TALBOT Elizabeth U23 5.12.74, Bedford & Co :
1500 - 4:25.32 (4:24.5-93), 3k - 9:45.7
TALBOT Nicola U23 17.02.72, Telford :
SP - 11.71 (11.74-93), DT - 49.92 (54.24-93)
TAPLIN Naomi U13 18.12.81, Oxford City :
75 - 10.2, 80 - 10.9, 100 - 13.0,
150 - 19.7, 200 - 26.5
TAYLOR Claire U20 6.08.76, Telford :
JT - 43.52 (48.00-92)
TAYLOR Gail U20 2.06.76, Glasgow :
HJ - 1.65i (1.65-92)
TAYLOR Kim-Anne U17 10.02.78, Dartford :
300H - 46.21
TAYLOR Lucinda 8.11.63, Trafford :
3k - 9:58.8 (9:18.42-90)
TAYLOR Lynn Caroline 5.08.67, Woking :
800 - 2:07.45 (2:06.5-93)
TAYLOR Patricia U17 14.03.79, Liverpool Pem :
Hepl - 3833
TEASDALE Kate U20 27.12.75, Elan Valley :
200 - 24.7/25.09 (24.6/24.63w-93/24.9w-92)
TELFORD Louise U13 7.01.82, Lochgelly :
JTM - 31.58
TELFORD Rebekah U20 4.11.76, Trafford :
PV - 2.60
TEREK Ann 22.09.64, Lisburn :
1500 - 4:31.9, 3k - 9:37.9
TERRY Sandra 28.04.69, Army :
DT - 36.78 (37.24-93)
THACKERAY Helen 26.06.71, Hull Spring :
SP - 11.26, JT - 40.76
THACKRAY Penny U23 18.08.74, Spen :
1500 - 4:26.5, 3k - 9:35.76
THIRKLE Kelly Michelle 29.03.71, Sale
(nee MASON) :
HJ - 1.80i/1.76 (1.88i-92/1.85-91)
THIRLWELL Tina M U13 5.09.81, Altrincham :
PenM - 2373
THOMAS Clare U17 26.08.79, Swansea :
1500 - 4:40.69
THOMAS Judy P. 20.01.63, Birchfield :
400 - 57.3 (54.58-89),
400H - 64.86 (63.99-93)
THOMAS Lisa U15 22.06.80, Shaftesbury B :
100 - 12.24w
THOMAS Michelle 16.10.71, Coventry Godiva :
100 - 12.25 (11.9-91/11.93w-89/12.03-91),
200 - 24.2/24.45 (24.29w-90/24.3-91),
400 - 55.83 (54.01-92)
THOMAS Paula 3.12.64, Trafford :
100 - 11.15 (11.13w-88), 200 - 22.69,
LJ - 5.71 (6.07w-88/6.01-86)
THOMAS Sonia U17 16.05.79, Wallsend :
1500 - 4:42.1
THOMAS Yvonne M. V35 31.03.57, London O :
Mar - 3:06:15
THOMPSON Alison Kate U23 11.02.74, Sale :
100 - 11.86db/11.88 (11.8w?-93),
200 - 24.5/24.95 (24.3w/24.48w-93/24.58-92)
THOMPSON Clara U15, Brecon :
DT - 33.00
THOMPSON Joanne V35 30.10.58, C of Bath :
1500 - 4:32.6 (4:30.4-92),
3k - 9:34.5mx/9:38.41 (9:15.54-93),
5k - 16:13.43, 10k - 33:56.04,
10MR - 55:20 (55:59-93)

THOMPSON Kimberley U23 5.01.73, Gate :
HT - 44.46
THOMPSON Lisa 12.07.62, Bromley :
800 - 2:06.9mx/2:07.38 (2:04.85-90)
THOMPSON Lisa U15 25.04.81, Colwyn Bay :
PenG - 2636
THOMPSON Margaret V40 8.07.54, Pott Mar :
Mar - 3:00:16 (2:59:01-90)
THOMSON Jan, Pitreavie :
Mar - 3:07:32
THOMSON Pamela U17 29.03.78, AUS :
DT - 36.26
THOMSON Trudi V35 18.01.59, Pitreavie :
HMar - 1:17:25, Mar - 2:43:18,
100kR - 7:42:17 (8:12:05-93)
THOMSON Wendy U13 28.06.82, Glasgow :
100 - 13.0/13.35, 150 - 20.3,
200 - 27.2/27.46
THORNE Alison U23 25.09.72, Windsor S & E :
400 - 55.33
THORNE Louretta U20 6.05.77, Wycombe :
100 - 12.1w/12.24 (12.2-93), 200 - 24.39,
400 - 54.27, LJ - 5.74w/5.46 (5.54-93)
THORNER Kate U13 13.01.82, Yeovil Oly :
70HM - 11.7
THORNER Rosie 7.08.67, Bris (nee BAGWELL) :
400 - 56.94, 400H - 64.0
THORP Angela Caroline U23 7.12.72, Wigan :
60 - 7.57i, 100 - 12.02,
60H - 8.3i/8.39i (8.35i-92),
100H - 13.32 (13.28-93)
THORPE Amanda 21.07.71, Hyndburn :
800 - 2:09.5,
1500 - 4:19.7mx/4:22.69 (4:22.48-93),
1M - 4:44.94,
3k - 9:17.4mx/9:40.17 (9:29.9-93)
THORPE Sophia 3.01.70, Queens Park :
TJ - 11.07
THURSTON Kathy U20 2.01.76, Warrington :
400H - 62.55
TIMMIS Irene 28.03.65, Southampton City :
SP - 11.88
TINDAL Jacqueline U17 21.01.79, Fife :
60H - 9.20i, 80HI - 11.9w/12.04,
HJ - 1.65i (1.61-92), Hepl - 4023
TITTERINGTON Helen 24.10.69,
Leics Cor/Loughborough Studnts :
5k - 16:48.2+e (15:40.14-89),
10k - 34:08.00 (32:36.09-89), 10kR - 34:36
TODD Charlotte U13 7.12.81, Edinburgh WM :
100 - 13.0, 70HM - 11.79
TOMLINSON Joanne U17 5.11.77, Deeside :
TJ - 10.44
TONKS Sharon J. 18.04.70, Bromsgrove & R :
3kW - 15:07.0 (14:50.0-89),
5kW - 25:47.26 (25:35.15-89),
5kWR - 25:27, 10kWR - 52:39
TOWN Anna U20 22.04.75, Verlea :
HT - 36.48
TOZER Lynsey U20 6.12.75, Birchfield :
3kW - 15:20.7, 5kW - 26:14.09,
5kWR - 25:49 (25:35-92),
10kWR - 53:28 (53:18-92)
TRAFFORD Sharon U23 10.08.73, Ashford :
400H - 65.0/65.63
TREBLE Katie U17 21.11.78, Cornwall AC :
300H - 46.9

TREMBLE Amanda U20 2.11.76, North S Poly :
800 - 2:12.5 (2:12.3-93),
1500 - 4:27.91, 3k - 9:56.3 (9:50.42-93)
TRIBE Leah U13 3.09.81, Portsmouth :
75 - 10.1, 150 - 20.3
TRISTRAM Zoe 15.11.69, Horsham BS :
DT - 37.60 (40.80-93)
TROWERS Kelly U17 12.07.79, Birchfield :
HJ - 1.65
TUCKER Laura U13 11.05.82, Yate :
1500 - 5:07.0
TUGWELL Emily U17 26.05.78, Cornwall AC :
TJ - 10.59
TUNALEY Sharon 2.09.68, Notts :
60 - 7.80i (7.74i-89), 100 - 12.1w,
200 - 24.4w?/25.0, 400 - 57.14
*TUOHY Teresa V35 1.06.59, London Oly/IRE :
10MR - 58:59 (58:24-92)
TURNBULL Claire U17 17.12.77, Sussex Sch :
JT - 35.82 (38.40-92)
TURNBULL Jessica U20 4.07.75, Bury :
3k - 9:56.57
TURNER Adele U20 10.08.76, Kendal :
JT - 39.96
TURNER Lesley 1.08.66, Rowheath :
HMar - 1:16:40 (1:15:48-93),
Mar - 2:45:16 (2:41:09-93)
TURNER Lorna U23 11.05.72, Essex L :
400H - 65.5, HJ - 1.65,
LJ - 5.65 (5.93w/5.77-88), TJ - 12.94
TURNER Natasha U23 8.11.74, Oxford City :
100H - 14.4 (14.23w/14.4-93/15.28-92),
400H - 61.9/66.43 (65.02-93),
HJ - 1.65i (1.67-91)
TURNER Nicola U20 26.09.75, Radley :
LJ - 5.69 (5.81w/5.80-93)

UNDERWOOD Diane R. V40 20.12.52, Cent :
10MR - 58:49 (58:00-93)
UPSON Hayley U20 16.04.77, Norfolk :
100 - 12.1/12.24w (12.58-93), 200 - 25.1

VAGGERS Melanie U13 16.06.82, Tav :
HJ - 1.45, JT - 22.20,
JTM - 33.32, PenM - 2125*
VANNET Lisa U23 8.11.74, Arbroath :
200 - 25.0, 400 - 56.11
VEEVERS Sara U23 26.04.74, Pendle :
HJ - 1.70 (1.73-89)
VENTON Nicola U20 26.11.75, Thurrock :
TJ - 11.25
VERNON Carean U15 2.06.80, Hercules W:
800 - 2:16.59, 1500 - 4:43.91
VETTRAINO Carol U17 16.10.77, Dundee HH :
1500 - 4:43.41, 3k - 10:20.38
VEYSEY Sarah U20 4.03.75, Stroud :
400H - 62.47 (62.31-93)
VINCENT Lisa U23 23.09.74, Havering/WarU. :
LJ - 5.55 (5.59-92), TJ - 11.33
VINE Kelly U17 26.07.78, Spenborough :
HJ - 1.64
VINES Samantha U20 28.02.77, Bournem'th :
3kW - 16:15.5
VINEY Elaine 20.12.71, Peterborough :
200 - 24.9/25.01 (24.2-90/24.78-91),
400 - 56.4/56.69
VINEY Gemma U13 7.01.83, Blackheath :
1500 - 5:08.1

VYFSCHAFT Jackie 15.12.64, Ballymena & A :
HJ - 1.65

WADE Kirsty Margaret 6.08.62, Blaydon :
800 - 2:05.60i (1:57.42-85),
1500 - 4:26.05i (4:00.73-87)
WAITE Amanda U17 1.02.78, Basildon :
100 - 12.3/12.55 (12.3-93/12.41-92),
200 - 24.70w/24.8/25.09
WAKEFIELD Denise V40 29.03.54, Sale :
Mar - 2:55:49
WALE Amanda 14.10.70, Wrexham :
Hep - 4302
WALKER Brenda V35 24.08.56, Western :
HMar - 1:16:42 (1:14:29-91)
WALKER Claire U23 8.10.72, Coventry RWC :
see CHILDS
WALKER Elizabeth U17 30.05.79, Barnsley :
300 - 40.10
WALKER Gail 7.12.71, Aberdeen (nee MURCHIE) :
60H - 8.94i (8.94i-93), 100H - 14.70
WALKER Hilary V40 9.11.53, Serpentine :
Mar - 3:05:41 (2:59:00-89),
100kR - 8:44:59 (7:50:01-93),
24HrT - 170.912
WALKER Jennifer 28.01.69, Shaftesbury B :
HJ - 1.65 (1.76-88)
WALKER Joanne U17 2.03.78, Loudon :
JT - 44.06
WALKER Marcia 27.05.70, Shaftesbury B :
200 - 24.4 (24.36w/25.17-93)
WALKER Melanie U17 29.04.79, Newbury :
SP - 10.62
WALLACE Ailsa U20 12.03.77, Barry :
HJ - 1.73i/1.70
WALLACE Andrea Maxine 22.11.66, Torbay :
5k - 16:47.4+e (15:28.63-92),
10kR - 33:09 (31:56-91),
10MR - 54:07+ (53:44-93),
HMar - 1:11:34 (1:09:39-93)
WALLACE Katie U17 19.09.78, Team Solent :
1500 - 4:43.43, 3k - 10:10.8
WALLACE Michelle U23 1.11.72, Notts :
DT - 41.26 (41.50-93)
WALLACE Sarah U23 31.05.73, Lincoln City :
1500 - 4:30.4 (4:25.99-91), 3k - 9:54.1
WALLACE Stacey U17 8.10.78, Woking :
1500 - 4:44.88, 3k - 10:33.4
WALLBANK Rebecca U17 17.06.78, S & NH :
HJ - 1.67
WALLEN Mary V40 9.06.52, Chiltern :
10kWR - 58:23
WALLHEAD Caroline U17 13.12.78, Norm Prk :
SP - 11.06
WALSH Caroline U15 29.04.80, Shaftesbury B :
1500 - 4:43.94
WARBURTON Angela 24.01.64, City of Hull :
400H - 64.00 (63.5-92)
WARD Alexandra U15 11.03.80, Hyndburn :
LJ - 5.38
WARD Emma U13 2.01.82, City of Stoke :
600 - 1:38.9, 800 - 2:23.9, 1500 - 5:02.2
WARD Hayley U20 3.03.77, Newcastle :
3k - 9:51.3mx/10:12.06
WARD Jennifer U17 22.09.78, Pitreavie :
800 - 2:13.65, 1500 - 4:38.26, 3k - 10:33.8
WARD Jenny U13, Liverpool Pembroke :
75 - 10.3

WARD Naomi U23 19.10.74, Hounslow :
400H - 63.72 (63.3-92)
WARREN Sally U17 29.01.78, Steyning :
3kW - 16:04.88
WARRILOW Hayley U15 10.04.80, C of Stoke :
PenG - 2996
WARRINGTON Clare U13 28.07.82, Macc :
JT - 24.70, JTM - 27.14
WATERS Elizabeth U20 19.02.77, Kettering :
400H - 63.66
WATSON Gillian 26.05.64, Sheffield RWC :
3kW - 15:05.7, 5kW - 25:54.0 (25:41.0-93),
5kWR - 26:15 (25:33-93),
10kW - 53:44.0, 10kWR - 55:10
WATSON Leslie V45 4.02.45, London O/Highgate :
Mar - 3:00:59 (2:44:18-82)
WATSON Louise Carole 13.12.71, GEC/Lough :
3k - 9:42.66 (9:16.45-92),
5k - 16:23.85i/16:39.79 (16:25.4-92),
10k - 34:36.83, 10kR - 33:58
WATSON Ruth U15 29.11.79, Camb & Col:
200 - 25.14w/25.58
WATSON Sylvia A. V45 29.09.47, Valley Str :
Mar - 2:58:40, 100kR - 8:24:30 (8:13:00-93)
WATT Fiona U23 29.01.73, Glasgow :
TJ - 11.63
WATTON Clare U17 23.12.77, Hereford :
HJ - 1.70
WEATHERILL Carolina 13.05.68, Chelmsford :
3k - 9:57.3 (9:31.80i-93)
WEBB Lucy U17 28.07.79, Oldham & Royton :
HJ - 1.65
WEBSTER Eve U17 7.10.77, East Grinstead :
TJ - 10.32
WEISS Patricia U17 24.12.77, Liverpool Pem :
200 - 24.88w/25.10, 300 - 41.4
WELBOURN Emma U17 14.02.79, C of Hull :
HT - 32.54
WELLS Sarah 11.08.69, Worthing :
800 - 2:12.3
WEMYSS Catherine U20 19.05.77, Dorch :
Hep - 3872
WEST Rebecca U23 9.09.74, Southampton C :
DT - 40.04
WESTON Abigail U15 8.03.80, Bracknell :
DT - 31.26
WESTON Claire U15 26.07.80, Broms& R :
60 - 7.97i
WHALLEY Michelle U15 1.10.80, Wigan :
1500 - 4:42.35
WHEELER Elizabeth U13 31.10.81, Derby L :
1500 - 5:06.2
WHEELER Michele Dawn 10.01.68, CovG :
see MARSELLA
WHIGHAM Lisa U15 14.08.80, Kirkintillock :
PenG - 2557
WHITCOMBE Andrea 8.06.71, Parkside :
1500 - 4:23.5 (4:14.56-90),
3k - 9:27.3 (8:58.59-91)
WHITE Caroline Helen 8.10.68, Trafford :
JT - 50.58 (56.50-91)
WHITE Catherine 9.03.66, Highgate :
see DAWSON
WHITE Jacqueline 12.01.71, Tamworth :
200 - 24.97 .
WHITE Laura U15 5.09.79, Hyndburn :
PenG - 2862

WHITE Rebecca U15 5.06.80, Blackburn :
LJ - 5.30
WHITEHALL Sarah U13 9.10.81, Cornwall AC :
LJ - 4.74
WHITEHEAD Fiona 31.05.70, Croydon/WLIHE :
HT - 48.68 (52.84-93)
WHITEHEAD Hayley U17 14.05.79, BHM :
800 - 2:16.13
WHITEHEAD Louise U20 26.03.75, Liv Pem :
200 - 24.54w/24.7/25.02 (24.1/24.54w-93),
400 - 56.5/57.36i
WHITEHEAD Suzanne U15 13.05.80, Barns :
LJ - 5.25
WHITEHOUSE Claire U17 11.04.79, Cov RWC :
3kW - 15:15.5, 5kW - 27:49.0
WHITEHURST Caroline V35 3.07.59, Hull Ach :
400H - 65.9
WHITFIELD Joanna U17 5.01.78, Bristol :
PV - 2.65io/2.40i/2.40
WHITLEY Meryl 12.04.69, Chester Le Street :
10k - 36:24.13
WHITLOCK Janine U23 11.08.73, Spen :
100H - 14.64w/14.8/14.90, PV - 3.10i
WHITNEY Paula U17 21.03.79, Warrington :
1500 - 4:43.6
WHITTAKER Kim U17 12.11.77, Sale :
100 - 12.21w/12.66
WHITTAKER Louise U13 29.11.82, Sale :
600 - 1:45.06, 1500 - 5:07.5
WHITTLE Elizabeth U20 23.06.75, Wigan :
DT - 38.94, HT - 37.96
WILDING Helen U20 25.10.76, Wirral :
SP - 13.17, DT - 42.26 (41.24-93), HT - 38.06
WILHELMY Sarah U15 2.02.80, Southend :
60 - 7.64i, 100 - 12.0/12.02,
200 - 23.99w/24.54,
LJ - 5.73i/5.55 (5.77w/5.70-93)
WILKIN Paula U23 28.03.74, City of Hull :
100H - 15.0w/15.33 (14.9w-93)
WILKINS Melanie U23 18.01.73, AF&D :
200 - 24.47w/24.7, 60H - 8.55i (8.55i-92),
100H - 13.6/13.65w/13.72 (13.67-93)
WILKINSON Michelle U23 1.01.73, Sale :
800 - 2:08.6 (2:06.3-90)
WILKINSON Tanya 1.04.70, City of Stoke :
400H - 64.7
WILLIAMS Donna Maria U17 7.10.78, Sale :
SP - 11.43, DT - 37.84
WILLIAMS Elizabeth U20 2.06.77, Walton :
400 - 56.39
WILLIAMS Evaun V55 19.02.37, Essex L :
HT - 37.36
WILLIAMS Evette U17 23.03.78, Dartford :
100 - 12.3/12.33, 200 - 24.7/25.13
WILLIAMS Kathryn U17 10.11.77, Swansea :
80HI - 11.72, 300H - 44.25
WILLIAMS L., :
HMar - 1:19:16
WILLIAMS Lisa U13 29.12.81, Chelmsford :
1500 - 4:56.3
WILLIAMS Rebecca U15 1.10.80, Exeter :
800 - 2:16.79
WILLIAMS Rebecca U13 13.02.82, Medway :
600 - 1:46.3
WILLIAMS Sharon 20.05.70, Essex L :
100 - 12.1 (11.90w-93/11.9-90/12.01-92)
WILLIAMS Shelley U17 4.10.77, Dacorum :
DT - 34.46

WILLIAMS Susan U20 2.06.77, Walton :
  100 - 12.0w (12.3/12.39-93),
  200 - 24.11w/24.27
WILLIAMS Wendy Jane 9.02.68, Salisbury :
  800 - 2:09.36 (2:08.55-90),
  1500 - 4:21.36 (4:19.9-92)
WILLIAMSON Kelly Louise U15 4.12.79, Derby L :
  75HG - 11.2/11.35, LJ - 5.66w/5.48,
  PenG - 2861
WILLIS Angela W. 22.07.69, Bournemouth :
  LJ - 5.75
WILLOUGHBY Joanne Roberta 30.11.63, Bris :
  LJ - 5.64 (6.38w?/6.32-89)
WILSON Amy U15 31.12.80, Ipswich :
  SPG - 11.96 (10.01-93)
WILSON Paula 20.11.69, Cannock & Stafford :
  PV - 3.45
WINCKLESS Sarah Katherine U23 18.10.73,
  Epsom & Ewell/Cambridge University :
  DT - 53.16, HT - 37.28
WINTERBOURNE Joanne U17 11.01.78, Reading :
  3k - 10:24.3
WISE Clare L. 22.08.69, AF&D :
  100H - 14.9, 400H - 61.84
WISE Hannah U23 8.10.74, Woking :
  HJ - 1.65 (1.68-92)
WISEMAN Victoria U20 14.11.76, Ilford :
  HJ - 1.65
WITTEKIND Anna L. 7.12.64, Parkside :
  see MOUTRIE
WOFFENDEN Laura 14.08.70, Leeds :
  3k - 9:56.46
WOOD Allison U23 30.12.72, Oxford Univ :
  HT - 41.32
WOOD Caroline U17 5.01.79, Cramlington :
  3k - 10:20.19
WOOD Hannah U13 17.11.81, Solihull & SH :
  100 - 13.2, 150 - 19.7, 200 - 27.1,
  600 - 1:37.5, 800 - 2:22.9
WOOD Joanna U23 2.10.72, Wigan :
  DT - 41.18
WOOD Laura U17 31.10.78, Trafford :
  DT - 34.28
WOODCOCK Sian U15 13.01.80, Bingley :
  2.5kW - 13:41.45
WOODHOUSE Serena U13 20.10.81, Derby L :
  100 - 13.2, 200 - 26.6
WOODLAND Paula U17 21.12.78, Radley :
  60H - 8.90i, 80HI - 11.64w/11.68, 300H - 46.8
WOODLAND-NASCIMENTO Michaela U23
  19.11.73, Norfolk : SP - 12.52, DT - 40.98
WOODS Kelly U20 28.05.75, Peterborough :
  400 - 57.20i (57.05-93)
WOODS Michelle U15 2.08.80, Basildon :
  SPG - 11.71 (11.18-93), DT - 32.52
WOOLRIDGE Maureen V35 25.11.58, N & P :
  5k - 17:22.69
WOOLGAR Deborah 10.03.65, Worthing :
  LJ - 5.65 (5.81-86), TJ - 11.43,
  SP - 13.12 (14.18-89),
  DT - 40.72 (40.92-91),
  Hep - 4783 (5434w-90/5380-89)
WOOLLEY Jessica U15 26.01.80, Bristol :
  800 - 2:16.7, 1500 - 4:45.9
WOOLRICH Sharon U20 1.05.76, Ports Far :
  HJ - 1.70
WORLD Ruth U23 19.03.74, Portsmouth Far :
  400H - 63.4

WRIGHT Alice U17 31.12.78, Rowntrees :
  300H - 44.92
WRIGHT Amanda 14.07.68, Tipton :
  1500 - 4:27.5, 3k - 9:19.67 (9:06.7-92),
  5k - 16:22.95 (16:04.51-92),
  10k - 34:19.51 (33:26.79-92),
  10kR - 33:54 (33:05-92), HMar - 1:15:15
WRIGHT Dawn-Alice U20 20.01.76, Milton K :
  PV - 3.10
WRIGHT Jackie V40 8.10.53, Bracknell :
  DT - 42.56
WRIGHT Lucy 17.11.69, Leeds :
  5k - 17:05.6 (16:58.5-93),
  10k - 36:05.78, 10kR - 34:32
WRIGHT Melanie 5.04.64, Nun (nee BROOKES) :
  3kW - 13:43.0, 5kW - 23:47.0, 5kWR - 23:58,
  10kW - 49:16.0 (49:15.2-92),
  10kWR - 48:58 (47:40sh-93/48:18-92)
WRIGHT Michelle U23 26.04.74, Solihull & SH :
  DT - 41.74 (44.32-93)
WRIGHT Rebecca U17 20.12.77, W S & E :
  300H - 46.96
WRIGHT Sharon U20 6.10.76, Holbeach :
  LJ - 5.59 (5.62-93), Hep - 4058
WYARD Elaine 6.04.70, Wakefield :
  see SUTCLIFFE
WYATT Julie U15 30.11.79, Kirkintilloch :
  DT - 31.28
WYETH Alison 26.05.64, Parkside :
  800 - 2:07.26 (2:04.5-93),
  1500 - 4:04.19 (4:03.17-93),
  1M - 4:30.24 (4:24.87-91),
  2k - 5:43.13 (5:38.50-93),
  3k - 8:45.76 (8:38.42-93),
  5k - 15:10.38, 10kR - 32:56
WYNTER-PINK Clover U17 29.11.77, Croy :
  60H - 9.22i, 80HI - 11.9, SP - 11.63,
  JT - 43.04 (44.20-93), Hepl - 4861

Y ARWOOD Cathy 17.06.69, Bolton :
  400H - 64.70 (64.4-93)
YAVARI Ellie U13 15.09.81, Wirral :
  600 - 1:45.5, 1500 - 5:03.8
YEARSLEY Fran U15 24.03.80, Dursley :
  PenG - 2671
YELLING Hayley U23 3.01.74, Hounslow :
  3k - 9:46.38, 5k - 17:30.2
YORWERTH Amanda E. 18.05.67, St Albans :
  Mar - 2:56:48
YOUDEN Nicola U17 2.11.77, Kilmarnock :
  300 - 40.70, 400 - 58.64i (59.0-93)
YOUDEN Sally U17 2.11.77, Kilmarnock :
  400H - 67.7 (67.5-93)
YOUNG Cathy U13, Stamford & Deeping :
  PenM - 2103
YOUNG Hayley U15 26.09.79, Stamford & D :
  HJ - 1.69, PenG - 2930
YOUNG Sally T. V35 29.09.55, Parkside :
  1500 - 4:31.0 (4:27.85-93), 3k - 9:34.47,
  5k - 16:48.8 (16:41.05-90),
  1.5kSt - 5:18.2mx,
  2kSt - 7:22.34 (7:04.7mx-93), 2KSTW - 7:00.7
YOUNG Wendy U23 3.02.74, Edinburgh WM :
  200 - 25.27 (24.63w-93/25.16-92)

Z AWADA Sarah U13 9.04.82, AF&D :
  80 - 10.6, 100 - 13.2,
  150 - 19.6, 200 - 26.7, 75HG - 12.8

TSB JUNIOR RANKINGS
Men Under 20

#	Name	County	Event	Points	#	Name	County	Event	Points
1.	Jason Gardener	Avon	(100)	1144	51.	Paul Cooper	Humber	(800)	980
2.	Mark Hylton	Berks	(300)	1108	52.	Richard Laws	Northumb	(HJ)	979
3.	Noel Levy		(400H)	1102	53.	Simon Heggie	Notts	(400)	977
4.	Larry Achike		(TJ)	1098	54.	Hugh Kerr		(400)	977
5.	Ian Mackie		(200)	1092	55.	Ian Wilding		(PV)	977
6.	Julian Golding	London	(100)	1088	56.	Craig Wheeler		(3KST)	975
7.	James Archampong		(110H)	1065	57.	Matt O'Dowd	Wilts	(3KST)	973
8.	Guy Bullock	Lancs	(400)	1064	58.	Andrew Lowe		(HJ)	971
9.	Eddie King		(800)	1059	59.	Paul Dovell	Dorset	(HJ)	971
10.	Stuart Ohrland	Essex	(HJ)	1056	60.	David Nolan		(HJ)	971
11.	Trevor Cameron		(100)	1054	61.	Bryn Middleton		(200)	971
12.	Darius Burrows		(3K)	1052	62.	Chris Hindley	Notts	(HJ)	971
13.	Nick Budden	Norfolk	(400)	1050	63.	Chris Stringer		(800)	970
14.	Mark Griffin		(800)	1050	64.	Michael Champion	Kent	(200)	969
15.	James Brierley	Shrops	(HJ)	1048	65.	Matthew Clarke	Northants	(800)	967
16.	Marlon Devonish	West Mid	(100)	1045	66.	Andrew Young		(800)	964
17.	Jared Deacon	Durham	(300)	1041	67.	Tony Gilhooly		(HJ)	964
18.	Bruno Witchalls	Surrey	(1500)	1038	68.	Matthew Bridle	Ches	(200)	963
19.	Kevin Mark	Mx	(100)	1036	69.	Peter Brend	Devon	(400)	962
20.	Tayo Erogbogbo	Bucks	(TJ)	1035	70.	Alan Tatham	Derbs	(1500)	960
21.	Mike Robbins	S. Yorks	(110HJ)	1033	71.	Geoff Dearman		(400)	960
22.	Nick Csemiczky	Berks	(110HJ)	1027	72.	Jason Fletcher	Northants	(100)	959
23.	Chris Blount		(800)	1027	73.	Marvin Bramble	Mx	(TJ)	957
24.	Simon McAree	Northumb	(110H)	1027	74.	Chris Woods	Cleve	(800)	957
25.	Rob Brocklebank	Lancs	(HJ)	1025	75.	Paul Gripton	Here & W	(110HJ)	956
26.	Neil Caddy	Cornwall	(1500)	1024	76.	Carl Foster	S. Yorks	(400H)	956
27.	Steve McHardy	West Mid	(400)	1022	77.	Ian Massey	Mersey	(HJ)	956
28.	Curtis Browne	West Mid	(100)	1018	78.	Jon Snade	Shrops	(110HJ)	956
29.	Chris Elliott	Hamps	(3KST)	1017	79.	Stuart Cavanagh	Hamps	(400)	955
30.	Damon Rutland	Cornwall	(HJ)	1017	80.	Richard Girvan		(800)	954
31.	Ben Reese	Mersey	(800)	1017	81.	Wayne Martin	Wilts	(400)	954
32.	Andrew Walcott	West Mid	(200)	1015	82.	Norman Ellis	Kent	(100)	954
33.	Stuart Smith	Warks	(HJ)	1010	83.	Tony Mason	Suffolk	(LJ)	953
34.	Mark Latham	Staffs	(HJ)	1010	84.	Mark Bailey		(110HJ)	953
35.	Karl Andrews	Avon	(HTJ)	1006	85.	Simon Rush	Surrey	(400H)	952
36.	Alex Hunte	Mx	(400H)	1006	86.	Daniel Money	Derbs	(200)	952
37.	Perry Batchelor	West Mid	(110HJ)	1004	87.	Bryan McCoy		(400)	952
38.	Des Roache		(800)	1002	88.	Matthew Winter	Lancs	(800)	951
39.	Scott West	Leics	(1500)	1001	89.	Dominic Shepherd	Ches	(PV)	951
40.	Quincy Douglas		(400)	1000	90.	Roger Hunter	W Yorks	(DECJ)	951
41.	James Egan	W Yorks	(200)	997	91.	Eric Crowther		(1500)	950
42.	Mark Ponting		(400)	994	92.	Tom Mayo	West Mid	(1500)	950
43.	Matthew Douglas	Bucks	(400H)	991	93.	Mark Bushell	Hamps	(110HJ)	950
44.	David Locker	Staffs	(800)	989	94.	James Leaver	Dorset	(HJ)	949
45.	Ian Bowden	W Yorks	(800)	985	95.	Simon Kett	Dorset	(HJ)	949
46.	Barry Middleton		(400H)	984	96.	Guy Clarke	Lancs	(800)	949
47.	Michael Nartey	Surrey	(100)	983	97.	Robert Scantlebury	Surrey	(400)	948
48.	Steve Lamb	Derbs	(400H)	983	98.	David Connelly		(3KST)	948
49.	Jamie Henthorn		(100)	983	99.	Chris Davidson	Kent	(LJ)	947
50.	Adrian Milnes		(100)	980	100.	Ian Mitchell	W Yorks	(1500)	947

Men Under 17

1.	Matthew Clements	Cambs	(110HJ)	1065
2.	Dean Macey	Essex	(OCTY)	1004
3.	Damien Greaves	Essex	(100HY)	994
4.	Mark Rowlands		(400HY)	993
5.	Dwain Chambers	Mx	(100)	991
6.	Ross Baillie		(100HY)	990
7.	Uvie Ugono	London	(200)	988
8.	Fyn Corcoran	Cornwall	(OCTY)	985
9.	C. Robertson-Adams	Shrops	(400HY)	983
10.	Scott Fraser		(100)	983
11.	Dean Park	London	(400HY)	979
12.	Ben Challenger	Leics	(HJ)	971
13.	Kevin Farrell	Essex	(200)	970
14.	Scott Walker	Ches	(OCTY)	956
15.	Christian Malcolm		(100)	954
16.	Ben Walker	Herts	(OCTY)	952
17.	Chris Blake		(200)	950
18.	Graham Beasley	Beds	(200)	948
19.	Emeka Udechuku	London	(SPY)	943
20.	Philip Perigo	S Yorks	(200)	940
21.	Martin Giraud	Surrey	(100)	936
22.	Michael Tietz	Derbs	(100)	936
23.	Mark Findlay	Essex	(LJ)	931
24.	Laurence Baird	Humber	(400)	926
25.	Mike Wright	N Yorks	(HJ)	926
26.	Andrew Penk		(HJ)	926
27.	Darren Joseph	West Mid	(HJ)	926
28.	Alan Rudkin	Lincs	(OCTY)	923
29.	Marcellas Peters	Derbs	(OCTY)	921
30.	Matthew Bell	Northants	(HTY)	914
31.	Ian Horsburgh		(400)	914
32.	Joel Calliste	Mx	(100)	914
33.	Richard Churchill	S Yorks	(100HY)	912
34.	Michael Combe		(800)	911
35.	Keith Oag		(HJ)	911
36.	Andrew Row	Northumb	(100)	911
37.	Mark Francis	Surrey	(JTY)	909
38.	Steve Mitchell	Surrey	(400HY)	908
39.	Robert Brown	Northumb	(1.5KST)	904
40.	Dale Canning		(800)	903
41.	Josef Bailey	Staffs	(100HY)	903
42.	Mark Anderson	Staffs	(400HY)	901
43.	Roger Morley	Lincs	(800)	901
44.	Yacin Yusuf	Surrey	(800)	898
45.	Michael Bell	West Mid	(400)	898
46.	Damien Slater	Beds	(HTY)	897
47.	Andrew Thomas	Mersey	(800)	896
48.	Gavin Cater	Hamps	(100)	894
49.	Tim Slocombe	Dorset	(400)	894
50.	Andrew Benn	Kent	(HTY)	893

Men Under 15

1.	Peter Waterman	Kent	(SPB)	884
2.	Edward Willers	Essex	(HJ)	858
3.	Matthew Brereton	Mersey	(HJ)	858
4.	Andre Duffus	Mx	(100)	850
5.	Clifton Green	Wilts	(JTB)	831
6.	Steven Daly	Mersey	(100)	831
7.	Kevin Drury	Shrops	(HJ)	828
8.	James Hawkins	Kent	(HTB)	824
9.	James Punch	Northants	(HTB)	821
10.	Tom Benn	Essex	(80HB)	819
11.	Jamie Hunt	Norfolk	(SPB)	817
12.	Marc Newton	Staffs	(PENB)	817
13.	Andy Castle	Somerset	(SPB)	813
14.	Andrew Smith	Hamps	(HJ)	813
15.	Jamie Dalton		(HJ)	813
16.	Dan Carter	Essex	(JTB)	807
17.	Robert Allenby	Humber	(200)	804
18.	Carl Myerscough	Lancs	(SPB)	803
19.	Wayne Gray	London	(100)	799
20.	Martin Lloyd	Kent	(HJ)	798
21.	Christian Linskey	S Yorks	(PV)	796
22.	Steven Wiggans	Lancs	(100)	794
23.	Stuart Smith	Lincs	(200)	793
24.	Patrick Brown	Northumb	(80HB)	786
25.	Kris Stewart		(400)	785
26.	Dan Reardon	West Mid	(HJ)	783
27.	Tom Bridgeman	Avon	(80HB)	780
28.	David O'Leary	Mersey	(80HB)	777
29.	Gary Neblett	Mx	(HJ)	775
30.	Robert Toms	Berks	(HJ)	775
31.	Lewis Erdman	London	(HJ)	775
32.	Ian Wilson	West Mid	(HJ)	775
33.	Neil Dixon		(HJ)	775
34.	David Naismith	Derbs	(400)	774
35.	Martin Wilson	Suffolk	(SPB)	774
36.	Sam Hartley	Wilts	(80HB)	773
37.	Russell Johnson	Essex	(100)	773
38.	Chris Low		(80HB)	772
39.	Michael Jones		(200)	771
40.	Chris Aherne		(HTB)	771
41.	Luke Dart		(200)	770
42.	William Kirkpatrick		(SPB)	769
43.	Paul Chantler	Mersey	(100)	768
44.	Neil Akester	Humber	(100)	768
45.	Richard McNab	S Yorks	(400)	765
46.	Daniel Hutchinson	Derbs	(TJ)	764
47.	David Parker	N Yorks	(JTB)	762
48.	Sam Stephenson	London	(80HB)	762
49.	Andrew Cresswell	Here & W	(HJ)	761
50.	Andrew Chaddock	Derbs	(HJ)	761

TSB JUNIOR RANKINGS
Women Under 20

1.	Diane Allahgreen	Mersey	(100H)	1129	51.	Helen Seery	W Yorks	(200)	984
2.	Catherine Murphy	Herts	(200)	1077	52.	Jo MacDonald	Surrey	(100H)	983
3.	Alice Braham		(3K)	1077	53.	Jo Burton		(JT)	982
4.	Allison Curbishley	Cleve	(400H)	1074	54.	Sally Evans		(200)	982
5.	Nicky Slater	Ox	(3K)	1066	55.	Kate Norman	Surrey	(400H)	980
6.	Louretta Thorne	Bucks	(400)	1056	56.	Keeley Butler		(200)	980
7.	Catherine Berry	Surrey	(3K)	1052	57.	Emma Symonds	Norfolk	(200)	977
8.	Vicki Jamison		(400H)	1051	58.	Teresa Andrews		(HJ)	976
9.	Sinead Dudgeon		(200)	1050	59.	Lindsay Evans	Suffolk	(HJ)	976
10.	Susan Williams	Surrey	(200)	1046	60.	Patricia Naughton		(100H)	976
11.	Debbie Mant	Dorset	(200)	1040	61.	Sarah Still		(200)	975
12.	Jeina Mitchell		(800)	1040	62.	Lucy Burrell	West Mid	(JT)	974
13.	Orla Bermingham	Essex	(100H)	1036	63.	Megan Jones		(100H)	974
14.	Ellana Ruddock	West Mid	(100)	1028	64.	Hayley Ward	Staffs	(3K)	974
15.	Jo Sloane	Here & W	(400)	1028	65.	Clare Hill		(400)	971
16.	Dorothea Lee		(800)	1026	66.	Nicola Davies		(400)	971
17.	Denise Bolton		(100H)	1021	67.	Hayley Parkinson		(3K)	971
18.	Fiona Hutchison		(100)	1020	68.	Hayley Upson	Norfolk	(100)	971
19.	Kirsty Morrison	Kent	(JT)	1017	69.	Samantha Jones	Berks	(200)	970
20.	Adele Forester	Durham	(LJ)	1015	70.	Kathryn Saunders	Berks	(400)	968
21.	Bev Christopher		(100)	1015	71.	Beverley Gray	Humber	(3K)	967
22.	Joanne Dear		(100)	1015	72.	Clare Bushby	Northumb	(100H)	965
23.	Leanne Eastwood	Lancs	(100)	1015	73.	Kelly Woods		(400)	963
24.	Rebecca Kilgour	Devon	(200)	1015	74.	Celia Brown	Essex	(400H)	963
25.	Louise Whitehead		(200)	1012	75.	Elizabeth Waters	Northants	(400H)	963
26.	Julia Sykes		(400H)	1011	76.	Rhonda MacPhee	Kent	(800)	963
27.	Alison Outram	Mx	(3K)	1011	77.	Claire Swift	Mersey	(3K)	962
28.	Victoria Shipman	Derbs	(200)	1011	78.	Rachel Briars	Mersey	(400H)	961
29.	Stacey Jacques	S Yorks	(400)	1011	79.	Emma Davies		(400H)	961
30.	Joanne Mahony	Mersey	(400H)	1006	80.	Sharon Price	West Mid	(100H)	960
31.	Shani Anderson		(100)	1003	81.	Jane Fuller	Bucks	(400H)	960
32.	Susan Hendry		(400)	1002	82.	Sarah Ramminger		(LJ)	958
33.	Julie Hollman	Lincs	(LJ)	1001	83.	Stephanie Dobson		(LJ)	958
34.	Sarah Simmons	Kent	(1500)	1001	84.	Jessica Turnbull		(3K)	958
35.	Louise Sharps		(100)	1000	85.	Kathryn Gray		(100)	955
36.	Claire Griffiths		(400H)	998	86.	Adele Foster	Humber	(100)	954
37.	Kate Teasdale	Mersey	(200)	998	87.	Juliette Oldfield	Northants	(1500)	953
38.	Katharine Eustace		(400)	996	88.	Sarah Bull		(800)	953
39.	Julie Crane	Notts	(HJ)	994	89.	Katherine Morris		(400)	953
40.	Lorraine Bell		(200)	994	90.	Sandra Cull		(LJ)	952
41.	Rachel King		(100H)	994	91.	Hannah Jenkin		(100H)	951
42.	Jannette Niccolls	London	(100)	992	92.	Jane Groves	Ches	(800)	951
43.	Sarah Veysey		(400H)	992	93.	Karen Manuel	Dorset	(400)	950
44.	Claire O'Connor		(3K)	990	94.	Hayley Martin	London	(LJ)	947
45.	Kathy Thurston	Ches	(400H)	990	95.	Fiona Sinclair		(100)	946
46.	Elizabeth Williams	Surrey	(400)	989	96.	Tammy McCammon	Mx	(LJ)	945
47.	Amanda Tremble	Northumb	(1500)	988	97.	Jenny Harnett	Kent	(800)	945
48.	Emily Feltham	Wilts	(200)	986	98.	Lisa Brown		(HJ)	943
49.	Sarah Ditchfield	Lancs	(400H)	986	99.	Leone Dickinson	W Yorks	(HJ)	943
50.	Katie Jones		(400H)	985	100.	Samantha Male	Surrey	(100H)	943

Women Under 17

1.	Tatum Nelson	Kent	(100)	1063
2.	Susan Jones		(HJ)	1054
3.	Laura Seston	Suffolk	(100)	1046
4.	Natasha Danvers	London	(100H)	1043
5.	Rebecca Drummond	Staffs	(100)	1041
6.	Lesley Owusu	Berks	(300)	1040
7.	Liz Fairs	Derbs	(80HI)	1019
8.	Lee McConnell		(HJ)	1019
9.	Lorraine Brackstone	Ches	(80HI)	1012
10.	Michelle Dunkley	Northants	(HJ)	1011
11.	Natalie Hynd		(100)	1010
12.	Lucy Chaffe	Essex	(300)	1009
13.	Julie Pratt	Essex	(80HI)	1008
14.	Philippa Roles		(DT)	1003
15.	Louise Colledge	Leics	(80HI)	1003
16.	Suzanne McGowan		(300)	1003
17.	Cathy Boulton	Ox	(HJ)	1002
18.	Rachael Forrest	Shrops	(HJ)	1002
19.	Evette Williams	Kent	(200)	998
20.	Jayne Ludlow		(TJ)	993
21.	Amanda Waite	Essex	(200)	991
22.	Elizabeth Hall	Here &W	(200)	991
23.	Kate Forsyth	Northumb	(80HI)	990
24.	Amanda Batt	Herts	(80HI)	988
25.	Paula Woodland	Ox	(80HI)	987
26.	Patricia Weiss	Mersey	(200)	987
27.	Claire Everett	Norfolk	(HJ)	984
28.	Susan Mary Douglas		(200)	983
29.	Kirsty Payne	Shrops	(200)	982
30.	Louise Eden		(LJ)	982
31.	Gillian Hegney		(100)	981
32.	Sharon Hollett		(300)	980
33.	Elizabeth Walker	S Yorks	(300)	980
34.	Kathryn Williams		(80HI)	980
35.	Rebecca Lewis	Ches	(200)	977
36.	Ruth Nicholson	Kent	(200)	977
37.	Dawn Rose	Warks	(100)	976
38.	Wooday Sidibe	London	(200)	973
39.	Amanda Gray	Derbs	(200)	973
40.	Sarah Hunter	Herts	(200)	972
41.	Hannah Paines		(100)	968
42.	Helen Parsons	Sussex	(400)	965
43.	Dawn Adams	Mersey	(1500)	965
44.	Gahlie Davis	Dorset	(100)	965
45.	Rachael Kennedy	Humber	(80HI)	965
46.	Delyth Jones	Ches	(100)	962
47.	Michelle Murray		(200)	962
48.	Rosalind Baker	Sussex	(300)	961
49.	Nina Rogers	Staffs	(300)	960
50.	Sarah Cootes	Essex	(300)	960

Women Under 15

1.	Sarah Wilhelmy	Essex	(200)	1042
2.	Maria Bolsover	S Yorks	(200)	1006
3.	Sarah Claxton	Essex	(100)	995
4.	Rachael Kay		(200)	987
5.	Amy Nuttell	Lincs	(PENG)	984
6.	Samantha Foster	Essex	(PENG)	978
7.	Ayeesha Charles	Ox	(200)	977
8.	Jade Johnson	London	(LJ)	970
9.	Karlene Palmer	Bucks	(200)	970
10.	Ruth Watson	Cambs	(200)	969
11.	Katherine Livesey	Lancs	(PENG)	968
12.	Helen Roscoe	Ches	(200)	961
13.	Lois Cresswell	West Mid	(200)	961
14.	Amanda Pritchard		(800)	960
15.	Jennifer Meadows		(200)	957
16.	Kelli Bailey	Shrops	(100)	955
17.	Nicola Hall	Suffolk	(75HG)	954
18.	Lindsay Impett	Dorset	(200)	953
19.	Lindsay Fleet	Kent	(200)	951
20.	Karen Johns	Durham	(800)	951
21.	Antonia Bemrose	Hamps	(HJ)	950
22.	Tracy Martin	West Mid	(200)	949
23.	Karen Gear	Devon	(200)	949
24.	Hayley Young	Lincs	(HJ)	941
25.	Hayley Warrilow	Staffs	(PENG)	939
26.	Dominique Coldwell	Humber	(200)	936
27.	Elizabeth Alder	Gloucs	(200)	931
28.	Sarah Todd		(100)	928
29.	Emma Alberts	Durham	(1500)	927
30.	Kelly Morgan	Wilts	(JT)	925
31.	Debbie Sinnott	Mersey	(100)	924
32.	Elizabeth Lloyd	Staffs	(100)	924
33.	Amanda Freeman	Beds	(100)	924
34.	Lisa Thomas	Mx	(100)	924
35.	Eve Miller	Herts	(100)	924
36.	Keira Stout	Essex	(HJ)	924
37.	Lynn Fairweather		(75HG)	923
38.	Natalie Kerr	West Mid	(DT)	922
39.	Alison Kerboas		(PENG)	922
40.	Laura McCabe	Ches	(800)	917
41.	Nadia Brewer	Kent	(HJ)	915
42.	Julie Davis		(80HI)	915
43.	Kelly Williamson	Derbs	(PENG)	913
44.	Laura White		(PENG)	913
45.	Leanda Adams	Staffs	(75HG)	912
46.	Iona Frazer		(HJ)	906
47.	Chloe Cozens	Beds	(PENG)	905
48.	Sonya Green	Cumbria	(100)	905
49.	Charlotte Barker	Suffolk	(200)	903
50.	Cheryl Kennedy	Durham	(75HG)	901

AMENDMENTS TO BRITISH ATHLETICS 1994

From Tony Miller and other members of NUTS

Men

200m
21.43un Tremayne Rutherford   Irvine, USA Jul
Under 20 : 22.05w Bryn Middleton Tilburg, HOL 17 Jul
Under 15 : 23.3 Daniel Bonich 1 Luton 23 May
Under 15 : 23.3 Robert Lewis 1 Havering 25 Jul
Under 15 : 23.5 Allan Penford 1 London (WP) 23 May
Under 15 : 23.5 Robert Allenby 1 Grimsby 27 Jun
Under 15 : 23.61w Christian Creaby 5s1 Blackpool 10 Jul

400m
48.4 Peter Maitland Cardiff 1 Sep

1500m
3:48.6 James Ellis-Smith Kansas 9 May

5000m
14:21.02 Rixon (not 14:20.2)

80mh
Under 15 : 11.2 Nick Dorsett 1P Stoke 18 Sep, Allen 2P
Under 15 : 11.76 P. Watts 1 Antrim 28 Aug

400mh
56.4 James Melville Jackson 24.01.74

Long Jump
Under 20 : 7.02 Nick Walne Tilburg, HOL 17 Jul

Triple Jump
Under 15 : 12.47 Ashley Fox 1 Welwyn 5 Jun

Discus
43.16 Peter Roberts Cardiff 19 May
Under 15 : 44.50 David Irwin 1 Tullamore 5 Jun

Javelin
60.88 Furst (not 63.88)

20k Walk
1:29:05 Mark Easton 25.05.63 1 Morecambe 4 Sep

50k Walk
Postions at Horsham - Johnson 3, Berwick 4, Beattie 7, Adams 8.

Women

100mh
14.8 Tracy Lewis Wrexham 27 Jun

300mh
44.0 Angela Bonner Cardiff 1 Sep

20Miles Road
1:57:58 Lynn Harding 18.08.61 1 South Shields 10 Oct
2:03:17 Lesley Turner 1.08.66 2 South Shields 10 Oct
2:11:15 Sandra Edwards 14.03.61 1 Hull 21 Mar
2:12:08 Alison Davidson   9.03.71 2 Hull 21 Mar

Amendment to British Athletics 1993

HT
Delete Masterman 40.76 (R Bonner's mark)

Many additions and corrections have been made to the index.
Any extra information for the index is always most welcome.

The Last Page

Rob Whittingham

Peter Matthews always thinks that every athletics statistical publication should be full to the the very last page. Indeed I always check the cover of the ATFS annual for any last minute information. Since I have recieved fewer corrections than normal this year I am faced with a blank last page so for the *information freaks* a little more :-

10000 Metres Walk - Track Extra Performances

44:09.1	Bell	2	Istanbul	22	May
44:06.93	Easton	2	Horsham	19	Jun

An Extra International Result

IAAF WORLD HALF MARATHON CHAMPIONSHIPS
Oslo, NOR 24 September 1994

Men

1.	Khalid Skah	MAR	60:27
2.	German Silva	MEX	60:28
3.	Ronaldo de Costa	BRA	60:54
4.	Godfrey Kiprotich	KEN	61:01
5.	Shem Kororia	KEN	61:16
6.	Andrew Masai	KEN	61:19
7.	Tendai Chimusasa	ZIM	61:26
8.	Fackson Nkandu	ZAM	61:30
9.	Moses Tanui	KEN	61:35
10.	Rolando Rodes	ECU	61:36
11.	Paul Tergat	KEN	61:37
12.	Martin Pitayo	MEX	61:38
13.	Badilu Kibret	ETH	61:40
14.	Benjamin Paredes	SPA	61:41
15.	Carsten Elch	GER	61:44
16.	Kamel Kohil	ALG	61:50
17.	Addis Abede	ETH	62:14
18.	Salah Hissou	MAR	62:20
19.	Samson Dingani	ZIM	62:21
20.	Meshack Mogotsi	RSA	62:26
29.	MARTIN McLOUGHLIN		62:45
47.	CARL UDALL		63:36
60.	ANDREW PEARSON		64:30
61.	MARK CROASDALE		64:41
dnf	DAVE PAYNE		

Women

1.	Elana Meyer	RSA	68:36
2.	Iulia Negura	ROM	69:15
3.	Anuta Catuna	ROM	69:35
4.	Albertina Dias	POR	69:57
5.	Elena Fidatov	ROM	70:13
6.	Hilde Stavik	NOR	70:21
7.	Merlene Renders	BEL	70:29
8.	Brynhild Synstnes	NOR	70:34
9.	Adriana Barbu	ROM	70:44
10.	Mari Tanigawa	JPN	70:49
11.	Fatuma Toba	ETH	71:00
12.	Natalya Galushko	BLS	71:02
13.	Alena Peterková	TCH	71:16
14.	Alla Zhilyayeva	RUS	71:16
15.	Nicole Levéque	FRA	71:24
16.	Klara Kashapova	RUS	72:04
17.	Martha Ernstdóttir	ISL	72:16
18.	Stella Castro	COL	72:23
19.	Mineko Watanabe	JPN	72:26
20.	Yukari Komatsu	JPN	72:30
29.	DANIELLE SANDERSON		73:13
31.	ANGIE HULLEY		73:19
46.	HEATHER HEASMAN		74:06
47.	CATH MIJOVIC		74:15
72.	MARIAN SUTTON		76:15

Men Team

1.	Kenya	3:03:36
2.	Mexico	3:03:47
3	Morocco	3:05:58
4.	Zimbabwe	3:06:59
5.	Ethiopia	3:07:07
6.	Brazil	3:07:47
12.	GREAT BRITAIN & NI	3:10:51

Women Team

1.	Romania	3:29:03
2.	Norway	3:33:36
3.	Japan	3:35:39
4.	Portgugal	
5.	Russia	
6.	South Africa	
9.	GREAT BRITAIN & NI	3:40:38